CANADIAN TORT LAW

CASES, NOTES AND MATERIALS

CANADIAN TORT LAW

CASES, NOTES AND MATERIALS

By

CECIL A. WRIGHT

Q.C., S.J.D., LL.D.
LATE DEAN AND PROFESSOR OF LAW, FACULTY OF LAW
UNIVERSITY OF TORONTO

and

ALLEN M. LINDEN

A JUSTICE OF THE SUPREME COURT OF ONTARIO

SEVENTH EDITION

TORONTO

BUTTERWORTHS

1980

© 1980 Butterworth & Co. (Canada) Ltd.
Printed and bound in Canada

CANADA:	BUTTERWORTH & CO. (CANADA) LTD. TORONTO: 2265 Midland Avenue, Scarborough, M1P 4S1
UNITED KINGDOM:	BUTTERWORTH & CO. (PUBLISHERS) LTD. LONDON: 88 Kingsway, WC2B 6AB
AUSTRALIA:	BUTTERWORTH PTY. LTD. SYDNEY: 586 Pacific Highway, Chatswood, NSW 2067 MELBOURNE: 343 Little Collins Street, 3000 BRISBANE: 240 Queen Street, 4000
NEW ZEALAND:	BUTTERWORTHS OF NEW ZEALAND LTD. WELLINGTON: 77-85 Custom House Quay, 1
SOUTH AFRICA:	BUTTERWORTH & CO. (SOUTH AFRICA) (PTY.) LTD. DURBAN: 152/154 Gale Street
NIGERIA:	BUTTERWORTH & CO. (NIGERIA) LTD. ILUPEJU: Palmgrove House, No. 1 Shagama Avenue

First Published 1954
Second Edition 1958
Third Edition 1963
Fourth Edition 1967
Fifth Edition 1970
First Reprint 1971
Second Reprint 1972
Sixth Edition 1975
Seventh Edition 1980

For "Acknowledgments" see p. xi

Canadian Cataloguing in Publication Data

Wright, Cecil A., 1904-1967.
    Canadian tort law

(Canadian legal casebook series)
Includes index.

ISBN 0-409-87805-7 pa.   ISBN 0-409-87804-9 bd.

1. Torts – Canada – Cases. I. Linden, Allen M., 1934- II. Title. III. Series.

KE1232.A7W74   346.7103   C80-094501-8

To my mother and father,
Lily and Louis,
with deepest gratitude.

Canadian Legal Casebook Series

CASTEL: *CONFLICT OF LAWS, Cases, Notes and Materials (4th ed.)*

PALMER AND WELLING: *CASES AND MATERIALS ON COMPANY LAW (2nd ed.)*

WRIGHT AND LINDEN: *CANADIAN TORT LAW, Cases, Notes and Materials (7th ed.)*

SCHMEISER: *CRIMINAL LAW, Cases and Comments (3rd ed.)*

WATSON, BORINS AND WILLIAMS: *CANADIAN CIVIL PROCEDURE, Cases and Materials (2nd ed.)*

CASTEL: *INTERNATIONAL LAW (3rd ed.)*

FODDEN: *CANADIAN FAMILY LAW, Cases and Materials*

GLASBEEK: *EVIDENCE, Cases and Materials*

WHYTE AND LEDERMAN: *CANADIAN CONSTITUTIONAL LAW, Cases, Notes and Materials (2nd ed.)*

SWAN AND REITER: *CONTRACTS, Cases and Materials*

WALKER AND ASH: *CASES AND MATERIALS ON DEBTOR-CREDITOR RELATIONS*

CLAYDON AND GALLOWAY: *LAW AND LEGALITY, MATERIALS ON LEGAL DECISION-MAKING, Cases, Notes and Materials*

PREFACE

Like its predecessors, this casebook is meant to furnish a basis for an introductory course in the law of torts. Because the book is used primarily in Canadian law schools, the bulk of the material is Canadian. Much of this new Canadian material is exciting, for it reflects a vitality and vibrance in our judges and scholars that matches the spirit of modern Canada. Indeed, for a change, others may well be able to learn from and emulate some of our solutions to thorny legal problems. It is impossible, however, to provide a complete understanding of tort principles without a detailed study of the English cases. Consequently, many of the leading ones are included, as are a few selected opinions from American and Commonwealth countries.

As in the last edition, I have tried to ask questions more than provide answers. I have done this for two reasons: (1) because it is much more stimulating to teach and to study torts in this way; and (2) because definitive answers to many of the fundamental issues of tort law are lacking.

This edition, like the last, retains the same basic organization adopted by Dean Wright in the first four editions. Although minor structural changes have been made, the flow of the material has not been altered. The intentional torts and the defences thereto are, in my view, still the best way for a law student to begin the study of torts. It eases the student gently into the materials, providing a glimpse of some history, some simple concepts and some everyday human problems that tort law has tried to solve. The bulk of this book is still concerned with negligence, which remains the most important part of the tort lawyer's work. The notion of strict liability, the third basis of tort liability, is then dealt with. Chapter 13, on products liability, focuses on a serious, modern problem and tort law's response to it. It also furnishes an excellent vehicle for reviewing some of the theoretical concepts explored during the earlier part of the course. The chapter on auto accident compensation raises the whole question of whether, in the light of our social welfare laws, tort law has any claim to survive in modern Canada. In response to suggestions from various colleagues across the country, three new chapters have been added to the book covering briefly the topics of Defamation, Nuisance and Business Torts.

The debate about tort law's relevance in the 1980's continues, perhaps with increased intensity. New Zealand has recently abolished the tort suit as a remedy for accidental injury and has established in its place, a comprehensive, government-operated, compensation scheme. This development, and others being discussed everywhere, forces us to consider, once again, whether tort law is worthy of survival in our time. If the exclusive function of the law of torts is compensation, as some believe, then perhaps it should be discarded. If, however, tort law serves other useful social functions then perhaps it deserves to survive. Questions are asked throughout this book to stimulate discussion about the role of tort law in the modern world. Does it deter? Does it educate? Does it restrain the abuse of power in society? Does it offer any psychological benefits? Does it provide any market deterrence? The answers to these questions, upon which the destiny of tort law rests, are by no means clear. It is a fascinating area for dialogue about the kind of society we want to build in Canada and the place of tort law in that society.

I should like once again to express my gratitude to the late Dean Wright, the late William Lloyd Prosser, the late Albert Ehrenzweig and John Fleming, whose influence on the shape of this book is visible to everyone. I should also like to thank the torts teachers of Canada, and elsewhere in the world, from whose work, some of which has been included or referred to herein, I have learned so much. My research assistants, Robert Kligman, Adrian Hill (Defamation), David Basskin (Intentional Torts) and Richard Hay (Products Liability), deserve my thanks for their contribution. A special thank you is due to my secretary, Benita Cadawas, for her superb assistance in preparing this manuscript for publication. Also I am greatly indebted to Marie Graham of Butterworths for her editorial assistance.

Finally, I want to express my deepest gratitude to my family and especially to my parents, Lily and Louis Linden, to whom I have dedicated this edition of the book, for all their support over the years.

Allen M. Linden
April 7, 1980

ACKNOWLEDGMENTS

A case book on such a wide subject necessarily contains a great deal of reference to the work of others in the field, in the cases, notes and text, and more especially in the selected reading. The authors and publishers of these articles and textbooks have been most generous in giving permission for the reproduction in this text of work already in print. References, of course, appear where necessary and possible in the text. It is convenient for us to list below, for the assistance of the reader, the publishers and, in several instances, the authors for whose courtesy we are most grateful.

A.P. Watt & Son	A.P. Herbert, *Uncommon Law* (1935). A.P. Herbert, *The Uncommon Law* (1978).
The Association of American Trial Lawyers	Marryott, "Testing the Criticisms of the Fault Concept" from *Justice and the Adversary System* (1968).
California Law Review	Ehrenzweig, "Negligence Without Fault" (1951), reprinted (1966), 54 Calif. L. Rev. 1422. Copyright © 1951, California Law Review, Inc., Reprinted by permission.
Canadian Bar Journal	W. David Griffiths, "Don't Abolish Tort Law in Auto Accident Compensation" (1969), 12 Can. Bar Rev. 187.
Canadian Bar Review	Fleming, "The Passing of Polemis" (1961), 39 Can. Bar Rev. 489. Lang, "The Activity-Risk Theory of Tort: Risk, Insurance and Insolvency" (1961), 39 Can. Bar Rev. 53. MacIntyre, "The Rationale of Last Clear Chance" (1940), 18 Can. Bar Rev. 665.
The Carswell Co. Ltd.	W.H. Charles, "A New Handbook on the Assessment of Damages in Personal Injury Cases from the Supreme Court of Canada" (1977-78), 3 C.C.L.T. 344, at p. 346.
Connecticut Law Review	Kalven, "A Schema of Alternatives to the Present Auto Accident Tort System". This article appeared in Vol. 1 of the Connecticut Law Review at p. 33 and is reprinted with the permission of the

Connecticut Law Review and Fred B. Rothman & Co. Copyright © 1968 by the University of Connecticut.

Doubleday & Co. Inc.

Ratcliffe, *The Good Samaritan and the Law* (1966)
Freedman, "No Response to the Cry for Help";
Gusfield, "Social Sources of Levites and Samaritans";
Honoré, "Law, Morals and Rescue";
Tunc, "The Volunteer and the Good Samaritan".

Duke University School of Law

L.L. Jaffe, "Damages for Personal Injury: The Impact of Insurance". Reprinted with permission from a symposium entitled The Federal Employers' Liability Act, pt. 1, appearing in Law and Contemporary Problems, Vol. 18, No. 2, at pp. 222-225 (Spring, 1953), published by Duke University School of Law, Durham, North Carolina. Copyright 1953 by Duke University.

George Weidenfeld and Nicolson Ltd.

Atiyah, *Accidents, Compensation and the Law* (2nd ed., 1975).

The Georgetown Law Journal

Joseph A. Page, "Of Mace and Men: Tort Law as a Means of Controlling Domestic Chemical Warfare" (1969), 57 Georgetown L.J. 1238. Reprinted with permission of the publisher; copyright © 1969 by The Georgetown Law Journal.

Harvard Law Review

Ames, "Law and Morals" (1908), 22 Harv. L. Rev. 97. Copyright 1908 by the Harvard Law Review Association.
Calabresi, "The Decision for Accidents: An Approach to Non-fault Allocation of Costs" (1965), 78 Harv. L. Rev. 713. Copyright 1965 by the Harvard Law Review Association.
MacIntyre, "The Rationale of Last Clear Chance" (1940), 53 Harv. L. Rev. 1225. Copyright 1940 by the Harvard Law Review Association.
Seavey, "Mr. Justice Cardozo and the Law of Torts" (1939), 52 Harv. L. Rev. 372. Copyright 1939 by the Harvard Law Review Association.

The Law Book Co. Ltd.

Fleming, *The Law of Torts* (5th ed., 1977).

The Law Society of Upper
Canada and Richard De
Boo Ltd.

Schroeder, "The Charge to the Jury"
Special Lectures of the Law Society of
Upper Canada on Jury Trials (1959),
pp. 339-341.

Little, Brown & Co.

Keeton, Robert H., and O'Connell, Jeffrey,
Basic Protection for the Traffic Victim,
pp. 1-3, 257-259. Little, Brown & Co.
(Boston, 1965).

Louisiana Law Review

Mansfield, "Informed Choice in the Law of
Torts" (1961), 22 La. L. Rev. 17.
Wade, "The Place of Assumption of Risk in
the Law of Negligence" (1961), 22 La.
L. Rev. 5.

Michigan Law Review

Green, "The Causal Relation Issue in
Negligence Law" (1962), 60 Mich. L.
Rev. 547.

Northwestern University Law
Review

Ehrenzweig, "A Psychoanalysis of Negligence". Reprinted by special permission
of the Northwestern University Law
Review, Copyright © 1953 by Northwestern University School of Law, Vol.
47, Rev. 855.

Osgoode Hall Law Journal

Haines, "The Medical Professions and the
Adversary Process" (1973), 11 O.H.L.J.
41.
Linden and Sommers, "The Civil Jury in
the Courts of Ontario: A Postscript to
the Osgoode Hall Study" (1968), 6
O.H.L.J. 252.

Oxford University Press

Hart and Honoré, *Causation in the Law*
(1959). By permission of Oxford
University Press.

Rutgers Law Review

Blumrosen, "Antidiscrimination Law in
Action in New Jersey: A Law-Sociology
Study" (1965), 19 Rutgers L. Rev. 189.
Reprinted with permission of Rutgers
Law Review.

Sijthoff & Noordhoff
International Publishers BV

Dawson, "Rewards for the Rescue of
Human Life" from Twentieth Century
Comparative Law and Conflicts Law.

Stanford Law Review

Malone, "Ruminations on Cause-in-Fact"
(1956), 9 Stan. L. Rev. 60. Copyright
1956 by the Board of Trustees of the
Leland Stanford Junior University.

Stanford University Press	Packer, *The Limits of the Criminal Sanction* (1968).
Stevens & Sons Ltd.	Glanville Williams, "The Aims of the Law of Tort"(1951), Current Legal Problems 137.
Sweet and Maxwell Ltd.	Salmond, *The Law of Torts* (17th ed., 1977, Heuston). *Winfield and Jolowicz on Tort* (10th ed., 1975, Rogers).
Tennessee Law Review	Plant "Strict Liability of Manufacturers for Injuries Caused by Defects in Products— An Opposing View" (1957), 24 Tenn. L. Rev. 938. Reprinted with permission of the Tennessee Law Review Assoc., Inc.
University of Chicago Law Review	Blum and Kalven, "Public Law Perspectives on a Private Law Problem—Auto Compensation Plans" (1964), 31 U. Chi. L. Rev. 646. Copyright 1964, University of Chicago Law Review. Blum and Kalven, "The Empty Cabinet of Dr. Calabresi: Auto Accidents and General Deterrence" (1967), 34 U. Chi. L. Rev. 239. Copyright 1967, University of Chicago Law Review.
The University of Chicago Press	Zimring and Hawkins, *Deterrence: The Legal Threat in Crime Control* (1973). Reprinted by permission of The University of Chicago Press.
University of Florida Law Review	Otto E. Lang, "The Nature and Potential of the Saskatchewan Insurance Experiment" (1962), 14 U. Fla. L. Rev. 352. Reprinted with the permission of the University of Florida Law Review. Copyright 1962.
University of Pennsylvania Law Review	Andenaes, "The General Preventive Effects of Punishment" (1966), 114 University of Pennsylvania Law Review 949. Reprinted by permission of The University of Pennsylvania Law Review and Fred B. Rothman & Co.
University of Toronto Law Journal	Ison, "Tort Liability and Social Insurance" (1969), 19 U. of T.L.J. 614. Weiler, "Defamation, Enterprise Liability and Freedom of Speech" (1967), 17 U. of T.L.J. 278, at p. 285. Reprinted by

permission of University of Toronto Press.

Utah Law Review

Green, "The Wagon Mound (No. 2)—Foreseeability Revised" (1967) Utah L. Rev. 197.

James, "Nature of Negligence" (1953), 3 Utah L. Rev. 275.

The Yale Law Journal

Calabresi, *Costs of Accidents: Legal and Economic* (1970).

Calabresi, "Fault, Accident and the Wonderful World of Blum and Kalven". Reprinted by permission of the Yale Law Journal Co. and Fred B. Rothman & Co. from The Yale Law Journal, Vol. 75, p. 26.

Eleanor S. Glass, "Restructuring Informed Consent: Legal Therapy for the Doctor-Patient Relationship". Reprinted by permission of The Yale Law Journal Co. and Fred B. Rothman & Co. from The Yale Law Journal, Vol. 79, p. 1533.

James, "Assumption of Risk". Reprinted by permission of The Yale Law Journal Co. and Fred B. Rothman & Co. from The Yale Law Journal, Vol. 61, p. 141.

Every effort has been made to contact authors and publishers to obtain permissions. If the publisher is made aware of any errors which may have been made in obtaining permissions, the publisher will take steps to ensure that proper credit be given at that time.

TABLE OF CONTENTS

TABLE OF CASES

[A page number in bold face (black) type indicates that the text of the case or a portion thereof is reproduced. A page number in light face type indicates that the case is merely referred to or mentioned.]

CHAPTER 1

INTRODUCTION: THE FUNCTIONS OF TORT LAW

LINDEN, CANADIAN TORT LAW
(2nd ed., 1977)

The law of torts hovers over virtually every activity of modern society. The driver of every automobile on our highways, the pilot of every aeroplane in the sky, and the capitain of every ship plying our waters must abide by the standards of tort law. The producers, distributors and repairers of every product, from bread to computers, must conform to tort law's counsel of caution. No profession is beyond its reach: a doctor cannot raise a scalpel, a lawyer cannot advise a client, nor can an architect design a building without being subject to potential tort liability. In the same way, teachers, government officials, police, and even jailers may be required to pay damages if someone is hurt as a result of their conduct. Those who engage in sports, such as golfers, hockey-players, and snowmobilers, may end up as parties to a tort action. The territory of tort law encompasses losses resulting from fires, floods, explosions, electricity, gas, and many other catastrophies that may occur in this increasingly complex world. A person who punches another person in the nose may have to answer for it in a tort case as well as in the criminal courts. Hence, any one of us may become a plaintiff or a defendant in a tort action at any moment. Tort law, therefore, is a subject of abiding concern not only to the judges and lawyers who must administer it, but also to the public at large, whose every move is regulated by it.

WRIGHT, INTRODUCTION TO CASES ON THE LAW OF TORTS
(4th ed., 1967)

While no definition of a "tort" has yet been made that affords any satisfactory assistance in the solution of the problems we shall encounter, the purpose, or function, of the law of torts can be stated fairly simply. Arising out of the various and ever increasing clashes of the activities of persons living in a common society, carrying on business in competition with fellow members of that society, owning property which may in any of a thousand ways affect the person or property of others—in short doing all the things that constitute modern living—there must of necessity be losses, or injuries of many kinds sustained as a result of the activities of others. The purpose of the law of torts is to adjust these losses and to afford compensation for injuries sustained by one person as the result of the conduct of another. Such a statement of the problem indicates that the law of torts must constantly be in a state of flux, since it must be ever ready to recognize and consider new losses arising in novel ways. The introduction of printing, by facilitating the manner in which a man's reputation might be injured by the dissemination of the printed word, had a tremendous effect on the law of defamation; the radio of today presents even more serious problems, as do also the aeroplane and the modern motor car.

The study of the law of torts is, therefore, a study of the extent to which the law will shift the losses sustained in modern society from the person affected to the shoulders of him who caused the loss or, more realistically in many fields, to the insurance companies who are increasingly covering the many risks involved in the conduct of business and individual activities.

SALMOND, THE LAW OF TORTS

(17th ed., 1977, Heuston)

Tort and Crime

A tort is a species of civil injury or wrong. The distinction between civil and criminal wrongs depends on the nature of the appropriate remedy provided by law. A civil wrong is one which gives rise to civil proceedings—proceedings, that is to say, which have as their purpose the enforcement of some right claimed by the plaintiff as against the defendant. Criminal proceedings, on the other hand, are those which have for their object the punishment of the defendant for some act of which he is accused. It is often the case that the same wrong is both civil and criminal—capable of being made the subject of proceedings of both kinds. Assault, libel, theft and malicious injury to property, for example, are wrongs of this kind. Speaking generally, in all such cases the civil and criminal remedies are not alternative but concurrent, each being independent of the other. The wrongdoer may be punished criminally by imprisonment or otherwise, and also compelled in a civil action to make compensation or restitution to the injured person. . . .

Tort and Contract

The distinction between tort and contract is that the duties in the former are primarily fixed by the law, while in the latter they are fixed by the parties themselves. Further, in tort the duty is towards persons generally; in contract it is towards a specific person or persons. . . .

Tort and Equity

No civil injury is to be classed as a tort if it is only a breach of trust or some other merely equitable obligation. The reason for this exclusion is historical only. The law of torts is in its origin a part of the common law, as distinguished from equity, and it was unknown to the Court of Chancery. . . .

We may accordingly define a tort as *a civil wrong for which the remedy is a common law action for unliquidated damages, and which is not exclusively the breach of a contract or the breach of a trust or other merely equitable obligation.*

NOTES

1. Winfield and Jolowicz, *Tort* (10th ed., 1975, Rogers) define tortious liability as that which "arises from the breach of a duty primarily fixed by the law; this duty is towards persons generally and its breach is redressible by an action for unliquidated damages".

2. Professor John G. Fleming, in his *Law of Torts* (5th ed., 1977) explains that the word *tort* derives from the Latin *tortus,* meaning twisted or crooked, and early found its way into the English language as a general synonym for the word "wrong". In general terms, Fleming concludes that a tort is a "civil wrong

other than a breach of contract, which the law will redress by an award of damages". Fleming is unhappy with a definition of tort law, preferring instead to "describe it in terms of the policies which have brought it into existence and contrasting these with the policies underlying other forms of liability".

3. Most definitions of a tort are almost as circular as saying that a tort is a tort. The only way in which a satisfactory description of tort law can be obtained is by focussing on function. In tort litigation, the courts must decide whether to shift the loss suffered by one person, the plaintiff, to the shoulders of another person, the defendant. The principles and rules of the law of torts which have been developed over the centuries assist the courts in this task. No definition could possibly depict the richness and variety of the subject matter of tort law. In order to know what tort law is, it is necessary to study in some detail what it aims to do and what it does in fact, as well as the basic principles incorporated within it.

It should be stressed that tort law is not one-dimensional; it serves several functions. The purpose of this chapter is to identify in a preliminary and tentative way the main aims of modern tort law. It will be seen that not all of its goals are harmonious, indeed some may be in conflict with others. It will also be noticed that not all the purposes of tort law are expressed openly in the case law. On the contrary, some of them are totally unrecognized or dimly perceived, or even vehemently denied. In sum, tort law serves a potpourri of objectives, some conscious and some unconscious.

See generally Linden, *Canadian Tort Law* (2nd ed., 1977), p. 2.

HOLMES, THE COMMON LAW

(1881)

A man need not, it is true, do this or that act—the term "act" implies a choice—but he must act somehow. Furthermore, the public generally profits by individual activity. As action cannot be avoided, and tends to the public good, there is obviously no policy in throwing the hazard of what is at once desirable and inevitable upon the actor.

The state might conceivably make itself a mutual insurance company against accidents, and distribute the burden of its citizens' mishaps among all its members. There might be a pension for paralytics, and state aid for those who suffered in person or estate from tempest or wild beasts. As between individuals it might adopt the mutual insurance principle *pro tanto*, and divide damages when both were in fault, as in the *rusticum judicium* of the admiralty, or it might throw all loss upon the actor irrespective of fault. The state does none of these things, however, and the prevailing view is that its cumbrous and expensive machinery ought not to be set in motion unless some clear benefit is to be derived from disturbing the *status quo*. State interference is an evil, where it cannot be shown to be a good. Universal insurance, if desired, can be better and more cheaply accomplished by private enterprise. The undertaking to re-distribute losses simply on the ground that they resulted from the defendant's act would not only be open to these objections, but, as it is hoped the preceding discussion has shown, to the still graver one of offending the sense of justice. Unless my act is of a nature to threaten others, unless under the circumstances a prudent man would have foreseen the possibility of harm, it is no more justifiable to make me indemnify my neighbor against the consequences, than to make me do the same thing if I had fallen upon him in a fit, or to compel me to insure him against lightning. . . .

The general principle of our law is that loss from accident must lie where it falls, and this principle is not affected by the fact that a human being is the instrument of misfortune. But relatively to a given human being anything is accident which he could not fairly have been expected to contemplate as possible, and therefore to avoid.

PROSSER, HANDBOOK OF THE LAW OF TORTS

(4th ed., 1971)

Perhaps more than any other branch of the law, the law of torts is a battleground of social theory. Its primary purpose, of course, is to make a fair adjustment of the conflicting claims of the litigating parties. But the twentieth century has brought an increasing realization of the fact that the interests of society in general may be involved in disputes in which the parties are private litigants. The notion of "public policy" involved in private cases is not by any means new to tort law, and doubtless has been with us ever since the troops of the sovereign first intervened in a brawl to keep the peace; but it is only in recent decades that it has played a predominant part. Society has some concern even with the single dispute involved in a particular case; but far more important than this is a system of precedent on which the entire common law is based, under which a rule once laid down is to be followed until the courts find good reason to depart from it, so that others now living and even those yet unborn may be affected by a decision made today. There is good reason, therefore, to make a conscious effort to direct the law along lines which will achieve a desirable social result, both for the present and for the future.

Individuals have many interests for which they claim protection from the law, and which the law will recognize as worthy of protection. Various interesting attempts have been made to classify these interests into categories, which of course have no virtue in themselves, and only serve to suggest the wide extent to which the law is concerned with human welfare. Men wish to be secure in their persons against harm and interference, not only as to their physical integrity, but as to their freedom to move about and their peace of mind. They want food and clothing, homes and land and goods, money, automobiles and entertainment, and they want to be secure and free from disturbance in the right to have these things, or to acquire them if they can. They want freedom to work and deal with others, and protection against interference with their private lives, their family relations, and their fellow men. The catalogue of their interests might be as long as the list of legitimate human desires; and not the least of them is the desire to do what they please, without restraint and without undue consideration for the interests and claims of others.

In any society, it is inevitable that these interests shall come into conflict. When they do, the primitive man determines who shall prevail with sword and club and tomahawk; and there is recent melancholy evidence that the law of the jungle is not yet departed from the affairs of nations. But in a civilized community, it is the law which is called upon to act as arbiter.

The administration of the law becomes a process of weighing the interests for which the plaintiff demands protection against the defendant's claim to untrammeled freedom in the furtherance of his own desires, together with the importance of those desires themselves. When the interest of the public is thrown into the scale and allowed to swing the balance for or against the plaintiff, the result is a form of "social engineering" that deliberately seeks to use the law as an instrument to promote that "greatest happiness of the greatest number" which by common consent is the object of society. This process of "balancing the interests" is by no means peculiar to the law of torts, but it has been carried to its greatest lengths and has received it most general conscious recognition in this field.

The process is not a simple one, and the problems which arise are complex, and seldom easy of solution. It is usually far easier to describe what has been done than to give a clear reason for it, and harder still to predict what the future may hold. It is a simple matter to say that the interests of individuals are to be balanced against one another in the light of those of the general public, but far more difficult to say where the public interest may lie. Most of the writers who have pointed out the process have stopped short of telling us how it is to be done. It is easy to say that the law will require of every man reasonable conduct not unduly harmful to his neighbors; but what is reasonable, and what is undue harm? In determining the limits of the protection to be afforded by the law, the courts have been pulled and hauled by many conflicting considerations, some of them ill defined and seldom expressed at all, no one of which can be said always to control. Often they have had chiefly in mind the justice of the individual case, which may not coincide with the social interest in the long run. If we are to have general rules, and the law is to have no favorites, occasional injustice is inevitable to someone who does not fit into the rule; and the constant struggle is to make the rule sufficiently flexible to allow for the particular circumstances, and yet so rigid that lawyers may predict what the decision may be, and men may guide their conduct by that prediction. It is only by a slow, halting, confused, and often painful progress that any agreement is reached as to the best general rule. Ultimately the law must coincide with public opinion, and cannot stand against it; but when the opinion is in a state of division and flux, it is not surprising that the courts' decisions reflect the battle which is raging about them. . . .

Factors Affecting Tort Liability

Among the many considerations affecting the decision as to which of the conflicting interests is to prevail, a few may be singled out for special mention, with the repeated caution that no one of them is of such supervening importance that it will control the decision of every case in which it appears.

Moral Aspect of Defendant's Conduct. One such factor is the moral aspect of the defendant's conduct—or in other words, the moral guilt or blame to be attached in the eyes of society to his acts, his motives, and his state of mind. Personal morals are of course a matter on which there may be differences of opinion; but it may be assumed that in every community there are certain acts and motives which are generally regarded as morally right, and others which are considered morally wrong. Of course such public opinion has its effect upon the decisions of the courts. The oppressor, the perpetrator of outrage, the knave, the liar, the scandal-monger, the man who does spiteful harm for its own sake, the egotist who deliberately disregards and overrides the interests of his neighbors, may expect to find that the courts of society condemn him no less than the opinion of society itself. In a very vague general way, the law of torts reflects current ideas of morality, and when such ideas have changed, the law has kept pace with them. . . .

[T]here are still many immoral acts which do not amount to torts, and the law has not yet enacted the golden rule. It is impossible to afford a lawsuit for every deed of unkindness or betrayal, and there is much evil in the world which must necessarily be left to other agencies of social control. The basest ingratitude is not a tort, nor is a cruel refusal of kindness or courtesy, or a denial of aid. The rich man is under no compulsion to feed his starving neighbor, and it is still the law that the owner of a boat who sees another drowning before his eyes may rest on his oars and let him drown — although perhaps in so extreme a case it is a reproach to the law that it is so. Petty insults, threats, abuse and lacerated feelings must be endured in a society not many centuries removed from the law of the club. To what extent the moral ideas of a future day may yet create new torts to deal with such misconduct, it is now impossible to say.

In short, it is undoubtedly true that in the great majority of the cases liability in tort rests upon some moral delinquency on the part of the individual. But quite often it is based upon considerations of public policy which have little connection with private morals. The ethical principles which underlie the law are "not the moral code of popular speech, but an artificial and somewhat sublimated morality, which is formulated by the law and is called morality only by a use of that term which is almost metaphorical". . . .

Historical Development. The shadow of the past still lies rather heavily on the law of torts. When the common law first emerged, its forms of procedure were rigidly prescribed, and the plaintiff could have no cause of action unless he could fit his claim into the form of some existing and recognized writ. These "forms of action we have buried, but they still rule us from their graves". At the beginning of the nineteenth century they still existed although somewhat blurred in their outlines, as the core of common law procedure. By the middle of the century they began to be modified, liberalized, and at last replaced to a great extent by the modern procedural codes. The old attitude still persisted, however, that the substance of the plaintiff's right is determined and limited by the possibility of a remedy under the common law forms. Thus even today, we find courts holding that blasting operations which cast rocks onto the plaintiff's land may be actionable where those which merely shake his house to pieces are not, on the basis of the old distinction between the action of trespass and the action on the case. Added to this is the devotion to precedent and the distrust of new ideas, which is by no means peculiar to the law but for which it often is reproached, and which has made it change slowly. There are not many rules in tort law as to which one may say that there is no better reason for their existence than that they were laid down by Lord Mildew three centuries since, at a time when the world was a very different place, but they do exist.

Nevertheless, change and development have come, as social ideas have altered, and they are constantly going on. The law of deceit has progressed from a point where it was assumed as a matter of course that every seller of goods will lie; the law of slander at one time held that mere "brabbling words" imputing harlotry to a woman were not actionable; and the same evolution is to be traced in the law of seduction, the right of privacy, and interference with contractual relations. More recently courts have recognized for the first time an action for prenatal injuries, a recovery by a wife for personal injury at the hands of her husband, new tort liabilities of municipal corporations, and a whole new field of actions for nervous shock and mental suffering. This process of development, of course, is not ended, and continues every year. . . .

Convenience of Administration. It does not lie within the power of any judicial system to remedy all human wrongs. The obvious limitations upon the time of the courts, the difficulty in many cases of ascertaining the real facts or of providing any effective remedy, have meant that there must be some selection of those more serious injuries which have the prior claim to redress and are dealt with most easily. Trivialities must be left to other means of settlement, and many wrongs which in themselves are flagrant—ingratitude, avarice, broken faith, brutal words, and heartless disregard of the feelings of others—are beyond any effective legal remedy, and any practical administration of the law.

The courts always have stood more or less in dread of a "flood of litigation" involving problems which they are not prepared to deal with. At one time they refused to permit any inquiry as to the state of a man's knowledge, or his belief or intentions, upon the ground that "they cannot be known". For many years they denied all recovery in cases of "mental suffering" involving fright or shock without physical impact, for fear it would "open a wide door for unjust claims, which cannot successfully be met". The refusal to extend the obligation of a contract to third parties was based upon the "infinity of actions" and the "most absurd and outrageous consequences" which might ensue, and this is still the chief obstacle to holding contractors liable to third persons. . . .

Capacity to Bear Loss. Another factor to which the courts have given weight in balancing the interests before them is the relative ability of the respective parties to bear the loss which must necessarily fall upon one or the other. This is not so much a matter of their respective wealth, although certainly juries, and sometimes judges, are not indisposed to favor the poor against the rich. Rather it is a matter of their capacity to absorb the loss or avoid it. The defendants in tort cases are to a large extent public utilities, industrial corporations, commercial enterprises, automobile owners, and others who by means of rates, prices, taxes or insurance are best able to distribute to the public at large the risks and losses which are inevitable in a complex civilization. Rather than leave the loss on the shoulders of the individual plaintiff, who may be ruined by it, the courts have tended to find reasons to shift it to the defendants. Probably no small part of the general extension of tort law to permit more frequent recovery in recent years has been due to this attitude. The development of the doctrine of strict liability "without fault" for dangerous conditions and activities has rested to some extent on this basis, as has that of vicarious liability for the torts of a servant; and the extension of the liability of a manufacturer to the ultimate consumer of his product has been favored by the feeling that he is best able to bear the loss. The same principle, of course, underlies such statutes as the workmen's compensation acts.

But there are obvious limitations upon the power of a defendant to shift the loss to the public, and the courts frequently have been reluctant to saddle an industry with the entire burden of the harm it may cause, for fear that it may prove ruinously heavy. This is particularly true where the liability may extend to an unlimited number of unknown persons, and is incapable of being estimated or insured against in advance. It is also likely to be true as to a new industry, which may be unduly hampered in its development, as is illustrated by the controversy over the liability of the aviation industry for damage to persons or property on the ground, which used to turn primarily on the policy of imposing such a burden upon a new enterprise.

Prevention and Punishment. The "prophylactic" factor of preventing future harm has been quite important in the field of torts. The courts are concerned not with only compensation of the victim, but with admonition of the wrongdoer. When the decisions of the courts become known, and defendants realize that they may be held liable, there is of course a strong incentive to prevent any occurrence of the harm. Not infrequently one reason for imposing liability is the deliberate purpose of providing that incentive. The rule of vicarious liability is intended, among other things, to result in greater care in the selection and instruction of servants than would otherwise be the case; the carrier which is held to the "highest practicable degree of care" toward its passengers will tend to observe it for their safety; the manufacturer who is made liable to the consumer for defects in his product will do what he can to see that there are no such defects. While the idea of prevention is seldom controlling, it very often has weight as a reason for holding the defendant responsible.

This idea of prevention shades into that of punishment of the offender for what he has already done, since one admitted purpose of punishment itself is to prevent repetition of the offense. There are those who believe that punishment or retaliation is an important and proper aim of the law in assessing damages, since what is paid to the plaintiff is taken away from the defendant. However this may be, it is not often mentioned in the award of compensatory damages, which usually are treated by the courts as a mere adjustment of the loss which has occurred in accordance with responsibility. To the extent that punitive damages are given, however, both prevention and retaliation become accepted objects of the administration of the law of torts.

FLEMING, THE LAW OF TORTS

(5th ed., 1977)

The history of the law of torts has centred around the search for an adjust-ment between two basic interests of individuals—the interest in security and the interest in freedom of action. The first requires that a person who has been hurt in consequence of another's action should be compensated by the other regardless of the latter's motivation and purpose; the second that a person who harms another should be held responsible only when his activity was intention-ally wrongful or indicated an undue lack of consideration for others. The former is content with imposing liability for faultless causation; the latter insists on 'fault' or 'culpability'. At any given time and place, the rules of tortious liability reflect a compromise between these two competing ideas.

Individual Responsibility

Primitive law stressed security. Pre-occupied with preserving the peace and providing a substitute for private vengeance, it looked to causation rather than fault: "not so much to the intent of the actor as the loss and the damage of the party suffering". Even so, notions of fault were not wholly excluded. For one thing, the failure of early law to require a finding as to the wrongdoer's state of mind may have been based on its inability or unwillingness to conceive the unintentional infliction of harm rather than a lack of concern with such intention. For another, the myth has lately been exposed that early English law ever adhered to an unqualified principle that a man acted at his peril and became responsible for all resulting harm. Yet liability, if not 'absolute', was nonetheless 'strict' and scant regard was paid to the moral quality of the defendant's conduct. Gradually, however, the law began to pay greater heed to exculpatory considerations and, partially under the influence of the moral philosophy of the Church, tended to progress in the direction of recognizing moral culpability as the proper basis for tort. This subjectivation of the test of civil liability necessarily tended to benefit the injurer and curtail the protection for the injured. During the nineteenth century, the 'moral advance' of tort law vastly accelerated. In response to doctrines of natural law and *laissez faire,* the courts attached increasing importance to freedom of action and ultimately yielded to the general dogma of 'no liability without fault'. This movement coincided with, and was undoubtedly influenced by the demands of the Industrial Revolution. It was felt to be in the better interest of an advancing economy to subordinate the security of individuals, who happened to become casualties of the new machine age, rather than fetter enterprise by loading it with the cost of 'inevitable' accidents. Liability for faultless causation was feared to impede progress because it gave the individual no opportunity for avoiding liability by being careful and thus confronted him with the dilemma of either giving up his projected activity or shouldering the cost of any resulting injury. Fault alone was deemed to justify a shifting of loss, because the function of tort remedies was seen as primarily admonitory or deterrent. An award against a tortfeasor served as a punishment for him and a warning to others; it was, in a sense, an adjunct to the criminal law designed to induce antisocial and inconsiderate persons to conform to the standards of reasonable conduct prescribed by law. The significance attached to the element of deterrence operated, of course, on the assumption that an adverse judgment would be paid out of the defendant's own pocket. Personal fortunes were regarded as the sole source of compensation, so that the deterrent lash would be both real and inescapable.

Today, we are in the process of revising this approach. The moral viewpoint will, of course, continue to dominate intentional injuries, and tort law (whatever its prospects of survival elsewhere) appears to have an assured future in this regard. However, in the core area of tort—accidents—our viewpoint has been changing drastically. It is being increasingly realized that human failures in a machine age exact a large and fairly regular toll of life, limb and property, which is not significantly reducible by standards of conduct that can be prescribed and enforced through the operation of tort law. Accident prevention is more effectively promoted through the pressure exerted by penal sanctions attached to safety regulations and such extra-legal measures as road safety campaigns, the practice of insurance companies to base the rate of premiums on the insured's accident rate, improvements in the quality of roads and motor vehicles and of production processes in industry. But despite all these controls, accidents and injuries remain, and it is the task of the modern law of torts to deal with them. Some no doubt are attributable to negligence in the conventional sense, others will be 'pure accidents'. In either case, however, they may fairly be ascribed, not just to the immediate participants, but to the activity or enterprise itself with which they are connected. The progress of society is linked to the maintenance and continuance of industrial operations and fast methods of transport, and must therefore suffer the harms associated with them. The question is simply, who is to pay for their cost, the hapless victim who may be unable to pin conventional fault on any particular individual, or those who benefit from the accident-producing activity? The effect of denying compensation to the casualty is "to take much from few, and something from all, in order that a special group may pay less". If rules of law can be devised that will require each industry or those sponsoring a particular activity, like drivers of motor-cars, to bear collectively the burden of its own operating cost, public policy will be better served than under a legal system which is content to leave the compensation of casualties to the fortuitous outcome of litigation based on outdated and unrealistic notions of fault. What is required is to assure accident victims of compensation and to distribute the losses involved over society as a whole or some portion of it.

Loss Spreading

This approach suggests that a proper function of tort law should be not so much the shifting as the distribution of losses *typically* involved in modern living. Acceptance of this viewpoint must inevitably change evaluations of what is a fair allocation of risks. We have seen that no social value attaches to the mere shifting of loss so long as its effect is merely to impoverish one individual for the benefit of another. In order to warrant such a result, the law had to find a cogent reason for subordinating the defendant's interests to the plaintiff's, and inevitably focused attention on the moral quality of the conduct of the individual participants in the accident. On the other hand, if a certain type of loss is looked upon as a more or less inevitable by-product of a desirable but dangerous activity, it may well be just to distribute its costs among all who benefit from that activity, although it would be unfair to impose it upon each or any one of those individuals who happened to be the faultless instruments causing it. Such a basis for administering losses has been variously described as 'collectivization of losses' or 'loss distribution'. It leads to the selection of defendants, not necessarily because they happen to be morally blameworthy, but because of their superior ability to absorb the cost of compensation. In this manner, attention is focused, not only on who has the greater capacity to bear the loss, but also on who occupies the most strategic position to administer the loss by passing it on to a wider section of the public, either through insurance or price calculation.

Sometimes, no doubt, this approach would point to the victim as the better loss-bearer, as in the case of business and fire losses. Usually, however, it points to the injurer. A good illustration is furnished by workmen's compensation. Towards the close of the last century, it had become obvious that the judicial policy of protecting industry from the impact of accident losses suffered by its workers no longer corresponded either with the growing sense of social responsibility or the needs of the economy. It was increasingly felt that, instead of the workman subsidizing the growth of industrial development at the cost of his life or broken limbs, industry itself should bear the cost of its accidents by writing it off as an overhead charge of its operations. In response to this change in attitude, the first system of social insurance was inaugurated, whereby the casualties of accidents suffered in the course of employment became entitled to compensation, regardless of whether negligence in the conventional sense could be established. Liability for compensation was placed on the employer who, in turn, had to cover himself against the risk by compulsory insurance. This meant that responsibility for industrial accidents was not simply allocated to the employer on account of his superior risk-bearing capacity, but also that he would be able to distribute the cost to that large segment of the public who bought his products. . . .

Liability Insurance

The most potent influence on the growing trend towards loss distribution is the modern prevalence of liability insurance. Nowadays "we assume that the defendant in an action in tort is insured unless the contrary appears". The existence of insurance has the effect that an adverse judgment no longer merely shifts a loss from one individual to another, but tends to distribute it among all policy holders carrying insurance on this type of risk. The person cited as defendant is, in reality, only a nominal party to the litigation, a mere 'conduit through whom this process of distribution starts to flow'.

The fact that, through this device of indemnity insurance, some of the benefits of a regime of 'collectivization of losses' are already being attained under our traditional rules of tort law, suggests several observations. In the first place, insurance cover eliminates completely whatever admonitory effect an adverse verdict would otherwise have had in deterring unreasonably dangerous conduct. There is no evidence, however, that this has fostered irresponsibility. On the contrary, the steady *proportional* decline in the accident rate both on the road and in factories points to the conclusion that the assumed deterrent value of tort damages has been somewhat overrated and that accident prevention can be as effectively promoted by other pressures among the most important of which are the instinct of self-preservation and increase of premiums in the light of an adverse accident record. This, in turn, casts some doubt on the traditional assumption that tort liability can be justified only if it serves to deter and admonish misconduct. Equally relevant has now become the inquiry how a particular risk (e.g. defective products) can best be absorbed in the light (*inter alia*) of its insurability. Secondly, it may suggest the need for re-evaluating rules of tort liability which were originally formulated on assumptions that are no longer valid. An obvious example is the marital immunity which was based on considerations that insurance renders irrelevant. Proceedings by a wife against her husband for injury sustained by her in a car accident as the result of his careless driving can no longer be treated as hostile in any real sense, and the continued recognition of the immunity in such cases would only have the unintended and undesirable consequence of conferring a windfall on the husband's insurer. Thirdly, it may be asked to what extent, if at all, the law is adjusting itself to this new reality? Legislation has been the main agent of change, ranging from compulsory insurance for motorists and industrial employers to the abolition of immunities, like that between spouses and of hospitals. A new technique is to 'channel' liability to one source of compensation alone, to the exclusion of other potential defendants, so as to obviate the wasteful need of multiple (pyramiding) insurance. What of reorientation by the courts? Judicial attitudes are mixed, but changing rapidly. The 'official line' no doubt still is that insurance is contingent on liability, not vice versa, and therefore irrelevant to the tort issue. In practice, however, it is an influential factor even when hidden, though indeed nowadays increasingly brought out into the open. Without it, one could neither explain nor justify the pervasive trend towards strict(er) liability which runs like a golden thread throughout this textbook.

Compensation Plans

Not that liability insurance is the only road to risk pooling. Its greatest drawback as a system of compensation is its link with tort liability; benefits being contingent on a prior determination of tort responsibility, often complex, contentious and protracted. This is not only directly prejudicial to the accident victim, but vastly increases the cost of the system so much that more than half the premium is lost to administrative expenses. By comparison, direct compensation is much more efficient, benefits flowing from the fund to the victim without reference to the injurer or his responsibility for the accident. This is the model of accident and social insurance which eventually may well displace tort liability for all unintended injury.

Already it has gained a substantial foothold. In most countries, including Great Britain, workmen's compensation is now a straight-out form of social insurance under which the employer no longer serves even as a formal defendant backed by compulsory *liability* insurance (as he still does in Australia). In New Zealand, this model has been applied not only to industrial injuries but to all personal injury from accident, completely displacing tort recovery. In Australia, an even more ambitious project, covering also congenital disability and sickness, was recently very close to adoption. The related model of first-party insurance is increasingly replacing tort and liability insurance for dealing with the toll of the road both in Australia and North America. The death knell of tort liability for accidents is indeed becoming ever more audible.

NOTES

1. See also Harper and James, *The Law of Torts* (1956), an excellent treatise expounding the loss distribution theory; Ehrenzweig, "Negligence Without Fault" (1951), reprinted (1966), 54 Calif. L. Rev. 1422; Friedman, "Social Insurance and the Principles of Tort Liability" (1950), 63 Harv. L. Rev. 241; Wright, "Adequacy of the Law of Torts", [1961] Camb. L.J. 44. For some judicial

support, see *Launchbury* v. *Morgans*, [1971] 2 Q.B. 245 (C.A.) revd. [1973] A.C. 127; *Nettleship* v. *Weston*, [1971] 2 Q.B. 691 (C.A.).

2. See generally Winfield, "The Foundation of Liability in Tort" (1927), 27 Colum. L. Rev. 1; Goodhart, "The Foundation of Tortious Liability" (1938), 2 Mod. L. Rev. 1; Glanville Williams, "The Foundation of Tortious Liability" (1939), 7 Camb. L.J. 111; Williams and Hepple, *Foundations of the Law of Tort* (1976); Stone, "Touchstones of Tort Liability" (1950), 2 Stan. L. Rev. 259; Malone, "Ruminations on the Role of Fault in the History of the Common Law of Torts" (1970), 31 La. L. Rev. 1.

CALABRESI, FAULT, ACCIDENTS AND THE WONDERFUL WORLD OF BLUM AND KALVEN

(1965), 75 Yale L.J. 26.

There is no need to go to great length in reiterating what the "general deterrence" thesis is. Essentially it is the notion that in our society what is produced is by and large the result of market choices by individuals. These choices are influenced by the relative prices of competing goods. To the extent that these prices reflect the costs of producing the product involved, people get as near to what they want as is possible in a fallible world; but to the extent that these prices understate the actual cost to society of producing a product, more of that product gets made and bought (relative to other goods) than we in fact want, and unnecessary costs are undertaken. And finally, accident costs are as much costs to society and as worthy of being considered in deciding what goods we want as, say, the cost of the metal it takes to make a product. Specifically, the thesis holds that although, for instance, we may not want the *safest* possible product, we do want the manufacturer to choose a means of production which may be somewhat more expensive in terms of materials used if this expense is made up by savings in accident costs. Similarly, although we do not wish to abandon cars altogether (they give us more pleasure than they cost us— despite accident costs), we may, if we are made to pay for car-caused accidents, drive less, or less at night, or less when we are of accident-prone ages, or with more safety devices, than if we are not made to pay for accident costs when we decide to use a car. I call this thesis general deterrence, because it seeks to diminish accident costs not by directly attacking specific occasions of danger, but (like workmen's compensation) by making more expensive those activities which are accident prone and thereby making more attractive their safer substitutes.

NOTES

1. This "general deterrence" theory, perhaps better described as "market deterrence", has been elaborated in several articles and finally in a book: Calabresi, *The Costs of Accidents* (1970). See infra, Chapter 15.

EHRENZWEIG, A PSYCHOANALYSIS OF NEGLIGENCE

(1953), 47 Nw. U.L. Rev. 855

THE FAULT RULE AND WHY WE CLING TO IT

Deterrence of other potential wrongdoers and the convicted wrongdoer's admonition are the accepted purposes of all sanction of blame-worthy conduct. Neither purpose can be used to rationalize our insistence on the fault rule.

As late as 1898 an English judge considered deterrence as the purpose of all legal sanctions and later yet an Austrian scholar called it "the signature of law in all fields". But, while deterrence would, indeed, presuppose a "wrongdoer's" fault at least in the eyes of those to be deterred, it cannot support a fault liability of lawful enterprise. Clearly, imposition of liability on the manufacturer for harm caused by his defective merchandise to the ultimate consumer despite all possible caution, is not designed to deter him or others from operations otherwise so effectively encouraged by society. Nor can, realistically, a higher premium he might become obligated to pay in consequence of greater losses, cause him to exercise greater care. Similar often repeated arguments for the retention of the fault rule in the adjustment of automobile losses have been repeatedly disproved. Indeed, deterrence and reformation, "the reasons usually given to justify punishment do not explain why it exists. They serve only to conceal the truth, that the scheme of punishment is a barbaric system of revenge, by which society tries to 'get even' with the criminal". And it is this barbaric system of revenge, in its more refined form of retaliation, which lies at the root of our fault rule. . . .

In addition to an irrational desire for relief from guilt feelings attending all coercive aggression, conceivably another factor may account in part for the fact that American society not only tolerates but seems anxious to preserve a situation in which popular confidence in the law itself is being sacrificed to the idol of fault as a sole or primary basis of all civil liability. Ruth Eisler in a captivating analysis of numerous individual cases has shown how purportedly solicitous parents have often, subconsciously but all-too-effectively, acted out their desire to see their children delinquent by a strange masochistic mechanism of self-punishment. It may not be too far-fetched to assume that the same self-punishing tendency underlies the toleration and promotion by the law of a chaos necessarily apt to undermine the very authority on which it is based. A maturing society will have to replace this fault formula by one less burdened with pseudo-moral considerations and more responsive to present needs, however devoid the new formula should prove of emotional satisfaction.

NOTES

1. See also Ehrenzweig, *Psychoanalytic Jurisprudence* (1971), at pp. 242 *et seq.*

ATIYAH, ACCIDENTS, COMPENSATION AND THE LAW
(2nd ed., 1975)

Certainly we could hardly remain satisfied indefintely with a system which regarded retribution as a legitimate purpose if we were satisfied that the public desire for it, even if demonstrated to exist, was always wrong in itself. But it is perhaps doubtful if we need go as far as this. Retribution in the law of torts is on a modest scale. We do not demand (or if we do, we certainly do not get) retribution by way of capital punishment, flogging or even imprisonment. Retribution here is on the prosaic level of hurting people by depriving them of some money; moreover the pain or penalty is not wholly gratuitous since— though this is not the object of the exercise — the receipt of the money by the injured party is no doubt always welcome enough. If this sometimes satisfies a desire for vengeance—a desire which if unsatisfied might lead to personal vengeance—must it always be condemned as wrong? The question is made more difficult by the fact that the desire for retribution cannot always or perhaps often, be separated from a less ignoble desire, namely that for public satisfaction and vindication.

When a person is involved in a dispute with another who he thinks has done wrong, and when that other refuses to admit that he has done wrong (and sometimes even when he does admit it), it may be a great satisfaction to the former to know that he has the right to summon the latter before one of Her Majesty's judges for a public confrontation in which the latter may be branded as in the wrong. This desire is probably compounded of many things. There is the desire for an 'official' decision to settle a dispute or an argument, a decision which will finally put an end to excuses, evasions and discussion. This sort of desire sometimes extends to the public at large who may have an interest in knowing the answer to certain questions of public import. Frequently this demand is met by setting up public inquiries of one kind or another. . . .

This sort of inquiry, it will be noted, is not a decision-making body. Its objects are merely to ascertain facts and, sometimes, to ascribe responsibility for them. It does not award damages or grant any other legal remedy, though doubtless its findings would usually be accepted for the purposes of negotiating a settlement of claims arising from the facts inquired into. But it is plain that this is not always felt to be a necessary adjunct of the process. The desire for the public confrontation, the opportunity to state one's case in public before impartial judges, the desire for a public judgment in which one is vindicated and another person condemned, all this is often sufficient in itself. And it may well be that if the tort system were eventually merged into the social security system there would be a greater need for public inquiries of this kind.

I indicated earlier that there are many situations in which this desire obviously goes hand in hand with the desire for retribution, and indeed it is often hard to separate the two. A person wants public vindication in order that he may have the satisfaction of public and official support, while his opponent has the hurt of being publicly condemned. How far, then, do these desires get satisfied by the compensation systems operating today? The answer is that in general there is not a great deal of scope in the law today for satisfying the desire for retribution or vindication, except by means of the criminal law and the sort of public inquiry we have just mentioned. Civil systems of compensation, personal insurance, the social security system and even the Criminal Injuries Compensation Board have really nothing to offer in the way of retribution and satisfaction. The compensation in these cases is sought from and paid by persons who are in no way responsible for the plaintiff's suffering or loss. The process is largely administrative, and even in the case of the Criminal Injuries Tribunal which is semi-judicial in procedure, the hearings are in private and the wrongdoer is not present.

The tort system may occasionally have something to offer the desire for retribution or vindication. The occasional award of damages against a bully or thug who has beaten up the plaintiff, even a mere finding of negligence on a long-controverted and important issue, may sometimes satisfy these desires. But we have already seen how, in the great majority of cases the 'real' defendant in a tort action is purely a financial body—someone who holds the purse strings out of which a judgment may be satisfied. It is possible that an injured pedestrian still gets a real satisfaction (quite apart from the compensation awarded to him) in hearing a judge in open court publicly absolve him from blame for his own injuries, and place that blame on some motorist, even though the motorist will not have to pay the damages and is unlikely to be in court. But even if this does sometimes happen, the law does not set a very high store by it, as is apparent from the fact that an injured plaintiff is not entitled to pursue this desire *at the cost of the defendant*. If the defendant offers sufficient compensation to the plaintiff by way of settlement of the claim, a plaintiff who rejects the offer and insists on his day in court, not because he finds the offer insufficient, but simply because of his desire for public satisfaction or vindication, will, in the majority of cases have to pay for this privilege. Nevertheless, it must be conceded that tort law does here have something of great value which other compensation systems do not have.

GLANVILLE WILLIAMS, THE AIMS OF THE LAW OF TORT

(1951), Current Legal Problems 137

An intelligent approach to the study of law must take account of its purpose, and must be prepared to test the law critically in the light of its purpose. The question that I shall propound is the end or social function or *raison d'être* of the law of tort, and particularly of the action in tort for damages.

It is commonly said that the civil action for damages aims at compensation, as opposed to the criminal prosecution which aims at punishment. This, however, does not look below the surface of things. Granted that the immediate object of the tort action is to compensate the plaintiff at the expense of the tortfeasor, why do we wish to do this? Is it to restore the *status quo ante?*—but if so, why do we want to restore the *status quo ante?* And could not we restore this *status* in some other and better way, for instance by a system of national insurance? Or is it really that we want to deter people from committing torts? Or, again, is it that the payment of compensation is regarded as educational, or as a kind of expiation for a wrong?

An inquiry of this nature is familiar in criminal law. Every lawyer knows the various theories of criminal punishment: propitiation of the victim, expiation, deterrence, incapacitation, reform. The question is whether any of these interpretations fits the sanction in tort, and if not whether there is some other that does so. In asking this question we must be prepared to find that there is no simple answer. No one theory adequately explains the whole of the criminal law, and it may be that the law of tort, also, refuses to open to a single key. Then again, we must bear in mind that any inquiry into the social justification of the law of tort is really three inquiries: a doctrinal inquiry, what purpose the law of tort has been commonly thought to serve, a sociological inquiry, what purpose it does in fact serve, and a philosophical inquiry, what purpose we ourselves think it ought to serve. It is possible for a rule to be designed to do one thing and in fact to do another, and we may think it ought to do something different from both. It is also possible for different rules of the law of tort to have different justifications. Thus there may be a difference between torts to the person and torts to property, or between intentional and negligent torts.

THE FOUR POSSIBLE BASES OF THE ACTION FOR DAMAGES IN TORT

There are four possible bases of the action for damages in tort: appeasement, justice, deterrence and compensation.

Appeasement. —Crime and tort have common historical roots. The object of early law is to prevent the disruption of society by disputes arising from the infliction of injury. Primitive law looks not so much to preventing crime in general as to preventing the continuance of this squabble in particular. The victim's vengeance is bought off by compensation, which gives him satisfaction in two ways: he is comforted to receive the money himself, and he is pleased that the aggressor is discomfited by being made to pay. By this means the victim is induced to 'let off steam' within the law rather than outside it.

In modern times the safety-valve function of the law of tort probably takes a subordinate place. We do not reckon on the recrudescence of family feuds as a serious possibility, or even that of duelling. However, it may be thought that unredressed torts would be a canker in society, and to that extent the law can still be regarded as having a pacificatory aim. . . .

Justice.—With the growth of moral ideas it came to be thought that the law of tort was the expression of a moral principle. One who by his fault has caused damage to another ought as a matter of justice to make compensation. Two variants of this theory may be perceived: (1) The first places emphasis upon the fact that the payment of compensation is an evil for the offender, and declares that justice requires that he should suffer this evil. This is the principal of ethical retribution, exemplified (in criminal law) by Kant's dictum about the moral necessity of executing even the last murderer. (2) The second variant looks at the same situation from the point of view of the victim; it emphasises the fact that the payment of compensation is a benefit to the victim of the wrong, and declares that justice requires that he should receive this compensation. We may call this ethical compensation.

It may be thought that these two variants are simply two different ways of stating the same thing, but that is not entirely true. (1) Many people who would not subscribe generally to the principle of ethical retribution would nevertheless assert the principle of ethical compensation. The principle of ethical retribution goes much beyond anything needed to justify the law of tort, because it requires the wrongdoer to be punished generally. Making him pay compensation is only one form of punishment. It is quite possible to take the view that the wrongdoer ought to make amends without thinking that he ought to suffer in any other way. Again, (2) one who asserts the principle of ethical compensation does not necessarily say that the wrongdoer must himself be afflicted. If no one else will pay the compensation, the wrongdoer must; but if someone (such as the State or an insurance company) steps in and pays for him, the requirement of recuperation is satisfied even though there is no ethical retribution against the offender.

Those who adopt the doctrine of ethical retribution do not, and cannot, refer it to any other principle. It is a postulate—an ultimate value-judgment which can only be accepted or rejected. Those who reject it include the utilitarians, many Christians (I should like to call them the true Christians), the determinists, and the psychologists (who have a shrewd idea that our notion of vindictive justice has a very earthly origin).

The case is far different with ethical compensation. This does serve a social purpose, independently of any doctrine of punishment or (for the matter of that) of deterrence. Imagine a small community of comparatively moral people who hardly need a deterrent legal system but who do occasionally commit acts of negligence or even of unruly temper. Even such a community would find educational value in a rule requiring the making of reparation for harm caused by fault. Whereas people do not voluntarily accept punishment for themselves (except for religious reasons by way of penance), good people do accept for themselves the necessity of paying compensation for harm that they have caused. It is not a question of punishment, but of showing in a practical way one's solicitude and contrition, and of obeying the golden rule that we should do as we would be done by.

The existence within us of the sentiment of justice pre-supposed by this theory can easily be shown by an example. Suppose that you have borrowed a friend's book and lost it. As a conscientious person you will naturally wish to replace the book. It is not a question of intimidating yourself from losing books in future, but merely of doing the decent thing. (In fact, you will want to replace the book even though the loss occurred without your negligence, though the law says that you are liable only in the event of negligence.)

It is even held by some that the notion of rightness in this respect takes no account of the fact that money may have different values for the wrongdoer and the victim. In de Maupassant's story of the necklace, the poor Loisels replace for their rich friend her necklace that they have lost, though they have to drudge for ten years to make up the sum they think it is worth. Replacement is a point of honour with them, even though the burden of replacement is heavy beyond all comparison with the pleasure that it gives to the recipient. . . .

Deterrence.—Ranged against the theory of tort as part of the moral order are those who believe that it is merely a regime of prevention. The action in tort is a 'judicial parable', designed to control the future conduct of the community in general. In England this view seems to have been first expounded by Bentham. Blackstone had expressed the opinion that civil injuries are 'immaterial to the public', but Bentham thought that such a contrast with criminal law could not be maintained, and that the underlying object of civil and criminal law was the same. Both criminal punishment and tort damages were sanctions and therefore evils: the only difference was in the degree of evil. The purpose of threatening them was to secure obedience to rules. Austin followed Bentham in this. The proximate end of the civil sanction, said Austin, is redress to the injured party; but its remote and paramount end is the same as that of the criminal sanction: the prevention of offences generally. Salmond adopted the same opinion. 'Pecuniary compensation', he wrote, 'is not in itself the ultimate object or a sufficient justification of legal liability. It is simply the instrument by which the law fulfils its purpose of penal coercion.'

The most vigorous exponent of the view in modern times is the Swedish jurist Lundstedt. According to him, the justification for the existence of civil law, like criminal law, is not morality but the fact that it is absolutely necessary for the existence of the community. Its object is to create a sense of safety and security, and this it does in two ways: first and foremost, by deterring from injurious and (from the point of view of the public benefit) useless acts, *i.e.*, by preventing these acts through its psychological effect on the prospective wrongdoer; and, secondly, by promising the injured party that he shall or probably will receive damages in reparation if the legal prohibition is ignored. Lawyers tend to focus their attention on the second—the reparative—aspect of the law of contract and tort; but in Lundstedt's view the more important social function is the first, the preventive. 'One stares one's eyes out at the *relatively rare* cases where injury really has been done, but forgets the infintely greater number of cases in which injury *has not been done* owing to the fact that a social order—including, among other things, criminal law and the law of torts— is operative.' Lundstedt points out that if, as is sometimes supposed, the community were naturally 'law-abiding' as a general rule independently of law, and the law of tort existed simply to impose liability for damage in the rare case where such damage was caused, it would be doubtful whether the usefulness of the law could counterbalance the disadvantage of the economic burden on the community involved in its maintenance. The truth is, he says, that 'law-abidingness' springs from the maintenance of law, and it is in the creation of this law-abidingness that civil law, like criminal law, finds its primary justification.

Lundstedt denies that there is necessarily a moral basis for the law of tort, even where liability is confined to cases of *culpa.* He seeks to prove his denial by an example. 'Through the negligence of a poor man a millionaire has suffered damage estimated at £500. Surely it would not be in accordance with the sentiment of justice that the poor man should eventually be forced to beg for his living in order that the millionaire might obtain his "satisfaction"?' In Lundstedt's opinion, not only is such a transfer unjust; it is, if regarded in isolation, socially undesirable. Only by taking a broad view can we discover it to be for the public good to maintain, without exception, a rule whereby damage ought regularly to be so transferred. . . .

Whatever the imperfections of the moral interpretation of tort, the deterrent theory itself fails to provide a perfect rationale. For one thing, it offends against the principle that deterrent punishment must be kept to the effective minimum. According to utilitarian philosophy, of which the deterrent theory is an application, a punishment must not be greater than is necessary to repress the mischief in question. Damages in tort, however, may be far greater than are needful as a warning. If, in a moment of rage, I assault a film actor and unluckily spoil his looks, so that he is compelled thereafter to confine himself to broadcast drama, I am liable for damages based on his loss of earnings, which may be enormous; yet in a criminal court the same assault may be thought deserving only of a fine of £50. If a fine of £50 is sufficient to deter me and others from such assaults in future, the film actor's damages of say £50,000 cannot be justified from the point of view merely of deterrence. They can, however, be defended by reference to a principle of justice which says that since his loss of salary must be borne by him or me, in all the circumstances it is more just that I should bear it than he. This objection to the deterrent theory is not necessarily an out-and-out refutation of it, but at least shows that the theory, like the ethical one, does not explain the whole of the law.

Looked at as a deterrent system, tort can be regarded as lagging far behind the law of crime. In criminal law we have learnt the necessity of individualising punishment, and even, in many cases, of refraining from punishment altogether; but tort still imposes an arbitrary, mechanical forfeiture. Tort still seeks 'the object all sublime—to make the punishment fit the crime' (or rather, the fortuitous result of the crime), when the criminal law is giving up the effort to do so. In general, tort does not even care about the degree of the offender's fault. For instance, in criminal law the punishment for an intentional crime is generally more severe than for a negligent crime, because a more severe sanction is thought to be necessary by way of example; yet in tort the measure of damages is almost the same whether the tort was intentional or negligent. All the objections to the criminal fine—that it is ineffective or harmful as applied to poor persons, that by impoverishing it may drive to further offences, and that it falls upon the offender's family as much as or more than it falls upon himself—apply with even greater force to tort damages, for (speaking generally) the amount of these damages is not under the control of the tribunal. Regarded merely as a deterrent system, the law of tort is nothing more than a crude rule of thumb, for the sanction will almost certainly be either too great or too little in any particular case.

Damages are particularly ineffective against poor persons, and for wrongs of acquisitiveness. A thief or cheat could do good business if he merely had to restore his gains on the occasions when he was found out. For torts of damage or destruction, however, the deterrent effect of damages may be considerable. Again, the civil indemnity is generally limited to cases where damage has been caused: it is inapplicable, for instance, to careless driving where no one is injured. On the other hand, the civil sanction is frequently more efficient than the criminal one in that there is a stronger inducement to sue than to prosecute. It also has the advantage that it may be settled without action; every criminal charge must go through the court. In some instances the admonitory effect of a money judgment is increased by the award of punitive damages. If we look from deterrence to prevention in general, it is arguable that compensation payable to the injured party is educationally superior to a fine: it teaches a moral lesson.

To say that the goal of the law of tort is deterrence (if that is true) is not the same as saying that it actually does deter. No one that I know of has investigated by mass observation or psycho-analysis or statistics whether it fulfils this function. On the face of things, for instance, it seems unlikely that the tort of enticement is responsible for the comparatively small number of 'eternal triangles' in society; other causes could be named that are probably far more important. However, this absence of experimental proof has been almost as true for the criminal law as for the law of tort. The sanctions of the criminal law were imposed on the assumption that they would repress crime, long before scientific methods of sociological investigation were thought of. In the case of some of them there is grave doubt whether they do in fact deter, or whether a less severe punishment might not have the same salutary effect. This doubt does not detract from the fact that the aim of the criminal legislator, however clumsy the means he uses, is to prevent crime. Moreover, most lawyers would be ready to affirm (even though it is only a guess on their part) that both the law of crime and the law of tort do actually deter in a large number of cases. For instance, employers now take many precautions for the safety of their employees that they did not take before the Factory Acts and similar legislation created criminal and civil sanctions for lack of such precautions. It is true that the civil sanction can be insured against, but an employer with a high accident ratio is not likely to get favourable terms from his insurers. Again, it is probable that the publicity accorded to libel suits, and the high damages awarded, have had the result of making some people careful in making statements about others; in fact the cramping effect of the libel law upon freedom of discussion has been made, rightly or wrongly, the subject of complaint. There are probably many owners of dangerous structures who have spent money in putting them safe because of the fear of actions for damages, or because it was only upon those terms that they could get insurance against liability. There are probably many business men who have been restrained from passing off their goods as other people's because of fear of the law of tort. The law is particularly effective when it can be expounded in advance in a solicitor's letter, the prospective victim having had notice of the other's intentions, or the tort being a continuing one. Probably the law of tort is least successful in checking casual acts of inadvertent negligence.

Realisation of the preventive role of tort has led to various proposals for the extension of the law. Thus, it has been suggested that there would be an increase of road safety if highway authorities were made liable for accidents resulting from their omission to repair highways. Judges have created the tort of breach of statutory duty partly because they have thought the criminal sanction provided by the statute to be insufficient. When the question recently arose whether employers' liability in tort should be wholly replaced by State insurance, the argument was advanced that the common-law remedy tended to make employers more vigilant for the safety of their employees. The same idea is at the back of the legislative maxim that a mischief should not be made a crime if the civil sanction is sufficient.

If the deterrent theory of tort is right, and even if deterrence is a mere by-product of compensation, the current definition of crime as a wrong resulting in punishment fails to define. Tort also, on this supposition, is a wrong resulting in punishment, for damages are punishment. A more careful definition of crime then becomes necessary if it is to be kept separate from the law of tort.

Compensation.—Finally there is the compensatory or reparative theory, according to which one who has caused injury to another must make good the damage whether he was at fault or not. This is the same as the theory of ethical compensation except that it does not require culpability on the part of the defendant. If valid, it justifies strict liability, which the theory of ethical compensation does not. The difficulty is, however, to state it in such a form as to make it acceptable. If it is said that a person who has been damaged by another ought to be compensated, we readily assent, moved as we are by sympathy for the victim's loss. But what has to be shown is not merely that the sufferer ought to be compensated, but that he ought to be compensated by the defendant. In the absence of any moral blame of the defendant, how is this demonstration possible?

It is fashionable to say that the question is simply one of who ought to bear the risk. This, however, is a restatement of the problem rather than a solution of it. A more satisfactory version is that known as the *entrepreneur* theory or, to speak English, the enterprise theory. This regards liability for torts connected with an enterprise as a normal business expense. Nothing can be undertaken without some risk of damage to others, and if the risk eventuates it must be shouldered by the undertaker in the same way as the cost of his raw materials. That this attitude has come into prominence in the present century, though not unknown in the last, is symptomatic of the general search for security at the cost, if need be, of freedom of enterprise. It would not have appealed to philosophers of the individualist school of the last century. Sidgwick, for example, wrote: 'It is fundamentally important for the general happiness of any society that its members should be acting strenuously and energetically in some way or other; and it would too seriously interfere with this to lay down the broad rule "that every man acts at his peril", and is responsible for any mischief that may result.' From this it looks as though the cry 'no liability without fault' comes from those who wish to maximise the national income, while the present apothesis of strict liability is the result of a majority preference for security and broad equality, even if this means some stifling of progress. However, the actual rules of strict liability are so haphazard that they can hardly be fitted into any rational pattern. If the enterprise theory were consistently applied it would result in strict liability in respect of all acts done in the course of manufacture or business; but, in fact, the law does not go so far as this.

ANDENAES, THE GENERAL PREVENTIVE EFFECTS OF PUNISHMENT

(1966), 114 U. Pa. L. Rev. 949

1. THE CONCEPT OF GENERAL PREVENTION

In continental theories of criminal law, a basic distinction is made between the effects of punishment on the man being punished—individual prevention or special prevention—and the effects of punishment upon the members of society in general—general prevention. The characteristics of special prevention are termed "deterrence," "reformation" and "incapacitation," and these terms have meanings similar to their meanings in the English speaking world. General prevention, on the other hand, may be described as the *restraining influences emanating from the criminal law and the legal machinery.*

By means of the criminal law, and by means of specific applications of this law, "messages" are sent to members of a society. The criminal law lists those actions which are liable to prosecution, and it specifies the penalties involved. The decisions of the courts and actions by the police and prison officials transmit knowledge about the law, underlining the fact that criminal laws are not mere empty threats, and providing detailed information as to what kind of penalty might be expected for violations of specific laws. To the extent that these stimuli restrain citizens from socially undesired actions which they might otherwise have committed, a general preventive effect is secured. While the effects of special prevention depend upon how the law is implemented in each individual case, general prevention occurs as a result of an interplay between the provisions of the law and its enforcement in specific cases. In former times, emphasis was often placed on the physical exhibition of punishment as a deterrent influence, for example, by performing executions in public. Today it is customary to emphasize the *threat* of punishment as such. From this point of view the significance of the individual sentence and the execution of it lies in the support that these actions give to the law. It may be that some people are not particularly sensitive to an abstract threat of penalty, and that these persons can be motivated toward conformity only if the penalties can be demonstrated in concrete sentences which they feel relevant to their own life situations.

The effect of the criminal law and its enforcement may be *mere deterrence*. Because of the hazards involved, a person who contemplates a punishable offense might not act. But it is not correct to regard general prevention and deterrence as one and the same thing. The concept of general prevention also includes the *moral* or *socio-pedagogical* influence of punishment. The "messages" sent by law and the legal processes contain factual information about what would be risked by disobedience, but they also contain proclamations specifying that it is *wrong* to disobey. Some authors extend the concept of deterrence so that it includes the moral influences of the law and is, thus, synonymous with general prevention. In this article, however, the term deterrence is used in the more restrictive sense.

The moral influence of the criminal law may take various forms. It seems to be quite generally accepted among the members of society that the law should be obeyed even though one is dissatisfied with it and wants it changed. If this is true, we may conclude that the law as an institution itself to some extent creates conformity. But more important than this formal respect for the law is respect for the values which the law seeks to protect. It may be said that from law and the legal machinery there emanates a flow of propaganda which favors such respect. Punishment is a means of expressing social disapproval. In this way the criminal law and its enforcement supplement and enhance the moral influence acquired through education and other non-legal processes. Stated negatively, the penalty neutralizes the demoralizing consequences that arise when people witness crimes being perpetrated.

Deterrence and moral influence may both operate on the conscious level. The potential criminal may deliberate about the hazards involved, or he may be influenced by a conscious desire to behave lawfully. However, with fear or moral influence as an intermediate link, it is possible to create unconscious inhibitions against crime, and perhaps to establish a condition of habitual lawfulness. In this case, illegal actions will not present themselves consciously as real alternatives to conformity, even in situations where the potential criminal would run no risk whatsoever of being caught.

General preventive effects do not occur only among those who have been informed about penal provisions and their applications. Through a process of learning and social imitation, norms and taboos may be transmitted to persons who have no idea about their origins—in much the way that innovations in Parisian fashions appear in the clothing of country girls who have never heard of Dior or Lanvin.

Making a distinction between special prevention and general prevention is a useful way of calling attention to the importance of legal punishment in the lives of members of the general public, but the distinction is also to some extent am artificial one. The distinction is simple when one discusses the reformative and incapacitative effects of punishment on the individual criminal. But when one discusses the deterrent effects of punishment the distinction becomes less clear. Suppose a driver is fined ten dollars for disregarding the speed limit. He may be neither reformed nor incapacitated but he might, perhaps, drive more slowly in the future. His motivation in subsequent situations in which he is tempted to drive too rapidly will not differ fundamentally from that of a driver who has not been fined; in other words a general preventive effect will operate. But for the driver who has been fined, this motive has, perhaps, been strengthened by the recollection of his former unpleasant experience. We may say that a general preventive feature and special preventive feature here act together.

Let me hasten to point out here that so far I have only presented a kind of conceptual framework. Determination of the extent to which such general preventive effects exist, and location of the social conditions that are instrumental in creating them, are empirical problems which will be discussed in this paper.

NOTES

1. See also Packer, *The Limits of the Criminal Sanction* (1968):

"The existence of a 'threat' helps to create patterns of conforming behavior and thereby to reduce the number of occasions on which the choice of a criminal act presents itself. Every one of us is confronted daily by situations in which criminal behavior is a possible alternative. Sometimes the presentation is sufficiently vivid that we think about it and reject the criminal alternative. More frequently and more significantly, we automatically and without conscious cognition follow a pattern of learned behavior that excludes the criminal alternative without even thinking about it. Indeed, the arguments for the efficacy of deterrence may become stronger the more one departs from a rational free-will model and the more one accepts an unconsciously impelled, psychological determinism as an accurate description of human conduct. There seems to be a paradox in the rejection by some psychologists of the idea that the threat of punishment (itself reflecting a legal model) can induce people unconsciously to adopt patterns of law-abiding behavior. Guilt and punishment are, after all, what the superego is all about.

The socializing and habit-forming effects of the threat of punishment are not limited to simple, literal observation of threats being made and carried out. There is heavy symbolic significance in the operation of the criminal sanction; for the process of ascribing guilt, responsibility, and punishment goes on day after day against the background of all human history. The vocabulary of punishment (itself heavily influenced by legal concepts and models) with which we become acquainted beginning in early childhood impresses us—some more than others—with the gravity of antisocial conduct. The ritual of the criminal trial becomes for all of us a kind of psychodrama in which we participate vicariously, a morality play in which innocence is protected, injury requited, and the wrongdoer punished. It is not simply the threat of punishment or its actual imposition that contributes to the total deterrent effect but the entire criminal process, standing as a paradigm of good and evil, in which we are reminded by devices far more subtle than literal threats that the wicked do not flourish. These public rituals, it is plausible to suppose, strengthen the identification of the majority with a value-system that places a premium on law-abiding behavior."

2. See also Zimring and Hawkins, *Deterrence: The Legal Threat in Crime Control* (1973):

"It is possible to distinguish at least three aspects of the operation of punishment in this didactic or educative role. In the first place, to put it in very simple terms, the association of forbidden behavior and bad consequences may lead individuals to view the behavior itself as bad. Thus, knowledge that people who steal are treated badly would lead to the association of wrongfulness with stealing, and ultimately to the conclusion that stealing is wrong. This is the point that the Report of the Royal Commission on Capital Punishment makes when it suggests that the use of capital punishment in the past may have created 'a strong association between murder and the death penalty in the popular imagination'."

In the second place, punishment by a legal system will communicate to the individual that the legal system views the threatened behavior as wrong, and this information will also affect the moral attitudes of the individual. The internal reasoning would go: 'The institutions I respect view this behavior as wrong; therefore, I should consider this behavior wrong.'

For it is a mistake to think that the only sort of respect inspired by the criminal law is that which is implied in the concept of mere deterrence. The criminal law is more than a neutral system of compulsion; respect for legal authority is different from mere response to threats. To ignore this confuses authority with coercive power. Although coercive power may sometimes be a necessary condition for the exercise of authority and for securing obedience, respect for authority depends on recognition of its legitimacy.

It is not necessary to consider here the various principles of legitimacy upon which authority is said to depend, nor to discuss their sociological and ideological bases. It is sufficient to note that in any society, if it is to continue in existence, there must be a general acceptance of authoritative regulation as a means of achieving social control. This affirmative attitude toward obedience to rules may be a more powerful factor than the fear of punishment in securing conformity. Moreover, the respect, or deference, which the law attracts makes it possible for the law to exercise a socializing influence by securing society's acceptance of rules and regulations in areas where custom, tradition, morality, or religion provide no final guidance. . . .

In the third place, threat and punishment may aid moral education by serving as an attention-getting or attention-focusing mechanism. The threat of punishment for stealing forces the individual to think about the moral nature of stealing. Such reflections might lead to the conclusion that stealing is wrong because it causes other people to suffer and underlines the security of a system of private property. In this last aspect, which Professor Andenaes calls 'punishment as an eye-opener', the threat of punishment provides only the occasion for reflection rather than any substantial moral precept."

3. Can tort law also serve as an "eye-opener"? See also Andenaes, "The Moral or Educative Influence of Criminal Law" (1971), J. Soc. Issues 17; Andenaes, "Deterrence and Specific Offences" (1971), 38 U. Chi. L. Rev. 537; Hawkins, "Punishment and Deterrence: The Educative, Moralizing and Habituative Effects", [1969] Wisc. L. Rev. 550; Thurman Arnold, "The Criminal Trial as a Symbol of Public Morality" in *Criminal Justice in Our Time* (1965, Howard ed.), at p. 141. Does the existence of liability insurance eliminate this as a possible function of tort law?

4. In *Rookes* v. *Barnard*, [1964] A.C. 1129, at p. 1227, Lord Devlin asserted that "it is necessary to teach a wrongdoer that tort does not pay".

5. Chief Justice Holt once declared, in *Ashby* v. *White* (1703), 2 Ld. Raym. 956, "Damages are designed not only as a satisfaction to the injured person, but likewise as a punishment to the guilty, to deter from any such proceeding for the future, and as a proof of the detestation of the jury to the action itself."

6. See generally Stoll, "Penal Purposes in the Law of Torts" (1970), 18 Am. J. Comp. L. 3; Jorgensen, "The Decline and Fall of the Law of Torts" (1970), 18 Am. J. Comp. L. 39; Hall, "Interrelations of Crime and Tort" (1943), 43 Colum. L. Rev. 753 and 967.

LINDEN, TORT LAW AS OMBUDSMAN

(1973), 51 Can. Bar Rev. 155

Introduction

These are turbulent times. People everywhere are refusing to submit docilely to the rule of distant bureaucrats and managers. Because of a longing for more control over their own lives citizens are demanding that governmental institutions and private organizations be more responsive to their wishes. Undoubtedly this struggle will continue during the coming decades and may well intensify.

Many techniques are being employed to render institutions more considerate of human needs. One weapon Canadians have deployed effectively is the vote; in the last few years, eight provincial governments have been turned out of office and the federal government has been severely rebuked. Citizen groups have sprung up everywhere and, on occasion, as in the Spadina Expressway battle, have met with astonishing success. Protest marches, consumer boycotts, mass meetings and publicity campaigns are being used to pressure mass institutions into being more attuned to the aspirations of ordinary people.

To assuage this insatiable appetite for justice, some modern governments have turned to an old Swedish institution—the ombudsman. The five provinces of Nova Scotia, New Brunswick, Quebec, Manitoba and Alberta have already established such an office, and the federal government is considering following suit. The primary function of the ombudsman is to protect ordinary people from the abuse of governmental power. An individual who feels ill-treated by some government department may complain to the ombudsman, who may investigate his complaint and suggest a remedy, if that is warranted. This is a useful instrument for supervising governmental activity, one that deserves our support. One problem with it, however, is that, like all bureaucracies, it will eventually become overworked and insensitive. Another shortcoming of the ombudsman is its unavailability as a check on private power.

There is no need to despair, however, because tort law may serve society in much the same way as an ombudsman. In fact, tort law may sometimes be more effective in this watchdog role than the ombudsman. The resources available to tort law are almost limitless, for every court and lawyer in the land may be called upon to participate in this noble work. Moreover, tort law may be used against private as well as public institutions.

Despite this, some authors are singing a requiem for tort law. They allege that it is obsolescent. Social insurance, they claim, can provide swifter, more efficient and more universal coverage for those who are injured as a result of the inevitable accidents of the industrial world. They denigrate the deterrent force of tort law and suggest that the abuse of power should be curbed by criminal law and administrative regulations. They contend that, because insurance covers most of these activities, there is rarely any sting left in tort liability.

It is true that the compensation function of tort law is waning in importance. New social welfare schemes are gradually rendering superfluous the need for tort reparation, at least for economic losses. Criminal and administrative law *can* curb deviant conduct more effectively than civil sanctions. Widespread insurance *does* diminish the deterrent force of civil liability. However, this does not necessarily doom tort law to extinction.

The law of torts may still serve in the years ahead as an instrument of social pressure upon centres of governmental, financial and intellectual power. The financial damages awarded against transgressors are no longer the only deterrent. Bad publicity may be more important. When a tort suit is launched, the glare of publicity may be focused upon it. The officials of the defendant government or company are drawn into the litigation. They are publicly under attack and are required to justify their conduct and their methods of operation to the judge and the jury. This can have a salutary effect, even though the amount of damages they must actually pay is insignificant.

1. *The Tort Action and the Publicity Sanction*

By means of a tort suit, an injured individual may be able to direct unfavourable publicity against a tort feasor. The use of this publicity sanction may have three effects. First, the adverse publicity can cost the defendant money. The amount involved may be far in excess of any possible damage award. For example, when Coca-cola is sued as a result of an exploding Coke bottle, this fact may be broadcast to millions of potential customers, some of whom may switch to Pepsi-cola or orange juice. Sales of Coke and other soft drinks will shrink and profits may sink. Even if the impact of this unfavourable publicity is only temporary, the cost to the company can be substantial. When Air Canada is sued because of an air crash, some passengers may choose to travel on other airlines or go by train. When an action is launched against a particular doctor or hospital, some patients may turn to other doctors or hospitals for their medical care.

Another way in which negative publicity causes financial loss is through diminution in the value of corporate shares. For example, when Richardson-Merrell, the producer of thalidomide and Mer/29, was sued by hundreds of people injured by these products, the value of its stock, which had been selling at twenty-five to thirty-five times its earnings, plunged to fifteen to twenty times its earnings. In other words, the paper value of the shares fell to almost half. The shareholders suffered enormous financial losses, largely because investors feared that the numerous law suits against the company might bankrupt it. Actually, these law suits hardly impaired the financial security of the company. Indeed, some stockbrokers, at the height of the scare, were suggesting to their clients that they would be wise to buy Richardson-Merrell stocks at the abnormally low prices.

The second effect of the publicity sanction is that it brings about a loss of prestige. Of course, this may also result in monetary loss, but it is important for its own sake. Even the managers of modern corporations are anxious to be held high in public esteem. They want to be proud of their company. Businesses spend millions on public relations campaigns to shine their corporate images. A much-publicized civil suit may tarnish a company's reputation for quality goods and service. It is, therefore, to be avoided at all costs. The repair of a damaged corporate reputation may require a great deal of money, time and effort, that might be used more profitably elsewhere.

Third, harmful publicity may also induce governmental intervention. This is something that most businesses and enterprises would prefer to avoid, if they possibly could. Nevertheless, if an action is brought against an organization engaged in some dangerous activity, the attention of governmental officials may be attracted to it. This may trigger a criminal prosecution or an administrative sanction. If the government agency has no authority to do anything, public opinion may be stirred up to such an extent that the politicians may be forced to enact new legislation to control the perceived abuse. Thus, a tort may lead to the creation of new regulatory schemes.

It is difficult to measure the power of the publicity sanction. It depends for its impact upon the reaction of individuals to information, something that is difficult to fathom. This is both a weakness and a strength. It is a weakness because there is no way of insuring that a tort suit will receive any media attention at all. In fact, most ordinary law suits do not attract any publicity. Moreover, the public may not think that the challenged conduct is very reprehensible. If this is the case, no one's conduct will be affected and public officials will not be spurred to action. Furthermore, some defendants, like a monopoly or a governmental agency, may be able to withstand some bad publicity, without being badly mauled. Other defendants may minimize the force of negative publicity by launching a counter-publicity campaign. Such a manoeuvre was employed by General Motors after the much-publicized United States Senate hearings about automobile safety in the mid-1960's. After it was shown how neglectful they were about auto safety, General Motors tried to convince the public, with their "Mark of Excellence" advertising, that their products were unimpeachable.

In some ways the indefinite nature of the publicity sanction may render it more powerful than a criminal prosecution or a civil suit. This is so because the amount of penal fines and damage awards are often easy to forecast, whereas the result of bad publicity is nearly impossible to prophesy. Some civil trials may drag on for weeks or even months under the glare of publicity. Newspapers, magazines, radio and television may give great coverage to the story. Politicians may be drawn into the fray. The defendant may be put out of business. It is no small wonder that corporate managers seem more concerned with the effect of negative publicity arising from law suits against them than they are about the actual penalties provided for by the law.

Perhaps the most advantageous aspect of the publicity sanction is that it is in the hands of ordinary citizens. It is both triggered by ordinary citizens and imposed by them. Thus anyone who feels injured by someone else may institute civil proceedings. He does not have to wait for some prosecutor or civil servant to take up his cause. Too often such public servants are reluctant to move. They may have only limited resources at their command. Politics may be involved. An aggrieved individual, however, labours under no such burden; he can unilaterally commence proceedings at any time, even if his case is by no means iron-clad.

Because of the ease with which civil litigation may be started, there is a danger of unfounded legal attacks upon innocent defendants. This hazard is minimized in several ways. First, totally unfounded actions may be struck out at the pleading stage. Moreover, an action properly pleaded may be dismissed at the trial before the defendant actually has to call evidence, if the plaintiff's evidence does not support the facts he has pleaded. Second, the technique of awarding costs against the losing side in litigation is a deterrent to spurious claims. Most claimants will not lightly undertake a law suit because, if they lose, it could cost them dearly. Third, the vexatious proceedings legislation may be used to deny access to the courts to some irresponsible persons. These measures do not remove the problem altogether, of course, but they do reduce it.

The application of the publicity sanction is also in the hands of ordinary citizens. Offenders are not jailed, nor do they lose their licences. If the people are repulsed by the conduct of the defendant they will change their purchasing habits and their attitudes. If they do not feel that anything seriously wrong has been done, they will not alter their conduct and the publicity sanction will be no sanction at all. . . .

Conclusion

Without doubt, this ombudsman role of tort law is a blunt and imperfect tool. Other weapons will also be needed to aid citizens in their struggle for more responsive institutions. But, however many governmental ombudsmen we appoint, however many criminal laws we pass, however many administrative regulations we enact, there will always remain grievances that are unresolved. The private tort suit is at the service of society as *one* way of rectifying some of these wrongs, or at least of exposing them to public view. Canadians would be wise to preserve the historic tort action as they may yet have need of it.

NOTES

1. See also Shapo, "Changing Frontiers in Torts: Vistas for the 70's" (1970),

22 Stan. L. Rev. 330: Rourke, "Law Enforcement Through Publicity" (1957), 24 U. Chi. L. Rev. 225; Fisse, "The Use of Publicity as a Criminal Sanction Against Business Corporations" (1971), 8 Melb. U.L. Rev. 107; Katz, "The Function of Tort Liability in Technology Assessment" (1969), 38 U. Cinc. L. Rev. 582, at p. 607; Sax, *Defending the Environment: A Strategy for Citizen Action* (1971). See generally, Linden, *Canadian Tort Law* (2nd ed., 1977), Chapter 1.

2. Professor Fridman in his book, *Introduction to the Law of Torts* (1978) expressed misgivings about tort law playing any role as Ombudsman:

"The actual, or potential growth in importance of these, and other torts, and the possibility of development of new forms of liability in the manner suggested earlier, has led one writer in Canada to put forward the idea that in the future the law of torts will play a new role. From having been the medium through which individuals obtained redress, in the form of damages, for wrongs suffered at the hands of others, the law of torts will become a tool for ensuring that those with various sorts of powers, whether arising at common law or under statute, and whether governmental, judicial, administrative, or otherwise, will not abuse those powers, and will be called to account if they do. In this way the law of torts will fulfill the role of an "ombudsman", that new-fangled inquisitor into the validity of official acts, spawned in Scandinavia but now to be found all over the world, designed originally for the supervision of civil servants and governments, but now found in other odd places, such as universities. This legitimate, or perhaps legitimized busybody may have a place in the scheme of state organization. To suggest that the law of torts should be made into his image, as it were, behave in accordance with the principles, and achieve the ends for which the ombudsman was invented, is a monstrous idea, which, it is hoped, will never be countenanced. There may be justification for the creation of an official, or an office, which is empowered and obliged to ensure that officials do not abuse their position or trust, and perform their tasks in the interests of the public whom they have been appointed to serve (which, it is suggested, indicates the unsuitability of such an office or official in other contexts, where the concept of appointment for the service of the public is alien, and those who govern, rule or regulate the particular group, organization or society do so under different auspices and for different purposes). This does not invite or necessitate the conclusion that such a role can and ought to be performed by a body of law, the law of torts, which emerged for totally different reasons, to serve utterly different purposes, and operates in a decidedly different fashion. The marriage of the "ombudsman concept" with the idea that misconduct which causes harm should give rise to a liability to compensate the victim by the payment of damages would be neither a marriage "made in heaven" nor a marriage of convenience. The law of torts is not independantly inquisitorial in character. It does not lend itself easily to the process of broad scale investigation into the validity or correctness of official or similar acts. If what the author of this proposition means is simply that the existence of the law of torts, the possibility that an abuse may give rise to liability to pay damages is something that may operate *in terrorem,* so as to keep officials and others from straying away from the path of valid, righteous conduct, then there can be no quarrel with his conception. Such has been the case for many centuries. There is nothing new in the idea that people's behaviour may be regulated and made to conform to reasonable standards, that the subjects of the law may be educated and led to the maintenance of what is required for civilized life to continue. If something more is inherent in the concept of the law of torts as ombudsman, however, then it is not possible to accept and accede to the suggestion."

Are Professor Fridman's criticisms well-founded, or does he misconceive the argument for tort law as an Ombudsman?

3. Professor Atiyah has also considered the potential of the role of tort law as an Ombudsman in *Accidents, Compensation and the Law* (2nd ed., 1975):

"The fact that any citizen has it in his power to initiate open and public discussion about the behaviour of another party by issuing a writ alleging negligence, and bringing him before the Courts, is an important consideration. Unfortunately, this power is clearly one which can lose in impact from over use, or use in everyday routine cases. It is a valuable power in rare cases, cases where it is desired, for example, to challenge some public authority or some large corporation over some aspect of its conduct. In this respect tort law has been likened to an ombudsman, and the analogy is apt. Examples of the use of tort law in this sort of way may be found in actions for negligence in respect of industrial disease where there is uncertainty about the medical causation of the disease; or in actions arising out of mass tragedies, such as the thalidomide affair, or some official action which it is desired to challenge, such as the policy of maintaining open Borstals. It does not follow that in cases of this nature it is desirable that the decision of the Courts should override that of public bodies; but the opportunity for a public airing of controversial issues is itself something of value. It is true that other similar procedures may sometimes be available if no action in negligence is possible. For example, public inquiries are often held under statutory powers into disasters in which people are injured or killed, such as aircraft or railway accidents. And of course there are the usual remedies open to any citizen who wishes to raise some issue, such as writing to his Member of Parliament in the hope of having the matter submitted to the real Ombudsman. But from the citizen's point of view, tort law has the inestimable advantage that the power of initiation lies with him, and that, if successful, he will be able to recover the costs of the proceedings. It would be strange if, at a time when the citizen's need for administrative remedies is more widely recognized than ever before, the disappearance of actions for negligence were to deprive him of this ombudsman-like weapon. The solution does not lie in the retention of the negligence action but in devising some new form of public inquiry in which the power of initiation—subject perhaps to some screening process—lies with the citizen and not some Minister. Something of this kind would seem to be an essential prerequisite of the abolition of actions for damages for negligence."

4. Professors Williams and Hepple have also dealt with this matter in *Foundations of the Law of Tort* (1976):

"It must be said, however, that an action in tort sometimes serves the valuable function of applying pressure on those in power to remedy a wrong. A recent example is the actions brought on behalf of the victims of the drug thalidomide. These actions dramatically brought to light the difficulties of proving negligence against the manufacturers of the drug and the disputed legal question whether a person can sue for damage done to him before his birth. The *Sunday Times* took a keen interest, and public pressure was aroused, so that the manufacturers—who had settled the claims of 65 victims for about £1m in 1968—were eventually compelled to set up a £20m trust fund for 410 children. The legal difficulties raised led the Lord Chancellor to ask the Law Commission to consider the question of antenatal injuries, and contributed to the Government's decision to set up a Royal Commission to investigate civil liability and compensation for personal injury. Attention was focused on the plight of other children with congenital disabilities, and, in addition to substantial subventions of taxpayers' money, a Minister for the Disabled was appointed in 1974. It is by no means certain that the same results would have occurred without a tort action to highlight the legal problems. . . .

Relatively few tort actions are capable of achieving this kind of publicity, and they are an expensive and indirect way of putting pressure on public authorities. Alternatives can be found through the development of administrative law. Examples are the Race Relations Act 1968 and the Sex Discrimination Act 1975. The former allows a person alleging that he has been the victim of racial discrimination to complain to a public body, the

Race Relations Board, which investigates the complaint and, if it finds a *prima facie* case of unlawful discrimination, attempts to conciliate and reach a settlement. If this fails the Board may institute civil proceedings against the respondent. This new kind of public law remedy which combines individual complaint with public enforcement provides a more effective means of combating racial discrimination than is possible through tort actions of the kind exemplified in *Constantine's* case. The Sex Discrimination Act gives a right of action to the individual but also allows the Equal Opportunities Commission to assist and represent complainants in appropriate cases, and itself to bring certain proceedings. This combination of the right of individual access to the courts with strategic functions assigned to a Commission responsible for enforcing the law in the public interest is an ambitious attempt to combine the virtues of tort and administrative law. The extension of public law remedies (such as *mandamus*) to enable individuals to compel public authorities to carry out their duties is another way in which a function imperfectly fulfilled by tort in the past could be given a new dimension.

Developments along these lines will reduce the importance of the law of tort and will in part replace it. But it is likely that the law of tort will retain residual importance for a long time to come, and there is no likelihood of intentional torts to the person being affected, particularly battery, wrongful interference and false imprisonment. A civil action for assault and battery at present provides a far better remedy than a criminal prosecution for assault, because the police are slow to interfere where serious injury is not caused, and magistrates also take a lenient view, whereas a civil action can give the complainant substantial damages. These torts to the person also serve the important public function of helping to control police powers, because the enforcement of the civil law is in no way in the hands of the police. Again, there is no reason to foresee the demise of the law of tort as a regulator of economic activity, for example in giving a remedy for negligent statements causing loss and for the passing off by the defendant of his products as the plaintiff's. Although, as already said, trade mark law now assists in giving this protection, products may be passed off without the infringement of a trade mark, and the tort remedy, which may lead to large damages, is far more efficacious than a prosecution for infringement of a trade mark. Again, the existence of administrative powers for the suppression of nuisances does not always mean that those powers will be effectively used, and the ability of the aggrieved citizen to bring proceedings himself is a valuable recourse. . . .

So, while we may see important advantages in superseding much of the law of tort, which may totally eliminate the tort action in accident cases, this will not represent the end of a body of law with a long tradition."

5. Is there a legitimate Ombudsman role for tort law to play in the Canada of the 1980's? How effective are the alternative techniques for social control? Does it depend on the type of activity being regulated?

6. Consider this observation in Linden, *Canadian Tort Law* (2nd ed., 1977):

"Like so many social institutions, tort law is being re-evaluated in the context of our times. It is assailed as a relic of a bygone age which has no purpose in contemporary society. If it is true that tort law no longer serves us, it should be buried along with the other fossils of the legal system. The mere assertion that tort law is useless, however, does not establish the truth of that indictment. There is a disturbing paucity of data relevant to the aims and efficacy of tort law. We are debating in the dark. What is more disconcerting is that we do not possess reliable techniques of measurement upon which to base valid conclusions. Unsubstantiated claims and counterclaims are no basis for rational choice. It may be that our society will ultimately choose to jettison tort law, but it should not be done until we have evaluated *all* of its benefits and *all* of its costs. It is too early for such a decision to be taken because our information is still fragmentary. We have barely begun to analyze the aims and functions of tort law. Empirical studies should be undertaken to measure the efficacy of tort law in achieving its goals. Only after these studies are concluded will we be able to make an informed decision about the destiny of tort law."

CHAPTER 2

INTENTIONAL INTERFERENCE WITH THE
PERSON AND PROPERTY

The idea of liability for the intentional infliction of injury to person or property seems quite simple. To be sure, it is one of the more settled and understandable areas of tort law. And yet it is not as easy as some textwriters and judges seem to indicate. There are occasions when courts "solve" novel problems by invoking a time-worn phrase, instead of applying themselves to a thorough study of the problem. Moreover, there is sometimes a failure to recognize the true nature of the interests being protected by tort law. Is this area of the law worth preserving in the world of the 1980's?

A. INTENT

WINFIELD AND JOLOWICZ ON TORT

(10th ed., 1975, Rogers)

To begin with, it is impossible for the law to do more than to infer a man's intention, or indeed any other mental state of his, from his conduct. The law may frequently attribute to him an intention which a metaphysician would at most consider very doubtful. Centuries ago, Brian C.J. said: "It is common knowledge that the thought of man shall not be tried, for the Devil himself knoweth not the thought of man." On the other hand, Bowen L.J. in 1885, had no doubt that "the state of a man's mind is as much a fact as the state of his digestion". There is no contradiction in these dicta. All that Brian C.J. meant was that no one can be perfectly certain of what passes in the mind of another person. But Brian would certainly not have dissented from the proposition that in law what a man thinks must be deduced from what he says and does; and that is all that Bowen L.J. meant.

GARRATT v. DAILEY

Supreme Court of Washington. (1955), 46 Wash. 2d 197; 279 P. 2d 1091

It was alleged that the defendant, aged 5 years, 9 months, pulled a lawn chair out from under the plaintiff as she was about to sit down on it. The trial judge dismissed the case, and the plaintiff appealed.

Hill J.: A battery would be established if it was proved that, when Brian moved the chair, he knew with substantial certainty that the plaintiff would attempt to sit down where the chair had been. . . . The mere absence of any intent to injure the plaintiff or to play a prank on her or to embarrass her, or to commit an assault and battery on her would not absolve him from liability if in fact he had such knowledge.

Case remanded for clarification.

NOTES

1. On the retrial, judgment was entered for the plaintiff, which decision was affirmed at (1956), 49 Wash. 2d 409, 304 P. 2d 681.

RESTATEMENT OF TORTS, SECOND

§8A. Intent

The word "intent" is used throughout the restatement of this Subject to denote that the actor desires to cause consequences of his act, or that he believes that the consequences are substantially certain to result from it.

Comment:

a. "Intent", as it is used throughout the *Restatement of Torts,* has reference to the consequences of an act rather than the act itself. When an actor fires a gun in the midst of the Mojave Desert, he intends to pull the trigger; but when the bullet hits a person who is present in the desert without the actor's knowledge, he does not intend that result. "Intent" is limited, wherever it is used, to the consequences of the act.

b. All consequences which the actor desires to bring about are intended, as the word is used in this *Restatement.* Intent is not, however, limited to consequences which are desired. If the actor knows that the consequences are certain, or substantially certain, to result from his act, and still goes ahead, he is treated by the law as if he had in fact desired to produce the result. As the probability that the consequences will follow decreases, and becomes less than substantial certainty, the actor's conduct loses the character of intent, and becomes mere recklessness. . . . As the probability decreases further, and amounts only to a risk that the result will follow, it becomes ordinary negligence. . . . All three have their important place in the law of torts, but the liability attached to them will differ.

NOTES

1. A throws a bomb into B's office for the purpose of killing B. A knows that C, B's stenographer, is in the office. A has no desire to injure C, but knows that his act is substantially certain to do so. C is injured by the explosion. Is A subject to liability to C for an intentional tort?

2. It is sometimes said that the intention here is "constructive" or that it has been "imputed" to the defendant.

CARNES v. THOMPSON

Supreme Court of Missouri. (1932), 48 S.W. 2d 903

Defendant attempted to evict from a house on his farm a former employee and his wife who had been living there. An argument developed, and defendant struck at the employee with a pair of pliers. The employee dodged the blow, and the defendant unintentionally hit the wife, who was standing near her husband. The wife brought an action, in which the jury returned a verdict for the plaintiff, finding no actual damages but $100 punitive damages. Defendant appeals.

Hyde C.: . . . Plaintiff's evidence, unquestionably, made a case for the jury. Defendant says that the evidence does not show that he at any time intended injury and harm to the plaintiff, and that he was never close enough to plaintiff's husband to strike him. However, plaintiff's evidence was sufficient to justify a finding that defendant struck at plaintiff's husband, in anger, with the pliers, and that, when he dodged the blow, plaintiff received it. If one person intentionally strikes at, throws at, or shoots at another, and unintentionally strikes a third person, he is not excused, on the ground that it was a mere accident, but it is an assault and battery of the third person. Defendant's intention, in such a case, is to strike an unlawful blow, to injure some person by his act, and it is not essential that the injury be to the one intended. . . .

NOTES

1. The doctrine of "transferred intent", depicted in the principal case, came to tort law from the criminal law. It is utilized not only where a different *person* is the victim of a particular nominate tort, but also where a different *tort* than the one intended results, as long as both torts are descendants of the old action of trespass. Thus, if the defendant intends to commit battery, assault, false imprisonment, trespass to land or trespass to chattels, he is liable for any of the others if they accidentally occur. See Prosser, "Transferred Intent" (1967), 45 Tex. L. Rev. 650; see also *Bunyan* v. *Jordan* (1937), 57 C.L.R. 1 (H.C. Aust.).

2. Donald shoots at Peter in order merely to frighten him. By accident, he hits Peter. What tort liability has arisen? What if Donald shoots at Peter in order to frighten him and he frightens a stranger, Paul? What if he shoots at Peter in order to frighten him and he hits the stranger, Paul?

SMITH v. STONE

King's Bench. (1647), Style 65; 82 E.R. 533

Smith brought an action of trespass against Stone, *pedibus ambulando*. The defendant pleads this special plea in justification, *viz.*, that he was carried upon the land of the plaintiff by force and violence of others, and was not there voluntarily, which is the same trespass for which the plaintiff brings his action. The plaintiff demurs to this plea. In this case, Rolle J. said that it is the trespass of the party that carried the defendant upon the land, and not the trespass of the defendant as he that drives my cattle into another man's land is the trespasser against him, and not I, who am owner of the cattle.

NOTES

1. What is the difference between voluntariness and intention? Is there such a thing as an intentional act that is not voluntary? Can voluntary conduct be unintentional?

2. Is it voluntary conduct if the defendant, while sleepwalking, enters another's property? See Fridman, "Mental Incompetency" (1964), 80 L.Q.R. 87.

3. The defendant, while asleep in the back of the plaintiff's car, pushed the driver's seat forward causing the plaintiff to lose control of the car. Liability? In *Stokes* v. *Carlson* (1951), 240 S.W. 2d 132 (Mo.), Commissioner Lozier stated:

> "A contraction of muscles which is purely a reaction to some outside force, convulsive movements of an epileptic, movements of the body during sleep, when will is in abeyance, and movements during periods of unconsciousness, are not 'acts' of the person, and the person will not be responsible for injuries inflicted thereby, since such movements are without volition."

4. What if the defendant is so drunk that he does not know what he is doing? See *D.P.P.* v. *Beard*, [1920] A.C. 479. Is drunkenness any different than sleepwalking? Does it matter whether the case is a civil one or a criminal one?

5. Twelve armed men, by threatening the defendant, compel him to enter the plaintiff's land to steal a horse. Is the defendant's conduct voluntary? Is it intentional? Should there be liability imposed? What are the conflicting policy goals? See *Gilbert* v. *Stone* (1648), Style 72, 82 E.R. 539.

6. Distinguish between motive and intention. An actor's motive is the reason

why he acts. Motive is seldom important in tort law. Does this shed any light on the above problem?

7. See Atrens, "Intentional Interference with the Person", in *Studies in Canadian Tort Law* (1968):

"It is a general condition of tort liability that the act of the defendant must be voluntary in the sense that it was directed by his conscious mind. Where the defendant is forcibly carried onto the land of the plaintiff there is no voluntary act, and he is not liable for trespass. There is no liability for the results of movements made while asleep. Similarly, to borrow an example from negligence cases, there is no liability for an accident which occurs when the driver of an automobile is rendered unconscious by sudden illness, which he could not, as a reasonable man, have anticipated. Volition, in the above sense, may be present even though the act was performed under pressure from circumstances beyond the control of the actor under conditions which negative liability; for example, where he acted in self defence. Whether an act is voluntary when the mind directing it is incapable, due to mental illness, of exercising normal control is a matter of definition. As will be seen later, the authorities indicate that such incapacity is no defence."

BASELY v. CLARKSON

Common Pleas. (1681), 3 Levinz 37; 83 E.R. 565

Trespass for breaking his closs called the *balk* and the *hade*, and cutting his grass, and carrying it away. The defendant disclaims any title in the lands of the plaintiff, but says that he hath a *balk* and *hade* adjoining to the *balk* and *hade* of the plaintiff, and in mowing his own land he involuntarily and by mistake mowed down some grass growing upon the *balk* and *hade* of the plaintiff, intending only to mow the grass upon his own *balk* and *hade*, and carried the grass, etc., *quae est eadem*, etc. *Et quod ante emanationem brevis* he tendered to the plaintiff 2s. in satisfaction, and that 2s. was a sufficient amends. Upon this the plaintiff demurred, and had judgment; for it appears the fact was voluntary, and his intention and knowledge are not traversable; they cannot be known.

NOTES

1. This is a case of mistake. Can you explain the result? Was the act voluntary? Was there an intention to intrude.

2. Why do you think the law was so strict in 1680? Should we preserve this rule? Is it as harsh in operation as it seems?

3. Defendant shoots the plaintiff's dog, believing it to be a wolf. Liability? Did the defendant "intend" to kill the dog? See *Ranson* v. *Kitner* (1888), 31 Ill. App. 241.

4. An anaesthetized patient, Y, is wheeled into the operating room. Doctor Z performs an appendectomy without negligence, believing reasonably that Y is X, who has consented to such treatment. Y, who was supposed to get a hernia operation, sues Dr. Z for battery. Result?

B. BATTERY

COLE v. TURNER

Nisi Prius. (1705), 6 Mod. 149; 87 E.R. 907

Holt C.J.: Upon evidence in trespass for assault and battery, declared:
First, that the least touching of another in anger is a battery.

Secondly, if two or more meet in a narrow passage, and without any violence or design of harm, the one touches the other gently, it will be no battery.

Thirdly, if either of them use violence against the other, to force his way in a rude inordinate manner, it will be a battery; or any struggle about the passage to that degree as may do hurt, will be a battery.

FILLIPOWICH v. NAHACHEWSKY ET AL.

Saskatchewan Queen's Bench. (1969), 3 D.L.R. (3d) 544

MacPherson J.: On October 21, 1965, the plaintiff got into a fight with the defendants, who are father and son. The plaintiff was injured and now sues for damages for assault.

That day the plaintiff discovered between 20 and 30 cattle in a barley field belonging to him. Some of the crop was uncut, some lying in swath. The plaintiff then went for assistance and came back with his brother-in-law, Fred Tataryn and his nephew, Wayne Gurski. They rounded up the cattle and started to drive them to the pound. As the plaintiff suspected, most of the cattle belonged to the defendants.

In order to get to the pound the cattle had to pass by the defendants' gate. The defendant, Nick Nahachewsky (the father), heard and recognized the cowbells on the roadway and ran out. He saw Tataryn by his gate and, some distance away—perhaps 200 or 300 yards—the plaintiff and Gurski driving the cattle toward him. Tataryn told him what they were doing and why.

The other defendant, Bill Nahachewsky, came to the gate shortly after his father and followed him along the road. They both ran toward the plaintiff but the father, having a considerable head start and a hotter head, got there first.

The defendant, Nick Nahachewsky, was then 70. He is below average height and weighed the same in 1965 as he does now, 135 lbs. But he appeared to me as a man who would not be deterred from action because of his age or weight. What there is of him is all muscle and he looks very fit and fearless. His son, the defendant Bill Nahachewsky, is in his forties, is 5'10", and weighed then 150 lbs.

The plaintiff at that time was 42 and weighed over 200 lbs. He is not as tall a man as Bill so I judge he must have been well overweight. He now weighs 153. Although the plaintiff was then much heavier than Bill, that additional weight was fat which he has since lost. I would think that in a fight between them neither would then have had an unfair advantage. Bill's greater reach and agility compensated for the plaintiff's greater weight.

Each of these three men was very strong.

Almost every time I have heard testimony about a physical fight, I have heard as many stories as there were participants and witnesses. Sometimes there is a tendency to brag. In the circumstances here I am prepared to accept most of what the plaintiff said. The various descriptions of what occurred here did not create as many problems in evidence as I expected.

As I stated, the defendant Nick Nahachewsky reached the plaintiff before his son got there. There were a few words spoken in Urkranian. Nick told the plaintiff that he would kill him. He then struck at the plaintiff. The plaintiff, with little effort because he was much the more powerful, pushed or struck Nick to the ground. At that moment the defendant Bill Nahachewsky arrived on the scene and if he had any patience left for the plaintiff it expired when he saw his father on the ground. He struck the plaintiff and a struggle started between them.

While these two were struggling the defendant, Nick Nahachewsky, struck the plaintiff twice with a stone. The first blow was partially avoided by the palintiff who saw it coming. It did little damage. The second was on the top of the plaintiff's head and he fell to the ground, momentarily stunned. I have no doubt this blow caused serious injury. With that the fight ended. The plaintiff walked to Tataryn's car and was taken for medical examination. I suppose the cattle never got to the pound.

The stone was about the size of a fist; a size that can easily be held in one hand. Very possibly Nick had it in his hand when he first approached the plaintiff.

Before I enter upon a discussion of the applicable law I should mention that the claim of the plaintiff's is in assault only and that battery is not mentioned. The distinction between these torts was not raised by either counsel and I think they were right. The distinction does remain in law but it is important only when the assault falls short of actual physical contact. Counsel here intended the word assault to include battery as, in fact, does popular language.

Battery is the intentional application of force to another person.

These blows by the father were not in self defence or done to protect his son. I have found as a fact that the defendant Nick struck the first blow and started the fracas. I feel that the son had a cooler head than the father. Even if it could be said that the plaintiff was the aggressor the defendant Nick would still be guilty of battery because there was no reasonable proportion between the aggression and the defense. The two defendants together could well have handled the plaintiff by ordinary blows and strength and without any weapon. "A man cannot justify a maim for every assault . . .": *Cook* v. *Beal* (1967), 1 Ld. Raym. 176 at p. 177, 91 E.R. 1014; *Clerk & Lindsell on Torts*, 12th ed., para. 452.

It was not argued or pleaded that the acts of the defendants were done in defence of their cattle. They knew that the cattle had trespassed and were being driven to the pound.

On these facts the liability of the defendant Nick Nahachewsky is clear. But I feel I must dismiss the action against his son. It cannot be said that the defendants conspired to injure the plaintiff. There was no time to conspire and, in fact, it is not pleaded. . . .

The injuries suffered by the plaintiff from blows other than with the stone were of no consequence. They were typical, I think, of the violence which unhappily erupts in our society every once in awhile and which our manly flesh is heir to; some scratches, perhaps, a black eye or a thick lip. All would cause amused discussion in a pub but no litigation and, certainly, nominal damages at most.

Winfield on Tort, 7th ed., p. 155, states:

"Every day scores of trivial assaults and batteries are committed which never find their way into the law courts, owing to the rough common sense and humour of mankind. It is not so much *de minimis non curat lex* as *de minimis non agit sapiens.*"

The blows with the stone were different. They constituted a complete departure from the ordinary in a fight between adult males, however annoyed they were with one another. I doubt if our civilization will every approach the point at which annoyed males will not occasionally breach the peace by striking out at one another. But it will forever frown on an unfair fight or the use of weapons capable of producing actual bodily harm.

It is this departure from the ordinary that should, I think, eliminate the defendant son from liability. Applying the rules in the Code, s. 21, I hold that he did nothing for the purpose of aiding his father to strike the injuring blows, and, whatever their common purpose, there is no evidence upon which I can hold that he knew or ought to have known that his father would use the stone as a weapon. . . . The defendant Bill, however, did not, in my view, intend that the action in concert with his father should go beyond bruising the plaintiff. There is a vast difference between bruising with a fist and maiming with a stone. When he used the stone the father was no longer acting in concert with his son. It was an act independent of the son on the evidence before me.

Mr. MacDonald argued vigorously that the plaintiff provoked this assault. With respect, I do not agree. I cannot and will not hold that one who is attempting to drive another's cattle to the pound is provoking an assault upon himself. The Stray Animals Act, R.S.S. 1953, c. 193 [later R.S.S. 1965, c. 210] is essential legislation. In this case the plaintiff was acting in accordance with its provisions and the defendant Nick Nahachewsky, being annoyed, started the fight.

Furthermore, provocation is not a defence to the torts of assault and battery. Provocation, if it existed, may, however, be taken into consideration in the assessment of damages as Bastin J. did in *Agar* v. *Canning* (1965), 54 W.W.R. 302, aff'd. 55 W.W.R. 384. See also Linden, *Studies in Canadian Tort Law* (1968), p. 414. . . .

I assess loss of income past and future resulting from the injury at $5,000.

For pain and suffering, inconvenience, and loss of enjoyment I assess a further $5,000.

Special damages have been agreed at $2,345.35 for which I express my thanks to counsel.

In the result therefore, the plaintiff will have judgment against the defendant Nick Nahachewsky for $12,345.35 and costs.

The action against William Nahachewsky is dismissed but without costs.

RESTATEMENT OF TORTS, SECOND

§13. Battery: Harmful Contact

An actor is subject to liability to another for battery if

(a) he acts intending to cause a harmful or offensive contact with the person of the other or a third person, or an imminent apprehension of such a contact, and

(b) a harmful contact with the person of the other directly or indirectly results.

NOTES

1. In *Stewart* v. *Stonehouse* (1928), 20 Sask. L.R. 459, McKay J.A. said:
   "I find defendant did grab plaintiff by the nose and did commit an assault upon him. There is no evidence that plaintiff was physically injured on this occasion, but he is entitled to damages, nevertheless, for the assault. To touch a person without his consent or some lawful reason is actionable. . . . Judge Salmond in his *Law of Torts*, 6th ed., at pp. 419-420 says: 'In respect of his personal dignity, therefore, a man may recover substantial damages for an assault which has done no physical harm whatever'."

Is it a battery if X kicks Y in the rear end? See *Soon* v. *Jong et al.* (1968), 70 D.L.R. (2d) 160. What about an unsolicited hug? See *Spivey* v. *Battaglia* (1972), 258 So. 2d 815.

2. Jones, with the intention of attracting the attention of Smith, taps him on the shoulder. Is this a battery? What if Jones is excited and taps Smith with considerable force? Compare with *Coward* v. *Baddeley* (1859), 4 H. & N. 478, 157 E.R. 927 (Ex.).

3. In *Morgan* v. *Loyacomo* (1941), 190 Miss. 656, 1 So. 2d 510, the defen-

dants forcibly seized a package from under the plaintiff's arm. Mr. Justice Griffiths stated:

"The authorities are agreed that, to constitute an assault and battery, it is not necessary to touch the plaintiff's body or even his clothing; knocking or snatching anything from plaintiff's hand or touching anything connected with his person, when done in a rude or insolent manner, is sufficient."

See also *Fisher* v. *Carrousel Motor Hotel* (1967), 424 S.W. 2d 627 (Tex.).

What if someone punches the horse you are riding on? What if someone kicks the tire of the car you are driving? What if someone intentionally bumps into the rear end of the car you are driving?

4. Can a kiss be a battery?

5. What if you are kissed while you are asleep and only find out about it later? What is the interest being protected here?

6. You are standing on a fast-moving bus and start to fall. You reach out and grab another passenger's leg. Battery? What if you grab the other bus passenger's leg not to steady yourself, but merely for enjoyment? Does it make any difference if it is a man grabbing a woman's leg or vice versa?

7. Is there a battery if the defendant hits the plaintiff with a club? If he throws a stone at the plaintiff? If he puts an overdose of pepper in the plaintiff's soup? If he throws a choclate cream pie into the plaintiff's face?

8. Paul is standing with his back to an open window. Donald knows this and moves menacingly toward him. Paul backs up and falls out of the window, breaking his leg on the ground below. Battery?

9. Is there a battery if the defendant spills water on someone? See *Soon* v. *Jong, supra.*

10. What if a defendant spits in a plaintiff's face? In *Alcorn* v. *Mitchell* (1872), 63 Ill. 553, the defendant spat in the face of the plaintiff. Mr. Justice Sheldon, in upholding a trial verdict in favour of the plaintiff, said:

"The act in question was one of the greatest indignity, highly provocative of retaliation by force, and the law, as far as it may, should afford substantial protection against such outrages, in the way of liberal damages, that the public tranquility may be preserved by saving the necessity of resort to personal violence as the only means of redress."

11. Is there a battery if the plaintiff, in advance, forbids the defendant from making a contact that would ordinarily be considered inoffensive?

BETTEL ET AL. v. YIM

Ontario County Court. (1978), 20 O.R. (2d) 617

The plaintiff and his friends threw lighted matches into the defendant's store, one of which, thrown by the plaintiff, caused a bag of charcoal to ignite. The defendant grabbed hold of the plaintiff with both hands and while shaking him the defendant's head came in contact with the plaintiff's nose, severely injuring it. The defendant's purpose in grabbing and shaking the plaintiff was to force him to confess that he had set the fire. The defendant had no intention to injure the plaintiff in the manner which he did although he did intend to grasp him firmly by the collar and to shake him.

Borins (County Court Judge): The plaintiff has framed his action in assault. Properly speaking the action should have been framed in battery which is the intentional infliction upon the body of another of a harmful or offensive contact. However, in Canada it would appear that the distinction between assault and battery has been blurred and when one speaks of an assault, it may include a battery: *Gambriell* v. *Caparelli* (1974), 7 O.R. (2d) 205, 54 D.L.R. (3d) 661. It is on the basis that this is an action framed in battery that I approach the facts in this case.

It would appear to be well established in this country (although not necessarily warmly received), following the dictum of Cartwright, J. (as he then was), in *Cook* v. *Lewis,* [1951] S.C.R. 830 at p. 839, [1952] 1 D.L.R. 1 at p. 15, that once the plaintiff proves that he was injured by the direct act of the defendant, the defendant is entitled to judgment only "if he satisfies the onus of establishing the absence of both intention and negligence on his part": *Dahlberg* v. *Naydiuk* (1969), 10 D.L.R. (3d) 319, 72 W.W.R. 210 (Man. C.A.), *per* Dickson, J.A. (as he then was), at pp. 328-9. On the defendant's evidence, his act in grabbing the plaintiff with both his hands and shaking him constituted the intentional tort of battery. It is obvious that he desired to bring about an offensive or harmful contact with the plaintiff for the purpose of extracting a confession from him. Viewed as such, the defendant's own evidence proves, rather than disproves, the element of intent is so far as this aspect of his physical contact with the plaintiff is concerned. Indeed, the defendant's admitted purpose in grabbing and shaking the plaintiff does not fit into any of the accepted defences to the tort of battery —consent, self-defence, defence of property, necessity and legal authority: Fleming, *Law of Torts,* 5th ed. (1977), p. 74 *et seq.* Furthermore, assuming the onus created by *Cook* v. *Lewis* requires the defendant to establish absence of negligence in the sense that he must show that his trespass was not careless (which, I readily concede, can be seen to be a contradiction in terms), it is my opinion that he has failed to do so. In grabbing the plaintiff and shaking him firmly, it ought to have been apparent to the defendant that in doing so he created the risk of injury to the plaintiff resulting from some part of the plaintiff's body coming into contact with some part of the defendant's body while the plaintiff was being shaken. If Cartwright, J., meant that the defendant must disprove negligence such as would give rise to an action in negligence, the defendant would be put in a very unusual position because, with respect, the element of negligence is, by definition, absent from the intentional tort of battery.

That there is no liability for accidental harm is central to the submission of defence counsel who argues that the shaking of the plaintiff by the defendant and the striking of the plaintiff by the defendant's head must be regarded as separate and distinct incidents. While he concedes that the defendant intentionally grabbed and shook the plaintiff, he submits that the contact with the head was unintentional. I have, of course, accepted the defendant's evidence in this regard. This, in my view, gives rise to the important question: Can an intentional wrongdoer be held liable for consequences which he did not intend? Another way of stating the problem is to ask whether the doctrine of foreseeability as found in the law of negligence is applicable to the law of intentional torts? Should an intentional wrongdoer be liable only for the reasonably foreseeable consequences of his intentional application of force or should he bear responsibility for all the consequences which flow from his intentional act?

To approach this issue one must first examine what interests the law seeks to protect. A thorough discussion of the history of the old actions of trespass and case is found in Prosser, *Law of Torts,* 4th ed. (1971), p. 28 *et seq.* Terms such as battery, assault and false imprisonment, which were varieties of trespass, have come to be associated with intent. The old action on the case has emerged as the separate tort of negligence. Today it is recognized that there should be no liability for pure accident, and that for there to be liability the defendant must be found at fault, in the sense of being chargeable with a wrongful intent, or with negligence. Thus, "with rare exceptions, actions for injuries to the person, or to tangible property, now require proof of an intent to inflict them, or of failure to exercise proper care": Prosser, *supra,* p. 30.

In discussing battery Fleming writes, *supra*, pp. 23-4:

Of the various forms of trespass to the person the most common is the tort known as battery, which is committed by intentionally bringing about a harmful or offensive contact with the person of another. The action, therefore, serves the dual purpose of affording protection to the individual not only against bodily harm but also against any interference with his person which is offensive to a reasonable sense of honour and dignity. The insult involved in being touched without consent has been traditionally regarded as sufficient to warrant redress, even though the interference is only trivial and not attended with actual physical harm. "The least touching of another in anger is a battery", and so is such offensive and insulting behaviour as spitting in another man's face, cutting his hair or kissing a woman. The element of personal indignity is given additional recognition in the award of aggravated damages to compensate for any outrage to the plaintiff's feelings . . .

. . . . .

Battery is an intentional wrong: the offensive contact must have been intended or known to be substantially certain to result. On the other hand, it is not necessary that the actor intended to inflict bodily harm, since we have seen that the legal injury is complete without it. Indeed it may be sufficient that he intended only to frighten but in a manner fraught with serious risk of bodily contact or harm.

. . . . .

With respect to injuries caused by the negligence of a defendant, it is often necessary to determine whether, or to what extent, the defendant must answer for the consequences which his conduct actually helped to produce. It is well established that a person is not legally responsible for all the consequences of his negligent conduct, and so to limit liability certain rules or principles have been established. Fleming discusses the policy considerations with respect to loss distribution arising from negligent conduct, *supra,* at p. 179:

There must be a reasonable connection between the harm threatened and the harm done. As a matter of practical politics, some limitation must be placed upon legal responsibility, because the consequences of an act theoretically stretch into infinity. The task is to select those factors which are of sufficient significance to justify the imposition of liability and to draw a boundary along the line of consequences beyond which the injured party must either shoulder the loss himself or seek reparation from another source. This inquiry . . . presents a much larger area of choice in which legal policy and accepted value judgments must be the final arbiter of what balance to strike between the claim to full reparation for the loss suffered by an innocent victim of another's culpable activity and the grievous burden that would be imposed on human activity if a wrongdoer were held to answer for all the consequences of his default.

The dominant limiting factor in modern negligence law is the "foreseeability" test as developed in *Overseas Tankship (U.K.) Ltd.* v. *Morts Dock & Engineering Co. Ltd.,* [1961] A.C. 388 (P.C.), and as explained in *Overseas Tankship (U.K.) Ltd.* v. *Miller Steamship Co. Pty. et al.,* [1967] 1 A.C. 617 (P.C.). For the purposes of this judgment, it is not necessary to explore the meaning and application of this test. It is only necessary to acknowledge it as a limiting factor to the ambit, or, indeed, the creation of liability arising from negligent conduct. The issue, here, is whether a similar limitation applies to intentional torts, such as battery.

This question has been the subject of discussion by legal academics who appear, on balance, to be of the view that the foreseeability test does not apply to intentional torts. Harper and James, after stating that by the fiction of "transferred intent" a defendant who intends to strike a third person is liable if his blow miscarries and he strikes the plaintiff, go on to say, *supra,* at pp. 218-9:

As has been pointed out, it is not easy to explain on logical principles the liability of one who, having directed a blow at one person, injures another, if he had no reason to believe the other was present and thus likely to be hurt. There is no intention to harm the plaintiff and no negligence toward him. The rule has been likened to that imposing liability without fault. A similar situation is involved in the rule that where the defendant intended to inflict a harmful or offensive contact, he is liable for the results even though they are unintended and unforeseeable. But as a matter of sound social policy, it is clearly better that the risk of such unintended and unforeseeable consequences should fall on the intentional wrongdoer than on his victim. The former is a tort-feasor and the latter is innocent. The wrongdoer, thus, should bear the loss.   . . . . .

It is my respectful view that the weight of opinion is that the concept of foreseeability as defined by the law of negligence is a concept that ought not to be imported into the field of intentional torts. While strong policy reasons favour determining the other limits of liability where conduct falls below an acceptable standard, the same reasons do not apply to deliberate conduct, even though the ultimate result in terms of harm caused to plaintiff is not what was intended by the defendant. In the law of intentional torts, it is the dignitary interest, the right of the plaintiff to insist that the defendant keep his hands to himself, that the law has for centuries sought to protect. In doing so, the morality of the defendant's conduct, characterized as "unlawful", has predominated the thinking of the Courts and is reflected in academic discussions. The logical test is whether the defendant was guilty of deliberate, intentional and unlawful violence or threats of violence. If he was, and a more serious harm befalls the plaintiff than was intended by the defendant, the defendant, and not the innocent plaintiff, must bear the responsibility for the unintended result. If physical contact was intended, the fact that its magnitude exceeded all reasonable or intended expectations should make no difference. To hold other-wise, in my opinion, would unduly narrow recovery where one deliberately invades the bodily interests of another with the result that the totally innocent plaintiff would be deprived of full recovery for the totality of the injuries suffered as a result of the deliberate invasion of his bodily interests. To import negligence concepts into the field of intentional torts would be to ignore the essential difference between the intentional infliction of harm and the un-intentional infliction of harm resulting from a failure to adhere to a reasonable standard of care and would result in bonusing the deliberate wrongdoer who strikes the plaintiff more forcefully than intended. For example, in the case of a deliberate blow to the eye liability should cover not only the black eye and the bloody nose but also the resultant brain damage caused when the plaintiff falls to the ground and strikes his head, even though the latter was never intended. Thus, the intentional wrongdoer should bear the responsibility for the injuries caused by his conduct and the negligence test of "foreseeability" to limit, or eliminate, liability should not be imported into the field of intentional torts.

Counsel for the defendant submits that the grabbing of the plaintiff and the subsequent striking of his nose by the defendant's head should be viewed as separate acts and that liability should end after the plaintiff was grabbed because what followed was accidental. I do not agree. On the facts of this case it is artificial to attempt to separate the two events which were part of one trans-action. The striking of the nose occurred while the defendant continued to hold the plaintiff and while the plaintiff was being shaken by the defendant. To adopt the views of the English Court of Appeal in *Gray* v. *Barr,* [1971] 2 Q.B. 554, where the Court was required to determine whether an unintended fatal injury following upon an intentional firing of a gun into the air to frighten the deceased was an accident within the meaning of a policy of insurance, the striking of the plaintiff's nose was not an accident. In that case, as in this case, there were two acts to consider—one deliberate and the other accidental— separated in time by a matter of seconds. To grab the plaintiff and shake him is undoubtedly a battery. It was this act that set in motion a chain of events. When something happens as a result of a chain of events deliberately set in motion by the defendant and at the end of that chain of events some act is done by the defendant that causes an unintended injury, it is not an accident. It is conduct for which the defendant must assume responsibility.

NOTES

1. Does Judge Borins' reasoning make sense to you? See also *Vosburg* v. *Putney* (1891), 50 N.W. 403 (Wis.). The extent of liability in negligence cases is dealt with below, Chapter 9, Remoteness and Proximate Cause.

2. Would the defendant have been liable if the plaintiff had died? What if he had been treated negligently by a doctor and then died?

TILLANDER v. GOSSELIN

Ontario High Court. [1967] 1 O.R. 203

The infant defendant, one week less than three years old, removed the infant baby from her carriage and dragged her over 100 feet, fracturing her skull and causing some brain damage.

Grant J.: The infant defendant at the time of this mishap was about one week less than 3 years of age. If he was capable of forming an intent to do what he did his actions would amount to an assault. The question to be decided is, can an infant of that age be held responsible in damages in such circumstances?

The action is framed in trespass. It cannot be said to be in negligence because the defendant had no right whatever to touch or remove the infant.

It is clear that a child of such tender years could not be guilty of negligence. The reasons for such conclusion is that such an infant is considered to be lacking in sufficient judgment to exercise that reasonable care that is expected of one. His normal condition is one of recognized incompetency and he is devoid of ability to make effective use of such knowledge as he may have at that early age. . . .

In recent years the weight of authority is to the effect that no action will lie in trespass if the act is not wrongful, either through wilfulness or as being the result of negligence. . . .

The law applicable is fully discussed by Clyne J. of the British Columbia Supreme Court in a very learned judgment in *Walmsley et al.* v. *Humenick*, [1954] 2 D.L.R. 232, who reviewed the many cases touching on the point in question. In that case injury had been sustained by one of two five-year-old boys who were playing with bows and arrows. The learned trial judge held that the infant defendant could not be found guilty of negligence because of his tender years and as it was admitted that there was no intention on his part to injure, the plaintiff could not succeed.

Section 12 of the Criminal Code is as follows:

> 12. No person shall be convicted of an offence in respect of an act or omission on his part while he was under the age of seven years.

The reason for such provision is that a child under that age is considered incapable of knowing the nature and consequence of his conduct and to appreciate that it is wrong.

Although there has been considerable agitation in legal circles for the adoption of a theory of strict liability in the cases where one individual suffers physical or financial damage as the direct result of another's act, the present state of the law recognizes no such rule. The result of the decisions in *Holmes* v. *Mather, supra; Stanley* v. *Powell, supra,* and *Walmsley et al.* v. *Humenick, supra,* and the unequivocal words of Cartwright J., of the Supreme Court of Canada in *Cook* v. *Lewis, supra,* is this: in an action for damages in trespass where the plaintiff proves that he has been injured by the direct act of the defendant, the onus falls upon the defendant to prove that his act was both unintentional and without negligence on his part. If he fails to do so, the plaintiff must succeed; but if he succeeds, he is entitled to judgment dismissing the claim. In this action, the defendant's tender age at the time of the alleged assault satisfies me that he cannot be cloaked with the mental ability of the ordinary reasonable man and hence negligence cannot be imputed to him. That same condition satisfies me that he cannot be said to have acted deliberately and with intention when the injuries were inflicted upon the infant plaintiff.

I do not believe that one can describe the act of a normal three-year-old child in doing injury to the baby plaintiff in this case as a voluntary act on his part. There is no evidence as to what instrument, if any, was used to inflict the injury. The infant plaintiff may have been struck by some object or she might have been dropped on a stone, but as indicated, the plaintiff's rights must be considered on the basis of an action for assault. The defendant child, however, would not have the mental ability at the age of three to appreciate or know the real nature of the act he was performing. A child of that age emulates or imitates the actions of those about him rather than making his own decisions. In the present case there could be no genuine intent formulated in his mind to do harm to the child plaintiff or to perform whatever act he did that caused the injury.

For these reasons the action must be dismissed, but under the circumstances without costs.

Action dismissed.

NOTES

1. Is the basis of this decision the lack of intention or the absence of a voluntary act?

2. Does battery require an intention to do "harm"?

3. Is there a battery if a 6-year-old child pushes another child who falls and breaks her leg? In *Baldinger* v. *Banks* (1960), 201 N.Y.S. 2d 629, Mr. Justice Baker imposed liability in such a case, saying:

". . . the proof clearly indicates that the defendant, despite his tender years, had the capacity of mind to know and did, in fact, know, as would any normal 6 year old child, that his act, under the circumstances disclosed in the proof, was offensive; and it is equally clear that it was so intended".

4. Should small children be held liable like adults for their conduct? What are the policies being served here? See Alexander, "Tort Liability of Children and Their Parents" in *Studies in Canadian Family Law* (1972), at p. 845.

LAWSON v. WELLESLEY HOSPITAL

Ontario Court of Appeal. (1975), 61 D.L.R. (3d) 445, 9 O.R. (2d) 677; affd. on another ground, [1978] 1 S.C.R. 893, 76 D.L.R. (3d) 688

The plaintiff, a non-psychiatric patient of the defendant hospital, sought damages for injuries sustained as the result of an attack by a psychiatric patient

(Coxall) with a history of violent conduct. The action against the hospital was founded on an alleged breach of contract to provide care and protection to the plaintiff and, alternately, on the negligence of the hospital in permitting Coxall to be at large without adequate control or supervision.

The County Court Judge held that the action was barred by s. 59 of The Mental Health Act, R.S.O. 1970, c. 269 which reads:

> No action lies against any psychiatric facility or any officer, employee or servant thereof for a tort of any patient".

The Court of Appeal reversed this ruling and a further appeal to the Supreme Court of Canada was dismissed on the ground that the section could not relieve the hospital of liability for its own negligence. The Supreme Court refrained from considering the matter of the mental element required to commit a tort.

The majority in the Court of Appeal, however, held that s. 59 would be inapplicable if it were found that the patient was incapable of intending to commit a tort.

Dubin J.A.: . . . I think it is now well established that if a mentally ill person is by reason of his illness incapable of the intent to assault a person, he is not liable in an action founded upon that assault.

In *Buckley and T.T.C.* v. *Smith Transport Ltd.,* [1946] O.R. 798 at p. 805, [1946] 4 D.L.R. 721 at p. 727, Roach, J.A., cited with approval the following quote [from Middleton, J., in *Slattery* v. *Haley* (1922), 52 O.L.R. 95 at p. 99, [1923] 3 D.L.R. 156 at p. 160]:

> "When a tort is committed by a lunatic, he is unquestionably liable in many circumstances, but under other circumstances the lunacy may shew that the essential *mens rea* is absent; but, when 'the lunacy of the defendant is of so extreme a type as to preclude any genuine intention to do the act complained of, there is no voluntary act at all, and therefore no liability:' Salmond, 5th ed., pp. 74 and 75."

In *Salmond on the Law of Torts,* 15th ed. (1969), p. 583, the proposition is stated as follows:

> (1) In wrongs based on malice or on some specific intent, like malicious prosecution, malicious libel on a privileged occasion, or deceit, insanity may be a good defence as disproving the existence of any such malice or intent.
>
> (2) In wrongs of voluntary interference with the person, property, reputation, or other rights of other persons, such as trespass, assault, conversion, or defamation, it is no defence that the defendant was under an insane delusion as to the existence of a sufficient legal justification. If he knew the nature and quality of his act it is no defence that he did not know that what he was doing was wrong, whatever the position may be in the criminal law. An insane person, therefore, who converts another's property to his own use under the delusion that it is his own, or who publishes a defamatory statement under the belief that it is true, is just as liable as if he were sane. If, however, the insanity of the defendant is of so extreme a type as to preclude any genuine intention to do the act complained of, there is no voluntary act at all, and therefore no liability.

[His Lordship then quoted from *Morriss* v. *Marsden et al.,* [1952] 1 All E.R. 925, *infra.*]

> I accept the principle that it is an essential element in the tort of assault that there be a voluntary act, the mind prompting and directing the act which is complained of. The authorities on that issue are fully canvassed in the judgment of McGregor, J., in *Beals* v. *Hayward,* [1960] N.Z.L.R. 131. However, in view of the observations in *Cook* v. *Lewis,* [1952] 1 D.L.R. 1,

[1951] S.C.R. 830, the onus of showing that the act was involuntary appears to be on the person who makes that assertion.

In the instant case, if the plaintiff establishes the averments in the statement of claim, *i.e.*, that the patient Rupert suffered from such a profound mental disorder that he was incapable of appreciating the nature or quality of his act, no action would lie against him at the suit of the plaintiff. It is sometimes said that mental illness excuses one from liability for the tort committed by him. See 87 Hals. 3rd ed., p. 134, para. 236:

> Persons suffering from mental disorder are not liable for their tortious acts where, by reason of their mental infirmity, they are unable to understand the nature and consequences of their acts or, where intention is an element of the tort, they are unable to form the necessary intention.

However, with respect, I think it more accurate to state that where a person, by reason of mental illness, is incapable of appreciating the nature or quality of his acts, such person has committed no tort since the intention, which is an essential element of the cause of action, is missing. Prosser, *Handbook of the Law of Torts,* 4th ed. (1971), p. 1001, puts it this way:

> It has been recognized, however, that his insanity may be such that he is incapable of entertaining the specific intent necessary for a particular tort, such as deceit, malicious prosecution, defamation, or even battery, and so he should not be liable simply because he has not committed the tort.

In any event, unless the act complained of is one for which redress will be awarded by way of damages, it is not a tort. That being so, I am respectfully of the opinion that the learned County Court Judge erred in dismissing the action on the preliminary question of law. He ought to have let the action proceed to trial where the ultimate determination would have to be made as to whether the conduct of the psychiatric patient constituted a tort. . . .

Appeal allowed;
Order directing that the action proceed to trial.

NOTES

1. What is the law concerning the mentally disabled and the requisite mental state required for the tort of battery? Did the court decide on the basis of lack of intention or lack of voluntariness?
2. Do you agree with this decision?

MORRISS v. MARSDEN

Queen's Bench Division. [1952] 1 All E.R. 925; 96 Sol. Jo. 281

The defendant made a violent attack on the plaintiff, manager of a Brighton hotel in which defendant had a room, while plaintiff was talking with a prospective guest. Plaintiff was struck on the head with a blunt instrument. Defendant was subsequently arrested on a charge of criminal assault but on medical evidence was found unfit to plead to the indictment and was directed to be detained to await Her Majesty's pleasure.

The plaintiff brought action for damages for assault and battery. The trial judge found that defendant's mind directed the blows he struck but that he was a catatonic schizophrenic and a certifiable lunatic who knew the nature and quality of his act but who, from disease of the mind, did not know what he was doing was wrong.

Stable J.: . . . Counsel for the defendant . . . submits that the test of civil re-

sponsibility is the application of the rules in *M'Naghten's Case* (1843), 10 Cl. &
Fin. 200, and that, since my finding as to his mental state would absolve him
from responsibility if this were a criminal charge tried on indictment, applying
the same yardstick, he is equally absolved from liability in a civil court. *White*
v. *White*, [1950] P. 39; [1949] 2 All E.R. 339, has been cited as an authority
binding me to hold that the M'Naghten rules are the only test, whether in a
civil or a criminal court, where the responsibility of a mentally sick person is in
question. In my view, that is not the law. . . . It cannot be suggested that the
M'Naghten rules are the appropriate test when the question is one of testa-
mentary capacity. In determining whether a contract is binding on a person
who was mentally sick at the time it was made, the consideration whether he
had a capacity to recognize that what he was doing was wrong seems to me to
be wholly inapt . . . .

   I do not think I need discuss the question referred to in argument—whether
the trend of our law is in the direction of culpability or compensation. Conflicting views on that matter have been expressed in various judgments. . . . I think
it is sufficient if I examine the essential facts which must be proved to establish
the cause of action on which the plaintiff relies. Counsel for the plaintiff says
in effect that where the action is an action of trespass in the highly technical
sense, no averment either of negligence or intention is essential to support it.
Counsel for the defendant, on the contrary, argues that, whatever the position
may have been 150 or 200 years ago, the whole trend of modern decisions is
that in an action, whether it be founded on trespass or on case, negligence or
intention must be averred. I cannot think that, if a person of unsound mind
converts my property under a delusion that he is entitled to do it or that it was
not property at all, that affords a defence. I can bring an action against him for
the recovery of my property, or, if it has been converted and destroyed, for its
value. Against that it may be said: "There all you are seeking is restitution,
either the return of your property or the equivalent. In this case what is being
asked for is damages, which is compensation and involves in a sense some punitive element." On the whole, I accept the view that an intention—*i.e.*, a voluntary act, the mind prompting and directing the act which is relied on, as in this
case, as the tortious act—must be averred and proved. For example, I think that,
if a person in a condition of complete automatism inflicted grievous injury, that
would not be actionable. In the same way, if a sleepwalker inadvertently, without intention or without carelessness, broke a valuable vase, that would not be
actionable. I agree that there is much force in the contention that, in those
cases where it has been held that an intention must be averred and proved, the
act in itself was a legitimate piece of behaviour: *e.g.*, in *Stanley* v. *Powell*, where
a man shooting pheasants shot the beater, and *Holmes* v. *Mather*, where the defendant was being driven in his carriage along a highway when the horse bolted.
Those cases may well be different from the present matter where the act complained of was a trespass, as direct an act of violence as possible. The injuries
were not the indirect result of a legitimate activity gone wrong, but were the
direct result of illegal behaviour, which was wrongful from the beginning and
could not conceivably be anything else. The distinction may be succinctly
stated as being between conduct tortious in its very essence and conduct innocent in itself, but becoming tortious by the addition of some ingredient such
as intention, heedlessness, or malice. But though the argument is extremely
attractive, I must hold that an intention to do the thing complained of must
be alleged and proved.

   The latest authority on this question is *National Coal Board* v. *J.E. Evans &
Co. (Cardiff), Ltd.* It may be said that in that case the Court of Appeal were
dealing with an act that was perfectly innocent and legitimate in itself and only

became actionable, if at all, because inadvertently it resulted in injury to the plaintiffs' property. It is possible that, if that court had been confronted, as I am, with an activity of a wholly different character, *viz.*, a violent assault and battery on a harmless man, they would have held that a different principle applied and that such considerations as intention and conception of right and wrong were wholly immaterial, the act of trespass being all that was required to support the cause of action. The matter is by no means free from doubt, but I think I ought to apply that decision, which is in accordance with my own view of the law though it is not directly in point. It appears that Denning L.J., does not agree with that aspect of the law: see *White* v. *White*. It is a matter of controversy. There is no authority directly in point, but I venture to think the weight of the *dicta* on the subject and the trend of authority point to the conclusion I have reached.

The next matter to consider is whether, granted that the defendant knew the nature and quality of his act, it is a defence in this action that, owing to mental infirmity, he was incapable of knowing that his act was wrong. If the basis of liability be that it depends, not on the injury to the victim, but on the culpability of the wrongdoer, there is considerable force in the argument that it is, but I have come to the conclusion that knowledge of wrongdoing is an immaterial averment, and that, where there is the capacity to know the nature and quality of the act, that is sufficient although the mind directing the hand that did the wrong was diseased.

NOTES

1. In *Phillips* v. *Soloway* (1957), 4 D.L.R. (2d) 570 (Man. Q.B.), the defendant attacked the plaintiff with a knife, cutting an eye so badly that the eyeball had to be removed. To a defence of insanity, Williams C.J.Q.B. stated that the *M'Naghten* rules "are not applicable in a civil action of tort". He also found that defendant knew the nature and quality of his act but held "that it makes no difference whether the defendant was or was not capable of knowing that his act was wrong". Plaintiff obtained judgment.

2. Mr. Justice Galligan has recently employed the *Morriss* v. *Marsden* test in *Squittieri* v. *de Santis* (1976), 15 O.R. (2d) 416, where the defendant, who stabbed someone to death, was sued by the family in tort, even though he was found not guilty in the criminal trial by reason of insanity. His Lordship imposed liability and explained:

". . . it appears to be clear on the authorities that regardless of whether or not a person because of insanity did not know that his act was wrong, if he intended to kill and appreciated the nature and quality of his acts, the defence of insanity is not available to him.

In this case, as I have indicated, he not only intended to kill but he appreciated that his conduct would result in the death and he knew and appreciated that at the time he was killing a man with a knife".

3. See also *Tindale* v. *Tindale*, [1950] 4 D.L.R. 363 (B.C.S.C.), where a mother, suffering under insane delusions, attacked her daughter with an axe. Macfarlane J. imposed liability on the mother. He assumed that the onus was on the defendant to establish that the insanity was "so extreme as to preclude any genuine intention to do the act complained of". The question of whether she "knew what she was doing was wrong for her to do or that her act was voluntary in the sense that she was capable of making a deliberate choice is much more difficult". He concluded by saying that the "child here is an innocent and unfortunate sufferer on whom no fault can possibly lie . . . [and] . . . the estate of the mother should be used, so far as it avails, to provide for the necessary medical expenses of the child . . . in her crippled condition".

4. In *Donaghy* v. *Brennan* (1900), 19 N.Z.L.R. 289, a defendant was held liable for shooting the plaintiff despite a finding that he was insane in the sense

of not understanding the nature and quality of his act or knowing that it was wrong. At the trial the jury were directed that if they found defendant insane, in the above sense, "damages should be limited to the actual injury and loss to the plaintiff, present and future", otherwise they could deal "liberally" with damages, for the assault was unprovoked and of a gross character. A verdict of £750 was returned.

5. In two early Ontario cases, *Stanley* v. *Hayes* (1904), 8 O.L.R. 81 and *Taggard* v. *Innes* (1862), 12 U.C.C.P. 77, the defence of insanity was held to be unavailable to a lunatic who burned down a barn. Three policy reasons were advanced by the court: (1) when one of two innocent parties must bear a loss, he must bear it whose act caused it; (2) if liability is imposed, the relatives of the lunatic might be under inducement to restrain him; (3) the vexing problems of the criminal law with regard to simulation of insanity might be kept out of tort law. Eventually, the Ontario courts reversed themselves and allowed the insanity plea in tort cases. Were they wise to do so?

6. See Bohlen, "Liability in Tort of Infants and Insane Persons" (1924), 23 Mich. L. Rev. 9; Robins, "Tort Liability of the Mentally Disabled", in Linden, *Studies in Canadian Tort Law* (1968) and in *Special Lectures of the Law Society of Upper Canada* (1963); Picher, "The Tortious Liability of the Insane in Canada" (1975), 13 Osgoode Hall L.J. 193; Fridman, "Mental Incompetency" Part II (1964), 80 L.Q.R. 84.

C. ASSAULT

I. DE S. & WIFE v. W. DE S.

(1348), Year-Book, Liber Assisarum, folio 99, p. 60

I. De S. & M. uxor ejus querunt de W. de S. de eo quod idem W. anno, &c., vi et armis, &c., apud S., in ipsam M. insultum fecit, et ipsam verberavit &c. And W. pleaded not guilty. And it was found by verdict of the inquest that the said W. came in the night to the house of the said I., and would have bought some wine but the door of the tavern was closed; and he pounded on the door with a hatchet, which he had in his hand, and the female plaintiff put her head out at a window and told him to stop; and he saw her and struck at her with the hatchet, but did not hit her. Whereupon the inquest said that it seemed to them that there was no trespass, since there was no harm done.

Thorpe C.J.: There is harm done, and a trespass for which they shall recover damages, since he made an assault upon the woman as it is found, although he did no other harm. Wherefore tax his damages, &c. and they taxed the damages at half a mark .... *Et sic nota*, that for an assault one shall recover damages, &c.

STEPHENS v. MYERS

Nisi Prius. (1830), 4 C. & P. 349; 172 E.R. 735

Assault. The declaration stated, that the defendant threatened and attempted to assault the plaintiff. Plea—not guilty.

It appeared, that the plaintiff was acting as chairman, at a parish meeting, and sat at the head of a table, at which table the defendant also sat, there being about six or seven persons between him and the plaintiff. The defendant having, in the course of some angry discussion which took place, been very vociferous, and interrupted the proceedings of the meeting, a motion was made, that he should be turned out, which was carried by a very large majority. Upon this, the defendant said, he would rather pull the chairman out of the chair than be turned out of the room; and immediately advanced with his fist clenched toward the chairman, but was stopped by the churchwarden, who sat next but one to the chairman, at a time when he was not near enough for any blow he might have meditated to have reached the chairman; but the witnesses said, that it seemed to them that he was advancing with intention to strike the chairman.

Spankie, Serjt., for the defendant, upon this evidence, contended, that no assault had been committed, as there was no power in the defendant, from the situation of the parties, to execute his threat—there was not a present ability—he had not the means of executing his intention at the time he was stopped.

Tindal C.J., in his summing up, said: It is not every threat, when there is no actual personal violence, that constitutes an assault, there must, in all cases, be the means of carrying the threat into effect. The question I shall leave to you will be, whether the defendant was advancing at the time, in a threatening attitude, to strike the chairman, so that his blow would almost immediately have reached the chairman, if he had not been stopped; then, though he was not near enough at the time to have struck him, yet if he was advancing with that intent, I think it amounts to an assault in law. If he was so advancing, that, within a second or two of time, he would have reached the plaintiff, it seems to me it is an assault in law. If you think he was not advancing to strike the plaintiff, then only can you find your verdict for the defendant; otherwise you must find it for the plaintiff, and give him such damages as you think the nature of the case requires.

Verdict for the plaintiff, damages 1 s.

TUBERVILLE v. SAVAGE

King's Bench. (1699), 1 Mod. 3; 2 Keble 545; 86 E.R. 684

Action of assault, battery and wounding. [The defendant pleaded the plaintiff began first; and the stroke he received, whereby he lost his eye, was on his own assault, and in defence of the defendant.—2 Keb. 545.] The evidence to prove a provocation was, that the plaintiff put his hand upon his sword and said, "If it were not assize-time, I would not take such language from you." The question was, if that were an assault.

The court agreed that it was not; for the declaration of the plaintiff was that he would not assault him, the judges being in town; and the intention as well as the act makes an assault. Therefore, if one strike another upon the hand or arm or breast, in discourse, it is no assault, there being no intention to assault; but if one, intending to assault, strike at another and miss him, this is an assault; so if he hold up his hand against another in a threatening manner and say nothing, it is an assault. In the principal case the plaintiff had judgment.

NOTES

1. Suppose the defendant said to the plaintiff, "Come one step closer, and I'll run you through." Assault? *Cf. Police* v. *Greaves*, [1964] N.Z.L.R. 295 (C.A.).

2. Suppose the defendant said, "I'll run you through, if you don't get out of here"? *Cf. Read* v. *Coker* (1853), 13 C.B. 850.

3. What if he said, "Give me all your money, or I'll run you through"? *Cf. Restatement of Torts, Second* §30; *Holcombe* v. *Whittaker* (1975), 318 So. So. 2d 289.

4. The defendant telephones the plaintiff and informs him that he is coming over to shoot him. The plaintiff, understandably, becomes apprehensive,

Assault? The defendant arrives and knocks on the door. Assault now? The plaintiff answers the door and sees the defendant standing there with a gun pointed in his direction. Is there an assault now?

5. Does it make any difference if the gun is not loaded? Compare *Blake* v. *Barnard* (1840), 9 C. & P. 626; *Regina* v. *St. George* (1840), 9 C. & P. 483; *Allen* v. *Hannaford* (1926), 138 Wash. 423, 244 P. 700. See the Criminal Code, s. 84(1) which reads: "Every one who, without lawful excuse, points a firearm at another person, whether the firearm is loaded or unloaded, is guilty of an . . . [offence]." What impact, if any, should this have on the issue of civil liability for assault?

6. Does it make any difference whether the plaintiff knew or did not know it was loaded? What interest is being protected here?

7. A points a gun at B while B is asleep intending to shoot him. He changes his mind and goes away. B, upon awakening, hears about the incident and suffers a heart attack. What arguments would you advance on behalf of B? On behalf of A? What do you think a court would do with the case?

8. Does the plaintiff have to be "afraid" of the defendant? Suppose a little man shakes his fist in the nose of a heavyweight champion, who merely laughs at him. Assault? See *Brady* v. *Schatzel,* [1911] Q.S.R. 206.

9. It is sometimes said that words alone cannot amount to an assault. See *Read* v. *Coker* (1853), 13 C.B. 850, 138 E.R. 1437. Is it an assault if you telephone someone and say, "I have put dynamite in the telephone you are now holding and I am pushing the plunger that will cause it to blow up this instant"? See Handford, "Tort Liability for Threatening or Insulting Words" (1976), 54 Can. Bar Rev. 563, who argues for the adoption of § 31, *Restatement of Torts Second,* which reads:

"Words do not make an actor liable for assault, unless together with other acts or circumstances they put the other in reasonable apprehension of an imminent harmful or offensive contact with his person".

10. It is now a criminal offence to convey a threat of death or injury by letter, telegram, telephone or radio. See Criminal Code of Canada, R.S.C. 1970, c. C-34, s. 331.

11. It is sometimes said that there must be some motion by the defendant before an assault is committed. Is it an assault if a gunman stands motionless but with a gun in his hand pointing at you?

12. Does tort law have any business trying to regulate this kind of conduct? Is not the criminal law sufficient? Are we wasting our time on trivia?

BRUCE v. DYER

Court of Appeal. [1970] 1 O.R. 482 (C.A.): affg. [1966] 2 O.R. 705

Ferguson J. (at trial): This is an action for damages for assault tried before me without a jury at the Toronto non-jury sittings. The plaintiff's case is that he was assaulted by the defendant on the highway near Barrie, Ontario . . . as a result of which he suffered severe physical injuries.

On the evening of May 18, 1964, the plaintiff and the defendant were returning to Toronto after spending the so-called May 24th weekend in the north at their respective cottages in the Georgian Bay area off Hwy. 103. The defendant was accompanied by his wife and five children, the eldest child at that date being about 14 years of age. The plaintiff was accompanied by his wife, who was sitting in the front seat with him, and a Miss Christina McNeil who was sitting in the back seat. In order to reach Hwy. 400, it was necessary for both the plaintiff and the defendant to proceed along Hwy. 103 and then for some short distance on Hwy. 12 and then on the extension of Hwy. 400. As they were proceeding along the extension of Hwy. 400, about 12 or 14 miles north of Barrie, Ontario, the defendant came upon a line of four cars ahead led by a panel truck, the plaintiff's car being next in line behind the panel truck, with an interval between said to be four or five car lengths. At this point the extension of Hwy. 400 is a two-lane road. Their speed is put by the evidence at an indefinite 45-60 m.p.h. The defendant came upon this line of cars and remained behind, keeping station with them when as they approached a grade, said to be at least 200 yards long, the fourth car pulled out of line and passed the three cars ahead of him and the panel truck. The defendant, being now somewhat nearer the grade, pulled to the left into the passing lane and proceeded to pass the traffic in front of him. I find on the evidence that when the defendant commenced to pass there was sufficient space between the panel truck and the plaintiff for the defendant to enter in safety. When the defendant reached the gap separating the panel truck from the plaintiff's vehicle, the glow from the headlights of an oncoming vehicle appeared over the crest of the grade. The defendant seeing the glow of the headlights of the approaching vehicle, proceeded to pull to the right into the space between the panel truck and the car driven by the plaintiff. At this point, he heard an unexpected blast of the horn of an automobile, and on glancing to his right he saw the plaintiff's vehcile to the right of the rear of his vehicle in the driving lane. The defendant says, and I believe him, that as he was passing the plaintiff, the plaintiff accelerated closing the gap between his car and the panel truck from four to five car lengths to two car lengths, thus preventing the defendant from entering this space, leaving him to face the oncoming car in the passing lane, thus endangering the life of the defendant and his family as well as his own.

The defendant being thus endangered and being unable to get in behind the panel truck applied his brakes and, fortunately for all concerned, there was then sufficient space between the plaintiff's vehicle and the next behind for the defendant to re-enter the driving lane safely. The plaintiff noticed the defendant pull out of the line behind him and admits that he, the plaintiff, knew the defendant was endeavouring to pass. He says, however, that the defendant was endeavouring to pass him while going up a hill, and that there was at the point in question, two white solid lines on the pavement. According to the plaintiff the defendant cut over and attempted to move into his lane. The front wheels were "just ahead of mine" which he says caused him some anxiety. He admits that he put his hand on the horn and that the defendant had to swing to his left to obtain room to drop back. He realized the defendant was in danger, but in spite of this he accelerated. There was no contact between the cars. He saw the lights of the oncoming vehicle coming over the hill and he admits that he knew it would create a danger to the defendant who, to his own observation, was pulling ahead and endeavouring to get into the driving lane. He was asked on cross-examination why he did not pull over or pull back instead of compelling the defendant to pull over on to the passing lane and drop back. He answered: "Why should I. It wasn't a passing zone and I had the right of way."

Understandably, I think, Dr. Dyer, the defendant, was highly annoyed at the actions of the plaintiff in accelerating and closing the gap ahead of his car from five to two car lengths and thus putting his life and that of his family in danger from the oncoming vehicle. The plaintiff says that when the defendant took his place behind, he then put his lights on high beam and "tailgated" him to about the northern outskirts of the town of Barrie, a distance which he described at different times as 12-14 miles, 12 miles and then 10 miles. By this time both cars were on the driving side of the southbound lane of Hwy. 400 some short way south of St. Vincent St. at which point the plaintiff signalled to the defendant by a wave of his hand and stopped his car on the pavement of the driving lane and so managed to bring the defendant's vehicle to a halt also. It is the plaintiff's contention that the traffic ahead of his car was halted at the time he stopped, but I cannot find such to be so, because, when the plaintiff got out of the vehicle which he proceeded to do, the traffic in the passing lane, which was very heavy, continued to flow by. At any rate the defendant's evidence, which I accept, is that there was no halted traffic in front of the plaintiff. The position was that the plaintiff had stopped in very heavy traffic, right on the driving lane of the southbound part of Hwy. 400 effectively blocking the defendant as the traffic at that hour of the evening, on a holiday week-end was very heavy and very fast. I accept the defendant's evidence on this point in preference to that of the plaintiff and his witnesses, not only because I believe him, but also because the defendant's evidence is corroborated to some extent by Constable Donald Burditte Byles of the Provincial Police who came to the scene. He said he saw no block in the traffic, and there had not been an accident. Moreover, there were no traffic lights or crossroads to block traffic either at that point or to the south.

The plaintiff contends that he stopped the car to get out and get the defendant's licence number to give it to the police. He says that he stood directly in front of the defendant's automobile which was stopped only some four or five feet behind his car. He says that he was bending over memorizing the number when the defendant got out of his car, and without hesitation struck him a violent blow on his jaw, fracturing it on both sides of the chin and also producing lesser fractures—more or less hair line fractures—in the condiles or shafts.

I find, however, that when the plaintiff and the defendant emerged from their respective automobiles, they met at the front left hand corner of the defendant's car where the plaintiff, according to his own admission, was gesticulating with his right hand. He says that his hand motions were for the purpose only of indicating to the defendant that he was not going to argue with the defendant. The defendant, however, says that the gesture made by the plaintiff was by no means an offer of peace, but on the contrary, was made with a clenched fist threatening violence. The defendant in fact alleges that the plaintiff made a similar threatening gesture with his fist from his seat in the car as he was about to stop on the highway. The plaintiff admits the gesture, but contends it was merely a polite friendly indication that he was about to stop and was not intended to be menacing. I think it no friendly gesture, for the plaintiff was moving towards the door of the defendant's car and had he reached it before the defendant got out, he would have had the defendant at a distinct disadvantage. I prefer the defendant's account of this part of the affray to that of the plaintiff's and his witnesses. The plaintiff had so little consideration for the lives and safety of the persons in the defendant's car that he deliberately accelerated and reduced the space ahead of him—that is between him and the panel truck, from four or five car lengths to two car lengths, asserting his right to do the same on the basis of some imaginary right of way rule in his favour. A person who deliberately endangers human life on the highway in that fashion has, I think, aside from all other defects, an insufferable arrogance and a disregard for the safety of others. If he was annoyed by the defendant's high lights, he could have avoided them, but he preferred to endanger all other traffic on the road by stopping wholly on the pavement, on a week-end holiday when the traffic on Hwy. 400 as is well known is very heavy indeed.

I think the plaintiff was guilty of dangerous driving in keeping the defendant's car in the passing lane and preventing it from getting back into the driving lane. It was the plaintiff's case that the defendant did not elevate his lights as a signal that he was about to pass but as a retaliation for the defeat of his first attempt to do so. The defendant's evidence is to the effect that he was in no sense retaliating, but that after the first episode he endeavoured to pass the plaintiff on several occasions before reaching Barrie. Each time he did so he signalled his intentions by elevating his lights to high beam as is the custom, but that each time he did so the plaintiff accelerated and prevented his passing in the heavy traffic. If the defendant elevated his lights in the manner complained of, he was wrong as the Highway Traffic Act, R.S.O. 1960, c. 172, prohibits driving within 200 ft. of another vehicle except in the act of overtaking and passing. The plaintiff, however, could easily have rid himself of the nuisance of the lights behind by not taking active steps to prevent the defendant passing, or he might have pulled to the shoulder of the road and stopped. He chose to do neither, but took the highly objectionable course of stopping on the pavement in heavy traffic, a stop which is prohibited by s. 89 [am. 1965, c. 46, s. 12] of the Highway Traffic Act.

There is no doubt that the defendant struck the plaintiff a violent blow on the chin, but the evidence satisfies me that the blow was not delivered at the side of the face, but directly at the point of the chin with the result that the chin was fractured in four places as I have indicated above. The circumstances were that the plaintiff, aged 57, had suffered from pyorrhea for some years and that this disease had the serious effect of causing a necrosis in a substantial portion of the jaw-bone causing it to die and disappear. In the course of treatment, all his teeth had been extracted. In all, the mandible had become thin and weak, quite below pugilistic qualifications. He knew of this condition yet nothing daunted, he gave the impression to Dr. Dyer of challenging him to combat. The shattered mandible was wired together, but infection set in. Four operations and a bone graft were necessary before the jaw healed. The condiles which had been fractured, but not displaced, healed so as to leave a malocclusion making it very difficult for the dental surgeon to make dentures with satisfactory occlusion or which would remain in place. He will suffer an appreciable amount of permanent disability in these respects for the rest of his life. Quite apart from the hospital expenses, he has suffered quite substantial damages including out-of-pocket expenses and because of thinness of his jaw-bone he has suffered discomfort. Needless to say, the defendant could never have anticipated such a condition in a man so arrogant, belligerent and determined.

The question for decision, therefore, is whether Dr. Dyer is liable in damages for the assault suffered by the plaintiff.

The law concerning assault goes back to earliest times. The striking of a person against his will has been, broadly speaking, always regarded as an assault. It has been defined in the 8th American Edition of *Russell on Crime* as "an attempt or offer with force and violence to do a corporal hurt to another". So an attempted assault is itself an assault; so an attempt to strike another is an assault even though no contact has been made.

Usually, when there is no actual intention to use violence there can be no assault. When there is no power to use violence to the knowledge of the plaintiff there can be no assault. There need not be in fact any actual intention or power to use violence, for it is enough if the plaintiff on reasonable grounds believes that he is in fact in danger of violence. So if a person shakes his fist at another the person so assaulted may strike back, if he, on reasonable grounds, believes that he is in danger.

When the plaintiff emerged from his vehicle waving his fist, I think the defendant had reasonable grounds for believing that he was about to be attacked and that it was necessary for him to take some action to ward it off.

In *Salmond on Torts*, 8th ed., p. 373, the following passage appears based on *R. v. St. George* (1840), 9 Car. & P. 483, 173 E.R. 921:

"There need be no actual intention or power to use violence, for it is enough if the plaintiff on reasonable grounds believes that he is in danger of it."

More modern cases point out that even if it later appears that no violence was intended, it is sufficient if the defendant or a reasonable man thinks that it is intended.

Bruce had not only emerged from his vehicle shaking his fist but in addition he blocked the defendant's passage on the road. In my opinion that blocking action on his part was an assault.

In *Innes* v. *Wylie* (1844), 1 Car. & K. 257, 174 E.R. 800, a plaintiff who had been expelled from a club attempted to enter the rooms of the club, but was prevented by a policeman who stood in the doorway and refused to move to let the plaintiff pass. Lord Denman C.J., instructing the jury, said [p. 263]:

> "You will say, whether, on the evidence, you think the policeman committed an assault on the plaintiff, or was merely passive. If the policeman was entirely passive like a door or a wall put to prevent the plaintiff from entering the room, and simply obstructing the entrance of the plaintiff, no assault has been committed on the plaintiff, and your verdict will be for the defendant. The question is, did the policeman take any active measures to prevent the plaintiff from entering the room, or did he stand in the door-way passive, and not move at all."

The jury returned a verdict for the plaintiff so presumably they found that the policeman had taken active measures to block the plaintiff's way. So the police, I think, commit an assault when they bar the way of a householder from entering his own house by standing in the gateway with an arm projecting from his body or without lawful authority bar the way of one's motor vehicle.

If the plaintiff in the case at bar had left his auto in some place where subsequently it had blocked the defendant's way, I have no doubt that the proper remedy would be an action on the case, but when, as here, he drove his car to a position on the roadway to block the defendant's vehicle, he took active steps to block the defendant and so committed an assault upon him. The defendant was then justified in defending himself from the assault thus imposed upon him: *Re Lewis* (1874), 6 P.R. (Ont.) 236, where Gwynne J. illustrates when the action is one for assault or on the case. When a person is assaulted he may do more than ward off a blow, he may strike back: *R.* v. *Morse* (1910), 4 Cr. App. R. 50.

The right to strike back in self-defence proceeds from necessity. A person assaulted has a right to hit back in defence of himself, in defence of his property or in defence of his way. He has, of course, no right to use excessive force and so cannot strike back in defence of his way if there is a way around. Here, however, the evidence is that the traffic from the rear was such that it would have been a highly dangerous manoeuvre for the defendant to emerge into it, and the Highway Traffic Act, at all events, prohibits proceeding off the pavement and on to the shoulder for the purpose of passing. The defendant was effectively blocked for the time being at least.

The law requires that the violence of defence be not disproportionate to the severity of the assault. It is, of course, a fact that severe damage was done to the plaintiff. In my opinion, the plea of self-defence is still valid. The defendant struck one blow only. The law does not require him to measure with nicety the degree of force necessary to ward off the attack even where he inflicts serious injury. This is not a case of "beating up". The defendant was highly provoked by the plaintiff's conduct which was unjustified in my view. The plaintiff knew the condition of his own physical state and one would have thought that he would have, for that reason alone, refrained from such highly provocative conduct. He invited the treatment he received.

If I had been instructing a jury in this instance, I would have left the general verdict to them, and I would have directed them that if they found for the defendant they should not attempt to assess the damages suffered by the plaintiff. Indeed, I should have directed them that it was open to them to find that the provocation was such as to reduce the damages to the vanishing point. That is the course which I now follow as my general verdict is for the defendant and so I dismiss the plaintiff's case accordingly. I think this is a proper case for the successful party to be deprived of his costs.

Aylesworth J.A. (Schroeder and McGillivray JJ.A. concurring, on appeal): The learned trial Judge upon all of the evidence has found that the plaintiff committed an assault upon the defendant. We perceive no ground upon which we ought to interfere with that finding supported as it is by ample evidence to which the learned trial Judge gave credence. It is not in controversy that the actions of the defendant complained of, so far as assault is concerned, is the striking of one blow. The learned trial Judge has found that that blow was struck validly in self-defence and further has said that in such circumstances the defendant in defending himself was not required to measure with nicety the degree of force employed in the blow. With this we agree, as well as with his conclusion that no excessive force was employed.

The appeal will be dismissed with costs.

NOTES

1. Is the conclusion of Mr. Justice Ferguson that the blocking amounted to an assault consistent with the authorities? If not, is it in error or is it a bold new breakthrough? How did the Ontario Court of Appeal deal with this problem?

2. Did Mr. Bruce commit an assault when he closed the gap and kept Dr. Dyer from re-entering the driving lane from the passing lane?

3. Would an assault have been committed if Dr. Dyer had "tailgated" Mr. Bruce with his lights on high beam as alleged?

4. Would any tort liability have arisen if, as a result of the punch, Dr. Dyer had broken his own fist instead of Mr. Bruce's jaw?

5. Plaintiff, by accident, damages the defendant's car. Defendant assaults him. Provocation? See *Golnick* v. *Geissinger* (1967), 64 D.L.R. (2d) 754 (B.C.S.C.).

6. In *Agar* v. *Canning* (1965), 54 W.W.R. 302, provocation was taken into account in assessing damages where, during a hockey game, the defendant hit the plaintiff with his stick after being hooked by him.

RESTATEMENT OF TORTS, SECOND

§21. Assault.
   (1) An actor is subject to liability to another for assault if
      (a) he acts intending to cause a harmful or offensive contact with the person of the other or a third person, or an imminent apprehension of such a contact, and
      (b) the other is thereby put in such imminent apprehension.
   (2) An action which is not done with the intention stated in Sub-section (1) (a) does not make the actor liable to the other for an apprehension caused thereby although the act involves an unreasonable risk of causing it and, therefore, would be negligent or reckless if the risk threatened bodily harm.

CRIMINAL CODE OF CANADA

R.S.C. 1970, c. C-34

244. A person commits an assault when, without the consent of another person or with consent, where it is obtained by fraud,

(a) he applies force intentionally to the person of the other, directly or indirectly, or

(b) he attempts or threatens by an act or gesture, to apply force to the person of the other, if he has or causes the other to believe upon reasonable grounds that he has present ability to effect his purpose.

NOTES

1. The Criminal Code distinguishes between a "common assault", which is an offence punishable on summary conviction, and "assault causing bodily harm", which is an indictable offence punishable by imprisonment of up to five years. The 1927 Criminal Code, which was replaced in 1955 by the present Code, contained provisions which released an accused from all further proceedings, both civil and criminal, if he were acquitted of common assault, if the assault was so trifling as to merit no punishment or if he was convicted and paid the fine or suffered the imprisonment. The constitutional validity of this provision was challenged on several occasions and conflicting decisions emerged from the various provinces. See (1941), 19 Can. Bar Rev. 379; (1948), 26 Can. Bar Rev. 1001. These provisions were omitted from the present Code. Should they be resurrected?

2. In British Columbia, the United Kingdom and in some Australian jurisdictions, a conviction or acquittal in a summary criminal proceeding for assault is a bar to further civil proceedings for the same cause. If there is a conviction, however, some Australian states authorize the magistrates to direct that a sum be paid to the aggrieved person by way of compensation. See Fleming, *The Law of Torts* (5th ed., 1977), p. 26. See also *Sindaco* v. *Stupka* (1977), 74 D.L.R. (3d) 148 (B.C.). But see *Nelson* v. *Sneed*, [1976] 1 W.W.R. 360 (Alta.).

3. The Criminal Code (s. 10) is as follows:
"No civil remedy for an act or omission is suspended or affected by reason that the act or omission is a criminal offence".
In exceptional circumstances, however, a civil action may be stayed pending the outcome of a criminal trial, but this is rare. See *Stickney* v. *Trusz* (1973), 45 D.L.R. (3d) 275; affd. (1974), 46 D.L.R. (3d) 80 and 82; *Demeter* v. *Occidental Insurance Co.* (1975), 11 O.R. (2d) 369 (H.C.).

4. The Criminal Code of Canada empowers a court that convicts someone of an indictable offence to order that person to pay an "amount by way of satisfaction or compensation for loss of or damage to property suffered by the applicant as a result of the commission of the offence". (See s. 653). This section has been held *intra vires* as part of the sentencing process, but orders should be given with restraint. See *R.* v. *Zelensky* (1978), 20 Crim. L.Q. 272 (S.C.C.); See also Chasse, "Restitution in Canadian Criminal Law" (1977), 36 C.R.N.S. 201. Is there any reason why this section is limited to compensation for loss of or damage to property?

5. In the granting of probation, a court may impose conditions on an accused person. One of the conditions that may be exacted is that the accused "make restitution or reparation to any person aggrieved or injured by the commission of the offence for the actual loss or damage sustained by that person as a result thereof". (Section 663(e).) What does this mean? Is the compensation limited to economic losses only? Why is this provision used so rarely? Should criminal courts make more use of these compensation provisions? How can they be encouraged to do so? See Linden, "Restitution, Compensation for Victims of Crime and Canadian Criminal Law" (1977), 19 Can. J. Crim. 49, also in Law Reform Commission of Canada, *Community Participation in Sentencing* (1976).

6. When someone punches another in the nose, *both* the tort of battery and the crime of assault are committed. The actor may be made to pay tort damages and may also be convicted and punished criminally. Although *theoretically* available, very few civil actions are *actually* launched by victims of assault against their attackers. *The Report of the Osgoode Hall Study on Compensation*

for Victims of Crime (1968) demonstrated that only 1.8% of the victims studied collected anything from their attackers, *i.e.,* three individuals out of the 167 respondents. Not only was tort recovery rare, but few victims ever considered suing, fewer consulted a lawyer and still fewer attempted to secure reparation. According to the Osgoode Hall Study, 14.9% considered suing, 5.4% consulted a lawyer and 4.8% actually tried to collect from their attackers. See Linden, "Victims of Crime and Tort Law" (1969), 12 Can. Bar J. 17. Why do you think so few people recovered or tried to recover?

7. In 1964, New Zealand established a plan to compensate victims of crime. Soon after, the United Kingdom followed suit. Today, there are eight such plans operating in Canada and several in Australia and in the United States. See Linden, *The Report of the Osgoode Hall Study on Compensation for Victims of Crime* (1968), for descriptions of some of these plans. See also Feeney, "Compensation for Victims of Crime: A Canadian Proposal" (1967), 2 Ott. L. Rev. 175; Eremko, "Compensation for Criminal Injuries in Saskatchewan" (1961), 33 Sask L. Rev. 41; Eremko, "Compensation of Criminal Injuries in Saskatchewan" (1969), 19 U. of T.L.J. 263; Bryan, "Compensation to Victims of Crime" (1968), 6 Alta. L. Rev. 202; Samuels, "Compensation for Criminal Injuries in Britain" (1967), 17 U. of T.L.J. 20; Burns and Ross, "A Comparative Study of Victims of Crime Indemnification in Canada, B.C. as Microcosm" (1973), 8 U. B. C. L. Rev. 105; Bennett, "Practice and Procedure Before the Law Enforcement Compensation Board" in *Special Lectures of the Law Society of Upper Canada* (1971), at p. 167; Miers, "The Ontario Criminal Injuries Compensation Scheme" (1974), 24 U. of T. L.J. 347; Veitch & Miers, "Assault on the Law of Tort" (1975), 38 Mod. L. Rev. 139; Miers, *Responses to Victimization* (1978).

THE COMPENSATION FOR VICTIMS OF CRIME ACT

Statutes of Ontario, 1971, c.51 as amended.

5. Where any person is injured or killed by any act or omission in Ontario of any other person occurring in or resulting from,

(a) the commission of a crime of violence constituting an offence against the *Criminal Code* (Canada), including poisoning, arson, criminal negligence and an offence under section 86 of that Act but not including an offence involving the use or operation of a motor vehicle other than assault by means of a motor vehicle;

(b) lawfully arresting or attempting to arrest an offender or suspected offender for an offence against a person other than the applicant or his dependant or against such person's property, or assisting a peace officer in executing his law enforcement duties; or

(c) preventing or attempting to prevent the commission of an offence or suspected offence against a person other than the applicant or his dependant or against such person's property,

the Board, on application therefor, may make an order that it, in its discretion exercised in accordance with this Act, considers proper for the payment of compensation to,

(d) the victim;

(e) a person who is responsible for the maintenance of the victim;

(f) where the death of the victim has resulted, the victim's dependants or any of them or the person who was responsible for the maintenance of the victim immediately before his death or who has, on behalf of the victim or his estate and not being required by law to do so, incurred an expense referred to in clause *a* or *e* of subsection 1 of section 7 arising from the act or omission.

6. An application for compensation shall be made within one year after the date of the injury or death but the Board, before or after the expiry of

the one-year period, may extend the time for such further period as it considers warranted.

7. (1) Compensation may be awarded for,

(a) expenses actually and reasonably incurred or to be incurred as a result of the victim's injury or death;

(b) pecuniary loss incurred by the victim as a result of total or partial disability affecting the victim's capacity for work;

(c) pecuniary loss incurred by dependants as a result of the victim's death;

(d) pain and suffering;

(e) maintenance of a child born as a result of rape;

(f) other pecuniary loss resulting from the victim's injury and any expense that, in the opinion of the Board, it is reasonable to incur.

(2) Where the injury to a person occurred in the circumstances mentioned in clause *b* or *c* of section 5 the Board may, in addition to the compensation referred to in subsection 1, award compensation to the injured person for any other damage resulting from the injury for which damages may be recovered at common law.

. . .

14. Where, . . .

(b) it appears to the Board that it will probably award compensation to the applicant,

the Board may, in its discretion, order interim payments to the applicant in respect of maintenance and medical expenses and, if compensation is not awarded, the amount so paid is not recoverable from the applicant.

. . .

16. (1) An order for compensation may be made whether or not any person is prosecuted for or convicted of the offence giving rise to the injury or death but the Board may, on its own initiative or upon the application of the Minister adjourn its proceedings pending the final determination of a prosecution or intended prosecution.

(2) Notwithstanding that a person for any reason is legally incapable of forming criminal intent, he shall, for the purposes of this Act, be deemed to have intended an act or omission that caused injury or death for which compensation is payable under this Act.

17. (1) In determining whether to make an order for compensation and the amount thereof the Board shall have regard to all relevant circumstances, including any behaviour of the victim that may have directly or indirectly contributed to his injury or death.

(2) In assessing pecuniary loss, the Board shall take into consideration any benefit, compensation or indemnity payable to the applicant from any source.

18. The Board may order compensation to be paid in a lump sum or in periodic payments, or both, as the Board thinks fit.

19. (1) The amount awarded by the Board to be paid in respect of the injury or death of one victim shall not exceed,

(a) in the case of lump sum payments, $15,000; and

(b) in the case of periodic payments, $500 per month,

and where both lump sum and periodic payments are awarded, the lump sum shall not exceed half of the maximum therefor prescribed in clause *a*. . . .

NOTES

1. One of the most interesting cases under this statute, *Re Sheehan and Criminal Injuries Compensation Board* (1973), 37 D.L.R. (3d) 336, arose out of the Kingston Penitentiary riots, during which the applicant was severely injured as a result of assaults by other prisoners. The Board, however, rejected

his application for three reasons: (1) the applicant had previously been guilty of criminal behavior; (2) conditions in Kingston Penitentiary were totally outside the power and jurisdiction of the Province of Ontario to deal with; and (3) the applicant had not applied to any other governmental agency for compensation.

The Divisional Court quashed the decision, holding that the tribunal had acted on the basis of irrelevant considerations. The issue of Sheehan's prior criminal behavior was totally irrelevant, because this behavior did not provoke the assaults. Since there was nothing in the Act which exlcudes prisoners as a class from recovery, the second consideration was similarly improper. Finally, the Act does not require an applicant to pursue his other remedies before applying for compensation; it merely allows the Board rights of subrogation if such remedies are subsequently sought, so that the third consideration was also irrelevant. In this case the court stated that it was unclear what other remedies could be available to the applicant. As none of the Board's considerations were relevant, the court quashed the decision and ordered a new hearing. See also *Re Fregeau and Criminal Injuries Compensation Board*, [1973] 2 O.R. 182, where the Divisional Court quashed a decision of the Criminal Injuries Compensation Board because there was an error of law on the face of the record. And see also *R. v. Criminal Injuries Compensation Board, Ex parte Laine*, [1967] 2 All E.R. 770.

2. The victim, an 18-year-old female, was assaulted by the wife of a man, with whom she had been keeping company. The offender was convicted and fined $100. The Board, relying on s. 17(1), denied the victim compensation. See Case No. 200-567, *Fifth Report*, Ontario Criminal Injuries Compensation Board, at p. 75.

3. The applicant picked up a strange woman at the Brown Derby Tavern in Toronto and accompanied her to the Rex Hotel, where he was assaulted by two men. Compensation? See Case No. 200-651, *ibid.*, at p. 76.

4. For a helpful discussion of the question of victim contribution see Miers, *Responses to Victimization* (1978), p. 169.

D. INTENTIONAL INFLICTION OF MENTAL SUFFERING

WILKINSON v. DOWNTON

Queen's Bench. [1897] 2 Q.B. 57; 66 L.J.Q.B. 493; 13 T.L.R. 388; 76 L.T. 493

Consideration by the trial judge of damages assessed by a jury. It was contended that as to damage caused by nervous shock the plaintiff had no cause of action.

Wright J.: In this case the defendant, in the execution of what he seems to have regarded as a practical joke, represented to the plaintiff that he was charged by her husband with a message to her to the effect that her husband was smashed up in an accident, and was lying at The Elms at Leytonstone with both legs broken, and that she was to go at once in a cab with two pillows to fetch him home. All this was false. The effect of the statement on the plaintiff was a violent shock to her nervous system, producing vomiting and other more serious and permanent physical consequences at one time threatening her reason, and entailing weeks of suffering and incapacity to her as well as expense to her husband for medical attendance. These consequences were not in any way the result of previous ill-health or weakness of constitution; nor was there any evidence of predisposition to nervous shock or any other idiosyncrasy.

In addition to these matters of substance there is a small claim for 1s. 10½d. for the cost of railway fares of persons sent by the plaintiff to Leytonstone in obedience to the pretended message. As to this 1s. 10½d. expended in railway fares on the faith of the defendant's statement, I think the case is clearly within the decision in *Pasley* v. *Freeman* (1789), 3 T.R. 51. The statement was a misrepresentation intended to be acted on to the damage of the plaintiff.

The real question is as to the £100, the greatest part of which is given as compensation for the female plaintiff's illness and suffering. It was argued for her that she is entitled to recover this as being damages caused by fraud, and therefore within the doctrine established by *Pasley* v. *Freeman* and *Langridge* v. *Levy* (1837), 2 M. & W. 519. I am not sure that this would not be an extension of that doctrine, the real ground of which appears to be that a person who makes a false statement intended to be acted on must make good the damage naturally resulting from its being acted on. Here there is no *injuria* of that kind. I think, however, that the verdict may be supported upon another ground. The defendant has, as I assume for the moment, wilfully done an act calculated to cause physical harm to the plaintiff—that is to say, to infringe her legal right to personal safety, and has in fact thereby caused physical harm to her. That proposition without more appears to me to state a good cause of action, there being no justification alleged for the act. This wilful *injuria* is in law malicious, although no malicious purpose to cause the harm which was caused nor any motive of spite is imputed to the defendant.

It remains to consider whether the assumptions involved in the proposition are made out. One question is whether the defendant's act was so plainly calculated to produce some effect of the kind which was produced that an intention it ought to be imputed to the defendant, regard being had to the fact that the effect was produced on a person proved to be in an ordinary state of health and mind. I think that it was. It is difficult to imagine that such a statement, made suddenly and with apparent seriousness, could fail to produce grave effects under the circumstances upon any but an exceptionally indifferent person, and therefore an intention to produce such an effect must be imputed, and it is no answer in law to say that more harm was done than was anticipated, for that is commonly the case with all wrongs. The other question is whether the effect was, to use the ordinary phrase, too remote to be in law regarded as a consequence for which the defendant is answerable. Apart from authority, I should give the same answer and on the same ground as the last question, and say that it was not too remote. Whether, as the majority of the House of Lords thought in *Lynch* v. *Knight* (1861), 9 H.L.C. 577, at pp. 592, 596, the criterion is in asking what would be the natural effect on reasonable persons, or whether, as Lord Wensleydale thought, the possible infirmities of human nature ought to be recognized, it seems to me that the connection between the cause and the effect is sufficiently close and complete. It is, however, necessary to consider two authorities which are supposed to have laid down that illness through mental shock is a too remote or unnatural consequence of an *injuria* to entitle the plaintiff to recover in a case where damage is a necessary part of the cause of action.

[The decision of the Privy Council in *Victoria Ry. Cmsrs.* v. *Coultas*, 13 App. Cas. 222, was considered and held not an authority in this case since it did not involve "any element of wilful wrong; nor perhaps was the illness so direct and natural a consequence of the defendant's conduct as in this case".]

A more serious difficulty is the decision in *Allsop* v. *Allsop*, 5 H. & N. 534, which was approved by the House of Lords in *Lynch* v. *Knight*. In that case it was held by Pollock C.B., Martin, Bramwell, and Wilde BB. that illness caused by a slanderous imputation of unchasity in the case of a married woman did not constitute such special damage as would sustain an action for such a slander. That case, however, appears to have been decided on the ground that in all the innumerable actions for slander there were no precedents for alleging illness to be sufficient special damage, and that it would be of evil consequence to treat it as sufficient, because such a rule might lead to an infinity of trumpery or groundless actions. Neither of these reasons is applicable to the present case. Nor could such a rule be adopted as of general application without results which it would be difficult or impossible to defend. Suppose that a person is in a precarious and dangerous condition, and another person tells him that his physician has said that he has but a day to live. In such a case, if death ensued from the shock caused by the false statement, I cannot doubt at this day the case might be one of criminal homicide, or that if a serious illness ensued damages might be recovered. I think, however, that it must be admitted that the present case is without precedent. . . . In *Smith* v. *Johnson & Co.*, unreported, decided in January last, Bruce J. and I held that where a man was killed in the sight of the plaintiff by the defendant's negligence, and the plaintiff became ill, not from the shock from fear of harm to himself, but from the shock of seeing another person killed, this harm was too remote a consequence of the negligence. But that was a very different case from the present.

There must be judgment for the plaintiff for £100. 1s. 10½d.

Judgment for plaintiff.

NOTES

1. In *Janvier* v. *Sweeney*, [1919] 2 K.B. 316, the defendant, a private detective, in order to obtain some letters from the plaintiff, made the following statement: "I am a detective from Scotland Yard and represent military authorities. You are the woman we want, as you have been corresponding with a German spy." The plaintiff, who was engaged to marry an interned German, sued for damages "for false statements wilfully and maliciously made by the defendant to the plaintiff, intended to cause and actually causing her physical injury". The plaintiff claimed to have sustained a severe shock and resulting neurasthenia. The plaintiff was held entitled to recover. See a criticism, from a medical point of view, in Smith and Solomon, *Traumatic Neuroses in Court* (1943), 30 Va. L. Rev. 87, at p. 124.

2. In *Brooker* v. *Silverthorne* (1919), 99 S.E. 350 (South Carolina S.C.), the defendant appealed from a judgment for the plaintiff for $2,000 damages for mental anguish and nervous shock caused by the following language addressed to the plaintiff by the defendant over the telephone: "You God damned woman! None of you attend to your business . . . . You are a God damned liar. If I were there, I would break your God damned neck." Evidence at the trial disclosed that the plaintiff was so shocked and unnerved that she was ill and unfit for duty and could not sleep for some time. The judgment was reversed on appeal since the defendant's language was "not of such nature or made under such circumstances as to put a person of ordinary reason and firmness in fear of bodily hurt. And it is not alleged that plaintiff was not a person of ordinary reason and firmness and that defendant knew it."

3. In *Clark* v. *Associated Retail Credit Men of Washington* (1939), 105 Fed. 2d 62 (U.S. Court of Appeals for Dist. of Col.), the plaintiff was suffering from arterial hypertension and had lost, but was recovering, his sense of sight, which required him to avoid excitement and worry. He claimed that the defendant, knowing these facts, in an effort to collect a debt of some $60, wrote him a number of threatening letters which aggravated his condition and injured him "both psychologically and physiologically" and caused him "mental and physical agony". The defendant demurred to this claim and the demurrer was sustained. On appeal to the District Court of Appeals, the judgment was reversed. Edgerton J., said:

"The law does not, and doubtless should not, impose a general duty of care to avoid causing mental distress. For the sake of reasonable freedom of action, in our own interest and that of society, we need the privilege of being careless whether we inflict mental distress on our neighbours. It is perhaps less clear that we need the privilege of distressing them intentionally and without excuse. Yet there is, and probably should be, no general principle that mental distress purposely caused is actionable unless justified. Such a principle would raise awkward questions of *de minimis* and of excuse. 'He intentionally hurt my feelings' does not yet sound in tort, though it may in a more civilized time.

But the law has long given redress, in some circumstances, for intended mental harm without more. For centuries it has permitted recovery, under the name of assault, for intentionally-induced fear of a contact either harmful or offensive. In such cases the plaintiff has not been required to show that the fear produced physical consequences. The legally protected interest in bodily integrity has not been infringed, but it has been threatened; and the prospect of physical consequences, though no such consequences followed, has been accepted as adding to the intended mental disturbance a physical color sufficient to call for redress.

For a long time the assault cases stood practically alone; but in recent years an analogous principle has begun to develop. Several cases in which there was no physical harm and no assault have allowed recovery for intended mental harm which was serious enough so that it might have been found that defendant's acts had created a risk of physical illness . . . . The advantage to society of preventing such harm seems greater than the advantage of leaving ill-disposed persons free to seek their happiness in inflicting it."

4. In *Bielitski* v. *Obadiak* (1922), 15 Sask. L.R. 153, 65 D.L.R. 627, the defendant over the telephone told a friend that Steve Bielitski had hanged himself. After a number of repetitions, Steve's mother finally heard the statement and, believing the report to be true, "sustained a violent shock and mental anguish, which brought on physical illness and incapacitated her for some time". In an action by her against the defendant, she was held entitled to recover, the court drawing the conclusion that the defendant made the statement with the intention it should reach the plaintiff and that any reasonable man would know that it would "in all probability cause her not only mental anguish but physical pain". See notes in 35 Harv. L. Rev. 348; 22 Colum. L. Rev. 86.

5. In *Purdy* v. *Woznesensky*, [1937] 2 W.W.R. 116 (Sask. C.A.), at a dance held at a rural school, defendant twice struck the male plaintiff on the head, knocking him down and rendering him unconscious. This was done in the presence of the female plaintiff, his wife, who suffered a severe shock, requiring prolonged medical care. At the trial, both plaintiffs obtained judgments against defendant which were upheld on appeal. Mackenzie J.A. said that as defendant should have foreseen that such a violent assault might upset his victim's wife "an intention to produce such an effect must . . . be imputed to him."

6. In *Blakely* v. *Shorttal's Estate* (1945), 236 Iowa 787, 20 N.W. 2d 28, Shortal, a friend of the plaintiff's, spent the night at their home. He was left in the house next day and when plaintiffs returned they found Shortal had cut his throat in the kitchen. In an action to recover damages from Shortal's estate for resulting shock and nervousness, the jury was directed to find for the defendant at the trial. On appeal a new trial was ordered in which the jury were to find whether Shortal's act was wilful, and if so found, the plaintiffs would recover. Wilful was defined as a "reckless disregard for the safety of others".

7. The defendant announces that he is going to shoot someone. He then goes into a neighbouring room and fires a revolver. The plaintiff, who has overheard the defendant's threats, is taken ill. Liability? *Cf. Bunyan* v. *Jordan* (1937), 57 C.L.R. 1 (High Court of Australia).

8. Believe it or not, the following tragedy was reported in the Toronto Daily Star:

"STREAKED TO DEATH

Merced, Calif. (AP)—A 71-year-old man collapsed and died after a middle-aged, pot-bellied man broke into his house and streaked through the living room, police said. Joseph Mello died of a heart attack soon after the man dashed through the house."

Tort liability? What if the streaker had been young and slim? What if the deceased had been only 25 years of age?

SAMMS v. ECCLES

Supreme Court of Utah. (1961), 11 Utah 2d 289; 358 P. 2d 344

Crockett Justice: Plaintiff Marcia G. Samms sought to recover damages from David Eccles for injury resulting from severe emotional distress she claims to have suffered because he persistently annoyed her with indecent proposals.

The parties presented their respective contentions to the court at pretrial. The court entered a pretrial order noting that, "plaintiff bases her cause of action on . . . the infliction of severe emotional distress by wilful and wanton conduct of an outrageous and intolerable nature", and dismissed the action upon the ground that plaintiff had shown no basis upon which relief could be granted. She appeals.

Plaintiff alleged that she is a respectable married woman; that she has never encouraged the defendant's attentions in any way but has repulsed them; that all during the time from May to December, 1957, the defendant repeatedly and persistently called her by phone at various hours including late at night, soliciting her to have illicit sexual relations with him; and that on one occasion came to her residence in connection with such a solicitation and made an indecent exposure of his person. She charges that she regarded his proposals as insulting, indecent and obscene; that her feelings were deeply wounded; and that as a result thereof she suffered great anxiety and fear for her personal safety and severe emotional distress for which she asks $1,500 as actual, and a like amount as punitive, damages.

A motion for summary judgment is in effect a demurrer to the claims of the plaintiff, saying: assuming they are true, no right to recover is shown. It is regarded as a harsh measure which the courts are reluctant to sanction because it deprives the adverse party of an opportunity to present the evidence concerning her grievance for adjudication. For this reason plaintiff's contentions must be considered in the light most to her advantage and all doubts resolved in favor of permitting her to go to trial; and only if when the whole matter is so viewed, she could, nevertheless, establish no right to recover, should the motion be granted.

Due to the highly subjective and volatile nature of emotional distress and the variability of its causations, the courts have historically been wary of dangers in opening the door to recovery therefor. This is partly because such claims may easily be fabricated: or as sometimes stated, are easy to assert and hard to defend against. They have, therefore, been reluctant to allow such a right of action unless the emotional distress was suffered as a result of some overt tort. Nevertheless, recognizing the reality of such injuries and the injustice of permitting them to go unrequited, in many cases courts have strained to find the other tort as a peg upon which to hang the right of recovery.

Some of these have been unrealistic, or even flimsy. For instance, a technical battery was found where an insurance adjuster derisively tossed a coin on the bed of a woman who was in hospital with a heart condition, and because of this tort she was allowed to recover for distress caused by his other attempts at intimidation in accusing her of gold-bricking and attempting to defraud his company; courts have also dealt with trespass where hotel employees have invaded rooms occupied by married couples and imputed to them immoral conduct; and other similar torts have been used as a basis for such recovery. But a realistic analysis of many of these cases will show that the recognized tort is but incidental and that the real basis of recovery is the outraged feelings and emotional distress resulting from some aggravated conduct of the defendant. The lengths to which courts have gone to find a basis for allowing such recoveries serves to emphasize their realization that justice demands that grossly wrong conduct which causes such an injury to another should be held accountable.

In recent years courts have shown an increasing awareness of the necessity and justice of forthrightly recognizing the true basis for allowing recovery for such wrongs and of getting rid of the shibboleth that another tort peg is necessary to that purpose. [Examples omitted.]

Our study of the authorities, and of the arguments advanced, convinces us that, conceding such a cause of action may not be based upon mere negligence, the best considered view recognizes an action for severe emotional distress, though not accompanied by bodily impact or physical injury, where the defendant intentionally engaged in some conduct toward the plaintiff, (a) with the purpose of inflicting emotional distress, or, (b) where any reasonable person would have known that such would result; and his actions are of such a nature as to be considered outrageous and intolerable in that they offend against the generally accepted standards of decency and morality. This test seems to be a more realistic safeguard against false claims than to insist upon finding some other attendant tort, which may be of minor character, or fictional.

It is further to be observed that the argument against allowing such an action because groundless charges may be made is not a good reason for denying recovery. If the right to recover for injury resulting from the wrongful conduct could be defeated whenever such dangers exist, many of the grievances the law deals with would be eliminated. That some claims may be spurious should not compel those who administer justice to shut their eyes to serious wrongs and let them go without being brought to account. It is the function of courts and juries to determine whether claims are valid or false. This responsibility should not be shunned merely because the task may be difficult to perform.

We quite agree with the idea that under usual circumstances the solicitation to sexual intercourse would not be actionable even though it may be offensive to the offeree. It seems to be a custom of long standing and one which in all likelihood will continue. The assumption is usually indulged that most solicitations occur under such conditions as to fall within the well-known phrase of Chief Judge Magruder that, "there is no harm in asking". The Supreme Court of Kentucky in *Reed* v. *Maley* [115 Ky. 816, 74 S.W. 1079] pertinently observed that an action will not lie in favor of a woman against a man who, without trespass or assault, makes such a request; and that the reverse is also true: that a man would have no right of action against a woman for such a solicitation.

But the situations just described, where tolerance for the conduct referred to is indulged, are clearly distinguishable from the aggravated circumstances the plaintiff claims existed here. Even though her complaint may not flawlessly state such a cause of action, the facts were sufficiently disclosed that the case she proposes to prove could be found to fall within the requirements hereinabove discussed. Therefore, the trial court erred in dismissing the action.

Reversed.

NOTES

1. The defendant asks a 12-year-old girl to go to bed with him. She gets very upset and becomes ill. Liability? The defendant asks a 25-year-old woman, who is nine months pregnant, to go to bed with him. She is so shocked she becomes extremely sick. Liability? What if a 35-year-old woman propositions an innocent lad of 14?

2. Suppose a 21-year-old woman is invited to have sexual relations by the dean of her college. She suffers a nervous breakdown. Liability? What if she is invited to do the same by a policeman in uniform who stops her on the street? Suppose that a woman law professor issues a similar request to one of her male students?

3. In *State Rubbish Collectors Association* v. *Siliznoff* (1952), 240 Pac. 2d 282, Mr. Justice Traynor of the Supreme Court of California stated:

"There are persuasive arguments and analogies that support the recognition of a right to be free from serious, intentional and unprivileged invasions of mental and emotional tranquility. If a cause of action is otherwise established, it is settled that damages may be given for mental suffering naturally ensuing from the acts complained of . . . and in the case of many torts, such as assault, battery, false imprisonment and defamation, mental suffering will frequently constitute the principal element of damages. . . . In cases where mental suffering constitutes a major element of damages it is anomalous to deny recovery because the defendant's intentional misconduct fell short of producing some physical injury.

It may be contended that to allow recovery in the absence of physical injury will open the door to unfounded claims and a flood of litigation, and that the requirement that there be physical injury is necessary to insure that serious mental suffering actually occurred. The jury is ordinarily in a better position, however, to determine whether outrageous conduct results in mental distress than whether that distress in turn results in physical injury. From their own experience jurors are aware of the extent and character of the disagreeable emotions that may result from the defendant's conduct, but a difficult medical question is presented when it must be determined if emotional distress resulted in physical injury. (See Smith, *Relation of Emotions to Injury and Disease*, 30 Va. L. Rev. 193, 303-306.) Greater proof that mental suffering occurred is found in the defendant's conduct designed to bring it about than a physical injury that may or may not have resulted therefrom. . .".

4. What is meant by "physical injury"? What is "mental suffering"? Will liability be imposed if no damage is suffered at all? Should it be? What kind of result is required for liability?

5. Should a poor tenant who lives in a dreadful slum dwelling be able to sue the landlord for intentional infliction of mental suffering? See Sax and Hiestand, "Slumlordism as a Tort" (1967), 65 Mich. L. Rev. 869; Blum and Dunham, "Slumlordism as a Tort — A dissenting View" (1968), 66 Mich. L. Rev. 451; Sax, "Slumlordism as a Tort — A Brief Response" (1968), 66 Mich. L. Rev. 465.

RESTATEMENT OF TORTS, SECOND

§46. Outrageous Conduct Causing Severe Emotional Distress

(1) One who by extreme and outrageous conduct intentionally or recklessly causes severe emotional distress to another is subject to liability for such emotional distress, and if bodily harm to the other results from it, for such bodily harm.

(2) Where such conduct is directed at a third person, the actor is subject to liability if he intentionally or recklessly causes severe emotional distress

    (a) to a member of such person's immediate family who is present at the time, whether or not such distress results in bodily harm, or

(b) to any other person who is present at the time, if such distress results in bodily harm.

Caveat:

The Institute expresses no opinion as to whether there may not be other circumstances under which the actor may be subject to liability for the intentional or reckless infliction of emotional distress.

NOTES

1. See generally Glasbeek, "Outraged Dignity: Do We Need a New Tort?" (1968), 6 Alta. L. Rev. 77; Prosser, "Insult and Outrage" (1956), 44 Calif, L. Rev. 40; Handford, "Tort Liability for Threatening or Insulting Words" (1976), 54 Can. Bar Rev. 563.

A NOTE ON PRIVACY

1. Although the right to privacy is well-entrenched in American tort law (see *Nader* v. *G.M.* (1970), 307 N.Y.S. 2d 647), the Canadian and English courts have been reluctant to recognize a separate right to privacy. (See Winfield, "The Right of Privacy" (1931), 47 L.Q.R. 23; Gibson, "Common Law Protection of Privacy: What To Do Until the Legislators Arrive" in Klar (ed.), *Studies in Canadian Tort Law* (1977); Burns, "The Law and Privacy: The Canadian Experience" (1976), 54 Can. Bar Rev. 1; See also *Re X*, [1975] 1 All E.R. 697, at p. 704 (C.A.) *per* Lord Denning, "We have as yet no general remedy for infringement of privacy."; *Victoria Park Racecourse* v. *Taylor* (1937), 58 C.L.R. 479, at p. 494.)

2. Legislation has been enacted in three provinces, however, that makes it a "tort, actionable without proof of damage, for a person wilfully and without a claim or right to violate the privacy of another". (See Privacy Act, S.B.C. 1968, c. 39, s. 2(1); *Davis* v. *MacArthur* (1970), 10 D.L.R. (3d) 250; revd. [1971] 2 W.W.R. 142, 17 D.L.R. (3d) 760; Privacy Act, S.M. 1970, c. 74; S.S. 1973-74, c. 80.) In addition, the federal government has forbidden the interception of private communications by electronic or mechanical devices, unless judicial authorization has been obtained. Violators of this legislation may, *inter alia,* be required to pay punitive damages to the person aggrieved. (See Protection of Privacy Act, Stat. Can. 1974, c. 50, amending the Criminal Code, R.S.C. c. C-34, s. 178.21. See also Beck, "Electronic Surveillance and the Administration of Justice" (1968), 66 Can. Bar Rev. 643): Manning, *The Protection of Privacy Act* (1974). There are other legislative provisions as well. See, for example, Consumer Reporting Act, Stat. Ont. 1973, c. 97; Telephone Act, R.S.O. 1970, c. 457, s. 112; Bell Telephone Company Act, R.S.C. 1970, c. 67, s. 25; Post Office Act, R.S.C. 1970, c. P-14, s. 58, forbidding interception of mail.

3. At common law, the nearest a Canadian court has come to the creation of a general right to privacy has been the refusal of Mr. Justice Parker to dismiss an action for the invasion of privacy at the pleading stage on the ground that it had not been shown to him that the court would not recognize a right to privacy. (See *Krouse* v. *Chrysler Canada Ltd.*, [1970] 3 O.R. 135.) The matter, therefore, remains open — the right of privacy may not be judicially recognized but neither is it denied absolutely.

4. In the United States, a separate right to privacy has existed for many years. (See Warren and Brandeis, "The Right to Privacy" (1890), 4 Harv. L. Rev. 193.) Dean Prosser has argued that privacy was not one tort, but a complex of four: (1) intrusion on the plaintiff's seclusion or into his private affairs; (2) public disclosure of embarrassing private facts about the plaintiff; (3) publicity which places the plaintiff in a false light in the public eye; and (4) appropriation of the plaintiff's name or likeness for the defendant's advantage. (See Prosser, "Privacy" (1960), 48 Calif. L. Rev. 383; *cf.* Bloustein, "Privacy As An Aspect of Human Dignity: An Answer to Dean Prosser" (1964), 39 N.Y.U.L.J. 962. See also Fried, "Privacy" (1968), 77 Yale L. Rev. 475; Kalven, "Privacy in Tort Law — Were Warren and Brandeis Wrong?" (1966), 31 Law and Cont. Prob. 325.)

5. Various aspects of the right to privacy have been protected in Canada and the Commonwealth under different legal theories, such as trespass, contract and defamation. (See for example *Green* v. *Minnes* (1891), 22 O.R. 177 and see Gibson *op. cit., supra,* note 1.) In Quebec, Art. 1053 of the Civil Code has been utilized to award damages to someone who was bothered by phone calls for three days. (See *Robbins* v. *C.B.C.* (1957), 12 D.L.R. (2d) 35.) The theory of "passing off" has been used to protect what might be considered an aspect of privacy. (See *Lord Byron* v. *Johnston* (1816), 2 Mer. 29; *cf. Clark* v. *Freeman* (1848), 11 Beav. 112, 50 E.R. 759; *Dackrell* v. *Dougall* (1899), 80 T.R. 556.) See also *Sim* v. *H.J. Heinz Co. Ltd.,* [1959] 1 W.L.R. 313 (C.A.); Mathieson, "Comment" (1961), 39 Can. Bar Rev. 409; J. Williams, *Legal Protection of Privacy* (1972), A Study by the Privacy and Computer Task Force; *Privacy and Computers* (1972), at p. 125, Report by the Department of Communications/ Department of Justice.

6. One important recent development has been the recognition of the tort of "appropriation of one's personality". In *Krouse* v. *Chrysler Canada Ltd.,* [1974] 1 O.R. 225 (C.A.), revg. [1972] 2 O.R. 133, an action photograph of a football game was used in some advertising material. The plaintiff could be identified as one of the players depicted in the photo. Since he had not consented to this use of his photo, he claimed damages. Mr. Justice Estey recognized that there was a tort of appropriation of one's personality, but dismissed the claim because the usefulness of the player's name had not been diminished and therefore there had been no infringement of his legal right. In a similar type of case, where a photograph of the plaintiff waterskiing was used by the defendant to promote its business without his consent, damages of $500, the commercial value of the photo, was awarded. See *Athans* v. *Canadian Adventure Camps* (1977), 4 C.C.L.T. 20 (Ont. H.C.) *per* Henry J. Rather than being an invasion of privacy, it has been suggested that this is a form of "publicity piracy". See Gibson, Note on *Athans* case, (1977), 4 C.C.L.T. 37, at p. 42.

7. See generally Westin, *Privacy and Freedom* (1967); Miller, *The Assault on Privacy* (1971); Sharp, *Credit Reporting and Privacy;* Brittan, "The Right of Privacy in England and the United States" (1963), 37 Tulane L. Rev. 235; Wade, "Defamation and the Right of Privacy" (1962), 15 Vand. L. Rev. 1093; Neill, "The Protection of Privacy" (1962), Mod L. Rev. 393; Weisstub and Gotlieb, *The Nature of Privacy* (1972), A Study by the Privacy and Computer Task Force; Pedrick, "Publicity and Privacy: Is It Any of Our Business?" (1970), 20 U.T.L.J. 391; J. Williams, "Invasion of Privacy" (1973), 11 Alta. L. Rev. 1; Rowan, "Privacy and the Law", in *Special Lectures of the Law Society of Upper Canada* (1973), at p. 259; Ont. Law Reform Commission, *Report on Protection of Privacy in Ontario* (1968); Marshall, "The Right to Privacy: A Skeptical View" (1975), 21 McGill L.J. 242.

E. FALSE IMPRISONMENT

BIRD v. JONES

Queen's Bench. (1845), 7 Q.B. 742; 115 E.R. 668

At a trial of an action of assault and false imprisonment with a jury the trial judge, Lord Denman C.J., had instructed the jury that the facts disclosed at the trial constituted an imprisonment of the plaintiff. The plaintiff obtained a verdict, and after a rule *nisi* for a new trial had been obtained on the ground of misdirection, the arguments and judgments related to the sole question whether the following facts, taken from the judgment of Williams J., constituted an imprisonment of the plaintiff by the defendant:

"A part of Hammersmith Bridge, which is generally used as a public footway, was appropriated for seats to view a regatta on the river, and separated for that purpose from the carriage way by a temporary fence. The plaintiff insisted upon passing along the part so appropriated, and attempted to climb over the fence. The defendant (clerk of the Bridge Company) pulled him back; but the plaintiff succeeded in climbing over the fence. The defendant then stationed two policemen to prevent, and they did prevent, the plaintiff from proceeding forwards along the footway in the direction he wished to go. The plaintiff, however, was at the same time told that he might go back into the carriage way and proceed to the other side of the bridge, if he pleased. The plaintiff refused to do so, and remained where he was so obstructed, about half an hour."

Coleridge J.: The plaintiff, being in a public highway and desirous of passing along it, in a particular direction, is prevented from doing so by the orders of the defendant, and . . . the defendant's agents for the purpose are policemen, from whom, indeed, no unnecessary violence was to be anticipated, or such as they believed unlawful, yet who might be expected to execute such commands as they deemed lawful with all necessary force, however resisted. But, although thus obstructed, the plaintiff was at liberty to move his person and go in any other direction, at his free will and pleasure: and no actual force or restraint on his person was used, unless the obstruction before mentioned amounts to so much.

I lay out of consideration the question of right or wrong between these parties. The acts will amount to imprisonment neither more nor less from their being wrongful or capable of justification.

And I am of opinion that there was no imprisonment. To call it so appears to me to confound partial obstruction and disturbance with total obstruction and detention. A prison may have its boundary large or narrow, visible and tangible, or, though real, still in the conception only; it may itself be moveable or fixed: but a boundary it must have; and that boundary the party imprisoned must be prevented from passing; he must be prevented from leaving that place, within the ambit of which the party imprisoning would confine him, except by prison-breach. Some confusion seems to me to arise from confounding imprisonment of the body with mere loss of freedom: it is one part of the definition of freedom to be able to go withersoever one pleases; but imprisonment is something more than the mere loss of this power; it includes the notion of restraint within some limits defined by a will or power exterior to our own. . . .

On a case of this sort, which, if there be difficulty in it, is at least purely elementary, it is not easy nor necessary to enlarge: and I am unwilling to put any extreme case hypothetically: but I wish to meet one suggestion, which has been put as avoiding one of the difficulties which cases of this sort might seem to suggest. If it be said that to hold the present case to amount to an imprisonment would turn every obstruction of the exercise of a right of way into an imprisonment, the answer is, that there must be something like personal menace or force accompanying the act of obstruction, and that, with this, it will amount to imprisonment. I apprehend that is not so. If, in the course of a night, both ends of a street were walled up, and there was no egress from the house but into the street, I should have no difficulty in saying that the inhabitants were thereby imprisoned; but, if only one end were walled up, and an armed force stationed outside to prevent any scaling of the wall or passage that way, I should feel equally clear that there was no imprisonment. If there were, the street would obviously be the prison; and yet, as obviously, none would be confined to it. [Williams J. agreed with Coleridge J.]

Lord Denman C.J. (dissenting): . . . There is some difficulty perhaps in defining imprisonment in the abstract without reference to its illegality; nor is it necessary for me to do so, because I consider these acts as amounting to imprisonment. That word I understand to mean any restraint of the person by force. . . .

I had no idea that any person in these times supposed any particular boundary to be necessary to constitute imprisonment, or that the restraint of a man's person from doing what he desires ceases to be an imprisonment because he may find some means of escape.

It is said that the party here was at liberty to go in another direction. . . . But this liberty to do something else does not appear to me to affect the question of imprisonment. As long as I am prevented from doing what I have a right to do, of what importance is it that I am permitted to do something else? How does the imposition of an unlawful condition shew that I am not restrained? If I am locked in a room, am I not imprisoned because I might effect my escape through a window, or because I might find an exit dangerous or inconvenient to myself, as by wading through water or by taking a route so circuitous that my necessary affairs would suffer by delay?

It appears to me that this is a total deprivation of liberty with reference to the purpose for which he lawfully wished to employ his liberty: and, being effected by force, it is not the mere obstruction of a way, but a restraint of the person. . . .

Rule absolute.

NOTES

1. Suppose the defendant locks the plaintiff in a room but there is a window open. The room is on the first floor of the house. Is this false imprisonment? Suppose the room is on the second floor? What if there is no ladder, but there is a rope, long enough to touch the ground? Does it matter if the plaintiff is an athletic young woman or a sick old man?

2. What if a woman agrees to let a man drive her home in his car. When she discovers that he is going in the opposite direction she remonstrates. He informs her, as he speeds along at 50 m.p.h., that the door of the car is not locked and that she is free to go. She chooses not to jump. Imprisonment?

3. The plaintiff goes for a swim in the nude, hiding his clothes in the bushes. The defendant takes the plaintiff's clothes so that he cannot leave without exposing himself. Imprisonment?

4. Suppose the plaintiff's purse is held by the defendant who tells the plaintiff she is free to go wherever she wants. Imprisonment? *Cf. Ashland Dry Goods Co.* v. *Wages* (1946), 302 Ky. 577, 195 S.W. 2d 312.

CHAYTOR ET AL. v. LONDON, NEW YORK AND PARIS ASSOCIATION OF FASHION LTD. AND PRICE

Supreme Court of Newfoundland. (1961), 30 D.L.R. (2d) 527

The plaintiffs, Vera Chaytor and John Delgado, Jr., were employees of Bowring Brothers Ltd., a department store in St. John's, Newfoundland. On the day in question they went across the street from Bowring's and entered the department store of the defendant, a competitor, in order to do some "comparison shopping". In other words, they wished to look over their competitor's goods and prices. They were stopped by the manager of the defendant store, Mr. Price, who called them spies, asked his own store detectives to watch them and called the police to arrest them as "suspicious characters". The plaintiffs accompanied the police in order to avoid embarrassment and because they felt compelled to do so. They were detained about 15 minutes at the police station and were then released without any charge being laid. They sued Price and his employer for false imprisonment.

Dunfield J.: . . . To treat generally, at this point of the question of what is called "comparison shopping", I think we must accept the situation that it is a normal practice among retailers. Reputable and competent witnesses have said that it is done here and in Great Britain and in Mainland Canada and in the United States; and apart from what they say, I think it is a matter of common knowledge. Retailing is a very competitive and catch-as-catch-can business, and a retailer who failed to keep a close watch on the goods and prices of his competitors would be likely to suffer for it. It has been sought to represent to me that it is a reprehensible practice, and amounts to stealing other people's ideas; but I do not accept this. Every branch of commerce must watch its competition. We all read, for example, of the many precautions taken by motor car manufacturers to conceal their tentative models, and by dressmakers to do the same, before they are ready for exhibition. I am strongly of the opinion that commercial enterprises spy on one another like nations; it is inevitable in acute competition and shares the general ethics of competition. And in any case, it is in practice impossible to prevent. A merchant admitted in evidence that his firm had private shoppers whose names were known to one person only in the firm. It would be the easiest possible thing for any of the large department stores here, where so many people pass through their service, to arrange for former employees, such as married women who had been in their service as girls, to tip them off regarding competitors' goods. Indeed, much could be done by keeping a careful watch on shop windows, and as Mrs. Chaytor humorously observed, she had once bought a hat for herself in The London Shop, which she had a perfect right to do; but obviously in the course of doing it she could have inspected and probably did inspect most of the hats in the shop. In my view, the close watching of competitors is a normal commercial practice and does not carry any opprobrium. Moreover, people like department managers and buyers are dependent for their own status within their own establishment upon being closely in touch with the competition, and even if they were not told to keep themselves in touch they would naturally do so.

Actually, I think that for a department head and a buyer, probably known to half the shop-hands on Water St., to go out and look round was an exceptionally open and aboveboard way of seeking information. Mrs. Chaytor said that she had occupied her present position for eight years and had often done this before and had never been challenged before. I gathered from another witness that it was an ordinary matter to recognise in the shop emissaries from another shop and, as it were, to tolerate them with a smile.

Now the proper course in my view for a shop manager who recognised such emissaries and did not want them in his shop would be to identify them and ask them politely to leave and, to wait a while and see whether they did so before taking any further measures; and further, in view of the well-recognised situation in the city, politeness would be in order and would be forthcoming from both sides. I think that any trouble there was brought on by the rather angry and hasty action of Mr. Price, which would, I feel, be not in accord with the common manners of the town. Whatever they may do in big cities among strangers, roughness and incivility are neither common nor necessary in this environment. . . .

. . .

I am quite satisfied that Mr. Delgado and Mrs. Chaytor were highly desirous of avoiding embarrassment to themselves, by being treated in a way which would make it look as if they were shoplifters or something of the kind, and also of avoiding embarrassment to their firm; and that they would have departed politely if they had been asked politely to do so; and that it was the rough behaviour of the store manager, together with the calling of the police, which brought about the whole trouble.

I consider therefore that there was what one might call a psychological type of imprisonment. In addition to this of course the plaintiffs were subjected to an objectionable form of public treatment. If they went to the Police Station voluntarily, I think it was because they felt they could hardly do otherwise; and by the mere operation of normal delays, they were psychologically compelled to remain there in the surroundings appropriate to suspected criminals for 15 or 20 minutes.

We find cases of this kind mostly in connection with shoplifting; and I refer to a few cases, some raised by counsel, some not.

In *Conn* v. *David Spencer Ltd.*, [1930] 1 D.L.R. 805, 42 B.C.R. 128, the plaintiff, who had been shopping in the self-service department of the defendant's departmental store in Vancouver, was tapped on the shoulder by a house detective and accused of having stolen a cake of soap and requested by her to leave the basement and go upstairs to one of the rooms. Plaintiff had not committed any theft, but still he thought it advisable in view of the crowded state of the store to give way without any exhibition of force on the part of the detective, so he went upstairs accompanied by her and her assistant and upon being searched satisfied them that a mistake had occurred. They went upstairs with the detective walking beside him and her assistant behind. The detective, Mrs. Kinser, was asked whether she was taking the plaintiff into custody when she took him upstairs and replied that she was taking him up there to question him. She was asked whether she intended to let the plaintiff out of the room and stated that she might not have been able to hold him but she would have done her best to prevent it when protecting the goods of her employer. Macdonald J., therefore, concludes that while physical force was not exerted to compel the plaintiff to leave the basement of the store and go to the room to remain and be searched, still that the control and detention arising out of a mistake was inexcusable and unwarranted, and he quotes Alderson B., in *Peters* v. *Stanway* (1835), 6 Car. & P. 737, at pp. 739-740, 172 E.R. 1142, where Baron Alderson says: 'The question therefore is, whether you think the going to the station-house proceeded originally from the plaintiff's own willingness, or from the defendant's making a charge against her; for it proceeded from the defendant's making a charge, the plaintiff will not be deprived of her right of action by her having willingly gone to meet the charge.' . . .

In *Sinclair* v. *Woodward's Stores Ltd.*, [1942] 2 D.L.R. 395, it is said by Ellis J., that the fact that actual force was not exercised by a store detective in compelling a customer suspected of shoplifting to come with him to a private room will not defeat an action for false arrest if the detective, to the customer's knowledge, was prepared to use force if necessary, so that the customer's act in accompanying the detective was not voluntary. So says the headnote; but I think it goes further than the facts. Plaintiff says that the store detective grabbed her by the arms and said she would force her. The shop detective swore she never put a hand on the plaintiff. The trend of the evidence quoted is that if plaintiff had not come along she would have been publicly humiliated. The Judge says he is convinced the plaintiff was not taken by the arm; and that few noticed the occurrence. The case is much nearer *Conn* v. *David Spencer Ltd., supra*, and our present case than would appear at first sight.

And, I observe, how is a person to know whether or not force will be used if he does not comply with the order given him. He can at best form an estimate of the probabilities . . . .

A point was made by Mr. Dawe, Q.C., for the defence that there is another exit from the area where Mrs. Chaytor was, by a stair which leads to the street.

But plaintiffs may not have known that. It is not the regular main entrance known to everybody. And indeed, I do not think that anybody who had done something to detain a person can say that she could, if she had insisted or resisted, or been clear about her rights and position, have effected an escape . . . I hardly think we need argue the pretty obvious point that there can be restraint of freedom without touching of the person. . . .

I therefore award (a) to Mr. Delgado against the London, New York and Paris Association of Fashion Ltd. $100 and against Mr. Richard Price $100 and (b) to Mrs. Vera Chaytor against the London, New York and Paris Association of Fashion Ltd. $100 and against Mr. Richard Price $100. If I thought that the plaintiffs' reputations had been seriously affected I might have allowed much more; but the whole street knows now about the affair and knows also that the plaintiffs are respectable people.

NOTES

1. Is a suspect who is asked to accompany a police officer in order to avoid a "scene which would be embarrassing" imprisoned? See *Campbell* v. *S.S. Kresge Co. Ltd.* (1976), 74 D.L.R. (3d) 717 (N.S.S.C.), *per* Hart J.

2. How, then, should a storekeeper handle these unwelcome guests? Can they be forcibly ejected if they refuse to leave when asked to do so?

3. A touching was once thought necessary for an arrest. See *Russen* v. *Lucas* (1824), 1 C. & P. 153, 171 E.R. 1141; *Genner* v. *Sparkes* (1704), 1 Salk. 79, 91 E.R. 74. This requirement seems to have been laid to rest. See *Warner* v. *Riddiford* (1858), 4 C.B.N.S. 180, 140 E.R. 1052.

4. The American cases are in accord. See, for example, *Martin* v. *Houck* (1906), 141 N.C. 317, 54 S.E. 295, where the defendant told the plaintiff to consider himself under arrest and that he had to go with him. The plaintiff said that he would go. Mr. Justice Walker explained the principle as follows:

> "In ordinary practice, words are sufficient to constitute an imprisonment, if they impose a restraint upon the person, and the party is accordingly restrained; for he is not obliged to incur the risk of personal violence and insult by resisting until actual violence be used. This principle is reasonable in itself, and is fully sustained by the authorities. Nor does it seem that there should be any very formal declaration of arrest. If the officer goes for the purpose of executing his warrant, and has the party in his presence and power, if the party so understands it, and in consequence thereof submits, and the officer, in the execution of the warrant, takes the party before a magistrate, or receives money or property in discharge of his person, it is in law an arrest, although he did not touch any part of the body. It is not necessary to constitute false imprisonment that the person restrained of his liberty should be touched or actually arrested. If he is ordered to do or not to do the thing, to move or not to move against his own free will, if it is not left to his option to go or stay where he pleases, and force is offered, or there is reasonable ground to apprehend that coercive measures will be used if he does not yield, the offense is complete upon his submission. A false imprisonment may be committed by words alone, or by acts alone, or by both, and by merely operating on the will of the individual, or by personal violence, or by both. It is not necessary that the individual be confined within a prison or within walls, or that he be assaulted. It may be committed by threats."

5. This principle has had some doubt cast on it by the Supreme Court of Canada in *R.* v. *Whitfield*, [1970] S.C.R. 46. A police constable called Kerr spotted Whitfield at the wheel of an automobile which had stopped for a red light on St. Clair Avenue, Toronto. Kerr, being aware of an outstanding warrant for the arrest of Whitfield, approached the car and informed Whitfield that he had a warrant for his arrest. Whitfield accelerated in an attempt to get away, but was slowed down by the traffic. Kerr reached through the window

of the car and grabbed Whitefield's shirt with both hands, saying, "You are under arrest." Whitfield accelerated, causing Kerr to release his hold on the shirt and the car and fall to the ground. Whitfield was apprehended shortly thereafter and charged with escaping from lawful custody. At trial he was convicted, but the Court of Appeal quashed the conviction, directing that a verdict of acquittal be entered. The Crown appealed to the Supreme Court of Canada successfully, the sole issue being whether the accused had been in lawful custody. Mr. Justice Judson (Fauteux, Martland, Ritchie and Pigeon JJ. concurring) relied on some of the older authorities to the effect that, if an officer is "near enough to touch him, and does touch him, and gives him notice of the writ, it is an arrest". These authorities were aimed at the preservation of the peace. Mr. Justice Judson concluded with these words:

"A police officer has the right to use such force as may be necessary to make an arrest. What kind of arrest are we to expect if it becomes a principle of law that a police officer, acting under a warrant of which he informs the accused, and who actually seizes the accused's person, is found not to have made an arrest because the accused is in the driver's seat of a motor car which enables him to shake off the arresting officer?"

Mr. Justice Hall (Spence J. concurring) dissented and argued that the majority judgment was based on a principle "applicable to situations arising 100 years after the situations to which they applied became obsolete". Mr. Justice Hall concluded:

"The dead hand of the past cannot reach that far. These outdated procedures evolved before the organization of police forces as we now know them and had no relation to the arrest or taking into custody of a person charged with a criminal offence.

Accordingly in my view this case does not fall to be decided upon the authority of cases applicable to the taking into custody under writs of *capeas ad satisfaciendum*, obsolete since 1869, civil in their nature, and not involving the criminal law doctrine of proof beyond a reasonable doubt but should be decided upon principles applicable to the circumstances obtaining in this century and particularly since Parliament has legislated in the very matter to cover both resisting lawful arrest and escaping from lawful custody as two distinct and separate offences.

In the instant case the police officer, Kerr, had a lawful right and duty to arrest Whitfield. There is no question as to the fact that a warrant was outstanding and Kerr's attempt to arrest was lawful. Whitfield accordingly was under a legal obligation to submit to the lawful arrest. It is only by the recognition of these corresponding duties and obligations that we can avoid the notion that the person being arrested has to be restrained physically before he can be said to be 'arrested'. I do not see that it should be necessary to touch or hold the person being arrested. He must, of course, be informed that he is being arrested. If he does not submit or tries to flee, the arresting officer may use such force as may reasonably be necessary to detain his man having regard to the nature of the offence for which the person is wanted. If the man flees and is not in fact detained he cannot be said to have been in lawful custody, but that does not mean he has not committed an offence. Parliament has legislated specifically in this regard."

6. A policeman phones X and tells him that he must come down immediately to the police station for questioning. X goes to the police station immediately. Imprisonment? What if X says he will be right down and then runs away? What if he refuses to go and runs away?

7. See Horkins, "False Arrest Today" in *New Developments in the Law of Torts, Special Lectures of The Law Society of Upper Canada* (1973), for a practitioner's view of some of the problems encountered in false arrest litigation.

HERRING v. BOYLE

Court of Exchequer. (1834), 1 Cr. M. & R. 377; 149 E.R. 1125

Trespass for assault and false imprisonment. Plea, the general issue. The plaintiff, who sued by his next friend, was an infant about ten years old. He was placed by his mother at a school kept by the defendant. On the 24th of December the plaintiff's mother went to the school and asked that the boy be permitted to come home with her. The defendant refused to permit it unless the tuition fee then due was paid. After repeated demands a writ of *habeas corpus* was sued out, thereupon the plaintiff was sent home seventeen days after the first request of his mother. No proof was given that the plaintiff knew of the denial to his mother, nor was there any evidence of actual restraint upon him. On these facts Gurney B., was of the opinion that there was no evidence of an imprisonment to go to the jury, and he nonsuited the plaintiff. A rule *nisi* was obtained, to set aside the nonsuit and for a new trial against which cause was now shown.

Bolland B.: . . . I cannot find anything upon the notes of the learned Judge which shows that the plaintiff was at all cognizant of any restraint. There are many cases which show that it is not necessary, to constitute an imprisonment, that the hand should be laid upon the person: but in no case has any conduct been held to amount to an imprisonment in the absence of the party supposed to be imprisoned. An officer may make an arrest without laying his hand on the party arrested; but in the present case, as far as we know, the boy may have been willing to stay; he does not appear to have been cognizant of any restraint, and there was no evidence of any act whatsoever done by the defendant in his presence. I think that we can not construe the refusal to the mother in the boy's absence, and without his being cognizant of any restraint, to be an imprisonment of him against his will; and therefore I am of opinion that the rule must be discharged.

[The concurring judgments of Alderson and Gurney BB. and Lord Lyndhurst are omitted.]

NOTES

1. Could it be contended that the mother, while at the school, was imprisoned by the defendant's conduct?

MEERING v. GRAHAME-WHITE AVIATION CO., LTD.

Court of Appeal. (1919), 122 L.T. 44

The plaintiff was an employee of the defendant company living with another employee, Lamb, in the latter's cottage adjoining the defendant's plant. Certain materials had been stolen from the defendant company's stock and some of the company's employees suspected it to be in Lamb's cottage. A search warrant was obtained, the cottage searched and Lamb was arrested by the police. The police told employees of the company that they would like to question the plaintiff away from Lamb's house in which certain of the stolen articles had been found and an employee, Prudence, was instructed to arrange to have the plaintiff at the company's office around 9 p.m. Prudence told two other employees to inform the plaintiff he was wanted at the office. The two men took different approaches to the house and one of them went in and told the plaintiff he was wanted at the office. He agreed to go. On the way the other employee joined the two and the plaintiff was invited to go to the waiting room.

As he reached this room he asked what he was there for and said if they did not tell him he should leave. He was told his evidence was wanted about some things that were stolen, and with that, he stayed. Prudence had meanwhile phoned the police and told them, "We have got him at the office." One or two employees stayed outside in the hall on to which the door of the waiting room opened. After about an hour the police, who had been investigating, arrived and arrested the plaintiff on a charge of theft.

The plaintiff, having been acquitted, sued the defendant company for damages for false imprisonment, his statement of claim referring only to imprisonment by the police acting at the instance and under the direction of the defendant company. At the trial attention was directed to the action of the company's employees before the police arrived and the trial judge left two questions to the jury: (1) Had the plaintiff been detained in the waiting room before the detectives arrived? and (2) Were the detectives when they formally arrested the plaintiff acting as agents and with the authority of the defendants? The jury answered "Yes" to both questions and awarded £250 damages for false imprisonment. [Consideration of the further claim against the defendant for damages for malicious prosecution is omitted. On that claim the jury awarded the plaintiff £1,250 damages.] The defendant appealed.

Warrington L.J. [after holding there was "ample evidence" justifying the jury's answer to the first question] : . . . I think that that evidence satisfies me that the officers of the defendant company did not give the plaintiff in charge, but that in that matter the Metropolitan Police acted on their own responsibility, and by virtue of the powers which were conferred upon them as police constables. That being so, the arrest of the plaintiff by them was not wrongful, because I think that they had at the time they arrested him sufficient reasonable ground for suspecting that a felony had been committed, and that the plaintiff had been involved in the commission of that felony. . . .

That being so, but for what Mr. Gregory has said on the plaintiff's behalf, a very difficult question would be involved, because the jury have made no distinction between the damages incurred by the false imprisonment, which only lasted something under an hour, and the subsequent formal arrest and its consequences. But Mr. Gregory, on the plaintiff's behalf, has agreed that, there being no wrongful imprisonment by the arrest on the part of the police constables, the only wrongful imprisonment being that by the officers of the company for a short time in the waiting-room, we may reduce the damages awarded by the jury to a nominal sum. That accordingly I think ought to be done. . . .

Duke L.J.: (dissenting on this point) . . . Can it be said upon what is affirmatively proved here that there is evidence upon which the jury could act that the plaintiff was so restrained as that he had not his liberty freely to go whither he would? To my mind there is a conclusive fact proved in the case with regard to the matter, which is, that the plaintiff himself does not show the slightest indication of a suspicion that he was restrained of his liberty to go if he had thought fit to go. . . .

Atkin L.J.: . . . It appears to me that a person could be imprisoned without his knowing it. I think a person can be imprisoned while he is asleep, while he is in a state of drunkenness, while he is unconscious, and while he is a lunatic. Those are cases where it seems to me that the person might properly complain if he were imprisoned, though the imprisonment began and ceased while he was in that state. Of course, the damages might be diminished and would be affected by the question whether he was conscious of it or not.

So a man might in fact, to my mind, be imprisoned by having the key of a door turned against him so that he is imprisoned in a room in fact although he does not know that the key has been turned. It may be that he is being detained in that room by persons who are anxious to make him believe that he is not in fact being imprisoned, and at the same time his captors outside that room may be boasting to persons that he is imprisoned, and it seems to me that if we were to take this case as an instance supposing it could be proved that Prudence had said while the plaintiff was waiting: "I have got him detained there waiting for the detective to come in and take him to prison" — it appears to me that that would be evidence of imprisonment. It is quite unnecessary to go on to show that in fact the man knew that he was imprisoned. . . .

At any rate, it appears to me that there are no doubt two inferences that the jury might draw from these circumstances — they might come to the conclusion from all those circumstances that all that happened was that Prudence would have restrained the liberty of the plaintiff if the plaintiff had sought to exercise his liberty by proceeding to the cottage; but they might, to my mind, infer also that Prudence had made up his mind from the time that the plaintiff was in the waiting-room that he should not exercise his liberty, and that he placed the policeman there for that purpose. . . .

[The Court of Appeal dismissed the defendant's appeal on the malicious prosecution issue and made an order changing the judgment for the plaintiff on false imprisonment to 1s. The defendant was awarded costs of the issue on false imprisonment as raised in the statement of claim, *i.e.,* in the trial court, and the defendant was directed to pay two-thirds of the costs of the appeal.]

NOTES

1. Is consciousness of confinement a requisite of false imprisonment on the basis of these two cases? Is there a holding on this point in either case?

2. Which is the better rule? See Prosser, "False Imprisonment — Consciousness of Confinement" (1955), 55 Colum. L. Rev. 847.

RESTATEMENT OF TORTS, SECOND

§35. False Imprisonment
   (1) An actor is subject to liability to another for false imprisonment if
      (a) he acts intending to confine the other or a third person within boundaries fixed by the actor, and
      (b) his act directly or indirectly results in such a confinement of the other, and
      (c) the other is conscious of the confinement or is harmed by it.
   (2) An act which is not done with the intention stated in Subsection (1, a) does not make the actor liable to the other for a merely transitory or otherwise harmless confinement, although the act involves an unreasonable risk of imposing it and therefore would be negligent or reckless if the risk threatened bodily harm.
Caveat:
   The Institute expresses no opinion as to whether the actor may or may not be subject to liability for conduct which involves an unreasonable risk of causing a confinement of such duration or character as to make the other's loss of freedom a matter of material value.

HERD v. WEARDALE STEEL, COAL AND COKE CO., LTD.

House of Lords. [1915] A.C. 67

The plaintiff was an employee of the defendant company under a verbal contract determinable on either side by fourteen days' notice, and worked in the company's colliery. The colliery was entered by a shaft and the men were raised from and lowered to the mine in a cage worked by machinery.

Working conditions were regulated by the Coal Mines Regulations Act and a collective labour agreement made between associations of mine owners and associations of mine workers. Times for raising and lowering were dealt with by the Act and agreement and notices of the times so fixed posted at the pit head. The cages furnished the only means of access or egress to or from the mine. The cages were used to convey workman and coal, but when coal was carried workmen were not allowed to enter.

The mine was worked on a shift system and at 9.30 a.m. on May 30, 1911, the plaintiff descended the mine. Ordinarily he would have been entitled to be raised at the end of the shift, about 4 p.m. The plaintiff and two other men were directed to do certain work, but they believed it was unsafe, and in breach of an arrangement reached with the owners, and consequently they refused to do the work. About 11 a.m. they and 29 men acting in sympathy with them requested the foreman to allow them to ascend the shaft by means of the cage as they wished to leave the mine. The foreman, on instructions from the manager, informed them that permission to use the cage would not be granted until the end of the shift. The cage came down several times in the morning but on many occasions it was used to hoist coal. At about 1 p.m. the cage came down carrying men and at the bottom of the shaft it was empty and available for the carriage of men. The 29 men were refused permission to enter, but some got in and refused to leave when ordered. By the manager's orders the cage was left stationary for about 20 minutes. Ultimately, at 1.30 p.m. permission was given the men to enter the cage. The plaintiff was then taken to the top.

In another proceeding, regulated by statute, the plaintiff was ordered to pay the defendant 5s. damages for breach of contract. The plaintiff thereafter sued the defendant for damages for false imprisonment. At a trial before Pickford J., the plaintiff obtained a judgment for 20s. with costs on the High Court scale. In delivering judgment Pickford J. stated: "The right, as I understand it, which was claimed by the defendant was this: that as, they say, the plaintiff had contracted to work for that shift and was impliedly to remain in the mine until the end of the shift they were entitled to retain him in the mine until the end of the shift, whether he wished to remain or not; in fact practically to enforce his performance of his contract by not allowing him to leave the mine until the end of the time when the performance had been made. It is only if that contention be good that they can justify detaining him in the circumstances in which they did in this case.

I do not think the defendants can maintain that proposition. I hold that it is not correct to say that, if miners go down for the purpose of working a shift and then decline to do so, even wrongfully, the mine owner is entitled to detain them against their will in the mine until the end of the shift comes, although the cage may have been in the mine and going to the surface in circumstances in which the miner would have been entitled to use it."

The defendant appealed.

Vaughan Williams L.J. (dissenting): . . . The case, to my mind, does not differ a jot from the case where there is a staircase instead of a lift and the manager has the key of the gate in his pocket, but, on being asked to open the gate which gives access to the stairs, refuses to produce the key, and thus of his own will prevents the men from using the staircase for no other reason whatsoever than his own will. . . . I shall be very much surprised if I hear that to detain a man by not allowing him to go out of a room or out of any other place is not false imprisonment, unless the detention can in some way or other be justified. I say, as I have already said, that it is an admitted fact in this case that the detention of these men was not for the purpose of carrying out the work of the company, but was a detention which would not have been ordered unless these men had refused to do this dangerous work. In my opinion that amounts to a false imprisonment. . . . I think that if this action had not been brought the men would have left the masters in the position of being able to say that they had the right to refuse to allow their workmen who refused to obey an order to come up to the surface. I wholly deny that any such right exists. I think that it is a legitimate conclusion from the admitted facts that the defendants refused permission to the men to use the lift as a penalty or punishment for their refusal to obey the order.

Buckley L.J.: . . . But is it true to say that the defendants compelled the plaintiff against his will to remain in the mine and imprisoned him? To my mind it is not. It is true that he could not leave the place; but he was detained there, not by any act of the defendants, but by a certain physical difficulty arising from the situation of the place, a difficulty which the plaintiff was, as between himself and his employers, contractually entitled to call upon them to remove for him at a time, but not at that time. What kept him from getting to the surface was not any act which the defendants did, but the fact that he was at the bottom of a deep shaft, and that there were no means of getting out other than the particular means which belonged to his employers and over which the plaintiff had contractual rights which at that moment were not in operation. He had no right to say to the defendants at that moment, "You are preventing me from getting out of the mine." The defendant's reply would be, "We are not preventing you from getting out; get out by all means if you can. But you are not entitled to call upon us to take you out when contractually, as between you and us, we are not bound to do so. You are calling upon us to assist you in your breach of contract by taking you out. We are bound by contract to do so at a time, but not at this time." From that it follows, in my opinion, that there was no imprisonment of the plaintiff by the defendants. . . .

The question may be tested in another way. Suppose that at the end of the shift, when there would be a contractual right on the part of the man to come up, the master were to say that it was not convenient to bring the man up at that time and that he must remain in the pit for another hour, the man would be entitled to damages for breach of contract, but would there be any false imprisonment? In my opinion there would not. The master has not imprisoned the man. He has not enabled him to get out as under the contract he ought to have done, but he has done no act compelling him to remain there.

[The plaintiff appealed to the House of Lords.]

Viscount Haldane L.C.: My Lords, by the law of this country no man can be restrained of his liberty without authority in law. That is a proposition the maintenance of which is of great importance; but at the same time it is a proposition which must be read in relation to other propositions which are equally important. If a man chooses to go into a dangerous place at the bottom of a quarry or the bottom of a mine, from which by the nature of physical circumstances he cannot escape, it does not follow from the proposition I have enunciated about liberty that he can compel the owner to bring him up out of it. The owner may or may not be under a duty arising from circumstances, on broad grounds the neglect of which may possibly involve him in a criminal charge or a civil liability. It is unnecessary to discuss the conditions and circumstances which might bring about such a result, because they have, in the view I take, nothing to do with false imprisonment.

My Lords, there is another proposition which has to be borne in mind, and that is the application of the maxim *volenti non fit injuria*. If a man get into an express train and the doors are locked pending its arrival at its destination, he is not entitled, merely because the train has been stopped by signal, to call for the doors to be opened to let him out. He has entered the train on the terms that he is to be conveyed to a certain station without the opportunity of getting out before that, and he must abide by the terms on which he has entered the train. So when a man goes down a mine, from which access to the surface does not exist in the absence of special facilities given on the part of the owner of the mine, he is only entitled to the use of these facilities (subject possibly to the exceptional circumstances to which I have alluded) on the terms on which he has entered. I think it results from what was laid down by the Judicial Committee of the Privy Council in *Robinson* v. *Balmain New Ferry Co.,* [1910] A.C. 295, that that is so. There there was a pier, and by the regulations a penny was to be paid by those who entered and a penny on getting out. The manager of the exit gate refused to allow a man who had gone in, having paid his penny, but having changed his mind about embarking on a steamer, and wishing to return, to come out without paying his penny. It was held that that was not false imprisonment; *volenti non fit injuria.* The man had gone in upon the pier knowing that those were the terms and conditions as to exit, and it was not false imprisonment to hold him to conditions which he had accepted. So, my Lords, it is not false imprisonment to hold a man to the conditions he has accepted when he goes down a mine. . . .

Now, my Lords, in the present case what happened was this. The usage of the mine — a usage which I think must be taken to have been notified — was that the workman was to be brought up at the end of his shift. In this case the workman refused to work; it may have been for good reasons or it may have been for bad — I do not think that question concerns us. He said that the work he had been ordered to do was of a kind that was dangerous, and he threw down his tools and claimed to come up to the surface. The manager, or at any rate the person responsible for the control of the cage, said: "No, you have chosen to come at a time which is not your proper time, and although there is a cage standing empty we will not bring you up in it," and the workman was in consequence under the necessity of remaining at the bottom of the shaft for about 20 minutes. There was no refusal to bring him up at the ordinary time which was in his bargain; but there was a refusal — and I am quite ready to assume that the motive of it was to punish him, I will assume it for the sake of argument, for having refused to go on with his work — by refusing to bring him up at the moment when he claimed to come. Did that amount to false imprisonment? In my opinion it did not. No statutory right under the Coal Mines Regulation Act, avails him. . . . Nor had he any right in contract. His right in contract was to come up at the end of his shift. Was he then falsely imprisoned? There were facilities which, in accordance with the conditions that he had accepted by going down, were not available to him until the end of his shift, at any rate as of right.

My Lords, under these circumstances I find it wholly impossible to come to the conclusion that the principle to which I have alluded, and on which the doctrine of false imprisonment is based, has any application to the case. *Volenti non fit injuria.* The man chose to go to the bottom of the mine under these conditions — conditions which he accepted. He had no right to call upon the employers to make use of special machinery put there at cost, and involving cost in its working, to bring him to the surface just when he pleased. . . .

. . . But what we are concerned with at the moment is this and this simply: that no conditions existed which enabled the miner in this case to claim the right which he asserted, and that there was nothing which comes within the definition well known in the law of England which amounts to false imprisonment.

Appeal dismissed.

NOTES

1. Would the House of Lords have decided *Herd* the same way if the elevator had been unused and available to raise the plaintiff at the time of his request to leave the mine? What would the court have done if the reason for the defendant's request to leave the mine was that he was seriously ill? Would *Herd* be decided in the same way today?

2. In *Robinson* v. *Balmain New Ferry Co.*, [1910] A.C. 295 (P.C.) the plaintiff entered a turnstile at a wharf and paid the usual penny for a ride on a ferry. On discovering that he missed the ferry, he sought to leave but he was told he had to pay another penny before he would be permitted to leave. A notice board stated that "a fare of one penny must be paid on entering and leaving the wharf. No exception will be made to this rule, whether the passenger has travelled by ferry or not." After 20 minutes the plaintiff escaped. He sued, *inter alia*, for false imprisonment. Liability was denied. Lord Loreburn L.C. felt that the defendants were entitled to impose a "reasonable condition before allowing him to pass through their turnstile from a place to which he had gone of his own free will".

3. At Honest Ed's, a discount department store in Toronto, there is a sign posted that reads "Everyone entering these premises agrees to be searched prior to exit." Plaintiff fails to read the sign upon entry. When he tries to leave, he is asked to submit to a search, but he refuses. He is detained for a time and is finally let go. Imprisonment?

4. A woman agreed to go from Syria to America on the defendant's yacht on the understanding that she would not be detained on board. Upon arrival the defendant refused to furnish her with a boat to enable her to leave the yacht. False Imprisonment? See *Whittaker* v. *Sandford* (1912), 110 Me. 77, 85 A. 399.

F. INTENTIONAL INTERFERENCE WITH LAND

ENTICK v. CARRINGTON

Common Pleas. (1765), 19 State Trials 1029

Action of trespass for breaking and entering plaintiff's house and carrying away papers, against persons who claimed to act under a warrant from a Secretary of State.

Lord Camden L.C.J.: The great end, for which men entered into society, was to secure their property. That right is preserved sacred and incommunicable in all instances where it has not been taken away or abridged by some public law for the good of the whole. The cases where this right of property is set aside by positive law, are various. Distresses, executions, forfeitures, taxes, etc., are all of this description; wherein every man by common consent gives up that law for the sake of justice and the general good. By the laws of England every invasion of private property, be it ever so minute, is a trespass. No man can set his foot upon my ground without any licence but he is liable to an action, though the damage be nothing; which is proved by every declaration in trespass where the defendant is called upon to answer for bruising the grass or even treading upon the soil. If he admits the fact, he is bound to show by way of justification, that some positive law has empowered or excused him. . . .

According to this reasoning, it is now incumbent upon the defendants to show the law by which this seizure is warranted. If that cannot be done, it is a trespass.

NOTES

1. In *Cooper* v. *Crabtree* (1882), 20 Ch. D. 589, 47 L.T.R. 5, 51 L.J.Ch. 544, defendant had placed two small poles and a piece of board on land owned by plaintiff but which at the time he had leased to a third person who was in occupation under the lease. Plaintiff brought action to enjoin defendant's conduct. The court held that plaintiff's action failed. The plaintiff could not base his claim on trespass since possession of the land was in his tenant; a claim in nuisance failed since plaintiff's use of land was not interfered with. If plaintiff could establish some damage of a permanent or substantial nature causing injury to the reversion he might have had a cause of action for such actual damage. Defendant had admitted that his object was the quite legitimate one of blocking the light of a window in a cottage on the land in order to prevent the acquisition of a right to light. The same result could have been achieved if the poles were on defendant's own land. See also *Townsview Properties* v. *Sun Construction* (1974), 7 O.R. (2d) 666.

2. In *Carr-Harris* v. *Schacter*, [1956] O.R. 994, 6 D.L.R. (2d) 225, defendant, an apartment-house builder, deliberately trespassed on plaintiff's residential property and excavated under plaintiff's land causing damage to flowerbeds, etc. In an action plaintiff recovered a judgment covering the cost of the repairs to his land and $5,000 as exemplary damages for the wilful trespass. See also *Starkman* v. *Delhi Court Ltd.* (1961), 28 D.L.R. (2d) 269 (Ont. C.A.); *Pretu* v. *Donald Tidey Co. Ltd.* (1965), 53 D.L.R. (2d) 504 (Ont.).

3. In Ontario, The Petty Trespass Act, R.S.O. 1970, c. 347, provides that:
   (1) Every person who unlawfully enters or in any other way trespasses upon another person's land, (*a*) that is enclosed; (*b*) that is a garden or lawn; or (*c*) with respect to which he has had notice by word of mouth, or in writing, or by posters or sign boards so placed as to be visible from every point of access to the land, not to trespass, and whether or not damage has been occasioned thereby, is guilty of an offence and on summary conviction is liable to a fine of not less than $10 and not more than $100.
It is further provided that if the offence is committed by means of a motor vehicle the driver and the owner of the car are both liable. It is further provided that nothing in the Act authorizes a justice of the peace to hear and determine a case of trespass in which the title to land or any interest therein is called in question; nor does the Act extend to a case where the person trespassing does so under a "fair and reasonable supposition that he had a right to do the act complained of".

4. In *Regina* v. *Burko and others* (1969), 3 D.L.R. (3d) 330, six univeristy students were found guilty under the Ontario Petty Trespass Act when they entered a collegiate without permission and disseminated radical literature. Although the public has a right to use the corridors in an ordinary and reasonable manner, the magistrate felt that the distribution of newspapers was not such a use. This activity had nothing to do with furnishing of education, the prime purpose of the institution. Rather, the accused were motivated by hostility toward the system of education at the school. The magistrate suggested that it would be all right for a parent to enter the school without permission to locate his child if he proceeded directly to the classroom where he was being taught. Would it make any difference if the students went to the school in question? Would it make any difference if the literature being distributed urged the students to attend church on Sunday? What if they distributed the literature in the school yard or on the street in front of the school? Magistrate Barron concluded by warning that "our society will not progress through anarchy or deliberate flouting of its laws when there are democratic means by which our society can be changed". It may be "cumbersome and slow" but it will not

"destroy those parts of society that are good . . . . [N]o minority has the right to try to impose its will on the majority no matter how well-meaning or sincere their thinking may be."

5. See also *Harrison* v. *Carswell* (1975), 62 D.L.R. (3d) 68 (S.C.C.), where picketers at a privately owned shopping centre were found guilty of violating the Petty Trespasses Act of Manitoba. Dickson J. for the majority stated:

"The submission that this Court should weigh and determine the respective values to society of the right to property and the right to picket raises important and difficult political and socio-economic issues, the resolution of which must, by their very nature, be arbitrary and embody personal economic and social beliefs. It raises also fundamental questions as to the role of this Court under the Canadian Constitution. The duty of the Court, as I envisage it, is to proceed in the discharge of its adjudicative function in a reasoned way from principled decision and established concepts. I do not for a moment doubt the power of the Court to act creatively — it has done so on countless occasions; but manifestly one must ask — what are the limits of the judicial function? There are many and varied answers to this question. Holmes, J., said in *Southern Pacific Co.* v. *Jensen* (1917), 244 U.S. 205 at p. 221: "I recognize without hesitation that judges do and must legislate, but they can do it only interstitially; they are confined from molar to molecular actions". . . .

Society has long since acknowledged that a public interest is served by permitting union members to bring economic pressure to bear upon their respective employers through peaceful picketing, but the right has been exercisable in some locations and not in others and to the extent that picketing has been permitted on private property the right hitherto has been accorded by statute. For example, s. 87 [since rep. & sub. 1975, c. 33, s. 21] of the *Labour Code of British Columbia Act,* 1973 (B.C.) (2nd Sess.), c. 122, provides that no action lies in respect of picketing permitted under the Act for trespass to real property to which a member of the public ordinarily has access.

Anglo-Canadian jurisprudence has transitionally recognized, as a fundamental freedom, the right of the individual to the enjoyment of property and the right not to be deprived thereof, or any interest therein, save by due process of law. The Legislature of Manitoba has declared in the *Petty Trespasses Act* that any person who trespasses upon land, the property of another, upon or through which he has been requested by the owner not to enter, is guilty of an offence. If there is to be any change in this statute law, if A is to be given the right to enter and remain on the land of B against the will of B, it would seem to me that such a change must be made by the enacting institution, the Legislature, which is representative of the people and designed to manifest the political will, and not by this Court".

Laskin J. dissented and declared:

"The considerations which underlie the protection of private residences cannot apply to the same degree to a shopping centre in respect of its parking areas, roads and sidewalks. Those amenities are closer in character to public roads and sidewalks than to a private dwelling. All that can be urged from a theoretical point of view to assimilate them to private dwellings is to urge that if property is privately owned, no matter the use to which it is put, trespass is as appropriate in the one case as in the other and it does not matter that possession, the invasion of which is basic to trespass, is recognizable in the one case but not in the other. There is here, on this assimilation, a legal injury albeit no actual injury. This is a use of theory which does not square with economic or social fact under the circumstances of the present case.

What does a shopping centre owner protect, for what invaded interest of his does he seek vindication in ousting members of the public from sidewalks and roadways and parking areas in the shopping centre? There is no challenge to his title and none to his possession nor to his privacy when members of the public use those amenities. Should he be allowed to choose what members of the public come into those areas when they have been opened to all without discrimination? Human rights legislation would prevent him from discriminating on account of race, colour or creed or national origin, but counsel for the appellant would have it that members of the public can otherwise be excluded or ordered to leave by mere whim. It is contended that it is unnecessary that there be a reason that can stand rational assessment. Disapproval of the owner, in assertion of a remote control over the "public" areas of the shopping centre, whether it be disapproval of picketing or disapproval of the wearing of hats or anything equally innocent, may be converted (so it is argued) into a basis of ouster of members of the public. Can the common law be so devoid of reason as to tolerate this kind of whimsy where public areas of a shopping centre are concerned?

If it was necessary to categorize the legal situation which, in my view, arises upon the opening of a shopping centre, with public areas of the kind I have mentioned (at least where the opening is not accompanied by an announced limitation on the classes of public entrants), I would say that the members of the public are privileged visitors whose privilege is revocable only upon misbehaviour (and I need not spell out here what this embraces) or by reason of unlawful activity. Such a view reconciles both the interests of the shopping centre owner and of the members of the public, doing violence to neither and recognizing the mutual or reciprocal commercial interests of shopping centre owner, business tenants and members of the public upon which the shopping centre is based.

The respondent picketer in the present case is entitled to the privilege of entry and to remain in the public areas to carry on as she did (without obstruction of the sidewalk or incommoding of others) as being not only a member of the public but being as well, in relation to her peaceful picketing, an employee involved in a labour dispute with a tenant of the shopping centre, and hence having an interest, sanctioned by the law, in pursuing legitimate claims against her employer through the peaceful picketing in furtherance of a lawful strike".

6. Is it a trespass if the defendant's tree is allowed to grow so that its branches extend over the plaintiff's land? Is the plaintiff liable if he snips off the branches that hang above his land? See *Pickering* v. *Rudd* (1815), 1 Starkie 56, 171 E.R. 400.

7. In *Ellis* v. *Loftus Iron Company* (1874), L.R. 10 C.P. 10, the defendant's horse put his head over a line fence and bit the plaintiff's mare. The defendant was held liable for "cattle trespass". Compare *Clifton* v. *Viscount Bury* (1887), 4 T.L.R. 8 (bullets crossing plaintiff's land at a height of 75 feet). And see *Big Point Club* v. *Lozon*, [1943] 4 D.L.R. 136, [1943] O.R. 491 (shot passing over and on plaintiff's land); *Kelsen* v. *Imperial Tobacco Co. Ltd.*, [1957] 2 All E.R. 343 (advertising sign above shop); *Woollerton* v. *Oostain*, [1970] 1 W.L.R. 412. What if the defendant's crane swings over the plaintiff's land? See *Woollerton & Wilson Ltd.* v. *Richard Costain Ltd.*, [1970] 1 All E.R. 483.

8. In *Turner* v. *Thorne* (1959), 21 D.L.R. (2d) 29 (Ont.), defendant delivered a number of parcels at the wrong address. He placed them in plaintiff's garage, believing that this was the garage of the consignee where he formerly delivered parcels addressed as these were. Plaintiff entered the garage after dark, fell over the parcels and sustained damage. McRuer C.J.H.C. held defendant liable, adopting ss. 158 and 163 of the American *Restatement of Torts.* The continued presence of chattels on the land of another is a trespass, and a trespasser "is liable for any harm to the possessor . . . irrespective of whether it was caused by conduct which, were the actor not a trespasser, would have subjected him to liability".

9. In *Mee* v. *Gardiner*, [1949] 3 D.L.R. 852, [1949] 1 W.W.R. 830 (B.C.C.A.), affg. [1948] 4 D.L.R. 871, [1948] 2 W.W.R. 813, an employee of the owner of a tourist camp permitted a tramp to sleep in a cabin, the exclusive use of which had, by contract, been given to the plaintiff. As a result of the tramp's occupancy, plaintiff contracted a skin disease. The defendant was held

liable in damages to the plaintiff for "physical injuries inflicted on him without lawful excuse". The trial judge had held that "the tramp was a trespasser, and, since defendant brought him onto the premises, . . . is as responsible for the consequences of his trespass as he is".

10. In *Wyant* v. *Crouse* (1901), 127 Mich. 158, 86 N.W. 527, defendant entered plaintiff's blacksmith shop as a trespasser and started a fire in the forge. He was not negligent in his supervision of the fire, but after he left, the building, in some way that could not be explained nor have been anticipated, caught fire and was destroyed. Defendant was held liable. "He was engaged in an unlawful act, and therefore was liable for all the consequences."

11. In *Wormald* v. *Cole,* [1954] 1 Q.B. 614, it was held that in an action for cattle trespass, the occupier of the land could recover for personal injuries caused by the trespassing animal acting in accord with its natural propensities. Guests of the occupier must prove negligence or *scienter. Per* Lord Goddard C.J., at p. 625: "Suppose, then, a trespasser on a dark or foggy night ran into the occupier in his drive and thereby caused him to fall and injure himself, or a trespasser in a building ran out as the occupier appeared and collided with him and, without intending to do so, caused him personal injury, it seems to me clear that the trespasser would be liable for the injury as part of the damage for the trespass." Singleton L.J., indicated that "it may seem odd" that plaintiff could recover but her servant (or friend) would not have been able to recover in the absence of negligence. Hodson L.J., said that "Since the decision in *Re Polemis*, no question of foreseeability arises, although this might otherwise have caused difficulty in considering remoteness of damage."

12. See generally Magnet, "Intentional Interference with Land" in Klar (ed.), *Studies in Canadian Tort Law* (1977).

ATLANTIC AVIATION v. NOVA SCOTIA
LIGHT & POWER CO. LTD.

Nova Scotia Supreme Court. (1965), 55 D.L.R. (2d) 554

Plaintiff owned land on the shore of a lake in Nova Scotia and was licensed under the Aeronautics Act to give flying instructions there. The defendant, on land to which it had acquired either title or easements to a right-of-way had, in 1959, erected 14 steel transmission towers along the shore of the lake and about 1,500 feet from it. The towers ranged in height from 125-300 feet. The plaintiff claimed that the presence of the transmission towers has affected and will in future affect his operations to the extent that pilots or students in training might collide with the towers or wires. The plaintiff claimed an injunction to restrain defendant from constructing or erecting towers or permitting him to maintain towers already erected in the position in which they were situated.

The defendant replied that the erection of the towers and wires was a lawful, reasonable and necessary use of defendant's air space and that flying aircraft over the defendant's land is unlawful.

MacQuarrie J.: . . . In my view of the law as it applies to the plaintiff's claim against the defendant in this case, the result is the same whether the plaintiff has succeeded or failed to show any loss sustained as a result of the erection of the defendant's transmission line.

Before the plaintiff can succeed, it must show that it as a member of the public had a right to use the air space blocked by the defendant's transmission line paramount to the right of the defendant to erect it. There are no English or Canadian authorities that I am aware of which deal with this type of problem, nor have any regulations been passed pursuant to the Aeronautics Act, which are relevant to this case. Section 4 (1) (*j*) [enacted R.S.C. 1952, c. 302, s. 1] of that Act provides that the Minister of Air Transport has power to make Regulations with respect to the height used and location of structures on land adjoining airports. No such zoning regulations have been passed with respect to Lake William. . . .

The question of the right of the landowner in relation to the rights, if any, in air space has been the subject of both legislation and judicial decision in the United States.

Fleming on Torts, 2nd ed., refers on pp. 47-48 to the four solutions set forth by the American Courts: "There are no English or Australian decisions which have explored the transient and harmless use of air-space over private land, but the preceding case law is not opposed to the right of flight at reasonable height which does not impair the enjoyment of subjacent soil. Indeed, such *dicta* as have adverted to the question support this view. The use of aircraft has become of such social importance that it is idle to speculate whether the courts might not inhibit it by an extravagant application of the *ad coelum* maxim; the question is rather how to adjust, with the least friction, the conflict between the competing claims of aircraft operators to reasonable scope for their activities and of landowners to unimpaired enjoyment of their property.

In the United States, four solutions have been put forward. First, that it is trespass only to fly within the zone of the landowner's 'effective possession' or such altitude up to which he might in the future make effective use of the air-space. Secondly, that there is no trespass unless the flight occurs within the zone of the landowner's *actual use.* This view, in effect, eliminates any concept of technical trespass justifying the recovery of nominal damages, and confers protection only against actual and substantial injury to the landowner in the enjoyment of the surface. Thirdly, that flight of aircraft is not trespass at all but that the proper remedy is in nuisance or negligence. This approach is practically identical with the second, except that it might forestall recovery for an isolated act, since nuisance ordinarily involves continuity or recurrence. Fourthly, that flight at any altitude is trespass save for a privilege of reasonable flight, analogous to the public right of navigation on navigable rivers. On this basis, an aviator is protected if he traverses the air-space of another for a legitimate purpose, in a reasonable manner and at such height so as not to interfere unreasonably with the possessor's enjoyment of the surface and the air-space above it, but he cannot enjoin the surface owner from putting up a structure, like a transmission line, which has the effect of preventing the landing of aircraft at a near-by aerodrome."

The case cited in the footnote at the end of the closing words in the citation . . . is *Guith et al.* v. *Consumers Power Co.* (1940), 36 F. Supp.21. In *Guith* the common law on the relative rights of the landowner and the aviator is stated by Tuttle D.J. as follows: "In the *Restatement of the Law of Torts* by The American Law Institute, the common law on the relative rights of the landowner and the aviator to the use of air-space above the surface of the earth is stated as follows:

Section 159, Comment e:
An unprivileged intrusion in the space above the surface of the earth, at whatever height above the surface, is a trespass.
Section 194 – Travel Through Air Space.
An entry above the surface of the earth, in the air space in the possession of another, by a person who is travelling in an aircraft, is privileged if the flight is conducted:
(a) for the purpose of travel through the air space or for any other legitimate purpose,
(b) in a reasonable manner,

(c) at such a height as not to interfere unreasonably with the possessor's enjoyment of the surface of the earth and the air space above it, and

(d) in conformity with such regulations of the State and federal aeronautical authorities as are in force in the particular State.

In my opinion, *Guith* is based on common law as well as on statute.

In Canada the common law position is unaffected by statute: Jack E. Richardson, "Private Property Rights in the Air Space at Common Law," 31 Can. Bar Rev. 117, at p. 119 (1953): "It has been established in the United States that obstructions to aircraft may be a public nuisance, as in *Commonwealth of Pennsylvania* v. *von Bestecki*, [1937] U.S. & C. Av.R.1; 30 Pa.County R. 137, *Tucker* v. *United Airlines Inc. and the City of Iowa*, [1936] U.S. & C. Av. R. 10 and *United Airports Company of California Ltd.* v. *Hinman*, [1940] U.S. & C. Av. R.1. In each of these cases, however, the court found that the obstructions were deliberately raised by the defendant on his own land for the purpose of obstructing or embarrassing aircraft taking off from and landing on an adjoining airfield and not for any necessary or incidental use or enjoyment of the defendant's land.

> "In *Guith* v. *Consumers Power Company* and *Strother* v. *Pacific Gas and Electric Company*, 211 P. 2d 624, the right of the landowner to erect structures on his land in the exercise of his use and enjoyment of his land, even if the obstructions interfered with the free passage of aircraft taking off and landing on an adjoining airfield, was affirmed." . . .

The point has been raised that the paramount right to navigate air space would depend on the actual use of the air space by aircraft prior to its use by the landowner.

In my opinion, highways in the air cannot be so established. . . .

The defendant's use of the land over which it acquired rights of way and was the lawful occupier was reasonable and necessary under the circumstances.

In my opinion, the only Canadian law which can prevent the defendant using its land (including land of which it is the lawful occupier) as it has would be zoning restrictions passed pursuant to the Aeronautics Act, with respect to land surrounding Lake William or land in the area of Lake William. No such zoning regulations have been passed.

The erection and use of the towers and wire by the defendant was a lawful, reasonable and necessary use of the defendant's air space.

In the result, the plaintiff's action will be dismissed with costs.

NOTES

1. In *Lacroix* v. *The Queen*, [1954] Ex C.R. 69, [1954] 4 D.L.R. 470, an owner of agricultural land on which there were no buildings, adjacent to the Dorval airport, claimed compensation from the Crown by reason of the latter's having established a "flightway" over his land and thus having appropriated the air and space over his land. Fournier J. denied the claim. "It seems to me that the owner of land has a limited right in the air space over his property; it is limited by what he can possess or occupy for the use and enjoyment of his land. By putting up buildings or other constructions the owner does not take possession of the air but unites or incorporates something to the surface of his land. This which is annexed or incorporated to his land becomes part and parcel of the property.

The Crown could not expropriate that which is not susceptible of possession. It is contrary to fact to say that by the so-called establishment of a flightway and the flying of planes it had taken any property belonging to the suppliant or interfered with his rights of ownership.

In this instance it did not appropriate any air or space over his land and did not interfere with his rights. I need go only so far as to say that the owner of land is not and cannot be the owner of the unlimited air space over his land, because air and space fall in the category of *res omnium communis*. For these reasons the suppliant's claim for damages by reason of the so-called establishment of a flightway over his land fails."

2. Problems similar to trespass to the air-space are raised by invasions below the surface. Such invasions have been held actionable: *Cox* v. *Glue* (1848), 5 C.B. 533. The limits of the protection given the interest of the surface owner have not been much debated. Suppose B places a sewer 150 feet below the surface of A's lot which is used for a residence? *Cf. Boehringer* v. *Montalto* (1931), 254 N.Y.S. 276.

3. Is it a trespass if an airplane's engine stops and it falls on the plaintiff's house? See *Rochester Gas & Electric Corp.* v. *Dunlop* (1933), 266 N.Y.J. 469. See also Bohlen, "Aviation under Common Law" (1934), 48 Harv. L. Rev. 216; Hackley, "Trespassers in the Sky" (1937), 21 Minn. L. Rev. 733.

4. If surface damage is caused by a foreign aircraft in flight or any person or thing falling therefrom, compensation is forthcoming by virtue of special legislation. See Foreign Aircraft Third Party Damage Act, R.S.C. 1970, c. F-28.

5. There are some cases in which trespass theory has been used to protect other property interests as well as the interest in privacy. See *Hickman* v. *Maisey*, [1900] 1 Q.B. 752; *Victoria Park Racecourse etc. Co. Ltd.* v. *Taylor* (1937), 58 C.L.R. 479. See also *Gross* v. *Wright*, [1923] S.C.R. 214, [1923] 2 D.L.R. 171; *Hurst* v. *Picture Theatres Ltd.*, [1915] 1 K.B.1, 30 T.L.R. 642.

G. INTENTIONAL INTERFERENCE WITH CHATTELS

EVERITT v. MARTIN

Supreme Court of New Zealand. [1953] N.Z.L.R. 298

Plaintiff, alighting from his car in a parking space, had his coat caught on a dilapidated fender of defendant's adjoining car. In an action for damages the court found that defendant was negligent in the sense that he, knowing of his car's condition, should have foreseen the likelihood of such an injury when parking his car in the heart of a big city. The defendant was held liable to plaintiff. The following related only to one of defendant's arguments.

F.B. Adams J.: . . . As to the suggestion that plaintiff committed an act of trespass, the argument was that defendant could not be under a duty to foresee and guard against harm that could be incurred only by an act of trespass. This is an application to chattels of the familiar doctrine that an occupier of premises owes, in general, no duty to take care for the protection of trespassers on his premises . . . . The first question is, of course, whether plaintiff was guilty of trespass in allowing his coat to come in contact with defendant's car. Counsel referred me to *Salmond on Torts*, 10th ed., 318, where it is said that trespass to chattels, defined as consisting in any act of direct physical interference without lawful justification, is actionable *per se*. It may be that this is not to be read as including merely accidental contacts; but, even if it be limited to intentional touchings, it is, with respect, questionable law. *Pollock on Torts*, 15th ed., 264, speaks much more guardedly, as also do *Winfield on Torts* and *Clerk and Lindsell on Torts*, 10th ed., 412. It would appear that (1906) 1 *Street's Foundations of Legal Liability*, 16, is to the contrary, and in 1 *Restatement of the Law of Torts*, para. 218, there is a clear and emphatic statement negativing liability unless there is damage to the chattel, substantial deprivation of use, or bodily harm ensuing: see also 33 *Halsbury's Laws of England*, 2nd ed., 22, and the old case of *Slater* v. *Swann* (1731), 2 Stra. 782; 93 E.R. 906, which is direct authority for the proposition that trespass to another man's horse is not actionable without "a special damage".

The matter being in doubt at this late stage of our legal history, I would hesitate to be the first to hold that there is a right of action for the mere touching of another's goods without damage or asportation. But, however this may be in the case of intentional contacts, a consideration of the material discussed above leads me to the conclusion that there is no right of action in the case of merely accidental contacts where no damage is done. I cannot imagine that plaintiff is liable, even for nominal damages, on account of the casual and unintended contact of his coat with defendant's car.

This being my view, I hold that plaintiff is not disentitled to recover on the ground that he was a trespasser, and that, in such circumstances as existed here, there is a duty resting on users of the highway to take reasonable care to avoid injuries to other users which may arise from casual and unintended contacts of the kind in question. It is accordingly unnecessary to decide whether the doctrine as to the duties, or absence of duties, on the part of occupiers of land towards trespassers is applicable to chattels, or how far, if at all, a person who touches a chattel intentionally, but without moving or damaging it, is to be regarded as a trespasser.

NOTES

1. Is there any reason why damage should be necessary in a trespass to goods action and not in an assault action? See Fleming, *The Law of Torts* (5th ed., 1977) at p. 50. See also *Marentille* v. *Oliver* (1808), 2 N.J.L. 358 (S.C.N.J.).

HOLLINS v. FOWLER

House of Lords. (1875), L.R. 7 H.L. 757; 44 L.J.Q.B. 169

One Bayley, by fraudulently representing he was acting as purchasing agent for a third person with good credit, obtained possession of 13 bales of the plaintiff, Fowler's cotton. Bayley offered it for sale to Hollins, a broker, who frequently purchased for prospective clients. Hollins sent a delivery note to Bayley stating that the cotton was bought by him for Micholls & Co. Hollins obtained the cotton from Bayley and delivered it to Micholls & Co. who spun the cotton into yarn at its plant. Bayley obtained the sale price from Hollins who was repaid by Micholls & Co. together with a brokerage commission. Learning of the fraud practised on him, and not having been paid, Fowler applied for the cotton to Hollins who informed him that Micholls & Co. had bought the cotton and used it. Fowler brought action against Hollins in trover.

At the trial before Willes J., he asked the jury whether (a) Hollins bought the cotton as agents, and (b) whether they dealt with the goods as agents for their principal. The jury answered both in the affirmative and Willes J. entered judgment for the defendant Hollins, reserving leave to the plaintiff to move for judgment. On a rule being granted, it was made absolute.

The defendant appealed to the Exchequer Chamber and, on equal division, the plaintiff's judgment was upheld. The defendant appealed to the House of Lords. The judges were summoned to give their opinions and the opinions so given were 4:2 in favour of the plaintiff. The House of Lords then dismissed the appeal. The following is the opinion of one of the four judges summoned to advise the House of Lords.

Blackburn J.: . . . However hard it may be on those who deal innocently and in the ordinary course of business with a person in possession of goods, yet, as long as the law, as laid down in *Hardman* v. *Booth*, 1 H. & C. 803, is unimpeached, I think it is clear law, that if there has been what amounts in law to a conversion of the plaintiff's goods, by any one, however innocent, that person must pay the value of the goods to the real owners, the plaintiffs.

And, accordingly, I think it has not been disputed by any one, that if the plaintiffs had sued Micholls, who has worked this cotton up into yarn, Micholls must have had judgment against him for the value of the cotton, and would be liable to pay the price over again, though he honestly transmitted the price to the defendants, Hollins, who honestly handed it to Bayley.

And I take it that if the defendants have done what amounts in law to a conversion, they also must be liable to pay the plaintiffs.

It is hard on them, I agree, but I do not think that it is harder than it would have been on Micholls . . . . When a loss has happened through the roguery of an insolvent, it must always fall on some innocent party; and that must be hardship . . . . I own that it is not always easy to say what does and what does not amount to a conversion . . . I think many cases which at first seem difficult are solved if the nature of the action is remembered.

It is generally laid down that any act which is an interference with the dominion and right or property of the plaintiff is a conversion, but this requires some qualification.

From the nature of the action, as explained by Lord Mansfield in *Cooper* v. *Chitty* (1756),1 Burr. 20, it follows that it must be an interference with the property which would not, as against the true owner, be justified, or at least excused, in one who came lawfully into the possession of the goods. . . .

There are some acts which from their nature are necessarily a conversion, whether there was notice of the plaintiff's title or not. There are others which if done in a bona fide ignorance of the plaintiff's title are excused, though if done in disregard of the title of which there was notice there would be a conversion. . . . Thus a demand and refusal is always evidence of a conversion. If the refusal is in disregard of the plaintiff's title, and for the purpose of claiming the goods either for the defendant or for a third person, it is a conversion. If the refusal is by a person who does not know the plaintiff's title, and having a bona fide doubt as to the title to the goods, detains them for a reasonable time, for clearing up that doubt, it is not a conversion. . . .

So the finder of goods is justified in taking steps for their protection and safe custody till he finds the true owner. And therefore it is no conversion if he bona fide removes them to a place of security. . . .

I can not find it anywhere distinctly laid down, but I submit to your Lordships that on principle, one who deals with goods at the request of the person who has the actual custody of them, in the bona fide belief that the custodier is the true owner, or has the authority of the true owner, should be excused for what he does, if his act is of such a nature as would be excused if done by the authority of the person in possession if he was a finder of the goods, or entrusted with their custody. . . . Thus a warehouseman with whom goods have been deposited is guilty of no conversion by keeping them, or restoring them to the person who deposited them with him, though that person turns out to have had no authority from the true owner. . . .

And the same principle . . . will enable us to answer a question put during the argument at your Lordships' bar. It was said: "Suppose that the defendant had sent the delivery order to Micholls, who had handed it to the railway company, requesting them by means of it to procure the goods in Liverpool, and carry them to Stockport, and the railway company had done so, would the railway company have been guilty of conversion?"

I apprehend the company would not, for merely to transfer the custody of goods from a warehouse at Liverpool to one at Stockport, is *prima facie* an act justifiable in any one who has the lawful custody of the goods as a finder, or bailee, and the railway company, in the case supposed, would be in complete ignorance that more was done. But if the railway company, in the case supposed, could have been fixed with knowledge that more was done than merely changing the custody, and knew that the company's servants were transferring the property from one who had it in fact to another who was going to use it up, the question would be nearly the same as that in the present case. It would, however, be very difficult, if not impossible, to fix a railway company with such knowledge . . . .

I think, however, it is but candid to admit that the principle I have submitted to your Lordships, though it will solve a great many difficulties, will not solve all.

In Comyns' Digest it is said: "If a man deliver the oats of another to B to be made oatmeal, and the owner afterwards prohibits him, yet B makes the oatmeal, this is a conversion. *Per* Berkly, 1638."

To this every one would agree: but suppose the miller had honestly ground the oats and delivered the meal to the person who brought the oats to him before he even heard of the true owner. How would the law be then? Or, suppose the plaintiffs in the case at your Lordships' bar had, for some reason, brought the action against Micholls' men who assisted in turning this cotton into twist? The principle I have suggested would hardly excuse such conversions; and yet I feel that it would be hard on them to hold them liable. If ever such a question comes before me, I will endeavour to answer it. I think it is not necessary now to do so; for I think that what the defendants are found to have done in the present case amounts to a conversion, and is not in any way excused.

I do not rely on the ground, taken in the earlier part of my Brother Cleasby's judgment below, that the defendants themselves were the purchasers from Bayley for though, if it were left to me to draw inferences of fact, I should draw that inference, I doubt if it is open to me so to do after the finding of the jury affirming that the defendants were agents. But though it is to be taken in favour of the defendants that they acted throughout as brokers, and only as brokers, for Micholls, I still think them guilty of a conversion.

The case against them does not rest on their having merely entered into a contract with Bayley, or merely having assisted in changing the custody of the goods, but on their having done both. They knowingly and intentionally assisted in transferring the dominion and property in the goods to Micholls, that Micholls might dispose of them as their own, and the plaintiffs never got them back. It is true they did it as brokers for Micholls, and not for any benefit for themselves; but that is not material. . . .

The conversion in the case of *Stephens* v. *Elwall* (1815), 4 M. & S. 259, consisted in assisting in transferring the goods from Deane to the defendant's master in America, with intent to transfer Deane's *de facto* property to the defendant's master. Deane's title was bad against the plaintiffs . . . though of that the defendant was ignorant, unavoidably ignorant, says Lord Ellenborough.

The conversion in the present case consists in, by means of the delivery order, transferring the goods from Bayley to Micholls with intent to transfer *de facto* Bayley's property to Micholls. Bayley's title was bad against the now plaintiffs, though of that the defendants were ignorant. I can see no possible distinction between the two cases.

NOTES

1. Conversion may be committed in several ways. In addition to the transfer of goods, one can also convert by taking a chattel, withholding or retaining it,

disposing of it, destroying, damaging or using it. See Fleming, *The Law of Torts* (4th ed., 1971), p. 51.

2. In *Fouldes* v. *Willoughby* (1841), 8 M. & W. 540, the defendant was manager of a ferry on which the plaintiff embarked with two horses after paying the usual fare. The plaintiff having misconducted himself after he came on board, the defendant told him that he would not carry the horses over and that he must take them on shore. The plaintiff refused to do so, and the defendant took the horses from the plaintiff, who was holding one of them by the bridle, put them on shore and turned them loose. Under a charge that the defendant's acts amounted to a conversion unless the plaintiff's conduct had justified his removal from the steamboat, the plaintiff had a verdict. Upon a rule *nisi*, a new trial was ordered on the ground that "a simple asportation of a chattel, without any intention of making any further use of it, although it may be a sufficient foundation for an action of trespass, is not sufficient to establish a conversion". If defendant's act of removing plaintiff's horses from the boat was done simply to induce the plaintiff to go on shore himself, "it was not exercising over the horses any right inconsistent with, or adverse to, the rights which the plaintiff had in them. . . ." Lord Abinger C.B. stated:

> "In order to constitute a conversion, it is necessary either that the party taking the goods should intend some use to be made of them, by himself or by those for whom he acts, or that, owing to his act, the goods are destroyed or consumed, to the prejudice of the lawful owner. As an instance of the latter branch of this definition, suppose, in the present case, the defendant had thrown the horses into the water, whereby they were drowned, that would have amounted to an actual conversion; or as in the case cited in the course of the argument, of a person throwing a piece of paper into the water; for, in these cases, the chattel is changed in quality, or destroyed altogether. But it has never yet been held that the single act of the removal of a chattel, independent of any claim over it, either in favour of the party himself or any one else, amounts to a conversion of the chattel."

Was a trespass committed?

3. One nightmare of a case, pointing out the complexities of the law of conversion, is *Penfolds Wines Proprietary Ltd.* v. *Elliott* (1946), 74 C.L.R. 204 (H.C. Aust.). The plaintiff made wine and sold it in bottles that were embossed with the words, "This bottle is the property of Penfolds Wines Ltd." Penfolds also delivered invoices to all their customers which forbade the use of their bottles for anything other than their own product. The defendant hotel-keeper sold bulk wine to customers who transported it in their own bottles. The defendant's brother brought him several Penfolds bottles and he filled them with his own wine. Penfolds argued that this was conversion and sought an injunction. The High Court of Australia, in a split decision, ultimately denied the injunction. Some judges thought that there had been a conversion, while others disagreed. Do you think that the defendant's use of these bottles was a conversion?

NOTES ON DAMAGES FOR INTENTIONAL TORTS AND PUNITIVE DAMAGES

1. The ordinary principles for assessment of damages apply to intentional torts. The plaintiff may recover any pecuniary losses, including medical expenses, loss of wages and increased living expenses. He may also recover non-pecuniary losses, such as pain and suffering and loss of enjoyment of life. See Atrens, "Intentional Interference with the Person" in *Studies in Canadian Tort Law* (1968).

2. Intentional torts are, however, unique in that punitive damages or exemplary damages may also be permitted in appropriate cases in order to punish the defendant for his high-handed, malicious or contemptuous conduct. The rationale for such damages was expressed by McRuer C.J.H.C. at trial in *Denison* v. *Fawcett,* [1957] O.W.N. 393, a case involving conspiracy to defraud and deceit, as follows:

"The text books and the authorities use different terminology to characterize damages awarded in excess of strict compensation for the injuries suffered. They are described as exemplary, vindictive, penal, punitive, aggravated and retributory damages. Their purpose is discussed and different views expressed as to the basis on which they are awarded. It is sometimes said that it is because of the difficulty in fixing compensation for the injury done, *e.g.*, in libel and slander actions. In other cases their foundation is based on punishment for wrong done or to make an example of the wrong-doer for the purpose of deterring others in the commission of like torts."

3. The Ontario Court of Appeal affirmed the trial decision awarding punitive damages at [1958] O.R. 312. Mr. Justice Schroeder indicated the scope of the punitive damage principle in these words:

"Exemplary or aggravated damages are not, broadly speaking, awarded in actions for breach of contract, since damages for breach of contract are in the nature of compensation, and the motives and conduct of the defendant are not considered relevant to the assignment of damages. The action for breach of promise of marriage and an action upon a contract against a banker for wrongfully refusing to pay his customers' cheques constitute exceptions to this rule. Generally, however, such damages may be awarded in actions of tort such as assault, trespass, negligence, nuisance, libel, slander, seduction, malicious prosecution and false imprisonment. If, in addition to committing the wrongful act, the defendant's conduct is 'high-handed, malicious, conduct showing a contempt of the plaintiff's rights, or disregarding every principle which actuates the conduct of a gentleman' (to quote a few examples taken from the authorities), his conduct is an element to be considered as a circumstance of aggravation which may, depending upon its extent or degree, justify an award to the injured plaintiff in addition to the actual pecuniary loss which he has sustained. I do not think that it can be stated with any precision what may be classed as aggravating circumstances but malice, wantonness, insult and persistent repetition have always been regarded as elements which might be taken into account."

In concluding, His Lordship stated:

"The conduct of the defendant was outrageous and scandalous and the circumstances clearly call for an award of retributory damages as an expression of the Court's strong aversion to the defendant's conduct. The element of conspiracy, as has been pointed out, is an aggravating circumstance which is not generally found in the ordinary action of deceit and brings the case within the ambit of the principle pronounced in *Klein* v. *Jenoves and Varley, supra* [[1932] O.R. 504, [1932] 3 D.L.R. 571]. The defendant's motive was grossly fraudulent and evil, and he consciously and deliberately manifested such a callous disregard of the rights of his partner towards whom he stood in a position of trust and confidence, that his conduct can properly be described as wilful and wanton. The learned Chief Justice rightly awarded aggravated damages in this case and I would dismiss the appeal with costs."

4. Punitive damages have been awarded in many different types of cases, as, for example, assault and unlawful arrest (*Basil* v. *Spratt* (1918), 44 O.L.R. 155 (App. Div.)); trespass to land (*Pollard* v. *Gibson* (1924), 55 O.L.R. 424 (App. Div.); *Pafford* v. *Cavotti* (1928), 63 O.L.R. 171 (App. Div.); *Patterson* v. *De Smit*, [1949] O.W.N. 338 (C.A.); *Carr-Harris* v. *Schacter*, [1956] O.R. 994 (H.C.); *Starkman* v. *Delhi Court Ltd.*, [1961] O.R. 467 (C.A.); *Cash & Carry Cleaners* v. *Delmas* (1974), 44 D.L.R. (3d) 315 (N.B.S.C.)); trespass to goods (*Owen and Smith* v. *Reo Motors* (1934), 151 L.T. 274); trespass to a ship (*Fleming* v. *Spracklin* (1921), 50 O.L.R. 289 (App. Div.); *Mackay* v. *Canada Steamship Lines* (1926), 29 O.W.N. 334 (H.C.)); defamation (*Ross* v. *Lamport*, [1957] O.R. 402 (C.A.)); conversion (*Grenn* v. *Brampton Poultry Co.* (1959), 18 D.L.R. (2d) 9 (C.A.)).

5. In England, the availability of punitive damages has recently been severely limited. In *Rookes* v. *Barnard*, [1964] A.C. 1129, [1964] 1 All E.R. 367, the House of Lords expressed the view that tort law ought to be primarily

aimed at compensation and not at punishment. It limited awards of exemplary damages (in addition to express statutory authorization, of course) to two situations: (1) where there was oppressive, arbitrary or unconstitutional action by servants of governments; (2) where the defendant's conduct was calculated by him to make a profit which may exceed the compensation payable to the plaintiff. "Aggravated" damages, however, as distinct from "exemplary" damages were said to remain available. *Rookes* v. *Barnard* was not received with enthusiasm. The courts in Canada, Australia and New Zealand, refused to follow it, but the English courts submitted, that is, at least, until *Broome* v. *Cassell & Co. Ltd.,* [1971] 2 All E.R. 187. In that case, although the facts of the case were actually within the second exception of *Rookes* v. *Barnard*, Lord Denning sought to overthrow the decision and urged that it no longer be followed. When the case was appealed, the House of Lords affirmed the result on the basis of the second exception, but used the occasion to reaffirm *Rookes* v. *Barnard* and to criticize the Court of Appeal "with studied moderation" for its course of conduct in defying them (see *Cassell & Co. Ltd.* v. *Broome*, [1972] 1 All E.R. 801). For a fine article on this topic, see Catzman, "Exemplary Damages: The Decline, Fall and Resurrection of *Rookes* v. *Barnard*", in *New Developments in the Law of Torts, Special Lectures of the Law Society of Upper Canada* (1973).

6. In the main, Canadian courts have refused to follow *Rookes* v. *Barnard* and have clung to the earlier Canadian authorities. See *McElroy* v. *Cowper-Smith* (1967), 62 D.L.R. (2d) 65 (S.C.C.); Catzman, *op. cit., supra.* One recent example of the current attitude of Canadian judges is *S.* v. *Mundy* (1969), 9 D.L.R. (3d) 446, where the defendant indecently assaulted and beat the plaintiff severely. No criminal charges were laid, but the plaintiff sued for assault. Cudney Co. Ct. J. awarded $1,500 exemplary damages. His Honour indicated that our courts had not differentiated between "aggravated" and "exemplary" damages, the words being used interchangeably. He suggested that "exemplary" or "punitive" damages may be awarded where there is a "wanton or intentional act" and when it "is necessary to teach the wrongdoer that tort does not pay". These damages are "preventive or deterrent in character and are over and above compensation". Since His Honour felt that the defendant's conduct was "outrageous", it was "deserving of punishment to deter him and others from attempting the same thing in future". Another judge has opined "I do not draw any distinction between punitive, exemplary or deterrent damages as I am satisfied there is no practical distinction". See Stevenson D.C.J. in *Dalsin* v. *T. Eaton Co.* (1975), 63 D.L.R. (3d) 565, at p. 567. *Cf. Banks* v. *Campbell* (1974), 44 D.L.R. (3d) 603 (N.S.S.C.), where Cowan C.J.T.D. refused to award punitive damages against the defendant who shot the plaintiff, but gave aggravated damages against him on the basis of *Rookes* v. *Barnard*.

7. Another example was where two football players who savagely beat up some people in a hotel, were required to pay exemplary damages because of their "outrageous and high-handed conduct". See *Delta Hotels et al.* v. *Magrum* (1975), 59 D.L.R. (3d) 126 (B.C.S.C.).

8. If the plaintiff provokes an assault, that may be taken into account in mitigation of the punitive damages awarded, but not the compensatory damages. See *Shaw* v. *Gorter* (1977), 2 C.C.L.T. 111 (Ont. C.A.); *Check* v. *Andrews Hotel Co. Ltd.,* [1975] 4 W.W.R. 370, 56 D.L.R. (3d) 364 (Man. C.A.); *Lane* v. *Holloway*, [1968] 1 Q.B. 379, [1967] 3 All E.R. 129; *Landry* v. *Patterson* (1978), 22 O.R. (2d) 335 (C.A.).

9. Do you believe that punitive damages have a legitimate role in modern tort law? Is not the criminal law the proper vehicle for punishing wrongdoers?

10. What if the defendant has been convicted of a criminal offence and sentenced? See *Loomis* v. *Rohan,* [1974] 2 W.W.R. 599; *Amos* v. *Vawter* (1969), 6 D.L.R. (3d) 234 (B.C.S.C.); *Radovskis* v. *Tomm* (1957), 65 Man. R. 61, 21 W.W.R. 658 (Q.B.); *Natonson* v. *Lexier,* [1939] 3 W.W.R. 289 (Sask. K.B.). See *Fenwick* v. *Staples* (1977), 18 O.R. (2d) 128 (Co. Ct.). What if he is convicted but given a conditional discharge? See *Loedel* v. *Eckert* (1977), 3

C.C.L.T. 145; *cf. Kenmuir* v. *Heutzelman* (1977), 3 C.C.L.T. 153, father suing. What if he was charged but acquitted?

11. X shoots Y and then shoots himself dead. In denying punitive damages to the family of Y in an action against X's estate, McLung J. doubted whether punitive damages would furnish any additional deterrent to others beyond that of the criminal law. His Lordship remarked that "his innocent beneficiaries are the real defendants". See *Breitkreutz* v. *Public Trustee* (1978), 6 C.C.L.T. 76 (Alta. S.C.). Do you agree?

12. See Fridman, "Punitive Damages in Tort" (1970), 48 Can. Bar Rev. 373, at p. 399; Atrens, *op. cit., supra,* at p. 411. See also Morris, "Punitive Damages in Tort Cases" (1931), 44 Harv. L. Rev. 1173.

ATRENS, INTENTIONAL INTERFERENCE WITH THE PERSON

Studies in Canadian Tort Law (1968)

The arguments for and against punitive damages cannot be considered in detail here. The main objection, and the one which found favour with Lord Devlin in *Rookes* v. *Barnard,* is that compensation, and not punishment, is the proper function of the law of torts. No one would suggest that punishment for its own sake is a justification for either a criminal sanction or punitive damages, but such justification may be found if it discourages antisocial behaviour. Theoretically, punitive damages may prevent antisocial behaviour in three ways: first, by deterring the defendant from repetition of the tortious behaviour; secondly, the example made of the defendant may dissuade others from similar conduct, and thirdly, the availability of punitive damages may encourage the injured party to seek a remedy in court, rather than resorting to private vengeance.

Assuming for the sake of argument that punitive damages can accomplish these deterrent objectives, is this a proper function of the law of torts? It has been argued that punitive damages may become an instrument of oppression because the law of torts denies the defendant certain safeguards which are available to him in the criminal law, for example, proof beyond a reasonable doubt and maximum penalties. Although this objection applies to any tort case, the absence of these safeguards is particularly objectionable where the purpose of the award of damages is not to compensate an innocent victim, but to use the defendant to promote a public policy of discouraging antisocial behaviour. Because an award of punitive damages is a windfall to the plaintiff, the danger is that, without effective controls, the plaintiff is unlikely to claim an award of punitive damages with a dispassionate concern for the public welfare.

Despite the persuasiveness of the above objections, it does not follow that punitive damages have no place in our legal system. The law of torts should, at least as a subsidiary aim, attempt to discourage certain forms of socially undesirable behaviour. To leave this function entirely to the criminal law would require a considerable extension of the existing law, bringing unnecessary restrictions on the freedom of the individual. If in borderline cases the choice is to be made between a criminal sanction and liability in tort, the latter should be chosen. An adverse civil judgment does not involve the possibility of imprisonment or the stigma of a criminal conviction. In most cases the admonitory function of the law of torts will be accomplished through an award of compensatory damages. As indicated above, such damages may be aggravated by the nature of the defendant's conduct. Where compensatory damages and the criminal law cannot perform an effective deterrent function, punitive damages may be considered.

REVIEW PROBLEM

Paul and Dick, both first year students at Osgoode Hall Law School, decided to spend a weekend camping together at Lake Muskoka. After arriving at the campsite on Friday evening, they pitched a tent, made a fire, had dinner, and drank a few beers. As darkness fell, Paul entered the tent to prepare for bed, but Dick, feigning a call of nature, excused himself.

Suddenly, a devilish gleam appeared in Dick's eye. When he and Paul had first discussed this camping trip, Dick, an inveterate practical joker, had learned about Paul's irrational fear of snakes. Dick had assured Paul that there were no longer any snakes to be found near the campsites in the Muskoka area. It was only then that Paul reluctantly agreed to accompany Dick on the trip. The moon was bright, the stars twinkled, and silence reigned over the dark forest. "Now," Dick thought, "it is time to have some fun with Paul," and hid behind a bush some 50 feet away. Dick then made a rattling sound that resembled the noise made by an angry rattlesnake, which he had learned to imitate as a Boy Scout years ago. Paul, hearing the sound and believing it to be a rattlesnake, began to feel rather uneasy. Again Dick made the rattling sound, this time from behind a tree only 20 feet away, which caused a trembling Paul to call out for Dick. Dick moved closer and hovered immediately outside the tent door. Inside, he could hear Paul nervously pacing the ground. Again, he uttered the fearsome sound of the "rattler". Paul, now almost frantic, whirled around to defend himself with an axe that he had picked up but twisted his ankle and fell, breaking his left leg. Dick burst into the tent, laughing, only to find his friend Paul writhing in pain and shaking uncontrollably on the ground.

Two months later, Paul retains you to sue his ex-friend, Dick. Paul is now fully recovered from the neurasthenia he suffered as a result of his experience in the tent, but his left leg is still in a cast.

Do you think Paul will succeed in recovering damages from Dick and, if so, on what theory of tort liability?

CHAPTER 3

DEFENCES TO INTENTIONAL TORTS

Conduct which would ordinarily result in liability may not do so for a number of different reasons. For example, if a plaintiff consents to an invasion of his person, he will not be allowed to claim the protection of the law. In this situation, no "wrong" has been done to him. In addition to consent, there are other reasons that may excuse an invasion of some interest of the plaintiff. These "privileges" may arise where the defendant is protecting himself, his property or some interest of a third person or of society generally. Here the courts must balance the interest being invaded and the interest being advanced by the defendant's conduct. Here, too, seemingly simple questions can become issues of serious social importance.

A. CONSENT

O'BRIEN v. CUNARD SS. CO.

Supreme Judicial Court of Massachusetts. (1891), 154 Mass. 272; 28 N.E. 266

Tort, for an assault, and for negligently vaccinating the plaintiff, who was a steerage passenger on the defendant's steamship. The trial court directed a verdict for the defendant, and the plaintiff brings exceptions.

Knowlton J.: This case presents two questions: first, whether there was any evidence to warrant the jury in finding that the defendant, by any of its servants or agents, committed an assault on the plaintiff; secondly, whether there was evidence on which the jury could have found that the defendant was guilty of negligence towards the plaintiff. To sustain the first count, which was for an alleged assault, the plaintiff relied on the fact that the surgeon who was employed by the defendant vaccinated her on ship-board, while she was on her passage from Queenstown to Boston. On this branch of the case the question is whether there was any evidence that the surgeon used force upon the plaintiff against her will. In determining whether the act was lawful or unlawful, the surgeon's conduct must be considered in connection with the surrounding circumstances. If the plaintiff's behaviour was such as to indicate consent on her part, he was justified in his act, whatever her unexpressed feelings may have been. In determining whether she consented, he could be guided only by her overt acts and the manifestations of her feelings. [Citations omitted.] It is undisputed that at Boston there are strict quarantine regulations in regard to the examination of emigrants, to see that they are protected from small-pox by vaccination, and that only those persons who hold a certificate from the medical officer of the steamship, stating that they are so protected, are permitted to land without detention in quarantine, or vaccination by the port physician. It appears that the defendant is accustomed to have its surgeons vaccinate all emigrants who desire it, and who are not protected by previous vaccination, and

3-1

give them a certificate which is accepted at quarantine as evidence of their protection. Notices of the regulations at quarantine, and of the willingness of the ship's medical officer to vaccinate such as needed vaccination, were posted about the ship in various languages, and on the day when the operation was performed the surgeon had a right to presume that she and other women who were vaccinated understood the importance and purpose of vaccination for those who bore no marks to show that they were protected. By the plaintiff's testimony, which, in this particular, is undisputed, it appears that about 200 women passengers were assembled below, and she understood from conversation with them that they were to be vaccinated; that she stood about 15 feet from the surgeon, and saw them form in a line, and pass in turn before him; that he "examined their arms, and, passing some of them by, proceeded to vaccinate those that had no mark"; that she did not hear him say anything to any of them; that upon being passed by they each received a card, and went on deck; that when her turn came she showed him her arm; he looked at it, and said there was no mark, and that she should be vaccinated; that she told him she had been vaccinated before, and it left no mark; "that he then said nothing; that he should vaccinate her again"; that she held up her arm to be vaccinated; that no one touched her; that she did not tell him she did not want to be vaccinated; and that she took the ticket which he gave her, certifying that he had vaccinated her, and used it at quarantine. She was one of a large number of women who were vaccinated on that occasion, without, so far as appears, a word of objection from any of them. They all indicated by their conduct that they desired to avail themselves of the provisions made for their benefit. There was nothing in the conduct of the plaintiff to indicate to the surgeon that she did not wish to obtain a card which would save her from detention at quarantine, and to be vaccinated, if necessary, for that purpose. Viewing his conduct in the light of the surrounding circumstances, it was lawful; and there was no evidence tending to show that it was not. The ruling of the court on this part of the case was correct. The plaintiff contends that, if it was lawful for the surgeon to vaccinate her, the vaccination was negligently performed, "There was no evidence of want of care or precaution by the defendant in the selection of the surgeon, or in the procuring of the virus or vaccine matter." Unless there was evidence that the surgeon was negligent in performing the operation, and unless the defendant is liable for this negligence, the plaintiff must fall on the second count. . . .

Exceptions overruled.

NOTES

1. What was the test used by the court in determining whether or not the plaintiff consented? Is this an acceptable test?

2. It is now clear that a defendant, who relies on the defence of consent, bears the onus of proving it. *Kelly* v. *Hazlett* (1976), 1 C.C.L.T. 1, *per* Morden J.; *Hambley* v. *Shepley* (1967), 63 D.L.R. (2d) 94, at p. 95, *per* Laskin J.A.; *Schweizer* v. *Central Hospital* (1974), 6 O.R. (2d) 606 (H.C.). *Allan* v. *New Mount Sinai Hospital et al.* (Feb. 20, 1980) *per* Linden J.

3. In an isolated town in rural Manitoba, where the social mores of a bygone era still flourish, Derek asks his date, Penny, for a kiss in the moonlight. Penny says nothing. Derek musters his courage and plants a kiss on her cheek. Liability?

4. Suppose Penny, in response to the request whispers "No", but at the same time sighs softly and looks lovingly at Derek. Derek kisses her on the cheek. Liability?

5. Donald tells Peter he is going to punch him in the nose. Peter stands his

ground. Donald punches him in the nose. Liability? Would it make any difference if, before the punch, Peter bravely said to Donald, "I'd like to see you try!"?

6. Can silence alone ever operate as consent? What else is normally needed?

7. In *Agar* v. *Canning* (1965), 54 W.W.R. 302 (Man. Q.B.), the defendant hockey player hit the plaintiff with his stick after being hooked by him. Bastin J., in dealing with the question of consent, stated:

"Neither counsel has been able to find a reported case in which a claim was made by one player against another for injuries suffered during a hockey game. Since it is common knowledge that such injuries are not infrequent, this supports the conclusion that in the past those engaged in this sport have accepted the risk of injury as a condition of participating. Hockey necessarily involves violent bodily contact and blows from the puck and hockey sticks. A person who engages in this sport must be assumed to accept the risk of accidental harm and to waive any claim he would have apart from the game for trespass to his person in return for enjoying a corresponding immunity with respect to other players. It would be inconsistent with this implied consent to impose a duty on a player to take care for the safety of other players corresponding to the duty which, in a normal situation, gives rise to a claim for negligence. Similarly, the leave and licence will include an unintentional injury resulting from one of the frequent infractions of the rules of the game.

The conduct of a player in the heat of the game is instinctive and unpremeditated and should not be judged by standards suited to polite social intercourse.

But a little reflection will establish that some limit must be placed on a player's immunity from liability. Each case must be decided on its own facts so it is difficult, if not impossible, to decide how the line is to be drawn in every circumstance. But injuries inflicted in circumstances which show a definite resolve to cause serious injury to another, even when there is provocation and in the heat of the game, should not fall within the scope of the implied consent. I have come to the conclusion that the act of the defendant in striking plaintiff in the face with a hockey stick, in retaliation for the blow he received, goes beyond the limit marking exemption from liability."

8. In *Wright* v. *McLean* (1956), 7 D.L.R. (2d) 253, the plaintiff, 12 years old, was participating with some other boys in a game that involved throwing mud balls and lumps of clay at each other. He was injured when hit on the side of his head by a lump thrown by the defendant, 14 years old. In dismissing the action, Mr. Justice MacFarlane stated:

"This pleading raises the issue of consent. It is contended that there is no plea here of *volens*, but I think this pleading is sufficient to raise that issue.

The subject is discussed in most text books and I might refer particularly to *Pollock on Torts,* 15th ed., pp. 112-116. The learned editor of Pollock there commences para. 10 on p. 112 with the words: 'Harm suffered by consent is, within limits to be mentioned, not a cause of civil action.' Very briefly, the purpose of that paragraph is that in sport where there is no malice, no anger and no mutual ill will, the combatants consent to take the ordinary risks of the sport in which they are engaged. In a note given at the foot of p. 114 in Pollock, there is a reference to an article in the Law Quarterly Review, vol. 6, pp. 111-112. In that article, the author uses this language: 'The reasonable view is that the combatants consent to take the ordinary risk of the sport in which they engage, the risks of being struck, kicked, or cuffed, as the case may be, and the pain resulting therefrom; but only while the play is fair, and according to rules, and the blows are given in sport and not maliciously. . . . If these tacit conditions of fair play and good temper are not kept the consent is at an end, and the parties are remitted to their rights.'

In all the circumstances where it is agreed that there was no ill will and where the evidence shows that the infant defendant was invited to join the game by the others, then I think that no liability arises apart from culpable carelessness. I think it is quite clear that there is no evidence of that in this case. . . .

In his discussion of the subject, the learned editor of Pollock says (p. 115): 'Trials of strength and skill in such pastimes as those above-mentioned afford, when carried on within lawful bounds, the best illustration of the principle by which the maxim *volenti non fit injuria* is enlarged beyond its literal meaning. A man cannot complain of harm (with the limits we have mentioned) to the chances of which he has exposed himself with knowledge and of his free will. Thus in the case of two men fencing, *volenti non fit injuria* would be assigned by most lawyers as the governing rule, yet the words must be forced. It is not the will of one player that the other should hit him; his object is to be hit as seldom as possible. But he is content that the other shall hit him as much as by fair play he can; and in that sense the striking is not against his will.'

I think the action must be dismissed with costs."

MANSFIELD, INFORMED CHOICE IN THE LAW OF TORTS

(1961), 22 La. L. Rev. 17

Why is it that the plaintiff cannot recover when the defendant acted on a reasonable belief that the plaintiff was willing to encounter the risk? "The maxim *volenti non fit injuria*", says Mr. Bohlen, "is a terse expression of the individualistic tendency of the common law, which, proceeding from the people and asserting their liberties, naturally regards the freedom of individual action as the keystone of the whole structure. Each individual is left free to work out his own destinies; he must not be interfered with from without, but in the absence of such interference he is held competent to protect himself. While therefore protecting him from external violence, from imposition, and from coercion, the common law does not assume to protect him from the effects of his own personality and from the consequences of his voluntary actions or of his careless misconduct." Terse the maxim is, but scarcely less terse is Mr. Bohlen's explanation of it. At the time he wrote, the prevailing climate of thought was so congenial to a doctrine that made individual choice decisive that any extended explanation of why this should be so seemed quite unnecessary. The doctrine was founded on a whole range of presuppositions thought to underlie a free society. Now that so many of these presuppositions have been called into question or altogether discarded, a fuller and more painstaking explanation is necessary.

All individual action bears mediately or immediately on the welfare of the community and any distinction between public and private interests is at best a matter of degree. Seizing on this truth, the law could define goals for individual and society and, in regard to all conduct, set forth rules judged likely to lead to their achievement. Not contenting itself with setting outer limits to individual choice, it could comprehensively catalogue the risks or injuries that a plaintiff ought to accept or reject in the pursuit of ends authoritatively approved. Of course the whole orientation of our law is otherwise and its ambitions, at least so far as the official organs of government are concerned, very much more modest. Embedded in our political philosophy is a fundamental judgment that events should be ordered according to individual choice. No comprehensive scheme of ends and means, either for the individual or for society, is attempted. Government is not thought competent to the task; it is too vast practically to be executed, and experience has shown that men are insufficiently endowed with wisdom to be entrusted with such extensive law-making

powers. The individual is closer to his own needs and better able to perceive
the goals he ought to pursue and the steps necessary to attain them. He is
thought capable of intelligent appraisal of these matters. Moreover, not only
does the diversity of men make the imposition of uniform goals and patterns
of conduct seem of doubtful wisdom, but it is a peculiarity of human nature
that the value of ends achieved depends very largely on their having been freely
defined and freely pursued.

Such, in any event, is the judgment to which the relatively restricted scope
of our official law-making bears witness, and it is a judgment manifested not
only in the relations between government and the citizen but also in the relations among the citizens themselves, where choice is habitually made a determining factor. When one considers the full range of human activities, it is apparent that, in specifying rules of conduct, government concerns itself with
only a small, though doubtless important, fragment of the whole. No more is
there ordinarily an authoritative view on what course it is best for an individual
to pursue when confronted with the necessity of suffering an injury or encountering a risk to achieve some goal than there is an authoritative view on
what provisions ought to be included in contracts. Reliance is placed for the
most part on the choice of individuals, singly or freely grouped in organizations
less than the whole community. Through this process it is thought the common
good is more likely to result than by a comprehensive scheme of governmental
regulation. The law rests in its self-denying ordinance on the fundamentals of
our political philosophy.

The most obvious consequences to be drawn from the premises are that a
plaintiff should not be compelled to do what he does not choose to do nor
prevented from doing what he does choose to do. If he chooses to suffer the
invasion of a normally protected interest or expose himself to an unusual risk,
he must not be held back. Nor, after he has acted, must he be deprived of the
fruits of his choice if he is satisfied with them. These consequences appertain
most directly to the plaintiff's freedom, and to withhold them would be to
suspend the operation of that very process of free choice upon which, as has
been said, the hopes of realizing the individual and common good are primarily
founded.

Less obvious is the consequence that the law will not compensate the plaintiff for those results of his choice that he finds undesirable. The plaintiff cannot see why such assistance would interfere with the benefits of a regime of
individual choice; indeed, why would it not contribute to the fuller realization
of his freedom by giving effect to a second choice to undo the unwanted consequences of the first? The answer is clear enough, at least in the situation we
are now considering, where the defendant was induced to act by a belief in the
plaintiff's willingness. Correlative to the plaintiff's freedom is the defendant's
freedom. If the plaintiff is not compelled to observe an authoritatively prescribed course of conduct, no more is the defendant. In particular, the defendant is not required to respond to the plaintiff's wish that he should act in a
certain manner. Our hopes for the realization of the common good are based
not exclusively on the fulfillment of the plaintiff's choice, but also on coopera-
tion between plaintiff and defendant in mutually acceptable action. Therefore,
so long as the defendant is not required to act, and so long as the only source of
compensation for the plaintiff is the wealth of the defendant (a limitation that
should not be taken for granted), the plaintiff's freedom must be less than perfect in order to assure that the choice of those in his position will be, for the
major part, effective. If defendants were bound to compensate whenever the
results of choice turned out disadvantageously, they might well cease to act at
all in response to the desires of willing plaintiffs. At least a plaintiff's chance of

inducing action would be significantly reduced. Thus, it is to the interest of willing plaintiffs as a class that a defendant who has been induced to act by a willing plaintiff be shielded from liability.

MULLOY v. HOP SANG

Alberta Court of Appeal. [1935] 1 W.W.R. 714

Jackson D.C.J.: The plaintiff's claim is for professional fees for an operation involving the amputation of the defendant's hand which was badly injured in a motor-car accident. The accident took place near the town of Cardston and the defendant was taken to the hospital there. The plaintiff, a physician and surgeon duly qualified to practise, was called to the hospital and the defendant, being a stranger and unacquainted with the plaintiff, asked him to fix up his hand but not to cut it off as he wanted to have it looked after in Lethbridge, his home city. Later on in the operating room the defendant repeated his request that he did not want his hand cut off. The doctor, being more concerned in relieving the suffering of the patient, replied that he would be governed by the conditions found when the anaesthetic had been administered. The defendant said nothing. As the hand was covered by an old piece of cloth and it was necessary to administer an anaesthetic before doing anything, the doctor was not in a position to advise what should be done. On examination he decided an operation was necessary and the hand was amputated. Dr. Mulloy said the wounds indicated an operation as the condition of the hand was such that delay would mean blood poisoning with no possibility of saving it. In this he was supported by the two other attending physicians. I am, however, not satisfied that the defendant could not have been rushed to Lethbridge where he evidently wished to consult with a physician whom he knew and relied on. Dr. Mulloy took it for granted when the defendant, a Chinaman without much education in English and probably not of any more than average mentality, did not rely or make any objection to his statement that he would be governed by conditions as he found them, that he had full power to go ahead and perform an operation if found necessary. On the other hand, the defendant did not, in my opinion, understand what the doctor meant, and he would most likely have refused to allow the operation if he did. Further, he did not consider it necessary to reply as he had given explicit instructions.

Under these circumstances I think the plaintiff should have made full explanations and should have endeavoured to get the defendant to consent to an operation, if necessary. It might have been different if the defendant had submitted himself generally to the doctor and had pleaded with him not to perform an operation and the doctor found it necessary to do so afterwards. The defendant's instructions were precedent and went to the root of the employment. The plaintiff did not do the work he was hired to do, and must, in my opinion, fail in his action.

The defendant has counterclaimed for damages in the sum of $400, being $150 for an artificial hand and the balance for loss of wages due to the operation and possibly general damages.

In my opinion the operation was necessary and performed in a highly satisfactory manner. Indeed, there was no suggestion otherwise. The damage and loss and the cost of an artificial hand are the results of the accident and not the unauthorized operation. The defendant, however, is, in my opinion entitled to damages because of the trespass to the person. . . . The damages are *per se* and should be more than nominal. Personally, I in a similar position might have been able to satisfy myself that the operation was necessary, and that I should be glad to pay the reasonable fee charged, but it was not my hand and the defendant will always no doubt feel that he might have saved the hand if he had consulted with a doctor he knew. While I might have been able to forego my rights, I cannot ask the defendant to do so and he is entitled to rely on his rights. There also must have been some shock to him when he found out his hand had been taken off in the manner in which it was, over and above the ordinary shock from an operation. His damages should, therefore be substantial but only sufficient to make them substantial rather than nominal. I place the amount at $50.

[The Alberta Court of Appeal dismissed an appeal by the plaintiff and a cross-appeal by the defendant without written reasons.]

NOTES

1. The plaintiff consents to an operation to examine her stomach, but expressly insists that nothing else be done. The defendant doctor proceeds to remove part of her stomach. Liability? See *Schloendorff* v. *Society of New York Hospital* (1914), 211 N.Y. 125, 105 N.E. 92.

A plaintiff who tells an anaesthetist not to use her left arm may recover in battery if the doctor ignores her instructions. See *Allan* v. *New Mount Sinai Hospital* (Feb. 20, 1980), where Linden J. said:

"While our courts rightly resist advising the medical profession about how to conduct their practice, our law is clear that the consent of a patient must be obtained before any surgical procedure can be conducted. Without consent, either written or oral, no surgery may be performed. This is not a mere formality, it is an important individual right to have control over one's own body, even where medical treatment is involved. It is the patient, not the doctor, who decides whether surgery will be performed, where it will be done, when it will be done and by whom it will be done."

2. Does a consent to remove one tooth allow a dentist to remove all the patient's upper teeth? See *Boase* v. *Paul,* [1931] O.R. 625, at p. 627.

3. Does a consent to a tonsillectomy also permit the removal of some rotten teeth? See *Parmley* v. *Parmley,* [1945] S.C.R. 635.

4. Does a patient who consents to an operation on his toe agree to a spinal fusion? See *Schweizer* v. *Central Hospital* (1974), 6 O.R. (2d) 606 (H.C.).

5. In *McNamara* v. *Smith,* [1934] O.R. 249, [1934] 2 D.L.R. 417, a surgeon was negligent in removing the plaintiff's tonsils and the negligence resulted in removing the plaintiff's uvula. In an action for damages, the Ontario Court of Appeal upheld a judgment dismissing the action on the ground that the plaintiff had failed to prove damage. *Per* Masten J.A.: "This is not an action for trespass to the person. The patient has voluntarily submitted to the operation and the action was properly framed in negligence. Under the old forms of action it would have been an action of trespass on the case." David J.A. dissented: "To unlawfully deprive the [plaintiff] of a part of her body gives rise to a claim for substantial damages." He would allow $500 for loss of the uvula despite evidence of medical men that they knew of no function of the uvula. Does this make sense?

6. For a stimulating and perceptive article that deals, *inter alia,* with the problem of consent, see Castel, "Some Legal Aspects of Human Organ Transplantations in Canada" (1968), 46 Can. Bar Rev. 345, at p. 361. See also, McCoid, "A Reappraisal of Liability for Unauthorized Medical Treatment" (1957), 41 Minn. L. Rev. 381; Rozovsky, "Consent to Treatment" (1973), 11 O.H.L.J. 103; Edwards, "Failure to Inform as Medical Malpractice" (1970), 23 Vand. L. Rev. 754: Sharpe, "Consent to Medical Treatment" (1974), 22 Chitty's L.J. 319; Picard, "The Tempest of Informed Consent" in Klar (ed.), *Studies in Canadian Tort Law* (1977).

MARSHALL v. CURRY

Nova Scotia Supreme Court. [1933] 3 D.L.R. 260; 60 Can. C.C. 136

Chisholm C.J.: The plaintiff, a master mariner residing at Clifton in the County of Colchester, brings this action in which he claims $10,000 damages against the defendant who is a surgeon of high standing, practising his profession in the City of Halifax.

The plaintiff in his statement of claim alleges:

(1) That after being employed to perform and while performing an operation on the plaintiff for the cure of a hernia and while plaintiff was under the influence of an anaesthetic, the defendant without the knowledge or consent of the plaintiff removed the plaintiff's left testicle;

(2) In the alternative, that the defendant was negligent in diagnosing the case and in not informing the plaintiff that it might be necessary in treating the hernia to remove the testicle; and

(3) In the further alternative, that in removing the testicle in the above-mentioned circumstances, the defendant committed an assault upon the plaintiff.

The defence, in addition to general denials, is, that the removal of the testicle was a necessary part of the operation for the cure of the hernia; that the necessity for removing the testicle could not have been reasonably ascertained by diagnosis before any operation was begun; and that consent to the further operation was implied by plaintiff's request to cure the hernia, and that the plaintiff's claim is barred by the Statute of Limitations . . . .

The plaintiff says with respect to the hernia:—"I simply told him (defendant) I wanted the hernia cured. He examined me. He said, 'all right'. That was his words."

The operation took place on July 19, 1929. A day or two later the plaintiff was informed by the defendant that the testicle had been removed because it might have caused trouble. He says he did not give consent to the removal and was never told that it might be necessary. After he became cognizant of what had been done, the plaintiff made no complaint until December, 1931.

The defendant states that plaintiff had asked him in July, 1929, what he thought of this hernia. The defendant replied that there was a reasonable chance of curing it; that he thought it was a case suitable for the ordinary hernia operation; the abdominal muscles were in a reasonably good condition. In the operation the defendant found the muscles very much weaker than he had anticipated. In opening the inguinal canal the testicle appeared and was found grossly diseased; it was enlarged, nodular and softened. In order to cure the hernia it was necessary in defendant's opinion to obliterate the canal completely so as not to leave any space. The defendant deemed it necessary to remove the testicle in order to cure the hernia, and also because it would be a menace to the health and life of the plaintiff to leave it. That he says was his best judgment in the circumstances. After the operation the defendant cut the testicle in two and found multiple abscesses in it. The defendant gave, as his opinion that if the testicle had not been removed, it might have become gangrenous, and the pus might be absorbed into the circulation, and condition of blood-poisoning have set up. . . .

The defendant called as witnesses three eminent surgeons to support the propriety of his procedure . . . . The defendant's professional skill was not challenged on the trial . . . . Nor could it be contended on the evidence that the operations conducted by him were not skillfully performed. The evidence of the medical witnesses supports the opinion that the condition of the testicle revealed by the operation could not reasonably have been anticipated before the operation was begun. That removes from the case the allegation that there was negligence on defendant's part; and, as I conceive the matter, leaves only the question of the assault.

The following findings are supported by the evidence:

1. That there was no express consent by plaintiff to the removal complained of;

2. That there was no implied consent thereto in the conversations between plaintiff and defendant before the operation; the exigent situation which arose was not then in the mind of either of them;

3. That the extended operation was necessary for the health and in the opinion of the defendant reasonably necessary to preserve the life of the plaintiff.

On these findings it becomes necessary to consider the questions in law which arise with respect to the rights and liabilities of the patient and surgeon and on what principle the action of the defendant must be justified. It seems to me that that justification must be found either in an assent implied by the circumstances which arose or in some other principle—broader than and outside of any consent—founded on philanthropic or humanitarian considerations. [A review of English and American authorities is omitted.]

In the cases these propositions of law find support:

1. That in the ordinary case where there is opportunity to obtain the consent of the patient it must be had. A person's body must be held inviolate and immune from invasion by the surgeon's knife, if an operation is not consented to. The rule applies not only to an operation but also to the case of mere examination. . . .

2. That such consent by the patient may be express or implied. If an operation is forbidden by the patient, consent is not to be implied; and . . . . "It must be constantly remembered that in this connection silence does not give consent, nor is compliance to be taken as consent."

3. That consent may be implied from the conversation preceding an operation or from the antecedent circumstances. It is said that if a soldier goes into battle with a knoweldge beforehand that surgeons attached to the army are charged with the care of the wounded, the consent of the patient may be implied therefrom for such operations as the surgeon performs in good faith upon the soldier.

I am unable to see the force of the opinion, that in cases of emergency where the patient agrees to a particular operation, and in the prosecution of the operation, a condition is found calling in the patient's interest for a different operation, the patient is said to have made the surgeon his representative to give consent. There is unreality about that view. The idea of appointing such a representative, the necessity for it, the existence of a condition calling for a different operation, are entirely absent from the minds of both patient and surgeon. The will of the patient is not exercised on the point. There is, in reality, no such appointment. I think it is better, instead of resorting to a fiction, to put consent altogether out of the case, where a great emergency which could not be anticipated arises, and to rule that it is the surgeon's duty to act in order to save the life or preserve the health of the patient; and that in the honest execution of that duty he should not be exposed to legal liability. It is, I think, more in conformity with the facts and with reason, to put a surgeon's justification in such cases on the higher ground of duty, as was done in the Quebec cases. . . .

The phrase "good surgery" has appeared in some of the cases. Its use is not helpful; it is general and vague and I think ambiguous. It may mean good execution by the surgeon, and in that meaning it does not touch the question of the surgeon's right to operate. In these emergency cases, it is not useful to strain the law by establishing consent by fictions—by basing consent on things that do not exist. Is it not better to decide boldly that apart from any consent the conditions discovered make it imperative on the part of the surgeon to operate, and if he performs the duty skillfully and with due prudence, that no action will lie against him for doing so; as I have stated, that is the jurisprudence established in the Province of Quebec, and I think it can well be adopted in other jurisdictions.

In the case at bar, I find that the defendant after making the incisions on plaintiff's body, discovered conditions which neither party had anticipated, and which the defendant could not reasonably have foreseen, and that in removing the testicle he acted in the interest of his patient and for the protection of his health and possibly his life. The removal I find was in that sense necessary, and it would be unreasonable to postpone the removal to a later date. I come to this conslusion despite the absence of expressed and possibly of implied assent on the part of the plaintiff.

A further defence raised is that plaintiff's case is barred by the Statute of Limitations, R.S.N.S. 1923, c. 238, s. 2 (1) (a) of which enacts that actions of assault and battery shall be commenced "within one year after the cause of such action arose".

The plaintiff's contention is that he had three years, and not one year, within which to bring the action by virtue of s. 32A of the Medical Act, R.S.N.S. 1923, c. 113, as enacted by 1930 (N.S.), c. 34, s. 1. That section is as follows:

> 32A. No person duly registered under this Chapter shall be liable to any action for negligence or malpractice by reason of professional services requested or rendered unless such action be commenced within three years from the date when in the matter complained of such professional services terminated.

The action is not one of negligence or malpractice, but one of assault and battery. The operation, if unlawful, was technically a surgical battery for which the defendant is liable. "The distinction ordinarily between an unauthorized operation amounting to assault and battery on the one hand, and negligence such as would constitute malpractice, on the other, is that the former is intentional, while the latter is unintentional:" *Hershey* v. *Peake* (1924), 115 Kan. 562.

The Statute of Limitations, s. 2 (1) (a), and not s. 32A of the Medical Act applies, and the plaintiff's claim is thereby barred.

The plaintiff's action will be dismissed with costs.

Action dismissed.

NOTES

1. Are *Mulloy* v. *Hop Sang* and *Marshall* v. *Curry* in conflict?

2. In *Murray* v. *McMurchy*, [1949] 2 D.L.R. 442, [1949] 1 W.W.R. 989, a surgeon, during a caesarian operation, discovered a number of fibroid tumors in the uterus wall. After consultation with another surgeon he tied off the Fallopian tubes to prevent the hazards of a second pregnancy. The plaintiff sued the surgeon and recovered $3,000 damages. Macfarlane J. distinguished the case where an operation was "necessary" as involving "urgency" and "immediate decision". In the present case the possibility of future hazard did not absolve the surgeon from obtaining consent no matter how "convenient or desirable" in order to prevent danger in a later contingency. That risk must be left to the decision of the plaintiff.

3. In *Tabor* v. *Scobee* (1952), 254 S.W. 2d 474 (Ky. C.A.), the plaintiff, 20 years of age, submitted to an operation for appendicitis. During the operation

the defendant surgeon discovered that plaintiff's Fallopian tubes were full of pus, swollen and sealed at both ends. The defendant proceeded to remove the tubes on the theory that they would have had to come out "within six months anyway if I was not mistaken". He feared the tubes would break and cause peritonitis. Other medical evidence approved his decision. The plaintiff's stepmother, in the hospital at the time, was not asked to give her consent. At a trial with a jury for the "unauthorized" act, the jury rendered a verdict for defendant. One of the instructions to the jury was to the effect that if the jury believed that the plaintiff's Fallopian tubes were in a diseased condition and if the defendant, in the exercise of ordinary care and skill considered that "such condition if not removed would have endangered plaintiff's life and health" then defendant was justified in removing the tubes even though no consent was obtained or given. On appeal by plaintiff, a new trial was directed, the court holding that such instruction was erroneous. On the new trial the jury should consider whether the evidence disclosed that the condition of plaintiff's tubes "was such that it would have endangered her life or her health to have let them stay in because they might immediately have ruptured or because a separate or later operation for their removal might unduly have endangered her life or her health and it was impracticable at the time . . . to obtain [plaintiff's] consent or [that of] her stepmother . . . before the removal of the tubes".

4. Upon admission for surgery to most hospitals today, it is customary to sign a consent form. St. Joseph's Hospital in Toronto, for example, has a form which reads as follows:

I HEREBY CONSENT TO A .... BEING
(Insert Name of Operation)

PERFORMED ON ME AND I FURTHER AUTHORIZE THE SURGEON TO CARRY OUT SUCH ADDITIONAL OR ALTERNATIVE OPERATIVE MEASURES AS IN HIS OPINION MAY BE FOUND ADVISABLE. THE NATURE OF THE SAID OPERATION AND THE MATTER OF ADDITIONAL OPERATIVE MEASURES HAVE BEEN EXPLAINED TO ME. I ALSO CONSENT TO THE ADMINISTRATION OF AN ANAESTHETIC AND A TRANSFUSION IF FOUND ADVISABLE.

Does this practice render cases like *Marshall* v. *Curry* irrelevant? Should the courts enforce such an agreement or should it be declared void as contrary to public policy?

5. Suppose Jane, a Jehovah's Witness, refuses to sign such a form upon admission to hospital because her religion forbids her to have a blood transfusion. It transpires that she needs a blood transfusion to save her life. She refuses to consent. So does her husband. The doctor asks you to advise him about whether he can legally proceed to administer a blood transfusion. Do so.

6. In *Application of President and Directors of Georgetown College* (1964), 118 U.S. App. D.C. 80, 331 F. 2d 1000, rehearing denied 118 U.S. App. D.C. 90, 331 F. 2d 1010, *certiorari* denied *Jones* v. *President, etc. of Georgetown College, Inc.,* 377 U.S. 978, 84 S.Ct. 1883, Mrs. Jones was brought to the Georgetown Hospital for emergency care having lost two-thirds of her blood from a ruptured ulcer. She relied solely on the hospital staff. Both she and her husband were Jehovah's Witnesses, whose teachings prohibited blood transfusions. When Mrs. Jones' death without blood became imminent the hospital applied to the District Court for permission to administer blood. This was refused and the present application to a judge of the Court of Appeals was made for an emergency writ to preserve the *status quo* pending an appeal. Neither Mr. nor Mrs. Jones would consent to a transfusion. The order was made authorizing blood transfusions "to save Mrs. Jones' life". The court by previous decisions recognized that a court could order medical treatment to save a child's life notwithstanding the parents' objection on religious grounds. The court considered the argument that if suicide is lawful or not made unlawful it could be argued that an individual's liberty to control himself extended to liberty to end his life. On the other hand, if self-homicide is a crime there is no exception for

those who believe the crime to be divinely ordained. In the present case, Mrs. Jones did not wish to die since she sought medical aid. The court felt that "it is not clear just where a patient would derive her authority to command her doctor to treat her under limitations which would produce death". On the facts here the order for the transfusion would merely preserve for Mrs. Jones the life she wanted without sacrifice of her religious beliefs.

7. The Criminal Code of Canada was amended by the 1972 Statutes of Canada, c. 13, s.16, to eliminate the offence of attempted suicide, but it is still an offence to counsel, aid or abet a person to commit suicide (s. 224). Does this change or affect your answer to the problem?

8. Assuming that you come to the conclusion that it would be a battery for the doctor to proceed, could you advise him to give the blood in any event? Would the doctor be helped by s. 45 of the Criminal Code which reads:

45. Every one is protected from criminal responsibility for performing a surgical operation upon any person for the benefit of that person if

(a) the operation is performed with reasonable care and skill, and

(b) it is reasonable to perform the operation, having regard to the state of health of the person at the time the operation is performed and to all the circumstances of the case.

What damages would be awarded against him if he were found liable civilly for battery? Would he be liable for anything that went wrong in the operation even without his negligence? See *Bettel* v. *Yim* (1978), 20 O.R. (2d) 617 *per* Borins C.C.J.; see also *Allan* v. *New Mount Sinai Hospital et al.* (Feb. 20, 1980) *per* Linden J. What penalty would be exacted if he were held responsible criminally for assault? What ethical problems arise here?

9. Consent to the surgical treatment of children and young people poses some problems. In an emergency situation, at least where there is no express refusal to consent, a doctor can probably do what is necessary to save a young patient's life. However, in non-emergency situations, the situation is more complicated. If the patient has reached 18, the age of majority in Ontario, the doctor is able to deal with the patient as a mature adult. If a young person is under the age of majority, however, a valid consent may still be given by him. In *Johnston* v. *Wellesley Hospital,* [1971] 2 O.R. 103, 17 D.L.R. (3d) 139 (H.C.), a 20-year-old underwent an acne treatment by a dermatologist. The age of majority at that time was 21 years of age. The court held that the consent was valid, even though the young person was not yet 21. Addy J. expressed the law as follows:

". . . Although the common law imposes very strict limitations on the capacity of persons under 21 years of age to hold, or rather to divest themselves of, property or to enter into contracts concerning matters other than necessities, it would be ridiculous in this day and age, where the voting age is being reduced generally to 18 years, to state that a person of 20 years of age, who is obviously intelligent and as fully capable of understanding the possible consequences of a medical or surgical procedure as an adult, would, at law, be incapable of consenting thereto. But, regardless of modern trend, I can find nothing in any of the old reported cases, except where infants of tender age or young children were involved, where the Courts have found that a person under 21 years of age was legally incapable of consenting to medical treatment. If a person under 21 years were unable to consent to medical treatment, he would also be incapable of consenting to other types of bodily interference. A proposition purporting to establish that any bodily interference acquiesced in by a youth of 20 years would nevertheless constitute an assault would be absurd. If such were the case, sexual intercourse with a girl under 21 years would constitute rape. Until the minimum age of consent to sexual acts was fixed at 14 years by a statute, the Courts often held that infants were capable of consenting at a considerably earlier age than 14 years.

I feel that the law on this point is well expressed in the volume on *Medical Negligence* (1957), by Lord Nathan, p. 176:

'It is suggested that the most satisfactory solution of the problem is to

rule that an infant who is capable of appreciating fully the nature and consequences of a particular operation or of particular treatment can give an
effective consent thereto, and in such cases the consent of the guardian is
unnecessary; but that where the infant is without that capacity, any apparent consent by him or her will be a nullity, the sole right to consent
being vested in the guardian.'

The plaintiff in the present case was, therefore, quite capable at law of
consenting."

See also *Booth* v. *Toronto General Hospital* (1910), 17 O.W.R. 118.

10. A serious problem has arisen in relation to young women with regard to
certain types of medical treatment such as birth control, venereal disease tests
and abortions. *In Re "D" and the Council of the College of Physicians and
Surgeons of B.C.* (1970), 11 D.L.R. (3d) 570 (B.C.S.C.), it was held that a
doctor, who inserted a birth control device in a 15-year-old female patient
without parental consent, was guilty of unprofessional conduct.

11. Ontario has issued regulations forbidding surgical operations unless there
is a written consent by a patient, who is either married or 16 years of age or by
a parent if the patient is unmarried or under 16 years of age. See O. Reg. 100/74,
49 and 49a under the Public Hospitals Act. See generally Gosse, "Consent to
Medical Treatment: A Minor Digression" (1974), 9 U.B.C.L. Rev. 56; Wadlington,
"Minors and Health Care: The Age of Consent" (1973), 11 O.H.L.J. 115; Skegg,
"Consent to Medical Procedures on Minors" (1973), 36 Mod. L. Rev. 370.
Picard, *Legal Liability of Doctors and Hospitals in Canada* (1978), p. 73. How
does this additional material affect the law as declared in *Johnston* v. *Wellesley
Hospital, supra*? What is the best way to handle these problems?

12. Should a parent be able to prohibit emergency medical treatment that
would save a child's life? A new born baby needs a blood tranfusion. His
parents, devout Jehovah's Witnesses, refuse to consent. Can the doctor proceed
to administer the blood? In *Raleigh -Fitkin—Paul Morgan Mem. Hospital* v.
Anderson (1964), 201 Atl. 2d 537 (S.C.N.J.), the plaintiff hospital sought
authority to administer blood transfusions to the defendant, Mrs. Anderson, in
the event that such transfusions should be necessary to save her life and the life
of her unborn child. Mrs. Anderson had notified the hospital that because of
her religious convictions she did not wish blood transfusions. The trial judge
held that the court would not intervene in the case of an adult or with respect
to an unborn child. On appeal this was reversed. It had already been held that
the State's concern for the welfare of an infant justified blood transfusions
notwithstanding objections of the parents based on religious beliefs. The court
held that an unborn child was entitled to the law's protection and an order
should be made to insure blood transfusions in the event they were necessary
in the opinion of the physician in charge. Whether an adult may be made to
submit to such medical procedures to save life is more difficult, but in the
present case it was unnecessary to decide the question since the welfare of the
mother and child were intertwined and inseparable. The court appointed a
guardian for the infant and ordered the guardian to consent to such blood
transfusions as might be necessary to preserve the lives of the mother and the
child. The mother was ordered to submit to such transfusions and the defendant husband was restrained from interfering therewith. See also *J.F.K.
Memorial Hospital* v. *Heston* (1971), 279 A. 2d 670 (N.J.S.C.). *Cf. Re Osborne*
(1972), 294 A. 2d 372 (D.C.C.A.).

13. The Child Welfare Act, R.S.O. 1970, c. 64 provides a method to protect
children in situations like the one above. It authorizes a hearing to determine if
a child is "in need of protection", which is defined by s. 20(1) (b) (x) as:

a child where the person in whose charge he is neglects or refuses to provide
or obtain proper medical, surgical or other recognized remedial care or treatment necessary for his health or well-being, or refuses to permit such care of
treatment to be supplied to the child when it is recommended by a legally
qualified medical practitioner, or otherwise fails to protect the child
adequately. . . .

A child is defined as one "actually or apparently under sixteen years of age". Under s. 26, when a judge finds that a child is in need of protection, he may make the child a ward of the children's aid society in the area, which may, in turn, give the consent to the medical treatment. Following this procedure the child is returned to the parents.

Is this a satisfactory solution to the "Jehovah's Witness" cases?

14. What if the C.A.S. decides that it wants to sterilize one of its mentally backward female wards, 11 years of age. Should the court authorize such an operation? See *Re D (A Minor),* [1976] 1 All E.R. 326.

KELLY v. HAZLETT

Ontario High Court. (1976), 15 O.R. (2d) 290, 1 C.C.L.T. 1, 75 D.L.R. (3d) 536

The plaintiff was referred to the defendant, an orthopedic surgeon, for treatment of rheumatoid arthritis in her right arm causing crookedness of the elbow and numbness. The defendant determined that the best procedure would be to perform an ulnar nerve transplant and a cleaning out of the joint. He did not think that an osteotomy, a breaking of the bone in the arm in an attempt to straighten it, would be advisable because the plaintiff's emotional state was such that she would be unable to cope with wearing a cast for the prolonged period that would be required after an osteotomy. The plaintiff executed a consent to the performance of the transplant and clean-out. Prior to the operation, and while under sedation, she also insisted on the osteotomy. The defendant advised against it, but finally agreed to do the transplant and the osteotomy. The plaintiff signed a second consent form for the osteotomy. The defendant did not explain the real risks of temporary or permanent stiffness in her arm which might result from the osteotomy. The operations were both performed, and, as a result of the osteotomy, the plaintiff developed permanent stiffness in her right arm. She sued for damages in battery and negligence.

Morden J.:

The Grounds of the Plaintiff's Claim

The plaintiff's case is based on several grounds. First, it is alleged that the plaintiff did not consent to the performance of the osteotomy and that the unauthorized performance of this operation constituted a battery. It was also submitted in argument that the manipulation was performed without the consent of the plaintiff, but this was not pleaded. Secondly, and alternatively, it is alleged that if she did consent to the osteotomy then the decision to perform it constituted negligence "in that the osteotomy was not medically required and the said defendant did not exercise proper professional skill and judgment in the performance of the said osteotomy". It is further alleged that the defendant was negligent in several other respects. At the conclusion of the evidence the plaintiff's case was narrowed down considerably to one of surgical battery or negligence in performing the operation or in failing to warn or advise the plaintiff "of the foreseeable nature and effects of the surgical repair aforesaid".

Before turning to the issues in contention I think it well to indicate clearly and simply what is now in issue. First, it is not now suggested that either of the osteotomy or the manipulation operations were negligently performed. As far as the osteotomy is concerned there could be no possible ground for coming to such a conclusion and, with respect to the manipulation, the refracture was an unfortunate misadventure but not, in itself, any evidence of negligence. The procedure was, in the circumstances, one of considerable difficulty in that, if sufficient force were not applied to the joint the purpose of achieving more motion could not be served.

The statement of claim further alleges that the manipulation was not a method of medical treatment dictated by the facts. The evidence is solidly against this allegation. Other allegations of negligence made, but not pursued— or proven, in my view—were that the defendant "failed to adequately examine the plaintiff prior to surgery", "permitted the plaintiff's right arm to be immobilized in a cast for too long a period of time" and, finally, "performed a joint clean-out by way of removing three bony ossicles and other debris in area of elbow in the course of surgery contrary to good medical practice thereby increasing the risk of stiffness".

This is an appropriate place to mention that the defendant raises no argument based on the language of the consent form. Specifically he places no reliance on "such additional operations or procedures as are considered necessary or desirable in the judgment of the surgeon" or on the patient certifying that she is "aware of the contents and significance of this statement."

Battery or Negligence?

Is the plaintiff entitled to succeed on the basis of a battery on the part of the defendant or in negligence in proceeding as he did, with or without her consent?

Broadly speaking, a battery is the intentional, unconsented to, touching of the person of the plaintiff by the defendant, while negligence (in the context of a case such as this) consists of the substandard execution of a duty of care by the doctor resulting in damage. The doctor's general duty of care includes not only the duty to exercise due skill and competence in diagnosis and treatment but also to give reasonable information and advice to the patient. This latter duty is one of variable content depending on the circumstances of the case and the determination of its proper scope is very often a matter of considerable difficulty.

The issue of "informed" consent can arise in both battery and negligence cases: with respect to the former a lack of proper information communicated by the doctor to the patient can vitiate an apparent consent while, with respect to the latter, failure to see to it that the patient is properly advised can amount, in certain circumstances, to an act of negligence. Quite apart from the nature of the doctor's conduct, the interest of the patient which the law seeks to protect is substantially the same in both kinds of cases: "Every human being of adult years and sound mind has a right to determine what shall be done with his own body": per Cardozo C.J. in *Schloendorff* v. *Society of The New York Hospital* (1914), 105 N.E. 92, 93; and see *Parmley* v. *Parmley,* [1945] S.C.R. 635, 645-46, [1945] 4 D.L.R. 81.

In Canada the great majority of cases involving the issues of consent and of informed consent have been pleaded and decided as battery cases (see Rozovsky, Consent to Treatment (1973), 11 Osgoode Hall Law Journal 103 at p. 104 and 25 Can. Abr. (2nd), pp. 209-212) but there have been notable exceptions (see, for example, *Male* v. *Hopmans,* [1966] 1 O.R. 647, 54 D.L.R. (2d) 592, affirmed with a variation of the portion of the judgment relating to damages [1967] 2 O.R. 457, 64 D.L.R. (2d) 105 (C.A.)). In the United States the predominant view, with respect to failure to disclose collateral risks of proposed treatment, is to regard such cases as ones of negligence rather than battery: Prosser, Law of Torts (1971, 4th ed.) pp. 105-106 and 165-166.

How the case is pleaded in many cases is more than a matter of mere academic interest. It will have important bearing on such matters as the incidence of the onus of proof, causation, the importance of expert medical evidence, the significance of medical judgment, proof of damage and, most important, of course, the substantive basis upon which liability may be found. . . .

It appears to me that it is reasonable to look at the matter of informed consent, as far as an alleged battery is concerned, from the point of view of what information was communicated. If the basic nature and character of the operation performed is substantially that of which the plaintiff was advised, and then agreed to, then there has not been an unconsented-to invasion of the person of the plaintiff, regardless of any failure to disclose any collateral risks flowing from the operation. However, such failure, if it can be shown to have resulted in damage to the patient, and was not justified by reasonable medical considerations, may properly be subject-matter for a claim based on negligence. This approach is helpfully explained and illustrated by Professor Plante in An Analysis of "Informed Consent" (1968), 36 Fordham Law Review 639 at pp. 648 et seq. It seems to me to strike a reasonable balance in the complex of interests, rights and duties subsisting in the patient-doctor relationship, as well as being consistent with basic concepts of the law of torts. (Reference should also be made to the landmark article of McCoid, A Reappraisal of Liability for Unauthorized Medical Treatment (1957), 41 Minnesota Law Review 381, which submits that the battery approach should be confined to those rare cases where the doctor engaged in an intentional deviation from practice not intended to be beneficial to the patient. The vast majority of unauthorized treatment cases should turn on a single basis of liability, a "deviation from the standard of conduct of a reasonable and prudent doctor of the same school of practice as the defendant under similar circumstances": (p. 434)).

However, it has to be recognized that this test has both its practical and, perhaps, its policy frailties. In some cases it may be difficult to distinguish, and separate out, the matter of consequential or collateral risks from the basic nature and character of the operation or the procedure to be performed. This may possibly have been the case in *Halushka* v. *University of Saskatchewan,* [(1965), 53 D.L.R. (2d) 436]. The more probable the risk the more it could be said to be an integral feature of the nature and character of the operation. Further, even if a risk is truely collateral, but still material, if it could be said that its disclosure is so essential to an informed decision to undergo the operation that lack of such disclosure should vitiate the consent. In Nathan's Medical Negligence at p. 158, although the point is not expressly dealt with, it appears to be the learned author's view that inadequate explanation of the effects and risks of an operation may result in an apparent consent being ineffective and, hence, not an answer to a claim for assault.

Was there Negligence apart from the Issue of Consent?

I shall address myself to the issue, briefly and inconclusively, of whether the defendant was negligent in deciding to perform the osteotomy, apart from the issue of the plaintiff's consent. I say briefly and inconclusively because I have difficulty separating the issue of the plaintiff's consent from the general question but, somewhat as a requirement of logically progressing through the issues which have been put before me, I shall consider it. It is clear that the operation caused damage to the plaintiff but the defendant cannot be liable therefor unless, in deciding to perform the operation, he failed to exercise "that degree of care and skill which could reasonably be expected of a normal, prudent practitioner of the same experience and standing, and if he holds himself out as a specialist, a higher degree of skill is required of him than one who does not profess to be so qualified by special training and ability." *Crits* v. *Sylvester,* [1956] O.R. 132, 143, 1 D.L.R. (2d) 502, affirmed [1956] S.C.R.

991, 5 D.L.R. (2d) 601. In short, I think the issue reduces itself to one of whether the risks involved were medically acceptable. In a frequently quoted statement of the Judicial Committee of the Privy Council the matter has been put this way "A defendant charged with negligence can clear his feet if he shows that he acted in accord with general and approved practice": *Vancouver General Hospital* v. *McDaniel,* [1934] 4 D.L.R. 593 at p. 597, [1934] 3 W.W.R. 619 (P.C.).

What medical evidence is there in this case bearing on these issues? [His Lordship considered the medical evidence.] . . .

The onus is on the plaintiff "to establish substandard conduct that amounts to negligence." (Linden, Canadian Negligence Law (1972), p. 48). This can be done, on a balance of probabilities, by reference to all the evidence in the case, regardless of which party produced it. In the circumstances of this case I am inclined to the view that there is insufficient affirmative medical evidence in the plaintiff's favour to justify my holding that the defendant was guilty of substandard conduct in deciding to perform the osteotomy, . . .

Was There an Informed Consent?

I have found that on 28th July the plaintiff was told that to straighten the crooked elbow would require the breaking of the bone in her arm followed by a period of time in a cast. The risk of stiffness may have been "mentioned" but certainly no more than that. The matter was then closed by the mutual decision that the ulnar nerve transplant and the joint clean-out only would be performed. On the following day when the plaintiff was under sedation as the result of an injection of 100 mgm. of Pethidine (a matter to which I shall return), and just prior to the intended operation, she demanded of the defendant that he not operate on her unless her crooked elbow was straightened. According to the defendant, and this was his view at that time, she was "a little more undependable" than she was previously, "irrational", "foolish" and "silly". In saying "irrational" the defendant meant "irrational from the point of view of not being able to think the way I was thinking which, I think, was more rational". He further elaborated on this. He said: "I thought that it was rational to be concerned about her paralyzed, weak hand. She was only interested in the appearance of her elbow". It may thus be seen that the defendant was concerned with her choice of priorities—between curing the paralysis and straightening the arm—and was not so much concerned with the risks of the osteotomy. . . .

I have rejected the plaintiff's evidence as to what transpired between the parties immediately prior to the signing of the consent but her evidence as to how she felt following the administration of the sedation is not inconsistent with what the defendant observed or, possibly with her confused and erroneous recollection of what did happen. If her state of mind was such that at the point of her conversation with the defendant she did not know the basic nature of the operation required to straighten her arm, and it may be noted that all she was asking for was a *result,* not a procedure, and she manifested this lack of knowledge to the defendant, then her apparent consent to the operation, notwithstanding her clear desire for the result, would be ineffective.

The onus is on the defendant to prove facts that indicate a valid consent as far as the basic nature of the operation is concerned. In this regard the evidence respecting the plaintiff being under sedation is not helpful to him. I say, with respect, the evidence relating to the various effects of Pethidine is not too detailed. What there is indicates that its main effects are to calm the patient and act as a pain killer. There is no evidence that it would have an anaesthetic effect. Dr. Sorbie said that it is not a hypnotic. Obviously its sedative purposes indicate that it must effect some blunting of the mental processes. The plaintiff said that she had a "funny sensation" a "high feeling" and she felt like she did not care, but she was still nervous. The defendant said that the drug is supposed to have a calming effect. It has an individual effect depending on the patient. The plaintiff was calm but more irrational than the day before. I do not think that it could be suggested otherwise than that the giving of a consent under such circumstances, at the very least, leaves the validity of the consent open to question (Rozovsky, Canadian Hospital Law (1974), p. 36 and *Beausoleil* v. *La Communaute Des Soeurs De La Charite De La Providence et al.* (1966), 53 D.L.R. (2d) 65) and that it would be incumbent on the defendant to prove affirmatively that the effect of the sedation probably did not adversely affect the patient's understanding of the basic nature of the contemplated operation. Notwithstanding these frailties in the defendant's position, I do find that, taking the conversation of the day before into account, that the defendant could reasonably have thought that the plaintiff, in asking to have her elbow straightened on 29th July was aware that this involved the fracturing and resetting of her arm under general anaesthetic. In other words—that the combination of the sedation, and her labile condition, had not blotted the information from her mind respecting the basic nature and character of the operation when she made her demand. In such circumstances he has shown a sufficient consent to avoid liability on the basis of battery. (I shall deal shortly with whether he could reasonably have thought at that time that she was aware of the special risks of the operation.)

This, clearly, would not be the result if the collateral risks of the operation were considered to be part and parcel of the proposed procedure or if the preferable approach were that a reasonable understanding of such risks, in itself, were considered to be essential to a valid consent asserted as a defence to a battery action.

I now consider these issues in the context of the claim based on negligence. In this area, I think that it is reasonable to conclude that when the plaintiff demanded the elbow-straightening on 29th July her decision was not based upon any knowledge or appreciation of the risk of stiffness associated with the procedure to be followed and, equally important, the defendant knew that her decision lacked this foundation. A valid consent involves both awareness and assent. In the course of a thorough and perceptive study in this area two American writers have put the following proposition, which seems to me to be a balanced and reasonable one: "To establish consent to a risk it must be shown that the patient was aware of the risk and that he assented to it. The hard question involves the kind of evidence that would be admitted to establish these elements. Preliminarily, it is obvious that a risk must have been understandably communicated before the element of awareness can be established": Waltz and Scheuneman, Informed Consent to Therapy (1969), 52 Northwestern University Law Review 628 at p. 643. In the present case it is obvious that awareness of the risk of stiffness had not been understandably communicated to the plaintiff and that the defendant knew this. There followed the ritual of the signing of the consent form.

Mr. Nelligan has put some stress on the failure of the defendant to warn the plaintiff of the risk of the manipulation procedure following the osteotomy as being a foreseeable result of this operation. (Dr. Sorbie had testified that in his view permanent stiffness was unlikely, one of the steps which would be taken to avoid this being manipulation under general anaesthetic.) I am not prepared to intrude into this area in such detail, and to such extent, as to hold that this particular failure, in itself amounts to a breach of duty. All that I can say is that if this warning had been given and brought home to the plaintiff it would have been good evidence that she had been properly informed of the stiffness risk.

I have found that the risk of stiffness both temporary and permanent, was a definite risk of the proposed osteotomy in the circumstances of the plaintiff's condition. It was a "special" risk relating to the nature of the operation, as opposed to being a usual risk incident to, or possible in, any operation (*Kenny* v. *Lockwood,* supra, at p. 161 and the passage in Nathan, Medical Negligence at p. 56 quoted above). Indeed, on the evidence, it was the only risk of this kind of the operation, and in my view it was the defendant's duty to be satisfied that it had been brought home to the patient before he could reasonably regard her apparent consent as being valid. I appreciate here that it would be quite unreasonable, and the law does not call for it, to expect the doctor to see into the mind of the patient to satisfy himself that the patient not only understands the risks but also puts the degree of emphasis on them which the doctor considers to be reasonable—but that is not the case here. The defendant could see that she was missing something rather fundamental: ". . . she didn't know the consequences". Whatever had been communicated to the plaintiff on 28th July and, in any event, I have found that the risk of stiffness had not really been brought home to her then, could not be resorted to by the defendant on 29th July, unless he was reasonably satisfied that at the time she executed the consent she then understood the special risks of the operation. "The medical man should always proceed upon the basis that it is his duty to make sure the patient consents to the treatment proposed": Nathan's, Medical Negligence, p. 159, and, consistent with this, in my view, is the duty to be reasonably satisfied that the patient is aware of those risks associated with the treatment of which he or she should be aware.

I take it to be the law in this jurisdiction that the duty to disclose the collateral risks inherent in any proposed procedure is substantially a matter of medical judgment as opposed to being one of absolute and invariable content (see *Male* v. *Hopmans,* supra), unlike the law in some U.S. jurisdictions where the duty is based upon the notion of what a reasonable patient might be expected to wish to hear in order to make up his mind—and that, therefore, normally, the duty would be determined with the assistance of expert medical evidence on what would be the proper scope of disclosure in the circumstances presented. In this case there is no such evidence but that is probably because the duty was not really put in issue by the defendant. It was not suggested on behalf of the defendant that this was a case which called for the exercise of any discretion relating to what the patient should be told. Having regard to the fact that the proposed operation was not emergency and that there was no danger in alarming the patient—indeed, since the operation was for cosmetic purposes only it would have been prudent to attempt to alarm the patient—and to the nature of the risks, I do not see any possible grounds for submitting that there was no duty in this case.

Finally, there is the matter of causation. In a claim based on negligence the plaintiff must show that the breach of the duty in question was an effective cause of the damages of which complaint is made. In the context of this case the plaintiff must satisfy me that if the defendant had properly informed her of the risk involved in the osteotomy and seen to it that she understood this risk then she would have foregone the operation and hence not suffered the alleged damage. It is implicit throughout her evidence that this would, no doubt, have been the case. I really do not think it would have strengthened her case if she put this position in express language. Of course, I have to be on guard against a naturally self-serving position on what is essentially a hypothetical question. (See *Smith* v. *Auckland Hospital Board,* [1965] N.Z.L.R. 191). However, I think the difficulties standing in the way of the plaintiff in this case, on this issue, are considerably less imposing than those facing plaintiffs in other possible cases where, for example, the undisclosed risks related to treatment intended to cure a serious condition and were not, possibly, as likely to materialize as in the present case. The evidence of the defendant himself is of considerable assistance in resolving this issue. He characterized the plaintiff's decisions as "foolish", "silly" and "unwise", since she did not know the consequences, with the clear implication that if she had known and understood the consequences her decision would have been otherwise. Obviously the plaintiff was interested in cosmesis. However, the osteotomy operation involved the necessary jettisoning of the joint clean-out which was intended to give her more movement in her elbow, and the risk, therefore, that confronted her involved not only more restriction of movement, rather than a possible improvement in this respect, *together* with cosmetic shortcomings which would be associated with a stiffened elbow. On all the evidence I think that it is more probable than not that if she had known and understood the risks of the osteotomy on 29th July such operation would not have been performed.

[The defendant was held liable in negligence.]

NOTES

1. What must a patient prove in order to recover from his doctor in battery? If he fails, does he still have a chance to recover in negligence? What difference does it make whether battery theory or negligence theory is employed? If you were a patient which approach would you prefer the court to use? See Picard, "The Tempest of Informed Consent" in Klar (ed.), *Studies in Canadian Tort Law* (1977); *cf.* Hertz, "Volenti Non Fit Injuria: A Guide", *ibid.* See generally Castel, "Nature and Effects of Consent with Respect to the Right to Life and the Right to Physical and Mental Integrity in the Medical Field: Criminal and Private Law Aspects" (1978), 16 Alta. L. Rev. 293.

2. In *Reibl* v. *Hughes* (1978), 6 C.C.L.T. 227, the Ontario Court of Appeal adopted the general approach of *Kelly* v. *Hazlett* to the issue of informed consent. The plaintiff suffered from hypertension and headaches. The defendant, a neurosurgeon, examined him and discovered a blockage in one of the arteries of his neck, which subjected him to the risk of a stroke, but it was not an emergency situation. The defendant advised that the blockage be removed surgically. There was evidence that there was a 4% risk of death and a 10% risk of neurological damage during the operation, but the doctor did not disclose this to the patient, thinking he was aware of them because of the questions he had asked. The operation was done and the plaintiff suffered a massive stroke which paralyzed the right side of his body.

The trial judge found the doctor liable on both battery and negligence theories, but the Court of Appeal ordered a new trial.

In explaining the decision, Brooke J.A. stated, at p. 246:

"In cases such as this, the notion of battery seems quite inappropriate. In the circumstances when the evidence is consistent only with the fact that the doctor has acted in good faith and in the interests of the patient, but in so doing was negligent in failing to make disclosure of a risk inherent in treatment which he recommends and as a result has caused his patient loss or damage, the action should properly be in negligence and not in battery. The finding then of battery cannot stand.

See also *Cobbs* v. *Grant* (1972), 502 P. 2d 1 (Calif.). Leave to appeal has been given by the S.C.C. in *Reibl.*

3. The factors a doctor must consider in deciding how much to tell his patient have been ably outlined by Woodhouse J. in *Smith* v. *Auckland Hospital Board,* [1964] N.Z.L.R. 241, revd. on other grounds [1965] N.Z.L.R. 191 as follows:

"As it seems to me, the paramount consideration is the welfare of the patient, and given good faith on the part of the doctor, I think the exercise of his discretion in the area of advice must depend upon the patient's overall needs. To be taken into account should be the gravity of the condition to be treated, the importance of the benefits expected to flow from the treatment or procedure, the need to encourage him to accept it, the relative significance of its inherent risks, the intellectual and emotional capacity of the patient to accept the information without such distortion as to prevent any rational decision at all, and the extent to which the patient may seem to have placed himself in his doctor's hands with the invitation that the latter accept on his behalf the responsibility for intricate or technical decisions. Finally, it cannot be overlooked that although the patient may not appreciate the specific risk in the particular treatment, he has lived like all of us with the knowledge that contingencies are inseparable from human affairs, and accordingly would recognize, without being told, that there can be no part of medical practice which is infallible. Even when some warning may seem necessary, however, I cannot think that there should be an inevitable elaboration of detailed risks. Nor can it be sufficient to show after the event that a doctor would have been wiser to say more. This duty appears to me to be governed by all the factors I have mentioned as they would be assessed and applied by a reasonably prudent medical practitioner; and the need to include descriptions of the adverse possibilities of treatment in the explanations must depend upon the significance which that prudent doctor in his patient's interests would reasonably attach to them in all the environment of the case. I certainly am not prepared to hold, in the absence of authority, that doctors should be distracted from their prime responsibility to care for the health of their patients by the thought that there is an almost automatic need to describe these possibilities in order to avoid a claim in negligence should something, by bad chance, go wrong."

4. The standard of care required of the doctor by this test is called the "professional disclosure" standard, which means that a doctor must disclose the risks that his professional colleagues would normally disclose in the circumstances. In doing so, however, he must assess his patient subjectively to determine his individual needs. See Picard, Note on *Lepp* v. *Hopp* (1979), 8 C.C.L.T. 261, at p. 262; see also discussion in *Reibl* v. *Hughes, supra,* at p. 243, *per* Brooke J.A.

5. In *Male* v. *Hopmans,* [1966] 1 O.R. 647; varied on other grounds [1967] 2 O.R. 457, a patient had a serious knee infection. He was given neomycin, even though his surgeon knew that this drug involved a 10-20% chance of hearing impairment. The doctor did not tell the patient about the risk. The patient was left totally deaf. Although liability was imposed on another ground, the court felt that there was no need to warn the patient about the possible adverse side effects of neomycin because (1) the patient was untrained in medicine, (2) his morale may have been adversely affected by knowledge of the drug's dangerous propensities, (3) he was in considerable pain and had a high fever at the time, and the court felt that it was "unrealistic to assume either that he could have fully appreciated the nature of the risks of the various alternatives or that he could have assisted in selecting a particular method of treatment".

Is this a subjective or objective patient standard? Do you agree with the reasoning of the court on the informed consent question?

6. A surgeon operates on a woman's protruding vagina, with the result that it is shortened to one-quarter of its normal size, making sexual intercourse impossible. Evidence is introduced that shows that some shortening of the vagina occurs in 25% of such operations and that in only 1% of the cases is the shortening as severe as occurred in this case. The doctor mentioned nothing of these risks and assured the plaintiff that intercourse would be possible after the operation. Battery?

See *Chipps* v. *Peters,* March 8, 1979, unreported (Ont. C.A.).

7. A patient suffered a loss of taste and smell after an operation to relieve the pain of migraine headaches. The neurosurgeon had had "many" complaints but still assured the plaintiff that if she had "lasting complications of importance" it would "be a first time". Informed consent? See *Koehler* v. *Cook* (1976), 65 D.L.R. (3d) 766 (B.C.).

8. Is a doctor obliged to tell his patient that it is his first time performing the particular operation he is recommending to him? See *Lepp* v. *Hopp* (1979), 8 C.C.L.T. 260 (Alta. C.A.).

9. Is a doctor required to tell a patient that, in case of complications arising during an operation, it would be safer to do it in a city hospital rather than in a small town hospital? See *Lepp* v. *Hopp* (1979), 8 C.C.L.T. 260. Should a dentist give a patient a choice of whether an operation should be done in the office or in the hospital? See *Kangas* v. *Parker,* [1976] 5 W.W.R. 75 (Sask. Q.B.) See also *Zimmer* v. *Ringrose* (1978), 89 D.L.R. (3d) 646 (Alta.).

10. When someone consents to surgery by one doctor, does this operate as a consent to administer anaesthesia by another doctor? See *Villeneuve* v. *Sisters of St. Joseph,* [1971] 2 O.R. 593, at p. 608; revd. in part [1972] 2 O.R. 119 (C.A.). Should a patient be asked whether he prefers a general or local anaesthetic where either would be acceptable for purposes of the operation? *Gorback* v. *Ting,* [1974] 5 W.W.R. 606 (Man. Q.B.).

11. Does an inquiry by the patient enlarge the amount of information that the doctor must supply? See *Lepp* v. *Hopp* (1979), 8 C.C.L.T. 260, at p. 297 (Alta. C.A.).

12. How many people really understand what they are consenting to when they agree to let doctors operate on them? Is this a valid reason for not being too stringent in requiring detailed explanations? How voluntary is a consent given by a seriously sick patient to a doctor upon whom he is relying for treatment?

13. Do doctors in large cities today know their patients well enough to decide intelligently the amount of information they should give their patients prior to signing a consent?

14. The problem of informed consent has received some attention in the field of experimentation with human beings. In *Halushka* v. *University of Saskatchewan* (1965), 53 D.L.R. (2d) 436, a student at the University of Saskatchewan had attended summer school in 1961. On August 21, 1961, he went to the employment office to find a job. At the employment office he was advised that there were no jobs available but that he could earn $50 by being the subject of a test at the University Hospital. The respondent said that he was told that the test would last a couple of hours and that it was "a safe test and there was nothing to worry about". He was told that electrodes would be attached to him, that an incision would be made in his left arm and that a catheter tube would be inserted into his vein. He then signed a consent which released the doctors and everyone else from liability for "untoward effects or accidents" due to the tests. When the plaintiff asked the meaning of this latter phrase, he was told it covered an accident like falling down the steps at home after the test.

The test contemplated . . . was to be conducted jointly by the appellants Wyant and Merriman, using a new anaesthetic agent known commercially as "Fluoromar". The agent had not been previously used or tested by the appellants in any way.

The respondent returned to the University Hospital on August 23, 1961, to undergo the test. The procedure followed was that which had been described to the respondent and expected by him, with the exception that the catheter, after being inserted in the vein in the respondent's arm, was advanced towards his heart. When the catheter reached the vicinity of the heart, the respondent felt some discomfort. The anaesthetic agent was then administered to him. The time was then 11.32 a.m. Eventually the catheter tip was advanced through the various heart chambers out into the pulmonary artery where it was positioned. . . .

At about 12.20 there were changes in the respondent's cardiac rhythm which suggested to the appellants Wyant and Merriman that the level of the anaesthetic was too deep. The amount of anaesthetic was then decreased, or lightened. At 12.23 the respondent suffered a complete cardiac arrest.

The appellants Wyant and Merriman and their assistants took immediate steps to resuscitate the respondent's heart by manual massage. To reach the heart an incision was made from the breastbone to the line of the arm-pit and two of the ribs were pulled apart. A vasopressor was administered as well as urea, a drug used to combat swelling of the brain. After one minute and 30 seconds the respondent's heart began to function again.

The respondent was unconscious for a period of four days. He remained in the University Hospital as a patient until discharged 10 days later. On the day before he was discharged the respondent was given fifty ($50) dollars by the appellant Wyant. At that time the respondent asked the appellant Wyant if that was all he was going to get for all he went through. The appellant said that fifty dollars was all that they had bargained for but that he could give a larger sum in return for a complete release executed by the respondent's mother or elder sister.

As a result of the experiment the appellants concluded that as an anaesthetic agent "Fluoromar" had too narrow a margin of safety and it was withdrawn from clinical use in the University Hospital.

The respondent brought action against the appellants, basing his claim for damages on two grounds, namely, trespass to the person and negligence. The action came on for trial before Balfour J., sitting with a jury. . . .

The jury found that (1) the plaintiff did not consent to the performance of the test made by the defendant doctors; (2) the doctors committed a trespass in performing the test; (3) the doctors were negligent in (a) failing to explain fully the test at the time of the so-called "consent"; (b) failing to obtain a medical history or to perform a physical examination of plaintiff; and (4) they assessed the damages at $22,500.

Mr. Justice Balfour stated:

"The main issue before the jury concerning the respondent's claim of trespass to the person was that of consent. The attachment of the electrodes, the administration of anaesthetic and the insertion of the catheter were each an intentional application of force to the person of the respondent. When taken as a whole they certainly constitute a trespass which would be actionable unless done with consent. . . . The appellants rely upon ex.D.1 and the conduct of the respondent as evidence of consent.

In ordinary medical practice the consent given by a patient to a physician or surgeon, to be effective, must be an 'informed' consent freely given. It is the duty of the physician to give a fair and reasonable explanation of the proposed treatment including the probable effect and any special or unusual risks. . . .

In my opinion the duty imposed upon those engaged in medical research, as were the appellants Wyant and Merriman, to those who offer themselves as subjects for experimentation, as the respondent did here, is at least as great as, if not greater than, the duty owed by the ordinary physician or surgeon to his patient. There can be no exceptions to the ordinary requirements of disclosure in the case of research as there may well be in ordinary medical practice. The researcher does not have to balance the probable effect of lack of treatment against the risk involved in the treatment itself. The example of risks being properly hidden from a patient when it is important that he should not worry can have no application in the field of research. The subject of medical experimentation is entitled to a full and frank disclosure of all the facts, probabilities and opinions which a reasonable man might be expected to consider before giving his consent. The respondent necessarily had to rely upon the special skill, knowledge and experience of the appellants, who were, in my opinion, placed in the fiduciary position described by Lord Shaw of Dunfermline in *Nocton* v. *Lord Ashburton,* [1914] A.C. 932 . . . .

Although the appellant Wyant informed the respondent that a 'new drug' was to be tried out, he did not inform him that the new drug was in fact an anaesthetic of which he had no previous knowledge, nor that there was risk involved with the use of an anaesthetic. Inasmuch as no test had been previously conducted using the anaesthetic agent 'Fluoromar' to the knowledge of the appellants, the statement made to the respondent that it was a safe test which had been conducted many times before, when considered in the light of the medical evidence describing the characteristics of anaesthetic agents generally, was incorrect and was in reality a non-disclosure.

The respondent was not informed that the catheter would be advanced to and through his heart but was admittedly given to understand that it would be merely inserted in the vein in his arm. While it may be correct to say that the advancement of the catheter to the heart was not in itself dangerous and did not cause or contribute to the cause of the cardiac arrest, it was a circumstance which, if known, might very well have prompted the respondent to withhold his consent. The undisclosed or misrepresented facts need not concern matters which directly cause the ultimate damage if they are of a nature which might influence the judgment upon which the consent is based."

15. Do you agree that the doctor's duty of disclosure to experimental subjects should be greater than to his sick patients? What about the situation where a doctor tries innovative techniques on his ill patients already in hospital?

16. In *Halushka,* the plaintiff was paid to participate in the experiment. For some sick, poor people and for prisoners in institutions, this may be one of the only sources of remuneration open to them. Is their consent then truly "free"? Should all experimentation with such people be prevented?

17. Renée C. Fox, in Katz, *Experimentation with Human Beings* (1972), at p. 631, indicates that there are positive as well as negative aspects to such experiments:

"Many patient-volunteers in this situation seem to enjoy what the psychiatrist would term 'secondary gains' from this role; some establish 'transference' relations with medical investigators from which they derive important emotional satisfactions. Or, as Leopold indicated, the comfort, privileges, and trust that he and his fellow-prisoners were granted as volunteers made them feel that they were 'on the same side of the fence. . . partners in a common endeavour' with the Army doctors for the benefit of society, which, in turn, gave them 'more solid, lasting satisfaction from what they were doing than many of them had known in some time'."

18. In response to some of the concerns about the reality of informed consent, Eleanor S. Glass has advocated a "patient's standard of care". In "Restructuring Informed Consent: Legal Therapy for the Doctor-Patient Relationship" (1970), 79 Yale L.J. 1533, at p. 1559, she has written:

"The decision about what is or is not relevant information upon which a patient can base an informed consent is a human judgment, not a determination requiring medical expertise. When the doctor makes this decision, he does not deserve the special protection afforded his professional activities by the professional standard of negligence. His lack of a sustained personal relationship with his patients deprives the professional of any special ability to perceive a reasonable patient's capacity or need to understand and evaluate a proposed intervention. The doctor should be judged as an ordinary reasonable man.

In assessing whether the doctor acted reasonably, courts should adopt a patient's, or layman's, standard of care. The jury would decide whether the doctor disclosed enough information for the reasonable patient to make an intelligent decision. The jury should not undertake a subjective inquiry into what the individual patient actually understood or whether he acted intelligently. Presumably the plaintiff will present evidence regarding material facts that were not disclosed. The jury's task is to determine whether the information actually withheld would have been relevant for the jury members themselves, for their judgment is by definition that of the reasonable patient. They make this determination in the light of the knowledge about a given procedure which is available to the medical profession. Thus whether a piece of undisclosed information would have been relevant for their own decision is the only question which the jury need resolve, unless the doctor claims that the patient was for some reason 'unreasonable'. If the jurors find the information irrelevant, the doctor acted reasonably in withholding it. If they find it relevant, the doctor acted unreasonably and will be held liable for failure to obtain informed consent. . . .

In addition to a different standard of care, the restructured law of informed consent also should have at its center formal rules of disclosure stipulating the minimum amount of information that a reasonable patient must be told before his consent is requested. The doctor ought to initiate discussion with his patient on the following substantive topics: the diagnosis; the physician's choice of treatment; the physician's experience with this treatment; the methods to be used; the risks involved, major and collateral; expected pain and discomfort; the benefits of this treatment; alternatives to this treatment; prognosis. Any omission from this list would constitute a *prima facie* violation of the physician's duty to disclose and liability would ensue. The physician must at least mention basic facts within each category. . . ."

What do you think of this approach?

HEGARTY v. SHINE

Irish Court of Appeal. (1878), 14 Cox C.C. 145

Ball C.: . . . Between the plaintiff and the defendant there had for about two years subsisted an illicit intercourse, and during its continuance, the plaintiff contracted from the defendant disease. As the questions to be decided by us arise upon the charge of the learned judge before whom the trial took place, in respect of the legal considerations applicable to a case of this character, I think it unnecessary to enter into the details of the evidence. There was a verdict for the plaintiff; but if the jury were misdirected, of course it cannot be upheld. The charge is reported by the learned judge in the terms which I shall now state: ". . . I in substance directed the jury, as matter of law, that an assault implied an act of violence, committed upon a person against his or her will, and that, as a general rule, when the person consented to the act, there was no assault; but that if the consent was obtained by the fraud of the party committing the act, the fraud vitiated the consent, and the act became in view of the law an assault, and that therefore if the defendant, knowing that he had venereal disease, and that the probable and natural effect of his having connection with the plaintiff would be to communicate to her venereal disease, fraudulently concealed from her his condition, in order to induce, and did thereby induce, her to have connection with him; and if but for that fraud she would not have consented to have had such connection; and if he had with her the connection so procured and thereby communicated to her such venereal disease, he had committed an assault, and one for which they might on the evidence award substantial damages". This charge, and the objections to it, were brought before the Queen's Bench Division, when a majority of the judges held that the views presented by the learned judge to the jury . . . were a misdirection, and they consequently awarded a new trial upon this ground. The propriety of their ruling we have now to examine.

The charge of the learned judge assumes that, in order to constitute an assault upon a person, the act done should be against his or her will, without his or her consent. With that proposition I entirely agree. To strike a person minaciously or in anger is a matter very different in character from a blow in sport or play. Sexual intercourse with the consent of the female (supposing no grounds to exist for holding the consent inoperative) cannot be an assault on the part of the male. The charge then proceeds to assert that, although consent be given, yet if that consent was obtained by the fraud of the party committing the act, the fraud vitiated the consent and the act became in view of the law an assault. From this proposition when laid down in reference to the particular facts of the present case I dissent. We are not dealing with deceit as to the nature of the act to be done, such as occurred in the case cited in argument, of the innocent girl who was induced to believe that a surgical operation was being performed. There was here a lengthened cohabitation of the parties, deliberate consent to the act or acts out of which the cause of action has arisen. If deceit by one of them as to the condition of his health suffices to alter the whole relation in which they otherwise were to each other, so as to transform the intercourse between them into an assault on the part of the defendant, why should not any other deceit have the same effect? Suppose a woman to live with her paramour under and with a distinct and reiterated promise of marriage not fulfilled, nor, it may be, intended to be fulfilled, is every separate act of intercourse an assault? Let the same happen in conjunction with a broken engagement to provide for her maintenance and protection against poverty, does a similar consequence here also follow? No one, I think, would be prepared to answer these questions in the affirmative. . . .

These reasons in my opinion justify the order of the Queen's Bench Division directing a new trial upon the ground of misdirection by the learned judge. I think it right to add that I also concur with the majority of that court in holding that an action of this character cannot be maintained. The consequence of an immoral act — the direct consequence — is the subject of complaint. Courts of justice no more exist to provide a remedy for the consequences of immoral or illegal acts and contracts than to aid or enforce those acts or contracts themselves.

[Judgments of Palles C.B., and Deasy L.J.A., to the same effect are omitted.]

NOTES

1. In *Agar* v. *Canning* (1966), 54 W.W.R. 302, affd. 55 W.W.R. 384, the court decided that a retaliatory blow struck during a hockey game "with resolve to cause serious injury" did not fall within the scope of implied consent inherent in the game. See also *Martin et al.* v. *Daigle* (1969), 6 D.L.R. (3d) 634 where the New Brunswick Court of Appeal awarded damages for a severe blow struck during a hockey game because it was "clearly intended to cause bodily hurt. It inflicted actual bodily harm and was therefore actionable."

How do these cases relate to *Hegarty* v. *Shine*?

2. In *R.* v. *Clarence* (1888), 22 Q.B.D. 23, the accused was charged with assaulting his wife, causing grievous bodily harm, and unlawfully and maliciously inflicting grievous bodily harm. The accused knew he had gonorrhea. His wife did not know and had she known would not have consented to the sexual intercourse which, under the circumstances, was the basis of the charge. By a majority of 9:4 it was held the accused could not be convicted.

Is it vital for the criminal law to parallel the civil law in this area?

3. If A consents to contact with a piece of metal and B knows, but A does not, that the metal is heavily charged with electricity, may A sue B for physical harm intentionally caused?

4. The plaintiff and defendant go out into the alley to have a fist fight. The defendant pulls out a knife and stabs the plaintiff. Liability? *Cf. Teolis* v. *Moscatelli* (1923), 119 Atl. 161 (R.I.S.C.). What if they agree to fight with knives? *Cf. Lykins* v. *Hamrick* (1911), 137 S.W. 852 (Ky.). See also *Lane* v. *Holloway*, [1967] 3 All E.R. 129.

5. What relevance to the outcome of this case is the immorality or illegality of the plaintiff's conduct? There is a Latin maxim that is sometimes invoked in cases such as this, *ex turpi causa non oritur actio*. See *Hartlen* v. *Chaddock* (1957), 11 D.L.R. (2d) 705 (N.S.S.C.). See also *Tomlinson* v. *Harrison*, [1972] 1 O.R. 670 in Chapter 11, Section D.

6. Can someone "consent" to the perpetration of an unlawful act upon him-

self? If a woman consents to a criminal abortion, can she later sue the doctor for battery? What are the policies at conflict here? What about the policy of discouraging abortions? What about the goal of encouraging disclosure of evidence of crime? *Cf. Sayadoff* v. *Warda* (1954), 25 Cal. App. 2d 626, 271 P. 2d 140 and *Millicken* v. *Heddesheimer* (1924), 110 Ohio. St. 381, 144 N.E. 264.

7. If a young virgin of 15 consents to carnal knowledge (an offence on the part of the man under s. 146 of the Criminal Code), can she recover damages against the man later? If she is permitted to do so, are we rewarding her for abandoning her virtue? See *Bishop* v. *Liston* (1924), 199 N.W. 825 (Neb.) where Mr. Justice Good declared:

"The purpose of the Legislature in changing the common law, as to the facts necessary to constitute rape, was to protect the virtue and chastity of female children of tender years who have not attained such a degree of mental development as to fully comprehend and realize the nature and effect of the immoral and unlawful act. The statute says that up to a certain age they are incapable of giving consent to the violation of their persons, with the consequent degradation, humiliation and shame, to which it will subject them. It further says to the libertine, who would rob a virtuous maiden, under the age of 18 years, of the priceless and crowning jewel of maidenhood, that he does so at his peril. There was no consent to the wrongful act of defendant because plaintiff was not legally capable of consent. His liability is the same as if he had accomplished his vile purpose by force and violence."

8. Compare with *Barton* v. *Bee Line* (1933), 238 App. Div. 501, 265 N.Y.S. 284, where the court stated:

"It is one thing to say that society will protect itself by punishing those who consort with females under the age of consent; it is another to hold that, knowing the nature of her act, such female shall be rewarded for her indiscretion. Surely public policy — to serve which the statute was adopted — will not be vindicated by recompensing her for willing participation in that against which the law has sought to protect her. The very object of the statute will be frustrated if by a material return for her fall 'we should unwarily put it in the power of the female sex to become seducers in their turn'. . . . Instead of incapacity to consent being a shield to save, it might be a sword to desecrate."

9. A and B agree to engage in a boxing match, contrary to the Criminal Code, s. 81, which makes a prizefight a crime unless gloves of at least five ounces are worn or it is held under permission of a provincial athletic board. Suppose the gloves weigh four ounces; or that the licence of the board is not obtained. If B defeats A, may the latter sue B for the hurts he received? *Cf. Hart* v. *Geysel* (1930), 159 Wash. 632, 294 P. 570. Should a "wrongdoer" be allowed to seek the help of the court if he is injured while participating in a crime? What policy choices are involved in this?

10. See Bohlen, "Consent as Affecting Liability for Breaches of the Peace" (1924), 24 Colum. L. Rev. 849.

GRAHAM v. SAVILLE

Ontario Court of Appeal. [1945] O.R. 301; [1945] 2 D.L.R. 489

The defendant, being then married, told the plaintiff he was a bachelor and induced her to agree to marry him. The plaintiff gave up a small business she operated and purchased wedding clothes. The parties went through a ceremony of marriage in July and lived as man and wife for 18 days. The defendant then left the plaintiff. A child was born the following March. The plaintiff sued alleging fraud in the representation of bachelorhood; complaining of "divers assaults upon her person by way of coition, she consenting thereto by her belief that she was the lawful wife of the defendant" and injury to her "character and reputation and great damage to her person by reason of the defendant's deceit and assaults". She claimed $5,000 damages.

The trial judge dismissed the action on the ground that no special damages were pleaded or claimed and general damages were not allowed in actions for false representations. The plaintiff appealed.

Laidlaw J.A.: . . . The wrong called deceit is not easily or satisfactorily defined. It consists in recklessly or wilfully causing another person to believe and act on a falsehood. . . . It has been said, *per* Lord Wensleydale in *Smith* v. *Kay* (1859), 7 H.L.C. 750, at p. 775: "Fraud gives a cause of action if it leads to any sort of damage." But "The only damage of which the law takes cognizance, in an action for misrepresentation, is actual and temporal damage — that is, some loss either of money or money's worth, or some physical injury, capable of being pecuniarily compensated, or some present or contingent liability, or tangible detriment, which admits of being quantified and assessed. Such damage does not include mere mental distress, or the mere loss of social advantages to which no money value can be attached:". (see *Spencer Bower on Actionable Misrepresentation*, 2nd ed., p. 151). . . .

It cannot be doubted that the plaintiff, under the circumstances of the present case, suffered actual and temporal damage. There was physical injury, pain and suffering, in consequence of her pregnancy and the birth of a child. There is likewise "present or contingent liability" and "tangible detriment which admits of being quantified and assessed." [Discussion of *Wilkinson* v. *Downtown*, is omitted.] It is sufficient for the purposes of the present case to decide that the plaintiff is entitled to recover damages sustained by her as a direct and natural consequence of the fraudulent misrepresentations of the defendant. On the basis discussed I would fix the general damages suffered by the plaintiff at the sum of $1,000.

Roach J.A.: . . . I think the damages should not be limited to compensation for "physical injury, pain, and suffering, in consequence of her pregnancy and the birth of a child", and the financial burden of maintaining that child. Supposing that the defendant's act of coition with the plaintiff had not resulted in her pregnancy, could it be said that, apart from the items included in the award of $860, she had suffered no damages recoverable under the law? In my opinion there would have been a violation of her person which would entitle her to substantial damages.

Then, too, there is the fact that the plaintiff's chances of marriage have been prejudiced by reason of her unfortunate relationship with the defendant including the fact that by him she is the mother of an illegitimate child. It is difficult to determine the extent to which those chances have been lessened and to assess reasonable compensation therefore. In addressing myself to that phase of this case, I am not thinking of her loss in terms of mental distress or social advantages, but rather of her loss in terms of the comfort of a home maintained by a husband as breadwinner of the household. All that is "actual and temporal damage", "the loss of money's worth". However difficult it may be to assess that damage, the court should nevertheless struggle to do so adequately.

In my opinion the plaintiff's total damages should be assessed at $4,000. I would, therefore, allow the appeal and direct that judgment be entered in her favour for that amount, together with costs throughout.

[Henderson J.A. agreed with Roach J.A. The court was unanimous that $860 should be allowed as special damages; being the amount of loss caused by the sale of a business and purchase of wedding clothes. Amendments of the pleadings were allowed since there was no surprise or prejudice and evidence had been offered at the trial without objection.]

NOTES

1. In *Smythe* v. *Reardon,* [1948] Q.S.R. 74, the defendant, already legally married, persuaded the plaintiff to go through a form of marriage with him. They lived together as man and wife for eight years. Discovering the earlier marriage, plaintiff brought action against defendant claiming £2,000 for fraudulent representation. Stanley J. held that damages "at large", and exemplary damages could not be given in an action for deceit. He indicated, however, that although defendant could not be convicted of rape "nevertheless he frequently assaulted the plaintiff because her consent to sexual intercourse was obtained by fraud". He refused to allow an action for deceit to be transformed into an action for assault since the rules as to damages in each were entirely different.

2. In *Papadimitropoulos* v. *The Queen* (1957), 98 C.L.R. 249, a woman with no knowledge of English was induced to believe she had married the accused at a registry office. As a matter of fact they had only made application for a subsequent marriage. During the next four days the woman and accused lived together and had sexual intercourse two or three times. The accused then departed and never again lived with the woman. On a charge of rape, the accused was convicted. The conviction was upheld by a majority in the Court of Criminal Appeal of Victoria. "What she was consenting to was a marital act, an act to which in her mistaken belief she was in duty bound to submit. What she got was an act of fornication — an act wholly different in moral character . . . the consent relied on is no real consent at all." On appeal to the High Court of Australia, the conviction was quashed. The court quoted with approval the editorial note to *R.* v. *Harms,* [1944] 2 D.L.R. 61, distinguishing "between the type of fraud which induces a consent that would not otherwise have been obtained but which is none the less a valid consent and the type of fraud which prevents any real consent from existing". The court concluded that "rape is carnal knowledge of a woman without her consent: carnal knowledge is the physical act of penetration; it is the consent to that which is in question; such a consent demands a perception as to what is about to take place, as to the identity of the man and the character of what he is doing. But once the consent is comprehending and actual the inducing causes cannot destroy its reality."

3. In *R.* v. *Harms,* [1944] 2 D.L.R. 61, 81 Can. C.C. 4 (Sask. C.A.), the accused induced a woman to have sexual intercourse with him on the fraudulent ground that the act would correct certain physical disorders. He was convicted of rape, notwithstanding evidence that the woman understood the meaning of carnal knowledge and its possible consequences. The Court of Appeal unheld the conviction stating that "the jury may well have decided that the nature and quality of the act so far as she was concerned (that is to say subjectively) was pathological and not carnal". Compare with the famous choirmaster case, *R.* v. *Williams,* [1923] 1 K.B. 340.

4. See also *R.* v. *Bolduc and Bird* (1967), 59 W.W.R. 103 (B.C.C.A.), where the defendant doctor examined the female patient's sexual organs in the presence of a curious friend in a white "lab coat", who was falsely represented as a qualified medical person. At trial, both defendants were found guilty of indecent assault. Mr. Justice Lord stated:

> "In my opinion the complainant's consent on this day involved only the doctor's right to examine her and lay hands on her in the presence of a medical intern or student. That was the nature and quality of the act to which she had consented. But when the examination and touching of her private parts takes place in the presence of a person who, aided by the doctor's deception, was present for no other reason than his own gratification, and who observed and had explained to him each step taken by the doctor during his examination, there is a drastic change in the nature and quality of the act, and, in my opinion, the consent she gave cannot be considered as a consent to the thing done to her and cannot be relied on by the appellants.

> The act consented to was not the act done. There was nothing indecent in the act she consented to but it became an indecent act and an unwarranted

and disgraceful invasion of her privacy to have her private parts exposed to such a person in the manner in which it was done."

This decision was reversed by the Supreme Court of Canada (1967), 60 W.W.R. 665, where Mr. Justice Hall, for the majority, stated:

"With respect, I do not agree that an indecent assault was committed within the meaning of this section. What Bolduc did was unethical and reprehensible in the extreme and was something no reputable medical practitioner would have countenanced. However, Bolduc's unethical conduct and the fraud practised upon the complainant do not of themselves necessarily imply an infraction of s. 141. It is common ground that the examination and treatment, including the insertion of the speculum, were consented to by the complainant. The question is: 'Was her consent obtained by false and fraudulent representations as to the nature and quality of the act?' Bolduc did exactly what the complainant understood he would do and intended that he should do, namely, to examine the vaginal tract and to cauterize the affected parts. Inserting the speculum was necessary for these purposes. There was no fraud on his part as to what he was supposed to do and in what he actually did. The complainant knew that Bird was present and consented to his presence. The fraud that was practised on her was not as to the nature and quality of what was to be done but was as to Bird's identity as a medical intern. His presence as distinct from some overt act by him was not an assault. However, any overt act either alone or in common with Bolduc would have transposed the situation into an unlawful assault, but Bird did not touch the complainant; he merely looked on and listened to Bolduc's comments on what was being done because of the condition then apparent in the vaginal tract. Bird was in a sense a 'peeping tom'."

Mr. Justice Spence, dissenting, explained that the complainant gave her consent "on the basis that Bird was a doctor intending to commence practice and who desired practical experience in such matters. . . . The indecent assault upon her was not the act to which she consented."

If the woman had sued for battery, could she have been successful? Are the policies being served by criminal law and tort law the same?

5. If A consents to B, a physician, rubbing her body with oil, may A sue in assault and battery if she discovers that B has no belief that what he was doing was of any medical value and was done merely for his own amusement? Compare *R. v. Rosinski* (1824), 1 Mod. C.C. 19.

6. Suppose the defendant persuades the plaintiff to have sexual intercourse with him by telling her that he plans to marry her. Would an action lie for battery or deceit? Is it rape?

7. Is there a battery if the defendant induces the plaintiff to go to bed with him in return for a counterfeit $20 bill? Is it rape? What if the defendant says he has had a vasectomy when he has not?

8. Can you articulate a rule for distinguishing fraud that goes to the nature and quality of the act and the lesser type of fraud that does not? Should the criminal law and civil law rules be the same?

9. Despite the light treatment of the material in the above pages, the problem is a very serious one. What can the law do to reduce the number of these incidents?

10. Donna points a pistol at Paul and tells him that she will shoot him if he does not "consent" to have sexual intercourse with her. He submits. Battery?

LATTER v. BRADDELL

Court of Appeal. (1881), 50 L.J.Q.B. 488; on appeal from 50 L.J.Q.B.
166; 44 L.T. 369

The plaintiff was a housemaid employed by Captain and Mrs. Braddell. Mrs. Braddell decided, after hearing certain gossip, that the plaintiff was pregnant.

She accused the plaintiff of this and told her to leave at once. The plaintiff denied the charge and Mrs. Braddell said, "The doctor will be here presently." The plaintiff cried, was forbidden to speak and told to go to her bedroom.

Dr. Sutcliffe had already been called and when he arrived he went to the plaintiff's bedroom. She was in tears and said she did not want to be examined. The doctor told her to remove her dress and when the plaintiff protested he said it would satisfy Mrs. Braddell and himself. At the request to remove each successive article of clothing, the plaintiff cried and said she did not like to. The doctor said "You must." When the plaintiff had removed all her clothing, Dr. Sutcliffe examined her — the plaintiff crying all the time. During the examination no one else was in the room. Dr. Sutcliffe said she was all right and he would speak to Mrs. Braddell. The latter, however, dismissed the plaintiff from her employ and refused to give her a character reference.

The plaintiff sued Captain and Mrs. Braddell and Dr. Sutcliffe for assault. At the trial, in addition to the evidence outlined, the plaintiff swore that what was done was not with her consent. The trial judge, Lindley J., at the end of the plaintiff's case, withdrew the case against Captain and Mrs. Braddell from the jury. The jury returned a verdict for Dr. Sutcliffe. A rule was obtained calling on the defendant to show cause why the verdict should not be set aside and a new trial granted.

Lopes J.: . . . I do not think it was correct to tell the jury that to maintain this action the plaintiff's will must have been overpowered by force or the fear of violence. This I understand was the direction given by the learned judge to the jury in summing up the case against the defendant Sutcliffe, and I presume this view of the law induced him to withdraw from the jury the case against Captain and Mrs. Braddell . . . .

The sending for a doctor by a master or mistress and directing him to examine a female servant, without first apprising her, is, in any circumstances, an arbitrary and high-handed proceeding, and cannot, in my opinion, be justified unless the servant's consent is voluntarily given. A submission to what is done, obtained through a belief that she is bound to obey her master and mistress; or a consent obtained through a fear of evil consequences to arise to herself, induced by her master's or mistress's words or conduct, is not sufficient. In neither case would the consent be voluntarily given; it would be a consent in one sense, but a consent to which the will was not a party. The plaintiff's case is stronger. She swears she did not consent. I know not what more a person in the plaintiff's position could do unless she used physical force. She is discharged without a hearing, forbidden to speak, sent to her room, examined by her mistress's doctor alone, no other female being in the room, made to take off all her clothes and lie naked on the bed. She complains of the treatment, cries continuously, objects to the removal of each garment and swears the examination was without her consent. Could it be said, in these circumstances, that her consent was so unmistakably given that her state of mind was not a question for a jury to consider? I cannot adopt the view that the plaintiff consented because she yielded without her will having been overpowered by force, or fear of violence. That, as I have said, is not, in my opinion, an accurate definition of consent in a case like this.

Lindley J.: . . . The plaintiff's case cannot be put higher than this, namely, that, without consulting her wishes, her mistress ordered her to submit to be examined by a doctor, in order that he might ascertain whether she (the plaintiff) was in the family way, and that she (the plaintiff) complied with that order reluctantly — that is, sobbing and protesting — and because she was told she must, and she did not know what else to do. There was, however, no evidence of any force or violence, nor of any illegal act done or threatened by the mistress beyond what I have stated; nor did the plaintiff in her evidence say that she was in fear of the mistress or of the doctor, or was in any way overcome by fear. She said she did not consent to what was done; but the sense in which she used this expression was not explained, and to appreciate it regard must be had to the other facts of the case. The plaintiff had it entirely in her own power physically to comply or not to comply with her mistress's orders, and there was no evidence whatever to show that anything improper or illegal was threatened to be done if she had not complied. It was suggested that her mistress ordered the examination with a view to see whether she could dismiss her without paying a month's wages. But there was no evidence of any threat to withhold wages, nor of any conversation on the subject of wages, until the plaintiff was paid when on leaving. The question, therefore, is reduced to this: Can the plaintiff, having complied with the orders of her mistress, although reluctantly, maintain this action upon the ground that what was done by the doctor was against her will, or might properly be so regarded by a jury? I think not. It is said that the jury ought to have been asked whether the plaintiff in effect gave her mistress leave to have her examined, or whether the plaintiff's will or mind went with what she did. But in my opinion, such questions inadequately express the grounds on which alone the defendants can be held liable. The plaintiff was not a child; she knew perfectly well what she did and what was being done to her by the doctor. She knew the object with which he examined her, and upon the evidence there is no reason whatever for supposing that any examination would have been made or attempted if she had told the doctor she would not allow herself to be examined. Under these circumstances, I am of opinion that there was no evidence of want of consent as distinguished from reluctant obedience or submission to her mistress's orders, and that in the absence of all evidence of coercion, as distinguished from an order which the plaintiff could comply with or not as she chose the action cannot be maintained. . . .

Rule discharged.

The plaintiff appealed.

Bramwell L.J.: I am of opinion that Mr. Justice Lindley was right; in fact, I may almost say that he was more than right, for it seems to me that he might have directed a verdict for the defendant, Dr. Sutcliffe; but if there was any evidence, his direction to the jury was right and their finding was right, although it may be a practical hardship. Very likely the plaintiff thought the defendants had a right to have her examined; but the truth is, she submitted to it, and it is impossible to say the jury were wrong in finding that she submitted. She may have submitted under an erroneous notion of law, but it was not through fear of violence. It seems to follow that if the verdict for Dr. Sutcliffe was right the other defendants are entitled to a verdict. I think Mr. Justice Lindley was right in telling the jury that there was no evidence against Captain and Mrs. Braddell. There could only be evidence against them if the plaintiff submitted through fear of violence, and if what was done was done by their order.

[Judgments of Baggallay and Brett L.JJ., to the same effect are omitted.]

Judgment affirmed.

NOTES

1. Would the same result have been reached if Dr. Sutcliffe had had sexual intercourse with the plaintiff in the same circumstances?

2. Would this case be decided in the same way today? Should economic

duress vitiate consent? See generally Bankier, "The Avoidance of Contracts for Economic Duress: Threats to Employment: American Developments and Anglo-Canadian Prospects" (1974), 22 Chitty's L.J. 73.

B. SELF-DEFENCE

COCKCROFT v. SMITH

Queen's Bench. (1705), 11 Mod. 43; 88 E.R. 872

Cockcroft, in a scuffle, ran her fingers towards Smith's eyes, who bit a joint off from the plaintiff's finger. The question was, Whether this was a proper defence for the defendant to justify in an action of Mayhem?

Holt C.J.: If a man strike another, who does not immediately after resent it, but takes his opportunity, and then — sometime after — falls upon him and beats him, in this case *son assault* is no good plea. Neither ought a man, in case of a small assault, give a violent or unsuitable return. But, in such cases, plead what is necessary for a man's defence; and not who struck first, though this (he said), has been the common practice. But this, he wished, was altered; for hitting a man a little blow with a little stick on the shoulder, is not a reason for him to draw a sword and cut and hew the other.

NOTES

1. A recent case demonstrating the application of these principles is *Mac-Donald* v. *Hees* (1974), 46 D.L.R. (3d) 720. The defendant, a former cabinet minister in the Diefenbaker government, was in Nova Scotia campaigning on behalf of the local P.C. candidate in the federal election of 1972. The plaintiff, a P.C. worker and a friend who wished to meet the defendant, went to the motel where the defendant was staying at around midnight. They knocked, and, finding the door unlocked, they entered the room. To their surprise, they discovered the defendant, who was tired after a hard day of campaigning, already retired for the night. The defendant, who had an early morning appointment, got out of bed, grabbed the plaintiff and threw him towards the door. His head struck the glass and he was injured. In holding the defendant responsible, Chief Justice Cowan rejected the defence of self-defence and explained:

"In my opinion, the defendant in this case was not required to use any force for the protection of himself. I find that, at no time did the plaintiff or his associate, Glen Boyd, do anything which could have led the defendant to believe that any force was to be used against the defendant. The defendant's evidence was to the effect that he saw that the plaintiff was smaller than he was; he agreed that the plaintiff did not pose a threat to him; that he was not afraid of the plaintiff or of his comrade and that he was not afraid of any physical violence to his person or property. I find that the defendant was not threatened in any way by the plaintiff or by Glen Boyd, and that the defendant was not under the impression that he was threatened in any way by the use of force. In addition, I find that the force which the defendant used in ejecting the plaintiff from his motel unit was not reasonable, and was far greater than could possibly be considered by any reasonable man to be requisite for the purpose of removing the plaintiff from the motel unit. I also find that the force used by the defendant in ejecting the plaintiff was entirely disproportionate to the evil to be prevented, *i.e.,* the continued presence of the plaintiff in the motel unit.

I am, therefore, of the opinion that the defence of justification on the ground of self-defence fails."

See also *McNeill* v. *Hill,* [1929] 2 D.L.R. 296 (Sask. C.A.), where Mr. Justice Martin stated:

"While the law recognized the right of self-defence, the right to repel force with force, no right is to be abused, and the right of self-defence is one which may easily be abused. The force employed must not be out of proportion to the apparent urgency of the occasion."

2. The onus of proof rests upon the person invoking the defence of self-defence. He must not only prove that the occasion was one which warranted defensive action, but also that the force used was not excessive. In *Mann* v. *Balaban* (1969), 8 D.L.R. (3d) 548 (S.C.C.), Mr. Justice Spence (Hall, Pigeon JJ. concurring) summarized the law on this issue as follows:

"In an action for assault, it has been, in my view, established that it is for the plaintiff to prove that he was assaulted and that he sustained an injury thereby. The onus is upon the plaintiff to establish those facts before the jury. Then it is upon the defendant to establish the defences, first, that the assault was justified and, secondly, that the assault even if justified was not made with any unreasonable force and on those issues the onus is on the defence."

See also *Miska* v. *Sivec* (1959), 18 D.L.R. (2d) 363 (Ont. C.A.); *Veinot* v. *Veinot* (1977), 81 D.L.R. (3d) 549 (N.S.C.A.). Cf. *McClelland* v. *Symons*, [1951] V.L.R. 157.

3. It is permissible to kill in self-defence, if it is necessary to preserve one's own life or to avoid serious bodily injury. *R.* v. *Smith* (1837), 8 C. & P. 160, 173 E.R. 441.

4. For a discussion of the necessity of retreating before applying, in self-defence, force that may kill, see Beale, "Retreat From a Murderous Assault" (1903), 16 Harv. L. Rev. 567. Some American cases have recognized the right to stand one's ground but the author submits that "no killing can be justified upon any ground, which was not necessary to secure the desired and permitted result; and it is not necessary to kill in self-defence when the assailed can defend himself by the peaceful though often distasteful method of withdrawing to a place of safety".

5. In defence of his own house, however, a man need not retreat before the threat of grievous bodily harm. See *R.* v. *Hussey* (1924), 18 Cr. App. R. 160.

6. What if the defendant kills someone whom he mistakenly, but reasonably, believes is about to kill him? See *Keep* v. *Quallman* (1887), 68 Wis. 451, 32 N.W. 233. Cf. *Ranson* v. *Kitner, supra.*

7. What if the defendant, who is, in fact, in danger of losing his life, shoots at his attacker but, without negligence, hits an innocent passerby? See *Morris* v. *Platt* (1864), 32 Conn. 75; *Shaw* v. *Lord* (1914), 41 Okl. 347, 137 P. 885. See generally, Forbes, "Mistake of Fact With Regard to Defences in Tort Law" (1970), 4 Ottawa L. Rev. 304.

8. Self-defence, which is a complete defence, should not be confused with provocation, which is not. The principle was correctly outlined by Mr. Justice Beck in *Evans* v. *Bradburn* (1915), 25 D.L.R. 611, 9 W.W.R. 281 as follows:

"The instinct of human nature is to resent insult in many cases by physical force; and, according to the circumstances, this is more or less generally approved or even applauded, but the law, probably wisely, does not recognize any provocation, short of an assault or threats creating a case for self-defence, as a justification for an assault, but only takes into account as a circumstance which may reduce culpable homicide from murder to manslaughter, and in all criminal cases involving an assault as a circumstance going in mitigation of punishment, and in civil cases in mitigation of damages."

9. Is it provocation to threaten someone? *Bruce* v. *Dyer*, [1966] 2 O.R. 705; affd. [1970] 1 O.R. 482. To swear at someone? *Check* v. *Andrews Hotel* (1974), 56 D.L.R. (3d) 364 (Man. C.A.). To make love to someone's spouse? *White* v. *Conolly*, [1927] Q.S.R. 75. To collide with another person's vehicle? *Golnik* v. *Geissinger* (1967), 64 D.L.R. (2d) 754 (B.C.). To legally drive another person's cattle to the pound? *Fillipowich* v. *Nahachewsky* (1969), 3 D.L.R. (3d) 544 (Sask.).

NOTE ON DEFENCE OF THIRD PERSONS

1. People are entitled to defend not only themselves but also other people who are being attacked or threatened. The early English law seemed to limit this privilege to husbands protecting their wives, or masters defending their servants and vice versa. Now it is clear that a mother may protect her son and a son his mother and that a policeman may protect a citizen and vice versa. See *Prior* v. *McNab* (1976), 1 C.C.L.T. 137 (Ont. H.C.) *per* Reid J.

2. If one defends another in the reasonable belief that he is in need of help, he may be excused from tort liability even if he is mistaken. In *Gambriell* v. *Caparelli* (1975), 7 O.R. (2d) 205 (Co. Ct.), a mother, believing her son was being choked by the plaintiff, shouted at him to stop, picked up a three-pronged garden cultivator, struck him three times on the shoulder with it, and finally hit him on the head with considerable force. The mother was relieved of liability on the ground that she really had few options open to her, given her lack of knowledge of English, and her size in relation to the plaintiff's. His Honour Judge Carter, relying on the Compensation for Victims of Crime Act, which he felt implied that the legislature "considered it meritorious to aid one's neighbour", explained:

"Where a person intervening to rescue another holds an honest (though mistaken) belief that the other person is in imminent danger of injury, he is justified in using force, provided that such force is reasonable."

Would the result have been the same if the defendant had stabbed the plaintiff in the chest with the cultivator? What if instead of beating up her son, the plaintiff was trying to kiss her daughter?

3. As in self-defence, the onus is on the person seeking to invoke this defence to prove both that he was reasonable and that he did not use excessive force. See *Prior* v. *McNab, supra,* note 1.

4. The Criminal Code, R.S.C. 1970, c. C-34, s. 37(1) provides that: Everyone is justified in using force to defend himself or any one under his protection from assault, if he uses no more force than is necessary to prevent the assault or the repetition of it.

Section 27 also provides that everyone is justified in using such force as is reasonably necessary: (a) to prevent the commission of an offence (i) for which, if it were committed, the person who committed it might be arrested without warrant, and (ii) that would be likely to cause immediate and serious injury to the person or property of anyone; or (b) to prevent anything being done that, on reasonable and probable grounds he believes would, if it were done, be an offence mentioned in paragraph (a).

What relevance, if any, do these sections have to tort law?

C. DEFENCE OF PROPERTY

GREEN v. GODDARD

Queen's Bench. (1704), 2 Salk. 641; 91 E.R. 540

Et per cur.: There is a force in law, as in every trespass *quare clausum fregit:* As if one enters into my ground, in that case the owner must request him to depart before he can lay hands on him to turn him out; for every *impositio manuum* is an assault and battery, which cannot be justified upon the account of breaking the close in law, without a request. The other is an actual force, as in burglary, as breaking open a door or gate; and in that case it is lawful to oppose force to force; and if one breaks down the gate, or comes into my close *vi et armis,* I need not request him to be gone, but may lay hands on him immediately, for it is but returning violence with violence: So if one comes forcibly and takes away my goods, I may oppose him without any more ado, for there is no time to make a request.

NOTES

1. In *Bigcharles* v. *Merkel et al.*, [1973] 1 W.W.R. 324 (B.C.S.C.), a group of burglars discovered by the defendant while committing a burglary of his premises took flight. The defendant fired one shot of his rifle after them into the darkness, and accidentally killed the plaintiff's husband who was one of the burglars. No intention to hit the deceased was attributed to the defendant but he was, nevertheless, held 25% liable for his negligence, with the deceased bearing 75% of the blame. Mr. Justice Seaton explained: "The act cannot be justified as preventing crime, preventing a continuance of a breach of the peace, a step in an arrest, protection of property, repelling a trespasser, protection of himself or those under his care, or preventing breaking in or breaking out of a dwelling." Under what circumstances would the killing have been justified?

2. In *MacDonald* v. *Hees, supra*, it was also contended by the defendant that he was merely preventing an unlawful entry and an invasion of his privacy. Chief Justice Cowan rejected the defence, and stated:

". . . a trespasser cannot be forcibly repelled or ejected until he has been requested to leave the premises and a reasonable opportunity of doing so peaceably has been afforded him. It is otherwise in the case of a person who enters or seeks to enter by force. . . . Even in such a case, however, the amount of force that may be used . . . must amount to nothing more than forcible removal and must not include beating, wounding, or other physical injury. . . . In the present case, I find that there was no forcible entry by the plaintiff. . . . Even if there had been forcible entry, the defendant did not request the plaintiff and his companion to leave and give them any reasonable opportunity of doing so, peaceably".

3. For an economic analysis of this problem, see Posner, "Killing or Wounding to Protect a Property Interest" (1971), 14 J. Law & Econ. 201. See also *Katko* v. *Briney* (1971), 183 N.W. 2d 657 (Iowa); Palmer, "The Iowa Spring Gun Case: A Study in American Gothic" (1971), 56 Iowa L. Rev. 1219.

4. There is now some authority indicating a possible shift on the ground of *ex turpi causa*, or *volenti non fit injuria*. See *Murphy* v. *Culhane*, [1976] 3 All E.R. 533 (C.A.), *per* Denning M.R.; *Cummings* v. *Granger*, [1976] 3 W.L.R. W.L.R. 842 (C.A.), where it is suggested that a householder who shoots a burglar may have a defence on either of these two grounds. Would this be a good idea?

BIRD v. HOLBROOK

Common Pleas. (1828), 4 Bing. 628; 130 E.R. 911

The defendant was the occupier of a walled garden in which he grew rare and expensive tulips. A short time before the accident in question someone had robbed his garden of flowers and roots of the value of £20. As a consequence the defendant placed a spring gun in the garden with wires crossing several paths at a height of about fifteen inches from the ground.

A witness to whom the defendant mentioned the fact of his having been robbed, and of having set a spring gun, proved that he had asked the defendant if he had put up a notice of such a gun being set, to which the defendant answered, that "he did not conceive that there was any law to oblige him to do so", and the defendant desired such person not to mention to any one that the gun was set, "lest the villain should not be detected". No notice was given of the spring gun having been placed in the garden.

On the 21st of March, 1825, between the hours of six and seven in the afternoon, it being then light, a pea-hen belonging to the occupier of a house in the neighbourhood had escaped, and finally alighted in the defendant's garden. A female servant of the owner of the bird was in pursuit of it, and the plaintiff (a youth of the age of 19 years), seeing her in distress from fear of losing the bird, said he would go after it for her; he accordingly got upon the wall at the back of the garden, and having called out two or three times to ascertain whether any person was in the garden, and waiting a short space of time without receiving any answer jumped down into the garden. The boy's foot came in contact with one of the wires, close to the spot where the gun was set, it was thereby discharged, and a great part of its contents, consisting of large swan shot, were lodged in and about his knee-joint, and caused a severe wound.

The question for the opinion of the court was whether the plaintiff was entitled to recover.

Best C.J.: I am of opinion that this action is maintainable. If any thing which fell from me in *Ilott* v. *Wilkes* (1820), 3 B. & Ald. 304, were at variance with the opinion I now express, I should not hestitate to retract it; but the ground on which the judgment of the court turned in that case, is decisive of the present; and I should not have laboured the point that the action was not maintainable in that case on the ground that the plaintiff had received notice unless I had deemed it maintainable if no notice had been given. . . . I am reported to have said, expressly, "Humanity requires that the fullest notice possible should be given, and the law of England will not sanction what is inconsistent with humanity."

It has been argued that the law does not compel every line of conduct which humanity or religion may require; but there is no act which Christianity forbids, that the law will not reach: if it were otherwise, Christianity would not be, as it has always been held to be, part of the law of England. I am therefore, clearly of opinion that he who sets spring guns, without giving notice, is guilty of an inhuman act, and that, if injurious consequences ensue, he is liable to yield redress to the sufferer. But this case stands on grounds distinct from any that have preceded it. In general, spring guns have been set for the purpose of deterring; the defendant placed his for the express purpose of doing injury; for, when called on to give notice, he said, "If I give notice, I shall not catch him." He intended, therefore, that the gun should be discharged, and that the contents should be lodged in the body of his victim for he could not be caught in any other way. On these principles the action is clearly maintainable, and particularly on the latter ground.

Burrough J.: . . . The present case is of a worse complexion than those which have preceded it; for if the defendant had proposed merely to protect his property from thieves, he would have set the spring guns only by night. The plaintiff was only a trespasser: if the defendant had been present, he would not have been authorized even in taking him into custody, and no man can do indirectly that which he is forbidden to directly. . . .

[The concurring judgment of Park J., is omitted.]

Judgment for the plaintiff.

NOTES

1. The Criminal Code, R.S.C. 1970, c. C-34, s. 231 (1) enacts:

"Every one who, with intent to cause death or bodily harm to persons, whether ascertained or not, sets or places or causes to be set or placed a trap, device or other thing whatsoever that is likely to cause death or bodily harm to persons is guilty of an indictable offence and is liable to imprisonment for five years."

What effect, if any, would a violation of this provision have on civil liability to someone injured thereby?

2. The defendant puts up a sign which warns trespassers that they will be

shot if they trespass. Is the defendant liable if he does, in fact, shoot a trespasser who has read and ignored the sign?

3. Suppose that the defendant does not shoot the trespasser, but merely points a gun at him and says, "Get off or I'll shoot you!" The trespasser departs in haste and sues for assault. Liability?

4. The defendant fires a gun at the ground behind a trespasser, whom he discovers on his land, trying to frighten him. Assault? What if the bullet ricochets and hits the trespasser? Liability? Compare with *Harris* v. *Wong* (1971), 19 D.L.R. (3d) 589 (Sask.), negligence liability.

5. The defendant keeps a large dog to protect his land from intruders. Peter intrudes and is chased off by the growling dog. Liability? What if the dog bites him? A landowner puts an electrically charged fence around his property which gives a trespasser a shock when he touches it. Liability? What if the electrical current is so strong that it kills the intruder? Can you articulate a rule that balances all the interests involved?

6. Suppose a visitor to your home becomes ill and wants to stay. Can you push him out into the cold? See *Depue* v. *Flatau* (1907), 100 Minn. 299, 111 N.W. 1 (S.C. Minn.). Would it make any difference if the visitor had a dangerous, infectious disease?

7. See Hart, "Injuries to Trespassers" (1931), 47 L.Q.Rev. 92; Bohlen and Burns, "The Privilege to Protect Property by Dangerous Barriers and Mechanical Devices" (1926), 35 Yale L.J. 527; *Sycamore* v. *Levy* (1932), 147 L.T. 342; Williams, *Liability for Animals* (1939), p. 350.

8. With regard to the privilege to protect personal property, see *Cresswell* v. *Sirl*, [1948] 1 K.B. 241, [1947] 2 All E.R. 730 (C.A.).

9. The privilege of recapture of property is closely related to defence of property. It was first recognized where there was a momentary interruption of possession and an immediate repossession. It was then extended to dispossession by fraud or force and where the pursuit was fresh. There are many difficult and confusing decisions in this area. See *Devoe* v. *Long,* [1951] 1 D.L.R. 203, 26 M.P.R. 357 (N.B.C.A.); *Hemmings & Wife* v. *Stoke Poges Golf Club Ltd.,* [1920] 1 K.B. 720, 36 T.L.R. 77 (C.A.); *Napier* v. *Ferguson* (1878), 18 N.B.R. 255 (N.B.C.A.); *Phillips* v. *Murray,* [1929] 3 D.L.R. 770 (Sask C.A.); *Wentzell* v. *Veinot,* [1940] 1 D.L.R. 536, 14 M.P.R. 323 (N.S.C.A.); see generally Branston, "The Forcible Recaption of Chattels" (1918), 28 L.Q.Rev. 262.

D. NECESSITY

DWYER v. STAUNTON

Alberta District Court. [1947] 4 D.L.R. 393; [1947] 2 W.W.R. 221

Sissons D.C.J.: The plaintiff sues for trespass and claims the sum of $500 as damages to his crop of special quality fall barley and $20 as damages to gates and fences, and also claims an injunction restraining the defendant from further trespass.

The plaintiff is a farmer and rancher residing near Lundbreck, Alberta. The defendant is a farmer and rancher living to the north of the plaintiff. The public highway running north and south past the farm of the plaintiff was on January 5, 1947, so blocked by snow drifts as to be impassable. On that day employees of an oil company operating in the area bulldozed a way to Lundbreck from a point some distance north of the plaintiff's farm, following the highway where possible and at other points going through the fields of the farmers and ranchers. The bulldozer was not able to follow the highway alongside the farm of the plaintiff and opened a way for about a quarter of a mile through the plaintiff's gates and fences and over his land. The bulldozer was followed by five trucks. The following morning, January 6th, taking advantage of the opened road, the defendant, in his car, with four or five other cars and trucks, started for Lundbreck. They were stopped by the plaintiff while following the way bulldozed across his farm. The plaintiff protested that his farm was not a road allowance and no one had any right to go over his land without his permission. There was some argument. The plaintiff says the defendant was the ringleader and was friendly, but insistent in his attitude. The plaintiff finally consented to the parties continuing their journey to town, but warned them that he would stop them if they attempted to return across his land. The defendant, and the others, while in town, interviewed the municipal authorities in regard to opening the highway, and were advised that the bulldozer of the municipality was broken and that the highway could not be ploughed out that day. The parties attempted to return home that evening by a different route, but could not get through, and then took the route across the plaintiff's land. They were stopped by the plaintiff at one of the gates. Following some argument, and the repeated refusal of the plaintiff to allow them to pass, the defendant drove his car through the two-strand barbed wire gate and was followed by the other cars and trucks. In reply to the plaintiff's protest, the defendant said he was able to pay for all the damage and took the position that he wished to see the case brought to court.

The real point in issue is whether the defendant, under the circumstances, had the right to leave the highway and proceed over the land of the plaintiff. A secondary point is whether the defendant, if he had such right, caused any unnecessary damage to the plaintiff in exercising that right.

My understanding of the law is that a traveller who is lawfully using a public road has the right to go upon private land at places where the public way is impassable.

> "Where a public way is foundrous, as such ways frequently were in former times, the public have by the common law a right to travel over the adjoining lands, and to break through the fences for the purpose:" *Williams on Real Property*, 24th ed., pp. 508-9.

> "Where a highway becomes impassable, travellers are entitled to deviate from the established road on to adjacent land, taking care to do no unnecessary damage:" 37 Cyc., p. 206.

Broom gives the principle upon which the right is based as that of *salus populi suprema lex* — "Regard for the public welfare is the highest law."

> "The maxim is, that a private mischief shall be endured, rather than a public inconvenience; and, therefore, if a highway be out of repair and impassable, a passenger may lawfully go over the adjoining land, since it is for the public good that there should be, at all times, free passage along thoroughfares for subjects of the realm:" *Broom's Legal Maxims*, 10th ed., p. 2.

Other authorities put the principle upon the doctrine of necessity.

> "In such case, an interference with private property is obviously dictated and justified *summa necessitate*, by the immediate urgency of the occasion, and a due regard to the public safety or convenience:" *Morey* v. *Fitzgerald* (1884), 56 Vt. 487, at p. 489. . . .

One of the leading English cases is that of *Taylor* v. *Whitehead* (1781), 2 Doug. K.B. 745. In that case the facts had to do with a private way, and it was held that in respect of such ways the right to deviate was rather limited, but Lord Mansfield went on to say: "Highways are governed by a different principle. They are for the public service, and if the usual tract is impassable, it is for the general good that people should be entitled to pass in another line." . . .

My conclusion is that the defendant was quite within his legal rights, under the circumstances, in leaving the highway and going through the gates and fences and over the land of the plaintiff. I find that the defendant did no unnecessary damage in so doing. . . . In the result, the action of the plaintiff is dismissed, with costs. . . . I have considerable sympathy with the plaintiff in his insistence on his private property rights. Those rights should be respected, but I must hold that there are higher rights — the rights of the public.

NOTES

1. Compare the resolutions of the Justices concerning *The King's Prerogative in Saltpetre* (1606), 12 Co. Rep. 12, 77 E.R. 1294. As the "defence of the realm" was involved, it was resolved that the prerogative extended to digging for Saltpetre, even as "it is lawful to come upon my land . . . to make trenches or bulwarks for the defence of the realm, for every subject hath benefit by it . . . but after the danger is over, the trenches and bulwarks ought to be removed, so that the owner shall not have prejudice in his inheritance; and for the commonwealth, a man shall suffer damage; as, for saving of a city or town, a house shall be plucked down if the next be on fire; and the suburbs of a city in time of war for the common safety shall be plucked down; and a thing for the commonwealth every man may do without being liable to an action."

2. In *Burmah Oil Co.* v. *Lord Advocate,* [1965] A.C. 75, [1964] 2 All E.R. 348, the House of Lords held that when the Crown, in furtherance of its war aims, deprived a person of property for the benefit of the state — in the instant case the destruction of plaintiff's oil installations near Rangoon, in order to prevent their falling into the hands of the enemy, Japan — the loss must be compensated for at public expense. Such loss did not include damage done in the course of an actual battle, but "battle damage" did not include the taking of property for long-range strategic purposes. The United States Supreme Court in *United States* v. *Caltex (Philippines) Inc.* (1952), 344 U.S. 149, reached a contrary conclusion, despite the Fifth Amendment which forbids taking "private property . . . for public use, without just compensation". Speaking for the majority, Vinson C.J., said that "the common law has long recognized that in times of imminent peril — such as when fire threatened a whole community — the sovereign could, with immunity, destroy the property of a few that the property of many and the lives of many more could be saved". See (1966), 79 Harv. L. Rev. 614.

3. Compare the case of general average contribution for goods jettisoned at sea to save the rest of the cargo. "In jettison, the rights of those entitled to contribution, and the corresponding obligations of the contributors, have their origin in the fact of a common danger which threatens to destroy the property of them all; and these rights and obligations are mutually perfected whenever the goods of some of the shippers have been advisedly sacrificed, and the property of the others has been thereby preserved." — Lord Watson in *Strang Steel & Co.* v. *A. Scott & Co.* (1899), 14 App. Cas. 601, 5 T.L.R. 705.

4. In *Surocco* v. *Geary* (1853), 3 Cal. 69, the "mayor" of the town ordered a building destroyed in order to prevent the spread of a fire that was raging. The owner of the building was denied recovery. Murray C.J. stated:

"This must, in some instances, be a difficult matter to determine. The necessity of blowing up a house may not exist, or be as apparent to the owner, whose judgment is clouded by interest, and the hope of saving his property, as to others. In all such cases the conduct of the individual must be regulated by his own judgment as to the exigencies of the case. If a building should be torn down without apparent or actual necessity, the parties concerned would undoubtedly be liable in an action of trespass. But in every case the necessity must be clearly shown. It is true, many cases of hardship may grow out of this rule, and property may often in such cases be destroyed, without necessity, by irresponsible persons, but this difficulty would not be obviated by making the parties responsible in every case, whether the necessity existed or not.

The legislature of the State possesses the power to regulate this subject by providing the manner in which buildings may be destroyed, and the mode in which compensation shall be made; and it is to be hoped that something will be done to obviate the difficulty and prevent the happening of such events as those supposed by the respondent's counsel.

In the absence of any legislation on the subject, we are compelled to fall back upon the rules of the common law.

The evidence in this case clearly establishes the fact, that the blowing up of the house was necessary, as it would have been consumed had it been left standing. The plaintiffs cannot recover for the value of the goods which they might have saved; they were as much subject to the necessities of the occasion as the house in which they were situate; and if in such cases a party was held liable, it would too frequently happen, that the delay caused by the removal of the goods would render the destruction of the house useless."

5. Metropolitan Fire Brigades Act, 1958, Victoria Statutes 1958, No. 6315, s. 33 provides that "for the purpose of extinguishing any fire, the Chief Officer of the Metropolitan Fire Brigades . . . may exercise the following [*inter alia*] power: (d) he may take any measures which appear to him necessary or expedient for the protection of life and property, and may cause any houses, buildings or tenements to be entered, taken possession of, pulled down or otherwise destroyed for the purpose of extinguishing or preventing the spread of fire." Section 54 provides that "any damage to property caused by the Chief Officer . . . in the lawful execution of any power conferred by this Act shall be deemed to be damage by fire within the meaning of any policy of insurance against fire covering the property so damaged notwithstanding any clause or condition to the contrary in any such policy." Fleming, *Torts* (4th ed., 1971), p. 92, indicates that there is uniform legislation throughout Australia to this effect.

6. See Williams, "The Defence of Necessity" (1953), 6 Current Legal Problems 216.

VINCENT v. LAKE ERIE TRANSPORTATION CO.

Supreme Court of Minnesota. (1910), 109 Minn. 456; 124 N.W. 221

Action to recover $1,200 for damage to the plaintiffs' wharf caused by defendant negligently keeping its vessel tied to it. The defendant alleged that after the discharge of the cargo the wind had attained so great a velocity that the master and crew were powerless to move the vessel. At the trial the jury returned a verdict of $500 for the plaintiffs. Defendant appealed from an order denying a motion for judgment notwithstanding the verdict of the jury.

O'Brien J.: The steamship Reynolds, owned by the defendant, was for the purpose of discharging her cargo on November 27, 1905, moored to plaintiffs' dock in Duluth. While the unloading of the boat was taking place a storm from the northeast developed, which at about ten o'clock p.m., when the unloading was completed, had so grown in violence that the wind was then moving at 50 miles per hour and continued to increase during the night. There is some evidence that one, and perhaps two, boats were able to enter the harbour that night, but it is plain that navigation was practically suspended from the hour mentioned until the morning of the twenty-ninth, when the storm abated, and during that time no master would have been justified in attempting to navigate his vessel, if he could avoid doing so. After the discharge of the cargo the Reynolds signalled for a tug to tow her from the dock, but none could be obtained because of the severity of the storm. If the lines holding the ship to the dock had been cast off, she would doubtless have drifted away, but, instead, the lines were kept fast, and as soon as one parted or chafed it was replaced, sometimes with a larger one. The vessel lay upon the outside of the dock, her bow to the east, the wind and waves striking her starboard quarter with such force that she was constantly being lifted and thrown against the dock, resulting in its damage, as found by the jury, to the amount of $500.

We are satisfied that the character of the storm was such that it would have been highly imprudent for the master of the Reynolds to have attempted to leave the dock or to have permitted his vessel to drift away from it. One witness testified upon the trial that the vessel could have been warped into a slip, and that, if the attempt to bring the ship into the slip had failed, the worst that could have happened would be that the vessel would have been blown ashore upon a soft and muddy bank. The witness was not present in Duluth at the time of the storm, and, while he may have been right in his conclusions, those in charge of the dock and the vessel at the time of the storm were not required to resort to every possible experiment which could be suggested for the preservation of their property. Nothing more was demanded of them than ordinary prudence and care, and the record in this case fully sustains the contention of the appellant that, in holding the vessel fast to the dock, those in charge of her exercised good judgment and prudent seamanship.

It is claimed by the respondent that it was negligence to moor the boat at an exposed part of the wharf, and to continue in that position after it became apparent that the storm was to be more than usually severe. We do not agree with this position. The part of the wharf where the vessel was moored appears to have been commonly used for that purpose. It was situated within the harbour at Duluth, and must, we think, be considered a proper and safe place, and would undoubtedly have been such during what would be considered a very severe storm. The storm which made it unsafe was one which surpassed in violence any which might have reasonably been anticipated.

The appellant contends by ample assignments of error that, because its conduct during the storm was rendered necessary by prudence and good seamanship under conditions over which it had no control, it cannot be held liable for any injury resulting to the property of others, and claims that the jury should have been so instructed. An analysis of the charge given by the trial court is not necessary, as in our opinion the only question for the jury was the amount of damages which the plaintiffs were entitled to recover, and no complaint is made upon that score.

The situation was one in which the ordinary rules regulating property rights were suspended by forces beyond human control, and if, without the direct intervention of some act by the one sought to be held liable, the property of another was injured, such injury must be attributed to the act of God, and not to the wrongful act of the person sought to be charged. If during the storm the Reynolds had entered the harbor, and while there had become disabled and been thrown against the plaintiffs' dock, the plaintiffs could not have recovered. Again, if while attempting to hold fast to the dock the lines had parted, without any negligence, and the vessel carried against some other boat or dock in the harbor, there would be no liability upon her owner. But here those in charge of the vessel deliberately and by their direct efforts held her in such a position that the damage to the dock resulted, and, having thus preserved the ship at the expense of the dock, it seems to us that her owners are responsible to the dock owners to the extent of the injury inflicted.

In *Depue* v. *Flatau,* 100 Minn. 299; 111 N.W. 1, this court held that where the plaintiff, while lawfully in the defendants' house, became so ill that he was incapable of travelling with safety, the defendants were responsible to him in damages for compelling him to leave the premises. If, however, the owner of the premises had furnished the traveller with proper accommodations and medical attendance, would he have been able to defeat an action brought against him for their reasonable worth?

In *Ploof* v. *Putnam* (Vt.) 71 Atl. 188, the Supreme Court of Vermont held that where, under stress of weather, a vessel was without permission moored to a private dock at an island in Lake Champlain owned by the defendant, the plaintiff was not guilty of trespass, and that the defendant was responsible in damages because of his representative upon the island unmoored the vessel, permitting it to drift upon the shore, with resultant injuries to it. If, in that case, the vessel had been permitted to remain, and the dock had suffered an injury, we believe the shipowner would have been held liable for the injury done.

Theologians hold that a starving man may, without moral guilt, take what is necessary to sustain life; but it could hardly be said that the obligation would not be upon such person to pay the value of the property so taken when he became able to do so. And so public necessity, in times of war or peace, may require the taking of private property for public purposes; but under our system of jurisprudence compensation must be made.

Let us imagine in this case that for the better mooring of the vessel those in charge of her had appropriated a valuable cable lying on the dock. No matter how justifiable such appropriation might have been, it would not be claimed that, because of the overwhelming necessity of the situation, the owner of the cable could not recover its value.

This is not a case where life or property was menaced by any object or thing belonging to the plaintiffs, the destruction of which became necessary to prevent the threatened disaster. Nor is it a case where, because of an act of God, or unavoidable accident, the infliction of the injury was beyond the control of the defendant, but is one where the defendant prudently and advisedly availed itself of the plaintiffs' property for the purpose of preserving its own more valuable property, and the plaintiffs are entitled to compensation for the injury done.

Order affirmed.

Lewis J. (dissenting): I dissent. It was assumed on the trial before the lower court that appellant's liability depended on whether the master of the ship might, in the exercise of reasonable care, have sought a place of safety before the storm made it impossible to leave the dock. The majority opinion assumes that the evidence is conclusive that appellant moored its boats at respondents' dock pursuant to contract and that the vessel was lawfully in position at the time the additional cables were fastened to the dock, and the reasoning of the opinion is that, because appellant made use of the stronger cables to hold the boat in position, it became liable under the rule that it had voluntarily made use of the property of another for the purpose of saving its own.

In my judgment, if the boat was lawfully in position at the time the storm broke, the master could not, in the exercise of due care, have left that position without subjecting his vessel to the hazards of the storm, then the damage to the dock, caused by the pounding of the boat, was the result of an inevitable accident. If the master was in the exercise of due care, he was not at fault. The reasoning of the opinion admits that if the ropes, or cables, first attached to the dock had not parted, or if, in the first instance, the master had used the stronger cables, there would be no liability. If the master could not, in the exercise of reasonable care, have anticipated the severity of the storm and sought a place of safety before it became impossible, why should he be required to anticipate the severity of the storm, and, in the first instance, use the stronger cables?

I am of the opinion that one who constructs a dock to the navigable line of waters, and enters into contractual relations with the owner of a vessel to moor the same, takes the risk of damage to his dock by a boat caught there by a storm, which event could not have been avoided in the exercise of due care, and further, that the legal status of the parties in such a case is not changed by renewal of cables to keep the boat from being cast adrift at the mercy of the tempest.

Jaggard J.: I concur herein.

NOTES

1. How does this differ from *Dwyer* v. *Staunton* and *Surocco* v. *Geary?* See Bohlen, "Incomplete Privilege to Inflict Intentional Invasion of Property and Personality" (1926), 39 Harv. L. Rev. 307.

2. To protect your property against flood water, you erect an embankment to keep out the water. The water thus repelled damages your neighbour's lands. Liability? *Gerrard* v. *Crowe*, [1921] A.C. 395, 37 T.L.R. 110, held there was no liability. In *Whalley* v. *Lancashire and Yorkshire Ry.* (1884), 13 Q.B.D. 131, 50 L.T. 472, a heavy rainfall accumulated on the defendant's land against an embankment. To protect the embankment the defendant cut timbers which carried the water off the defendant's land and on to the plaintiff's land. The defendant was held liable in damages to the plaintiff.

3. In *Romney Marsh* v. *Trinity House* (1870), L.R. 5 Exch. 204, the defendant's ship was, without negligence, thrown on the plaintiff's sea wall. The defendant did not break up the ship until all valuable property had been removed. During this period the ship could have been broken up, and because it was not removed it caused additional damage to the sea wall, for which damage the plaintiff brought action. *Held*, for the defendant. "There was no duty to sacrifice the vessel in the plaintiff's interests."

4. In *Manor & Co. Ltd.* v. *M. V. "Sir John Crosbie"* (1965), 52 D.L.R. (2d) 48 (Nfld.), affd. [1967] 1 Ex. 94, on facts similar to those in the principal case, damage caused to a wharf by defendant's ship remaining moored thereto during a storm of hurricane force, were claimed only in negligence. The court held that in light of the dangers involved in moving the ship, there had been no negligence and, therefore, the owner of the wharf could not recover. See Sussman, "The Defence of Private Necessity and the Problem of Compensation" (1967-68), 2 Ottawa L. Rev. 184.

5. Necessity is no defence, however, where in similar circumstances, the captain of the ship negligently contributes to the creation of the risk. See *Bell Canada* v. *The Ship Mar-Tirenno* (1974), 52 D.L.R. (3d) 702 (Fed. Ct.).

6. In *Read* v. *Smith* (1836), 2 N.B.R. 288, defendant's logs were driven by a storm on to plaintiff's land. The defendant went on the plaintiff's land and caused damage in removing the logs. In an action of trespass the court held there would be no justification for the trespass without a previous request, and in any event the defendant should pay for actual damage done; "It being the defendant's property, it was their affair to take it away without doing wrong to the plaintiff, for 'no man shall do a tort to another to ease himself'." "The defendant . . . must go the whole length of contending for the right to damage without making compensation for . . . if the right were but a qualified one, the plea should have been adapted to it." See also *Anthony* v. *Haney*, 8 Bing. 186, 131 E.R. 372.

7. In *Esso Petroleum Co. Ltd.* v. *Southport Corp.*, [1956] A.C. 218, [1955] 3 All E.R. 864; revg. [1954] 2 Q.B. 182, [1954] 2 All E.R. 561; revg. [1953] 2 All E.R. 1204, a tanker, approaching an estuary, developed a steering defect and stranded on a revetment wall. To save the vessel and crew from grave danger the master jettisoned four hundred tons of oil which became deposited on plaintiff's foreshore causing damage. In an action for trespass, nuisance and negligence, the trial judge, Devlin J., said: "I am not prepared to hold without further consideration that a man is entitled to damage the property of another without compensating him merely because the infliction of such damage is necessary to save his own property. I doubt whether the court in such circum-

stances can be asked to evaluate the relation of the damage done to the property saved, by inquiring, for example, whether it is permissible to do £5,000 worth of damage to a third party in order to save property worth £10,000. . . . The safety of human lives belongs to a different scale of values from the safety of property. The two are beyond comparison and the necessity for saving life has at all times been considered a proper ground for inflicting such damage as may be necessary on another's property." With this passing reference to the problem of an intentional act done with a view to, or a "substantial certainty" of, causing harm, the case proceeded through all courts as one where the issue of negligence ("risk") only was involved.

8. In *Swan-Finch Oil Corp.* v. *Warner-Quinlan Co.* (1933), 167 Atl. 211, 171 Atl. 800 (Sup. Ct. N.J.), and see 32 Mich. L.R. 713, the defendant moored a barge with 6,000 gallons of crude oil to its dock. Lightning struck the barge and ignited the oil. After attempting to fight the fire, the defendant's servants cut the barge loose and a tug pushed it across the stream. Some eight hours later the barge collided with the plaintiff's dock and set it afire. The plaintiff was held entitled to recover. "While it cannot be said that it was intended by the casting adrift of this barge to set on fire the property of the plaintiff or any one else, nevertheless it is clear that the intent of the defendant was to save its own property, irrespective of any danger or consequence to the property of others. The law cannot allow one deliberately to cast upon another any dangerous instrumentality, even in self-defence, without being answerable for the natural consequences which follow." The court also found that using a wooden barge for the storing of oil, mooring it in proximity to other shipping, and then casting it adrift was "not the exercise of the care which ordinary prudence required under the circumstances".

9. Is the defence of necessity available to excuse the taking of life? In *R.* v. *Dudley* (1884), 15 Cox C.C. 624, 14 Q.B.D. 273, four survivors of a shipwreck were adrift in an open boat, a thousand miles from land, and dying of hunger. Two survivors killed one of the other survivors and ate him. They were held criminally liable for his death, but the sentence was commuted to six months in prison.

10. In *United States* v. *Holmes* (1842), 1 Wall Jr. 1, a passenger ship had hit an iceberg and sunk. Nine members of her crew and 32 passengers were adrift in a badly overloaded lifeboat. The wind freshened, the sea began to rise, and the boat was in imminent danger of being swamped. The crew then threw overboard six of the passengers to lighten the boat. The following morning the survivors were rescued by a passing ship. Holmes, who had taken a leading part in throwing the passengers over, was tried for manslaughter, convicted, and sentenced to hard labour for a long term, which the court subsequently reduced to six months. Considerable public sentiment arose in favor of Holmes, and there was much pressure upon President Tyler for a pardon. He refused to grant it because the court did not join in the request, but later changed his mind and remitted the sentence. See Fuller, "The Case of the Speluncean Explorers" (1949), 62 Harv. L. Rev. 616.

SOUTHWARK LONDON BOROUGH COUNCIL v. WILLIAMS AND ANDERSON

Court of Appeal. [1971] 2 W.L.R. 467

The defendants, who were in dire need of housing, made an orderly entry into two empty houses owned by the local authority. The authority owned hundreds of empty houses in areas that were awaiting redevelopment for public housing that would be supplied, on completion, to some of the thousands of people on the local authority's housing list. The authority secured an order for possession against the defendants who appealed to the Court of Appeal.

Edmund Davies L.J.: Nobody of even ordinary sensitivity could have read the affidavit evidence presented in this case without experiencing a feeling of deep depression. It serves to illustrate afresh the extent of the grave social problem presented by the dire shortage of adequate housing accommodation. But in fairness it has to be remembered that the circumstances present great difficulties to the local authorities concerned as well as to the benighted who are living in deplorable conditions or who may even be lacking a roof over their heads. The one question presented by these appeals is whether the defendants have shown that a triable issue has been raised in answer to the action for possession brought by the plaintiffs — that and nothing else has now to be determined. If there be a triable issue, leave would have to be granted and the appeals allowed. . . .

But when and how far is the plea of necessity available to one who is *prima facie* guilty of tort? Well, one thing emerges with clarity from the decisions, and that is that the law regards with the deepest suspicion any remedies of self-help, and permits those remedies to be resorted to only in very special circumstances. The reason for such circumspection is clear — necessity can very easily become simply a mask for anarchy. As far as my reading goes, it appears that all the cases where a plea of necessity has succeeded are cases which deal with an urgent situation of imminent peril: for example, the forcible feeding of an obdurate suffragette, as in *Leigh* v. *Gladstone* (1909), 26 T.L.R. 139, 142, where Lord Alverstone C.J. spoke of preserving the health and lives of the prisoners who were in the custody of the Crown; or performing an abortion to avert a grave threat to the life, or, at least, to the health of a pregnant young girl who had been ravished in circumstances of great brutality, as in *Rex* v. *Bourne,* [1939] 1 K.B. 687; or as in the case tried in 1500 where it was said in argument that a person may escape from a burning gaol notwithstanding a statute making prison-breach a felony, "for he is not to be hanged because he would not stay to be burnt." Such cases illustrate the very narrow limits with which the plea of necessity may be invoked. Sad though the circumstances disclosed by these appeals undoubtedly are, they do not in my judgment constitute the sort of emergency to which the plea applies.

Finally, even if necessity could be invoked in such circumstances as the present, it could surely at most justify merely an initial entry into premises in such circumstances as those to which I have referred. I do not see how it could possibly be permitted to extend to and authorise continuing in occupation for an indefinite period of time, which was the understandable aim of the appellants when entering these premises. I therefore have to concur with Lord Denning M.R. in holding that the public weal demands that these appeals be dismissed.

Lord Denning M.R.: . . . I will next consider the defence of "necessity". There is authority for saying that in case of great and imminent danger, in order to preserve life, the law will permit of an encroachment on private property. That is shown by *Mouse's Case* (1609), 12 Co. Rep. 63, where the ferryman at Gravesend took 47 passengers into his barge to carry them to London, A great tempest arose and all were in danger. Mouse was one of the passengers. The defendant threw a casket belonging to the plaintiff (Mouse) overboard so as to lighten the ship. Other passengers threw other things. It was proved that, if they had not done so, the passengers would have been drowned. It was held by the whole court "that in case of necessity, for the saving of the lives of the passengers it was lawful for the defendant, being a passenger to cast the casket of the plaintiff out of the barges . . ." The court said it was like pulling down of a house, in time of fire, to stop it spreading, which has always been held justified *pro bono publico.*

The doctrine so enunciated must, however, be carefully circumscribed. Else necessity would open the door to many an excuse. It was for this reason that it was not admitted in *Reg.* v. *Dudley and Stephens* (1884), 14 Q.B.D. 273, where the three shipwrecked sailors, in extreme despair, killed the cabin boy and ate him to save their own lives. They were held guilty of murder. The killing was not justified by necessity. Similarly, when a man, who is starving, enters a house and takes food in order to keep himself alive. Our English law does not admit the defence of necessity. It holds him guilty of larceny. Lord Hale said that "if a person, being under necessity for want of victuals, or clothes, shall upon that account clandestinely, and *animo furandi,* steal another man's food, it is felony . . .": *Hale, Pleas of the Crown,* i. 54. The reason is because, if hunger were once allowed to be an excuse for stealing, it would open a way through which all kinds of disorder and lawlessness would pass. So here. If homelessness were once admitted as a defence to trespass, no one's house could be safe. Necessity would open a door which no man could shut. It would not only be those in extreme need who would enter. There would be others who would imagine that they were in need, or would invent a need, so as to gain entry. Each man would say his need was greater than the next man's. The plea would be an excuse for all sorts of wrongdoing. So the courts must, for the sake of law and order, take a firm stand. They must refuse to admit the plea of necessity to the hungry and the homeless: and trust that their distress will be relieved by the charitable and the good.

NOTES

1. What criticisms can you offer of the court's reasoning in this case? Of what relevance is the availability of social welfare services here? What if the temperature had been below zero? Just how much can the courts do to alleviate the problem dramatized in the principal case?

2. On November 8, 1972, there was an airplane crash in the Yukon. In order to keep from starving, the pilot, one Marten Hartwell, had to eat the flesh of one of his passengers who had died. Necessity?

E. LEGAL AUTHORITY

LEBRUN v. HIGH-LOW FOODS, LTD.

British Columbia Supreme Court. (1968), 69 D.L.R. (2d) 433

Jelstad, the manager of the defendant supermarket at which the plaintiff was a regular customer, became suspicious over the plaintiff's habit of leaving the store and returning in the course of shopping. The manager and several employees therefore watched the plaintiff during a shopping trip that lasted about an hour. At the beginning of his visit to the supermarket, the plaintiff picked up a carton of cigarettes. He subsequently made a trip to his car and returned. When he checked out the cigarettes were not among his purchases. The manager called the defendant, Constable Parry, told him that several employees had seen the plaintiff pick up the cigarettes, that they had not been returned and had not been paid for. The constable came to the store and stopped the plaintiff's car as it was leaving the parking lot.

The constable told the plaintiff: "There appears to be a mixup in your order. The store believes that you have something for which you have not paid." Constable Parry then asked the plaintiff to move his car over near where the police car was parked. The plaintiff complied. The plaintiff was then asked for his driver's licence and was asked for his name. The constable then spoke to him and said: "I have to check the car. Do you mind?" The plaintifff replied: "By all means go ahead."

The police officer asked the plaintiff if he could search the vehicle. The plaintiff replied, "Go ahead. I'd like to get this cleared up". The constable then proceeded to search the main area of the car, the glove compartment, the trunk and the back seat.

The police officer was polite and almost apologetic for the inconvenience he was causing. The plaintiff was co-operative, polite, calm and was not visibly upset. The plaintiff made no attempt to leave and made no request to be allowed to leave. The plaintiff did not deny this but said that he felt he had no alternative but to submit to the search, that he unlocked the trunk of his car at the request of Constable Parry because he felt he would be arrested if he refused.

The cigarettes were still not located. The plaintiff claimed he had put them back on the rack at the front of the store after having found that he did not have enough money to pay for them. His trip to the car, he said, was to get a package of cigarettes. The manager admitted that the plaintiff had gone to the rear of the store and disappeared for 30 seconds.

Macfarlane J.: The first question which I am called upon to decide is whether there was, in the circumstances of this case, an imprisonment or arrest of the plaintiff. . . . I have no doubt, notwithstanding the plaintiff's acquiescence, that he was imprisoned or arrested in all the circumstances of this case. He stated that he thought that he had no alternative but to submit to the search, and was under total restraint, and I so find.

Counsel for the defendant contended that there was no "arrest" here because the plaintiff submitted voluntarily to what was done. *Cannon* v. *Hudson's Bay Co., Stephens* v. *Hudson's Bay Co.,* [1939] 4 D.L.R. 465, [1939] 3 W.W.R. 179, 54 B.C.R. 293, was cited in support of that proposition. That case, however, can be distinguished on the ground that there a store employee was approached by another employee, a personnel superintendent, and was questioned regarding a suspected theft.

Here we have a police officer, in uniform, stopping the plaintiff, telling him to move his car to a given spot, inferring an accusation of theft, and searching his vehicle. Consent by the plaintiff in these circumstances is not, in my view, a genuine consent at all.

I find that the plaintiff was imprisoned within the meaning of the authorities.

The next question for decision is whether Constable Parry is liable for damages for false imprisonment. Counsel for the defendant Parry argues that the said defendant is relieved by virtue of the provisions of ss. 25 and 435 of the Criminal Code, 1954-54 (Can.), c. 51. Those sections read as follows:

> 25(1) Every one who is required or authorized by law to do anything in the administration or enforcement of the law
>   *(a)* as a private person,
>   *(b)* as a peace officer or public officer,
>   *(c)* in aid of a peace officer or public officer, or
>   *(d)* by virtue to his office,
> is, *if he acts on reasonable and probable grounds,* justified in doing what he is required or authorized to do and in using as much force as is necessary for that purpose.

(The emphasis is mine.)

> 435. A peace officer may arrest without warrant
>   *(a)* a person who has committed an indictable offence or who, *on reasonable and probable grounds,* he believes, has committed or is about

to commit an indictable offence or is about to commit suicide, or
(b) a person whom he finds committing a criminal offence.

(The emphasis is mine.)

In this case when Constable Parry received the telephone call from Mr. Jelstad he was required, as a matter of duty, in his capacity as a constable to attend at the scene to investigate. This was so if he had reasonable and probable grounds upon which to act.

Did he have reasonable and probable grounds upon which to act? He knew Jelstad as the manager of the defendant's store. He had received several telephone calls from him before about thefts at the store and had attended the store on each of these other occasions. In each case the investigation resulted in a charge of theft or in the disclosure of circumstances which would have justified a charge of theft. He spoke to Jelstad on the telephone for about five minutes and I find as a fact that he was told during that conversation that a carton of cigarettes had disappeared from the store and had last been seen in the possession of the plaintiff. I find as a fact that he was told that the plaintiff had been seen by several employees to pick up a carton of cigarettes, that he did not return them to the rack and that he left the store without paying for them. This information surely justified Constable Parry in investigating the matter, and in fact, it was his duty to do so. . . .

The report of Mr. Jelstad gave Constable Parry reasonable and probable grounds for believing that the plaintiff had committed an indictable offence, namely, the theft of a carton of cigarettes.

Constable Parry was therefore justified in doing what he did and I find that he is not liable in damages for false imprisonment. He acted most reasonably in the circumstances of this case, and is to be commended for his polite, although firm, approach to the plaintiff.

I now proceed to determine whether the plaintiff is entitled to damages against the defendant High-Low Foods Ltd.

In *Broughton* v. *Jackson* (1852), 18 Q.B. 378, at p. 385, 118 E.R. 141, Lord Campbell C.J., said:

"The defendant, in a case of this kind, must shew reasonable grounds of suspicion for the satisfaction of the Court; it is not enough to state that he himself reasonably suspected. But he is not bound to set forth all the evidence; it is enough if he shews facts which would create a reasonable suspicion in the mind of a reasonable man."

Apparently Mr. Jelstad, the manager of the defendant's store, had convinced himself that the plaintiff had been stealing from the store. The only ground for his belief was that he had observed the plaintiff on other occasions leaving the store, going to his car and then returning to complete his shopping.

On the occasion in question he had the plaintiff under surveillance and had six other employees of the store watching him also. While he states positively that the plaintiff did not return the carton of cigarettes to any cigarette rack in the store, he nevertheless admits that he lost sight of the plaintiff for 30 seconds. It is possible that the plaintiff did return the carton of cigarettes to the rack and was not seen by the store manager or by any of the other employees.

In any event, the store manager saw the plaintiff leave the store both times. He watched him closely and he is not prepared to say that he had any reason to believe that the plaintiff had the carton of cigarettes on his person at that time. He also watched him go to his automobile and he is not prepared to say that he saw or had any reason to believe that the plaintiff took a carton of cigarettes or anything else out of his pockets or out of his jacket and placed it in the car. If he had a reasonable suspicion that the plaintiff was removing goods from the store without paying for them, why did he not question the plaintiff before he left the store? I find that the store manager, Mr. Jelstad, did not have reasonable grounds for suspecting that the plaintiff had removed any goods from the store without paying for them. He had a suspicion, it is true, but it was not based upon any facts which would create a reasonable suspicion in the mind of a reasonable man.

The case of *Hucul* v. *Hicks* (1965), 55 D.L.R. (2d) 267, 54 W.W.R. 442, which was cited to me, is quite a different case than the present one. In that case a storekeeper who had seen the plaintiff in the vicinity from which a wallet had disappeared, became suspicious when the plaintiff would not empty out a pocket which contained an ominous bulge. He called the police, but when the police arrived and searched the man the bulge was gone and the wallet could not be found. The learned trial judge found that the defendant had reasonable cause for his suspicion because of the refusal by the plaintiff to empty the bulging pocket.

I do not believe that the defendant store can be so relieved here. Its manager chose to call the police and to bring about the constructive arrest of the plaintiff and it is therefore responsible to the plaintiff in damages.

Apparently the plaintiff was not seen on this occasion by any one he knew or anybody who knew him, and I think the damages should be nominal. I award the plaintiff the sum of $250 damages and he will of course have his costs against the defendant High-Low Foods Ltd.

The action of the plaintiff against Constable Parry is dismissed with costs.

NOTES

1. For a similar case, see *Dendekker* v. *F.W. Woolworth Co.,* [1975] 3 W.W.R. 429 (Alta. S.C.), where the defendant company and two security officers employed by them were held liable to the plaintiff for detaining her as a suspected thief of two brassieres. Shannon J. stated that "security officers employed to guard against thefts of merchandise have no higher rights of arrest than those conferred on citizens generally".

2. The onus is on the defendant to show "lawful justification" for an arrest. See *Kariogiannis* v. *Poulos & T. Eaton Co.,* [1976] 6 W.W.R. 197, at p. 198 (B.C.S.C.), *per* Rae J. See also *Carpenter* v. *MacDonald* (1979), 21 O.R. (2d) 165 (Dist. Ct.).

3. In *Walters* v. *Smith & Sons, Ltd.,* [1914] 1 K.B. 595, 110 L.T. 345, the plaintiff, after having been acquitted of a criminal charge of the theft of some books, sued his employer who had handed him over to the police. The defendant was held liable by Sir Rufus Isaacs C.J. who summarized the common law rules as follows:

"Interference with the liberty of the subject, and especially interference by a private person, has ever been most jealously guarded by the common law of the land. At common law a police constable may arrest a person if he has reasonable cause to suspect that a felony has been committed although it afterwards appears that no felony has been committed, but that is not so when a private person makes or causes the arrest, for to justify his action he must prove, among other things, that a felony has actually been committed: see *per* Lord Tenterden C.J. in *Beckwith* v. *Philby,* 6 B. & C. 635. I have come to the conclusion that it is necessary for a private person to prove that the same felony had been committed for which the plaintiff had been given into custody. . . .

When a person, instead of having recourse to legal proceedings by applying for a judicial warrant for arrest or laying an information or issuing another process well known to the law, gives another into custody, he takes a risk upon himself by which he must abide, and if in the result it turns out that the person arrested was innocent, and that therefore the arrest was wrongful, he cannot plead any lawful excuse unless he can bring himself within the proposition of law which I have enunciated in this judgment."

4. Section 33 of the old Criminal Code of Canada had enacted the *Walters* v. *Smith & Sons, Ltd.,* principle into the law, but this section was repealed by the new Code, which came into effect in 1955. There remains some uncertainty about the scope of a private person's privilege to arrest. It can be argued either that the matter of civil liability has been left for the courts to determine, or that the privilege has been altered by the new Criminal Code, ss. 449 and 450.

5. In *Hucul* v. *Hicks* (1965), 55 D.L.R. (2d) 267 (Sask.), the defendant storekeeper, having had several thefts from his store, placed a wallet in a show window to trap the guilty party. The plaintiff, seeing some duck decoys in the window, entered the store and went to the show window to examine the decoys. The defendant came from the rear of the store and noticed the wallet was missing. He told the plaintiff not to leave the store and that he would have to be searched. The plaintiff turned out his side pockets and right hip pocket and then, becoming annoyed, left the store. The defendant, not being satisfied with regard to the plaintiff's left hip pocket, called a constable who questioned the plaintiff who was then asked to go back to the store with him. All the plaintiff's pockets were this time emptied and the constable then departed. The plaintiff brought action for false imprisonment. Sirois J., held that there had been a restraint on the plaintiff's liberty when the defendant called the constable. Up until then there were no threats, no intent to use force, and no preventing the plaintiff from leaving the store, which he in fact did. The plaintiff having refused "to avail himself of a golden opportunity to completely exonerate himself", the defendant was "forced" to arrive at the logical conclusion that the wallet was in the left hip pocket. "The plaintiff, in the vernacular, was asking for it." While a private person can lawfully arrest only if he can prove that a felony has been committed and that he had reasonable grounds for suspecting the person arrested to have committed that felony, "here the evidence indicated that, the wallet having disappeared from the window, a crime had in fact been committed by someone, and the defendant had reasonable grounds to suspect from the plaintiff's conduct that the latter was the offender". The plaintiff's action failed. No reference is made to the Criminal Code and "proof of the felony" is covered by the language quoted. Does this case equate the private citizen's privilege and that of a peace officer?

6. In *Regina* v. *Yehl* (1964), 44 D.L.R. (2d) 504 (B.C.C.A.), A had been ejected from a beer parlour by the bartender. C, a police officer, entered the beer parlour shortly afterwards and found A intoxicated and arguing with the bartender. C asked A to come outside and when he refused to do so, pushed him out. When he got outside, A became very profane and belligerent, thereby drawing a crowd. C's partner, B, another police officer, then informed A he was under arrest and when he grabbed A's arm the latter became violent and assaulted B. A was charged and convicted of assaulting a police officer in the execution of his duty. This conviction was upheld on appeal. There was no arrest in the beer parlour, and if there had been, it would have been illegal since A was not at the time committing a disturbance and a police officer would only have been justified in arresting without a warrant for a summary conviction offence if the accused was found committing it. In pushing A outside, C was only using reasonable force to eject a trespasser. When A created a disturbance outside, B was justified in arresting him and A was, therefore, properly convicted of assaulting B in the execution of his duty.

7. Does it make sense to hold liable the private citizen in *Lebrun* and at the same time relieve the policeman of liability? Should private citizens be encouraged or discouraged to assist in law enforcement? What are the advantages and disadvantages of their participation?

8. The problem of shoplifting is no joke: millions of dollars worth of articles are stolen from self-service stores each year. Most efforts by commercial establishments to reverse the trend have failed. Cases like *Lebrun* do not assist

the storekeeper in his battle to protect his goods. Although the innocent shoppers appear to be well protected by such a rule, they pay the price in the long run by increased prices for goods. Should we consider granting to merchants a new privilege of temporary detention for investigation? What are the conflicting values here? Should an honest person object to waiting for a few minutes in order to clear up a misunderstanding? What are the dangers involved? Can we avoid them by specifying certain limitations of time, place and manner? Is the problem really in the way that we define false imprisonment?

9. In the United States such a new privilege is beginning to emerge. See Prosser, *Handbook of the Law of Torts* (4th ed., 1971), p. 121. Can this be looked upon merely as an extension of the privilege of protection or recapture of property? There is a fine student note on this topic, "Shop-lifting and the Law of Arrest: The Merchant's Dilemma" (1953), 62 Yale L.J. 788.

10. Who should bear the cost of these errors? The shops? The individuals suspected? The customers of the shops? The police departments? The taxpayers?

11. In *Bahner* v. *Marwest Hotel Co. Ltd., et al.* (1969), 6 D.L.R. (3d) 322; affd. (1970), 12 D.L.R. (3d) 646 (B.C.C.A.), Mr. Bahner took two friends to dinner at Trader Vic's restaurant operated by the defendant Marwest in the Bayshore Inn, Vancouver. At 11:30 p.m. the waiter asked if the party would care for another bottle of wine. A second bottle was brought, opened and left at the table but by 11:50 had not been touched. At this time the waiter informed the plaintiff that according to law the bottle of wine must be consumed by midnight. The plaintiff said this could not be done and refused to pay for the second bottle. When he said he would take it elsewhere to drink, he was told that this was against the law, which it was. The plaintiff attempted to leave the restaurant after having offered to give his name and address but was prevented from doing so by the restaurant's security officer who blocked the exit and informed the plaintiff that he could not leave. After some discussion the police were called and the defendant constable ordered the plaintiff to pay for the wine or face arrest. The plaintiff still declined to pay and was arrested, taken to the Police Station and lodged in a cell. The police officer believed that the plaintiff had committed the offence of obtaining goods by false pretenses but when he discovered that this was an error, he then laid an unfounded charge of intoxication which was subsequently dismissed.

Wilson C.J.S.C. stated:

"I cannot take very seriously the argument of counsel for the hotel company that there were other exits from the cafe unbarred and that the plaintiff might have escaped through one of them. The plaintiff, commanded by a security officer to stay, and prevented by that officer from leaving by the ordinary exit, behaved with admirable restraint in making no forcible attempt to pass the security officer. After what the officer had said and done he could reasonably expect to be restrained by force if he tried to leave by any exit and he was not required to make an attempt to run away."

Mr. Justice Wilson continued as follows:

"It seems to me that there were here two false imprisonments. When Rocky, the Pinkerton man, barred the exit from the cafe and told the plaintiff he could not leave, there was false imprisonment by the defendant Mar-West Hotel Co. Ltd. When Muir, without a warrant took into custody and gaoled the plaintiff, who was not committing an offence, and whom the constable had no reasonable cause to believe to be guilty of an offence, there was a second false imprisonment. There was no reasonable and probable cause for imprisonment in either case. As I have said, it must be assumed that the reason in Muir's mind justifying the arrest was the plaintiff's refusal to pay for the second bottle of wine, and the plaintiff also knew that his refusal to pay was almost certainly the reason for his arrest. But I find as a fact that Muir did not, at the moment of arrest, disclose to the plaintiff the reason for his arrest. I think that Muir had in his mind some confused notion that a failure to pay for a thing ordered was a crime, but did not know what crime it was. The attitude of the manager and house detective of this grand caravanserai, both of whom seemed to have thought that failure to pay was a crime, may have influenced Muir's thinking.

But the fact that he was publicly humiliated by detention by the security officer in the hotel in the presence of the staff and a dozen guests, and by subsequent interrogation and arrest by a uniformed policeman was known to a considerable number of people, who have in all probability and very naturally, told other persons about it. It is hard to calculate how far news of this kind may spread and what harm it may have done. Few persons who witnessed his arrest are likely to be aware of his subsequent acquittal. The ripples from the boulder thrown in the water by the defendants may spread far. The degradation consequent upon the experience suffered by the plaintiff is sore and not easily forgotten."

His Lordship then proceeded to award $3,500 in damages against Marwest, (including $1,000 punitive damages) and $2,500 against Muir (including punitive damages). In addition, the $75 legal fee that the plaintiff spent on his legal defence in Police Court was awarded against Muir.

On the appeal, Mr. Justice Tysoe affirmed the result. With regard to the defendant hotel, His Lordship indicated that he thought the purpose of the detention was "to frighten the respondent into paying for the wine he had ordered and into paying for it there and then". He just could not believe that the hotel could possibly have believed that the respondent had committed a criminal offence. After affirming against the policeman, Mr. Justice Tysoe stated that his conduct was "simply outrageous". He did not think that the courts should "hold their hand until it is seen what the police commission sees fit to do in the way of disciplining a member of the police force".

Is this a good way of supervising police behaviour?

For a surprisingly similar case, see *Perry* v. *Fried et al.* (1972), 32 D.L.R. (3d) 589 (N.S.S.C.) *per* Cowan C.J.

12. Police officers are wise to avoid interfering in what are essentially civil disputes between innkeepers and their guests or between landlords and their tenants. Where an innkeeper is charged by the police with breaking and entering and possession of stolen goods, when he was only exercising his legal rights under the Innkeeper's Act in relation to certain goods belonging to some guests, both false imprisonment and malicious prosecution are committed, since the officers should have realized that no crime had been perpetrated. See *Carpenter* v. *MacDonald* (1979), 21 O.R. (2d) 165 (Dist. Ct.).

13. Where an individual merely informs the police of certain events, and the police decide themselves to make an arrest, that is not false arrest by the informer. If, however, the police are told by the informer to "stop" an individual, and they do, they are not acting on their own initiative and the informer is responsible for causing the arrest. See *Roberts* v. *Buster's Auto Towing Service Ltd.* (1976), 70 D.L.R. (3d) 716 (B.C.S.C.).

14. The Supreme Court of Canada has adopted the following definition of malicious prosecution:

". . . in an action for malicious prosecution the plaintiff has to prove, first, that he was innocent and that his innocence was pronounced by the tribunal before which the accusation was made; secondly, that there was a want of reasonable and probable cause for the prosecution, or, as it may be otherwise stated, that the circumstances of the case were such as to be in the eyes of the judge inconsistent with the existence of reasonable and probable cause; and, lastly, that the proceedings of which he complains were initiated in a malicious spirit, that is, from an indirect and improper motive, and not in furtherance of justice.

See *Meyer* v. *General Exchange Insce. Corp.* (1962), 31 D.L.R. (2d) 689, at p. 695, [1962] S.C.R. 193, quoting from *Abrath* v. *N. Eastern R. Co.* (1883), 11 Q.B.D. 440, at p. 455 (no malice shown).

Punitive damages may be awarded against persons who are found liable for malicious prosecution, as where someone laid a phony charge of common assault against some police officers out of "revenge" or "spite", after they were properly arrested by those police officers. See *Tedford* v. *Nitch* (1976), 13 O.R. (2d) 471, *per* Phelan Co. Ct. J.

15. A provincial probation officer, negligently believing that the plaintiff had failed to report as required by his probation order, has a warrant issued for the arrest of the plaintiff. The plaintiff is arrested and spends a weekend in jail before the error is discovered. Is this false imprisonment by the probation officer? Is this malicious prosecution by the probation officer? See *Willan* v. *The Queen* (1978), 20 O.R. (2d) 587, *per* Waisberg Co. Ct. J. *cf. Reid* v. *Webster* (1966), 59 D.L.R. (2d) 189 (P.E.I.S.C.), setting in motion legal proceedings does not amount to false arrest. See also *Austin* v. *Dowling* (1870), L.R. 5 C.P. 534.

16. The police power of arrest under s. 450(1)(b) of the Criminal Code has been held to have application to a situation in which a person is "apparently" committing a summary conviction offence, even though he is subsequently acquitted of the offence for which he was arrested: *R.* v. *Biron* (1975), 59 D.L.R. (3d) 409 (S.C.C.). Martland J., speaking for the majority, stated:

> "If the words 'committing a criminal offence' are to be construed in [a restrictive manner] para. (*b*) becomes impossible to apply. The power of arrest which that paragraph gives has to be exercised promptly, yet, strictly speaking, it is impossible to say than an offence is committed until the party arrested has been found guilty by the Courts. If this is the way in which this provision is to be construed, no peace officer can ever decide, when making an arrest without a warrant, that the person arrested is 'committing a criminal offence'. In my opinion the wording used in para. (*b*), which is over simplified, means that the power to arrest without a warrant is given where the peace officer himself finds a situation in which a person is apparently committing an offence."

Laskin C.J.C., in a strong dissent, refused to accept this construction and held that if the offence for which the accused was arrested had not in fact been committed, then the arrest was unlawful, and the accused was justified in resisting that arrest. He further remarked:

> ". . . a constable's lot is a heavy and even unenviable one when he has to make an on-the-spot decision as to an arrest. But he may be overzealous as well as mistaken, and it may be too that when a charge or charges come to be laid, the Crown attorney or other advising counsel may mistake the grounds and thus lay a charge which does not support the arrest. We cannot go on a guessing expedition out of regret for an innocent mistake or a wrong-headed assessment. Far more important, however, is the social and legal, and indeed political, principle upon which our criminal law is based, namely, the right of an individual to be left alone, to be free of private or public restraint, save as the law provides otherwise. Only to the extent to which it so provides can a person be detained or his freedom of movement arrested."

FLETCHER v. COLLINS

High Court of Ontario. (1968), 70 D.L.R. (2d) 183

Plaintiff was arrested on a warrant issued for the arrest of a man with an identical name. The description of the true suspect on the back of the warrant fitted plaintiff in a general way. When questioned by the officers possessing the warrant, plaintiff adopted a hostile, truculent and belligerent attitude, refused to answer questions as to his former employment which would have cleared him of suspicion after proper inquiry, and subjected the officers to verbal abuse and profanity. Plaintiff's conduct reinforced the officer's belief that he was in fact the suspect. Plaintiff was detained approximately four hours, when it was determined that he was innocent of any offence. He was then released and driven home. An apology was made.

Lacourciere J.: . . . I turn now to the question of reasonable and probable cause; under s. 28(1) of the Criminal Code where a person who is authorized to

execute a warrant to arrest believes, in good faith and on reasonable and probable grounds, that the person whom he arrests is the person named in the warrant, he is protected *from criminal responsibility* in respect thereof as if the
person were the person named in the warrant. The emphasis is added above to
show that civil liability is not affected by the above section: at common law, a
constable who arrests the wrong person under a warrant, or even the right
person under the wrong name is liable in damages for false imprisonment:
Newell on Malicious Prosecution (1892), p. 77:

> "It is almost unnecessary to say that an officer should be careful to arrest
> the right person, for if he arrests one person upon a writ against another he
> becomes liable in an action for false imprisonment. And this is true notwith-
> standing the similarity and even the identity of the names. Lord Ellen-
> borough said that process ought regularly to describe the party against whom
> it is meant to be issued, and the arrest of one person cannot be justified
> under a writ sued out against another."

It would appear that the common law regarded the arrest of an innocent
person bearing the identical name as the person named in the warrant as false
imprisonment, but admitted evidence of good faith in mitigation of damages:
Sinclair v. *Broughton and Government of India* (1882), 47 L.T. 170. . . .

Because of s. 25 and s. 435 (*a*) [rep. & sub. 1960-61 (Can.), c. 43, s. 14] of
the Criminal Code, I am of opinion that the situation of absolute liability on
the part of a constable does not obtain in Canada: a police officer proceeding
to make what he believes to be a lawful arrest under a warrant, is justified if he
acts "in good faith and on reasonable and probable grounds".

In Ontario, the judgment of the Court of Appeal in *Kennedy* v. *Tomlinson*
(1959), 20 D.L.R. (2d) 273, 126 C.C.C. 175, makes it clear that the issue of
reasonable and probable cause, in an action for false arrest, is for the Judge
where the facts are undisputed. Schroeder J.A., points out at p. 299, D.L.R.,
pp. 206-207, C.C.C.:

> "The point must not be overlooked that in actions of false imprisonment
> and malicious prosecution, the question whether, on the facts, the defendant
> acted without reasonable and probable cause is for the Judge, but the facts
> on which his decision depends must, if disputed, be found by the jury: *West*
> v. *Baxendale* (1850), 9 C.B. 141, 137 E.R. 846. In that case it was stated by
> Maule J. at p. 152: "It was for the jury to say whether the facts pleaded
> were proved, and for the judge to determine whether or not they amounted
> to reasonable and probable cause, — reasonable and probable cause, not for
> suspecting, but for imprisoning the plaintiff.
>
> At pp. 152-3, Maule J. directed that the rule must be made absolute for a
> new trial on the ground of misdirection, stating "if the direction of the Lord
> Chief Justice in substance was, that the jury were to consider whether the
> facts stated in the plea were true, and whether they amounted to reasonable
> and probable cause, then, no doubt, the direction was wrong."

This is in accordance with modern English practice, recently illustrated in
Dallison v. *Caffery*, [1964] 4 All E.R. 610, at p. 616. Lord Denning M.R., in
his judgment says:

> "Thirdly, the issue of 'reasonable cause' is for the judge. He is not bound
> to leave to the jury every single issue of fact which may bear on it. He is en-
> titled to make his own findings of fact. He need only leave to the jury the
> issues on which he feels he needs their help. . . ."

In accordance with the cases cited, the court must rule on the question of
reasonable and probable cause; I am entirely satisfied that the defendants were
at all times acting bona fide; it was never suggested by anyone that they acted

under the influence of an indirect or improper motive. They were not actuated by malice in the sense of spite or hatred against the plaintiff. The identity of the plaintiff's name with the suspect, the physical resemblance coupled with the plaintiff's uncooperative attitude and the other circumstances mentioned here, in my opinion justified the arrest and the holding of the plaintiff for identification. The detention was not unduly prolonged and was followed by an apology. I believe the test to be applied is whether the facts relied upon by the officers were such as to create a reasonable suspicion in the mind of a reasonable man that the person arrested was the person described in the warrant. That test, adapted to the facts of this case, is the test, as I understand it, described in *Kennedy* v. *Tomlinson, supra,* at p. 299, D.L.R., pp. 206-7, C.C.C., in giving the meaning of "reasonable and probable grounds" in ss. 25(1) and 435(*a*) of the Criminal Code. Assisted by the jury's answers, I am of opinion that the defendants have met the required test, and were justified in arresting and detaining the plaintiff.

The action will therefore be dismissed, but in the circumstances, without costs.

NOTES

1. Another case of arrest under a warrant of the wrong person is *Crowe* v. *Noon,* [1971] 1 O.R. 530, 16 D.L.R. (3d) 22. In this case, the suspect had been identified by the complainant as the man who had given him a worthless cheque. The warrant was for a person with the identical name and of the same age. Notwithstanding that the plaintiff was proved to be the wrong person at the criminal trial, Mr. Justice Pennell dismissed his case against the constable.

His Lordship pointed out that the "onus of proving affirmatively the existence of 'reasonable and probable' grounds for the arrest is upon the defendant since arrest is *prima facie* a tort and demands justification". Mr. Justice Pennell explained:

"The test whether the circumstances relied upon by the defendant Noon, having regard to all the circumstances known to him at the time, were such as to create a reasonable suspicion that the alleged offence had been committed, and the plaintiff had committed it, is an objective one. . . a peace officer is not bound to test every possible relevant fact before he effects an arrest."

Mr. Justice Pennell offered these concluding remarks:

"I add a concluding observation, though I cannot tell whether it will be useful. It is evident that the conclusion I have reached will result, if effect is given to it, in leaving the plaintiff without compensation for 12 days of imprisonment which he has undeservedly suffered. The remedy, assuming I have reached the correct decision, lies outside a Court of law. In the circumstances, I am tempted to paraphrase the words of Justice Robert Jackson of the Supreme Court of the United States: The final protection against the invasion of individual liberty by members of officialdom is the attitude of society and of its political forces rather than its legal machinery.

It is perhaps hardly necessary to add that I have neither the duty nor the right to inquire into the merits of a moral right to compensation. I have only jurisdiction to deal with points of law raised before me and to determine to the best of my ability whether there is a claim in law. But I do not believe that I breach the canons of legal propriety by respectfully suggesting that the law officer of the Crown might wish to consider whether this is a case in which justice might be done by way of *ex gratia* payment."

2. The plaintiff, recovering from breast surgery, was arrested in a Toronto hospital and taken to police headquarters. The police were acting under a warrant for the arrest of a dancer with the same first name as the plaintiff whom they believed to be in the hospital. Actually, the person being pursued had been released from the hospital a week earlier. Further, she was a white woman,

whereas the plaintiff was black. Reasonable and probable grounds? Is the seriousness of the offence a relevant consideration? The person being sought was charged with putting on an indecent performance. Would the police have been justified if the offence was murder? The matter ended with a public apology. What purpose would a court action have served here? Should there be a public scheme to compensate victims of mistaken arrests? See also for an arrest of the wrong person, *Schuck* v. *Stewart,* [1978] 5 W.W.R. 279 (B.C.S.C.).

3. Suppose the wrong person is arrested because of a reasonable mistake? The error is then discovered, but the police take 15-30 minutes before they release the person. Is this false imprisonment? See *Romilly* v. *Weatherhead* (1975), 55 D.L.R. (3d) 607 (B.C.S.C.).

4. Where there is no dispute on the facts, the question of whether there was reasonable and probable cause is for the Judge, not the jury. See *Schuck* v. *Stewart, supra.*

CHRISTIE AND ANOTHER v. LEACHINSKY

House of Lords. [1947] A.C. 573; [1947] 1 All E.R. 567: on appeal
from [1946] 1 K.B. 1242; [1945] 2 All E.R. 295

Leachinsky was a dealer in "rags" or "waste" who bought supplies from time to time from Michaelson in Leicester. In August, 1942, he bought three bales of waste, and in picking them up asked Michaelson if he had any "remnants" from which he might make a dress for his wife. Michaelson said he had, and Leachinsky bought a considerable number of remnants and had them packed in a single bale. The four bales were shipped to Leachinsky's warehouse in Liverpool and they were all described as "waste". At the time of the purchase of the remnants war-rationing restrictions on the purchase and sale of cloth were in effect.

When the goods arrived in Liverpool the police, being suspicious, examined the goods and discovered that one of the bales contained cloth and not waste. When Leachinsky commenced to unload the bales, he himself set aside the bale of cloth. Christie and Morris, police officers, then questioned Leachinsky about a bale of cloth and the latter professed to know nothing about such cloth. The officers, not satisfied with the explanation, arrested Leachinsky under the provisions of the Liverpool Corporation Act, 1921. This Act provided that if a person's name and address were unknown, he could be arrested and brought before the court to give an explanation of his possession of goods believed to have been stolen by someone, although not necessarily by the person arrested — the charge usually referred to as "unlawful possession". The two police police officers knew Leachinsky's name and address and later, in evidence, Christie admitted that he knew he had no power to arrest under the Liverpool Corporation Act and made the arrest in this way simply because it was "more convenient".

Leachinsky was charged in police court with "unlawful possession" and after spending a night in jail was brought before a magistrate on September 1, when a remand of one week in custody was granted. During this period the police had seen Michaelson in Leicester and the latter had denied that he had sold the goods to Leachinsky and claimed that they had been taken from him without his authority. When Leachinsky was brought before the magistrate on September 8, a further remand was granted of one week, under bail, and at the hearing on September 15 the police withdrew the charge of unlawful possession and Leachinsky was discharged. Before he could leave the court he was re-arrested for theft of the remnants. At his subsequent trial, he was acquitted and

Michaelson was proved to have been lying. Leachinsky brought action against Michaelson for libel and recovered £250. Leachinsky then brought action for false imprisonment against Christie and Morris.

At the trial before Stable J., the defendants obtained judgment, the trial judge taking the view that the two police officers had reasonable grounds for suspecting Leachinsky of theft, and although the arrest on the "unlawful possession" charge was improper, they could justify the arrest by their state of mind at the time of the arrest. As he put it, "Why did they arrest him? If they arrested him because they believed he had committed a felony and there were reasonable grounds for so believing, they do not lose the protection of the law." Leachinsky appealed and the Court of Appeal (Scott and Uthwatt L.JJ., Lawrence L.J. dissenting) allowed the appeal and entered judgment for the plaintiff for the false imprisonment with damages to be assessed. Christie and Morris appealed to the House of Lords.

Lord Simonds: . . . I proceed on the basis that, when the appellants arrested the respondent . . . they, in fact, suspected that he had stolen a bale of cloth, or had received it knowing that it was stolen, and, further, that they had reasonable grounds for that suspicion. . . . If, then, the appellants reasonably suspected that the respondent had committed a felony, was it not their right to arrest him without a warrant? And, if they did so arrest him, is it that the arrest can be branded as illegal and an action for false imprisonment lie against them? My Lords, it is here that the crux of the matter lies and it is not easy so to state the law as not, on the one hand, to impinge upon the liberty of the subject, or, on the other hand, to make more difficult the duty of every subject of the King to preserve the King's peace. It was, I think, this difficulty that led Lawrence L.J., to the conclusion that the appellants were not precluded from pleading their reasonable suspicion of felony, which would have justified arrest, by the fact that they at no time charged the respondent with anything but a misdemeanor, which in the circumstances did not justify arrest. The learned Lord Justice states his view of the law thus:

> "It is argued that it is unfair not to let the person arrested know what the charge against him is and no doubt it is desirable that he should be informed as soon as possible of the facts which are said to constitute a crime on his part and ultimately when the indictment is framed what the actual charge is. But the undoubted fact that the charge may be altered seems to me to show that the right to know the charge only comes into existence when the indictment is finally drawn."

My Lords, in my opinion this statement of the law, which the learned Lord Justice proceeds to apply with perfect logic to the present case, cannot be accepted without qualification.

First, I would say that it is the right of every citizen to be free from arrest unless there is in some other citizen, whether a constable or not, the right to arrest him. I would say next that it is the corrollary of the right of every citizen to be thus free from arrest that he should be entitled to resist arrest unless that arrest is lawful. How can these rights be reconciled with the proposition that he may be arrested without knowing why he is arrested? It is to be remembered that the right of the constable in or out of uniform is, except for a circumstance irrelevant to the present discussion, the same as that of every other citizen. Is citizen A bound to submit unresistingly to arrest by citizen B in ignorance of the charge made against him? I think, my Lords, that cannot be the law of England. Blind, unquestioning obedience is the law of tyrants and of slaves. It does not yet flourish on English soil. I would, therefore, submit the general proposition that it is a condition of lawful arrest that the man arrested should be entitled to know why he is arrested, and then, since the affairs of life seldom admit an absolute standard or an unqualified proposition, see whether any qualification is of necessity imposed on it. This approach to the question has, I think, a double support. In the first place, the law requires that, where arrest proceeds on a warrant, the warrant should state the charge on which the arrest is made. I can see no valid reason why this safeguard for the subject should not equally be his when the arrest is made without a warrant. The exigency of the situations, which justifies or demands arrest without a warrant, cannot, as it appears to me, justify or demand either a refusal to state the reason of arrest or a mis-statement of the reason. Arrested with or without a warrant, the subject is entitled to know why he is deprived of his freedom, if only in order that he may without a moment's delay take such steps as will enable him to regain it. . . .

If, then, this is, as I think it is, the fundamental rule, what qualification, if any, must be imposed upon it? The cogent instances given by Lawrence L.J. are conclusive that an arrest does not become wrongful merely because the constable arrests a man for one felony, say, murder, and he is subsequently charged with another felony, say, manslaughter. It is not enough to say that in such a case the accused man could not recover any damages in an action for false imprisonment. It is more than that. It is clear that the constable has not been guilty of an illegal arrest, if he reasonably suspected that murder had been done. Again, I think it is clear that there is no need for the constable to explain the reason of arrest if the arrested man is caught redhanded and the crime is patent to high Heaven. Nor, obviously, is explanation a necessary prelude to arrest where it is important to secure a possibly violent criminal. Nor, again, can it be wrongful to arrest and detain a man on a charge of which he is reasonably suspected with a view to further investigation of a second charge on which information is incomplete. In all such matters a wide measure of discretion must be left to those whose duty it is to preserve the peace and bring criminals to justice.

These and similar considerations lead me to the view that it is not an essential condition of lawful arrest that the constable should at the time of arrest formulate any charge at all, much less the charge which may ultimately be found in the indictment, but this, and this only, is the qualification which I would impose on the general proposition. It leaves untouched the principle, which lies at the heart of the matter, that the arrested man is entitled to be told what is the act for which he is arrested. The "charge" ultimately made will depend on the view taken by the law of his act. In ninety-nine cases out of a hundred the same words may be used to define the charge or describe the act, nor is any technical precision necessary — for instance, if the act constituting the crime is the killing of another man, it will be immaterial that the arrest is for murder and at a later hour the charge of manslaughter is substituted. The arrested man is left in no doubt that the arrest is for that killing. This is, I think, the fundamental principle, that a man is entitled to know what, in the apt words of Lawrence L.J. are "the facts alleged to constitute crime on his part. If so, it is manifestly wrong that a constable arresting him for one crime should profess to arrest him for another. Of what avail is the prescribed caution if it is directed to an imaginary crime? And how can the accused take steps to explain away a charge of which he has no inkling? . . .

It is clear then that, whatever may have been the secret thought of the constables at the time of the arrest and detention, they allowed the respondent to think that he was being arrested for being "in unlawful possession" of certain goods, an offence, if it be an offence, which was at the most a misdemeanour within the Liverpool Act and could not, except under conditions which did not here obtain, justify an arrest without a warrant, and was described in terms not calculated to bring home to him that he was suspected of stealing or receiving the goods. In these circumstances the initial arrest and detention were wrongful. He was not aware and was not made aware of the act alleged to constitute his crime, but was misled by a statement which was calculated to suggest to his uneasy conscience that he was guilty of a so-called black market offence. It is no answer that the constables had no sinister motive. They had from the administrative point of view a perfectly good motive. It will be found in an answer to a question, which, though it related to a later stage of the proceedings, is equally applicable to the earlier: "Why did you not then charge him with larceny?" To this the revealing answer was: "Because that larceny was committed at Leicester and it would then be a matter of withdrawing one charge and handing him over to Leicester. Unlawful possession was the most convenient charge at the time until he could be handed over to the Leicester City Police."

My Lords, the liberty of the subject and the convenience of the police or any other executive authority are not to be weighed in the scales against each other. This case will have served a useful purpose if it enables your Lordships once more to proclaim that a man is not to be deprived of his liberty except in due course and process of law.

KOECHLIN v. WAUGH AND HAMILTON

Ontario Court of Appeal. (1957), 11 D.L.R. (2d) 447

Laidlaw J.A.: This is an appeal by the plaintiffs from a judgment pronounced by His Honour Judge Shea, in the County Court of the County of York, on May 21, 1956, dismissing with costs an action brought by the plaintiffs for damages for alleged unlawful arrest and imprisonment. . . .

On the evening of October 11, 1955, the infant plaintiff, aged about 20 years, and his friend Victor Wassilgew, attended a picture show in the Township of Scarborough. The show ended about midnight. They went to a restaurant for coffee and, afterwards, started to walk on the sidewalk on Kingston Road in the direction of the home of Wassilgew. They were stopped by the defendants, who are police officers of the Township of Scarborough. The police officers were in plain clothes and were in a police cruiser car. The police called the infant plaintiff and his companion to their car and asked for their identification. Wassilgew gave his identification at once and told the police officers that they were on their way home after the show. The infant plaintiff objected to giving his identification unless the police officer, Hamilton, who spoke to him, first identified himself. The defendant Hamilton produced a badge and said he was a police officer, but the infant plaintiff was not satisfied with that identification and requested the name and number of the officer. The officer did not give his name, but his number was on the badge. The infant plaintiff continued to refuse to identify himself, and a scuffle ensued during which the infant plaintiff fell into a deep ditch. Subsequently, force was used by the police officer and other officers who were called to the scene to put the infant plaintiff into a police car. He was not told any reason for his arrest. He was taken to the police station and told that he would be charged with assault of a police officer . . . .

The learned judge stated in reasons given by him that the police officers stopped the infant plaintiff and his companion because they were sauntering along the street, and because of "their dress". There was in fact nothing distinctive about the dress of the infant plaintiff, but his companion was wearing rubber-soled shoes and a jacket. The learned judge referred also to the fact that there had been a number of "break-ins" in the neighbourhood a few nights before and that the police had reported that a person wearing rubber-soled shoes was involved in one or more of those break-ins. After referring to the reasons for stopping the infant plaintiff and his companion and asking for identification, the learned judge said: "Then, from then on, the actions of Koechlin, and his words, would in my opinion justify the officers in believing that this man either had or was about to commit a crime." Later, he said, referring to Koechlin — "his refusal to co-operate — made the officers still more suspicious and firm in the belief, as I said, that something was wrong."

Counsel for the appellants in this court based his case on the ground that the police officers had no reasonable or probable grounds for believing that the infant plaintiff had committed or was about to commit an indictable offence. We are satisfied, after perusal of the evidence, that neither of the police officers had such grounds. We do not refer in detail to the evidence, but observe from the evidence given by the defendant Waugh that the reason for him believing the infant plaintiff and his companion were about to commit an offence was "the way they were dressed and the way they were walking — sauntering along the sidewalk". We observe, also, that he said in his evidence: "We were going to take him up to the station and find out who he was . . . . The reason we were going to take him to the station; we thought it would be better to take the man up to the station than argue out on the street."

A police officer has not in law an unlimited power to arrest a law-abiding citizen. The power given expressly to him by the Criminal Code to arrest without warrant is contained in s. 435, but we direct careful attention of the public to the fact that the law empowers a police officer in many cases and under certain circumstances to require a person to account for his presence and to identify himself and to furnish other information, and any person who wrongfully fails to comply with such lawful requirements does so at the risk of arrest and imprisonment. None of these circumstances exist in this case. No unnecessary restriction on his power which results in increased difficulty to a police officer to perform his duties of office should be imposed by the court. At the same time, the rights and freedom under law from unlawful arrest and imprisonment of an innocent citizen must be fully guarded by the courts. In this case, the fact that the companion of the infant plaintiff was wearing rubber-soled shoes and a wind-breaker and that his dress attracted the attention of the police officers, falls far short of reasonable and probable grounds for believing that the infant plaintiff had committed an indictable offence or was about to commit such an offence. We do not criticize the police officers in any way for asking the infant plaintiff and his companion to identify themselves, but we are satisfied that when the infant plaintiff, who was entirely innocent of any wrongdoing, refused to do so, the police officer has no right to use force to compel him to identify himself. It would have been wise and, indeed, a duty as a good citizen, for the infant plaintiff to have identified himself when asked to do so by the police officers. It is altogether likely that if the infant plaintiff had been courteous and co-operative, the incident giving rise to this action would not have occurred, but that does not in law excuse the defendants for acting as they did in the particular circumstances.

We direct attention to an important fact. The infant plaintiff was not told by either of the police officers any reason for his arrest. The infant plaintiff was entitled to know on what charge or on suspicion of what crime he was seized. He was not required in law to submit to restraint on his freedom unless he knew the reason why that restraint should be imposed . . . .

Finally, we are not in accord with the view expressed by the learned trial judge that the actions of the infant plaintiff in resisting the efforts of the police officers can be regarded as justification for their belief that he "either had or was about to commit a crime". In the particular circumstances he was entitled in law to resist the efforts of the police officers, and they have failed in this case to justify their actions.

It was stated in the course of giving oral reasons for judgment that the courts would strive diligently to avoid putting any unnecessary obstacle in the way of the detection of crime or the lawful arrest of persons in the proper performance of the duties of a police officer. We repeat an expression of that policy of the courts. Nothing in these reasons for judgment should be taken as encouragement to any person to resist a police officer in the performance of his duties; on the contrary, it is not only highly desirable, but vitally important, that every person should co-operate to the utmost with police officers for the good of the public and to ensure the preservation of law and order in his community.

In this case the police officers exceeded their powers and infringed the rights of the infant plaintiff without justification. Therefore, the appeal will be allowed with costs.

NOTES

1. Section 29 of the Criminal Code now provides that it is the "duty of every one who arrests a person, whether with or without warrant, to give notice to that person, where it is feasible to do so, of (a) the process or warrant under which he makes the arrest, or (b) the reason for the arrest. . .".

In *Sandison* v. *Rybiak* (1974), 1 O.R. (2d) 74, the police refused to inform the plaintiff of the reason why they were arresting his friend, when he asked them. They also refused to tell the friend why she was being arrested. A scuffle ensued and the plaintiff was charged with obstructing the police. After both the plaintiff and the friend were acquitted of the charges against them, the plaintiff brought an action for assault, false imprisonment and malicious prosecution. He was successful on all theories before Mr. Justice Parker who explained:

"The prisoner or someone speaking for him or her is entitled to know the reasons for the arrest and make a statement in answer to it. The exercise of such a right cannot be converted into obstruction unless it is intemperate, unduly persistent, irrelevant or made in an unreasonable manner. . . .

The accused is not required to submit to a restraint of his freedom until he is told that he is under arrest and the reason for the restraint. . . .

If an arrest is unlawful then any restriction on the liberty of the subject is false imprisonment."

Do these cases restore some of your faith in the power of the law to control the police? What are the practical problems encountered in law suits against the police?

2. On the question of the speed with which an arrested person must be taken before a justice of the peace, see Criminal Code, R.S.C. 1970, c. C-34, s. 452; *John Lewis & Co. Ltd.* v. *Tims,* [1952] A.C. 676, [1952] 1 All E.R. 1203; *Dallison* v. *Caffery,* [1964] 2 All E.R. 610.

3. For a superb analysis of this problem see Weiler, "The Control of Police Arrest Practices: Reflections of a Tort Lawyer", in Linden, *Studies in Canadian Tort Law* (1968). See also Wood, "Powers of Arrest in Canada Under Federal Law" (1970), 9 West. Ont. L. Rev. 55.

REYNEN v. ANTONENKO ET AL.

Alberta Supreme Court. (1975), 54 D.L.R. (3d) 124, 20 C.C.C. (2d) 342, [1975] 5 W.W.R. 10, 30 C.R.N.S. 135

The plaintiff was arrested by the defendant police officers on suspicion of possession of narcotics. They took him to a hospital in order to have a rectal search done. The plaintiff co-operated with the defendant physician in this examination, and, as a result, two condoms containing heroin were recovered. The plaintiff then brought suit for assault and battery against the physician and the police officers.

McDonald D.C., J.: The plaintiff's sole complaint is with the procedure that took place at the hospital. He contends that the examination of his anal canal, constituted assault and battery, alleging it was done without consent, in the absence of any emergency and without legal justification . . . .

The question in this case is whether or not the police officers were required or authorized by law to search for the drugs which were removed from the plaintiff, employing medical assistance to search through the anus into the rectum of the plaintiff.

A general power of search of a person under arrest is given by common law. . . .

It seems clear . . . that the police in this case had not only the right but also a duty to conduct a search of the plaintiff for drugs, and to seize any drugs found as evidence to be presented to the Court. In making this search and seizure the police are clearly authorized to use such force as is reasonable, proper and necessary to carry out their duty, providing that no wanton or unnecessary violence is imposed. It is also clear that what is reasonable and proper in any particular case will depend on all the circumstances of that particular case, it being impossible to lay down any hard and fast rule to be applied to all cases, except the test of reasonableness.

Under the *Narcotic Control Act,* R.S.C. 1970, c. N-1, it is not only the duty of the police to arrest persons who they have good reason to believe are in breach of the Act but also to seize drugs that may be evidence of such breach as is specifically provided for in s. 10 (1) (c).

The decision in this case is therefore to be based on whether or not the actions of the police were reasonable under the circumstances.

The evidence showed that Constable Hudon told Dr. Antonenko that the plaintiff at the airport had consented to the search at the hospital. I find that although Constable Hudon may have misinterpreted the statement or response of the plaintiff, yet he had some reason to believe that the plaintiff had indicated consent, and that Constable Hudon acted in good faith. It is true that the plaintiff did not give his written consent or explicit verbal consent, for that matter, to the examination by the doctor, but neither was he asked for it.

In his evidence-in-chief, the plaintiff testified that in the examining room at the hospital he was asked by the doctor to position himself and that he did so believing "he had no choice". . . .

It is clear from the plaintiff's own evidence and that of Dr. Antonenko that the plaintiff co-operated fully with the doctor in the conduct of the examination. Without the plaintiff's full co-operation the doctor made it clear that the examination would not have been made.

No doubt the plaintiff suffered some discomfort during the examination but he was not injured in any way by the examination. The total result of the examination was that the police obtained the heroin the plaintiff had secreted in his rectum. No doubt this induced the plaintiff to plead guilty to the charge later laid against him.

The examination being conducted in a hospital under conditions of high standard by an eminently qualified medical practitioner indicates that the police exercised every care to assure that the plaintiff was not subjected to any unreasonable force. The examination was only possible with his co-operation. . . .

Under the circumstances of this case I find that the action of the police officers in obtaining the medical examination of the plaintiff's rectum was done in a reasonable and proper manner and without any unreasonable force or threat to the health and well-being of the plaintiff. I therefore dismiss the action of the plaintiff with costs. . . .

Action dismissed.

NOTES

1. This case may be contrasted to *Re Laporte* v. *The Queen* (1972), 29 D.L.R. (3d) 651 (Que., Hugessen J.), in which a search warrant, authorizing a surgical search of accused's body for police bullets months after his arrest, was quashed on the ground *inter alia* that the human body could not be said to be a "place" or "receptacle" within the meaning of s. 443 of the Criminal Code.

2. The police, while arresting someone on a narcotics charge see him put something in his mouth. They grab his throat in order to prevent him from swallowing. They find nothing. Liability? What if they get him to spit out some heroin? See *Scott* v. *The Queen* (1975), 61 D.L.R. (3d) 130 (Fed. C.A.).

3. What if a policeman puts his fingers in the suspect's mouth to search it? What if the suspect bites them? See *R.* v. *Brezack* (1949), 96 C.C.C. 97, [1950] 23 D.L.R. 265, [1949] O.R. 888 (C.A.).

4. At the time he is arrested, the accused swallows something, which the police believe is narcotics. They take him to the hospital and have his stomach pumped. Liability? Does it make any difference if the procedure turns up some narcotics or if it does not?

5. Can the police, aside from statutory authority, have a blood test made? What about an X-ray?

6. Although prison guards may use reasonable force in moving an inmate, they are not permitted to beat him up while doing so. See *Dodge* v. *Bridge* (1977), 4 C.C.L.T. 83, *per* Keith J., varied as to damages (1978), 6 C.C.L.T. 71 (Ont. C.A.).

7. The police seem to have some power to interfere with individual rights in order to prevent violence. In *Humphries* v. *Connor* (1864), 17 Ir. C.L.R. 1, the defendant police officer removed an orange lily from the clothes of the plaintiff because he feared that it was provoking a crowd to possible violence against the plaintiff. Mr. Justice Hayes, on a demurrer by the plaintiff, explained:

". . . When a constable is called upon to preserve the peace, I know no better mode of doing so than that of removing what he sees to be the provocation to the breach of the peace; and when a person deliberately refuses to ac-quiesce in such removal, after warning so to do, I think the constable is authorized to do everything necessary and proper to enforce it. It would seem absurd to hold that a constable may arrest a person whom he finds committing a breach of the peace, but that he must not interfere with the individual who has wantonly provoked him to do so. But whether the act which he did was or was not, under all the circumstances, necessary to pre-serve the peace, is for the jury to decide."

8. In *Thomas* v. *Sawkins*, [1935] 2 K.B. 249, 153 L.T. 419, the defendant, a constable, attended a meeting, advertised to the public to discuss a matter of public interest, after being refused admittance. The plaintiff, in occupation of the premises, having requested the defendant to withdraw, which the defendant refused to do, attempted to eject the defendant and the latter used reasonable force in resisting the ejection. In proceedings for assault and battery, it was held that the defendant was not liable since, as a police officer, he had reason to believe that if he and other police officers were not present a serious breach of the peace might have ensued. *Per* Lawrence J: "If a constable in the execu-tion of his duty to preserve the peace is entitled to commit an assault, it appears to me that he is equally entitled to commit a trespass." *Per* Avory J.: "No ex-press statutory authority is necessary [to empower police to enter] where the police have reasonable grounds to apprehend a breach of the peace." On the general problem see Goodhart, *"Thomas* v. *Sawkins:* A Constitutional Innova-tion" (1936), 6 Camb. L.J. 22.

9. The police are privileged to enter private premises without a warrant to make an arrest (1) if they believe on reasonable and probable grounds that the person they are looking for is present, and (2) if they make a proper announcement to the occupier. Normally, the police should knock, identify themselves and give the reason for their entry. Such an announcement may not be required in circumstances where it is impracticable to do so. See *Eccles* v. *Bourque et al.* (1974), 41 D.L.R. (3d) 392 (B.C.C.A.), affd. 27 C.R.N.S. 325 (S.C.C.) *per* Dickson J. See also *Levitz* v. *Ryan* [1972] 3 O.R. 783 (C.A.). Has tort law a valuable role to play in supervising police misconduct?

WEILER, THE CONTROL OF POLICE ARREST PRACTICES: REFLECTIONS OF A TORT LAWYER

in Linden, *Studies in Canadian Tort Law* (1968)

Hence the real burden of deterrence appears to be thrown on the law of torts. Now tort law, ordinarily, appears to be institutionally unsuited for its so-called "admonitory" function. Imposition of sanctions depends on the fact of somebody being hurt, not just a breach of the rules, on the person hurt making the unilateral decision to seek legal redress, and on the effectiveness of his resources alone to establish the breach. The sanction itself is not rationally related to the enormity of the defendant's conduct but rather to the seriousness of the plaintiff's loss. Reasons such as these, together with other inadequacies in this junction of civil and criminal law, *e.g.*, burden of proof, double jeopardy, windfall to the plaintiff, etc., have led to a radical decrease, in England, of the incidence of punitive damages in tort cases (although not "aggravated" damages). The ruling in *Rookes* v. *Barnard,* however, does not appear to strike at the use of punitive tort damages to sanction abuses of police arrest powers. Moreover, the arguments are not necessarily decisive when countervailing considerations are articulated. There are a vast number of occasions in our society when wilful abuse of discretionary power, both public and private, inflicts substantial, but not inordinate, harm on individuals. Taken by itself no such instance appears to warrant the use of the overworked criminal process as a sanction. However, collectively, such instances could render social life quite intolerable if we had to depend on purely voluntary adherence to legal and social mores. The *least deficient* of all solutions may well be punitive tort law. This confers on private individuals the competence to decide whether they have been hurt enough by some such abuse to make them want to undertake the trouble and expense of inflicting a necessary penalty on the defendant. Allowing punitive damages may well be considered a tolerable incentive, however deficient in relation to a utopian ideal, to increase the incidence of such legal actions and penalties.

However, it must be recognized that there are substantial institutional difficulties in using tort law as a means for achieving the ends for which we strive. These stem primarily from the fact that tort law operates after the fact of the breach to award a monetary amount to the plaintiff, in some way related to his loss. This is quite an adequate process when the harm for which the award is made is in some way economic (either out-of-pocket expenses, loss of profits, loss of earning capacity, etc.), and can be rationally reduced into pecuniary terms, but these conditions rarely exist here. . . .

A simple remedy to this problem has been suggested to remove the occasion for such prejudice and to enhance the effectiveness of the tort remedy by creating a substantial incentive for its use. Not only should the full solicitor-client costs be awarded (and legal aid provided liberally for those unable to afford counsel), but also a minimum figure ($1,000; $5,000) should be legally required in any judgment where an illegal abuse of police power is found, which should be awarded against both the officer and the public body which employs him. This proposal demonstrates in the most blatant form the change in the function of the tort law suit, from compensation to punishment. In effect, the legislature is asked to create a monetary fine to be enforced by a private individual who is affected by the official's unlawful conduct. Such a device is not unheard of in the law, as is shown by the analogous example of the "informer's share" or triple damage suits in antitrust cases. If it is frankly recognized that this is what we are doing, we must ask the question of whether the civil or criminal burden of proof is most appropriate and how we can insure that the officer will not be unfairly subjected to "double jeopardy". Is the conduct of the officer sufficiently "outrageous" that it should warrant such a penalty?

It may be that such problems are unreal because the officer's employer will pay anyway, especially if made strictly and/or vicariously liable. Seen from this perspective, the suggested basis of the tort action becomes "enterprise liability". There are two important social purposes served by a system of enterprise liability in tort, whose theoretical validity I have assessed elsewhere. Suffice it for now to say that the policies of both risk distribution and general deterrence are relevant to governmental liability for police torts. The justification for risk distribution in this context is that, instead of the losses due to mistakes in the enforcement of criminal justice being borne completely by the innocent victim, they should be distributed in small portions over a large group of taxpayers who support the police officer's employer. There are two problems in the policy of risk distribution: first, why single out the victims of this type of loss as the beneficiaries of compulsory governmental insurance; second, why make the innocent taxpayer the victim even of a small portion of a loss which is no-one's fault, rather than treating it as one of the inevitable costs of living in an organized society.

It is here that the policy of general deterrence enters, as a buttress for the legal regime of enterprise liability. Losses (economic, physical and psychic) caused by mistaken arrests are an inevitable (almost statistically predictable) incident to the administration of justice. If they are borne by the scattered, innocent victims of this activity or enterprise, then the latter is subsidized to a certain extent. Some of the actual costs of various types of police practices are hidden from the sight of those who make the judgment that such practices are desirable. For instance, if one of the reasons for the use of arrests rather than summons (where the latter is feasible on legitimate law enforcement grounds) is the extra cost in police resources of obtaining, serving and certifying a summons, the rational allocation of the costs of law enforcement is distorted when the extra cost to citizens of arrest is not put in the balance. Hence enterprise liability, by imposing the costs of obtaining a lawyer, posting bail, etc. on governmental unit, gives the latter the incentive to analyse the different possible enforcement practices in the light of *all* of the social costs of each. The result will be "general deterrence" of any one type of activity to precisely the extent which is desirable in the light of the relative benefits to be achieved. The taxpayer to whom the loss is distributed receives the benefits of the law enforcement practices to which it is necessarily incident. Hence it is fair to ask him to bear the costs of the activity to the extent to which his representatives feel it is still rational to engage in a particular practice.

There are logical problems in the reasoning behind enterprise liability. I have concluded elsewhere that such a basis for strict liability may be appropriate where we feel that some patterns of activity are unnecessarily dangerous or involve unreasonably excessive costs, that reasonable substitutes are available but are not employed because of reluctance to shoulder the immediate extra cost to the enterprise, and that imposing all of the costs on the activity would be an effective lever to overcome this reluctance, and thus substantially reduce the total social costs of the practice. Strict liability also assumes that the social costs of an activity cannot meaningfully be minimized by "specific deterrence" of instances of faulty conduct within the activity, *via* individually-directed sanctions. It appears to me that these conditions for enterprise liability may well obtain as far as police enforcement practices are concerned, at least with regard to the economic costs of this activity (lost wages, legal fees, etc.).

It should be recognized, though, that we are using tort law to impose a tax which it is hoped will induce a desired redirection of human conduct, and this involves problems of both fairness and efficiency. The tax must be distributed among those citizens who benefit in a significant way from the particular law enforcement system to which the tort losses are incident. Moreover, those who are responsible for the institution of different types of enforcement practice must be confronted with the tort bill when they make their institutional decisions. Hence, a recent proposal to shift the tax burden for the administration of justice from a municipality to the province of Ontario, if it would include these costs of arrest practices, would seriously threaten a fair and efficient allocation of the risk.

JOSEPH A. PAGE, OF MACE AND MEN: TORT LAW AS A MEANS OF CONTROLLING DOMESTIC CHEMICAL WARFARE

(1969), 57 Georgetown L.J. 1238

The hazards created by the public sale of chemical sprays may be said to constitute a consumer protection problem and hence raise issues which are politically popular and "safe" for legislators and administrators. Existing state and federal laws provide a basis for the exercise of some degree of regulation over these weapons. Additional federal legislation may be forthcoming. The use of sprays by the police presents a considerably more difficult problem. There are no laws regulating the manufacture or use of police sprays, and the present delicacy of the "law-and-order" issue militates against the passage of such legislation.

This leaves the courts as a final barrier to the unfettered production and use of chemical sprays for law enforcement. The judicial process has the capability to provide a forum both for the dispassionate resolution of the factual issues which underlie the MACE controversy and for the imposition of rational public restraints upon the manufacture and use of these weapons. The substantive rules to be applied in damage actions and suits for equitable relief provide an adequate means of achieving these results. How judges and jurors will apply these rules is the crucial question. Whether the courts will accept the challenge and the extent to which the judicial process can regulate the utilization of chemical warfare technology by domestic law enforcement agencies will reflect to a significant degree the law's role and relevance in dealing with the pressures which are presently straining at the seams of the American social fabric.

NOTES ON TRESPASS AB INITIO

Professor Fleming, in his *Law of Torts* (5th ed., 1977) describes the doctrine as follows:

"... a person who entered another's land by authority of law and subsequently abused his privilege by committing an affirmative tort to the person, chattels or land of the possessor, forfeited his immunity for the original lawful entry. By fiction, he was retrospectively treated as if he had been a trespasser from the outset, however innocent his conduct up to the moment of his default."

There were three limitations upon the rule. First, it was confined to licences given by law and not extended to any granted by the possessor himself. See *Delta Hotels* v. *Magrum* (1976), 52 D.L.R. (3d) 126 (B.C.S.C.). This has been justified on the ground that, as a landowner may choose his own licensee, he should assume the risk that the privilege might be abused. The more convincing reason, however, is that the doctrine was intended primarily to curb abuses of authority by public officials which might lead to the oppression of the subject.

Secondly the doctrine was applied only to acts of misfeasance as distinct from mere omissions. Thus in the leading case which established the doctrine, six carpenters entered an inn, and after consuming bread and wine, refused to pay their bill of eightpence. This was held not to be a trespass *ab initio,* 'because not doing is no trespass'.

Thirdly the scope of the rule was substantially circumscribed by holding it inapplicable to cases where the original entry can be justified on an independent ground to which the abuse has no reference.

The doctrine has been condemned everywhere and may even be dead. In *Chic Fashions (West Wales) Ltd.* v. *Jones,* [1968] 2 W.L.R. 201 (C.A.), the court dismissed an action against police who entered premises under a search warrant and seized goods that were not covered by the warrant. Denning M.R. said that "at one time a man could be made a trespasser *ab initio* by the doctrine of relation back. But that is no longer true. . . . [The doctrine] was a by-product of the old forms of action. Now that they are buried, it can be interred with their bones."

REVIEW PROBLEMS

1. While on her way to the corner of Eglinton and Yonge Street where she planned to spend the morning selling copies of Watchtower and Awake, Penny, a devout Jehovah's Witness, negligently slipped and fell cutting herself severely. Penny lay there in a pool of blood calling for someone to telephone the J.W. Ambulance Service, a service owned by Jehovah's Witnesses. An ambulance soon arrived but it had "AAA Ambulance" written on the side of it. Penny saw this sign as the men came for her with the stretcher and declared, "I will not go into your ambulance. I want J.W. and I want to go to the J.W. Hospital for Jehovah's Witnesses". Just then Penny fainted from loss of blood. The A.A.A. attendants placed the unconscious Penny on the stretcher and into the ambulance and rushed her to the nearest hospital, the T.G. Hospital.

Penny came to in the emergency room as Donald, an intern, approached her with the blood transfusion equipment. She looked around, realized that she was not in the J.W. Hospital and what was about to happen and objected, "I am a Jehovah's Witness and would rather die than take a blood transfusion. Let me out of here and get me to the J.W.!" She fainted again from loss of blood. Donald, assessing rightly that this woman was doomed without an immediate transfusion, administered the required blood which saved Penny's life, sewed up the cut she suffered, put her into a private room and called Penny's husband, Paul.

Paul arrived with a J.W. ambulance, went up to Penny's room and angrily demanded his wife's release.

When Donald appeared, he stated that she could not be released unless the hospital bill of $35 was paid first. Paul refused to pay and insisted upon the immediate release of Penny, who was now awake and overheard everything. When Donald refused again, Paul picked up his wife and triumphantly carried her out to the waiting J.W. ambulance. What tort liabilities have arisen?

2. Penelope was a photography bug who loved to take pictures of Ontario scenery. One Sunday she drove down to the Scarborough Bluffs and began to take pictures. She noticed that one particularly fantastic view of the coastline might be seen from inside the confines of one of the private dwellings along the coast owned by Dimwit. Desperately wanting this photograph for a contest that she had entered, Penelope parked her car and sneaked up to the high fence that surrounded the property. She noticed two signs on the fence. One read: "Trespassers will be shot." and the other stated: "This fence is electrically charged — Beware."

Penelope was undeterred, mainly because she was incredulous. She reached over and touched the fence prior to climbing over it, but received a slight jolt of electrical juice. Penelope then got wise; she put on a pair of rubber gloves and shoes and, thus insulated, climbed over the fence. When she alighted on the other side, she hurried over to the edge of the cliff and took some glorious photographs.

Suddenly she heard a voice behind her say that, "If you are not off my land in one minute, I shall blow your brains out." Penelope wheeled around and observed Dimwit standing there menacingly with a large shotgun aimed at her. Realizing that Dimwit meant business, Penelope sprinted back to the fence, received another electric jolt because she forgot to put her rubber gloves and shoes back on, and finally climbed back over to safety.

What tort liabilities, if any, have arisen?

CHAPTER 4

NEGLIGENCE: THE STANDARD OF CARE

Negligence is by far the most important field of tort liability at present. Its principles regulate most of the activities of our society. Tort lawyers spend most of their time working on negligence actions. It is, therefore, understandable why the bulk of this book deals with problems of negligence law.

Negligence is not a state of mind but conduct which falls below the standard accepted in the community. There is not a single nominate tort of negligence; rather negligence is a basis of liability which protects some interests and not others.

The word negligence has two meanings, a restricted one and a broader one. In its narrow sense, it refers to certain *conduct* that falls below the standard required by society. In this context, negligence connotes more than a mere state of mind. The second and wider meaning of negligence makes reference to a *cause of action for negligence*. Negligence in the first sense is only one fragment of this expanded meaning of negligence.

To establish a cause of action for negligence several elements must be present. There is disagreement, however, over the number of these components. Perhaps the most commonly accepted formulation has been called the "A.B.C. rule". According to this rule, a plaintiff in a negligence action is entitled to succeed if he is able to establish three things to the satisfaction of the court: (A) a duty of care exists; (B) there has been a breach of that duty; and (C) damage has resulted from that breach. This is the traditional English approach to negligence liability, and it has been repeated countless times in the cases. The trouble with the A.B.C. rule is its beguiling simplicity. It blurs together issues that should not be treated under one rubric. Complexities that should be illuminated are disguised. Thus, when the English courts are forced to consider the problem of the extent of liability, none of the three elements seem to cover the issue satisfactorily. Duty, remoteness and proximate cause may be utilized interchangeably without any explanation.

Professor Gibson, in his perceptive article, "A New Alphabet of Negligence", in Linden, *Studies in Canadian Tort Law* (1968) attacked the traditional A.B.C. Rule. He proposes instead to utilize the "functional type of analysis often employed in other areas of tort". The three main variables, according to Professor Gibson, are: (1) the type of conduct involved; (2) the degree of mental participation required of the defendant; and (3) the nature of the detriment suffered by the plaintiff. Professor Gibson's new "analytical trinity" is a valiant attempt to restructure negligence law. He may succeed one day, but it would be unwise to be overly optimistic.

Another division of the subject of negligence is that advocated by the American scholars. They suggest that there are four elements in a cause of action for negligence: (1) duty; (2) failure to conform to the standard required; (3) a reasonably close causal connection between the conduct and the resulting injury, sometimes termed "proximate cause"; (4) actual loss or damage resulting to the interest of another. This categorization also produces difficulties. A court sometimes handles the proximate cause question in terms of duty or remoteness, which leads to a blending of the first and third elements. Similarly, a court sometimes confuses the first and second components. Another deficiency is that this approach neglects the consideration of the conduct of the plaintiff, as an element to be assessed in the process. Professor Fleming, in his masterful text, overcomes this last criticism by adumbrating five elements of a cause of action for negligence. To the four listed above, he adds a fifth component, the absence of any conduct by the injured party which would preclude him from recovering. Consequently, the defences of contributory negligence and voluntary assumption of risk are considered as one of the five elements.

This work will utilize a six-part division of negligence in order to facilitate an examination of the subject from all possible angles. A cause of action for negligence arises if the following elements are present: (1) the defendant's conduct must be negligent, that is, in breach of the standard of care set by the law; (2) the claimant must suffer some damage; (3) the damage suffered must be caused by the negligent conduct of the defendant; (4) there must be a duty recognized by the law to avoid this damage; (5) the conduct of the defendant must be a proximate cause of the loss or, stated in another way, the damage should not be too remote a result of the defendant's conduct; (6) the conduct of the plaintiff should not be such as to bar his recovery, that is, he must not be guilty of contributory negligence and he must not voluntarily assume the risk.

A. UNREASONABLE RISK

BOLTON & OTHERS v. STONE

House of Lords. [1951] A.C. 850; [1951] 1 All E.R. 1078

The defendants were the committee and members of a cricket club. During a match, a batsman hit a ball which went over a fence seven feet high and 17 feet above the cricket pitch, and hit the plaintiff who was standing on the adjoining highway. The distance to the fence from the batsman was 78 yards and, to where the plaintiff was hit, 100 yards. The ground had been used for about 90 years and no one had been injured before in this way, although on about six occasions over a period of 30 years a ball had been hit into the highway. A witness, Mr. Brownson, said that five or six times during the last few years a ball had hit his house or come into his yard. His house was closer to the cricket grounds than the spot where the plaintiff was hit. The plaintiff brought action for damages for negligence and nuisance. At the trial her claim was dismissed on the ground that there was no evidence of negligence and nuisance was not established. On appeal to the Court of Appeal judgment was given the plaintiff on the basis of negligence, Somervell L.J. dissenting. The majority held ([1949] 2 All E.R. 851), there was a foreseeable risk of a ball being hit in to the road and defendants had failed to take reasonable care to avoid injury to anyone in the road. The defendant appealed. In the House of Lords the plaintiff conceded that unless negligence were established, the claim in nuisance must fail.

Lord Reid: My Lords, it was readily foreseeable that an accident such as befell the respondent might possibly occur during one of the appellants' cricket matches. Balls had been driven into the public road from time to time, and it was obvious that if a person happened to be where a ball fell that person would receive injuries which might or might not be serious. On the other hand, it was plain that the chance of that happening was small. The exact number of times a ball has been driven into the road is not known, but it is not proved that this has happened more than about six times in about 30 years. If I assume that it has happened on the average once in three seasons I shall be doing no injustice to the respondent's case. Then there has to be considered the chance of a person being hit by a ball falling in the road. The road appears to be an ordinary side road giving access to a number of private houses, and there is no evidence to suggest that the traffic on this road is other than what one might expect on such a road. On the whole of that part of the road where a ball could fall there would often be nobody and seldom any great number of people. It follows that the chance of a person ever being struck even in a long period of years was very small.

This case, therefore, raises sharply the question what is the nature and extent of the duty of a person who promotes on his land operations which may cause damage to persons on an adjoining highway. Is it that he must not carry out or permit an operation which he knows or ought to know clearly can cause such damage, however improbable that result may be, or is it that he is only bound to take into account the possibility of such damage if such damage is a likely or probable consequence of what he does or permits, or if the risk of damage is such that a reasonable man, careful of the safety of his neighbour, would regard that risk as material? I do not know of any case where this question has had to be decided or even where it has been fully discussed. Of course there are many cases in which somewhat similar questions have arisen, but, generally speaking, if injury to another person from the defendant's acts is reasonably foreseeable the chance that injury will result is substantial and it does not matter in which way the duty is stated . . . .

I think that reasonable men do, in fact, take into account the degree of risk and do not act on a bare possibility as they would if the risk were more substantial . . . . For example, in *Fardon* v. *Harcourt-Rivington*, 146 L.T. 391, Lord Dunedin said: "This is such an extremely unlikely event that I do not think any reasonable man could be convicted of negligence if he did not take into account the possibility of such an occurrence and provide against it . . . people must guard against reasonable probabilities, but they are not bound to guard against fantastic possibilities."

I doubt whether Lord Dunedin meant the division into reasonable proba- bilities and fantastic possibilities to be exhaustive so that anything more than a fantastic possibility must be regarded as a reasonable probability. What happened in that case was that a dog left in a car broke the window and a splinter from the glass entered the plaintiff's eye. Before that had happened it might well have been described as a fantastic possibility and Lord Dunedin did not have to consider a case nearer the border-line . . . .

Counsel for the respondent in the present case had to put his case so high as to say that, at least as soon as one ball had been driven into the road in the ordinary course of a match, the appellants could and should have realized that that might happen again, and that, if it did, someone might be injured, and that that was enough to put on the appellants a duty to take steps to prevent such an occurrence. If the true test is foreseeability alone I think that must be so. Once a ball has been driven on to a road without there being anything extra- ordinary to account for the fact, there is clearly a risk that another will follow and if it does there is clearly a chance, small though it may be, that somebody may be injured. On the theory that it is foreseeability alone that matters it would be irrelevant to consider how often a ball might be expected to land on the road and it would not matter whether the road was the busiest street or the quietest country lane. The only difference between these cases is in the degree of risk. It would take a good deal to make me believe that the law has departed so far from the standards which guide ordinary careful people in ordinary life. In the crowded conditions of modern life even the most careful person cannot avoid creating some risks and accepting others. What a man must not do, and what I think a careful man tries not to do, is to create a risk which is substantial . . . . In my judgment, the test to be applied here is whether the risk of damage to a person on the road was so small that a reasonable man in the position of the appellants, considering the matter from the point of view of safety, would have thought it right to refrain from taking steps to prevent the danger. In considering that matter I think that it would be right to take into account, not only how remote is the chance that a person might be struck, but also how serious the consequences are likely to be if a person is struck, but I do not think that it would be right to take into account the difficulty of remedial measures. If cricket cannot be played on a ground without creating a substantial risk, then it should not be played there at all. I think that this is in substance the test which Oliver J. applied in this case. He considered whether the appellants' ground was large enough to be safe for all practical purposes and held that it was. This is a question, not of law, but of fact and degree. It is not an easy question, and it is one on which opinions may well differ. I can only say that, having given the whole matter repeated and anxious consideration, I find myself unable to decide this question in favour of the respondent. I think, however, that this case is not far from the border-line. If this appeal is allowed, that does not, in my judgment, mean that in every case where cricket has been played on a ground for a number of years without accident or complaint those who organize matches there are safe to go on in reliance on past immunity. I would have reached a different conclusion if I had thought that the risk here had been other than extremely small because I do not think that a reasonable man, considering the matter from the point of view of safety, would or should disregard any risk unless it is extremely small . . . . In my judgment, the appeal should be allowed.

NOTES

1. What are the factors that the court took into account in deciding that the risk created was not an unreasonable one? Why did the court refuse to take into account the difficulty of remedial measures? Do you think this factor should be worthy of some weight? Did the court really fail to consider it?

2. Would the court have reached the same conclusion if the ball went over the fence 6 times a year? 6 times a day? 6 times an hour? Would it make any difference if the cricket pitch adjoined Picadilly Circus?

3. Would the court have reached the same conclusion if, instead of a cricket ball, the offending object was a bullet or a stick of dynamite?

4. Professor John Fleming has written that "not only the greater risk of injury, but also the risk of greater injury is a relevant factor". See Fleming, *The Law of Torts* (5th ed., 1977), p. 115.

5. What does the court mean when it talks about a "reasonable probability"? Does it mean 51 percent? 25 percent? 10 percent? Can one chance in a thousand be considered a "reasonable probability"?

Consider the statement by Lord Reid in *Southern Portland Cement Ltd.* v. *Cooper*, [1974] 2 W.L.R. 152 (P.C.):

"Chance probability or likelihood is always a matter of degree. It is rarely capable of precise assessment. Many different expressions are in common use. It can be said that the occurrence of a future event is very likely, rather likely, more probable than not, not unlikely, quite likely, not improbable, more than a mere possibility, etc."

6. One need not weep for Mrs. Stone, who was paid her damages and costs by the defendants following the decision in her favour by the Court of Appeal. After the House of Lords reversed the decision, the defendants, who were supported by the cricketers association in conducting the litigation because they felt an important principle was involved, decided not to pursue Mrs. Stone for repayment of the money they had paid to her. Mrs. Stone had to pay her own costs in the House of Lords, however. See Note (1952), 68 L.Q.R. 3. Do you believe that there was a matter of important principle involved here? See also concerning the problem of injunction *Miller and another* v. *Jackson and another*, [1977] 3 All E.R. 338 (C.A.).

7. In *Paris* v. *Stepney Borough Council*, [1951] A.C. 367, [1951] 1 All E.R. 42, the plaintiff was employed in the defendant's garage. To the defendant's knowledge he had the use of only one eye. While using a hammer to remove a bolt on the undercarriage of a truck, a chip of metal flew into his good eye with the result that he became totally blind. The plaintiff claimed damages alleging negligence in the failure of the defendant to supply him with goggles. The evidence was overwhelming that the usual practice in trades of this nature was not to supply goggles for men engaged in this work, at least if they were two-eyed men. At the trial plaintiff recovered. The Court of Appeal, [1949] 2 All E.R. 843, reversed this judgment. Accepting the evidence of the trade as indicating that to normal employees the defendant owed no duty to supply goggles because the risk was not one against which a reasonable employer was bound to take precautions, the court held that the plaintiff's disability could be relevant only if it increased the risk. Asquith L.J. stated: "A one-eyed man is no more likely to get a splinter or a chip in his eye than is a two-eyed man. This risk is no greater, but the damage is greater to a man using his only good eye . . . *quantum* of damage is one thing . . . scope of duty is another. The greater risk of injury is not the same thing as the risk of greater injury, and the first thing seems to me relevant here." The House of Lords (3:2) reversed the judgment of the Court of Appeal holding that the gravity of the harm likely to be caused would influence a reasonable man and, therefore, even though no duty was owed a two-eyed man, the duty of care to a one-eyed employee should require the supply of goggles. In considering negligence, two factors must be considered: the magnitude of the risk and the likelihood of injury being caused. The dissenting law lords felt that loss of an eye to a two-eyed man was so serious that there should be liability to all employees, two- or one-eyed, or to none at all. It was not a case of trivial as against grave injury.

8. The great American Justice Learned Hand attempted to explain the concept of unreasonable risk in terms of a mathematical equation in *United States* v. *Carroll Towing Co.* (1947), 159 F. 2d 169:

"[T]he owner's duty, as in other similar situations, to provide against resulting injuries, is a function of three variables: (1) The probability that she [a barge tied to a dock] will break away; (2) the gravity of the resulting injury, if she does; (3) the burden of adequate precautions. Possibly it serves to bring this notion into relief to state it in algebraic terms: if the probability be called P; the injury L; and the burden B; liability depends upon whether B is less than L multiplied by P; *i.e.*, whether B is less than PL."

Does this cast any additional light on the problem? Is the burden side of the equation sufficiently broken down? Would it be preferable to split up the burden element (B) into object and cost (OC)? See Linden, *Canadian Tort Law* (1977), p. 83.

9. See Posner, *Economic Analysis of Law* (1972), p. 69, referring to Judge Learned Hand's formula:

"This is an economic test. The burden of precautions is the cost of avoiding the accident. The loss multiplied by the probability of the accident is the cost that the precautions would have averted. If a larger cost could have been avoided by incurring a smaller cost, efficiency requires that the smaller cost be incurred."

Should decisions such as these be made on the basis of an economic test?

PRIESTMAN v. COLANGELO & SMYTHSON

Supreme Court of Canada. [1959] S.C.R. 615; 19 D.L.R. (2d) 1

Cartwright J. (dissenting): On August 1, 1955, Smythson, then 17 years of age, stole a new Buick automobile, which was red in colour and bore dealers' licence plates, from a dealer's lot on Danforth Ave. in the Township of East York. Priestman, the appellant, a police officer of the township, was in a police car driven by his senior, Constable Ainsworth. They were on patrol duty when, shortly before 8.30 p.m. while it was still broad daylight, they received a message on the radio telephone reporting the theft and giving the description and licence number of the stolen car. Almost immediately they saw a motor vehicle which they believed to be — and which later turned out to be — the stolen vehicle, driven by Smythson. The stolen vehicle was travelling west on Cosburn, turned south at the intersection with Donlands and continued southerly on Donlands Ave. at about 20 m.p.h. It came to a stop about 2 ft. from the west curb by reason of a red traffic light at the corner of Donlands and Mortimer Aves. The police car pulled up alongside the stolen car and Priestman ordered Smythson to stop. Both officers were in uniform and Smythson, no doubt, realized that they were police officers. Instead of stopping he pulled around the corner quickly and drove west on Mortimer Ave. at a high rate of speed. The police car followed and on three occasions attempted to pass the stolen car in order to cut it off, but each time Smythson pulled to the south side of the road and cut off the police car. On the third occasion the police car was forced over the south curb on to the boulevard and was compelled to slow up in order to avoid colliding with a hydro pole on the boulevard. Following this third attempt and as the police car went back on to the road, Priestman fired a warning shot from his .38 calibre revolver into the air. The stolen car increased its speed and when the police car was one and a half to two car lengths from the stolen car Priestman aimed at the left rear tire of the stolen car and fired. The bullet hit the bottom of the frame of the rear window, shattered the glass, ricocheted and struck Smythson in the back of the neck, causing him to lose consciousness immediately. The stolen car went over the curb on the south side of the road, grazed a hydro pole, crossed Woodycrest Ave. — an intersecting street — went over the curb on the southwest corner, through a low hedge about 2 ft. high, struck the verandah of the house, coming to a stop somewhere near the northwest corner of the house. On its course along the side of the house it struck and killed Columba Colangelo and Josephine Shynall, who were waiting for a bus.

On October 14, 1955, the administrator of Josephine Shynall commenced an action against Smythson and Priestman claiming damages under the Fatal Accidents Act, R.S.O. 1950, c. 132. On November 8, 1955, the administrator of Columba Colangelo commenced a similar action. On February 1, 1956, Smythson commenced an action against Priestman for damages for personal injuries. As mentioned above, these three actions were tried together.

The learned trial judge was of opinion that Smythson's action against Priestman failed on two grounds, (i) that the force used by Priestman was not more than was necessary to prevent Smythson's escape by flight and that Priestman was justified in firing as he did by the terms of s. 25 (4) of the Criminal Code, and (ii) that the action, not having been commenced within 6 months of the act complained of, was barred by s. 11 of the Public Authorities Protection Act, R.S.O. 1950, c. 303.

Smythson's appeal in that action was dismissed. All members of the Court of Appeal agreed with the learned trial judge as to the second ground on which he proceeded. Laidlaw J.A. was also of opinion that Priestman was justified in using his revolver to prevent Smythson's escape and had acted without negligence. No appeal was taken by Smythson from the judgment of the Court of Appeal in that action.

In the Shynall and Colangelo actions the learned trial judge held (i) that the fatalities were caused by the negligence of Smythson, and (ii) that Priestman was justified in using the force he did use and that as against him the actions must be dismissed. In each action he assessed the damages at $1,250 and gave judgment accordingly against Smythson for the amount with costs, dismissed the action as against Priestman with costs and directed that the plaintiff should add to his judgment against Smythson the costs payable by him to Priestman.

From these judgments the plaintiffs and Smythson appealed to the Court of Appeal, the plaintiffs asking that Priestman also be found negligent and that the damages be increased, and Smythson asking that he be absolved from the finding of negligence made against him and that Priestman be found solely to blame for the fatalities.

The Court of Appeal were unanimous in upholding the finding that Smythson was guilty of negligence causing the fatalities and in refusing to increase the damages awarded. The majority held that Priestman also was guilty of negligence and that the blame should be apportioned equally between Smythson and Priestman. Laidlaw J.A., dissenting in part, would have dismissed the appeal. In the result, judgment was directed to be entered in each action against Smythson and Priestman jointly and severally for $1,250 damages and providing that as between them each should be liable to the extent of 50%.

From these judgments Priestman appeals to this court, pursuant to special leave granted by the Court of Appeal, asking that the judgment of the learned trial judge be restored. The plaintiff in each action cross-appeals asking that the damages be increased. Smythson cross-appeals in each action asking that he be absolved from the finding of negligence made against him and that Priestman be held solely to blame.

At the conclusion of the argument of Smythson's counsel on his cross-appeal, the court was unanimously of opinion that the finding of negligence against Smythson should not be disturbed and counsel for the other parties were not called upon on that point.

Two main grounds are urged in support of Priestman's appeal: first, that Priestman, in firing his revolver as he did, used only as much force as was necessary to prevent the escape of Smythson by flight, that his escape could not have been prevented by reasonable means in a less violent manner, that Priestman was therefore justified in acting as he did by s. 25 (4) of the Criminal Code, that that justification relieved him from civil liability not only as regards Smythson but also as regards the plaintiffs, and that the Court of Appeal erred in holding that the question whether he was liable to the plaintiffs fell to be decided in accordance with the rules of the common law as to the duty of reasonable care; secondly, that even if the Court of Appeal were right in holding that the last-mentioned question fell to be decided in accordance with the rules of the common law as to the duty of reasonable care, they erred in holding that Priestman had acted negligently. . . .

It is clear that Priestman was a peace officer who was proceeding lawfully to arrest Smythson, without warrant, for an offence for which he might be arrested without warrant, and that Smythson had taken to flight to avoid arrest; Priestman was therefore justified in using as much force as was necessary to prevent the escape by flight unless the escape could be prevented by reasonable means in a less violent manner. . . . For the purposes of this branch of the matter, I will assume, without deciding, that Smythson's escape could not have been prevented by reasonable means in a less violent manner and that

as between Priestman and Smythson the former was justified in using his
revolver as he did. . . .

The question of difficulty is whether the justification afforded by the subsection is intended to operate only as between the peace officer and the
offender who is in flight or to extend to injuries inflicted, by the force used for
the purpose of apprehending the offender, upon innocent bystanders unconnected with the flight or pursuit otherwise than by the circumstance of their
presence in the vicinity. The words of the subsection appear to me to be
susceptible of either interpretation and that being so I think we ought to
ascribe to them the more restricted meaning. In my opinion, if Parliament
intended to enact that grievous bodily harm or death might be inflicted upon
an entirely innocent person and that such person or his dependants should be
deprived of all civil remedies to which they would otherwise have been
entitled, in circumstances such as are present in this case, it would have used
words declaring such intention without any possible ambiguity. . . .

I conclude that the first main ground upon which Priestman's appeal is
based fails and pass to the second, which raises the question whether the two
fatalities were contributed to by negligence on the part of Priestman.

Under s. 45 of the Police Act, R.S.O. 1950, c. 279, Priestman was charged
with the duty of apprehending Smythson. . . . This duty to apprehend was not,
in my opinion, an absolute one to the performance of which Priestman was
bound regardless of the consequences to persons other than Smythson. Co-
existent with the duty to apprehend Smythson was the fundamental duty
alterum non laedere, not to do an act which a reasonable man placed in
Priestman's position should have foreseen was likely to cause injury to persons
in the vicinity.

The identity of the persons likely to be injured or the precise manner in
which the injuries would be caused, of course, could not be foreseen; but, in
my opinion, that the car driven by Smythson would go out of control as a
result of the shot fired by Priestman was not "a mere possibility which would
never occur to the mind of a reasonable man" — to use the words of Lord
Dunedin in *Fardon v. Harcourt-Rivington* (1932), 146 L.T. 391, at p. 392 — it
was rather a reasonable probability; that causing a car travelling at a speed of
over 60 m.p.h. on a street such as Mortimer Ave. to be suddenly thrown out of
control would result in injury to persons who happened to be upon the street
also seems to me to be a probability and not a mere possibility. To hold, as has
been done by all the Judges who have dealt with this case, that Smythson
should have foreseen the harm which was caused and at the same time to hold
Priestman ought not to have foreseen it would, it seems to me, involve an inconsistency. In my opinion, Priestman's act in firing without due regard to the
probabilities mentioned was an effective cause of the fatalities and amounted
to actionable negligence unless it can be said that the existence of the duty to
apprehend Smythson robbed his act of the negligent character it would otherwise have had.

The question which appears to me to be full of difficulty is how far, if at all,
the duty which lay upon Priestman to apprehend Smythson required him to
take, or justified him in taking, some risk of inflicting injury on innocent persons. Two principles are here in conflict, the one *alterum non laedere,* above
referred to, the other *salus populi est suprema lex.* It is undoubtedly in the
public interest than an escaping criminal be apprehended and the question is to
what extent innocent citizens may be called upon to suffer, without redress, in
order that that end may be achieved. In spite of the diligence of counsel, little
helpful authority has been brought to our attention. I have already made it
clear that for the purposes of this branch of the matter I am assuming that

Priestman could not have prevented Smythson's escape otherwise than by firing his revolver, and, on this assumption, it appears to me that the question for the court is: "Should a reasonable man in Priestman's position have refrained from firing although that would result in Smythson escaping, or should he have fired although foreseeing the probability that grave injury would result therefrom to innocent persons?" I do not think an answer can be given which would fit all situations. The officer should, I think, consider the gravity of the offence of which the fugitive is believed to be guilty and the likelihood of danger to other citizens if he remains at liberty; the reasons in favour of firing would obviously be far greater in the case of an armed robber who has already killed to facilitate his flight than in the case of an unarmed youth who has stolen a suitcase which he has abandoned in the course of running away. In the former case it might well be the duty of the officer to fire if it seemed probable that this would bring down the murderer even though the firing were attended by risks to other persons on the street. In the latter case he ought not, in my opinion, to fire if to do so would be attended by any foreseeable risk of injury to innocent persons.

In the particular circumstances of the case at bar I have, although not without hesitation, reached the conclusion that Priestman ought not to have fired as he did and that he was guilty of negligence in so doing. . . .

I would dismiss the appeals with costs and the cross-appeals without costs.

Locke J.: The performance of the duty imposed upon police officers to arrest offenders who have committed a crime and are fleeing to avoid arrest may, at times and of necessity, involve risk of injury to other members of the community. Such risk, in the absence of a negligent or unreasonable exercise of such duty, is imposed by the statute and any resulting damage is in my opinion, *damnum sine injuria.* In the article in the last edition of *Broom's Legal Maxims,* p. 1, dealing with the maxim *salus populi est suprema lex* where the passage from the judgment of Buller J. in the *British Cast Plate* case is referred to, the learned author says: "This phrase is based on the implied agreement of every member of society that his own individual welfare shall, in cases of necessity, yield to that of the community; and that his property, liberty, and life shall, under certain circumstances, be placed in jeopardy or even sacrificed for the public good."

Assuming a case where a police officer sees a pickpocket stealing from a person in a crowd upon the street and the pickpocket flees through the crowd in the hope of escaping arrest, if the officer in pursuit unintentionally collides with some one, is it to be seriously suggested that an action for trespass to the person would lie at the instance of the person struck? Yet, if the test applied in the cases which are relied upon is adopted without restriction, it could be said with reason that the police officer would probably know that, if he ran through a crowd of people in an attempt to arrest a thief, he might well collide with some members of the crowd who did not see him coming. To take another hypothetical case, assume a police officer is pursuing a bank robber known to be armed and with the reputation of being one who will use a gun to avoid capture. The escaping criminal takes refuge in a private house. The officer, knowing that to enter the house through the front door would be to invite destruction, proceeds to the side of the house where through a window he sees the man and fires through the window intending to disable him. Would an action lie at the instance of the owner of the house against the officer for negligently damaging his property? If an escaping bank robber who has murdered a bank employee is fleeing down an uncrowded city street and fires a revolver at the police officers who are pursuing him, should one of the officers return the fire in an attempt to disable the criminal and, failing to hit the man, wound a pedestrian some distance down the street of whose presence he is unaware, is the officer to be found liable for damages or negligence?

The answer to a claim in any of these suppositious cases would be that the act was done in a reasonable attempt by the officer to perform the duty imposed upon him by the Police Act and the Criminal Code, which would be a complete defence, in my opinion. As contrasted with cases such as these, if an escaping criminal ran into a crowd of people and was obscured from the view of a pursuing police officer, it could not be suggested that it would be permissible for the latter to fire through the crowd in the hope of stopping the fleeing criminal.

The difficulty is not in determining the principle of law that is applicable but in applying it in circumstances such as these. . . . Police officers in this country are furnished with fire-arms and these may, in my opinion, be used when, in the circumstances of the particular case, it is reasonably necessary to do so to prevent the escape of a criminal whose actions, as in the present case, constitute a menace to other members of the public. I do not think that these officers having three times attempted to stop the fleeing car by endeavouring to place their car in front of it were under any obligation to again risk their lives by attempting this. No other reasonable or practical means of halting the car has been suggested than to slacken its speed by blowing out one of the tires. . . .

The cause of action pleaded is in negligence which, in the case of an officer attempting to perform his duty in these difficult circumstances, is to be constructed, in my opinion, as meaning that what was done by him was not reasonably necessary and not a reasonable exercise of the constable's powers under s. 25 in the circumstances. As Laidlaw J.A. has pointed out, to find the constable guilty of negligence in the manner in which the revolver was fired, as distinct from firing at all, would necessitate finding that Priestman should have anticipated that his arm might be jolted at the instant he fired. That learned judge was not willing to make that finding nor am I.

I consider that the statement in Broom to which I have referred accurately states the law and that it is applicable in the present circumstances. . . . In my opinion, the action of the appellant in the present matter was reasonably necessary in the circumstances and no more than was reasonably necessary, both to prevent the escape and to protect those persons whose safety might have been endangered if the escaping car reached the intersection with Pape Ave. So far as Priestman was concerned, the fact that the bullet struck Smythson was, in my opinion, simply an accident. As to the loss occasioned by this lamentable occurrence, I consider that no cause of action is disclosed as against the appellant.

For these reasons, I would allow these appeals and set aside the judgments entered in the Court of Appeal. In accordance with the provisions of the orders granting leave to appeal to this court, no costs should be awarded against the respondents Colangelo and Shynall. I would dismiss the cross-appeals without costs. The appeal of Smythson should be dismissed and without costs.

[Taschereau J. agreed with Locke J., Fauteux J. agreed with the result reached by Locke J., and Martland J. concurred with Cartwright J.]

NOTES

1. What were the key factors relied on by the Supreme Court in dismissing the case? How does this treatment compare with the way that the difficulty of remedial measures was handled in *Bolton* v. *Stone*?

2. In *Bittner* v. *Tait-Gibson Optometrists Ltd.* (1964), 44 D.L.R. (2d) 113 (Ont. C.A.), a finding of contributory negligence on the part of the plaintiff, a police officer, who was injured by slipping on ice negligently permitted to accumulate in front of defendant's store was set aside by the Ontario Court of Appeal. At the time of the fall, the plaintiff was moving quickly to the store in the belief that some unauthorized person was in the store. His duty to detect crime and apprehend offenders outweighed any risk of speedy movement. "If there was a risk the end to be achieved outweighed that risk." Do you agree?

3. In *Daborn* v. *Bath Tramways Motor Co. Ltd.*, [1946] 2 All E.R. 333 (C.A.), the plaintiff was driving an ambulance (in England) with a left-hand drive and with a driving mirror on the left-hand side. The ambulance was shut in at the back and this would prevent her seeing anyone about to pass to the right. Unaware of a motor omnibus close behind and about to pass, the plaintiff made a signal with her left hand and started to move to the right. A collision occurred with the omnibus in which the plaintiff was injured. In an action for damages it was found the defendant was negligent and the issue concerned contributory negligence on the plaintiff's part. It was held she was not negligent. *Per* Asquith L.J.: "In determining whether a party is negligent . . . a relevant circumstance . . . may be the importance of the end to be served by behaving in this way or that. As has often been pointed out if all the trains in this country were restricted to a speed of 5 miles an hour there would be fewer accidents but our national life would be intolerably slowed down . . . . During the war . . . it was necessary for many highly important operations to be carried out by means of motor vehicles with left-hand drives, no others being available . . . . It would be demanding too high and an unreasonable standard of care from the drivers of such cars to say to them: 'Either you must give signals which the structure of your vehicle renders impossible or you must not drive at all.' " Do you agree?

4. In *Watt* v. *Hertfordshire County Council*, [1954] 2 All E.R. 368 (C.A.), the defendant's fire station had a heavy jack to be used in case of need. It stood on wheels and only one vehicle was properly equipped to carry it safely and properly. While that vehicle was out on other service an emergency call was received to rescue a woman trapped under a heavy vehicle. The officer in charge ordered the jack loaded on a lorry on which there was no way of properly securing it. On the way to the scene of the accident the driver of the lorry had to stop suddenly and the jack rolled and injured the plaintiff, a foreman, who sued for damages caused by the defendant's negligence in failing to use reasonable care in supplying safe appliances and working conditions. The plaintiff's action failed. *Per* Denning L.J.: "It is well settled that in measuring due care one must balance the risk against the measures necessary to eliminate the risk. To that proposition there ought to be added this. One must balance the risk against the end to be achieved. If this accident had occurred in a commercial enterprise without any emergency, there could be no doubt that the servant would succeed. But the commercial end to make profit is very different from the human end to save life or limb. The saving of life or limb justifies taking considerable risk . . . I quite agree that fire engines, ambulances and doctor's cars should not shoot past the traffic lights when they show a red light. That is because the risk is too great to warrant the incurring of the danger. It is always a question of balancing the risk against the end." Should the existence of an emergency situation be taken into account in determining whether a risk is unreasonable?

5. Are the hypothetical cases posed by Mr. Justice Locke involving the pickpocket and the two bank robbers analogous to the principal case? Would the dissenting judge have disagreed with Mr. Justice Locke's disposition of them? Do you?

6. Do you prefer the majority opinion of Mr. Justice Locke or the dissenting views of Mr. Justice Cartwright? Is the difference between them one of principle or merely in the application of a principle?

7. In *Beim* v. *Goyer* (1966), 57 D.L.R. (2d) 253 (S.C.C.), liability was

imposed when a policeman's gun accidentally fired and struck an unarmed car thief who was being chased on foot over rough ground in circumstances where there was no danger to the policeman.

In *Woodward* v. *Begbie,* [1962] O.R. 60, a similar result ensued when the plaintiff prowler was accidentally shot by one of two policemen who fired their pistols intending to hit the ground near the fleeing suspect. Mr. Justice McLennan stated that, "more force was used than was necessary and the escape could have been prevented by the more reasonable means of overtaking the plaintiff . . .".

Are these two cases consistent with the principal case? See Weiler, "Groping Towards a Canadian Tort Law: The Role of the Supreme Court" (1971), 21 U. of T. L.J. 264.

8. What do you think of the way s. 25 (4) of the Criminal Code was handled by the Supreme Court? It reads as follows:

(4) A peace officer who is proceeding lawfully to arrest, with or without warrant, any person for an offence for which that person may be arrested without warrant, and every one lawfully assisting the peace officer, is justified, if the person to be arrested takes flight to avoid arrest, in using as much force as is necessary to prevent the escape by flight, unless the escape can be prevented by reasonable means in a less violent manner.

Should it be relevant at all in a civil case? See McDonald, "Use of Force by Police to Effect Lawful Arrest" (1966-67), 9 Crim. L.Q. 435.

9. In *Poupart* v. *Lafortune* (1974), 41 D.L.R. (3d) 720 (S.C.C.), the Supreme Court held that s. 25 applied to exempt a police officer from liability for a gun shot wound he accidentally inflicted on an innocent bystander, when some armed robbers opened fire on him after he tried to apprehend them. Fauteux C.J.C. stated:

"First, I should say that if only because of the decision of this Court in the *Priestman* case, *supra*, there is no reason to doubt, in my view, that the justification created by the aforementioned provisions of s. 25 relieves the police officer of any civil or criminal liability, not only in respect of the fugitive but also in respect of any person who accidentally becomes an innocent victim of the force used by such an officer in the circumstances described in those provisions. . . .

. . . in contrast with the driver of an automobile, Lafortune was not engaged merely in performing an act permitted by law, but, which is quite a different matter . . . he was engaged in the hazardous performance of a grave duty imposed on him by law. In carrying out such a duty a peace officer must undoubtedly refrain from making any unjustifiable use of the powers relating to it. . . .

However, while a police officer is not relieved of a duty to take reasonable care, that is care the degree of which must be determined in relation to the particular circumstances of the case to be decided, the actions of Lafortune cannot, in a case like that before the Court, be evaluated as they would be if it were a case in which the precautions to be taken in accordance with the duty not to injure others were not conditioned by the requirements of a public duty. In short, the police officer incurs no liability for damage caused to another when without negligence he does precisely what the legislature requires him to do: see *Priestman* case, *supra*. Interpreted otherwise the justification provided by s. 25 (4) would be reduced to a nullity."

How does this case fit in with the above cases? If the court had found Lafortune negligent, would s. 25 have been of any help to him? What is the effect of s. 25 in tort cases?

10. In *Howley* v. *The Queen* (1973), 36 D.L.R. (3d) 261 (Fed. Ct.), the court held that it was reasonable to separate the guards in a prison dormitory from the inmates for security reasons, even though the result was a delay in their reaction time when an inmate was attacked.

11. In *Hogan* v. *McEwan; Royal Insce. Co.* (1975), 64 D.L.R. (3d) 37 (Ont.

H.C.) the defendant driver, suddenly confronted by a large German Shepherd dog on the road, swerved to the right and ended up in an accident injuring the plaintiffs who were passengers. Mr. Justice Henry explained:

"On the evidence, he was presented with the three choices I have mentioned—to turn left, to hit the dog, or to turn right. All of these courses contained a risk. Any sudden swerve to avoid an impact, particularly on a wet roadway, would create an immediate hazard to the vehicle and its occupants. He rejected the first two choices and their attendant risks for the reasons already stated, and chose the third, which, as he saw it, presented the least danger of the three. I find that in so doing he acted reasonably in the emergency and that his conduct meets the standard of care required by the law in such a situation."

See also *Neufeld* v. *Landry* (1974), 55 D.L.R. (3d) 296 (Man. C.A.); *Coderre* v. *Ethier; Gachot* v. *Ethier* (1978), 19 O.R. (2d) 503, 85 D.L.R. (3d) 621 (H.C.), vehicle must make way for ambulance.

12. In *Molson* v. *Squamish Transfer Ltd.* (1969), 7 D.L.R. (3d) 553 (B.C.S.C.), a plaintiff, who suddenly stopped her car in an intersection to avoid hitting a small animal, was held 50% contributorily negligent, when the defendant negligently collided with the rear of her vehicle. Wilson C.J.S.C. stated:

". . . a reaction based on instinct is not enough, there must be a process of reasoning. The reaction of any driver who sees an object on a highway is to avoid striking it. Natural compassion makes him wish to avoid killing an animal, whether a squirrel or a horse. Natural caution makes him wish to avoid running over say a small carton, which may contain glass or steel. But in our world regard for human life and safety must always come first and it is not reasonable that a driver should risk human life or himself in order to preserve the life of an animal. There is no suggestion in this case of any danger to the plaintiff or to other persons in running over the small unidentified animal she saw, but only of danger to the animal. She should have had it in her mind that stopping her car in that forbidden spot, where a stop was not to be expected by a following driver, did create a risk to the following driver. She could not expect, as she might have expected if the emergency arose from the sudden appearance in the intersection of a person or vehicle, that the need to stop would be apparent to the following driver as well as to her. I think she is 50% to blame for in this accident".

Why is this case different than the *Hogan* case? Why differentiate between an animal and a person?

13. The defendant is driving a truck loaded with heavy pipe along the road, when a little child wanders out in front of him. If he stops suddenly, the pipe will shift forward and crush him. What should he do? Would it make any difference to your answer if he had a passenger in his truck? Compare with *Thurmond* v. *Pepper* (1938), 119 S.W. 2d 900 (Tex.).

B. THE REASONABLE PERSON

VAUGHAN v. MENLOVE

Common Pleas. (1837), 3 Bing. N.C. 467; 132 E.R. 490

Plaintiff was the owner of two cottages. The defendant owned land, with certain buildings and a hayrick thereon, near the said cottages. Owing to the spontaneous ignition of this hayrick, fire was communicated to the defendant's buildings. This fire spread to the plaintiff's cottages, which were thereby consumed.

At the trial it appeared that the rick in question had been made by the defendant near the boundary of his own premises; that the hay was in such a state when put together, as to give rise to discussions on the probability of fire;

that though there were conflicting opinions on the subject, yet during a period of five weeks the defendant was repeatedly warned of his peril; that his stock was insured; and that upon one occasion, being advised to take the rick down to avoid all danger, he said, "he would chance it." He made an aperture or chimney through the rick; but in spite, or perhaps in consequence of this precaution, the rick at length burst into flames from the spontaneous heating of its materials, the flames communicated to the defendant's barn and stables and thence to the plaintiff's cottages, which were entirely destroyed.

Patterson J.: before whom the case was tried, told the jury that the question for them to consider was, whether the fire had been occasioned by gross negligence on the part of the defendant adding, that he was bound to proceed with such reasonable caution as a prudent man would have exercised under such circumstances.

A verdict having been found for the plaintiff a rule *nisi* for a new trial was obtained, on the ground that the jury should have been directed to consider, not, whether the defendant had been guilty of gross negligence with reference to the standard of ordinary prudence, a standard too uncertain to afford any criterion; but whether he had acted bona fide to the best of his judgment; if he had, he ought not to be responsible for the misfortune of not possessing the highest order of intelligence. The action under such circumstances, was of the first impression. . . .

Tindal C.J.: I agree that this is a case *primae impressionis*; but I feel no difficulty in applying to it the principles of law as laid down in other cases of a similar kind. Undoubtedly this is not a case of contract such as a bailment or the like where the bailee is responsible in consequence of the remuneration he is to receive. But there is a rule of law which says you must so enjoy your own property as not to injure that of another; and according to that rule the defendant is liable for the consequence of his own neglect. And though the defendant did not himself light the fire, yet mediately he is as much the cause of it as if he had himself put a candle to the rick; for it is well known that hay will ferment and take fire if it be not carefully stacked. It has been decided that if an occupier burns weeds so near the boundary of his own land that damage ensues to the property of his neighbour, he is liable to an action for the amount of injury done, unless the accident were occasioned by a sudden blast which he could not foresee: *Tuberville* v. *Stamp*, 1 Salk. 13. And put the case of a chemist making experiments with ingredients, singly, innocent, but when combined, liable to ignite; if he leaves them together and injury is thereby occasioned to the property of his neighbour, can any one doubt that an action on the case would lie?

It is contended, however, that the learned judge was wrong in leaving this to the jury as a case of gross negligence; and that the question of negligence was so mixed up with reference to what would be the conduct of a man of ordinary prudence that the jury might have thought the latter the rule by which they were to decide; that such a rule would be too uncertain to act upon; and that the question ought to have been whether the defendant had acted honestly and bona fide to the best of his own judgment. That, however, would leave so vague a line as to afford no rule at all, the degree of judgment belonging to each individual being infinitely various. And though it has been urged that the care which a prudent man would take is not an intelligible proposition as a rule of law, yet such has always been the rule adopted in cases of bailment, as laid down in *Coggs* v. *Bernard,* 1 Ld. Rym. 909. The care taken by a prudent man has always been the rule laid down; and as to the supposed difficulty of applying it, a jury has always been able to say, whether, taking that rule as their guide, there has been negligence on the occasion in question.

Instead, therefore, of saying that the liability for negligence should be co-extensive with the judgment of each individual, which would be as variable as the length of the foot of each individual, we ought rather to adhere to the rule which requires in all cases a regard to caution such as a man of ordinary prudence would observe. That was in substance the criterion presented to the jury in this case, and therefore the present rule must be discharged.

[Park Vaughan and Gaselee JJ. concurred.]

Rule discharged.

NOTES

1. What was the standard employed by the court in evaluating the conduct of the defendant? Is it a subjective or objective standard? What reason did the court give for adopting this standard? What other policy reasons could be given in support of this approach?

2. Should any allowance be made in negligence law for stupid people? How can it be said that the defendant was "at fault" when he did his best?

3. How should tort law treat awkward individuals and those who are accident-prone? See James and Dickinson, "Accident Proneness and Accident Law" (1950), 63 Harv. L. Rev. 769.

4. In his book, *The Common Law* (1881), Oliver Wendell Holmes justified the principle in this way:

"The standards of the law are standards of general application. The law takes no account of the infinite varieties of temperament, intellect, and education which make the internal character of a given act so different in different men. It does not attempt to see men as God sees them, for more than one sufficient reason. In the first place, the impossibility of nicely measuring a man's powers and limitations is far clearer than that of ascertaining his knowledge of law, which has been thought to account for what is called the presumption that every man knows the law. But a more satisfactory explanation is, that, when men live in society, a certain average of conduct, a sacrifice of individual peculiarities going beyond a certain point, is necessary to the general welfare. If, for instance, a man is born hasty and awkward, is always having accidents and hurting himself or his neighbours, no doubt his congenital defects will be allowed for in the courts of Heaven, but his slips are no less troublesome to his neighbours than if they sprang from guilty neglect. His neighbors accordingly require him, at his proper peril, to come up to their standard, and the courts which they establish decline to take his personal equation into account.

The rule that the law does, in general, determine liability by blameworthiness, is subject to the limitation that minute differences of character are not allowed for. The law considers, in other words, what would be blameworthy in the average man, the man of ordinary intelligence and prudence, and determines liability by that. If we fall below the level in those gifts, it is our misfortune; so much as that we must have at our peril, for the reasons just given. But he who is intelligent and prudent does not act at his peril, in theory of law. On the contrary, it is only when he fails to exercise the foresight of which he is capable, or exercises it with evil intent, that he is answerable for the consequences."

BLYTH v. BIRMINGHAM WATER WORKS CO.

Court of Exchequer. (1856), 11 Ex. 781; 156 E.R. 1047

Defendants had installed a fire-plug made according to the best known system. Due, however, to an exceptionally severe frost in 1855, damage was caused to the plug resulting in the plaintiff's premises being flooded. The plug had worked satisfactorily for 25 years. The judge left it to the jury to consider whether the company had used proper care to prevent the accident. . . .

Alderson B.: I am of opinion that there was no evidence to be left to the jury. The case turns upon the question, whether the facts proved show that the defendants were guilty of negligence. Negligence is the omission to do something which a reasonable man, guided upon those considerations which ordinarily regulate the conduct of human affairs, would do, or doing something which a prudent and reasonable man would not do. The defendants might have been liable for negligence, if, unintentionally, they omitted to do that which a reasonable person would have done, or did that which a person taking reasonable precautions would not have done. A reasonable man would act with reference to the average circumstances of the temperature in ordinary years. The defendants had provided against such frosts as experience would have led men, acting prudently, to provide against; and they are not guilty of negligence, because their precautions proved insufficient against the effects of the extreme severity of the frost of 1855, which penetrated to a greater depth than any which ordinarily occurs south of the polar regions. Such a state of circumstances constitutes a contingency against which no reasonable man can provide. The result was an accident, for which the defendants cannot be held liable.

[Judgments to the same effect by Martin B. and Bramwell B. are omitted.]

NOTES

1. What was the standard employed by the court to measure the defendant's conduct? Does it differ from the test used in *Vaughan* v. *Menlove*?

2. The reasonable person is a familiar figure in the law. A number of different adjectives have been used to express the same idea, for example, "prudent and reasonable", "reasonable and prudent", "reasonably careful", "reasonably prudent and careful", "typically prudent" and "average person of ordinary prudence".

3. Would the court have come to the same conclusion if this frost had occurred in Saskatoon rather than in England?

4. Does a reasonable person have to take steps to guard against lightning? Against an earthquake? Would it make a difference if he lived in Ottawa or San Francisco?

5. What knowledge should a reasonable person possess? Must he know that a worn tire may blow out? See *Delair* v. *McAdoo* (1936), 324 Pa. 392, 199 A. 181. Must he know about the law of gravity? Must he be aware that bulls are dangerous? See (1939), 23 Minn. L. Rev. 628. May a reasonable person forget something that he has learned about? See *Ferrie* v. *D'Arc* (1959), 31 N.J. 92, 155 A. 2d 257.

6. Does a reasonable person, who is ignorant of relevant facts, ever have an obligation to make enquiries? Suppose you are visiting Africa and encounter a purple traffic signal. What should you do? Suppose you have a large elm tree with overhanging branches on your property. Can you rely on your own judgment about whether the tree needs lopping or must you consult an expert? Compare *Caminer* v. *Northern and London Investment Trust Ltd.*, [1951] A.C. 88, [1950] 2 All E.R. 486 with *Quinn* v. *Scott*, [1965] 2 All E.R. 588. A guest at a hunting lodge tries to start a fire in his fireplace with something he wrongly believes to be furnace oil. The something is gasoline and the cabin burns down. Liability? See *Cone* v. *Welock* (1970), 10 D.L.R. (3d) 257 (S.C.C.).

7. What level of competence should be expected of a beginner? Should a fledgling driver have to perform as well as an experienced one? See Denning M.R. in *Nettleship* v. *Weston*, [1971] 3 All E.R. 581, at p. 586.

8. Should any allowance be made for the physically disabled? For example, should a blind man be expected to live up to the same standard of care as a

sighted individual? See *Carroll and Carroll* v. *Chicken Palace Ltd.*, [1955] O.R. 23 (H.C.). Should special precautions be taken to protect the blind? See *Haley* v. *London Electricity Board*, [1965] A.C. 778; [1964] 3 All E.R. 185 (H.L.). A deaf-mute? See *Dziwenka* v. *The Queen in Right of Alberta* (1972), 25 D.L.R. (3d) 12 (S.C.C.). Other physically disabled people? See Lowrey, "The Blind and the Law of Tort; The Position of a Blind Person as Plaintiff in Negligence" (1972), 20 Chitty's L.J. 253.

9. Can the opening of a door give rise to liability in negligence? Suppose a judge opens the door of his office and it strikes a secretary, who is making tea, and injures her. Liability? What about contributory negligence by the secretary? See *O'Connor* v. *State of South Australia* (1976), 14 S.A.S.R. 187.

10. Does a person have to walk carefully? If someone does not look where he is walking and knocks another person over, can there be liability for negligent walking?

11. Can an actor be held liable for negligent acting? Suppose, because of his incompetence as an actor, an actor delays the making of a movie by weeks, costing the producer thousands of dollars in expenses. Liability?

12. If someone makes it necessary for the police to chase him in an automobile and a collision ensues between the police vehicle and a stationary object, is he negligent? See *A.G. Ont.* v. *Keller* (1978), 19 O.R. (2d) 695 *per* Hollingworth J. Does it make any difference if the chasing vehicle hits the vehicle being chased? What about the onus in these cases?

A. P. HERBERT, UNCOMMON LAW

(1935)

The Common Law of England has been laboriously built about a mythical figure — the figure of "The Reasonable Man." In the field of jurisprudence this legendary individual occupies the place which in another science is held by the Economic Man, and in social and political discussions by the Average or Plain Man. He is an ideal, a standard, the embodiment of all those qualities which we demand of the good citizen. No matter what may be the particular department of human life which falls to be considered in these courts, sooner or later we have to face the question: Was this or was it not the conduct of a reasonable man? Did the defendant take such care to avoid shooting the plaintiff in the stomach as might reasonably be expected of a reasonable man? Did the plaintiff take such precautions to inform himself of the circumstances as any reasonable man would expect of an ordinary person having the ordinary knowledge of an ordinary person of the habits of wild bulls when goaded with gardenforks and the persistent agitation of red flags?

I need not multiply examples. It is impossible to travel anywhere or to travel for long in that confusing forest of learned judgments which constitutes the Common Law of England without encountering the Reasonable Man. He is at every turn, an ever-present help in time of trouble, and his apparitions mark the road to equity and right. There never has been a problem, however difficult, which His Majesty's judges have not in the end been able to resolve by asking themselves the simple question, "Was this or was it not the conduct of a reasonable man?" and leaving that question to be answered by the jury.

This noble creature stands in singular contrast to his kinsman the Economic Man, whose every action is prompted by the single spur of selfish advantage, and directed to the single end of monetary gain. The Reasonable Man is always thinking of others; prudence is his guide, and "Safety First", if I may borrow a contemporary catch-word, is his rule of life. All solid virtues are his, save only that peculiar quality by which the affection of other men is won. For it will not be pretended that socially he is much less objectionable than the Economic Man. While any given example of his behaviour must command our admiration, when taken in the mass his acts create a very difficult set of impressions.

He is one who invariably looks where he is going, and is careful to examine the immediate foreground before he executes a leap or a bound; who neither star-gazes nor is lost in meditation when approaching trapdoors or the margin of a dock; . . . who never mounts a moving omnibus and does not alight from any car while the train is in motion; who investigates exhaustively the bona fides of every mendicant before distributing alms, and will inform himself of the history and habits of a dog before administering a caress; who believes no gossip, nor repeats it, without firm basis for believing it to be true; who never drives his ball till those in front of him have definitely vacated the putting-green which is his own objective; who never from one year's end to another makes an excessive demand upon his wife, his neighbours, his servants, his ox, or his ass; who in the way of business looks only for the narrow margin of profit which twelve men such as himself would reckon to be "fair", and con-templates his fellow-merchants, their agents, and their goods with that degree of suspicion and distrust which the law deems admirable; who never swears, gambles, or loses his temper, who uses nothing except in moderation, and even while he flogs his child is mediating only on the golden mean. Devoid, in short, of any human weakness, with not one single saving vice, sans prejudice, procrastination, ill-nature, avarice, and absence of mind, as careful for his own safety as he is for that of others, this excellent but odious creature stands like a monument in our Courts of Justice, vainly appealing to his fellow citizens to order their lives after his own example.

NOTES

1. Would it be proper for this statement to be included in a Canadian judge's charge to a jury? If not, what is wrong with it?

2. See James, "Nature of Negligence" (1953), 3 Utah L. Rev. 275 where the author states:

"Now this reasonably prudent man is not infallible or perfect. In fore-sight, caution, courage, judgment, self-control, altruism and the like he represents, and does not excel, the general average of the community. He is capable of making mistakes and errors of judgment, of being selfish, of being afraid — but only to the extent that any such shortcoming embodies the normal standard of community behavior. . . .

In striking this balance — that is, in weighing the likelihood of harm, the seriousness of the injury and the value of the interest to be sacrificed — the law judges the actor's conduct in the light of the situation as it would have appeared to the reasonable man in his shoes at the time of the act or omis-sion complained of. Not what actually happened, but what the reasonably prudent person would then have foreseen as likely to happen, is the key to the question of reasonableness."

3. One of the best judicial pronouncements about the reasonable person was issued by Mr. Justice Laidlaw in *Arland and Arland* v. *Taylor*, [1955] O.R. 131, at p. 142:

"The standard of care by which a jury is to judge the conduct of parties in a case of the kind under consideration is the care that would have been taken in the circumstances by 'a reasonable and prudent man'. I shall not attempt to formulate a comprehensive definition of 'a reasonable man' of whom we speak so frequently in negligence cases. I simply say he is a mythical creature of the law whose conduct is the standard by which the Courts mea-sure the conduct of all other persons and find it to be proper or improper in particular circumstances as they may exist from time to time. He is not an extraordinary or unusual creature; he is not superhuman; he is not required to display the highest skill of which anyone is capable; he is not a genius who can perform uncommon feats, nor is he possessed of unusual powers of foresight. He is a person of normal intelligence who makes prudence a guide to his conduct. He does nothing that a prudent man would not do and does not omit·to do anything a prudent man would do. He acts in accord with general and approved practice. His conduct is guided by considerations which ordinarily regulate the conduct of human affairs. His conduct is the standard 'adopted in the community by persons of ordinary intelligence and prudence'."

4. See Green, *Judge and Jury* (1930), for this insight:
"The man of ordinary prudence can only serve his function as an abstraction. In this way he is a mere caution pointing the jury in as dramatic a way as possible the directions their deliberations should take. The judge through him can indicate to the jury that they are dealing with society's power and not their own; therefore, they should act reasonably and not let their own desires run riot. The formula is as much for controlling the jury's deliberations as for measuring the party's conduct. Its beauty is that it can be used for both purposes without committing the judge to anything and without telling the jury anything that amounts to more than a sobering caution. It does exactly what any good ritual is designed to do; its function is psychological. It serves as a prophylaxis. Nothing more should be expected of it."

5. Would it be proper to ask the jury to put themselves in the place of the defendant and to ask themselves what they would have done in the circumstances? See *Arland* v. *Taylor*, [1955] O.R. 131, [1955] 3 D.L.R. 358; *Eyres* v. *Gillis & Warren Ltd.* (1941), 48 Man. R. 164. Is it proper for the judge to use himself as a measuring rod? See *Edwards* v. *Smith*, [1941] 1 D.L.R. 741, 56 B.C.R. 61.

6. Do you know a "reasonable person"? Is there such a beast in captivity anywhere?

7. Professor Leon Green has written in his *Judge and Jury* that "we may have a process for passing judgment in negligence cases, but practically no 'law of negligence' beyond the process itself". Do you agree? If so, is this a good thing? What are the advantages and disadvantages?

8. Are you satisfied with the reasonable person test? Is it fair to minority groups? Can you think of a better yardstick with which to measure conduct? What about the "humane" person? See *Southern Portland Cement Ltd.* v. *Cooper*, [1974] 2 W.L.R. 152 (P.C.), *per* Lord Reid. Is this standard any different than the reasonable person test? Can someone be reasonable and not humane?

9. See Seavey, "Negligence — Subjective or Objective" (1927), 41 Harv. L. Rev. 1; Green, "The Negligence Issue" (1928), 37 Yale L.J. 1029; James, "The Qualities of the Reasonable Man in Negligence Cases" (1951), 16 Mo. L. Rev. 1; Terry, "Negligence" (1915), 29 Harv. L. Rev. 45; Millner, *Negligence in Modern Law* (1967).

WARE'S TAXI LTD. v. GILLIHAM

Supreme Court of Canada. [1949] S.C.R. 637; [1949] 3 D.L.R. 721

The infant plaintiff, aged 5 years, attended a kindergarten school. The defendant taxi company transported the children to and from school under contract with the school. Children carried ranged from 3-6 years of age with a few up to 8. The taxi in question was a normal 4-door sedan. Each door was equipped with a handle for opening the door and a push button which, when down, locked the door and prevented it being opened from within or without.

The driver of the taxi said she was always careful to see that the button was down before starting the car.

On the day in question the taxi had seven or eight children passengers. After delivering two or three the driver noticed the plaintiff playing with the push button on the left rear door. The driver told her to stand away from the door and she did. The driver then made certain the push button was down and continued. Shortly afterwards, the left rear door opened and the infant plaintiff fell out and was injured.

An action for damages was dismissed at the trial: [1948] 1 W.W.R. 1111. The Alberta Supreme Court, Appellate Division, reversed this judgment and gave the plaintiff judgment for damages to be assessed. The defendant appealed.

Estey J.: . . . This push button was within easy reach of every child in the rear seat of the automobile. Moreover, that it could be raised up and pushed down was made evident to each child every time the driver of the automobile opened or closed that door. The operation of the push button and the handle were being constantly brought to their attention. In these circumstances it would be expected that the children would be drawn toward them and "heedlessly to put them in operation".

Moreover, that there is a danger or a circumstance of peril when children are placed in the rear seat of a 4-door sedan is supported by the evidence. Some parents take the precaution to purchase the 2-door type. Other parents, however, equip their 4-door sedans with safety devices and prior to the war and again at least in 1947 some of these devices were upon the market. Three of them were before the Court at the trial. An automobile could be equipped with the most expensive of these for about $10. Moreover, these devices were not complicated and anyone with mechanical ability could place a workable device upon an automobile which would insure the door remaining closed even if the children should meddle or play with the push button and the handle.

A representative of another taxi company called as a witness said: "We have at times transported children" from two other kindergartens without either a safety device upon the rear doors or any supervision. A taxi owner called as a witness stated that he had transported children for two organizations in Calgary, one for a period of 2 years and the other 8 months, using 8 cars and making 4 trips per day. He had only the push buttons without any safety device upon the rear doors. The children, however, that he transported were of ages from 4 to 10 years. He stated that the younger children were placed in the front seat with the driver, and then: "We do make a point to have the older children look after the doors", or as he again stated: "We put a couple of the older kiddies to watch it." The appellants took the precaution of placing the younger children in the front seat but this left children usually up to 6 years of age entirely by themselves in the back seat with only such supervision as the driver in the circumstances might find it possible to exercise.

The foregoing indicates that parents and at least one taxi owner appreciate the need for either safety devices or supervision when young children are being conveyed in a 4-door sedan. That these devices have been developed and placed upon the market would suggest that the apprehension of danger is generally recognized.

The possibility of an automobile rear door opening without being meddled with is very remote. The precautions suggested above are taken because of the propensity of small children to meddle with that which attracts them. It would, therefore, appear that a reasonable man, assuming an obligation to transport children from the ages of about 3 to 6 years in a 4-door sedan equipped with push button and door handle, as in this case, would foresee the possibility of these small children meddling or playing with the push button and the handle and foresee the danger or peril consequent upon their doing so and would take such precautions as would either prevent them playing with the push button and the handle, or if they did so, remove the possibility of dangerous consequences ensuing. . . .

The appellants also submitted that they were using taxicabs with standard or approved equipment which would negative the negligence here alleged on their part. That they were using the standard or approved equipment for the transportation of other than young children is not here in issue. . . . The evidence does not establish either that there is any "general approved practice" or that there is what may be properly described as standard equipment for the transportation of young children in 4-door sedan automobiles. . . .

Neither can the appellants' submission that they were acting in accord with the custom among taxi companies in using this 4-door sedan in the transportation of these children be accepted. It is true that evidence of established practice or custom may be adduced for the purpose of rebutting an allegation of negligence but in order to establish such it must have been a practice over a long period of years. . . . The evidence here does not establish any such custom or practice.

It would appear that *Shrimpton* v. *Hertfordshire County Council* (1911), 104 L.T. 145, is more in point. There a child was injured while being transported in a school conveyance. The jury found that it was negligence not to provide supervision other than that of the driver. The Lord Chancellor (Loreburn) stated at p. 147: "They [the jury] have found that it was not a reasonable and proper way for the county council to convey children to school in this vehicle without a conductor or some adult person to take care of them. It is said that there is no evidence in support of this finding. To my mind it is a question which any man of the world can answer by the exercise of his own common sense and his knowledge of life."

It would therefore appear that the appellants in conveying the children in the above described 4-door sedan, without safety devices and no greater degree of supervision than could be exercised under the circumstances by the driver, were negligent.

Rand J. (dissenting): . . . Both the school authorities and the parents of the respondent, as well, I have no doubt, as all the other parents, were fully aware that the children were being carried in a taxicab with ordinary safety devices, though under the care and oversight of a selected chauffeur. . . . Ordinarily a reasonably intelligent person can be taken to foresee all risks likely or remotely possible to his young child in any situation more sensitively than another and if we find parents uniformly, freely and voluntarily accepting a course of conduct in others involving risks to their young children, could there be a better test of the reasonableness or sufficiency of the actual care in the particular case? . . .

Now, although the acquiescence by the parents in the carriage of their children in the manner adopted here may not be conclusive of that standard, yet when associated as it is with the acceptance of similar services both in Calgary and other places in Canada and in the absence of a syllable of evidence against it, I feel bound to find its security to be reasonable: it was adequate to the risks.

If it had been feasible by adding a convenient device that had become generally used as an additional precaution, a new element in the realized standard would have been added; but although two or three mechanisms have appeared on the market, which were claimed not to have been available during the time in question, the public have not taken them up. The door, of course, might be locked with a key, but there are flaws in all perfection of one dimension, and in that case there would be not only intolerable inconvenience but also new dangers in case of accident.

It is an everyday occurrence in Canada and the United States that parents set off in their automobiles with young children in the rear seat. It is frequent that little ones "pile in" for a short pleasure trip. The doors uniformly, as in this case, have double catches and safety lock and within that protection they enjoy the ride. It would confound a neighbour who with the consent of the parent had taken a young child along with his own for a short run to find himself the victim of a crippling lawsuit because in a moment of wantonness the young child had opened a car door and fallen out. And the duty of care toward such a child in that case would in this respect be the same as in this. Settled over this physical security of lock and catches is the presence of the adult who exercises the authority and oversight of the parent. That was the case here. But the most assiduous surveillance is not absolute insurance against impulse or perversity; there is always an irreducible margin. With insignificant exceptions, children are sufficiently within control by what was furnished here just as they are within their own home, and no other accident of this nature, so far as known, had ever before happened in Alberta; and the searches of counsel have not revealed a similar reported instance in the many services of this sort carried on in the United States.

The injury to the child may be a permanent scar upon a young life, but unfortunately in the multiplying risks and perils of this age these misfortunes occasionally happen as their inevitable result. But I can imagine no sounder or more realistic appraisal of reasonable safety than the long continued acceptance by parents of protective conditions against hazards into which they allow their children to be taken by strangers. Even hind-sight supports that here because for some time after the accident the child continued to be carried under the same conditions in the taxi.

I agree, therefore, with McLaurin J., who tried the case. The appeal must be allowed and the action dismissed with costs throughout.

[Rinfret C.J.C. and Kerwin J. agreed with Estey J. Locke J. agreed with Rand J.]

NOTES

1. What is the basis of this decision? How will it affect taxi companies in the future? Who should bear the cost of such accidents?

2. Do you agree with the dissent of Mr. Justice Rand? Should parents and neighbours be expected to live up to the same standard of care as a taxi company? What are the reasons for and against?

3. Was there a custom established here?

C. CUSTOM

CAVANAGH v. ULSTER WEAVING CO. LTD.

House of Lords. [1960] A.C. 145

The plaintiff, an employee of the defendant, fell from a crawling ladder on a roof while carrying a bucket of cement. The ladder had no handrails. At the time, the plaintiff was wearing a pair of rubber boots provided by his employer, the soles of which were wet and slippery. As a result of the accident, his right arm had to be amputated above the elbow.

Although the plaintiff argued that it was negligent not to have handrails, he led no evidence that this was in violation of the custom of the trade. The defendant, however, called an expert who stated that the operation was "perfectly in accord with good practice". Nevertheless, the jury found for the plaintiff. The Court of Appeal in Northern Ireland reversed this verdict and the plaintiff appealed to the House of Lords.

Viscount Simonds: The evidence given by the expert called for the defence in regard to what was called "the set-up", which was not seriously or, perhaps, at all challenged, was of very great weight, but I cannot say that it was so conclusive as to require the learned trial judge to withdraw the case from the jury. There were other matters also which they were entitled to take into consideration, and it was for them to determine whether in all the circumstances the respondents had taken reasonable care. I do not think that the learned judges of the Court of Appeal were justified in concluding that reasonable men might not find the verdict which this jury found. If I may respectfully say so, I think that the error of the majority of the court lay in treating as conclusive evidence which is not conclusive, however great its weight, particularly where it has to be weighed against other evidence. But that does not mean that the familiar words of Lord Dunedin in *Morton* v. *Wm. Dixon Ltd.,* which have been so often quoted both in Scottish and English cases, are not to be regarded as of great authority in determining what is in all the circumstances reasonable care. It would, I think, be unfortunate if an employer who has adopted a practice, system or set-up, call it what you will, which has been widely used without complaint, could not rely on it as at least a *prima facie* defence to an action for negligence, and I would say with the greatest respect to those who think otherwise, that it would put too great a burden on him to require him to prove that the circumstances of his own case were "precisely" similar to those of the general practice that I have assumed. But these are not questions that arise on the present appeal, and I am content to move that the appeal be allowed with costs here and below.

Lord Tucker: . . . I would . . . desire to express my agreement with what was said by my noble and learned friend, Lord Cohen, in *Morris'* case where . . . he said: "I think that the effect of their Lordships' observations is that when the court finds a clearly established practice 'in like circumstances' the practice weighs heavily in the scale on the side of the defendant and the burden of establishing negligence, which the plaintiff has to discharge, is a heavy one" . . . .

For these reasons I would allow this appeal on the ground that the jury's verdict on common law negligence should not have been disturbed.

[Lord Keith of Avonholm and Lord Somervell of Harrow agreed.]

NOTES

1. How did the House of Lords treat the evidence of custom in this case? Should evidence of compliance with the general practice in a trade be conclusive of due care? There are some older *dicta*, now discredited, to the effect that "a defendant charged with negligence can clear his feet if he shows that he acted in accord with general and approved practice". See *Vancouver General Hospital* v. *McDaniel,* [1934] 4 D.L.R. 593 (P.C.), *per* Lord Alness. See also *Marshall* v. *Lindsey County Council,* [1935] 1 K.B. 516; affd. [1937] A.C. 97 where Maugham L.J. stated: "An act cannot, in my opinion, be held to be due to a want of reasonable care if it is in accordance with the general practice of mankind. What is reasonable in a world not wholly composed of wise men and

women must depend on what people presumed to be reasonable constantly do."

What, if anything, is objectionable about this statement? Is there any danger in judicial abdication from the control over private conduct?

2. Mr. Justice Coyne in *Anderson* v. *Chasney*, [1949] 4 D.L.R. 71, at p. 81; affd. [1950] 4 D.L.R. 223 (S.C.C.) declared that if common practices were blindly adhered to, the "expert witnesses would, in effect, be the jury to try the question of negligence. That question, however, must continue to be one for the petit jury empanelled to try the case, if it is a jury case, and the court, where it is not." His Lordship went on to warn that if this were not the case, "there will hardly be a railway, motor or other accident case where the same argument cannot be advanced that it be similarly decided by the railway, motor or other experts". Experts may "aid or hinder the court in reaching a sound decision. They are never allowed to decide the case . . .", said Mr. Justice Dysart, at p. 92. Mr. Justice Schultz, in *Penner* v. *Theobald* (1962), 35 D.L.R. (2d) 700, at p. 712, stated: "It is the courts and not the particular profession concerned which decide whether negligence is established in a particular case."

Mr. Justice Matas of the Manitoba Court of Appeal has reiterated that evidence of compliance with custom "is not conclusive" in a situation where there was an explosion during a school chemistry experiment that was done in the same way as other schools did it. See *James* v. *River East School Division No. 9.*, [1976] 2 W.W.R. 577, 64 D.L.R. (3d) 338 (Man. C.A.). Do you agree or disagree with these statements?

3. Why should the courts rely on custom or general practice at all? Does it have anything to do with the expectations of mankind? Is there an element of morals involved? Does it assure that the courts do not demand of citizens impossible or economically unfeasible standards?

4. Does the use of custom facilitate judicial administration? See Linden, "Custom in Negligence Law" (1968), 11 Can. Bar J. 151.

5. If compliance with custom were held to be dispositive of the negligence issue, would the development of safer techniques be hampered? Professor Paul Weiler has written that a plaintiff should be permitted to go to court as a "one-man lobby to demand recognition of the need for the safety device, and for a decision that the earlier failure to adopt it was indeed against contemporary mores, if not practice". See "Groping Towards a Canadian Tort Law: The Role of the Supreme Court of Canada" (1971), 21 U. of T. L.J. 264, at p. 319.

6. Although the courts recognized quite early that custom could not always be conclusive, the test originally used to challenge a common practice was an extremely narrow one. In *Morton* v. *William Dixon Ltd.*, [1909] S.C. 807, Lord President Dunedin stated:

"Where the negligence of the employer consists of what I may call a fault of omission, I think it is absolutely necessary that the proof of that fault of omission should be one of two kinds, either — to shew that the thing which he did not do was a thing which was commonly done by other persons in like circumstances, or — to shew that it was a thing which was so obviously wanted that it would be folly in anyone to neglect to provide it."

Eventually, this "trenchant" test was relaxed. Lord Keith of Avonholm, in *Canavagh* v. *Ulster Weaving Co.*, *supra*, declared: "There is no magic in the word 'folly'. It gives the formula the characteristic that was described by Lord Normand in *Paris* v. *Stepney Borough Council* as 'trenchant'. But the language could be phrased otherwise without any loss of meaning. Lord Dunedin might equally have said: 'It would be stupid not to provide it', or 'that no sensible man would fail to provide it', or 'that common sense would dictate that it should be provided'. Lord Cooper himself, who was particularly averse from watering down Lord Dunedin's language, on three separate occasions in his judgment in *Gallagher* used 'inexcusable' as the equivalent of 'folly'. With this may be read the passage from Lord Normand's judgment in *Paris* v. *Stepney Borough Council* that the formula 'does not detract from the test of the conduct and judgment of the reasonable and prudent man'."

7. Modern courts have refused to be ruled by custom. In *King* v. *Stolberg*

et al. (1968), 70 D.L.R. (2d) 473, for example, Mr. Justice Rae stated, ". . . no amount of repetition of a careless practice will make it any less careless. The negligent driver is not any the less negligent by reason of being ubiquitous". See also *Drewry* v. *Towns*, [1951] 2 W.W.R. 217 (Man. K.B.); *Kauffman* v. *T.T.C.*, [1960] S.C.R. 251; affg. [1959] O.R. 197, at p. 205; *Mercer* v. *Commissioners for Road Transport & Tramways* (1937), 56 C.L.R. 580 (Aust. H.C.).

8. Compliance with custom, however, normally will be held to be reasonable. For example in *Karderas* v. *Clow*, [1973] 1 O.R. 730, Cromarty J. relieved a defendant doctor of liability because he "followed standard, approved and widely accepted procedures . . . ." See also *Savickas* v. *City of Edmonton,* [1940] 2 W.W.R. 675 (Alta.); *MacLeod* v. *Roe,* [1947] S.C.R. 420.

9. Just as compliance with custom is not conclusive of due care, so too deviation from custom is not conclusive of negligence. It does, however, provide a welcome guideline for the court.

The House of Lords in *Brown* v. *Rolls Royce Ltd.*, [1960] 1 All E.R. 577, [1960] 1 W.L.R. 210 had occasion to consider this matter. A workman, who contracted dermatitis from exposure to oil during his work, sued the defendant relying upon its omission to supply barrier cream to its employees, although this was alleged to be the common practice elsewhere. The trial decision for the plaintiff was reversed on two grounds: first, there was no proof that the barrier cream would have prevented dermatitis, that is, evidence of causation was lacking; second, since evidence of noncompliance with custom was not conclusive and since the defendant relied on competent medical evidence in not supplying this cream, he could be exonerated. Lord Denning stated that "if the defenders do not follow the usual precautions, it raises a *prima facie* case against them in this sense, that it is evidence from which negligence 'may' be inferred, but not in the sense that it 'must' be inferred unless the contrary is proved. At the end of the day, the court has to ask itself whether the defenders were negligent or not." Lord Keith of Avonholm contended that "a common practice in like circumstances not followed by an employer may no doubt be a weighty circumstance to be considered by judge or jury in deciding whether failure to comply with this practice, taken along with all the other material circumstances in the case, yields an inference of negligence on the part of the employers". In the last analysis, however, "the ultimate test is lack of reasonable care for the safety of the workman in all the circumstances of the case".

10. Are the words "prima facie" helpful to the court or jury in deciding the weight to be accorded evidence of custom? Is this formula giving sufficient weight to this evidence? Should the same weight be given to evidence of the violation of all customs? Compare with the problems on violation of statute, *infra*.

11. See *Adderly* v. *Bremner*, [1968] 1 O.R. 621 (Brooke J. reported only as to evidentiary point) for a case of liability for deviation from the "accepted procedure" of inoculation for flu. See generally Morris, "Custom and Negligence" (1942), 42 Colum. L. Rev. 1147; Fricke, "General Practice in Industry" (1960), 23 Mod. L. Rev. 653; Alexander, "Recent Developments in the Law of Torts", *Special Lectures of the Law Society of Upper Canada* (1966); Linden, "Custom in Negligence Law" (1968), 11 Can. Bar J. 151.

D. THE MENTALLY DEFICIENT

BUCKLEY & T.T.C. v. SMITH TRANSPORT LTD.

Ontario Court of Appeal. [1946] O.R. 798; [1946] 4 D.L.R. 721

Taylor was employed by defendant company as a motor transport driver. On the day in question he drove his truck past a stop sign and into a through street directly ahead of a street car, of which plaintiff was the operator. In the resulting accident plaintiff sustained damages for which he sued the defendant.

The street car company also sued for property damage. There was no doubt that the manner in which the transport truck was driven was the sole cause of the accident. The defence was that Taylor, suddenly and without warning, had become insane and was labouring under an insane delusion that the transport unit was under remote electrical control from the defendant's head office as a result of which he could not control the speed of the vehicle or stop it. The defendant, therefore, pleaded unavoidable accident. Immediately after the accident, Taylor was found to be suffering from syphilis of the brain. He died in a mental hospital, less than a month after the accident, from general paresis.

At the trial, the plaintiffs obtained judgment, the trial judge finding that, as Taylor, in the split second before impact, had made a frenzied effort to avoid collision by a quick turn, he was not under the influence of the insane delusion. The defendant appealed.

Roach J.A. (after finding that the "almost automatic" act of self-preservation in turning just before impact did not show that Taylor had escaped from the insane delusion under which he was labouring): The fact that [Taylor] was suffering from that particular delusion does not conclude the question of liability.

In *Slattery* v. *Haley*, 52 O.L.R. 95, at p. 99, Middleton J., whose judgment was later sustained by this court, said: "I think that it may now be regarded as settled law that to create liability for an act which is not wilful and intentional but merely negligent it must be shewn to have been the conscious act of the defendant's volition. He must have done that which he ought not to have done, or omitted that which he ought to have done, as a conscious being."

He continues in the next paragraph, as follows:

> "When a tort is committed by a lunatic, he is unquestionably liable in many circumstances, but under other circumstances the lunacy may shew that the essential *mens rea* is absent; but, when 'the lunacy of the defendant is of so extreme a type as to preclude any genuine intention to do the act complained of, there is no voluntary act at all, and therefore no liability': Salmond, 5th ed., pp. 74 and 75."

Although that latter statement is only *obiter* in that case, it is supported by English decisions and texts to which that learned judge refers, and I subscribe to it. In my opinion the question of liability must in every case depend upon the degree of insanity.

Supposing a man who was labouring under the insane delusion that his wife was unfaithful to him, but who was otherwise mentally normal, due to the manner in which he operated a motor vehicle on the highway injured some other person on the highway, no one would suggest that he would not be liable in damages simply because of the fact that he had that one particular insane delusion. Then, add to that one delusion the further delusion that his next-door neighbour was conspiring against him to burn down his house, would he still be liable? I entertain no doubt that he might be liable. . . . In particular, notwithstanding those delusions, he might still understand and appreciate the duty which rested upon him to take care. That surely must be the test in all cases where negligence is the basis of the action. If that understanding and appreciation exists in the mind of the individual, and delusions do not otherwise interfere with his ability to take care, he is liable for the breach of that duty. It is always a question of fact to be determined on the evidence, and the burden of proving that a person was without that appreciation and understanding and/or ability is always on those who allege it. Therefore, the question here, to my mind, is not limited to the bare inquiry whether or not Taylor at the time of the collision was labouring under this particular delusion, but whether or not he understood and appreciated the duty upon him to take care, and whether he was disabled, as a result of any delusion, from discharging that duty.

The delusion or delusions may manifest the fact that due to mental disease the individual's mind has become so deteriorated or dilapidated or disorganized that he has neither the ability to understand the duty nor the power to discharge it. If I have correctly stated the law, as I think I have, then the question is: What was the extent of Taylor's insanity? Did he understand the duty to take care, and was he, by reason of mental disease, unable to discharge that duty?

To the police constable, within 20 minutes after the collision, he told the story of this remote electrical control. Later that same evening in the police station, he told another officer who interrogated him "that electricity had pushed him down the hill and he could not stop with this electricity". He said: "It turned me around some loop away out the highway somewhere and that was where the electricity did the damage." . . .

He was seen at the police station the night of the collision by an official of the defendant company, to whom he said: "That machine was under remote control and when you people put the power on I could not do anything." Taylor had a vacant look in his eyes, and his appearance and the nature of his conversation, were such that that official was frightened.

Having regard to all the evidence, I have reached the conclusion that at the time of the collision Taylor's mind was so ravaged by disease that it should be held, as a matter of reasonable inference, that he did not understand the duty which rested upon him to take care, and further that if it could be said that he did understand and appreciate that duty, the particular delusion prevented him from discharging it. Therefore no liability for the damages which he caused could attach to him.

Then, is the defendant company liable? The defendant could only be liable if it put Taylor in charge of this vehicle with knowledge of his mental condition. . . .

In my opinion, no liability could attach to the defendant. I would therefore allow the appeal with costs and direct that judgment be entered dismissing the action, with costs.

NOTES

1. Should there be any exception made for the mentally disabled? Should there be a different rule for the dull-witted than there is for the insane?

2. Is the test enunciated by Mr. Justice Roach a workable one? Does even a normally intelligent person always "understand the duty that rests upon him to take care"?

3. In criminal law the *McNaghten* test excuses from criminal responsibility those who do not understand what they are doing or those who do not realize that what they are doing is wrong. Why does tort law not follow the criminal law test? Should the tests be the same? Should one be stricter than the other? Is the widespread existence of insurance relevant here?

4. *The Restatement of Torts, Second,* §283B provides that "unless the actor is a child, his insanity or other mental deficiency does not relieve the actor from liability for conduct which does not conform to the standard of a reasonable man under like circumstances". See *Johnson* v. *Lambotte* (1961), 363 P. 2d 165; *Sforza* v. *Green Bus Lines* (1934), 268 N.Y.S. 446. What are the policies competing for recognition?

5. In *White* v. *White*, [1950] P. 39, [1949] 2 All E.R. 339, the Court of Appeal considered the effect of insanity as a ground for divorce. In the course of his judgment Denning L.J. made the following observations: "In the case of torts such as trespass and assault it is also settled that a person of unsound

mind is responsible for wrongful conduct . . . even though it has since become apparent that such conduct was influenced by mental disease . . . and this is so even if the mental disease was such that he did not know what he was doing or that what he was doing was wrong. The reason is that the civil courts are concerned not to punish him, but to give redress to the person he has injured. . . . I am aware that these rules of law have been criticized by some jurists who would make responsibility in contract depend on real consent, and liability in tort depend on blameworthiness, but I venture to think that this criticism is somewhat out of date. Recent legislative and judicial developments show that the criterion of liability in tort is not so much culpability, but on whom the risk should fall. Notable examples occur in the liability of a master for, or to, his servant, and in the escape of dangerous things. I can understand, of course, that where a specific intent is a necessary ingredient of the wrong, a man may not be responsible if he was suffering at the time from a disease which made him incapable of forming that intent. . . . But the cases which I have cited show that assault and trespass, to which I would add negligence, do not fall within that exception."

6. Should a person who suffers a sudden heart attack while driving a car be civilly responsible for an accident that follows? In *Slattery* v. *Haley* (1922), 52 O.L.R. 95, [1923] 3 D.L.R. 156, the defendant driver of a motor car, without any previous symptoms, was suddenly taken ill and became unconscious. The car ran up on the sidewalk killing a boy of 15. The plaintiff brought action under the Ontario Fatal Accidents Act (Lord Campbell's Act) to recover damages resulting from death. The court held there was no liability. The only ground for liability resulting from a lawful use of the highway is negligence and a negligent act "must be shown to have been the conscious act of the defendant's volition". Do you agree with this? See also *Lawson* v. *Wellesley Hospital* (1975), 61 D.L.R. (3d) 445 (Ont. C.A.), *per* Dubin J.A., affd. on other grounds [1978] 1 S.C.R. 893. See *supra.*

7. Does it matter if the defendant had a heart condition which he knew could cause a heart attack at any time? See *Gordon* v. *Wallace* (1974), 2 O.R. (2d) 202.

8. Can an epileptic ever take a car onto the highway? Should he be able to? What does it depend upon?

9. Suppose a man, who is so drunk that he does not know what he is doing, crashes into someone. Is he liable? Why? What if he is high on L.S.D.? Are these people any different than someone in a state of automatism? See *Michael* v. *Pennsylvania R. Co.* (1938), 331 Pa. 584, 1 A. 2d 242; *Morriss* v. *Marsden, supra*, at p. 35.

10. Does it make any difference if the person became drunk or under the influence of drugs involuntarily and without his knowledge? For example, suppose David is given an injection at a dentist's office which he does not realize will make him sleepy. He falls asleep at the wheel while driving home and injures somebody. Is he liable?

11. Should David have asked the dentist about the possible effects of the drug? Should the dentist have allowed him to leave his office without warning? Compare *The Queen* v. *King*, [1962] S.C.R. 746.

12. In *Boomer* v. *Penn* (1965), 52 D.L.R. (2d) 673 (Ont.), the plaintiff was injured when the defendant's motor car crossed the centre line of the highway and struck the plaintiff's car. The defendant alleged that the accident was an "inevitable accident" and was the result of an insulin reaction which was completely unanticipated. On this point Evans J., used the following language: "If an accident is caused by negligence then the defendant can avoid the consequences of the negligent act, if he can establish a defence of inevitable accident. That is by showing that the cause of the collision was a cause not produced by him, but a cause the result of which he could not avoid. A driver claiming inevitable accident must discharge the onus upon him of rebutting by a preponderance of evidence and on the balance of probabilities the presumption of negligence arising from his manner of driving. The test to be applied is whether

the faculties of judgment of the driver became impaired to such a degree that a reasonable person could not regard his operation of the motor vehicle in the manner complained of as the conscious act of his will. The onus of establishing that the acts or omissions were not conscious acts or omissions of the driver rests upon the driver, and it is not discharged if the court is left in doubt on that subject. The evidence must disclose the probability that the driver's acts and omissions were not conscious acts of his volition and that what he did or failed to do was not done or omitted by him as a conscious being."

13. For an extremely helpful article see Robins, "Tort Liability of the Mentally Disabled" printed in Linden, *Studies in Canadian Tort Law* (1968), at p. 76 as well as in the *Special Lectures of the Law Society of Upper Canada* (1963). See also Bohlen, "Liability in Tort of Infants and Insane Persons" (1924), 23 Mich. L. Rev. 9; Cook, "Mental Deficiency in Relation to Tort" (1921), 21 Colum. L. Rev. 333.

14. The Civil Code of the Province of Quebec is rather specific on this problem:

Art. 1053. Toute personne capable de discerner le bien du mal, est responsable du dommage causé par sa faute à autrui, soit par son fait, soit par imprudence, négligence ou inhabilité. (Every person capable of discerning right from wrong is responsible for the damage caused by his fault to another, whether by positive act, imprudence, neglect or want of skill.)

15. In Holmes, *The Common Law* (1881) the author stated:

". . . the general purpose of the law of torts is to secure a man indemnity against certain forms of harm to person, reputation, or estate, at the hands of his neighbors, not because they are wrong, but because they are harms. The true explanation of the reference of liability to a moral standard, in the sense which has been explained, is not that it is for the purpose of improving men's hearts, but that it is to give a man a fair chance to avoid doing the harm before he is held responsible for it. It is intended to reconcile the policy of letting accidents lie where they fall, and the reasonable freedom of others with the protection of the individual from injury." What is the best solution?

E. THE YOUNG

1. Liability of the Young

HEISLER v. MOKE

Ontario High Court of Justice. [1972] 2 O.R. 446, 25 D.L.R. (3d) 670

Addy J. (orally): In this particular case I shall not bother reviewing the facts. They are rather simple and the issue is a very narrow one as to whether there was any negligence on the part of the infant child causing the second injury, and, if there was such negligence, what was the resulting degree of that negligence. . . .

In the case of adults, when one is considering the question of whether the person was negligent, the test to be applied is purely an objective one. It is that of the proverbial reasonable man. One must not ask oneself whether the particular individual whose conduct is under investigation having regard to his education, his ability, and his general knowledge and his physical or mental attributes, acted reasonably under the circumstances, but whether a reasonable man acting reasonably under those circumstances would have acted in that particular fashion. Where an individual whose conduct is under investigation (unless he is not at all responsible for his action) has not the physical or mental attributes of a normal person, he cannot escape a finding of negligence on the basis that, although a reasonable man would be expected to act in a certain manner, he, because of his natural failings must not be expected to do so.

The test, I repeat, is therefore clearly an objective one.

In the case of children, however, other considerations enter into play. There are two separate questions to be determined. The first one is whether the child, having regard to his age, his intelligence, his experience, his general knowledge and his alertness is capable of being found negligent at law in the circumstances under investigation. In other words, we consider here the particular child. As has been stated frequently, there is no absolute rule as to age in order to determine this question. Age is merely one of the factors, although the age of seven is often regarded as the crucial or critical age where normally a child may be expected to assume responsibility for his actions.

The test in order to determine this preliminary question is therefore a very subjective one. All of the qualities and defects of the particular child and all of the opportunities or lack of them which he might have had to become aware of any particular peril or duty of care must be considered.

In the case at bar I have found the plaintiff child to be fully capable of being found negligent. He is a bright, alert child and was nine years of age at the time of the accident. His recollection of events which occurred over three years ago was very good and he gave his evidence most clearly — much better as a matter of fact than many adults would.

One must next consider the second question, namely, whether he was negligent at all and, if so, to what degree?

In the case of infants the law clearly does not assume that full knowledge and responsibility occurs all of a sudden and, that at a given time in a child's development, once that child has attained the age of reason or an age where some degree of negligence can be attributed to him, then the test to be applied is the test of the reasonable man. At the very least, one must ask oneself what a reasonable child of that particular age could reasonably be expected to do and to foresee under those particular circumstances.

This test, which is still a very objective one, in the sense that the child's conduct is analysed in the light of that of a reasonable child of that age, seems to have been applied in the English case of *Gough* v. *Thorne,* [1966] 3 All E.R. 398, at p. 400. I am reading at p. 400 from the judgment of Lord Justice Salmon:

> "The question as to whether the plaintiff can be said to have been guilty of contributory negligence depends on whether any ordinary child of 13½ could be expected to have done any more than this child did. I say, 'any ordinary child'. I do not mean a paragon of prudence; nor do I mean a scatter-brained child; but the ordinary girl of 13½."

This fairly objective test was also applied in the Australian case of *McHale* v. *Watson* (1966), 39 A.L.J.R. 459, which was quoted in the text of Wright and Linden, *Law of Torts*, 5th ed. (1970), at p. 199, and I am reading from that text at p. 199 and also at p. 200. At p. 199 the judgment of Mr. Justice Kitto reads as follows:

> "I take this to mean that the test to be applied in determining whether the appellant's injury resulted from a breach of duty owed to her by the respondent should be stated not in terms of the reasonable foresight and prudence of an ordinary [person, but in terms of the reasonable foresight and prudence of an ordinary boy of twelve; and that the respondent should succeed because an ordinary] boy of twelve would not have appreciated that any risk to the appellant was involved in what he did."

At p. 200 it clearly states as follows:

"The principle is of course applicable to a child. The standard of care being objective, it is no answer for him, any more than it is for an adult, to say that the harm he caused was due to his being abnormally slow-witted, quick-tempered, absent-minded or inexperienced. But it does not follow that he cannot rely in his defence upon a limitation upon the capacity for foresight or prudence, nor as being personal to himself, but as being characteristic of humanity at his stage of development and in that sense normal."

Now if I were not otherwise bound by authority I would think that is the proper test to be applied to negligence on the part of a child. It seems, however, that in Canada, the test is considerably more subjective in determining this question.

The question as to whether there was, in fact, negligence on the part of the child and the degree of that negligence was considered in the leading case of *McEllistrum* v. *Etches,* [1956] S.C.R. 787, 6 D.L.R. (2d) 1. That case seems to base the test on that of a child of like age, intelligence and experience. I will read from the report at p. 793 S.C.R., pp. 6-7 D.L.R.; this is a judgment, of course, of the Supreme Court of Canada; it was delivered by Chief Justice Kerwin who, at the time, was delivering judgment on behalf of the court. It reads as follows:

"The present view of the law is summarized by Glanville L. Williams in his work on Joint Torts and Contributory Negligence, 1951, s. 89, p. 355. It should now be laid down that where the age is not such as to make a discussion of contributory negligence absurd, it is a question for the jury in each case whether the infant exercised the care to be expected from a child of like age, intelligence and experience."

It . . . therefore, seems to be quite clear, on the authority of the Supreme Court of Canada, in our province the test would be based not only on the age but on the intelligence of that particular child or a child of similar intelligence and also on the question of the experience of the child.

In the present case the child was warned against jumping. It is not clear on the evidence who warned him. It was not brought out in examination-in-chief or in cross-examination. The second injury occurred while he was pressing down with his leg on the clutch of a tractor while holding on to the steering wheel to brace himself. Although an adult might be expected to realize that this was a dangerous act having regard to the recent injury to the leg and that such action might exert as much force, if not more force, on the leg than jumping on it, it certainly cannot find applying either the objective test of a reasonable child of nine or the more subjective test of that particular child considering his intelligence and experience and what he had been told, that the plaintiff could possibly be guilty of negligence, for he could not be expected to realize or foresee the consequences of his act. Thus, I attribute no negligence to the infant defendant.

NOTES

1. Should there be any allowance made for children who cause accidents? Is a child any different than an ignorant person or a mentally deficient one? What are the policy considerations?

2. Is the Supreme Court's test, employed by Mr. Justice Addy, a workable one?

3. Do you prefer the test propounded by Mr. Justice Kitto in *McHale* v. *Watson* that is referred to by Mr. Justice Addy? Mr. Justice Kitto explained his choice of the test in these words:

"In regard to the things which pertain to foresight and prudence — experience, understanding of causes and effects, balance of judgment, thought-fulness — it is absurd, indeed it is a misuse of language, to speak of normality in relation to persons of all ages taken together. In those things normality is, for children, something different from what normality is for adults; the very concept of normality is a concept of rising levels until "years of discretion" are attained. The law does not arbitrarily fix upon any particular age for this purpose, and tribunals of fact may well give effect to different views as to the age at which normal adult foresight and prudence are reasonably to be expected in relation to particular sets of circumstances. But up to that stage the normal capacity to exercise those two qualities necessarily means the capacity which is normal for a child of the relevant age."

4. Are these tests subjective or objective or do they contain elements of subjectivity as well as objectivity?

5. It is clear that children of "tender age", which probably includes children of up to five or six, are totally immune from liability and are also incapable of being contributorily negligent. The standard expressed in *Heisler* v. *Moke* comes into play only after children reach five or six years of age and is employed until they are well into their teens. At some point in their later teens, children begin to be judged by the ordinary adult standard. There have been no precise border-lines drawn between these categories. The statutory age of majority that has been enacted in Ontario, for example, was not specifically made to apply for purposes of tort law, but anyone over 18 years of age should be expected to be treated as an adult. See Linden, *Canadian Tort Law* (2nd ed., 1977), p. 101.

6. In *Gough* v. *Thorne*, [1966] 3 All E.R. 398, the Court of Appeal con-sidered a finding of contributory negligence on the part of a girl 13½ years of age. In the language of Lord Denning M.R., concurred in by Danckwerts L.J.: "A very young child cannot be guilty of contributory negligence. An older child may be; but it depends on the circumstances. A judge should only find a child guilty of contributory negligence if he or she is of such an age as reason-ably to be expected to take precautions for his or her own safety; and then he or she is only to be found guilty if blame should be attached to him or her. A child has not the road sense or the experience of his or her elders. He or she is not to be found guilty unless he or she is blameworthy.

In this particular case I have no doubt that there was no blameworthiness to be attributed to the plaintiff at all. Here she was with her elder brother crossing a road. They had been beckoned on by the lorry driver. What more could you expect the child to do than to cross in pursuance of the beckoning? It is said by the judge that she ought to have leant forward and looked to see whether any-thing was coming. That indeed might be reasonably expected of a grown-up person with a fully developed road sense, but not of a child of 13½."

Salmon L.J., said that the question was "whether any ordinary child of 13½ could be expected to have done more than this child did". *Cf. Whitehorse* v. *Fernley* (1964), 47 D.L.R. (2d) 472, where a child of six was held 25 percent responsible when he rode his tricycle into the middle of the highway and was struck by a car.

7. Should we enact legislation to sort this all out? Can you formulate an acceptable principle? The Ontario Law Reform Commission, in its *Report on Family Law, Part I, Torts* (1969) decided to make no recommendation on the matter on the ground that there was "no practical alternative to the existing law". It concluded that "the age of responsibility is best left to the courts to determine in each case owing to the great variety of circumstances that can exist". Do you agree?

8. Should the same test be used whether the child is a plaintiff or a defen-dant? What can be said for a different rule in the two situations? In practice, would a jury be as strict with an infant plaintiff as with an infant defendant?

DELLWO v. PEARSON

Supreme Court of Minnesota. (1961), 259 Minn. 452, 107 N.W. 859

Loevinger Justice: This case arises out of a personal injury to Jeanette E. Dellwo, one of the plaintiffs. She and her husband, the other plaintiff, were fishing on one of Minnesota's numerous and beautiful lakes by trolling at a low speed with about 40 to 50 feet of line trailing behind the boat. Defendant, a 12-year-old boy, operating a boat with an outboard motor, crossed behind plaintiffs' boat. Just at this time Mrs. Dellwo felt a jerk on her line which suddenly was pulled out very rapidly. The line was knotted to the spool of the reel so that when it had run out the fishing rod was pulled downward, the reel hit the side of the boat, the reel came apart and part of it flew through the lens of Mrs. Dellwo's glasses and injured her eye. Both parties then proceeded to a dock where inspection of defendant's motor disclosed 2 to 3 feet of fishing line wound about the propeller.

The case was fully tried to the court and jury and submitted to the jury upon instructions which, in so far as relevant here, instructed the jury that: (1) In considering the matter of negligence the duty to which defendant is held is modified because he is a child, a child not being held to the same standard of conduct as an adult and being required to exercise only that degree of care which ordinarily is exercised by children of like age, mental capacity, and experience under the same or similar circumstances; . . . .

The jury returned a general verdict for defendant, and plaintiffs appeal.

[The court first found error in other instructions to the jury on proximate cause, and reversed for that reason. The opinion continues:]

Since the case must be retried, it is appropriate for us to indicate the principles which should govern the submission upon a second trial. . . .

A more important point involves the instruction that defendant was to be judged by the standard of care of a child of similar age rather than of a reasonable man. There is no doubt that the instruction given substantially reflects the language of numerous decisions in this and other courts. However, the great majority of these cases involve the issue of contributory negligence and the standard of care that may properly be required of a child in protecting himself against some hazard. The standard of care stated is proper and appropriate for such situations.

However, this court has previously recognized that there may be a difference between the standard of care that is required of a child in protecting himself against hazards and the standard that may be applicable when his activities expose others to hazards. Certainly in the circumstances of modern life, where vehicles moved by powerful motors are readily available and frequently operated by immature individuals, we should be skeptical of a rule that would allow motor vehicles to be operated to the hazard of the public with less than the normal minimum degree of care and competence.

To give legal sanction to the operation of automobiles by teenagers with less than ordinary care for the safety of others is impractical today, to say the least. We may take judicial notice of the hazards of automobile traffic, the frequency of accidents, the often catastrophic results of accidents, and the fact that immature individuals are no less prone to accidents than adults. While minors are entitled to be judged by standards commensurate with age, experience, and wisdom when engaged in activities appropriate to their age, experience, and wisdom, it would be unfair to the public to permit a minor in the operation of a motor vehicle to observe any other standards of care and conduct than those expected of all others. A person observing children at play with toys, throwing balls, operating tricycles or velocipedes, or engaged in other childhood activities may anticipate conduct that does not reach an adult standard of care or prudence. However, one cannot know whether the operator of an approaching automobile, airplane, or powerboat is a minor or an adult, and usually cannot protect himself against youthful imprudence even if warned. Accordingly, we hold that in the operation of an automobile, airplane, or powerboat, a minor is to be held to the same standard of care as an adult.

Undoubtedly there are problems attendant upon such a view. However, there are problems in any rule that may be adopted applicable to this matter. They will have to be solved as they may present themselves in the setting of future cases. The latest tentative revision of the *Restatement of Torts* proposes an even broader rule that would hold a child to adult standards whenever he engages "in an activity which is normally undertaken only by adults, and for which adult qualifications are required". However, it is unnecessary to this case to adopt a rule in such broad form, and, therefore, we expressly leave open the question whether or not that rule should be adopted in this state. For the present it is sufficient to say that no reasonable grounds for differentiating between automobiles, airplanes, and powerboats appear, and that a rule requiring a single standard of care in the operation of such vehicles, regardless of the age of the operator, appears to us to be required by the circumstances of contemporary life.

Reversed and remanded for a new trial.

NOTES

1. This concept has been adopted by the *Restatement Torts, Second,* § 283A and by Mr. Justice Goodman, in *Ryan* v. *Hickson* (1974), 7 O.R. (2d) 352, where in a case involving 12 and 14-year-olds driving snowmobiles, he stated:

"... Snowmobiles, unlike automobiles, are most often used off the highways but they are no less a lethal weapon in the places in which they are used, in the hands of an inexperienced or careless person or a person lacking the skill, or strength or judgment for their proper operation resulting in their improper use, than the automobile on the highway. Statutory restrictions with respect to the age of a person who may drive these vehicles in places other than on a highway are nonexistent. ... I am of the opinion that the principles set forth [above] ... are equally as applicable to snowmobiles as to automobiles and whether or not such vehicles are in use on or off the highway."

See also Linden, *Canadian Tort Law* (2nd ed., 1977), p. 104. What do you think of this principle?

2. Liability for the Young

RYAN et al. v. HICKSON et al.

Ontario High Court. (1974), 7 O.R. (2d) 352, 55 D.L.R. (3d) 196

The 9-year-old plaintiff was riding on the back of a snowmobile driven by the 12-year-old defendant. The vehicle struck a snow bank as the plaintiff turned to wave to a trailing snowmobile driven by the 14-year-old defendant. As a result of the impact, the plaintiff was thrown from his snowmobile into the path of the other. The court held both drivers negligent as well as the plaintiff contributorily negligent. The court then considered the liability of the fathers of the two drivers.

Goodman J.: I now direct my attention to the claims of the plaintiffs against Edward Cummings and Thomas Hickson, the fathers of the infants James Cummings and Michael Hickson respectively. The claims of the plaintiffs in this regard are founded primarily on allegations of negligence on the part of the respective fathers in that in each case the father allowed the son to operate the snowmobile without having given proper instructions to and without having provided proper supervision of the son. . . .

The law is well settled that a parent is not liable in damages for the torts of his child committed without his knowledge, consent or sanction and not in the course of his employment of the child: *Eversley's Law of the Domestic Relations,* 4th ed. (1926), p. 581; 21 Hals., 3rd ed., p. 150, para. 335. Where, however, a child causes injury to others by the use of dangerous things, the parent or any other person in charge of the child may be liable if the parent or other person has control of the dangerous thing which causes the injury or is negligent, either in permitting the child to use a thing which is dangerous in itself or *known to be dangerous or capable of causing danger to others,* or in not exercising proper control and supervision of the child (Halsbury's Laws of England, same citation as above). Parents are required to supervise their children reasonably, although they are not vicariously responsible on the ground of their family relationship alone: Linden—*Canadian Negligence Law,* p. 24; *Thibodeau* v. *Cheff* (1911), 24 O.L.R. 214 at p. 218.

To put it in another way, "Without going so far as to attach vicarious liability, the common law insists that parents at least exercise reasonable care, commensurate with their peculiar ability to keep their offspring under discipline and supervise their activities for the sake of public safety": Fleming, *The Law of Torts,* 4th ed. (1971), at p. 147. That is to say a parent may incur responsibility for failing in his personal duty to control the child's activities. The standard exacted by the law is that of reasonable care and has regard to the practices and usages prevailing in the community and the common understanding of what is practicable: *Hatfield* v. *Pearson* (1956), 6 D.L.R. (2d) 593, 20 W.W.R. 580.

In considering the desirability of permitting children to engage in activities for the purposes of amusement and training which are not perfectly safe, without rendering a parent or other person in charge liable for damages caused by such children in pursuing such activities, a Court should weigh the risk to others resulting from such activities.

Where a child, to a parent's actual knowledge, has a propensity to misbehave in a particular way, such knowledge will give rise to a duty to use reasonable care, but the parent will not be liable for the damage caused by such child unless the parent could reasonably have done something, which he failed to do, to control the child on the occasion in question. But just because a child has never exhibited a propensity to misbehave in a particular manner, might not excuse a parent, if there is a well-known general propensity of children to act in a certain way with respect to certain objects or certain types of activity. The distinction is between a propensity common to most children in a certain age group of which parental knowledge is assumed, and a propensity peculiar to a particular child, of which parental knowledge is not assumed, but must be proved by the plaintiff: *Carmarthenshire County Council* v. *Lewis,* [1955] A.C. 549, *per* Lord Reid at p. 563. Knowledge of a propensity to misbehave, whether imputed or actual, gives rise to a parental duty because of the reasonable foreseeability of harm to the child himself, or others, arising from the child's conduct (see note of E.R. Alexander, Faculty of Law, University of Ottawa, 16 *U. of T. Law Jo.* 165 at pp. 168 and 172). I am of the opinion that where a parent creates an unreasonable risk to other persons by giving to a child possession of an object the use of which is likely to create a recognizable risk to other persons, then such parent should be liable for any damages suffered by such persons as a result of the use by the child of such object. . . .

Although a snowmobile is not *per se* a dangerous thing, I am of the opinion that it is a thing which is known to be dangerous or capable of causing danger to others. Although a snowmobile is not a weapon, its careless use makes it just as dangerous as a weapon in so far as the personal injury it can cause and, indeed, even more dangerous in so far as the property damage it can cause. I am of the opinion that it is an act of negligence to give to a young boy care and control of a snowmobile which is a thing known to be dangerous or capable of causing danger to others, unless it is proved (a) that he was properly and thoroughly trained in its use, with particular regard to using it safely and carefully, and (b) that the boy was of an age, character and intelligence such that the father might safely assume the boy would apprehend and obey the instructions given to him (see *Starr et al.* v. *Crone,* [1950] 4 D.L.R. 433 at p. 438, [1950] 2 W.W.R. 560, *per* Wilson J., which case dealt with the matter of a father allowing a son to use an air rifle).

In so far as a snowmobile is concerned, I am of the opinion that the parent must, in addition to the above requirements, prove not only that he could safely assume that the child would apprehend and obey the instructions given to him, but that he was physically capable of safely following those instructions and also of safely operating the vehicle: *School Division of Assiniboine South No. 3* v. *Hoffer et al.* (1971), 21 D.L.R. (3d) 608 at p. 612, [1971] 4 W.W.R. 746, 1 N.R. 34 [affirmed [1973] S.C.R. vi, 40 D.L.R. (3d) 480*n*, [1973] 6 W.W.R. 765]. I am satisfied that at the conclusion of the case for the plaintiff and for the defendants Steven Ryan and Richard Ryan there was a *prima facie* case of negligence made out against the defendant Edward Nathan Cummings and there was not sufficient evidence before me to rebut that *prima facie* case and, accordingly, the motion made on his behalf for nonsuit must be dismissed.

[The court found the fathers negligent for failure to give adequate instruction with regard to the dangers associated with the operation of a snowmobile, as well as for failure to properly supervise the activities of their sons.]

. . . Accordingly, Edward Nathan Cummings is jointly responsible with his son James Cummings for 33 1/3% of the damage incurred by the plaintiffs and Thomas Hickson is jointly responsible with his son Michael Hickson for 33 1/3% of the damages incurred by the plaintiffs.

Judgment for the plaintiff

NOTES

1. This case raises the problem of parents' liability for the acts of their children. There are many cases involving the use of guns by young people. See *Edwards* v. *Smith,* [1941] 1 D.L.R. 736; *Sullivan* v. *Creed,* [1904] 2 I.R. 317; *Floyd* v. *Bowers* (1978), 6 C.C.L.T. 65; *Bishop* v. *Sharrow* (1975), 8 O.R. (2d) 649 (H.C.); *Ingram* v. *Lowe* (1975), 55 D.L.R. (3d) 292 (Alta. C.A.); *cf. Hatfield* v. *Pearson* (1956), 6 D.L.R. (2d) 593 (B.C.C.A.). See *infra,* Chapter 9. Liability depends on whether in the circumstances the parents were negligent in the way they trained their children or in the way they supervised them.

2. Would a parent be liable for letting a 16-year-old son, who was convicted twice for traffic offences and was also involved in an unexplained auto accident, drive a car which got into an accident? See *Le Large* v. *Blakney* (1978), 92 D.L.R. (3d) 440 (N.B.C.A.).

3. Can a teacher be responsible for a pupil who causes an accident injuring some third person? It is sometimes said that the standard of care expected of a teacher is that of "a careful parent to his child". See *Moffat* v. *Dufferin County Board of Education* (1973), 31 D.L.R. (3d) 143 (Ont. C.A.). Is this a fair standard? What about the large number of students a teacher must supervise compared with the small number a parent usually has?

4. Suppose a poorly supervised child of 3 runs out onto the road. A passing motorist, caught totally by surprise, swerves to avoid hitting the child and hits a tree, injuring himself. Can the driver recover from the parents?

5. What if in the above circumstances the child is injured when it is struck by the car? Can the parents be held negligent? Can the driver and the parents share liability?

6. This is the problem of liability *to* children. In the case of *Teno* v. *Arnold* (1976), 11 O.R. (2d) 585; varied (1978), 3 C.C.L.T. 272 (S.C.C.). Zuber J.A. held a mother partially to blame for an accident in which her child was injured by an automobile while returning from purchasing ice cream from a street vendor. This decision was reversed by the Supreme Court on the facts. Zuber J.A. also held the ice cream vendor partially to blame, explaining "A pied piper cannot plead his inability to take care of his followers when it was he who played the flute." This aspect of the case was affirmed by the Supreme Court. See also *Gambino* v. *DiLeo*, [1971] 2 O.R. 131 (H.C.); *Harris* v. *T.T.C.*, [1967] S.C.R. 460.

7. Is a teacher responsible for supervising students in a gym class to keep them from being injured? Should the careful parent standard be employed here? What type of evidence is required for liability to be imposed? See *Myers* v. *Peel County Board of Education* (1978), 5 C.C.L.T. 271 (Ont. C.A.).

8. See Alexander, "Tort Responsibility of Parents and Teachers for Damage Caused by Children" (1965), 16 U. of T.L.J. 165; Dunlop, "Torts Relating to Infants" (1966), 5 West. L. Rev. 116; Shulman, "The Standard of Care Required for Children" (1927-28), 37 Yale L.J. 618; Bohlen, "Liability in Tort of Infants and Insane Persons" (1924), 23 Mich. L. Rev. 9.

F. PROFESSIONAL NEGLIGENCE

CHALLAND v. BELL

Alberta Supreme Court. (1959), 18 D.L.R. (2d) 150, 27 W.W.R. 182

Riley J.: On Sunday morning, August 16, 1953, about the hour of 9.30 a.m., the plaintiff fell while working in his cattle barn on his farm. He farms in the vicinity of Leeside in the Province of Alberta. In falling, he broke his left forearm, fracturing both the radial and ulnar bones at the mid-third of the forearm. Either the radius or the ulna punctured the flesh causing a compound or open fracture. The plaintiff was then taken to the defendant for medical treatment. The defendant is a general practitioner at the town of Rimbey in the Province of Alberta. He graduated with a medical degree in 1949 and commenced the practice of his profession at Rimby in the year 1951.

The defendant looked at the plaintiff's fracture about the hour of 11.30 a.m. on the same day. The defendant looked at the wound which was oozing blood. The arm was x-rayed. The plaintiff was put under an anaesthetic. The defendant spread the wound with forceps but did not observe any foreign material in the wound. The tissue which he saw looked alive and with the blood oozing, the defendant's judgment was that the wound was a clean one. Very probably from the bone perforating from within out and the absence of any sign of foreign material, the defendant was led to the conclusion that the wound had not been contaminated. The defendant soaked gauze in merthiolate and applied it around the wound and the sharp edges of the wound. The defendant then proceeded to set the fracture and the arm was placed in a cast. The defendant made periodic checks of the plaintiff and instructed a dosage of 400,000 units of penicillin and one-half gram of streptomycin twice a day. On the same Sunday afternoon he noted some swelling of the arm which he concluded was not excessive and noted that when he, the defendant, touched the plaintiff's hand, the return of colour seemed to be adequate. The defendant personally checked the patient's condition on the Monday morning between 9 and 10 a.m., noted the circulation was probably not so good as it should be, noted excessive swelling, and made a saw cut in the upper and lower ends of the cast so as to loosen the same. On the same

Monday afternoon, he made a further cut in the cast because the circulation still had not improved.

On Tuesday morning, the defendant became somewhat alarmed about the circulatory changes in the plaintiff's hand, concluded the plaintiff was running into considerable difficulty probably with spasms of blood vessels following the injury, concluded the plaintiff needed the services of a specialist, telephoned Dr. Gordon Wilson, a specialist in orthopaedic surgery, and arranged that the plaintiff be taken to the University Hospital, Edmonton, Alberta, for an examination by the said Dr. Wilson. The plaintiff arrived at the University Hospital on the same Tuesday afternoon, was seen by Dr. Wilson, who diagnosed acute fulminating gas gangrene and immediately amputated the plaintiff's arm at a point some three inches below the elbow.

The plaintiff alleges that the arm was lost as a result of negligent treatment by the defendant at the Rimbey Hospital. While many grounds of negligence are alleged in the statement of claim, at the trial the alleged negligence relied on was:

1. The defendant failed or neglected to properly clean out or debride the wound caused by the bone puncturing the plaintiff's skin. 2. The defendant failed to watch the circulation in the plaintiff's arm and failed to remove the cast and improve the circulation in the arm when he knew or ought to have known that the circulation of the arm was impaired.

The evidence shows that gas gangrene bacteria (bacillus welchii), are commonly found in soil contaminated by farm animals, and also upon the clothing and skin of farmers working around cattle. Farms are their natural habitat and where a fracture has been open to the air in a barn, it is particularly susceptible to gas gangrene infection. Gas gangrene bacteria flourish in dead and devitalized tissue as in such dead tissue there is a shortage of oxygen. Where such conditions exist, the bacteria if present thrive. The means commonly used to prevent such a condition from existing is debridement. Debridement or excision of the wound is the making of an incision and the removal of any dead and devitalized tissue to give all parts of the wound an adequate blood supply with sufficient oxygen.

As is not unusual in this type of case, the plaintiff, in support of his case, relief on the evidence of Dr. John E. Mitchell who is a specialist in the practice of surgery in the city of Red Deer, his evidence being supported by several authoritative text books; and the defendant called two learned and eminent specialists, Dr. E.P. Scarlett of the Calgary Associate Clinic, and Dr. Wilson to whom I previously made reference.

Before pinpointing the evidence of the experts, it might be useful to review briefly the law relating to the standard of care required of a general practitioner. In *Salmond on Torts,* 12th ed., pp. 420-1, it is stated:

"Doctors, surgeons, and dentists owe to their patients a duty in tort as well as in contract. It is expected of such a professional man that he should show a fair, reasonable and competent degree of skill, it is not required that he should use the highest degree of skill, for there may be persons who have higher education and greater advantages than he has, nor will he be held to have guaranteed a cure."

Fleming in his book, *The Law of Torts,* 1957, states at p. 128: "Thus a surgeon is expected to apply the degree of care which a normally skilled member of his profession may reasonably be expected to exercise."

And on p. 129: "The skill required of beginners presents an increasingly difficult problem in modern society. While it is necessary to encourage them, it is equally evident that they cause more than their proportionate share of accidents. The paramount social need for compensating accident victims, however, clearly outweighs all competing considerations, and the beginning is, therefore, held to the standard of those who are reasonably skilled and proficient in that particular occupation or calling."

An early Canadian case laying down the standard to be observed by a medical practitioner is *Town* v. *Archer* (1902), 4 O.L.R. 383, in which Falconbridge, C.J., said at pp. 387-8: "The burthen of proof is upon the plaintiff in an action of this character, to show that there was a want of due care, skill, and diligence on the part of the defendant, and also that the injury was the result of such want of care, skill, and diligence. The general rule of skill required of a medical practitioner was thus ably summed up by Erle, C.M., in *Rich* v. *Pierpont* (1862), 3 F. & F. 35, at p. 40: 'A medical man was certainly not answerable merely because some other practitioner might possibly have shown greater skill and knowledge: but he was bound to have that degree of skill which could not be defined, but which, in the opinion of the jury, was a competent degree of skill and knowledge. What that was, the jury were to judge. It was not enough to make the defendant liable that some medical men, of far greater experience or ability, might have used a greater degree of skill, nor that even he might possibly have used some greater degree of care. The question was whether there had been a want of competent care and skill to such an extent as to lead to the bad result.' "
. . .

The most authoritative Canadian decision is that of the Supreme Court of Canada in *Wilson* v. *Swanson,* 5 D.L.R. (2d) 113, [1956] S.C.R. 804. In that case a skilled surgeon operating at the Vancouver General Hospital embarked on radical surgery after receiving a pathologist's report during the course of the operation. His judgment was proved to have been wrong in that the lesion was not malignant and consequently there had been an unnecessary resection of a large portion of the stomach, pancreas and spleen. In the British Columbia Court of Appeal [(1956), 2 D.L.R. (2d) 193] the surgeon was held liable. In the Supreme Court of Canada the appeal was allowed and the trial judgment [[1955] 3 D.L.R. 171] was restored (*per* Rand, Abbott and Nolan, JJ., with Locke, J., and Kerwin, C.J.C., dissenting).

At pp. 119-20 Rand, J., (Nolan, J., concurring) said:

"In the presence of such a delicate balance of factors, the surgeon is placed in a situation of extreme difficulty; whatever is done runs many hazards from causes which may only be guessed at; what standard does the law require of him in meeting it? What the surgeon by his ordinary engagement undertakes with the patient is that he possesses the skill, knowledge and judgment of the generality or average of the special group or class of technicians to which he belongs and will faithfully exercise them. In a given situation some may differ from others in that exercise, depending on the significance they attribute to the factors in the light of their own experience. The dynamics of the human body of each individual are themselves individual and there are lines of doubt and uncertainty at which a clear course of action may be precluded.

There is here only the question of judgment; what of that? The test can be no more than this: was the decision the result of the exercise of the surgical intelligence professed? or was what was done such that, disregarding it may be the exceptional case or individual, in all the circumstances, at least the preponderant opinion of the group would have been against it? If a substantial opinion confirms it, there is no breach or failure. . . .

An error in judgment has long been distinguished from an act of unskillfulness or carelessness or due to lack of knowledge. Although universally accepted procedure must be observed, they furnish little or no assistance in resolving such a predicament as faced the surgeon here. In such a situation a decision must be made without delay based on limited known and unknown factors; and the honest and intelligent exercise of judgment has long been recognized as satisfying the professional obligation."

The test laid down by the Supreme Court of Canada is a threefold one:

1. The surgeon undertakes that he possesses the skill, knowledge and judgment of the average. 2. In judging that average, regard must be had to the special group to which he belongs. From a general practitioner at a rural point, a different standard is exacted than from a specialist at an urban point. 3. If the decision was the result of exercising that average standard, there is no liability for an error in judgment.

The evidence shows that cases of gas gangrene are rare. Dr. Scarlett indicated that the average general practitioner might have one case in his whole practising lifetime, and that a surgical specialist might have one, two or three times over a period of 10 years. Further, gas gangrene in its early stages is difficult if not impossible to diagnose. The doctor doubts if anybody could have diagnosed gas gangrene. Dr. Mitchell agreed that gas gangrene was very uncommon and stated the average general practitioner maybe would encounter such a case once or twice in a lifetime. In point of fact, the defendant had never previously encountered a case of gas gangrene.

The plaintiff's expert witness, Dr. Mitchell, was critical of both the initial and the follow-up treatment given by the defendant to the plaintiff. The learned doctor felt that while the plaintiff was under the general anaesthetic, amongst other things, the wound should have been irrigated with a saline solution and the wound be excised and any damage to muscle or tissues in the depths of the wound would be removed. He further was of the opinion that after the cast was applied, upon pain and swelling becoming excessive and the hand becoming discoloured and the fingers stiff, that the cast should have been split in its entire length through its thickness, and if that had not relieved the situation in an hour or two, the other side of the cast should have been split and the entire front half of the cast removed.

Dr. Mitchell did admit that there was a field for individual judgment by the doctor in attendance; that one would not necessarily have excisions of the wound in every compound fracture; that excision was much more necessary when the puncture was from the outside in rather than from the inside out as in the case at bar; that in any compound fracture he would anticipate pain, swelling and darkening of the colour of the skin; that frequently patients do claim that a cast is too tight when in fact it is not; that swelling will be caused by "tissue tension" and that the practitioner in attendance is in the best position to judge as to the tightness of the cast.

Dr. Wilson, as a specialist, would not have debrided or irrigated the wound and termed such a procedure "meddlesome surgery".

Dr. Scarlett states that the defendant's treatment would be given by nine out of ten country practitioners.

Where the experts disagree but some of them support the treatment given, then surely the treatment given by the general practitioner should not be criticized, and one must always keep in mind the importance of viewing the treatment and seeing matters through the eyes of the attending physician.

Dr. Wilson stated that as a specialist he had on many occasions treated similar injuries in the way the defendant treated this one. In other words, the defendant's treatment was not only correct for a general practitioner but in fact did not differ from that which a specialist would have given.

All of the medical witnesses agreed that following an injury such as this, the patient suffers from "tissue tension" and that complaints of a tight cast are common when in fact such is not the case. Thus the statements by the lay witnesses, relatives of the plaintiff, that the cast was too tight are of little significance. Further, another circulatory condition was present—Volkmann's ischemic paralysis—due to the trauma of the injury itself and not due to a tight cast.

It is impossible for this Court not to feel a profound sympathy for the plaintiff in his great misfortune, but "we must not condemn as negligence that which is only misadventure". No medical practitioner becomes an insurer that he will effect a cure, nor do the Courts condemn an honest exercise of judgment even though other practitioners may disagree with that judgment. It appears, too, that the text books quoted to this Court may generalize too much and that the need for debriding may depend on such things as the size of the wound and its nature. Was it a small puncture, one from within as in the case at bar, or a dirty, contused contaminated mess from without?

In the result the plaintiff's action must necessarily be dismissed.

NOTES

1. What is the standard of care that a doctor must live up to? Is it objective or subjective? Does it provide sufficient protection for patients? Is it too demanding for medical practitioners? Do you agree with the result of *Challand* v. *Bell*?

2. Another formulation of the standard was articulated by Schroeder J.A. in *Crits et al.* v. *Sylvester*, [1956] O.R. 132, affd. [1956] S.C.R. 991, where he said:

". . . Every medical practitioner must bring to his task a reasonable degree of skill and knowledge and must exercise a reasonable degree of care. He is bound to exercise that degree of care and skill which could reasonably be expected of a normal, prudent practitioner of the same experience and standing, and if he holds himself out as a specialist, a higher degree of skill is required of him than of one who does not profess to be so qualified by special training and ability.

I do not believe that the standard of care required of a medical practitioner has been more clearly or succinctly stated than by Lord Hewart C.J. in *Rex* v. *Bateman* (1925), 41 T.L.R. 557, at 559: If a person holds himself out as possessing special skill and knowledge and he is consulted, as possessing such skill and knowledge, by or on behalf of a patient, he owes a duty to the patient to use due caution in undertaking the treatment. If he accepts the responsibility and undertakes the treatment and the patient submits to his direction and treatment accordingly, he owes a duty to the patient to use diligence, care, knowledge, skill and caution in administering the treatment. . . . The law requires a fair and reasonable standard of care and competence."

3. How should a fledgling doctor on his first case be treated? An intern? A resident? What are the competing policies? See *Jones* v. *Manchester Corporation*, [1952] 2 Q.B. 852; *McKeachie* v. *Alvarez* (1971), 17 D.L.R. (3d) 87 (B.C.S.C.) (novice surgeon). In *Vancouver General Hospital* v. *Fraser*, [1952] 2 S.C.R. 36, at p. 46, Rand J. said that an intern "must use the undertaken degree of skill, and that cannot be less than the ordinary skill of a junior doctor in appreciation of the indications and symptoms of injury before him, as well as an appreciation of his own limitations and of the necessity for caution in anything he does". What does this mean?

4. Should a higher standard of performance be required of a city doctor than a country doctor? In *McCormick* v. *Marcotte* (1971), 20 D.L.R. (3d) 345 (S.C.C.) in an *obiter dictum,* Abbott J. said that doctors must possess and use "that reasonable degree of learning and skill ordinarily possessed by practitioners *in similar communities* in similar cases" (emphasis added). Do you agree? Are not all the doctors in a province licensed by the same body? Would this disparity have been more justified in an earlier time when transportation and communications were less advanced? See *Town* v. *Archer* (1902), 4 O.L.R. 383, at p. 388; Waltz, "The Rise and Gradual Fall of the Locality Rule in Medical Malpractice Litigation" (1969), 18 de Paul L. Rev. 408. See Picard, *Legal Liability of Doctors and Hospitals in Canada* (1978), p. 118.

5. An incorrect diagnosis may or may not lead to liability. In *Dale* v. *Munthali*

(1978), 21 O.R. (2d) 554 (C.A.) a doctor was found liable for wrongly diagnosing as flu a case of meningitis, from which the patient died. What if the disease being diagnosed is a rare and unusual one? See *Tiesmaki* v. *Wilson,* [1974] 4 W.W.R. 19 (Alta. S.C.); *Bell* v. *The Queen* (1974), 44 D.L.R. (3d) 549 (Fed. Ct.). Suppose a doctor suspects that a uterine lump is a tumour, operates and discovers not a tumour but that the patient is pregnant. Liability? See *Finlay* v. *Hess* (1974), 3 O.R. (2d) 91.

6. Must doctors always use the latest and most up-to-date surgical techniques? See *Eady* v. *Tenderenda* (1974), 41 D.L.R. (3d) 706 (N.S.S.C.); revd. [1975] 2 S.C.R. 599.

7. Can a doctor rely on a patient to behave reasonably in following his instructions with regard to medication? Does a doctor have to check up on whether the patient is taking or not taking medication as prescribed? Can a patient be contributorily negligent along with a doctor? See *Crossman* v. *Stewart* (1977), 5 C.C.L.T. 45 (B.C.S.C.), plaintiff was two-thirds at fault for getting medication illegally and taking it beyond the period he should have, doctor was one-third to blame.

8. What if a doctor *expressly* agrees to cure an ailment? See *Town* v. *Archer* (1902), 4 O.L.R. 383, at p. 388; *Guilmet* v. *Campbell* (1971), 385 Mich. 57.

9. A fine review of the law in this area appears in *MacDonald* v. *York County Hospital,* [1972] 3 O.R. 469, *per* Addy J.; affd. in part (1974), 1 O.R. (2d) 653 (C.A.); affd. [1976] 2 S.C.R. 825. See also the excellent treatise on the subject , Picard, *Legal Liability of Doctors and Hospitals in Canada* (1978); Nathan, *Medical Negligence* (1952); Meredith, *Malpractice Liability of Doctors and Hospitals* (1956); Louisell and Williams, *Trial of Malpractice Cases* (1960); McCoid "The Care Required of Medical Practitioners" (1959), 12 Vand L. Rev. 549; Sherman, "The Standard Care in Malpractice Cases" (1966), 4 O.H.L.J. 222; Linden, "The Negligent Doctor" (1973), 11 O.H.L.J. 31; Hoyt, "Professional Negligence", Law Society of Upper Canada, *Special Lectures on New Developments in the Law of Torts* (1973), pp. 137 *et seq.;* Sharpe and Sawyer, *Doctors and the Law* (1978).

HAINES v. BELLISSIMO

Ontario High Court. (1977), 82 D.L.R. (3d) 215, 18 O.R. (2d) 177, 1 L.M.Q. 292

The family of a mental patient, who committed suicide, sued a psychiatrist, a psychologist and a hospital. The mental patient had been under the care of a psychiatrist and a psychologist as an out-patient of a hospital in Hamilton, Ontario. The doctors had concluded during their treatment of the deceased in the three years or so before his death that he suffered from chronic schizophrenia, with aspects of depression. In the beginning of 1974 there was a marked deterioration of his mental health and there appeared the symptoms of acute mental disorder. He was voluntarily admitted as a patient to the hospital for a two-week period, but then he was released and he continued being treated as an out-patient. In June of 1974, he purchased a shotgun. His wife discovered this and she telephoned the psychologist who then telephoned the psychiatrist to discuss the matter. They agreed that the gun should be taken away from the deceased and the psychiatrist asked the psychologist to bring the patient into the hospital for a complete check-up in order to see if there were any suicidal tendencies. The deceased gave up his shotgun and told the psychologist that he had no present suicide plans. The psychologist, after his investigation, formed the opinion that it was in the deceased's best interest to continue being treated as an out-patient and let him go. The next day the deceased bought himself another shotgun, and killed himself two days later.

The action brought against the psychiatrist, the psychologist and the hospital by the widow and her three children was dismissed, because the court held that the psychiatrist behaved in an acceptable way in delegating the responsibility to the psychologist and that the psychologist exercised his judgment in a reasonable and responsible fashion in deciding that it would be better not to hospitalize the patient.

Griffiths J.: The plaintiff contends that the defendants were negligent in failing to hospitalize Robert Haines on the night of June 28, 1974, thereby protecting him from the reasonably apprehended danger of suicide. It is common ground that, had Dr. Bellissimo elected to hospitalize Mr. Haines, it would have been a relatively easy matter to arrange for his admission on a voluntary basis or, if he had resisted admission, to arrange to have Dr. Cleghorn or the resident psychiatrist commit him to hospital on an involuntary basis, under the provisions of the *Mental Health Act,* R.S.O. 1970, c. 269. Had Mr. Haines been hospitalized he would have been kept under close supervision for 24 to 48 hours or longer if the staff felt the risk of suicide remained, given such psychotherapy or medication as his condition warranted and, if necessary, electro-convulsive therapy.

The duty and standard of care imposed on Dr. Cleghorn as a psychiatrist is, in my view, the same as required of physicians in all fields of medicine and surgery. In my opinion, the same legal principles should apply to Dr. Bellissimo as a clinical psychologist applying a healing art in a specialized capacity in a hospital environment. Those principles are set out in the leading cases of *Wilson* v. *Swanson,* [1956] S.C.R. 804, 5 D.L.R. (2d) 113, and *Crits and Crits* v. *Sylvester et al.,* [1956] O.R. 132 at pp. 143-4, 1 D.L.R. (2d) 502 at pp. 508-9 (C.A.); affirmed [1956] S.C.R. 991, 5 D.L.R. (2d) 601.

Having undertaken to treat Robert Haines, the defendants owed to him a duty to exercise that degree of reasonable skill, care, and knowledge possessed by the average of like professionals. If the patient's mental condition and actions were such that a reasonably prudent psychiatrist or psychologist would under the circumstances have anticipated a suicide attempt, then the concept of "reasonable care" in treatment requires the therapist to take all reasonable steps including hospitalization of the patient, if necessary, to prevent or reduce the risk of self-destruction. To this should be added the fundamental principle of law that governs all professionals that the psychiatrist or psychologist who makes a diagnostic mistake or error in judgment does not incur liability whatever the harm, provided he exercised reasonable care and skill and took into consideration all relevant factors in arriving at his diagnosis or judgment. Psychology and psychiatry are inexact sciences and the practice thereof should not be fettered with rules so strict as to exact an infallibility on the part of the practitioners which they could not humanly possess.

It seems to me as well that, where a Court is called upon to analyze the judgment of a therapist who concluded that his patient was not suicidal, regard must be had to the undoubted advantage he enjoyed in his direct relationship with the patient at the time, over those who would attempt to second-guess him after the event. From the evidence it is clear to me that the assessment of a suicidal intent requires not only the recognition of florid or overt signs of mental disturbance, but depends on the art of the therapist to interpret subtler signs: the appearance of the patient, his reactions, his thoughts, his tone of voice, the inflection, the meaning of silences, and the significance of words implying reservations on the patient's part. All of the experts who testified at the trial agreed that, assuming his competence, Dr. Bellissimo was in the best position of all to make the assessment on the evening of June 28, 1974.

With regard to Dr. Cleghorn, it is submitted on behalf of the plaintiff that he was negligent in failing to assume a direct responsibility for the care of Mr.

Haines in this, his first life-threatening situation. Having delegated the responsibility of assessing the suicidal risk to Dr. Bellissimo, it was his duty, in light of the seriousness of the situation and the relative inexperience of Dr. Bellissimo, to follow up and to find out what eventually transpired. The evidence establishes that by 1974 Dr. Bellissimo had extensive experience in the treatment and assessment of mentally ill patients. He had for two years been treating approximately 30 out-patients a week. He had occasion previously to deal with suicidal patients, some of which had to be hospitalized. There is no question that Dr. Bellissimo had the qualifications, training, and experience and was competent to make a suicidal assessment. I can find no negligence on the part of Dr. Cleghorn in delegating this task to Dr. Bellissimo and, in assuming that Dr. Bellissimo would, if in doubt as to the proper course to be taken, consult his superior. Dr. Wickware, who gave evidence on behalf of the plaintiff, testified that in his opinion the instructions given by Dr. Cleghorn to Dr. Bellissimo on the evening of June 28, 1974, were clear, concise, unambiguous, and not open to misinterpretation. . . .

The expert evidence established that the competent therapist, in the assessment of suicidal intention and in determining whether or not the patient should be hospitalized, must weigh the advantages and disadvantages of hospitalization against the advantages of continuing out-patient treatment. Obviously, if the therapist feels that there is a real risk of suicide or is in doubt about this, he should opt for hospitalization. On the other hand, modern psychiatry recognizes that close observation, restrictions, and restraint of the patient may be anti-therapeutic and aggravate the feelings of worthlessness which, in themselves, intensify the risk of suicide. In this case, there was the risk that hospitalization, whether voluntary or involuntary, would have been a blow to Mr. Haines' self-esteem and pride, would have interfered with his long-term vocational rehabilitation and, most significantly, would have destroyed the strong therapeutic bond that existed between Mr. Haines and Dr. Bellissimo.

Doctor Bellissimo made a decision not to hospitalize Mr. Haines based on his opinion that there was no immediate risk of suicide and that to continue the psychotherapy of Mr. Haines as an out-patient was preferable to the dubious advantages of hospitalization.

Doctor Wickware expressed the view, no doubt influenced by his opinion that there was present a serious depressive illness, that the majority of therapists would, in the circumstances existing on the evening of June 28th, have hospitalized Mr. Haines. Dr. Lowy testified that he was not certain what he might have done in the circumstances, but placing himself in Dr. Bellissimo's shoes, after carrying out a complete assessment as Dr. Bellissimo did, if he had concluded that there was no immediate risk once the gun was surrendered, then he would have followed the same course as Dr. Bellissimo. Dr. Sakinofsky, with a particular expertise in the treatment of suicidal patients, and Dr. Preston both expressed the opinion that in the circumstances described they would have made the same decision as Dr. Bellissimo. Dr. Preston, in particular, emphasized that in his opinion what Dr. Bellissimo did was "fully reasonable" and quite in accord with the accepted practice of psychology and psychiatry at the time.

Action dismissed.

NOTES

1. Is there a different standard of care required of a specialist than of a general practitioner? See also *Karderas* v. *Clow*, [1973] 1 O.R. 730, *per* Cromarty J. (gynaecologist). Should a psychologist be expected to live up to the same standard as a psychiatrist? Do they charge the same fees? Does the public expect as much from them?

2. Can a doctor rely on other doctors and professional personnel? What if a surgeon relies on a resident to close up after an operation and a sponge is left behind inside the patient? *Kaderas* v. *Clow, supra.* Can a doctor rely on the nurses to supervise a very sick patient properly and not go out for coffee? See *Laidlaw* v. *Lions Gate Hospital* (1969), 8 D.L.R. (3d) 730 (B.C.S.C.); *Krujelis* v. *Esdale* (1971), 25 D.L.R. (3d) 557 (B.C.S.C.). Can a doctor rely on a nurse to warn a patient about the possible side-effects of a drug? See *Crichton* v. *Hastings,* ˈ1972] 3 O.R. 859 (C.A.). What standard of care should be exacted from para-medical personnel? How is the scope of their role to be defined? What other legal problems are created by this concept of "team medicine" and how are they to be handled by the courts?

3. Must a G.P. consult a specialist if he gets out of his depth? See Dubin J.A. in *McDonald* v. *York County Hospital* (1974), 1 O.R. (2d) 653; affd. [1976] 2 S.C.R. 825. Must one specialist call in another if he gets out of his field?

4. Do you agree with the result of the *Haines* decision?

5. What if the specialist is acting outside his field of expertise? How should an older specialist be treated if his field of specialization has been broken down into several sub-categories over the years? Is he to be regarded as an expert in all of them?

6. What standard should tort law exact from a genius brain surgeon from Vienna or from a heart transplant expert from South Africa? See Castel, "Some Legal Aspects of Human Organ Transplantation in Canada" (1968), 46 Can. Bar Rev. 345, at p. 357. Does it depend on what he holds himself out to be? See *Rann* v. *Twitchell* (1909), 82 Vt. 79, 71 A. 1045. What about a general practitioner who acts as an anaesthetist? See *Villeneuve* v. *Sisters of St. Joseph,* [1971] 2 O.R. 593 (H.C.); appeal allowed in part, [1972] 2 O.R. 119 (C.A.); appeal allowed in part, (1974), 47 D.L.R. (3d) 391 (S.C.C.). What about a specialist who holds himself out only as a general practitioner? See *Harris* v. *Fall* (1910), 177 F. 79; *MacDonald* v. *York County Hospital, supra;* What about a Christian Science healer? See *Spead* v. *Tomlinson* (1904), 73 N.H. 46, 59 A.376. What about a jeweller who pierces ears?

7. What standard of care is expected of an anaesthetist? If as a result of having consumed a cup of coffee three hours earlier a patient dies because of complications during the anaesthetizing procedures prior to an operation for ingrown toenails is the anaesthetist negligent for not having personally questioned the patient on the subject? What if the patient had already been given strict warnings not to eat or drink anything within five hours of the operation and had failed to reveal the fact that he had drunk the coffee? See *Webster et al.* v. *Armstrong et al.,* [1974] 2 W.W.R. 709 (B.C.S.C.) (no liability).

8. The problems of proof in a medical malpractice case are enormous, mainly because of the need for expert witnesses. According to some, the dif-ficulties are compounded by a "conspiracy of silence" among doctors. Others deny that any such phenomenon exists. They explain that any hesitancy among doctors to testify stems from the uncertainty of medical science and the importance of judgmental factors in treatment.

In 1971, a team from the Osgoode Hall Law School circulated a medical-legal questionnaire to Ontario doctors. One of the questions asked concerned the physician's response if he were to witness some grossly negligent conduct by another doctor and that other doctor were sued by his patient because of it. Of the 1835 responses, 2.3 percent said they would *volunteer* the informa-tion they had to the patient or to his lawyer; 22.2 percent stated they would disclose the information if *asked* about it; 1.5 percent claimed they would refuse to disclose the information or to co-operate even if asked; 72.1 percent declared they would disclose the information in court if subpoenaed, but only if subpoenaed; while 2.0 percent thought they would refuse to disclose the in-formation in court even if subpoenaed. On the basis of this evidence, do you believe there is a "conspiracy" of silence? How willing would one lawyer be to testify in a malpractice suit against another lawyer? See generally *Report of*

the Attorney-General's Committee on Medical Evidence in Civil Cases (1965);
Sharpe, "The Conspiracy of Silence Dilemma" (1973), 40 Ont. Med. Rev. 25.

9. If a doctor, in giving treatment, complies with the standard practice in
his field, he almost invariably escapes liability. In *Johnston* v. *Wellesley
Hospital* (1971), 17 D.L.R. (3d) 139, the plaintiff suffered more pain than was
usual from a dermatological treatment designed to remove some of his scars
caused by acne. No liability was imposed by Mr. Justice Addy who held that
the defendant doctor ". . . acted throughout in accordance with generally
accepted good medical practice in the field of dermatology. He, possessed of
the required skill and knowledge, acting in accordance with his medical judgment, after due examination of the patient and with the knowledge that he
had carried out this procedure hundreds if not thousands of times previously
with favourable results, decided that, in order to achieve the desired effect an
exposure of 15 seconds would be proper. His judgment proved to be wrong in
the light of subsequent developments, but I cannot find that it was a negligent
exercise of judgment. It was an error in judgment, but no more."

A similar result occurred in *Ostrowski* v. *Lotto* (1970), 15 D.L.R. (3d) 402
(Ont. C.A.); affd. (1972), 31 D.L.R. (3d) 715, where the Court of Appeal endorsed the view that "a doctor is not guilty of negligence if he has acted in
accordance with a practice accepted as proper by a responsible body of medical
men skilled in that particular art".

Should compliance with general practice absolve a doctor from all liability?
Does a custom of a professional body deserve any more weight than that of an
ordinary profit-making industry?

10. The question of the importance of expert testimony and of evidence of
general practice has generated some difficulty. In *Gent* v. *Wilson*, [1956] O.R.
257, 2 D.L.R. (2d) 160, the evidence of skilled and experienced witnesses was
said to govern the matter of a vaccination made on the inner aspect of the left
arm when the plaintiff had an inflamed thumb. See also *Mahon* v. *Osborne*,
[1939] 2 K.B. 14, [1939] 1 All E.R. 535. On the other hand, there are some
accidents where expert evidence may not be needed. In *Sylvester* v. *Crits*,
[1956] S.C.R. 991, 5 D.L.R. (2d) 601, an explosion occurred during an operation by reason of a spark of electricity setting aflame an ether-oxygen mixture.
The court indicated that, although steps in the procedure may be governed by
"standard practice", the avoidance of danger from static electricity is not a
question to be decided by such a criterion and, indeed, a practice may involve
such an unnecessary risk as to be held improper. In *Taylor* v. *Gray*, 11 M.P.R.
588, [1937] 4 D.L.R. 123, the Court of Appeal for New Brunswick dealt with
a claim against a surgeon for negligence, based on the fact that forceps were
discovered in the abdomen of the plaintiff after an operation conducted by the
defendant. The court used the following language: "While men eminent in their
profession have given evidence of their system of practice, yet every system put
forward must stand the test of judicial examination and, possibly, of reproba-
tion by a jury. There is no question here of skill displayed in the operation
itself, nor of the technique employed in performing it. In such matters we have
to be governed by the best professional opinion we can get. But in a case which
involves none of these elements but simply whether or not the defendant has
shown that he was not negligent in respect to the non-removal of the instrument from the abdominal cavity, the opinion of one man is about as good as
that of another."

11. In a similar vein, in *Chasney* v. *Anderson*, [1950] 4 D.L.R. 223
(S.C.C.), the Chief Justice of Manitoba had this to say in the Court of Appeal:
"While the method in which the operation was performed may be purely a
matter of technical evidence, the fact that a sponge was left in a position
where it was or was not dangerous is one which the ordinary man is competent
to consider in arriving at a decision as to whether or not there was negligence."
The Supreme Court merely concluded: "Since the appellant had not used
sponges with tapes attached, which were available, or had a count kept by the
nurse in attendance of the number used and removed, it was his clear duty to

make a thorough search following the operation to determine whether any sponges remained in the cavity. We agree . . . that the proper inference to be drawn from the evidence is that the appellant failed in the discharge of this duty and that the death of the child was attributable to this failure."

12. Should medical malpractice cases be tried by a jury? What are the policy considerations on both sides? See *Smith* v. *Rae* (1919), 46 O.L.R. 518, at p. 520; *Hodgins* v. *Banting* (1906), 12 O.L.R. 117.

13. Are malpractice claims a very large problem for Canadian doctors, as opposed to American doctors? In the United States, many thousands of malpractice claims are begun each year. About two out of every nine doctors in the United States have been sued for negligence. See *Annual Report, American Medical Association* (1969), J.A.M.A. 210. Some may wonder if this phenomenon is being transported into Canada. The Canadian Medical Protective Association which insured 32,175 doctors (over 80 percent of Canadian doctors), handled 323 malpractice writs in 1978. This number is part of an increasing trend. Until 1969, about 65 writs were issued against members each year. In 1970, the figure rose to 80 and in 1974 to 220. See *Annual Report, Canadian Medical Protective Association* (1979). Even with this new trend, Canadian doctors are sued far less frequently than American. The C.M.P.A. membership fee is only $250 per annum, as a result. What are the reasons for this difference? Is the Canadian situation preferable?

14. Some Canadian courts have evinced a reluctance to second-guess doctors in the practice of their profession. Mr. Justice Gould recently declared: "The less the courts try to tell the doctors how to practise medicine the better." See *McLean* v. *Weir* (1977), 3 C.C.L.T. 801. Do you agree with this attitude? What about the patients who are damaged by medical error?

15. Should doctors be subject to malpractice suits at all? Mr. Justice Haines thinks not. He would prefer the use of no-fault insurance to cover all medical "accidents". See "The Medical Profession and the Adversary Process" (1973), 11 O. H. L. J. 41:

"Doctors do not take kindly to the adversary system. It is entirely foreign to their way of settling disputes. When they disagree on a diagnosis or a treatment technique, they attempt to resolve it by obtaining the assistance of more experienced scientists and each joins in an objective search for the truth. It would be unthinkable for them to refer the matter to an independent layman, whether he be a judge or jury. Even if they did, there are no specialist judges in malpractice matters and the majority have no training in basic anatomy and physiology. The courts seem to dislike calling an expert assistant to sit with the judge and assist him in understanding the evidence. Leaving aside those few cases of such obvious error that the law implies negligence from the event (*res ipsa loquitur*), the great bulk of bad results from medical care arise in a terribly grey area where the law may see negligence but medicine sees merely an unexpected occurrence in a very inexact art. Here we must recognize the difference in thinking between lawyers and doctors. The lawyer is armed with the most accurate diagnostic instrument, the 'retroscope'. With twenty-twenty vision he seizes on the unfortunate result, second-guesses the doctor and charges him with fault, although at the time of treatment the symptoms and the various tests presented a very foggy picture and resulted in a complex, differential diagnosis.

However, the major objection of the doctor to a malpractice action is the confirmed belief of the medical profession that the suit is a reflection on his professional abilities and standing. The very name 'malpractice' repels him, and in the minds of some denotes quasi-criminal or unethical conduct, a loss of standing with his colleagues in the medical profession, degradation in the eyes of his patients and the community in which he practices, or loss of possible promotion and staff privileges in local hospitals."

See also Ehrenzweig, "Hospital Accident Insurance: A Needed First Step Towards the Displacement of Liability for Medical Malpractice" (1964), 31 U. Chi. L. Rev. 279; O'Connell, "Expanding No-Fault Beyond Auto Insurance"

(1973), 59 Va. L. Rev. 749; R. Keeton, "Compensation for Medical Accidents" (1973), 121 U. Pa. L. Rev. 590.

16. Do you think the medical malpractice action should be abolished? If we did, would there remain enough independent supervision of medical practice? Is professional self-regulation adequate? Are coroners' inquests sufficient? Is the role of the hospital important here? Should tort law seek to upgrade the quality of medical practice? See Kretzmer, "The Malpractice Suit: Is it Needed?" (1973), 11 O.H.L.J. 55.

17. What do you think of the following quote from Linden, "Tort Law as Ombudsman" (1973), 51 Can. Bar Rev. 155, at p. 160:

"All professional groups come under the aegis of tort law. The expertise of doctors, lawyers, engineers and accountants may be impugned in a tort suit. Of course, negligence law normally adopts as its own the standards that the professions require of themselves. But this does not make negligence law redundant, because professional groups are less than zealous in policing themselves. Hardly ever does a doctor, for example, lose his licence to practice medicine because of his incompetence or professional misconduct. It is far more common for a physician to be sued by a patient injured by his malpractice. Consequently, it is the judges, not the College of Physicians and Surgeons, who by default become regulators of the quality of medical practice.

The courts can encourage the medical profession to develop safer procedures. In *Chasney* v. *Anderson* an action was brought because a child suffocated on a sponge left behind in its throat after a tonsillectomy. No sponge count had been done. Nor were strings attached to the sponges that were used. Still worse, the search that had been conducted did not discover anything. Liability was imposed. Following this decision, two articles were written in the *Canadian Medical Association Journal* warning doctors about the need for special precautions in relation to sponges. It is not unlikely that these articles, coupled with the publicity in the daily press at the time, had some impact on the habits of medical men.

There is reason to suspect that, when malpractice actions are successfully brought against doctors for negligently performing an operation, administering an anaesthetic or putting on a cast, other physicians are alerted to the dangers involved in those medical procedures and the need for utmost care. The impact of these decisions is amplified because reports of them are published in the annual report of the Canadian Medical Protective Association, something that is received by almost every doctor in Canada. Even if the law suit is not successful, it will still be reported and will serve to remind doctors of the wisdom of caution.

Thus, medical malpractice actions serve a useful function, despite the fact that doctors do not pay the awards personally. It is the publicity that carries the sting. However, this sanction is not as severe on the individual doctor as might be expected. His practice generally survives the litigation. In fact, so small a threat is the civil action to the profession that the Ontario Committee on the Healing Arts dismissed it as almost useless in controlling the quality of medical practice. This body, however, failed to appreciate the educational value of malpractice litigation. No doubt malpractice actions are a costly and cumbersome way of dramatizing the risks of medical practice, but they should provide incentives to care. True, the medical profession could do a much better job of regulating the quality of medical practice if it would exert itself more in this area. True, a medical ombudsman would assist greatly in exposing some acts of wrongdoing. In their absence, however, the malpractice action stands as a temporary ombudsman, constantly reminding doctors of the risks involved in their acts. Other professional groups are in much the same position as doctors, and stand to learn in the same way."

See also Prichard, "Professional Civil Liability and Continuing Competence", in Klar (ed), *Studies in Canadian Tort Law* (1977).

18. The Pearson Commission, after considering the various alternative reform possibilities, concluded that they would make no major recommendations for reforming the way in which medical malpractice claims are handled by the courts. The only change it suggested was that volunteers for research and clinical trials should be allowed to sue on a strict liability basis. The Commission also urged that developments elsewhere should be studied and assessed in the event that changing circumstances indicated that a no-fault plan should be instituted. See *Report of the Royal Commission on Civil Liability and Compensation for Personal Injury* (1978). Are you disappointed about this?

BRENNER v. GREGORY

Ontario High Court. [1973] 1 O.R. 252

The plaintiff agreed to purchase four town lots after several inspections thereof. The defendant, Gregory, a lawyer, was retained to search the title and to close the transaction which he did. It turned out that a building on the land in question encroached on the street. The vendor had warned the plaintiff of this danger before closing, but only a survey could prove if this was correct, and none was done. The plaintiff sued his lawyer *inter alia.*

Grant, J.: . . . As against the defendant Gregory, the plaintiffs allege that he was negligent in not obtaining a survey or warning the plaintiffs of the danger of purchasing such a property without a survey. It is admitted by all parties that there was no discussion between the purchasers and Mr. Gregory at any time prior to the closing of the transaction in regard to the necessity of acquiring a survey. Mr. Gregory knew that the purchasers had seen the property on a number of occasions before purchasing. It was apparent to the purchasers that the building had stood on that location for many years. There is no doubt in my mind that the purchasers knew there was some question as to whether or not the store was out in the street because of the conversations with him about the closing and the conveyance of the one-half of the street. The fact that they said nothing to Mr. Gregory in these circumstances indicates that they were prepared to deal with the matter themselves and did not rely upon their solicitor therefor.

Mr. Robert E. Mountain Q.C., a solicitor who has practised extensively in Stratford since 1954 with considerable experience in the closing of real estate transactions, stated that in the circumstances of this case a reasonably competent and diligent solicitor in that area acting for a purchaser would not be expected either to secure a survey or to advise his client to do so and his failure to do so would not amount to negligence. In any event, I cannot see that the plaintiffs have lost anything by reason of the failure to advise them about a survey because prior to the commencement of this action it was abundantly clear to them that they could have all of the land on which the building is supposed to have encroached with more to the north thereof.

In an action against the solicitor for negligence it is not enough to say that he has made an error of judgment or shown ignorance of some particular part of the law, but he will be liable in damages if his error or ignorance was such that an ordinarily competent solicitor would not have made or shown it: *Aaroe and Aaroe* v. *Seymour et al.,* [1956] O.R. 736, 6 D.L.R. (2d) 100, [1956-60] I.L.R. 1010*n.*

The obligation of a solicitor to exercise due care in protecting the interests of a client who is a purchaser in a real estate transaction will have been discharged if he has acted in accordance with the general and approved practice followed by solicitors unless such practice is inconsistent with prudent precautions against a known risk, as where particular instructions are given which the solicitor fails to carry out: *Winrob and Winrob* v. *Street and Wollen* (1959), 19 D.L.R. (2d) 172, 28 W.W.R. 118. In a recent case of *Grima et al.* v. *MacMillan,* [1972] 3 O.R. 214, 27 D.L.R. (3d) 666, Parker J. found that it was not the usual practice for solicitors to make a search to find out if a party was alive before issuing a writ of summons against him in a personal injury claim. Thus, where the defendant had died previous to the issue of the writ and the same was then a nullity and the limitation period had expired, the solicitor was not negligent. The responsibility of a solicitor is set out in *Charlesworth on Negligence*, 4th ed. (1962), pp. 1032-1035, para. 1034, as follows:

> "The standard of care and skill which can be demanded from a solicitor is that of a reasonably competent and diligent solicitor. Lord Ellenborough has said: 'An attorney is only liable for *crassa negligentia.*' Again, Lord Campbell in discussing the essential elements to sustain an action for negligence has said: 'What is necessary to maintain such an action? Most undoubtedly that the professional adviser should be guilty of some misconduct, some fraudulent proceeding, or should be chargeable with gross negligence or with gross ignorance. It is only upon one or other of those grounds that the client can maintain an action against the professional adviser.' This, however, does not mean that the standard of care imposed upon a solicitor is below that imposed on other professional men; it only means that it is not enough to prove that the solicitor has made an error of judgment or shown ignorance of some particular part of the law, but that it must be shown that the error or ignorance was such that an ordinary competent solicitor would not have made or shown it."

I have therefore come to the conclusion that there was no negligence in this case on the part of Mr. Gregory.

The action therefore should be dismissed as against all the defendants, with costs.

Action dismissed.

NOTES

1. What standard of care is imposed on solicitors? Are they liable only for "gross" negligence? Should they be? Is the court more likely to impose liability for bungling routine procedures, such as failing to issue a writ before a limitation period expires? *Aaroe & Aaroe* v. *Seymour et al.*, [1956] O.R. 736, at p. 740; *Page* v. *A Solicitor* (1971), 20 D.L.R. (3d) 532.

2. Must the plaintiff establish that had the writ been issued on time his action would have been successful? *Fyk et al.* v. *Millar et al.* (1974), 41 D.L.R. (3d) 684 (Ont. H.C.). Does he have to show he suffered some damages? See *Gouzenko* v. *Harris* (1976), 72 D.L.R. (3d) 293 (Ont. H.C.); *Messineo* v. *Beale* (1978), 5 C.C.L.T. 235 (Ont. C.A.); *Charette* v. *Provenzano* (1979), 7 C.C.L.T. 23 (Ont. H.C.).

3. What is the role of custom here? *Winrob and Winrob* v. *Street and Wollen* (1959), 19 D.L.R. (2d) 172 (B.C.S.C.); *Grima* v. *MacMillan,* [1972] 3 O.R. 214 (S.C.)

4. Are the problems and costs of proving negligence against a lawyer a deterrent to frivolous actions? Will the court be hesitant to impose liability because of the judgmental and hurried nature of the practice of law in all its aspects? Will other lawyers be willing to take a case against a colleague for a plaintiff?

5. Does the degree of care expected of a criminal lawyer or a tax lawyer differ from that of a lawyer in general practice? Should the court recognize the *de facto* specialization of lawyers by holding specialists to a higher standard just as their counterparts in medicine are so held? What are the problems of

doing so? Should a Queen's Counsel be expected to have a greater degree of skill than the average lawyer? Should less be demanded of a country lawyer than a city lawyer?

6. Should a continuing solicitor-client relationship impose a duty on the solicitor to warn his client or to undertake preventive action when circumstances change? For example, should he advise a client to alter his will after a divorce?

7. Although barristers and solicitors in the United Kingdom are immune from tort liability for errors made during the conduct of litigation (see *Rondel* v. *Worsley*, [1967] 3 All E.R. 993 (H.L.), *Saif Ali* v. *Sydney Mitchell & Co.*, [1978] 3 All E.R. 1033 (H.L.), the Canadian courts make no such distinction, holding lawyers liable equally for errors in litigation and in other fields of practice. See *Demarco* v. *Ungaro et al.* (1979), 21 O.R. (2d) 673 (Krever J.). Which is the preferable principle? See *infra*, Chapter 7.

8. What about other methods of controlling the quality of a lawyer's conduct? See The Law Society Act, R.S.O. 1970, c. 238, s. 34 outlining disciplinary procedures for professional misconduct. See generally, Bastedo, "A Note on Lawyer's Malpractice" (1970), 7 O.H.L.J. 311; Wade, "The Attorney's Liability for Negligence" (1959), 12 Vand. L. Rev. 755.

9. Are other professional groups expected to use a special degree of care? See Glos, "Note on the Doctrine of Professional Negligence" (1963), 41 Can. Bar Rev. 140: "Professional men are expected and bound to exercise that degree of care and skill which is displayed by the average practitioner in that profession." See also Eddy, *Professional Negligence* (1955); Roady and Andersen, *Professional Negligence* (1960), reprinted from (1959), 12 Vand. L. Rev. 549; Tallin, "Liability of Professional Men in Negligence and Malpractice" (1960), 3 Can. Bar J. 230.

10. Is the liability of a professional person to a client founded on contract or on tort? Does it make any difference? See *Smith* v. *McInnis* (1978), 4 C.C.L.T. 154 (S.C.C.), Pigeon J. dissenting; *Halvorson* v. *McLellan & Co.*, [1973] S.C.R. 65, at p. 74; *Schwebel* v. *Telekes*, [1967] 1 O.R. 541, at p. 543; *Messineo* v. *Beale* (1978), 5 C.C.L.T. 235 (Ont. C.A.) *cf.* Arnup J.A. at p. 241 (contract), with Zuber J.A. at p. 247 (contract or tort). See also *Esso Petroleum* v. *Mardon*, [1976] 2 All E.R. 5; *Dabous* v. *Zuliani* (1976), 12 O.R. (2d) 230. If this responsibility is a contractual one, how is it that third persons can sue for losses they suffer as a result of professional negligence? See *Haig* v. *Bamford*, [1976] 3 W.W.R. 331 (S.C.C.); *Whittingham* v. *Crease & Co.* (1978), 6 C.C.L.T. 1 (B.C.S.C.). If the responsibility is contractual, could a doctor who supplied free medical attention to an indigent patient be liable to him if he was negligent?

11. For cases on the standard of care of an engineer, see *King* v. *Stolberg* (1968), 70 D.L.R. (2d) 473 (B.C.S.C.); *Carl M. Halvorson Inc.* v. *Robert McLellan & Co. Ltd.* (1973), 29 D.L.R. (3d) 455 (S.C.C.); *Dom. Chain Ltd.* v. *Eastern Construction* (1974), 2 O.R. (2d) 481. See also Laidlaw, *Engineering Law* (4th ed., 1951); an architect, *Clayton* v. *Woodman & Son (Builders) Ltd.*, [1962] 2 All E.R. 33; *Nowlan et al.* v. *Brunswick Construction Ltée* (1973), 34 D.L.R. (3d) 422 (N.B.S.C.); a surveyor, *MacLaren-Elgin Corp. Ltd. et al.* v. *Gooch* (1972), 23 D.L.R. (3d) 394 (Ont. H.C.); a real estate agent, *Burstein* v. *Crisp Devine Ltd.* (1973), 36 D.L.R. (3d) 674 (Ont. H.C.).

12. Should someone who does carpentry work at home be held to the standard of a professional carpenter? See *Wells* v. *Cooper*, [1958] 2 Q.B. 263; [1958] 2 All E.R. 527.

13. Should there be established a special standard of care for professional truck drivers who have chauffeur's licences and have years of experience driving trucks on our highways? Or should they be treated in exactly the same way as a newly licenced automobile driver? What are the considerations, pro and con?

G. DEGREES OF NEGLIGENCE

THE HIGHWAY TRAFFIC ACT

1975 (Alta.), c. 56, s. 160

160. (1) No person transported by the owner or driver of a motor vehicle as his guest without payment for the transportation has any cause of action for damages against the owner or driver for injury, death or loss, in case of accident, unless

(a)   the accident was caused by the gross negligence or wilful and wanton misconduct of the owner or operator of the motor vehicle, and

(b)   the gross negligence or willful and wanton misconduct contributed to the injury, death or loss for which the action is brought.

(2)   This section does not relieve

(a)   any person transporting passengers for hire or gain, or

(b)   any owner or operator of a motor vehicle that is being demonstrated to a prospective purchaser,

of responsibility for any injury sustained by a passenger being transported for hire or gain or sustained by any such prospective purchaser.

(3)   Where the owner of a motor vehicle is being driven in his own motor vehicle by another person, subsection (1) applies as if the owner were the guest of the driver.

MUNICIPAL ACT

R.S.O. 1970, c. 284, s. 427

427. − (1) Every highway and every bridge shall be kept in repair by the corporation the council of which has jurisdiction over it or upon which the duty of repairing it is imposed by this Act and, in case of default, the corporation, subject to *The Negligence Act*, is liable for all damages sustained by any person by reason of such default.

(4) Except in case of gross negligence, a corporation is not liable for a personal injury caused by snow or ice upon a sidewalk.

NOTES

1. There has been much criticism of the idea of drawing distinctions between acts of negligence. Baron Rolfe once said that gross negligence was merely ordinary negligence "with the addition of a vituperative epithet". See *Wilson* v. *Brett* (1843), 11 M. & W. 113. Some courts have even denied the existence of different types of negligence. *Pentecost* v. *London District Auditor*, [1951] 2 K.B. 759, at p. 764. Nevertheless, certain legislation such as the two sections above have utilized language which requires the courts to employ different standards of negligence in civil cases.

The concept of gross negligence is the most frequently used in Canadian statutes, and, despite the groans of some commentators, the courts have managed to handle these various standards (in addition to the criminal standards that exist).

The guest passenger section of Alberta is fairly typical of that used in most provinces. A few provinces, notably Ontario and British Columbia, after much criticism and after much dilution of the gross negligence standard (see *Engler* v. *Rossignol* (1975), 10 O.R. (2d) 721 (C.A.)), have abolished their guest passenger legislation, permitting them to recover for ordinary negligence like anyone else. In Ontario, 1977, c. 54, s. 16, repealed s. 132(3) of the Highway Traffic Act, which required guest passengers to prove gross negligence in order to succeed against their drivers. Guest passengers were barred from recovery totally in Ontario from 1935 to 1967.

2. The leading case defining gross negligence is *Cowper* v. *Studer*, [1951] S.C.R. 450, where Mr. Justice Locke defined it as "very great negligence in the circumstances of a particular case". See also *Kingston* v. *Drennan* (1896), 27 S.C.R. 46; *Holland* v. *Toronto*, [1927] 1 D.L.R. 99.

3. Perhaps it is not as difficult to understand the difference as some have made out. Judge Magruder is reputed to have explained the difference among negligence, gross negligence and recklessness as being the distinction among a fool, a damned fool and a God-damned fool. Would a charge to a Canadian jury incorporating this language be acceptable?

4. In *Girling* v. *Howden*, [1949] 3 D.L.R. 622, [1949] 2 W.W.R. 772, the British Columbia Court of Appeal (Sidney Smith J.A., dissenting) held that a driver who fell asleep at the wheel of his car was guilty of "gross negligence". O'Halloran J.A. said that the magnitude of the foreseeable risk involved in falling to sleep imposed a duty "to take more than ordinary care" not to do so while driving. It was reckless indifference to existing and foreseeable risks in which loss of life was almost inevitable. Compare with *McDonald* v. *Little* (1970), 14 D.L.R. (3d) 114 (Alta. S.C.), where a driver who fell into a hypnoidal state was not held to be grossly negligent. See also *Ewashko* v. *Desiatnyk* (1973), 35 D.L.R. (3d) 318 (Man. C.A.) and *Atkins et al.* v. *Urlichsen et al.* (1973), 37 D.L.R. (3d) 368 (B.C.S.C.).

5. In a 30 m.p.h. zone, is driving at 50 m.p.h. gross negligence? What does it depend upon?

6. In *Gordon* v. *Nutbean*, [1969] 2 O.R. 420, Mr. Justice Haines stated:

"Gross negligence is a question of fact. It must be established that the conduct in question, if there is not a conscious wrongdoing, is a marked departure from the standard by which responsible and competent people in charge of motor-cars govern themselves. See Duff C.J.C. in *McCulloch* v. *Murray*, [1942] S.C.R. 141, [1942] 2 D.L.R. 179. In considering the conduct alleged to be gross, the court should consider the cumulative effect of all the factors producing the casualty and not fall into the error where there are several factors, of considering them individually. Taken alone, in a given set of circumstances, excessive speed, improper lookout, breach of the rules of the road, lack of control, and many others, may or may not amount to gross negligence, but when considered together their totality may be overwhelming.

In this case, considering the cumulative effect of the negligence of the defendant, Lawrence Nutbean, I find that his gross negligence has been established on the following facts.

1. He was driving at an excessive rate of speed.

2. He was driving with bald rear tires which, on that highway and under such circumstances, made his car very difficult to control.

3. He attempted to overtake and pass northbound traffic when southbound traffic was so close that he could not possibly do so without very great danger to southbound traffic and his own passengers.

4. In my opinion, this manoeuvre was the act of a man who either did not care or was utterly reckless. The moment he swung out, disaster was both apparent and inevitable.

5. On getting on to the west side of the highway, he failed to control his automobile in cutting back into the east side so that he lost control and a collision resulted.

6. That on the occasion in question, he drove with a reckless state of mind and was indifferent to the rights of others."

7. In *Roy* v. *McEwan*, [1969] 2 O.R. 530 the defendant who had been drinking and driving at an excessive rate of speed at night ran into a car, the tail-lights of which he should have seen. Mr. Justice Lacourciere stated:

"On the evidence I am not prepared to say that the defendant's ability to drive was impaired by his consumption of alcohol in any criminal sense. This has not been observed and is not pleaded. However, consumption of alcohol is a definite factor to be weighed with the other obvious acts of negligence; the speed and the failure to keep a look-out, running into the rear of the southbound vehicle and then pulling away. The cumulative effect of all such factors leads me to the inescapable conclusion that the conduct of the defendant exhibited a very marked departure from the standard of responsible and competent drivers and that, therefore, the defendant was guilty of gross negligence as defined in the leading cases cited to me."

See also *Avgeropoulos et al.* v. *Karanasos*, [1969] 2 O.R. 521 (D.C.J.); *Wright* v. *Burrell* (1973), 32 D.L.R. (3d) 334 (Ont. C.A.). A helpful article on this issue is MacArthur, "Gross Negligence and the Guest Passenger" (1960), 38 Can. Bar Rev. 47. See also Singleton, "Gross Negligence and the Guest Passenger" (1973), 11 Alta. L. Rev. 165. As for the role of appellate courts in reviewing trial judges' decisions on gross negligence, see *Goulais* v. *Restoule* (1975), 48 D.L.R. (3d) 285 (S.C.C.) *per* Dickson J., dissenting.

8. The courts have avoided the use of the absolute and partial bars against guest passengers whenever they could. Many varied and imaginative theories have been invented to enable judges to circumvent the subsection. In the leading case *Harrison* v. *Toronto Motor Car and Krug*, [1945] O.R. 1, at p. 13, [1945] 1 D.L.R. 286, at p. 294, the court limited the operation of the subsection to the abolition of the newly-created liability of an owner *qua* owner, but did not "bar a right of action due to some other relationship". Much ink has been spilled in describing the extent of these "other relationships", which have included master and servant, express or implied contracts, statutory relations and others. See Wright, "Comment on *Harrison* v. *Toronto Motor Car*" (1945), 23 Can. Bar Rev. 344; Morton, "Comment on *Duchaine* v. *Armstrong*" (1958), 36 Can. Bar Rev. 414; Linden, "Comment on *Dorosz* v. *Koch*" (1962), 40 Can. Bar Rev. 284; Linden, "Comment on *Feldstein* v. *Alloy Metal Sales*" (1963), 41 Can. Bar Rev. 593; Gibson, "Gratuitous Passenger Discrimination" (1968), 6 Alta. L. Rev. 211; Mendes da Costa, "Husband and Wife in The Law of Torts" in Linden, *Studies in Canadian Tort Law* (1968), 524 *et seq.* and Linden, *Canadian Tort Law* (2nd ed., 1977), p. 515.

9. In *Ouellette* v. *Johnson*, [1963] S.C.R. 96, Mr. Justice Cartwright outlined the test for determining whether a vehicle was "operated in the business of carrying passengers for compensation". This clause is sometimes called the "exception within the exception". The plaintiff had paid a fixed fee of $2 each way to the defendant for the week-end trip on which he was injured. The amount was not based on the cost of gas and oil. His Lordship declared that ". . . once it has been determined that the arrangement between the parties was of a commercial nature the manner in which the amount of the fee to be paid was decided upon becomes irrelevant". See also *Platt* v. *Katz* (1971), 15 D.L.R. (3d) 296 (Ont. C.A.). Compare with *Teasdale* v. *MacIntyre* (1969), 69 D.L.R. (2d) S.C.C. where an agreement to share gas expenses on a holiday was held not to come within the test of *Ouellette* v. *Johnson*. See also *Larente* v. *Thibeault*, [1968] 1 O.R. 285 (C.A.).

10. Another important "relationship" is that of contract. A court may hold that there has been a contract of carriage established between the passenger and the defendant. Often an arrangement to drive someone somewhere is *both* a contract of carriage *and* brings the vehicle under the language of the "exception within the exception" discussed above. Confusion has arisen here by the courts' failure to distinguish the two distinct techniques for avoiding the application of the guest passenger section. In *Co-operators Insurance Association* v. *Kearney*, [1965] S.C.R. 106, an insurance salesman passenger was injured while driven by the defendant adjuster during the course of their employment for the defendant insurance company. The driver was excused of liability because of the wording of the section, but Mr. Justice Spence, writing for the majority, held the company responsible. His Lordship recognized the difference between the contract theory and the "exception within the exception" theory and stated that "Certainly, the vehicle was not 'operated in the business of carrying passengers for compensation'." Nevertheless, His Lordship

held that there is a "duty by implied term of contract to the servant . . . to take reasonable care to provide for the safety of that servant when he is engaged in the course of his employment". See also *Dorosz* v. *Koch*, [1961] O.R. 442, affd. [1962] O.R. 105, 31 D.L.R. (2d) 139 (C.A.); *Holowenko* v. *Kosloski* (1966), 56 D.L.R. (2d) 529, at p. 537 (*per* Disberry J.); *Noger* v. *Bellinger*, [1971] 1 O.R. 403, at p. 407, 15 D.L.R. (3d) 433 (*per* Wilson J.), *cf. Manuge* v. *Dominion Atlantic Ry. Co.* (1973), 32 D.L.R. (3d) 49 (S.C.C.); *Feldstein* v. *Alloy Metal Sales*, [1962] O.R. 476.

H. NECESSITY OF DAMAGE

1. Negligent conduct alone is not enough to visit liability upon an actor; some damage must be caused by the negligent conduct before a cause of action may arise. Although damage is not always a necessary component for a criminal prosecution or for a tort action arising out of the writ of trespass, it is a vital requirement in a negligence action which stems from the writ of trespass on the case. Mr. Justice Guy of the Manitoba Court of Appeal has explained in *Long* v. *Western Propellor Co. Ltd.* (1968), 67 D.L.R. (2d) 345 that "In negligence actions . . . there is no 'cause to sue' until the third requirement of the A, B, C, rule — *i.e.*, the damage, has occurred." Mr. Justice Laskin echoed this view in *Schwebel* v. *Telekes*, [1967] 1 O.R. 541, a case that was held to be a contract action, when he stated, "where a claim for personal injuries is made, proof of damage would be required to complete the cause of action". The requirement of damage is not based on history alone; there are policy reasons that support it. In *Pfiefer* v. *Morrison* (1974), 42 D.L.R. (3d) 314, Wilson J., in dismissing an action, stated:

> "In this highly mobile age collisions between motor vehicles occur in great numbers every day. Many of them have grave consequences in injury to persons and damage to property. In other instances, more numerous, slight damage or no damage is caused to the vehicles and there is no injury to persons. If, in the latter class of cases, a litigant claiming damages for personal injury is able to establish a cause of action and a right to at least nominal damages merely by proving negligence then, I say, needless law-suits must proliferate, each one giving damages and costs to persons who have suffered no injury. Such actions would proceed to trial, at no risk to the plaintiff of failure and penalty costs, and with the assurance that he would recover costs. The undesirability of such a state of affairs is self-evident."

2. When a limitation period is measured from the time when a cause of action in negligence arose, therefore, it begins to run on the date the damage is suffered. See Limitations Act, R.S.O. 1970, c. 246, s. 45; Ontario Highway Traffic Act, R.S.O. 1970, c. 202, s. 146. Thus, in the case of *Roberts* v. *Read* (1812), 16 East 215, 104 E.R. 1070 (K.B.), the plaintiff complained that the defendant, a municipal surveyor, in May 1810, so undermined and exposed his boundary wall that it fell on January 31, 1811. The plaintiff's action was commenced on April 13, 1811. The defendant argued that this action was too late by virtue of a special statutory provision to the effect that an action "for anything done or acted in pursuance of this Act" must be commenced within three months "after the fact committed". At the trial, the plaintiff obtained judgment, but the defendant moved to set it aside. Lord Ellenborough C.J. stated:

> "It is sufficient that the action was brought within three months after the wall fell, for that is the gravamen: the consequential damage is the cause of action in this case. If this had been trespass, the action must have been

brought within three months after the act of trespass comaplined of; but being an action on the case for the consequential damage, it could not have been brought till the specific wrong had been suffered; and that only happened within three months before the action was brought."

3. Sometimes the courts can be quite harsh in determining when the damage occurs. In *Archer* v. *Catton & Co. Ltd.*, [1954] 1 All E.R. 896, for example, an employee contracted a disease of the chest from inhalation of dust alleged to be caused by the negligence of his employer. The employee first discovered the disease three years after he left his employment. His action for damages was brought nine years after he left his employment but within six years of discovering the disease. The court held that the action was barred by the Statute of Limitations. The cause of action accrued when the plaintiff was exposed to the dust, not when he knew or should have known that he suffered injury as a consequence.

4. Sometimes legislation alters the common law and sets out the occasion from which time will run in more specific terms. When a statute directs that the time begins to run from some other event, rather than the time the damage occurred, that of course governs. For example, the new Ontario Health Disciplines Act, 1974 (Ont.), c. 47, s. 17 states:

No duly registered member of a College is liable to any action arising out of negligence or malpractice in respect of professional services requested or rendered unless such action is commenced within one year from the date when the person commencing the action knew or ought to have known the fact or facts upon which he alleges negligence or malpractice.

What problems, if any, does this new section create for doctors?

5. This provision has certainly improved the lot of patients who once had to sue within one year of the date the "services terminated". (See Medical Art, R.S.O. 1970, c. 268, s. 48.) Sometimes patients were barred from suing even though they knew nothing about the malpractice. The Ontario Law Reform Commission had recommended some of these changes in its *Report on Limitation of Actions* (1969). What problems, if any, remain for the patients?

6. One way of extending the time period, in appropriate fact situations, may be to sue for battery. This will depend on the respective limitation periods operative for negligence and battery in the province in which the action is commenced. In Ontario, for example, the Limitations Act, R.S.O. 1970, c. 246, s. 45(1)(j) gives four years from the time the cause of action arose to bring an action for battery. See McLaren, "Of Doctors, Hospitals and Limitations—'The Patient's Dilemma' " (1973), 11 O.H. L.J. 85.

7. Limitation periods set out in the Limitations Act do not normally run against infants or the mentally disabled. See, for example, Limitations Act, R.S.O. 1970, c. 246, s. 47. However, the time does run against children and the mentally disabled when the period within which the action may be brought is enacted in a special statute such as the Medical Act, R.S.O. 1970, c. 268, s. 48. See *Philippon et al.* v. *Legate et al.*, [1970] 1 O.R. 392 (C.A.).

8. See generally McLaren, "The Impact of Limitations Periods on Actionability in Negligence" (1969), 7 Alta. L. Rev. 241; Bowker, "Limitation of Actions in Tort in Alberta" (1962), 2 Alta. L. Rev. 41; Williams, *Limitation of Actions in Canada* (1972).

9. At one time it was possible to bring two separate causes of action as a result of one negligent act. In the now discredited case of *Brunsden* v. *Humphrey* (1884), 14 Q.B. D. 141, the plaintiff was permitted to sue for damages to his cab in one action and for the personal injuries suffered in the same accident in another action. See also *Sandberg* v. *Giesbrecht* (1963), 42 D.L.R. (2d) 107 (B.C.). This is no longer permitted since *Cahoon* v. *Franks*, [1967] S.C.R. 455.

An action was commenced for damage to the plaintiff's automobile within the time period allotted. After the expiry of the limitation period, the plaintiff was allowed to amend his pleadings to include a claim for personal injuries. The Supreme Court of Canada decided that this was not a new cause of action. Mr. Justice Hall quoted at length from an excellent opinion of Porter J.A. of the Alberta Court of Appeal:

... "The factual situation which entitles the plaintiff here to recover damages from the defendant is the tort of negligence, a breach by the defendant of the duty which he owed to the plaintiff at common law which resulted in damage to the plaintiff. The injury to the person and the injury to the goods, and perhaps the injury to the plaintiff's real property and the injury to such modern rights as the right to privacy flowing from the negligence serve only as yardsticks useful in measuring the damage which the breach caused. . . .

To deny this plaintiff the opportunity to have a court adjudicate on the relief which he claims merely because it lacks ancient form would be to return to those evils of practice which led to judicial amendment and the ultimate legislative abolition of the 'form of action' . . . . The decision in *Brunsden* v. *Humphrey* may well have persisted in Great Britain largely because the courts were governed by it. Free as we are to apply reasons unhampered by precedent, I am of the opinion that the principle of *Brunsden* v. *Humphrey* ought not to be adopted."

Mr. Justice Hall concluded that *"Brunsden* v. *Humphrey* is not now good law in Canada and it ought not to be followed".

CHAPTER 5

PROOF OF NEGLIGENCE

The trial of a negligence case is usually more concerned with facts and evidence than it is with substantive law. Historically, a negligence trial was conducted before a judge and a jury. This is still the case in some jurisdictions, notably Ontario, British Columbia and the United States, but in many areas the use of the jury is diminishing. Where a jury is utilized, the judge does not become irrelevant. He still exercises a good deal of control over the jury by ruling on the evidence, by instructing the jury about the law, by commenting on the evidence and by deciding whether there is sufficient evidence to be considered by a jury.

Concerning motor car accidents and resulting litigation, it has often been said that the case actually tried by a jury is a case that never in fact took place, since frequently the evidence is either contradictory or in many cases non-existent. It is here that procedural devices and questions of proof play a large part. *Res ipsa loquitur* is one concept that must be considered in this context. The effect given to the operation of *res ipsa loquitur* may lead away from negligence to a liability without fault. In other cases the ease of dividing fault on a 50-50 basis, made possible by contributory negligence statutes, has led many judges — and probably more juries — into the theoretical error of fixing liability on two motorists where the evidence is, in a sense, completely neutral. Sometimes by statute, we have placed the onus of disproof of negligence on a motorist in circumstances where the happening of the accident itself furnishes no rational basis for the inference of negligence. The truth is that under the guise of "fault-finding" the courts often move in reality, despite the theory, close to a principle of liability without fault.

It is significant that in England, where juries have practically disappeared in negligence cases, *res ipsa loquitur* has, in effect, operated to shift the burden of disproof of negligence to the defendant. Perhaps this is inevitable in light of the fact that the same person who decides that the facts are such as to make the principle of *res ipsa loquitur* applicable, is also faced with the additional problem of determining the actual outcome of the issue of liability on those facts. Once having decided that the facts give rise to an inference of negligence, it is understandable that a judge would require something in the way of proof in order that his mind should be changed. The situation, however, in jurisdictions with juries is entirely different. There, it is the jury which assesses the weight of the inference to be drawn and the jury should, in theory, not be bound by the inference which a judge may initially have drawn. This distinction may explain the difference between many English and Canadian cases. If it does, it is an additional indication of a move towards liability without fault, since an onus of disproof of negligence automatically gives a benefit to a plaintiff at the expense of a defendant who must bear that burden.

If, as Maine said, substantive law was in the early days "secreted in the interstices of procedure", it is no less true today that under the guise of procedure courts are able to shift imperceptibly into forms of liability without fault, while speaking the language of negligence. In the tradition of the common law, effect is frequently given to policies without mentioning them or, perhaps, even recognizing them. The cases in the present section, therefore, while exploring some of the problems of proof in negligence actions, provide further material for a study of the basic objectives and policies of loss-shifting — or loss distribution. Further, difficult problems of proof are a salutary check on the naive but common belief of students that "black-letter" law is more important than the facts to which it must be applied.

A. THE ONUS OF PROOF

WAKELIN v. THE LONDON & S.W. RY. CO.

House of Lords. (1886), 2 App. Cas. 41

Action brought by the administratrix of Henry Wakelin for damages arising from the death of Wakelin due to the alleged negligence of the defendant railway.

At the trial the evidence showed that deceased left his house shortly after ten and was not seen until his body was found on the railway line near a crossing. There was no evidence as to the circumstances under which he got on the line. The defendant admitted Wakelin was struck by one of its trains. The plaintiff put in evidence defendant's answers to interrogatories showing that pedestrians had a clear view of the track and that the company did not give any special signal at the crossing. The defendant called no evidence at the trial and submitted there was no case. The trial judge left the case to the jury who returned a verdict of £800 for the plaintiff. On appeal the Divisional Court set aside the verdict and entered judgment for defendant. The Court of Appeal affirmed this decision. The plaintiff appealed.

Lord Halsbury L.C.: My Lords, it is incumbent upon the plaintiff in this case to establish by proof that her husband's death has been caused by some negligence of the defendants, some negligent act, or some negligent omission, to which the injury complained of in this case, the death of the husband, is attributable. That is the fact to be proved. If that fact is not proved the plaintiff fails, and if in the absence of direct proof the circumstances which are established are equally consistent with the allegation of the plaintiff as with the denial of the defendants, the plaintiff fails, for the very simple reason that the plaintiff is bound to establish the affirmative of the proposition. . . .

If the simple proposition with which I started is accurate, it is manifest that the plaintiff, who gives evidence of a state of facts which is equally consistent with the wrong of which she complains having been caused by — in this sense that it could not have occurred without — her husband's own negligence as by the negligence of the defendants, does not prove that it was caused by the defendants' negligence. She may indeed establish that the event has occurred through the joint negligence of both, but if that is the state of the evidence the plaintiff fails, because *in pari delicto potior est conditio defendentis*. It is true that the onus of proof may shift from time to time as matter of evidence, but still the question must ultimately arise whether the person who is bound to prove the affirmative of the issue, *i.e.*, in this case the negligent act done, has discharged herself of that burden. I am of opinion that the plaintiff does not do this unless she proves that the defendants have caused the injury in the sense which I have explained.

In this case I am unable to see any evidence of how this unfortunate calamity occurred. One may surmise, and it is but surmise and not evidence, that the unfortunate man was knocked down by a passing train while on the level crossing; but assuming in the plaintiff's favour that fact to be established, is there anything to shew that the train ran over the man rather than that the man ran against the train? I understand the admission in the answer to the sixth interrogatory to be simply an admission that the death of the plaintiff's husband was caused by contact with the train. If there are two moving bodies which come in contact, whether ships, or carriages, or even persons, it is not uncommon to hear the person complaining of the injury describe it as having been caused by his ship, or his carriage, or himself having been run into, or run down, or run upon; but if a man ran across an approaching train so close that he was struck by it, is it more true to say that the engine ran down the man, or that the man ran against the engine? Neither man nor engine were intended to come in contact, but each advanced to such a point that contact was accomplished. . . . The peculiarity about this case is that no one knows what the circumstances were. The body of the deceased man was found in the neighbourhood of the level crossing on the down line, but neither by direct evidence nor by reasonable inference can any conclusion be arrived at as to the circumstances causing his death.

It has been argued before your Lordships that we must take the facts as found by the jury. I do not know what facts the jury are supposed to have found, nor is it, perhaps, very material to inquire, because if they have found that the defendants' negligence caused the death of the plaintiff's husband, they have found it without a fragment of evidence to justify such a finding.

Under these circumstances, I move that the judgment appealed from be affirmed, and the appeal dismissed.

[The speeches of Lord Watson and Lord Fitzgerald to the same effect are omitted. Lord Blackburn concurred.]

NOTES

1. Do you think that it is wise to require the plaintiff to establish by proof that the defendant's negligence caused his loss? Why not place the onus of disproof upon the defendant?

2. How is it that the jury found for the plaintiff in this case? Is this an argument for the abolition of the civil jury? Is it an argument for greater judicial control over the jury?

3. Is it enough for the plaintiff to lead medical evidence to the effect that an accident was a *possible* cause of his depression? Should such evidence be allowed to go to the jury at all or is it enough if the jury is warned about its limitations? See *Danjanovich* v. *Buma*, [1970] 3 O.R. 604 (C.A.), *per* Gale C.J.O., at p. 605.

4. If both plaintiff and defendant are at fault the plaintiff no longer loses. See, *infra*, Chapter 11.

5. In order that students may (1) become familiar with the difficulties of proof; (2) appreciate the distinction between laying a foundation for reasonable "inference" as opposed to mere conjecture; (3) form some opinion of the possibility of widely split judicial opinion overruling a jury's opinion, it is suggested they read and compare with the *Wakelin* case, *Jones* v. *Gt. West Ry.* (1930), 47 T.L.R. 39, 144 L.T. 194 (H.L.) and *Danley* v. *C.P.R.*, [1940] S.C.R. 290, [1940] 2 D.L.R. 145 (S.C.C.). Both involved a railway accident. In both the accident resulted in death of the person for whose death damages were claimed. In both a jury at the trial found the railway negligent. In the *Jones* case, the Court of Appeal said there was no evidence on which a jury could find negligence causing death. In the House of Lords four out of five Law

Lords held there was such evidence: a total count of five judges in favour of the jury's verdict, four opposed. In the *Danley* case, the trial judge entered judgment for plaintiff. Four judges in the Saskatchewan Court of Appeal held there was no evidence to support the plaintiff's claim and reversed the judgment. In the Supreme Court of Canada by a 3:2 judgment, the trial judgment was restored: a total count of six judges opposed to a finding of negligence and four in favour.

6. On the function of judges and juries in negligence actions, Lord Cairns stated in *Metropolitan Railway Co.* v. *Jackson* (1877), 3 App. Cas. 193, 37 L.T. 679:

> "The judge has a certain duty to discharge and the jurors have another and a different duty. The judge has to say whether any facts have been established by evidence from which negligence may be reasonably inferred; the jurors have to say whether, from those facts, when submitted to them, negligence ought to be inferred. It is, in my opinion, of the greatest importance in the administration of justice that these separate functions should be maintained, and should be maintained distinct. It would be a serious inroad on the province of the jury, if in a case where there are facts from which negligence may reasonably be inferred, the judge were to withdraw the case from the jury upon the ground that, in his opinion, negligence ought not to be inferred; and it would, on the other hand, place in the hands of the jurors a power which might be exercised in the most arbitrary manner, if they were at liberty to hold that negligence might be inferred from any state of facts whatever. To take the instance of actions against railway companies: a company might be unpopular, unpunctual, and irregular in its service; badly equipped as to its staff; unaccommodating to the public; notorious, perhaps for accidents occurring on the line; and when an action was brought for the consequences of an accident, jurors, if left to themselves, might, upon evidence of general carelessness, find a verdict against the company in a case where the company was really blameless."

7. Compare with the dictum of Evatt J., in *Davis* v. *Bunn* (1936), 56 C.L.R. 246, at p. 264:

> "The whole theory of review of juries' verdicts rests upon the postulate that they are at liberty to reject the judges' view of the facts of the case and of their relative importance. Unless this applies to actions of negligence . . . the jury system will be defeated. Moreover, the over-emphasis or under-emphasis by a judge of mere heads of negligence should never detract from a finding of a jury which proceeds upon a view of the facts differing from that of the judge. Even if the judge's view of the facts is sounder, this principle applies. There is, however, little reason to suppose that the hypothesis just made is always or even usually correct."

FOWLER v. LANNING

Queen's Bench Division. [1959] 1 Q.B. 426; [1959] 1 All E.R. 290

The plaintiff sought damages for "trespass to the person", alleging in his statement of claim that "the defendant shot the plaintiff" and that by reason thereof the plaintiff sustained personal injuries and has suffered loss and damage. In a preliminary motion, the defendant objected that the statement of claim disclosed no cause of action since the plaintiff did not allege that the shooting was either intentional or negligent.

Diplock J.: . . . The alleged injuries were, I am told, sustained at a shooting party; it is not suggested that the shooting was intentional. The practical issue is whether, if the plaintiff was in fact injured by a shot from a gun fired by the defendant, the onus lies upon the plaintiff to prove that the defendant was negligent, in which case, under the modern system of pleading, he must so plead and give particulars of negligence . . . or whether it lies upon the defendant to prove that the plaintiff's injuries were not caused by the defendant's negligence, in which case the plaintiff's statement of claim is sufficient and discloses a cause of action.

I am much indebted to counsel on both sides for their diligence and erudition — tracing the history of the distinction between trespass *vi et armis* and trespass on the case. . . . Pausing . . . at the convenient date of 1852, when the Common Law Procedure Act was passed, it was well established that where personal injury was caused to the plaintiff by the direct act of the defendant himself, alternative remedies in trespass to the person and in negligence were available.

[His Lordship reviewed the historical development of trespass *vi et armis* and trespass on the case.]

Little assistance is to be obtained from any later cases. Since *Stanley* v. *Powell*, and perhaps as a result of that decision, there appears to be no case in the reports where unintentional trespass to the person has been relied upon as distinct from negligence, despite the encouragement of the learned authors of the article on Trespass and Negligence in the Law Quarterly Review in 1933 (45 Law Quarterly Review 359), and the continued appearance in successive editions of Bullen and Leake of a precedent of a pleading in trespass to the person in which neither intention nor negligence is alleged. No doubt in many cases it is the master who is sued for the act of his servant, and here trespass as opposed to case would never lie; but in the 68 years which have passed since *Stanley* v. *Powell* there must have been many cases where the injury to the plaintiff was the direct consequence of the act of the defendant himself. But no practitioner seems to have thought, and certainly no court has decided, that to do so would affect the onus of proof.

I think that what appears to have been the practice of the profession during the present century is sound in law. I can summarize the law as I understand it from my examination of the cases as follows: (1) Trespass to the person does not lie if the injury to the plaintiff, although the direct consequence of the act of the defendant, was caused unintentionally and without negligence on the defendant's part. (2) Trespass to the person on the highway does not differ in this respect from trespass to the person committed in any other place. (3) If it were right to say with Blackburn J. in 1866 that negligence is a necessary ingredient of unintentional trespass only where the circumstances are such as to show that the plaintiff had taken upon himself the risk of inevitable injury (*i.e.*, injury which is the result of neither intention nor carelessness on the part of the defendant), the plaintiff must today in this crowded world be considered as taking upon himself the risk of inevitable injury from any acts of his neighbour which, in the absence of damage to the plaintiff, would not in themselves be unlawful — of which discharging a gun at a shooting party in 1957 or a trained band exercise in 1617 are obvious examples. For Blackburn J., in the passage I have quoted from *Fletcher* v. *Rylands*, was in truth doing no more than stating the converse of the principle referred to by Lord Macmillan in *Read* v. *J. Lyons & Co., Ltd.*, [1947] A.C. 156, 170, that a man's freedom of action is subject only to the obligation not to infringe any duty of care which he owes to others. (4) The onus of proving negligence, where the trespass is not intentional, lies upon the plaintiff, whether the action be framed in trespass or in negligence. This has been unquestioned law in highway cases ever since *Holmes* v. *Mather*, and there is no reason in principle, nor any suggestion in the decided authorities, why it should be any different in other cases. It is, indeed, but an illustration of the rule that he who affirms must prove, which lies at the root of our law of evidence.

I am glad to be able to reach this conclusion, and to know that the Supreme Court of British Columbia has recently done the same (*Walmsley* v. *Humenick*, [1954] 2 D.L.R. 232), for "while admiring the subtlety of the old special pleaders our courts are primarily concerned to see that rules of law and procedure should serve to secure justice between the parties": *per* Lord Simon in *United Australia Ltd.* v. *Barclays Bank Ltd.*, [1941] A.C. 1, [1940] 4 All E.R. 20.

If, as I have held, the onus of proof of intention or negligence on the part of the defendant lies upon the plaintiff, then, under the modern rules of pleading, he must allege either intention on the part of the defendant, or, if he relies upon negligence, he must state the facts which he alleges constitute negligence. Without either of such allegations the bald statement that the defendant shot the plaintiff in unspecified circumstances with an unspecified weapon in my view discloses no cause of action.

This is no academic pleading point. It serves to secure justice between parties. If it is open to the plaintiff — as [Mr. McCreery] must, I think, contend — on the pleadings as they at present stand to prove that the defendant shot him deliberately, failure to allege such intention deprives the defendant of his right to apply to stay the action pending prosecution for the felony (*Smith* v. *Selwyn*, [1914] 3 K.B. 98). I should repeat that there is, of course, in fact no suggestion that the shooting was intentional, and thus felonious. But if [Mr. McCreery] be right, proof of intention would be open under the pleading in its present form.

Turning next to the alternative of negligent trespass to the person, there is here the bare allegation that on a particular day at a particular place "the defendant shot the plaintiff". In what circumstances, indeed with what weapon, from bow and arrow to atomic warhead, is not stated. So bare an allegation is consistent with the defendant's having exercised reasonable care. It may be — I know not — that, had the circumstances been set out with greater particularity, there would have been disclosed facts which themselves shouted negligence, so that the doctrine of *res ipsa loquitur* would have applied. In such a form the statement of claim might have disclosed a cause of action even although the word "negligence" itself had not been used, and the plaintiff in that event would have been limited to relying for proof of negligence upon the facts which he had alleged. But I have today to deal with the pleading as it stands. As it stands, it neither alleges negligence in terms nor alleges facts which, if true, would of themselves constitute negligence. [If, Mr. McCreery is right, he would be entitled to prove that the defendant's gun was to his knowledge defective or even that he was short-sighted and had left his spectacles at home, nor would the plaintiff be bound at any time before the trial to disclose to the defendant what facts he relies upon as constituting negligence.]

I do not see how the plaintiff will be harmed by alleging now the facts upon which he ultimately intends to rely. On the contrary, for him to do so will serve to secure justice between the parties. It offends the underlying purpose of the modern system of pleading that a plaintiff, by calling his grievance "trespass to the person" instead of "negligence", should force a defendant to come to trial blindfold; and I am glad to find nothing in the authorities which compels justice in this case to refrain from stripping the bandage at least from the defendant's eyes.

I hold that the statement of claim in its present form discloses no cause of action.

NOTES

1. The heavy hand of history plays an important role in modern law. Courts

usually have difficulty shedding traditional methods of solving legal problems. *Fowler* v. *Lanning* is a rare example of judicial boldness in discarding a time-worn concept. It has been followed in another context in *Letang* v. *Cooper*, [1965] 1 Q.B. 232, [1964] 2 All E.R. 929 (C.A.) where Lord Justice Denning stated:

"The truth is that the distinction between trespass and case is obsolete. We have a different sub-division altogether. Instead of dividing actions for personal injuries into *trespass* (direct damage) or *case* (consequential damage), we divide the causes of action now according as the defendant did the injury intentionally or unintentionally. If one man intentionally applies force directly to another, the plaintiff has a cause of action in assault and battery, or, if you so please to describe it, in trespass to the person. 'The least touching of another in anger is a battery.' If he does not inflict injury intentionally, but only unintentionally, the plaintiff has no cause of action today in trespass. His only cause of action is in negligence, and then only on proof of want of reasonable care. If the plaintiff cannot prove want of reasonable care, he may have no cause of action at all. Thus, it is not enough nowadays for the plaintiff to plead that 'the defendant shot the plaintiff' [see *Fowler* v. *Lanning*, [1959] 1 Q.B. 426]. He must also allege that he did it intentionally or negligently. If intentional, it is the tort of assault and battery. If negligent and causing damage, it is the tort of negligence.

The modern law on this subject was well expounded by my brother Diplock J., in *Fowler* v. *Lanning* with which I fully agree. But I would go this one step further: when the injury is not inflicted intentionally, but negligently, I would say that the only cause of action is negligence and not trespass. If it were trespass, it would be actionable without proof of damage; and that is not the law today."

2. What is the practical effect of this new approach? Does it advance or impede the policy of loss distribution? Will it have any effect on accident prevention? Is the change primarily a theoretical one?

GOSHEN v. LARIN

Nova Scotia Court of Appeal. (1974), 46 D.L.R. (3d) 137; revd (1975), 56 D.L.R. (3d) 719 (N.S.C.A.); leave to appeal to S.C.C. refused Dec. 17/74.

The defendant was a referee at a wrestling match who made an unpopular decision as far as the crowd was concerned. After leaving the ring he proceeded toward the dressing room escorted by the police amidst a mass of thrown objects. He was struck on the head by one of these objects and fell to his knees, a bit stunned. He got up and continued out of the arena with his right arm shielding his face. Although no one saw him strike anybody, the plaintiff alleged that the defendant pushed him down causing him to fracture his wrist. The defendant appeals from a decision for the plaintiff in an action for battery.

Macdonald J.A.: . . . The action was originally framed in assault. The learned trial Judge permitted counsel for the respondent to amend the statement of claim to include an allegation that the injury complained of was caused by the appellant who "directly either intentionally or negligently caused physical contact with the person of the plaintiff without the plaintiff's consent". In other words, the action is one of battery, being a trespass to the person.

In *Fowler* v. *Lanning,* [1959] 1 All E.R. 290, Diplock, J., then of the Queen's Bench Division, held that the onus of proving negligence, where the trespass is *not* intentional, lies upon the plaintiff, whether the action be framed in trespass or in negligence. Lord Denning in *Letang* v. *Cooper,* [1964] 2 All E.R. 929 (C.A.), said at p. 932:

"If he does not inflict injury intentionally, but only unintentionally, the plaintiff has no cause of action today in trespass. His only cause of action is in negligence, and then only on proof of want of reasonable care."

The English judicial view, as above expressed, appeals to me as being a fair and just one. I am, however, bound by the decision of the Supreme Court of Canada in *Cook* v. *Lewis,* [1952] 1 D.L.R. 1, [1951] S.C.R. 830, in which Cartwright, J., said (p. 15 D.L.R., p. 839 S.C.R.):

"In my view, the cases collected and discussed by Denman J. in *Stanley* v. *Powell,* [1891] 1 Q.B. 86, establish the rule . . . that where a plaintiff is injured by force applied directly to him by the defendant his case is made by proving this fact and the onus falls upon the defendant to prove 'that such trespass was utterly without his fault'. In my opinion *Stanley* v. *Powell* rightly decides that the defendant in such an action is entitled to judgment if he satisfies the onus of establishing the absence of both intention and negligence on his part."

Cook v. *Lewis, supra,* has been followed and applied in various jurisdictions: see *Walmsley et al.* v. *Humenick et al.,* [1954] 2 D.L.R. 232 (B.C.S.C.); *Tillander* v. *Gosselin* (1967), 60 D.L.R. (2d) 18, [1967] 1 O.R. 203 (Ont. H.C.) [affirmed 61 D.L.R. (2d) 192*n* (Ont. C.A.)] ; *Dahlberg* v. *Naydiuk* (1970), 10 D.L.R. (3d) 319, 72 W.W.R. 210 (Man. C.A.).

The law in Canada at present is this: In an action for damages in trespass where the plaintiff proves that he has been injured by the direct act of the defendant, the onus falls upon the defendant to prove that his act was both *unintentional and without negligence* on his part, in order for him to be entitled to a dismissal of the action.

The learned trial Judge found that the appellant "actually did shove or push the defendant, Jacob Goshen, to the floor . . ." but that there was no malice and no intention on the part of the appellant to wilfully injure the respondent, but that the injuries occurred through his negligence. As to what he considered the negligence of the appellant to be, the learned trial Judge said [46 D.L.R. (3d) 137 at pp. 140 and 142] :

". . . it seems to me that even though the defendant did not intend to do any harm to the plaintiff he did not take sufficient precaution to prevent harm befalling the plaintiff through the defendant's actions. *The defendant blindly proceeded up the corridor with one arm in front of his face . . .*

. . .

. . . there is considerable evidence to indicate that the defendant actually conducted himself in a negligent manner by not taking care to avoid striking persons who were lawfully on the premises and who were not in any way threatening him . . ."

(Emphasis added.)

These extracts from the decision of the learned trial Judge must be viewed in light of the following remarks which he also made [at pp. 138-9] :

"The crowd had become hostile and chairs and other objects were being thrown at the referee and at the two wrestlers, Frederick Prosser, sometimes known as Frederick Sweetan, and Eric Pomeroy. They were being escorted by three police officers from the City of Halifax Police Force and two or three security guards through the crowd, many of whom shouted and hurled insults at them as they went by. The plaintiff emphatically testified that he took no part in this demonstration, and there is no evidence to indicate that he did.

Donald Larin, the defendant, and the referee in the bout was preceded by a police officer, and on his left side he was being conducted and held by the left arm by Sergeant John Mitchell of the Halifax Police Force. He held his right arm before his eyes and in front of him in order, as he said, to protect his eyes and at the same time to fend off any blows or objects that were hurled at him."

I accept, of course, the learned trial Judge's finding of facts. I respectfully disagree, however, as to the inference of negligence on the part of the appellant. This inference is a conclusion on the trial Judge's part from the facts by which, in my opinion, we are not bound.

Negligence has been said to be the omission to do something which a reasonable man, guided upon those considerations which ordinarily regulate the conduct of human affairs, would do, or doing something which a prudent and reasonable man would not do: see *Blyth* v. *Birmingham Waterworks Co.* (1856), 11 Ex. 781, 156 E.R. 1047, *per* Baron Alderson, followed and applied in *Gebbie* v. *Saskatoon,* [1930] 4 D.L.R. 543, 25 Sask. L.R. 7, [1930] 2 W.W.R. 625 (Sask. C.A.).

Of course, the question of liability for negligence cannot arise at all until it is established that the man who has been negligent owed some duty to the person who seeks to make him liable for his negligence. In the present case, I assume that there was a duty to take care on the part of the appellant with respect to the respondent.

Negligence being the failure to take due care according to the circumstances, in determining whether the appellant exercised due care, the test or standard is whether or not he acted as a reasonable and prudent person would act. As was stated in *Ratcliffe* v. *Whitehead,* [1933] 3 W.W.R. 447, 41 Man. R. 570, the test is whether a person charged with negligence has acted in such a way as reasonably could be required in such a case.

. . .

I accept, of course, the finding of the learned trial Judge that the respondent received his injuries by being pushed unintentionally by the appellant. It is my opinion, however, that, due to the circumstances that existed at the time, the appellant was perfectly justified in proceeding up the corridor with his right arm in front of his face which, in all probability, is the reason he made contact with the respondent. Indeed, he was in protective police custody at the time and the police officers themselves had to push people away. Certainly, it could not be said that the police, in so doing, were guilty of assault or trespass to the person, unless, of course, they used excessive force. Although it is not necessary to decide this point, and I expressly refrain from doing so, it might well be argued that even if the appellant pushed the respondent intentionally, he was doing so in aid of and in consort with the peace officers, in achieving the common purpose of the police officers, namely, to get the appellant and the two wrestlers safely to their respective dressingrooms.

In the result, it is my opinion that the actions of the appellant did not amount to negligence under the circumstances, from which it follows that he has discharged the onus of showing that the respondent's injuries were not caused by his negligence.

The appeal should be allowed with costs, both here and in the Court below.

Appeal allowed;
action dismissed.

NOTES

1. In *Ellison* v. *Rogers* (1967), 67 D.L.R. (2d) 21 (Ont. S.C.), the plaintiff was struck by a golf ball driven by the defendant, 100 yards away, which "hooked" inexplicably. The plaintiff pleaded trespass, as well as negligence. Brooke J., in dismissing the action, explained the law as follows:

"The plaintiff contends in his submissions to me that if I find that the plaintiff was indeed struck by the golf ball as alleged, that the onus of proof then shifts to the defendant to show that this striking was caused neither by his negligence nor was it intentional. That is to say, as to these two elements, either of which may be elements of a trespass as an actionable wrong, the onus is on the defendant to disprove that the striking was either negligent or intentional if the plaintiff succeeds in proving that he was struck.

I think this submission is correct.

. . .

In the circumstances then, the defendant Rogers has satisfied me by a preponderance of evidence which I believe that he was not negligent in the circumstances. Accordingly, the action as against both of the defendants will be dismissed."

See also *Hollebone* v. *Barnard,* [1954] O.R. 236, [1954] 2 D.L.R. 278.

2. The vitality of this principle is evinced in *Dahlberg* v. *Naydiuk* (1970), 10 D.L.R. (3d) 319 (Man. C.A.). The action, framed in both negligence and trespass, arose when a farmer was accidentally shot by a hunter who fired over his land. Mr. Justice Dickson referred to the onus shift as "one of those strange anomalies of the law" and quoted Dean Wright's critique of the rule as "irrational and unnecessary". Nevertheless, he held that "[i]f such a change is to be made in the law it must be made by a court higher than this". An insight into the policy rationale behind the stubborn longevity of this principle is provided by this statement of Mr. Justice Dickson:

"Hunters must recognize that firing over land without permission of the owner constitutes a trespass to land and if injury to person results, trespass to person. A hunter who fires in the direction in which he knows or ought to know farm buildings are located must accept full responsibility for resultant damage to person or property. It is no answer to say he thought the buildings were unoccupied. There are vast areas of western Canada in which deer abound and where no farming activities are carried on. Even in farming areas there are often hills from which one can fire at game in the valley below without risk of injury to others. If a hunter chooses to hunt in a farming area he must do so in full awareness of the paramount right of the farmer to carry on his lawful occupation without risk of injury from stray bullets."

See also *Teece et al.* v. *Honeybourn et al.* (1975), 54 D.L.R. (3d) 549 (B.C.S.C.), where the deceased was shot by the police as they pursued him on foot in connection with a stolen car problem. In an action by the family of the deceased, Rae J. found one of the defendant policemen 20% at fault and the deceased 80% to share. *Cook* v. *Lewis* and *Dahlberg* v. *Naydiuk* were relied upon because His Lordship felt bound to do so, but he indicated that he found the reasoning in *Fowler* v. *Lanning* and *Letang* v. *Cooper* "persuasive".

3. See also *Tillander* v. *Gosselin,* [1967] 1 O.R. 203; *Bell Canada* v. *Bannermount Ltd.,* [1973] 2 O.R. 811 (C.A.), buried cable damaged during digging, onus on defendant not discharged; *Venning* v. *Chin* (1974), S.A.S.R. 299, trespass still available though of "dubious justice or utility". See generally Fridman, "Trespass or Negligence" (1971), 9 Alta. L. Rev. 250; Winfield and Goodhart, "Trespass and Negligence" (1933), 49 L.Q.R. 359; Trindade, "Comment" (1971), 49 Can. Bar Rev. 612.

4. Why have the Canadian courts taken this line? Are they more conservative than the English? Are they more cowardly? Or are they more progressive in that they are concerned with practical results rather than with theorizing?

5. In *Bell Canada* v. *Cope (Sarnia) Ltd.* (1980), 11 C.C.L.T. 170, Mr. Justice Linden stated:

"Despite many attacks by judges and scholars, the trespass action has survived in Canada, even though it has long ago been eclipsed both in the United Kingdom and in the United States. The trespass action still performs several functions, one of its most important being a mechanism for shifting the onus of proof of whether there has been intentional or negligent wrongdoing to the defendant, rather than requiring the plaintiff to prove fault. The trespass action, though perhaps somewhat anomalous, may thus help to smoke out evidence possessed by defendants, who cause direct injuries to plaintiffs, which should assist courts to obtain a fuller picture of the facts, a most worthwhile objective."

Does this make any sense? Is this a good methodoly to adopt in achieving this goal? What is wrong with it?

6. Another holdover from days gone by is the defence of inevitable accident. Although perhaps meaningful as a defence to the old action for trespass, it seems to have no place in modern negligence law. The theory of the defence is that the defendant can escape liability if he shows one of two things: (1) "the cause of the accident, and . . . the result of that cause was inevitable", or (2) "all the possible causes, one or other of which produced the effect, and . . . with regard to every one of these possible causes that the result could not have been avoided". See *The Merchant Prince*, [1892] P. 179, *per* Fry L.J.

7. Mr. Justice Devlin in *Esso Petroleum Co. Ltd.* v. *Southport Corporation*, [1953] 2 All E.R. 1204; revd. [1954] 2 All E.R. 561; revd. [1956] A.C. 218, [1955] 3 All E.R. 864, commenting on *The Merchant Prince* stated:

"I do not find *The Merchant Prince* an easy case to apply. One must distinguish, I think, between a case where inevitable accident has to be proved as a matter of defence and a case of *res ipsa loquitur*. Take, for example, trespass to which inevitable accident may be a defence. When the plaintiff proves the trespass (I am dealing now with the ordinary case and not with trespass arising from use of the highway) his cause of action is complete, and the defendant fails unless he proves his defence. But when the cause of action is negligence, the plaintiff must prove negligence; *res ipsa loquitur* is a principle which helps him to do so. If one looks at the classic statement of the rule by Erle C.J., in *Scott* v. *London Dock Co.*, one finds that it says no more than that the happening of an accident may in certain circumstances itself be reasonable evidence of negligence; and when there is reasonable evidence of negligence put forward by the plaintiff and no explanation put forward by the defendant, the plaintiff is, of course, entitled to succeed. If the defendant offers a plausible explanation consistent with his diligence, the plaintiff is back where he was before and must show the greater probability of negligence. The distinction is seen at once in pleading. In trespass the defendant must plead inevitable accident. . . . In negligence he need only plead a denial. . . .

8. In *United Motors Service Inc.* v. *Hutson*, [1937] S.C.R. 294, [1937] 1 D.L.R. 737, Duff C.J. said:

"The phrase *res ipsa loquitur* is, however, used in connection with another class of case where, by force of a specific rule of law, if certain facts are established, then the defendant is liable unless he proves that the occurrence out of which the damage has arisen falls within the category of inevitable accident. The rule of law in such a case is set forth by Fry L.J., in *The Merchant Prince*, [1892] P. 172 . . . . [In such case] the onus is on the defendant to establish affirmatively inevitable accident or, in other words, absence of negligence on his part."

9. In *Sinclair* v. *Maillett*, [1951] 3 D.L.R. 216, 27 M.P.R. 335 (N.B.), Harrison J., said:

"In the present case the plaintiff alleges injury by the negligence of the defendant. The defendant denies negligence. The burden of establishing his case is upon the plaintiff. The plaintiff proved a *prima facie* case of negligence; the defendant gave evidence to show that the accident was not due to his negligence. If the court, after all the evidence is in, is left in doubt, the decision must be against the plaintiff who has the burden of establishing his case. . . .

In the present case this question is complicated if it is considered that the defendant is setting up the defence of inevitable accident. He did plead inevitable accident in the alternative, but this was unnecessary. He could set up the defence of inevitable accident under his plea denying negligence. It is not necessary to plead inevitable accident affirmatively. . . .

Text-book writers have frequently stated that where the defence is inevitable accident the burden of proof is on the defendant. This can mean only burden of proof in the secondary sense of burden of adducing evidence to meet the *prima facie* case of the plaintiff. . . .

The burden of proof in the sense of establishing the case still rests on the party alleging negligence, though the burden of proof in the sense of adducing evidence is upon the party raising the defence of inevitable accident."

10. In *Gootson* v. *The King*, [1948] 4 D.L.R. 33, a car operated by a servant of the Crown mounted the sidewalk and struck the plaintiff. Witnesses called by the plaintiff proved that the driver had fainted and so lost control of the car. In the Supreme Court of Canada, Kerwin J. dealt with the case on the assumption that this was the only evidence before the court. He admitted that the plaintiff could rely on *res ipsa loquitur* upon proof of the car mounting the sidewalk. There was, however, the additional evidence of fainting and loss of control. "This circumstance fulfilled the only obligation that would otherwise have rested upon the [defendant] *i.e.*, of showing facts which produced an explanation equally consistent with negligence and no negligence: *United Motors Service* v. *Hutson*, [1937] S.C.R. 294." To the argument that the defendant ought to have shown affirmatively that the servant was not subject to epileptic fits, Kerwin J. said, "this would impose upon the [defendant] a greater onus than is recognized as devolving upon a defendant in circumstances where the maxim applies". Compare, however, *Dessaint* v. *Carrière* (1958), 17 D.L.R. (2d) 222 (Ont. C.A.), where, in a similar case, Laidlaw J.A. said that evidence of a sudden dizzy spell and loss of consciousness might not be sufficient, since the defendant must prove affirmatively that he exercised all reasonable care, and *semble* this may require proof that he could not reasonably foresee a dizzy spell.

11. A bee lands on D as he drives on the highway. D is so preoccupied with the bee that he fails to negotiate a curve, crosses the centre line and collides with P. Inevitable accident? See *Sinclair* v. *Nyehold* (1972), 5 W.W.R. 461 (B.C.C.A.). What if the bee had stung D? See also *Aubrey* v. *Harris* (1957), 7 D.L.R. (2d) 545.

LEGISLATIVE ASSEMBLY OF ONTARIO, SELECT COMMITTEE ON AUTOMOBILE INSURANCE, FINAL REPORT (1963)

THE DEFENCE OF INEVITABLE ACCIDENT

In its submission to the Committee, the special committee on trial of damage claims, appointed by the Law Society of Upper Canada made the following observations (pages 84-86, Committee proceedings for October 26, 1962):

> "With so many older models of cars on the highway, the condition of the brakes, mechanical equipment and tires is often not of the best, but nonetheless the condition is often not known to the owner. Suddenly there might be a breakdown and in a few cases the car goes out of control and injures someone. When sued by the innocent sufferer, the owner's insurer raises the defence of unavoidable accident. This defence sometimes succeeds, although more often it is denied. It is submitted the owner should be responsible for all defects in his motor vehicle, and The Highway Traffic Act should be amended accordingly.

RESPONSIBILITY FOR PHYSICAL OR MENTAL CONDITION OF OPERATOR

It has been established in Ontario that if without negligence on his part the operator loses consciousness, or dies, or becomes insane and causes injury the innocent sufferer cannot recover. This disability in the operator is something that should be assumed by the insurer of the vehicle rather than by the person suffering injury. It could be assumed with probably no increase in the insurance rates."

The Committee feels that justice will be better served if the defence of inevitable accident is eliminated and recommends that appropriate legislative steps be taken to do so. There is, after all, no reason why any party should suffer financial ruin by reason of an unavoidable accident which stems either from a sudden defect of a motor vehicle or the illness or death of the driver of a motor vehicle. The Committee believes that such admittedly rare occurrences should be absorbed in the existing insurance arrangements even if the result is a very minor increase in premium rates or, in the case of an uninsured vehicle, should be borne by the Motor Vehicle Accident Claims Fund.

NOTES

1. To date this recommendation has been ignored. Why? Is it worthy of adoption?

B. RES IPSA LOQUITUR: ORIGIN AND SCOPE

BYRNE v. BOADLE

Exchequer. (1863), 2 H. & C. 722; 159 E.R. 299

In an action for negligence, the evidence for the plaintiff was to the effect that as he was walking past the shop of the defendant, a dealer in flour, a barrel of flour fell from a window above the shop and seriously injured him. The defendant submitted that there was no evidence of negligence for the jury, and the Assessor being of that opinion non-suited the plaintiff, reserving leave to the latter to move the Court of Exchequer to enter a verdict for him for £50 damages, the amount assessed by the jury. The plaintiff obtained a rule *nisi.*

Charles Russell now shewed cause. . . . There was no evidence that the defendant, or any person for whose acts he would be responsible, was engaged in lowering the barrel of flour. It is consistent with the evidence that the purchaser of the flour was superintending the lowering of it by his servant, or it may be that a stranger was engaged to do it without the knowledge and authority of the defendant. [Pollock C.B.: The presumption is that the defendant's servants were engaged in removing the defendant's flour; if they were not it was competent to the defendant to prove it.] Surmise ought not to be substituted for strict proof when it is sought to fix a defendant with serious liability. The plaintiff should establish his case by affirmative evidence.

Secondly, assuming the facts to be brought home to the defendant or his servants, these facts do not disclose any evidence for the jury of negligence. The plaintiff was bound to give affirmative proof of negligence. But there was not a scintilla of evidence, unless the occurrence is of itself evidence of negligence. . . . [Pollock C.B.: There are certain cases of which it may be said *res ipsa loquitur*, and this seems one of them. . . .] On examination of the authorities, that doctrine would seem to be confined to the case of a collision between two trains upon the same line, and both being the property and under the management of the same company. . . .

Pollock C.B.: We are all of opinion that the rule must be absolute to enter the verdict for the plaintiff. The learned counsel was quite right in saying that there are many accidents from which no presumption of negligence can arise, but I think it would be wrong to lay down as a rule that in no case can presumption of negligence arise from the fact of an accident. Suppose in this case the barrel had rolled out of the warehouse and fallen on the plaintiff, how could he possibly ascertain from what cause it occurred? It is the duty of persons who keep barrels in a warehouse to take care that they do not roll out, and I think that such a case would, beyond all doubt, afford *prima facie* evidence of negligence. A barrel could not roll out of a warehouse without some negligence, and to say that a plaintiff who is injured by it must call witnesses from the warehouse to prove negligence seems to me preposterous. So in the building or repairing of a house, or putting pots on the chimneys, if a person passing along the road is injured by something falling upon him, I think the accident alone would be *prima facie* evidence of negligence. Or if an article calculated to cause damage is put in a wrong place and does mischief, I think that those whose duty it was to put it in the right place are *prima facie* responsible, and if there is any state of facts to rebut the presumption of negligence, they must prove them. The present case upon the evidence comes to this, a man is passing in front of the premises of a dealer in flour, and there falls down upon him a barrel of flour. I think it apparent that the barrel was in the custody of the defendant who occupied the premises, and who is responsible for the acts of his servants who had the control of it; and in my opinion the fact of its falling is *prima facie* evidence of negligence, and the plaintiff who was injured by it is not bound to show that it could not fall without negligence, but if there are any facts inconsistent with negligence, it is for the defendant to prove them.

[The judgments of Bramwell, Channell and Pigott BB., to the same effect are omitted.]

NOTES

1. This case is the first one in which the phrase *res ipsa loquitur* was used. What did Chief Baron Pollock mean by these words? Did he believe he was relying on some established legal principle in employing this Latin phrase? Did he believe he was establishing a new legal doctrine?

2. Did *Byrne* v. *Boadle* decide that the plaintiff no longer had to prove negligence? What did it decide?

3. What kind of evidence was that adduced in *Byrne* v. *Boadle*? Should courts rely on this type of evidence? What are the dangers of doing so? What are the advantages?

4. Is it not possible that a tramp entered the building and rolled the barrel out of the window? How should the court treat this possibility?

5. Chief Justice Erle explained the principal case in *Scott* v. *London & St. Katherine Docks Co.* (1865), 3 H. & C. 596, 159 E.R. 665: "There must be reasonable evidence of negligence; but where the thing is shown to be under the management of the defendant or his servants, and the accident is such as in the ordinary course of things does not happen if those who have the management use proper care, it affords reasonable evidence, in the absence of explanation by the defendants, that the accident arose from want of care." Does this make sense?

6. In *Shawinigan Carbide Co.* v. *Doucet* (1909), 42 S.C.R. 281, at p. 330, the Supreme Court of Canada, in an *obiter dictum*, stated that *res ipsa loquitur* is applicable:

". . . when the injury has been caused by something wholly within the control of the defendant or of persons for whose actions he was responsible, and the occurrence to which the injury was due was not of such a character as would ordinarily take place in the absence of negligence. Given these conditions, the inference in the absence of explanation is a plain one, but the question whether the inference is, or is not, permissible, is in truth, not a question of law at all. Apart from the specific rule it is merely a question of right thinking".

7. One of the clearest expositions of the doctrine was by Dean C.A. Wright

in his article "*Res Ipsa Loquitur*", in *Studies in Canadian Tort Law* (1968), at p. 46, to this effect:

"What is required is a situation where the happening of the accident in itself will afford the basis from which an inference can be drawn as a matter of ordinary experience that there was negligence and that the defendant was the person who was negligent."

See also *Richer* v. *A. J. Freiman Ltd.*, [1965] 2 O.R. 750 (C.A.), *per* McGillivray J.A.

8. Another fine articulation of the doctrine occurs in *Lloyde* v. *West Midlands Gas Bd.*, [1971] 1 W.L.R. 749, at p. 755 where Megaw L.J. stated:

"I doubt whether it is right to describe *res ipsa loquitur* as a 'doctrine'. I think that it is no more that [*sic*] an exotic, although convenient, phrase to describe what is in essence no more than a common sense approach, not limited by technical rules, to the assessment of the effect of evidence in certain circumstances. It means that a plaintiff *prima facie* establishes negligence where: (i) it is not possible for him to prove precisely what was the relevant act or omission which set in train the events leading to the accident; but (ii) on the evidence as it stands at the relevant time it is more likely than not that the effective cause of the accident was some act or omission of the defendant or of someone for whom the defendant is responsible, which act or omission constitutes a failure to take proper care for the plaintiff's safety."

9. There is a good deal of literature on *res ipsa loquitur*. Among the better articles are: Wright, "*Res Ipsa Loquitur*", in *Studies in Canadian Tort Law* (1968); Prosser, "*Res Ipsa Loquitur* in California" (1949), 37 Calif. L. Rev. 183, 223; Fridman, "The Myth of *Res Ipsa Loquitur*" (1954), 10 U. of T.L.J. 233; Jaffe, "*Res Ipsa Loquitur* Vindicated" (1951), 1 Buff. L. Rev. 1; Paton, "*Res Ipsa Loquitur*" (1936), 14 Can. Bar Rev. 480; Seavey, "*Res Ipsa Loquitur* in England and Australia" (1972), 35 Mod. L. Rev. 337; Schiff, "A *Res Ipsa Loquitur* Nutshell" (1976), 26 U. of T.L.J. 451.

KIRK ET AL. v. McLAUGHLIN COAL & SUPPLIES LTD.

Ontario Court of Appeal. (1967), 66 D.L.R. (2d) 321

Evans J.A. (orally): This is an appeal by the plaintiffs from the judgment of W. A. C. Hall Co. Ct. J. in the 8th Division Court of the County of Ontario on October 25, 1966, dismissing the plaintiffs' action with costs.

The action arises from a claim by the plaintiffs for damages caused to their home in the City of Oshawa as the result of two explosions which occurred in their oil furnace on February 21 and March 6, 1966.

The facts as found by the trial judge are as follows: The furnace was converted by the installation of an oil burner about 12 years ago and thereafter the defendant supplied oil to the plaintiffs and as part of the arrangement agreed to service the furnace, and also clean it annually.

On January 7, 1966, some repairs were made to the furnace by the defendant. On February 21st, the first explosion occurred. The furnace was put back in operating order by the defendant and on March 6th the second explosion took place.

The trial judge accepted the evidence of the plaintiffs that they did not touch the furnace other than the thermostatic control to increase or decrease heat and that no one other than the defendant serviced the furnace.

The plaintiffs could not establish the cause of the explosions and were unable to establish any specific act of negligence which might cast responsibility upon the defendant. It was argued on their behalf that the circumstances surrounding the two accidents were such that the happenings in themselves formed a basis for inferring negligent conduct on the part of the defendant and was a situation where the maxim of *res ipsa loquitur* was applicable. The learned trial judge rejected this submission, being of the view that exclusive control of the furnace by the defendant was a prerequisite to the application of the doctrine and further that to hold the defendant liable would be to make it an insurer of the plaintiff.

With the greatest respect to the trial judge, I must disagree. I am of the opinion that all the circumstances surrounding the incidents created a situation where *res ipsa loquitur* comes into operation. It is common knowledge that oil furnaces do not normally explode. The trial judge accepted the evidence of the plaintiffs that they had done nothing nor had they permitted anything to be done, which might cause the explosions and we are then faced with the problem as to whether the explosions occurred under such circumstances that it is so improbable that they occurred without negligence on the part of the defendant that their occurrences alone immediately give rise to the inference that the defendant was in fact negligent. Having ruled out intervention on the part of the plaintiffs and having accepted the evidence that the defendants alone serviced the furnace, the trial judge in my opinion was forced to conclude that effective "control" was in the hands of the defendant. I do not consider "control" to mean physical custody or possession. It is sufficient to establish "control" if it is demonstrated that the servicing and repairing of the furnace was the exclusive province of the defendant and that no other agency intervened.

Res ipsa loquitur is no more than a specific instance of circumstantial evidence which may or may not be sufficient to raise an inference. In the present case, I believe that a situation was established where the happening of the explosions in themselves founded a basis from which an inference can be reasonably and properly drawn as a matter of common experience that the explosions resulted from negligence and that the negligence is properly attributed to the defendant.

Whatever procedural advantages the rule may have it does not relieve the plaintiffs of their primary burden of proving their case against the defendant. The defendant may avoid liability if it can meet the inference of negligence by giving an explanation showing the exercise of reasonable care in the maintenance and servicing of the furnace. In my opinion the evidence on behalf of the defendant fails to reach that standard and the inference of negligence raised by the plaintiffs is sufficient to discharge the onus placed on them of proving their case on the balance of probabilities.

I recognize that it is not the function of the defendant to disprove negligence on its part. It is only required to give an explanation that is consistent with the exercise of due care on its part and then the explanation is weighed against the inference arising from the happening of the accident and the liability is determined on the balance of probabilities.

The appeal is allowed with costs fixed at $25. The judgment below is set aside and judgment will issue in favour of the plaintiffs for $394.43 together with costs and a counsel fee of $25.

Appeal allowed.

CLAYTON v. J.N.Z. INVESTMENTS LTD.

Ontario Court of Appeal. (1968), 1 D.L.R. (3d) 440

Gale C.J.O.: This is an appeal from the judgment of I. M. Macdonnell Co. Ct. J. of the County Court of the County of York allowing damages to the plaintiff in an amount to be assessed. The assessment has not yet taken place.

The action arises by reason of an unfortunate incident which took place on November 22, 1964. The plaintiff moved into an apartment in a large apartment building approximately five and a half months before that date. The building had been completed in February, 1964, and the plumbing therein had been installed by the defendants. On September 15th the heat for the fall term of 1964 was turned on and, inexplicably, one of the lead pipes leading to a radiator in the plaintiff's apartment burst on November 22nd causing damage to some of his furnishings and fixtures.

In the pleadings the plaintiff asserted that his loss had been caused by negligence on the part of the defendants. It is to be noted at once that neither the owners nor those responsible for maintaining the building were made parties to the action.

When the case came on for trial the only fact really proved by the plaintiff was to the effect that the pipe burst on November 22, 1964, at an elbow with a V-shaped fracture and that he did not tamper with the fixture personally. The section of the pipe including the burst was not produced and there was no expert evidence which might have aided the court as to the cause of the mishap.

The defendants elected to call no evidence.

The learned judge came to the conclusion that on the evidence which had been adduced he was justified in finding that there was a *prima facie* case of negligence. With great respect we cannot agree with that finding as against these defendants. There was no evidence as to when the installation of the plumbing took place, nor whether the defendants supplied the pipe in question. The court was not informed as to what happened with respect to the maintenance or condition of the plumbing between the time of the completion of its installation and November 22nd and, in our opinion, we cannot bring ourselves to agree that the mere statement of the plaintiff to the effect that the pipe had burst constitutes evidence of negligence on the part of the defendants. Any number of causes might have been the underlying reason for the failure of the pipe and we do not think it was sufficient in the circumstances for the plaintiff merely to show that the fracture had occurred and that damage resulted from it.

It might have been otherwise had the owners or those responsible for the maintenance of the apartment also been made parties to the action.

It is our view, therefore, and we are in as good a position as the trial judge to assess the evidence, that the action ought to have been dismissed. Accordingly, the appeal will be allowed and the action dismissed. Costs here and below, of course, follow the event.

Appeal allowed; action dismissed.

NOTES

1. Are the *Kirk* and *Clayton* cases in conflict? Can you rationalize them?

2. On V.J. day, August 14, 1945, one Larson was walking on the sidewalk outside the St. Francis Hotel in San Francisco when he was struck on the head by a heavy stuffed armchair. Although no one saw where the chair came from, it was assumed that it came out of the hotel. San Franciscans are known for their exuberance during such celebrations. Should *res ipsa loquitur* be invoked? Does a hotel have control over its furniture? Would such an accident occur without negligence on the part of the hotel? See *Larson* v. *St. Francis Hotel* (1948), 83 Cal. App. 210, 188 P. 2d 513 (D.C.A.).

3. Plaintiff is riding on a horse when the saddle slips and he falls to the ground. The saddle was fastened by the defendant, but it was not clear on the evidence whether the accident occurred because of the negligence of the defendant or because the plaintiff leaned to the left while the galloping horse

was making a right hand turn. Does this accident speak of negligence? If so, was the horse and saddle under the "control" of the defendant? See *Saillant* v. *Smith* (1973), 33 D.L.R. (3d) 61 (Ont. C.A.).

4. There is a great variety of situations where accidents have been held to speak of negligence. Following *Byrne* v. *Boadle*, there are a number of cases dealing with an assortment of falling objects such as a lump of coal, a bag of sugar, a mirror and some plaster. For example, in *Saccardo* v. *City of Hamilton et al.*, [1971] 2 O.R. 479, the plaintiff was injured when a Christmas decoration, a four foot star, fell from a hydro pole in downtown Hamilton, Ontario. In imposing liability on the contractor, Mr. Justice Osler stated:

"Things properly secured do not simply fall of their own weight in the absence of negligence or intervention by some third person."

5. Explosions of various kinds have been held to bespeak negligence. See *Colvilles Ltd.* v. *Devine*, [1969] 1 W.L.R. 475 (H.L.); *Corsini* v. *City of Hamilton*, [1931] O.R. 598 (C.A.); *Rideau Lawn Tennis Club* v. *Ottawa*, [1936] O.W.N. 347 (C.A.); *cf. Collier* v. *City of Hamilton* (1914), 32 O.L.R. 214 (C.A.). Negligence was also thought to be present in air crashes (*Malone* v. *T.C.A.*, [1962] O.R. 453: ". . . with experienced and careful pilots and proper equipment, a passenger has the right to expect that he will be carried safely to his destination", *per* Robertson C.J.O., (Comment (1942), 20 Can. Bar Rev. 705); *cf. Tataryn* v. *Co-operative Trust Co.* (1975), 54 D.L.R. (3d) 154 (Sask. Q.B.), where a dual-controlled private Cessna airplane crashed in circumstances where the co-pilot or even the other passenger, who was "within reach of the controls", may have been responsible for the crash; unexplained fires (*United Motors Service Inc.* v. *Hutson*, [1937] S.C.R. 294; *Hutterly* v. *Imperial Oil*, [1956] O.W.N. 681 (H.C.)); *Carter* v. *Steelgas Utilities Ltd.* (1974), 52 D.L.R. (3d) 377 (Man. C.A.) and defective product cases (*Arendale* v. *Canada Bread*, [1941] O.W.N. 69 (C.A.)). See for a more detailed discussion, Linden, *Canadian Tort Law* (2nd ed., 1977), p. 227.

6. Would *res ipsa loquitur* be invoked if a stone is found in a baker's bun? Does it depend on the size of the stone? See *Chaproniere* v. *Mason* (1905), 21 T.L.R. 633. If chemicals are found in underwear? See *Grant* v. *Australian Knitting Mills*, [1936] A.C. 85. If some yogurt is found on the floor of a supermarket? (*Ward* v. *Tesco Stories*, [1976] 1 All E.R. 219). What if a car turns over as a result of sudden braking? (see *Andanoff* v. *Smith et al*, [1935] O.W.N. 415 (C.A.)) or moves forward unexpectedly while the defendant is in the driver's seat? (see *Lawson* v. *Watts* (1957), 7 D.L.R. (2d) 758 (B.C.)) or begins suddenly to gyrate wildly? (see *Jackson* v. *Millar*, [1976] 1 S.C.R. 225). What if the door of a vehicle opens suddenly? (see *Gallagher* v. *Green*, [1958] O.W.N. 442; affd (1959), 19 D.L.R. (2d) 490 (S.C.C.) (truck); *Petrie* v. *Speers Taxi*, [1952] O.R. 731 (C.A.) (taxi).)

7. What if a runaway automobile crashes into a building? (See *C. & S. Tire Service (1961) Ltd. et al.* v. *The Queen* (1972), 29 D.L.R. (3d) 492 (Fed. Ct.)). Does *res ipsa* apply if a T.V. set inexplicably catches fire? (See *Wylie* v. *R.C.A. Victor* (1973), 5 N. & P.E.I.R. 147 (Nfld.), manufacturer held liable; *cf. Gladney* v. *Simpson-Sears* (1975), 10 N. & P.E.I.R. 424 (P.E.I.), repairer not liable since not clear that fire originated within T.V. set.).

8. Does *res ipsa loquitur* apply if an unexplained fire breaks out in a cottage while the inhabitants are away? (see *Katterback* v. *Setrakov*, [1971] 2 W.W.R. 308 (Sask. C.A.); *cf. Wyant* v. *Crouse* (1901), 127 Mich. 158, 86 N.W. 527; *Turner* v. *Thorne* (1959), 21 D.L.R. (2d) 29 (Ont. H.C.). What if a steering mechanism on a car jams? (see *Brad's Transport Ltd.* v. *Stevenson & MacEachern Ltd.* (1974), 7 N. & P.E.I.R. 232 (P.E.I.); affd (1976), 9 N. & P.E.I.R. (P.E.I.C.A.)). What if a ladder gives away when climbed? (see *McHugh* v. *Reynolds Extension Co.* (1974), 7 O.R. (2d) 366, no liability because explanation adequate). What if someone is burned during a permanent wave hair treatment? (see *David Spencer Ltd.* v. *Field*, [1939] S.C.R. 36).

9. What if a part of a moving truck breaks off and lands on the car behind? See *Procter & Gamble Co.* v. *Cooper's Crane Rental Ltd.* (1973), 33 D.L.R. (3d)

148 (Ont. C.A.).

10. *Res ipsa loquitur* may provide evidence not only of negligence but also of gross negligence in appropriate circumstances. In *Walker* v. *Coates*, [1968] S.C.R. 599, a Volkswagen in which the plaintiff was a guest passenger, went across the centre of the road at a high rate of speed and collided with a road sign, killing the driver and injuring the plaintiff. Mr. Justice Ritchie declared:

"If the rule of *res ipsa loquitur* is accepted in cases where proof of 'negligence' is in issue, I can see no logical reason why it should not apply with equal force when the issue is whether or not there was 'very great negligence' provided, of course, that the facts of themselves afford 'reasonable evidence, in the absence of explanation by the defendant, that the accident arose' as a result of 'a very marked departure from the standards' [of the reasonable person]."

This decision has been followed in several cases including *Doxtator* v. *Burch*, [1972] 1 O.R. 321 (*per* Lieff J.); *Tucker* v. *Latt*, [1972] 2 O.R. 409; *Jackson* v. *Millar*, [1976] 1 S.C.R. 225.

11. *Res ipsa loquitur* has recently been employed in a case where the plaintiff was held to be contributorily negligent. In *Westlake* v. *Smith Transport Ltd.*, [1973] 2 O.R. 258 (*per* Lieff J.), a tire on a truck exploded while a repairman was attempting to remove it for repairs. Evidence that the plaintiff was negligent in failing to protect himself was held not to have constituted an explanation consistent with no negligence, but only to have demonstrated contributory negligence by the plaintiff. Mr. Justice Lieff stated:

"Tires do not normally 'blow' when changed according to a procedure employed many times previously without incident."

Defendant was held 65 percent at fault and plaintiff 35 percent to blame.

MAHON v. OSBORNE

Court of Appeal. [1939] 2 K.B. 14; [1939] 1 All E.R. 535

The defendant performed an emergency abdominal operation on one Thomas Mahon. During the operation swabs were used to pack off adjacent organs from the area of the operation. About three months after the operation the patient became seriously ill, and when operated on, it was found that a swab had been left in his abdomen at the first operation. The patient died, and the present action was brought under the relevant English statutes claiming damages against the defendant for negligence in the conduct of the first operation.

The plaintiff obtained a verdict and judgment at the trial before Atkinson J. with a jury. The defendant appealed.

Goddard L.J.: . . . The plaintiff, beyond proving facts necessary to establish damage and putting in answers to interrogatories, called no further evidence. She proved by the interrogatories that the swab had been left in at the operation performed by the defendant, and that was enough to call upon him for an explanation. And here, as I understand the court is not unanimous on the point, I think it right to say that in my opinion the doctrine of *res ipsa loquitur* does apply in such a case as this, at least to the extent I mention below.

The surgeon is in command of the operation, it is for him to decide what instruments, swabs and the like are to be used, and it is he who uses them. The patient, or, if he dies, his representatives, can know nothing about this matter. There can be no possible question but that neither swabs nor instruments are ordinarily left in the patient's body, and no one would venture to say that it is proper, although in particular circumstances it may be excusable, so to leave them. If, therefore, a swab is left in the patient's body, it seems to me clear that the surgeon is called on for an explanation, that is, he is called on to show not necessarily why he missed it but that he exercised due care to prevent it being left there. It is no disparagement of the devoted and frequently gratuitous service which the profession of surgery renders to mankind to say that its members may on occasion fall short of the standard of care which they themselves, no less the law, require, and, if a patient on whom had befallen such a misfortune as we are now considering were not entitled to call on the surgeon for an explanation, I cannot but feel that an unwarranted protection would be given to carelessness, such as I do not believe the profession itself would either expect or desire. . . .

Scott L.J. (dissenting on this point): . . . It is difficult to see how the principle of *res ipsa loquitur* can apply generally to actions of negligence against a surgeon for leaving a swab in a patient, even if in certain circumstances the presumption may arise. If it applied generally, plaintiff's counsel, having by a couple of answers to interrogatories proved that the defendant performed the operation and that a swab was left in, would be entitled to ask for judgment, unless evidence describing the operation was given by the defendant. Some positive evidence of neglect of duty is surely needed. It may be that a full description of the actual operation will disclose facts sufficiently indicative of want of skill or care to entitle a jury to find neglect of duty to the patient. It may be that expert evidence in addition will be requisite. But to treat the maxim as applying in every case where a swab is left in the patient seems to me an error of law. The very essence of the rule when applied to an action for negligence is that on the mere fact of the event happening, for example, an injury to the plaintiff, there arise two presumptions of fact: (1) that the event was caused by a breach by somebody of the duty of care towards the plaintiff, and (2) that the defendant was that somebody. The presumption of fact only arises because it is an inference which the reasonable man knowing the facts would naturally draw, and that is in most cases for two reasons: (1) because the control over the happening of such an event rested solely with the defendant, and (2) that in the ordinary experience of mankind such an event does not happen unless the person in control has failed to exercise due care. The nature even of abdominal operations varies widely, and many considerations enter it — the degree of urgency, the state of the patient's inside, the complication of his disorder or injury, the condition of his heart, the effects of the anaesthetic, the degree and kind of help which the surgeon has (for example, whether he is assisted by another surgeon), the efficiency of the theatre team of nurses, the extent of the surgeon's experience, the limits of wise discretion in the particular circumstances (for example, the complications arising out of the operation itself, and the fear of the patient's collapse). In the present case, all the above considerations combined together to present a state of things of which the ordinary experience of mankind knows nothing, and therefore to make it unsafe to beg the question of proof. I cannot see how it can be said that the first essentials of the rule, if it can be called a rule, apply.

It is not necessary to enter on any analysis of the rule which, as Lord Shaw said in *Ballard* v. *North British Railway Co.*, [1923] S.C. (H.L.) 43, 56, nobody would have called a principle if it had not been in Latin. . . .

[Only those parts of the case are given which relate to *res ipsa loquitur.* MacKinnon L.J. apparently agreed with Goddard L.J., because he stated that if the defendant had persisted in his contention that the plaintiff's evidence made out no case, "the judge would have rightly over-ruled it".]

NOTES

1. Do you prefer the reasoning of Scott L.J. or Goddard L.J.? What are the conflicting policies being promoted in the two approaches?

2. For a time, the Canadian courts refused to employ *res ipsa loquitur* in

medical malpractice cases (see *Clark* v. *Wansborough*, [1940] O.W.N. 67, at p. 72), but eventually they had a change of heart. In *Nesbitt* v. *Holt*, [1953] 1 S.C.R. 132, [1953] 1 D.L.R. 671; affg. [1951] O.R. 601, [1951] 4 D.L.R. 478, the defendant, an oral surgeon, was extracting teeth of a patient under a general anaesthetic when, unknown to the defendant, a sponge lodged in the patient's windpipe causing suffocation. In the Ontario Court of Appeal, Mr. Justice Laidlaw rejected the earlier rule and declared:

"It would give doctors, dentists and members of other professions an unfair and unwarranted protection in actions where their conduct in the exercise of their profession is called into question. It would permit them to refuse to give an explanation in a court of justice of a happening which has caused injury to a person, even though the occurrence was of such a kind and description that a reasonable man would naturally infer from it that it was caused by some negligence or misconduct. It would place them in a position in the courts that in a case such as the present one the defendant could unfairly and unjustly say: 'I alone am responsible for all that happened in the course of the operation. I know all the facts from which it can be decided whether or not I used due care. I can explain the happening, but I refuse to do so.' To permit a defendant to take such a position in a court of law would be, in my opinion, a denial of justice to a person who knows nothing of the matter that caused his injury and seeks to recover for the loss suffered by reason of it from the person who possesses full knowledge of the facts."

The Supreme Court of Canada affirmed. Mr. Justice Kerwin stated simply:

"It [*res ipsa loquitur*] may apply in malpractice cases depending upon the circumstances and for the reasons already given, it applies here."

3. Canadian courts have been cautious in their application of *res ipsa* to medical mishap situations. Mr. Justice Ritchie, of the Supreme Court of Canada, has explained this policy in *Wilcox* v. *Cavan* (1975), 50 D.L.R. (3d) 687 as follows:

"It appears to me that in medical cases where differences of expert opinion are not unusual and the sequence of events often appears to have brought about a result which has never occurred in exactly the same way before to the knowledge of the most experienced doctors, great caution should be exercised to ensure that the rule embodied in the maxim *res ipsa loquitur* is not construed so as to place too heavy a burden on the defendant. Each such case must of necessity be determined according to its own particular facts and it seems to me that the rule should never be applied in such cases by treating the facts of one case as controlling the result in another, however similar those facts may be."

Do you agree with this philosophy? What are its advantages and disadvantages?

4. A similar view was evinced in *Girard* v. *Royal Columbian Hospital* (1976), 66 D.L.R. (3d) 676 (B.C.S.C.), where the plaintiff was given a spinal anaesthetic by the defendant anaesthetist in preparation for an operation with the result that the anaesthetic caused permanent partial paralysis of the legs. Andres J. sounded an important warning about the application of *res ipsa loquitur* in medical malpractice suits.

"The human body is not a container filled with a material whose performance can be predictably charted and analysed. It cannot be equated with a box of chewing tobacco or a soft drink. Thus, while permissible inferences may be drawn as to the normal behaviour of these types of commodities the same kind of reasoning does not necessarily apply to a human being. Because of this medical science has not yet reached the stage where the law ought to presume that a patient must come out of an operation as well or better than he went into it. From my interpretation of the medical evidence the kind of injury suffered by the plaintiff could have occurred without negligence on anyone's part. Since I cannot infer there was negligence on the part of the defendant doctors the maxim of *res ipsa loquitur* does not apply."

In the result the action was dismissed.

5. In *Hobson* v. *Munkley* (1976), 1 C.C.L.T. 163 (Ont. C.A.), the plaintiff had

a tubal ligation operation performed on her by the defendant surgeon. As a result
of the operation, the plaintiff's ureter was damaged, but no evidence was brought
to show how this might have occurred. Krever J. refused to apply *res ipsa*
loquitur because neither common experience nor the evidence available in the
case indicated that the mere happening of the accident was an indication that
reasonable care had not been used. He explained:

"It would, I think, be wrong, in the circumstances of this case, to fasten on
the defendant's admission that he could not explain how the plaintiff's ureter
was damaged in the operation and, invoking res ipsa loquitur, to draw the
inference that the injury to the ureter was caused by the defendant's negligence.
The risk which the defendant runs in failing to advance an explanation, which
is equally consistent with the absence of negligence as with negligence, only
comes into play if, as I have indicated, common experience or the evidence in
the case indicates that the mere happening of the injury may be considered as
evidence that reasonable care has not been used. It cannot be said, as a matter
of common experience, that a ureter is not damaged in the course of the
surgical removal of an ovary, fallopian tube and connecting endometrial tissue
and the placing of a mattress suture to control bleeding, unless the surgeon
fails to use reasonable care. Nor does the evidence in this case give rise to an
inference that the defendant was negligent. Indeed, the expert witnesses
called for the plaintiff and for the defendant gave evidence from which no
other conclusion is reasonable than that the defendant acted reasonably in the
carrying out of the surgical procedure which he performed."

Do you agree with this analysis? For a severe critique of this case, see Teplitsky &
Weisstub, Comment, (1978), 56 Can. Bar Rev. 122. See also *Kapur v. Marshall*
(1978), 4 C.C.L.T. 204; *Holmes v. Board of Hospital Trustees of the City of*
London (1979), 5 C.C.L.T. 1.

6. Would *res ipsa loquitur* be applied where forceps are left in the abdomen
of a patient? See *Taylor v. Gray*, [1937] 4 D.L.R. 123, 11 M.P.R. 588 (N.B.).
Where sodium pentathol, injected intravenously, leaks into surrounding tissue?
See *Hughston v. Jost*, [1943] 1 D.L.R. 402. *Cf., Villeneuve v. Sisters of St.*
Joseph, [1971] 2 O.R. 593; revd. in part [1972] 2 O.R. 119 (C.A.); *Martel v.*
Hotel-Dieu St. Vallier (1970), 14 D.L.R. (3d) 445 (S.C.C.). Where a dentist
leaves part of a wisdom tooth in the jaw? See *Fish v. Kapur*, [1948] 2 All E.R.
176. Where a woman emerged from an operation on her neck with a serious
voice impairment? See *Finlay v. Auld*, [1975] S.C.R. 338. For a fine judicial
examination of *res ipsa loquitur* in the medical context, see Addy J. in *MacDonald*
v. *York County Hospital*, [1972] 3 O.R. 469; affd (1974), 1 O.R. (2d) 653; affd
[1976] 2 S.C.R. 825. A thorough academic analysis appears in Picard, *Legal*
Liability of Doctors and Hospitals in Canada (1978), p. 204.

7. In *Morris v. Winsbury-White*, [1937] 4 All E.R. 494, the defendant had
operated on the plaintiff. The post-operative treatment involved the insertion
into his body of tubes and their frequent replacement. The tubes were originally inserted by the defendant during the operation but replacements were
made subsequently by resident doctors and nurses. Sometime after his discharge from hospital a portion of a tube was found in the plaintiff's bladder.
In an action for negligence against the defendant, Tucker J. held that *res ipsa*
loquitur did not apply because while at the hospital, he was treated by
numerous doctors and nurses, and was not in the control or charge of the
defendant for the whole period.

8. In *Ybarra v. Spangard* (1944), 154 P. 2d 687 (Cal.), in the course of an
operation for appendicitis, the patient suffered an injury to his shoulder which
developed into paralysis of the muscles. He brought suit in one action against
the diagnostician, the surgeon, the anaesthetist, the owner of the hospital, and
two nurses. At the trial the plaintiff was non-suited. On appeal the non-suit
was set aside and the case sent back for trial invoking the doctrine of *res ipsa*
loquitur. "Without the aid of the doctrine a patient who received permanent
injuries of a serious character, obviously the result of someone's negligence,
would be entirely unable to recover unless the doctors and nurses in attendance

voluntarily chose to disclose the identity of the negligent person and the facts establishing liability."

Is this a dangerous decision? Can it be justified because of the so-called "conspiracy of silence" among doctors? See Seavey, *"Res Ipsa Loquitur: Tabula in Naufragio"* (1950), 63 Harv. L. Rev. 643, and compare Prosser, *"Res Ipsa Loquitur* in California" (1949), 37 Cal. L. Rev. 183, 223.

9. In *Roe* v. *Ministry of Health*, [1954] 2 Q.B. 66, [1954] 2 All E.R. 131, the plaintiff was operated on in the defendant hospital and a spinal anaesthetic of Nupercaine was administered by defendant, Dr. Graham, an anaesthetist. After the operation, the plaintiff developed spastic paraplegia resulting in paralysis from the waist down. The plaintiff brought an action against the hospital and/or Dr. Graham contending that *res ipsa loquitur* applied since paralysis ordinarily did not follow a properly administered anaesthetic. Assuming Dr. Graham (a) to have been a servant of the hospital, (b) not a servant but acting independently for plaintiff, does *res ipsa loquitur* apply? Finding that (a) was the true situation, the Court of Appeal held the principle applicable but on the evidence given by the defendants, exonerated them from liability. Had (b) been the situation, Somervell and Morris L.JJ. expressly refrained from expressing an opinion. Denning L.J. expressed the view that the hospital and Dr. Graham could not avoid giving an explanation by each throwing responsibility on the other. "If an injured person shows that one or other of two persons injured him, but cannot say which of them it was, he is not defeated altogether. He can call on each of them for an explanation."

How does this case differ from *Ybarra*? See *Leaman* v. *Rae, infra.*

C. PROCEDURAL EFFECT OF RES IPSA LOQUITUR

INTERLAKE TISSUE MILLS CO. LTD. v. SALMON & BECKETT

Ontario Court of Appeal. [1948] O.R. 950; [1949] 1 D.L.R. 207

The plaintiff was a paper manufacturer. The defendant Salmon was a moving contractor and defendant Beckett was in his employ as foreman. The defendant Salmon had agreed with plaintiff to move a heavy steel roller from a paper machine and instal another in its place. The plaintiff alleged that the defendant Beckett or other workmen while installing the new roller had negligently damaged a fine copper screen in the machine. The plaintiff alleged that Beckett or other workmen did this by pushing a plank against the wire. *Res ipsa loquitur* was also specifically pleaded. The jury found in reply to questions, that there was no negligence on the part of defendants. The plaintiff appealed.

Roach J.A.: . . . At the trial counsel for the defendant did not call any witnesses. Counsel for the plaintiff, in the absence of the jury, then submitted to the trial judge that he should therefore take the case from the jury and enter judgment for the plaintiff because, so he urged, on the evidence already adduced by him, it should be held that the principle *res ipsa loquitur* applied, raising a presumption of fact that the damage to the screen was caused by the negligence of the defendants, and that this presumption had not been rebutted by the defendants. The learned trial judge having indicated that he would not accede to that submission, counsel for the plaintiff then submitted that the learned trial judge should direct the jury to return a verdict in favour of the plaintiff. The learned trial judge rejected both those submissions, and in doing so said: "I don't think this is a proper case for giving judgment on the evidence we have heard so that judgment will be given purely on the question of *res ipsa loquitur*. I think it is a case which is supremely suited for a jury to decide on the evidence which has been submitted and I would therefore dismiss the motion of counsel for the plaintiffs and let the jury decide the question of liability."

One of the grounds on which counsel for the plaintiff rested this appeal is that the trial judge erred in refusing to grant the plaintiff's motion for judgment or alternatively for a directed verdict. I deal with that ground at once.

The trial judge was right in refusing both motions, but what he said in doing so calls for comment. There was no direct evidence of negligence on the part of any of the persons engaged in the removal of the old dryer and the installation of the new one; that is to say, there was no evidence of any specific act of negligence on their part. There was no case at all to go to the jury unless *res ipsa loquitur* applied and I cannot understand what the trial judge meant when he said that this was not a case where judgment "will be given purely on the question of *res ipsa loquitur*."

There was definitely no case against the defendant Beckett to go to the jury and the trial judge, far from acceding to either motion on behalf of the plaintiff, should have taken the case as against Beckett from the jury and dismissed the action as against him. The reason for that course is plain. If *res ipsa loquitur* applied then it would raise an inference that some one or more of the persons engaged on the job was negligent. It would not raise that inference against any particular one of them.

In *Cole* v. *De Trafford*, [1918] 2 K.B. 523, at pp. 528-529, Pickford L.J., dealt with that precise question when he said: "In the well-known case always cited for this principle of *Byrne* v. *Boadle* (1863), 2 H. & C. 722, the fall of the barrel was more consistent with negligence on the part of the defendant or his servants than with any other cause, but if it had been necessary to show that the barrel fell by the personal negligence of the defendant I do not think the mere fact of the accident would have been evidence of such negligence."

If the trial judge meant, by what he said, that, in a case where the maxim *res ipsa loquitur* applies and there is no evidence of any specific act of negligence, the trial judge either could or should therefore take the case from the jury and enter judgment for the plaintiff or alternattively direct the jury to retrun a verdict for the plaintiff, he was wrong. Where the maxim is applicable, instead of that fact being a reason for taking the case from the jury it is a reason for leaving it with them. Furthermore where the maxim applies the question whether the *res* justifies an inference of negligence is a question of fact for the jury alone to determine.

The learned trial judge instructed the jury in part as follows:

> "The defendant is charged with negligence. I have before me the statement of claim of the plaintiffs and in that statement of claim they charge that there was negligence which caused the damage to part of their plant. Now it is a well-known principle that when the plaintiff charges negligence, negligence must be proved, so the first thing you have to decide is whether there was any negligence that caused this damage — whether there was any negligence on the part of the defendants. That's your first duty.
>
> If you find that there was negligence then you are asked a subsequent question to say in what respect they were negligent, so that you have not only to find that they were negligent but you have to state for the benefit of the court what they did to constitute that negligence.
>
> Now that is the first and second question to be dealt with. You have heard the evidence as to the whole transaction between the parties. You have heard the evidence of the setting-up of the repair machine and you will have noted, no doubt, that throughout the whole evidence of the plaintiff there is no evidence, no direct evidence of any act or omission which would constitute neglect on their part. Therefore you have to look to some other source to come to the conclusion that there is neglect on their part. Has the

plaintiff given you any evidence by which you might draw a reasonable conclusion that there must have been negligence to cause this accident and moreover have they given you evidence that satisfies you that they were the ones that were responsible for the accident? That is the first question and the second question falls in the same line as my remarks."

On the retirement of the jury counsel for the plaintiff made several objections to the trial judge's charge. The trial judge refused to recall the jury. Counsel for the appellant rested his appeal on those objections and argued that the trial judge erred in those parts of his charge to which objections were taken and erred further in refusing to recall the jury for the purpose of correcting his first error.

In recording his objections to the trial judge counsel said: "Now my position is already known to your Honour in that *res ipsa loquitur* applies and the plaintiff does not have to prove negligence in that case and I object to the charge on that ground."

The objection thus recorded is so absolutely devoid of merit that I have wondered whether or not counsel meant what he then said. The plaintiff having alleged negligence, of course it had to prove it to the reasonable satisfaction of the jury, and the trial judge was right in charging the jury as he did in the first paragraph which I have quoted. The principle *res ipsa loquitur* does not alter the general principle of law that the onus of proving his case always rests on the plaintiff. A plaintiff alleging negligence may be unable to adduce evidence of any specific act of negligence but that does not relieve him from the necessity of proving that there was some act or omission amounting to negligence on the part of the defendant or those for whom the defendant is responsible. This he may do by proving that the accident occurred under circumstances where it is so improbable that it would have happened without the negligence of the defendant that the mere happening of the accident immediately gives rise to the inference that the defendant was in fact negligent. If a plaintiff does that much then he thereby gives reasonable evidence of negligence. It is therefore, a contradiction to say that where *res ipsa loquitur* applies the plaintiff is not required to prove negligence, because until he has adduced evidence of such circumstances the maxim does not apply and when he has adduced evidence of such circumstances he has already proved negligence.

It is a question of law whether there is or is not evidence which permits of the application of the maxim. If the evidence is such that clearly the maxim applies then the trial judge should instruct the jury concerning it. There may be cases, and this is one of them, where the evidence may or may not result in the principle being applicable, depending entirely on the view the jury takes of that evidence. Since the trial judge cannot tell in advance what view the jury may take of it, he should in such cases, also instruct them with respect to the principle. . . .

The plaintiff's counsel sought to establish by evidence that between August 4th and August 8th none of the members of the maintenance crew was in the immediate neighbourhood of the screen. Of course, if that were a fact, then the damage to the screen could not have been caused by them, or any of them. He also sought to show in evidence that with the exercise of reasonable care the old dryer could have been removed, and the new one installed, without the risk of damage to the screen. If the evidence proved those two facts, then the maxim *res ipsa loquitur* would apply.

Whether or not the evidence proved those two facts was a question entirely for the jury, properly instructed, to determine. . . .

[A detailed examination of the evidence is omitted. It showed that the roller was moved while the plant was closed but about 10-12 maintenance men were in the mill walking about but "having no occasion" to go near the dryer. A witness for the plaintiff testified that damage to the screen could have been caused by "negligence" or "by an accident". He rather doubted the latter but he had considered in advance that the screen might be injured by an accident: it was, in fact, in close proximity to the heavy roller.]

Now, whether or not the plaintiff establishes as part of its case such circumstances as made the maxim *res ipsa loquitur* applicable depended on what view the jury took of the evidence to which I have referred. In any event, I think the evidence was such that there was a duty on the trial judge to instruct the jury with respect to that principle, and because he failed to do so there must be a new trial limited to the question of the liability of the defendant Salmon. The trial judge should have instructed the jury that if they felt that it had been reasonably established (a) that with the exercise of reasonable care the new dryer could have been installed without damage to the screen and (b) that those engaged in its installation were the only persons in the immediate area at the time the screen was damaged, those two circumstances, would lead to the inference not only that the damage was the result of negligence, but also that the negligence consisted of some act or omission on the part of those engaged on the job.

Since there is to be a new trial, it may be salutary to point out that in a case where a plaintiff is relying on the principle *res ipsa loquitur* and there is no evidence of any specific act of negligence, it is improper to submit a question like Question 2. Indeed, for a trial judge to submit such a question and tell the jury, as the trial judge did here, that if they find the defendant negligent they must answer that question by specifying the negligence, may prevent the jury from applying the principle. . . .

Finally, it may also be salutary to say that in a case where *res ipsa loquitur* applies it is not proper for the trial judge to instruct the jury that before they can find a verdict for the plaintiff, it is necessary that there be evidence from which they may "draw a reasonable conclusion that there must have been negligence to cause" the accident. That is the equivalent of telling the jury that the burden is on the plaintiff of proving negligence beyond a reasonable doubt. In a civil case the burden on a plaintiff is not so onerous. All the plaintiff is required to do in order to succeed in such a case is to satisfy the jury that on the balance of probabilities an inference of negligence should be made.

For the reasons I have stated, the appeal as against the defendant Beckett should be dismissed with costs. The appeal as against the defendant Salmon should be allowed with costs and a new trial directed limited to his liability, if any, and the amount thereof.

NOTES

1. In *Cudney* v. *Clements Motor Sales Ltd.,* [1969] 2 O.R. 209 (Ont. C.A.), the plaintiff died when his jeep left the highway and rolled in a ditch. The highway was straight for some miles and tire marks showed that the plaintiff had gone onto the shoulder several times before leaving the road altogether. Inspection of the jeep after the accident showed that the four steering arm bolts had broken off. These bolts had been replaced by the defendant when he had repaired the steering mechanism of the jeep less than a month before the accident. At trial, the administratix of the deceased's estate had been successful. The defendant appealed. In allowing the defendant's appeal, Kelly J.A. stated: "It is unquestionable that, when the facts established by direct evidence or admitted by the defendant are such that, in the light of ordinary common experience, negligence on the part of the defendant may be inferred, the onus of proof passes from the plaintiff to the defendant until it returns to the plaintiff by

reason of the defendant putting forward a theory, consistent with the facts, of a way in which the accident may have happened without negligence on his part; when the defendant has done so, the cogency of the facts by themselves disappears and the plaintiff is left as he began in that he must show negligence." [Citations omitted.]

Does the procedural effect accorded *res ipsa loquitur* in *Cudney* differ from that in *Interlake Tissue Mills?* If so, how? Which treatment yields the best result?

2. In *MacDonald* v. *York County Hospital,* [1972] 3 O.R. 469; revd. in part (1974), 1 O.R. (2d) 653; affd [1976] 2 S.C.R. 825, Mr. Justice Addy, in a *dictum,* discussed the problem of the shifting burden of proof as follows:

"Many of the cases inadequately distinguish between an 'evidential burden of proof' and the legal burden of proof. In an action for negligence the plaintiff has the legal burden of proving that the accident was caused by the defendant's negligence. This legal burden of proof does not shift. At the conclusion of the evidence the court must be satisfied that, on a balance of probabilities, the accident was caused by the negligence of the defendant; if not, the plaintiff's action fails. However, in the course of the trial the application of the doctrine of *res ipsa loquitur* may raise a *prima facie* inference against the defendant and unless he introduces some evidence to rebut this inference he will lose. This is the sense in which there can be said to be an "evidential burden of proof" on the defendant. As stated previously, the defendant can satisfy this evidential burden by introducing a reasonable explanation of the happening of the accident, that is consistent with the proven facts, and is as consistent with there being no negligence on his part as with the inference that there is negligence. *Res ipsa loquitur* does not have the effect of shifting the legal burden of proof to the defendant so that he must disprove negligence on his part."

Does this treatment of *res ipsa* differ from that in *Cudney?* If so, which do you prefer?

3. See also *Everatt et al.* v. *Elgin Electric Ltd.,* [1973] 3 O.R. 691, at p. 710, where Mr. Justice Lerner stated:

"It is not essential that the defendant should prove that the accident did in fact happen in the way suggested. It is sufficient, in order to meet the operation of *res ipsa loquitur,* if the defendant gives a reasonable explanation of the way in which the accident *may* have happened. . . . the maxim does not operate to take the onus of proof from a plaintiff to prove negligence and make it a burden upon a defendant to disprove negligence."

See also *Erison* v. *Higgins* (1975), 4 O.R. (2d) 631 (C.A.), where Mr. Justice Arnup declared:

"The onus can be satisfied by showing an explanation of the cause of the mishap which is equally consistent with the existence or non-existence of negligence on the part of the defendant upon whom the onus lies."

4. In *Jackson* v. *Millar,* [1973] 1 O.R. 399 (C.A.); revd [1976] 1 S.C.R. 225, the plaintiff, a gratuitous passenger, was injured when the car he was driving in went out of control on the highway. The trial judge found that *res ipsa loquitur* raised a "presumption" of negligence which was left intact, in spite of the defendant's explanation. The Court of Appeal reversed this decision on the ground that *res ipsa* does not create a "presumption" of negligence but only an "inference" thereof which had been displaced by the explanation given. Evans J.A. explained:

"I believe the trial judge was in error when he failed to distinguish between a 'presumption' which is a deduction the law requires a trier of facts to make and an 'inference' which is a deduction which the trier may or may not make according to his own conclusions. The former is mandatory while the latter is permissible. A presumption would necessarily cast an onus on the defendant which he would be required to disprove by preponderance of evidence which is another way of stating that the onus shifts from plaintiff to defendant. In my opinion, there is no shifting of the onus of proof and the doctrine does no more than grant to the plaintiff a procedural advantage which could lead to a discharge of the burden of proof in the absence of an explanation.

On the facts of the case under review I am satisfied that in the final analysis *res ipsa loquitur* had no application. Whatever force it may have had, and I believe it to be a limited one, was spent and exhausted once an explanation was proffered by the defendant which was consistent with the exercise of due care on his part. This is not a case in which there was no explanation given which was consistent with the absence of negligence. The defendant, in effect, says:

> I was driving properly and the car skidded as I made a gradual turn to the left to avoid stones on the pavement.

The immediate cause of the accident becomes known and with the cause known *res ipsa loquitur* is no longer appropriate."

The Supreme Court of Canada reversed and restored the trial judge's decision. Spence J. indicated that *res ipsa* was not a "doctrine" but only a "rule of evidence". He felt that the trial judge was correct when he considered the explanation given and found that it was "not a valid explanation" and that the maxim therefore applied.

5. Most of the confusion surrounding the doctrine of *res ipsa loquitur* turns on the procedural effect accorded it. This is understandable because of the difficulty we have had generally with presumptions and burdens of proof. See Morgan, "Instructing the Jury on Presumptions and Burdens of Proof" (1933), 47 Harv. L. Rev. 59; Denning, "Presumptions and Burdens" (1945), 61 L.Q.Rev. 379; Sopinka and Lederman, *The Law of Evidence in Civil Cases* (1974), p. 395.

6. Most judicial and academic opinion prefers the *Interlake Tissue* approach in all cases. In *Temple* v. *Terrace Transfer Ltd.* (1966), 57 D.L.R. (2d) 631, for example, Mr. Justice Tysoe of the British Columbia Court of Appeal stated:

> "In recent years the trend in England seems to have been to increase the defendant's burden in *res ipsa loquitur* cases. Leading examples are *Barkway* v. *South Wales Transport Co. Ltd.,* [1948] 2 All E.R. 460, and *Moore* v. *R. Fox & Sons,* [1956] 1 All E.R. 182. I do not find it necessary to discuss these cases at any length as, . . . so far as I am aware, they have not been applied in Canada, to enlarge the onus on a defendant beyond that stated by Duff C.J.C., in *United Motors Service Inc.* v. *Hutson, supra.*
>
> In the two English cases which I have mentioned the maxim *res ipsa loquitur* when applicable appears to have been treated as giving rise to a legal presumption of negligence on the part of the defendant which must be rebutted by the defendant. . . .
>
> With the greatest of respect, it is my opinion that the doctrine of *res ipsa loquitur* when it is applicable does not create a legal presumption of negligence, but merely operates to justify the tribunal of fact inferring negligence on the part of the defendant from the proven circumstances if the tribunal thinks it right and proper to do so. . . .
>
> It appears to me, then, that it is error to regard the maxim *res ipsa loquitur* as operating to change the burden on a plaintiff to prove negligence into a burden on a defendant to disprove negligence. In my view the plaintiff commences with an onus of establishing negligence on the part of the defendant resting upon him. If he proves, to the satisfaction of the tribunal, facts which bring the maximum into operation, then unless the defendant produces an explanation 'equally consistent with negligence and with no negligence', to use the words of Duff C.J.C., in *United Motors Service, Inc.* v. *Hutson, supra,* the plaintiff will succeed. But where the defendant comes forward with such an explanation, the burden of establishing negligence still remains with the plaintiff. If the tribunal is left in doubt whether, on the mass of evidence, negligence on the part of the defendant ought to be inferred, the plaintiff should fail."

7. In *Hellenus* v. *Lees,* [1971] 1 O.R. 273, at p. 288: affd. [1972] S.C.R. 165, 20 D.L.R. (3d) 369, Mr. Justice Laskin (as he then was) stated that *res ipsa*

loquitur "means only that there is circumstantial evidence from which an inference of negligence is warranted". In affirming, Mr. Justice Ritchie, at p. 373 in D.L.R., said, "The so-called rule embodied in the Latin phrase *res ipsa loquitur* is nothing more than a rule of evidence and states no principle of law."

8. If these statements are accurate, why must the defendant offer any explanations at all?

9. At least one court has indicated that it is not enough for a defendant to give an explanation equally consistent with no negligence in order to relieve himself of liability under *res ipsa*. In *Interprovincial Pipe Line Co.* v. *Seller's Oil Field Service Ltd.* (1976), 58 D.L.R. (3d) 719 (Man. Q.B.), Wilson J. held, in a fire case, that it was not enough for the defendant to "recite the possible mechanisms or agencies by which plaintiff's loss could have occurred without his . . . negligence. . . . He must go beyond that, and demonstrate not only the probability that the mechanism or agent to which he points could have caused the loss, but also the probability of the presence of that mechanism or agent. . . . 'It is not enough for the defendant to point out other *possible* explanations. For example, it is not enough to say that it might have been caused by lightning.'" In concluding, Wilson J. held that while several agents suggested were "capable of starting a fire", the evidence fell "short of establishing, or even suggesting, the presence of any of these factors. And so, whatever the theoretical chance of fire from any of those causes, there is no evidence to raise any of them beyond the level of a guess."

Is this a bold new breakthrough? Is it a retrogressive step? Or is it just a mistaken view of the procedural effect of *res ipsa*?

10. See also *Zerka* v. *Lau-Goma Airways Ltd.*, [1960] O.W.N. 166, at p. 167 (C.A.) *dictum* where Laidlaw J.A. stated:

"[it is] not sufficient to show that there were several hypothetical causes of an accident consistent with an absence of negligence. A defendant must go further and must show either that there was no negligence or must give an explanation of the cause of the accident which did not connote negligence."

See also *Nystedt* v. *Wings Ltd.*, [1942] 1 W.W.R. 39 (Man.) *per* Dysart J.; *Wylie* v. *R.C.A. Limited* (1973), 5 N. & P.E.I.R. 147 (Nfld. S.C.), *per* Furlong C.J.: [*Res ipsa* establishes a] "prima facie case and the onus shifts to the defendant to show that the cause was either known to him or not within his knowledge. It will not necessarily follow from this shift of the onus that if he fails to discharge the task the case must go against him. But it certainly strengthens a prima facie case if it remains unanswered and a Court, if satisfied that the cause can be attributed only to some unexplained defect in the apparatus itself, is entitled to find for the plaintiff."

Is it possible that greater force is being accorded to *res ipsa* in these cases because they deal with fires and air crashes? See Linden, *Canadian Tort Law* (2nd ed., 1977) pp. 238-247.

11. Sometimes *res ipsa loquitur* appears to shift the burden of proof to the defendant.

In *Zeppa* v. *Coca-Cola, Ltd.*, [1955] O.R. 855, [1955] 5 D.L.R. 187, in an action by a consumer against a soft drink manufacturer for injuries sustained from particles of glass in a bottled soft drink, the Ontario Court of Appeal held that on proof that glass particles were in the product when it left the manufacturer, there was "a presumption of negligence on the part of the manufacturer and a burden upon him of disproving negligence on his part to the satisfaction of the jury". As the trial judge had charged the jury that the plaintiff had the burden of proving negligence by a preponderance of credible evidence, and the jury found no negligence on defendant, a new trial was ordered. See also *Varga* v. *John Labatt* (1957), 6 D.L.R. (2d) 336. Is this a "progressive" decision or is it a reactionary one? Is it a proper or improper use of *res ipsa loquitur* theory? Is it wise to distort legal principles in order to achieve just aims? See also *Brad's Transport* v. *Stevenson & MacEachern Ltd.* (1974), 7 N. & P.E.I.R. 232, at p. 241 (P.E.I. S.C.) *per* Nicholson J. In relation to a jammed steering mechanism,

Nicholson J. held that the defendant did not satisfy "the onus which that doctrine casts upon it".

12. The future of *Zeppa* v. *Coca-Cola Ltd.* is uncertain. Mr. Justice Laskin has commented in parenthesis, in *Hellenius* v. *Lees, supra,* note 5, "I leave to another occasion consideration of the extent or trend to reliance on *res ipsa loquitur* as a means of shifting the burden of proof or of imposing strict liability for defectively manufactured products." Mr. Justice Schroeder has also remarked in *Phillips* v. *Ford Motor Co.* (1971), 18 D.L.R. (3d) 641, at p. 658, ". . . *res ipsa loquitur* has no effect on the burden of proof, and that the plaintiff has to establish negligence on a balance of probabilities. It does not cast upon the defendant the burden of disproof of negligence, for this would come dangerously close to a fictional use of the maxim as a foundation for the doctrine of strict liability". Although *Phillips* was a products liability case, there was no mention of *Zeppa.* What do you think would happen if the Supreme Court of Canada had to decide this question?

13. In *Moore* v. *R. Fox & Sons,* [1956] 1 Q.B. 596, [1956] 1 All E.R. 182, in an action by an employee against an employer for damages sustained in an explosion in the defendant's plant, the trial judge had held that *res ipsa loquitur* applied but the plaintiff failed in his action because the defendant, while unable to show how the accident happened, was able to give an explanation satisfactory to the court which indicated that the accident was just as likely to have occurred without negligence as with it. On appeal the court held this to be incorrect. In a case to which *res ipsa loquitur* applies, the onus of proof is on the defendant to explain the accident so as to absolve himself from the implication of negligence. See also *Scrimgeour* v. *Bd. of Management, etc. of America Lutheran Church,* [1947] 1 D.L.R. 677. Can it be that the Canadian position differs from the English? Could it have anything to do with the fact that civil jury trial is now very rare in the United Kingdom?

14. A rather strange new concept, "latent defect", has surfaced recently in the United Kingdom which seems to shift the onus of disproof of negligence to the defendant. In *Pearce* v. *Round Oak Steelworks,* [1969] 3 All E.R. 680 (C.A.), the plaintiff was working with a machine when a bolt broke, causing the machine to fall on him. The court imposed liability, but did not rely on *res ipsa loquitur.* Nevertheless, it held that there was a burden on the defendant to rebut the evidence of want of reasonable care, which it failed to do, because it refused to give evidence. The court confessed its "pleasure at being able to arrive at such a conclusion in conformity with the decided cases in circumstances where a workman is injured. . . and the defendants furnish no explanation at all of why that accident occurred". So too, in *Henderson* v. *Henry E. Jenkins & Sons et al.,* [1969] 3 All E.R. 756 (H.L.), the brakes on a truck failed when the pipe carrying the brake fluid corroded. Liability was imposed on the theory of latent defect, because the defendant failed to rebut the onus upon it to disprove negligence. It had to adduce evidence of the entire history of the vehicle, which it failed to do.

Does this concept have anything to do with *res ipsa loquitur?*

15. Several American jurisdictions apply *res ipsa loquitur* in favour of a passenger of a common carrier against the latter where the carrier and another vehicle collided with resulting injury to the passenger. See, *e.g., Capital Transit Co.* v. *Jackson* (1945), 149 F. 2d 839, where the U.S. Court of Appeals for the District of Columbia spoke of a carrier of passengers being "subject to certain definite responsibilities which, without a showing that these were discharged, will justify an inference of negligence". See Prosser, "*Res Ipsa Loquitur;* Collisions of Carriers with Other Vehicles" (1936), 30 Ill. L. Rev. 983.

16. Must *res ipsa loquitur* always be given the same procedural effect? What are the arguments pro and con?

17. What do you think of the comment in Prosser, "*Res Ipsa Loquitur* in California" (1949), 37 Cal. L. Rev. 183, where, after reviewing the chaotic condition of authorities, he suggests "What is needed is a recognition that there is, and should be, no uniform procedural effect of a '*res ipsa* case'; that where the

facts bespeak negligence beyond dispute a verdict should be directed in the absence of sufficient evidence to the contrary; that there are special relations which should require the defendant to sustain the burden of proof; and that there are some cases in which the court has moved or is moving in the direction of strict liability." Seę Prosser, "The Procedural Effect of *Res Ipsa Loquitur*" (1936), 20 Minn. L. Rev. 241.

18. Compare with *Easson* v. *L.N.E. Ry. Co.,* [1944] K.B. 421, [1944] 2 All E.R. 425, where Du Parcq L.J. said: "The words *res ipsa loquitur* . . . are a figure of speech, by which sometimes is meant that certain facts are so inconsistent with any view except that the defendant has been negligent that any jury which, on proof of those facts, found that negligence was not proved would be giving a perverse verdict. Sometimes, the proposition does not go so far as that, but is merely that on proof of certain facts an inference of negligence may be drawn by a reasonable jury. . . ."

19. Professor Fleming has expressed the same idea: ". . . the facts of an accident may speak in a whisper or shout aloud." See *Law of Torts* (5th ed., 1977), p. 312.

20. See also Wright, *"Res Ipsa Loquitur",* in *Special Lectures of the Law Society of Upper Canada on Evidence* (1955), reprinted in Linden, *Studies in Canadian Tort Law* (1968), where he says, "It is true that the *res* does not always speak with the same voice. This is merely to say that the happening of some accidents furnishes a much stronger inference of negligence than some others. . . .While, as a general rule, I would therefore submit that *res ipsa loquitur* has nothing to do with burden of proof, it may well be that certain policy considerations should enter into some situations. In other words, *res ipsa loquitur* does furnish a convenient disguise for legislation by the courts." Do you agree? If so, is this such a terrible thing?

21. It is advisable to plead *res ipsa loquitur* (*Johnson* v. *Schneon,* [1943] O.W.N. 673; *Petrie* v. *Speers Taxi Ltd.,* [1952] O.R. 731), although it is not strictly required (*Greschuk* v. *Kolodychuk* (1958-59), 27 W.W.R. 157 (Alta. C.A.); *Bennett* v. *Chemical Construction (GB) Ltd.,* [1971] 3 All E.R. 822, p. 825), as long as the factual groundwork is laid in the pleadings. Courts have been known to refuse to allow claimants to re-cast their cases on appeal so as to avail themselves of the doctrine. (*David Spencer Ltd.* v. *Field,* [1939] S.C.R. 36.) If a plaintiff is unable to prove specific acts of negligence, it is permissible to fall back on *res ipsa loquitur.* (*Neal* v. *T. Eaton Co.,* [1933] O.R. 573.)

22. The proper place for referring to *res ipsa loquitur* is in the instructions to the jury. The jury should not be asked questions relating to *res ipsa loquitur.* See *Polinski* v. *Griffin* (1973), 36 D.L.R. (3d) 685 (Ont. C.A.), where the following instructions to a jury in an air crash case were held to be correct:

"1. Was there negligence on the part of the late Richard Griffin which caused or contributed to the airplane crash on June 12th 1968?

2. If your answer to question 1 is 'Yes', are you able to specify particulars of such negligence?

3. If your answer to question 2 is 'Yes', give particulars of such negligence."

D. EXTENSIONS OF RES IPSA LOQUITUR

LEAMAN v. RAE

New Brunswick Supreme Court, Appeal Division. [1954] 4 D.L.R. 423

Appeals by the plaintiff and defendant from a decision of the trial judge dismissing their claim and counterclaim respectively for damages sustained in a collision between their motor vehicles.

Harrison J.: This case arose out of a collision between two passenger cars, one owned and driven by the defendant, Rea, and the other owned by the plaintiff Leaman, and driven by one Crossman, with the plaintiff, Smith and Collier as passengers.

The plaintiff's car was proceeding northerly towards Moncton and the defendant proceeding southerly on a gravel road, the travelled portion of which was 26 feet wide. The road had some ice and snow on it but was in good driving condition.

The collison occurred about 7.30 a.m. on the south edge of the crest of a blind knoll on a straight road. According to the evidence of plaintiff and others in the plaintiff's car, they were travelling between 35 and 40 m.p.h. and first saw the defendant at a distance of some 50 yards. They say he was approaching at about the same speed on the plaintiff's side of the road, that is to say the eastern side. They also testified that, when he was only 30 feet distant the defendant tried to go over to his own side. While proceeding crosswise to the road, the left front of the defendant's car collided with the left front of the plaintiff's car. This collision, they said, took place on the plaintiff's side of the road. After the collision the defendant's car was almost at right angles to the road with the rear wheels in the west ditch and the front wheels on the shoulder, pointing roughly south-east. The plaintiff's car was also at an angle across the road with its rear end some 3 feet from the east ditch.

The defendant gave evidence that he was travelling on his own side of the road in going over the knoll and that when he saw the plaintiff's car it was distant about 100 feet and was travelling on the defendant's side of the road. He said that the plaintiff's driver first went to his own side (the east) and "then as he got to me he cut her in again and hit the left front of my car". Some anti-freeze liquid which came from the plaintiff's radiator was found on the road after the collision some 6 or 8 feet from the west side of the highway, also some glass and mud, and the trial judge found that the impact occurred slightly west of the centre of the highway. The learned trial judge also said: "My guess is that both cars were proceeding over the knoll in the centre of the highway and neither driver saw the other in time to completely avoid a collision. But after considerable thought I am unable to reach to the necessary degree of certainty in conclusion as to how the accident happened or who was at fault. Accordingly I must hold that neither party has established his case and, therefore, the claim and the counterclaim are both dismissed."

In the case of *Bray* v. *Palmer*, [1953] 2 All E.R. 1449, a case of collision between a motorcycle and a motor car, the trial judge took the view that the accident must have been due to the exclusive negligence of one or the other side. He rejected the possibility of both sides being to blame and being unable to make up his mind which was the right story, dismissed both the claim and the counterclaim. In the Court of Appeal, it was held that the judge was not entitled to dismiss the claim and the counterclaim on the ground that he was unable to decide which party was in the right. It was his duty to come to some conclusion on the evidence and he should not have excluded the possibility of both parties being in some measure to blame, and therefore, there must be a new trial.

In the cases of *Baker* v. *Market Harborough, etc., Soc., Wallace* v. *Richards (Leicester) Ltd.,* [1953] 1 W.L.R. 1472, two motor vehicles travelling in opposite directions collided and both drivers were killed. The evidence disclosed that the two motor vehicles were proceeding in opposite directions, both coming down hill. At the trial of the *Wallace* case Sellers J. said that it was clearly established that "these vehicles came together with the off-side of one vehicle against the off-side of the other in the centre of the roadway," and added that the two vehicles overlapped by some 2 or 3 feet at least in what must have been practically a straight head-on collision. Sellers J. held that the facts gave rise to the inference that both drivers were negligent in failing to keep a proper look-out and that both were therefore equally to blame for the accident which resulted therefrom. Denning L.J. said at pp. 1476-7:

"It is pertinent to ask, what would have been the position if there had been a passenger in the back of one of the vehicles who was injured in the collision? He could have brought an action against both vehicles. On proof of the collision in the centre of the road, the natural inference would be that one or other or both were to blame. If there was no other evidence given in the case, because both drivers were killed, would the court, simply because it could not say whether it was only one vehicle that was to blame or both of them, refuse to give the passenger any compensation? The practice of the courts is to the contrary. Every day, proof of the collision is held to be sufficient to call on the two defendants for an answer. Never do they both escape liability..One or the other is held to blame, and sometimes both. If each of the drivers were alive and neither chose to give evidence, the court would unhesitatingly hold that both were to blame. They would not escape simply because the court had nothing by which to draw any distinction between them. So, also, if they are both dead and cannot give evidence, the result must be the same. In the absence of any evidence enabling the court to draw a distinction between them, they must be held both to blame, and equally to blame.

Now take this case where there is no passenger, but both drivers are killed. The natural inference, again, is that one or other was, or both were, to blame. The court will not wash its hands of the case simply because it cannot say whether it was only one vehicle which was to blame or both. In the absence of any evidence enabling the court to draw a distinction between them, it should hold them both to blame, and equally to blame.

It is very different from a case where one or other only is to blame but clearly not both. Then the judge ought to make up his mind between them, as this court said recently in *Bray* v. *Palmer*, [1953] 1 W.L.R. 1455. But when both may be to blame, the judge is under no such compulsion and can cast the blame equally on each."

The Court of Appeal in both cases apportioned the responsibility equally on both parties.

In the case before this court the same principles would apply and, in the absence of any evidence enabling the court to draw a distinction between the parties, they must be held both to blame and equally to blame. The damages assessed by the learned trial judge do not differ substantially in amount and the result of holding both parties to blame may not be greatly different from dismissing both claims, but in principle, where there is clearly fault, since we have a collision in broad daylight between two cars travelling in opposite directions on a road the travelled portion of which is 26 feet wide, both parties must be held liable and in equal degree.

The appeal should be allowed with full costs and judgment entered for the plaintiff for 50 per cent of his damages as assessed by the trial judge with 50 per cent of his costs. Judgment should also be entered for the defendant for 50 per cent of his damages as assessed, with 50 per cent of his costs of trial.

Bridges J.: I concur in the judgment of Harrison J. It is my opinion that where there has been a collision between two motor vehicles under such circumstances that there must have been negligence on the part of one or both drivers and the court is unable to distinguish between such drivers as to liability, both drivers should be found equally at fault.

In the last part of the All England Reports received by me, there is a case reported *France* v. *Parkinson,* [1954] 1 All E.R. 739, where a motor collision took place between two motor vehicles in the middle of crossroads of equal status. The trial judge dismissed the action on the ground that no negligence had been proven. His judgment was reversed on appeal, the court holding that in the absence of special circumstances the inference should be drawn that both drivers were equally negligent.

The appeal should be allowed with costs and judgments entered for the plaintiff and defendant as directed by Harrison J. with costs as allowed by him.

[Richards C.J. concurred with Harrison J.]

NOTES

1. Is this an instance of *res ipsa loquitur?*

2. See Prosser, "*Res Ipsa Loquitur* in California" (1949), 37 Calif. L. Rev. 183, 207: "There is room for a conclusion of the jury that when two vehicles collide and injure a third person the great probability is that *both* drivers were at fault. Certainly that is the experience of liability insurance companies. . . ." Do you agree?

3. In *Wood* v. *Thompson* (1957), 11 D.L.R. (2d) 452 (Man.), the plaintiff's husband was a passenger driven in Thompson's car when it collided with a car driven by Tomko. The plaintiff's husband, Thompson, and Tomko, were all killed in the accident and there were no witnesses to the accident. The plaintiff brought action for damages accruing from her husband's death against the personal representatives of Thompson and Tomko. The trial judge, Campbell J., found that both cars were in good operating condition; there were no skid-marks to show the course of the cars and the only evidence was some glass near the centre of the roadway and the ultimate position of both cars some 48-50 feet from this spot. Citing *Baker* v. *Market Harborough*, [1953] 1 W.L.R. 1472, Campbell J. said: "I find the defendants equally to blame. If I be wrong in this then sec. 4(3) of the Tortfeasors and Contributory Negligence Act, R.S.M. 1954, c. 266 applies." Judgment for $16,000 was entered against both defendants. Section 4(3) of the Act referred to reads: If it is not practicable to determine the respective degree of negligence as between the plaintiff and defendant to an action they shall be deemed equally negligent.

4. In *Davison* v. *Leggett* (1969), 133 J.P. 552 (C.A.), the trial judge dismissed a head-on collision case because he could not tell who was at fault and it was feasible that neither party was negligent. On appeal, Lord Justice Denning said that counsel wrongly tried to revive the "fallacy" that the "plaintiff must prove that the defendant was negligent". His Lordship declared: "*Prima facie* one or other or both are to blame. If the judge cannot say which it was, he should find that they are both to blame and equally to blame." Lord Justice Sacks agreed that this was a "salutary rule without which the law would be in a sad condition in relation to passengers in cars as well as drivers". See also *Nettleship* v. *Weston*, [1971] 3 All E.R. 581.

5. It should be emphasized that there must be some evidence that *both* parties were negligent; if the proof indicates that *one or other* of the parties were to blame, but *not both,* the action must be dismissed.

In *Wotta* v. *Haliburton Oil Well Cementing Co., Ltd.,* [1955] S.C.R. 377, [1955] 2 D.L.R. 785, two large motor vehicles, proceeding in opposite directions collided. The only witnesses of the accident were the two drivers and their evidence was conflicting. It appeared that the forward part of each vehicle passed the other and contact occurred between the rear parts of both trucks. There were no marks on the road to assist in determining the respective positions of the trucks. In an action and counterclaim for damages, the trial judge held he could not make any finding of negligence and dismissed the action and the counterclaim. This judgment was upheld by the Saskatchewan Court of Appeal and by the Supreme Court of Canada. Taschereau J. held that if *Leaman* v. *Rea* meant that where the evidence shows that *one* of two drivers was negligent and the court is unable to distinguish between them, then both should be found equally at fault, it should be overruled. There is no principle on which a person may be held liable unless his negligence is proved. There was no evidence

here, as there was in *France* v. *Parkinson* and *Baker* v. *Market Harborough* from
which an inference could be drawn that *both* parties were negligent. Locke J.
indicated that, in *Leaman* v. *Rea,* the evidence disclosed a collision in the centre
of the road, from which it could be inferred there was negligence on both
drivers. Here, as the forward parts of both vehicles were on the proper side of
the road, something occurred to produce a collision of the rear parts. There was
no evidence to justify an inference that both drivers were negligent and liability
cannot be imposed on the basis that one or other of the drivers was negligent.
Does this case conflict with *Leaman* v. *Rae?*

6. A trial judge must consider not only the guilt of *each* of the parties but
also the possibility that *both* parties were negligent. In *Fogel* v. *Satnik* (1960),
23 D.L.R. (2d) 630 (Ont. C.A.), the trial judge dismissed a motor vehicle action
saying, "if [plaintiff's witness] A's version is correct, the defendant is entirely
to blame; and conversely, if the defendant is to be believed, the plaintiff's negligence was the sole cause of action. . . . I am completely unable to make a finding as to credibility." The Court of Appeal found this procedure wanting and
ordered a new trial on the ground that the trial judge "did not consider the possibility of *both* drivers of the vehicles being at fault" and it was "quite open to
the learned trial judge to find that both the plaintiff and the defendant were
negligent".

7. One should not be deluded into thinking that all automobile collision
claims will now be successful. In *Haswell* v. *Enman* (1961), 28 D.L.R. (2d) 537
(B.C.C.A.), one party died, the other party had amnesia and other evidence was
almost non-existent. The court dismissed both actions. Davey J.A. stated that
"the cause of the collision is surrounded by so much speculation and conjecture
that it is impossible to find that either party discharged the burden of proving
negligence resting upon him". This was a case of "absence of evidence" rather
than one of "the probabilities being evenly divided". A similar result obtained
in *Binda* v. *Waters Const. Co.* (1960), 24 D.L.R. (2d) 431 (Man. C.A.), where
the plaintiff motorist, proceeding north, collided with a tractor that was
travelling south. The accident occurred in a dense cloud of smoke or steam blown
across the highway by a nearby railway locomotive. There being ample room
for both vehicles to pass on the highway, the crucial fact issue at the trial was
on which side of the highway the accident occurred. The trial judge, after stating that there was "no evidence", found that both parties were equally responsible, purportedly in accordance with the contributory negligence legislation.
The Manitoba Court of Appeal said that this was improper and sent the case
back for a new trial. The court did not cite any of the cases referred to here,
not even the *Wood* v. *Thompson* case decided in the same province. Mr. Justice
Freedman stated:

> "The statutory provision is not a substitute for a judicial finding of negli-
> gence, nor does its existence obviate the need of the tribunal making such a
> judicial finding. Admittedly the learned trial judge faced a difficult problem.
> But the resolution of that problem called for a judicial decision on the issue
> of negligence. Only then could the statutory provision be called into play.
> Instead the learned trial judge resorted to the section and found equal re-
> sponsibility on the basis thereof. His use of the section in these circum-
> stances involved him — altogether innocently of course — in an abdication
> of the judicial task which he was required to perform."

Tritschler J.A. would have dismissed the action on the ground that the trial
judge had really said he could not find on the evidence that the defendant was
negligent. "To grant a new trial is to give the plaintiff a second chance to persuade another court to come to a different conclusion of fact."

8. The High Court of Australia has reached the same conclusion. In *Nester-
czuk* v. *Mortimore* (1965-66), 39 A.L.J.R. 288, two vehicles headed in opposite
directions struck one another a glancing blow. Each party claimed that the
other had crossed the centre line. The trial judge decided that neither party had
established that the other was to blame and this was affirmed. Mr. Justice
Windeyer explained that "very seldom would the proper inference from the

mere fact of a collision in the centre of a road be that the drivers were equally to blame". Many other circumstances are involved. The trial judge did not have to be persuaded by either party, nor did he have to hold both parties to blame, if he could not decide which one was at fault. "Doubtless the facts spoke for themselves, and eloquently, of negligence: but of whose negligence they had nothing to say. And when the parties themselves spoke, what they said left the learned trial judge still in doubt." Mr. Justice Owen cast some doubt upon the statements of Lord Justice Denning. He agreed that an unexplained collision in the centre of the road leads to a reasonable inference of negligence, but he would not accept the "view that there is some principle of law which insists that both parties must be held to be blameworthy when that hypothesis is not a more probable one than that one or the other was wholly responsible". He added that "no court is entitled to make a finding which is not justified by the evidence". The dissenting judge, McTiernan A.C.J., thought that the "probabilities are that neither of the parties was keeping a proper look out, and that each was driving in dangerous proximity to the other vehicle".

9. In *Wing* v. *London Gen'l Omnibus Co.*, [1909] 2 K.B. 652, at pp. 663-4, Fletcher Moulton L.J. said:

> "Without attempting to lay down any exhaustive classification of the cases in which the principle of *res ipsa loquitur* applies, it may generally be said that the principle only applies when the direct cause of the accident, and so much of the surrounding circumstances as was essential to its occurrence, were within the sole control and management of the defendants, or their servants, so that it is not unfair to attribute to them a *prima facie* responsibility for what happened. An accident in the case of traffic on a highway is in marked contrast to such a condition of things. Every vehicle has to adapt its own behaviour to the behaviour of other persons using the road, and over their actions those in charge of the vehicle have no control. Hence the fact that an accident has happened either to or through a particular vehicle is by itself no evidence that the fault, if any, which led to it was committed by those in charge of that vehicle. Exceptional cases may occur in which the peculiar nature of the accident may throw light upon the question on whom the responsibility lies, but there is nothing of the kind here."

Is this reasoning still sound?

10. Compare these cases with *Ybarra* v. *Spangard, supra.*

THE HIGHWAY TRAFFIC ACT

R.S.O. 1970, c. 202, s. 133(1)

133. (1) When loss or damage is sustained by any person by reason of a motor vehicle on a highway, the onus of proof that such loss or damage did not arise through the negligence or improper conduct of the owner or driver of the motor vehicle shall be upon the owner or driver.

(2) This section shall not apply in case of a collision between motor vehicles on the highway nor to an action brought by a passenger in a motor vehicle in respect of any injuries sustained by him while a passenger.

NOTES

1. The purpose of the "onus" section, as this provision has been called, has been well-explained by Matheson C.C.J. in *MacDonald* v. *Woodard* (1973), 2 O.R. (2d) 438, at p. 440, as follows:

> "This section was enacted in order to overcome difficulties experienced by plaintiffs in obtaining and presenting sufficient evidence of a motorist's negligence to avoid a non-suit at the close of their case. Knowledge of relevant acts and circumstances leading up to an accident might be in the possession only of the defendant and injustice might result if a plaintiff was unable to overcome the initial obstacle of a *prima facie* case and to avoid having his case

determined before all the evidence was before the Court. Hence the introduction of a type of statutory *res ipsa loquitur* doctrine under which the owner or driver is *prima facie* liable for damage caused by his motor vehicle unless he satisfied the Court on a preponderance of evidence that he was not in fact negligent.

A plaintiff must therefore show, in order that the section may apply, that his damages were occasioned by the presence of a motor vehicle on the highway.

This does not mean that before the onus begins to operate, the plaintiff must first prove that the effective cause of the collision was the conduct of the driver; he need only show that the collision—not the conduct of the driver —was the cause of the damage: *Stewart* v. *Ottawa Electric R. Co. and Hollis,* [1945] O.W.N. 639, [1945] 4 D.L.R. 400; affirmed [1948] 2 D.L.R. 800, 62 C.R.T.C. 272; *Mann* v. *Hilton,* [1953] O.W.N. 908.''

With regard to the procedural effect of the section, do you agree that the section creates a type of statutory *res ipsa loquitur* doctrine which operates as suggested by Matheson C.C.J.?

2. What is the procedural effect of this section? See *Winnipeg Electric Co.* v. *Geel,* [1932] A.C. 690, where the Privy Council considered the application of such a section. Lord Wright, quoting Duff J., stated: "The statute creates, as against the owners and drivers of motor vehicles, in the conditions therein laid down, a rebuttable presumption of negligence. The onus of disproving negligence remains throughout the proceedings. If, at the conclusion of the evidence, it is too meagre or too evenly balanced to enable the tribunal to determine this issue as a question of fact, then, by force of the statute, the plaintiff is entitled to succeed." Lord Wright also noted: "The position of the defendants under the statute is thus analogous to the position of the defendant in a case to which the principle often called *res ipsa loquitur* applies." Do you agree? What is the difference between the effect of the statute and the way the rule of *res ipsa loquitur* usually operates?

3. This onus section has been used primarily by pedestrians who are run down. Do you think it is of any practical use? The *Osgoode Hall Study on Compensation for Victims of Automobile Accidents* (1965), found that 54 percent of the injured pedestrians received some tort compensation while only 43 percent of all those injured recovered. Is any of this due to the onus section?

4. In *Foster* v. *Registrar of Motor Vehicles* (1961), 28 D.L.R. (2d) 561 (Ont. C.A.), the plaintiff motorist, while driving northerly, was injured by a piece of metal debris left on the street from an earlier collision, which was thrown through his open window by a car driven southbound by an unidentified driver (represented by the Registrar of Motor Vehicles). At the trial, the court held that s. 106(1) [now s. 133(1)] of the Ontario Highway Traffic Act did not apply to place the burden of disproof of negligence on the defendant driver. In any event, on a consideration of all the evidence, the trial judge decided that the defendant was not negligent in law. On appeal, this judgment was reversed by a majority of the Court of Appeal and judgment was entered for the plaintiff. The court was unanimous that s. 106(1) [now s. 133(1)] applied to place the onus of disproof on the defendant, since the plaintiff's injury arose by reason of a motor vehicle on the highway and the facts did not bring the plaintiff within s. 106(2) [now s. 133(2)].

5. Would a bicyclist be able to claim the advantage of s. 133(2)? See *Hutcheon* v. *Storey,* [1935] 4 D.L.R. 684. What about a motorcyclist? See generally, Horsley, *Manual of Motor Vehicle Law* (1963), p. 275; MacIntyre, "Liability Incident to the Ownership of a Motor Car" (1940-42), 4 Alta. L.Q. 3; Phelan, "Onus Under the Highway Traffic Act", in *Special Lectures of the Law Society of Upper Canada on Evidence* (1955).

6. It is not necessary for the plaintiff to plead negligence if he is relying on the onus section. See *Finnie* v. *Webster,* [1941] O.R. 167, [1941] 3 D.L.R. 499. However, where the owner or operator of a motor car is suing for damage caused otherwise than by another motor vehicle, it has been held in Ontario

that the plaintiff has the burden of proving that his damage was not caused by his own negligence or improper conduct: *Wright* v. *C.N.R.,* [1938] O.R. 66, [1938] 1 D.L.R. 496; *Groves* v. *County of Wentworth,* [1939] O.R. 138, [1939] 2 D.L.R. 375; *Kielb* v. *C.N.R.,* [1941] 3 D.L.R. 665.

7. The questions usually put to the jury in a pedestrian case were outlined by Mr. Justice Schroeder in "The Charge to the Jury", *Special Lectures of the Law Society of Upper Canada* (1955), as follows:

"Q1. Has the defendant satisfied you on the whole evidence that the loss or damage sustained by the plaintiff did not arise through the negligence or improper conduct of the defendant, the owner (or driver) of the motor vehicle?

Ans. Yes or No.

Q2. Was there negligence on the part of the plaintiff which caused or contributed to the accident?

Ans. Yes or No.

Q3. If your answer to question No. 2 is Yes, then state fully and clearly the particulars of such negligence."

8. The trial judge may direct the jury in an onus case to specify negligent acts or omissions that caused the accident, but this power has been sparingly, if ever, exercised. See Ontario Judicature Act, R.S.O. 1970, c. 228, s. 67 (2); Schroeder, "The Charge to the Jury," *op cit., supra,* at p. 330; Phelan, "Onus Under the Highway Traffic Act", *Special Lectures of the Law Society of Upper Canada* (1955), at p. 215.

9. Proof of contributory negligence has created some difficult problems of interpretation of the onus section, the wording of which differs in some jurisdictions. See *Dearing* v. *Hebert,* [1957] S.C.R. 843, 11 D.L.R. (2d) 97; *Feener* v. *McKenzie,* [1972] S.C.R. 525; *Gordon* v. *Trottier,* [1974] S.C.R. 158, *Hartman* v. *Fisette* (1976), 66 D.L.R. (3d) 516, at p. 522 (S.C.C.), proof of contributory negligence not a complete excuse.

REVIEW PROBLEM

Paul owned a 1961 Chevrolet automobile. One winter morning his engine refused to start. Clem, his mechanic, told him that he needed a new battery. Paul went down to Simpson's Department Store and purchased a new Power battery and had Simpson's install it for him. It was an ordinary-looking black battery with 2 steel knobs protruding from the top of it. It was attached to the automobile by 2 rubber-covered wires which were screwed on to these 2 steel knobs. Printed on the side of the battery were these words "More Power and More Safety: Manufactured by the Power Battery Company". No other writing appeared on the battery, and no other written or oral directions were given.

The next day, Paul's new battery refused to work, and the car still would not start. Paul lifted the hood of the car and decided that he would recharge the battery with his own battery-charger. Paul removed the 2 rubber-covered wires and affixed his battery-charger to the 2 steel knobs on the battery. Paul turned on the electrical current and suddenly the battery exploded. Paul was severly injured.

On investigation, it appears that automobile battery manufacturers know that batteries explode on occasion. They offer no satisfactory explanation for this. However, the explosions frequently occur while a battery is being charged. The manufacturers of these batteries do not issue any warnings to their wholesalers, retailers or to the general public because they say that "no useful purpose would be served by this".

Paul sued only the Power Battery Company. The trial judge granted a nonsuit on motion by the defendant. You are retained to argue the appeal to the Court of Appeal. Do so.

CHAPTER 6

NEGLIGENCE AND VIOLATION OF
CRIMINAL STATUTES

The common law treatment of legislation has never been happy. The way in which statutes are used (or abused) in determining the incidence of tort liability is no exception. There is much confusion, uncertainty and downright injustice. Much of the difficulty is of the courts' own making, although, being human, they generally blame the legislatures for creating the problem. One of the major obstacles to clarity stems from the insistence of some judges on a search for a legislative intention to confer a cause of action where any objective observer can see that no such intent has been expressed. Another difficulty is that, after they have decided to employ a statute, the courts are uncertain about the procedural effect to give it. As a result, this area has become one of the most unsatisfactory in the entire field of tort law. The outcome of the cases defies prediction. This is unfortunate because legislative activity is expanding rapidly and civil courts are, consequently, being called upon more frequently to grapple with statutory material. The common law must learn to live in harmony with legislation.

This chapter is designed to move us in the direction of a better understanding of the true problems involved in this complex area. Here we shall concentrate on the use of legislation in the standard of care context. Chapter 7 deals with penal statutes as a factor in the creation of new tort duties.

A. WHY CIVIL COURTS RELY ON PENAL STATUTES

PHILLIPS v. BRITANNIA HYGIENIC LAUNDRY CO. LTD.

Court of Appeal. [1923] 2 K.B. 832; 129 L.T. 177; 93 L.J.K.B.5

While the defendant's servant was driving their motor lorry, one of the axles broke, a wheel came off and struck and damaged the plaintiff's van. The defendants had sent their lorry to be overhauled and repaired by a reputable firm. That firm replaced one worn axle and rethreaded and annealed the other which was seen to be defective; they did not consider it necessary to replace it with a new axle. The defendants received the lorry back, two days before the accident.

The trial judge held that the defendants were not negligent, but he did hold them liable by reason of violating art. II, cl. 6 of the Motor Cars (Use and Construction) Order, 1904, made by the Local Government Board pursuant to the Locomotives on Highways Act, 1896. This regulation provided that "the motor car and all the fittings thereof shall be in such a condition as not to cause, or to be likely to cause, danger to any person in the motor car or on any highway."

A Divisional Court reversed the trial judgment and entered judgment for the defendants: [1923] 1 K.B. 539. The plaintiff appealed.

Atkin L.J.: . . . This is an important question, and I have felt some doubt upon it, because it is clear that these regulations are in part designed to promote the safety of the public using highways. The question is whether they were intended to be enforced only by special penalty attached to them in the Act. In my opinion, when an Act imposes a duty of commission or omission, the question whether a person aggrieved by a breach of the duty has a right of action depends on the intention of the Act. Was it intended to make the duty one which was owed to the party aggrieved as well as to the State, or was it a public duty only? That depends on the construction of the Act and the circumstances in which it was made and to which it relates. One question to be considered is: Does the Act contain reference to a remedy for a breach of it? *Prima facie*, if it does that is the only remedy. But that is not conclusive. The intention as disclosed by its scope and wording must still be regarded, and it may still be that, though the statute creates the duty and provides a penalty, the duty is nevertheless owed to individuals . . . .

To my mind, and in this respect I differ from McCardie J., the question is not to be solved by considering whether or not the person aggrived can bring himself within some special class of the community or whether he is some designated individual. The duty may be of such paramount importance that it is owed to all the public. It would be strange if a less important duty, which is owed to a section of the public, may be enforced by an action, while a more important duty owed to the public at large cannot. The right of action does not depend on whether a statutory commandment or prohibition is pronounced for the benefit of the public or for the benefit of a class. It may be conferred on any one who can bring himself within the benefit of the Act, including one who cannot be otherwise specified than as a person using the highway. Therefore, I think McCardie J. is applying too strict a test when he says: "The Motor Car Acts and Regulations were not enacted for the benefit of any particular class of folk. They are provisions for the benefit of the whole public, whether pedestrians or vehicle users, whether aliens or British citizens, and whether working or walking or standing upon the highway." . . . The question is whether these regulations, viewed in the circumstances in which they were made and to which they relate, were intended to impose a duty which is a public duty only or whether they were intended, in addition to the public duty, to impose a duty enforceable by an individual aggrieved. I have come to the conclusion that the duty they were intended to impose was not a duty enforceable by individuals injured, but a public duty only, the sole remedy for which is the remedy provided by way of a fine. They impose obligations of various kinds, some are concerned more with the maintenance of the highway than with the safety of passengers; and they are of varying degrees of importance; yet for breach of any regulation a fine not exceeding £10 is the penalty. It is not likely that the Legislature in empowering a department to make regulations for the use and construction of motor cars, permitted the department to impose new duties in favour of individuals and new causes of action for breach of them in addition to the obligations already well provided for and regulated by the common law of those who bring vehicles upon highways. In particular it is not likely that the Legislature intended by these means to impose on the owners of vehicles an absolute obligation to have them roadworthy in all events even in the absence of negligence. For these reasons I think the appeal should be dismissed.

NOTES

1. What was the main reason the court gave for refusing to use the penal statute in this case? How did it determine what the Legislature intended with regard to civil liability? Is there any merit in the public duty notion? See *Pugliese* v. *National Capital Commission* (1977), 3 C.C.L.T. 18 (Ont. C.A.); varied (1979), 25 N.R. 498 (S.C.C.).

2. If a legislature intends the violation of one of its penal statutes to give rise to civil liability, can it not write this into the legislation? For examples of express provisions imposing civil liability, see Railway Act, R.S.C. 1970, C-234, ss. 336, 339, 370; Liquor Licence Act, R.S.O. 1970, c. 250, s. 68. See *Menow v. Jordan House Hotel Ltd.*, [1970] 1 O.R. 54 (Haines J.) affd. [1971] 1 O.R. 129, affd. [1974] S.C.R. 239. Can you think of any reasons why this is so seldom done?

3. What do you think were the real reasons for denying liability in *Phillips*? Did it have anything to do with a mistrust of the type of body that the legislative enactment emanated from? See *Silver Line Taxi Co. v. Souch*, [1952] 4 D.L.R. 751, 6 W.W.R. (N.S.) 154 (Man. C.A.). Did it have anything to do with the general nature of the provision? Did it have anything to do with an antagonism toward strict liability? Did it have anything to do with the size of the criminal penalty imposed? Do you agree with the result?

4. This intention rationale for utilizing criminal violations in tort suits has a long history. In *Couch v. Steel* (1854), 3 E. & Bl. 402, 118 E.R. 1193 the court, in imposing liability, relied on the Statute of Westminster II and Comyns' Digest. In *Atkinson v. Newcastle Waterworks* (1877), 2 Ex. D. 441 liability was denied on the ground that it was not called for "on the purview of the legislature". In *Groves v. Winborne*, [1898] 2 Q.B. 402 the court purported to follow both these earlier cases and imposed liability on the intention theory. The trouble was that little guidance was given about how the legislative intention was to be determined. Reliance was placed in two conflicting presumptions — one that a private right would exist unless removed — the other that the private rights would not exist unless inserted. The courts could, therefore, choose the approach they would use depending on the result they wished to reach. Confusion resulted and fog still fills the air. This is explored more fully in Linden, "Tort Liability for Criminal Nonfeasance" (1966), 44 Can. Bar Rev. 25.

5. Sometimes courts find that there is an intention to confer a cause of action and sometimes they do not. It is usually impossible to discover why they reach the conclusions they do. In *Cunningham v. Moore*, [1972] 3 O.R. 369; affd. [1973] 1 O.R. 358, for example, it was held that a violation of the Ontario Landlord and Tenant Act, R.S.O. 1970, c. 236, s. 96(1) gave rise to a cause of action. The plaintiff-tenant sued the defendant-landlord in tort for damages resulting from a fire that he alleged occurred as a result of defective wiring in an electric stove. Although there was no cause of action at common law in these circumstances, he alleged that s. 96(1) created a new cause of action. Section 96(1) reads:

A landlord is responsible for providing and maintaining the rented premises in a good state of repair and fit for habitation during the tenancy and for complying with health and safety standards, including any housing standards required by law, and notwithstanding that any state of non-repair existed to the knowledge of the tenant before the tenancy agreement was entered into.

The defendant sought a determination of a question of law before trial on this issue. Scott Co. Ct. J. held that by introducing s. 96(1), "the intention of the legislation was to create a cause of action in favour of a particular class, to wit, tenants". His Honour explained that "the remedies provided are wholly inadequate and do not represent adequate compensation should damages be suffered". On appeal, Mr. Justice Holland agreed with Judge Scott and stated: "If a duty is imposed by statute then *prima facie*, the plaintiff is entitled to succeed upon showing a breach of that statutory duty resulting in injury or damage to the plaintiff." He concluded that "from a fair reading of s. 96 it was the intention of the Legislature to establish civil liability. . . ."

See also *Fleischmann v. Grossman Holdings* (1976), 79 D.L.R. (3d) 142 (Ont. C.A.); *Dye v. McGregor* (1978), 20 O.R. (2d) 1 (C.A.); *Lindstrom v. Basset Realty* (1978), 90 D.L.R. (3d) 238 (N.S.).

A different result, however, flows when a guest of a tenant is injured, rather than the tenant himself. (See *Alexander v. Candy* (1974), 57 D.L.R. (3d) 654 Goodman J. (Ont.). (It should also be noted that a landlord will not be absolutely liable under this section if he had no knowledge of the defect and no reasonable opportunity to acquire such knowledge. (See *McQuestion* v. *Schneider* (1975), 57 D.L.R. (3d) 537 (Ont. C.A.).)

6. Another case in which liability was imposed is *In re MacIssac and Beretanos* (1972), 25 D.L.R. (3d) 610. The plaintiff-tenant sought damages from the defendant-landlord who illegally entered his apartment in contravention of s. 46 of the British Columbia Landlord and Tenant Act which forbids entry except in an emergency or upon 24 hours written notice. There was no penalty provided in the statute for a violation of this section. Levey Prov. Ct. J. concluded *inter alia* that it was "undoubtedly clear that the Legislature intended that a breach of s. 46 of the Act gives rise to damages, otherwise the Legislature would have inserted a penalty provision". Do you think that a different conclusion would have been reached if a fine of up to $1000 had been permitted by the legislation? Any difference if the fine were only $10?

7. A contrary view was expressed in an *obiter dictum* in *Henzel* v. *Brussels Motors Ltd.* (1972), 31 D.L.R. (3d) 131. The plaintiff purchased a truck from the defendant and was involved in an accident a short time later. It was proved that the brakes of the vehicle were defective and that this caused the collision. The plaintiff sued the defendant, *inter alia*, for breach of a stautory duty. The Highway Traffic Act, R.S.O. 1960, c. 172, s. 49 required a dealer in used motor vehicles to give the purchaser a certificate of mechanical fitness. The regulations passed pursuant to the Act required that all wheels be removed for inspection of the brakes prior to the issuance of such a certificate. The defendant admitted in evidence that this inspection was not carried out as required. Fogarty Co. Ct. J. held the defendant liable on a warranty theory, but rejected the contention that there was a cause of action for breach of statutory duty and stated:

"The question in every case is one as to the intention of the Legislature in creating the duty, and no action for damages will appear to lie, if, on the true construction of the statute, the intention is that some other remedy, civil or criminal, shall be the only one available. One of the means of determining the intention of the statute, is to ascertain whether the duty is owed primarily to the state or community, and only incidentally to the individual, or primarily to the individual or class of individuals and only incidentally to the state or community: see *Solomons* v. *R. Gertzenstein Ltd.*, [1954] 2 Q.B. 243 at p. 265. If the statute imposes a duty for the protection of particular citizens or a particular class of citizen, it *prima facie* creates at the same time a correlative right vested in those citizens and *prima facie*, therefore, they will have a remedy for the enforcement of that right, namely, an action for damages in respect to any loss occasioned by the violation of it. The law of England is replete with situations where breaches of statutory duties give rise to actions being brought by those in a special group of persons intended to be affected; for example, workers under the Factories Act, and miners under the Mines and Quarries Act. In these instances, the court has, in the main, held for absolute liability in favour of such workers as a particular class or classes of persons intended to be protected under the relevant Act. This liability has been found notwithstanding that there is a penalty section in the various acts by which the employer may be prosecuted for failure to take certain safety precautions.

In the case at bar, the Ontario Highway Traffic Act provides for a penalty, in the event that there is failure to issue a certificate of mechanical fitness or in the event that the certificate is improperly issued arising out of failure to conform to the standards of inspection as set out in the Regulation. The Act, however, gives no express cause of action to the purchaser of a motor vehicle but is silent on the point. Notwithstanding the presence of the penalty section, I would have no hesitation in finding liability on the basis of the breach of the statutory condition alone, if I could bring myself to the view that the purchasers of used motor vehicles constitute a class or classes in the community which are intended to be protected by s. 49 of the Highway Traffic Act. In my view, a class of persons intended to be protected by a statute must be an identifiable group of persons and not a vague group of people who from time to time would fall into some special category known as purchasers of used motor vehicles. Such a group of persons can hardly be similar to a group of workers such as industrial employees, miners, etc. The group is just too vague, in my view, to be considered a class within the usual legal meaning of that term. I do not believe that the circumstances of this case can be strained to such an extent and clearly against the general view of the courts which is opposed to the construction of penal statutes to create torts.

Quite apart from the inability to define "purchasers of used cars" as a distinct class which the legislation might be intended to protect, I am frankly of the view that such legislation as we have here is not only intended to protect the purchasers of used vehicles, but to ensure safety on our roadways and hence to protect the numbers of the public generally. If a vehicle goes out of control by reason of defective brakes, it is a hazard not only to the driver of that vehicle but to any member of the public who might have the misfortune to be in its path. In the case at bar it was another car and driver which were its victims. It could just as easily have been a pedestrian, on the road, on the sidewalk, or a member of the public on the limits of his own property. For this further reason, I cannot find that a separate class exists which was intended solely to be the beneficiary of this legislation, but rather am of the view that such legislation is intended primarily to benefit the State generally and any duty under such a statute is owed to the State."

Are you impressed with the analysis of Judge Fogarty? Would the opposite conclusion have been preferable?

8. The intention theory is not only unhelpful, it can also be harmful. For example, it can draw courts into constitutional debates. Because the B.N.A. Act grants to the provinces the jurisdiction over property and civil rights, there have been doubts expressed about whether the federal government can "create" civil rights by passing penal legislation. See *Wasney* v. *Jurazsky*, [1933] 1 W.L.R. 616, 41 Man. R. 46: *Fowell* v. *Grafton* (1910), 22 O.L.R. 550; 20 O.L.R. 639; *Placatka* v. *Thompson*, [1941] 2 D.L.R. 320, [1941] 1 W.W.R. 528 (Alta.); *Transport Oil Co.* v. *Imperial Oil Co.*, [1935] O.R. 111, 215, [1935] 2 D.L.R. 500, affirming [1935] 1 D.L.R. 751; See Finkleman, Comment, (1935), 13 Can. Bar Rev. 517; *Philco Products Ltd.* v. *Thermionics Ltd.*, [1940] S.C.R. 501, [1940] 4 D.L.R. 1; *Direct Lumber Co. Ltd.* v. *Western Plywood Co. Ltd.*, [1962] S.C.R. 646, 35 D.L.R. (2d) 1; *Heimler* v. *Calvert Caterers Ltd.* (1975), 4 O.R. (2d) 667; affd (1975), 8 O.R. (2d) 1 (C.A.). See generally, *MacDonald* v. *Vapor Canada Ltd.* (1976), 66 D.L.R. (3d) 1 (S.C.C.); Hogg, Comment (1976), 54 Can. Bar Rev. 361. Would this problem disappear if the intention theory were jettisoned?

9. Other theories have been utilized to justify judicial reliance on penal statutes in tort cases. Professor Thayer, in an article called "Public Wrong and Private Action" (1914), 27 Harv. L. Rev. 317, at p. 321, suggested that, if the legislature forbids certain conduct as "dangerous" and "unreasonable", it would be an "unjust reproach to the ordinary prudent man to suppose he would do such a thing in the teeth of the ordinance". In other words, since reasonable people obey the law, someone who violates a legislative provision cannot be said to have acted reasonably. This view was once expressed by Mr. Justice Schroeder in a *dictum* in *Horne* v. *Fortalsky*, [1952] O.W.N. 121, at p. 122, as follows:

"The Highway Traffic Act is a statute which is designed to control and regulate the use of the public highways in this province by motorists and others. Certain requirements are laid down as to what shall be done and what shall not be done, and the provisions are in all respects most salutary; and no doubt the reasonable, prudent man will endeavour, so far as practicable to comply with the requirements of the Act, because it may be said to set a standard of care which should be observed by the reasonable, prudent man who ventures upon the public highway. . . ."

What do you think of this rationale, which has been considered to be "inade-

quate" to explain the "action upon the statute" by Fricke, "The Juridical
Nature of the Action Upon the Statute" (1960), 76 L.Q.Rev. 240, at p. 243?

10. Another basis for using legislation is the "public wrong" theory. Since
someone who violates the provisions of a penal statute is guilty of a "public
wrong", he should be held responsible for all of the consequences of his act.
This rationale has been described as the "statutory nuisance" theory. It has
been invoked on occasion in judicial pronouncements. Mr. Justice Chute, for
example, in *Kerr* v. *Townsend* (1917), 12 O.W.N. 166, at p. 167, imposed liability on a defendant who violated a speeding statute, because his conduct
amounted to an "illegal act". More recently, Mr. Justice Haines offered this
theory as an alternative basis of liability in *Menow* v. *Honsberger & Jordan
House Hotel Ltd.,* [1970] 1 O.R. 54, where the defendant was held civilly
liable for serving alcohol to an intoxicated patron who was then injured in a
car accident. His Lordship reasoned that "by committing this unlawful act, the
corporate defendant has not only committed an offence under the relevant
liquor statutes, but it has also breached a common law duty to the plaintiff".
What are the deficiencies of this theory?

11. Does a civil court have any business at all relying upon criminal statutes
in deciding whether civil liability will be imposed? What policy arguments can
be advanced in favour of the use of penal statutes in tort cases? What about the
desirability of consistency between the criminal law and the civil law? Is the
legislature better equipped with expertise than the judiciary to make decisions
about the appropriate standards of conduct to be adhered to? Can the force of
penal enactments be rendered more powerful by their adoption in tort cases?
Does the reliance on criminal legislation simplify the administration of the reasonable care test by the judge and jury? Does the use of statutory standards
move us closer to a regime of strict liability?

12. What policy reasons can be offered in opposition to the use of statutes
in civil cases? Does this practice offend the principle of deference to the legislature by going beyond its expressed will? Can civil liability impose too onerous
a burden upon the violator of a minor piece of legislation? What about the
matter of double jeopardy? Can the expertise of the legislature be over-esti-
mated? Is it wise to control too closely the operation of the judge and jury in
the daily administration of negligence law? Is it advisable to depart from "fault"
liability in this area? See generally, Linden, *Canadian Tort Law* (2nd ed., 1977),
pp. 155-169.

13. The basis for judicial reliance on penal statutes was the subject of a perceptive comment by Dixon J. of the High Court of Australia in *O'Connor* v.
S.P. Bray Ltd. (1937), 56 C.L.R. 464 at p. 477 to this effect:

"It is a question of some difficulty whether a civil remedy is given to a
person injured in consequence of the breach of [the statute]. Such a person
may, of course, maintain an action of negligence and rely upon the failure to
comply with the statutory regulations as evidence of negligence. But it is a
different question whether the enactment itself confers a distinct cause of
action. The received doctrine is that when a statute prescribes in the interests
of the safety of members of the public or a class of them a course of conduct
and does no more than penalize a breach of its provisions, the question
whether a private right of action also arises mus. be determined as a matter
of construction. The difficulty is that in such a case the legislature has in
fact expressed no intention upon the subject, and an interpretation of the
statute, according to ordinary canons of construction, will rarely yield a
necessary implication positively giving a civil remedy.

As an examination of the decided cases will show, an intention to give, or
not to give, a private right has more often than not been ascribed to the
legislature as a result of presumptions or by reference to matters governing
the policy of the provision rather than the meaning of the instrument. Sometimes it almost appears that a complexion is given to the statute upon very
general considerations without either the authority of any general rule of
law or the application of any definite rule of construction . . . . Perhaps in

the end, a principle of law will be acknowledged as the foundation of the cases. In the absence of a contrary legislative intention, a duty imposed by statute to take measures for the safety of others seems to be regarded as involving a correlative private right, although the sanction is penal, because it protects an interest recognized by the general principles of the common law. . . .

Whatever wider rule may ultimately be deduced, I think it may be said that a provision prescribing a specific precaution for the safety of others in a matter where the person upon whom the duty laid is, under the general law of negligence, bound to exercise due care, the duty will give rise to a correlative private right, unless from the nature of the provision or from the scope of the legislation fo which it forms a part a contrary intention appears. The effect of such a provision is to define specifically what must be done in furtherance of the general duty to protect the safety of those affected by the operations carried on."

Similar recognition of the creative role of civil courts in this area was articulated in *Placatka* v. *Thompson,* [1941] 2 D.L.R. 320, at p. 324 (Alta. C.A.); the dissenting opinion of Trueman J. in *Wasney* v. *Jurazsky* (1933), 41 Man. R. 46, [1933] 1 W.W.R. 155 (C.A.).

14. In discussing the use of motor vehicle legislation in tort cases, Mr. Justice Rand in *Bruce* v. *McIntyre,* [1955] S.C.R. 251, at p. 254, stated:

"The appearance of automobiles upon our highways has obviously created crowding dangers and hazards undreamt of in 1840. The speed and the momentum of these vehicles and the complexity of their operations are such that it has become necessary to place every person concerned with or who may be affected by them under a greatly heightened exercise of care and imagination to stimulate awareness and anticipation. The elaborate and detailed requirements that are now set out in the statutes dealing with speed, lights, signals, positions, parking and other details of management and operation combine to create more than a mere duty of abstention from affirmative action which may cause damage or injury to others; they may require action either by way of precautionary warning or by removing one's self or property from a range of danger which theoretically the prudent conduct of others would make unnecessary. They give rise to a responsibility for greater foresight than the mere first stage of minimum or formal measures of one's own proper conduct: they are intended to promote reciprocal, even overlapping, precautions. Always depending on the surrounding circumstances and subject to other demands of safety, they bind us to contemplate carelessness or oversight in others regardless of their duty under the rules of the road, and they require us to act within the limits of alerted reasonableness to ensure, in the interest of the public, the practicable maximum of generalized and mutual protection against injury to person and damage to property. The scandal of the ravages of our holidays from this cause is the more than sufficient justification for the insistence on the drastic measure to which our highway authorities have been aroused. . . ."

15. On the effect of criminal or penal legislation, see Thayer, "Public Wrong and Private Action" (1914), 27 Harv. L. Rev. 313; Lowndes, "Civil Iability Created by Criminal Legislation" (1932), 16 Minn. L. Rev. 361: Morris, "The Relation of Criminal Statutes to Tort Liability" (1933), 46 Harv. L. Rev. 453; Morris, "Role of Criminal Statutes in Negligence Actions" (1949), 49 Colum. L. Rev. 21; Williams, "The Effect of Penal Legislation in the Law of Tort" (1960), 23 Mod. L. Rev. 233; Fricke, "The Juridical Nature of the Action Upon the Statute" (1960), 76 L.Q.Rev. 240; James, "Statutory Standards and Negligence in Accident Cases" (1950), 11 La. L. Rev. 95; Alexander, "Legislation and the Standard of Care in Negligence" (1964), 42 Can. Bar Rev. 243; Linden, "Tort Liability for Criminal Nonfeasance" (1966), 44 Can. Bar Rev. 25.

B. WHEN CIVIL COURTS RELY ON PENAL STATUTES: THE LIMITATIONS

GORRIS v. SCOTT

Exchequer Court. (1874), L.R. 9 Ex. 125; 43 L.J. Ex. 92; 30 L.J. 431

Kelly C.B.: This is an action to recover damages for the loss of a number of sheep which the defendant, a shipowner, had contracted to carry, and which were washed overboard and lost by reason (as we take it to be truly alleged) of the neglect to comply with a certain order made by the Privy Council, in pursuance of the Contagious Diseases (Animals) Act, 1869. The Act was passed merely for sanitary purposes, in order to prevent animals in a state of infectious disease from communicating it to other animals with which they might come in contact. Under the authority of that Act, certain orders were made; amongst others, an order by which any ship bringing sheep or cattle from any foreign port to ports in Great Britain is to have the place occupied by such animals divided into pens of certain dimensions, and the floor of such pens furnished with batiens or foot-holds. The object of this order is to prevent animals from being overcrowded, and so brought into a condition in which the disease guarded against would be likely to be developed. This regulation has been neglected, and the question is, whether the loss, which we must assume to have been caused by that neglect, entitles the plaintiffs to maintain an action.

The argument of the defendant is, that the Act has imposed penalties to secure the observance of its provisions, and that, according to the general rule, the remedy prescribed by the statute must be pursued; that although, when penalties are imposed for the violation of a statutory duty, a person aggrieved by its violation may sometimes maintain an action for the damage so caused, that must be in cases where the object of the statute is to confer a benefit on individuals, and to protect them against the evil consequences which the statute was designed to prevent, and which have in fact ensued; but that if the object is not to protect individuals against the consequences which have in fact ensued, it is otherwise; that if, therefore, by reason of the precautions in question not having been taken, the plaintiffs had sustained that damage against which it was intended to secure them, an action would lie, but that when the damage is of such a nature as was not contemplated at all by the statute, and as to which it was not intended to confer any benefit on the plaintiffs they cannot maintain an action founded on the neglect. The principle may be well illustrated by the case put in argument of a breach of a railway company of its duty to erect a gate on a level crossing, and to keep the gate closed except when the crossing is being actually and properly used. The object of the precaution is to prevent injury from being sustained through animals or vehicles being upon the line at unseasonable times; and if by reason of such a breach of duty, either in not erecting the gate, or in not keeping it closed, a person attempts to cross with a carriage at an improper time, and injury ensues to a passenger, no doubt an action would lie against the railway company, because the intention of the legislature was that, by the erection of the gates and by their being kept closed individuals should be protected against accidents of this description. And if we could see that it was the object, or among the objects of this Act, that the owners of sheep and cattle coming from a foreign port should be protected by the means described against the danger of their property being washed overboard, or lost by the perils of the sea, the present action would be within the principle.

But, looking at the Act, it is perfectly clear that its provisions were all enacted with a totally different view; there was no purpose, direct or indirect, to protect against such damage; but, as is recited in the preamble, the Act is directed against the possibility of sheep or cattle being exposed to disease on their way to this country. The preamble recites that "it is expedient to confer on Her Majesty's most honourable Privy Council power to take such measures as may appear from time to time necessary to prevent the introduction into Great Britain of contagious or infectious diseases among cattle, sheep, or other animals, by prohibiting or regulating the importation of foreign animals," and also to provide against the "spreading" of such diseases in Great Britain. Then follow numerous sections directed entirely to this object. Then comes sec. 75, which enacts that "the Privy Council may from time to time make such orders as they think expedient for all or any of the following purposes." What, then, are these purposes? They are "for securing for animals brought by sea to ports in Great Britain a proper supply of food and water during the passage and on landing," "for protecting such animals from unnecessary suffering during the passage and on landing," and so forth; all the purposes enumerated being calculated and directed to the prevention of disease, and none of them having any relation whatever to the danger of loss by the perils of the sea. That being so, if by reason of the default in question the plaintiffs' sheep had been caused unnecessary suffering, and so had arrived in this country in a state of disease, I do not say that they might not have maintained this action. But the damage complained of here is something totally apart from the object of the Act of Parliament, and it is in accordance with all the authorities to say that the action is not maintainable.

NOTES

1. Is this a wise limitation for the civil courts to place upon their use of penal statutes? Why?

2. A boy runs into a pointed ornament on a stationary car and injures himself. The defendant contravened a statute that forbids the use of any ornament "which extends or protrudes to the front of the face of the radiator grill". Liability? See *Hatch* v. *Ford Motor Co.* (1958), 163 Cal. App. 2d 293, 329 P. 2d 605.

3. The defendant violates a war-time speed limit of 35 m.p.h. and collides with the plaintiff on the highway. The purpose of the statute was found to be the conservation of gasoline, not safety. Liability? See *Cooper* v. *Hoeglund* (1946), 221 Minn. 446, 22 N.W. 2d 450.

4. Penelope was blinded by a small particle of a broken wire that was flung out of a machine she was operating. David, the defendant and owner of the factory, violated a statute that required unsafe machines to be securely fenced. If it were impossible to fence, it was permissible to provide a device which would "prevent the operator from coming into contact with that part". Would a civil court rely on the violation of this statute in a tort suit? Would it make any difference to your answer if the statute said nothing about the reason for the fencing requirement? Aside from the statutory breach, is David liable for negligence? Does it depend on how frequently this type of accident occurred in the past? Compare with *Kilgollan* v. *William Cooke & Co. Ltd.,* [1956] 2 All E.R. 294 (C.A.). See also *Keeting* v. *Elvan Reinforced Concrete Co. Ltd. et al.,* [1968] 1 W.L.R. 722 (C.A.); *Thordarson* v. *Zastre* (1968), 70 D.L.R. (2d) 91 (Alta. S.C.); *Beauchamp* v. *Ayotte et al.* [1971] 3 O.R. 21 (Lacourciere J.).

5. Not only must the accident be of a type the statute was meant to prevent, but the claimant must be someone whom the statute was designed to protect. In *Kelly* v. *Henry Muhs Co.* (1904), 71 N.J.L. 358, 59 A. 23 a statute aimed at protecting employees was violated when the defendant failed to place a guard rail or trapdoor on an elevator shaft. The plaintiff, a fireman who came to put out a fire in the building fell down an unguarded elevator shaft. He was denied recovery on the basis of the statutory breach. Policemen and other visitors have

been treated in the same way. See *Davey* v. *Greenlaw* (1957), 101 N.H. 134, 135 A. 2d 900. Is this a wise limitation?

6. In *Paulsen* v. *C.P.R.* (1963), 40 D.L.R. (2d) 761 (Man. C.A.), a section of the Railway Act required a railway to erect and maintain 4 ft. 6 in. fences on each side of the railway. "Such fences shall be suitable and sufficient to prevent cattle and other animals from getting on the railway lands." A child of 27 months was struck by a train operated by defendant railway. The Manitoba Court of Appeal held that the absence of a fence was a cause of the child's injuries and the defendant was, accordingly, liable in damages. The defendant's argument that the section was passed "for the safe passage of trains" was not adopted nor was the argument that infant trespassers were not intended to be protected by the statute. Is this decision consistent with *Kelly?* With *Gorris* v. *Scott?*

7. A tavernkeeper serves liquor to an intoxicated patron, in violation of a Liquor Control Act. As a result of this additional liquor, the drunken patron punches another patron of the tavern in the nose. Is the fact of the violation of the statute relevant in an action against the tavernkeeper? (See *Stachniewicz* v. *Mar-Cam Corp.* (1971), 259 Oregon 583, 488 P. 2d 436.) Would the result be any different if the drunken patron hit an employee of the tavern rather than a fellow patron? Would the result vary if, instead of punching the other patron, the intoxicated person tripped and fell on him? What would the result be if there were no statute? Should the courts be liberal or narrow in their assessment of the purpose of these statutes? What is the danger associated with a broad interpretation?

8. Someone leaves a car, engine running, outside a beer parlour. A thief takes the car and collides with the plaintiff. The plaintiff sues, relying on a statute making it an offence to leave a car standing or parked without having stopped the engine, locked the ignition, removed the key and braked the vehicle. Liability? See *Stavast* v. *Ludwar,* [1974] 5 W.W.R. 380 (B.C.); *Ross* v. *Hartman* (1943), 139 F. 2d 14. Would the result be any different without the statutory provision? See *Hewson* v. *City of Red Deer* (1975), 63 D.L.R. (3d) 168 (Alta.). Would the result vary if the collision took place a week after the theft of the car? Compare *Justus* v. *Wood* (1961), 349 S.W. 2d 793 (Tenn.).

9. The conduct in violation of the enactment must cause the injury. *Schofield* v. *Town of Oakville* (1968), 69 D.L.R. (2d) 441 (Ont. C.A.), *per* McGillivray J.A. The Supreme Court of Canada in *Odlum & Sylvester* v. *Walsh,* [1939] 2 D.L.R. 545 stated that it was open to the jury to find that excess speed was "not in whole or in part a direct cause of the accident". See also *dictum* in *McKenzie* v. *Robar,* [1953] 1 D.L.R. 449 (S.C.C.) and *Service Fire Insurance* v. *Larouche,* [1956] Que. Q.B. 294, at p. 296 where Mr. Justice Martineau concluded, "Il n'y a aucun lien de causalité entre sa vitesse et la collision." A similar conclusion was reached in *Wright* v. *Ruckstahl,* [1955] O.W.N. 728, at p. 729 where Mr. Justice Spence held that "no part of the accident is due to the plaintiff's speed". See Linden, "Speeding as Negligence" (1967), 10 Can. Bar. J. 94.

10. Would there by any liability if the defendant, who is in violation of a vehicle lighting statute, collides with another automobile in a brightly lit intersection? See *Collins* v. *General Service Transport* (1927), 38 B.C.R. 512, 2 D.L.R. 353; *Peacock* v. *Stephens,* [1927] 3 W.W.R. 570 (Sask. C.A.). What if the defendant, driving with defective brakes, strikes a pedestrian who darts out in front of his car before he has an opportunity to apply the brakes. See *Johnson* v. *Sorochuk,* [1941] 1 W.W.R. 445 (Alta. S.C.); *Payne* v. *Lane,* [1949] O.W.N. 284 (H.C.).

GODFREY v. COOPER

Appellate Division, Supreme Court of Ontario
(1920), 46 O.L.R. 565; 51 D.L.R. 455

The plaintiffs had paid one Flemming to drive them in his car. They were injured by reason of a collision between Flemming's car and that of the defendant. The Motor Vehicles Act, R.S.O. 1914, c. 207, s. 4, provided that "No person shall, for hire, pay or gain, drive a motor car on a highway" unless a licence was issued to the driver for that purpose. Flemming was not so licenced. The plaintiffs obtained a judgment at the trial against the defendant who was found to be negligent. The defendant appealed.

Middleton J.: . . . The contention is that Flemming in driving the car for hire was unlawfully upon the highway, and the passenger . . . by participating in his illegal act, became unlawfully upon the highway, and the negligence of the defendant resulting in their injury affords them no right of action.

I disagree with every element of this contention. In my opinion, a mere failure to obtain a licence does not deprive the driver of any right of action he would otherwise have against any person who injures him by negligence. Nor can a defendant rely upon any breach of the provisions of the statute unless he can show that the breach of the statute was a proximate cause of the accident. Nor can any such defence avail against a passenger in the car. He is not so identified with the driver as to be disentitled to recover by the fault of the driver.

The question is very widely different from that which arises in an action against the municipality for damages by reason of the non-repair of a highway. There there is no wrongful act resulting in injury, but a mere failure to perform a statutory duty; and before the plaintiff can succeed, he must shew that the defendant owed a duty to him, and he fails in this when it appears that by reason of some fact he is not lawfully upon the highway. The obligation to repair a highway is an obligation to those lawfully upon the highway. An example of the application of this principle is found in *Sercombe* v. *Township of Vaughan*, 45 O.L.R. 142; 46 D.L.R. 131.

The doctrine relied upon by the defendant has the assent of the Courts of Massachusetts . . . . [I]n that State the automobile, if unregistered, and "all its occupants are trespassers upon the highway and have no rights against other travellers except to be protected from reckless or wanton injury" . . . and it logically follows that a person injured by an unregistered car "can recover damages in an action against the operating owner without proving that he was negligent in operating the car, his liability being that of a wrongdoer maintaining a nuisance on the highway" . . . . This effect is attributed to the provision of the statute that no automobbile shall be operated on the streets unless registered. . .

. . . The whole scope of the [Motor Vehicles] Act indicates that it is intended to require those operating vehicles upon the highway to observe its requirements, and failure to do so subjects the offender to certain penalties, but does not make him a trespasser in the sense that he is an "outlaw" within the meaning of the Massachusetts cases . . . .

Further, I can find no English law to justify the proposition that the rule laid down as to the obligation of owners of land to trespassers can be applied to highway accidents. . . .

When the foundation of the doctrine as to the right of a trespasser is looked at, it will be seen that it rested upon the right of the owner to do as he pleases upon his own property, assuming that no one will violate his property-right, and that the limitation is that he must not wilfully injure one who he knows is trespassing . . . . This standard cannot be applied to persons using the highway, for there is upon them the common law duty to care for others; and, in the case of motor vehicles, there is the duty to observe all the requirements of the statute. The existence of this duty shews how inapplicable the suggested principle is.

Meredith C.J.C.P. (dissenting): . . . The driver of the car in which the plaintiffs were, was driving in defiance of the statutory prohibition to which I have referred. He was unlawfully driving upon the highway. And that unlawful state of affairs was caused by the plaintiffs. They hired and paid, or were to pay, him for so driving . . . .

The statutory prohibition was passed for the benefit of those lawfully upon the highway: for their safety, benefit, and convenience: a benefit which the courts have no right to cut down, not to speak of putting the wrongdoer in the same position in all respects, as those having the highest rights in the highway, notwithstanding such prohibition, as the judgment in appeal does.

[Latchford J. agreed with Middleton J.]

NOTES

1. In *Field* v. *Supertest Petroleum Corp.*, [1943] O.W.N. 482, the statement of claim against a motorist alleged that "he was not a skilled or reasonably skilled operator [and did not hold an operator's licence as required by the Highway Traffic Act]". On a motion before the Master the clause in brackets was struck out.

2. In *City of Vancouver* v. *Burchill*, [1932] S.C.R. 620, [1932] 4 D.L.R. 200, the plaintiff, a taxi driver, had failed to obtain a licence from the municipality in which he was operating, as provided by the British Columbia Motor Vehicle Act. He was injured because of the non-repair of the highway. The Supreme Court of Canada held that he was entitled to recover against the municipality notwithstanding his failure to hold a licence. *Per* Rinfret J.: "After all, we are concerned here with an action founded on negligence and, in actions of that kind, the guiding principle — we should say the inevitable principle — is the principle of cause and effect. The liability in such a case is based — and can only be based — upon the casual connection between the tort and the resulting damage. Failure by the plaintiff to comply with a statute, in no way contributing to the accident, will not, in the absence of a specific provision to that effect, defeat the right of recovery of the plaintiff . . . . The municipality, in respect of its streets, does not stand in the same position as a landowner with regard to his property." See also *Roy Swail Ltd.* v. *Reeves* (1956), 2 D.L.R. (2d) 326 (S.C.C.); *Leask Timber* v. *Thorne* (1961), 106 D.L.R. 33.

3. Do you agree with the holdings in *Godfrey, Field* and *Burchill*? Do you prefer the dissent of Meredith C.J.C.P.? Which of tort law's policy goals would be served by it? Which would be rendered a disservice?

4. Would the courts take a different view if the alleged negligence was the poor driving ability of the defendant? What if the defendant had actually tried to get a driver's licence and failed the test? What if he failed ten times?

5. The defendant has a learner's licence which permits him to drive only if he is accompanied by another fully-licenced driver. He takes a car onto the road alone, in violation of the legislation, and collides with someone. Is the evidence of his violation of the statute relevant to whether or not he was negligent? What if one of the allegations of negligence was that he had not noticed the plaintiff and that he would have if he had been accompanied by someone else? *Cf. Feener* v. *McKenzie*, [1972] S.C.R. 525.

6. What if an unlicenced person, posing as a doctor, inflicts some injury on a patient during unauthorized treatment? *Cf. Brown* v. *Shyne* (1926), 151 N.E. 197 and *Whipple* v. *Grandchamp* (1927), 158 N.E. 270.

7. Summarizing the matters to be considered in deciding whether legislation will be relied on in a tort case, Chief Justice Howland in *Pugliese* v. *National Capital Commission* (1977), 3 C.C.L.T. 18 stated:

"In determining whether there is a right of action by a member of the public for breach of a statutory duty, four considerations may be relevant:

(a) Was the object of the statutory provision to prevent damage of the nature which occurred? See *Gorris* v. *Scott* (1874), L.R. 9 Exch. 125.

(b) Was the provision enacted to impose a public duty only, or was it enacted to impose in addition to the public duty a duty which could be enforced by an individual who was aggrieved? See *Phillips* v. *Britannia Hygienic Laundry Co.,* [1923] 2 K.B. 832 at 840-41.

(c) Were the statutory remedies of punishment by way of criminal prosecution or by action at the instance of the ministry intended to be the only remedies available? See *Phillips* v. *Britannia Hygienic Laundry Co.,* ibid.

(d) Would the contemplated beneficiaries of the performance of the duty be without an effective remedy unless a remedy is implied from the statutory provisions? See *McCall* v. *Abelesz,* [1976] 2 W.L.R. 151, [1976] 1 All E.R. 727."

Is this an accurate outline of the law? How would you alter it, if at all?

C. HOW CIVIL COURTS USE PENAL STATUTES: PROCEDURAL EFFECTS

1. The Possible Alternatives

SATTERLEE v. ORANGE GLENN SCHOOL DISTRICT

Supreme Court of California. (1947), 177 P. 2d 279

The California Vehicle Code provides that if two motor vehicles enter an intersection at the same time, the vehicle on the right has the right of way. Plaintiff's car collided with a bus of the defendant at an intersection and the plaintiff brought action for damages for his own injuries and those arising from the death of his wife.

At the trial, with a jury, the trial judge instructed the jury as follows:

"I told you that when two automobiles enter an intersection at the same time the automobile or motor vehicle, whether bus or lighter vehicle, on the right, has the right of way, and if one motor vehicle enters an intersection before the other, that motor vehicle has the right of way, but that the right of way is not an absolute right to barge through ignoring any danger to the other motorists or to the barging motorist. One cannot arbitrarily rely on the right of way and expect to scatter from his path all of those who have lesser rights. In other words, the same general rule applies, and the test is: What would a reasonably prudent person do under the same or similar circumstances? It is possible for one who has the right of way to be negligent in the operation of his automobile."

From a judgment for plaintiff the defendant appealed, relying on what he claimed to be the erroneous instruction to the jury.

Edmonds J.: . . . [The trial judge] refused to adopt the standard of care established by the Legislature and did not instruct the jury that violation of the statutory standard constituted *prima facie* evidence of negligence which could be rebutted by evidence of justification or excuse. Instead, upon the issue of contributory negligence, the court adopted the reasonable man standard of care exclusively, and allowed the jury to determine what constituted due care under the circumstances. The question presented for decision upon this aspect of the case is, therefore, whether the trial court arrived at a proper standard.

By the instruction which adopted the reasonable man standard of care, the jury, in effect, was told that the school district and its driver had the burden of establishing the failure of Satterlee to act as a reasonable man under the circumstances, although he had violated a statute and such violation proximately caused the accident. That is not the law. The presumption created by proof of failure to comply with a statute or ordinance relieves a defendant from the burden of proving that the plaintiff failed to act as a reasonably prudent man. All that the defendant need prove to establish contributory negligence is that plaintiff's violation of the statute in question proximately caused the accident. The burden cast upon the defendant where such violation is relied upon, is therefore more easily established than a failure to act as would a reasonably prudent man under similar circumstances. If there was a violation of the applicable statute, the burden of going forward is then cast upon the plaintiff, if the defendant is relying upon contributory negligence, to present evidence justifying an excuse for violation. If the jury does not believe that the evidence is sufficient to excuse violation, it must find for the defendant.

For these reasons the adoption by the trial court of the standard of care imposed by a statute or ordinance becomes an important factor in imposing liability. The instruction given by the court on its own motion had the effect of minimizing, if not completely negativing the code provision. It was, therefore, erroneous and considering the direct conflict in the evidence, constituted "a miscarriage of justice" . . . .

The judgment is reversed.

Traynor J. (dissenting in part): I concur in the judgment. I cannot agree, however, with the doctrine set forth in the majority opinion that an act or a failure to act in violation of a statute like the Vehicle Code is merely "presumptive evidence of negligence", which may be rebutted by showing that the act or omission was justifiable or excusable under the circumstances, with the excuse or justification a question of fact for the jury. This doctrine is in effect a modified form of the doctrine that the violation of a statute (herein used to include an ordinance) is merely evidence of negligence. Under the ordinary evidence-of-negligence doctrine the jury, while obliged to consider the statutory standard, is free to substitute a standard of its own. Under the majority opinion it is likewise free to do so, if the one violating the statute offers evidence of excuse or justification. Since it is a question of fact for the jury whether the excuse or justification is sufficient, the result is that one violating the statute need only offer proof that he acted as a reasonably prudent person under the circumstances and the jury is then free to conclude therefrom that he was justified in violating the statute unless "reasonable men can draw but one inference . . . pointing unerringly to . . . negligence".

The statement is frequently found in the cases that an act in violation of a statute "is presumptively an act of negligence, and while the defendant is permitted to rebut such presumption by showing that the act was justifiable or excusable under the circumstances, until so rebutted it is conclusive". . . .

The vice of such a statement is that it leaves to the jury the determination of the effect of a statute, a question of law that properly belongs to the court. Presumptions are used in ascertaining what the facts are, not in determining what the law is. . . . If the "presumption" can be rebutted merely by showing that one charged with violating the statute acted as a reasonably prudent person under the circumstances, the controlling standard is no longer the statutory rule, but the view of the jury as to what constitutes reasonable conduct.

The vital question, presented at the outset, is whether the statutory standard is applicable at all. If it is, conduct of the parties must be measured by that standard, and the jury is not free to determine what a reasonably prudent person would have done under the circumstances. If there is sufficient excuse or justification, there is ordinarily no violation of a statute, and the statutory standard is inapplicable. If a statute is so drawn as not to be susceptible of such a construction, so that it would impose liability without fault, the statutory standard is ordinarily not an appropriate one in a negligence case and should be rejected by the court . . . see Morris, "Criminal Statutes and Tort Liability", 46 Harv. L. Rev. 453, 457. It is needlessly circuitous and confusing, and productive of caprice and conflict in decisions, to instruct the jury that they should first determine whether the conduct in question fell below the statutory standard and that they should then determine whether such conduct was justifiable under the circumstances. It is a question of law in each case whether the acts were in violation of the statute, or excepted therefrom, or if not excepted, whether liability without fault would be imposed by adopting the statutory standard. It is of course a question of fact whether the alleged acts occurred.

A majority of American courts have adopted the doctrine that the violation of a statute constitutes negligence *per se* towards persons harmed as a result of acts or omissions constituting such violation, if the statute was designed to protect such persons against that kind of harm, even though the statute provides criminal sanctions only and makes no reference to civil liability. . . .

It is clear that the legislative standard is controlling if the statute expressly provides for civil liability. Confusion has arisen in the past from a failure to understand why the legislative standard governs civil liability when the statute prescribes criminal sanctions only. The reason is simply that the courts under common law principles make the legislative standard controlling and take the formulation of a standard from the jury, when they find that the criminal statute has been enacted not merely in the interest of the community as a whole but to protect a general class of persons, of which the party invoking the statute is a member, against the kind of harm that has been sustained. The decision as to what should be the controlling standard is made by the court, whether it instructs the jury to determine what would have been due care of a man of ordinary prudence under the circumstances or to follow the standard formulated by a statute. The latter standard determines civil liability, not because the Legislature has so provided, but because the courts recognize that, with respect to the conduct in question, the duties of the parties are determined by the statute. The legislative standard may be controlling even in situations in which there is technically no crime. . . . If the forbidden conduct were merely evidence of negligence, the jury would be free to substitute its own standard of reasonable conduct, and to approve conduct that the Legislature has declared so dangerous as to call for criminal punishment. "Negligence is failure to exercise the care required by law. Where a statute defines the standard of care and the safeguards required to meet a recognized danger, then, as we have said, no other measure may be applied in determining whether a person has carried out the duty of care imposed by law. Failure to observe the standard imposed by statute is negligence, as matter of law." Lehman J., in *Tedla* v. *Ellman* (1939), 280 N.Y. 124, 19 N.E. 2d 987, 990. "By the very terms of the hypothesis, to omit, wilfully or heedlessly, the safeguards prescribed by law for the benefit of another that he may be preserved in life or limb, is to fall short of the standard of diligence to which those who live in organized society are under a duty to conform. . . . Jurors have no dispensing power, by which they may relax the duty that one traveller on the highway owes under the statute to another. It is error to tell them that they have." Cardozo J., in *Martin* v. *Herzog* (1920), 228 N.Y. 164, 126 N.E. 814, 815.

Extraordinary circumstances may justify conduct that appears to violate the letters of a statute but which is impliedly excepted therefrom, if obedience is substantially impossible or deviation from the letter of the statute is necessary to serve its purpose. "If a criminal statute or ordinance which prohibits a particular act is construed to permit such an act to be done under conditions without criminal responsibility such an act may be done under the same conditions without creating civil liability under the statute or ordinance. Many statutes and ordinances are so worded as apparently to express a universal obligatory rule of conduct. Such enactments, however, may in view of their purpose and spirit be properly construed as intended to apply only to ordinary situations and to be subject to the qualification that the conduct prohibited thereby is not wrongful if, because of an emergency or the like, the circumstances justify an apparent disobedience to the letter of the enactment. Thus, the statutory prohibition against parking an automobile on the travelled part of a highway is not applicable to one which has broken down and is incapable of motion and thus remains on the highway while the driver is diligently seeking assistance to remove it. The provisions of statutes, intended to codify and supplement the rules of conduct which are established by a course or judicial decision or by custom, are often construed as subject to the same limitations and exceptions as the rules which they supersede. Thus, a statute or ordinance requiring all persons to drive on the right side of the road may be construed as subject to an exception permitting travellers to drive upon the other side, if so doing is likely to prevent rather than cause the accidents which it is the purpose of the statute or ordinance to prevent." . . .

The jury should have been instructed in accordance with the foregoing rules.

The trial court's instruction . . . did not advise the jury that the question as to who was at fault was to be determined under the right-of-way provisions, if both cars properly approached the intersection and one was there first or one car came from the right, if they both arrived at the intersection at the same time. The instruction was inadequate in not advising the jury that one cannot gain the right of way by racing for it or otherwise violating the law. The effect of the instruction was to advise the jury that the provisions of the Vehicle Code dealing with the right of way were of no consequence, and that if an ordinary prudent person under the circumstances would have violated the statute, the violation was excused. Instead of describing the scope of the statutory standard the court rejected that standard and in its place adopted the reasonable man standard, leaving it to the jury to determine what was proper conduct under the circumstances.

In cases of this sort the choice of the wrong theory, either as a basis of instruction to the jury or as a rule of decision for the trial court sitting without a jury, may have serious consequences. Any doctrine that allows uncontrolled discretion in the jury or trial court to disregard statutory standards cannot fail to bring about a similar disregard of the standards by those whose conduct is regulated.

Carter J.: I dissent. The issue in this case is whether or not a purported violation of the traffic law right of way at intersections constitutes negligence *per se*; that is, whether the court should adopt it as the invariable standard of care or the test should be that of the conduct of a person of ordinary prudence. The latter is preferable for the reason that the rule is not capable of precise application.

A violation of the rule may or may not be negligence depending upon the circumstances. That is conceded by the opinion prepared by Justice Edmonds and is supported by the authorities. It is clear that there may be factors indicating that the violation of the rule may not be negligence, such as excuse, emergency, justification, the speed of the vehicles, and their distance from the intersection and the nature of the intersection. . . .

Being dependent upon the circumstances in the particular case, we have nothing more, in effect, than an application of the ordinary prudence standard, and the provision of the statute should not be made an absolute standard for the determination of either the issue of negligence or contributory negligence.

The right of way rule does not lend itself to practical application. It is only in the rare theoretical situation that it can be applied. It must be supposed that the two vehicles are travelling at the identical speed and enter the intersection at precisely the same time, and that the view of oncoming vehicles is equal to both drivers. There must be no disturbing elements or sudden emergencies. Justice Edmonds treats the matter as creating a *prima facie* case of negligence and then shifts the burden of going forward to the opponent to show exculpatory circumstances. That leads only to confusion of the jury. If there may be such circumstances then the test actually being used is the conduct of a person of ordinary prudence. Hence the jury should be so instructed thus avoiding the complication of shifting the burden of proceeding which must inevitably result in confusion. . . .

The majority opinion purports to lay down the rule that the violation of a statute or ordinance may be a proximate cause of the accident, and therefore constitutes negligence *per se*, and yet may be excused or justified. Such a rule can only lead to confusion worse confounded. How such a rule can be applied in a trial forum is difficult to understand. Negligence cases are presented by the plaintiff first making out a *prima facie* case of negligence on the part of the defendant which was a proximate cause of the accident. The defendant then presents his defence by attempting to show absence of negligence on his part or contributory negligence on the part of the plaintiff. When the evidence is concluded the court instructs the jury that so far as the burden of proof is concerned, such burden is on the plaintiff to prove defendant's negligence and the burden is on the defendant to prove any contributory negligence on the part of plaintiff unless such contributory negligence affirmatively appears from the evidence presented by the plaintiff. Accepting the theory advanced in the majority opinion that the violation of a statute or ordinance is negligence *per se,* and assuming that there was evidence of a violation of a statute or ordinance by either party, the court could very simply instruct the jury that if they believe that either party was guilty of a violation of a statute or ordinance and that such violation was a proximate cause of the accident the violator was guilty of negligence *per se* unless such violation was excused or justified. This is, in effect, what the trial court did in the case at bar except that it added that a person who violates a statute is not guilty of negligence if he acted as a reasonably prudent person, which is the equivalent of saying that the violation was excused or justified. There is no basis in such a case for talk about the "burden of going forward" or that it is easier to establish contributory negligence by proving that plaintiff violated a statute than to prove that his conduct was not that of a reasonably prudent person, as all of the evidence has been already introduced and the function of the jury is to weigh that evidence and arrive at a conclusion based upon the law contained in the instructions of the court.

It should be obvious that the moment the absolute standard which makes violation of a statute or ordinance negligence *per se*, is relaxed, by permitting a showing of excuse, justification, emergency, etc., the inevitable result is that the issue of negligence is determined by the trier of fact giving consideration to evidence relating to the conduct of the parties. While the standard provided in the statute or ordinance is a factor to be considered, the ultimate fact to be determined is whether or not the person charged with negligence or contributory negligence failed to exercise that degree of care which a reasonably prudent person would have exercised under similar circumstances. Hence, the standard applied is the conduct which would be expected of a reasonably prudent person. Experience has shown that this is the standard applied by juries in the general run of negligence cases. Little heed is given to technical and artificial standards which have no practical application, as jurors are familiar with traffic rules and are more capable of applying them to the facts of a particular case than the members of this court.

For the reasons above discussed a violation of the traffic law right of way as constituting negligence *per se* is peculiarly inadequate to test civil liability, and the instruction in the case at bar applying the test of a reasonably prudent person was proper. The judgment should be affirmed.

[Gibson C.J. and Shank, Schauer and Spence JJ. concurred with Edmonds J.]

NOTES

1. What procedural effect was given to the violation of the statute by Mr. Justice Edmonds for the majority, by Mr. Justice Traynor in his concurrence and by Mr. Justice Carter in his dissent? What was the underlying reason for their disagreement? Does this argument have any practical significance? Which of the three formulae do you prefer?

2. How did Mr. Justice Traynor handle the problem of excused violation? How did the other judges deal with this question? Which method is the best?

3. Should the courts always consider evidence of an excuse for the statutory infraction? Under what circumstances, if any, would it be appropriate to exclude such evidence? What about factory safety acts? See *Koenig* v. *Patrick Construction Corp.* (1948), 298 N.Y. 313, 83 N.E. 2d 133. What about child labour acts? See *Krutlies* v. *Bulls Head Coal Co.* (1915), 249 Pa. 162, 94 A. 459. What about pure food acts and statutes prohibiting the sale of firearms to minors? What are the policy considerations?

4. The negligence *per se* approach of Mr. Justice Traynor is the one used in most American jurisdictions. About one-half dozen States accept the evidence of negligence treatment of Mr. Justice Carter. Only California and one or two others use the presumption of negligence technique of the majority. The Canadian courts, as we shall see below, tend to vacillate from one of these approaches to the other without appearing to recognize that they are doing so.

5. Should evidence of a statutory violation always be treated in exactly the same way by a civil court? Would it be advisable to accord varying procedural effects to different statutes in different situations? What are the dangers of such an eclectic approach?

6. In the 1957 edition of their casebook on the law of torts, Green, Malone, Pedrick and Rahl wrote:

It would seem that negligence *per se* performs very much the same function in cases of so-called statutory negligence as *res ipsa loquitur* does in common law negligence. The violation of a statute approximates the same dramatic characteristic of a *res ipsa loquitur* situation in that it speaks for itself. How decisively it speaks and what it says is something else, though it would seek to speak of want of care on the part of the violator. Its possible weight as in *res ipsa loquitur* would seem to run the whole gamut from being merely the basis of an inference to a conclusive presumption in absence of satisfactory explanation. It is only on this basis that what seems to be confusing, and frequently contradictory, language of the courts makes much sense.

7. Occasionally, a legislature will direct the civil courts to utilize evidence of a violation of one of its statutes in a particular way. Such aid, though welcome, is all too rare. One such provision is the United Kingdom Road Traffic Act, 1960, s. 74(5) which states:

A failure on the part of a person to observe a provision of the Highway Code shall not of itself render that person liable to criminal proceedings of any kind, but any such failure may, in any proceedings (whether civil or criminal. . .), be relied upon by any party to the proceedings as tending to establish or to negative any liability which is in question in those proceedings.

In *Powell* v. *Phillips,* [1972] 3 All E.R. 864 (C.A.), the plaintiff, a pedestrian walking on a poorly-lit street, was struck by a speeding car and suffered severe injuries. Although it was proved that she was in breach of the Highway Code, by not wearing anything white or reflective and by not being on the proper side of the road facing on-coming traffic, she recovered 100 percent of her damages. Stephenson L.J.stated at p. 868:

"In law a breach of the Highway Code has a limited effect. . . . It is . . . clear . . . that a breach [by the plaintiff[creates no presumption of negligence calling for an explànation, still less a presumption of negligence making a real contribution to causing an accident or injury. The breach is just one of the circumstances on which one party is entitled to rely in establishing the negligence of the other and its contribution to causing the accident or injury. . . . [I]t must be considered with all the other circumstances including the explanation. . . . It must not be elevated into a breach of statutory duty which gives a right of action to anyone who can prove that his injury resulted from it."

Would the court have come to the same conclusion without s. 74(5) of the Road Traffic Act?

2. Prima Facie Evidence of Negligence

STERLING TRUSTS CORP. v. POSTMA & LITTLE

Supreme Court of Canada. [1965] S.C.R. 324; 48 D.L.R. (2d) 423

Brown and his wife were driving in an easterly direction in Brown's car about 5.30 p.m. in December, 1959. Postma was proceeding westerly on the same highway when, after breasting a knoll, he finally noticed what turned out to be a westbound truck owned by F.H. Little and driven by F.A. Little. The truck was engaged in making a proper turn across the highway into their own driveway. Postma applied his brakes, skidded some 120 feet, then veered to the left where he collided with the Brown vehicle. Mrs. Brown was killed and Mr. Brown severely injured. An action was brought against Postma and the two Littles for damages. At the trial, plaintiff obtained judgment for some $166,000 which were apportioned on the basis of 1/3 of the negligence to Fred A. Little and 2/3 to Postma. On appeal to the Ontario Court of Appeal the judgment so far as the Littles were concerned, was dismissed, and Postma was, therefore, alone held liable. The personal representative of Mrs. Brown and Mr. Brown appealed to the Supreme Court of Canada.

The only ground of negligence alleged against the Littles that survived the trial and the judgment of the Ontario Court of Appeal was that the tail light of the truck was not lighted as required by the Highway Traffic Act. At the trial, the trial judge had held the onus was on the Littles to show the tail light was lighted. The Ontario Court of Appeal held that this was erroneous and found on the evidence that the light was unlighted. In so doing they acted on what was admitted by all members of the court to be inadmissible evidence.

Cartwright J.: . . . There is in the written record evidence on which it might be found that the tail light was lighted and there is also evidence on which the contrary could be found. In my respectful view, it would be mere guess-work to make either finding from the written record; the only tribunal by which such a finding can safely be made is one that has seen and heard the witnesses. For this reason I have reluctantly reached the conclusion that a new trial should be directed, unless a further argument of the respondents to be dealt with hereafter is entitled to prevail.

If it were established that the tail light was not lighted, it would be my opinion that there was evidence to support the finding of the learned trial judge that this failure was an effective cause of the collision. If at the new trial it is found as a fact that the tail light was not lighted it will be for the judge on the evidence adduced before him to decide whether or not that failure was an effective cause of the collision.

The further argument of counsel for the respondents referred to above is that even if, contrary to their submission, it should be found that the tail light was not lighted and that the failure to have it lighted was an effective cause of the collision the respondents are not to be found liable in the absence of evidence that the driver of the truck knew or ought to have known that the tail light was out. In my opinion this argument is not entitled to prevail.

The decision of the House of Lords in *London Passenger Transport Board* v. *Upson,* [1949] A.C. 155, appears to me to proceed on the basis that the breach by the driver of a motor vehicle of a statutory provision which is designed for the protection of other users of the highway gives a right of action to a user of the highway who is injured as a direct result of that breach. The statutory provision requiring a motor vehicle to have a lighted tail light when it is travelling on a highway after dark is designed for the protection of other users of the highway, particularly the drivers of overtaking vehicles. Its primary purpose is to prevent the occurrence of such a disaster as that out of which this case arises.

In my opinion, the law on this question is so well settled that it is unnecessary to multiply citations of authority. There have been differences of opinion as to whether an action for breach of a statutory duty which involves the notion of taking precautions to prevent injury is more accurately described as an action for negligence, or in the manner suggested by Lord Wright, in the *Upson case,* in the following words: "A claim for damages for breach of a statutory duty intended to protect a person in the position of the particular plaintiff is a specific common law right which is not to be confused in essence with a claim for negligence. The statutory right has its origin in the statute, but the particular remedy of an action for damages is given by the common law in order to make effective, for the benefit of the injured plaintiff, his right to the performance by the defendant of the defendant's statutory duty. It is an effective sanction. It is not a claim in negligence in the strict or ordinary sense. . . ."

I do not find it necessary in this case to attempt to choose between these two views as to how this cause of action should be described. I think it plain that once it has been found (i) that the respondents committed a breach of the statutory duty to have the tail light lighted, and (ii) that the breach was an effective cause of the appellant's injuries, the respondents are *prima facie* liable for the damages suffered by the appellants. I wish to adopt two observations made in the House of Lords in *Lochgelly Iron & Coal Co., Ltd.* v. *M'Mullan,* [1934] A.C. 1, as applicable to the case at bar.

At p. 23, Lord Wright said: "In such a case as the present the liability is something which goes beyond and is on a different plane from the liability for breach of a duty under the ordinary law, apart from the statute, because not only is the duty one which cannot be delegated but, whereas at the ordinary law the standard of duty must be fixed by the verdict of a jury, the statutory duty is conclusively fixed by the statute. . . ." At p. 9, Lord Atkin said: "I cannot think that the true position is, as appears to be suggested, that in such cases negligence only exists where the tribunal of fact agrees with the Legislature that the precaution is one that ought to be taken. The very object of the legislation is to put that particular precaution beyond controversy."

I have used above the expression that once it is found that the breach of the statute was committed and was an effective cause of the collision the respondents are *prima facie* liable to the appellants. The question then arises whether the respondents can absolve themselves from liability by showing that they had done everything that a reasonable man could have done under the circumstances to prevent the occurrence of the breach. A passage in the judgment of Lord Uthwatt in the *Upson case,* seems to suggest that this can be done by showing that under the circumstances it was impossible for the defendants to avoid committing the breach so that the maxim *lex non cogit ad impossibilia,* takes effect. On the other hand, in *Galashiels Gas Co. Ltd.* v. *O'Donnell or Millar,* [1949] A.C. 275, the House of Lords held the statutory duty there under consideration to be absolute.

I do not find it necessary in this case to decide whether the statutory duty to have the tail light lighted was an absolute one or, if it be not absolute, to attempt to define the extent of the burden cast upon a person who has committed the breach because, even if it is not so heavy as Lord Uthwatt seems to suggest, I do not think it can be said that in the case at bar the respondents have discharged it. The position of the respondents is not that there was a sufficient explanation to account for and excuse the fact that the light was not lighted, their position is that the light was in fact lighted at all relevant times. If the burden could be discharged simply by showing that the person upon whom it lay neither intended nor knew of the breach, the protection which it is the purpose of the statute to afford would in most cases prove illusory.

Before parting with this phase of the matter I think it desirable to refer to all three cases which were chiefly relied on by counsel for the respondents. These are *Falsetto* v. *Brown,* [1933] O.R. 645; *Grubbe* v. *Grubbe,* [1953] O.W.N. 626, and *Fuller* v. *Nickel,* [1949] S.C.R. 601.

In *Falsetto* v. *Brown* an automobile had run into the rear of a stationary truck in darkness. Kingstone J., the trial judge, found that the tail light of the truck was not lighted. He found that the driver of the automobile was negligent in driving too fast under the weather conditions and in not keeping a proper look-out. He found both parties equally to blame. . . . An appeal by the owner and driver of the truck was allowed by the Court of Appeal. . . .

Davis J.A. examined the evidence in considerable detail and reached the following conclusion: "I am satisfied that the negligence of the driver of the sedan was solely responsible for the accident which gave rise to the damages sued for in these actions." However, Davis J.A. gave an additional reason for allowing the appeal which is summarized in the following sentence: "The statutory duty to have a red tail lamp burning at certain times imposed by the statute is a public duty only to be enforced by the penalty imposed for a breach of it, and it was not the intention of the Legislature that everyone injured through a breach of any statutory requirements should have a right of civil action against the owner for damages."

While this statement was not necessary for the decision of the appeal, it was a ground on which Davis J.A. based his decision and cannot be regarded as having been said *obiter*. It was not, however, the judgment of the court. . . . Latchford C.J., refrained from agreeing with it and proceeded on the other ground on which Davis J.A. founded his judgment. . . .

Later in the same year a similar question came before the Court of Appeal in *Irvine* v. *Metropolitan Transport Co.,* [1933] O.R. 823. The breach of statutory duty committed by the defendant was leaving its truck parked on the travelled portion of the highway contrary to s. 35a of the Highway Traffic Act then in force. The plaintiff's vehicle ran into the parked truck from behind. The trial judge found both parties at fault and apportioned the blame 75 percent to the defendant and 25 percent to the plaintiff. . . . The defendant's appeal was dismissed, Riddell J.A. dissenting. In dealing with the question whether the defendant's breach of the statutory provision gave the plaintiff a right of action, Masten J.A. said:

> "In considering this phase of the appeal, I have not overlooked sub-s. 4 of s. 35a which imposes a penalty for violation of any of the provisions of the section.
>
> Upon a consideration of the whole section, I think that, notwithstanding that it prescribes a penalty for breach of the duty imposed, it also creates a cause of action in favour of a particular class of persons, namely, those who are travelling on the highway and suffer damage from breach of the statute. My reasons are (1) that the legislation is for the protection of one particular class of the community; (2) that the penalty is not payable to the party injured; (3) that a penalty of $5 up to $50 would in most cases be a wholly inadequate compensation for the damages suffered." . . .

I think it clear that the majority of the court must have disagreed with the proposition of law on the point now under consideration stated by David J.A., in *Falsetto* v. *Brown.* In my respectful view the reasoning of Masten J.A. on this point in the *Irvine* case is to be preferred to that of Davis J.A. in the *Falsetto* case.

In *Grubbe* v. *Grubbe,* [1933] O.W.N. 626, the plaintiff had run into the rear of the defendant's motor vehicle which had stopped on the highway without a lighted tail light. The trial judge found the defendant solely to blame. The Court of Appeal reversed this judgment and held that the negligence of the plaintiff in driving too fast and not having his motor vehicle under proper control was "the sole cause of the damages suffered by the parties". The following passage in the reasons of Laidlaw J.A., who delivered the unanimous judgment of the court, appears to lend some support to the view expressed by Davis J.A. in the *Falsetto* case: . . .

> "With much respect for the judgment of the learned trial judge, I express the view that he has not approached the determination of the issues in this case in a proper manner. I accept his finding of fact that the rear light of the defendant's vehicle was not lighted when the vehicle stopped on the highway. But it appears to me that the learned judge was improperly influenced to the conclusion that there was negligence on the part of the defendant merely because the rear light of his vehicle was out. That fact alone does not impose liability on the defendant: *Falsetto* v. *Brown et al.* . . . ."

The note of the case does not show whether the judgment was delivered at the conclusion of the argument. The reasons refer to no authority other than the *Falsetto* case. Reading the reasons as a whole I think that it appears that the *ratio* of the decision was that on the facts the absence of a tail light was not a *causa causans* of the collision. I cannot think that the court intended to depart from the principles enunciated in the *Irvine* case, *supra,* and in *London Passenger Transport Board* v. *Upson, supra,* when the reasons make no reference to either of these decisions. . . .

I would allow the appeal, set aside the judgment of the Court of Appeal and the judgment at the trial except in so far as they find Postma liable to the appellants and direct that a new trial be had of the questions (i) whether the respondents are liable to the appellants (ii) if the respondents are found liable to the appellants, the degrees of fault as between the respondents and Postma, and (iii) the quantum of the appellants' damages.

Spence J.. . . . I agree with my brother Cartwright, whose reasons I have had the privilege of reading, that if the court upon the retrial were to find that the tail light was unlit and that such unlit condition was an effective cause of collision, there is a *prima facie* liability upon the defendants Olive Russell Little and

Frederick H. Little. I am not prepared to say that that liability is an absolute one and that the said defendants would be unable to discharge it by showing that such condition occurred without negligence for which they are in law responsible as all of the evidence which I have perused in reference to the tail light was not addressed to the question of whether it was lit or unlit. I agree with my brother Cartwright that such evidence is not even relevant upon the issue of whether the tail light, if unlit, was unlit due to any negligence.

I therefore agree that there must be a new trial upon the questions as outlined by my brother Cartwright.

[Hall J. agreed with the reasons and conclusions of Cartwright J. Ritchie J. dissented, Judson J. concurring, on the ground that in view of the time element and other considerations there would be no point in relitigating the issue of the Littles' liability, and he, therefore agreed with dismissing the action against them. In the course of his judgment, while pointing out it was unnecessary to consider the effect of the breach of the statutory duty, he did, however, "adopt the analysis of the conflicting decisions . . . contained in the reasons of Cartwright J." and held that "once it is found that the tail light was unlit, the problem then is one of causation".]

NOTES

1. What procedural effect did the Supreme Court of Canada favour giving to a breach of the penal statute involved in this case? How does this formula compare with the three alternative approaches that were outlined in the *Satterlee* case?

2. How did the Supreme Court treat the problem of excused violation? Did Mr. Justice Cartwright agree with Mr. Justice Spence on this issue? Did Mr. Justice Cartwright agree with Mr. Justice Spence on the matter of who bears the onus of proof on the question of excuse? Is there a holding of the Supreme Court on this point or is it still an open question?

3. Distinguish between: (1) evidence of breach is conclusive of negligence and no excuse will be countenanced; (2) evidence of a breach imposes upon the violator the onus of proving he could not possibly have conformed to the statute; (3) evidence of a breach imposes upon the violator the onus of proving he was not at fault with respect to the violation. Which, if any, of these procedural effects was supported by Mr. Justice Cartwright? By Mr. Justice Spence? See Alexander, "The Fate of *Sterling Trusts Corp.* v. *Postma*" (1968), 2 Ottawa L.J. 441, at p. 458.

4. Which of these three methods of handling an excused violation do you think best promotes the policy of deterrence, of loss distribution, of jury control, of administrative simplicity? Which approach do you prefer?

5. Did the Supreme Court of Canada give us any guidance on the juridical nature of the civil action for violation of penal legislation? Did Mr. Justice Cartwright rely on the intention theory? It has been suggested that His Lordship did take this "traditional approach" without appreciating that he was relying on the inconsistent case of *Upson,* on the one hand, and *Falsetto* and *Irvine,* on the other. See Alexander, "The Fate of *Sterling Trusts Corp.* v. *Postma*", *supra,* note 3. Do you agree? If the intention theory was in fact employed, why did Mr. Justice Cartwright not adopt the negligence *per se* formula rather than the *prima facie* negligence technique. Why is the rationale behind the use of these statutes so important?

6. Should the *Sterling Trusts* formula be used for lighting equipment legislation only? Should it be applied to all equipment regulation violations? Should it be employed for breaches of all motor vehicle legislation? Should it be utilized for all statutory violations? Compare Alexander, *op. cit., supra,* at p. 460 with Linden, "Comment on *Sterling Trusts*" (1967), 45 Can. Bar Rev. 125, at p. 140.

7. The Supreme Court of Canada has used this *prima facie* negligence formula in a case where a motorist failed to keep to the right in violation of the statute. See *Jordan* v. *Coleman* (1975), 57 D.L.R. (3d) 256 (S.C.C.), at p. 259, *per* Ritchie J. See also *Gagnon* v. *R.,* [1970] Ex. C.R. 714, at p. 736, "presumption".

QUEENSWAY TANK LINES LTD. v. MOISE

Court of Appeal. [1970] 1 O.R. 535

The plaintiff's northbound tractor trailer collided with the defendant's southbound dump truck a short distance south of a narrow bridge on County Road 16 in the County of Stormont on a rainy morning. There was a solid white line painted on the highway, but it did not divide the pavement equally, in that the northbound lane, in which the plaintiff's trailer was travelling, was wider than the southbound lane in which the defendant's dump truck was. The defendant's truck appeared to pass the plaintiff's trailer, but then it swerved over and collided with the trailer. The jury's answers indicated that the defendant was negligent in that he allowed his vehicle to veer to the left across the centre line and into the plaintiff's truck, which was close to but not over the centre line. At the trial all parties proceeded on the assumption that the white line dividing the highway into two unequal lanes would govern the rights of the parties insofar as the rules of the road requiring vehicles meeting other vehicles to leave one-half of the road free was concerned. The trial judge gave judgment for the plaintiff and dismissed a counter claim by the defendant. The defendant appealed to the Court of Appeal.

MacKay J.A.: On these facts I would dismiss the defendant's appeal. There is, however, a further matter to which I should give consideration.

On the argument on appeal, although it was not among the grounds of appeal in his notice of appeal, counsel for the appellant made the submission that the learned trial judge erred in law in reading s. 76(a) of the Highway Traffic Act (the section relating to a highway that has been divided into clearly marked lanes for traffic) to the jury and instructing them that it applied to this case.

I agree that in so doing the learned trial judge erred. His attention was not drawn to the case of *Newton* v. *Skretteberg,* [1958] O.W.N. 155, in which this court held that this section did not apply to two lane highways, so I have now to consider whether this error could have resulted in a miscarriage of justice which would warrant a new trial being directed.

This is an action founded on the tort of negligence. From time to time attempts have been made to found actions arising out of motor vehicle collisions on "breach of a statute" where the breach was a cause or one of the causes of the accident. One of the earliest of these cases was *Hall* v. *Toronto-Guelph Express Co.* (1928), 63 O.L.R. 355, [1929] S.C.R. 92, a case where a tail light on a truck was not burning contrary to the requirements of the statute and a car collided with the rear of the truck. At that time the then s. 41(1) of The Highway Traffic Act was as follows:

> The owner of a motor vehicle shall be responsible for any violation of this Act or of any regulation prescribed by the Lieutenant-Governor in Council, unless at the time of such violation the motor vehicle was in the possession of some person other than the owner or his chauffeur, without the owner's consent, and the driver of a motor vehicle not being the owner shall be responsible for any such violation.

An amendment to the Ontario Highway Traffic Act was passed in 1930

Statutes of Ontario, c. 48, s. 41(a). This section is now s. 105 of the present Highway Traffic Act and reads as follows:

> The owner of a motor vehicle is liable for loss or damage sustained by any person *by reason of negligence* in the operation of the motor vehicle on a highway unless the motor vehicle was without the owner's consent in the possession of some person other than the owner or his chauffeur, and the driver of a motor vehicle not being the owner is liable to the same extent as the owner. (Italics mine).

While the purpose of this section would appear to require that in Ontario civil actions for damages arising out of motor vehicle collisions could only be founded on negligence, subsequent cases are not all in agreement as to whether proof of breach of a statutory provision that was a cause of the accident of itself gave a right of action. Two of these cases decided by the Ontario Court of Appeal in 1933 in at least some of the judgments reached different conclusions. They are *Falsetto* v. *Brown et al.,* [1933] O.R. 645 and *Irvine* v. *Metropolitan Transport Co. Ltd.,* [1933] O.R. 823.

I do not propose to review all the cases. They have been fully reviewed and discussed by the Supreme Court of Canada in *Sterling Trust Corp.* v. *Postma & Little* (1965), 48 D.L.R. (2d) 423 and by Professor Allen Linden in a very interesting commentary in (1967), 45 Canadian Bar Review, pages 122 to 140.

Having read all of the cases referred to in the *Sterling Trust* case and in Professor Linden's commentary, I would put the matter this way. In a negligence action the traditional legal test of liability is whether the party against whom negligent conduct is alleged acted as a reasonably prudent and careful person in all the circumstances.

Under this standard of care there would be a duty on the part of a motorist to maintain his vehicle and its equipment in a safe condition and in compliance with the regulations as to equipment and to comply with the traffic rules and regulations in the operation of his vehicle and to have regard for such other circumstances and conditions existing at the time as a reasonably prudent person would take into consideration. If the person failed to have his car equipped or operating in accordance with the Act or regulations, or contravened any of the rules of the road, and such conduct was shown to be a cause of the accident, it would, as Cartwright J., as he then was, said in the *Sterling Trust* case, be *prima facie* evidence of negligence and unless he could show by the evidence that the failure of his equipment or breach of the traffic rules occurred through no fault or want of care on his part, he would be liable.

In the case of *Aubrey* v. *Harris et al.,* [1957] O.W.N. 133, the defendant's truck crossed the centre line of the highway and collided with an oncoming car. His defence was that his steering gear had failed. This defence was raised on his own evidence and was not supported by expert or other evidence. Roach J.A., after reviewing a number of cases, held, reversing the trial judge, that such a defence could not succeed unless the defendant could prove that the *greatest* care had been exercised to see that the vehicle was maintained in a safe operating condition and that the defendant had failed to do so, and further that the evidence of the driver alone without some supporting evidence could not be accepted as proving that the steering gear had failed.

I do not regard this judgment as in any way altering the legal standard of care. I regard it rather as a statement of the factual standard of care to be expected of a reasonably prudent and careful man under modern traffic conditions of high speeds and congested traffic.

When the breach of a statute causing the accident has occurred because of a failure of the mechanism or equipment of the vehicle of which the person charged has control and management, having regard to modern traffic conditions it is not perhaps asking too much to say that a reasonably prudent and careful man would and should take the greatest care to see to it that his vehicle is in a safe mechanical condition and that all equipment required by law is in proper working condition. What Roach J.A. in effect held was that if such a person fails to prove that he exercised the greatest care in these respects, he will be liable on the ground that he did not act as a reasonably prudent and careful man. . . .

I am of the opinion that on the point now raised the type of charge recommended by the California Jury Instructions (Civil) would have been appropriate in this case if counsel had brought to the attention of the trial judge the *Newton* v. *Skretteberg* case. This recommended charge is as follows:

> If a party violated the statute just read to you, a presumption arises that he was negligent. This presumption is not a conclusive one. It may be overcome by other evidence showing that under all the circumstances surrounding the event the conduct in question was excusable, justifiable and such as might reasonably have been expected from a person of ordinary prudence. (In this connection, you may assume that a person of ordinary prudence will reasonably endeavour to obey the law and will do so unless causes, not of his own intended making, induce him, without moral fault, to do otherwise.)

If so charged, the jury, if there was evidence which they accepted that the plaintiff's vehicle was over the mathematical centre of the highway but not over the white line, would have to consider whether the driver of the vehicle acted as a reasonably prudent and careful man in taking the white line painted on the highway to be the line dividing his half of the travelled portion of the highway from that of the approaching vehicle of the defendant. In the circumstances of this case, the only reasonable answer a jury could give to this question would be that he did act reasonably in taking the white painted line to be the dividing line between his lane of traffic and the approaching traffic.

. . . Where there is a white line dividing a two lane highway, a motorist could not reasonably be required at all times to scrutinize the surface of the highway immediately in front of him or to get out and measure the highway to make certain that the line painted by the highway authorities was in the exact centre of the highway.

Under the circumstances of this case, I am unable to say that the misdirection of the learned trial judge, concurred in by counsel, created any miscarriage of justice and I would not direct a new trial on the ground of the learned trial judge's misdirection.

NOTES

1. Did Mr. Justice MacKay eliminate the confusion surrounding the *Sterling Trusts* case? Did His Lordship follow the approach of Mr. Justice Cartwright, Mr. Justice Spence or neither? Does the quotation from the California Jury Instructions help or hinder our understanding of this area of the law?

2. In *Blakney* v. *LeBlanc et al.* (1971), 13 D.L.R. (3d) 180 (N.B.C.A.), the defendant experienced some difficulty with her generator while driving at night on a dark highway. She parked on the side of the road, leaving her lights on, but without placing a portable reflector unit at a distance of approximately 100 feet to the rear of the motor vehicle as required by the New Brunswick Motor Vehicles Act. The plaintiff's vehicle ran into the back of the defendant's car causing injuries. Bridges C.J.N.B. found that the defendant's breach of statute was an "effective cause" of the collision and, following *Sterling Trusts* v. *Postma,* he declared that "the party committing the breach is *prima facie* liable to one who as a result of the breach has suffered a loss." The plaintiff

was also held 50 percent at fault. Limerick J.A. (dissenting) although he agreed with the Chief Justice's statement of the law, felt that the evidence did not "establish that the failure to set out the reflector was an effective cause of the collision."

3. In *Morrison* v. *Leyenhorst* (1968), 70 D.L.R. (2d) 469 (Div. Court), the defendant heard peculiar noises coming from the front of his car. It was an old car, with high mileage and mechanical problems. He got out and checked the wheels but discovered nothing. He proceeded further along the road for 20 feet, when his front wheel came off, lodged under the plaintiff's car and did some damage to the undercarriage. Leach Co. Ct. J. referred to the Ontario Highway Traffic Act which forbade anyone from driving a vehicle that "is in such a dangerous or unsafe condition as to endanger. . . any person upon the highway". He explained that this section created a "statutory duty, the breach of which provides *prima facie* evidence of negligence, providing, of course, it is the proximate cause of the accident". His Honour went on to point out that the owner of a motor vehicle is not an "insurer of its mechanical perfection", but he must take reasonable care that it is fit for the road. Judge Leach then concluded that the defendant was negligent in failing to check the wheel properly and in proceeding on to the highway knowing that the vehicle was defective. Was the evidence of the violation of the statute necessary for this decision? Did it help?

4. In *Moore* v. *Maxwells of Emsworth Ltd.*, [1968] 1 W.L.R. 1077 (C.A.), the plaintiff ran into the back of the defendant's unlighted truck which was parked on the road as the driver was attempting to repair the tail light which had suddenly gone out. The driver had checked the lights at the start of the journey and again at lighting up time, but there was no evidence of regular servicing of the lighting system. There was no discussion about any statutory violation. Harman L.J. thought that an explanation was needed, but that the evidence was sufficient to "discharge the burden" of the defendant and rebut the "presumption of negligence". Diplock L.J. agreed and stated: "The presence of an unlighted vehicle in a road is *prima facie* evidence of negligence on the part of the driver, and it is for him to explain how it came to be unlighted. . . .[T]he person responsible for its being there must show that he has taken all reasonable steps to avoid creating or prolonging of that danger." His Lordship felt that the defendants succeeded in this and dismissed the action. Are these two opinions inconsistent? Would the existence of a lighting statute have made any difference to the outcome of this case? See also *Kelly* v. *W.R.N. Contracting Ltd.*, [1968] 1 W.L.R. 921 (Q.B.D.); *Schofield* v. *Town of Oakville* (1968), 69 D.L.R. (2d) 441 (Ont. C.A.).

5. Suppose A's car crashes into B's car injuring B. It is established that A's brakes were defective, in contravention of the Ontario Highway Traffic Act provision referred to in *Leyenhorst, supra*. Does A escape liability if he proves (1) that he did not know that his brakes were defective? (2) that he checked his brakes bi-annually as recommended in his car owner's manual? (3) that he had his brakes repaired the preceding day at a reliable garage? Should any or all of these be a complete defence to tort liability? See Linden, "Automobile Equipment Legislation and Tort Liability" (1967), 5 Western L. Rev. 76. See also *Clarke* v. *Brims*, [1947] K.B. 497, [1949] 1 All E.R. 242; *Taber* v. *Smith* (1930), 26 S.W. 2d 722 (Tex.); *Lopresto* v. *Golding* (1957), 31 Aust. L.J. 851.

6. Would it make any difference in the above three situations if the legislation violated specifically required a vehicle to be equipped with brakes "adequate to control" and "to stop" the vehicle? See *Spalding* v. *Waxler* (1965), 205 N.E. 2d 890 (Ohio), strict liability; compare with *Davison* v. *Williams* (1968), 242 N.E. 2d 101 (Indiana), reasonable care standard adopted; *Maloney* v. *Rath* (1968), 71 Cal. Rptr. 897, 445 P. 2d 513, reasonable care standard, but non-delegable duty.

7. In *Fontaine et al.* v. *Thompson et al.* (1967), 64 D.L.R. (2d) 611, the British Columbia Court of Appeal (Davey C.J.B.C., dissenting) held that the defendant driver, who violated a statute requiring him to keep to the right, could displace the *prima facie* case of negligence against him by producing "an

explanation at least equally consistent with negligence, and no negligence". If this is done, it is then for the plaintiff "to prove negligence in the ordinary way". The defendant's evidence that a deer suddenly jumped in front of his truck forcing him to turn slightly as he applied the brakes to slow down was accepted by the majority and the action against him was dismissed. Is this case consistent with *Sterling Trusts* and *Queensway Tank Lines*? Does it give sufficient weight to the fact of a violation of statute?

3. Negligence Per Se

OSTASH v. SONNENBERG ET AL.

Alberta Court of Appeal. (1968), 67 D.L.R. (2d) 311

A contractor installed a natural gas water-heater and a natural gas furnace burner in a house that had been heated by coal for 30 years. Both units were vented into the chimney without an adequate inspection to determine the amount of soot accumulated in the chimney although the contractor was aware that the burning of gas could dislodge soot and mortar. In this respect and in certain others the contractor was in breach of the provisions of the Installation Code for gas burning appliances and equipment made under the Gas Protection Act, R.S.A. 1955, c. 129, and having the effect of Regulations by virtue of s. 9 of the Act. A provincial gas inspector whose duty it was under the Act to carry out inspections and require compliance with the Code also failed adequately to inspect the chimney and to direct the contractor to remedy the departures from the Code. Some two years later a subsequent purchaser of the house and his family suffered carbon monoxide poisoning as a result of the accumulation of dislodged soot and mortar in the bottom of the chimney to a level above the heater and furnace vents, which blocked the vents, caused incomplete combustion of the natural gas and prevented the escape of the resulting carbon monoxide which accumulated in the house. On the day when the family became ill a physician was called and attended three times at the house. He considered the possibility of natural gas poisoning but as there was no odour he dismissed it. He did not think of any other kind of gas and considered that the symptoms indicated influenza, which was prevalent in the community. Three of the four children in the family later died and the purchaser of the house suffered prolonged illness and the loss of a leg. Actions were brought against the contractor, the Crown and the doctor. The contractor and the Crown were held liable but the doctor was not.

Smith C.J.A.: The risk in the case at bar was most grave if the duty should not be fulfilled. The case of dangerous things is "a special instance of negligence where the law exacts a degree of diligence so stringent as to amount practically to a guarantee of safety" (Lord Macmillan in *M'Alister (or Donoghue)* v. *Stevenson*, [1932] A.C. 562 at pp. 611-12).

Was there a duty at common law on the part of the installer and the inspector towards these people who might use this house in the foreseeable future? It may be more suitable to paraphrase Lord Macmillan's words in *M'Alister (or Donoghue)* v. *Stevenson* at p. 620 and say "to all potential users of the house".

It is clear to me that all potential users of this house stood in the position of being the neighbours in law of the installer and the inspector, as they were "persons who are so closely and directly affected by my act that I ought reasonably to have been in contemplation as being so affected when I am directing my mind to the acts or omissions which are called in question" (Lord Atkin in *M'Alister (or Donoghue)* v. *Stevenson* at p. 580).

In *Dominion Natural Gas Co. Ltd.* v. *Collins and Perkins,* [1909] A.C. 640, Lord Dunedin, at p. 646, said in respect of the case of articles dangerous in themselves "there is a peculiar duty to take precaution imposed upon those who send forth or install such articles when it is necessarily the case that other parties will come within their proximity". In my view it is quite clear that there was a duty at common law on the part of the installer and the inspector towards potential users of the house to use the degree of care and skill required of persons installing equipment for the use of natural gas previously spoken of. In my view neither the installer nor the inspector used the degree of care and skill required. . . .

But in my view there is an additional ground upon which the appellants can be found to have been under a duty to the respondents and to have failed to fulfil that duty. In *Direct Lumber Co. Ltd.* v. *Western Plywood Co. Ltd.,* 35 D.L.R. (2d) 1, [1962] S.C.R. 646, 40 C.P.R. 9, Judson J., on behalf of the Supreme Court of Canada at p. 3 quoted the following statement of Duff J. (later C.J.C.) in *Orpen* v. *Roberts,* [1925] 1 D.L.R. 1101 at p. 1106, [1925] S.C.R. 364:

> "But the object and provisions of the statute as a whole must be examined with a view to determining whether it is a part of the scheme of the legislation to create, for the benefit of individuals, rights enforceable by action; or whether the remedies provided by the statute are intended to be the sole remedies available by way of guarantees to the public for the observance of the statutory duty, or by way of compensation to individuals who have suffered by reason of the non-performance of that duty."

In the *Direct Lumber Co.* case in this Division, 32 D.L.R. (2d) 227 at p. 230, 37 W.W.R. 177, Johnson J.A., on behalf of this Division said, in referring to an article by Glanville Williams in 23 Modern Law Review, p. 233, entitled "The Effect of Penal Legislation in the Law of Tort":

> "As he pointed out, if the statute or Regulation made under a statute is one which seeks to provide safer working conditions for employees, Courts have found little difficulty in finding that the legislation intended to create a cause of action for workmen who were injured because of a breach."

[*Lochgelly Iron & Coal Co. Ltd.* v. *M'Mullan,* [1934] A.C. 1 was discussed.]

I have no doubt that the provisions of the Gas Protection Act and the Regulations made under it and the Installation Code adopted and brought into force pursuant to it, were all enacted for the protection of persons in the position of the Ostash family amongst others. The duty to take care to avoid injury was therefore established; the particular standard of care was thereby established. The duty to the injured person to take care was prescribed by the statute, Regulations and Code. The breach was proven. All the essentials of negligence in my opinion are present.

I have no doubt that Reid was under a duty to follow the provisions of the Installation Code. He failed in his duty. My view is that the reasonable and sensible course for Reid to follow was to find or put into the chimney a clean out door and at least to clean out or have cleaned out the accumulation of soot and material below the vent or to install a liner.

The duty of the inspector, in my view, was clearly to see that there was a clean out in existence and that the space in the chimney below the clean out was entirely clear of soot and other material or to make sure that a liner was installed. He could have enforced proper safety measures being taken by reason of two provisions. The first was s. 10(2) [enacted 1957, c. 26, s. 3(b)] of the Gas Protection Act, R.S.A. 1955, c. 129, which is as follows:

10(2). If an inspector finds a gas installation that is dangerous to life or property he may disconnect the gas supply thereto or require the person supplying the gas to disconnect the gas supply.

The second was para. 1(d) of the Regulations Governing Gas Permits and Inspection Fees [O.C. 1981/57, Alta. Reg. 636/57] under the Gas Protection Act, which was as follows:

1. *General*
   (d) Issuance of a permit shall not entitle the holder thereof to install any facilities for the use of gas which is not in accordance with the Gas Protection Act Regulations, and notwithstanding anything which may be written in the permit, the Inspection Branch may order such changes or additions as may be required to bring the work into conformity with such Regulations as may be in force.

Each of the installer and the inspector in my view failed to carry out his respective duty under the provisions of the Gas Protection Act and the Regulations made under it and the Code established pursuant to it.

It is clear to me that the object of the provisions of the Gas Protection Act and the Regulations made under it and the Installation Code established pursuant to it, was to provide as part of the scheme of the legislation the creation for the benefit of individuals such as the Ostash family of rights enforceable by action. The full title of the Gas Protection Act is "An Act to Provide for the Protection of Persons from Injury and Property from Damage in the Installation, Transmission, Distribution, Supply or Use of Gas, Including Liquefied Petroleum Gas, in the Province." The Lieutenant-Governor in Council is authorized by s. 5 to make Rules and Regulations of various kinds including Regulations [s. 5(*m*)] "relating to any other matter or thing . . . (11) that has for its object the avoidance of danger to life and property by reason of the installation, repair or use of any gas equipment. . .". I have already quoted extensively from the Installation Code. I know of no reason why the principles laid down in *Lochgelly Iron & Coal Co. Ltd.* v. *M'Mullan,* [1934] A.C. 1, cannot properly be applied in cases other than those dealing with legislation enacted to provide safer working conditions for employees, where the legislation in question is obviously enacted for the protection of a particular class of people. I would affirm the judgment against the installer.

NOTES

1. In *Van Oudenhove* v. *D'Aoust et al.* (1970), 8 D.L.R. (3d) 145 (Alta. C.A.), an eight-year-old boy was electrocuted under the defendant's cottage as a result of the failure of the two defendants to ground a wire properly. The defendant occupier was found 50 percent liable on a theory of occupier's liability. The defendant electrician, who did the work involved, was also found to be 50 percent liable, because *inter alia,* his failure to connect the ground wire was a breach of the Regulations adopted under the Electrical Protection Act of Alberta. Allen J.A. cited *Ostash* v. *Sonnenberg et al.* and concluded:

"Without going exhaustively into the cases dealing with the question as to whether a breach of statutory duty gives rise to an action I think it is sufficient to say only that a breach of these particular Regulations having as one of their expressed objects the protection of life is evidence of negligence [sic]."

Was the use of the word "evidence" a mere slip of the pen or was this procedural effect actually intended by the court?

2. In *Northern Helicopters Ltd.* v. *Vancouver Soaring Association et al.* (1972), 31 D.L.R. (3d) 321 (B.C.S.C.), a helicopter collided in mid-air with a glider, killing both pilots. Both pilots had violated the Air Regulations passed under the authority of the Aeronautics Act, R.S.C. 1952, c. 2. Mr. Justice

Berger rationalized his use of these provisions as follows:

"We have the *Air Regulations*. They lay down a set of rules governing aircraft. They can be applied to the case at bar. They establish a reasonable standard of care. In my view, the court ought to apply those Regulations in a sensible way that takes into account the nature of flight and the special characteristics of the aircraft that collided here. . . . To apply the law as developed in automobile cases or in collisions at sea, would involve the risk of introducing rules that might well be arbitrary and insensitive to the peculiarities of flight.

Now, the *Air Regulations* are not a code governing civil liability on aircraft collisions. But they do represent a reasonable standard of care to be observed. A failure to observe that standard is negligence."

In this case, both pilots were in breach of their statutory duty and liability was split 66-2/3 against the plaintiff and 33-1/3 against the defendant. Which procedural effect has Mr. Justice Berger accorded these Air Regulation? What do you think of His Lordship's reasoning?

3. In *Maynes* v. *Galicz* (1976), 62 D.L.R. (3d) 385 (B.C.) a 7-year-old child was injured by a wolf at a zoo when she climbed over a barrier which did not comply with certain regulations and put her fingers into the wire mesh cage which contained the wolf. McKay J., in imposing liability, stated:

"In my view, the secondary barrier does not comply with the Regulations. It would not *prevent* an excited or inquisitive youngster from reaching the enclosure. It certainly did not in this case. I agree with counsel for the defendant that a breach of the Regulations does not *ipso facto* create liability. It is my view, however, that the Regulation in question sets a minimum standard of care that the public is entitled to expect from those who display wild and dangerous animals for financial gain."

4. Do *Ostash* v. *Sonnenberg, Van Oudenhove* v. *D'Aoust, Northern Helicopters Ltd.* v. *Vancouver Soaring Association* and *Maynes* v. *Galicz* have anything in common that might distinguish them from *Sterling Trusts* v. *Postma* and *Moise* v. *Queensway Tank Lines*?

5. Some courts are more hesitant to use the negligence *per se* theory. See, for example, *School Division of Assiniboine South No. 3* v. *Hoffer et al.* (1970), 16 D.L.R. (3d) 703; affd [1971] 4 W.W.R. 746 (C.A.); affd [1973] 6 W.W.R. 765 (S.C.C.), where an explosion was caused when a snowmobile negligently collided with an unguarded gas riser pipe. Dickson J.A., as he then was, stated that he did not wish to "rest a finding of negligence or, as it has often been termed 'statutory negligence', against the [defendant] gas company upon breach by it of the Public Utility Board Regulations", which regulated the guards on gas riser pipes.

6. Is it wise to have an assortment of procedural effects to accord penal statutes? How will the court decide which method to sue? Will it have a free hand in every case?

7. What procedural effect should be given to the breach of a pure food statute? See *infra*, Chapter 13, Section F.1. See *Curll* v. *Robin Hood Multifoods* (1974), 56 D.L.R. (3d) 129 (Cowan C.J.T.D. N.S.). Cf. *Heimler* v. *Calvert Caterers Ltd.* (1975), 4 O.R. (2d) 667 (Stortini Co. Ct. J.); affd (1975), 56 D.L.R. (3d) 643 (C.A.).

8. In *Curtis* v. *Jacques* (1978), 20 O.R. (2d) 552, partial liability was imposed on a boat owner who failed to use his lights at night contrary to the regulations under the Canada Shipping Act. Mr. Justice Steele stated that "anyone disobeying the law with respect to navigational lighting must bear the consequences and risks that are incurred by such violation". This was so even though there was evidence that boaters in the area customarily did not use their lights. What procedural effect has Mr. Justice Steele accorded the regulations here?

9. In *National Capital Commn.* v. *Pugliese* (1979), 8 C.C.L.T. 69, Pigeon J. said "The statute has defined what is reasonable" and consequently anyone pumping over 10,000 gallons of water per day is liable both in negligence and in nuisance for damage caused to another's property. Explain.

D. COMPLIANCE WITH THE STATUTE
CHIPCHASE v. BRITISH TITAN PRODUCTS CO.
Court of Appeal. [1956] 1 Q.B. 545; [1956] 1 All E.R. 613

Appeal by the plaintiff, a painter employed by defendant, from a judgment for defendant in an action for damages sustained as a result of a fall from a staging on which he was working. The plaintiff had sued for breach of statutory regulation and for negligence at common law.

Denning L.J.: Counsel for the plaintiff says that if the plaintiff had been working six feet six inches above the ground, he would, as he had a paint bucket up there beside him, have had to have planks at least thirty-four inches wide. That is provided by reg. 22 (c) of the Building (Safety, Health and Welfare) Regulations, 1948. Counsel agrees that the present case is not within the regulations because the plaintiff was working only six feet above the ground; but he argues that, as it was so nearly within the regulation, the court ought to take the regulation into account and hold that there ought to have been a plank wider than nine inches. I do not think that that argument is correct. The commissioner was clearly right in saying that the common law claim must be considered independently of the regulations. Undue complications would be brought into these cases if, whenever the courts were considering common law obligations, they had to consider all the statutory regulations which nearly apply but which do not in fact apply.

As a matter of common sense, the question, therefore, is — Ought there to have been a wider staging? On all the evidence in the case the commissioner thought not, and I see no reason why this court should interfere with his decision. . . .

Morris L.J.: . . . In the present case, if the regulation were an indication of anything in particular, it was an indication of that which everyone knows, namely, that if one falls one may hurt oneself, and if one falls from a great height one may hurt oneself more than if one falls from a lower height. The commissioner was not unmindful of that, and he said that he approached the case independently of any regulation. He put to himself the test whether the employer had failed to take that degree of reasonable care for the safety of his workmen which is required by the standards laid down at common law. I can see no error at all in that approach, and . . . I agree with the judgment delivered by the commissioner which it seems to me was wholly admirable judgment.

[Parker L.J., concurred.]

NOTES

1. In *Thatcher* v. *C.P.R.*, [1947] O.W.N. 965, 61 C.R.T.C. 162, plaintiff was injured in a level-crossing accident. In an action against defendant railway the jury found defendant negligent in that "speed was not being properly reduced with relation to the approach to a thickly populated area." Section 309 of the Railway Act provided that no train shall pass through "any thickly populated portion of any city" at a greater speed than 10 m.p.h. The accident occurred close to but outside a city, and the evidence showed that the speed of the train was such at the place of the accident that it could not have been reduced to the statutory maximum on entering the city. The Ontario Court of Appeal upheld a judgment based on the jury's finding. Hogg J.A., dissented on the ground that the railway's duty could not be enlarged to embrace persons with whom the section of the Act was not concerned.

2. Can these two cases be reconciled? Which do you prefer?

3. If a car is driven at 45 m.p.h. in a 50 m.p.h. zone, can civil liability be im-

posed on the ground of excessive speed? See *Martin* v. *Powell* (1928), 62 O.L.R. 436. What if it is foggy or icy? What if there is a lot of traffic? What if the defendant is driving an old jalopy? See Linden, "Speeding as Negligence" (1967), 10 Can. Bar J. 94.

4. In *Weiss* v. *Larson* (1965), 55 D.L.R. (2d) 330 (Alta. C.A.), it was held that compliance with the precautions legislatively prescribed for a railroad cannot amount to negligence, unless "special circumstances of danger" or "unusual or extraordinary conditions" exist. The Supreme Court of Canada reaffirmed this principle in *Paskivski et al.* v. *Canadian Pacific Ltd. et al.* (1976), 57 D.L.R. (3d) 280, where a child, waiting at a crossing for a train to pass, slipped on ice and fell under the train, losing both his legs as a result. Even though the railway had complied with its statutory obligations under the Railway Act, R.S.C. 1970, c. R-2, it was held liable in negligence because of the "exceptional circumstances". Dickson J. for the majority of the Supreme Court explained:

"The *McKay* case was decided over seventy years ago, when Canada was, to quote Sedgewick J., in that case, 'a young and only partially developed territory'. Davies, J., in the same case expressed concern that railway development not be impeded. The past seventy years have wrought many changes within Canada and today one might perhaps be inclined to question the relevance and validity of a rule of law which limits the common law duty of care of a railway to the special case or the exceptional case, particularly if those words are to receive a strict or narrow construction. It may well be that the interests of a young and undeveloped nation are best served by a minimum of impediment to industrial growth and economic expansion but in a more developed and populous nation this attitude of *laissez faire* may have to yield to accommodate the legitimate concern of society for other vital interests such as the safety and welfare of children. But if the test to be met is that of exceptional or special circumstances, it appears to me it was open to the trial Judge to find upon all of the evidence that the appellant had met that test."

See also *Sdraulig* v. *C.P.R.* (1969), 5 D.L.R. (3d) 177 (S.C.C.).

5. In *School Division of Assiniboine South No. 3* v. *Hoffer et al.* (1970), 16 D.L.R. (3d) 703; affd [1971] 4 W.W.R. 746 (C.A.); affd [1973] 6 W.W.R. 765 (S.C.C.), the principle concerning compliance with legislation was well-expressed by Deniset J., at trial as follows:

"An ordinary person, even while following regulations, is not relieved of responsibility to take care and to think, and to try and foresee, as a responsible man, what may well be the consequences of his actions."

In the Court of Appeal, Dickson J.A. (as he then was) agreed, explaining that:

"Evidence of compliance or non-compliance with a statutory Rule undoubtedly has a decided bearing on civil recovery . . . [a defendant] is under a common-law duty to take care, apart from any duty arising under the regulation. . . ."

6. In *Bux* v. *Slough Metals Ltd.*, [1974] 1 All E.R. 262 (C.A.), the plaintiff injured his eye when he was splashed by some molten metal which he was removing from a furnace. The evidence indicated that if he had been wearing the safety goggles which the employer was required by Regulation to supply, he would not have been injured. The goggles had been provided to the workers but, to the employer's knowledge, they were not used because the lenses tended to mist up very quickly. The employer did not enforce the wearing of the goggles. The court found that there was no breach of statutory duty but, nevertheless, held the employer negligent at common law for not forcing the employees to use the goggles or for not providing better ones. The employer argued that compliance with the statutory duty absolved him from any breach of his common law duty. In response to this, Stephenson L.J. said, at pp. 272-273:

"There is, in my judgment, no presumption that a statutory obligation abrogates or supersedes the employer's common law duty or that it defines or measures his common law duty either by clarifying it or by cutting it down — or indeed by extending it. It is not necessarily exhaustive of that duty or co-extensive with it and I do not, with all due respect to counsel for the defendants' argument, think it possible to lay down conditions in which it is exhaustive or to conclude that it is so in this case. The statutory obligation may exceed the duty at common law or it may fall short of it or it may equal it. The court has always to construe the statute or statutory instrument which imposes the obligation, consider the facts of the particular case and the allegations of negligence in fact made by the particular workman and then decide whether, if the statutory obligation has been performed, any negligence has been proved. In some cases such proof will be difficult or impossible; in others it may be easy.

In imposing statutory duties whose breach may give an injured workman a right of action against his employer, Parliament cannot be presumed to have intended to take from the courts their duty of deciding whether his employer has taken reasonable care of the workman and what the extent of that duty is. In this case, and I venture to think in every case where a plaintiff has alleged a breach of statutory duty, he is entitled to allege negligence at common law and to ask the court to answer the question whether he has proved negligence, irrespective of his having proved a breach of statutory duty. In this case the plaintiff, having failed to prove a breach of statutory duty, can certainly ask the court to decide whether a prudent employer ought to have done more for his safety by way of persuading, instructing or ordering him to wear goggles than his employers did."

The court also held that the plaintiff was contributorily negligent to the extent of 40 percent.

CLINKSCALES v. CARVER

Supreme Court of California. (1943), 22 Cal. 2d 72; 136 P. 2d 777

The defendant went through a stop sign that was put up without proper legal authorization and collided with the plaintiff. From a judgment for the plaintiff, the defendant appeals.

Traynor J.: [The contention of the defendant] would make the question of negligence *per se* turn upon the irregularity of the authorization. Whatever the effect of the irregularity on defendant's criminal liability it cannot be assumed that the conditions that limit it also limit civil liability. The propriety of taking from the jury the determination of negligence does not turn on defendant's criminal liability. A statute that provides for a criminal proceeding only does not create a civil liability; if there is no provision for a remedy by civil action to persons injured by a breach of the statute it is because the Legislature did not contemplate one. A suit for damages is based on the theory that the conduct inflicting the injuries is a common-law tort, in this case the failure to exercise the care of a reasonable man at a boulevard stop. The significance of the statute in a civil suit for negligence lies in its formulation of a standard of conduct that the court adopts in the determination of such liability. [Citations omitted.]

The decision as to what the civil standard should be still rests with the court, and the standard formulated by a legislative body in a police regulation or criminal statute becomes the standard to determine civil liability only because the court accepts it. In the absence of such a standard the case goes to the jury, which must determine whether the defendant has acted as a reasonably prudent man would act in similar circumstances. The jury then has the burden of deciding not only what the facts are but what the unformulated standard is of reasonable conduct. When a legislative body has generalized a standard from the experience of the community and prohibits conduct that is likely to cause harm, the court accepts the formulated standards and applies them [citations omitted] except where they would serve to impose liability without fault. [Citations omitted.]

Even if the conduct cannot be punished criminally because of irregularities in the adoption of the prohibitory provisions, the legislative standard may nevertheless apply if it is an appropriate measure for the defendant's conduct. When the court accepts the standard it rules in effect that the defendant's conduct falls below that of a reasonable man as the court conceives it. It does no more than it does in any ruling that certain acts or omissions amount as a matter of law to negligence. *Restatement: Torts,* sec. 285. An appellate court is concerned with determining whether the trial court arrived at a proper standard in a paticular case. In this case the trial court rightly instructed the jury that measured by the standard set up by the resolution of the board of supervisors and the Vehicle Code it was negligence as a matter of law to disregard the stop-sign. Failure to observe a stop-sign is unreasonably dangerous conduct whether or not the driver is immune from criminal prosecution because of some irregularity in the erection of the stop-sign. If a through artery has been posted with stop-signs by the public authorities in the customary way and to all appearances by regular procedure, any reasonable man should know that the public naturally relies upon their observance. If a driver from a side street enters the ostensibly protected boulevard without stopping, in disregard of the posted safeguards, contrary to what drivers thereon could reasonably have expected him to do, he is guilty of negligence regardless of any irregularity attending the authorization of the signs. [Citations omitted.] Such irregularity does not relieve a person from the duty to exercise the care of a reasonable man under such circumstances. Otherwise a stop-sign would become a trap to innocent persons who rely upon it.

The judgment is affirmed.

[The dissenting opinion of Shenk J., in which Edmonds J. concurred, is omitted.]

NOTES

1. In *Littley* v. *Brooks and Canadian National Railway,* [1930] S.C.R. 416, [1930] 4 D.L.R. 1, in an action for damages arising from a level crossing accident, the plaintiff tendered in evidence an order of the Ontario Railway and Municipal Board declaring that the railway speed at this crossing should be 5 m.p.h. At the time of the accident the railway had been taken over by the Canadian National Railways under a Dominion statute and had, therefore, ceased to be subject to the legislative authority of the Province. The Order was rejected at the trial and on appeal, but the Supreme Court of Canada declared it admissible "not as a rule that could be enforced against the railway company, but as affording evidence of an adjudication by a competent tribunal upon the dangerous character of the crossing — a matter of public concern — at the time the Order was pronounced (*Taylor on Evidence,* 10th ed., pp. 442-443 and 1213) and presenting a standard of reasonableness upon which a jury might act."

2. Do these cases make sense? How can they be reconciled with *Chipchase?*

REVIEW PROBLEM

Peter, whose driver's licence has expired at midnight on January 31, was driving home from his girlfriend's house in Camelot, at 3:00 a.m. on February 1, in the dark.

Because it was very foggy out, he was travelling at 12 m.p.h. He peered out his windshield, watching most carefully, to see that he did not collide with anybody ahead of him. His blazing headlights were not of much use to him in the thick fog, enabling him to see only 20 feet in all directions. The speed limit in force was 30 m.p.h.

Unexpectedly, Peter caught a glimpse of a shadowy object, slammed his brakes and crashed into the rear of Dodo's car, which was travelling in the same direction as Peter, but at only 8 m.p.h.

Despite a Highway Traffic Act, requirement that "2 red tail lights on every vehicle must be lit between dusk and dawn", the tail lights on Dodo's vehicle were not lit. The evidence clearly indicates that, if these lights had been on, they would have been seen by Peter in time to stop his automobile without colliding with Dodo, but Dodo swears that he did not know his lights were unlit and that, when he had checked them earlier that day, they were operating perfectly.

Peter was injured quite severely in the crash and was hospitalized. When he is released from hospital he retains you to sue Dodo.

Can Peter recover from Dodo?

CHAPTER 7

DUTY

Even if the conduct of a defendant is considered to be negligent, he will not necessarily be held liable for that conduct. The court must conclude that he owes a duty to avoid acting carelessly, before it will affix responsibility. Esher M.R., in *Le Lievre* v. *Gould,* [1893] 1 Q.B. 491, at p. 497, stated: "A man is entitled to be as negligent as he pleases towards the whole world if he owes no duty to them."

Because the duty issue is a question of law for the court to decide, it enables courts to check the propensity of juries to award damages in circumstances where it is felt to be inappropriate. Moreover, an attack on the pleadings by a defendant may snuff out an unfounded action if the court concludes that there is no duty owed.

The trouble with the duty notion, however, is that it is more a statement of a conclusion than a guideline for decision-making. The concept of foreseeability is of great importance in determining whether a duty exists, but it will be seen that it by no means solves all the duty issues.

A. THE CONCEPT OF DUTY GENERALLY

M'ALISTER (OR DONOGHUE) v. STEVENSON

House of Lords. [1932] A.C. 562

The appellant, a shop assistant, sought to recover from the respondent, an aerated water manufacturer, on the ground of his alleged negligence, £500 as damages for the injurious effects alleged to have been produced on her by the presence of a snail in a bottle of ginger beer manufactured by the respondent and ordered for the appellant in a shop in Paisley by a friend of the appellant. In consequence of her having drunk part of the contaminated contents of the bottle the appellant alleged that she contracted a serious illness. The bottle was stated to have been dark opaque glass, so that the condition of its contents could not be ascertained by inspection, and to have been closed with a metal cap, while on the side was a label bearing the name of the respondent.

The Lord Ordinary rejected the respondent's plea in law that the appellant's averments were irrelevant and insufficient to support the conclusions of the summons and allowed a proof. The Second Division, by a majority (the Lord Justice-Clerk, Lord Ormidale, and Lord Anderson; Lord Hunter dissenting), recalled the interlocutor of the Lord Ordinary and dismissed the action.

Lord Atkin: The sole question for determination in this case is legal: Do the averments made by the pursuer in her pleading, if true, disclose a cause of action? I need not restate the particular facts. The question is whether the manufacturer of an article of drink sold by him to a distributor in circumstances which prevent the distributor or the ultimate purchaser or consumer from discovering by inspection any defect is under any legal duty to the ultimate purchaser or consumer to take reasonable care that the article is free from defect likely to cause injury to health. I do not think a more important problem has occupied your Lordships in your judicial capacity, important both because of its bearing on public health and because of the practical test which it applies to the system of law under which it arises. The case has to be determined in accordance with Scots law, but it has been a matter of agreement between the experienced counsel who argued this case, and it appears to be the basis of the judgments of the learned judges of the Court of Session, that for the purposes of determining this problem the law of Scotland and the law of England are the same . . . The law of both countries appears to be that in order to support an action for damages for negligence the complainant has to show that he has been injured by the breach of a duty owed to him in the circumstances by the defendant to take reasonable care to avoid such injury. In the present case we are not concerned with the breach of the duty; if a duty exists, that would be a question of fact which is sufficiently averred and for the present purposes must be assumed. We are solely concerned with the question whether as a matter of law in the circumstances alleged the defender owed any duty to the pursuer to take care. . .

At present I content myself with pointing out that in English law there must be, and is, some general conception of relations giving rise to a duty of care, of which the particular cases found in the books are but instances. The liability for negligence, whether you style it such or treat it as in other systems as a species of "culpa", is no doubt based upon a general public sentiment of moral wrongdoing for which the offender must pay. But acts or omissions which any moral code would censure cannot in a practical world be treated so as to give a right to every person injured by them to demand relief. In this way rules of law arise which limit the range of complainants and the extent of their remedy. The rule that you are to love your neighbour becomes in law, you must not injure your neighbour, and the lawyer's question, Who is my neighbour? receives a restricted reply. You must take reasonable care to avoid acts or omissions which you can reasonably foresee would be likely to injure your neighbour. Who, then, in law, is my neighbour? The answer seems to be — persons who are so closely and directly affected by my act that I ought reasonably to have them in contemplation as being so affected when I am directing my mind to the acts or omissions which are called in question. . . .

Lord Macmillan.: . . . The law takes no cognizance of carelessness in the abstract. It concerns itself with carelessness only where there is a duty to take care and where failure in that duty has caused damage. In such circumstances carelessness assumes the legal quality of negligence and entails the consequences in law of negligence. What then are the circumstances which give rise to this duty to take care? In the daily contacts of social and business life human beings are thrown into or place themselves in an infinite variety of relationships with their fellows, and the law can refer only to the standards of the reasonable man in order to determine whether any particular relationship gives rise to a duty to take care as between those who stand in that relationship to each other. The grounds of action may be as various and manifold as human errancy, and the conception of legal responsibility may develop in adaptation to altering social conditions and standards. The criterion of judgment must adjust and adapt itself to the changing circumstances of life. The categories of negligence are never closed. The cardinal principle of liability is that the party complained of should owe to the party complaining a duty to take care and that the party complaining should be able to prove that he has suffered damage in consequence of a breach of that duty. Where there is room for diversity of view is in determining what circumstances will establish such a relationship between the parties as to give rise on the one side to a duty to take care and on the other side to a right to have care taken. . . .

Appeal allowed.

[This excerpt concentrates on the duty problem. A much fuller treatment of this case as it affects products liability is done below, see Chapter 13. The judgments of Lord Thankerton, concurring, and Lords Buckmaster and Tomlin, dissenting, are omitted.]

NOTES

1. See Green, "The Duty Problem in Negligence Cases" (1928), 28 Colum. L. Rev. 1014; Wright, "Negligent 'Acts or Omissions'" (1941), 19 Can. Bar Rev. 465; Morison, "A Re-examination of the Duty of Care" (1948), 11 Mod. L. Rev. 9; Dias, "The Duty Problem in Negligence" (1955), Camb. L.J. 198; Symmons, "The Duty of Care in Negligence: Recently Expressed Policy Elements" (1971), 34 Mod. L. Rev. 394 and 528; J.C. Smith, "The Mystery of Duty", in Klar (ed.) *Studies in Canadian Tort Law* (1977).

NOVA MINK LTD. v. TRANS-CANADA AIRLINES

Nova Scotia Supreme Court. [1951] 2 D.L.R. 241; 26 M.P.R. 389

An aircraft, operated by defendant, on a scheduled flight, flew to the south of its usual line of flight over an approved Airway in order to avoid clouds. While flying contact, with the approval of the airport authorities preparatory to landing, it passed over a hill beyond which lay a mink ranch owned by plaintiff. The female mink had just whelped and the noise of the aircraft caused them to devour their young resulting in a loss of 175-200 animals. Evidence as to the height of the plane was conflicting but there was no doubt that it observed all statutory regulations in that regard. The plaintiff's ranch had been marked in accordance with a Circular to pilots advising that such markings were mink ranches and should be avoided. The defendant had not been advised of the location of plaintiff's ranch nor was the pilot aware of its existence. The pilot on the day in question was not keeping any lookout for farms on the ground. The plaintiff brought action against the defendant for damages alleged to have resulted from the negligent operation of defendant's aircraft. At the trial, with a jury, the latter found defendant's employees negligent in "flying directly over mink ranch, thus creating such a noise that the mink became panicky thus causing them to devour their young". From a judgment for plaintiff, defendant appealed.

MacDonald J.. . . . Does the evidence establish that the defendant was under a legal duty to use care to avoid injury to the plaintiff's business as a mink ranch operator? If so, was there a breach of that duty by the defendant?

Unless both of these questions are answered in the affirmative, the plaintiff must fail in his action; for it is immaterial that the defendant's conduct caused him loss unless that conduct was wrongful as being a violation of a duty imposed upon the defendant by law.

In considering these questions it is material to keep in mind that the law of negligence has developed through the discharge by judges and juries of their respective functions. It is the function of the judge to determine whether there is any duty of care imposed by the law upon the defendant and if so, to define the measure of its proper performance; it is for the jury to determine, by reference to the criterion so declared, whether the defendant has failed in his legal duty. In every case, the judge must decide the question: Is there a duty of care in this case owing by the defendant to the plaintiff and, if so, how far does that duty extend? This question relates both to the existence of a duty and to its quantum; for the case can only go to the jury on the issue of breach of duty, if duty has been found to exist in law, and the jury can only determine that issue if it has been provided with a statement of the standard of care required by the law in performance of that duty . . .

The common law yields the conclusion that there is such a duty only where the circumstances of time, place, and person would create in the mind of a reasonable man in those circumstances such a probability of harm resulting to other persons as to require him to take care to avert that probable result. This element of reasonable prevision of expectable harm soon came to be associated with a fictional reasonable man whose apprehensions of harm became the touchstone of the existence of duty, in the same way as his conduct in the face of such apprehended harm became the standard of conformity to that duty.

And so it came about that the initial question of the existence and quantum of duty, though a question of law for the judge, is to be decided by him by reference to what the notional reasonable man would have foreseen in the way of danger or risk in the circumstances and what he would have done about it. In this way it was felt that the question would be decided by reference to a standard of prevision and conduct grounded in normality and practicality rather than in judicial technicality or diversity of view. Thus, in the present case, we are to determine this question by reference to our assumptions as to what the reasonable man would have foreseen as to the probable consequences of flying over the defendant's ranch and what he would have done in the circumstances; and to declare, accordingly, whether the defendant was under a duty of care in respect of it or not . . . .

Such a question, though one of law, "is essentially a jury question" . . .

When upon analysis of the circumstances and application of the appropriate formula, a court holds that the defendant was under a duty of care, the court is stating as a conclusion of law what is really a conclusion of policy as to responsibility for conduct involving unreasonable risk. It is saying that such circumstances presented such an appreciable risk of harm to others as to entitle them to protection against unreasonable conduct by the actor. It is declaring also that a cause of action can exist in other situations of the same type, and *pro tanto* is moving in the direction of establishing further categories of human relationships entailing recognized duties of care. No doubt it is true, as Lord Macmillan said in *M'Alister (or Donoghue)* v. *Stevenson* that "the categories of negligence are never closed" and that there will always remain "room for diversity of view . . . in determining what circumstances will establish such a relationship . . . as to give rise, on the one side to a duty to take care, and on the other side to a right to have care taken". It is no less true that every case of a duty established in respect of a given situation-pattern establishes a legal duty in similar situation-patterns as they may arise. This process was strikingly manifested in *Donoghue* v. *Stevenson* itself and in the later cases which applied its principle to varying aspects of the manufacturer-ultimate consumer situation.

Accordingly there is always a large element of judicial policy and social expediency involved in the determination of the duty-problem, however it may be obscured by use of the traditional formulae . . . .

Many attempts have been made to generalize the circumstances which create a legal duty of care . . . What is common . . . is the idea of a *relationship between parties attended by a foreseeable risk of harm* . . . That relationship may arise out of circumstance of physical proximity; but it is not that circumstance *per se* which gives rise to duty but the probability of harm inhering in the relationship of parties, spatial or otherwise. If such a relationship does exist in fact, or in contemplation, and is fraught with the likelihood of harm to another in that relationship, the basis of duty exists; and it is immaterial that the locus or date of the occurrence of the apprehended harm be unknown. . . .

Another influential attempt to state the circumstances which give rise to duty was that of Cardozo C.J., in *Palsgraf* v. *Long Island R.R. Co.*, who based it on relational hazards apparent to the "eye of reasonable vigilance" . . . And, as he was careful to point out, the range of apprehension and the orbit of the duty are affected by the presence or absence of knowledge of any circumstance which in fact increased or diminished the apparent risk. Indeed this element was crucial in the decision; for it was the fact that the explosive which there did the damage was encased in a package harmless to outward seeming and gave no notice that it had in it the potency of peril to persons far removed from the locus of its fall, that chiefly defeated the plaintiff.

The present approach to the duty-problem is exemplified in two closely-reasoned cases in the House of Lords. [Discussion of *Bourhill* v. *Young,* [1943] A.C. 92, and *Glasgow Corporation* v. *Muir,* [1943] A.C. 448, is omitted.]

This catalogue of quotations and citations leads to certain conclusions:

1. That the existence of a legal duty of care by a defendant depends upon whether the hypothetical reasonable man would foresee the risk of harm to a person in the situation of the plaintiff *vis-a-vis* himself and his activities.

2. That the envisagement of the reasonable man as to the probability of danger must include whatever notice of the plaintiff's situation (*e.g.,* his proximity or location) the facts afford; and that if there is nothing in the circumstances, as known to the defendant, to suggest the likelihood of harm to the plaintiff from the defendant's activity there is no duty to the plaintiff in respect of it.

3. That in the absence of knowledge as to any special susceptibility of the plaintiff to harm from mere noise, there can be no duty to refrain from making a kind or degree of noise which would otherwise be harmless. (*Cf.* Lord Wright in *Bourhill* v. *Young, supra; Salmond on Torts,* p. 435.)

4. That whatever circumstances suggest the probability of harm if care be not taken, also define the measure of care to be taken.

5. That if there is insufficient evidence to justify a declaration of duty and of its extent, or if there is no evidence from which the jury could reasonably infer a breach of duty, *i.e.,* if it affords no criterion by which the reasonableness of his conduct could be judged, there is no case for the jury . . .

The Circular gave no indication as to how many of such farms there were in Canada or in Nova Scotia, or as to where any of them lay; nor did it define what was meant, in terms of lateral distance, by the word "avoided" . . . So far, at least, as . . . the company were concerned, no information as to the existence and location of the plaintiff's ranch was given by the plaintiff or was in their possession . . . I cannot regard this Circular as giving such notice of the existence of the plaintiff's mink ranch as to impose upon the defendant company the duty (initially and periodically) to survey the terrain beneath its airway in order to discover what, if any, fur farms existed thereon and to plot their location and advise its pilots thereof . . .

So far as the pilots were concerned, it is contended that as they were aware of the Circular, they were bound thereby to keep a look-out for farms marked in conformity with it and to avoid such a farm as the plaintiff's altogether, or to avoid low flying over it . . . But the common law imposes duty only when the circumstances manifest a probability of danger. The only additional circumstance which knowledge of the Circular would afford to a pilot was that of the possibility of there being fur farms under his course. Accordingly I cannot conclude that there was any duty to look for fur farms on this regularly flown route.

Moreover, the duty, if there were one, would be merely to look for fur farms likely to be affected by the flight of the plane in unreasonable proximity to it. The Circular gave no data as to the distance from a fur farm — vertically or horizontally — at which a danger of a plane disturbing the animals would arise.

Accordingly I find that knowledge of the Circular *per se* imposed no duty on the company or its servants to keep any farther away from this fur farm than from any other farm.

It seems quite clear to me that where the situation presented no foreseeable risk of contact with the defendant's farm or physical injury to it and no such thing occurred, a duty to pass the plaintiff's farm at a greater distance than would normally be harmless must be based on the defendant's knowledge of the special nature of the farm and of the special susceptibility of its inmates to noise. Lacking such knowledge the duty would arise only out of harm to be expected in respect of a normal farm . . . Here there was no more reason for the pilot to envisage the presence of noise-conscious mink as within the orbit of danger than there was in *Bourhill* v. *Young* for the cyclist to foresee the proximity of a pregnant fish-wife. Statistically, of course, one may know that in any concourse of people there may be a pregnant woman or that in any rural area there may be a mink ranch; but the authorities do not require prevision of the proximity of abnormal people nor, I submit, of abnormal farms. As Lord Wright said in the *Bourhill* case: "The test of the plaintiff's extraordinary susceptibility, if *unknown to the defendant,* would in effect make him an *insurer.*"

In short, I hold that the circumstances apparent to the defendant and its servants in this case did not suggest a probability of harm to the plaintiff's ranch as to give rise to a duty of care to avoid it by any greater distance than ordinary prudence would suggest in the case of an ordinary farm. Indeed to say that there was such a duty would be futile; for there is no evidence upon which one could define the spatial limits of the duty. There are no data in this case upon which one could found a conclusion as to how far the reasonable man (or a reasonable pilot) would keep away from the ranch in order to avoid apprehended harm to the mink even if he knew of their existence and propensities. What is the hearing range or sensitivity of mink to sounds from a plane? What volume (or amplitude or pitch) of noise will frighten them? At what distance may a transit plane pass over them or near them without alarming them? How far does the speed of a plane and particular atmospheric conditions affect the audibility of plane noises from the ground?

To these and similar questions the evidence affords no answer; yet it is the postulate of duty that it arises out of circumstances of reasonably foreseeable harm *avoidable by reasonable care.*

It would be unthinkable for a court to hold a litigant bound to take care in respect of a condition of affairs of which the facts give no warning. . . . It would be equally absurd to hold one bound to exercise a degree of care incapable of ascertainment; for in this case even the "hypothetical reasonable man" could not exercise reasonable care in respect of the mink without knowledge of their hearing powers and of the complex factors entering into the physical laws of sound.

I hold, therefore, that in law the defendant owed no duty of care to the plaintiff in respect of the harm of which he complains and the case should have been withdrawn from the jury as matter of law.

Further, I hold that the case should have been withdrawn from the jury on the ground that there was not sufficient evidence from which the jury could reasonably infer a breach of duty by the defendant. . . .

In my view the appeal should be allowed, the verdict and the order based thereon set aside, and the action dismissed, with costs of the action and appeal to the defendant.

[The judgments of Ilsley C.J., and Parker J. are omitted. The former said there was no duty to the plaintiff to keep a careful look-out since there was no evidence that keeping a look-out would have been effective. "The plaintiff, if relying on a duty to keep a look-out, has the burden of showing that doing so . . . would have done some good." He further found that if there were such a duty, "there is no evidence that the breach of it . . . caused the loss". Parker J. found that the defendant's pilot owed a duty to keep a look-out; that he failed in his duty to the plaintiff; there was no evidence to show that, no matter how vigilant the pilot might have been, the plaintiff's ranch, could have been seen in time to avoid the damage. On these findings he held there was no evidence of any negligence causing damage to be submitted to the jury and the case should have been withdrawn from the jury's consideration. MacQuarrie J. concurred with Parker J., and Currie J., concurred with MacDonald J.]

HOME OFFICE v. DORSET YACHT CO. LTD.

House of Lords. [1970] 2 All E.R. 294

Lord Reid: My Lords, on 21st September 1962, a party of borstal trainees were working on Brownsea Island in Poole Harbour under the supervision and control of three borstal officers. During that night seven of them escaped and went aboard a yacht which they found nearby. They set this yacht in motion and collided with the respondents' yacht which was moored in the vicinity. Then they boarded the respondents' yacht. Much damage was done to this yacht by the collision and some by the subsequent conduct of these trainees. The respondents sue the appellant, the Home Office, for the amount of this damage.

The case comes before your Lordships on a preliminary issue whether the Home Office or these borstal officers owed any duty of care to the respondents capable of giving rise to a liability in damages. So it must be assumed that the respondents can prove all that they could prove on the pleadings if the case goes to trial. The question then is whether on that assumption the Home Office would be liable in damages. It is admitted that the Home Office would be vicariously liable if an action would lie against any of these borstal officers.

The facts which I think we must assume are that this party of trainees was in the lawful custody of the governor of the Portland Borstal Institution and was sent by him to Brownsea Island on a training exercise in the custody and under the control of the three officers with instructions to keep them in custody and under control. But in breach of their instructions these officers simply went to bed leaving the trainees to their own devices. If they had obeyed their instructions they could and would have prevented these trainees from escaping. They would therefore be guilty of the disciplinary offences of contributing by carelessness or neglect to the escape of a prisoner and to the occurrence of loss, damage or injury to any person or property. All the escaping trainees had criminal records and five of them had a record of previous escapes from borstal institutions. The three officers knew or ought to have known that these trainees would probably try to escape during the night, would take some vessel to make good their escape and would probably cause damage to it or some other vessel. There were numerous vessels moored in the harbour, and the trainees could readily board one of them. So it was a likely consequence of their neglect of duty that the respondents' yacht would suffer damage.

The case for the Home Office is that under no circumstances can borstal officers owe any duty to any member of the public to take care to prevent trainees under their control or supervision from injuring him or his property. If that is the law then enquiry into the facts of this case would be a waste of time and money because whatever the facts may be the respondents must lose. That case is based on three main arguments. First, it is said that there is virtually no authority for imposing a duty of this kind. Secondly, it is said that no person can be liable for a wrong done by another who is of full age and capacity and who is not the servant or acting on behalf of that person. And thirdly, it is said that public policy (or the policy of the relevant legislation) requires that these officers should be immune from any such liability.

The first would at one time have been a strong argument. About the beginning of this century most eminent lawyers thought that there were a number of separate torts involving negligence each with its own rules, and they were most unwilling to add more. They were of course aware from a number of leading cases that in the past the courts had from time to time recognised new duties and new grounds of action. But the heroic age was over, it was time to cultivate certainty and security in the law; the categories of negligence were virtually closed. The learned Attorney-General invited us to return to those halcyon days, but, attractive though it may be, I cannot accede to his invitation.

In later years there has been a steady trend towards regarding the law of negligence as depending on principle so that, when a new point emerges, one should ask not whether it is covered by authority but whether recognised principles apply to it. *Donoghue* v. *Stevenson* may be regarded as a milestone, and the well-known passage in Lord Atkin's speech should I think be regarded as a statement of principle. It is not to be treated as if it were a statutory definition. It will require qualification in new circumstances. But I think that the time has come when we can and should say that it ought to apply unless there is some justification or valid explanation for its exclusion. For example, causing economic loss is a different matter; for one thing it is often caused by deliberate action. Competition involves traders being entitled to damage their rivals' interests by promoting their own, and there is a long chapter of the law determining in what circumstances owners of land can, and in what circumstances they may not, use their proprietary rights so as to injure their neighbours. But where negligence is involved the tendency has been to apply principles analogous to those stated by Lord Atkin (*cf. Hedley Byrne & Co. Ltd.*, v. *Heller & Partners Ltd.*). And when a person has done nothing to put himself in any relationship with another person in distress or with his property mere accidental propinquity does not require him to go to that person's assistance. There may be a moral duty to do so, but it is not practicable to make it a legal duty. And then there are cases, *e.g.*, with regard to landlord and tenant, where the law was settled long ago and neither Parliament nor this House sitting judicially has made any move to alter it. But I can see nothing to prevent our approaching the present case with Lord Atkin's principles in mind. . . .

If the carelessness of the borstal officers was the cause of the respondents' loss what justification is there for holding that they had no duty to take care? The first argument was that their right and power to control the trainees was purely statutory and that any duty to exercise that right and power was only a statutory duty owed to the Crown. I would agree but there is very good authority for the proposition that, if a person performs a statutory duty carelessly so that he causes damage to a member of the public which would not have happened if he had performed his duty properly, he may be liable. In *Geddis* v. *Proprietors of Bann Reservoir* Lord Blackburn said:

> "For I take it, without citing cases, that it is now thoroughly well established that no action will lie for doing that which the legislature has authorized, if it be done without negligence, although it does occasion damage to anyone; but an action does lie for doing that which the legislature has authorized, if it be done negligently."

The reason for that is, I think, that Parliament deems it to be in the public interest that things otherwise unjustifiable should be done, and that those who do such things with due care should be immune from liability to persons who may suffer thereby. But Parliament cannot reasonably be supposed to have licensed those who do such things to act negligently in disregard of the interests of others so as to cause them needless damage.

Where Parliament confers a discretion the position is not the same. Then there may, and almost certainly will, be errors of judgment in exercising such a discretion and Parliament cannot have intended that members of the public should be entitled to sue in respect of such errors. But there must come a stage when the discretion is exercised so carelessly or unreasonably that there has been no real exercise of the discretion which Parliament has conferred. The person purporting to exercise his discretion has acted in abuse or excess of his power. Parliament cannot be supposed to have granted immunity to persons who do that. The present case does not raise that issue because no discretion was given to these borstal officers. They were given orders which they negligently failed to carry out. But the county court case of *Greenwell* v. *Prison Comrs* was relied on and I must deal with it. Some 290 trainees were held in custody in an open borstal institution. During the previous year there had been no less than 172 escapes. Two trainees escaped and took and damaged the plaintiff's motor truck; one of these trainees had escaped on three previous occasions from this institution. For three months since his last escape the question of his removal to a more secure institution had been under consideration but no decision had been reached. The learned judge held that the authorities there had been negligent. In my view, this decision could only be upheld if it could be said that the failure of those authorities to deal with the situation was so unreasonable as to show that they had been guilty of a breach of their statutory duty and that this had caused the loss suffered by the plaintiff.

Governors of these institutions and other responsible authorities have a difficult and delicate task. There was some argument whether the present system is fully authorised by the relevant statutes, but I shall assume that it is. That system is based on the belief that it assists the rehabilitation of trainees to give them as much freedom and responsibility as possible. So the responsible authorities must weigh on the one hand the public interest of protecting neighbours and their property from the depreciations of escaping trainees and on the other hand the public interest of promoting rehabilitation. Obviously there is much room here for differences of opinion and errors of judgment. In my view there can be no liability if the discretion is exercised with due care. There could only be liability if the person entrusted with discretion either unreasonably failed to carry out his duty to consider the matter or reached a conclusion so unreasonable as again to show failure to do his duty. It was suggested that these trainees might have been deliberately released at the time when they escaped and then there could have been no liability. I do not agree. Presumably when trainees are released either temporarily or permanently some care is taken to see that there

is no need for them to resort to crime to get food or transport. I could not imagine any more unreasonable exercise of discretion than to release trainees on an
island in the middle of the night without making any provision for their future
welfare. . . .

I think the fears of the Home Office are unfounded; I cannot believe that
negligence or dereliction of duty is widespread among prison or borstal officers.

Finally, I must deal with public policy. It is argued that it would be contrary
to public policy to hold the Home Office or its officers liable to a member of
the public for this carelessness — or indeed any failure of duty on their part.
The basic question is who shall bear the loss caused by that carelessness — the
innocent respondents or the Home Office who are vicariously liable for the conduct of their careless officers? I do not think that the argument for the Home
Office can be put better than it was put by the Court of Appeals of New York
in *Williams* v. *New York State:*

> ". . . public policy also requires that the State be not held liable. To hold
> otherwise would impose a heavy responsibility upon the State, or dissuade
> the wardens and principal keepers of our prison system from continued ex-
> perimentation with minimum security work details — which provide a means
> for encouraging better-risk prisoners to exercise their senses of responsibility
> and honor and so prepare themselves for their eventual return to society.
> Since 1917, the Legislature has expressly provided for out-of-prison work,
> Correction Law, § 182, and its intention should be respected without foster-
> ing the reluctance of prison officials to assign eligible men to minimum
> security work, lest they thereby give rise to costly claims against the State,
> or indeed inducing the State itself to terminate this 'salutary procedure'
> looking toward rehabilitation."

It may be that public servants of the State of New York are so apprehensive,
easily dissuaded from doing their duty, and intent on preserving public funds
from costly claims, that they could be influenced in this way. But my experience leads me to believe that Her Majesty's servants are made of sterner stuff.
So I have no hesitation in rejecting this argument. I can see no good ground in
public policy for giving this immunity to a government department. I would
dismiss this appeal.

Viscount Dilhorne (dissenting): . . . . Apart from one decision in the Ipswich
county court in 1951 to which I shall refer later, among the thousands of reported cases not a single case can be found where a claim similar to that in this
case has been put forward. No case in this country has been found to support
the contention that such a duty of care exists under the common law. . . .

Lord Atkin in defining the elements common to all cases where a breach of
a duty of care gives rise to liability cannot have intended his words to mean
that in every case failure to take reasonable care to avoid acts or omissions
which could reasonably be foreseen as likely to injure one's neighbour as defined by him was actionable. He cannot, for instance, have meant that a person
is liable in negligence if he fails to warn a person nearby whom he sees about
to step off the pavement into the path of an oncoming vehicle or if he fails to
attempt to rescue a child in difficulties in a pond. In both these instances — and
they could be multiplied — it can be said that he could reasonably have foreseen
that they would be likely to suffer injury by his omission to take action and
that they were so closely and directly affected by his omission to do so that he
ought to have had them in contemplation.

If, applying Lord Atkin's test, it be held that a duty of care existed in this
case, I do not think that such a duty can be limited to being owed only to those
in the immediate proximity of the place from which the escape is made. In

Donoghue v. *Stevenson* the duty was held to be owed to consumers wherever they might be. If there be such a duty, it must, in my view, be owed to all those who it can reasonably be foreseen are likely to suffer damage as a result of the escape. Surely it is reasonably foreseeable that those who escape may take a succession of vehicles, perhaps many miles from the place from which they escaped, to make their getaway. Surely it is reasonably foreseeable that those who escape from prisons, borstals and other places of confinement will, while they are on the run, seek to steal food for their sustenance and money and are likely to break into premises for that purpose.

If the foreseeability test is applied to determine to whom the duty is owed, I am at a loss to perceive any logical ground for excluding liability to persons who suffer injury or loss, no matter how far they or their property may be from the place of escape if the loss or injury was of a character reasonably foreseeable as the consequence of failure to take proper care to prevent the escape. . . .

I think that it is clear that the *Donoghue* v. *Stevenson* principle cannot be regarded as an infallible test of the existence of a duty of care; nor do I think that if that test is satisfied, there arises any presumption of the existence of such a duty. . . .

Lord Denning MR in the course of his judgment in this case said that he thought that the absence of authority was "because, until recently, no lawyer ever thought such an action would lie" on one of two grounds, first that the damage was far too remote, the chain of causation being broken by the act of the person who had escaped; and, secondly, on the ground that the only duty owed was to the Crown.

Whatever be the reasons for the absence of authority, the significant fact is its absence and that leads me to the conclusion, despite the disclaimer of counsel for the respondents of any such intention, that we are being asked to create in reliance on Lord Atkin's words an entirely new and novel duty and one which does not arise out of any novel situation.

I, of course, recognise that the common law develops by the application of well established principles to new circumstances but I cannot accept that the application of Lord Atkin's words, which, though they applied in *Deyong* v. *Shenburn* and might have applied in *Comr for Railways* v. *Quinlan*, were not held to impose a new duty on a master to his servant or on an occupier to a trespasser, suffices to impose a new duty on the Home Office and on others in charge of persons in lawful custody of the kind suggested.

No doubt very powerful arguments can be advanced that there should be such a duty. It can be argued that it is wrong that those who suffer loss or damage at the hands of those who have escaped from custody as a result of negligence on the part of the custodians should have no redress save against the persons who inflicted the loss or damage who are unlikely to be able to pay; that they should not have to bear the loss themselves whereas if there is such a duty, liability might fall on the Home Office and the burden on the general body of taxpayers. However this may be, we are concerned not with what the law should be but with what it is. The absence of authority shows that no such duty now exists. If there should be one, that is, in my view, a matter for the legislature and not for the courts. . . .

There is no authority for the existence of such a duty under the common law. Lord Denning M.R. in his judgment in the Court of Appeal, I think, recognised this for he said: "It is, I think, at bottom a matter of public policy which we, as judges, must resolve" and "What then is the right policy for the judges to adopt?" He went on to say:

"Many, many a time has a prisoner escaped — or been let out on parole — and done damage. But there is never a case in our law books when the prison authorities have been liable for it. No householder who has been burgled, no person who has been wounded by a criminal, has ever recovered damages from the prison authorities; such as to find a place in the reports. The householder has claimed on his insurance company. The injured man can now claim on the compensation fund. None has claimed against the prison authorities. Should we alter all this? I should be reluctant to do so if, by so doing, we should hamper all the good work being done by our prison authorities."

Where I differ is in thinking that it is not part of the judicial function 'to alter all this'. The facts of a particular case may be a wholly inadequate basis for a far reaching change of the law. We have not to decide what the law should be and then to alter the existing law. This is the function of Parliament.

As in my opinion no such duty can exist now under the common law my answer to the question raised in this preliminary issue is in the negative and I would allow the appeal.

Lord Diplock: . . . . The specific question of law raised in this appeal may therefore be stated as: is any duty of care to prevent the escape of a borstal trainee from custody owed by the Home Office to persons whose property would be likely to be damaged by the tortious acts of the borstal trainee if he escaped? This is the first time that this specific question has been posed at a higher judicial level than that of a country court.

Your Lordships in answering it will be performing a judicial function similar to that performed in *Donoghue* v. *Stevenson* and more recently in *Hedley Byrne & Co. Ltd.* v. *Heller & Partners Ltd.*, of deciding whether the English law of civil wrongs should be extended to impose legal liability to make reparation for the loss caused to another by conduct of a kind which has not hitherto been recognised by the courts as entailing any such liability.

This function, which judges hesitate to acknowledge as law-making, plays at most a minor role in the decision of the great majority of cases, and little conscious thought has been given to analysing its methodology. Outstanding exceptions are to be found in the speeches of Lord Atkin in *Donoghue* v. *Stevenson* and of Lord Devlin in *Hedley Byrne & Co. Ltd.* v. *Heller & Partners Ltd.* It was because the former was the first authoritative attempt at such an analysis that it has had so seminal an effect on the modern development of the law of negligence.

It will be apparent that I agree with Lord Denning MR that what we are concerned with in this appeal "is...at bottom a matter of public policy which we, as judges, must resolve". He cited in support Lord Pearce's *dictum* in *Hedley Byrne & Co. Ltd.* v. *Heller & Partners Ltd.*:

"How wide the sphere of the duty of care in negligence is to be laid depends ultimately on the courts' assessment of the demands of society for protection from the carelessness of others."

The reference in this passage to "the courts" in the plural is significant for —

"As always in English law the first step in such an inquiry is to see how far the authorities have gone, for new categories in the law do not spring into existence overnight;" *per* Lord Devlin.

The justification of the courts' role in giving the effect of law to the judges' conception of the public interest in the field of negligence is based on the cumulative experience of the judiciary of the actual consequences of lack of care in particular instances. And the judicial development of the law of negligence rightly proceeds by seeking first to identify the relevant characteristics that are common to the kinds of conduct and relationship between the parties which are involved in the case for decision and the kinds of conduct and relationships which have been held in previous decisions of the courts to give rise to a duty of care.

The method adopted at this stage of the process is analytical and inductive. It starts with an analysis of the characteristics of the conduct and relationship involved in each of the decided cases. But the analyst must know what he is looking for; and this involves his approaching his analysis with some general conception of conduct and relationships which *ought* to give rise to a duty of care. This analysis leads to a proposition which can be stated in the form: "In all the decisions that have been analysed a duty of care has been held to exist wherever the conduct and the relationship possessed each of the characteristics A, B, C, D etc., and has not so far been found to exist when any of these characteristics were absent."

For the second stage, which is deductive and analytical, that proposition is converted to: "In all cases where the conduct and relationship possess each of the characteristics A, B, C, D etc., a duty of care arises." The conduct and relationship involved in the case for decision is then analysed to ascertain whether they possess each of these characteristics. If they do the conclusion follows that a duty of care does arise in the case for decision.

But since *ex hypothesi* the kind of case which we are now considering offers a choice whether or not to extend the kinds of conduct or relationships which give rise to a duty of care, the conduct or relationship which is involved in it will lack at least one of the characteristics A, B, C or D etc. And the choice is exercised by making a policy decision whether or not a duty of care ought to exist if the characteristic which is lacking were absent or redefined in terms broad enough to include the case under consideration. The policy decision will be influenced by the same general conception of what ought to give rise to a duty of care as was used in approaching the analysis. The choice to extend is given effect to by redefining the characteristics in more general terms so as to exclude the necessity to conform to limitations imposed by the former definition which are considered to be inessential. The cases which are landmarks in the common law, such as *Lickbarrow* v. *Mason, Rylands* v. *Fletcher, Indermaur* v. *Dames, Donoghue* v. *Stevenson,* to mention but a few, are instances of cases where the cumulative experience of judges has led to a restatement in wide general terms of characteristics of conduct and relationships which give rise to legal liability.

Inherent in this methodology, however, is a practical limitation which is imposed by the sheer volume of reported cases. The initial selection of previous cases to be analysed will itself eliminate from the analysis those in which the conduct or relationship involved possessed characteristics which are obviously absent in the case for decision. The proposition used in the deductive stage is not a true universal. It needs to be qualified so as to read: "In all cases where the conduct and relationship possess each of the characteristics A, B, C and D etc., *but do not possess any of the characteristics Z, Y or X etc., which were present in the cases eliminated from the analysis,* a duty of care arises." But this qualification, being irrelevant to the decision of the particular case, is generally left unexpressed.

This was the reason for the warning by Lord Atkin in *Donoghue* v. *Stevenson* itself when he said:

"... in the branch of the law which deals with civil wrongs, dependent in England at any rate entirely upon the application by the judges of general principles also formulated by judges, it is of particular importance to guard against the danger of stating propositions of law in wider terms than is necessary, lest essential factors be omitted in the wider survey and the inherent adaptability of English law be unduly restricted. For this reason it is very necessary in considering reported cases in the law of torts that the actual decision alone should carry authority, proper weight, of course, being given to the *dicta* of the judges."

The respondents' argument in the present appeal disregards this warning. It seeks to treat as a universal not the specific proposition of law in *Donoghue* v. *Stevenson* which was about a manufacturer's liability for damage caused by his dangerous products but the well-known aphorism used by Lord Atkin to describe a "general conception of relations giving rise to a duty of care":

"You must take reasonable care to avoid acts or omissions which you can reasonably foresee would be likely to injure your neighbour. Who, then, in law is my neighbour? The answer seems to be — persons who are so closely and directly affected by my act that I ought reasonably to have them in contemplation . . . when I am directing my mind to the acts or omissions which are called in question."

Used as a guide to characteristics which will be found to exist in conduct and relationships which give rise to a legal duty of care this aphorism marks a milestone in the modern development of the law of negligence. But misused as a universal it is manifestly false.

The branch of English law which deals with civil wrongs abounds with instances of acts and, more particularly, of omissions which give rise to no legal liability in the doer or omitter for loss or damage sustained by others as a consequence of the act or omission, however reasonably or probably that loss or damage might have been anticipated. The very parable of the good Samaritan which was evoked by Lord Atkin in *Donoghue* v. *Stevenson* illustrates, in the conduct of the priest and of the Levite who passed by on the other side, an omission which was likely to have as its reasonable and probable consequence damage to the health of the victim of the thieves, but for which the priest and Levite would have incurred no civil liability in English law. Examples could be multiplied. One may cause loss to a tradesman by withdrawing one's custom although the goods which he supplies are entirely satisfactory; one may damage one's neighbour's land by intercepting the flow of percolating water to it even though the interception is of no advantage to oneself; one need not warn him of a risk of physical danger to which he is about to expose himself unless there is some special relationship between one and him such as that of occupier of land and visitor; one may watch one's neighbour's goods being ruined by a thunderstorm although the slightest effort on one's part could protect them from the rain and one may do so with impunity unless there is some special relationship between one and him such as that of bailor and bailee.

In *Hedley Byrne & Co. Ltd.* v. *Heller & Partners Ltd.*, which marked a fresh development in the law of negligence, the conduct in question was careless words not careless deeds. Lord Atkin's aphorism, if it were of universal application, would have sufficed to dispose of this case, apart from the express disclaimer of liability. But your Lordships were unanimous in holding that the difference in the characteristics of the conduct in the two cases prevented the propositions of law in *Donoghue* v. *Stevenson* from being directly applicable. Your Lordships accordingly proceeded to analyse the previous decisions in which the conduct complained of had been careless words, from which you induced a proposition of law about liability for damage caused by careless words which differs from the proposition of law in *Donoghue* v. *Stevenson* about liability for damage caused by careless deeds.

In the present appeal, too, the conduct of the Home Office which is called in question differs from the kind of conduct discussed in *Donoghue* v. *Stevenson* in at least two special characteristics. First, the actual damage sustained by the respondents was the direct consequence of a tortious act done with conscious volition by a third party responsible in law for his own acts and this act was interposed between the act of the Home Office complained of and the sustention of damage by the respondents. Secondly, there are two separate "neighbour relationships" of the Home Office involved, a relationship with the respondents and a relationship with the third party. These are capable of giving rise to conflicting duties of care. This appeal, therefore, also raises the lawyer's question "Am I my brother's keeper"? A question which may also receive a restricted reply.

From the previous decisions of the English courts, in particular those in *Ellis* v. *Home Office* and *D'Arcy* v. *Prison Comrs,* which I accept as correct, it is possible to arrive by induction at an established proposition of law as respects one of those special-relations: *viz* A is responsible for damage caused to the person or property of B by the tortious act of C (a person responsible in law for his own acts) where the relationship between A and C has the characteristics: (1) that A has the legal right to detain C in penal custody and to control his acts while in custody; (2) that A is actually exercising his legal right of custody of C at the time of C's tortious act; and (3) that A if he had taken reasonable care in the exercise of his right of custody could have prevented C from doing the tortious act which caused damage to the person or property of B; and where also the relationship between A and B has the characteristics; (4) that at the time of C's tortious act A has the legal right to control the situation of B or his property as respects physical proximity to C; and (5) that A can reasonably foresee that B is likely to sustain damage to his person or property if A does not take reasonable care to prevent C from doing tortious acts of the kind which he did.

On the facts which your Lordships are required to assume for the purposes of the present appeal the relationship between the Home Office, A, and the borstal trainees, C, did possess characteristics (1) and (3) but did not possess characteristic (2); while the relationship between the Home Office, A, and the respondents, B, did possess characteristic (5) but did not possess characteristic (4). What your Lordships have to decide as respects each of the relationships is whether the missing characteristic is essential to the existence of the duty or whether the facts assumed for the purposes of this appeal disclose some other characteristic which if substituted for that which is missing would produce a new proposition of law which *ought* to be true.

As any proposition which relates to the duty of controlling another man to prevent his doing damage to a third deals with a category of civil wrongs of which the English courts have hitherto had little experience it would not be consistent with the methodology of the development of the law by judicial decision that any new proposition should be stated in wider terms than are necessary for the determination of the present appeal. Public policy may call for the immediate recognition of a new sub-category of relations which are the source of a duty of this nature additional to the sub-category described in the established proposition; but further experience of actual cases would be needed before the time became ripe for the coalescence of sub-categories into a broader category of relations giving rise to the duty, such as was effected with respect to the duty of care of a manufacturer of products in *Donoghue* v. *Stevenson.* Nevertheless, any new sub-category will form part of the English law of civil wrongs and must be consistent with its general principles. . . .

It is common knowledge, of which judicial notice may be taken, that borstal training often fails to achieve its purpose of reformation, and that trainees when they have ceased to be detained in custody revert to crime and commit tortious damage to the person and property of others. But so do criminals who have never been apprehended and criminals who have been released from custody on completion of their sentences or earlier pursuant to a statutory power to do so. The risk of sustaining damage from the tortious acts of criminals is shared by the public at large. It has never been recognised at common law as giving rise to any cause of action against anyone but the criminal himself. It would seem arbitrary and therefore unjust to single out for the special privilege of being able to recover compensation from the authorities responsible for the prevention of crime a person whose property was damaged by the tortious act of a criminal, merely because the damage to him happened to be caused by a criminal who had escaped from custody before completion of his sentence instead of by one who had been lawfully released or who had been put on probation or given a suspended sentence or who had never been previously apprehended at all. To give rise to a duty on the part of the custodian owed to a member of the public to take reasonable care to prevent a borstal trainee from escaping from his custody before completion of the trainee's sentence there should be some relationship between the custodian and the person to whom the duty is owed which exposes that person to a particular risk of damage in consequence of that escape which is different in its incidence from the general risk of damage from criminal acts of others which he shares with all members of the public.

What distinguishes a borstal trainee who has escaped from one who has been duly released from custody, is his liability to recapture, and the distinctive added risk which is a reasonably foreseeable consequence of a failure to exercise due care in preventing him from escaping is the likelihood that in order to elude pursuit immediately on the discovery of his absence the escaping trainee may steal or appropriate and damage property which is situated in the vicinity of the place of detention from which he has escaped.

So long as Parliament is content to leave the general risk of damage from criminal acts to lie where it falls without any remedy except against the criminal himself, the courts would be exceeding their limited function in developing the common law to meet changing conditions if they were to recognise a duty of care to prevent criminals escaping from penal custody owed to a wider category of members of the public than those whose property was exposed to an exceptional added risk by the adoption of a custodial system for young offenders which increased the likelihood of their escape unless due care was taken by those responsible for their custody.

I should therefore hold that any duty of a borstal officer to use reasonable care to prevent a borstal trainee from escaping from his custody was owed only to persons whom he could reasonably foresee had property situate in the vicinity of the place of detention of the detainee which the detainee was likely to steal or to appropriate and damage in the course of eluding immediate pursuit and recapture. Whether or not any person fell within this category would depend on the facts of the particular case including the previous criminal and escaping record of the individual trainee concerned and the nature of the place from which he escaped.

So to hold would be a rational extension of the relationship between the custodian and the person sustaining the damage which was accepted in *Ellis* v. *Home Office* and *D'Arcy* v. *Prison Comrs* as giving rise to a duty of care on the part of the custodian to exercise reasonable care in controlling his detainee. In those two cases the custodian had a legal right to control the physical proximity of the person or property sustaining the damage to the detainee who caused it.

The extended relationship substitutes for the right to control the knowledge which the custodian possessed or ought to have possessed that physical proximity in fact existed.

In the present appeal the place from which the trainees escaped was an island from which the only means of escape would presumably be a boat accessible from the shore of the island. There is thus material, fit for consideration at the trial, for holding that the respondents, as the owners of a boat moored off the island, fell within the category of persons to whom a duty of care to prevent the escape of the trainees was owed by the officers responsible for their custody.

If therefore it can be established at the trial of this action: (1) that the borstal officers in failing to take precautions to prevent the trainees from escaping were acting in breach of their instructions and not in bona fide exercise of a discretion delegated to them by the Home Office as to the degree of control to be adopted: and (2) that it was reasonably foreseeable by the officers that if these particular trainees did escape they would be likely to appropriate a boat moored in the vicinity of Brownsea Island for the purpose of eluding immediate pursuit and to cause damage to it, the borstal officers would be in breach of a duty of care owed to the respondents and the respondents would, in my view, have a cause of action against the Home Office as vicariously liable for the 'negligence' of the borstal officers.

I would accordingly dismiss the appeal on the preliminary issue of law and allow the case to go for trial on those issues of fact.

Appeal dismissed.

[Lords Morris of Borth-y-Gest and Pearson wrote concurring opinions.]

NOTES

1. For a fine discussion of this case, see Weinrib, "The Dorset Yacht Case: Causation, Care and Criminals" (1971), 4 Ottawa L. Rev. 389.

2. A youth was involved in an automobile accident in a stolen vehicle the day after his escape from custody. No liability was found against the juvenile authorities, the police who gave chase, nor against the owner of the vehicle. See *O'Reilly* v. *C.*, [1979] 3 W.W.R. 124 (Man. C.A.). What if the accident occurred shortly after the escape in the vicinity of the custodial institution?

3. On the question of duty, Lord Wilberforce, in *Anns* v. *Merton London Borough Council*, [1977] 2 W.L.R. 1024 had this to say:

"Through the trilogy of cases in this House—*Donoghue* v. *Stevenson*, [1932] A.C. 562, *Hedley Byrne & Co. Ltd.* v. *Heller & Partners Ltd.*, [1964] A.C. 465, [1963] 2 All E.R. 575, and *Dorset Yacht Co. Ltd.* v. *Home Office*, [1970] A.C. 1004, [1970] 2 All E.R. 294, the position has now been reached that in order to establish that a duty of care arises in a particular situation, it is not necessary to bring the facts of that situation within those of previous situations in which a duty of care has been held to exist. Rather the question has to be approached in two stages. First one has to ask whether, as between the alleged wrongdoer and the person who has suffered damage there is a sufficient relationship of proximity or neighbourhood such that, in the reasonable contemplation of the former, carelessness on his part may be likely to cause damage to the latter—in which case a prima facie duty of care arises. Secondly, if the first question is answered affirmatively, it is necessary to consider whether there are any considerations which ought to negative, or to reduce or limit the scope of the duty or the class of person to whom it is owed or the damages to which a breach of it may give rise: . . . ."

See also *Batty* v. *Metropolitan Property Realizations*, [1978] 2 W.L.R. 500 (C.A.); *Barratt* v. *North Vancouver* (1978), 5 C.C.L.T. 303 (B.C.C.A.), municipality not liable for potholes since discretionary.

4. In *Dutton* v. *Bognor Regis Building Co.*, [1972] 1 All E.R. 462 (C.A.), the plaintiff's house that was built on an old rubbish tip was damaged when it subsided, as a result *inter alia* of the failure of the council's inspector to discover the danger. One of the problems to be dealt with was whether the council owed a duty to warn the plaintiff. [Another part of this case is excerpted below.]

Lord Denning M.R.: . . . 10. *Policy*

This case is entirely novel. Never before has a claim been made against a council or its surveyor for negligence in passing a house. The case itself can be brought within the words of Lord Atkin in *Donoghue* v. *Stevenson*; but, it is a question whether we should apply them here. In *Home Office* v. *Dorset Yacht Co. Ltd.* Lord Reid said that the words of Lord Atkin expressed a principle which ought to apply in general "unless there is some justification or valid explanation for its exclusion". So did Lord Pearson. But Lord Diplock spoke differently. He said that it was a guide but not a principle of universal application. It seems to me that it is a question of policy which we, as judges, have to decide. The time has come when, in cases of new import, we should decide them according to the reason of the thing.

In previous times, when faced with a new problem, the judges have not openly asked themselves the question: what is the best policy for the law to adopt? But the question has always been there in the background. It has been concealed behind such questions as: Was the defendant under any duty to the plaintiff? Was the relationship between them sufficiently proximate? Was the injury direct or indirect? Was it foreseeable, or not? Was it too remote? And so forth.

Nowadays we direct ourselves to considerations of policy. In *Rondel* v. *Worsley* we thought that, if advocates were liable to be sued for negligence, they would be hampered in carrying out their duties. In *Home Office* v. *Dorset Yacht Co. Ltd.* we thought that the Home Office ought to pay for damage done by escaping borstal boys, if the staff was negligent, but we confined it to damage done in the immediate vicinity. In *SCM (United Kingdom) Ltd.* v. *W. J. Whittall & Son Ltd.* some of us thought that economic loss ought not to be put on one pair of shoulders, but spread amongst all the sufferers. In *Launchbury* v. *Morgans* we thought that, as the owner of the family car was insured, she should bear the loss. In short, we look at the relationship of the parties; and then say, as a matter of policy, on whom the loss should fall. What are the considerations of policy here? I will take them in order.

First, Mrs Dutton has suffered a grievous loss. The house fell down without any fault of hers. She is in no position herself to bear the loss. Who ought in justice to bear it? I should think those who were responsible. Who are they? In the first place, the builder was responsible. It was he who laid the foundations so badly that the house fell down. In the second place, the council's inspector was responsible. It was his job to examine the foundations to see if they would take the load of the house. He failed to do it properly. In the third place, the council should answer for his failure. They were entrusted by Parliament with the task of seeing that houses were properly built. They received public funds for the purpose. The very object was to protect purchasers and occupiers of houses. Yet, they failed to protect them. Their shoulders are broad enough to bear the loss.

Next I ask: is there any reason in point of law why the council should not be held liable? Hitherto many lawyers have thought that a builder (who was also the owner) was not liable. If that were truly the law, I would not have thought it fair to make the council liable when the builder was not liable. But I hold that the builder who builds a house badly is liable, even though he is himself the owner. On this footing, there is nothing unfair in holding the council's surveyor also liable.

Then, I ask: if liability were imposed on the council, would it have an adverse effect on the work? Would it mean that the council would not inspect at all, rather than risk liability for inspecting badly? Would it mean that inspectors would be harassed in their work or be subject to baseless charges? Would it mean that they would be extra cautious, and hold up work unnecessarily? Such considerations have influenced cases in the past (as in *Rondel* v. *Worlsey*). But here I see no danger. If liability is imposed on the council, it would tend, I think, to make them do their work better, rather than worse.

Next, I ask: is there any economic reason why liability should not be imposed on the council? In some cases the law has drawn the line to prevent recovery of damages. It sets a limit to damages for economic loss, or for shock, or theft by escaping convicts. The reason is that, if no limit were set, there would be no end to the money payable. But I see no such reason here for limiting damages. In nearly every case the builder will be primarily liable. He will be insured and his insurance company will pay the damages. It will be very rarely that the council will be sued or found liable. If it is, much the greater responsibility will fall on the builder and little on the council.

Finally, I ask myself: if we permit this new action, are we opening the door too much? Will it lead to a flood of cases which the council will not be able to handle, nor the courts? Such considerations have sometimes in the past led the courts to reject novel claims. But I see no need to reject this claim on this ground. The injured person will always have his claim against the builder. He will rarely allege — and still less be able to prove — a case against the council.

All these considerations lead me to the conclusion that the policy of the law should be, and is, that the council should be liable for the negligence of their surveyor in passing work as good when in truth it is bad. I would therefore dismiss this appeal.

5. The British Courts have granted an immunity from tort liability to advocates during the conduct of litigation. See *Rondel* v. *Worsley,* [1969] A.C. 191 (H.L.); Catzman, Comment (1968), 46 Can. Bar Rev. 505. This immunity which relies on barristers acting "honourably in accordance with the recognized standards of their profession" (see Lord Reid), is not a blanket protection against all the errors that an advocate may make. It will not apply to errors while giving advice or while drafting documents, etc. Nor will it excuse a barrister from liability for failing to sue a particular defendant. See *Saif Ali* v. *Sydney Mitchell & Co.,* [1978] 3 All E.R. 1033 (H.L.); Catzman, Comment (1979), 57 Can. Bar Rev. 339. The policy grounds upon which the House of Lords relied in supporting the immunity were:

"first, the proper administration of justice demands that lawyers carry out their duties fearlessly; second, justice would not be served if it were necessary to retry law suits in order to evaluate the conduct of the counsel; and third, it is unfair to make a barrister civilly responsible when he cannot refuse to accept a brief."

6. The British rule was resoundingly rejected by Krever J. in *Demarco* v. *Ungaro et al.* (1979), 21 O.R. (2d) 673. The defendants, who were lawyers, brought a motion to strike out a statement of claim alleging negligence against them for losing a case on the ground that they failed to call certain evidence that they should have called. In a learned judgment dismissing the motion, Mr. Justice Krever held that the immunity afforded a British lawyer has no place in Ontario. He explained:

"I have come to the conclusion that the public interest . . . in Ontario does not require that our Courts recognize an immunity of a lawyer from action for negligence at the suit of his or her former client by reason of the conduct of a civil case in Court. It has not been, is not now, and should not be, public policy in Ontario to confer exclusively on lawyers engaged in Court work an immunity possessed by no other professional person. Public policy and the public interest do not exist in a vacuum. They must be examined against the background of a host of sociological facts of the society concerned. Nor are they lawyers' values as opposed to the values shared by the rest of the community. In the light of recent developments in the law of professional negligence and the rising incidence of 'malpractice' actions against physicians (and especially surgeons who may be thought to be to physicians what barristers are to solicitors), I do not believe that enlightened, non-legally trained members of the community would agree with me if I were to hold that the public interest requires that litigation lawyers be immune from actions for negligence. I emphasize again that I am not concerned with the question whether the conduct complained about amounts to negligence. Indeed, I find it difficult to believe that a decision made by a lawyer in the conduct of a case will be held to be negligence as opposed to a mere error of judgment. But there may be cases in which the error is so egregious that a court will conclude that it is negligence. The only issue I am addressing is whether the client is entitled to ask a Court to rule upon the matter.

Many of the sociological facts that are related to public policy and the public interest may be judicially noticed. The population of Ontario is approximately eight and a quarter million people. In 1978 there were approximately 12,300 lawyers licensed by the Law Society of Upper Canada to practise law in Ontario. All of them have a right of audience in any Court in Ontario as well as in the Federal Court of Canada and the Supreme Court of Canada. The vast majority of these lawyers are in private practice and, as such, are required to carry liability insurance in respect of negligence in the conduct of their clients' affairs. No distinction is made in this respect between those exclusively engaged in litigation and all other lawyers. The current rate of increase in the size of the profession is approximately 1,000 lawyers annually. It is widely recognized that a graduating class of that size places such an enormous strain on the resources of the profession that the articling experience of students-at-law is extremely variable. Only a small percentage of lawyers newly called to the Bar can be expected to have had the advantage of working with or observing experienced and competent counsel. Yet very many of those recently qualified lawyers will be appearing in Court on behalf of clients. To deprive these clients of recourse if their cases are negligently dealt with will not, to most residents of this Province, appear to be consistent with the public interest.

It is with a great sense of deference that I offer a few brief remarks on the grounds and consideration which formed the basis of the public policy as expressed by the House of Lords in *Rondel* v. *Worsley*. I am only concerned with the applicability of those considerations to Ontario conditions and have no hesitation in accepting them as entirely valid for England. With respect to the duty of counsel to the Court and the risk that, in the absence of immunity, counsel will be tempted to prefer the interest of the client to the duty to the Court and will thereby prolong trials, it is my respectful view that there is no empirical evidence that the risk is so serious that an aggrieved client should be rendered remediless. Between the dates of the decisions in *Leslie* v. *Ball*, 1863, and *Rondel* v. *Worsley*, 1967, immunity of counsel was not recognized in Ontario and negligence actions against lawyers respecting their conduct of Court cases did not attain serious proportions. Indeed, apart from the cases I have cited I know of no case in which a lawyer was sued for negligence by his or her client in the conduct of a case in Court. A very similar argument is advanced in many discussions of the law of professional negligence as it applies to surgeons. Surgeons, it is claimed, are deterred from using their best judgment out of fear that the consequence will be an action by the patient in the event of an unfavourable result. This claim has not given rise to an immunity for surgeons. As to the second ground—the prospect of relitigating an issue already tried, it is my view that the undesirability of that event does not justify the recognition of lawyers' immunity in Ontario. It is not a contingency that does not already exist in our law and seems to me to be inherently involved in the concept of *res judicata* in the recognition that a party, in an action *in personam,* is only precluded from relitigating the same matter against a person who was a party to the earlier action. I can find no fault with the way in which Hagarty, C.J., dealt with this consideration in *Wade* v. *Ball et. al.* (1870), 20 U.C.C.P. 302 at p. 304: 'Practically, such a suit as the present may involve the trying over again of *Wade* v. *Hoyt*. This cannot be avoided.' Better that than that the client should be without recourse.

The third consideration related to the obligation of a lawyer to accept any client. Whether that has ever been the universally accepted understanding of a lawyer's duty in Ontario is doubtful. In any event, I do not believe such a duty exists in the practice of civil litigation and that is the kind of litigation with which I am now concerned."

What do you think of this decision? Are you, as a future lawyer, afraid? Can anything be said in favour of the retention of the advocate's immunity? See Laskin, *The British Tradition in Canadian Law* (1969), p. 26; Linden, *Canadian Tort Law* (2nd ed., 1977), p. 111; Hutchinson, Comment (1979), 57 Can. Bar Rev. 346.

7. There are several other situations where the duty technique has been utilized to limit liability for negligent conduct. These will be dealt with in Chapter 9, Remoteness and Proximate Cause.

JOSEPH C. SMITH, THE MYSTERY OF DUTY

in Klar (ed.), *Studies in Canadian Tort Law* (1977)

I Introduction

Lawyers, judges and academics generally take one of two approaches to the concept of duty of care in the law of negligence. There are those whom I would call "the true believers". They take the concept seriously. This is to say that they believe that the concept of duty of care is a meaningful doctrine of the law of negligence. It has three aspects: foreseeability, limitation in regard to the scope of the law of negligence, and limitation to the scope of recovery. Somehow these three are aspects of one unity—duty of care. Like the mystery of the Holy Trinity, three in one, yet not one but three. This is a confused position which leads to ambiguity in the law.

Then there are those whom I would term "the sceptics". For them, duty of care is so much jargon which can cover a variety of different policy issues and is resorted to by judges when they are unable to clearly articulate the policies at stake or the reasons for taking one alternative rather than another in decision-making. This approach leads to uncertainty in the law, and prediction of decisions becomes impossible. Some sceptics such as Lord Denning recommend banishing the term altogether from the language of negligence. In dealing with the difficult question of recovery for economic loss he writes:

> "The more I think about these cases, the more difficult I find it to put each into its proper pigeon-hole. Sometimes I say: 'There was no duty.' In others I say: 'The damage was too remote.' So much so that I think the time has come to discard those tests which have proved so elusive. It seems to me better to consider the particular relationship in hand, and see whether or not, as a matter of policy, economic loss should be recoverable, or not."

As much as this might be desirable, I doubt that it will happen within the near future as the term and concept are too firmly entrenched in the jurisprudence of this subject. We may at least, however, be able to dispel the mystery with careful analysis.

There are certain ideas or notions which are basic to the concept of negligence, whether within or without the law. We say of a person that he is negligent when he acts without due care and attention in regard to harmful consequences of his actions. The concept of negligence thus assumes the notion of risk, and the notion of risk entails the idea of foreseeable harm. When we say that a person has been negligent we are passing a normative judgment on or about him. We are saying that he acted in a way that he ought not to have acted. This assumes that we know how he ought to have acted. The way in which we consider that he ought to have acted is the norm or standard which entitles us to condemn him for being negligent when he fails to comply with it. When a person complies with the norm or standard of care expected of him, he cannot be judged to be at fault or found to be negligent.

Where a person's actions do not comply with the standard of care expected of him and injury to others results, we say of the person at fault that he 'caused' the damage. When a person causes injury to someone else through the doing of an act which he ought not to have done, we consider him to blame or responsible for the damage. This responsibility is the basis or justification for the law requiring the person at fault to compensate the other party for his loss.

There are also certain steps which must be taken before we can reach the conclusion that a person has been negligent, and decide what legal consequences ought therefore to result. To begin with, a decision must be made as to whether the law of negligence even covers or applies to a particular kind of situation. It must then be ascertained whether the defendant has created a risk of harm which would be recognized as negligence in the legal sense. Next, it must be determined whether or not the negligence was the cause of the loss. Finally, it must be decided whether the particular kind of loss suffered is recoverable under the law, and if so, how that loss is to be measured in monetary terms. Each of these steps raises particular kinds of legal problems, and most are closely interrelated with the basic ideas or notions which are a constitutive part of the concept of negligence.

I have identified above certain ideas or notions, such as 'risk', 'foreseeability', 'standard of care', 'causation' and 'responsibility', which are entailed in, are a constitutive part of, or are related to the concept of negligence. I have also enumerated a number of steps which must be followed before it can be decided that a particular person is liable in the law of negligence to pay another person a specified amount in damages. Is the concept of 'duty' equivalent to any of these ideas or notions? If not, is it an independent idea or concept in its own right which is entailed in or related to the concept of negligence? If so, how is it to be explained? Does it refer to a particular step in an action of negligence? If so, which one?

The fact that an answer to these questions is not obvious indicates that the concept of 'duty of care' is confusing and ambiguous. It is so because it is not entailed by or assumed in the concept of negligence, nor does it refer to a particular step in reaching a conclusion as to whether a person has been negligent and what his liability will be. Rather, it is often used as equivalent to a number of the notions or ideas related to the concept of negligence, and as well, is used to refer to several of the different steps in a negligence action.

If the confusion stemming from the use of the ambiguous concept 'duty of care' is to be clarified and not perpetuated, the problem must be tackled in terms of categories and concepts which are independent of duty language. . . .

I am not necessarily advocating that lawyers argue cases without resort to duty language. If a judge wants to know whether or not the defendant owed the plaintiff a duty of care, then counsel must be prepared to argue the case in those terms; but at least we need not be prisoners of our own concepts. If we are able to pierce the mystery of duty of care and have our own analogies and understanding of the problems at issue, we can use the right cases and make the right policy arguments, dressing them in duty language if needs be. . . .

III The Ambiguity of the Duty Concept

There are at least four different kinds of questions which can be isolated in terms of the analysis of an action in negligence set out in the previous section, each of which can be, and often is, phrased in terms of duty of care language. One kind of question raises issues of extension of the limits to the law of negligence. Another raises the issue of the presence of a foreseeable risk of harm. A third raises the issue of what standard of care ought to be taken in regard to the risk, and a fourth raises the issue of remoteness.

When issues in the law of negligence are framed in duty of care language, problems of extension, foreseeability of harm, standard of care, and remoteness become muddled. The failure to distinguish the basic kinds of problems leads to the use of tests and policy considerations which are not appropriate to the real issue before the court. Thus, considerations relevant only to problems of risk are used to solve remoteness issues, and problems of remoteness are dealt with in terms of policies and considerations relevant only to questions of extension. Much of the conceptual confusion in the law of negligence can be traced to this failure to distinguish between these various basic problems. Once these questions are separated, an examination of the relevant policies can then be made.

The reason that duty of care language has been used to refer to at least four different kinds of problems (with the result that we fail to distinguish between them) lies, I think, in the distinction which the common law historically made between questions of fact and questions of law. Under the traditional common law theory regarding the distinction between the role of the judge and that of the jury, questions of law were to be decided by the judge and questions of fact by the jury. If, however, the judge wished to take from or keep a case from being put to the jury, he could do so by framing the issue in terms of a question of law which was then conceived to be only appropriate for the judge to decide. This way of conceiving of legal problems has remained, although for all practical purposes the jury system has nearly ceased to exist as far as civil actions are concerned. This historical pattern, plus the fact that psychologically a question of law appears to be susceptible of a more decisive and certain answer than does a question of fact, has led the common law judge to express decisions wherever possible in terms of responses to issues of law rather than to issues of fact. The presence or absence of a duty of care has always been considered to be a matter of law, consequently, any issue which can be phrased as a matter of duty of care becomes a question of law.

a) DUTY LANGUAGE USED TO DEAL WITH ISSUES OF EXTENSION

There are . . . certain areas of human activity with which the courts will not interfere on grounds of public policy. That is, they will not impose any standard of care on a person in regard to a particular kind of activity or a particular kind of loss. Where the judge feels that no standard of care ought to be imposed on a particular kind of activity, the court will rule that, as a matter of law (and this is a true question of law and not of fact) no duty of care is owed by the defendant. Thus, duty of care language is used to deal with problems of extension, or the limits of the law of negligence.

For example, public bodies such as municipalities and public officials or employees were generally not held liable for damages caused by a failure to act. The English Court of Appeal radically departed from the old line of precedents in *Dutton* v. *Bognor Regis Urban District Council* when they held a municipal body liable for damages resulting from the failure of a municipal building inspector to inspect properly the foundations of a house. When the members of the Court raised and dealt with the issue of whether the municipality and the inspector owed a duty of care to a subsequent purchaser of a house, the Court was grappling with a problem of extension, and its finding that a duty exists means no more than that the law of negligence now extends to such bodies and persons in the sense that the law will impose a standard of care upon them not only in regard to risks arising from their actions, but for risks which they did not create, but failed to remove. A similar issue of extension was raised in *Home Office* v. *Dorset Yacht Co. Ltd.,* where the House of Lords ruled that the Home Office was liable for damage to a yacht caused by inmates of a borstal institution when supervision became lax. Lord Diplock first stated the issue in terms of duty of care language, then interpreted the question as a problem as to the perimeters or limits of the law of negligence.

> "The specific question of law raised in this appeal may therefore be stated as: Is any duty of care to prevent the escape of a Borstal trainee from custody owed by the Home Office to persons whose property would be likely to be damaged by the tortious acts of the Borstal trainee if he escaped?
>
> This is the first time that this specific question has been posed at a higher judicial level than that of a county court. Your Lordships in answering it will be performing a judicial function similar to that performed in *Donoghue* v. *Stevenson* [1932] A.C. 562 and more recently in *Hedley, Byrne & Co. Ltd.* v. *Heller & Partners Ltd.* [1964] A.C. 465 of deciding whether the English law of civil wrongs should be extended to impose legal liability to make reparation for the loss caused to another by conduct of a kind which has not hitherto been recognised by the courts as entailing any such liability.
>
> This function, which judges hesitate to acknowledge as law-making, plays at most a minor role in the decision of the great majority of cases, and little conscious thought has been given to analysing its methodology. Outstanding exceptions are to be found in the speeches of Lord Atkin in *Donoghue* v. *Stevenson* and of Lord Devlin in *Hedley, Byrne & Co. Ltd.* v. *Heller & Partners Ltd.* It was because the former was the first authoritative attempt at such an analysis that it has had so seminal an effect upon the modern development of the law of negligence.
>
> It will be apparent that I agree with the Master of the Rolls that what we are concerned with in this appeal 'is . . . at bottom a matter of public policy which we, as judges, must resolve.' . . ."

b) DUTY LANGUAGE USED TO DEAL WITH ISSUES OF RISK

Given that the case deals with conduct where the courts will impose a standard of care, the next question is whether or not a reasonable person would have foreseen a risk of harm. If the judge believes that he would not, he will often express this conclusion by saying that the defendant owes no duty of care to the plaintiff. This would be the case, not because the defendant's conduct was the kind where courts will not impose any standard of care, but because the court believes there was in fact no foreseeable risk of harm, he often expresses this by saying that the defendant owed the plaintiff a duty of care.

This use of duty language may be illustrated by the judgment of *Nova Mink Ltd.* v. *Trans-Canada Airlines* where the court held that a pilot was not negligent in causing female mink to eat their young as the result of the noise of the aircraft which he flew overhead, because he did not know and could not reasonably have foreseen that there were mink farms in the district. The issue of whether there was a foreseeable risk of harm was stated and answered in duty language. MacDonald J. first asks, "Does the evidence establish that the defendant was under a legal duty to use care to avoid injury to the plaintiff's business as a mink ranch operator?" He frames the test of the existence of a duty in the following words:

> "The common law yields the conclusion that there is such a duty only where the circumstances of time, place, and person would create in the mind of a reasonable man in those circumstances such a probability of harm

resulting to other persons as to require him to take care to avert that probable result."

He states further:

"Many attempts have been made to generalize the circumstances which create a legal duty of care . . . . What is common . . . is the idea of a *relationship between parties attended by a foreseeable risk of harm* . . . . That relationship may arise out of circumstances of physical proximity; but it is not that circumstances per se which gives rise to duty but the probability of harm inhering in the relationship of parties, spatial or otherwise. If such a relationship does exist in fact, or in contemplation, and is fraught with the likelihood of harm to another in that relationship, the basis of duty exists; and it is immaterial that the locus or date of the occurrence of the apprehended harm be unknown."

Lord Atkin's famous dictum in *Donoghue* v. *Stevenson* is the classic formulation of the risk issue in terms of duty language:

"At present I content myself with pointing out that in English law there must be, and is, some general conception of relations giving rise to a duty of care, of which particular cases found in the books are but instances . . . You must take reasonable care to avoid acts or omissions which you can reasonably foresee would be likely to injure your neighbour."

c) DUTY LANGUAGE USED TO DEAL WITH ISSUES OF STANDARD OF CARE

Even though there might be a reasonably foreseeable risk of harm, the judge may believe that on the facts the defendant did all that could reasonably be expected to prevent the harm. This conclusion is often expressed in the form of a ruling that the defendant did not have a duty to take the particular action which would have prevented the risk of harm from materializing. If, on the other hand, the court is of the opinion that it is reasonable to expect the defendant to guard against the risk the conclusion could be expressed as a finding that the defendant owed a duty of care.

Deyong v. *Shenburn* furnishes us with a paradigm case of this kind of usage. That case dealt with whether an employer was liable to an employee for the theft of some clothing due to the employer's failure to provide lockers. It is clear that theft of articles is a very foreseeable risk. It is equally clear that acts or failures to act which make theft possible can constitute negligence. The basic issue in these cases is whether a person can reasonably be expected to take whatever care is necessary to prevent the theft. This problem was discussed as follows by Du Parcq L.J.:

"It is not true to say that wherever a man finds himself in such a position that unless he does a certain act another person may suffer, or that if he does something another person will suffer, then it is his duty in the one case to be careful to do the act and in the other case to be careful not to do the act. Any such proposition is much too wide. One has to find that there has been a breach of a duty which the law recognises and to see what the law recognises one can only look at the decisions of the courts. There has never been a decision that a master must, merely because of the relationship which exists between a master and servant, take reasonable care for the safety of his servant's belongings in the sense that he must take steps to insure, so far as he can, that no wicked person shall have an opportunity of stealing the servant's goods. That duty is the duty which is contended for here, and there is not a shred of authority which suggests that any such duty exists or ever has existed. Probably the case in which one would have expected to find decisions on the point is that of the domestic servant and his or her master. Nobody has ever suggested, and in my opinion it is clearly not the law, that if the master of the house leaves the house unattended and empty, or if he forgets to shut a window at night or properly to secure it or if the locks on the door have ceased to be secure, by reason of which lack of care a housebreaker enters and steals, among other things, the goods of a domestic servant living in the house, then the master is liable to his servant for negligence. Certainly if one looks at the older cases . . . it is quite plain that in earlier days, at any rate, the courts would have thought such a claim to border on the ridiculous, and in my judgment the law on this particular matter is no different today."

Tucker L.J. dealt with the issue in a similar fashion, stating:

"This case raises a question as to whether the defendant was under any duty to the plaintiff to take reasonable steps to protect the property of the plaintiff from theft."

Or, in other words, ought the court to impose a sufficiently high standard of care on the defendant so as to require him to remove the risk?

d) DUTY LANGUAGE USED TO DEAL WITH ISSUES OF REMOTENESS

We judge a person negligent when, as a result of failing to take due care in his actions, he creates a foreseeable risk of harm. But as it is so often pointed out, negligence and risk are terms of relation. The relation is between an act or failure to act and its foreseeable consequences in terms of a particular kind of harm happening to particular persons. Often, however, other things happen than those which are entailed within the ambit of the risk. A different kind of harm may result. Thus A, by his action, creates a risk of harm x to B, but B may suffer harm y as well as, or in place of harm x. Or harm may result to someone other than, or as well as, the person who is the subject of the risk; as well as, or instead of B, C may suffer either harm x or harm y. The courts will not always give full damages for all injuries or losses resulting from the acts of a negligent person as obvious policy reasons dictate that there must be some limits placed on a person's legal liability. Where a judge feels that a particular loss falls outside these limits he can express this conclusion by holding that the defendant did not owe a duty of care in regard to the particular kind of harm or to the particular person where he considers that either the harm or the person who suffers it, or both, fall outside the limits which must be placed on the defendant's legal liability. Duty language in such instances is thus used to deal with problems of remoteness.

The so-called foreseeability test of remoteness furnishes us with a classic example of the confusion which can arise from multiple uses of 'duty' language. The issue of whether a particular injury to a particular person is too remote is stated in terms of whether or not the defendant owed a duty of care to that person in regard to the particular loss. The judge or court then surreptitiously shifts to a usage of the term duty appropriate for the issue of the presence of a reasonably foreseeable risk of harm. The test of foreseeability of harm, appropriate for dealing with an issue of risk, is then introduced as a test of remoteness.

This pattern appears in several of the judgments of members of the House of Lords in *Bourhill* v. *Young.* In that case a cyclist, through his negligence, caused an accident which resulted in nervous shock to the plaintiff. There was no question of the defendant's negligence; consequently, no issue in regard to standard of care arose. The Court clearly saw the issue as one of remoteness and dealt with it in terms of duty language.

Each member of the Court discussed the question of the limits of liability for damages resulting from the defendant's negligence (this is what is at stake in a

true remoteness issue) in terms of a duty of care in the sense of the creation of a
risk of harm. Lord Porter, for example, states:

> "In the case of a civil action there is no such thing as negligence in the
> abstract. There must be neglect of the use of care towards a person towards
> whom the defendant owes the duty of observing care, and I am content to
> take the statement of Lord Atkin in *Donoghue* v. *Stevenson* as indicating the
> extent of the duty."

He then quotes the passage from Lord Atkin's judgment which I have quoted in
b) above and applies that definition of duty in terms of risk to the problem of
remoteness, explaining:

> "Is the result of this view that all persons in or near the street down which
> the negligent driver is progressing are potential victims of his negligence?
> Though from their position it is quite impossible that any injury should
> happen to them and though they have no relatives or even friends who might
> be endangered, is a duty of care to them owed and broken because they
> might have been but were not in a spot exposed to the errant driving of the
> peccant car? I cannot think so. The duty is not to the world at large. It must
> be tested by asking with reference to each several complainant: Was a duty
> owed to him or her? If no one of them was in such a position that direct
> physical injury could reasonably be anticipated to them or their relations or
> friends normally I think no duty would be owed, and if, in addition, no shock
> was reasonably to be anticipated to them as a result of the defender's
> negligence, the defender might, indeed, be guilty of actionable negligence to
> others but not of negligence towards them."

. . .

VII Conclusion

I doubt whether, in the foreseeable future, the legal profession will give up
the use of duty language in negligence cases. Judges like to use it because with it
they can turn a factual question or a difficult policy problem into the legal issue,
"Did the defendant owe the plaintiff a duty of care?" Such a question can be
answered with a decisive "Yes!" or "No!", and the conclusion, whatever it is, has
the appearance of being reached by an inevitable pattern of legal logic. Even
though a judge may realize that it is circular reasoning to conclude that there is
no liability because the defendant did not owe the plaintiff a duty of care, or
that there is because he does, it is easier for the judge to sneak in his conclusion
in the disguise of a premise about the existence of a duty, than to attempt to
articulate some of the policy premises which were the actual bases of his decision.
Few judges dare be a Denning. In any case, the duty language is so ingrained in
the jurisprudence of negligence that it is unlikely that a precedent-oriented conservative profession such as ours will make such a change lightly. And as long as
the judge asks counsel, "Did the defendant owe the plaintiff a duty of care?",
then the lawyer must be prepared to deal with the case in that manner. In consequence, those who teach torts to the budding lawyer must equip him to deal
with a problem in duty language.

The issue, as I see it, is not whether or not we continue to use duty language,
but whether we are to be masters of the language or be caught up in the morass.

The purpose of this analysis is to enable one to recognize the separate fundamental steps or problems in a negligence action and the basic policies which are
at stake in each, and to deal with them clearly. Then it doesn't matter whether
or not the conclusion is stated in terms of the existence of a duty of care. Presumably both judge and counsel can better serve justice and the ends of the law
if they recognize the basic issues and can muster the right precedents and policies.
Surely a lawyer will be more effective if he is able to distinguish among questions

about the perimeters of the law of negligence, questions of risk of harm, questions of standard of care, and questions about remoteness. A judge has to be more competent or proficient if he focuses his attention on the policy which leads the law to favour recovery for rescuers than he does if he is trying to decide whether or not the rescuer is foreseeable.

Judges and practitioners who function within the law of negligence are continually going to be faced with shocked mothers, prenatally injured infants, explosions, cricket balls hitting heads, snails in bottles, toes in chewing tobacco, weird chains of events, and simple crushing, breaking, burning and cutting of the human body. A decision must be reached and given as to whether a loss will be shifted from the person suffering the loss to the actor who may have caused it. That decision must be justified in terms of 'the Law'. If that justification is to be meaningful and not mere empty words we must at least have a theory about "duty of care". The above is offered for that purpose.

Since it is unlikely that either judge or academic will exorcize the "spirit" or "ghost" of duty from the law, we must be satisfied with attempting to banish the mystery surrounding the concept and the way it functions in the law.

NOTES

1. See also J.C. Smith, "Clarification of Duty-Remoteness Problems Through a New Physiology of Negligence: Economic Loss, A Test Case" (1974), 9 U.B.C. L. Rev. 213.

B. THE UNFORESEEABLE PLAINTIFF

HAY (or BOURHILL) v. YOUNG

House of Lords. [1943] A.C. 92; [1942] 2 All E.R. 396; 167 L.T. 261

Plaintiff had alighted from a bus and was engaged in removing her fish-basket from the driver's platform, when a speeding motor-cyclist passed on the other side of the bus and collided with a motor-car at an intersection forty-five to fifty feet ahead of the bus. The plaintiff heard a crash and said she "just got in a pack of nerves". She saw and heard nothing until the noise of the impact. Later, after the cyclist's dead body had been removed, plaintiff saw the blood left in the roadway. As a result of the shock, the plaintiff claimed to have sustained a wrenched back and about a month later her child was still-born, which she attributed to shock and reaction to the event. Plaintiff sued the cyclist's executor. A judgment for defendant was affirmed by the Second Division of the Court of Session. Plaintiff appealed to the House of Lords.

Lord Wright: . . . [The] general concept of reasonable foresight as the criterion of negligence or breach of duty (strict or otherwise) may be criticized as too vague, but negligence is a fluid principle, which has to be applied to the most diverse conditions and problems of human life. It is a concrete, not an abstract, idea. It has to be fitted to the facts of the particular case. Willes J. defined it as absence of care according to the circumstances . . . It is also always relative to the individual affected. This raises a serious additional difficulty in the cases where it has to be determined, not merely whether the act itself is negligent against someone, but whether it is negligent *vis-a-vis* the plaintiff. This is a crucial point in cases of nervous shock. Thus, in the present case John Young was certainly negligent in an issue between himself and the owner of the car which he ran into, but it is another question whether he was negligent *vis-a-vis* the appellant. In such cases terms like "derivative" and "original" and "primary" and "secondary" have been applied to define and distinguish the type of the negligence. If, however, the appellant has a cause of action it is because of a wrong to herself. She cannot build on a wrong to someone else. Her interest, which was in her own bodily security, was of a different order from the interest of the owner of the car . . . .

The present case, like many others of this type, may, however, raise the different question whether the appellant's illness was not due to her peculiar susceptibility. She was eight months gone in pregnancy. Can it be said, apart from everything else, that it was likely that a person of normal nervous strength would have been affected in the circumstances by illness as the appellant was? Does the criterion of reasonable foresight extend beyond people of ordinary health or susceptibilities, or does it take into account the peculiar susceptibilities or infirmities of those affected which the defendant neither knew of nor could reasonably be taken to have foreseen? Must the manner of conduct adapt itself to such special individual peculiarities? If extreme cases are taken, the answer appears to be fairly clear, unless, indeed, there is knowledge of the extraordinary risk. One who suffers from the terrible tendency to bleed on slight contact, which is denoted by the term "a bleeder", cannot complain if he mixes with the crowd and suffers severely, perhaps fatally, from being merely brushed against. There is no wrong done there. A blind or deaf man who crosses the traffic on a busy street cannot complain if he is run over by a careful driver who does not know of and could not be expected to observe and guard against the man's infirmity. These questions go to "culpability, not compensation", as BANKES, L.J., said in the *Polemis* case. No doubt, it has long ago been stated and often restated that if the wrong is established the wrongdoer must take the victim as he finds him. That, however, is only true, as the *Polemis* case shows, on the condition that the wrong has been established or admitted. The question of liability is anterior to the question of the measure of the consequences which go with the liability. That was the second point, decided not for the first time, but merely reiterated in the *Polemis* case. It must be understood to be limited, however, to "direct" consequences to the particular interest of the plaintiff which is affected . . .

What is now being considered is the question of liability, and this, I think, in a question whether there is duty owing to members of the public who come within the ambit of the act, must generally depend on a normal standard of susceptibility. This, it may be said, is somewhat vague. That is true, but definition involves limitation which it is desirable to avoid further than is necessary in a principle of law like negligence which is widely ranging and is still in the stage of development. It is here, as elsewhere, a question of what the hypothetical reasonable man, viewing the position, I suppose *ex post facto*, would say it was proper to foresee. What danger of particular infirmity that would include must depend on all the circumstances, but generally, I think, a reasonably normal condition, if medical evidence is capable of defining it, would be the standard. The test of the plaintiff's extraordinary susceptibility, if unknown to the defendant, would in effect make him an insurer. The lawyer likes to draw fixed and definite lines and is apt to ask where the thing is to stop. I should reply it should stop where in the particular case the good sense of the jury or of the judge decides. I should myself be disposed, as at present advised, to say that it should have stopped short of judgment for the plaintiff in *Owens* v. *Liverpool Corporation*. The particular susceptibility there was to my mind beyond any range of normal expectancy or of reasonable foresight. . .

I cannot accept that John Young could reasonably have foreseen, or, more correctly, the reasonable hypothetical observer could reasonably have foreseen, the likelihood that anyone placed as the appellant was, could be affected in the manner in which she was. In my opinion, John Young was guilty of no breach of duty to the appellant, and was not in law responsible for the hurt she sustained. I may add that the issue of duty or no duty is, indeed, a question for the court, but it depends on the view taken of the facts. In the present case both courts below have taken the view that the appellant has, on the facts of the case, no redress, and I agree with their view.

[Lord Porter, during the course of his judgment stated that, "In the case of a civil action there is no such thing as negligence in the abstract. There must be neglect of the use of care towards a person towards whom the defendant owes the duty of observing care. The duty is not to the world at large. It must be tested by asking with reference to each several complainant: was a duty owed to him or her? If no one of them was in such a position that physical injury could reasonably be anticipated to them or their relations or friends normally I think no duty would be owed. . . ." Lord Macmillan agreed that the defendant was under "no duty to foresee that his negligence in driving at an excessive speed and consequently colliding with a motor-car might result in injury to her, for such a result could not reasonably and probably be anticipated."

Lords Thankerton and Russell wrote concurring opinions.]

NOTES

1. See *Palsgraf* v. *Long Island Railroad Co.* (1928), 162 N.E. 99, *infra.* The defendant's guard, in trying to assist a man who was rushing for a departing train, pushed him, thereby knocking from his arms a package of fireworks. Somehow an explosion ensued, which knocked over a scale, which in turn hit the woman plaintiff who was standing some distance away. She was denied recovery on the ground that she was beyond the range of foreseeable danger. Mr. Justice Cardozo rationalized the position as follows:

"The conduct of the defendant's guard, if a wrong in its relation to the holder of the package, was not a wrong in its relation to the plaintiff standing far away. Relatively to her it was not negligence at all . . . . If no hazard was apparent to the eye of ordinary vigilance, an act innocent and harmless, at least to outward seeming, with reference toward her, did not take to itself the quality of a tort because it happened to be a wrong, though apparently not one involving the risk of bodily insecurity, with reference to someone else. 'In every instance before negligence can be predicated of a given act, back of the act must be sought and found a duty to the individual complaining' . . . . The plaintiff sues in her own right for a wrong personal to her, and not as the vicarious beneficiary of a breach of duty to another . . . ."

Mr. Justice Andrews, who spoke for the dissenting minority, rejected this view and argued:

"Every one owes to the world at large a duty of refraining from those acts which unreasonably threaten the safety of others. Such an act occurs. Not only is he wronged to whom harm might reasonably be expected to result, but he also who is in fact injured, even if he be outside . . . the danger zone. There needs to be duty due the one complaining but this is not a duty to a particular individual because as to him harm might be expected."

See Prosser, "Palsgraf Revisited" (1952), 52 Mich. L. Rev. 1.

2. Why should negligence not be transferred like intent is transferred?

3. In *Farrugia* v. *Gt. Western R.,* [1947] 2 All E.R. 565, the defendant had loaded a lorry so high that in passing an overhead bridge a container was knocked off and fell on plaintiff. Plaintiff, shortly before the accident, had been on the lorry as a trespasser and at the time of injury he was running slightly behind the lorry preparatory to stealing a second ride. It was argued that as defendant's driver had no reason to foresee or expect that plaintiff would be running behind the lorry attempting to get on it he could owe no duty toward him. For this reliance was placed on *Bourhill* v. *Young,* [1943]

A.C. 92. The Court of Appeal held that the duty was one "to anybody who happened to be at the crucial moment in the neighbourhood of this dangerous thing". Anyone in the area in which the container would fall was in the area of potential danger.

4. In *Law* v. *Visser,* [1961] Queensland R. 46, the defendant motorist driving at night at a fast rate of speed saw in the light of his headlights a large object which looked like an abandoned bundle or, possibly, an animal killed by a passing car. The defendant made no effort to avoid the object and ran over it. The object proved to be the plaintiff, asleep on the road in a drunken stupor. The court held the defendant liable. It was no excuse that he did not know the nature of the object. He took his chance that it might be more valuable than he thought, or even a human being.

DUVAL v. SEGUIN

Ontario Court of Appeal. [1972] 2 O.R. 689; affd. (1974), 1 O.R. (2d) 482

The plaintiff, Ann Duval, was *en ventre sa mère* at the time of an automobile accident. Thirty-one weeks had elapsed from the time of conception until the time of the accident. Some two or three weeks after the accident, Ann Duval was born prematurely, weighing 2 lbs. 14¼ oz. She was found to be physically disabled and mentally retarded as a result of the accident.

Fraser J. (at trial): The question of whether a person can recover damages for prenatal injuries has been much discussed but I was not referred to any authorities which are decisive in this jurisdiction. That being so it may be helpful to refer briefly to the legal position of unborn children in other jurisdictions and in other branches of the law. For some purposes the law has long recognized an unborn infant as a person.

Blackstone's Commentaries, 15th ed., vol. 1, p. 129, stated the relevant criminal law as follows:

> "Life is the immediate gift of God, a right inherent by nature in every individual; and it begins in contemplation of law as soon as an infant is able to stir in the mother's womb. For if a woman is quick with child, and, by a potion or otherwise, killeth it in her womb; or if any one beat her, whereby the child dieth in her body and she is delivered of a dead child; this, though not murder (7), was by the ancient law homicide or manslaughter. But the modern law doth look upon this offence in quite so atrocious a light (8), but merely as a heinous misdeameanor.
> (7) The distinction between murder and manslaughter or felonious homicide, in the time of Bracton, was in a great degree nominal. The punishment of both was the same; for murder as well as manslaughter, by the common law, had the benefit of clergy.
> (8) But if the child be born alive, and afterwards die in consequence of the potion or beating, it will be murder; and of course those who, with a wicked intent, administered the potion or advised the woman to take it, will be accessories before the fact, and subject to the same punishment as the principal."

This law was applied in *R.* v. *Senior* (1832), 1 Mood. 346, 168 E.R. 1298, a case in which a midwife by some gross negligence so injured a child before it was born it died shortly after. She was convicted of manslaughter. A child *en ventre sa mère* by a legal fiction was also deemed a person in being for certain purposes connected with property. This fiction was more commonly applicable when it was for the benefit of the infant. I refer to an article on "The Unborn Child" by P.H. Winfield, 4 U. of T.L.J. 278 (1942), reprinted 8 Camb. L.J. 76. In contract there seems to be no authority for contracting on behalf of an unborn child. The article by Winfield, referred to above, points out some of the obvious reasons that this is so.

By the civil law, generally speaking, a child *en ventre sa mère* was considered as alive when to do so was for its benefit. In *Montreal Tramways Co.* v. *Leveille*, [1933] S.C.R. 456, [1933] 4 D.L.R. 337, 41 C.R.C. 291, an appeal from Quebec and in which the civil law was therefore applicable, a child *en ventre sa mère* was injured by the fault of the defendant, respondent. Two months later the child was born with club feet which, in the facts, was held to be atrributable to injuries received in the accident and the defendant was held liable (Smith J. dissenting). I will be referring to this case again as it contains a very helpful discussion of the common law. In *Pinchin et al., N.O.* v. *Santam Ins. Co. Ltd.*, [1936] 2 S. Africa 254, the civil law was reviewed, including the *Leveille* case. After discussing the authorities, civilian, American and others, Hiemstra J. held that a child could recover damages for brain injury caused by the fault of the defendant while the plaintiff was *en ventre sa mère*.

[His Lordship then discussed the United States and Commonwealth authorities.]

The article of Professor Winfield, *supra*, reviewed the English and American case law and literature on this question up to 1942. He also commented on *Montreal Tramways* v. *Leveille*, pp. 287-9 inclusive. He concluded that the weight of American authority was against recovery in such cases and that no one knew what the English law was. He then suggested that he saw no good reason that an action should not lie for prenatal injury which resulted in post-natal harm and that it would be unjust to deny it.

To constitute the tort of negligence there must be a duty to take care owed by the defendant to the plaintiff, a breach of that duty and resulting damage to the plaintiff. *Winfield on Torts*, 8th. ed. (1967), pp. 42 *et seq.*, gives a convenient analysis of the elements of this tort. As already indicated *M'Alister (or Donoghue)* v. *Stevenson, supra*, and the cases following it make it clear that the resulting damage may be separated in time or place or both from the wrongful act or omission.

Distillers Co. (Biochemicals) Ltd. v. *Thompson*, [1971] 2 W.L.R. 441, is a recent case in the Privy Council on appeal from the Court of Appeal of New South Wales. The plaintiff was a thalidomide baby and the defendant was the manufacturer of the drug containing it.

The only question before the Privy Council was whether the action could be brought in Australia under an Australian Procedure Act. However, in the judgment there is a discussion at pp. 448-49 of when a tort of negligence is complete and of cases where the negligence and the damages are separated in time and place.

While it does not assist to a decision in the present case it is interesting to note that in *S. et al.* v. *Distillers Co. (Biochemicals), Ltd.*, [1969] 3 All E.R. 1412, the Queen's Bench Division recently approved of a substantial settlement to be paid to certain children born with defects due to their mother having used thalidomide. This was done without admission of liability.

Ann's mother was plainly one of a class within the area of foreseeable risk and one to whom the defendants therefore owed a duty. Was Ann any the less so? I think not. Procreation is normal and necessary for the preservation of the race. If a driver drives on a highway without due care for other users it is foreseeable that some of the other users of the highway will be pregnant women and that a child *en ventre sa mère* may be injured. Such a child therefore falls well within the area of potential danger which the driver is required to foresee and take reasonable care to avoid.

In my opinion it is not necessary in the present case to consider whether the unborn child was a person in law or at which stage she became a person. For negligence to be a tort there must be damages. While it was the foetus or child *en ventre sa mère* who was injured, the damages sued for are the damages suffered by the plaintiff Ann since birth and which she will continue to suffer as a result of that injury.

In *Watt* v. *Rama*, a judgment delivered December 14, 1971, and so far as I am aware not yet reported [since reported, [1972] V.R. 353], an Australian appeal Court was called upon to decide an issue very similar to the one now under discussion. My understanding is that it is being appealed to the Privy Council. In that case the statement of claim alleged that on May 15, 1967, the defendant negligently caused the collision of a motor vehicle and that in it the plaintiff's mother was so injured that she became a quadraplegic, that at the time the plaintiff's mother was pregnant and that on January 4, 1968, she gave birth to the plaintiff who suffered brain damage from (a) damages to her while unborn and (b) the inability of the mother to carry and deliver the plaintiff normally as a result of the accident. The fault was admitted but liability and damages disputed. The matter went to the court on stated points of law. In the result it was held that the defendant owed a duty to the plaintiff and that the damages alleged were not too remote.

The reasons given in this case contain a comprehensive analysis of all the relevant cases and literature. The members of the court held that the cause of action was not complete until after the birth of the plaintiff when the damages were suffered.

Some of the older cases suggest that there should be no recovery by a person who has suffered prenatal injuries because of the difficulties of proof and of the opening it gives for perjury and speculation. Since those cases were decided there have been many scientific advances and it would seem that chances of establishing whether or not there are causal relationships between the act alleged to be negligent and the damage alleged to have been suffered as a consequence are better now than formerly. In any event the courts now have to consider many similar problems and plaintiffs should not be denied relief in proper cases because of possible difficulties of proof.

To refuse to recognize such a right would be manifestly unjust and unreasonable. In my opinion, and for the reasons I have tried to formulate, such a refusal would not be consonant with relevant legal principles as they have developed and have been applied in the last 50 years. Under the doctrine of *M'Alister (or Donoghue)* v. *Stevenson, supra*, and the cases cited, an unborn child is within the foreseeable risk incurred by a negligent motorist. When the unborn child becomes a living person and suffers damages as a result of prenatal injuries caused by the fault of the negligent motorist the cause of action is completed. A tortfeasor is as liable to a child who has suffered prenatal injury as to the victim with a thin skull or other physical defect. In the instant case the plaintiff sues, as a living person, for damages suffered by her since her birth as a result of prenatal injury caused by the fault of the defendant. In my opinion she is entitled to recover such damages. I refrain from expressing any opinion as to what, if any, are the legal rights of a child *en ventre sa mère* or of a foetus. Many difficult problems in this area of the law remain to be resolved.

Schroeder J.A. (on appeal): . . . We have given earnest consideration to the careful reasons of the learned trial judge which led him to the conclusion that at common law there is also a right of recovery by an infant child in such circumstances. There is a dearth of authority upon the question, but the view taken by the learned trial judge is wholly in accord with the view held by

present-day legal writers and commentators. The most recent decision upon
this point is *Watt* v. *Rama*, [1972]V.R. 353, a judgment of the Supreme Court
of Victoria. In that case it was held that a plaintiff who at and after birth
suffers injuries caused by the neglect of the defendant in driving his motor
vehicle, this act of neglect preceding the birth of the plaintiff in point of time,
has a cause of action in negligence against the defendant in respect of those
injuries. The reasoning in that case is most persuasive and it is evident that
great weight was given to it by the learned trial judge. We do not feel that we
can usefully add anything to what has been so well and clearly stated by the
learned trial judge in support of his conclusion that at common law the infant
plaintiff is entitled to recover damages in the present case. We adopt that conclusion and the reasons upon which it is founded.

NOTES

1. The holding in this case has now been enshrined in legislation in Ontario as
follows:

> No person shall be disentitled from recovering damages in respect of
> injuries incurred for the reason only that the injuries were incurred before his
> birth.

See Family Law Reform Act, S.O. 1978, c. 2, s. 67 (enacted originally in S.O.
1975, c. 41, s. 4); see also U.K. Congenital Disabilities (Civil Liability) Act,
1976, c. 28.

2. See Winfield, "The Unborn Child" (1942), 4 U. of T.L.J. 278, reprinted
8 Camb. L.J. 76; Gordon, "The Unborn Plaintiff" (1965), 63 Mich. L. Rev. 579;
Bennett, "The Liability of the Manufacturers of Thalidomide to the Affected
Children" (1965), 39 Aust. L.J. 256; Samuels, "Injuries to Unborn Children"
(1974), 12 Alta. L. Rev. 266.

C. FAILURE TO ACT

There has been much written and said about the problem of the Good
Samaritan and more particularly the Bad Samaritan, who fails to come to the
aid of someone in peril. Whether this is a worse problem today in the large
urban areas than it was in years gone by is problematical. Some contend that
the media are merely making us more aware of these shocking incidents and
that their frequency has not increased. It is hard to know.

The law of torts is relevant to the problem of the Good Samaritan. By
awarding or withholding damages, it may encourage or discourage Good
Samaritanism. Historically, the common law may well have served to discourage
citizens from offering help to one another. In most countries of Europe, where
it is an offence to withhold succour when it is needed, the law is in marked
contrast. Whether Canadian law should be altered to reflect more closely the
European tradition is an issue that raises many questions about the inter-
relation of law and morals. The answers are not as self-evident as they may
seem.

Tort law treats this problem as one of "duty". Unless the court finds that
there was a "duty" on the defendant to take positive action, there will be no
liability imposed, even if harm to someone else is foreseeable and preventable
by him. Lawyers and judges use the terms "nonfeasance" and "misfeasance";
there is no liability for mere nonfeasance, but there is liability for misfeasance.
There is "no duty" in the former case, but there is in the latter.

However, it is not as simple as that. The difference *in principle* between a
failure to act to prevent or mitigate a threatened harm and positive conduct
that creates a risk of harm is not hard to grasp. *In practice*, however, it is more

difficult to distinguish them because a failure to act can sometimes take on the attributes of positive conduct. Moreover, in certain circumstances there *can* be liability imposed for failure to act. In particular instances, legislatures have evinced a willingness to require someone to give aid and the common law courts have not hesitated to follow their lead by imposing civil liability for breach of these statutes. This chapter provides background material indicating how the courts have handled these problems and poses the question of what legal steps, if any, should be taken to encourage altruism.

1. "Nonfeasance" and "Misfeasance"

THE HOLY BIBLE

Luke, 10:30 - 10:37

. . . A certain man went down from Jerusalem to Jericho, and fell among thieves, which stripped him of his raiment, and wounded him, and departed, leaving him half dead.

And by chance there came down a certain priest that way; and when he saw him, he passed by on the other side.

And likewise a Levite, when he was at the place, came and looked on him, and passed by on the other side.

But a certain Samaritan, as he journeyed, came where he was; and when he saw him he had compassion on him.

And went to him, and bound up his wounds, pouring in oil and wine, and set him on his own beast, and brought him to an inn, and took care of him.

And on the morrow, when he departed, he took out two pence, and gave them to the host, and said unto him, "Take care of him; and whatsoever thou spendest more, when I come again, I will repay thee."

Which now of these, thinkest thou, was neighbour unto him that fell among the thieves?

And he said, "He that shewed mercy on him." Then said Jesus unto him, "Go, and do thou likewise".

NOTES

1. Professor Honoré, in his article "Law, Morals and Rescue," printed in Ratcliffe, *The Good Samaritan and The Law* (1966), comments on this story as follows:

"This story in Luke, Chapter 10, is simple enough. Jesus is questioned by a lawyer who asks what is necessary to inherit eternal life. When Jesus asks him what the law on the matter is, it turns out the lawyer can recite the law perfectly, but — the nature of lawyers being apparently everywhere the same — he wants to argue the interpretation of one of the words in it.

The law is this: 'Love the Lord thy God with all thy heart and with all thy soul and with all thy strength; and thy neighbor as thyself.' The lawyer wants to know: 'Who *is* my neighbor?' Whereupon Jesus tells the story of the Samaritan. . . .

This story, like many traditional stories at the time, turns upon the differing responses of priest, Levite, and layman. But typically in such stories, the layman as well as the other two would be Jews. Jesus, however, substitutes a Samaritan, a geographical neighbor but one who was despised and hated by the Jews of the time as being uncouth, unclean, immoral, and heretical. Thus the story as told by Jesus was intended to teach most emphatically that love of neighbor is so universal, so unqualified a principle as to include even the meanest of men being neighbor to the most self-righteous of enemies. The Gospel source also emphasizes *acting* as a neighbor, *decision* rather than legalistic classification. Finally, and of highest importance, the story has to do with eternal life, personal salvation — not with problems of keeping the public order.

When I say that this parable is concerned with the ultimate question of personal salvation through personal decision and unqualified commitment, I have in mind the other side of the coin: whether my soul is saved or not is none of the state's business. Let Caesar regulate his own affairs: keeping the public order and the public well-being. My soul is *my* affair. This was Jesus' teaching; it is also central to our own political tradition."

HORSLEY ET AL. v. MacLAREN ET AL.
"THE OGOPOGO"

[1969] 2 O.R. 137, revd. [1970] 2 O.R. 487 (C.A.), affd. (1972),
22 D.L.R. (3d) 545 (S.C.C.) See *infra*, at p. 9-54

Lacourciere J. (at trial): . . . It is still the modern law of negligence that, there is no general duty to come to the rescue of a person who finds himself in peril from a source completely unrelated to the defendant, even where little risk or effort would be involved in assisting: thus a person on a dock can with legal impunity ignore the call for help of a drowning person, even refusing to throw a life ring. The law leaves the remedy to a person's conscience.

Jessup J.A. (in the Court of Appeal): . . . Conceived in the forms of action and nurtured by the individualistic philosophies of past centuries, no principle is more deeply rooted in the common law than that there is no duty to take positive action in aid of another no matter how helpless or perilous his position is. In this area the Civil law has shown more regard for morality. It is a principle which is not reached by the doctrine of *Donoghue* v. *Stevenson*, [1932] A.C. 562 since that case leaves open only the categories of neighbours to whom there is owed a duty not to cause harm; its ratio has not yet been extended to enlarge the class to whom there is owed a duty to confer a benefit. So, despite the moral outrage of the text writers, it appears presently the law that one can, with immunity, smoke a cigarette on the beach while one's neighbour drowns and, without a word of warning, watch a child or blind person walk into certain danger . . . .

Even the legislatures of our collectivist society, while readily assuming for the state the care of the individual, have not moved often to burden him with the care of his neighbour. Section 143a(1) (b) of The Highway Traffic Act is almost unique. It was not until 1934 that what is now Section 526(1) of the Canada Shipping Act, R.S.C. 1952, Ch. 29 was enacted:

> 526.(1) The master or person in charge of a vessel shall, so far as he can do so without serious danger to his own vessel, her crew and passengers, if any, render assistance to every person, even if that person be a subject of a foreign state at war with Her Majesty, who is found at sea and in danger of being lost, and if he fails to do so he is liable to a fine not exceeding one thousand dollars.

NOTES

1. In *Hurley* v. *Eddingfield* (1901), 156 Ind. 416, 59 N.E. 1058, the deceased became dangerously ill and sent for the defendant, his family doctor. The messenger told the doctor of the illness, tendered his fee for his services and stated that no other physician was procurable in time. Without any reason whatsoever, the doctor refused to render aid to the deceased. When death ensued, the deceased's family sued the doctor. A demurrer was granted and sus-

tained on appeal. Baker J. stated, "In obtaining the state's license (permission) to practice medicine, the state does not require, and the licensee does not engage, that he will practice at all or on other terms than he may choose to accept."

2. In *Osterlind* v. *Hill* (1928), 263 Mass. 73, 160 N.E. 301, the defendant rented a canoe to the deceased, who went out in it. When the canoe overturned, the deceased hung on to it for half an hour, making loud calls for assistance before he let go and drowned. The defendant heard and ignored these calls. Mr. Justice Brayley sustained the demurrer of the defendant and said: "The failure of the defendant to respond to the intestate's outcries is immaterial. No legal right of the intestate was infringed."

3. In *Buch* v. *Amory Manufacturing Co.* (1897), 69 N.H. 257, 44 Atl. 809, the court stated: "With purely moral obligations the law does not deal. For example, the priest and the Levite who passed by on the other side were not, it is supposed, liable at law for the continued suffering of the man who fell among thieves, which they might and morally ought to have prevented or relieved." He may be called a "moral monster" or a "ruthless savage", but he is not liable in damages.

4. Chief Justice Best once stated in another context — "there is no act which Christianity forbids, that the law will not reach: if it were otherwise, Christianity would not be, as it has always been held to be, part of the law of England". See *Bird* v. *Holbrook* (1828), 4 Bing. 628, 130 E.R. 911. Is not the Good Samaritan tale a part of Christianity?

5. See Ames, "Law and Morals" (1908), 22 Harv. L. Rev. 97, where the following appears:

". . . however revolting the conduct of the man who declined to interfere, he was in no way responsible for the perilous situation, he did not increase the peril, he took away nothing from the person in jeopardy, he simply failed to confer a benefit upon a stranger. As the law stands today there would be no legal liability, either civilly or criminally, in any of these cases. The law does not compel active benevolence between man and man. It is left to one's conscience whether he shall be the good Samaritan or not."

6. Can you think of any reasons why such a rule is desirable? What about encouraging self-reliance?

7. Should the law try to enforce morality? Does this smack of undue paternalism or excessive interference with individual freedom? Can law make people altruistic and unselfish? How should law and morality interact?

8. What about the danger to the person who tries to help someone being attacked or someone drowning? Can we define the degree of danger one should encounter for one's fellow man?

9. Are there any problems of administration? How does one select which person on the crowded beach will be held liable for failing to rescue a drowning child? Who in the city of Toronto is liable if someone starves to death on Bay St.? When does the duty to the rescued person terminate? If you feed a starving person, do you have to continue feeding him forever?

10. Is there really a problem in Canada of citizens failing to help one another? How much of this is merely something the newspapers have generated?

11. Are we wise to want people to help one another? Some policemen say that they would prefer it if untrained personnel did not interfere with their work. Do we want to develop a nation of intermeddlers and "stool pigeons"? What is so wrong with minding one's own business?

12. Why do people refrain from helping others when they are in danger? Dr. L. Z. Freedman, a professor of psychiatry, in an essay entitled — "No Response To The Cry For Help", attempted to answer this question. See *The Good Samaritan and the Law* (1966), at p. 175:

"Let us speculate, rather more systematically, on what happens when someone does *not intercede* in the crisis of another human being in trouble.

Let me say at the outset that in my view apathy and indifference are the least likely primary psychic vectors in response to such an event. The sequence as I see it is, first, the intense emotional shock — characterized predominantly, but not exclusively, by anxiety; second, the cognitive perception and awareness of what has happened; third, an inertial paralysis of reaction, which as a non-act becomes in fact an act, and fourth, the self-awareness of one's own shock anxiety, non-involvement which is followed by a sense of guilt and intra-psychic and social self-justification.

I do not assume that these things happen in such neat sequence. For all practical purposes they seem to occur simultaneously. Not all the things I am to discuss happen to everyone; when they do occur, if they do occur, their relative strength and importance appear in the unique proportions of each idiosyncratic individual. I am talking about emotions as well as ideas, fantasies as well as accurate perceptions, subjective experiences which are unconscious as well as those that are conscious."

OKE v. WEIDE TRANSPORT LTD. & CARRA

Manitoba Court of Appeal. (1963), 41 D.L.R. (2d) 53

Defendant driver, without negligence, knocked down a traffic sign located in the middle of a gravel strip dividing the eastbound and westbound lanes of a highway. Defendant stopped his vehicle and removed the debris except for a metal post, which was too securely imbedded, which was left bent over and projecting at right angles towards the near side of the eastbound lane. Defendant subsequently mentioned the accident to a garage attendant and evidenced an intention to report it to the authorities but was dissuaded from doing so by the attendant. The next day deceased driver, while using the gravel strip to pass a vehicle in the eastbound lane, which was forbidden, passed over the metal post and was fatally injured when he was "speared" by the post which was deflected upwards and through the floor boards and pierced his chest. At trial defendant, and his employer, were held liable for the death on grounds of negligence in failing to notify the police of the hazardous condition created by the projecting metal post so that action could be taken to remove such hazards. The majority of the Court of Appeal dismissed the action on grounds of lack of foresight.

Freedman J.A. (dissenting): . . . Counsel for the defendant advanced another argument that I must now consider. Starting from the premise that the defendant's collision with the sign-post was not the result of his negligence, he urged that thereafter the defendant was under no duty whatever with respect to the broken sign. Without such a duty towards other motorists, including the plaintiff, no negligence could be ascribed to him. His position, it was argued, was no different from that of any other motorist who, driving by and observing the broken sign, did nothing about it.

Concerning this argument I have two observations to make. In the first place, no such other motorist is before the court as a defendant in this case and it is therefore unnecessary to consider what his position might have been. In the second place, even if we assume that such other motorist would not be liable, it is wrong to think that the defendant's position is on all fours with his. Indeed it is decidely different. Our other motorist did not collide with the sign; the defendant did, even if it was without negligence. The former, if observing the broken sign-post at all, could do so only fleetingly, while in the act of driving by; the latter stood at the very spot, where he could see the precise results of the collision and the hazard they created. The former, having had no part in the destruction of the sign, was never anything more than an innocent passer-by who might not be under a legal duty to take active steps to control the situation; the defendant on the other hand participated in the creation of the hazard, recognized his obligation to do something by way of rectification, and in fact took some steps in that direction — the removal of debris, the resolve to inform the police — but then failed to go far enough. It is entirely unrealistic, in my view, to try to assimilate his position to that of some passing motorist.

I accordingly agree with the learned trial Judge that the defendant Carra (and his co-defendant vicariously through him) must be held liable for the accident. Nor would I disturb the award of damages.

I would dismiss the appeal with costs, and would dismiss the cross-appeal without costs.

Appeal allowed.

JORDAN HOUSE LTD. v. MENOW & HONSBERGER

Supreme Court of Canada. (1973), 38 D.L.R. (3d) 105

Laskin J.: This is a case of first instance. The principal issue is whether the operator of a hotel may be charged with a duty of care to a patron of the hotel beverage room who becomes intoxicated there, a duty to take reasonable care to safeguard him from the likely risk of personal injury if he is turned out of the hotel to make his way alone. If such a duty may be imposed, it falls to determine the nature or scope of the duty to the intoxicated patron. This determination must then be related to the present case by inquiring whether, on its facts, there has been a breach of the duty by the appellant hotel so as to engage its liability to the respondent plaintiff for personal injuries. I shall refer later in these reasons to another issue raised on behalf of the respondent Honsberger.

There are concurrent findings of fact in this case by the trial judge Haines J. [7 D.L.R. (3d) 494, [1970] 1 O.R. 54], and by the Ontario Court of Appeal in favour of Menow [14 D.L.R. (3d) 545, [1971] 1 O.R. 129], on the basis of which he was awarded damages against the appellant hotel and against the respondent Honsberger under an equal apportionment of fault among all three parties. Honsberger was the driver of a car which struck Menow as he was walking east near the centre line of Highway No. 8, after having been ejected from the hotel. Neither the quantum of damages nor the apportionment of fault is in issue in this appeal.

The hotel premises front on Highway No. 8, a much-travelled two-lane highway running east and west between Hamilton and Niagara Falls, Ontario. The road is asphalt, 21 ft. wide, and, at the material time, January 18, 1968, the shoulders were icy, with snowbanks beyond them, and the pavement itself was wet, although not slippery. Menow was employed by a fruit farmer and lived alone on his employer's farm which was on a side road about two and one-half miles east of the hotel. The direct route to his abode was along the highway and then north along the side road.

Menow was a frequent patron of the hotel's beverage room, where beer was served, and was well-known to the owner-operator of the hotel, one Fernick. He was often there in the company of his employer and the latter's foreman, also well known to Fernick. Menow had a tendency to drink to excess and then act recklessly, although ordinarily he was courteous and mannerly. The hotel management and the beverage room employees knew of his propensities, and, indeed, about a year before the events out of which this case arose he had been barred from the hotel for a period of time because he annoyed other customers, and thereafter the hotel's employees were instructed not to serve him unless he was accompanied by a responsible person.

On January 18, 1968, Menow, his employer and the foreman arrived at the hotel at about 5:15 p.m. and drank beer. The employer and the foreman departed within a short time, leaving the plaintiff there alone. Fernick came on duty at about 7 p.m. and saw that the plaintiff was then sober. He was served with beer from time to time, and there is a finding that towards 10 p.m. Fernick was aware that Menow was drinking to excess and that he had become intoxicated, the hotel having sold beer to Menow past the point of visible or apparent intoxication. At about 10 p.m. or 10:15 p.m. Menow was seen wandering around the other tables in the beverage room and consequently was ejected from the hotel by employees thereof, Fernick then knowing that the plaintiff was unable to take care of himself by reason of intoxication and that he would have to go home, probably by foot, by way of a main highway.

No excessive force was used in turning Menow out of the hotel. The evidence shows that he was put out on a dark and rainy night and that he was wearing dark clothes not readily visible to motorists. It appears that Menow, when he was outside the hotel, was picked up by an unknown third person and taken part of the way home, being let out on Highway No. 8 at 13th St. The ride had not been arranged by the hotel. It was while continuing in an easterly direction and, indeed, while walking beyond 11th St., his turn-off point (because, according to his testimony, he was looking for a friend), that Menow was struck by the Honsberger vehicle. It is unnecessary to detail the circumstances attending the accident because Honsberger does not challenge in this court the finding of negligence and the apportionment of one-third fault against him. It is enough to say that the accident occurred within half an hour after Menow was ejected from the hotel, and that he was staggering near the centre of the highway when he was hit by the Honsberger vehicle which was travelling east.

On the foregoing facts, Haines J. found that the hotel owed and was in breach of a common law duty of care to Menow. The duty of care was first put on two grounds, each related but in different ways, in the assessment of the duty and of its breach, to certain statutes. Adverting to s. 53(3) of the Liquor Licence Act, R.S.O. 1960, c. 218 [now R.S.O. 1970, c. 250, s. 56(3)], and to s. 81 of the Liquor Control Act, R.S.O. 1960, c. 217 [now R.S.O. 1970, c. 249, s. 69], Haines J. held that in contravening those provisions the hotel was in breach of a common law duty to Menow not to serve him intoxicating drink when he was visibly intoxicated. He thus relied on these enactments as indicating a standard upon which a common law duty could be founded. Second, although in the view of the trial judge, s. 53(4) and (6) [now s. 56(4) and (6)] of the Liquor Licence Act, imposes a duty on a licensed hotel operator to eject an intoxicated patron and empowers his forcible removal if he refuses to leave on request, he held that this authority is qualified by a duty not to subject that patron to danger of personal injury, foreseeable as a result of eviction. In the present case, Haines J. found that the hotel was vicariously liable for the actions of its employees who were in breach of a common law duty of care not to eject Menow as they did when they knew or ought to have known that he would thereby be placed in a position of danger to his personal safety.

The trial judge took a third position in imposing liability on the hotel by holding that [7 D.L.R. (3d) at p. 504] "the defendant's employees undertook affirmative action to remove the plaintiff from the premises. In so doing, they assumed a duty of care to take reasonable precautions to ensure that his safety was not endangered as a result of their actions." I may say at once that I do not regard this assessment as adding anything to the first two grounds upon which Haines J. proceeded. The affirmative action of removal did not in itself result in any injury to the plaintiff, as might have been the case if excessive force had been used against him (which is not suggested in the present case), nor was it followed by any breach of duty raised by and resulting from the affirmative action *per se*; hence, it can only be considered in the present case as wrapped up in the duty of care, if any, resting upon the hotel towards an intoxicated patron.

In its brief oral reasons supporting the judgment of Haines J. the Ontario Court of Appeal stated [14 D.L.R. (3d) at p. 546] that "we place our dismissal of the appeal on the simple ground that, so far as the hotel is concerned, there was a breach of the common law duty of care owed to the plaintiff in the circumstances of this case."

The following are the statutory provisions referred to by the trial judge in the course of his reasons relating to the hotel's liability to Menow:

Liquor Licence Act, s. 53(3):

> 53(3) No liquor shall be sold or supplied on or at any licensed premises to or for any person who is apparently in an intoxicated condition.
>
> (4) No person holding a licence under this Act shall permit or suffer in the premises for which the licence is issued,
>
> > (b) any gambling, drunkenness or any riotous, quarrelsome, violent or disorderly conduct to take place;
>
> (6) Any person holding a licence under this Act who has reasonable grounds to suspect from the conduct of any person who has come upon the premises in respect of which such licence is issued that such person, although not of notoriously bad character, is present for some improper purpose or is committing an offence against this Act or the regulations, may request such person to leave the licensed premises immediately and, unless the requestion is forthwith complied with, such person may be forcibly removed.

Section 67 [now s. 68] :

> 67. Where any person or his servant or agent sells liquor to or for a person whose condition is such that the consumption of liquor would apparently intoxicate him or increase his intoxication so that he would be in danger of causing injury to his person or injury or damage to the person or property of others, if the person to or for whom the liquor is sold while so intoxicated,
>
> > (a) commits suicide or meets death by accident, an action under The Fatal Accidents Act lies against the person who or whose servant or agent sold the liquor; or
> >
> > (b) causes injury or damage to the person or property of another person, such other person is entitled to recover an amount to compensate him for his injury or damage from the person who or whose servant or agent sold the liquor.

Liquor Control Act, s. 81:

> 81. No person shall sell or supply liquor or permit liquor to be sold or supplied to any person under or apparently under the influence of liquor.

Section 67 of the Liquor Licence Act has no direct application to the facts of the present case, and the trial judge did not attempt to apply it even indirectly as pointing to a standard of care resting upon the hotel. Counsel for the appellant hotel urged, however, that the express provision for civil liability upon a breach of s. 67 reflected a legislative policy precluding the founding of a cause of action upon breach of the other terms of the Liquor Licence Act (or of the Liquor Control Act) invoked by the trial judge. In my opinion, this is to mistake the use to which the trial judge put s. 53(3) of the Liquor Licence Act and s. 81 of the Liquor Control Act. I do not read his reasons as holding that the mere breach of those enactments and the fact that Menow suffered personal injury were enough to attach civil liability to the hotel. He regarded them rather as crystallizing a relevant fact situation which because of its authoritative source, the court was entitled to consider in determining, on common law principles, whether a duty of care should be raised in favour of Menow against the hotel.

Before dealing in more detail with this central question, I wish to refer to an issue raised by counsel for Honsberger in reliance on s. 67(b) of the Liquor Licence Act. If the judgments below stand so far as the hotel's liability is concerned, Honsberger would have the benefit of the Ontario Negligence Act, R.S.O. 1970, c. 296, in respect of any claim over against the hotel for the damages assessed against both defendants. But on the assumption that the hotel is exonerated here, the submission on behalf of Honsberger is that the unappealed affirmation of the judgment against him amounts to "injury or damage to the . . . property" of Honsberger, within s. 67(b), and thus entitles him to recover from the hotel the amount for which he has been held liable to Menow. The court did not require counsel for the hotel to respond to this submission. It was of the opinion that s. 67(b) cannot be so interpreted. That provision does not entitle a blameworthy defendant to cast himself in the role of a plaintiff claiming, not for damage suffered by it, but rather for that suffered by the intoxicated person and for which it is in part responsible. This is entirely apart from the attempt to read the word "property" in a sense which is entirely foreign to its ordinary meaning as well as to the context in which it is used in s. 67(b).

I return to the main issue. The common law assesses liability for negligence on the basis of breach of a duty of care arising from a foreseeable and unreasonable risk of harm to one person created by the act or omission of another. This is the generality which exhibits the flexibility of the common law; but since liability is predicated upon fault, the guiding principle assumes a nexus or relationship between the injured person and the injuring person which makes it reasonable to conclude that the latter owes a duty to the former not to expose him to an unreasonable risk of harm. Moreover, in considering whether the risk of injury to which a person may be exposed is one that he should not reasonably have to run, it is relevant to relate the probability and the gravity of injury to the burden that would be imposed upon the prospective defendant in taking avoiding measures. *Bolton et al.* v. *Stone*, [1951] A.C. 850, in the House of Lords and *Lambert et al.* v. *Lastoplex Chemicals Co. Ltd. et al.* (1971), 25 D.L.R. (3d) 121, [1972] S.C.R. 569, in this court illustrate the relationship between the remoteness or likelihood of injury and the fixing of an obligation to take preventive measures according to the gravity thereof.

In the present case, it may be said from one point of view that Menow created a risk of injury to himself by excessive drinking on the night in question. If the hotel's only involvement was the supplying of the beer consumed by Menow, it would be difficult to support the imposition of common law liability upon it for injuries suffered by Menow after being shown the door of the hotel and after leaving the hotel. Other persons on the highway, seeing Menow in an intoxicated condition, would not, by reason of that fact alone, come under any legal duty to steer him to safety, although it might be expected that good Samaritan impulses would move them to offer help. They would, however, be under a legal duty, as motorists for example, to take reasonable care to avoid hitting him, a duty in which Honsberger failed in this case. The hotel, however, was not in the position of persons in general who see an intoxicated person who appears to be unable to control his steps. It was in an invitor-invitee relationship with Menow as one of its patrons, and it was aware, through its employees, of his intoxicated condition, a condition which, on the findings of the trial judge, it fed in violation of applicable liquor licence and liquor control legislation. There was a probable risk of personal injury to Menow if he was turned out of the hotel to proceed on foot on a much-travelled highway passing in front of the hotel.

There is, in my opinion, nothing unreasonable in calling upon the hotel in such circumstances to take care to see that Menow is not exposed to injury because of his intoxication. No inordinate burden would be placed upon it in obliging it to respond to Menow's need for protection. A call to the police or a call to his employer immediately come to mind as easily available preventive measures; or a taxi-cab could be summoned to take him home, or arrangements made to this end with another patron able and willing to do so. The evidence shows that the hotel has experience with or was sensitive to the occasional need to take care of intoxicated patrons. The operator had, in other like instances, provided rides. He also had spare rooms at the time into one of which Menow could have been put.

Given the relationship between Menow and the hotel, the hotel operator's knowledge of Menow's propensity to drink and his instruction to his employees not to serve him unless he was accompanied by a responsible person, the fact that Menow was served, not only in breach of this instruction, but as well in breach of statutory injunctions against serving a patron who was apparently in an intoxicated condition, and the fact that the hotel operator was aware that Menow was intoxicated, the proper conclusion is that the hotel came under a duty to Menow to see that he got home safely by taking him under its charge or putting him under the charge of a responsible person, or to see that he was not turned out alone until he was in a reasonably fit condition to look after himself. There was, in this case, a breach of this duty for which the hotel must respond according to the degree of fault found against it. The harm that ensued was that which was reasonably foreseeable by reason of what the hotel did (in turning Menow out), and failed to do (in not taking preventive measures).

The imposition of liability upon the hotel in the circumstances that I have recounted has roots in an earlier decision of this court when related to the evolutionary principles stemming from *Donoghue* v. *Stevenson*, [1932] A.C. 562, which have become part of this court's course of decision. The affinity of *Dunn* v. *Dominion Atlantic Ry. Co.* (1920), 52 D.L.R. 149, 60 S.C.R. 310, with the present case, is sufficiently shown by the folowing three sentences from the reasons of Anglin J. who was one of the plurality of this court which allowed the appeal of the administrator of the estate of a deceased passenger, killed by a passing train when put off at a closed and unlighted station in a drunken condition [at p. 154]:

> "The right of removal of a disorderly passenger which is conferred on the conductor [under a railway by-law] is not absolute. It must be exercised reasonably. He cannot under it justify putting a passenger off the train under such circumstances that, as a direct consequence, he is exposed to danger of losing his life or of serious personal injury."

I do not regard the *Dunn* case as turning on the fact that the defendant was a common carrier, any more than I regard it as relevant here whether or not the defendant hotel was under innkeeper's liability in respect of the operation of its beverage room.

The risk of harm to which Menow was exposed by the hotel was not abated to its exoneration by reason of the fortuitous circumstance that Menow obtained a ride part of the way home. The short period of time that elapsed between the time that he was removed from the hotel and the time of the accident is telling in this respect, as is the fact that the risk was not increased or changed in kind when he was dropped off at 13th St. Counsel for the appellant did not argue on causation, but did contend that any duty that the hotel might have had evaporated because of voluntary assumption of risk. The argument is untenable, whether put on the basis of Menow's self-intoxication or on the basis of the situation that faced him when he was put out of the hotel. In his condition, as found by the trial judge, it is impossible to say that he both appreciated the risk of injury and impliedly agreed to bear the legal consequences. However, the trial judge did find Menow contributorily negligent in becoming intoxicated, adverting in this connection to s. 80(2) [now s. 68(2)] of the Liquor Control Act, which enjoins any person against being in an intoxicated condition in a public place. This finding has not been attacked.

The result to which I would come here does not mean (to use the words of the trial judge [at p. 503]), that I would impose "a duty on every tavern-owner to act as a watch dog for all patrons who enter his place of business and drink to excess". A great deal turns on the knowledge of the operator (or his employees) of the patron and his condition where the issue is liability in negligence for injuries suffered by the patron.

I would dismiss the appeal with costs.

[Martland and Spence JJ. concur with Laskin J.]

Ritchie J.: I agree with my brother Laskin that this appeal should be dismissed.

For my part, however, the circumstances giving rise to the appellant's liability were that the innkeeper and his staff, who were well aware of the respondent's propensity for irresponsible behaviour under the influence of drink, assisted or at least permitted him to consume a quantity of beer which they should have known might well result in his being incapable of taking care of himself when exposed to the hazards of traffic. Their knowledge of the respondent's somewhat limited capacity for consuming alcoholic stimulants without becoming befuddled and sometimes obstreperous, seized them with a duty to be careful not to serve him with repeated drinks after the effects of what he had already consumed should have been obvious.

In my view, it was a breach of this duty which gave rise to liability in the present case.

[Judson J. concurs with Ritchie J.]

NOTES

1. What was the basis of Mr. Justice Laskin's decision? How did Mr. Justice Ritchie's reasons differ?

2. Is this a case of "nonfeasance" or "misfeasance"?

Sometimes something that looks like nonfeasance is in reality misfeasance. Donald is driving his car along and sees Penelope on the road in front of him. He fails to apply his brakes and runs her over. Is this a case of "nonfeasance"? See *Kelly* v. *Metropolitan Ry. Co.*, [1895] 1 Q.B. 94. Dick is driving along and decides to make a left turn in front of Paul, who is coming toward him in the opposite direction. Dick fails to signal and collides with Paul. Is this "nonfeasance"? See generally Wright, "Negligent 'Acts or Omissions' " (1941), 19 Can. Bar Rev. 465.

3. A, a passenger on the B Ry. Co., is intoxicated when his station is reached. The conductor leads him off the train, starts him up a flight of stairs leading to the street level, and leaves him halfway up. A falls and is seriously injured. Is the B Ry. Co. liable? See *Black* v. *New York, New Haven & Hartford Ry. Co.* (1907), 79 N.E. 797 (Mass.); *Fagan* v. *Atlantic Coast Line Ry. Co.*

(1917), 115 N.E. 704 (N.Y.). Compare *Dunn* v. *Dominion Atlantic Ry. Co.,* [1920] 2 W.W.R. 705, 52 D.L.R. 199, 60 S.C.R. 310; *Howe* v. *Niagara, St. Catharines and Toronto Ry. Co.,* [1925] 2 D.L.R. 115, 56 O.L.R. 202.

4. Do you think that the hotel would have been liable if, Menow had wandered out of the hotel rather than being ejected?

5. Would the hotel have been liable if Menow had entered the hotel in an intoxicated state and had been ejected immediately before he could buy another drink? What if he had come to the door drunk and had been truned away before he could enter?

6. If he could be found, would the unidentified driver who picked Menow up and later dropped him be partially liable?

7. Would Menow's friend, the foreman, have been partially to blame if he had not left earlier but had remained in his seat until and after Menow was ejected?

8. If the same thing that occurred in the hotel had transpired in a private home, would the same result have followed? *Cf. Brockett* v. *Kitchen Boyd Motor Co.* (1972), 100 Cal. Rptr. 753.

9. What effect, if any, would the *Menow* case have on the conduct of tavern keepers across Canada? Several reports of this case appeared in the journal of the Ontario Hotels Association which helped to finance the defendant's legal costs. A report of the decision in this case was written up in *Time* magazine and on the front page of the *Toronto Daily Star.* In the next few days, several students at the Osgoode Hall Law School did a survey of 28 tavernkeepers in the Toronto area. Over 70 percent of them had read a media story about the decision. In one bar, the story from the newspaper had been clipped out and posted on the employees' notice board. When asked if they had altered their conduct as a result of this case, they denied it, insisting that they never served drunk patrons and that, if an intoxicated person would somehow make his way into their bar, they would send him home in a taxi. Do you believe them? Is this an area where tort law may be a more powerful force for social control than the criminal law?

10. X lends his car to Y who is intoxicated. Y promptly collides with a tree. Is X liable? Compare with *Hempler* v. *Todd* (1970), 14 D.L.R. (3d) 637. What if X instructs an incompetent driver who has failed his driving test several times, to drive an automobile which is involved in a one-car collision? See *O.H.S.C.* v. *Borsoski* (1973), 54 D.L.R. (3d) 339 (Ont.) (Lerner J.); What if X lends a motorcycle to a young, unlicenced driver, who gets involved in a collision? See *Stermer* v. *Lawson* (1977), 79 D.L.R. (3d) 366 (B.C.) (Fulton J.) percentage varied (1979), 11 C.C.L.T. 76. What about contributory negligence here?

11. The nonfeasance limitation does not apply if there exists a positive duty to act based on some relationship such as contract, bailment or the like. See *Turner* v. *Stallibras,* [1898] 1 Q.B. 56, 67 L.J.Q.B. 52; *Kelly* v. *Metropolitan Railway Co.,* [1895] 1 Q.B. 944, 11 T.L.R. 366; *Hayn Roman & Co.* v. *Culliford* (1879), 4 C.P.D. 182, 48 L.J.Q.B. 372; *Lee Cooper, Ltd.* v. *C.H. Jenkins & Sons, Ltd.,* [1965] 1 All E.R. 280. *The Restatement of Torts, Second,* § 314A lists several other relationships which give rise to a duty to aid, that is, common carriers, innkeepers, possessors of land held open to the public and those who have custody of another person. § 314B states that a master is under a duty to assist an employee who is in danger or in a helpless condition.

12. The master of a ship is obligated to go to the aid of one of his passengers if he falls overboard: *Horsley* v. *MacLaren,* [1970] 2 O.R. 487; affd. (1972), 22 D.L.R. (3d) 545 (S.C.C.), revg. *Vanvalkenberg* v. *Northern Navigation Co.* (1913), 30 O.L.R. 142, 19 D.L.R. 649 (Ont. C.A.).

13. If one *negligently* injures another, there has always been imposed a duty to render aid. See *Northern Cent. R. Co.* v. *State of Maryland, Use of Adeline Price* (1868), 29 Md. 420; *Trombley* v. *Kolts* (1938), 29 Cal. App. 2d 699, 85 P. 2d 451; *Rains* v. *Hedenfels Brothers* (1969), 443 S.W. 2d 280.

14. If someone is in charge of an instrumentality that, without fault, causes injury, should he be obligated to help? See *L. S. Ayres* v. *Hicks* (1942), 40 N.E.

2d 334, which supports such a rule. See also *Restatement of Torts, Second*, §322. Denying liability are *Turbeville* v. *Mobile Light & R. Co.* (1930), 127 So. 519 (Ala.); *Union Pacific R. Co.* v. *Cappier* (1903), 66 Kan. 649, 72 P. 281; *Griswold* v. *Boston & Marine R. Co.* (1903), 183 Mass. 434, 67 N.E. 354.

15.   Custodians of prisoners have a duty to protect them from injury. (See *Daoust* v. *The Queen*, [1969] 2 Ex. C.R. 129, prison doctor negligent; *Danard* v. *The Queen*, [1971] F.C. 417, prisoners required to mow grass on hill; *MacLean* v. *The Queen*, [1973] S.C.R. 2, bale of straw hit prisoner, but there will be no liability if there is no negligence. See *Ellis* v. *Home Office*, [1953] 2 All E.R. 149; *Howley* v. *The Queen*, [1973] F.C. 184, no liability for stabbing; *Timm* v. *The Queen*, [1965] 1 Ex. C.R. 174, prisoner fell from truck.) Schools must take care to protect their students. (*Dziwenka* v. *The Queen*, [1972] S.C.R. 419.) See generally Barnes, "Tort Liability of School Boards to Pupils", in Klar (ed.), *Studies in Canadian Tort Law* (1977), p. 189. So too, hospitals must use reasonable precautions to safeguard their patients. (*Lawson* v. *Wellesley Hospital* (1977), 76 D.L.R. (3d) 688 (S.C.C.).) Also, occupiers of land may be required to take active steps to protect people on their land from danger. (See *Pridgen* v. *Boston Housing Authority* (1974), 308 N.E. 2d 467 (Mass.); *cf. Handiboe* v. *McCarthy* (1966), 151 S.E. 2d 905 (Georgia).)

2. Undertakings and Reliance

ZELENKO v. GIMBEL BROS.

Supreme Court of New York. (1935), 287 N.Y.S. 134

Motion to dismiss amended complaint on the ground that it does not state facts sufficient to constitute a cause of action.

Lauer J.: The general proposition of law is that if a defendant owes a plaintiff no duty, then refusal to act is not negligence. . . .But there are many ways that a defendant's duty to act may arise. Plaintiff's intestate was taken ill in defendant's store. We will assume that defendant owed her no duty at all — that defendant could have let her be and die. But if a defendant undertakes a task, even if under no duty to undertake it, the defendant must not omit to do what an ordinary man would do in performing the task.

Here the defendant undertook to render medical aid to the plaintiff's intestate. Plaintiff says that defendant kept his intestate for six hours in an infirmary without any medical care. If defendant had left plaintiff's intestate alone, beyond doubt some bystander, who would be influenced more by charity than by legalistic duty, would have summoned an ambulance. Defendant segregated this plaintiff's intestate where such aid could not be given and then left her alone.

The plaintiff was wrong in thinking that the duty of a common carrier of passengers is the same as the duty of this defendant. The common carrier assumes its duty by its contract of carriage. This defendant assumed its duty by meddling in matters with which legalistically it had no concern. The plaintiff is right in arguing that when the duty arose, the same type of neglect is actionable in both cases. The motion is denied.

NOTES

1. This decision was affirmed without reasons in (1936), 287 N.Y.S. 136.

SOULSBY v. CITY OF TORONTO

High Court of Ontario. (1907), 15 O.L.R. 13; 9 O.W.R. 871

Britton J.: On the 30th October, 1906, the plaintiff was employed as the driver of a baker's delivery waggon, and was delivering bread to customers in the western part of the city. On that day the plaintiff entered High Park, and drove along the road through the park, which leads out of the park, across the tracks of the Grand Trunk Railway and to the Lake Shore Road. Within the park and near the railway crossing, the city has erected gates, and during the season when the park is most frequented, the city keeps a watchman at the gate nearest the crossing keeping it open for users of the road when there is no danger from passing trains, and closing it when trains are approaching this crossing. The statement of claim alleges that the plaintiff on the day mentioned was approaching the crossing along the road in High Park, intending to proceed to the Lake Shore Road. When he arrived at the crossing, he found the gate open, and, relying upon that fact as notice to him that no train was approaching, he proceeded to cross the tracks, and while so crossing was struck by a train and seriously injured.

At the close of the evidence, counsel for the defendants asked that the action be dismissed, on the grounds that no actionable negligence had been shewn, and that the plaintiff was guilty of contributory negligence. It was then agreed that the only thing to be left to the jury was the assessment of damages, and that I should dispose of all other questions, subject to the rights of parties to appeal. The jury assessed the plaintiff's damages, contingent upon his right to recover, at $1,000.

In my opinion no duty was cast upon the defendants of erecting or maintaining the gate or of keeping the watchman at the crossing where the accident happened. . . .

It was argued that even if the defendants were not compelled to establish the gate and employ the watchman, having undertaken it, the plaintiff was entitled to rely on its continuance, at least until notice, actual or constructive, to the contrary. . . .

The plaintiff relied upon *Baxter* v. *Jones* (1903), 6 O.L.R. 360, and upon cases cited in *Anson on Contracts*, 10th ed., p. 98. One case is where a person undertook gratuitously to effect insurance upon another person's house, and, having failed to do so, was held liable. These cases, which are cases of mandate, and nothing of the kind exists here, are said to rest upon this broad ground . . . that if a person undertakes to perform a voluntary act, he is liable if he performs it improperly, but not if he neglects to perform it. The charge here is that a watchman employed did not do his duty properly. He was not at the gate at all. He was, as to the plaintiff and the public, when this accident happened, the same as during the night time — or during the rest of the year after October — when withdrawn from the gate.

I do not think the defendants are liable for merely leaving the gate open, as there is not, in my opinion, any duty to keep the gate closed at the time of approaching or passing trains. The plaintiff's own account of the accident is as follows: . . . "I ventured to cross, thinking every other time the watchman came out and either put out his stick or flag, and not seeing him do this, I thought he was in the cabin . . . I thought my track was clear. . . . The gates were kept up when the track was clear." "I looked; that is the reason I thought my track was clear." "When I saw the gate up I started to go across." "This was about 4 o'clock in the afternoon." . . .

This all goes to show that the unfortunate plaintiff had the means of knowing, and did, in fact, know, as much as the gate-keeper would have known had he been at the time in his cabin.

Baker (the watchman) had no time-tables. He was not in communication with the railway people, but simply upon hearing or seeing a train approaching he was accustomed to close the gate. Suppose he had been at his post, and had not seen or heard more than the plaintiff did — the plaintiff could hardly impute that as negligence. The only means Baker had of knowing when to close the gate was to look and listen. The plaintiff had that same opportunity; he did look — his only complaint is that he did not get the warning or prohibition implied by a closed gate.

The accident is, like others, a very regrettable one, and I would be very glad if the defendants could see their way to assist the plaintiff in some way, but, as I think the plaintiff not entitled in law to recover, I must dismiss the action, and I do so without costs.

NOTES

1. In *Mercer* v. *S. E. & C. Ry. Co.*, [1922] 2 K.B. 549, 92 L.J.K.B. 25, 127 L.T. 723, the defendants had made a practice of keeping a wicket gate locked to pedestrians when a train was passing. This practice was known to the plaintiff who was injured by a passing train when, owing to carelessness of the defendants' servant, the gate was left unlocked. The defendants were held liable. *Per* Lush J.: "To those who knew of the practice this was a tacit invitation to cross the line . . . . It may seem a hardship on a railway company to hold them responsible for the omission to do something which they were under no legal obligation to do, and which they only did for the protection of the public. They ought, however, to have contemplated that if a self-imposed duty is ordinarily performed, those who knew of it will draw an inference if on a given occasion it is not performed. If they wish to protect themselves against the inference being drawn they should do so by giving notice, and they did not do so in this case."

Can you reconcile *Soulsby* and *Mercer*? See also *Loader* v. *London & India Docks Joint Committee* (1891), 8 T.L.R. 5.

2. In *Barnett* v. *Chelsea and Kensington Hospital Management Committee*, [1968] 1 All E.R. 1068 (Q.B.D.), a watchman, after drinking some "tea" which made him vomit, went to the casualty department of the defendant's hospital. The watchman "entered the . . . hospital without hindrance, . . . made complaints to the nurse who received them and she in turn passed [them] on to the medical casualty officer and he sent a message through the nurse purporting to advise the [watchman]" to go home and see his own doctor. He died some hours later from arsenical poisoning. Although Mr. Justice Nield found that the negligence of the defendant's employees did not cause the death, he said in a *dictum* that because there was a "close and direct relationship between the hospital and the [plaintiff] . . . there was imposed on the hospital a duty of care. . . ." Mr. Justice Nield distinguished this case from a case of a casualty department that closes its doors and says that no patients can be received".

3. The Supreme Court of Canada has recently indicated that an undertaking and reliance thereon may lead to the establishment of a legal duty to take care, at least in the case of government safety activity. In *R.* v. *Nord-Deutsche et al.*, [1971] S.C.R. 849, employees of the Crown negligently permitted a set of range lights, upon which pilots relied, to become displaced, and thereby contributed to a collision between two ships. At trial, Mr. Justice Noel based liability on the ground that the Crown had "engendered reliance on the guidance afforded by [the lights]", and was therefore required to keep them in good working order or, failing that, to warn about the danger. In the Supreme Court of Canada, Mr. Justice Ritchie divided liability among the Crown and the two shipowners and explained that there was a "breach of duty on the part of the servants of the

Crown responsible for the care and maintenance of the range lights . . . upon which lights mariners were entitled to place reliance". *Cf. Cleveland-Cliffs S.S. v. R.,* [1957] S.C.R. 810; *O'Donnell* v. *R.* [1972] F.C. 966, no liability for certificate of airworthiness when crash not caused by conduct and where duty to supply information belonged to plaintiff, not to Crown.

4. Similarly, in *Grossman and Sun* v. *R.,* [1952] 1 S.C.R. 571, the Crown was held liable when a maintenance foreman at an airfield negligently failed to place warning flags around a ditch on the runway, causing damage to an aeroplane and injury to a passenger. Mr. Justice Kellock indicated that a duty was owed by the employee not only to his employer, but also to pilots, who were "entitled to rely" on its proper discharge.

5. Another case, in which liability was imposed on the Crown is *Hendricks* v. *R.,* [1970] S.C.R. 237, where the applicant's wife was drowned in a boating accident. The Crown employees negligently omitted to replace signs warning boaters "Danger—Falls Ahead", which had been knocked over. Because of this, as well as the contributory negligence of the suppliant and his wife, the falls were not noticed until too late. The boat went over the falls and capsized. An additional reason for imposing liability on the Crown was that it had actually created the danger to navigation by building the obstruction below the water level.

6. A Department of Highways was recently held liable when an 18" median strip it had erected on a highway proved inadequate to prevent an automobile accident. In *Malat* v. *Bjornson (No. 2),* [1975] 5 W.W.R. 429 (B.C.), Ruttan J. found that the Department was aware of the inadequacy of the 18" barrier and had already decided to replace it with a 30" barrier, "which would have prevented the accident and which could be done simply with no great expense or inconvenience". Since the defendant had taken the "operational" step of erecting the 18" barrier, it had a duty to use reasonable care which it breached by its "misfeasance". See also *R.* v. *Coté,* [1976] 1 S.C.R. 595, indicating that there may be an obligation on a Department of Highways to do something about particularly dangerous sections of an icy road. There is no general obligation, however, to salt or sand icy roads. See *Simms* v. *Metro Toronto* (1978), 4 C.C.L.T. 214 (Ont. C.A.) criticizing *Landriault* v. *Pinard* (1976), 1 C.C.L.T. 216 (Ont. C.A.).

BAXTER & CO. v. JONES

Ontario Court of Appeal. (1903), 6 O.L.R. 360; 2 O.W.R. 573

Plaintiffs applied to defendant, a general insurance agent, who had placed other insurance for them, to procure additional fire insurance on their mill. Defendant placed the insurance and as plaintiffs' manager was signing the formal application and paying the premium he asked the defendant to give the other companies notice of the insurance. Defendant said he would do so. Defendant failed to do so and when a fire occurred, the other companies availed themselves of the defence of failure to receive notice of additional insurance and refused to pay. Plaintiffs finally settled with them for $1,000 less than they would otherwise have been obliged to pay. Plaintiffs brought action to recover their loss against defendant for negligence in failing to give notice. He obtained judgment at the trial (4 O.L.R. 541) and defendant appealed.

Osler J.A.: . . . If the defendant's employment and promise was entire to do both acts, *viz.,* to procure the new insurance and to give the notices, then, even if it was, as it has been held in the court below, a gratuitous promise, yet having proceeded upon his employment the defendant would be liable for negligently performing it in such a manner as to cause loss or injury to the plaintiffs. He knew the importance of giving the notices, and the effect of the omission to do so, upon the plaintiffs' other policies. To stop when he had only obtained the insurance was simply to go as far with the business as to cause a direct injury to the plaintiffs if he failed to follow it up by notice to the other insurers, and cannot be regarded otherwise than as actionable negligence.

It would rather appear that nothing was said of giving notice when the defendant was first employed or instructed to procure the insurance, but before the business was complete, and while the plaintiffs might have still withdrawn, they requested the defendant and the latter undertook to give it. Defendant might have refused to assume that duty, and the plaintiffs would then have known that they must look after it themselves, or could have withdrawn their application and sought insurance elsewhere. But the whole business having been ultimately entrusted to and assumed by the defendant before any part of it had been completed, the plaintiffs have a right to complain that the defendant negligently proceeded with it only so far as to be detrimental to them.

I think the learned judge rightly regarded the transaction as one of mandate so that if the defendant had not entered upon the execution of the business entrusted to him he would have incurred no liability: *Coggs* v. *Bernard* (1703), 2 Ld. Raym. 909; 1 Smith's L.C. 11th ed., p. 173, but "it is well established that one who enters upon the performance of a mandate or gratuitous undertaking on behalf of another, is responsible not only for what he does, but for what he leaves unfulfilled, and cannot rely on the want of consideration as an excuse for the omission of any step that is requisite for the protection of any interest intrusted to his care". . . .

Maclennan J.A.: . . . If the defendant had been acting solely for the insurance company in effecting the insurance, his promise to give the notices would have stood by itself, and the breach of it would not have been actionable. But because he was procuring the insurance at the request of the plaintiffs, to that extent he was acting for them, which makes it necessary to consider how far, if at all, he was bound to give the notices, although all that he did was as between him and the plaintiffs purely voluntary. In *Coggs* v. *Bernard*, the defendant promised to hoist some hogsheads of brandy from one cellar and deposit them in another. In doing so a cask was staved, and the contents were lost. There the negligence was in doing the very act which was to be done, and the defendant was held to be liable though he was not to have any reward for what he undertook to do. That was a case of bailment, inasmuch as the defendant had taken the goods into his possession. But the judgment was not rested wholly upon that circumstances. At p. 181, Lord Holt in his elaborate judgment, refers to the case of a carpenter having undertaken to build a house, but who had not done it, and it was adjudged the action would not lie (*i.e.*, the promise having been voluntary) and he adds: "But then the question was put to the court — what if he had built the house unskilfully — and it is agreed in that case an action would have lain." . . . In *Skelton* v. *The London & North-Western R.W. Co.* (1867), L.R. 2 C.P. 631, at p. 636, Willes J., said the result of the decision in *Coggs* v. *Bernard* was that "if a person undertakes to perform a voluntary act, he is liable if he performs it improperly, but not if he neglects to perform it". . . .

Now, in this case, unless notice of the new insurance was given to the existing insurers, the new policy was certain to work injury to the plaintiffs by making void the existing policies. This the defendant knew, and as part of his undertaking to procure the new insurance, I think that he undertook and agreed that it should not be done injuriously to the plaintiffs. His omission to give notices has that effect. It put the plaintiffs at the mercy of the former insurers, when the loss occurred, and compelled them to accept whatever they chose to pay, which was $1,000 less than they would, as I think, having read the evidence, have received. Upon the whole I think the judgment is right and should be affirmed.

[Moss C.J.O., and Garrow J.A. concurred.]

NOTES

1. Is *Baxter* v. *Jones* a reliance case? Is it a case of an undertaking? Is it a misfeasance case? Is it a contract case? Is it based on more than one of these theories? See also *Myers* v. *Thompson et al.* (1967), 63 D.L.R. (2d) 476; *Siegal* v. *Spear & Co.* (1925), 138 N.E. 414 (N.Y.).

2. Do you agree with the decision? What if there had been no contractual relation, but a mere gratuitous undertaking? Compare with *Thorne* v. *Deas* (1809), 4 Johns. 84, where Chief Justice Kent stated, ". . . . by the common law . . . one who undertakes to do an act for another, without reward, is not answerable for omitting to do the act, and is only responsible when he attempts to do it, and does it amiss".

3. A husband makes an agreement with a doctor to look after his wife during her confinement. Although called, the doctor is not present when the baby is born. The baby dies and the wife suffers physical injury, pain, etc. Can the wife recover if the doctor's absence is found to be due to his carelessly overlooking the call? Is a contract with the wife a necessary prerequisite for liability? Compare with *Smith* v. *Rae* (1919), 46 O.L.R. 518.

4. Does a bailee have a duty to warn his bailor if he does not carry insurance? See *Mason* v. *Morrow's Moving* (1978), 5 C.C.L.T. 59 (B.C.C.A.).

5. Is a boatowner contributorily negligent for floating his boat before checking whether insurance was taken out as promised by the defendant? See *Truman* v. *Sparling Real Estate* (1977), 3 C.C.L.T. 205 (B.C.).

6. The liability of a Good Samaritan, once he commences a rescue attempt, is still clouded in uncertainty. According to some authorities, he must "worsen" the condition of the rescued person before he will be held liable. The leading case is *East Suffolk Rivers Catchment Board* v. *Kent*, [1940] 4 All E.R. 527 (H.L.). A public authority began to fix a damaged sea wall, which had permitted the plaintiff's land to be flooded. It delayed in doing the work and the plaintiff's land was submerged for a much longer period than it would have been if the work had been done properly. The defendant agency was, nevertheless, relieved of liability, because the plaintiff's position was not worsened by its actions. Viscount Simon L.C. indicated that if they had "inflicted fresh injury", such as flooding more land or prolonging the period of flooding beyond what it would have been if they had never interfered, they would be liable. They did not "cause the loss; it was caused by the operations of nature, which the appellants were endeavouring, not very successfully to counteract." The court resisted holding the public authority liable because it did not wish to put a strain on its limited resources.

Does the result of this case have anything to do with the fact that the defendant was a public authority?

See also *Neabel* v. *Town of Ingersoll* (1967), 63 D.L.R. (2d) 484 (Ont. H.C.); *Sheppard* v. *Glossop Corp.*, [1921] 3 K.B. 132; *Stevens-Willson* v. *City of Chatham*, [1933] O.R. 305, [1933] 2 D.L.R. 407; affd. [1934] S.C.R. 353. See Friedman, "Statutory Powers and Legal Duties of Local Authorities" (1945), 8 Mod. L. Rev. 31.

7. The leading American case on this issue is *H. R. Moch Co.* v. *Rensselaer Water Co.* (1928), 159 N.E. 896, where Mr. Justice Cardozo of the New York Court of Appeals stated:

"It is ancient learning that one who assumes to act, even though gratuitously, may thereby become subject to the duty of acting carefully, if he acts at all . . . . The plaintiff would bring its case within the orbit of that principle. The hand once set to a task may not be withdrawn with impunity though liability would fail if it had never been applied at all. A time-honoured formula often phrases the distinction as one between misfeasance and nonfeasance. Incomplete the formula is, and so at times misleading: Given a relation involving in its existence a duty of care irrespective of a contract, a tort may result, as well from acts of omission as of commission in the fulfilment of the duty thus recognized by law . . . . What we need to know is not so much the conduct to be avoided when the relation and its attendant duty are established as existing. What we need to know is the conduct that engenders the relation. It is here that the formula, however incomplete, has its value and significance.

If conduct has gone forward to such a stage that inaction would commonly result, not negatively merely in withholding a benefit, but positively or actively in working an injury, there exists a relation out of which arises a duty to go forward. Bohlen, *Studies in the Law of Torts*, p. 87. So the surgeon who operates without pay is liable, though his negligence is the omission to sterilize his instruments . . .; the engineer, though his fault is in the failure to shut off steam . . .; the maker of automobiles, at the suit of some one other than the buyer, though his negligence is merely in inadequate inspection . . . . The query always is whether the putative wrongdoer has advanced to such a point as to have launched a force or instrument of harm, or has stopped where inaction is at most a refusal to become an instrument for good . . . ."

8. This problem surfaced, but was not resolved, in *Horsley* v. *MacLaren*, [1970] 2 O.R. 487 (C.A.), affd. (1972), 22 D.L.R. (3d) 545 (S.C.C.). See *infra*. A passenger on a private yacht, Matthews, fell overboard and the owner of the boat began a rescue attempt by backing up towards him. Expert evidence was adduced to the effect that this was the wrong procedure. A rescuer died as a result and his widow sued. At trial, Mr. Justice Lacourcière exacted the standard of reasonable care usually demanded from a rescuer and asked, "What could the reasonable boat operator do in the circumstances . . .?" Because the defendant used the "wrong procedure" in backing the boat up and because of his "excessive consumption of alcohol", Mr. Justice Lacourcière held that he was negligent and, therefore, liable. The Court of Appeal, however, reversed the trial judge and decided that the defendant was guilty only of an error in judgment, which did not amount to negligence. Mr. Justice Jessup relied upon the *Kent* case and adopted its test for these rescue cases. He contended that "where a person gratuitously and without any duty to do so undertakes to confer a benefit upon or go to the aid of another, he incurs no liability unless what he does worsens the condition of the others". Mr. Justice Jessup rejected the rationale used by the trial judge and argued: "I think it is an unfortunate development in the law which leaves the Good Samaritan liable to be mulcted in damages, and apparently in the United States, it is one that has produced marked reluctance of doctors to aid victims." Mr. Justice Schroeder echoed this view and argued that "if a person embarks upon a rescue, and does not carry it through, he is not under any liability to the person to whose aid he has come so long as discontinuance of his efforts did not leave the other in a worse condition than when he took charge". Since MacLaren's rescue effort had not worsened Matthew's position, even though it may not have complied with the standard of "textbook perfection", he was relieved of responsibility. In the Supreme Court of Canada, the majority did not deal with this point, and Mr. Justice Laskin, dissenting, left it to be decided on another occasion. Mr. Justice Laskin said:

"Whether a case involving the exercise of statutory powers (but not duties) by a public authority should govern the issue of liability or non-liability to an injured rescuer is a question that need not be answered here."

For a thorough analysis of *Horsley* v. *MacLaren* see Alexander, "One Rescuer's Obligation to Another: The Ogopogo Lands in the Supreme Court of Canada" (1972), 22 U. of T.L.J. 98.

9. What are the policy reasons behind the application of the *Kent* rule in the rescue situation? What can be said for the opposing view? Should the *Kent*

rule be limited to situations involving municipalities and other public authorities?

10. Doctors sometimes say that they are afraid to stop at the scene of an accident because they fear being sued by the person they treat if something goes wrong. Do they really have much to worry about in the light of these cases?

11. Is this an effective way of encouraging rescue efforts? Can you think of any other better ways of fostering Good Samaritanism? See Linden, "Rescuers and Good Samaritans" (1971), 34 Mod. L. Rev. 241.

12. When is there an "undertaking" by affirmative action? Donald sees Percy drowning and shouts "Don't worry! I'll save you!" Donald gets the life buoy and throws it in. He misses. He throws it in again. He pulls Percy five feet closer to shore and then decides to abandon the rescue attempt. Percy sinks and is seen no more. Is Donald liable? What if there were dozens of other potential rescuers around? What if there was no one else in sight?

13. The *Restatement of Torts, Second* §§ 323, 324 limits its rule to cases where the plaintiff is left in a worse position as by increasing the danger, by depriving him of a chance of other aid or by inducing him to forego it in reliance upon the undertaking. Would Donald be relieved of liability under this rule? Should he be?

14. Consider here the notion of promissory estoppel. Can one bring an action for "detrimental reliance"? See Cheshire, Fifoot and Furmston, *The Law of Contract* (8th ed., 1972), at p. 84; Wilson, "Recent Developments in Estoppel" (1951), 67 L.Q.Rev. 330. See also Millner, *Negligence in Modern Law* (1967), at p. 142.

15. See Seavey, "Reliance Upon Gratuitous Promises or Other Conduct" (1951), 64 Harv. L. Rev. 913; Gregory, "Gratuitious Undertaking and the Duty of Care" (1951), 1 De Paul L. Rev. 30.

3. The Impact of Criminal Legislation

MONK v. WARBEY

Court of Appeal. [1935] 1 K.B. 75

The defendant Warbey permitted his motor vehicle to be used by Knowles who allowed a third person, May, to use it. Although the owner was himself insured against third party risks neither Knowles nor May were. Legislation required that they be so insured. May negligently caused injury to the plaintiff Monk who sued Knowles, May and Warbey. Interlocutory judgments were secured against Knowles and May but they could not satisfy them. The matter proceeded against Warbey on the theory that his breach of the statute gave rise to civil liability. The trial judge accepted this view and the defendant appealed.

Greer L.J.: . . . The Road Traffic Act, 1930, under which the question arises, was passed in these circumstances: it had become apparent that people who were injured by the negligent driving of motor cars were in a parlous situation if the negligent person was unable to pay damages. Accordingly two statutes were passed, one for the purpose of enabling persons who were thus injured to recover, in the case of the bankruptcy of an insured defendant the money which would be payable to him by the insurance company. Parliament enacted that in such circumstances the insurance money should go not to the general creditors of the bankrupt defendant but to the injured person; in other words the injured person, although not a party to the insurance could make the insurance company liable. That Act — the Third Parties (Rights against Insurers) Act, 1930, did not meet the whole difficulty that had arisen because motor car owners sometimes lent their cars to uninsured persons, and if a person who borrowed a car and in driving it caused injury to a third person the remedy provided by that Act did not avail the injured person. Consequently the Road Traffic Act, 1930, was passed for the very purpose of making provision for third parties who suffered injury by the negligent driving of motor vehicles by uninsured persons to whom the insured owner had lent such vehicles. How could Parliament make provision for their protection from such risks if it did not enable an injured third person to recover for a breach of s. 35? That section which is in Part II of the Act headed "Provision against third-party risks arising out of the use of motor vehicles", would indeed be no protection to a person injured by the negligence of an uninsured person to whom a car had been lent by the insured owner, if no civil remedy were available for a breach of the section. The Act requires every person who runs a car to have an insurance on the use of the car, and to provide himself with a certificate stating the terms of the insurance. Sect. 35, sub-s. 1, says that "subject to the provisions of this Part of this Act, it shall not be lawful for any person to use, or to cause or permit any other person to use, a motor vehicle on a road unless there is in force in relation to the user of the vehicle by that person or that other person, as the case may be, such a policy of insurance or such a security in respect of third-party risks as complies with the requirements of this Part of this Act". There is no dispute that the appellant committed a breach of the section, but it is argued that taking the Act as a whole it is clear that it was not intended to confer a right upon an injured third person to claim damages for such a breach. It seems to me that the situation is exactly within the language of A. L. Smith L.J. in *Groves* v. *Lord Wimborne,* where he said: "The Act in question" — the Factory & Workshop Act, 1878 — "which followed numerous other Acts *in pari materia,* is not in the nature of a private legislative bargain between employers and workmen, as the learned judge seemed to think, but is a public Act passed in favour of the workers in factories and workshops to compel their employers to do certain things for their protection and benefit". The Lord Justice then said: "Could it be doubted that, if s. 5 stood alone, and no fine were provided by the Act for contravention of its provisions, a person injured by a breach of the absolute and unqualified duty imposed by that section would have a cause of action in respect of that breach? Clearly it could not be doubted. That being so, unless it appears from the whole 'purview' of the Act, to use the language of Lord Cairns in the case of *Atkinson* v. *Newcastle Waterworks Co.,* that it was the intention of the Legislature that the only remedy for breach of the statutory duty should be by proceeding for the fine imposed by s. 82, it follows that upon proof of a breach of that duty by the employer and injury thereby occasioned to the workman, a cause of action is established." The result of the above construction may be stated as follows: *prima facie* a person who has been injured by the breach of a statute has a right to recover damages from the person committing it unless it can be established by considering the whole of the Act that no such right was intended to be given. So far from that being shown in this case, the contrary is established. To prosecute for a penalty is no sufficient protection and is a poor consolation to the injured person though it affords a reason why persons should not commit a breach of the statute.

Maugham L.J.: . . . On the whole, therefore, I have come to the conclusion that in this case there is nothing in the Act to show that a personal action is precluded by reason of the existence of the special remedy provided for a breach; and further that there is sufficient ground for coming to the conclusion that s. 35 was passed for the purpose of giving a remedy to third persons who might suffer injury by the negligence of the impecunious driver of a car. It is true to say that it is only if there is negligence in the driving of the car that the third party is given a right, but I cannot help thinking that when the Act was passed it was within the knowledge of the Legislature that negligence in the driving of cars was so common an occurrence with the likelihood of injury to third persons that it was necessary in the public interest to provide machinery whereby those third persons might recover damages. Sub-s. 4 of s. 35 also tends strongly in favour of the view that civil rights were being considered by the Legislature, that sub-section indicating that a person who has deposited a sum of £15,000 is not legally bound to take out a policy of insurance which will protect third parties. A personal right of action for a breach of s. 35 therefore in my opinion lies and it lies on the assumption that the policy of insurance was one which would give a third party some measure of indemnity in the event of the person using the car being guilty of negligence. Incidentally this also disposes of the point as to remoteness of damage. With regard to the other point I have nothing to add.

Roche L.J.: Notwithstanding the able argument of Mr. Monier-Williams I am clearly of opinion that the judgment of Charles J. was right and should be affirmed. I desire to add that I also am not uninfluenced by sub-s. 4 of s. 35, which seems to point to the conclusion that it was within the purview of the Act to render effective civil remedies for the mischiefs being dealt with in the section and that it was not intended to exclude a person who suffered damage through a breach of a statutory duty from his civil remedy merely because penalties of a criminal nature are imposed.

Appeal dismissed.

NOTES

1. Does the decision really have anything to do with "legislative intention"? What are the real reasons for the decision? Are they articulated?

2. Do you think that this case was "an improper type of judicial intervention"? See Glanville Williams, "The Effect of Penal Legislation in the Law of Tort" (1960), 23 Mod. L. Rev. 233. See also Gregory, "Breach of Criminal Licensing Statutes in Civil Litigation" (1951), 36 Cornell L.Q. 622.

3. Do you think Professor Fleming's criticism of this case as "a most blatant arrogation of legislative authority", "difficult to justify on any account", and as stretching judicial discretion "beyond . . . legitimate bounds" is accurate? See Fleming, *The Law of Torts* (4th ed. 1971), at p. 126 and (2nd ed., 1961) at p. 134. Why do you think Professor Fleming, who is an advocate of negligence *per se*, strict liability and the loss distribution theory of tort law, became so alarmed? Is he being inconsistent? Is he worried that courts will refuse to use penal legislation altogether if they are pressed too far?

COMMERFORD v.
BOARD OF SCHOOL COMMISSIONERS OF HALIFAX

Nova Scotia Supreme Court. [1950] 2 D.L.R. 207

Ilsley J.: The following preliminary point of law was set down for argument before me, *viz.*: "Whether a breach of the provisions of ss. 42-49 inclusive of Ordinance No. 3 of the Ordinances of the City of Halifax respecting streets, makes the owner, agent, lessee or occupier of abutting premises liable in damages to any person injured because of such breach."

Of the sections of Ordinance 3 in question, those which have special application are the following:

42. (1) Within the area comprised within the boundaries hereinafter set

out the owner, agent or occupier of any premises shall remove the snow
from the sidewalk, pathway and gutter in front of the same. In the case of
any unoccupied lot, the snow shall be removed by the owner or person
having charge of the same.

48A. Within the area as described in Subsection (2) of Section 42 hereof,
the owner, agent, lessee or occupier of any premises shall, whenever the
sidewalk in front of such premises is in a dangerous condition, arising from
the presence of ice thereon, place ashes, sand, calcium chloride, common
salt or a mixture of these materials on the sidewalk. The amount to be so
placed shall not exceed the minimum quantity required to remedy the
dangerous condition.

49. Every person who contravenes or fails to comply with the provisions
of this ordinance respecting the removal of snow or ice shall for every such
offence be liable to a penalty not exceeding two dollars, and in default of
payment to imprisonment for a period not exceeding ten days. Every day
that snow is allowed to remain after the first twenty-four hours shall
constitute a fresh offence. . . .

Ordinance 3 was made by the City Council under s. 589 of the City Charter,
1931, the relevant provisions of which are as follows:

589. The Council may from time to time make, alter or repeal ordinances
in respect to: . . .

(e) the removal of snow and ice by the owners or occupiers of properties,
and the measures to be taken by such owners or occupiers for the abatement
of dangerous conditions arising from the presence of snow and ice. . .

By s. 942 of the Charter it is provided that:

The power to make ordinances or by-laws or regulations in respect to
any matter comprised in any Part of this Act, . . . shall include:

(b) the power to impose a money penalty for the contravention of or
failure to comply therewith. . . .

. . . I agree, that the right of action does not depend on whether a statutory
commandment or prohibition is pronounced for the benefit of the public or for
the benefit of a class. . . . Surely a more important consideration than whether
the action is brought by a member of a particular class for the benefit of which
the statute or Ordinance was passed is whether it is brought by a person
pointed out on a fair construction of the Act as being one whom the Legislature (or perhaps the Council) desired to protect. . . . In the case at bar it can,
I think, be fairly said that s. 48A of the Ordinance pointed out pedestrians, of
whom the female plaintiff was one, as being those whom the Council desired
to protect — and to protect from the same kind of accident as the one alleged.
But there is nothing in my opinion to indicate that there was any similar intention in reference to s. 42 (1). The reason for requiring snow removal may have
had nothing to do with danger to pedestrians at all. On the principle of *Gorris*
v. *Scott* (1874), L.R. 9 Ex. 125, a difference in the rights arising under the two
sections is suggested, although as I shall indicate there is in my opinion really
no such difference. . . .

As stated above the question is one of intention and I have come to the conclusion that neither the Charter nor the Ordinance discloses an intention on
the part of either the Legislature or the Council that there should be any
liability for damages for breach of the Ordinance, and indeed that a contrary
intention is disclosed. . . .

But does the Charter empower the Council to impose liability for damages?
The intention to confer a power to alter civil rights by Ordinance should
certainly not be lightly assumed. See *Orpen* v. *Roberts*, [1925] 1 D.L.R., at

pp. 1106-7; S.C.R., at pp. 370-1; where Duff J., quotes with approval the remark of Meredith C.J., in *Tomkins* v. *Brockville Rink Co.*, 31 O.R. 124, that when one considers the different kinds of acts and conduct which municipal councils in Ontario are by statute permitted to prohibit or regulate, and the multiplicity of duties they have authority to impose upon property owners and others within their jurisdiction, one is rather startled by the proposition that in each case a duty is imposed for the failure to perform which an action lies by one who is injured owing to the non-performance of it. The Legislature of course did not expressly confer on the Council the power to impose liability for damages . . . [and] it is reasonable to infer that with regard to violations of provisions of the Ordinances, remedies do not exist unless expressly authorized. . . .

But whether this conclusion is correct or not, I think that the intention of the Council as disclosed by the Ordinance was not to impose, and that there should not be, any such liability. . . . One remedy and one alone is provided for contravention of ss. 42 to 48A inclusive — the recovery of a small penalty. If s. 42 (1) were the only section in question, there could be little doubt in my opinion that it was not intended that there would be an action for damages for personal injuries for contravention of that section because there is nothing in it to indicate that personal injury is the mischief aimed at as it is in s. 48A. But the two sections are put on the same footing as to remedies by s. 49 — an indication that there was to be no liability for damages for the violation of either, that the two sections are both for the protection of the public as a whole, s. 42 (1) probably envisaging public convenience and s. 42A public safety, and one common remedy being provided for the public's protection. That this remedy is conspicuously inadequate does not I think show that the Council intended that there should be other remedies. It may rather indicate a benevolence toward property owners and occupiers more understandable than appreciated by pedestrians; or it may indicate a desire to be lenient in the imposition of penalties on owners and occupiers in view of the casting on them of duties assumed in many towns and cities by the municipal authorities. . . .

. . . I cannot think that modern developments in the law of negligence have overthrown the carefully developed jurisprudence on recovery for breaches of statutory duty. And the fact that the duty of abutting owners and occupiers to remove snow and put sand on ice in streets is completely non-existent at common law, confirm me in the view that liability for damages for breach of a purely statutory obligation should not be found to exist except on well-established grounds. . . .

The answer to the question propounded is in the negative.

NOTES

1. In *Cutler* v. *Wandsworth Stadium Ltd.*, [1949] A.C. 398, [1949] 1 All E.R. 544, 65 T.L.R. 170, a statute had been passed legalizing betting by "totalisators" at dog-races and declaring that when a totalisator was being operated, the occupier of the track shall not exclude bookmakers, but shall take steps to reserve available space for such persons where they can carry on bookmaking. Penalties were provided for conviction of the offence created by the contravention of the statute. The plaintiff, a bookmaker, brought action against the defendant, claiming that the latter had committed a breach of the Act in not providing him with available space for the carrying on of bookmaking. The House of Lords held that the plaintiff had no cause of action, the general rule being that if an Act enforces an obligation in a particular way, performance may not be enforced in any other manner unless the "scope and language" of the Act establish an exception. In the present case, the Act was

for the benefit of the public and not for the benefit of any particular group of persons who had in the past or might in the future wish to do business at the defendant's track — a vague and uncertain class. Lord du Parcq spoke caustically of the failure of Parliament "to state explicitly what its intention is" in these matters instead of "obscuring" or "concealing" that intention and leaving the courts to say what it "may be supposed probably to be". Lord Simonds said that the statute is not "the charter of the bookmakers". The court concluded by proclaiming that the penalties provided were "effective sanctions" and stood "in no need of aid from civil proceedings".

2. Is *Monk* v. *Warbey* in conflict with *Cutler* v. *Wandsworth* and with *Commerford*?

3. How would you go about reconciling the three decisions? Does it depend on the policies advanced by the particular statutes and whether the courts feel them worthy of advancement? What policy considerations do you think distinguish these three cases? Would you have decided them all as did the courts? See Linden, "Tort Liability for Criminal Nonfeasance," (1966), 44 Can. Bar Rev. 25, at p. 64.

4. The Ontario Highway Traffic Act, R.S.O. 1970, c. 202, s. 140, states:
(1) Where an accident occurs on a highway, every person in charge of a vehicle or car of an electric railway that is directly or indirectly involved in the accident shall,
    (a) remain at or immediately return to the scene of the accident;
    (b) render all possible assistance; and
    (c) upon request, give in writing to anyone sustaining loss or injury, or to any constable or other police officer or to any witness, his name and address, and also the name and address of the registered owner of such vehicle, and the number of the permit.
(2) Every person who contravenes any of the provisions of this section is guilty of an offence and on summary conviction is liable to a fine of not less than $100 and not more than $500 or to imprisonment for a term of not more than six months, or to both, and in addition his licence or permit may be suspended for a period of not more than two years.

See also Criminal Code, R.S.C. 1970, c. C-34, s. 233(2) for a similar provision. Would a violation of s. 140(1) of the Highway Traffic Act, or of s. 233(2) of the Criminal Code give rise to tort liability? What are the problems? What would be the benefits?

5. In *Brooks* v. *E. J. Willig Truck Transport Co.* (1953), 255 P. 2d 802, (S.C. Cal.), Gibson C.J., in a hit and run case, stated:
"One who negligently injures another and renders him helpless is bound to use reasonable care to prevent any further harm which the actor realizes or should realize threatens the injured person. This duty existed at common law although the accident was caused in part by the contributory negligence of the person who was injured . . . . Sections 480 and 482 of the Vehicle Code require an automobile driver who injures another to stop and render aid. This duty is imposed upon the driver whether or not he is responsible for the accident, and a violation gives rise to civil liability if it is a proximate cause of further injury or death. . . . Failure to stop and render aid constitutes negligence as a matter of law, in the absence of a legally sufficient excuse or justification."

See also *Summers* v. *Dominguez* (1938), 84 P. 2d 237, at p. 239 (D.C.A. 3d Dist. Calif.). See *Rains* v. *Hedenfels Brothers* (1969), 443 S.W. 2d 280. And see generally Linden, "Tort Liability for Criminal Nonfeasance" (1966), 44 Can. Bar Rev. 25, at p. 48.

6. What policy reasons have prompted the U.S. courts to rely on the criminal hit-and-run legislation in imposing civil liability? Are the same rationales applicable in Canada?

7. In *Colonial Coach Lines* v. *Bennett and C.P.R.* (1967), 66 D.L.R. (2d) 396 (Ont. C.A.), the plaintiff's bus was damaged when it collided with a cow that had escaped from a farmer's land onto the highway through a defective

fence along the railway's right of way. Mr. Justice Laskin held that the railway was partially responsible to the plaintiff. He relied on ss. 277 and 392 of the Railway Act. Section 277 created an obligation to erect fences "suitable to prevent cattle . . . from getting on the railway lands". Section 392 imposed civil liability for failing to do so. Although s. 392 could not be applied in this case because the loss did not occur on "railway lands", Mr. Justice Laskin reasoned as follows:

"I am of opinion that having regard to the statutory duty to fence resting upon the railway under s. 277, there was a foreseeable risk of harm from escaping cattle to persons or property on the adjoining highway so as to impose a duty upon the railway for the breach of which it was liable at common law for the damage that occurred in this case.

. . . Lest this matter be thought settled in this case by default, I think it proper to say that the railway's liability for the loss of Bennett's cow may be founded on the ordinary law of negligence. There is a similarity to the liability of a municipality for injury arising from disrepair of a highway where, having notice of a want of repair or being chargeable therewith, the municipality is in default in its statutory duty to keep the highway in repair. I take the evidence in this case to support a finding that the railway had adequate notice of the disrepair of the fence along its right of way and time enough to correct the defect. There was a foreseeable risk of harm if escape through the defective fence to the railway right of way occurred. By reason of what it knew and of its statutory duty to maintain fences, the railway was negligent and must respond for the loss of the cow.

Equally, there was a foreseeable risk of harm from cattle to traffic on the adjoining highway if they escaped through the defective fence to the railway right of way. Again, I take the evidence to support a finding that the railway knew or ought to have known of the presence of Bennett's cattle in the field adjoining its right of way. This, coupled with the notice of disrepair of the fence, already adverted to, and awareness of the open access from the right of way to the highway adjoining on the other side, cast a common law duty on the railway to travellers on the highway to maintain the fence; failure to do so in the present case was a contributing cause of the damage to the motor coach, and for this the railway was liable. . . .

The explicit provision for civil redress under s. 392 cannot, in my view, be taken to limit the application of common law principles of liability for negligence in situations which fall outside the section but are none the less within those principles. Hence, even if the scope of a railway's strict liability under s. 392 extends generally to injury on the railway right of way arising from a failure to fence, it may incur liability beyond this scope for injury off the right of way which, by reason of what it knew or ought to have known, could reasonably be foreseen as likely to occur if it failed to keep in repair a fence known to it to be defective. This liability for negligence is not founded merely on breach of a statutory duty to fence, but proceeds on the footing of a state of facts comprehending maintenance of a fence to prevent the escape, from the adjoining land, of cattle which, if not contained, might stray on to a highway open from the right of way and expose oncoming traffic to the risk of injury. The triggering elements of liability are the railway's awareness of the defective condition of the fence and failure to take remedial measures to avert injury which could be reasonably foreseen. Existence of a statutory obligation to fence and actual assumption thereof by the railway were simply factors in the raising of a duty of care to the plaintiff by the railway when it knew that the obligation had not been met.

It follows that the jury's finding of fault against the railway should be reinstated."

In what way has Mr. Justice Laskin used the statute in this case? Was it really relevant? What about *Gorris* v. *Scott*?

8. In *Stermer* v. *Lawson* (1977), 79 D.L.R. (3d) 366 (B.C.) percentage varied (1979), 11 C.C.L.T. 76, someone lent his motorcycle to an unlicensed driver in

violation of s. 69 of the B.C. Motor-vehicle Act which read: "Every person who, being in possession or control of a motor-vehicle, permits the motor-vehicle to be driven or operated by a minor who is not the holder of a subsisting licence permitting such operation is guilty of an offence against this Act." Fulton, J., *inter alia,* stated:

"While breach of a statutory provision is not conclusive evidence of negligence at common law, it is a factor which the Court is entitled to consider in deciding whether or not in the particular case a duty is owed."

9. In *Stewart* v. *Park Manor Motors* (1968), 66 D.L.R. (2d) 143 (Ont. C.A.), an employee sued a former employer for vacation pay that was owed under the Hours of Work and Vacations with Pay Act. The statute made non-compliance with the Act a summary conviction offence and also required the judge, upon conviction, to order a delinquent employer to reimburse the employee for his unpaid wages. The Ontario Court of Appeal held that these statutory remedies did not foreclose a private civil action. Mr. Justice Schroeder stated:

". . . [the] summary remedy was provided as a matter of convenience or, perhaps, policy, but in my view it was at most an optional remedy which was never intended to replace the ancient remedy available in the Superior, District or County Courts."

His Lordship further explained:

"Where a statute creates a liability not existing at common law and provides a particular remedy for enforcing it, the question is raised as to whether the particular remedy provided is the only remedy or whether there is, in addition, a right of action for damages or other relief based on the breach of the statutory duty. As statutory duties deal with a great variety of matters of varying degrees of importance and are directed to a number of different objects it is impossible to give a simple, affirmative or negative answer to this question. Everything depends upon the object or intention of the statute."

Three factors were taken into account by the court in discerning the intention of the legislature:

(1) ". . . whether the action is brought in respect of the kind of harm which the statute was intended to prevent"; (2) ". . . if the person bringing the action is one of the class which the statute was designed to protect"; and (3) ". . . if the special remedy provided by the statute is adequate for the protection of the person injured".

All three factors were satisfied here, the first two being merely the requirements of *Gorris* v. *Scott.* The third, whether the statutory remedy was insufficient by itself, was met since an employee could be reluctant to prosecute criminally his employer, there was the possibility of technical grounds defeating a criminal prosecution and there was the problem of the expiry of a six-month limitation period.

What do you think of all this? See Hunter, "Civil Actions for Discrimination" (1977), 55 Can. Bar Rev. 106.

10. In *Schacht* v. *The Queen* (1973), 30 D.L.R. (3d) 641 (C.A.), a well-lighted barrier that marked a detour around some highway construction was knocked over by a car at night so that it was no longer visible to other motorists on the highway. The Ontario Provincial Police came and investigated the accident, but failed to take steps to warn the traffic about the danger on the road. The plaintiff was injured when he drove his automobile into the unmarked excavation. The Police Act of Ontario required that the O.P.P., *inter alia,* "shall maintain a traffic patrol . . .". The Highway Traffic Act, R.S.O. 1970, c. 202, s. 86, empowered the police officers to "direct traffic" in order to "ensure orderly movement" and "to prevent injury or damage to persons or property". Mr. Justice Schroeder allowed the plaintiff to recover 50 percent of his damages against the police administration. He recognized that the case was a novel one and stated:

"Police forces exist in municipal, provincial, and federal jurisdictions to exercise powers designed to promote the order, safety, health, morals, and general welfare of society. It is not only impossible but inadvisable to attempt to frame a definition which will set definite limits to the powers and duties of police officers appointed to carry out the powers of the state in relation to individuals who come within its jurisdiction and protection. The duties imposed on them by statute are by no means exhaustive. It is infinitely better that the courts should decide as each case arises whether, having regard to the necessities of the case and the safeguards required in the public interest, the police are under a legal duty in the particular circumstances. . . .

Section 55 of the Police Act which sets out the duties of members of a municipal police force declares that they 'have generally all the powers and privileges and they are liable to all the duties and responsibilities that belong to constables'. This is a legislative recognition of the fact that while constables have certain duties imposed upon them by statute, they are, in addition, subject to the traditional duties of police officers of which cognizance is taken under the common law.

The respondent police officers were under a statutory duty to maintain a traffic patrol of the highway in question. The word 'patrol' is used in reference to police passing along or over highways or streets in the performance of their duties. The word is sometimes used to refer to duties assigned to soldiers in reference to a camp, or to the duties of a caretaker of large buildings to protect the property against fire and burglary. There is a definite purpose in requiring the police to patrol the highways under their jurisdiction, namely, to ensure that traffic laws will be obeyed, to investigate road accidents, and to assist injured persons. All this is directed to the prevention of accidents and the preservation of the safety of road users. If an unlighted truck or other large obstruction presenting a danger to traffic were on a highway after nightfall any traffic officer, sensible of his duty, would feel obligated to adopt reasonable means of ensuring that adequate warning was given of their presence on the highway. A cavity such as existed here would be even less visible to a road user, and clearly presented a much greater hazard than an obstruction located above the road surface.

Negligence as commonly defined includes both acts and omissions which involve an unreasonable risk of injury. In earlier times the common law furnished redress only for injury resulting from affirmative misconduct, and inaction was regarded as too remote to furnish a ground for the imposition of legal liability. Much as the humanitarian spirit which motivated the conduct of the good Samaritan has been lauded, it was rooted in a moral philosophy, hence from the legal standpoint the *laissez-faire* attitude of the priest and the Levite was condoned. A member of a traffic detachment of the Ontario Provincial Police in the situation of Constable Boyd and Corporal Johnston is in an entirely different position from the ordinary citizen or the priest and the Levite. These officers were under a positive duty by virtue of their office to take appropriate measures in the face of a hazardous condition such as they encountered here to warn approaching traffic of its presence.

It is undoubtedly true that the nuisance was created in the first instance by the northbound motorist, Blancke, but the removal of the important large signs brought about by Blancke's act imperatively required officers patrolling the highway to deal with the dangerous situation so caused in an effective manner. The means of guarding against the danger of motorists driving into the excavation before the Department of Highways workmen could replace the large illuminated signs were readily available, since each of the defendant police officers was driving a police cruiser equipped with a revolving flashing light on the roof and nothing more was necessary than to place a cruiser across the highway at the southerly edge of the depression or to place a cruiser at both the south and north limits thereof.

Looked upon superficially the passivity of these two officers in the face of the manifest dangers inherent in the inadequately guarded depression across the highway may appear to be nothing more than non-feasance, but in the case of public servants subject not to a mere social obligation, but to what I feel bound to regard as a legal obligation, it was non-feasance amounting to misfeasance. Traffic officers are subject to all the duties and responsibilities belonging to constables. The duties which I would lay upon them stem not only from the relevant statutes to which reference has been made, but from the common law, which recognizes the existence of a broad conventional or customary duty in the established constabulary as an arm of the State to protect the life, limb and property of the subject.

I am not here concerned with the provisions of s. 86 of the Highway Traffic Act which confers a right upon a police officer, if he deems it advisable or necessary, to direct the movement of traffic and requires motorists to obey his directions. Although this section is couched in permissive language there may be circumstances in which a failure to act as provided by s. 86 may be legally censurable. However, the plaintiff's cause of action does not rest on a breach of s. 86, but is properly founded on the broader basis which I have attempted to outline. . . .

. . . Each case must, in the final analysis, depend upon its own peculiar circumstances, but to hold that the proven neglect attributed by the learned judge to both defendant police officers in the most emphatic terms was not an actionable wrong which attracted liability to the plaintiff in the degrees apportioned by the learned judge would be to make the phrase 'police protection' hollow and meaningless."

The Supreme Court of Canada affirmed in *O'Rourke* v. *Schacht* (1974), 55 D.L.R. (3d) 96, although it excused one of the several police officers involved. Mr. Justice Spence quoted at length from Mr. Justice Schroeder's opinion, which he described as "forthright and enlightened" and concluded:

"I have the same view as to the duty of a police officer under the provisions of the said s. 3(3) of the Police Act in carrying out police traffic patrol. In my opinion, it is of the essence of that patrol that the officer attempt to. make the road safe for traffic. Certainly, therefore, there should be included in that duty the proper notification of possible road users of a danger arising from a previous accident and creating an unreasonable risk of harm."

In a dissenting opinion, Martland J., Judson and Pigeon JJ. concurring, stated that he found nothing in the legislation that would "indicate an intention on the part of the Legislature to impose a liability upon a member of that Force who fails to carry out a duty assigned to him under the statute".

11. In *Millette* v. *Coté et al.,* [1971] 2 O.R. 155; revd. in part, [1972] 3 O.R. 224; revd. in part *R.* v. *Coté* (1974), 51 D.L.R. (3d) 244 (S.C.C.), Mr. Justice Galligan at trial held the provincial police partly to blame for a car accident because they failed to notify the Department of Highways about a dangerous icy condition on a highway. He stated:

"[T]here is a basic and fundamental duty on the part of the police officer to observe and report dangerous conditions seen by him on his patrol. . . .

In my opinion, [the police officer] was negligent in both his observation and report. He was negligent in my opinion in failing to recognize on his earlier visit to the scene that the situation was dangerous and a great hazard to motorists. He was negligent in the report he gave to the Department of Highways by not impressing upon them that the situation was one of extreme danger and of emergency. In my opinion, on the balance of probabilities this negligence was a contributing factor to the loss and damage in this case."

On appeal, the Court of Appeal did not pass upon the duty of the police, but reversed the decision against the police on the ground that there was no causal connection between their failure to notify and the accident. In other words, if they had warned the Department of Highways, it would have made no difference in preventing the accident. The decision was affirmed on this point by the Supreme Court of Canada (Nov. 27, 1974).

As for the liability of the Department of Highways, the trial judge had held it and the police 75 percent at fault. The Court of Appeal affirmed, but the Supreme Court of Canada reduced the liability of the Department of Highways to 25 percent, the defendant driver bearing 75 percent of the blame. The Supreme Court of Canada relied upon the provisions of the Highway Improvement Act, now R.S.O. 1970, c. 201, s. 30. Mr. Justice Dickson warned, however, that the decision "does not import recognition of any general duty to salt or sand highways, failure in the discharge of which would expose the Minister to civil claims", but was limited to the extremely dangerous conditions at that particular location about which the Department should have known. (The trial judge had described it as a "killer strip".)

See also on liability for condition of roads, *Millar & Brown Ltd.* v. *Vancouver* (1965), 56 D.L.R. (2d) 190 (B.C.S.C.), liability for overhanging tree; *Levine* v. *Morris*, [1970] 1 All E.R. 144 (C.A.), liability for negligent design of highway; *cf. Cox* v. *Town of Sydney Mines* (1969), 4 D.L.R. (3d) 341, no liability for condition of road at railway crossing. See generally Fitzpatrick et al., *The Law and Roadside Hazards* (1974).

12. In *County of Parkland* v. *Stetar*, [1975] 2 S.C.R. 884, a warning sign which was erected by a county fell down and thereby contributed to a collision. Although there was no obligation on the county to erect the sign, there was a statutory duty to keep the road in a reasonable state of repair. In holding the county partially to blame, Mr. Justice Dickson said:

". . . having erected a warning sign, the county came under a duty to make adequate and proper inspections to ensure the proper maintenance of the sign and to re-erect it when the county knew or ought to have known that the sign was not in its proper position to give warning to [the traffic]."
See also *Earl* v. *Bourdon* (1975), 65 D.L.R. (3d) 646 (B.C.).

13. Compare with *McRae* v. *White*, [1973] 1 W.W.R. 542, revd (1975), 56 D.L.R. (3d) 525 (B.C.C.A.), where an inspector was relieved of liability for inadequately inspecting a building that later collapsed. Berger J. had held him liable at trial on the ground *inter alia* that a municipal by-law had required certain inspections. The Court of Appeal, however, reversed on the ground that a duty to inspect arose only where notice under the by-law was given to the inspector that he was required to do so. Since the inspector received no notification in this instance, he was not obligated to make the inspection. Would the result have differed if the notice had been given pursuant to the by-law? See also *Kwong* v. *R.*, [1979] 2 W.W.R. 1 (Alta. C.A.); affd. S.C.C.

14. Does a municipality have a duty to protect a citizen who has been threatened with violence? If the citizen is injured, will a civil suit be available against the municipality? See *Riss* v. *New York* (1968), 240 N.E. 2d 860 (no liability).

15. Can an employer sue an employee for damages resulting from the violation of a labour relations statute? See Arthurs, "Tort Liability for Strikes in Canada" (1960), 38 Can. Bar Rev. 346, at p. 361.

16. What about a civil suit for pollution against someone who contravenes anti-pollution legislation? Actions such as these open up exciting new vistas for tort lawyers. Should tort law be used as a private citizen's weapon to enforce the criminal law?

17. An employee complains that she has been wrongfully dismissed from her job on the basis of sex discrimination contrary to the Ontario Human Rights Code, R.S.O. 1970, c. 318. Can she recover for wrongful dismissal relying on this statute? Does she have to rely on the Code at all? See *MacDonald* v. *283076 Ontario Inc.* (1979), 23 O.R. (2d) 185 (*per* Griffiths J.), revd C.A. Sept. 28, 1979. What if, rather than being fired, the employee is denied a promotion because of her sex or her colour? See Hunter, *supra*, note 9.

18. Most provinces now have human rights codes which forbid discrimination in employment and accommodation. Would the violation of one of these statutes give rise to tort liability? See *Crawford* v. *Kent* (1960), 341 Mass. 125, 167 N.E. 2d 620. Professor Blumrosen, in his article, "Antidiscrimination Law in Action

in New Jersey: A Law-Sociology Study" (1965), 19 Rutgers L. Rev. 189, concluded:

"The thesis suggested here is that the antidiscrimination provision of the New Jersey Constitution establishes such a standard and, therefore intentional discrimination on grounds of race constitutes a wrong for which a civil action may be brought. I do not expect that recognition of such a tort action will cause great changes in human behavior, or produce much litigation. Few persons injured by discrimination will sue and fewer will recover. We know that the traditional Anglo-American complaint-oriented judicial process will not be utilized by most Negroes. However, judicial recognition of the tort will generate certain pressures in connection with the race relations problems. One may be in the direction of furthering conformity to the law. Another may be to channel discrimination problems exclusively through the administrative process. These pressures could result in the improvement of the administrative process in racial discrimination cases."

See also Colley, "Civil Actions for Damages Arising Out of Violations of Civil Rights" (1965), 17 Hastings L.J. 189; Molot, "The Duty of Business to Serve the Public: Analogy to the Innkeeper's Obligation" (1968), 46 Can. Bar Rev. 612; see generally Tarnopolsky, *The Canadian Bill of Rights* (2nd ed., 1975). See Hunter, "Civil Actions for Discrimination" (1977), 55 Can. Bar Rev. 106.

19. In *Bhadauria* v. *Board of Governors of the Seneca College of Applied Arts and Technology* (1979), 11 C.C.L.T. 121 (Ont. C.A.), the plaintiff, a highly educated East Indian woman, qualified to teach in Ontario, alleged that she had applied for 10 openings on the teaching staff of the defendant college, but was not interviewed for any of them. She alleged that this was because of her ethnic origin. Rather than filing a complaint under the Ontario Human Rights Code, she sued the defendant, which moved to strike out her Statement of Claim as disclosing no cause of action. Although the action was initially struck out, the Ontario Court of Appeal reversed that decision and sent the matter on to trial.

Madam Justice Bertha Wilson (Houlden, Morden concurring) cited the principle of *Ashby* v. *White* to the effect that "If the plaintiff has a right, he must of necessity have a means to vindicate and maintain it, and a remedy if he is injured in the execution or enjoyment of it; and indeed it is a vain thing to imagine a right without a remedy; for want of right and want of remedy are reciprocal." The court held that the facts alleged gave rise to a cause of action at common law and explained:

"While no authority cited to us has recognized a tort of discrimination, none has repudiated such a tort. The matter is accordingly *res integra* before us. . . .

I think there can be no doubt that the interests of persons of different ethnic origins are entitled to the protection of the law. The preamble to *The Ontario Human Rights Code* reads as follows:

'Whereas recognition of the inherent dignity and the equal and inalienable rights of all members of the human family is the foundation of freedom, justice and peace in the world and is in accord with the Universal Declaration of Human Rights as proclaimed by the United Nations;

And Whereas it is public policy in Ontario that every person is free and equal in dignity and rights without regard to race, creed, colour, sex, marital status, nationality, ancestry or place of origin;

And Whereas these principles have been confirmed in Ontario by a number of enactments of the Legislature;

And Whereas it is desirable to enact a measure to codify and extend such enactments and to simplify their administration;

Therefore, Her Majesty, by and with the advice and consent of the Legislative Assembly of the Province of Ontario, enacts as follows:'

I regard the preamble to the Code as evidencing what is now, and probably has been for some considerable time, the public policy of this Province respecting fundamental human rights. If we accept that 'every person is free and equal in dignity and rights without regard to race, creed, colour, sex, marital status, nationality, ancestry or place of origin', as we do, then it is appropriate that these rights receive the full protection of the common law.

The plaintiff has a right not to be discriminated against because of her ethnic origin and alleges that she has been injured in the exercise or enjoyment of it. If she can establish that, then the common law must, on the principle of *Ashby* v. *White et al., supra,* afford her a remedy.

I do not regard the *Code* as in any way impeding the appropriate development of the common law in this important area. While the fundamental human right we are concerned with is recognized by the *Code,* it was not created by it. Nor does the *Code,* in my view, contain any expression of legislative intention to exclude the common law remedy. Rather the reverse since s. 14(1) appears to make the appointment of a board of inquiry to look into a complaint made under the *Code* a matter of ministerial discretion.

It is unnecessary, in view of the finding that a cause of action exists at common law, to determine whether or not the *Code* gives rise to a civil action." What is the legal basis for this action?

20. Shortly after the *Seneca College* case, another came down, *Aziz* v. *Adamson* (1979), 11 C.C.L.T. 134, in which the plaintiff, a "Green Hornet", a parking control officer, sued the Chief of Police of Metropolitan Toronto, alleging that he was discriminated against, in being rejected on 5 different occasions when he applied to become a police constable. Following *Seneca College,* which he described as an "eminently sensible decision", Linden J. said:

"By enacting these principles in the preamble of the Code, the Legislature of Ontario has chosen to underscore its commitment to equal rights for all of our citizens and its opposition to all forms of discrimination. The Court of Appeal made it clear, however, that this new tort action for discrimination did not depend for its life on *The Ontario Human Rights Code,* but rather was based on the common law. The public policy against racial and other discrimination existed in Ontario before the enactment of the Human Rights Code and was not created by the *Code.* The *Code* merely recognizes that preexisting policy in its preamble and then establishes an agency and procedures that seek to eliminate or reduce the number of incidents of discrimination in this province. The courts of Ontario should cooperate with the Legislature, where possible, in promoting the public policy enshrined in *The Ontario Human Rights Code.* I, therefore, find that the plaintiff's statement of claim does allege facts which, if proved, could support a cause of action in tort for discrimination.

The Court of Appeal did not have to decide in *Seneca College* whether the *Code* gives rise to a civil cause of action. There is no need in this case either to discuss that question, because no violation of any of the substantive provisions of *The Ontario Human Rights Code* was pleaded in the statement of claim. Doubtless, the courts will have some regard to these legislative terms in fleshing out the content of the new tort of discrimination. In the past they have relied on statutory enactments in crystallizing the standard of care in negligence cases. (See *Sterling Trusts* v. *Postma,* [1965] S.C.R. 324. See also Fleming, *The Law of Torts* (5th ed., 1977), p. 122.) Similarly, the courts have considered legislative provisions as relevant in determining whether certain conduct is excusable. (See *Priestman* v. *Colangelo,* [1959] S.C.R. 615; *Poupart* v. *Lafortune,* [1973] S.C.R. 175; cf. *Beima* v. *Goyer,* [1965] S.C.R. 638.) So too, reliance has been placed on legislation by the courts in recognizing new tort duties. (See *Monk* v. *Warbey,* [1935] 1 K.B. 75; *Brooks* v. *Willig Transport Co.* (1953), 266 P. 2d 802; *O'Rourke* v. *Schacht* (1975), 55 D.L.R. (3d) 96 (S.C.C.) *per* Spence J., at p. 120.) Consequently, legislation may be considered by the courts in cases such as this by analogy, but it is not controlling, unless there is specific language to that effect. The legislation, therefore, does not fix the standards to be employed by the common law courts; it may, however, serve as a useful guide to the courts in arriving at their own views as to the appropriate standards to be employed in the cases before them.

The enforcement machinery set out in the *Code* is not exclusive, as indicated by Madam Justice Wilson. A person who feels aggrieved is not forced to complain to the Ontario Human Rights Commission; a person may choose to seek redress in the courts. Although most victims would certainly prefer to proceed before the Commission because there are no legal costs to the complainant, they are free to avail themselves of a civil action in the courts, if they are willing to risk the potential costs involved in such action.

The availability of these alternative procedures can be useful in appropriate cases. As was pointed out by Professor Hunter in his article on Civil Actions for Discrimination, *supra*, there are situations where the complainant may prefer a court action to a commission resolution. Sometimes the complainant's interest and that of the Commission may diverge. For example, although the Commission may honestly conclude that there is no proof of discrimination, the complainant may still feel he was discriminated against and may wish to have "his day in court". He should be allowed that opportunity. Further, the Commission is required by law to effect a settlement of the matter complained of if it can do so. On occasion, a complainant may be unhappy with such a proposed settlement and may insist on the continuation of a public inquiry. (See *Amber* v. *Leder,* Report of Board of Inquiry under Professor W.S. Tarnopolsky dated April 10, 1969, as clarified on May 1, 1970). As Professor Hunter suggests, "If the complainant is intransigent in rejecting even a reasonable settlement, it seems more sensible that he be allowed to attempt to vindicate his position at his own, rather than public expense." (As to the paradoxes involved in these cases, see *Ruest* v. *International Brotherhood of Electrical Workers,* Report of Board of Inquiry under Professor H.W. Arthurs, dated April 9, 1968 at p. 24). There are, then, valid reasons for permitting complainants to avail themselves of private actions, if these appear preferable to them than commission proceedings."
Does this case add anything to the *Seneca College* case?

21. Should actions such as these be allowed? Is it better to give the Human Rights Commission a monopoly over these problems? What sort of damages would have to be proved? See Gibson, Comment (1979), 11 C.C.L.T. 141.

4. Possible Solutions

THE EMERGENCY MEDICAL AID ACT

R.S.A. 1970, c. 122, s. 3

Where, in respect of a person who is ill, injured or unconscious as the result of an accident or other emergency,

(*a*) a physician or registered nurse voluntarily and without expectation of compensation or reward renders emergency medical services or first aid assistance and the services or assistance are not rendered at a hospital or other place having adequate medical facilities and equipment, or

(*b*) a person other than a person mentioned in clause (*a*) voluntarily renders emergency first aid assistance and that assistance is rendered at the immediate scene of the accident or emergency,

the physician, registered nurse or other person is not liable for damages for injuries to or the death of that person alleged to have been caused by an act or omission on his part in rendering the medical services or first aid assistance, unless it is established that the injuries or death were caused by gross negligence on his part.

NOTES

1. What can we do to encourage people to be Good Samaritans? What extra-legal measures can be adopted? What legal measures can be enacted?

2. What do you think about a statute to relieve from tort liability anyone who attempts a rescue? Over 30 states in the United States provide either a

total or partial immunity to doctors and/or nurses who render emergency treatment at the scene of an accident. See Louisell & Williams, *The Trial of Malpractice Cases* (1960), s. 594.2. Alberta and Nova Scotia are the only Canadian provinces with such legislation in effect. Both the Ontario Law Reform Commission (Annual Report, 1971, p. 13) and the Manitoba Law Reform Commission (Report on the Advisability of a Good Samaritan Law, Report #11, March 8, 1973) have recommended against enacting a statute.

Several private members bills have been introduced in Ontario, but so far all have died on the order paper. See, for example, Bill 117, 1st session, 28th legislature, 17 Eliz. II, 1968.

3. Would such legislation be effective to increase the frequency of doctors offering help at the roadside? Do doctors refuse to assist *because* of fear of liability or do they just *say* they do? Is this merely their rationalization for decisions taken on other grounds? See "Note", 51 Calif. L. Rev. 816. See Gray and Sharpe, "Doctors, Samaritans and the Accident Victim" (1973), 11 O.H.L.J. 1, at p. 27.

4. Are there any dangers in exonerating doctors and/or nurses from liability? What are they? Do they outweigh the potential benefits?

5. Should the state compensate rescuers who offer assistance and are injured in the attempt? If the person being rescued was placed in the position of peril by a negligent person or was negligent himself, the rescuer is entitled to recover in tort. If there is no negligence, however, or insolvency, there is no compensation available. Some jurisdictions grant compensation to those injured by criminal acts. See *supra*. Consequently, if the rescuer is injured by criminal conduct, he may claim compensation from one of these funds, but not if there is no crime.

6. The Canadian Bankers Association gives rewards to those injured while trying to prevent bank robberies. Recently, in Toronto, a dentist who was shot while chasing a bank robber, was granted $5,000 by the C.B.A. Sometimes a municipality will make a gratuitous award to a person injured while doing some heroic act. On occasion the publicity generated by such acts prompts citizens to send small money gifts to the hero or his family. Is this a better way of dealing with this problem?

7. Should we reward rescuers on a contract or restitution basis? Paul saves Dennis from drowning. Dennis says, "Thank you. I promise to give you $1,000." The next day Dennis changes his mind. Can Paul recover in contract? Is this "past consideration"? What if Dennis had called out from the water for help? See generally, on this problem Dawson, "Rewards for the Rescue of Human Life," printed in *XXth Century Comparative and Conflicts Law:*

". . . And so we come to the ultimate, painful question — should the life-salvor on land have a civil remedy to reimburse him for his losses against the person whom he attempted by appropriate means to save from imminent peril, whether or not the attempt succeeded? My own answer is an inclusive no. To me the difficulty is not merely that American law has failed to adopt the generalizations of *negotiorum gestio*; for our own law of restitution, backward as it seems to most European observers, could be extended to fill at least part of this gap. Perhaps there would be no great injustice in allowing recovery against the victim for minor injuries to the person or property of the rescuer — medical care for frostbite suffered in a mountain rescue, or repairs to a car that is driven off the road to avoid colliding with a pedestrian. If the person rescued, inspired by gratitude, subsequently promises a reward or indemnity to his rescuer, it should be possible to find enough moral obligation to justify enforcement of the promise, even though the traditional tests of bargain consideration are not satisfied. But where no such promise has been made as a distinct ground and measure of liability, it seems grossly unjust that a drowning woman, herself without fault, should be required (jointly with her husband) to support the widow of the drowned rescuer for the rest of the widow's life, and the children of the rescuer until their majority. . . .

As to resort to the national treasury, it seems to me unlikely that we shall follow the example of Austria and provide state funds from which grants can be made to saviours of life. We would all applaud our great foundations if they gave not only Carnegie medals but cash awards to heroes or one could have recourse to the social security system, as in Germany whose legislation, already described, awards health, accident, and survivors' insurance at the normal rates to any person who saves or undertakes to save another from present danger to life, with danger to his own life, body or health, even though the person who attempts the rescue is not employed in an insured occupation. This seems, indeed, an attractive solution, for if mutual aid in the conservation of human life serves the interests of the community and even becomes a duty enforceable within limits by the criminal law, one feels a strong impulse to spread the cost over the widest possible group of contributors. But even this group is not large enough, for in truth the whole community should pay. . . .

My own conclusion, nevertheless, is that private law remedies are misapplied when they create liability without fault in the person whose life or health is saved. Whatever merit they may have in other contexts, the doctrines of *negotiorum gestio* do not compel this result. . . .

Perhaps it is right that the deviant individual who refuses aid when it can be rendered without serious risk should be punished by the criminal law and also made liable by the law of tort. But it seems to me a different question whether the one who conforms to or exceeds his duty should receive from another in desperate need either reward or indemnity for the aid he gives.

Perhaps this means that we must confess at this point a major failure of legal techniques. But I believe that even those who have the techniques — the doctrines of *negotiorum gestio* — should hesitate long before establishing rules of such broad reach and consequence. Remedies and doctrines of private law are ill adapted to measuring the value of human life. I see no compelling reason why they should be used to transfer the risks of our life together in a perilous world or to limit the price we all must pay for the privilege of being human beings."

8. Should we impose a general civil duty to render aid? See Ames, "Law and Morals" (1908), 22 Harv. L. Rev. 97:

"But ought the law to remain in this condition? Of course any statutory duty to be benevolent would have to be exceptional. The practical difficulty in such legislation would be in drawing the line. But that difficulty has continually to be faced in the law. We should all be better satisfied if the man who refuses to throw a rope to a drowning man or to save a helpless child on the railroad track could be punished and be made to compensate the widow of the man drowned and the wounded child. We should not think it advisable to penalize the surgeon who refused to make the journey. These illustrations suggest a possible working rule. One who fails to interfere to save another from impending death or great bodily harm, when he might do so with little or no inconvenience to himself, and the death or great bodily harm follows as a consequence of his inaction, shall be punished criminally and shall make compensation to the party injured or to his widow and children in case of death."

See also the rule proposed by Rudolph, "The Duty to Act: A Proposed Rule" (1965), 44 Neb. L. Rev. 499:

"A person has a duty to act whenever:

1. The harm or loss is imminent and there is apparently no other practical alternative to avoid the threatened harm or loss except his own action;
2. Failure to act would result in substantial harm or damage to another person or his property and the effort, risk, or cost of acting is disproportionately less than the harm or damage avoided; and
3. The circumstances placing the person in a position to act are purely fortuitous."

What is the proper function of the court here? See Weiler, "Legal Values and

Judicial Decisionmaking" (1970), 48 Can. Bar Rev. 1.

9. Sould we brand the failure to assist a person in peril as criminal conduct? One American state and some 14 European countries including Portugal, Italy, Netherlands, Norway, Russia, Denmark, Poland, Germany, Rumania, France, Hungary, Czechoslovakia, Switzerland and Belgium have done so. See Rudzinski, "The Duty to Rescue: A Comparative Analysis", printed in *The Good Samaritan and The Law* (1966); Franklin, "Vermont Requires Rescue" (1972), 25 Stan. L. Rev. 51; see also Gray and Sharpe, *supra,* note 3, at p. 26.

Professor Tunc described the French law in his article, "The Volunteer and the Good Samaritan," printed in *The Good Samaritan and The Law* (1966) as follows:

"The provision of main concern to us, however, is Article 63, Paragraph 2, according to which a person who abstains from giving assistance to somebody in danger, when he can give this assistance without risk to himself or to other persons, either by his personal action or by prompting the rescue, incurs a punishment of three months at least and five years at most in jail, and a fine of 360 francs at least and 15,000 francs at most.

The conditions under which the punishment is incurred are reasonably clear. Comparable conditions may be found in most European legislations. First, a person must be in danger. The law does not provide for protection of things; only for the rescue of people. The reason for the danger is of no importance. The man to be rescued may be a victim of his own fault as well as of the fault of somebody else. The crime of abstention is committed even if a physician can state afterward that assistance would have had no effect and that the victim was injured or sick to the point where he could no longer be saved. On the other hand, no crime is committed if the victim is already dead at the time when the rescue is refused.

The second element of the crime of abstention is the possibility of a rescue. A person who feels powerless, and actually is powerless, to help a man in danger cannot be sentenced. Nor can a person who commits a mistake in the form of assistance he gives to the victim. On the other hand, the fact that a person may be unable to render assistance personally does not exempt him; he should at least prompt assistance by means which appear reasonable in the circumstances.

The third element of the crime is the absence of risk in the rescue, either for the person who has failed to help or for a third party. The courts have to consider whether there was any real risk in rescuing the victim. Of course, mere inconvenience is not risk. Somebody may have to jump into a river, even if he finds it unpleasant, if by doing this he can save somebody else without appreciable risk.

The last element of the crime is the voluntary character of abstention. The law does not punish only the person who looks upon the distress of another with ill will or indifference; it also punishes the coward. However, abstention is not considered a crime if it is involuntary. For instance, no crime is committed by the passer-by who does not see the victim, or who does not understand that he is in danger; nor even by the physician or the nurse who does not understand that somebody calling for him is in urgent need of care and who defers his visit. . . .

The impact of the 1941 and 1945 statutes on the civil consequences of a failure to rescue was twofold.

First, when the failure to rescue constitutes a crime, it can no longer be disputed that civil liability is incurred. The person who could have rescued the victim and did not do so must pay for the consequences of his failure. Of course, the casual connection between tort and damage does not appear here in its usual setting. Even before the law was passed, however, it could already be strongly argued, on the basis of human liberty, that such casual connection existed. Since casual connection is now undisputed in the application of penal law, it can no longer be disputed in the application of civil law.

Furthermore, the change in criminal law has brought with it a larger change in attitude towards omission. A number of cases have led to broader *dicta* than that of 1924. It is now recognized that the criterion of fault in cases of omission, as well as in cases of commission, is behaviour different from that of a reasonable man, careful and mindful of others, in similar circumstances. Therefore, even when circumstances are such that a failure to rescue does not constitute a crime, civil liability will be incurred whenever it is the judgment of the court that a reasonable man, careful and mindful of others, would have acted and, as the case may be, would have rescued the victim or prevented the damage."

10. Would the imposition of a criminal sanction be preferable to a tort laibility? Should there be both criminal and civil liability imposed?

11. A survey done in the United States has indicated that 75 percent of the respondents felt that assistance should remain only as a matter of conscience. In Germany it was 62 percent and in Austria 42 percent. Zeisel, "An International Experiment on The Effects of a Good Samaritan Law," printed in *The Good Samaritan and The Law* (1966). Does this affect your answer?

12. Will criminal or tort sanctions help to encourage Good Samaritanism? Joseph Gusfield, a Professor of Sociology wrote this:

"Americans are often accused of solving difficult problems of morality by passing laws and then disobeying them. While there is probably a great deal of truth to this characterization, it misses an important point. Laws are statements of public policy and opinion as well as instruments for courts to implement and police to enforce. The very passage of a law is an act of public definition of what is moral or immoral. The suggestions we consider today for revision in the law of nonfeasance may have their most important effect in underlining the moral obligations of the citizen toward his fellow anonymous citizen, rather than in the particular sanctions which they entail.

Law may do a great deal in the cases of indecency where the accomplished swimmer sits on the boat deck and watches the novice drown when he might easily have saved him. We cannot escape the impression that in the kinds of cases which we have been discussing, where a more heroic act is called for, these will not yield easily to legal solutions. The citizen does not act because he is afraid of what may happen to him in the immediate future, because he is afraid of violent reprisals, and because he cannot depend upon the immediacy of police intervention. He does not act because he has no role which will obligate him to act in any specific and definitely expected form, a form that carries its sanctions and rewards to the immediate group around him. The city is a plurality of circles of involvement surrounded by areas of 'no-man's land'. The urbanite does not venture into new involvements without strong inducements and pressures. Legal sanctions are distant, vague, and uncertain; the danger is here and now."

See "Social Sources of Levites and Samaritans" printed in *The Good Samaritan and The Law* (1966).

13. See also Honoré, Law, Morals and Rescue " printed in *The Good Samaritan and The Law* (1966).

"The law cannot make men good, but it can, in the sphere of duty at least, encourage and help them to do good. It not only can but should reinforce the sanctions of public opinion, for the reasons given, unless it would be oppressive or impracticable to do so. I need say little of the practicability of imposing a duty to aid those in peril. France, Germany, and other countries have tried it out and found that it works reasonably well. But would it be oppressive? The mere fact that the majority is shocked at certain conduct does not, in my view, justify them in imposing civil or criminal liability unless there is also a balance of advantage in doing so. Difficult as it may be to strike a balance, we have in the case of rescue to add to the evils of injustice, disrespect, and want of guidance (should the law impose no duty to act) the possible benefit to those in peril if such duty is imposed. Then we must subtract the hardship of making people conform to accepted standards of neighborliness or suffer penalties. If the balance is positive, the law not merely may, but should intervene."

REVIEW PROBLEM

As Macbeth drove his new car without negligence along the main street of a small Ontario town called Elsinore, Ophelia, who had lost her mind, suddenly stepped onto the road into his path. He had no chance to avoid her. He applied the brakes promptly, but Ophelia was hit and fell down on the road. She lay there very still, bleeding profusely from her left arm. Macbeth panicked and drove off, contrary to s. 140(1) of the Highway Traffic Act.

A crowd gathered. Hamlet, a rookie policeman, shouted "I'll help you", raced to the scene, lifted Ophelia from the road, and placed her on the sidewalk. He then ran to a nearby telephone and called the Elsinore Ambulance Service, which owned the only ambulance in the area. He was informed that it was the ambulance driver's day off and that, therefore, they could not help.

Brutus, a storekeeper in the neighbourhood, watched the entire proceedings through his store window. He had just sold a chocolate bar to Ophelia, whom he knew quite well, and wondered what she was doing wandering around alone, something he knew she never was permitted to do. Even though he was a volunteer first aid instructor, he did not lift a hand to help. Brutus explained that he did not "want to get involved". Besides, the policeman, Hamlet, "seemed to have things under control".

Macduff, a psychiatrist, stopped to help the bleeding girl. Although he had been a psychiatric specialist for 30 years, he realized that a tourniquet was required. He stupidly removed his shoelace, tied it around Ophelia's arm, stopped the bleeding and took her to the hospital. Ophelia's life was saved by the shoelace, but, alas, her arm was infected by it, and had to be amputated. Expert evidence is available to the effect that any general practitioner of medicine should know that a shoe-lace must never be used for a tourniquet because it is generally germ-ridden.

Can Ophelia recover reparation from any of the other actors in this tragedy?

CHAPTER 8

CAUSATION

A. CAUSE-IN-FACT

HART & HONORÉ, CAUSATION IN THE LAW
(1959) at p. 26

CAUSE AND EFFECT: THE CENTRAL NOTION

Human beings have learnt, by making appropriate movements of their bodies, to bring about desired alterations in objects, animate or inanimate, in their environment, and to express these simple achievements by transitive verbs like push, pull, bend, twist, break, injure. The process involved here consists of an initial immediate bodily manipulation of the thing affected and often takes little time. Men have, however, learnt to extend the range of their actions and have discovered that by doing these relatively simple actions they can, in favourable circumstances, bring about secondary changes, not only in the objects actually manipulated, but in other objects. Here the process initiated by bodily movements and manipulation may be protracted in space or time, may be difficult to accomplish and involve a series of changes, sometimes of noticeable different kinds. Here we use the correlative terms "cause" and "effect" rather than simple transitive verbs: the effect is the desired secondary change and the cause is our action in bringing about the primary change in the things manipulated or those primary changes themselves. So we cause one thing to move by striking it with another, glass to break by throwing stones, injuries by blows, things to get hot by putting them on fires. Here the notions of cause and effect come together with the notion of means to ends and of producing one thing by doing another. . . .

Human action in the simple cases, where we produce some desired effect by the manipulation of an object in our environment, is an interference in the natural course of events which *makes a difference* in the way these develop. In an almost literal sense, such an interference by human action is an intervention or intrusion of one kind of thing upon another distinct kind of thing. Common experience teaches us that, left to themselves, the things we manipulate, since they have a "nature" or characteristic way of behaving, would persist in states or exhibit changes different from those which we have learnt to bring about in them by our manipulation. The notion, that a cause is essentially something which interferes with or intervenes in the course of events which would normally take place, is central to the commonsense concept of cause, and at least as essential as the notions of invariable or constant sequence so much stressed by Mill and Hume. Analogies with the interference by human beings with the natural course of events in part control, even in cases where there is literally no human intervention, what is to be identified as the cause of some occurrence;

the cause, though not a literal intervention, is a *difference* to the normal course which accounts for the difference in the outcome.

GREEN, THE CAUSAL RELATION ISSUE IN NEGLIGENCE LAW

(1962), 60 Mich. L. Rev. 547

The causal relation issue in a negligence litigation is greatly simplified by the fact that it is restricted to the conduct of the parties; in the first instance to that of the defendant. It does not initiate an exploratory search for *all* the causes that contributed to the victim's injury, or a search for *the* cause, or the *proximate* or the *legal* cause. Nor does it initiate a search of the *why* of the defendant's conduct, *i.e.*, a search for the motive, reason, impulse or other accounting in explanation of his conduct. A philosophic or scientific exploration of defendant's conduct may be relevant to other issues but not to the causal relation issue. The inquiry is limited to the fact of defendant's contribution to the injury. The search for proximate, legal or other causes is designed to determine whether the defendant's conduct should be condemned and he be made to compensate for his victim's injury. Numerous lawyers and judges use proximate cause when they mean causal relation but that is only one of several confusing usages of the term. The only relevance the consideration of other cause factors may have in the determination of the causal relation issue is the light they may shed on whether defendant's conduct contributed to the injury.

Also it is well to understand that it is not important to the causal relation issue that defendant's conduct in whole or in part was lawful, unlawful, intentional, unintentional, negligent, or non-negligent. The moment some moral consideration is introduced into the inquiry the issue is no longer one of causal relation. Causal relation is a neutral issue, blind to right and wrong, It is so easy to think and speak of defendant's *negligence* as the cause of a victim's hurt that it is frequently overlooked that causal relation is the beginning point of liability and must be established or tentatively assumed before issues involving duty, negligence, damages, and the defensive issues can be determined. There may be causal relation but no basis for the later inquiries, but in absence of causal relation plaintiff has no case, and all other inquiries become moot.

There is great advantage in considering the causal relation issue *first*. This was done in the recent cigarette-cancer case with excellent results. Conduct is a factual concept; the victim's hurt is a factual concept; causal relation is a factual concept. Duty, negligence, and damages are legal concepts and depend upon different considerations from those involved in the determination of causal relation. Only after liability has been determined can negligence be merged with conduct, and even then for clarity's sake the merger should be called *negligent conduct.*

In the overwhelming number of cases it is very clear that a defendant's conduct contributed to the victim's hurt, but in what respect the conduct was negligent, if at all, may be a serious problem. For example, in a highway collision case defendant may be charged with driving his automobile at excessive speed, with bad brakes, inadequate lights, failure to keep a lookout or to give a signal, driving while intoxicated, or the violation of any combination of traffic regulations. If it is shown that defendant in driving the automobile collided with the victim, the causal relation issue between defendant's conduct and the hurt is settled once and for all, irrespective of the violation of any police regulation or common-law rule. Whether defendant's violation of any one or more of the regulations was negligent is another and distinct problem.

MALONE, RUMINATIONS ON CAUSE-IN-FACT

(1956), 9 Stan. L. Rev. 60

For nearly a century judges and writers have struggled to unravel the tangled skein of fact and policy. Even today the search is on for a judging and language technique that will enable courts to deal with those two components separately and effectively. In tort controversies the focal point for scrutiny in this respect has been the issue of causation. At the close of the last century courts used the term "cause" indiscriminately to express either their conclusion as to "what happened" or as a means of explaining what law "ought to do about it". As it became increasingly obvious that no single expression could fully support the burden of both inquiries without confusion, legal science began to recognize two separate notions — cause-in-fact, and "proximate" or "legal" cause. This was generally regarded as a major triumph of analysis. Writers of opinion undertook to explain in detail that the two types of cause perform entirely separate functions in the resolution of a tort dispute and that they are associated only by a vague common denominator — a confusing language similarity.

"Proximate" or "legal" cause has claimed the lion's share of attention, while cause-in-fact, or "simple" cause, is always regarded as though it raises only a question of fact. The judge, it is commonly said, can do no more than propound the inquiry on causation. It is wholly within the jury's province when it becomes an issue at all.

Certainly it is true in a sense that simple cause is a question of fact. The production of testimony, often in lavish and conflicting detail, is essential to the effort to establish or refute simple cause. Frequently it is necessary to know not only what happened, but what *might* have happened if the defendant's conduct had been other than what it actually was. Sometimes the services of experts must be enlisted for this purpose. Certainly, also, the issue of simple cause is for the consideration of the jury whenever the evidence affords ground for reasonable difference of opinion. Instructions on the weight of evidence must be given as in other factual disputes, and the power of the court to nonsuit or direct a verdict exists here as in other contests concerning facts.

Nevertheless, I find that even with reference to this issue of simple cause the mysterious relationship between policy and fact is likely to be in the foreground. . . .

[P]olicy may often be a factor when the issue of cause-in-fact is presented sharply for decision, much as it is when questions of proximate cause are before the court. The presence of policy factors is obscured by the accidental circumstance that the word "cause" is one that the law has borrowed from the layman's terminology, and the child of the street, unlike the artificial creatures of our professional vocabulary, simply will not behave. It refuses to submit to any effort at classification and it insists upon spilling itself throughout every area of the controversy.

A cause is not a fact in the sense that its existence can be established merely through the production of testimony. Although evidentiary data must supply the raw material upon which a finding of cause or no-cause will be based, yet something must first be done with this data by the trier, be he judge or juryman. He must refer the facts presented by the testimony to some judging capacity within himself before he can venture the conclusion that a cause exists. He must arrange the events established by the evidence into a relationship of some kind and he must satisfy himself that the relationship can properly be labeled "cause". The most that can be said is that the trier is making a deduction from evidentiary facts. This operation is not self-performing. It calls into play a variety of intellectual functions that are peculiar to the trier as an individual. It is these that play the decisive role in reaching an answer, and it is clear that they are no integral part of the raw fact data upon which the operation is being performed. . . .

Much misunderstanding between lawyers and physicians could be obviated if members of both professions would realize that "simple" causation is not merely an abstract issue of fact and that the resolution of the cause problem depends largely upon the purpose for which cause is to be used. What *is a* cause for the judge need not *be a* cause for the physician. It is through the process of selecting what is to be regarded as a cause for the purpose of resolving a legal dispute that considerations of policy exert their influence in deciding an issue of cause-in-fact. . . .

In an effort to lend some sense of definiteness and finality to the process, the courts have evolved several tests, the most frequently used of which is the "but-for" test. One fact or event, it is said, is a cause of another when the first fact or event is indispensable to the existence of the second. In the trial of controversies this means that a defendant should not be charged with responsibility for a plaintiff's harm unless we can conclude with some degree of assurance that the harm could not have occurred in the absence of the defendant's misconduct. It is noteworthy that this very announcement is a statement of legal policy. It marks an effort to point out the bare minimum requirement for imposing liability. Unless we can go this far, we must dismiss the claim without further ado. If we do reach this point, we are warranted in investigating further under the guise of determining proximate cause.

One might ask why the minimal relationship was established at this point, rather than at some other. Perhaps the answer is that the but-for test seems to be the best the law can do in its effort to offer an approximate expression of an accepted popular attitude toward responsibility. In passing homely judgments on everyday affairs we assume that we should not blame a person whose conduct "had nothing to do with" some unfortunate occurrence that followed. Some such attitude as this, however it may be expressed, is essential if we are to pass judgments at all, for if we were to adopt any other position we could never know whom to blame for what, or we would blame everybody for everything. If judgment is to be selective, if it is to have any salutary effect on future conduct, it must begin from some such point. Hence, we are willing to exonerate a suspected person whenever we decide that his conduct "had nothing to do with" the event in which we are interested. . . .

[T]he but-for test has a marked peculiarity which recommends it strongly for legal usage. Like other legal formulas, it is not self-executing. It calls upon the judge or jury-man to determine what would have happened if the defendant had not been guilty of the conduct charged against him. At times this determination is made so automatically that the cause issue is little more than a bit of formalism in the trial. But at other times the same test demands the impossible. It challenges the imagination of the trier to probe into a purely fanciful and unknowable state of affairs. He is invited to make an estimate concerning facts that concededly never existed. The very uncertainty as to what *might* have happened opens the door for conjecture. But when conjecture is demanded it can be given a direction that is consistent with the policy considerations that underlie the controversy.

The permissible range for conjecture is unlimited. We can never be absolutely certain that our estimate is correct. The point at which we might be satisfied can be expressed in many ways, such as "barely possible," "possible," "not unlikely," "as possible as not," "probable," "highly probable," or "virtually certain". Language is very rich for this purpose and demands but a minimum of commitment on our part.

Since the issue of causation is commonly regarded as an issue of fact, it lends itself readily to the techniques that control the proof of factual matters. Cause is established by "probabilities" or by that even more noncommunicative phrase, "the weight of the evidence," or by conflicting testimony or inferences upon which reasonable minds may differ. Again, consistent with the analogy of establishing facts, courts retain the power to nonsuit or direct a verdict whenever they feel that the jury's conjecture with reference to the nonexistent state of affairs would not be acceptable to the law. Thus, the judge is vested with authority to conjecture upon the very process of conjecture itself. His own estimate, in turn, is subject to the check of the appellant court. Here, then, is a complex of machinery and formulas that affords the greatest possible latitude for the rendering of a judgment tailored to meet the needs of the occasion.

NOTES

1. In the recent case of *Horsley* v. *MacLaren*, [1969] 2 O.R. 137, revd. on another point, [1970] 2 O.R. 487, affd. (1972), 22 D.L.R. (3d) 545 (S.C.C.), Mr. Justice Lacourcière, the trial judge, was concerned with the claim of the widows of two men who fell off a yatch into Lake Ontario and died. One of the problems that confronted the court was whether the death of the deceased, Matthews, was caused by the failure of the defendant to effectuate a prompt rescue. In denying liability, Mr. Justice Lacourcière explained:

"It is trite law that liability does not follow a finding of negligence, even where there exists a legally recognized duty, unless the defendant's conduct is the effective cause of the loss: *Cork* v. *Kirby MacLean, Ltd.* [1952] 2 All E.R. 402, at p. 407, *per* Denning, L.J.:

'Subject to the question of remoteness, causation is, I think, a question of fact. If you can say that the damage would not have happened for a particular fault, then that fault is in fact a cause of the damage; but if you say that the damage would have happened just the same, fault or no fault, then the fault is not a cause of the damage.'

In the present case the burden is on the plaintiff to prove by a preponderance of evidence that the defendant's negligence was the effective cause of Matthew's death. Obviously the defendant is not responsible for Matthew's fall overboard. There is no evidence in the present case that Matthews was ever alive after falling in the water: all witnesses agree that he was motionless and staring. Bearing in mind that Horsley, a younger man than Matthews, in the opinion of the pathologist probably died of shock immediately or shortly after his immersion, it is reasonable to think that Matthews, 16 years older, did not survive longer, and after he hit the water there never was a sign of life or consciousness. It was impossible in the present case to discharge this burden by a pathologist's report; in the case of a missing body, witnesses' evidence of some struggle or sign of life on the part of the deceased during rescue operations would be required. I am reluctantly forced to the conclusion that, on the balance of probabilities, it has not been shown that Matthews' life could have been saved. The defendant's negligence therefore was not the cause of Matthews' death and there can be no liability."

2. In *Kauffman* v. *T.T.C.*, [1960] S.C.R. 251, 22 D.L.R. (2d) 97; affg. [1959] O.R. 197, 18 D.L.R. (2d) 204, the plaintiff was injured when she fell while ascending an escalator in a Toronto subway station, after two scuffling youths ahead of her fell back on a man who in turn fell back on her. The jury found for the plaintiff, but the Court of Appeal reversed the decision and this

was affirmed by the Supreme Court of Canada. In addition to the negligence issues, there were two problems of causation raised in the case: (1) would the presence of a better handrail have prevented the accident? (2) would the presence of an attendant have avoided the accident? Mr. Justice Morden answered both of these questions in the negative:

"The theory advanced by the plaintiff's counsel to quote his own words was that 'in the operation of an escalator, particularly in a public transit system where large crowds are to be expected, if a person near the top falls backward (for whatever reason) against the person behind him, each person will fall gainst the other knocking him down in much the same fashion as a row of dominoes'. But there was a total absence of evidence that the man immediately ahead of the plaintiff or the two reckless and irresponsible youths ahead of him were grasping or attempted to grasp the hand rail before or in the course of the scuffle and consequent falling. Nor was there any evidence that in the circumstances the plaintiff would not have fallen if her hands had been grasping a rubber oval hand rail. In my opinion, there was no evidence to justify a finding that the type of hand rail in use at the St. Clair Ave. station was a contributing cause of the plaintiff's unfortunate and serious accident. It is a fundamental principle that the causal relation between the alleged negligence and the injury must be made out by the evidence and not left to the conjecture of the jury. . . The first finding of negligence in view of the evidence in this case does not justify a verdict against the defendant.

The second ground of negligence found by the jury was that 'the defendant failed to supply supervision'. Counsel for the appellant made a vigorous attack upon this finding. He submitted that if it meant the defendant should have provided attendants whose duty it would be to prevent passengers jostling (as pleaded in para. 4(d)) then it was not a good finding in law. The respondent's counsel submitted that the jury meant the failure of the defendant to have an attendant immediately beside the escalator whose duty it would have been to stop the escalator at the time the riders fell (para. 4(a)). There was evidence that the plaintiff suffered the greater part of her injuries after her fall and as she was being carried up the escalator lying under the bodies of two or three persons. For the purposes of this appeal, I am prepared to construe liberally this finding of the jury and accept the interpretation the respondent's counsel places on it.

The learned trial judge told the jury that if 'there is reasonable ground for apprehending danger from any external cause, such as acts of third persons, the defendant is bound to guard against them according to the best practical means at its disposal', and in discussing the allegation that the defendant failed to provide an attendant, instructed the jury to ask themselves, would an attendant have been an effective measure? Taking a broad interpretation of the finding, it then becomes evident that the jury were of the opinion that if an attendant had been present, the plaintiff would not have sustained the injuries she did. Again with respect to this answer I hold the view that the jury did not direct their minds to the real issue on this branch of the case, *viz.,* — was the defendant under a duty to the plaintiff and the travelling public to have attendants at this escalator and in fact at all their escalators? It must first be determined whether there was a duty to provide an attendant and if there was, then — would the presence of an attendant have prevented this accident?"

3. In *Reed* v. *Ellis* (1916), 38 O.L.R. 123, 32 D.L.R. 592, the plaintiff jewellery polisher sued his employer to recover damages for tuberculosis that he alleged he contracted as a result of dust and fumes getting into his lungs during 26 years on the job. Meredith C.J.C.P., reversing a jury verdict in his favour, stated:

"The first thing that strikes me as to it is the paucity of the testimony, in the plaintiff's behalf, adduced with a view to connecting the admitted illness with the alleged cause of it. The plaintiff's family physician alone was called to give professional evidence upon the subject; and he was not asked even to state that, in his opinion, the negligence complained of was the cause of the plaintiff's present diseased condition. In the circumstances of the case, and having regard to the nature of the disease, it is hardly possible that any intelligent, truthful person could say more than this witness did in his patient's behalf: that the things complained of by the plaintiff would make one more liable to the disease by producing an irritated condition of the throat and that they would interfere with normal resistance, and that the evidence which struck him most was the quantity of dust, and people expectorating who had tuberculosis, that allowing that sputum to dry and become mixed with the dust is an ideal condition for producing tuberculosis and is recognized as the most common cause. . . .

It is common knowledge, in these days, that inanimate dirt does not breed disease, nor is it the lurking place of the germs of disease; but that such germs are bred in animate beings and distributed by those who are possessed of them; and so none, no matter who or what or where they are, can be sure of avoiding them. Also, it is impossible for any reasonable person to say more than it may be that lowered resistance caused by some of the things complained of, or caused by other of very many things which might have a depressing physical defect, may have been a cause of the plaintiff's present diseased condition — and may not have been. Whether too remote a cause in such a case as this need not be considered until proved to be more than a possible or probable cause.

So, too, such evidence as there was upon the subject indicated that the death-rate from tuberculosis of the persons employed in this factory, while the plaintiff was employed there, was a good deal below the death-rate from the same cause throughout the Province.

Therefore, if the jury meant that lack of proper and reasonable precautions by some mechanical device for disposing of fumes and dust was the proximate cause of the plaintiff's disease, I have no hesitation in saying that there was no evidence upon which reasonable men could so find."

See also *Barnett* v. *Chelsea & Kensington Hospital Management Committee*, [1968] 2 W.L.R. 422; *York* v. *The Canada Atlantic SS. Co.* (1893), 22 S.C.R. 167; *Richard* v. *C.N.R. Co.* (1970), 15 D.L.R. (3d) 732 at p. 739. (P.E.I.S.C.).

4. In *McGhee* v. *National Coal Board*, [1972] 3 All E.R. 1008 (H.L.), the plaintiff contracted dermatitis while employed by the defendants to clean out brick kilns. The medical evidence indicated that the dermatitis was caused by the dusty working conditions in the kilns. Moreover, it was also known that, since the plaintiff had to exert himself bicycling home after work with brick dust adhering to his skin, this added materially to the risk of dermatitis. The plaintiff alleged that, because the defendants failed in their duty to supply adequate washing facilities, he was unable to wash prior to going home and that, therefore, the defendants' breach of duty contributed to his contracting the disease. There was evidence that the provision of such facilities was common practice in the industry.

The original action was dismissed by the Lord Ordinary, which decision was upheld on appeal by the First Division. The plaintiff appealed to the House of Lords. At this level the defendants admitted that their failure to supply adequate washing facilities was a breach of their duty and that the disease was attributable to the work performed by the plaintiff. They insisted, however, that it has not been proved that failure to supply washing facilities caused the onset of the disease.

The House of Lords unanimously allowed the appeal. Lord Reid could see no difference between a finding that the respondents' breach of duty had materially increased the risk of injury to the plaintiff and a finding that the breach of duty had materially contributed to this injury. Lord Reid explained that a pursuer succeeds if he can show that the fault of the defender "caused or materially contributed to his injury. There may have been two separate causes but it is enough if one of the causes arose from the fault of the defender.

The pursuer does not have to prove that this cause would of itself have been enough to cause him injury. . . it has often been said that the legal concept of causation is not based on logic or philosophy. It is based on the practical way in which the ordinary man's mind works in every-day affairs of life."

In his discussion of this issue, Lord Wilberforce stated:

". . . merely to show that a breach of duty increases the risk of harm is not, *in abstracto,* enough to enable the pursuer to succeed. . . . But the question remains whether a pursuer must necessarily fail if, after he has shown a breach of duty, involving an increase of risk of disease, he cannot positively prove that this increase of risk caused or materially contributed to the disease while his employees cannot positively prove the contrary. In this intermediate case there is an appearance of logic in the view that the pursuer, on whom the onus lies, should fail — a logic which dictated judgments below. The question is whether we should be satisfied in factual situations like the present, with this logical approach. In my opinion, there are further considerations of importance. First, it is a sound principle that where a person has, by breach of duty of care, created a risk, and injury occurs within the area of that risk, the loss should be borne by him unless he shows that it had some other cause. Secondly, from the evidential point of view, one may ask, why should a man who is able to show that his employer should have taken certain precautions, because without them there is a risk, or an added risk of injury or disease, and who in fact sustains exactly that injury or disease, have to assume the burden of proving more: namely, that it was the addition to the risk, caused by the breach of duty, which caused or materially contributed to the injury? In many cases of which the present is typical, this is impossible to prove, just because honest medical opinion cannot segregate the cause of an illness between compound causes. And if one asks which of the parties, the workman or the employers should suffer from this inherent evidential difficulty, the answer as a matter in policy or justice should be that it is the creator of the risk who, *ex hypothesi,* must be taken to have foreseen the possibility of damage, who should bear its consequences."

See Weinrib, "A Step Forward in Factual Causation" (1975), 38 Mod. L. Rev. 518.

5. The *McGhee* case was considered in *Powell* v. *Guttman,* [1978] 5 W.W.R. 228, a malpractice case, in which one doctor was held liable for a fracture that occurred during an operation by another doctor, an operation which should have been done sooner. O'Sullivan J.A., relying on *McGhee,* stated: ". . . [T]he law in Canada is that, where a tortfeasor creates or materially contributes to a significant risk of injury occurring and injury does occur which is squarely within the risk thus created or materially increased, then unless the risk is spent the tortfeasor is liable for injury which follows from the risk, even though there are other subsequent causes which also cause or materially contribute to that injury." Is this approach preferable to that in *Reed* v. *Ellis*? Is it dangerous?

6. What kind of evidence is necessary to prove causation? Is expert evidence necessary? What about judicial notice?

Suppose someone drowns in a swimming pool at which there is no lifeguard. Would the presence of a lifeguard have prevented the drowning? Suppose someone falls down some steps that are poorly lit. Would proper lighting have prevented the fall? How do we go about deciding these questions?

7. The plaintiff is cut by some broken glass. He develops skin cancer at the spot where he was cut. A doctor testifies that the cut *could* have caused the cancer, but that he could not say that it *did in fact cause* it. Another doctor said he did not think that the trauma caused cancer because, if so, nearly every person would suffer from cancer. Causation? Compare with *Kramer Service Inc.* v. *Wilkins* (1939), 184 Miss. 493, 186 So. 625.

8. What if a doctor stated that the cut played a substantial part in producing the cancer? What if a doctor says that an accident was a "possible" cause of depression? Should the jury be allowed to hear such evidence at all? See

Danjanovich v. *Buma*, [1970] 3 O.R. 604 (C.A.).

9. As for evidence about future loss or damage that an injured person will suffer as a result of his injury, the courts are not as strict in the quality of proof required. In *Schrump* v. *Koot* (1977), 18 O.R. (2d) 337 (C.A.) an expert testified, in a back injury case, that there was a 25-50% probability that future surgery would be required. The trial judge allowed this to go to the jury. Counsel for the defendant argued on appeal that this was evidence of a mere possibility and that the jury ought to have been told to exclude it from their consideration. Mr. Justice Lacourciere disagreed and explained:

"In this area of the law relating to the assessment of damages for physical injury, one must appreciate that though it may be necessary for a plaintiff to prove, on the balance of probabilities, that the tortious act or omission was the effective cause of the harm suffered, it is not necessary for him to prove, on the balance of probabilities, that future loss or damage *will* occur, but only that there is a reasonable chance of such loss or damage occurring. The distinction is made clear in the following passages in 12 Hals., 4th ed., pp. 437, 483-4:

1137. *Possibilities, probabilities and chances.* Whilst issues of fact relating to liability must be decided on the balance of probability, the law of damages is concerned with evaluating in terms of money, future possibilities and chances. In assessing damages which depend on the court's view as to what will happen in the future, or would have happened in the future if something had not happened in the past, the court must make an estimate as to what are the chances that a particular thing will happen or would have happened and reflect those chances, *whether they are more or less than even*, in the amount of damages which it awards.

. . . . .

1199. *Proof of damage.*

. . . . .

The plaintiff must prove his damage on a balance of probabilities. In many cases, however, the court is called upon to evaluate chances, such as the chance of a plaintiff suffering further loss or damage in the future; in these cases the plaintiff need only establish that he has a *reasonable*, as distinct from a *speculative*, chance of suffering such loss or damage, and the court must then assess the value of that chance.
(Emphasis added.)

The principle concisely stated in the passage quoted is directly applicable in this case. Speculative and fanciful possibilities unsupported by expert or other cogent evidence can be removed from the consideration of the trier of fact and should be ignored, whereas substantial possibilities based on such expert or cogent evidence must be considered in the assessment of damages for personal injuries in civil litigation. This principle applies regardless of the percentage of possibility, as long as it is a substantial one, and regardless of whether the possibility is favourable or unfavourable. Thus, future contingencies which are less than probable are regarded as factors to be considered, provided they are shown to be substantial and not speculative: they may tend to increase or reduce the award in a proper case."

COOK v. LEWIS

Supreme Court of Canada. [1951] S.C.R. 830, [1951] 1 D.L.R. 1

Defendants Cook and Akenhead were, together with a third person, in one party hunting for grouse. Plaintiff Lewis, with two others, was in another party in the same vicinity also engaged in grouse hunting. Lewis was injured by gun shot when his party came close to that of the defendants. Lewis brought action against Cook and Akenhead claiming that they had negligently injured him by discharging their guns knowing he was in the vicinity or without making sure he was not in their line of fire.

The evidence at the trial showed that shortly after the defendants had seen some of the plaintiff's party both Cook and Akenhead had fired but, according to the evidence, at different birds, and in different directions, and that plaintiff was injured as a result.

The trial judge submitted questions to the jury and they were answered as follows:

"Q. Was the plaintiff shot by either of the defendants? A. Yes. Q. If so, by which one? (No answer.) Q. If the plaintiff was shot by one of the defendants are you able to decide by which one? A. No. Q. Were the plaintiff's injuries caused by the negligence of either of the defendants? A. No. Q. Damages. (Not answered.)"

The trial judge, after argument, then dismissed the action against both defendants.

On plaintiff's appeal to the British Columbia Court of Appeal, [1950] 4 D.L.R. 136, a new trial was ordered, the court being of the opinion that as one of the defendants had shot and injured the plaintiff a finding that neither was negligent was perverse.

Defendant Cook appealed to the Supreme Court of Canada.

Rand J.: I agree with the Court of Appeal that the finding of the jury exculpating both defendants from negligence was perverse and it is unnecessary to examine the facts on which that conclusion is based.

There remains the answer that, although shots from one of the two guns struck the respondent, the jury could not determine from which they came. . . . The essential obstacle to proof is the fact of multiple discharges so related as to confuse their individual effects: it is that fact that bars final proof. But if the victim, having brought guilt down to one or both of two persons before the court, can bring home to either of them a further wrong done him in relation to his remedial right of making that proof, then I should say that on accepted principles, the barrier to it can and should be removed.

The Court of Appeal of England has laid down this principle: that if A is guilty of a negligent act towards B, the total direct consequences of that act are chargeable against A notwithstanding that they arise from reactions unforeseeable by the ordinary person acting reasonably: *Re Polemis & Furness, Withy & Co.,* [1921] 3 K.B. 560. . . .

Similarly would that result follow where, instead of an unforeseen potentiality, an element is introduced into the scene at the critical moment of which or its probability the negligent actor knows or ought to have known. That element becomes, then, one of the circumstances in reaction with which the consequences of his act manifest themselves, among which, here, is the confusion of consequences. If the new element is innocent, no liability results to the person who introduces it; if culpable, its effect in law remains to be ascertained.

What, then, the culpable actor has done by his initial negligent act is, first, to have set in motion a dangerous force which embraces the injured person within the scope of its probable mischief; and next, in conjunction with circumstances which he must be held to contemplate, to have made more difficult if not impossible the means of proving the possible damaging results of his own act or the similar results of the act of another. He has violated not only the victim's substantive right to security, but he has also culpably impaired the latter's remedial right of establishing liability. By confusing his act with environmental conditions, he has, in effect, destroyed the victim's power of proof.

The legal consequence of that is, I should say, that the onus is then shifted to the wrongdoer to exculpate himself; it becomes in fact a question of proof between him and the other and innocent member of the alternatives, the burden of which he must bear. The onus attaches to culpability, and if both acts bear that taint, the onus or *prima facie* transmission of responsibility attaches to both, and the question of the sole responsibility of one is a matter between them. . . .

Assuming, then, that the jury have found one or both of the defendants here negligent, as on the evidence I think they must have, and at the same time have found that the consequences of the two shots, whether from a confusion in time or in area, cannot be segregated, the onus on the guilty person arises. This is a case where each hunter would know of or expect the shooting by the other and the negligent actor has culpably participated in the proof-destroying fact, the multiple shooting and its consequences. No liability will, in any event, attach to an innocent act of shooting, but the culpable actor, as against innocence, must bear the burden of exculpation.

These views of the law were not as adequately presented to the jury as I think they should have been.

I would, therefore, dismiss the appeal with costs.

Locke J. (dissenting): . . . On the argument before us, it was contended for the respondent that in the circumstances there was a presumption of fault against the defendants and that the onus was on them to prove by affirmative evidence that they had exercised due care, but clearly this contention cannot be supported. There were here no circumstances which could, in my opinion, raise any such presumption.

The answers to Qq. 2 and 3 are decisive that upon the evidence the jury could not find which one of the defendants had fired the shot which caused the damage. The claim against Cook was, therefore, left in this position that either he or Akenhead had fired the shot which injured the unfortunate plaintiff, and upon such a finding it was clearly impossible to enter a verdict against him unless he was liable for the act of Akenhead, whether the claim pleaded sounded in negligence or in trespass. As I understand the contention of the respondent, it is that since Cook and Akenhead were hunting together, using the same dog, under an arrangement whereby the bag would be divided equally between them, each was liable for the negligence of the other. Thus, if but one of them had fired, both would be liable. As pointed out in *Clerk and Lindsell on Torts,* 10th ed., p. 100, an agent who commits a tort on behalf of his principal and the principal are joint tortfeasors, as are the servant who commits a tort in the course of his employment and his master, and an independent contractor and his employer in those cases in which the law holds the employer absolutely liable. The learned author further says that so are persons whose respective shares in the commission of a tort are done in furtherance of a common design, but that mere similarity of design on the part of independent actors causing independent damage is not enough. There must be concerted action towards a common end. . . . The facts in the present matter do not, however, in my opinion, support a claim upon this basis. Cook and Akenhead were merely hunting in each other's company: there was no common design in the sense that that expression is used in the passage quoted: they were rather each pursuing their own design of shooting grouse, as they were lawfully entitled to do. I am unable to understand how the fact that, like most hunters, they at the end of the day divided up the bag, the more fortunate sharing his luck with the other, can be a basis for any legal liability. . . .

In my opinion, this is decisive of the present appeal since, in the absence of a finding that the respondent was shot by Cook and since the latter is not liable if the damage was caused by the act of Akenhead, the action was properly dismissed. In the judgment appealed from, however, a new trial has been ordered on the ground that the jury's answer to the fourth question was perverse, in view of the finding that it was one or other of the defendants who fired the shots causing the damage. With great respect, it appears to me that in view of the failure of the plaintiff to obtain a finding from the jury as to which fired the shot this question did not arise. A finding that one or other of the defendants was negligent would clearly not have furthered the matter in view of the answer to the third question. . . .

This appeal should be allowed with costs here and in the Court of Appeal and the judgment at the trial restored.

Cartwright J.: . . . It is first necessary to consider the finding of the jury in their answer to the fourth question, that the plaintiff's injuries were not caused by the negligence of either of the defendants, for obviously if this finding stands the action must fail. In my opinion the Court of Appeal were right in deciding that this finding should be set aside. With the greatest respect, I think that the learned trial judge did not charge the jury correctly in regard to the onus of proof of negligence. While it is true that the plaintiff expressly pleaded negligence on the part of the defendants he also pleaded that he was shot by them and in my opinion the action under the old form of pleading would properly have been one of trespass and not of case. In my view, the cases collected and discussed by Denman J., in *Stanley* v. *Powell,* [1891] 1 Q.B. 86, establish the rule (which is subject to an exception in the case of highway accidents with which we are not concerned in the case at bar) that where a plaintiff is injured by force applied directly to him by the defendant his case is made by proving this fact and the onus falls upon the defendant to prove "that such trespass was utterly without his fault". In my opinion *Stanley* v. *Powell* rightly decides that the defendant in such an action is entitled to judgment if he satisfies the onus of establishing the absence of both intention and negligence on his part.

Owing to the fact that as Akenhead has not appealed, the order directing a new trial must stand so far as he is concerned, I do not find it necessary to discuss whether a jury, properly instructed as to onus, could have absolved him from negligence if they had found that it was he who shot the plaintiff. I think that if the jury found that it was Cook whose shot struck the plaintiff there was no evidence on which, acting judicially, they could have absolved him from negligence. . . .

For these reasons, I respectfully agree with the Court of Appeal that the jury's answer to Q. 4 should be set aside.

This, however, is not enough to dispose of the appeal. It is necessary to consider the answer to the third question in which the jury have indicated that they were unable to find which of the two defendants did fire the shot which did the damage.

The general rule is, I think, stated correctly in *Starkie on Evidence,* 4th ed. p. 860, quoted with approval by Patterson J.A., in *Moxley* v. *Can. Atlantic Ry.* (1887), 14 O.A.R. 309, at p. 315. " 'Thus in practice, when it is certain that one of two individuals committed the offence charged, but it is uncertain whether the one or the other was the guilty agent, neither of them can be convicted.' "

This rule, I think, is also applicable to civil actions so that if at the end of the case A has proved that he was negligently injured by either B or C but is unable to establish which of the two caused the injury, his action must fail against both unless there are special circumstances which render the rule inapplicable.

The respondent argues that such circumstances exist in this case. It is said that Akenhead and Cook were joint tortfeasors being engaged in a joint enterprise under such circumstances that each was liable for the acts of the other. Reliance is placed on the fact that they were hunting together and had agreed to divide the bag evenly.

I am unable to find any authority for the proposition that the mere fact that a party of persons are hunting together and have agreed to divide the bag renders each liable for the tortious acts of all the others. The American case of *Summers* v. *Tice,* 5 A.L.R. 2d 91, relied upon by the respondents is, I think, properly distinguished. . . . The decisive finding of fact in that case was that both of the defendants had shot in the direction of the plaintiff when they knew his location. There is no such finding in the case at bar. . . .

The judgments of the Court of Appeal in *The "Koursk",* [1924] P. 140, are of only limited assistance. . . . At p. 155, Scrutton L.J., says: "The substantial question in the present case is: What is meant by 'joint tortfeasors'? and one way of answering it is: 'Is the cause of action against them the same?' Certain classes of persons seem clearly to be 'joint tortfeasors': The agent who commits a tort within the scope of his employment for his principal, and the principal; the servant who commits a tort in the course of his employment, and his master; two persons who agree on common action, in the course of, and to further which, one of them commits a tort. These seem clearly joint tortfeasors; there is one tort committed by one of them on behalf of, or in concert with another." . . .

There was, I think, no evidence in the case at bar on which it could be found that the relationship of principal and agent or of master and servant or of partners existed between Akenhead and Cook. They were engaged in a lawful pursuit. Neither had any reason to anticipate that the other would act negligently, Neither had in fact either the right or the opportunity to control the other. Neither appears to have assisted or encouraged the other to commit a breach of any duty owed to the plaintiff. It is argued, however, that *Summers* v. *Tice, supra,* should be followed and that under the principles stated in that judgment the jury might properly have found both Akenhead and Cook liable for the plaintiff's injury if in their view of the evidence both of them fired in the direction of the clump of trees in which the plaintiff in fact was, under such circumstances that the conduct of each constituted a breach of duty to the plaintiff. I have not been able to find any case in the courts of this country, or of England in which consideration has been given to certain propositions of law laid down in *Summers* v. *Tice.* The underlying reason for the decision appears to me to be found in the following quotation from the case of *Oliver* v. *Miles* (1926), 110 So. Rep. 666, at p. 668:

> "We think that . . . each is liable for the resulting injury to the boy, although no one can say definitely who actually shot him. *To hold otherwise would be to exonerate both from liability, although each was negligent, and the injury resulted from such negligence."*

The judgment in *Summers* v. *Tice* (5 A.L.R. 2d 91) reads in part as follows (p. 96);

> "When we consider the relative position of the parties and the results that would flow if plaintiff was required to pin the injury on one of the defendants only, a requirement that the burden of proof on that subject be shifted to defendants becomes manifest. They are both wrongdoers — both negligent towards plaintiff. They brought about a situation where the negligence of one of them injured the plaintiff, hence, it should rest with them each to absolve himself if he can. The injured party has been placed by defendants in the unfair position of pointing to which defendant caused the harm. If one

can escape the other may also and plaintiff is remediless. Ordinarily defendants are in a far better position to offer evidence to determine which one caused the injury. This reasoning has recently found favour in this court."

I do not think it necessary to decide whether all that was said in *Summers* v. *Tice* should be accepted as stating the law of British Columbia, but I am of opinion, for the reasons given in that case, that if under the circumstances of the case at bar the jury, having decided that the plaintiff was shot by either Cook or Akenhead, found themselves unable to decide which of the two shot him because in their opinion both shot negligently in his direction, both defendants should have been found liable. I think that the learned trial judge should have sent the jury back to consider the matter further with a direction to the above effect in view of their answer to Q. 3. . . .

It may be that at the new trial no question of the application of the rule laid down in *Summers* v. *Tice,* will arise. I respectfully agree with the Court of Appeal that the jury should have been able to decide which one of the defendants fired the shot which struck the plaintiff.

In my respectful opinion the perverse finding on the question of negligence following the insufficient direction on the question of onus, the failure of the jury to reach a finding as to who fired the shot which struck the plaintiff and the failure of the learned trial judge to send them back for reconsideration of this question with the added direction indicated above, made it proper for the Court of Appeal to direct a new trial.

[Estey and Fauteux JJ., concurred with Cartwright J.]

NOTES

1. Is this a proof of negligence or proof of causation problem? How does this case compare with *Leaman* v. *Rae, supra*? See also *Joseph Brant Memorial Hospital* v. *Koziol* (1977), 2 C.C.L.T. 170 (S.C.C.), at p. 180.

2. In *Beecham* v. *Henderson,* [1951] 1 D.L.R. 628 (B.C.), two men engaged in work adjoining a highway each threw a handful of sand at a bus carrying high school students. The sand came through a window of the bus and hit the plaintiff in the eye. It was impossible to say which of the defendants threw the sand that hit the plaintiff. Coady J., held both defendants liable as "joint tortfeasors and not independent tortfeasors" but he also added, "unless one or other of them can establish that his wrongful act did not cause the injury."

3. In *Woodward* v. *Begbie et al.,* [1962] O.R. 60 (H.C.), two police officers shot at an escaping suspect, but only one bullet hit him. Not being able to decide which officer's bullet did the damage, Mr. Justice MacLennan held both of them liable.

4. Although this principle has withstood the test of time, it will not be lightly extended. In *Lange* v. *Bennett,* [1964] 1 O.R. 233, the 18-year-old plaintiff was hunting with two 16-year-old friends. He knelt down and then suddenly stood up in the line of fire of the other two boys. A bullet shot by one of them struck him, but it could not be determined which defendant was responsible. Mr. Justice McRuer found that, since the plaintiff was himself contributorily negligent, *Cook* v. *Lewis* would not apply. He explained:

"Negligence must necessarily be relative to the circumstances in each case and to the ages of the parties in question. The plaintiff at the time of the accident was two years older than the defendants. He kneeled down to shoot and knew that he was in the approximate line of fire of two younger boys, shooting from behind him. He was unquestionably negligent in standing up without warning and putting himself into the line of fire. He must be taken to have known that he might have been struck by a shot fired by either of them and it would be difficult to say in such circumstances which boy fired the shot that struck him. He had himself participated as a 'negligent actor' in 'the proof destroying fact.' To hold on these facts that the one who may have done him no harm should pay damages because he could not clear him-self from blame would be grossly unjust. These are not special circum-stances. . .".

Do you agree with Mr. Justice McRuer's disposition of the case and his reasoning?

5. There is some indication that *Cook* v. *Lewis* might even be employed in strict liability and nuisance cases. See *dictum* of Dubinsky J. in *MacDonald* v. *Desourdy Construction* (1972), 27 D.L.R. (3d) 144, at p. 159.

B. MULTIPLE CAUSES

THE NEGLIGENCE ACT

R.S.O. 1970, c.296

2. (1) Where damages have been caused or contributed to by the fault or neglect of two or more persons, the court shall determine the degree in which each of such persons is at fault or negligent, and . . . where two or more persons are found at fault or negligent, they are jointly and severally liable to the person suffering loss or damage for such fault or negligence, but as between themselves, in the absence of any contract express or implied, each is liable to make contribution and indemnify each other in the degree in which they are respectively found to be at fault or negligent.

NOTES

1. This section first appeared in the 1930 revision of the original 1924 Ontario Contributory Negligence Act which dealt only with fault on the part of a plaintiff (see the 1924 Act in R.S.O. 1927, c. 103). When originally enacted in 1930 (Ont. Statutes, c. 27) the present section provided for contri-bution "where two or more persons are found to be liable". A section similar to Ontario's s. 2(1) appears in the Contributory Negligence Acts of Alberta, British Columbia, New Brunswick, Newfoundland, Nova Scotia, Prince Edward Island, and Saskatchewan.

2. When two defendants are both liable jointly or severally to the plaintiff, the plaintiff is entitled to collect his entire damages from either of the defendants, who are individually liable for all of the damages caused by them. As Dickson J. stated in *County of Parkland* v. *Stetar*, [1975] 2 S.C.R. 884, "the plaintiff may elect to recover the full amount of his damage from a tortfeasor only partly to blame". Of course, he cannot recover more than the total of the damages assessed.

3. Tortfeasors are now allowed to recover contribution and indemnity from one another, although at common law they could not. See *Merryweather* v. *Nixan* (1799), 8 Term Rep. 186, 101 E.R. 1537. Both tortfeasors, however, must be liable for the loss in order to be able to recover; if one is not liable, he is not subject to an action for contribution or indemnity. See *Giffels Associates* v. *Eastern Construction Co. Ltd.* (1978), 4 C.C.L.T. 143 (S.C.C.); *County of Parkland* v. *Stetar, supra*.

4. It is still unclear whether there can be contribution under this section in a contractual setting. See Laskin C.J.C. in *Giffels Associates, supra*. The better view is that the section permits one tortfeasor to recover from another person even though the obligation of that other person arises out of a contract on the theory that a violation of a contract can also be "fault or negligence". See *De Meza* v. *Apple*, [1975] 1 Lloyd's Rep. 498 (C.A.); *Groves-Raffin Construction Ltd.* v. *Bank of Nova Scotia* (1975), 51 D.L.R. (3d) 380; revd on another point (1976), 64 D.L.R. (3d) 78 (B.C.C.A.); Jessup J.A. in *Dominion Chain* v. *Eastern Construction* (1976), 12 O.R. (2d) 201; affd on other grounds, S.C.C. *supra*. See also Pigeon J., dissenting, in *Smith* v. *McInnis* (1978), 4 C.C.L.T. 154; *Truman* v. *Sparling Real Estate* (1977), 3 C.C.L.T. 205 (B.C.C.A.). There is, however, authority to the contrary. See *Dabous* v. *Zuliani* (1976), 12 O.R. (2d) 230 (C.A.);

Allcock Laight v. *Patten,* [1967] 1 O.R. 18 (C.A.). These latter decisions make little sense since apportionment in contract law was permitted, even before the contributory negligence legislation. It would be paradoxical, to say the least, for legislation which was meant to *permit* contribution among tortfeasors to *forbid* contribution among those who are in breach of contracts. See Pigeon J. in *Smith* v. *McInnis, supra;* Weinrib, "Contribution in a Contractual Setting" (1975), 54 Can. Bar Rev. 338.

    5. For an excellent article explaining all of this, see Klar, "Contributory Negligence and Contribution Between Tortfeasors" in Klar (ed.), *Studies in Canadian Tort Law* (1977), p. 145. See also Cheifetz, *Apportionment of Damages under the Ontario Negligence Act* (1980).

ARNEIL v. PATTERSON & ANOTHER

House of Lords. [1931] A.C. 560

Viscount Hailsham: My Lords, this is an appeal from a decision of the Court of Session reversing the decision of the Sheriff-Substitute. The point at issue is a very short one, and the facts are not in dispute. It appears that the appellants are farmers who own a flock of black-faced sheep on a farm in Scotland. The respondent is the owner of a dog, and in the early morning of January 21, 1930, the respondent's dog, in company with another dog belonging to the other defender, who has not entered any appearance, attacked the flock of sheep belonging to the appellants. The statement in the condescendence is in these terms: "On the morning of Tuesday, January 21, 1930, about six o'clock, two dogs, a cross-airedale belonging to the first-named defender and a collie belonging to the second-named defender, trespassed on the pursuers' farm where the said ewes were grazing. The said dogs, acting together, attacked the pursuers' sheep, hunted and chased them, and severely bit, mauled and worried seventeen of them." To that condescendence the answer is made: "For the purpose of this action this defender admits that his dog, along with the other defender's dog, trespassed on the pursuers' farm, and that seventeen sheep were mauled and worried by the said two dogs acting together, and that ten of the sheep have died." The damages for the total damage done to the sheep were agreed for the purposes of this action at a sum of £60, and at the hearing before the Sheriff-Substitute, judgment was given against the present respondent for that amount. On appeal to the Court of Session, the Court of Session held that the respondent was liable only for half of the amount on the ground that there were two dogs who were jointly concerned in attacking and damaging the sheep, and that in the absence of any evidence as to how much of the damage was done by either of the dogs the damage must be apportioned equally between the two defenders. It is from that decision that this appeal is brought. . . .

    Once liability is established, then the ordinary measure of damage has to be applied. It has to be ascertained how much injury "that dog" has done to the cattle — in this case the pursuers' sheep. I think that each of the dogs did in law occasion the whole of the damage which was suffered by the sheep as the result of the action of the two dogs acting together. If that be so, then each of the owners of the two dogs is responsible for the whole of the damage which has been done, and judgment can be obtained against either of them. . . .

    In this case we have an admission that the two dogs were acting together, and, when that admission is made, then I think that in law each of the two owners is responsible for the whole of the damage, because each dog did in the eye of the law occasion the whole of the injury of which the pursuers complain.

    It follows that, in my opinion, the decision of the Court below was wrong and that the judgment of the Sheriff-Substitute should be restored, and I move your Lordships accordingly.

Viscount Dunedin: My Lords, I concur. From the very first moment in this case it seemed to me that the fallacy of the First Division's judgment was that they did not consider whether really each dog was, I will not say responsible, because that is an adjective which is more applicable to a human being than to a dog, but at least was the cause of what had happened. I think the fallacy of their view cannot be better exposed than by supposing only one sheep had been worried. Would we then have to hold that each dog had half killed the sheep, and that therefore each owner should pay for half the value of the sheep?

[The opinion of Lord Atkin is omitted. Lords Warrington and Thankerton concurred.]

NOTES

1. *Lambton* v. *Mellish*, [1894] 3 Ch. 163 was an action for nuisance against two merry-go-round operators because of the maddening noise made by their organs. Injunctions were granted on the ground that both were liable individually for nuisance, but, in a *dictum,* Mr. Justice Chitty went further:

"If a man shouts outside a house for most of the day, and another man, who is his rival (for it is to be remembered that these defendants are rivals), does the same, has the inhabitant of the house no remedy? It is said, that that is only so much the worse for the inhabitant. On the ground of common sense it must be the other way. Each of the men is making a noise and each is adding his quantum until the whole constitutes a nuisance. Each hears the other, and is adding to the sum which makes up the nuisance. In my opinion each is separately liable, and I think it would be contrary to good sense, and, indeed, contrary to law, to hold otherwise. It would be contrary to common sense that the inhabitants of the house should be left without remedy at law. . . . If the acts of two persons, each being aware of what the other is doing, amount in the aggregate to what is an actionable wrong, each is amenable to the remedy against the aggregate cause of complaint. The defendants here are both responsible for the noise as a whole so far as it constitutes a nuisance affecting the plaintiff, and each must be restrained in respect of his own share in making the noise."

2. In *Corey* v. *Havener* (1902), 182 Mass. 250, the plaintiff, in a horse and wagon, was passed by two motorists at a high rate of speed, one on each side. The horse took fright and the plaintiff was injured. Although the defendants acted independently, judgment was given against both for the full amount of the plaintiff's damages. "If each contributed to the injury, that is enough to bind both."

3. In *Duke of Buccleuch* v. *Cowan* (1866), 5 Macph. 214 (Court of Session): the plaintiff sued several defendants, mill-owners, for an injunction against polluting a stream flowing past his, and their, premises. In charging the jury, the trial judge directed them that "it is not indispensable for each of the pursuers to prove that any of the mills would of itself, if all the other mills were stopped, be sufficient to pollute the river, to the effect of creating a nuisance to him; that it is sufficient to entitle the pursuer to a verdict on any one of the issues, to prove that the river is polluted by the mills belonging to the defenders generally, to the effect of producing a nuisance to him, and that the defenders in that issue materially contribute to the production of the nuisance to him". On appeal this direction was upheld as correct. See the following language of Lord Benholme: "Now, in this world there are but few important effects, I take it, either in physics or in morals, that may not be said to have been occasioned by several causes. It is in general from a combination of causes that most great events are produced; and where you are merely considering the extent of an effect, it is quite obvious that every contributing cause must be held to be a

cause of that resulting combined effect. If it were not so, you would be in this position, that there are many important effects that have no cause at all, although, they certainly are produced by a combination of causes. That was put in this way in argument by the pursuers, and I think very fairly put — suppose this stream is polluted to the lower heritor, by the mills of A and B. A says — 'My mill is not enough to pollute this stream, and therefore you cannot reach me'; B says the same thing — 'My mill is not sufficient of itself to pollute the stream, and you cannot reach me' but the fact is, that the mills of A and B together have polluted the stream. And the result is that there is no remedy, because you cannot say that either of them has polluted the stream! Why, when this was put to the able counsel who argued the case on the part of the defenders, I think the solution which he attempted was this — You may attack the last; if A is the first transgressor, and he has not polluted so much as to cause an injury, you are not to attack him; but if B afterwards erects his mill, although it may be a much smaller and less pernicious mill, you are to attack him, because he is the person who has created the nuisance. This solution involves the fallacy that the original act of A is a legal act. But his act may not have been a legal one, and he may have been enabled to continue it, only because hitherto no one had sufficient interest to object to it, or could shew sufficient damage. The moment that that quality of his act ceases — the moment it can be said by any one, that what he does contributes materially to, although it may not altogether cause the injury to a lower proprietor — has that lower proprietor no redress? Can it be said that there is no redress to get rid of an alleged act, the effect of which, along with other illegal acts of the same kind, injures the property of that lower proprietor? Now, I apprehend that the direction given by your Lordship applicable to such a situation is founded upon common sense. It is an application of the law in this way, that what is illegal may be put down, whenever it is a contributing cause to an injury."

See also *Blair and Sumner* v. *Deakin* (1887), 57 L.T. 522, 3 T.L.R. 757 and *Michie* v. *Great Lakes Steel* (1974), 495 F. 2d 213 (U.S.C.A.), to the same effect.

4. What would be the result if the evidence in *Arneil* v. *Paterson* demonstrated that one dog killed three of the sheep by himself and that the other dog killed seven on his own? Compare with *Williams* v. *Woodworth* (1899), 32 N.S.R. 271; *Allan* v. *Popika* (1946), 54 Man. R. 379.

5. Donald and Dick negligently, but independently, shoot in the direction of Peter. Donald's bullet injures Peter's arm and Dick's bullet hits him in the leg. Who pays for what? Does it depend on whether the court is capable of apportioning the damages? See *McAllister* v. *Pennsylvania R.R. Co.* (1936), 324 Pa. 65, 187 A. 415. If the court has difficulty apportioning the damage that each has caused, should the claimant lose or should both the defendants be held liable for all the loss? What are the policy factors here? See *Maddux* v. *Donaldson* (1961), 362 Mich. 425, 108 N.W. 2d 33. See also *Johnston et al.*, v. *Burton et al.* (1971), 16 D.L.R. (3d) 660 (Man. Q.B.).

6. Suppose Donald's bullet hit Peter in the head and Dick's bullet hit him in the heart. Peter dies as a result of both of these injuries. Who pays for what? Can death be apportioned? Is the "but for" test helpful here?

7. Derek and David negligently start fires in the forest. Both fires spread and head toward Penelope's cottage. The fires both reach the cottage at the same time and consume it. Who is liable for the damage? Does the "but for" test work here? What if David's fire was only a tiny one and was engulfed in Derek's much larger blaze?

MALONE, RUMINATIONS ON CAUSE-IN-FACT

(1956), 9 Stan. L. Rev. 60

I have already suggested that the but-for test frequently fails as a means for determining whether the minimal requirements for causal relationship have been met. Sometimes defendant's conduct is regarded as a cause of the damage even though the same loss would have occurred without it. In such cases another and less exacting minimum must be established. The very fact that a new definition of cause is needed in many situations indicates clearly that the but-for rule does not always meet the policy requirements of law.

One group of situations where courts have felt themselves obliged to reject the but-for test is familiar to every first-year law student: Two noisy motorcycles simultaneously pass the horse on which plaintiff is riding, frightening the animal and causing it to run away and injure plaintiff. Neither cyclist in such a situation can escape liability by showing that the noise made by the other would have produced the same result alone. Similarly, a fire started through the negligence of a railroad may merge with a fire of undetermined origin and the two together destroy plaintiff's property. Under such facts the wrongdoer will not be allowed to show that his fire was not a cause by establishing that the other fire would have destroyed the property even without his participation. Our senses have told us that he *did* participate. We are not obliged to make deductions in order to reach this conclusion. In the language of the layman, the defendant's fire "had something to do with" the burning of plaintiff's property. The affinity between his conduct and the destruction is recognized as being close enough to bring into play the well-established rules that prohibit the setting into motion of a destructive force. The but-for test has failed in such cases to justify itself policywise, so we search for other language that will allow us to do what we feel is right and proper. We demand that we be allowed to judge as we observe. Drama has triumphed over the syllogism.

In the combined force cases courts do not abandon the effort to define cause. They merely re-establish the point of acceptable affinity between misconduct and loss lower on the scale. There must be evidence that the force set in motion by defendant was a "substantial factor" in bringing about the damage before the cause issue will be submitted to the jury. Thus courts retain the power to determine the proper adjustment between policy and fact. Again, as with the but-for test, the judge's resolution of the issue appears as an answer to a factual inquiry: How did the size of the defendant's fire compare with that of the fire of unknown origin? Or, how much noise was made by each of the motorcycles, respectively, that frightened the plaintiff's horse? The estimate of factual likelihood required under the but-for test has merely been supplanted by an estimate of quantity. The question, "How clear was the proof?" gives way to the question, "How much did the defendant's participation contribute to the destruction?" In either case the answer is, "Enough (or not enough) to warrant holding the defendant liable in this case, or, at least, enough (or not enough) to warrant going further into the matter."

NOTES

1. In *Cork* v. *Kirby MacLean*, [1952] 2 All E.R. 402 (C.A.), a workman was killed when he suffered an epileptic seizure while working on a high platform and fell to his death. The platform did not conform to the regulations. The workman had not told his employer that he suffered from epilepsy. In the action under the Fatal Accidents Act, Denning L.J. held the employer and the employee equally at fault for the accident and explained:

"Subject to the question of remoteness, causation is, I think, a question of fact. If you can say that the damage would not have happened but for a particular fault, then that fault is in fact a cause of the damage; but if you say that the damage would have happened just the same, fault or no fault, then the fault is not a cause of the damage. It often happens that each of the parties at fault can truly say to the other: "But for your fault, it would not have happened." In such a case both faults are in fact causes of the damage.

In this case, on the facts, I am clearly of opinion that both faults were causes of the damage. The man's fault (in not telling his employers he was forbidden to work at heights) was clearly one of the causes of his death. But for that fault on his part, he would never have been on this platform at all and would never have fallen. The employers' fault (in not providing a guard-rail or toe-boards) is more doubtful a cause. One cannot say that but for that fault the accident *would* not have happened. All that can be said is that it *might* not have happened. A guard-rail and toe-boards *might* have saved him from falling. If this was a very remote possibility, it could not be said to be a cause at all. But the judge did not so regard it. He thought that it probably would have saved him. On that view the employers' fault was also one of the causes of the man's death."

BAKER v. WILLOUGHBY

House of Lords. [1970] 2 W.L.R. 50; [1969] 3 All E.R. 1528

The plaintiff's leg was injured in a motor vehicle accident, for which he was held 25 percent at fault. He was later shot during a robbery in the same leg, which had to be amputated as a result. He now had an artificial limb, whereas he would have had a stiff leg. The trial judge assessed the general damages at £1,600, refusing to lower the amount because of the later injury. The Court of Appeal reversed assessing the general damages at a lower figure. The House of Lords restored the trial judge's assessment.

Lord Reid: The appellant argues that the loss which he suffered from the car accident has not been diminished by his second injury. He still suffers the same kind of loss of the amenities of life and he still suffers from reduced capacity to earn though these may have been to some extent increased. And he will suffer these losses for as long as he would have done because it is not said that the second injury curtailed his expectation of life.

The respondent on the other hand argues that the second injury removed the very limb from which the earlier disability had stemmed, and that therefore no loss suffered thereafter can be attributed to the respondent's negligence. He says that the second injury submerged or obliterated the effect of the first and that all loss thereafter must be attributed to the second injury. The trial judge rejected this argument which he said was more ingenious than attractive. But it was accepted by the Court of Appeal.

The respondent's argument was succinctly put to your Lordships by his counsel. He could not run before the second injury; he cannot run now. But the cause is now quite different. The former cause was an injured leg but now he has no leg and the former cause can no longer operate. His counsel was inclined to agree that if the first injury had caused some neurosis or other mental disability, that disability might be regarded as still flowing from the first accident; even if it had been increased by the second accident the respondent might still have to pay for that part which he caused. I agree with that and I think that any distinction between a neurosis and a physical injury depends on a wrong view of what is the proper subject for compensation. A man is not compensated for the physical injury: he is compensated for the loss which he suffers as a result of that injury. His loss is not in having a stiff leg: it is in his inability to lead a full life, his inability to enjoy those amenities which depend on freedom of movement and his inability to earn as much as he used to earn or could have earned if there had been no accident. In this case the second injury did not diminish any of these. So why should it be regarded as having obliterated or superseded them?

If it were the case that in the eye of the law an effect could only have one cause then the respondent might be right. It is always necessary to prove that any loss for which damages can be given was caused by the defendant's negligent act. But it is a commonplace that the law regards many events as having two causes: that happens whenever there is contributory negligence for then the law says that the injury was caused both by the negligence of the defendant and by the negligence of the plaintiff. And generally it does not matter which negligence occurred first in point of time.

I see no reason why the appellant's present disability cannot be regarded as having two causes, and if authority be needed for this I find it in *Harwood* v. *Wyken Colliery Co.,* [1913] 2 K.B. 158. That was a Workmen's Compensation Act case. But causation cannot be different in tort. There an accident made the man only fit for light work. And then a heart disease supervened and it also caused him only to be fit for light work. The argument for the employer was the same as in the present case. Before the disease supervened the workman's incapacity was caused by the accident. Thereafter it was caused by the disease and the previous accident became irrelevant: he would have been equally incapacitated if the accident had never happened. But Hamilton L.J. said, at p. 169:

"... he is not disentitled to be paid compensation by reason of the supervention of a disease of the heart. It cannot be said of him that partial incapacity for work has not resulted and is not still resulting from the injury. All that can be said is that such partial incapacity is not still resulting 'solely' from the injury." ...

If any assistance is to be got, it is I think from *The Haversham Grange,* [1905] P. 307 where neither collision rendered the vessel unseaworthy. The damage from the first collision took longer to repair than the damage from the second and it was held that the vessel responsible for the second collision did not have to contribute towards payment for time lost in repairs. In my view the latter would have had to pay for any time after the repairs from the first damage had been completed because that time could not be claimed from the first wrongdoer. The first wrongdoer must pay for all damage caused by him but no more. The second is not liable for any damage caused by the first wrongdoer but must pay for any additional damage caused by him. That was the ground of decision in *Performance Cars Ltd.* v. *Abraham,* [1962] 1 Q.B. 33. There a car sustained two slight collisions: the first necessitated respraying over a wide area which included the place damaged by the second collision. So repairing the damage caused by the first collision also repaired the damage done by the second. The plaintiff was unable to recover from the person responsible for the first collision and he then sued the person responsible for the second. But his action failed. The second wrongdoer hit a car which was already damaged and his fault caused no additional loss to the plaintiff: so he had nothing to pay.

These cases exemplify the general rule that a wrongdoer must take the plaintiff (or his property) as he finds him: that may be to his advantage or disadvantage. In the present case the robber is not responsible or liable for the damage caused by the respondent: he would only have to pay for additional loss to the appellant by reason of his now having an artificial limb instead of a stiff leg.

It is argued — if a man's death before the trial reduces the damages why do injuries which he has received before the trial not also reduce the damages? I think it depends on the nature and result of the later injuries. Suppose that but for the first injuries the plaintiff could have looked forward to 20 years of working life and that the injuries inflicted by the defendant reduced his earning capacity. Then but for the later injuries the plaintiff would have recovered for loss of earning capacity during 20 years. And then suppose that later injuries were such that at the date of the trial his expectation of life had been reduced to two years. Then he could not claim for 20 years of loss of earning capacity because in fact he will only suffer loss of earning capacity for two years. Thereafter he will be dead and the defendant could not be required to pay for a loss which it is now clear that the plaintiff will in fact never suffer. But that is not this case: here the appellant will continue to suffer from the disabilities caused by the car accident for as long as he would have done if his leg had never been shot and amputated.

If the later injury suffered before the date of the trial either reduces the disabiities from the injury for which the defendant is liable, or shortens the period during which they will be suffered by the plaintiff, then the defendant will have to pay less damages. But if the later injuries merely become a concurrent cause of the disabilities caused by the injury inflicted by the defendant, then in my view they cannot diminish the damages. Suppose that the plaintiff has to spend a month in bed before the trial because of some illness unconnected with the original injury, the defendant cannot say that he does not have to pay anything in respect of that month: during that month the original injuries and the new illness are concurrent causes of his inability to work and that does not reduce the damages.

Finally. I must advert to the pain suffered and to be suffered by the appellant as a result of the car accident. If the result of the amputation was that the appellant suffered no more pain thereafter, then he could not claim for pain after the amputation which he would never suffer. But the facts with regard to this are not clear, the amount awarded for pain subsequent to the date of the amputation was probably only a small part of the £1,600 damages and counsel for the respondent did not make a point of this. So in these circumstances we can neglect this matter.

I would allow the appeal and restore the judgment of Donaldson J.

Lord Pearson: . . . The second question is, as my noble and learned friend has said, more difficult. There is a plausible argument for the defendant on the following lines. The original accident, for which the defendant is liable, inflicted on the plaintiff a permanently injured left ankle, which caused pain from time to time, diminished his mobility and so reduced his earning capacity, and was likely to lead to severe arthritis. The proper figure of damages for those consequences of the accident, as assessed by the judge before making his apportionment, was £1,600. That was the proper figure for those consequences if they were likely to endure for a normal period and run a normal course. But the supervening event, when the robbers shot the plaintiff in his left leg, necessitated an amputation of the left leg above the knee. The consequences of the original accident therefore have ceased. He no longer suffers pain in his left ankle, because there no longer is a left ankle. He will never have the arthritis. There is no longer any loss of mobility through stiffness or weakness of the left ankle, because it is no longer there. The injury to the left ankle, resulting from the original accident, is not still operating as one of two concurrent causes both producing discomfort and disability. It is not operating at all nor causing anything. The present state of disablement, with the stump and the artificial leg on the left side, was caused wholly by the supervening event and not at all by the original accident. Thus the consequences of the original accident have been submerged and obliterated by the greater consequences of the supervening event.

That is the argument, and it is formidable. But it must not be allowed to succeed, because it produces manifest injustice. The supervening event has not made the plaintiff less lame nor less disabled nor less deprived of amenities. It has not shortened the period over which he will be suffering. It has made him more lame, more disabled, more deprived of amenities. He should not have less damages through being worse off than might have been expected.

The nature of the injustice becomes apparent if the supervening event is treated as a tort (as indeed it was) and if one envisages the plaintiff suing the robbers who shot him. They would be entitled, as the saying is, to "take the plaintiff as they find him". (*Performance Cars Ltd.* v. *Abraham,* [1962] 1 Q.B. 33.) They have not injured and disabled a previously fit and able-bodied man. They have only made an already lame and disabled man more lame and disabled. Take, for example, the reduction of earnings. The original accident reduced his earnings from £x per week to £y per week, and the supervening event further reduced them from £y per week to £z per week. If the defendant's argument is correct, there is as Mr. Griffiths has pointed out, a gap. The plaintiff recovers from the defendant the £x-y not for the whole period of the remainder of his working life, but only for the short period up to the date of the supervening event. The robbers are liable only for the £y-z from the date of the supervening event onwards. In the Court of Appeal an ingenious attempt was made to fill the gap by holding that the damages recoverable from the later tortfeasors (the robbers) would include a novel head of damage, *viz.,* the diminution of the plaintiff's damages recoverable from the original tortfeasor (the defendant). I doubt whether that would be an admissible head of damage: it looks too remote. In any case it would not help the plaintiff, if the later tortfeasors could not be found or were indigent and uninsured. These later tortfeasors cannot have been insured in respect of the robbery which they committed.

I think a solution of the theoretical problem can be found in cases such as this by taking a comprehensive and unitary view of the damage caused by the original accident. Itemisation of the damages by dividing them into heads and sub-heads is often convenient, but is not essential. In the end judgment is given for a single lump sum of damages and not for a total of items set out under heads and sub-heads. The original accident caused what may be called a "devaluation" of the plaintiff, in the sense that it produced a general reduction of his capacity to do things, to earn money and to enjoy life. For that devaluation the original tortsfeasor should be and remain responsible to the full extent, unless before the assessment of the damages something has happened which either diminishes the devaluation (*e.g.,* if there is an unexpected recovery from some of the adverse effects of the accident) or by shortening the expectation of life diminishes the period over which the plaintiff will suffer from the devaluation. If the supervening event is a tort, the second tortsfeasor should be responsible for the additional devaluation caused by him.

The solution which I have suggested derives support from a passage in the judgment of Buckley L.J., in *Harwood* v. *Wyken Colliery Co.,* [1913] 2 K.B. 158, 166, 167 and from a passage in a judgment given in the Court of Appeal of British Columbia in *Long* v. *Thiessen and Laliberte* (1968), 65 W.W.R. 577. Shortly these were the facts of this latter case. On November 27, 1964, Long as the driver of his motor vehicle was stopped at a street intersection when his vehicle was struck in the rear by the vehicle of the first defendant. As a result he suffered injuries to his neck and shoulder. On April 23, 1966, Long suffered similar injuries when his stationary vehicle was struck in the rear by a motor vehicle driven by the second defendant. There were separate actions, but each defendant admitted liability and the actions came to trial together for assessment of damages and there was an appeal as to the assessment. In the course of a judgment with which Nemetz J.A. concurred, Robertson J.A. said, at p. 591:

"Because the injuries inflicted in the second accident were super-imposed upon the then residual effects of the injuries inflicted in the first accident, it is a matter of the greatest difficulty to determine what damages should be awarded for each set of injuries. The plaintiff should not receive more in respect of the first accident than he would if the second had not occurred; nor should he receive less because it did occur. . . . I think that the way in which justice can best be done here is: (*a*) to assess as best one can what the plaintiff would have recovered against the Thiessens had his action against them been tried on April 22, 1966 (the date before the second accident), and to award damages accordingly; (*b*) to assess global damages as of the date of the trial in respect of both accidents; and (*c*) to deduct the amount under (*a*) from the amount under (*b*) and award damages against Laliberte in the amount of the difference. I think that nothing I have said in this paragraph is inconsistent with *Baker* v. *Willoughby,* [1969] 1 Q.B. 38 or any of the cases referred to there."

The last sentence was referring to the judgment of Donaldson J. at first instance in the present case.

I would allow the appeal and restore the judgment of Donaldson J. both in respect of the total amount of the damages and in respect of his apportionment.

NOTES

1. If the original injury had been caused in the robbery and the subsequent one by the negligent motorist, should the same result follow? If so, would this not deny the injured person most of his recompense? Why not joint liability? What effect should the existence of a victim of crime compensation scheme have on all this? What if either of the injuries resulted from a non-culpable source, such as an Act of God?

See *Stene* v. *Evans et al.* (1958), 14 D.L.R. (2d) 73 (Alta C.A.); *Dingle* v. *Associated Newspapers Ltd.,* [1961] 2 Q.B. 162 (C.A.); affd. [1964] A.C. 371; *Long* v. *Thiessen & Laliberté* (1968), 65 W.W.R. 577 (B.C.C.A.); *Harwood* v. *Wyken Colliery Co.,* [1913] 2 K.B. 158.

2. What should be done when a plaintiff is injured by two successive, unrelated acts of negligence? In *Hicks* v. *Cooper* (1973), 1 O.R. (2d) 221, the Ontario Court of Appeal adopted the *Baker* approach. Gale C.J.O. assessed the damages against the first tortfeasor as of the day before the second accident occurred. The second tortfeasor was required to pay the balance of the "global damages" resulting from both accidents.

3. A similar approach has been taken in a case where the plaintiff was injured in three successive, unrelated accidents. In *Berns* v. *Campbell et al.* (1974), 8 O.R. (2d) 680, Hughes J. assessed the general damages against the first defendant as of the day before the second accident at $6,000. His Lordship assessed the general damages as of the day before the third accident at $15,000, deducted from this $6,000, and awarded the $9,000 difference against the second defendant. He then assessed the global damages of all three accidents at $23,000, deducted $15,000 (6,000 plus 9,000) from that, and awarded the difference of $8,000 against the third defendant. Does this make sense? Can you think of a better way to do it?

4. If three months work would have been missed, even if there had been no accident, because of a heart problem, the plaintiff cannot recover for this three-month period from the wrongdoer who injured him. *Baker* was said to deal with a situation where the circumstances were culpable whereas here they were non-culpable. See *Penner* v. *Mitchell* (1978), 6 C.C.L.T. 132 (Alta. C.A.).

5. In *Dillon* v. *Twin State Gas & Electric Co.* (1932), 85 N.H. 449, 163 A. 111, a 14-year-old boy was killed in strange circumstances. While he was playing on a bridge he lost his balance, and reached for a wire to save himself. The electrical current in the wire killed the boy. If he had not grabbed the wire, he would have fallen, either to his death, or to serious injury below. Mr. Justice

Allen of the Supreme Court of New Hampshire stated that he had not been deprived of a normal life expectancy but only of a few moments of life, "too short to be given pecuniary allowance". If it were shown that he would only have been injured in the fall, he should be awarded just the value of the loss to the earning capacity he would have retained in his crippled or maimed condition.

6. The plaintiff is dying from an incurable disease. The defendant negligently kills him. What loss has the defendant caused?

7. The deceased, who is suffering from cirrhosis of the liver and cancer, incurs minor injuries in an accident caused by the defendant's negligence. His life expectancy prior to the accident was about two and one-half years. He dies three months after the accident. The evidence shows that his death was hastened by the accident. Is the defendant liable to the plaintiff's heirs for the hastening of his death? How could one go about assessing damages in such a case? See *Windrim* v. *Wood* (1974), 7 O.R. (2d) 211.

8. For a brief and clear treatment of some of these problems, see Strachan, "The Scope and Application of the 'But For' Causal Test" (1970), 33 Mod. L. Rev. 386. See also Peaslee, "Multiple Causation and Damage" (1934), 47 Harv. L. Rev. 1127; Carpenter, "Concurrent Causation" (1935), 83 U. Pa. L. Rev. 941; Street, "Supervening Events and the Quantum of Damages" (1962), 78 L.Q. Rev. 70; Wagner, "Successive Causes and the Quantum of Damages in Personal Injury Cases" (1972), 10 O.H. L.J. 369.

CHAPTER 9

REMOTENESS AND PROXIMATE CAUSE

Our law has never reached the stage where all losses caused by negligent conduct attract liability. Certain losses are felt to be beyond the sphere of protection that the law should afford, even though such harms result from negligent conduct. Various techniques, such as "duty of care", "remoteness of damage" and "proximate cause" have been used to place limits on the liability for negligent conduct. The present chapter is designed to bring into focus these concepts, which are among the most complex in the law of torts.

One of the difficulties which has plagued the law of negligence is the fact that many courts, and many more text-writers, have taken the language of these various concepts as separate and distinct dogmas which dictated specific results. One consequence was to segregate discussion of "duty of care" from "proximate cause" and "remoteness" and, at times, to state that the two concepts bore no relation one to the other. The fact is that they are related, often being different ways of looking at the same problem.

As negligent conduct is conduct which creates an unreasonable risk, the question arises, "risk to whom" and "risk of what"? When a question arises concerning the person who may be considered within a risk created by the defendant's conduct, courts have tended to use the concept of "duty". See *supra* chapter 7, B. While "foreseeability" is sometimes spoken of as determining this question, it is important to realize at an early stage that "foreseeability" will not solve all problems of "duty". This is apparent if one considers the rescue cases.

When one passes from the persons within a risk to the ways in which a risk may culminate in harm or the interests which may be invaded by conduct which is "negligent", it is more difficult to employ the term "duty", and courts have tended to use the concepts of "proximate cause" and "remoteness".

None of the devices presently used are altogether satisfactory. No simple answer can be given to questions of this kind. These cases, rather than explaining everything, should serve as a warning against dogmatising.

A. THE ALTERNATIVE APPROACHES

IN RE AN ARBITRATION BETWEEN POLEMIS AND FURNESS, WITHY & CO. LTD.

Court of Appeal. [1921] 3 K.B. 560; 90 L.J.K.B. 1353

The owners of the steamship *Thrasyvoulos* chartered the ship to Furness Withy. Clause 21 of the charterparty contained the usual exemption from liability for "act of God, the King's enemies, loss or damage from fire on board, etc."

While discharging cargo at Casablanca, a heavy plank fell into the hold in which petrol was stored. An explosion followed and the ship was completely destroyed. The owners claimed the loss from the charterers alleging negligence by the charterer's servants. The charterers contended the fire was an excepted peril; there was no negligence since to drop a plank into the hold of the ship could do no harm to the ship; the danger and/or damage was too remote. The claim was referred to arbitration.

The arbitrator found (a) the ship was lost by fire; (b) the fire arose from a spark igniting petrol vapour in the hold; (c) the spark was caused by the falling board coming in contact with some substance in the hold; (d) and (e) the fall was caused by the negligence of workmen who were servants of the charterers; (f) the causing of the spark could not reasonably have been anticipated from the falling of the board, though some damage to the ship might reasonably have been anticipated. Damages were assessed at £196,165. 1s. 11d., which were awarded the owners subject to an opinion of the court on any question of law. Sankey J., affirmed the award. The charterers appealed.

Bankes L.J.: . . . These findings are no doubt intended to raise the question whether the view taken, or said to have been taken, by Pollock C.B. in *Rigby* v. *Hewitt,* 5 Ex. 243, and *Greenland* v. *Chaplin,* 5 Ex. 248, or the view taken by Channel B. and Blackburn J. in *Smith* v. *London and South Western Ry. Co.,* L.R. 6 C.P. 21 is the correct one . . . . Assuming the Chief Baron to have been correctly reported in the Exchequer Reports, the difference between the two views is this: According to the one view, the consequences which may reasonably be expected to result from a particular act are material only in reference to the question whether the act is or is not a negligent act; according to the other view, those consequences are the test whether the damages resulting from the act, assuming it to be negligent, are or are not too remote to be recoverable. . . .

In the present case the arbitrators have found as a fact that the falling of the plank was due to the negligence of the defendant's servants. The fire appears to me to have been directly caused by the falling of the plank. Under these circumstances I consider that it is immaterial that the causing of the spark by the falling of the plank could not have been reasonably anticipated. The appellant's junior counsel sought to draw a distinction between the anticipation of the extent of damage resulting from a negligent act, and the anticipation of the type of damage resulting from such an act. He admitted that it could not lie in the mouth of a person whose negligent act had caused damage to say that he could not reasonably have foreseen the extent of the damage, but he contended that the negligent person was entitled to rely upon the fact that he could not reasonably have anticipated the type of damage which resulted from his negligent act. I do not think that the distinction can be admitted. Given the breach of duty which constitutes the negligence, and given the damage as a direct result of that negligence, the anticipations of the person whose negligent act has produced the damage appear to me to be irrelevant. I consider that the damages claimed are not too remote. . . .

Warrington L.J.: . . . The presence or absence of reasonable anticipation of damage determines the legal quality of the act as negligent or innocent. If it be thus determined to be negligent, then the question whether particular damages are recoverable depends only on the answer to the question whether they are the direct consequence of the act. . . .

Scrutton L.J.: . . . The second defence is that the damage is too remote from the negligence, as it could not be reasonably foreseen as a consequence. On this head we were referred to a number of well known cases in which vague language, which I cannot think to be really helpful, has been used in an attempt to define the point at which damage becomes too remote from, or not sufficiently directly caused by the breach of duty, which is the original cause of action, to be recoverable. For instance, I cannot think it useful to say the damage must be the natural and probable result. This suggests that there are results which are natural but not probable, and other results which are probable but not natural. I am not sure what either adjective means in this connection; if they mean the same thing, two need not be used; if they mean different things, the difference between them should be defined . . . . To determine whether an act is negligent, it is relevant to determine whether any reasonable person would foresee that the act would cause damage; if he would not, the act is not negligent. But if the act would or might probably cause damage, the fact that the damage it in fact causes is not the exact kind of damage one would expect is immaterial, so long as the damage is in fact directly traceable to the negligent act, and not due to the operation of independent causes having no connection with the negligent act, except that they could not avoid its results. Once the act is negligent, the fact that its exact operation was not foreseen is immaterial . . . .In the present case it was negligent in discharging cargo to knock down the planks of the temporary staging, for they might easily cause some damage either to workmen, or cargo, or the ship. The fact that they did directly produce an unexpected result, a spark in an atmosphere of petrol vapour which caused a fire, does not relieve the person who was negligent from the damage which his negligent act directly caused.

For these reasons the experienced arbitrators and the judge appealed from came, in my opinion, to a correct decision, and the appeal must be dismissed with costs.

PALSGRAF v. LONG ISLAND RAILROAD CO.

New York Court of Appeals. (1928), 248 N.Y. 339; 162 N.E. 99

Action by Helen Palsgraf against the Long Island Railroad Company. Judgment entered on the verdict of a jury in favour of the plaintiff was affirmed by the Appellate Division by a divided court (222 App. Div. 166; 225 N.Y.S. 412), and defendant appeals.

Cardozo C.J.: Plaintiff was standing on a platform of defendant's railroad after buying a ticket to go to Rockaway Beach. A train stopped at the station, bound for another place. Two men ran forward to catch it. One of the men reached the platform of the car without mishap, though the train was already moving. The other man, carrying a package, jumped aboard the car, but seemed unsteady as if about to fall. A guard on the car, who had held the door open, reached forward to help him in, and another guard on the platform pushed him from behind. In this act, the package was dislodged, and fell upon the rails. It was a package of small size, about 15 inches long, and was covered by a newspaper. In fact it contained fireworks, but there was nothing in its appearance to give notice of its contents. The fireworks when they fell exploded. The shock of the explosion threw down some scales at the other end of the platform, many feet away. The scales struck the plaintiff, causing injuries for which she sues.

The conduct of the defendant's guard, if a wrong in its relation to the holder of the package, was not a wrong in its relation to the plaintiff, standing far away. Relatively to her it was not negligence at all. Nothing in the situation gave notice that the falling package had in it the potency of peril to persons thus removed. Negligence is not actionable unless it involves the invasion of a legally protected interest, the violation of a right. "Proof of negligence in the air, so to speak, will not do" (Pollock, *Torts* [11th ed.], p. 455; *Martin* v. *Herzog,* 228 N.Y. 164, 170; *cf.* Salmond, *Torts* [6th ed.], p. 24). "Negligence is the absence of care, according to the circumstances" (Willes J., in *Vaughan* v. *Taff Vale Ry. Co.,* 5 H. & N. 679; 1 Beven, *Negligence* [4th ed.], 7). The plaintiff as she stood upon the platform of the station might claim to be protected against intentional invasion of her bodily security. Such invasion is not charged. She might claim to be protected against unintentional invasion by conduct involving in the thought of reasonable men an unreasonable hazard that such invasion would ensue. These, from the point of view of the law, were the bounds of her immunity, with perhaps some rare exceptions, survivals for the most part of ancient forms of liability, where conduct is held to be at the peril of the actor. If no hazard was apparent to the eye of ordinary vigilance, an act innocent and harmless, at least to outward seeming, with reference to her, did not take to itself the quality of a tort because it happened to be wrong, though apparently not one involving the risk of bodily insecurity, with reference to some one else. "In every instance before negligence can be predicated of a given act, back of the act must be sought and found a duty to the individual complaining, the observance of which would have averted or avoided the injury." . . . "The ideas of negligence and duty are strictly correlative" (Bowen L.J. in *Thomas* v. *Quartermaine,* 18 Q.B.D. 685, 694). The plaintiff sues in her own right for a wrong personal to her, and not as the vicarious beneficiary of a breach of duty to another.

A different conclusion will involve us, and swiftly too, in a maze of contradictions. A guard stumbles over a package which has been left upon a platform. It seems to be a bundle of newspapers. It turns out to be a can of dynamite. To the eye of ordinary vigilance, the bundle is abandoned waste, which may be kicked or trod on with impunity. Is a passenger at the other end of the platform protected by the law against the unsuspected hazard concealed beneath the waste? If not, is the result to be any different, so far as the distant passenger is concerned, when the guard stumbles over a valise which a truckman or a porter has left upon the walk? The passenger far away, if the victim of a wrong at all, has a cause of action, not derivative, but original and primary. His claim to be protected against invasion of his bodily security is neither greater nor less because the act resulting in the invasion is a wrong to another far removed. In this case, the rights that are said to have been invaded, are not even of the same order. The man was not injured in his person nor even put in danger. The purpose of the act, as well as its effect, was to make his person safe. If there was a wrong to him at all, which may very well be doubted, it was a wrong to a property interest only, the safety of his package. Out of this wrong to property, which threatened injury to nothing else, there has passed, we are told, to the plaintiff by derivation or succession a right of action for the invasion of an interest of another order, the right to bodily security. The diversity of interests emphasizes the futility of the effort to build the plaintiff's right upon the basis of a wrong to some one else. The gain is one of emphasis, for a like result would follow if the interests were the same. Even then, the orbit of the danger as disclosed to the eye of reasonable vigilance would be the orbit of the duty. One who jostles one's neighbour in a crowd does not invade the rights of others standing at the outer fringe when the unintended contact casts a bomb upon the ground. The wrongdoer as to them is the man who carries the bomb, not the one who explodes it without suspicion of the danger. Life will have to be made over, and human nature transformed, before prevision so extravagant can be accepted as the form of conduct, the customary standard to which behaviour must conform.

The argument for the plaintiff is built upon the shifting meanings of such words as "wrong" and "wrongful", and shares their instability. What the plaintiff must show is "a wrong" to herself, *i.e.,* a violation of her own right, and not merely a wrong to some one else, nor conduct "wrongful" because unsocial, but not a "wrong" to any one. We are told that one who drives at reckless speed through a crowded city street is guilty of a negligent act and, therefore, of a wrongful one irrespective of the consequences. Negligent the act is, and wrongful in the sense that it is unsocial, but wrongful and unsocial in relation to other travellers, only because the eye of vigilance perceives the risk of damage. If the same act were to be committed on a speedway or a race course, it would lose its wrongful quality. The risk reasonably to be perceived defines the duty to be obeyed and risk imports relation; it is risk to another or to others within the range of apprehension (Seavey, Negligence, Subjective or Objective; 41 Harv. L. Rev. 6; *Boronkay* v. *Robinson & Carpenter,* 247 N.Y. 365). This does not mean, of course, that one who launches a destructive force is always relieved of liability if the force, though unknown to be destructive, pursues an unexpected path. "It was not necessary that the defendant should have had notice of the particular method in which an accident would occur, if the possibility of an accident was clear to the ordinary prudent eye" (*Munsey* v. *Webb,* 231 U.S. 150, 156; *Condran* v. *Park & Tilford,* 213 N.Y. 341, 345; *Robert* v. *U.S.E.F. Corp.,* 240 N.Y. 474, 477). Some acts, such as shooting, are so imminently dangerous to any one who may come within reach of the missile, however unexpectedly, as to impose a duty of prevision not far from that of an insurer. Even today, and much oftener in earlier stages of the law, one acts sometimes at one's peril (Jeremiah Smith, "Tort and Absolute Liability", 30 Harv. L. Rev. 328; Street, *Foundations of Legal Liability,* Vol. 1. pp. 77, 78). Under this head, it may be, fall certain cases of what is known as transferred intent, an act wilfully dangerous to A resulting in misadventure in injury to B (*Talmage* v. *Smith,* 101 Mich. 370, 374). These cases aside, wrong is defined in terms of the natural or probable, at least when unintentional (*Parrot* v. *Wells-Fargo Co.* [The Nitro-Glicerine Case] 15 Wall. [U.S.] 524). The range of reasonable apprehension is at times a question for the court, and at times, if varying inferences are possible, a question for the jury. Here, by concession, there was nothing in the situation to suggest to the most cautious mind that the parcel wrapped in newspaper would spread wreckage through the station. If the guard had thrown it down knowingly and wilfully, he would not have threatened the plaintiff's safety, so far as appearances could warn him. His conduct would not have involved, even then, an unreasonable probability of invasion of her bodily security. Liability can be no greater when the act is inadvertent.

Negligence, like risk, is thus a term of relation. Negligence in the abstract, apart from things related, is surely not a tort, if indeed it is understandable at all (Bowen L.J., in *Thomas* v. *Quartermaine,* 18 Q.B.D. 685, 694). Negligence is not a tort unless it results in the commission of a wrong, and the commission of a wrong imports the violation of a right, in this case, we are told, the right to be protected against interference with one's bodily security. But bodily security is protected, not against all forms of interference or aggression, but only against some. One who seeks redress at law does not make out a cause of action by showing without more that there has been damage to his person. If the harm was not wilful, he must show that the act as to him had possibilities of danger so many and apparent as to entitle him to be protected against the doing of it though the harm was unintended. Affront to personality is still the keystone of the wrong. Confirmation of this view will be found in the history and development of the action on the case. Negligence as a basis of civil liability was unknown to mediaeval law (8 Holdsworth, *History of English Law,* p. 449; Street, *Foundations of Legal Liability,* vol, 1, pp. 189, 190). For damage to the person, the sole remedy was trespass, and trespass did not lie in the absence of aggression, and that direct and personal (Holdsworth, *op. cit.,* p. 453; Street, *op. cit.* vol. 3, pp. 258, 260, vol. 1, pp. 71, 74). Liability for other damage, as where a servant without orders from the master does or omits something to the damage of another, is a plant of later growth (Holdsworth, *op. cit.* 450, 457; Wigmore, *Responsibility for Tortious Acts,* vol. 3. *Essay in Anglo-American Legal History,* 520, 523, 526, 533). When it emerged out of the legal soil, it was thought of as a variant of trespass, an offshoot of the parent stock. This appears in the form of action, which was known as trespass on the case (Holdsworth, *op. cit.* p. 449; *cf. Scott* v. *Shepherd,* 2 Wm. Black 892; Green, *Rationale of Proximate Cause,* p. 19). The victim does not sue derivatively, or by right of subrogation, to vindicate an interest invaded in the person of another. Thus to view his cause of action is to ignore the fundamental difference between tort and crime (Holland, *Jurisprudence* (12th ed.), p. 328). He sues for breach of a duty owing to himself.

The law of causation, remote or proximate, is thus foreign to the case before us. The question of liability is always anterior to the question of the measure of the consequences that go with liability. If there is no tort to be redressed, there is no occasion to consider what damage might be recovered if there were a finding of a tort. We may assume, without deciding, that negligence, not at large or in the abstract, but in relation to the plaintiff, would entail liability for any and all consequences, however novel or extraordinary. [Citations omitted.]

There is room for argument that a distinction is to be drawn according to the diversity of interests invaded by the act, as where conduct negligent in that it threatens an insignificant invasion of an interest in property results in an unforeseeable invasion of an interest of another order, as, *e.g.,* one of bodily security. Perhaps other distinctions may be necessary. We do not go into the question now. The consequences to be followed must first be rooted in a wrong.

The judgment of the Appellate Division and that of the Trial Term should be reversed, and the complaint dismissed, with costs in all courts.

Andrews J. (dissenting): . . . Negligence may be defined roughly as an act or omission which unreasonably does or may affect the rights of others, or which unreasonably fails to protect one's self from the dangers resulting from such acts. Here I confine myself to the first branch of the definition. Nor do I comment on the word "unreasonable". For present purposes it sufficiently describes that average of conduct that society requires of its members . . . .

But we are told that "there is no negligence unless there is in the particular case a legal duty to take care, and this duty must be one which is owed to the plaintiff himself and not merely to others". (Salmond, *Torts* (6th ed.), 24.) This, I think too narrow a conception. Where there is the unreasonable act, and some right that may be affected there is negligence whether damage does or does not result. That is immaterial. Should we drive down Broadway at a reckless speed, we are negligent whether we strike an approaching car or miss it by an inch. The act itself is wrongful not only to those who happen to be within the radius of danger but to all who might have been there — a wrong to the public at large. Such is the language of the street. Such the language of the courts when speaking of contributory negligence. Such again and again their language in speaking of the duty of some defendant and discussing proximate cause in cases where such a discussion is wholly irrelevant on any other theory (*Perry* v. *Rochester Line Co.,* 219 N.Y. 60). As was said by Mr. Justice Holmes many years ago, "the measure of the defendant's duty in determining whether a wrong has been committed is one thing, the measure of liability when a wrong has been committed is another". (*Spade* v. *Lynn & Boston R.R. Co.,* 172 Mass. 488.) Due care is a duty imposed on each one of us to protect society from unnecessary danger, not to protect A, B or C alone.

It may well be that there is no such thing as negligence in the abstract. "Proof of negligence in the air, so to speak, will not do." In an empty world negligence would not exist. It does involve a relationship between man and his fellows. But not merely a relationship between man and those whom he might reasonably expect his act would injure. Rather, a relationship between him and those whom he does in fact injure. If his act has a tendency to harm some one, it harms him a mile away as it does those on the scene. We now permit children to recover for the negligent killing of the father. It was never prevented on the theory that no duty was owing to them. A husband may be compensated for the loss of his wife's services. To say that the wrongdoer was negligent as to the husband as well as to the wife is merely an attempt to fit facts to theory. An insurance company paying a fire loss recovers its payment of the negligent incendiary. We speak of subrogation — of suing in the right of the insured. Behind the cloud of words is the fact they hide, that the act, wrongful as to the insured, has also injured the company. Even if it be true that the fault of father, wife or insured will prevent recovery, it is because we consider the original negligence not the proximate cause of the injury. Pollock, *Torts*, 12th ed., 463.

In the well-known *Polemis* case, [1921] 3 K.B. 560, Scrutton L.J. said that the dropping of a plank was negligent for it might injure "workman or cargo or ship". Because of either possibility the owner of the vessel was to be made good for his loss. The act being wrongful the doer was liable for its proximate results. Criticized and explained as this statement may have been, I think it states the law as it should be and as it is.

The proposition is this. Every one owes to the world at large the duty of refraining from those acts that may unreasonably threaten the safety of others. Such an act occurs. Not only is he wronged to whom harm might reasonably be expected to result, but he also who is in fact injured, even if he be outside what would generally be thought the danger zone. There needs be duty due the one complaining but this is not a duty to a particular individual because as to him harm might be expected. Harm to some one being the natural result of the act, not only that one alone, but all those in fact injured may complain. We have never, I think, held otherwise . . . .

What is a cause in a legal sense, still more what is a proximate cause, depends in each case upon many considerations, as does the existence of negligence itself. Any philosophical doctrine of causation does not help us. A boy throws a stone into a pond. The ripples spread. The water level rises. The history of that pond is altered to all eternity. It will be altered by other causes also. Yet it will be forever the resultant of all causes combined. Each one will have an influence. How great only omniscience can say. You may speak of a chain, or, if you please, a net. An anology is of little aid. Each cause brings about future events. Without each the future would not be the same. Each is proximate in the sense it is essential. But that is not what we mean by the word. Nor on the other hand do we mean sole cause. There is no such thing.

Should analogy be thought helpful, however, I prefer that of a stream. The spring, starting on its journey, is joined by tributary after tributary. The river, reaching the ocean, comes from a hundred sources. No man may say whence any drop of water is derived. Yet for a time distinction may be possible. Into the clear creek, brown swamp water flows from the left. Later, from the right comes water stained by its clay bed. The three may remain for a space, sharply divided. But at last inevitably no trace of separation remains. They are so commingled that all distinction is lost.

As we have said, we cannot trace the effect of an act to the end, if end there is. Again, however, we may trace it part of the way. A murder at Sarajevo may be the necessary antecedent to an assassination in London 20 years hence. An overturned lantern may burn all Chicago. We may follow the fire from the shed to the last building. We rightly say that fire started by the lantern caused its destruction.

A cause, but not the proximate cause. What we do mean by the word "proximate" is that, because of convenience, of public policy, of a rough sense of justice, the law arbitrarily declines to trace a series of events beyond a certain point. This is not logic. It is practical politics. Take our rule as to fires. Sparks from my burning haystack set on fire my house and my neighbour's. I may recover from a negligent railroad. He may not. Yet the wrongful act as directly harmed the one as the other. We may regret that the line was drawn just where it was, but drawn somewhere it had to be. We said the act of the railroad was not the proximate cause of the neighbour's fire. Cause it surely was. The words we used were simply indicative of our notions of public policy. Other courts think differently. But somewhere they reach the point where they cannot say the stream comes from any one source.

Take the illustration given in an unpublished manuscript by a distinguished and helpful writer on the law of torts. A chauffeur negligently collides with another car which is filled with dynamite, although he could not know it. An explosion follows. A, walking on the sidewalk nearby, is killed. B, sitting in a window of a building opposite is cut by flying glass. C, likewise sitting in a window a block away, is similarly injured. And a further illustration: A nursemaid ten blocks away, startled by the noise, involuntarily drops a baby from her arms to the walk. We are told that C may not recover but A may. As to B it is a question for court or jury. We will all agree that the baby might not. Because, we are again told, the chauffeur had no reason to believe his conduct involved any risk of injuring either C or the baby. As to them he was not negligent.

But the chauffeur, being negligent in risking the collision, his belief that the scope of the harm he might do would be limited is immaterial. His act unreasonably jeopardized the safety of any one who might be affected by it. C's injury and that of the baby were directly traceable to the collision. Without that, the injury would not have happened. C had the right to sit in his office, secure from such dangers. The baby was entitled to use the sidewalk with reasonable safety.

The true theory is, it seems to me, that the injury to C, if in truth he is to be denied recovery, and the injury to the baby, is that their several injuries were not the proximate result of the negligence. And here not what the chauffeur had reason to believe would be the result of his conduct, but what the prudent would foresee, may have a bearing — may have some bearing, for the problem of proximate cause is not to be solved by any one consideration. It is all a question of expediency. There are no fixed rules to govern our judgment. There are simply matters of which we may take account. We have in a somewhat different connection spoken of "the stream of events". We have asked whether that stream was deflected — whether it was forced into new and unexpected channels: *Donnelly* v. *H.C. & A.I. Piercy Contracting Co.,* 222 N.Y. 210; 118 N.E. 605. This is rather rhetoric than law. There is in truth little to guide us other than common sense.

There are some hints that may help us. The proximate cause, involved as it may be with many other causes, must be, at the least, something without which the event would not happen. The court must ask itself whether there was a natural and continuous sequence between cause and effect. Was the one a substantial factor in producing the other? Was there a direct connection between them, without too many intervening causes? Is the effect of cause on result not too attenuated? Is the cause likely, in the usual judgment of mankind, to produce the result. Or, by the exercise of prudent foresight, could the result be foreseen? Is the result too remote from the cause, and here we consider remoteness in time and space: *Bird* v. *St. Paul & M. Ins. Co.,* 224 N.Y. 47; 120 N.E. 86; 13 A.L.R. 875, where we passed upon the construction of a contract — but something was also said on this subject. Clearly we must so consider, for the greater the distance either in time or space, the more surely do other causes intervene to affect the result. When a lantern is overturned, the firing of a shed is a fairly direct consequence. Many things contribute to the spread of the conflagration — the force of the wind, the direction and width of streets, the character of intervening structures, other factors. We draw an uncertain and wavering line, but draw it we must as best we can.

Once again, it is all a question of fair judgment, always keeping in mind the fact that we endeavour to make a rule in each case that will be practical and in keeping with the general understanding of mankind.

Here another question must be answered. In the case supposed, it is said, and said correctly, that the chauffeur is liable for the direct effect of the explosion although he had no reason to suppose it would follow a collision. "The fact that the injury occurred in a different manner than that which might have been expected does not prevent the chauffeur's negligence from being in law the cause of the injury." But the natural results of a negligent act — the results which a prudent man would or should foresee — do have a bearing upon the decision as to proximate cause. We have said so repeatedly. What should be foreseen? No human foresight would suggest that a collision itself might injure one a block away. On the contrary, given an explosion, such a possibility might be reasonably expected. I think the direct connection, the foresight of which the courts speak, assumes prevision of the explosion, for the immediate results of which, at least, the chauffeur is responsible.

It may be said this is unjust. Why? In fairness he should make good every injury flowing from his negligence. Not because of tenderness toward him we say he need not answer for all that follows his wrong. We look back to the catastrophe, the fire kindled by the spark, or the explosion. We trace the consequences, not indefinitely, but to a certain point. And to aid us in fixing that point we ask what might ordinarily be expected to follow the fire or the explosion.

This last suggestion is the factor which must determine the case before us. The act upon which defendant's liability rests is knocking an apparently harmless package onto the platform. The act was negligent. For its proximate consequences the defendant is liable. If its contents were broken, to the owner; if it fell upon and crushed a passenger's foot, then to him; if it exploded and injured one in the immediate vicinity, to him also as to A in the illustration. Mrs. Palsgraf was standing some distance away. How far cannot be told from the record — apparently 25 to 30 feet, perhaps less. Except for the explosion, she would not have been injured. We are told by the appellant in his brief, "It cannot be denied that the explosion was the direct cause of the plaintiff's injuries." So it was a substantial factor in producing the result — there was here a natural and continuous sequence — direct connection. The only intervening cause was that, instead of blowing her to the ground, the concussion smashed the weighing machine which in turn fell upon her. There was no remoteness in time, little in space. And surely, given such an explosion as here, it needed no great foresight to predict that the natural result would be to injure one on the platform at no greater distance from its scene than was the plaintiff. Just how no one might be able to predict. Whether by flying fragments, by broken glass, by wreckage of machines or structures no one could say. But injury in some form was most probable.

Under these circumstances I cannot say as a matter of law that the plaintiff's injuries were not the proximate result of the negligence. That is all we have before us. The court refused to so charge. No request was made to submit the matter to the jury as a question of fact, even would that have been proper upon the record before us.

The judgment appealed from should be affirmed, with costs.

[Pound, Lehman and Kellogg JJ., concurred with Cardozo C.J. Crane and O'Brien JJ., concurred with Andrews J.]

NOTES

1. See Goodhart, "The Unforeseeable Consequences of a Negligent Act" (1930), 39 Yale L.J. 449, reprinted in Goodhart, *Essays in Jurisprudence and the Common Law,* 1936, Ch. VII; Green, "The Palsgraf Case" (1930), 30 Colum. L. Rev. 789; Gregory, "Proximate Cause in Negligence — a Retreat from Rationalization" (1938), 6 U. Chi. L. Rev. 36; Wright, "The Law of Torts: 1923-1947" (1948), 26 Can. Bar Rev. 46; Prosser, "Palsgraf Revisited" (1953), 52 Mich. L. Rev. 1; Fleming, "Remoteness and Duty: The Control Devices in Liability for Negligence" (1953), 31 Can. Bar Rev. 471.

SEAVEY, MR. JUSTICE CARDOZO AND THE LAW OF TORTS

(1939), 52 Harv. L. Rev. 372, 48 Yale L.J. 390, 39 Colum. L. Rev. 20, reprinted in *Selected Essays on the Law of Torts* (1959)

There are perhaps three factors which are to be considered in determining whether the approach of Cardozo or that of Andrews is to be preferred in this type of situation.

1. Which is the more consistent with our sense of justice in the particular case? Personally, I would find it hard to answer this question. An innocent person has been hurt; some one must bear the loss. The defendant's employee was negligent, although only slightly. The fact that neither he nor his innocent employer had reason to believe that a momentary clumsiness might lead to great liability is not of itself sufficient to deny it. The law is not squeamish about imposing liability upon even innocent wrongdoers, as the defamation and conversion cases show; only by the unlawful act of the jury can damages be minimized when fault is slight or absent. On the other hand, it is universally agreed that the fact that a loss has resulted from the defendant's negligent conduct is not enough to impose liability. A momentary lapse does not transform the defendant into a man whom we wish to punish. He is not disentitled to take advantage of rules which may limit his liability.

2. Which view is more consistent with the underlying theory of negligence? On the existing cases, the issue seems clear. Even intentionally bad acts do not necessarily result in liability to the actor for harm thereby caused. One who, while carefully driving an automobile with which he is kidnapping a child, runs over and kills a pedestrian is not civilly liable for the death, even though he may be guilty of murder. In the *Palsgraf* case, the defendant's act was wrongul only because it created a risk — that is, an unreasonable risk — of harm to the package. *Prima facie* at least, the reasons for creating liability should limit it. In fact, whatever expressions have been used to define the limits of liability in this type of case, exceptability has always been in the background. Rules have frequently cut liability below this point. Thus in some states, New York included, there is

no liability for negligently causing a mental disturbance which later, through internal causes, leads to physical harm. The New York fire rules, and the rule in the waterworks cases (discussed below), are further illustrations of this. However, except as to consequences immediately following the tortious impact, seldom have the courts extended liability beyond the field in which there is an appreciable risk of harm. Interpretation of the innumerable statutes fixing a standard of care, such as those defining the rules of the road, is such that an injured person is protected only if it is found that the statute makers intended to protect a person in his class against a statutory violation, and then only if the harm he suffered is within the risk which the statute was intended to minimize. Likewise the owner of a dog, known to be vicious, who would be liable without fault if it should bite a person after escaping, is not (apart from statute) liable to a person whom the dog clumsily knocks down, since the risk created by the dog was only that of being bitten. I would assume that a court which would impose liability for harm resulting from an unexplained explosion of a large quantity of explosives, would not hold liable the possessor of a pile of bored explosives if, without his negligence, the boxes were to fall upon and crush the foot of a privileged visitor ignorant of the danger inherent in the pile. The risk is one of explosion and not of crushing.

In the modern negligence cases, the fact that the harm is directly caused by an intervening act of a stranger induced by the defendant's negligent conduct prevents the imposition of liability upon the first wrongdoer only if the type of intervention was not within the risk. Thus if the defendant were to leave open a bulkhead adjacent to a slippery sidewalk and a crowd of rowdies so jostled the plaintiff that he fell into the bulkhead, the defendant would be liable for the harm; if, however, the plaintiff were pushed in by an enemy, there would be no liability. The risk was that a traveller might slip in or be inadvertently pushed in, and not that he might be thrown in. On the other hand, one who negligently knocks over a wagon filled with goods would be liable to the owner for losses caused by thievery which the collision made expectable.

These results represent the normal reaction of courts to the various situations where the basic wrong is the creation of an unreasonable risk. Cardozo rationalizes the results, making them consistent with the fundamental conception of negligence. Andrews, as do all the philosophic proponents of the legal cause approach, rationalizes the results only by going back to the elementary basis of all proper legal decisions, by stating that the test is whether the result found by the court accords with our sense of justice. If we are to have the Chancellor's foot as a unit of measurement, we may reasonably expect the Chancellor to have feet of normal size; the result reached by Andrews is contrary to the great weight of American decisions, as I understand them.

3. The final question is which of the two approaches can be more easily applied. If we accept the Andrews opinion at its face value there can be little said in favor of its ease of application. It is difficult to apply a rule which is based upon a "rough sense of justice"; which "arbitrarily declines to trace a series of events beyond a certain point"; which has "no fixed rule to govern our judgment"; which gives "little to guide us other than common sense" or, if there are guides, a rule by which the answer depends upon whether there was "a natural and continuous sequence between cause and effect". We certainly do not desire arbitrariness, and the term "practical politics" as applied to negligence has no very definite connotation. No reason is obvious, and none is given why intervening events, time or space should play a part, aside from their expectability. One who leaves percussion caps where he should know a child will find them should not be and is not relieved from liability for harm where the child who finds them places them with his treasures carefully concealed from

adult eyes and six months later trades them to another child in another city who, in playing with them, causes an explosion, harming whom you will. Even Andrews invokes expectability in the *Palsgraf* case by asking what might be expected from the dropping of a package, but in order to make the result expectable, he begins his "chain of events" or his "direct sequence" by assuming an explosion as the beginning of the series. Those using the test of directness are merely playing with a metaphor; if directness is meant to connote the comparative absence of external forces not set in motion by the defendant, it is not responsive to the decisions either as a test of inclusion or exclusion. The phrases "natural and continuous sequence" and undeflected "stream of events" mean nothing except so far as they have reference to expectability by persons who know some of the facts but not all of them — that is, the reasonably prudent and intelligent person at the time and place — and this of course brings us back to risk. The connection between the act of the person who fails to insert a cotter pin in the mechanism of an automobile and the harm to a guest in the car six months later in another part of the country (facts corresponding to the *Buick* case), is direct only in the sense that the result is within the risk created by the failure. If we go beyond Andrews and use other well-known phrases and similes, we fare no better. Had the defendant's force been continuously active? In the use of the word, active is again but a metaphor, unless by "active" we mean pregnant with danger. Was the defendant's act a condition rather than the cause? This phrase can be interpreted only if we know what distinguishes condition from cause, or in other words, if we have already answered the problem. For many years chains and nets were supposed to have something to do with liability and although Andrews preferred not to use them, I suggest that by their use the situation is described no more inaccurately, if less vividly, than by the phrases which have displaced them in the favor of the modern Andrews School.

In place of word paintings and purported reasons, Cardozo in the three opinions here reviewed substituted "risk", a word which has a meaning, not merely to the legal student, trained in the use of fictions, but also to the jurors to whom, in most cases, the decisions will be entrusted. If it is complained that "risk" is a word of no definite import, it may be answered that at least it is more descriptive than the other phrases used, which in this type of case at least, always resolve themselves ultimately into rules dealing with expectability. If it is observed that the risk conception limits liability in situations like the *Palsgraf* case, it may be answered that it also widens it as in the *Buick* case, and that in both cases it makes the penalty fit the offense of the negligent person. It is consistent with this approach to carry liability further when the risk is to many and not merely to a few, a result which would be illogical were we relying merely upon "an unbroken stream of events" to carry the plaintiff to his destination of recovery. . . .

The courts, like the *Restatement,* have frequently tried to ride two horses, but I have faith that the simplicity, logic, and justice of the approach made prominent by Cardozo will ultimately prevail.

NOTES

1. In *Smith* v. *London & S.W. Ry. Co.* (1870), L.R. 6 C.P. 14 the Court of Exchequer Chamber affirmed a judgment for the plaintiff whose cottage was burned as a result of sparks emitted by a locomotive some distance away. Kelly C.B. stated:

"... It may be that they did not anticipate, and were not bound to anticipate, that the plaintiff's cottage would be burnt as a result of their negligence; but I think the law is, that if they were aware that these heaps were lying by the side of the rails and that it was a hot season, and that therefore by being left there the heaps were likely to catch fire, the defendants were bound to provide against all circumstances which might result from this, and were responsible for all the natural consequences of it. I think then, there was negligence in the defendants in not removing these trimmings, and that they thus become responsible for all the consequences of their conduct, and that the mere fact of the distance of this cottage from the point where the fire broke out does not affect their liability. . . ."

Channell B. said:

". . . When it has been once determined that there is evidence of negligence, the person guilty of it is equally liable for its consequences, whether he could have foreseen them or not."

Are the approaches of Kelly C.B. and Channell B. consistent? Are they consistent with *Polemis* or the *Palsgraf* case? Which of these approaches to the remoteness problem do you prefer? Do you accept Professor Seavey's analysis concerning the merits and demerits of the risk-duty approach? Can any formula be totally successful in solving all the problems that may arise?

2. Lord Justice Denning, in *Roe* v. *Ministry of Health,* [1954] 2 Q.B. 66, at p. 85, [1954] 2 All E.R. 131, at p. 138 said:

"The three questions, duty, causation, and remoteness, run continually into one another. It seems to me that they are simply three different ways of looking at one and the same question which is this: Is the consequence fairly to be regarded as within the risk created by the negligence? If so, the negligent person is liable for it: but otherwise not . . . . Instead of asking three questions, I should have thought in many cases it would be simple and better to ask the one question: Is the consequence within the risk? and to answer it by applying ordinary plain common sense."

3. A similar view has been expressed by Clement J.A. of the Alberta Court of Appeal in *Abbott et al.* v. *Kasza,* [1976] 4 W.W.R. 20, at p. 29 where he said:

"The question raised is whether in cases such as the present there is an appreciable difference in law in the projection of the reasonably foreseeable between remoteness of damage and duty and causation. For myself, I think that the law does not compel any distinction to be drawn and that the interests of a workable jurisprudence militate against it. As Denning L.J. points out, each component of liability is only a facet of the whole, and judgment must be on the entirety, not piecemeal on refractions from each facet."

THE WAGON MOUND (NO. 1)
OVERSEAS TANKSHIP (U.K.) LTD. v. MORTS DOCK & ENGINEERING CO. LTD.

Privy Council. [1961] A.C. 388; [1961] 1 All E.R. 404

Appeal from an order of the Full Court of the Supreme Court of New South Wales (Owen, Maguire and Manning JJ.) dismissing an appeal by the appellants, Overseas Tankship (U.K.) Ltd., from a judgment of Kinsella J. exercising the Admiralty Jurisdiction of that court in an action in which the appellants were defendants and the respondents, Morts Dock & Engineering Co., Ltd. were plaintiffs.

The following facts are taken from the judgment of the Judicial Committee: In the action the respondents sought to recover from the appellants compensation for the damage which its property known as the Sheerlegs Wharf, in Sydney Harbour, and the equipment thereon had suffered by reason of fire which broke out on November 1, 1951. For that damage they claimed that the appellants were in law responsible.

The relevant facts can be comparatively shortly stated inasmuch as not one of the findings of fact in the exhaustive judgment of the trial judge had been challenged.

The respondents at the relevant time carried on the business of ship-building, ship-repairing and general engineering at Morts Bay, Balmain, in the Port of Sydney. They owned and used for their business the Sheerlegs Wharf, a timber wharf about 400 feet in length and 40 feet wide, where there was a quantity of tools and equipment. In October and November, 1951, a vessel known as the *Corrimal* was moored alongside the wharf and was being refitted by the respondents. Her mast was lying on the wharf and a number of the respondents' employees were working both upon it and upon the vessel itself, using for that purpose electric and oxy-acetylene welding equipment.

At the same time the appellants were charterers by demise of the *S.S. Wagon Mound,* an oil-burning vessel, which was moored at the Caltex Wharf on the northern shore of the harbour at a distance of about 600 feet from the Sheerlegs Wharf. She was there from about 9 a.m. on October 29 until 11 a.m. on October 30, 1951, for the purpose of discharging gasolene products and taking in bunkering oil.

During the early hours of October 30, 1951, a large quantity of bunkering oil was, through the carelessness of the appellants' servants, allowed to spill into the bay, and by 10.30 on the morning of that day it had spread over a considerable part of the bay, being thickly concentrated in some places and particularly along the foreshore near the respondents' property. The appellants made no attempt to disperse the oil. The *Wagon Mound* unberthed and set sail very shortly after.

When the respondents' works manager became aware of the condition of things in the vicinity of the wharf he instructed their workmen that no welding or burning was to be carried on until further orders. He inquired of the manager of the Caltex Oil Company, at whose wharf the *Wagon Mound* was then still berthed, whether they could safely continue their operations on the wharf or upon the *Corrimal.* The results of the inquiry coupled with his own belief as to the inflammability of furnace oil in the open led him to think that the respondents could safely carry on their operations. He gave instructions accordingly, but directed that all safety precautions should be taken to prevent inflammable material falling off the wharf into the oil.

For the remainder of October 30 and until about 2 p.m. on November 1 work was carried on as usual, the condition and congestion of the oil remaining substantially unaltered. But at about that time the oil under or near the wharf was ignited and a fire, fed initially by the oil, spread rapidly and burned with great intensity. The wharf and the *Corrimal* caught fire and considerable damage was done to the wharf and the equipment upon it.

The outbreak of fire was due, as the judge found, to the fact that there was floating in the oil underneath the wharf a piece of debris on which lay some mouldering cotton waste or rag which had been set on fire by molten metal falling from the wharf; that the cotton waste or rag burst into flames: that the flames from the cotton waste set the floating oil afire either directly or by first setting fire to a wooden pile coated with oil, and that after the floating oil became ignited the flames spread rapidly over the surface of the oil and quickly developed into a conflagration which severely damaged the wharf.

The judgment of their Lordships was delivered by

Viscount Simonds: The trial judge also made the all-important finding which must be set out in his own words: "The *raison d'être* of furnace oil is, of course, that it shall burn, but I find that the defendant did not know and could not reasonably be expected to have known that it was capable of being set afire when spread on water." This finding was reached after a wealth of evidence, which included that of a distinguished scientist, Professor Hunter. It receives strong confirmation from the fact that at the trial the respondents strenuously maintained that the appellants had discharged petrol into the bay on no other ground than that, as the spillage was set alight, it could not be furnace oil. An attempt was made before their Lordships' Board to limit in some way the finding of fact, but it is clear that it was intended to cover precisely the event that happened.

One other finding must be mentioned. The judge held that apart from damage by fire the respondents had suffered some damage from the spillage of oil in that it had got upon their slipways and congealed upon them and interfered with their use of the slips. He said: "The evidence of this damage is slight and no claim for compensation is made in respect of it. Nevertheless it does establish some damage, which may be insignificant in comparison with the magnitude of the damage by fire, but which nevertheless is damage which, beyond question, was a direct result of the escape of the oil." It is upon this footing that their Lordships will consider the question whether the appellants are liable for the fire damage. . . .

It is inevitable that first consideration should be given to the case of *In re Polemis and Furness, Withy & Co. Ltd.*, [1921] 3 K.B. 560; 37 T.L.R. 940, which will henceforward be referred to as *Polemis*. For it was avowedly in deference to that decision and to decisions of the Court of Appeal that followed it that the Full Court was constrained to decide the present case in favour of the respondents. In doing so Manning J., after a full examination of that case, said: "To say that the problems, doubts and difficulties which I have expressed above render it difficult for me to apply the decision in *In re Polemis* with any degree of confidence to a particular set of facts would be a grave understatement. I can only express the hope that, if not in this case, then in some other case in the near future, the subject will be pronounced upon by the House of Lords or the Privy Council in terms which, even if beyond my capacity fully to understand, will facilitate, for those placed as I am, its everyday application to current problems." This *cri de coeur* would in any case be irresistible, but in the years that have passed since its decision *Polemis* has been so much discussed and qualified that it cannot claim, as counsel for the respondents urged for it, the status of a decision of such long standing that it should not be reviewed. . . .

There can be no doubt that the decision of the Court of Appeal in *Polemis* plainly asserts that, if the defendant is guilty of negligence, he is responsible for all the consequences whether reasonably foreseeable or not. The generality of the proposition is perhaps qualified by the fact that each of the Lords Justices refers to the outbreak of fire as the direct result of the negligent act. There is thus introduced the conception that the negligent actor is not responsible for consequences which are not "direct", whatever that may mean. It has to be asked, then, why this conclusion should have been reached. The answer appears to be that it was reached upon a consideration of certain authorities, comparatively few in number, that were cited to the court. Of these, three are generally regarded as having influenced the decision. The earliest in point of date was *Smith* v. *London & South Western Railway Co.* (1870), L.R. 6 C.P. 14. In that case it was said that "when it has been once determined that there is evidence of negligence, the person guilty of it is equally liable for its consequences, whether he could have foreseen them or not"; see *per* Channell B. Similar observations were made by other members of the court. Three things may be noted about this case: the first, that for the sweeping proposition laid down no authority was cited; the second, that the point to which the court directed its mind was not unforeseeable damage of a different kind from that which was foreseen, but more extensive damage of the same kind; and the third, that so little was the mind of the court directed to the problem which has now to be solved that no one of the seven judges who took part in the decision thought it necessary to qualify in any way the consequences for which the defendant was to be held responsible. It would perhaps not be improper to say that the law of negligence as an independent tort was then of recent growth and that its implications had not been fully examined.

[His Lordship went on to consider *H.M.S. London,* [1914] P. 72 and *Weld-Blundell* v. *Stephens,* [1920] A.C. 956, 983] ...

Before turning to the cases that succeeded it, it is right to glance at yet another aspect of the decision in *Polemis.* Their Lordships, as they have said, assume that the court purported to propound the law in regard to tort. But up to that date it had been universally accepted that the law in regard to damages for breach of contract and for tort was, generally speaking, and particularly in regard to the tort of negligence, the same. Yet *Hadley* v. *Baxendale* (1854), 9 Exch. 341, was not cited in argument nor referred to in the judgments in *Polemis.* This is the more surprising when it is remembered that in that case, as in many another case, the claim was laid alternatively in breach of contract and in negligence. If the claim for breach of contract had been pursued, the charterers could not have been held liable for consequences not reasonably foreseeable. It is not strange that Sir Frederick Pollock said that Blackburn and Willes JJ. would have been shocked beyond measure by the decision that the charterers were liable in tort: see *Pollock on Torts,* 15th ed., p. 29. Their Lordships refer to this aspect on the matter not because they wish to assert that in all respects today the measure of damages is in all cases the same in tort and in breach of contract, but because it emphasizes how far *Polemis* was out of the current of contemporary thought. The acceptance of the rule in *Polemis* as applicable to all cases of tort directly would conflict with the view theretofore generally held.

If the line of relevant authority had stopped with *Polemis,* their Lordships might, whatever their own views as to its unreason, have felt some hesitation about overruling it. But it is far otherwise. It is true that both in England and in many parts of the Commonwealth that decision has from time to time been followed; but in Scotland it has been rejected with determination. It has never been subject to the express scrutiny of either the House of Lords or the Privy Council, though there have been comments upon it in those Supreme Tribunals. Even in the inferior courts judges have, sometimes perhaps unwittingly, declared themselves in a sense adverse to its principle.

[Several examples were given.] ...

Enough has been said to show that the authority of *Polemis* has been severely shaken though lip-service has from time to time been paid to it. In their Lordships' opinion it should no longer be regarded as good law. It is not probable that many cases will for that reason have a different result, though it is hoped that the law will be thereby simplified, and that in some cases, at least, palpable injustice will be avoided. For it does not seem consonant with current ideas of justice or morality that for an act of negligence, however slight or venial, which results in some trivial foreseeable damage the actor should be liable for all consequences however unforeseeable and however grave, so long as they can be said to be "direct". It is a principle of civil liability, subject only to qualifications which have no present relevance, that a man must be considered to be responsible for the probable consequences of his act. To demand more of him is too harsh a rule, to demand less is to ignore that civilized order requires the observance of a minimum standard of behaviour.

This concept applied to the slowly developing law of negligence has led to a great variety of expressions which can, as it appears to their Lordships, be harmonized with little difficulty with the single exception of the so-called rule in *Polemis*. For, if it is asked why a man should be responsible for the natural or necessary or probable consequences of his act (or any other similar description of them) the answer is that it is not because they are natural or necessary or probable, but because, since they have this quality, it is judged by the standard of the reasonable man that he ought to have foreseen them. Thus it is that over and over again it has happened that in different judgments in the same case, and sometimes in a single judgment, liability for a consequence has been imposed on the ground that it was reasonably foreseeable or, alternatively, on the ground that it was natural or necessary or probable. The two grounds have been treated as coterminous, and so they largely are. But, where they are not, the question arises to which the wrong answer was given in *Polemis*. For, if some limitation must be imposed upon the consequences for which the negligent actor is to be held responsible — and all are agreed that some limitation there must be — why should that test (reasonable foreseeability) be rejected which, since he is judged by what the reasonable man ought to foresee, corresponds with the common conscience of mankind, and a test (the "direct" consequence) be substituted which leads to nowhere but the never-ending and insoluble problems of causation. "The lawyer," said Sir Frederick Pollock, "cannot afford to adventure himself with philosophers in the logical and metaphysical controversies that beset the idea of cause." Yet this is just what he has most unfortunately done and must continue to do if the rule in *Polemis* is to prevail. A conspicuous example occurs when the actor seeks to escape liability on the ground that the "chain of causation" is broken by a *"nova causa"* or *"novus actus interveniens"*.

The validity of a rule or principle can sometimes be tested by observing it in operation. Let the rule in *Polemis* be tested in this way. In the case of the *Liesbosch,* [1933] A.C. 449; 49 T.L.R. 289, the appellants, whose vessel had been fouled by the respondents, claimed damages under various heads. The respondents were admittedly at fault; therefore, said the appellants, invoking the rule in *Polemis,* they were responsible for all damage whether reasonably foreseeable or not. Here was the opportunity to deny the rule or to place it secure upon its pedestal. But the House of Lords took neither course; on the contrary, it distinguished *Polemis* on the ground that in that case the injuries suffered were the "immediate physical consequences" of the negligent act. It is not easy to understand why a distinction should be drawn between "immediate physical" and other consequences, nor where the line is to be drawn. It was perhaps this difficulty which led Denning L.J., in *Roe* v. *Ministry of Health,* [1954] 2 Q.B. 66, 85; [1954] 2 W.L.R. 915; [1954] 2 All E.R. 131, to say that foreseeability is only disregarded when the negligence is the immediate or *precipitating* cause of the damage. This new word may well have been thought as good a word as another for revealing or disguising the fact that he sought loyally to enforce an unworkable rule.

In the same connection may be mentioned the conclusion to which the Full Court finally came in the present case. Applying the rule in *Polemis* and holding therefore that the unforeseeability of the damage by fire afforded no defence, they went on to consider the remaining question. Was it a "direct" consequence? Upon this Manning J., said: "Notwithstanding that, if regard is had separately to each individual occurrence in the chain of events that led to this fire, each occurrence was improbable and, in one sense, improbability was heaped upon improbability. I cannot escape from the conclusion that if the ordinary man in the street had been asked, as a matter of common sense, without any detailed analysis of the circumstances, to state the cause of the fire at

Mort's Dock, he would unhesitatingly have assigned such cause to spillage of oil by the appellant's employees." Perhaps he would, and probably he would have added, "I never should have thought it possible." But with great respect to the Full Court this is surely irrelevant, or, if it is relevant, only serves to show that the *Polemis* rule works in a very strange way. After the event even a fool is wise. But it is not the hindsight of a fool; it is the foresight of the reasonable man which alone can determine responsibility. The *Polemis* rule by substituting "direct" for "reasonably foreseeable" consequence leads to a conclusion equally illogical and unjust.

At an early stage in this judgment their Lordships intimated that they would deal with the proposition which can best be stated by reference to the well-known *dictum* of Lord Sumner: "This however goes to culpability not to compensation." It is with the greatest respect to that very learned judge and to those who have echoed his words, that their Lordships find themselves bound to state their view that this proposition is fundamentally false.

It is, no doubt, proper when considering tortious liability for negligence to analyse its elements and to say that the plaintiff must prove a duty owed to him by the defendant, a breach of that duty by the defendant, and consequent damage. But there can be no liability until the damage has been done. It is not the act but the consequences on which tortious liability is founded. Just as (as it has been said) there is no such thing as negligence in the air, so there is no such thing as liability in the air. Suppose an action brought by A for damage caused by the carelessness (a neutral word) of B, for example, a fire caused by the careless spillage of oil. It may, of course, become relevant to know what duty B owed A, but the only liability that is in question is the liability for damage by fire. It is vain to isolate the liability from its context and to say that B is or is not liable, and then to ask for what damage he is liable. For his liability is in respect of that damage and no other. If, as admittedly it is, B's liability (culpability) depends on the reasonable foreseeability of the consequent damage, how is that to be determined except by the foreseeability of the damage which in fact happened — the damage in suit? And, if that damage is unforeseeable so as to displace liability at large, how can the liability be restored so as to make compensation payable?

But, it is said, a different position arises if B's careless act has been shown to be negligent and had caused some foreseeable damage to A. Their Lordships have already observed that to hold B liable for consequences however unforeseeable of a careless act, if, but only if, he is at the same time liable for some other damage however trivial, appears to be neither logical nor just. This becomes more clear if it is supposed that similar unforeseeable damage is suffered by A and C but other foreseeable damage, for which B is liable, by A only. A system of law which would hold B liable to A but not to C for the similar damage suffered by each of them could not easily be defended. Fortunately, the attempt is not necessary. For the same fallacy is at the root of the proposition. It is irrelevant to the question whether B is liable for unforeseeable damage that he is liable for foreseeable damage, as irrelevant as would the fact that he had trespassed on Whiteacre be to the question whether he has trespassed on Blackacre. Again, suppose a claim by A for damage by fire by the careless act of B. Of what relevance is it to that claim that he has another claim arising out of the same careless act? It would surely not prejudice his claim if that other claim failed: it cannot assist it if it succeeds. Each of them rests on its own bottom, and will fail if it can be established that the damage could not reasonably be foreseen. We have come back to the plain common sense stated by Lord Russell of Killowen in *Bourhill* v. *Young.* As Denning L.J., said in *King* v. *Phillips,* [1953] 1 Q.B. 429, 441: "there can be no doubt since *Bourhill* v. *Young* that the test of *liability for shock* is foreseeability of *injury by shock*". Their Lordships substitute the word "fire" for "shock" and endorse this statement of the law.

Their Lordships conclude this part of the case with some general observations. They have been concerned primarily to displace the proposition that unforeseeability is irrelevant if damage is "direct". In doing so they have inevitably insisted that the essential factor in determining liability is whether the damage is of such a kind as the reasonable man should have foreseen. This accords with the general view thus stated by Lord Atkin in *Donoghue* v. *Stevenson:* "The liability for negligence, whether you style it such or treat it as in other systems as a species of 'culpa', is no doubt based upon a general public sentiment of moral wrongdoing for which the offender must pay." It is a departure from this sovereign principle if liability is made to depend solely on the damage being the "direct" or "natural" consequence of the precedent act. Who knows or can be assumed to know all the processes of nature? But if it would be wrong that a man should be held liable for damage unpredictable by a reasonable man because it was "direct" or "natural", equally it would be wrong that he should escape liability, however "indirect" the damage, if he foresaw or could reasonably foresee the intervening events which led to its being done: *cf. Woods* v. *Duncan,* [1946] A.C. 401, 442. Thus foreseeability becomes the effective test. In reasserting this principle their Lordships conceive that they do not depart from, but follow and develop, the law of negligence as laid down by Baron Alderson in *Blyth* v. *Birmingham Waterworks Co.* (1856), 11 Exch. 781, 784.

It is proper to add that their Lordships have not found it necessary to consider the so-called rule of "strict liability" exemplified in *Rylands* v. *Fletcher* (1868), L.R. 3 H.L. 330, and the cases that have followed or distinguished it. Nothing that they have said is intended to reflect on that rule.

One aspect of this case remains to be dealt with. The respondents claim, in the alternative, that the appellants are liable in nuisance if not in negligence. Upon this issue their Lordships are of opinion that it would not be proper for them to come to any conclusion upon the material before them and without the benefit of the considered view of the Supreme Court. On the other hand, having regard to the course which the case has taken, they do not think that the respondents should be finally shut out from the opportunity of advancing this plea, if they think fit. They therefore propose that on the issue of nuisance alone the case should be remitted to the Full Court to be dealt with as may be thought proper.

Their Lordships will humbly advise Her Majesty that this appeal should be allowed, and the respondents' action so far as it related to damage caused by the negligence of the appellants be dismissed with costs, but that the action so far as it related to damage caused by nuisance should be remitted to the Full Court to be dealt with as that court may think fit. The respondents must pay the costs of the appellants of this appeal and in the courts below.

FLEMING, THE PASSING OF POLEMIS

(1961), 39 Can. Bar Rev. 489

Viscount Simonds' declaration should be accepted for what it is: not as an inexorable conclusion derived by a process of logical reasoning from a rigid premise concerning the "true nature" of negligence, but as a conscious choice of policy between competing ideals. It does not, because it cannot, purport to deny the *validity* of the opposing standpoint that, as between one who unjustifiably created an unreasonable risk and his innocent victim, the balance of equities should favour the latter rather than him who by his own negligence has set the whole thing in motion, even if it means that the sanction may sometimes be incommensurate with his original fault. True it is that, to the extent of this disparity, liability would assume an element of "strictness", but this is not (as Goodhart seems to be earnestly claiming) *logically* incompatible with linking it to merely negligent conduct. Even if we concede that negligence is a "term of relation", in the sense at least that an act does not assume the quality of negligence except by reference to foreseeably harmful consequences, it does not necessarily follow that liability should be restricted to such consequences alone. Conduct, once labelled negligent because fraught with risk of some particular harm, may well be thought to carry with it deserved responsibility for other or additional loss it caused, whether it was foreseeable or not. The question is one of policy, not logic; its resolution lies in the realm of values, and "what you choose depends on what you want".

In terms of kerb-stone morality, there is as much (and no more) to be said in favour of the innocent plaintiff as the hapless defendant. Who would gainsay that the harshness of burdening the actor with potentially far-reaching responsibility for a mere trivial lapse does not find its counterpart in the injustice of denying his victim redress and letting the loss lie where it happened to fall? Quite frankly, both arguments appear to cancel out, and this notwithstanding Viscount Simonds' seeming indifference to the latter. If depart we must then from the authoritative script and venture into the market place of ideas, are there any other pertinent factors which might fairly claim to influence our choice? Most relevant, clearly, in the context of contemporary tort law, are those bearing upon accident prevention and loss distribution.

The element of deterrence has traditionally played, and will undoubtedly continue to play, a vital role in the formulation of legal norms. Its influence has not surprisingly been strongest in the area of intentional wrongs which are most closely akin to conventional crimes. One such manifestation, of peculiar interest to the present inquiry, is the unsympathetic response to pleas by trespassers and others guilty of intentional aggression that they be excused for unexpected harm following in the wake of their transgressions. . . .

Enough has been said, I believe, to carry the point that, for the sake of more effective deterrence, courts have not shrunk in appropriate cases from imposing the most far-reaching liability and subordinating the "equities" of defendants to the demands of a more exacting policy. Nor is there any warrant in the *Wagon Mound* for anticipating a reversal of this trend; for, as already mentioned, it expressly refrained from any commitment with respect to torts other than negligence. The question persists, however, whether our contemporary scale of social values would accord to accident-prevention a weight corresponding to deterrence of intentional wrongdoing. It is of course hardly open to serious debate that this policy has exerted an influence, more vital and pervasive probably than any other, on the progressive development of our accident law. The vast proliferation of duties of care which has today reached a point in Anglo-American law where few, if any, islands of immunity remain; the noticeable rise in the standards of care, supplemented by the judicial doctrine of statutory negligence which has the effect of requiring "strict" conformity with an ever-increasing volume of legislative safety standards; and not least the statutory and common law extensions of strict liability, so poignantly illustrated by the contemporary American trend of discarding the privity requirement in warranty actions in relation to food, drugs and other highly dangerous commodities, like automobiles — none of these dramatic changes in the reallocation of risks incident to modern life in the highly complex societies of the Western world can be adequately accounted for except on the basis of a growing awareness of the need to conserve our human and material resources by applying the pressure of liability at those strategic points where accident-prevention can be most effectively promoted.

But after all this is said, it still remains highly problematical whether the policy of accident prevention can claim to make a serious contribution to the debate of where to stake the outer boundaries of liability for admitted negligence. Its proper function revolves primarily around the question whether a particular type of activity or conduct should be discouraged by the spectre of legal liability, and seems to be near exhaustion once that decision has been made. It is, of course, arguable that the prospect of more extensive liability may exert a correspondingly greater deterrent pressure on the would-be actor, but the force of this exceedingly speculative claim is in any event reduced to the vanishing point by the fact that we must assume such additional liability to be *ex hypothesi* unforeseeable and therefore, presumably, beyond the range of practical calculation.

Though we are reluctantly forced, therefore, to discount the relevance of accident-prevention, the policy of loss-distribution has a more obvious claim to attention in the present inquiry. Its advocates set out to re-emphasize that traditionally one, if not the most important, aim of the law of torts has been to afford compensation to those who have suffered harm at another's hands. True it is that this policy has always had to compete with countervailing considerations, especially the anxiety lest the impact of liability exert an undue deterrence on human activity and enterprise. In certain periods of the past, particularly during the nineteenth century, these apprehensions were accorded the fullest recognition in the interest of an acquisitive society bent on expansion and inclined to make light of the incidental cost to human and material assets. The subordination of the individual's security was deemed a necessary toll for achieving the more valuable goal of rapid industrial development and expolitation of the seemingly inexhaustible store of available resources. If injuries went without redress, it was but the victim's admission fee to participation in the larger benefits secured by advancing civilization. The current philosophy of laissez-faire, aligned to these economic tenets, lauded the virtues of individualism and self-reliance and viewed the task of tort law as primarily confined to its admonitory, rather than compensatory, function. But with the passage of time, these social postulates have undergone a drastic revision. The individualistic fault dogma is being eroded by the mid-twentieth century quest for social security, the welfare state replacing an outmoded order where man was expected and encouraged to fend for himself. Enhanced social consciousness has today led to the broad acceptance of the view that society can no longer afford to turn its back on the hapless victims of disaster or accident, leaving us only with the practical task of devising the economically least burdensome methods for redressing or mitigating their misfortune.

In promoting this object, the law of torts has its own part to play, and an important one at that; for to the extent that it ensures compensation for the injured, it is participating in the process of welfare economics and performing a task that would otherwise fall to social security. The renewed emphasis on the compensatory function of tort law has been aided by a growing recognition that an award of damages will result not merely in the shifting of a loss from plaintiff to defendant but in its further distribution, if the latter is either insured or otherwise in a position to pass it on as a small fraction of the cost of his goods or services. In this manner an adverse verdict, far from spelling likely ruin to the defendant, will be painlessly absorbed and its cost eventually spread over a large segment of the community so thin as to be barely noticed. Acceptance of this viewpoint naturally focuses attention more on a defendant's loss-bearing capacity and less on conventional considerations of fault. Indeed, even its most sanguine opponents are generally prepared to make at least the reluctant concession that it disposes convincingly of those heart-rending pleas by defendants which have often in the past persuaded courts to distort the law by creating special privileges and immunities (including the negation of duties of care) in the belief that the impact of ordinary responsibility would expose them to intolerable burdens. Its advocates, on the other hand, would go further and strive towards an eventual replacement of the fault criterion by strict liability in all those areas of accident law where defendants offer a suitable focus for channelling off and distributing the losses incident to their enterprise. The doctrine of vicarious liability, the modern trend pronounced in most jurisdictions of postulating standards of care from motorists and employers which often strain the verbal link with negligence to breaking point, the proliferation of safety statutes in industry combined with the judicial doctrine of negligence *per se* which at least in England and Australasia have rewritten in large measure the law of employers' liability, the concurrent weakening of the traditional defences of voluntary assumption of risk and contributory negligence — all these developments in our time have contributed their share in giving some substance to the claim that the fault dogma is already far on the path of decline in many significant areas of accident law.

Viewed from this perspective, the Privy Council's opinion in the *Wagon Mound* may seem a retrograde step, ill-attuned to general trends in the law of torts. For, if it is to have any practical effect on the future course of adjudication at all, it will be by setting somewhat narrower limits to the range of recovery than heretofore, and to that extent impairing the process of shifting and distributing losses. It is therefore at least open to argument whether Viscount Simonds correctly gauged the tenor of "current ideas of justice or morality" in expressing the belief that it would be "out of consonance" and "too harsh" to countenance liability beyond the ambit of foreseeable risks. On the face of it, at any rate, it is a trifle paradoxical that the apotheosis of foresight had to await a moment of decision when the very notion of fault liability was already under the lengthening shadow of decline and, as happens not infrequently, the acceptance of a rule is so long deferred that its destined role is merely to impede the next stage of legal progress. However that may be, the Board's opinion does not seem to have been uninfluenced by the noticeable trend towards stricter liability, and its sympathetic reference to the predicament of defendants who are held responsible for an "act of negligence, however slight or venial", involving the risk of but "trivial foreseeable damage", rather suggests an inclination to temper a little the wind to the shorn lamb. But previous experience in the judicial handling of the foresight test, both in relation to the issue of initial culpability (breach of duty) and remoteness of damage in cases involving "indirect" consequences, lends scant support to sanguine expectations of any appreciable change in the future direction of the law. This impression is reinforced by the fact that, as already noted, very few cases indeed ever fell to be decided on the basis of the defunct *Polemis* rule — a telling index of the very limited practical effect to be anticipated form the decision [of *The Wagon Mound (No. 1)*].

NOTES

1. *The Wagon Mound* case has been the subject of much academic discussion. See Williams, "The Risk Principle" (1961), 77 L.Q.Rev. 179, Joseph C. Smith, "Requiem for *Polemis*" (1965), 2 U.B.C.L. Rev. 159 and "The Limits of Tort Liability in Canada: Remoteness, Foreseeability and Proximate Cause" printed in Linden, *Studies in Canadian Tort Law*" (1968), at. p. 88; Gibson, "*The Wagon Mound* in Canadian Courts" (1963), 2 O.H. L.J. 416; McLaren,

"Negligence and Remoteness — The Aftermath of *Wagon Mound*" (1967), 1 Sask. L.J. 45; Honoré, Comment (1961), 39 Can. Bar Rev. 267.; Green, "Foreseeability in Negligence Law" (1961), 61 Colum. L. Rev. 1401.

2. Although most Canadian Courts followed the *Wagon Mound (No. 1)* those of Saskatchewan refused to. In *Shulhan* v. *Peterson, Howell & Heather (Canada) Ltd. et al.* (1966), 57 D.L.R. (2d) 491 (Sask.), plaintiff used his car as a salesman for a company selling pianos and organs. Due to the negligence of defendant, his car was damaged. Normally repairs would have been made in two to four weeks. Due to a strike at the plant of the company that made plaintiff's car, replacement parts could not be obtained and plaintiff was deprived of the use of his car for over 15 weeks. He rented a car for this period and paid insurance on it. In an action for damages, Disbery J., held plaintiff could recover these amounts paid. Defendant argued that on the basis of *The Wagon Mound*, damages enhanced by the strike were not recoverable. Disbery J., held that *Re Polemis* was still good law in Saskatchewan. He refused to apply *The Wagon Mound* which, in attempting to avoid hardship on negligent defendants, now visits such hardship on the innocent victims of negligence. Further, "no court has ever taken into account the element of foreseeability when measuring the quantum of damages." "Remoteness of damage is one thing and the measure of damages is another."

3. A similar result was recently reached, using the foresight analysis of *The Wagon Mound (No. 1)*, in *Penman et al.* v. *St. John Toyota* (1972), 30 D.L.R. (3d) 88 (N.B.C.A.). Limerick J.A. allowed a claim for the cost of renting a car to replace the plaintiff's car which was damaged by the defendant in an accident. The repairs took six months to complete because of a strike at the General Motors plant which delayed delivery of the required parts. In allowing the claim, Limerick J.A. stated: "The certainty, not the mere probability of the car being laid up for repair was foreseeable as a result of a collision. It is the nature of the injury or damages not the extent thereof which must be foreseeable. Counsel contends 'a strike was not foreseeable'. What if the strike was in progress at the time of the accident? Should damages be allowed if a strike started the day before the accident and not allowed if the strike started the day following the accident? What would the entitlement to damages be if it were generally known that the labour dispute existed between management and the employees of General Motors and that a strike was possible or that a strike was probable?

In the condition of today's economy the possibility of a strike in any industry particularly in the automobile manufacturing industry is foreseeable."

B. RETREAT FROM THE WAGON MOUND (No. 1)

1. The Thin-Skull Problem

SMITH v. LEECH BRAIN & CO.

Queen's Bench Division. [1962] 2 Q.B. 405; [1961] 3 All E.R. 1159

The defendant's negligence resulted in a piece of molten metal striking and burning the lip of plaintiff's husband. At the time, the burn was treated as a normal burn. Ultimately the place where the burn had been began to ulcerate and cancer was diagnosed. After radium treatments and several operations plaintiff's husband died. In an action for damages it was proved that the burn was a cause of the cancer and death.

Lord Parker C.J.: The third question is damages. Here I am confronted with the recent decision of the Privy Council in *Overseas Tankship (U.K.) Limited* v. *Morts Dock and Engineering Co. Ltd. (The Wagon Mound).* But for that case, it seems to me perfectly clear that, assuming negligence proved, and assuming that the burn caused in whole or in part the cancer and the death, the plaintiff would be entitled to recover. It is said on the one side by Mr. May that although I am not strictly bound by the *Wagon Mound* since it is a decision of the Privy Council, I should treat myself as free, using the arguments to be derived from that case, to say that other cases in these courts — other cases in the Court of Appeal — have been wrongly decided, and particularly that *In re Polemis and Furness Withy & Co.* was wrongly decided, and that a further ground for taking that course is to be found in the various criticisms that have from time to time in the past been made by members of the House of Lords in regard to the *Polemis* case.

It is said, on the other hand, by Mr. Martin Jukes, that I should hold that the *Polemis* case was rightly decided and, secondly, that even if that is not so I must treat myself as completely bound by it. Thirdly, he said that in any event, whatever the true view is in regard to the *Polemis* case, *The Wagon Mound* has no relevance at all to this case.

For my part, I am quite satisfied that the Judicial Committee in *The Wagon Mound* case did not have what I may call, loosely, the thin skull cases in mind. It has always been the law of this country that a tortfeasor takes his victim as he finds him. It is unnecessary to do more than refer to the short passage in the decision of Kennedy J. in *Dulieu* v. *White & Sons,* where he said: "If a man is negligently run over or otherwise negligently injured in his body, it is no answer to the sufferer's claim for damages that he would have suffered less injury, or no injury at all, if he had not had an unusually thin skull or an unusually weak heart."

To the same effect is a passage in the judgment of Scrutton L.J., in *The Arpad.* But quite apart from those two references, as is well known, the work of the courts for years and years has gone on on that basis. There is not a day that goes by where some trial judge does not adopt that principle, that the tortfeasor takes his victim as he finds him. If the Judicial Committee had any intention of making an inroad into that doctrine, I am quite satisfied that they would have said so.

It is true that if the wording in the advice given by Lord Simonds in *The Wagon Mound* case is applied strictly to such a case as this, it could be said that they were dealing with this point. But, as I have said, it is to my mind quite impossible to conceive that they were and, indeed, it has been pointed out that they disclose the distinction between such a case as this and the one they were considering when they comment on *Smith* v. *London & South Western Railway Company.* Lord Simonds, in dealing with that case said: "Three things may be noted about this case: the first, that for the sweeping proposition laid down no authority was cited; the second, that the point to which the court directed its mind was not unforeseeable damage of a different kind from that which was foreseen, but more extensive damage of the same kind." In other words, Lord Simonds is clearly there drawing a distinction between the question whether a man could reasonably anticipate a type of injury, and the question whether a man could reasonably anticipate the extent of injury of the type which could be foreseen.

The Judicial Committee were, I think, disagreeing with the decision in the *Polemis* case that a man is no longer liable for the type of damage which he could not reasonably anticipate. The Judicial Committee were not, I think, saying that a man is only liable for the extent of damage which he could anticipate, always assuming the type of injury could have been anticipated. I think that view is really supported by the way in which cases of this sort have been dealt with in Scotland. Scotland has never, so far as I know, adopted the principle laid down in *Polemis,* and yet I am quite satisfied that they have throughout proceeded on the basis that the tortfeasor takes the victim as he finds him.

In those circumstances, it seems to me that this is plainly a case which comes within the old principle. The test is not whether these employers could reasonably have foreseen that a burn would cause cancer and that he would die. The question is whether these employers could reasonably foresee the type of injury he suffered, namely, the burn. What, in the particular case, is the amount of damage which he suffers as a result of that burn, depends upon the characteristics and constitution of the victim.

Accordingly, I find that the damages which the widow claims are damages for which the defendants are liable.

NOTES

1. The thin-skull rule has clearly survived *The Wagon Mound (No. 1)*. It applies equally if there is a pre-existing susceptibility or if the injury renders someone vulnerable to additional loss. Some recent cases are *Bates* v. *Fraser* (1963), 38 D.L.R. (2d) 30, [1963] 1 O.R. 539; *Negretto* v. *Sayers,* [1963] S.A.S.R. 313; *Leonard* v. *B.C. Hydro* (1965), 50 W.W.R. 546; *Elloway* v. *Boomars* (1968), 69 D.L.R. (2d) 605 (B.C.H.C.); *La Brosse* v. *City of Saskatoon* (1968), 65 W.W.R. 168 (Sask. Q.B.); *Warren* v. *Scruttons Ltd.,* [1962] 1 Ll. R. 497; *Corrie* v. *Gilbert,* [1965] S.C.R. 457; *Peacock* v. *Mills et al.* (1965), 50 W.W.R. 626 (Alta. C.A.); *Winteringham* v. *Rae* (1966), 55 D.L.R. (2d) 108; *Robinson* v. *Post Office,* [1974] 1 W.L.R. 1176 (C.A.).

2. Although the defendant must compensate for thin-skull injuries, he need not pay full damages as if there were no thin skull, for a thin skull is less valuable than a normal one. In *Smith* v. *Maximovitch* (1968), 68 D.L.R. (2d) 244 (Sask. Q.B.), the plaintiff lost eight teeth in a collision. Because his remaining teeth were in poor condition, as a result of pyorrhea, they were unsuitable to anchor bridgework and, therefore, all the teeth had to be extracted and dentures put in. The claimant received damages for all the teeth, except that they were evaluated in accordance with their worth at the time of loss. Mr. Justice Disbery stated that the duty to use care on the highway extends not only to the healthy but also to "persons afflicted with disease or a weakness. . . . [T]he plaintiff was entitled to keep his natural teeth no matter how neglected and loose they might be, and to refrain from seeking the pleasures of the dentist's chair. So also he was entitled to continue to keep and 'enjoy', if that word may be used, his pyorrhea, even though such was detrimental to his health."

3. Is the thin-skull rule an exception to the *Wagon Mound (No. 1)* or is it consistent with the foresight principle?

In *Stephenson* v. *Waite Titeman Ltd.,* [1973] 1 N.Z. L.R. 152 (C.A.), Richards J.A. explained the thin-skull rule's operation as follows:

"1. In cases of damage by physical injury to the person the principles imposing liability for consequences flowing from the pre-existing special susceptibility of the victim and/or from new risk or susceptibility created by the initial injury remain part of our law.

2. In such cases the question of foreseeability should be limited to the initial injury. The tribunal of fact must decide whether that injury is of a kind, type or character which the defendant ought reasonably to have foreseen as a real risk.

3. If the plaintiff establishes that the initial injury was within a reasonably foreseeable kind, type or character of injury, then the necessary link between the ultimate consequences of the intial injury and the negligence of the defendant can be forged simply as one of cause and effect—in other words by establishing an adequate relationship of cause and effect between the initial injury and the ultimate consequence."

Compare with *Negretto* v. *Sayers,* [1963] S.A.S.R. 313, where a woman whose pelvis was fractured had a post-concussional psychosis as a result of a "pre-existing tendency to mental disorder". In applying the thin-skull rule, the court tried to explain that the principle is not inconsistent with foresight for the "consequences of even the simplest accident are unpredictable". One must foresee any consequence "between a negligible abrasion and permanent incapacity or death". Mr. Justice Chamberlain admitted that the defendant did not expect to run down anyone, let alone someone with a personality defect, yet one should foresee that a pedestrian might be hit "with quite possible disastrous consequences of one sort or another".

4. What policy reasons can be advanced in support of the thin-skull rule? Does it foster the compensatory aim of tort law? Does it deter? Does it obviate the administrative problems associated with distinguishing between foreseeable injuries and unforeseeable ones? See *Toronto Railway* v. *Toms* (1911), 44 S.C.R. 268, at p. 276 (*per* Davies C.J.). What can be said against the thin-skull rule?

5. Mental suffering flowing from physical injury is compensable under the thin-skull rule. In *Malcolm* v. *Broadhurst*, [1970] 3 All E.R. 508, a husband and wife were both injured physically and mentally in a car accident caused by the negligence of the defendant. The husband's serious head injuries led to his intellectual deterioration and diminution of his learning powers. His personality changed so that he became bad-tempered and violent. This changed behaviour of the husband caused additional nervous symptoms in the wife by aggravating a pre-existing nervous condition. In awarding the wife damages for these aggravated nervous symptoms, Geoffrey Lane J. stated:

"The defendant must take the wife as he finds her and there is no difference in principle between an egg-shell skull and an egg-shell personality, *Love* v. *Port of London Authority*, [1959] 2 Ll. R. 541. Exacerbation of her nervous depression was a readily foreseeable consequence of injuring her. Does the fact that it was caused, or caused to continue, by reaction to the husband's pathological bad-temper (itself the result of the defendant's negligence) put a stop to the defendant's liability? I think not. Once damage of a particular kind, in this case psychological, can be foreseen, as here it could, the fact that it arises or is continued by reason of an unusual complex of events does not avail the defendant, *Hughes* v. *Lord Advocate*, [1963] A.C. 837. Moreover, it is not beyond the range of reasonable anticipation to foresee that if one does severe injury to husband and wife, when the wife is temperamentally unstable, her instability may be adversely affected by the injury done to her husband."

The wife also claimed damages for loss of employment. She was absent from her full-time employment for six months and was compensated for this. In addition, she sought damages for the loss of a part-time job as her husband's secretary, which ended because her husband could no longer conduct his business. In rejecting this latter head of damage, Geoffrey Lane J. remarked:

"It seems to me that the only way in which the defendant could be made liable under this head would be by saying that he must take his victims as he finds them not only in relation to their physical infirmities but also in relation to their infirmities of employment. That would be an extension, and in my judgment an unwarranted extension of the present law. To make the defendant liable for the unforeseeable effect of the accident on the special and unforeseeable circumstances of the wife's employment would be to go beyond the proper limits of compensation."

6. Is the distinction between infirmities of employment and physical infirmities a valid one? Should we differentiate between physical and mental infirmities?

7. In *Duwyn* v. *Kaprelian* (1978), 7 C.C.L.T. 121 (Ont. C.A.), a child injured in an accident was treated in a way that caused it additional mental suffering by a parent who had guilt feelings about the accident. Recovery was allowed by Morden J.A. who likened the ineffective parental care with improper medical treatment and consequently "within the limits of foreseeability".

8. If an injured person suffers traumatic neurosis, compensation is payable.

See *Canning* v. *McFarland,* [1954] O.W.N. 467 (Ont. H.C.); *Dvorkin* v. *Stuart,* [1971] 2 W.W.R. 70 (Alta. S.C.). Depression as a result of a physical injury was held reasonably foreseeable, but not if it flows from worry over financial losses. See *Regush* v. *Inglis* (1962), 38 W.W.R. 245 (B.C.S.C.). See also generally *Beiscak* v. *National Coal Board,* [1965] 1 All. E.R. 895 (Karminski J.); *Blowes* v. *Hamilton,* [1970] 1 O.R. 310; *Sullivan* v. *Riverside Rentals Ltd.* (1973), 36 D.L.R. (3d) 538, at p. 559 (*per* Cowan C.J.T.D.). But *cf. Ostrowski* v. *Lotto* (1968), 2 D.L.R. (3d) 440, revd. on another point, [1971] 1 O.R. 372, affd. 31 D.L.R. (3d) 715 (S.C.C.); *Dietelbach* v. *Public Trustee* (1973), 37 D.L.R. (3d) 621.

9. Changes in personality, a common problem, are compensable under the thin-skull rule. In *Marconato et al.* v. *Franklin,* [1974] 6 W.W.R. 676 (B.C.), a woman injured slightly in a car accident also developed symptoms of depression, hostility, anxiety, tension, hysteria and some characteristics of paranoia. She underwent a personality change, from a happy and contented woman to a very unhappy woman. She was allowed recovery for these damages by Aikins J. who explained:

"One would not ordinarily anticipate, using reasonable foresight, that a moderate cervical strain with soft tissue damage would give rise to the consequences which followed for Mrs. Marconato. These arose, however, because of her pre-existing personality traits. She had a peculiar susceptibility or vulnerability to suffer much greater consequences from a moderate physical injury than the average person. The consequences for Mrs. Marconato could no more be foreseen than it could be foreseen by a tortfeasor that his victim was thin-skulled and that a minor blow to the head would cause very serious injury. It is plain enough that the defendant could foresee the probability of physical injury. It is implicit, however, in the principle that a wrongdoer takes his victim as he finds him, that he takes his victim with all the victim's peculiar susceptibilities and vulnerabilities. The consequences of Mrs. Marconato's injuries were unusual but arose involuntarily. Granted her type of personality they arose as night follows day because of the injury and the circumstances in which she found herself because of the injury."

10. What if, as a result of an injury, the plaintiff is unable to engage in a rare leisure activity? In *Watson* v. *Grant* (1970), 72 W.W.R. 665 (B.C.S.C.), an injured person was unable to finish building a sailboat and sought the cost of hiring help to complete the job. Aikins J. stated:

". . . I start out by saying that I have considerable doubt that building a boat, even quite a large one, at home is a wholly uncommon spare time project. However, the submission is that it was not reasonably foreseeable that the plaintiff might be engaged in such an activity. The argument may be dealt with shortly. If a person is injured so that, say, he has lost the use of an arm, it is reasonably foreseeable that he will be prevented from engaging in any activity that requires the use of the hurt arm. It is not, in my opinion, necessary that the injured person, in order to bring his loss within the foreseeability rule, take the next step and establish that it was reasonably foreseeable that he engaged in this or that leisure-time activity, whether ordinary or out-of-the-ordinary, before he was hurt. Indeed, I cannot see in a personal injury case that there could be any reasonable basis on which it could be foreseen what particular leisure-time pursuit or pursuits the victim followed. I put it somewhat rhetorically: How could it ever be reasonably foreseen that the victim in a motor-accident case was a scuba diver, mountain climber, was building a boat in his spare time, or whatever. It is enough that it be reasonably foreseeable that injury will hinder or prevent the victim from carrying on a spare-time activity regardless of how ordinary or bizarre that activity may be. The plaintiff, in my opinion, is entitled to compensation in respect to inability to continue building his boat."

11. Should a person with a thin-skull ever be considered contributorily negligent for exposing himself to risks which endanger him but would not endanger an ordinary person? See *Murphy* v. *McCarthy* (1974), 9 S.A.S.R. 424, where

Zelling J. declined to so hold, but he commented as follows:

"Where a plaintiff such as this one, with the disabilities which she had, goes as pillion passenger on a scooter, perhaps the real answer is that it ought to be treated as contributory negligence rather than as a problem in causation in damages. Contributory negligence was not pleaded in this case and the matter is only before me for assessment, but it may be that in some subsequent case the emphasis in argument may have to shift from the question of the impact of *The Wagon Mound* upon the "eggshell skull" cases to the question of whether or not the plaintiff exhibited due care for his or her own safety when, knowing of his or her pre-existing disability, he or she exposed themselves to the risk of accident, with predictable consequences much graver to themselves than to a plaintiff without the pre-existing disabilities."

12. See generally Linden, "Down With Foreseeability: Of Thin Skulls and Rescuers" (1969), 47 Can. Bar Rev. 545; Linden, "Foreseeability in Negligence Law" in Law Society of Upper Canada, *Special Lectures on New Developments in the Law of Torts* (1973), at p. 69; Linden, *Canadian Tort Law* (2nd ed., 1977), p. 322.

2. Type of Damage

HUGHES v. LORD ADVOCATE

House of Lords. [1963] A.C. 837; [1963] 1 All E.R. 705

This was an appeal from a decision of the First Division of the Court of Session (The Lord President (Lord Clyde), Lord Sorn and Lord Guthrie; Lord Carmont dissenting, reported [1961] S.C. 310). The court affirmed an interlocutor of the Lord Ordinary (Lord Wheatley), who had held that the respondent was not liable for injuries suffered by a boy of eight years of age on the ground that, although danger to children was reasonably foreseeable in the circumstances, the particular accident that happened was not reasonably foreseeable.

The following statement of facts is taken from the speech of Lord Guest: "In November, 1958, some Post Office employees had opened a manhole in Russell Road, Edinburgh, for the purpose of obtaining access to a telephone cable. The manhole from which the cover had been removed was near the edge of the roadway. A shelter tent had been erected over the open manhole. The manhole was some nine feet deep, and a ladder had been placed inside the manhole to give access to the cable. Around the area of the site had been placed four red warning paraffin lamps. The lamps were lit at 3.30 p.m. About 5 p.m. or 5.30 p.m. the Post Office employees left the site for a tea break for which purpose they went to an adjoining Post Office building. Before leaving they removed the ladder from the manhole and placed it on the ground beside the shelter and pulled a tarpaulin cover over the entrance to the shelter, leaving a space of two feet to two feet six inches between the lower edge of the tarpaulin and the ground. The lamps were left burning. After they left, the appellant, aged eight, and his uncle, aged ten, came along Russell Road and decided to explore the shelter. According to the findings of the Lord Ordinary (Lord Wheatley), the boys picked up one of the red lamps, raised up the tarpaulin sheet and entered the shelter. They brought the ladder into the shelter with a view to descending into the manhole. They also brought a piece of rope which was not the Post Office equipment, tied the rope to the lamp and, with the lamp, lowered themselves into the manhole. They both came out carrying the lamp. Thereafter, according to the evidence, the appellant tripped over the lamp, which fell into the hole. There followed an explosion from the hole with flames reaching a height of 30 feet. With the explosion the appellant fell into the hole and sustained very severe burning injuries.

In an action by the pursuer directed against the Lord Advocate, as representing the Postmaster-General, on the ground that the accident was due to the fault of the Post Office employees in failing to close the manhole before they left or to post a watchman while they were away, the Lord Ordinary assoilzied the respondent. His judgment was affirmed by a majority of the First Division, Lord Carmont dissenting. Before the Lord Ordinary and the First Division a preliminary point was taken by the respondent that the appellant was a trespasser in the shelter and that the Post Office employees therefore owed no duty to take precautions for his safety. This point was not persisted in before this House and it is therefore unnecessary to say anything about it.

The Lord Ordinary, after a very careful analysis of the evidence, has found that the cause of the explosion was as a result of the lamp which the appellant knocked into the hole being so disturbed that paraffin escaped from the tank, formed vapour and was ignited by the flame. The lamp was recovered from the manhole after the accident; the tank of the lamp was half out and the wickholder was completely out of the lamp. This explanation of the accident was rated by the experts as a low order of probability. But as there was no other feasible explanation it was accepted by the Lord Ordinary and this House must take it as the established cause.

Lord Reid: . . . It was argued that the appellant cannot recover because the damage which he suffered was of a kind which was not foreseeable. That was not the ground of judgment of the First Division or of the Lord Ordinary and the facts proved do not, in my judgment, support that argument. The appellant's injuries were mainly caused by burns and it cannot be said that injuries from burns were unforeseeable. As a warning to traffic the workmen had set lighted red lamps round the tent which covered the manhole, and if boys did enter the dark tent it was very likely that they would take one of these lamps with them. If the lamp fell and broke it was not at all unlikely that the boy would be bruned and the burns might well be serious. No doubt it was not to be expected that the injuries would be as serious as those which the appellant in fact sustained. But a defender is liable, although the damage may be a good deal greater in extent than was foreseeable. He can only escape liability if the damage can be regarded as differing in kind from what was foreseeable.

So we have (first) a duty owed by the workmen, (secondly) the fact that if they had done as they ought to have done there would have been no accident, and (thirdly) the fact that the injuries suffered by the appellant, though perhaps different in degree, did not differ in kind from injuries which might have resulted from an accident of a foreseeable nature. The ground on which this case has been decided against the appellant is that the accident was of unforeseeable type. Of course the pursuer has to prove that the defender's fault caused the accident and there could be a case where the intrusion of a new and unexpected factor could be regarded as the cause of the accident rather than the fault of the defender. But that is not this case. The cause of this accident was a known source of danger, the lamp, but it behaved in an unpredictable way. The explanation of the accident which has been accepted, and which I would not seek to question, is that, when the lamp fell down the manhole and was broken, some paraffin escaped, and enough was vaporized to create an explosive mixture which was detonated by the naked light of the lamp. The experts agreed that no one would have expected that to happen: it was so unlikely as to be unforeseeable. The explosion caused the boy to fall into the manhole: whether his injuries were directly caused by the explosion or aggravated by fire which started in the manhole is not at all clear. The essential step in the respondent's argument is that the explosion was the real cause of the injuries and that the explosion was unforeseeable. . . . This accident was caused by a known source of danger, but caused in a way which could not have been foreseen, and in my judgment that affords no defence. I would therefore allow the appeal.

Lord Jenkins: . . . It is true that the duty of care expected in cases of this sort is confined to reasonably foreseeable dangers, but it does not necessarily follow that liability is escaped because the danger actually materialising is not identical with the danger reasonably foreseen and guarded against. Each case must depend on its own particular facts. For example (as pointed out in the opinions), in the present case the paraffin did the mischief by exploding, not burning, and it is said that, while a paraffin fire (caused, *e.g.*, by the upsetting of the lighted lamp or otherwise allowing its contents to leak out) was a reasonably foreseeable risk so soon as the pursuer got access to the lamp, an explosion was not. To my mind the distinction drawn between burning and explosion is too fine to warrant acceptance. Supposing the pursuer had on the day in question gone to the site and taken one of the lamps, and upset it over himself, thus setting his clothes alight, the person to be considered responsible for protecting children from the dangers to be found there would presumably have been liable. On the other hand, if the lamp, when the boy upset it, exploded in his face, he would have no remedy, because the explosion was an event which could not reasonably be foreseen. This does not seem to me to be right. I think, that in these imaginary circumstances the danger would be a danger of fire of some kind, *e.g.*, setting alight of his clothes or causing him bodily hurt. If there is a risk of such fire as that I do not think that the duty of care prescribed in *Donoghue* v. *Stevenson* is prevented from coming into operation by the presence of the remote possibility of the more serious event of an explosion.

I would allow this appeal.

Lord Morris of Borth-y-Gest: . . . Exercising an ordinary, and certainly not an over-exacting, degree of prevision the workmen should, I consider, have decided, when the tea-break came, that someone had better be left in charge who could repel the intrusion of inquisitive children. . . .

When the children did appear they found good scope for moments of adventure. Then came disaster for the pursuer. A risk that he might in some way burn himself by playing with a lamp was translated into reality. In fact he was very severely burned. Though his severe burns came about in a way that seems surprising, this only serves to illustrate that boys can bring about a consequence which could be expected but yet can bring it about in a most unusual manner and with unexpectedly severe results. After the pursuer tripped against the lamp, and so caused it to fall into the manhole, and after he contrived to be drawn into or to be blown into or to fall into the manhole, he was burned. His burns were, however, none the less burns, although there was such an immediate combustion of paraffin vapour that there was an explosion. The circumstance that an explosion as such would not have been contemplated does not alter the fact that it could reasonably have been foreseen that a boy, who played in and about the canvas shelter and played with the things that were thereabouts, might get hurt and might in some way burn himself. That is just what happened. The pursuer did burn himself, though his burns were more grave than would have been expected. The fact that the features or developments of an accident may not reasonably have been foreseen does not mean that the accident itself was not foreseeable. The pursuer was in my view injured as a result of the type or kind of accident or occurrence that could reasonably have been foreseen. In agreement with Lord Carmont I consider that the defenders do not avoid liability because they could not have foretold the exact way in which the pursuer would play with the alluring objects that had been left to attract him or the exact way in which in so doing he might get hurt. . . .

My Lords, in my view there was a duty owed by the defenders to safeguard the pursuer against the type or kind of occurrence which in fact happened and which resulted in his injuries, and the defenders are not absolved from liability because they did not envisage "the precise concatenation of circumstances which led up to the accident". For these reasons, I differ with respect from the majority of the First Division and I would allow the appeal.

Lord Guest: . . . In dismissing the appellant's claim the Lord Ordinary and the majority of the judges of the First Division reached the conclusion that the accident which happened was not reasonably foreseeable. In order to establish a coherent chain of causation it is not necessary that the precise details leading up to the accident should have been reasonably foreseeable: it is sufficient if the accident which occurred is of a type which should have been foreseeable by a reasonably careful person. . . . An explosion is only one way in which burning can be caused. Burning can also be caused by the contact between liquid paraffin and a naked flame. In the one case paraffin vapour and in the other case liquid paraffin is ignited by fire. I cannot see that these are two different types of accident. They are both burning accidents and in both cases the injuries would be burning injuries. On this view the explosion was an immaterial event in the chain of causation. It was simply one way in which burning might be caused by the potentially dangerous paraffin lamp. I adopt with respect Lord Carmont's observation in the present case: "The defender cannot, I think, escape liability by contending that he did not foresee all the possibilities of the manner in which allurements — the manhole and the lantern — would act upon the childish mind."

I have therefore reached the conclusion that the accident which occurred and which caused burning injuries to the appellant was one which ought reasonably to have been foreseen by the Post Office employees and that they were at fault in failing to provide a protection against the appellant entering the shelter and going down the manhole.

I would allow the appeal.

Lord Pearce: . . . The defenders are liable for all the foreseeable consequences of their neglect. When an accident is of a different type and kind from anything that a defender could have foreseen he is not liable for it (see *The Wagon Mound,* [1961] A.C. 388). But to demand too great precision in the test of foreseeability would be unfair to the pursuer since the facets of misadventure are innumerable. . . . In the case of an allurement to children it is particularly hard to foresee with precision the exact shape of the disaster that will arise. The allurement in this case was the combination of a red paraffin lamp, a ladder, a partially closed tent, and a cavernous hole within it, a setting well-fitted to inspire some juvenile adventure that might end in calamity. The obvious risks were burning and conflagration and a fall. All these in fact occurred, but unexpectedly the mishandled lamp instead of causing an ordinary conflagration produced a violent explosion. Did the explosion create an accident and damage of a different type from the misadventure and damage that could be foreseen? In my judgment it did not. The accident was but a variant of the foreseeable. It was, to quote the words of Denning L.J. in *Roe* v. *Ministry of Health,* [1954] 2 Q.B. 66, "within the risk created by the negligence". No unforeseeable extraneous, initial occurrence fired the train. The children's entry into the tent with the ladder, the descent into the hole, the mishandling of the lamp, were all foreseeable. The greater part of the path to injury had thus been trodden, and the mishandled lamp was quite likely at that stage to spill and cause a conflagration.

Instead, by some curious chance of combustion, it exploded and no conflagration occurred, it would seem, until after the explosion. There was thus an unexpected manifestation of the apprehended physical dangers. But it would be, I think, too narrow a view to hold that those who created the risk of fire are excused from the liability for the damage by fire, because it came by way of explosive combustion. The resulting damage, though severe, was not greater than or different in kind from that which might have been produced had the lamp spilled and produced a more normal conflagration in the hole.

I would therefore allow the appeal.

NOTES

1. What is the effect of this case on *The Wagon Mound (No. 1.)*?

2. In *Doughty* v. *Turner Manufacturing Co. Ltd.*, [1964] 1 All E.R. 98, one of the defendant's servants either knocked an asbestos and cement compound cover of a heating bath (containing molten liquid of a heat of 800° centigrade), into the liquid, or allowed it to slide in. In a short time there was an erruption of the liquid which seriously injured the plaintiff, a bystander. It was later discovered that the asbestos cement compound would at the high temperature undergo a chemical change releasing water which would produce an explosion. The defendants did not appreciate that the immersion of the lid would produce an explosion and, indeed, similar covers had been used in England and the United States for some 20 years, and there was no blame in failing to appreciate that the immersion of the cover would produce an explosion. It was argued that knocking a cover into the liquid gave rise to a foreseeable risk of burning the plaintiff since there was a foreseeable risk of splashing. As the plaintiff was burned, the actual damage was of the same kind as could be foreseen by knocking in the lid; hence it was argued that even though the risk of explosion was unforeseeable, the defendant should be liable. Reliance was placed on *Hughes* v. *Lord Advocate*. The Court of Appeal held, however, that the only duty owed to the plaintiff was in relation to the foreseeable risk of splashing. Merely knocking in the lid, or putting it in intentionally was no breach of duty to plaintiff since in the state of existing knowledge mere immersion of the cover could not be foreseen as likely to injure anyone. The plaintiff's argument was supported by *Re Polemis,* but that case was no longer law. In the *Hughes* case the defendants created a risk of burning by failure to guard an allurement. That risk materialised although the combination of the circumstances by which the burns were more serious than they might have been expected to be could not reasonably have been foreseen. The burns were, however, a consequence of "defendants' breach of duty". In the present case the only duty related to splashing and there was no evidence of any splash and hence no breach of duty.

Is this an acceptable distinction in your opinion? Is the result just?

3. In *Lauritzen* v. *Barstead* (1965), 53 D.L.R. (2d) 267 (Alta.), the plaintiff asked the defendant for a ride in his car to a nearby town. While in the town the defendant did considerable drinking and eventually became intoxicated. He asked the plaintiff to drive the car back. On the way back the defendant decided he wanted more beer and ordered the plaintiff to take a turn-off into the first town. The plaintiff refused and continued on the highway. The defendant grabbed at the steering wheel which put the car out of control and off the road. While the plaintiff was out of the car investigating the situation the defendant made an attempt to drive back on the road but this merely resulted in the car becoming more precariously situated on the bank of a ditch some 30 ft. in depth. The plaintiff tried to walk to town for help but was forced to turn back because of the cold. The plaintiff and the defendant agreed to stay in the car overnight. While the plaintiff slept, the defendant drove the car across the prairie towards a river intending to drive to town on the frozen surface but the car went into a hole and became hopelessly stuck. The plaintiff made several other efforts to go for help but was turned back by wind and the cold. About

36 hours after they left the road the plaintiff walked several miles down river where he was found by a farmer. Frost-bite necessitated the amputation of parts of both feet. In an action by the plaintiff for damages it was argued that *The Wagon Mound (No. 1)* prevented recovery for the plaintiff's injuries. Kirby J., held the defendant liable. He ought to have foreseen "the dangerous consequences likely to flow from his negligent act in grabbing the steering-wheel. It does not seem to me that . . . the *Wagon Mound* case implies that recovery of damages should be conditional upon foreseeability of the particular harm and the precise manner or sequence of events in which it occurred."

Is this consistent with *The Wagon Mound (No. 1)*? Is it just?

4. In *Oke* v. *Weide Transport Ltd.* (1963), 41 D.L.R. (2d) 53 (Man. C.A.), the defendant motorist, who had knocked over a metal post on a strip of gravel between two highway lanes, left the post bent over and the plaintiff's deceased, improperly using the strip for the purpose of passing another car, was killed when the post came up through the floor boards of his car and impaled him. The majority of the Manitoba Court of Appeal held the defendant not liable, purporting to follow *The Wagon Mound (No. 1)*. Defendant could not have anticipated that someone would endeavour to pass a car at a point where it was wrong to do so, or that the damaged post would come up through the floor of the car and cause a fatal accident. It was a "freak accident" and the defendant could not reasonably have foreseen such an unusual occurrence. Freedman J.A., dissenting, said it was not necessary to foresee "either the precise manner in which the accident would occur or that its consequences would be so tragic . . . . It is enough that he ought to have foreseen that [the post] left in the state it was, could be a source of danger to a motorist . . . and become the cause of . . . an automobile accident of some kind."

Is this consistent with *The Wagon Mound (No. 1)*? Is the result a just one?

5. In *Weiner* v. *Zoratti* (1970), 11 D.L.R. (3d) 598 (Man. Q.B.), the defendant driver negligently collided with a fire hydrant and sheared it off, with the result that the basement of the plaintiff's pharmacy was flooded, damaging his stock-in-trade and personal effects. Matas J. held that damages were recoverable and explained:

". . . it is not necessary to engage in speculation about the specific foreseeability of each specific event from the moment of impact to the damage to the [plaintiff's] property; nor is it necessary to embark ôn an exercise in metaphysical subtleties. The plaintiff's loss was a direct, probable and foreseeable result of the negligent breaking of the hydrant just as much as if a piece of the broken hydrant had been propelled by the impact through the window of the [plaintiff's] shop or had struck a passing pedestrian causing physical injury."

Can you formulate a distinction between injury to a passing pedestrian and water damage to a pharmacist's stock? Would liability be imposed if someone had been sleeping in the basement and had been drowned in the flood? See also *Kennedy* v. *Hughes Drug (1969) Inc.* (1974), 47 D.L.R. (3d) 277 (P.E.I.).

6. In *Bradford* v. *Robinson Rentals,* [1967] 1 All E.R. 267, the plaintiff, a mobile radio and television service engineer, was exposed to prolonged periods of extreme cold and considerable fatigue, in consequence of which he suffered permanent damage to his hands and feet from frostbite, an unusual condition in England. He recovered damages from his employer before Mr. Justice Rees, who rationalized his decision as follows:

"It was strongly argued on behalf of the defendants that injury to his health suffered by the plaintiff in this case by 'frostbite' or cold injury was not reasonably foreseeable. There was no evidence that before the plaintiff started the journey either the plaintiff himself or the defendants' servants actually contemplated that the plaintiff might suffer from 'frostbite' if he were required to carry out the journey. However, I am satisfied that any reasonable employer in possession of all the facts would have realised — and [they] must have realised — that if the plaintiff was required to carry out the journey he would certainly be subjected to a real risk of some injury to his health arising from prolonged exposure to an exceptional degree of cold. No doubt the kinds of injury to health due to prolonged exposure to an exceptional degree of cold are commonly thought to include, for example, that the victim might suffer from a common cold or in a severe case from pneumonia, or that he might suffer from chilblains on his hands and feet. The question which I have to consider is whether the plaintiff has established that the injury to his health by 'frostbite' (and I use the lay term for convenience), which is admittedly unusual in this country, is nevertheless of the type and kind of injury which was reasonably foreseeable. . . .

In all these circumstances I hold that the defendants did, by sending the plaintiff out on this journey, expose him to a reasonably foreseeable risk of injury arising from exposure to severe cold and fatigue. This breach of duty caused the plaintiff to suffer from 'frostbite' or cold injury with serious consequences. Even if there had been — and there is not — evidence that the plaintiff was abnormally susceptible to 'frostbite' as opposed to the more common sequels of prolonged exposure to severe cold and fatigue, he would be entitled to succeed on the ground that a tortfeasor must take his victim as he finds him (see . . . *Smith* v. *Leech Brain & Co. Ltd.*).''

Do you agree with this analysis?

7. In *Tremain* v. *Pike*, [1969] 3 All E.R. 1303, the plaintiff, a farm hand, contracted Weil's disease while working on the defendant's farm. This rare disease was spread by contact with the urine of rats. The more usual diseases caused by rats came from rat bites or from food contaminated by rats. Lord Justice Payne held that there was no negligence in the control of the rats. In an *obiter dictum,* His Lordship stated:

"The kind of damage suffered here was a disease contracted by contact with rats' urine. This, in my view, was entirely different in kind from the effect of a rat-bite, or food poisoning by the consumption of food or drink contaminated by rats. I do not accept that all illness or infection arising from an infestation of rats should be regarded as the same kind. [His Lordship then referred to *Smith* v. *Leech Brain* and *Bradford* v. *Robinson Rentals*]. The distinction between those two cases and the present case is crystal clear. There the risk of injury from a burn in the first case and from extreme cold in the second was foreseeable, and it was only the degree of injury or the development of the *sequelae* which was not foreseeable. In this case, the risk or the initial infection of the plaintiff, was, in my view, not reasonably foreseeable."

Is the distinction "crystal clear" to you?

8. In *School Division of Assiniboine South, No. 3* v. *Hoffer, Hoffer and Greater Winnipeg Gas Co. Ltd.,* [1971] 1 W.W.R. 1; affd. [1971] 4 W.W.R. 746; affd. [1973] 6 W.W.R. 765 (S.C.C.), a 14-year-old boy started his father's snowmobile in a negligent manner, causing it to escape from his control. It collided with a defective and unprotected gas-riser pipe. This caused some gas to escape and enter a nearby school building through a window where it exploded. The school sued the young operator of the snowmobile, his father and the Gas Company that had improperly installed the gas-riser pipe. All three defendants were found liable for the damage, and as between themselves, 50 percent Gas Company, 25 percent son, 25 percent father.

In discussing the liability of the boy, Dickson J.A. (as he then was) stated:

"It is enough to fix liability if one could foresee in a general way the sort of thing that happened. The extent of the damage and its manner of incidence need not be foreseeable if physical damage of the kind which in fact ensues is foreseeable. In the case at bar, I would hold that the damage was of the *type* or *kind* which any reasonable person might foresee. Gas-riser pipes on the outside of . . . buildings are common. Damage to such a pipe is not of a kind that no one could anticipate. When one permits a power tobaggan to run at large, or when one fires a rifle blindly down a city street, one must not define narrowly the outer limits of reasonable prevision. The ambit of foreseeable damage is indeed broad."

With reference to the liability of the gas company, Dickson J.A. explained:

".... It is true that persons are not bound to take extravagant precautions but they must weigh the probability of injury resulting and the probable seriousness of the injury. Although the probability of the gas-riser being struck by an automobile, a motorcycle or an auto toboggan was not great, the pipe being tucked into the corner of the building, the probable seriousness of any injury was very great. Against this must be weighed the cost and difficulty of the precautions which could have been taken. Protective pipes could have been installed at small cost and little difficulty. The duty to take protective measures increases in direct proportion to the risk. In these circumstances the gas company failed to exercise a high degree of care."

See also *Worker's Compensation Bd.* v. *Schmidt* (1977), 80 D.L.R. (3d) 696 (Man. Q.B.), where it was found to be foreseeable that a workman might burn to death after mistakenly pouring a pail of cleaning fluid over himself while trying to put out a negligently started fire.

9. The test of *Wagon Mound (No. 1)* as expanded in *Hughes* v. *Lord Advocate* has been well-articulated by Mr. Justice Dickson of the Supreme Court of Canada in *R.* v. *Coté* (1974), 51 D.L.R. (3d) 244, at p. 252:

"It is not necessary that one foresee the 'precise concatenation of events'; it is enough to fix liability if one can foresee in a general way the class or character of injury which occurred . . . ."

10. A similar use of the test was in *Prasad* v. *Prasad* (1974), 54 D.L.R. (3d) 451 (B.C.). A father allowed his son to play with a knife which was apparently left on a sofa. The plaintiff came to visit the father, sat down on the sofa and leaned back, only to be pierced in the back by the knife. The father was held responsible for this rather bizarre accident on the ground that he was negligent in failing to supervise his child properly in the handling of the knife. Mr. Justice Rae stated "the harm occasioned the plaintiff here, it seems to me, was of such a class or general character as to be within the scope of the foreseeable risk. What occurred was but a variant of the foreseeable: . . . It was not necessary that the precise manner of its occurrence should have been envisioned. . . ."

11. In the case of *Harsim Construction Limited* v. *Olsen* (1973), 29 D.L.R. (3d) 121, an electrician negligently caused a short circuit while replacing a subsidiary circuit breaker. The main circuit breaker, which should have "blown" or "kicked out" and cut off the power, failed to do so. The power continued to flow and a fire resulted. MacDonald J. of the Alberta Supreme Court held that the plaintiff's damages should be limited to the costs of replacing the main circuit breaker, and not for the entire damages caused by the fire because the latter were "too remote". His Lordship explained:

"There was no reason for the defendant to foresee that the circuit breaker would not work or might not work, although that proved possible. However, the fact that the circuit breaker did not work would be considered as improbable. The responsibility of the defendant was for damage that would not be improbable or that would not be unpredictable to a reasonable man under the same circumstances."

Does this make sense to you?

12. One unhappy use of the foresight test occurred in *Wade* v. *C.N.R.* (1978), 80 D.L.R. (3d) 214 (S.C.C.), where a dull-witted eight-year-old, who was playing in some sand near an unfenced railway line, lost his leg trying to steal a ride on a train. In a jury trial, the railway, having been aware of children in the area, was found negligent in failing to warn, in failing to fence and in failing to remove the sand piles which were attractive to children. The boy was held incapable of contributory negligence because of his limited intelligence. The Nova Scotia Court of Appeal affirmed the finding of negligence against the railway, but held the boy 50% to blame as well. The Supreme Court of Canada (6-3) dismissed the action on the ground that no duty was owed to the boy. There were many issues in the case, but on this issue Mr. Justice de Grandpré said:

". . . I conclude that no reasonable occupier could have reasonably foreseen that a child playing on a pile of sand some 50 ft. from the track when the engine went by, would leave this place of safety, run towards the track and attempt to jump on the ladder of a boxcar."

Is it necessary to foresee an accident in such detail? What is the proper role of a Court of Appeal in these cases? Is it better for appellate courts to actively intervene in trial decisions on foresight, or should they restrain themselves as much as possible? What are the competing costs and benefits?

13. Defendant negligently maintains a wooden hydro pole so that it becomes rotten and weak. A car collides with the pole, which topples over and injures a pedestrian. Should the defendant be liable to the pedestrian? Should it make any difference if the car was driven negligently? What if the car was intentionally driven into the pole? Compare with *Gibson* v. *Garcia* (1950), 216 P. 2d 9 (Cal. D.C.A.).

14. Defendant's dogs escape creating a risk that someone will be bowled over by them. Someone is bitten. Liability? Compare with *Draper* v. *Hodder*, [1972] 2 All E.R. 210 (C.A.), at p. 222 (*per* Edmund Davies L.J.).

15. How can one tell if an accident is of the same type or kind as the one that is threatened? Is the reasoning process fully logical? How important is the verbal dexterity of counsel in classifying the accident? What role, if any, should policy considerations play? See Fridman and Williams, "The Atomic Theory of Negligence" (1971), 45 Aust. L.J. 117.

3. Possibility of Damage

THE WAGON MOUND (NO. 2)

OVERSEAS TANKSHIP (U.K.) LTD. v. THE MILLER STEAMSHIP CO. PTY. LTD.

Privy Council. [1966] 2 All E.R. 709

Appeal by Overseas Tankship (U.K.) Ltd. and a cross-appeal by The Miller Steamship Co. Pty. Ltd., and R.W. Miller & Co. Pty. Ltd., by leave of the Supreme Court of New South Wales, from the judgment of Walsh J. wherein judgment was entered against the appellant in favour of the respondents for £80,000 and £1,000 respectively. The circumstances which gave rise to the actions were the same as those which came before the Judicial Committee in *The Wagon Mound (No. 1)*. The plaintiffs in *The Wagon Mound (No. 1)* were the owners of a wooden wharf known as Sheerlegs Wharf which was damaged by the fire. Each of the plaintiffs in the present action was the owner of a ship which at the material time was lying at Sheerlegs Wharf and was damaged by the fire.

Lord Reid: . . . In the present case the respondents sue alternatively in nuisance and in negligence. Walsh J., had found in their favour in nuisance but against them in negligence. Before their Lordships the appellant appeals against his decision on nuisance and the respondents appeal against his decision on negligence. . . .

Comparing nuisance with negligence the main argument for the respondent was that in negligence foreseeability is an essential element in determining liability, and therefore it is logical that foreseeability should also be an essential element in determining the amount of damages: but negligence is not an essential element in determining liability for nuisance, and therefore it is illogical to bring in foreseeability when determining the amount of damages. It is quite true that negligence is not an essential element in nuisance. Nuisance is a term to cover a wide variety of tortious acts or omissions, and in many negligence in the narrow sense is not essential. An occupier may incur liability for the emission of noxious fumes or noise, although he has used the utmost care in building and using his premises. The amount of fumes or noise which he can lawfully emit is a question of degree, and he or his advisers may have miscalculated what can be justified. Or he may deliberately obstruct the highway adjoining his premises to a greater degree than is permissible hoping that no one will object. On the other hand the emission of fumes or noise or the obstruction of the adjoining highway may often be the result of pure negligence on his part: there are many cases (*e.g., Dollman* v. *Hillman,* [1941] 1 All E.R. 355) where precisely the same facts will establish liability both in nuisance and in negligence. And although negligence may not be necessary, fault of some kind is almost necessary and fault generally involves foreseeability, *e.g.,* in case like *Sedleigh-Denfield* v. *O'Callaghan,* [1940] A.C. 880, the fault is in failing to abate a nuisance of the existence of which the defender is or ought to be aware as likely to cause damage to his neighbour. (Their Lordships express no opinion about cases like *Wringe* v. *Cohen,* [1940] 1 K.B. 229, on which neither counsel relied.) The present case is one of creating a danger to persons or property in navigable waters (equivalent to a highway) and there it is admitted that fault is essential — in this case the negligent discharge of the oil.

"But how are we to determine whether a state of affairs in or near a highway is in danger? This depends, I think, on whether injury may reasonably be foreseen. If you take all the cases in the books you will find that if the state of affairs is such that injury may reasonably be anticipated to persons using the highway it is a public nuisance." (*per* Denning L.J., in *Morton* v. *Wheeler* (1956), unreported.) So in the class of nuisance which includes this case foreseeability is an essential element in determining liability.

It could not be right to discriminate between different cases of nuisance so as to make foreseeability a necessary element in determining damages in those cases where it is a necessary element in determining liability, but not in others. So the choice is between it being a necessary element in all cases of nuisance or in none. In their Lordship's judgment the similarities between nuisance and other forms of tort to which *The Wagon Mound (No. 1)* applies far outweigh any differences, and they must therefore hold that the judgment appealed from is wrong on this branch of the case. It is not sufficient that the injury suffered by the respondents' vessels was the direct result of the nuisance, if that injury was in the relevant sense unforeseeable.

It is now necessary to turn to the respondents' submission that the trial judge was wrong in holding that damage from fire was not reasonably foreseeable. In *Wagon Mound (No. 1)* the finding on which the Board proceeded was that of the trial judge: ". . . [the appellants] did not know and could not reasonably be expected to have known that [the oil] was capable of being set afire when spread on water". In the present case the evidence led was substantially different from the evidence led in *Wagon Mound (No. 1)* and the findings of Walsh J. are significantly different. That is not due to there having been any failure by the plaintiffs in *Wagon Mound (No. 1)* in preparing and presenting their case. The plaintiffs there were no doubt embarrassed by a difficulty which does not affect the present plaintiffs. The outbreak of the fire was consequent on the act of the manager of the plaintiffs in *Wagon Mound (No. 1)* in resuming oxy-acetylene welding and cutting while the wharf was surrounded by this oil. So if the plaintiffs in the former case had set out to prove that it was foreseeable by the engineers of the Wagon Mound that this oil could be set alight they might have had difficulty in parrying the reply that then this must also have been foreseeable by their manager. Then there would have been contributory negligence and at that time contributory negligence was a complete defence in New South Wales.

The crucial finding of Walsh J., in this case is in finding (v): that the damage was "not reasonably foreseeable by those for whose acts the defendant would be responsible". That is not a primary finding of fact but an inference from the other findings, and it is clear from the learned judge's judgment that in drawing this inference he was to a large extent influenced by his view of the law. The vital parts of the findings of fact which have already been set out in full are (i) that the officers of the Wagon Mound "would regard furnace oil as very difficult to ignite on water" — not that they would regard this as impossible, (ii) that their experience would probably have been "that this had very rarely happened" — not that they would never have heard of a case where it had happened, and (iii) that they would have regarded it as a "possibility, but one which could become an actuality only in very exceptional circumstances" — not as in *Wagon Mound (No. 1)* that they could not reasonably be expected to have known that this oil was capable of being set afire when spread on water. The question which must now be determined is whether these differences between the findings in the two cases do or do not lead to a different result in law.

In *Wagon Mound (No. 1)* the Board were not concerned with degrees of foreseeability because the finding was that the fire was not foreseeable at all. So Viscount Simonds has no cause to amplify the statement that the "essential factor in determining liability is whether the damage is of such a kind as the reasonable man should have foreseen". Here the findings show, however, that some risk of fire would have been present to the mind of a reasonable man in the shoes of the ship's chief engineer. So that first question must be what is the precise meaning to be attached in this context to the word "foreseeable" and "reasonably foreseeable".

Before *Bolton v. Stone*, [1951] A.C. 850, the cases had fallen into two classes: (i) those where, before the event, the risk of its happening would have been regarded as unreal either because the event would have been thought to be physically impossible or because the possibility of its happening would have been regarded as so fantastic or far-fetched that no reasonable man would have paid any attention to it — "a mere possibility which would never occur to the mind of a reasonable man" (*per* Lord Dunedin in *Fardon v. Harcourt-Rivington*, [1932] All E.R. 81) — or (ii) those where there was a real and substantial risk or chance that something like the event which happens might occur and then the reasonable man would have taken the steps necessary to eliminate the risk.

Bolton v. Stone posed a new problem. There a member of a visiting team drove a cricket ball out of the ground on to an unfrequented adjacent public road and it struck and severely injured a lady who happened to be standing in the road. That it might happen that a ball would be driven on to this road could not have been said to be a fantastic or far-fetched possibility: according to the evidence it had happened about six times in twenty-eight years. Moreover it could not have been said to be a far-fetched or fantastic possibility that such a ball would strike someone in the road: people did pass along the road from time to time. So it could not have been said that, on any ordinary meaning of the words, the fact that a ball might strike a person in the road was not foreseeable or reasonably foreseeable. It was plainly foreseeable; but the chance of its happening in the foreseeable future was infinitesimal. A mathematician given the data could have worked out that it was only likely to happen once in so many thousand years. The House of Lords held that the risk was so small that in the circumstances a reasonable man would have been justified in disregarding it and taking no steps to eliminate it.

It does not follow that, no matter what the circumstances may be, it is justifiable to neglect a risk of such a small magnitude. A reasonable man would only neglect such a risk if he had some valid reason for doing so: e.g., that it would involve considerable expense to eliminate the risk. He would weigh the risk against the difficulty of eliminating it. If the activity which caused the injury to Miss Stone had been an unlawful activity there can be little doubt but that *Bolton* v. *Stone* would have been decided differently. In their Lordships' judgment *Bolton* v. *Stone* did not alter the general principle that a person must be regarded as negligent if he does not take steps to eliminate a risk which he knows or ought to know is a real risk and not a mere possibility which would never influence the mind of a reasonable man. What that decision did was to recognise and give effect to the qualification that it is justifiable not to take steps to eliminate a real risk if it is small and if the circumstances are such that a reasonable man, careful of the safety of his neighbour, would think it right to neglect it.

In the present case there was no justification whatever for discharging the oil into Sydney Harbour. Not only was it an offence to do so, but also it involved considerable loss financially. If the ship's engineer had thought about the matter there could have been no question of balancing the advantages and disadvantages. From every point of view it was both his duty and his interest to stop the discharge immediately.

It follows that in their Lordships' view the only question is whether a reasonable man having the knowledge and experience to be expected of the chief engineer of the Wagon Mound would have known that there was a real risk of the oil on the water catching fire in some way: if it did, serious damage to ships or other property was not only foreseeable but very likely. Their Lordships do not dissent from the view of the trial judge that the possibilities of damage "must be significant enough in a practical sense to require a reasonable man to guard against them", but they think that he may have misdirected himself in saying "there does seem to be a real practical difficulty, assuming that some risk of fire damage was foreseeable, but not a high one, in making a factual judgment as to whether this risk was sufficient to attract liability if damage should occur". In this difficult chapter of the law decisions are not infrequently taken to apply to circumstances far removed from the facts which give rise to them, and it would seem that here too much reliance has been placed on some observations in *Bolton* v. *Stone* and similar observations in other cases.

In their Lordships' view a properly qualified and alert chief engineer would have realised there was a real risk here, and they do not understand Walsh J., to deny that; but he appears to have held that, if a real risk can properly be described as remote, it must then be held to be not reasonably foreseeable. That is a possible interpretation of some of the authorities; but this is still an open question and on principle their Lordships cannot accept this view. If a real risk is one which would occur to the mind of a reasonable man in the position of the defendant's servant and which he would not brush aside as far-fetched, and if the criterion is to be what that reasonable man would have done in the circumstances, then surely he would not neglect such a risk if action to eliminate it presented no difficulty, involved no disadvantage and required no expense.

In the present case the evidence shows that the discharge of so much oil on to the water must have taken a considerable time, and a vigilant ship's engineer would have noticed the discharge at an early stage. The findings show that he ought to have known that it is possible to ignite this kind of oil on water, and that the ship's engineer probably ought to have known that this had in fact happened before. The most that can be said to justify inaction is that he would have known that this could only happen in very exceptional circumstances; but that does not mean that a reasonable man would dismiss such risk from his mind and do nothing when it was so easy to prevent it. If it is clear that the reasonable man would have realised or foreseen and prevented the risk, then it must follow that the appellants are liable in damages. The learned judge found this a difficult case: he said that this matter is "one on which different minds would come to different conclusions". Taking a rather different view of the law from that of the learned judge, their Lordships must hold that the respondents are entitled to succeed on this issue.

The judgment appealed from is in the form of a verdict in favour of the respondents on the claim based on nuisance, a verdict in favour of the appellant on the claim based on negligence, and a direction that judgment be entered for the respondents in the sums of £80,000 and £1,000 respectively. The result of their Lordships' findings is that the direction that judgment be entered for the respondents must stand, but that the appeal against the verdict in favour of the respondents and the cross-appeal against the verdict in favour of the appellant must both be allowed.

Accordingly their Lordships will humbly advise Her Majesty that the appeal and the cross-appeal should be allowed and that the judgment for the respondents in the sums of £80,000 and £1,000 should be affirmed. The appellant must pay two-thirds of the respondents' costs in the appeal and cross-appeal.

[The Judicial Committee of the Privy Council that decided *The Wagon Mound (No. 1), supra,* was composed of Viscount Simonds, Lord Reid, Lord Radcliffe, Lord Tucker and Lord Morris of Borth-y-Gest.

The Judicial Committee of the Privy Council that decided *The Wagon Mound (No. 2), supra,* was composed of Lord Reid, Lord Morris of Borth-y-Gest, Lord Pearce, Lord Wilberforce and Lord Pearson.]

NOTES

1. What, if anything, does *The Wagon Mound (No. 2)* do to *The Wagon Mound (No. 1)*? Did it strike a "mortal blow"? See J.C. Smith, "The Passing of *The Wagon Mound*" (1967), 45 Can. Bar Rev. 336; Glasbeek, "*Wagon Mound II — Re Polemis* Revived; Nuisance Revised" (1967), 6 West. L. Rev. 192. Or is its impact more limited? How important were the different findings of fact? To what type of activity is *The Wagon Mound (No. 2)* confined? Is *The Wagon Mound (No. 2)* a remoteness case or is it a standard of care problem? See Green. "*The Wagon Mound No. 2* —Foreseeability Revised" (1967), Utah L. Rev. 197. Compare with *Bolton* v. *Stone, supra.*

2. This test for determining the limits of liability for negligent conduct—that of foresight of a *possibility* of damage, rather than its "reasonable probability"— as enunciated in *The Wagon Mound (No. 2),* has lain largely dormant for years, while *The Wagon Mound (No. 1)* occupied centre stage. Hailed by some scholars, it has been viewed rather skeptically by others. Some have argued that *The Wagon Mound (No. 2)* test is little different than the *Re Polemis* test, since all "direct" consequences must be considered foreseeable as "possible". Others have suggested that the place of *The Wagon Mound (No. 2)* is limited only to conduct that is "unlawful", "unjustifiable" and totally devoid of any social utility, such as the act of illegally spilling oil into the water in Sydney harbour, as occurred in *The Wagon Mound (No. 2)* case.

3. There have been several instances recently where courts have used the language of "possibility" based on *The Wagon Mound (No. 2).* It is too early to tell whether a significant shift is coming, but it is worth noting these instances. For example, Mr. Justice Dickson has explained *The Wagon Mound (No. 2)* as follows:

> "These words would suggest that recovery may be had, provided the event giving rise to the damage is not regarded as 'impossible', and even though it 'very rarely happened', 'only in very exceptional circumstances'. The test of foreseeability of damage becomes a question of what is possible rather than what is probable."

See *Hoffer* v. *School District of Assiniboine South* (1971), 21 D.L.R. (3d) 608, at p. 613; affd [1973] 6 W.W.R. 765 (S.C.C.). See also *McKenzie* v. *Hyde* (1967), 64 D.L.R. (2d) 362 (Man. Q.B.), at p. 376:

"The injury complained of was of a class or character foreseeable as a possible result of the negligence."

4. Mr. Justice Ruttan of the British Columbia Supreme Court relied on this statement and *The Wagon Mound (No. 2)* when he recently held liable the government of British Columbia for negligent highway construction in building a centre median only 18" high instead of 30" high so that it did not prevent an accident. He concluded:

"So here there was a real risk, however remote, and it was very simple to remove the risk with no great expense or inconvenience."

See *Malat* v. *Bjornson* (1978), 6 C.C.L.T. 142 (B.C.), at p. 152.

5. The most recent reliance on this possibility test was that of Arnup J.A. in *Price* v. *Milawski* (1977), 82 D.L.R. (3d) 130 (Ont. C.A.), where he stated:

"[A] person doing a negligent act may, in circumstances lending themselves to that conclusion, be held liable for future damages arising in part from the subsequent negligent act of another, and in part from his own negligence, where such subsequent negligence and consequent damage were reasonably foreseeable as a *possible* result of his own negligence." [Emphasis added.]

6. In *Shirt* v. *Wyong Shire Council,* [1978] 1 N.S.W.L.R. 631, the court, relying on *Wagon Mound (No. 2),* concluded:

"It could not be said that the kind of injury the plaintiff suffered is remote according to the accepted tests. There was evidence which would have entitled the jury to hold that, if a skier is induced by negligent conduct to ski in water the depth of which varies from 3 feet 6 inches to 4 feet, there is a foreseeable possibility that, if he is thrown off his skis and precipitated headfirst into the water, he may suffer injury of the kind which occurred."

See also *Leonard* v. *Knott et al.,* [1978] 5 W.W.R. 511 (B.C.), rare medical reaction found "possible" and not "far-fetched".

7. Should this development be encouraged or discouraged? What are the advantages and disadvantages? Does it more accurately reflect the position the courts have *actually* taken in most of these remoteness cases? Is it any more "honest" than *The Wagon Mound (No. 1)* test? Would the "possibility" test lead to more or fewer remoteness cases being decided in favour of plaintiffs? Would it stimulate more or less safety effort by those engaged in risky activities?

8. In *McKenzie et al.* v. *Hyde et al.* (1967), 64 D.L.R. (2d) 362 (Man. Q.B.), liability was imposed on someone who, during digging operations, broke a gas line permitting gas to seep into a nearby basement window, ignite and explode. Mr. Justice Dickson held that these consequences were "reasonably foreseeable". His Lordship confessed that he could not say that the damage and the explosion were "freakish" or "one in a million". In *Abbott et al.* v. *Kasza,* [1975] 3 W.W.R. 163, at p. 170; varied [1976] 4 W.W.R. 20 (Alta. C.A.). McDonald J. used the words "fantastic or improbable" to convey the idea. What do you think of these words as aids in determining for which results a defendant should pay?

9. *The Restatement of Torts, Second,* § 435 reads:

Foreseeability of Harm or Manner of Its Occurrence

(1) If the actor's conduct is a substantial factor in bringing about harm to another, the fact that the actor neither foresaw nor should have foreseen the extent of the harm or the manner in which it occurred does not prevent him from being liable.

(2) The actor's conduct may be held not to be a legal cause of harm to another where after the event and looking back from the harm to the actor's negligent conduct, it appears to the court highly extraordinary that it should have brought about the harm.

Does this test help? See also § 442 and § 443.

10. See Green, "*The Wagon Mound (No. 2)* – Foreseeability Revised" (1967), Utah L. Rev. 197:

"The chief criticism that can be leveled at Lord Reid's formula is his overloading of the foreseeability concept. Foreseeability is a delightful and useful fiction with no restrictions in itself, and when linked with the fictitious reasonable man as a jury formula to determine whether a defendant failed to exercise reasonable care to avoid the risk to his victim, it serves in every case to call forth a fresh judgment. As a judge's formula it is perhaps too glaringly fictitious unless given substantive additives so as to convert it into a meaningful concept for the assessment of policy factors. That a court, exercising the function of a jury in the determination of the issue of negligence, should take into account the risks a defendant should have taken into account when engaged in conduct hurtful to the plaintiff is sensible, but it is hardly an adequate formula for determining the 'measure of damages' or extent of duty after the victim has suffered injury. Many foreseeable risks do not fall within the scope of any duty owed a plaintiff while many unforeseeable risks do fall within the duty owed him. After the event hindsight takes over and becomes the basis of judgment in measuring the adjustment that should be made; foreseeability becomes what should have been foreseen, not what was foreseen; what should have been foreseen becomes what the defendant should be liable for, and this brings into consideration the policy factors that give rationality to the law. This progression in meaning can scarcely be labeled foreseeability. There must be some more serviceable term available for describing the process of judgment in the practical affairs of everyday life."

11. This skepticism about the foresight doctrine has been echoed by Haines J. in *Attorney-General for Ontario* v. *Crompton* (1976), 74 D.L.R. (3d) 345 (Ont.), at p. 349, where an action was brought to recover the expense incurred to fight a fire caused by a car accident. Haines J. wrote:

"It has been a frequent criticism of writers and jurists alike that the foreseeability concept is a strained mode of analysis, a fiction at best justifiable as a jury formula, but one too transparent for meaningful use by Judges."

12. Professor Joseph C. Smith concludes his article "The Limits of Tort Liability in Canada: Remoteness, Foreseeability and Proximate Cause" in Linden, *Studies in Canadian Tort Law* (1968) as follows:

"The majority of negligence cases do not present problems of remoteness. Such problems only arise where there is a risk of harm which materializes and which results, as well, in damage that, because of its extent, kind, other factors bearing a cause-effect relationship, or because of its unforeseeable nature, presents a problem of proportion in relation to the degree of fault.

The underlying principle in remoteness cases appears to be that, as between a person without fault who has suffered a loss and one who has fault and his departure from the norm bears a cause-effect relationship between the damage and the departure, the one with the fault should bear the loss, except where the fault is insignificant or the damage is so extensive that it is out of all proportion in comparison with the fault. There can be no objective test for deciding when these two factors are so out of proportion that liability ought not to be imposed. This decision will be a value judgment largely dependent upon the unique facts of each particular case. The decision of the Privy Council in *The Wagon Mound (No. 2)*, for this reason, is far more significant for the law of remoteness than its decision in *The Wagon Mound (No. 1)*, since in the second *Wagon Mound* case the court articulated some of the factors relevant to its decision rather than attempting to apply a rule of thumb test. This is probably what Canadian courts do in fact, though not in word, in dealing with remoteness problems. The unique nature of each particular case would become more evident, however, if the courts would articulate the factors upon which their decision is based rather than attempting to justify their decisions in traditional terms of proximate cause or foreseeability."

LINDEN, FORESEEABILITY IN NEGLIGENCE LAW

Special Lectures of the Law Society of Upper Canada on
New Developments in the Law of Torts (1973).

A NEW APPROACH TO REMOTENESS

It must now be apparent to everyone that there are no easy answers to the remoteness and proximate cause issues. *Polemis* has been discarded. *The Wagon Mound (No. 1)* has been largely undermined. Similarly, all future attempts to resolve these cases with an automatic formula are doomed. There is no magic phrase that can furnish automatic answers to all of the freakish and bizarre situations that arise in negligence cases. These "flukes", by their very nature, cannot be tamed by legal rules.

Not every accident, however, is unique. Certain events tend to recur from time to time. For such recurring situations, we should develop stable legal rules. It should be easy to forecast the outcome of a thin-skull case, for example, because these cases recur and the rules are settled. . . .

Understandably, the courts have encountered the most difficulty in handling the results that are uncommon. On occasion, courts have been bewitched by the word foresight and, as a result, have arrived at unsatisfactory decisions. They must resist the allure of foreseeability, because its power is largely an illusion. It can be as broad or as narrow as the beholder wishes to make it. It can disguise value choices as much as causation did. If we must use the term foreseeability, we must not allow it to blind us. Foresight does not excuse courts from the onerous responsibility of making difficult decisions.

Simply stated, the remoteness problem is concerned with whether the defendant, whose conduct has fallen below the accepted standard of the community, should be relieved from paying for damage that his conduct helped to bring about. By formulating the question in this way, we spotlight the value choices that are present in the case. We should not disguise the fact that some intuition and feeling are and should be involved in this determination.

We must admit that these freakish accidents do not lend themselves to effortless resolution by the application of ready-made rules. In the memorable words of Mr. Justice Andrews in *Palsgraf* v. *Long Island Railway Co.,* what is involved here "is not logic. It is practical politics". The "policy factors that give rationality to the law" are more important considerations than foreseeability. This does not mean that foresight should be an irrelevant consideration. It suggests only that other matters, in addition to foreseeability, deserve attention. The courts, according to Mr. Justice Andrews, consider a variety of matters, like was there a "natural and continuous sequence between the cause and effect", was the conduct a "substantial factor" in producing the result, was there a "direct connection" and was the result "too remote . . . in time and space". He concluded by explaining:

> "[We] draw an uncertain and wavering line, but draw it we must as best we can. . . . It is all a question of fair judgment, always keeping in mind the fact that we endeavour to make a rule in each case that will be practical and in keeping with the general understanding of mankind."

Consequently, the courts must assess certain policy factors in the process of decision-making. If the case deals with a personal injury rather than a property loss, this should be considered. If the defendant is an industrial undertaking rather than some private citizen, this should be evaluated. The probability of insurance coverage cannot be ignored. The potential for deterrence must be examined. If there remains any prophylatic power in tort law, it would be strengthened by forcing enterprisers to pay for all the costs of their negligent activities, including the unforeseeable results, so that they will be stimulated to exercise greater care. In addition, perhaps the occasional huge award for some bizarre event will dramatize publicly the importance of safety measures. Lastly, some market deterrence may be accomplished by transferring the entire cost of mishaps to the activity which produces them. It is only after full consideration of all of these policy matters and after the deployment of each of the available tests that the courts should try to decide the case. Even then it might be wise to put the matter to the jury to solve.

In sum, it is hard to escape the conclusion that the best we can ever do is to rely on the common sense of the judge and jury. It is not an admission of defeat to admit that these judgments lie "in the realm of values and what you choose depends on what you want". It is merely being realistic.

NOTES

1. A similar view has been expressed by Morden J.A. in *Duwyn* v. *Kaprelian* (1978), 7 C.C.L.T. 121 as follows:

"Obviously there is a significant element of experience and value judgment in the ultimate application of the foresight requirement."

2. This idea has also been given support by Clement J.A. of the Alberta Court of Appeal when he said, in *Abbott et al.* v. *Kasza*, [1976] 4 W.W.R. 20, at p. 28:

"The common law has always recognized that causation is a concept that in the end result must be limited in its reach by a pragmatic consideration of consequences: the chain of cause and effect can be followed only to the point where the consequences of an act will be fairly accepted as attributable to that act in the context of the social and economic conditions then prevailing and the reasonable expectations of members of the society in the conduct of each other. . . .

The precise point at which an original cause ceases to have a consequential legal effect cannot be determined by didactic structures. . . .

. . . [T]he reach of causation is limited by what the court determines is reasonably foreseeable."

3. A helpful discussion of this problem can be found in two cases, arising out of the same facts, decided by the United States Court of Appeals, Second Circuit: *Petition of Kinsman Transit Co. "Kinsman No. 1"* (1964), 338 F. 2d 708 and *Petition of Kinsman Transit Co. "Kinsman No. 2"* (1968), 388 F. 2d 821. A ship that was negligently moored in the Buffalo River, near Buffalo, N.Y., broke loose and drifted downstream toward a drawbridge. Despite frantic telephone calls the bridge was not raised in time to prevent the ship from colliding with it and bringing it down. As a result, the river flooded, causing damage to various people. The plaintiffs in *"Kinsman No. 1"* suffered property damage as a result of the flooding. Their action was successful and an appeal was dismissed. Friendly, Circuit Judge, explained in this way:

"We see no reason why an actor engaging in conduct which entails a large risk of small damage and a small risk of other and greater damage, of the same general sort, from the same forces, and to the same class of persons, should be relieved of responsibility for the latter simply because the chance of its occurrence, if viewed alone, may not have been large enough to require the exercise of care. By hypothesis the risk of the lesser harm was sufficient to render his disregard of it actionable; the existence of a less likely additional risk that the very forces against whose action he was required to guard would produce other and greater damage than could have been reasonably anticipated should inculpate him further rather than limit his liability. This does not mean that the careless actor will always be held for all damages for which the forces that he risked were a cause in fact. Somewhere a point will be reached when courts will agree that the link has become too tenuous that what is claimed to be consequence is only fortuity. Thus, if the destruction of the Michigan Avenue Bridge had delayed the arrival of a doctor, with consequent loss of a patient's life, few judges would impose liability on any of the parties here, although the agreement in result might not be paralleled by similar unanimity in reasoning; perhaps in the long run one returns to Judge Andrews' statement in *Palsgraf,* 248 N.Y. at 354-355, 162 N.E. at 104 (dissenting opinion). "It is all a question of expediency, . . . of fair judgment, always keeping in mind the fact that we endeavor to make a rule in each case that will be practical and in keeping with the general understanding of mankind." It would be pleasant if greater certainty were possible, [Citation omitted.] but the many efforts that have been made at defining the *locus* of the "uncertain and wavering line," 248 N.Y. at 354, 162 N.E. 99, are not very promising; what courts do in such cases makes better sense than what they, or others, say. Where the line will be drawn will vary from age to age; as society has come to rely increasingly on insurance and other methods of loss-sharing, the point may lie further off than a century ago. Here it is surely more equitable that the losses from the operators' negligent failure to raise the Michigan Avenue Bridge should be ratably borne by Buffalo's taxpayers than left with the innocent victims of the flooding; yet the mind is also repelled by a solution that would impose liability solely on the City and exonerate the persons whose negligent acts of commission and omission were the precipitating force of the collision with the bridge and its sequelae. We go only so far as to hold that where, as here, the damages resulted from the same physical forces whose existence required the exercise of greater care than was displayed and were of the same general sort that was expectable, unforeseeability of the exact developments and of the extent of the loss will not limit liability. Other fact situations can be dealt with when they arise."

4. In "*Kinsman No. 2*", a claim was made by the owners of some wheat stored aboard another ship berthed in the harbour below the bridge. The plaintiff's wheat was not damaged, but as a result of the accident, it could not be unloaded because the ship could not be moved to the grain elevator which was located above the bridge. This entailed additional costs for extra transportation and storage costs as well as for the purchase of replacement wheat. Kaufman, Circuit Judge, in "*Kinsman No. 2*", observed:

"On the previous appeal we stated aptly: 'somewhere a point will be reached when courts will agree that the result has become too tenuous — that what is claimed to be consequence is only fortuity.' [Citation omitted.] We believe that this point has been reached with [these] claims. . . . The instant claims occurred only because the downed bridge made it impossible to move traffic along the river. Under all the circumstances of this case, we hold that the connection between the defendants' negligence and the claimants' damages is too tenuous and remote to permit recovery. 'The law does not spread its protection so far.' Holmes J., in *Robins Dry Dock & Repair Co.* v. *Flint* (1927), 275 U.S. 303 at 309.

In the final analysis the circumlocution whether posed in terms of "foreseeability", "duty", "proximate cause", "remoteness", etc, seems unavoidable. . . . We return to Judge Andrews' frequently quoted statement in *Palsgraf* v. *Long Island R.R.* "It is all a question of expediency, . . . of fair judgment, always keeping in mind the fact that we endeavor to make a rule in each case that will be practical and in keeping with the general understanding of mankind."

See *infra*, Chapter 10, Section B, Economic Losses.

5. Commenting on proximate cause and the role of the jury, Mr. Justice Magruder (1st Circuit) stated in *Marshall* v. *Nugent* (1955), 222 F. 2d 604:

"Speaking in general terms, the effort of the courts has been, in the development of this doctrine of proximate causation, to confine the liability of a negligent actor to those harmful consequences which result from the operation of the risk, or of a risk, the foreseeability of which rendered the defendant's conduct negligent.

Of course, putting the inquiry in these terms does not furnish a formula which automatically decides each of an infinite variety of cases. Flexibility is still preserved by the further need of defining the risk, or risks, either narrowly, or more broadly, as seems appropriate and just in the special type of case.

Regarding motor vehicle accidents in particular, one should contemplate a variety of risks which are created by negligent driving. There may be injuries resulting from a direct collision between the carelessly driven car and another vehicle. But such direct collision may be avoided, yet the plaintiff may fall and injure himself in frantically racing out of the way of the errant car . . . . Or the plaintiff may be knocked down and injured by a human stampede as the car rushes toward a crowded safety zone . . . Or the plaintiff may faint from intense excitement stimulated by the near collision, and in falling sustain a fractured skull. . . . Or the plaintiff may suffer a miscarriage or other physical illness as a result of intense nervous shock incident to a hair-raising escape . . . . This bundle of risks could be enlarged indefinitely with a little imagination. In a traffic mix-up due to negligence, before the disturbed waters have become placid and normal again, the unfolding of events between the culpable act and the plaintiff's eventual injury may be bizarre indeed; yet the defendant may be liable for the result . . . . In such a situation, it would be impossible for a person in the defendant's position to predict in advance just how his negligent act would work out to another's injury. Yet this in itself is no bar to recovery . . . .

When an issue of proximate cause arises in a borderline case, as not infrequently happens, we leave it to the jury with appropriate instructions. We do this because it is deemed wise to obtain the judgment of the jury, reflecting as it does the earthy viewpoint of the common man — the prevalent sense of the community — as to whether the causal relation between the negligent act and the plaintiff's harm which in fact was a consequence of the tortious act is sufficiently close to make it just and expedient to hold the defendant answerable in damages. That is what the courts have in mind when they say the question of proximate causation is one of fact for the jury. It is similar to the issue of negligence, which is left to the jury as an issue of fact . . . .

In dealing with these issues of negligence and proximate causation, the trial Judge has to make a preliminary decision whether the issues are such that reasonable men might differ on the inferences to be drawn. This preliminary decision is said to be a question of law, for it is one which the Court has to decide, but it is nevertheless necessarily the exercise of a judgment on the facts."

Should questions such as these be left to a Canadian jury to decide? Can this be done if the issue is classified as one of duty or of remoteness, rather than one of proximate cause?

Study again the excerpt from J.C. Smith, *The Mystery of Duty, supra.*

C. INTERVENING FORCES

HARRIS v. T.T.C. AND MILLER

Supreme Court of Canada. [1967] S.C.R. 460

The infant appellant sustained injuries when he was a passenger in a bus owned by the respondent Transit Commission and operated by its servant, the second respondent Miller. As the bus in question pulled away from a bus stop, it brushed against a steel pole which was set in the sidewalk some 5½ inches from the curb with the result that the infant appellant's arm, which he had extended through a window in order to point out some object to his companion, was crushed and broken. In an action for damages brought on behalf of the infant appellant, the trial judge found that the negligence of the bus operator was a proximate cause of the collision but that the appellant was also guilty of negligence in putting his arm out of the window of the bus, having regard to the fact that a by-law of the respondent Commission, of which the appellant was aware, prohibited passengers from doing this and was posted in the bus together with a sign below the window reading: "Keep arm in". The trial judge divided the fault equally between the parties. On appeal, the Court of Appeal found that on the facts of the case there could be no recovery. With leave, an appeal was brought to the Supreme Court of Canada.

Ritchie J. (Cartwright, Martland, Spence JJ., concurring): . . . The decision of the Court of Appeal was rendered orally by Laskin J.A. at the conclusion of the argument. The learned judge did not refer to any authorities but reached his conclusion on the following grounds:

> "We are of the opinion that there was no negligence in this case attributable to the defendants which, as a matter of law, operated in favour of the infant plaintiff. On the facts, he was the author of his own misfortune. We do not think that the bus operator could reasonably be expected to foresee that the infant plaintiff would have his arm in the position in which it was outside the window when he pulled away from the curb. The evidence is clear that the infant plaintiff knew of the warning which was posted on the window ledge to keep his arm in, and it was his carelessness for his own safety and not any carelessness that may have existed in the way in which the driver pulled away from the curb that was the operative cause of the accident. . . ."

[The court felt there was no voluntary assumption of risk.]

It will also be observed that Mr. Justice Laskin did not consider that the bus driver could reasonably be expected to foresee that the little boy's arm would have been out of the window.

In my opinion we are relieved from the task of speculating on whether the bus driver could reasonably have foreseen such a thing by reason of the fact that he indicates in his own evidence that he was aware of the propensity of children on his own bus to put their arms and indeed their heads out of the window, notwithstanding the warning which the Commission had posted. . . .

I have no difficulty in drawing the conclusion from [the] evidence that the bus driver knew that children had a tendency to put their arms out of the windows and that he could therefore reasonably be expected to foresee that such a thing would happen in the case of the infant plaintiff. . . .

The relevant by-law of the respondent Commission, which was approved by the Ontario Municipal Board and therefore has the force of law by virtue of s. 167 of The Railway Act, R.S.O. 1950, c. 331, provided as follows:

> No person shall ride or stand on any exterior portion of any car or bus operated by the Commission nor lean out of or project any portion of his body through any window of such car or bus nor enter any such bus at other than the designated entries.

It was contended on behalf of the respondent that by passing this by-law and otherwise giving notice to its passengers of the danger of projecting any portion of their body through any window of the bus, the respondent Commission had fully discharged its duty of care in relation to the dangers involved in such conduct and that it owed no further duty to them in this regard. There may be circumstances in which a public carrier can discharge its duty to its passengers in relation to a specific danger by passing such a by-law and giving such notice, but when, as in this case, the respondent's negligence was an effective cause of the accident and its driver should have foreseen the likelihood of children passengers extending their arms through the window notwithstanding the warning, different considerations apply and in my opinion it becomes a case where the damages should be apportioned in proportion to the degree of fault found against the parties respectively. . . .

[Judson J. dissented.]

NOTES

1. Is this case a remoteness case or a standard of care problem? Is there a duty issue? Could it possibly be treated as any one of these? If so, which is preferable and why?

2. When ice cream is sold to children from trucks on city streets, are the ice cream vendors obligated to protect their young customers from the danger of traffic? See *Gambino* v. *Dileo*, [1971] 2 O.R. 131; *Arnold* v. *Teno* (1978), 3 C.C.L.T. 272 (S.C.C.). Are parents required to take steps to protect their children in these circumstances? *(Ibid.).* Are schools responsible for supervising children during their various activities to prevent injury to them? See *Dziwenka* v. *R.,* [1972] S.C.R. 419; *Thornton* v. *Board of School Trustees of School Dist. No. 57 (Prince George)* (1978), 3 C.C.L.T. 257 (S.C.C.). Can a school be liable if a child on one of its buses runs into the path of a car after being let off at a dangerous place? See *Mattinson* v. *Wonnacott* (1975), 8 O.R. (2d) 654. Can a teenager be liable for lending his motorcycle to another unlicensed teenager who negligently injures himself? (See *Stermer* v. *Lawson* (1977), 79 D.L.R. (3d) 366, *per* Fulton J. percentage varied (1980), 11 C.C.L.T. 76 (C.A.)). What if he lends it to a drunken person, who would be competent if sober? *Ibid.* See also *Hempler* v. *Todd* (1970), 14 D.L.R. (3d) 637 (Man. Q.B.)). What about contributory negligence?

3. In *Hatfield* v. *Pearson* (1956), 6 D.L.R. (2d) 593 (B.C.C.A.), the defendant kept an unloaded rifle in his basement on a beam seven feet above the floor. Ammunition was kept in a kitchen drawer. The defendant's son, 13½ years old, in deliberate disobedience to his father's orders, took the gun and some ammunition and so carelessly handled the gun that the plaintiff was injured. The defendant had allowed his son, during the six months since he purchased the gun, to fire it on four different occasions while under the defendant's supervision. The defendant had instructed his son as to the use and danger of the gun and the son had been told more than once not to touch it. The son was intelligent and obedient, and capable of realizing the danger involved in handling a gun. Further, the son had promised not to touch the gun. In an action for damages the defendant was held not liable. While the defendant anticipated a risk of the son's use of the gun, he had guarded against it sufficiently by his order not to touch it, the resulting promise, and keeping the gun in a way to exclude thoughtless intermeddling. There was no reason to anticipate the failure of these precautions and the defendant had, therefore, acted as a reasonably prudent man.

4. Compare *Sullivan* v. *Creed,* [1904] 2 Ir. R. 317, where the defendant after a hunting trip left his loaded gun on the path leading from his house to the road. His son, aged 15-16, picked it up and pointed the gun at the plaintiff. It went off and struck the plaintiff in the eye.

Gibson J. stated: "The question before us is whether, under the circumstances proved in the case, having regard to place, time, and persons likely to see the weapon, a prudent person ought to have foreseen danger to others from the gun being left where it was, exposed on full cock." Although the evidence was meagre, liability was imposed on the directness theory, the court concluding:

"The circumstances of alleged negligence directly causing the misfortune are these: the gun was left at full cock, beside and in the view of a footpath where it would be seen by anyone using the path. It was an inviting position to any person, who noticed it; the day and hour would tend to convey that the gun was unloaded. Defendant's son, of fifteen years of age, took it up in that mistaken belief, and tricking with it caused the injury. The boy was not of tender years, but his age was such . . . as to make it desirable not to place dangerous articles, such as loaded firearms, in his way, without caution or warning. Boys of fifteen are just as mischievous and likely to play with guns as children of ten or twelve."

See also *Bishop* v. *Sharrow* (1975), 8 O.R. (2d) 649.

See generally Alexander, "Tort Responsibility of Parents and Teachers for Damage Caused by Children" (1965), 16 U. of T.L.J. 165; Dunlop, "Torts Relating to Infants" (1966), 5 West. L. Rev. 116. See also *Ryan* v. *Hickson* (1974), 7 O.R. (2d) 352, where Mr. Justice Goodman held two fathers negligent for the way they supervised their sons in the operation of snowmobiles. See also *Hoffer* v. *School District of Assiniboine*, [1971] 4 W.W.R. 746; affd [1973] 6 W.W.R. 765 (S.C.C.).

5. In *Scott* v. *Philp* (1922), 52 O.L.R. 513, the defendant, a doctor, parked his car in front of a patient's house by turning his front wheels into the kerb. He did not set his brakes. A boy of nine got in the car in his absence and as a result of his action the car rolled down an incline and damaged the plaintiff's house. The defendant was not held liable. The court said that if the car had been set in motion by the movement of traffic the defendant might have been liable. The court also said that "in order to prove negligence" a finding was necessary that the defendant ought to have anticipated the event that put the car in motion.

6. What if the car had been parked in front of a school? See *Hewson et al.* v. *Red Deer et al.* (1975), 63 D.L.R. (3d) 168 (Alta.), where a tractor, owned by the city, was being used to level and stockpile gravel near a street, and near Red Deer College, which was in session. The operator left the tractor with the key in the ignition and the cab unlocked. When he returned it was gone. He traced the tracks and found that it had crashed into the plaintiff's house. The defendant argued, *inter alia,* that the actions of an unknown person constituted a break in the chain of causation. Kirby J. rejected this contention and said:

> "It seems to me that it was reasonably foreseeable that any one of such persons [students or staff of the college or persons using the street] might become aware that the tractor was being left at the stockpile unattended and might be tempted to put it in motion. The elementary precautions referred to above [i.e., remove ignition key, engage safety lever or lock cab door] were not taken to prevent this happening. I am of the view, therefore, that the maxim *novus actus interveniens* is not applicable."

Compare with *Wright* v. *McCrea*, [1965] 1 O.R. 300 (C.A.), where the defendant's bulldozer was set in motion by a stranger, damaging the plaintiff's house. In dismissing the action, Schroeder J.A. explained:

> "There is nothing in the evidence in the present case which supports the view that the defendant should have anticipated interference by third persons with the operation of the bulldozer. To set it in motion was a complicated procedure and while the manufacturer had not equipped the bulldozer with a locking device, nevertheless, the appellant had shut off the motor, had lowered the blade into the ground and had done everything that could reasonably have been required of him to prevent any interference with the machine by unauthorized strangers. In a period of 16 years he had never encountered a similar experience and the evidence strongly suggests that he was not bound to anticipate such intervention on the part of strangers as gave rise to the occurrence in question. The act which caused the plaintiff's damages was, therefore, not the act of the defendant but the act of unauthorized strangers which constitutes a *novus actus interveniens,* which, in my view, was not reasonably foreseeable."

Are these cases in conflict or is it just that the circumstances were different?

7. In *Bradford* v. *Kanellos*, [1971] 2 O.R. 393, 18 D.L.R. (3d) 60 (C.A.); affd. (1974), 40 D.L.R. (3d) 578 (S.C.C.), a flash fire was negligently caused in a restaurant. An employee activated an extinguisher system which released some gas and created a hissing sound. On hearing this, a patron shouted that gas was escaping and that there was a danger of an explosion. A stampede of patrons followed in which the plaintiff was injured. The original wrongdoer was ultimately relieved of liability, although held liable initially.

At trial, Lane Co. Ct. J. stated: "Whoever yelled that out almost qualifies in my opinion for that type of idiotic person. But this is foreseeable; human nature is rather unstable in emergencies and must be recognized as being unstable in emergencies. . . . The panic in the restaurant could have been foreseen."

Reversing the trial judgment, Mr. Justice Schroeder said: ". . . The *causa proxima* of the plaintiff's injuries was the unauthorized and unforeseeable act of the patron who made the exclamation referred to and the disorderly exit made by the other customers who took sudden flight. This affords a clear example of a *novus actus interveniens*".

In the Supreme Court of Canada, Mr. Justice Martland (Judson and Ritchie JJ. concurring) declared that the injuries "resulted from the hysterical conduct of a customer which occurred when the safety appliance properly fulfilled its function. Was that consequence fairly to be regarded as within the risk created by the respondent's negligence in permitting an undue quantity of grease to accumulate on the grill? The Court of Appeal has found that it was not and I agree with that finding."

Mr. Justice Spence (Laskin J., concurring), dissented and observed: "I am not of the opinion that the persons who shouted the warning of what they were certain was an impending explosion were negligent. I am, on the other hand, of the opinion that they acted in a very human and usual way and that their actions . . . were utterly foreseeable and were a part of the natural consequence of events leading inevitably to the plaintiff's injury . . . Even if the actions of those who called out 'gas' and 'it is going to explode' were negligent. . . then I am of the opinion that the plaintiffs would still have a right of action against the defendants. . . ."

Which of these opinions do you prefer? What if no one had shouted but the plaintiff had seen the fire, attempted to escape and had fallen, injuring herself? Compare with *Mauney* v. *Gulf Refining Co.* (1942), 9 So. 2d 780 (Miss S.C.) and *Zervobeakos* v. *Zervobeakos* (1970), 8 D.L.R. (3d) 377 (N.S.C.A.).

8. Compare with *Goodyear Tire & Rubber Co. of Canada Ltd.* v. *MacDonald* (1974), 51 D.L.R. (3d) 623 (N.S.C.A.), where a sign that fell off the defendant's truck caused a collision, damaging the plaintiff's vehicle. The plaintiff's driver was unable to stop the plaintiff's vehicle in time to avoid the accident because of a patch of fresh tar 15 feet long on the road. The defendant argued that the presence of this tar was a *novus actus interveniens* which absolved him of liability. Mr. Justice Cooper of the Nova Scotia Court of Appeal rejected this argument and explained that a *novus actus interveniens* was a "conscious act of human origin intervening between a negligent act or omission of a defendant and the occurrence by which the plaintiff suffers damage . . . . There was no such intervening act here."

9. Plaintiff and his car are being transported by ship across some water. A voice says, "We're here." Thinking wrongly that it was an attendant speaking, plaintiff backs his car up, but, because they were not in fact at the dock, ends up in the water. Liability? Compare with *Richard* v. *C.N.R.* (1970), 15 D.L.R. (3d) 732 (P.E.I.S.C.).

10. In *M'Kenna* v. *Stephens and Hall*, [1932] 2 I.R. 112, the defendant company were contractors and, in the course of building, it became necessary for them to erect a hoarding on a public thoroughfare. By the operation of a statute, no hoarding blocking a sidewalk was to be erected until a timber platform, provided with a strong hand-rail, was substituted for the way blocked off. In the present case the defendant company failed to provide a platform and hand-rail. As the hoarding blocked the sidewalk the plaintiff was forced to walk on the carriage-way past the hoarding. While so doing, she was struck by a motor lorry driven by the defendant Stephens. The plaintiff brought action against both Stephens and the defendant company alleging negligence against both. At the trial the jury found Stephens was negligent in driving the motor lorry, and that the defendant company was negligent in not taking reasonable precautions in providing a safe footway for persons lawfully passing in front of their premises, and in not complying with the statute.

Stephens obtained judgment on the ground that the action against him had not been brought within the proper limitation period. Judgment was entered against the defendant company. On appeal the judgment was upheld. "There ought to have been a footway. To protect them form what? What is the risk? The risk of being run down. . . . One is not entitled to make obvious occasions for the negligence of another." O'Connor L.J., dissented: "Being on the street [is not] the direct cause of a collision with a vehicle negligently driven. The negligence is the cause: not the presence on the spot when the negligence is operative."

11. Does a motorist have to foresee the negligence of another motorist? Can a driver going through a green light be partially to blame for not avoiding a collision with another vehicle which has gone through a red light? See *Smith* v. *Sambuco* (1978), 5 C.C.L.T. 215 (Ont. Co.Ct.).

12. In *Canphoto Ltd. et al.* v. *Aetna Roofing (1965) Ltd. et al.*, [1965] 3 W.W.R. 116 (Man. Q.B.), the employees of the defendant company left three propane gas tanks in a public laneway over a weekend. In so doing, they breached a provincial regulation concerning the storage of such tanks with respect to the required distances which they should be kept from buildings and fences. They were also found to be negligent in failing to chain the tanks closed and in an upright position. During the night someone apparently meddled with the tanks, causing a serious fire which damaged the plaintiff's premises.

Wilson J. gave judgment for the plaintiff, rejecting the contention of the defendants that the meddling with the tanks constituted an intervening act which broke the chain of causation. Citing Greer L.J. in *Haynes* v. *Harwood*, [1953] 1 K.B. 146, he stated: "If what is relied upon as *novus actus interveniens* is the very kind of thing which is likely to happen if the want of care which is alleged takes place, the principle embodied in the maxim is no defence. . . ." Referring to Lush J., in another case, Mr. Justice Wilson found that the intervention was not a "fresh, independent cause" of the damage and that ". . . the person guilty of the original negligence will still be the effective cause if he ought reasonably to have anticipated such interventions. . . ".

13. Defendant mistakenly delivers some highly inflammable material to plaintiff's premises. Someone comes along, lights a cigarette and quite innocently drops the match into the material. A fire breaks out. Is the defendant liable? What if the person, as a joke, drops the match into the material in order to see if it will burn? What if the match is dropped maliciously? Compare with *Philco Radio & Television Corp.* v. *J. Spurling Ltd.*, [1949] 2 K.B. 33, [1949] 2 All E.R. 882 (C.A.).

14. Would the prison authorities be liable if some inmates escaped and did damage to the plaintiff's property during the course of the escape? *Dorset Yacht* v. *Home Office*, [1970] 2 All E.R. 294 (H.C.). Would they be liable if a dangerous prisoner injured another prisoner? See *MacLean* v. *R.*, [1973] S.C.R. 2; *cf. Ellis* v. *Home Office*, [1973] 2 All E.R. 149. See also *Lawson* v. *Wellesley Hospital*, [1978] 1 S.C.R. 893, hospital can be liable for mental patient injuring another. Would the prison authorities be liable if a prisoner, let out on a day pass, negligently drove his vehicle and injured the plaintiff? What does it depend upon? See *Toews* v. *MacKenzie* (1977), 81 D.L.R. (3d) 302 (B.C., Hutcheon J.).

STANSBIE v. TROMAN

Court of Appeal. [1948] 2 K.B. 48; [1948] 1 All E.R. 599

Appeal from Birmingham county court.

On January 14, 1947, the plaintiff, Stansbie, a decorator, was at work in the house of the defendant, Troman. Between 1.30 and 2 p.m. Mrs. Troman, the householder's wife, left the house, having called up to the decorator that she was going out. The decorator was thus left alone in the house. At about half past three he went out to a neighbouring shop to buy a roll of wallpaper. On leaving the house he fastened back by its catch the latch of the yale lock on the front door, and pulled the door to. The door was then unlocked, but held to by its ordinary mortise lock with a handle, and it was only necessary to turn the handle to open the door. The decorator had some difficulty in obtaining the paper, and did not return until about 5.15 p.m. He then found the front door open. He waited until 8 p.m. and afterwards learnt from the householder that a quantity of articles, including a diamond bracelet and clothes, had been stolen. The value of those articles, £334 15s., was the subject of counter-claim by the householder in an action by the decorator for the price of work done.

The county court judge, in a reserved judgment, stated that the first question which he had to investigate was whether any duty was owed by the plaintiff decorator to the defendant householder; secondly, whether there had been any breach of that duty; and, thirdly, whether the damage had resulted from that breach. With regard to the first question, after referring to *Donoghue* v. *Stevenson* he said: "But I think that when the decorator was left alone in the house he was in a position to exercise control over access into the house, and this put him in such a relation to the householder that, in exercising such control, he ought to have had in mind the safety of the householder's goods which were in the house." He therefore gave judgment for the householder. The decorator now appealed.

Tucker L.J.: It was argued for the decorator that no duty was owed, that the duty must arise from the relationship between the parties, and that it must be a duty within the scope of the contractual relationship existing between them. I agree that the duty must be within the scope of the contractual relationship between these two persons, but I think that that contractual relationship did impose a duty on the plaintiff decorator to take reasonable care with regard to the state of the premises if he left them during the performance of his work. That, I think, was the measure of the duty.

The next question is whether there was a breach of that duty. If I am right as to the existence of the duty, I think that there can be no question but that there was a breach of it, for I do not think that it was acting reasonably, that it was taking reasonable care, to leave this empty house for a period of two hours with the front door in that condition. The county court judge, in considering that matter, applied the test of the ordinary reasonable man, quoting the words of Greer L.J., in *Hall* v. *Brooklands Auto Racing Club,* [1933] 1 K.B. 205: "the man who takes the magazines at home, and in the evenings pushes the lawn mower in his shirt sleeves", and said that he thought that the decorator "having fastened back the latch of the yale lock, ought not to have left the house more than a few moments, if at all, and in staying away for as long as two hours was guilty of negligence". I agree with that finding.

With regard to the third question, the judge said that he had found considerable difficulty and that his view had wavered, and continued: "It seems clear that the negligence of the decorator was not the direct cause of the householder's loss. The direct cause was the crime of the thief. The decorator plaintiff was no party to the crime, which was a thing that he never intended. On the other hand, the main purpose of the latch is to keep out thieves, so far as the latch will serve. If the latch be fastened back, the house needs watching; and therefore the negligence of the decorator really consisted in failure to take reasonable care to guard against the very thing that happened. Forcing a door or breaking a window takes time and may attract attention. The decorator's negligence increased the problematic risk of the theft; and the risk matured into a certainty."

[Counsel for the decorator] referred to *Weld-Blundell* v. *Stephens,* [1920]

A.C. 956, and, in particular to the following passage in the speech of Lord Sumner: "In general (apart from special contracts and relations and the maxim *respondeat superior*), even though A is in fault, he is not responsible for injury to C which B, a stranger to him, deliberately chooses to do. Though A may have given the occasion for B's mischievous activity, B then becomes a new and independent cause." I do not think that Lord Sumner would have intended that very general statement to apply to the facts of a case such as the present where, as the judge points out, the act of negligence itself consisted in the failure to take reasonable care to guard against the very thing that in fact happened. The reason why the decorator owed a duty to the householder to leave the premises in a reasonably secure state was because otherwise thieves or dishonest persons might gain access to them; and it seems to me that if the decorator was, as I think he was, negligent in leaving the house in this condition, it was as a direct result of his negligence that the thief entered by the front door, which was left unlocked, and stole these valuable goods. Except that I would have phrased the nature of the duty somewhat differently from the way in which the county court judge put it, I am in entire agreement with his judgment, and in my view the appeal fails.

[Somervell L.J., and Roxburgh L.J., concurred.]

NOTES

1. Would the decorator have been liable if an arsonist had entered the house and burned it down while he was gone? What if a murderer had entered and killed one of the children who were left unattended? Would it make any difference if it was generally known that an arsonist or a murderer was on the loose in the area?

2. Donald leaves Peter's car on a lonely street with the keys in it. Someone comes along and helps himself to the vehicle. Liability to Peter for the loss of his car? Cf. *Walker* v. *De Luxe Cab Ltd.,* [1944] 3 D.L.R. 175; Wright, "Note" (1944), 22 Can. Bar Rev. 725; *Thiele et al.* v. *Rod Service (Ottawa)* (1964), 45 D.L.R. (2d) 503 (Ont. C.A.). If the car thief negligently runs someone down, is Donald liable to that person? Would it make any difference if the thief had been drunk and the car had been left in front of the tavern in which he had been drinking? See *Hergenrether* v. *East* (1964), 61 Cal. 2d 440, 393 P. 2d 164. *Cf. Richards* v. *Stanley* (1954), 43 Cal. 2d 60, 271 P. 2d 23; *Schaff* v. *R.W. Claxton, Inc.* (1944), 144 F. 2d 532. Would a criminal statute that forbids leaving a car unlocked make any difference? See *Ross* v. *Hartman* (1943), 139 F. 2d 14. *Cf. Cornits* v. *Wittkop* (1959), 355 Mich. 170, 93 N.W. 2d 906.

3. A railroad carried a young girl past her station, letting her off near a hobo encampment, which was known to be full of criminal types. On her way back to town, she was raped by two different individuals. Is the railway liable? See *Hines* v. *Garrett* (1921), 131 Va. 125, 108 S.E. 690.

4. Could the police be held liable to the family of an informer who is killed as a result of inadequate protection afforded to him by the police? See *Schuster* v. *City of New York* (1958), 5 N.Y. 2d 75, 180 N.Y.S. 2d 265, 154 N.E. 2d 534.

5. An insurance company issued a policy on the life of a small child, payable to her aunt as beneficiary. The aunt had no insurable interest in the child and so the policy was void. The aunt murdered the child, was tried and executed. Could the parents of the child succeed in an action against the insurance company? See *Liberty Nat. Life Ins. Co.* v. *Weldon* (1958), 267 Ala. 171, 100 So. 2d 696; *Ramey* v. *Carolina Life Ins.* Co. (1964), 244 S.C. 16, 135 S.E. 2d 362. Is an airport insurance vending company liable if someone buys insurance from it, boards a plane, and causes it to crash? See *Galanis* v. *Mercury Int. Ins.* (1967), 247 Cal. App. 2d 690, 55 Cal. Rptr. 890.

6. Can a psychiatrist be liable if his patient confides to him that he plans to kill someone and then does so? See Fleming and Maximov, "The Patient or His

Victim: The Therapist's Dilemma" (1974), 62 Cal. L. Rev. 1025. See *Tarasoff* case 529 P. 2d 553. What if a patient kills himself? See *Haines* v. *Bellissimo* (1977), 82 D.L.R. (3d) 215 (Ont.).

D. RECURRING SITUATIONS

1. Rescue

HORSLEY et al. v. MACLAREN et al.

"The Ogopogo"

Supreme Court of Canada. (1972), 22 D.L.R. (3d) 545;
11 D.L.R. (3d) 277 (C.A.); 4 D.L.R. (3d) 557

The defendant, MacLaren, owned a cabin cruiser named The Ogopogo. On May 7, 1961, a cool spring day, he invited some friends to accompany him on a cruise on Lake Ontario. After visiting the Port Credit Yacht Club, they headed out into the harbour to return to Oakville, from where the cruise began. Brisk winds came up and made the water choppy, driving most of the passengers below. Matthews remained on the deck for a while, but he soon got up and proceeded toward the stern of the boat. For no apparent reason, he lost his footing and fell off the boat into the 44°F. water of the lake. This mishap was not caused by the negligence of anyone. Another passenger, Jones, exclaimed, "Roly's overboard." The craft had reached a point 40 to 50 feet beyond Matthews, and the appellant put the motor into reverse and backed the cruiser at once toward the man in the water. When it was within 4 or 5 feet of Matthews the engine was put into neutral position, but the wind caused the boat to drift away towards the port side. When Matthews was 10 feet from the vessel the appellant again put the engine into reverse and reached a point within 3 or 4 feet of him and he was drifting down towards the boat. At this juncture the passenger Marck was attempting to retrieve Matthew's body with a pikepole, but his efforts were unsuccessful.

Matthews had been in the water for a period estimated at approximately 3 to 4 minutes and at all times he was motionless, his head was well above the surface of the water and his arms were extended in front of him in a slightly elevated position, but his eyes were glassy. A life ring or life jacket thrown to him went unobserved and he was not making the slightest effort to assist himself. Marck came within 1 or 2 feet of him with the pikepole but Matthews did not react in any way and presented every appearance of having lost consciousness.

The appellant had no knowledge of Horsley's experience with watercraft and in the early stages of the journey had therefore warned him to remain in the cockpit or cabin and not to go on deck. When Horsley observed the difficulty which was being experienced in the effort to rescue Matthews, he removed his trousers and dived into the water, emerging from his dive approximately 10 feet away from Matthews who, at this time, was 3 or 4 feet from the vessel. A few seconds after Horsley's act of diving into the water Matthew's body sank below the surface and under the bottom of the boat on its starboard side near the stern. It disappeared from view and has never been recovered.

On observing what had happened to Matthews, Mrs. Jones, an experienced cold-water swimmer, plunged into the water in an effort to keep Matthews's head above water but she never had an opportunity to afford him this aid. Fearing for his wife's safety Jones, who was himself an experienced boatman, took the controls and caused the boat to describe a circle, moved it forward and brought its starboard side alongside his wife. She was thrashing about in the water and extended her arms towards MacLaren and Marck who succeeded in grasping her. Jones, responding to a call from MacLaren and Marck, came to their assistance and the trio succeeded in bringing her aboard.

MacLaren then resumed control of the vessel and drove it in a forward direction towards Horsley whose body was also retrieved from the water. From the moment that he re-appeared after his dive into the water, although he was known to have some ability as a swimmer, Horsley made no effort to help himself; his feet were down, he was floating with his head well above the surface of the water and his arms were extended forward, but when the rescuers reached him his head went under the water at that precise moment. The water of Lake Ontario is very cold in the hottest season of the year, but on the day in question it was bitterly cold.

A pathologist found that Horsley's death was caused by shock resulting from sudden immersion in the cold water.

Since the body of Matthews was never recovered, the exact cause of death remained unknown, but it was believed that he also died of a heart attack.

There had been some consumption of beer and champagne but there was no finding that any one was intoxicated as a result.

At the trial, Matthew's family was denied recovery on the ground that there was no evidence of causal relation between his death and MacLaren's conduct. Horsley's family, however, was successful. On appeal, the Ontario Court of Appeal reversed the decision and dismissed the Horsley action. [The Matthews did not appeal.] The Supreme Court of Canada affirmed this disposition in a three-two decision.

Lacourcière J. (at trial): I turn now to the claim made on behalf of the deceased Horsley, which rests on different legal considerations: Horsley, who was at the stern and witness to the abortive rescue attempts, voluntarily dived in to assist his friend Matthews. The question is whether Horsley's generous impulse was the natural and probable result of the defendant's negligence in effecting Matthews' rescue, or in other words, was Horsley's voluntary rescue attempt within the ambit of risk created by the defendant's negligence, in a reasonably foreseeable way? . . . . The leading decision which comes to mind is the one of the Court of Appeals of New York in *Wagner v. International Ry. Co.* (1921), 133 N.E. 437. In that case the plaintiff had fallen off a bridge in attempting the rescue of a fellow passenger who had fallen overboard off an electric railway car. The Court decided that the question of the defendant's negligence toward the rescuer was a question for the jury. The oft-quoted words of Cardozo J., speaking for the Court, appear at pp. 437-8:

"Danger invites rescue. The cry of distress is the summons to relief. The law does not ignore these reactions of the mind in tracing conduct to its consequences. It recognizes them as normal. It places their effects within the range of the natural and probable. The wrong that imperils life is a wrong to the imperiled victim; it is a wrong also to his rescuer. The state that leaves an opening in a bridge is liable to the child that falls into the stream, but liable also to the parent who plunges to its aid. . . . The railroad company whose train approaches without a signal is a wrongdoer toward the traveler surprised between the rails, but a wrongdoer also to the bystander who drags him from the path. . . . The risk of rescue, if only it be not wanton, is born of the occasion. The emergency begets the man. The wrongdoer may not have foreseen the coming of a deliverer. He is accountable as if he had."

The decision quoted, while not binding on this Court, sets out a principle which has been accepted by English and Canadian Courts. . . .

Before fastening liability on the defendant, this Court must decide whether Horsley's action was a "futile sacrifice" or a "wanton exposure to danger that was useless" to use the words in *Wagner* v. *International Ry. Co.,* 133 N.E. 437. Again, quoting the words of Cardozo J. in meeting this defence, at p. 438:

> "Rescue could not charge the company with liability if rescue was condemned by reason. 'Errors of judgment', however, would not count against him if they resulted 'from the excitement and confusion of the moment'."

In the excitement of the emergency, I am of opinion that Horsley's conduct was not futile, reckless, rash, wanton or foolhardy; that Horsley was not guilty of contributory negligence, and that the plaintiffs are not debarred because, in the light of present knowledge, it is doubtful if Matthews could be helped. ". . . a rescuer is not condemned of contributory negligence, unless his attempt was utterly foolhardy": *Fleming on Torts,* 3rd ed., p. 167, quoting *Baker* v. *Hopkins,* [1959] 3 All E.R. 225; *Morgan* v. *Aylen,* [1942] 1 All E.R. 489.

The following allegations of negligence were made against Horsley in the statement of defence:

> "6. This Defendant states that the unfortunate death of the said John Horsley, deceased, was caused solely by reason of his own negligence, particulars of which negligent acts are as follows:
>
> > (a) He voluntarily assumed the risk of injury to himself in diving into the water under the circumstances which existed at that time which made his own rescue improbable;
> > (b) He failed to seek permission from this Defendant, the master of the vessel, before entering the water;
> > (c) He took an extremely imprudent and unseamanlike course under the circumstances at that time;
> > (d) He failed to take proper precautions for his own safety in wearing a life jacket or securing himself to the vessel by a rope or by having others on the vessel stand by him;
> > (e) When he saw that the deceased, Roland Edgar Matthews, was in difficulty in the water he placed himself in the same position as the said deceased, Matthews, by entering the water which was so cold which would render his presence useless in the water."

Wearing a life-jacket or securing himself to a life line would indeed have been more prudent, but Horsley's impulsive act without such precautions was the result of the excitement, haste and confusion of the moment, and cannot be said to constitute contributory negligence.

I find also that the defence based on *volenti non fit injuria,* or voluntary assumption of risk, cannot prevail: although it was suggested in argument, it is not pleaded (for obvious reasons) that the deceased Horsley, knowing that the defendant was under the influence of liquor, voluntarily assumed the risk attendant upon his operation of the boat, and even if pleaded, I would not be prepared to find that " 'the plaintiff freely and voluntarily, with full knowledge of the nature and extent of the risk he ran, impliedly *agreed* to incur it' " (in the words of Wills J. in *Osborne* v. *London & North Western Ry. Co.* (1888), 21 Q.B.D. 220 at pp. 223-4, quoted and adopted as the proper test by the Supreme Court of Canada in *Car & General Ins. Corp. Ltd.* v. *Seymour and Maloney,* [1956] S.C.R. 322 at p. 331, 2 D.L.R. (2d) 369 at p. 378). This defence is met by the decision of *Haynes* v. *Harwood,* [1935] 1 K.B. 146, where Greer L.J., quotes with approval at pp. 156-7 an article of Professor Goodhart ["Rescue and Voluntary Assumption of Risk", Cambridge Law Journal, Vol. V., p. 192]:

> " 'The American rule is that the doctrine of the assumption of risk does not apply where the plaintiff has, under an exigency caused by the defendant's wrongful misconduct, consciously and deliberately faced a risk, even

of death, to rescue another from imminent danger of personal injury or death, whether the person endangered is one to whom he owes a duty of protection, as a member of his family, or is a mere stranger to whom he owes no such special duty.' In my judgment that passage not only represents the law of the United States, but I think it also accurately represents the law of this country."

I hold therefore that the defendant's negligence in effecting Matthews' rescue induced Horsley to come to the rescue and that this was within the risk created by the defendant's negligent conduct, and I must hold that such negligence was the effective cause of Horsley's death.

Jessup J.A. (in the Court of Appeal): This unique case, the facts of which might have been contrived for a bar exam, raises several questions of first instance. . . .

If MacLaren had a duty to render assistance to Matthews and to use reasonable care in so doing, there remains the question of whether Horsley's rescue attempt with consequent injury to him was within the ambit of risk resulting from MacLaren's negligence. *Haynes* v. *Harwood,* [1935] 1 K.B. 146, *Baker* v. *T.E. Hopkins and Sons Limited,* [1959] 1 W.L.R. 966 and *Videan* v. *British Transport Commission,* [1963] 2 Q.B. 650 establish the principle that where one creates a situation of peril through negligence it is a foreseeable consequence that a rescuer will go to the aid of a person in danger from the peril with resulting liability to the rescuer, for any injury sustained by him, of the person responsible for the peril. Here, of course, MacLaren did not create the peril of drowning but, for all that was apparent to the actors in the drama, his negligence prolonged Matthews' exposure to it permitting a potential risk of death to actualize and I consider that the principle of the cases cited logically and properly extends to such a situation. However, while MacLaren reasonably should have foreseen the intervention of a rescue attempt by one of his passengers as a consequence of his own negligently mishandled effort, the evidence is he had earlier warned Horsley to remain in the cockpit or cabin because he was unaware if Horsley had any experience with boating. By that command I think MacLaren, as effectively as he could, insulated Horsley from such perils of the voyage as were eventually encountered and put it beyond his reasonable contemplation that Horsley in particular would engage in the intervention he in fact undertook. On that narrow ground I would allow the appeal.

Schroeder J.A. (MacGillivray concurring): The learned trial judge, in a carefully reasoned judgment, found the appellant liable for Horsley's mishap on the theory which has been applied in a series of rescue cases, in which the principle has been enunciated that if A by his negligence causes B to be in a position of danger, he should foresee the probability that a third person C, "acting bravely and promptly and subjugating any timorous over-concern for his own well-being or comfort, may attempt a rescue. . .".

It is not contended, nor is there any basis for the contention, that Matthews was imperilled in the first instance by any act or omission on the part of the appellant. The respondents' theory is that in the circumstances there was a legal duty cast upon the appellant, even if Matthews's position of danger was brought about by Matthews's own fault or negligence, to use reasonable care in rescuing his passenger; that the appellant was negligent in reversing the engine and backing the boat towards Matthews's body rather than circling it and proceeding bow onward into the wind and drawing the boat alongside to a point where the body could be reached; that the delay which ensued by reason of the alleged improper conduct of the appellant in carrying out the rescue operation created a desperate situation and put Matthews in such a position of peril that the appellant should have foreseen that under the exigency caused by his alleged misconduct Horsely, or one of the other passengers, acting instinctively, would risk injury or death to themselves by diving into the water to rescue Matthews from the imminent danger created or increased by the appellant's alleged negligence. . . .

To establish a breach of duty on the defendant's part the plaintiff relied on the evidence of two expert witnesses, Captain Livingstone and Captain Mumford. They testified as to the proper rescue procedures to be followed in case a man fell overboard. They both agreed that the procedure of reversing the engines and backing towards the man in the water should never be adopted except in a confined area where the boat could not be turned around. They stated that this procedure should be automatic and ought to be known to every person who undertakes the operation of a boat such as The Ogopogo; that the man in the water should be approached "bow on", and that to bear down upon him stern first was evidence of incompetence. The defendant MacLaren admitted that this was recognized by him as the correct procedure, but maintained that on the spur of the moment and in the emergency which presented itself he had done what he thought would be most conducive to an early rescue.

Captain Mumford would not state that there was no reasonable chance of picking up a person in the water by backing the boat, but stated that there was a better chance of doing it by the method which he proposed, adding that it was a matter for the master to decide. Captain Livingstone stated that it was inadvisable for a person to remove his clothing before entering very cold water. In fact, he disapproved of anyone jumping into the water in the course of a rescue operation since one would be "compounding the situation by having two persons in the water instead of one".

In my respectful opinion the evidence of the two experts spells out a standard of text-book perfection given at a time when all the evidence had been sifted and all the facts ascertained in the calm and deliberate atmosphere of a judicial investigation. It is ever so easy to be wise after the event and to state *ex post facto* that the conduct of the appellant, who had to rely upon the co-operation of the other passengers in effecting the rescue of Matthews, fell short of the standard of reasonableness. He is surely entitled to be judged in the light of the situation as it appeared to him at the time and in the context of immediate and pressing emergency, even if a duty of using reasonable care in effecting the rescue of Matthews was properly cast upon him. . . .

This leads me to the precise ground of liability on the part of the appellant urged by counsel for the respondents. Assuming that the appellant's conduct in the rescue operation was blameworthy to such a degree as to attract liability on his part towards Matthews, can it be said that the appellant, who was not primarily negligent and hence responsible for Matthews's plight in the first instance, having failed to carry out a supposed duty to rescue Matthews with the care and promptitude, ought to have foreseen the probability that Horsley, obeying a commendable beneficial instinct of humanity, would be thereby induced to jump into the water and expose himself to the same peril as that in which Matthews was involved? I should think that no such thought would ever have occurred to the appellant or to any reasonable person standing in his position especially under the conditions of emergency that prevailed. The temperature of the water and the continuing efforts of all on board to bring Matthews to the safety of the vessel all militated against such an act on the part of any of the passengers as a probability to be reasonably anticipated. Nothing in the evidence points to Horsley's knowledge of the proper operation of a boat in an emergency of this kind, nor is there any evidence which suggests that he had any valid reason for supposing that MacLaren's conduct in the circumstances was not what it ought to be. Moreover, MacLaren had told Horsley to confine himself to the cockpit or cabin. It is not suggested that Horsley had made his intention known to MacLaren, and it would scarcely be anticipated in any event that any passenger would dive into the water without at least taking precautions for his own safety by donning a life jacket or attaching a rope to himself, especially when he could see the effect that the very cold water had had upon Matthews.

No case has been cited to us in which a defendant was held liable to a rescuer in a case in which the defendant's negligence had not imperilled the person whose recue the plaintiff attempted. To find negligence on the part of the defendant in relation to his rescue efforts with respect to Matthews and to treat his conduct as a basis of liability to Horsley would involve an unwarranted extension of the principle laid down in any of the known recue cases. The evidence does not support a finding that anything done or left undone by the defendant caused his rescue efforts to fail. Furthermore, if the appellant erred in backing instead of turning the cruiser and proceeding towards Matthews "bow on", the error was one of judgment and not of negligence, and in the existing circumstances of emergency ought fairly to be excused.

Appeal allowed.

Ritchie J. (Spence and Judson JJ. concurring, in the Supreme Court of Canada): . . . If, upon Matthews falling overboard, Horsley had immediately dived to his rescue and lost his life, as he ultimately did upon contact with the icy water, then I can see no conceivable basis on which the respondent could have been held responsible for his death.

There is, however, no suggestion that there was any negligence in the rescue of Horsley and if the respondent is to be held liable to the appellants, such liability must in my view stem from a finding that the situation of peril brought about by Matthews falling into the water was thereafter, within the next three or four minutes, so aggravated by the negligence of MacLaren in attempting his rescue as to induce Horsley to risk his life by diving in after him.

I think that the best description of the circumstances giving rise to the liability to a second rescuer such as Horsley is contained in the reasons for judgment of Lord Denning M.R., in *Videan* v. *British Transport Commission*, [1963] 2 Q.B. 650, where he said, at p. 669:

"It seems to me that, if a person *by his fault* creates a situation of peril, he must answer for it to any person who attempts to rescue the person who is in danger. He owes a duty to such a person above all others. The rescuer may act instinctively out of humanity or deliberately out of courage. But whichever it is, so long as it is not wanton interference, if the rescuer is killed or injured in the attempt, he can recover damages *from the one whose fault has been the cause of it.*"

The italics are my own.

In the present case a situation of peril was created when Matthews fell overboard, but it was not created by any fault on the part of MacLaren, and before MacLaren can be found to have been in any way responsible for Horsley's death, it must be found that there was such negligence in his method of rescue as to place Matthews in an apparent position of increased danger subsequent to and distinct from the danger to which he had been initially exposed by his accidental fall. In other words, any duty owing to Horsley must stem from the fact that a new situation of peril was created by MacLaren's negligence which induced Horsley to act as he did. . . .

The finding of the learned trial judge that MacLaren was negligent in the rescue of Matthews is really twofold. On the one hand he finds that there was a failure to comply with the "man overboard" rescue procedure recommended by two experts called for the plaintiff, and on the other hand he concludes that MacLaren "was unable to exercise proper judgment in the emergency created because of his excessive consumption of alcohol". In the course of his reasons for judgment in the Court of Appeal, Mr. Justice Schroeder expressly found that there was nothing in the evidence to support the view that MacLaren was incapable of proper management and control owing to the consumption of liquor, the question was not seriously argued in this Court, and like my brother Laskin, I do not think there is any ground for saying that intoxicants had anything to do with the fatal occurrences. . . .

I share the view expressed by my brother Laskin when he says, in the course of his reasons for judgment, that:

"Encouragement by the common law of the rescue of persons in danger would, in my opinion, go beyond reasonable bounds if it involved liability of one rescuer to a succeeding one where the former has not been guilty of any fault which could be said to have induced a second rescue attempt."

In the present case, however, although the procedure followed by MacLaren was not the most highly recommended one, I do not think that the evidence justifies the finding that any fault of his induced Horsley to risk his life by diving as he did. In this regard I adopt the conclusion reached by Mr. Justice Schroeder in the penultimate paragraph of his reasons for judgment where he says [at p. 287]:

". . . if the appellant erred in backing instead of turning the cruiser and proceeding towards Matthews 'bow on', the error was one of judgment and not negligence, and in the existing circumstances of emergency ought fairly to be excused."

I think it should be made clear that, in my opinion, the duty to rescue a man who has fallen accidentally overboard is a common law duty, the existence of which is in no way dependent upon the provisions of s. 526(1) of the Canada Shipping Act, R.S.C. 1952, c. 29 [now s. 516 (1), R.S.C. 1970, c. S-9].

I should also say that, unlike Jessup J.A., the failure of Horsley to heed MacLaren's warning to remain in the cockpit or cabin plays no part in my reasoning.

For all these reasons I would dismiss this appeal with costs.

Laskin J. (dissenting, Hall J. concurring): In this court, counsel for the appellants relied on three alternative bases of liability. There was, first, the submission that in going to the aid of Matthews, as he did, MacLaren came under a duty to carry out the rescue with due care in the circumstances, and his failure to employ standard rescue procedures foreseeably brought Horsley into the picture with the ensuing fatal result. The second basis of liability was doubly founded as resting (a) on a common law duty of care of a private carrier to his passengers, involving a duty to come to the aid of a passenger who has accidentally fallen overboard, or (b) on a statutory duty under s. 526(1) of the Canada Shipping Act, R.S.C. 1952, c. 29 [now s. 516(1), R.S.C. 1970, c. S-9], to come to the aid of a passenger who has fallen overboard. There was failure, so the allegation was, to act reasonably in carrying out these duties or either of them, with the foreseeable consequence of Horsley's encounter of danger. The third contention was the broadest, to the effect that where a situation of peril, albeit not brought about originally by the defendant's negligence, arises by reason of the defendant's attempt at rescue, he is liable to a second rescuer for ensuing damage on the ground that the latter's intervention is reasonably foreseeable.

None of the bases of liability advanced by the appellants is strictly within the original principle on which the "rescue" cases were founded. That was the recognition of a duty by a negligent defendant to a rescuer coming to the aid of the person imperilled by the defendant's negligence. The evolution of the law on this subject, originating in the moral approbation of assistance to a person in peril, involved a break with the "mind your own business" philosophy. Legal protection is now afforded to one who risks injury to himself in going to the rescue of another who has been foreseeably exposed to danger by the unreasonable conduct of a third person. The latter is now subject to liability at the suit of the rescuer as well as at the suit of the imperilled person, provided, in the case of the rescuer, that his intervention was not so utterly foolhardy as to be outside of any accountable risk and thus beyond even contributory negligence.

Moreover, the liability to the rescuer, although founded on the concept of duty, is now seen as stemming from an independent and not a derivative duty of the negligent person. As *Fleming on Torts,* 3rd ed. (1965), has put it (at p. 166), the cause of action of the rescuer in arising out of the defendant's negligence, is based "not in its tendency to imperil the person rescued, but in its tendency to induce the rescuer to encounter the danger. Thus viewed, the duty to the rescuer is clearly independent . . . ." This explanation of principle was put forward as early as 1924 by Professor Bohlen (see his *Studies in the Law of Torts,* at p. 569) in recognition of the difficulty of straining the notion of foreseeability to embrace a rescuer of a person imperilled by another's negligence. Under this explanation of the basis of liability, it is immaterial that the imperilled person does not in fact suffer any injury or that, as it turns out, the negligent person was under no liability to him either because the injury was not caused by the negligence or the damage was outside the foreseeable risk of harm to him: *cf. Videan* v. *British Transport Commission,* [1963] 2 Q.B. 650. It is a further consequence of the recognition of an independent duty that a person who imperils himself by his carelessness may be as fully liable to a rescuer as a third person would be who imperils another. In my opinion, therefore, *Dupuis* v. *New Regina Trading Co. Ltd.,* [1943] 4 D.L.R. 275, [1943] 2 W.W.R. 593, ought no longer to be taken as a statement of the common law in Canada in so far as it denies recovery because the rescuer was injured in going to the aid of a person who imperilled himself. The doctrinal issues are sufficiently canvassed by the late Dean Wright in 21 Can. Bar Rev. 758 (1943); and see also *Ward* v. *T.E. Hopkins & Son, Ltd.; Baker* v. *T.E. Hopkins & Son Ltd.,* [1959] 3 All E.R. 225.

I realize that this statement of the law invites the conclusion that Horsley's estate might succeed against that of Matthews if it was proved that Matthews acted without proper care for his own safety so that Horsley was prompted to come to his rescue. This issue does not, however, have to be canvassed in these proceedings since the estate of Matthews was not joined as a co-defendant.

The thinking behind the rescue cases, in so far as they have translated a moral impulse into a legally protectible interest, suggests that liability to a rescuer should not depend on whether there was original negligence which created the peril and which, therefore, prompted the rescue effort. It would appear that the principle should be equally applicable if, at any stage of the perilous situation, there was negligence on the defendant's part which induced the rescuer to attempt the rescue or which operated against him after he had made the attempt. If this be so, it indicates the possibility of an action by a second rescuer against a first. On one view of the present case, this is what we have here. It is not, however, a view upon which, under the facts herein, the present case falls to be decided.

The reason is obvious. MacLaren was not a random rescuer. As owner and operator of a boat on which he was carrying invited guests, he was under a legal duty to take reasonable care for their safety. This was a duty which did not depend on the existence of a contract of carriage, nor on whether he was a common carrier or a private carrier of passengers. Having brought his guests into a relationship with him as passengers on his boat, albeit as social or gratuitous passengers, he was obliged to exercise reasonable care for their safety. That obligation extends, in my opinion, to rescue from perils of the sea where this is consistent with his duty to see to the safety of his other passengers and with concern for his own safety. The duty exists whether the passenger falls overboard accidentally or by reason of his own carelessness.

I would hold that *Vanvalkenburg* v. *Northern Navigation Co.* (1913), 19 D.L.R. 649, 30 O.L.R. 142, should no longer be considered as good law in so far as it declared that operators of a ship were not under any legal duty to a seaman in their employ to go to his rescue when he fell overboard through his own carelessness. The Ontario Appellate Division in that case saw the facts through the classifications of non-feasance and misfeasance, and was not prepared to read the contract of hiring as imposing an affirmative obligation to protect the drowning seaman from the consequences of his own carelessness. Since the ship operators did not create any unreasonable risk of harm, the Appellate Division could not find any ground for holding them liable.

I do not accept this reasoning, based as it was on the state of the law of torts that did not yet know even *M'Alister (or Donoghue)* v. *Stevenson*, [1932] A.C. 562. Affirmative duties of care arise out of the relationship of employer and employee and out of the relationship of carrier and passenger, to take two examples. Where these relationships occur on board a ship at sea, the employee or passenger, who falls overboard from whatever cause, should be entitled to look for succour to the operators of the ship because of necessary dependency on them for return to shore. Such a duty of rescue was recognized in *Harris* v. *Pennsylvania Railroad Co.* (1931), 50 F. 2d 866, and in *The "Cappy", Hutchinson* v. *Dickie* (1947), 162 F. 2d 103; *cert.* denied, 332 U.S. 830, a case to which I will return because it is so strikingly similar on its facts to the present case.

I do not rest the duty to which I would hold MacLaren in this case on s. 526 (1) of the Canada Shipping Act, even assuming that its terms are broad enough to embrace the facts herein. That provision, a penal one, is as follows:

> 526(1) The master or person in charge of a vessel shall, so far as he can do so without serious danger to his own vessel, her crew and passengers, if any, render assistance to every person, even if that person be a subject of a foreign state at war with Her Majesty, who is found at sea and in danger of being lost, and if he fails to do so he is liable to a fine not exceeding one thousand dollars.

I do not find it necessary in this case to consider whether s. 526(1), taken alone, entails civil consequences for failure to perform a statutory duty; or, even, whether it fixes a standard of conduct upon which the common law may operate to found liability. There is an independent basis for a common law duty of care in the relationship of carrier to passenger, but the legislative declaration of policy s. 526(1) is a fortifying element in the recognition of that duty, being in harmony with it in a comparable situation.

It follows from this assessment that MacLaren cannot be regarded as simply a good Samaritan. Rather it is Horsley who was in that role, exposing himself to danger upon the alleged failure of MacLaren properly to carry out his duty to effect Matthews' rescue. The present case is, therefore, not one to which the principles propounded in *East Suffolk Rivers Catchment Board* v. *Kent*, [1941] A.C. 74, are applicable. In the Court of Appeal, both Schroeder J.A., and

Jessup J.A., referred to this case with approval. The former relied on it to support his rejection of the trial judge's holding that MacLaren was liable when, having undertaken to rescue Matthews, he failed to use reasonable care in the rescue operation. In the opinion of Schroeder J.A., as noted earlier in these reasons, there was no basis for holding that MacLaren's rescue efforts, even if improperly carried out, worsened Matthews' condition and thus induced Horsley to come to his rescue. Jessup J.A. would have applied this test of liability if the case, for him, had turned on the voluntary undertaking by MacLaren of rescue operations. Since, on the view taken by Jessup J.A. MacLaren had an antecedent or original duty to render assistance, the *East Suffolk Rivers Catchment Board* case did not apply.

Whether a case involving the exercise of statutory powers (but not duties) by a public authority should govern the issue of liability or non-liability to an injured rescuer is a question that need not be answered here. It has been widely noted that there is some incongruity in imposing liability upon a good Samaritan when he who passes by does not attract it. Legislation has been called in aid in some jurisdictions: see Note, 64 Col. L. Rev. 1301 (1964). However, the problem raised by the rescue cases with respect to the *East Suffolk Rivers Catchment Board* principles is the more ramified if the issue thereunder is one of liability to a rescuer as well as to a rescuee, and if it turns on an independent rather than on a derivative duty to the rescuer by the volunteer defendant. There is, hence, all the more reason to leave the problem to be considered on facts which raise it squarely.

On the view that I take of the issues in this case and, having regard to the facts, the appellants cannot succeed on the first of their alternative submissions on liability if they cannot succeed on the second ground of an existing common law duty of care. Their third contention was not clearly anchored in any original or supervening duty of care and breach of that duty; and, if that be so, I do not see how their counsel's submission on the foreseeability of a second rescuer, even if accepted, can saddle a non-negligent first rescuer with liability either to the rescuee or to a second rescuer. Encouragement by the common law of the rescue of persons in danger would, in my opinion, go beyond reasonable bounds if it involved liability of one rescuer to a succeeding one where the former has not been guilty of any fault which could be said to have induced a second rescue attempt.

If the appellant's third contention was based on any element of fault, it could only be fault in carrying out the attempt at rescue; and, moreover, it would have to be founded on a wide view of Lord Denning's statement in the *Videan* case, *supra,* at p. 669 where he said that "if a person by his fault creates a situation of peril, he must answer for it to any person who attempts to rescue the person who is in danger". There is no factual basis upon which to consider the extension of Lord Denning's proposition which underlies the appellants' third submission in the alternative view of it that I have taken. In so far as it rests on an allegation that fault arose only in the bungling of the rescue attempt (there being no anterior duty), no such finding is warranted. Beyond this, it invites a return to the principles of the *East Suffolk Rivers Catchment Board* case, and I do not wish to repeat what I have already said with respect to them.

The present case is thus reduced to the question of liability on the basis of (1) an alleged breach of a duty of care originating in the relationship of carrier and passenger; (2) whether the breach, if there was one, could be said to have prompted Horsley to go to Matthews' rescue; and (3) whether Horsley's conduct, if not so rash in the circumstances as to be unforeseeable, none the less exhibited want of care so as to make him guilty of contributory negligence.

Whether MacLaren was in breach of his duty of care to Matthews was a question of fact on which the trial Judge's affirmative finding is entitled to considerable weight. That finding was, of course, essential to the further question of a consequential duty to Horsley. Lacourciere J., came to his conclusion of fact on the evidence, after putting to himself the following question: "What would the reasonable boat operator do in the circumstances, attributing to such person the reasonable skill and experience required of the master of a cabin cruiser who is responsible for the safety and rescue of his passengers?" (see 4 D.L.R. (3d) 557 at p. 564, [1969] 2 O.R. 137). It was the trial judge's finding that MacLaren, as he himself admitted, had adopted the wrong procedure of rescuing a passenger who had fallen overboard. He knew the proper procedure, and had practised it. Coming bow on to effect a rescue was the standard procedure and was taught as such.

MacLaren's answer to the allegation of a breach of duty was that he had been guilty merely of an error of judgment. This was the view taken by the majority in the Ontario Court of Appeal who were moved by the element of emergency. What makes this view vulnerable is that this was not a case where MacLaren had failed to execute the required manoeuvre properly, but rather one where he had not followed the method of rescue which, on the uncontradicted evidence, was the proper one to employ in an emergency. There was no external reason for his failure to do so. Jones demonstrated that in the rescue of his wife. Further, after MacLaren's first abortive attempt at rescue, over a period of time which the evidence indicated would have been sufficient to effect a bow-on rescue, he made a second attempt with the wrong procedure. It was only then, with the lapse of three or four minutes after Matthews had fallen overboard, that Horsley went to his rescue. I note also that after MacLaren resumed control of his boat from Jones he went bow on to rescue Horsley.

I do not see how it can be said that the trial judge's finding against MacLaren on the issue of breach of duty is untenable. In relation to Horsley's intervention, the finding stands unembarrassed by any question of causation in relation to Matthews. This, at least, distinguishes the present case from *Hutchinson* v. *Dickie, supra.*

There, as here, an invited guest on a cabin cruiser fell overboard and drowned during a lake cruise. The owner and operator of the boat was blameless in respect of the fall overboard, but the trial judge founded liability for wrongful death on breach of duty to act reasonably to effect a rescue. There, as here, the owner-operator, on hearing the cry "man overboard", reversed and backed astern towards the drowning man. He was then about 75 ft. away from the boat. Two life rings were thrown to Dickie, the drowning man, one falling within 20 ft. and the other within six feet of him, but he paid no attention to them. A boat hook was then made ready for use, but Dickie disappeared when the boat was 20 to 25 ft. away. The trial judge found negligence, *inter alia*, in the failure to turn the boat and come bow on. On appeal the action was dismissed on several grounds. The appellate Court held that there was "an entire lack of evidence that anything appellant did or left undone caused his efforts at rescue to fail". This was enough to dispose of the case, as it was enough to dispose of the Matthews' action. On a question more germane to the present case, the court agreed that there was a duty of rescue owed to Dickie, but held that a breach was not established by the backing-up procedure that was employed; and, if there was an error, it was one of judgment only in dealing with an emergency. The court noted that there was a conflict of evidence on the issue of coming bow on or backing up, and this too distinguishes *Hutchinson* v. *Dickie* (which, moreover, was not an action by a rescuer's estate) from the present case which was decided more than 20 years later.

I turn to the question whether the breach of duty to Matthews could properly be regarded in this case as prompting Horsley to attempt a rescue. Like the trial judge, I am content to adopt and apply analogically on this point the reasoning of Cardozo J., as he then was, in *Wagner* v. *International R. Co.,* (1921), 133 N.E. 437, and of Lord Denning M.R., in *Videan* v. *British Transport Commission, supra.* To use Judge Cardozo's phrase, Horsley's conduct in the circumstances was "within the range of the natural and probable". The fact, moreover, that Horsley's sacrifice was futile is no more a disabling ground here than it was in the *Wagner* case, where the passenger thrown off the train was dead when the plaintiff went to help him, unless it be the case that the rescuer acted wantonly.

In the Ontario Court of Appeal, Schroeder J.A., as previously noted, took the view that Horsley was not justified in going to the rescue of Matthews unless MacLaren worsened Matthews' situation through want of reasonable care. I need say no more on this view than that it proceeds on the basis of the *East Suffolk Rivers Catchment Board* principles which are not applicable to the facts of the present case.

Of more concern here is the position taken by Jessup J.A., which, to put it again briefly, was that whoever MacLaren should have foreseen as a rescuer, it could not be Horsley. I cannot agree with this ground of exoneration of MacLaren when it is founded merely on his having told Horsley to confine himself to the cabin and cockpit. MacLaren's evidence on this matter was that he had not previously met Horsley, he did not know his experience with boating and with water, and hence he did not want him on deck. In my opinion, this evidence is no more telling against Horsley as a rescuer than it would be against Horsley as a rescuee if he had come on deck and had then fallen overboard. Moreover, the considerations which underlie a duty to a rescuer do not justify ruling out a particular rescuer if it be not wanton of him to intervene. The implication of Jessup J.A.'s position is that Horsley required MacLaren's consent to go to Matthews' rescue. This is not, in my view, a sufficient answer in the circumstances which existed by reason of MacLaren's breach of duty. To quote again Judge Cardozo in the *Wagner* case, "The law does not discriminate between the rescuer oblivious of peril and the one who counts the cost. It is enough that the act whether impulsive or deliberate is the child of the occasion." (133 N.E. 437 at p. 438.)

In responding as he did, and in circumstances where only hindsight made it doubtful that Matthews could be saved, Horsley was not wanton or foolhardy. Like the trial judge, I do not think that his action passed the point of brave acceptance of a serious risk and became a futile exhibition of recklessness for which there can be no recourse. There is, however, the question whether Horsley was guilty of contributory negligence. This was an alternative plea of the respondent based, *inter alia,* on Horsley's failure to put on a life-jacket or secure himself to the boat by a rope or call on the other passengers to stand by, especially in the light of the difficulties of Matthews in the cold water. The trial judge rejected the contentions of contributory negligence, holding that although "Wearing a life-jacket or securing himself to a lifeline would have been more prudent . . . . Horsley's impulsive act without such precautions was the result of the excitement, haste and confusion of the moment, and cannot be said to constitute contributory negligence" (see 4 D.L.R. (3d) at p. 569). In view of its conclusions on the main issue of MacLaren's liability, the Ontario Court of Appeal did not canvass the question of contributory negligence.

The matter is not free from difficulty. About two minutes passed after Matthews had fallen overboard and MacLaren made his first abortive attempt at rescue by proceeding astern. Two life-jackets had been successively thrown towards Matthews without any visible effort on his part to seize them. Then came the second attempt at rescue by backing the boat, and it was in progress when Horsley dived in. Horsley had come on deck at the shout of "Roly's over-board" and was at the stern during MacLaren's first attempt at rescue, and must have been there when the life-jackets were thrown towards Matthews. However, in the concern of the occasion, and having regard to MacLaren's breach of duty, I do not think that Horsley can be charged with contributory negligence in diving to the rescue of Matthews as he did. I point out as well that the evidence does not indicate that the failure to put on a life-jacket or secure himself to a lifetime played any part in Horsley's death.

NOTES

1. Although the American case of *Wagner* v. *International Railway* Co. (1921), 133 N.E. 437 (N.Y.C.A.) and the English case of *Haynes* v. *Harwood*, [1935] 1 K.B. 146 (C.A.) are usually referred to as the leading cases, the Canadian courts had much earlier recognized a duty to the rescuer. In *Seymour* v. *Winnipeg Electric Ry.* (1910), 13 W.L.R. 566 (Man. C.A.), the court on a demurrer declared that a rescuer could recover. Mr. Justice Richards recognized that "the promptings of humanity towards the saving of life are amongst the noblest instincts of mankind. . ." and concluded that "The trend of modern legal thought is toward holding that those who risk their safety in attempting to rescue others who are put in peril by the negligence of third parties are entitled to claim such compensation from such third parties for injuries they may receive in such attempts. . . ." This is particularly the case if "those whom it is sought to rescue are infirm or helpless". As an afterthought, Mr. Justice Richards added that the company had "notice" that "some brave man is likely to risk his own life to save the helpless", which indicates that the idea of notice or knowledge (or foresight if you will) was a relevant consideration.

2. What was the narrow ground of the decision of Mr. Justice Ritchie in *Horsley* v. *MacLaren*? On this point, what did Mr. Justice Laskin conclude? Are there any other issues upon which the majority and minority disagreed? See Alexander, "One Rescuer's Obligation to Another: The 'Ogopogo' Lands in the Supreme Court of Canada" (1972), 2 U of T.L.J. 98.

3. How did the Supreme Court deal with the foresight issue upon which the Ontario Court of Appeal based its decision?

4. Does a rescued person owe a duty to his own rescuer to avoid placing himself in a position of peril? See *Baker* v. *Hopkins*, [1958] 3 All E.R. 147; affd. [1959] 3 All E.R. 225 (C.A.) where, at trial, Mr. Justice Barry stated:

> "Although no one owes a duty to anyone else to preserve his own safety, yet if, by his own carelessness a man puts himself into a position of peril of a kind that invites rescue, he would in law be liable for any injury caused to someone whom he ought to have foreseen would attempt to come to his aid."

See also *C.N.R.* v. *Bakty* (1977), 18 O.R. (2d) 481 (Co. Ct.); *Chapman* v. *Hearse* (1961), 106 C.L.R. 112 (H.C. Aust.), rescued person held 25 percent liable to rescuer who was hit by negligently driven vehicle. The case of *Dupuis* v. *New Regina Trading Post*, [1943] 4 D.L.R. 275, [1943] 2 W.W.R. 593 (Sask. C.A.), which indicated that there was no such duty, has been discredited by Mr. Justice Laskin in *Horsley* v. *MacLaren*. Could Mrs. Horsley have recovered from Matthews? What would it depend upon? Why do you think she refrained from suing?

5. If someone is injured trying to rescue himself or in escaping injury to himself, the person who negligently placed him in that position will be held liable. See *Tuttle* v. *Atlantic City Ry.* (1901), 49 Atl. 450 (N.J.), where the plaintiff walking on the street, saw a street car careering off the tracks towards her. The plaintiff, frightened, started to run, and 200 yards away fell and broke a leg. The defendant street railway was held liable to the plaintiff for negligently causing her damage. See also *Sayers* v. *Harlow Urban District Council*, [1958] 2 All E.R. 342 (C.A.); *Winnipeg Electric Ry. Co.* v. *Canadian Northern Ry. Co.* (1920), 59 S.C.R. 352, at p. 367 (*per* Duff J.), where plaintiff either jumped or

fell from the back of a streetcar when it was negligently driven in front of an approaching train.

6. In *Holomis* v. *Dubuc* (1975), 56 D.L.R. (3d) 351 (B.C.), the defendant was the pilot of an amphibious flying boat carrying eight other passengers. Because landing at the desired destination was impossible, it became necessary to attempt a landing on an unmarked, fog-shrouded wilderness lake. While taxiing along the water, the plan collided with an unseen obstacle, which tore a hole in the hull. The water began rushing in and three of the passengers panicked and jumped out into the lake. Two were rescued, but one drowned. In an action by the administratrix of the deceased's estate, judgment for 50% of the damages was rendered against the defendant for failing to warn the passengers with regard to the plan to land, and for failing to give instructions about handling an emergency when the craft was water-borne. Distinguishing the *Wagon Mound (No. 1)* as a case in which "improbability was piled on improbability", Verchere J. concluded:

">. . . There is, in my view, nothing improbable in the fact that a person within a ruptured vessel that is rapidly filling with water would seek to get out of it, and neither does it seem improbable to me that such a person might, for some reason peculiar to himself, decline to pause long enough to take up a life-jacket or, alternatively, that he might forget about it altogether. In my view, then, the probability that a surprised and frightened passenger would leap from a sinking aircraft is entirely within the foresight of the reasonable man, and as such, it should of course have been foreseeable to the defendant."

The plaintiff's recovery was reduced by 50% on the ground that the deceased was contributorily negligent for failing to use one of the clearly available life-jackets.

7. Does one rescuer owe a duty to another potential rescuer to use care? Should a rescuer of a rescuer be able to recover from the negligent person who created the initial danger?

8. Should a rescuer of property be entitled to recover for personal injury to himself? See *Connel* v. *Prescott* (1892), 2 O.A.R. 49; affd. 22 S.C.R. 147; *Hutterly* v. *Imperial Oil*, [1956] 3 D.L.R. (2d) 719; *Hyett* v. *G.W.Ry.*, [1948] 1 K.B. 345 (C.A.). What if the damage suffered during the attempt is to property only? See *Thorn* v. *James* (1903), 14 Man. R. 373.

9. Should the cost of putting out a fire caused by the negligent driving of the defendant be recoverable? Does it make any difference if there is a contractual obligation to put out the fire, or if it is done by the provincial authority that owns the roadway? See *A.-G. (Ont.)* v. *Crompton* (1976), 1 C.C.L.T. 81 (Ont. Haines J.).

10. What about a futile rescue attempt? For example, what if the person being rescued is already dead? Does it make any difference if the plaintiff reasonably believes he is not dead? What if the person being rescued is not really in any danger? Does it make any difference if the rescuer reasonably believes he is?

11. In *Moddejonge et al.* v. *Huron County Board of Education et al.*, [1972] 2 O.R. 437, an employee of the defendant school board took some young people for a swim. Two girls were carried out into deep water by a surface current which was caused by a fresh breeze that suddenly developed. Geraldine Moddejonge immediately swam to their assistance, rescued one of them but drowned while trying to save the other girl. The parents of both deceased girls successfully sued the board for negligence. In discussing the liability to the rescuer, Mr. Justice Pennell stated:

"There is no general duty to assist anyone in peril. It is a great reproach to our legal institutions that rescuers for many years were denied recovery by a train of reasoning based on the concept of voluntary assumption of the risk. Eventually justice comes to live with men rather than with books. It fell to Justice Cardozo to allow the claim of humanity. I borrow, with respectful gratitude, a passage from his judgment in *Wagner* v. *Int'l R. Co.* [His Lordship quoted the famous passage beginning "Danger invites rescue".]

The principle thus established has been followed since. It was delicately argued that the efforts of Geraldine Moddejonge constituted a rash and futile gesture; that reasonableness did not attach to her response. Upon this, the rescue of Sandra Thompson is sufficient answer. One must not approach the problem with the wisdom that comes after the event. Justice is not to be measured in such scales. To Geraldine Moddejonge duty did not hug the shore of safety. Duty did not give her a choice. She accepted it. She discharged it. More need not be said. The law will give her actions a sanctuary.

The initial act that set the events in motion was the negligence of the defendant. One of the links of causation was that someone might thereby be exposed to danger and that someone else might react to the impulse to rescue.

For these reasons I am of opinion that the claim of the plaintiff, John Moddejonge, is well founded."

12. What about a rescue attempt that is utterly foolish, as where someone standing on Lion's Gate Bridge leaps off to save a child he sees drowning 500 feet below?

13. What if the conduct of the rescuer is not foolhardy but merely negligent? What about the contributory negligence technique? In *Sayers* v. *Harlow Urban District Council*, [1958] 2 All E.R. 342 the plaintiff was negligently locked into a public lavatory. In attempting to extricate herself from her predicament by climbing out of the stall, she was injured. Lord Justice Morris stated:

"The conduct being examined has to be tested and considered in the light of the circumstances. The question in the present case is whether the injury sustained by the plaintiff resulted either entirely or partly from the defendants' breach of duty. The defendants assert that, as the plaintiff was in no danger and was in no serious inconvenience, she acted unreasonably in doing what she did, so that she and she alone was the authoress of the injury that befell her.

I do not think that the plaintiff should be adjudged in all the circumstances to have acted unreasonably or rashly or stupidly. As to nearly everything that she did, in my judgment she acted carefully and prudently. Indeed, she showed a very considerable measure of self-control. My Lord has fully recited the facts, and there is no need for me to refer to them again. The learned Judge has found them carefully, and the only advantage that he has over us is that he actually saw the plaintiff herself. Subject to that advantage which in the present is comparatively slight, we are in as good a position as the Judge to determine this matter. What did the plaintiff do? First, she did her best to operate the lock. She tried with her finger to see whether there was any way of making it work. There was not. She then tried to get her hand through the window. She was unable to do that. She then banged on the door. Nobody came. She shouted. There was no response. Ten or fifteen minutes went by. The situation could not have been an agreeable one. What did she then do? It appears to me on the evidence that what she did was to explore the possibility of climbing over the door. That I cannot think was unwise or imprudent, or rash or stupid. I have therefore come to the same conclusion as that expressed by my Lord. Like my Lord, I feel that the plaintiff cannot entirely be absolved from some measure of fault — the fault described by my Lord — and I am in agreement that that measure should be marked by depriving her of one-quarter of that to which she would otherwise be entitled. I consider that the appeal should be allowed to the extent that my Lord has indicated."

If the plaintiff did not act "unreasonably" but "carefully and prudently", why deprive her of one-quarter of her damages? What is the best rule to use in judging the conduct of the rescuer?

14. Should a father who donates a kidney to his daughter, who lost hers as a result of the negligence of a doctor, recover damages from that doctor? Is he like a rescuer? Is this foreseeable? See *Urbanski* v. *Patel* (1978), 84 D.L.R. (3d) 650 (Man. Q.B.), at p. 671, *per* Wilson J.

15. How long does the duty to a rescuer last? When does it begin? X is in

danger. He telephones his friend Y to come over to help. Y responds and, while running towards his car, falls and breaks his leg. Is he entitled to recover? What if Y gets into a car accident on the way over to X's place? What if Y arrives at X's place, rescues him, and gets into an accident on the way to the hospital? What if Y trips and falls on his way out of the hospital?

16. In *Corothers et al.* v. *Slobodian et al.* (1973), 36 D.L.R. (3d) 597 (Sask. C.A.); revd. in part (1975), 51 D.L.R. (3d) 1 (S.C.C.) the plaintiff Bonnie Corothers was driving along the highway when the vehicle in front of her, driven by Anton Hammerschmid, collided with a vehicle being driven negligently by one Neil Poupard, who was killed in the accident. The plaintiff stopped her car and went over to assist. Seeing several severely injured people, she decided that she should try to get help. She ran along the highway intending to get aid. At this point, about 50 feet down the road, a semi-trailer truck, driven by Slobodian, approached. Slobodian, on seeing the plaintiff, Bonnie Corothers, put on his brakes, but the truck jack-knifed, went into the ditch and injured her.

The plaintiff's actions against both Slobodian and the estate of the late Neil Poupard were dismissed at trial. The Saskatchewan Court of Appeal affirmed.

With regard to the action against Poupard, Woods J.A. observed:

". . . the female plaintiff had completed all that she was going to do at the scene of the collision before the arrival of the truck driven by Slobodian. She had left the scene of the accident and her activities had reached a new stage. The situation of peril created by Poupard had ended. The plaintiff was not then acting in danger nor anticipating any danger created by acts of Poupard. The injury suffered arose from a new act or circumstance, which was not one that ought reasonably to have been foreseeable by Poupard. . . ."

As to the defendant Slobodian, Woods J.A. explained that he came upon an "unusual situation not of his own creation. The standards to be applied are not those of perfection. If he made a mistake of judgment, it is excusable in the circumstances".

The Supreme Court of Canada unanimously reversed the decision as against Poupard but the majority affirmed as against Slobodian. With regard to Poupard, Mr. Justice Ritchie explained that Mrs. Corothers' acts "in attempting to flag down the approaching traffic were, in my view, perfectly normal reactions to the cry of distress. . .". It was a "reasonably foreseeable consequence of Poupard's negligence which in my view was a cause, if not the only cause, of Mrs. Corothers' injury". In relation to Slobodian, Mr. Justice Ritchie stated that "faced with a gesticulating woman on the side of the highway . . . he was acting in a moment of imminent emergency" so that "his error of judgment" was not actionable negligence.

Mr. Justice Pigeon, for the minority, felt that both Poupard and Slobodian should be liable. On the issue of Poupard's liability, His Lordship stated:

"I just cannot accept that this can be said not to be foreseeable by the author of the first collision. Multiple collisions are such frequent occurrences that dangerous emergency manoeuvres to avoid them are to be expected.

. . . To say that [Mrs. Corothers] was not acting in danger nor anticipating any danger created by the acts of Poupard is to ignore the realities of the situation. What she was doing was nothing but the proper reaction to those acts and an attempt to avoid or to mitigate some of their dreadful consequences."

See Binchi, "Comment" (1974), 52 Can. Bar Rev. 292.

17. Is any duty owed to a person who arrives at the scene of an accident as an avenger, rather than as a rescuer? One night X "borrows" a car from Y, his brother-in-law, without Y's consent. When Y finds out, he gives chase in another car. As he is driving along, Y sees his car in a field at the side of the road. He stops his car, runs into the field toward his car and steps on a live hydro wire. Can he collect from X, if it is shown that X was negligent? Does Y's state of mind at the time he entered the field matter? What if he intended to beat up X if he was unhurt, but to take him to the hospital if he was injured? Would there be any liability to Z, a curious onlooker, who stopped to observe the accident

and stepped on the hydro wire? Do curious onlookers ever become rescuers? Are any of these situations any more or less foreseeable than any of the others? How should the court handle these situations? Compare with *Jones* v. *Wabigwan*, [1968] 2 O.R. 837; revd. [1970] 1 O.R. 366, where Mr. Justice Schroeder, in reversing a trial judgment which had dismissed the action, observed:

"With much deference to the view expressed by the learned trial judge we are respectfully of the opinion that in determining the test of foreseeability he confined his consideration within too narrow a compass. He would appear to have directed his mind to the plaintiff and his actions and as to what might have been anticipated by the defendant vis-à-vis the plaintiff, and the plaintiff only, rather than to anyone who might be in the immediate neighbourhood when the danger was created and continued to exist. . . .

In our view a reasonable man in the position of the defendant should have anticipated that if he negligently collided with the hydro pole it was a probable consequence that the pole and the live electric wires would fall to the ground; that persons travelling along the highway in proximity to this point might be attracted to the field where the damaged vehicle, with its lights burning was visible, and that they might reasonably be expected to come in contact with the live wires attached to the broken hydro pole and sustain serious personal injury. If this conclusion be valid as to any person who might pass along that highway at the time that the danger created by the defendant materialized, whether that person entered the field moved by a natural curiosity or a desire to render needed assistance, then the defendant's conduct was a proximate cause of the plaintiff's injuries and damages in the sense that they were reasonably foreseeable and not too remote."

18. In *Videan* v. *British Transport Commission*, [1963] 2 Q.B. 650, [1963] 2 All E.R. 860, a station master was killed, while rescuing his own child, Richard, from an approaching train. The child, though saved, was injured. The child and his mother, the widow, both sued, but their cases were dismissed at trial. Both plaintiffs appealed. The appeal of Richard, the infant, failed since all members of the Court of Appeal were of the opinion that "it could not reasonably be foreseen" that Richard "would be on the line". As Richard was a trespasser whose presence could not be anticipated, there was no duty owing to him however the duty of an occupier to trespassers was defined. The Court of Appeal was unanimous, however, in allowing the widow's appeal. Harman L.J. and Pearson L.J. rested their opinions largely on the ground that the danger to the station master, as an employee of the defendant, was foreseeable. Denning M.R. agreed with the result but he took a different approach:

". . . In order to establish it, the widow must prove that Souness [the trolley driver] owed a duty of care to the stationmaster, that he broke that duty, and that, in consequence of the breach, the stationmaster was killed. Counsel for the defendants says that the widow can prove none of these things. All depends, he says, on the test of foreseeability; and, applying that test, he puts the following dilemma: If Souness could not reasonably be expected to foresee the presence of the child, he could not reasonably be expected to foresee the presence of the father. He could not foresee that a trespasser would be on the line. So how could he be expected to foresee that anyone would be attempting to rescue him? Counsel for the defendants points out that, in all the rescue cases that have hitherto come before the courts . . . the conduct of the defendant was a wrong to the victim or the potential victim. How can he be liable to the rescuer when he is not liable to the rescued?

I cannot accept this view. The right of the rescuer is an independent right, and is not derived from that of the victim. The victim may have been guilty of contributory negligence — or his right may be excluded by contractual stipulation — but still the rescuer can sue. So, also, the victim may, as here, be a trespasser and excluded on that ground, but still the rescuer can sue. Foreseeability is necessary, but not foreseeability of the particular emergency that arose. Suffice it that he ought reasonably to foresee that, if he did not take care, some emergency or other might arise, and that someone or other might be impelled to expose himself to danger in order to effect a rescue. Such is the case here. Souness ought to have anticipated that some emergency or other might arise. His trolley was not like an express train which is heralded by signals and whistles and shouts of 'keep clear'. His trolley came silently and swiftly on the unsuspecting quietude of a country station. He should have realised that someone or other might be put in peril if he came too fast or did not keep a proper look-out; and that, if anyone was put in peril, then someone would come to the rescue. As it happened, it was the stationmaster trying to rescue his child; but it would be the same if it had been a passer-by. Whoever comes to the rescue, the law should see that he does not suffer for it. It seems to me that, if a person by his fault creates a situation of peril, he must answer for it to any person who attempts to rescue the person who is in danger. He owes a duty to such a person above all others. The rescuer may act instinctively out of humanity or deliberately out of courage. But whichever it is, so long as it is not wanton interference, if the rescuer is killed or injured in the attempt, he can recover damages from the one whose fault has been the cause of it."

What do you think of this reasoning? Does it hinge on foresight or something else?

19. See also *Chadwick* v. *British Transport Commission*, [1967] 2 All E.R. 945 (Q.B.D.), where someone who suffered an anxiety neurosis after helping in rescue operations after a train wreck received compensation. Would he have recovered if he had been a mere observer rather than a rescuer? See *infra*. Compare with *Elverson* v. *Doctor's Hospital* (1975), 49 D.L.R. (3d) 196 (C.A.); affd (1976), 65 D.L.R. (3d) 382 (S.C.C.), where a husband, with a weak back, voluntarily assisted the nurses to raise his wife's hospital bed in order to place blocks under it. The husband's action was dismissed. Evans J.A. distinguished *Chadwick* and said: "This was a common, everyday occurrence, completely devoid of any inherent danger, and the particular susceptibility of the plaintiff was beyond the range of normal expectancy, or of reasonable foresight on the part of the nurse." Would it have made any difference if the wife had been in danger as a result of the nurse's negligence?

20. See Linden, "Down With Foreseeability! Of Thin Skulls and Rescuers" (1969), 47 Can. Bar Rev. 545:

"In these rescue cases the same decisions have been reached whatever formula was used. This is because the courts have decided to use tort law to encourage rescuers by rewarding them if they are injured. In addition, the courts are hopeful that they will deter, both specifically and generally, enterprisers who cause accidents. If someone knows that he will be liable not only to those he injures but to their rescuers, he may be more careful. It is also better for an activity to pay its way by being required to reimburse not only those injured by the activity directly but also the rescuers of those injured. Furthermore, the loss distribution and social welfare goals of tort law are served by spreading liability. Foreseeability disguises this analysis and, therefore, I say down with foreseeability!" Do you agree?

2. Second Accident

WIELAND v. CYRIL LORD CARPETS, LTD.

Queen's Bench Division. [1969] 3 All E.R. 1006

On October 4, 1965, the plaintiff was injured in a bus accident due to the negligence of the defendant. She was X-rayed in the hospital and told to return two days later. She did and was fitted with a collar for her neck. On leaving the hospital, she felt "rather muzzy", as though her head was useless. She was also in a nervous condition, both because of the accident and the visit to the doctor. The plaintiff wore bi-focal glasses and had done so for ten years. The collar on her neck deprived her of the ability to adjust herself to the use of the bi-focals. The combination of these factors produced some unsteadiness.

She called on her son at his office to ask him to take her home. He saw her as she reached the first floor of his office building. He told her to stay where she was and he would come down to her. This he did, and together they descended the stairs and on reaching the last step or about the last step, the plaintiff fell, because she did not show her habitual skill in descending the stairs when wearing bi-focal glasses.

Eveleigh J.: In those circumstances, I have to value this claim. On behalf of the defence it has been argued that this plaintiff's fall and the injury to the ankles resulting therefrom was not caused by the defendant's negligence. Alternatively it is said, if that injury was so caused then it was not foreseeable and reliance is placed on *Overseas Tankship (U.K.), Ltd.* v. *Morts Dock & Engineering Co., Ltd., The Wagon Mound (No. 1)*. As to the first contention, I find that the fall and the resulting injury was caused by the defendant's negligence. I find that it was the result of the injury inflicted in that accident. The plaintiff's ability to negotiate stairs was impaired and this resulted in a fall, which was a fall, in my view, in one of the ordinary activities of life for which she had been rendered less capable than she previously was. . . .

I think it is also important in the present case to bear in mind that her fall occurred very soon after she was fitted with the collar. The position might have been different if a person were to persist in wearing bi-focal glasses for a long time after an injury such as this and then sustain another injury. The effect of the original accident might be more difficult to demonstrate.

It has long been recognised that injury sustained in one accident may be the cause of a subsequent injury. The injury sustained by accident victims on the operating table is an example of that situation. So too are cases of suicide resulting from a mental condition produced by an accident. . . . It is always a question of course for the court in each case to determine whether or not on the facts of that case the accident did cause the second injury or death as the case might be. . . .

So now I turn to the second part of the defendants' argument, namely that the fall and the resulting injury was something that was not foreseeable and therefore does not attract damages. . .

I do not read *The Wagon Mound (No. 1)* as dealing with the extent of the original injury or the degree to which it has affected the plaintiff. Still less do I regard it as requiring foreseeability of the manner in which that original injury has caused harm to the plaintiff. Indeed the precise mechanics of the way in which the negligent act results in the original injury does not have to be foreseen. . . .

Once actionable injury is established, compensation is rarely if ever a valuation of the injury simpliciter. It is a valuation of harm suffered as a result of that injury. The valuation which the law adopts is the valuation of that injury with its attendant consequences to the victim. Consequences of a kind which human experience indicates may result from an injury are weighed in the scale of valuation to a greater or less extent depending on the probability of their materialising. When they have materialised they attract full value. When they are only a risk they attract less value. But in determining liability for those possible consequences it is not necessary to show that each was within the foreseeable extent or foreseeable scope of the original injury in the same way that the possibility of injury must be foreseen when determining whether or not the defendant's conduct gives a claim in negligence. . . .

I think that it is perfectly permissible in the present case to say that it is no answer to the claim for damages, that she would not have suffered had she not had eyesight that required her to wear bi-focal lenses. . . .

In the present case I am concerned with the extent of the harm suffered by the plaintiff as a result of actionable injury. In my view the injury and damage suffered because of the second fall are attributable to the original negligence of the defendants so as to attract compensation. If necessary I think the plaintiff's case can also be put against the defendant in another way. It can be said that it is foreseeable that one injury may affect a person's ability to cope with the vicissitudes of life and thereby be a cause of another injury and if foreseeability is required, that is to say, if foreseeability is the right word in this context, foreseeability of this general nature will, in my view, suffice. . . .

Judgment for the plaintiff.

McKEW v. HOLLAND et al.

House of Lords. [1969] 3 All E.R. 1621

The plaintiff's leg had been weakened in an accident for which the defendants were liable. As a result, his leg would give way beneath him occasionally. One day, as he commenced to descend some steep stairs, unassisted and without holding on, his leg collapsed and he began to fall downstairs. He pushed his daughter, who was with him, out of the way and tried to jump so as to land in a standing position, rather than falling down the stairs. On landing, he broke his ankle, a much more serious injury than the original one.

Lord Reid: . . . The appellant's case is that this second accident was caused by the weakness of his left leg which in turn had been caused by the first accident. The main argument for the respondents is that the second accident was not the direct or natural and probable or foreseeable result of their fault in causing the first accident.

In my view the law is clear. If a man is injured in such a way that his leg may give way at any moment he must act reasonably and carefully. It is quite possible that in spite of all reasonable care his leg may give way in circumstances such that as a result he sustains further injury. Then that second injury was caused by his disability which in turn was caused by the defender's fault. But if the injured man acts unreasonably he cannot hold the defender liable for injury caused by his own unreasonable conduct. His unreasonable conduct is *novus actus interveniens.* The chain of causation has been broken and what follows must be regarded as caused by his own conduct and not by the defender's fault or the disability caused by it. Or one may say that unreasonable conduct of the pursuer and what follows from it is not the natural and probable result of the original fault of the defender or of the ensuing disability. I do not think that foreseeability comes into this. A defender is not liable for a consequence of a kind which is not foreseeable. But it does not follow that he is liable for every consequence which a reasonable man could foresee. What can be foreseen depends almost entirely on the facts of the case, and it is often easy to foresee unreasonable conduct or some other *novus actus interveniens* as being quite likely, But that does not mean that the defender must pay for damage caused by the *novus actus.* It only leads to trouble if one tries to graft on to the concept of foreseeability some rule of law to the effect that a wrongdoer is not bound to foresee something which in fact he could readily foresee as quite likely to happen. For it is not at all unlikely or unforeseeable that an active man who has suffered such a disability will take some quite unreasonable risk. But if he does he cannot hold the defender liable for the consequences.

So in my view the question is whether the second accident was caused by the appellant doing something unreasonable. It was argued that the wrongdoer must take his victim as he finds him and that that applies not only to a thin skull but also to his intelligence. But I shall not deal with that argument because there is nothing in the evidence to suggest that the appellant is abnormally stupid. This case can be dealt with equally well by asking whether the appellant did something which a moment's reflection would have shown him was an unreasonable thing to do.

He knew that his leg was liable to give way suddenly and without warning. He knew that this stair was steep and that there was no handrail. He must have realised, if he had given the matter a moment's thought, that he could only safely descend the stair if he either went extremely slowly and carefully so that he could sit down if his leg gave way, or waited for the assistance of his wife and brother-in-law. But he chose to descend in such a way that when his leg gave way he could not stop himself. I agree with what the Lord Justice-Clerk says at the end of his opinion and I think that this is sufficient to require this appeal to be dismissed.

But I think it right to say a word about the argument that the fact that the appellant made to jump when he felt himself falling is conclusive against him. When his leg gave way the appellant was in a very difficult situation. He had to decide what to do in a fraction of a second. He may have come to a wrong decision; he probably did. But if the chain of causation had not been broken before this by putting himself in a position where he might be confronted with an emergency, I do not think that he would put himself out of court by acting wrongly in the emergency unless his action was so utterly unreasonable that even on the spur of the moment no ordinary man would have been so foolish as to do what he did. In an emergency it is natural to try to do something to save oneself and I do not think that his trying to jump in this emergency was so wrong that it could be said to be no more than an error of judgment. But for the reasons already given I would dismiss this appeal.

Appeal dismissed.

NOTES

1. Are *Wieland* v. *Cyril Lord Carpets Ltd.* and *McKew* v. *Holland et al.* in conflict? How can they be rationalized?

2. In *Block* v. *Martin*, [1951] 4 D.L.R. 121, someone who had been negligently injured fell while fishing and fractured his leg. Mr. Justice MacDonald of Alberta held that the fracture would not have occurred unless the earlier injury was unhealed and that it was a "definite, contributing, predisposing cause". See also *Boss* v. *Robert Simpson Eastern Ltd.* (1969), 2 D.L.R. (3d) 114 (N.S.S.C.); *Goldhawke* v. *Harder* (1977), 74 D.L.R. (3d) 721. *Cf. Armstrong* v. *Stewart* (1978), 7 C.C.L.T. 164 (Ont.), where a falling accident one and one-half years after the initial injury was held to be *novus actus interveniens*.

3. In *Priestley* v. *Gilbert*, [1972] 3 O.R. 502, the plaintiff's leg was seriously injured as a result of an accident in which the defendant driver was found to be grossly negligent. At a Christmas party, the plaintiff, after becoming quite intoxicated, began dancing, and, as his leg was still weak from the injury, he fell and broke it again. In refusing the claim for damages arising from this second break, Osler J. stated:

"... there is an onus upon a person who knows or should know of a physical weakness to act reasonably and carefully and to protect himself from harm. . . . [T]o get up and dance on this occasion was not a reasonable action in his condition . . . and the principle of *novus actus interveniens* protects the defendant from responsibility for that injury".

What if he had been dancing while sober and fell? What if he was drunk, but not dancing? What about contributory negligence here?

4. Plaintiff suffers a back injury in an accident caused by a negligent defendant. The plaintiff returns to his work, which involves heavy lifting. In moving some heavy marble, his condition is aggravated. Liability? See *Saccardo* v. *City of Hamilton*, [1971] 2 O.R. 479 (Osler J.).

5. In *Lucas* v. *Juneau* (1955), 127 F. Supp. 730 (Alaska), the defendant negligently injured the plaintiff. After confinement in an Alaska hospital, it was decided that he should be taken to Seattle for treatment. While he was being transported in an ambulance, the driver had an epileptic fit, the ambulance went off the road, and plaintiff was injured. The court declared: "I conclude, therefore, that the risk which must be borne by the original wrongdoer includes not only negligent medical treatment but also negligent transportation of the plaintiff to a place where treatment of the kind indicated by the nature of the injury may be obtained. A corollary of this conclusion is that the first tortfeasor is in no position to avoid liability for an aggravation sustained by the plaintiff in taking one of the steps necessary to obtain further treatment." In accord is *State ex. rel. Smith* v. *Weinstein* (1965), 398 S.W. 2d 41 (Mo.), where the ambulance had a collision. Do you agree? What if the ambulance had been hit by lightning?

6. Is a negligent defendant liable if the second "accident" is the theft of an injured person's property?

In *Patten* v. *Silberschein*, [1936] 3 W.W.R. 169, 51 B.C.R. 133, the defendant motorist negligently struck the plaintiff rendering him unconscious. While unconscious he lost $80 which was in his pocket. D.A. McDonald J., said he had thought this claim for damages was not the natural and probable consequence of the defendant's negligence but *Salmond on Torts* 7th ed., p. 153, said that *In re Polemis* had decided that damages were recoverable whether probable or not. Upon this authority he held the defendant liable. In *Duce* v. *Rourke* (1951), 1 W.W.R. 305 (N.S.) (Alta.), Egbert J., disapproved of *Patten* v. *Silberschein*, and held a defendant who had negligently injured the plaintiff, not liable for tools stolen from the plaintiff's car while the car was standing in the highway after plaintiff's removal to a hospital. The theft "was the consequence of some conscious intervening independent act, for which the defendant was in no wise responsible". While approving of *In re Polemis*, Egbert J., held that the intervention of a *novus actus* was outside the rule in that case.

In *Brower* v. *N.Y. Central & Hudson River R.R. Co.* (1918), 103 Atl. 166 (N.J. Court of Error and Appeals), the defendant railway negligently collided with the plaintiff's horse and wagon at a crossing. The horse was killed, the wagon destroyed, and barrels which filled the wagon were lost. It appeared that the contents of the wagon were scattered by the collision and, the driver having been stunned in the collision, the barrels were stolen by people at the scene of the accident. The defendant by a divided court (7:5) was held liable for the loss of the barrels as well as the horse and wagon. The "natural and probable" result of depriving the plaintiff of his driver's protection of the property in the street of a large city was its disappearance.

What is the difference between these cases and *Stansbie* v. *Troman (supra)*? Does the conflict in the cases bother you? What is the best way to handle these situations? Is it more important for the defendant to get his victim to a hospital or to stay and guard the property at the scene of the accident?

3. Medical Mishaps

MERCER v. GRAY

Ontario Court of Appeal. [1941] O.R. 127; [1941] 3 D.L.R. 564

The judgment of the court was delivered by **McTague, J.A.**: This is an appeal from the judgment of Urquhart J. after trial by jury. Since I have reached the conclusion that there must be a new trial, I shall try to refrain from stating any views on the facts that may prove prejudicial on a new trial.

The action is for damages for negligence. The defendant was driving his auto-mobile on Ontario Street in the City of Sarnia and came into collision with the infant Naomi Mercer, who was crossing an intersection, as a result of which she was seriously injured. The jury in answer to questions gave damages to all three plaintiffs. The plaintiffs appeal on the ground that the damages awarded were inadequate by reason of the learned judge's faulty charge to the jury, and also by reason of the admission of evidence not properly admissible. A new trial is asked. . . .

The main difficulty in the case results from the evidence tendered by the defendant in respect to the amount of damages for which the defendant was liable. The child, as I have already intimated, was very seriously injured. The family physician was called in and he in turn called in a surgical specialist. No direct attack was made on the qualifications or general good repute of the medical men employed. From the evidence their general qualifications appear to be excellent. The child's both legs were fractured. Reductions under a fluoroscope were done in the recognized manner and the legs put in a cast. As sometimes happens, not always, swelling under the cast took place and the condition became much aggravated. Defendant introduced evidence to show that the doctors had not cut the cast early enough once a cyanosed condition became evident, and that therefore a great part of the damage resulted from the lack of skill or negligence in treatment and that for that part the defendant could not be liable.

The case went to the jury on that simple basis, and judging from the amount of damages awarded, particularly in respect of the father's out-of-pocket expenses, the jury gave strong effect to the defendant's contention.

With all due respect to the learned trial judge, I am of opinion that the matter is not so simple. Even if in the circumstances here the evidence were admissible at all the matter should have gone to the jury in a completely different way.

It seems to me that if reasonable care is used to employ a competent physician or surgeon to treat personal injuries wrongfully inflicted, the results of the treatment, even though by an error of treatment the treatment is unsuccessful, will be a proper head of damages. As Gahan in *Law of Damages,* at p. 141, points out, this principle always seems to have been conceded in England without argument. This also appears to be the case in Ontario. In Nova Scotia it was adopted in *Small* v. *Westville* (1898), 40 N.S.R. 226. Examples of adoption of the same principle in the United States are *Ryder* v. *Findley,* 195 N.Y.A.D.R. 731; *Reed* v. *Detroit,* [108 Mich. Rep. 224] , and *Pullman Palace Car Co.* v. *Bluhm,* 109 Illinois Reports, p. 20.

In *Beven on Negligence,* 4th edition, it is dealt with in the following terms, at p. 104; "It follows from what has been said that an injured person is not bound to employ the most skilful surgeon who can be found, nor yet to incur lavish expenditure of any kind in the treatment of the injuries he has sustained. If his medical man treats him erroneously, no claim to exoneration of the wrong-doer from full liability is thereby established, if only the medical man employed is of good standing and repute."

In *Denton on Municipal Negligence,* at p. 360, it is put: "Where the damages are increased owing to the physician's negligence, it is difficult to see why such negligence should be attributed to the plaintiff so long as there is no negligence on the plaintiff's part in the selection of his physician. The negligence of another person co-operating with the municipality in producing the injury in the first instance would not relieve the corporation from the consequences of its neglect so there is no reason why the subsequent negligence of a third person increasing the injury should tend to relieve the municipality. A plaintiff is bound to act in good faith and to resort to such reasonable means and methods within his reach as will make his damages as small as he can, and so long as he does this, if the injuries are enhanced by the negligence of a physician, the plaintiff is not disentitled to recover the whole damage."

In general the above, I think, may be taken as the correct general principle, although I am inclined to think that perhaps it may be a little too broadly stated by Judge Denton. There may be cases where the medical or surgical treatment is so negligent as to be actionable. This would be in effect *novus actus interveniens* and the plaintiff would have his remedy against the physician or surgeon. But this the defendant would have to prove in the proper forum, and as in Ontario the proper forum for actions of malpractice is a judge without a jury, if such a defence were set up there would be ample reason for dispensing with a jury. At any rate no proper instruction as to law on this subject was given to the jury, and a new trial must be had.

NOTES

1. In *Watson* v. *Grant* (1970), 72 W.W.R. 665 (B.C.S.C.), the negligently injured plaintiff was given some unnecessary medical treatment, in the form of two unneeded operations. In awarding damages against the original tortfeasor for the loss incurred as a result, Mr. Justice Aikins dealt with the foreseeability test of *The Wagon Mound (No. 1)* as follows:

"I commence with the proposition that if A. injures B, it is reasonably foreseeable that B. will seek advice and treatment for his injuries. It seems to me equally obvious that it is foreseeable that B. will seek advice and treatment from a person who is qualified and authorized to diagnose and treat injuries, namely a qualified doctor. The reasonable man, in my opinion, would be aware that a doctor may err in diagnosis or in treatment, or both, without the patient, who has done all he can reasonably be expected to do in going to a qualified person for help, having any reason to suppose he is being badly advised or treated. Returning to my example, if A. injures B. thereby putting B. in the position where he has to have medical help, there is inherent risk that B. may suffer further loss or injury because of *bona fide* error on the part of the doctor. I may, I think, properly assume that the great majority of people who are injured or are ill are well aware that the doctor chosen may make some mistake in diagnosis or treatment, but are driven by necessity to accept this risk. It seems to me plain that it is reasonably foreseeable that a person injured to the extent that medical help is required, is driven to accept the risk of medical error.

In my opinion, it is reasonably foreseeable that an injured person who seeks medical help may, not will, suffer further loss or damage because of error in medical treatment.

I wish to make it clear that I am not expressing an opinion on the position as to remoteness or foreseeability if it had been established that Dr. Jain had been negligent in respect to the last two operations. In conclusion on this branch of this case, I hold that the defendants are liable in respect to the last two operations."

See also *David* v. T.T.C. (1977), 77 D.L.R. (3d) 717 ((Ont.) *per* Parker J.).

2. In *Thompson et al.* v. *Toorenburgh et al.* (1972), 29 D.L.R. (3d) 608 (B.C.); affd (1975), 50 D.L.R. (3d) 717; affd S.C.C. Nov. 6, 1973, a woman with a minor heart condition received injuries in an accident which resulted from the defendant's negligence. She was treated at the hospital for lacerations then released. She returned to the hospital later the same evening and died of a pulmonary edema precipitated by the accident. It was clear from the evidence that proper medical treatment at the time of the readmission could have saved her life. Kirke Smith J. held that the defendant was liable for the death: "That there was such error [of medical treatment] here is not open to question; but I

think . . . there was no break, in the circumstances of this case, in the chain of causation." There was no specific finding, however, indicating whether the medical error was a negligent or a non-negligent one. In the Court of Appeal, Robertson J.A. stated:

> ". . . not only were the right procedures not followed, but certain harmful procedures were followed. The harmful procedures may have hastened the patient's death, but, if they did (upon which I express no opinion), they did not cause it. Death was the result of acute pulmonary edema and the edema was brought on by the collision. Mrs. Thompson would almost certainly have recovered if proper treatment had been applied speedily; the doctors failed to apply that treatment and so failed to save her life, but they did not cause her death. They failed to provide an *actus interveniens* that would have saved her life, but that is not the same as committing an *actus interveniens* that caused her death."

See also *Winteringham* v. *Rae* (1966), 55 D.L.R. (2d) 108 (Parker J.), where a reaction to an injection was held to be compensable. There was no allegation of malpractice. Mr. Justice Parker treated the case as one of abnormal susceptibility, an "exception" to *The Wagon Mound (No. 1)*. And see also *Robinson* v. *Post Office*, [1974] 1 W.L.R. 1176 (C.A.).

3. The burden of proof in these cases rests on the defendant who must establish the facts of intervening negligent treatment. See *Papp* v. *Leclerc* (1977), 77 D.L.R. (3d) 536 (Ont. C.A.) where Lacourciere J.A. stated:

> "Every tortfeasor causing injury to a person placing him in the position of seeking medical or hospital help, must assume the inherent risks of complications, *bona fide* medical error or misadventure, and they are reasonably foreseeable and not too remote . . . It is for the defendant to prove that some new act rendering another person liable has broken the chain of causation. This was not done in the present case."

4. Why should the result be different if the doctor is negligent in his treatment? Is malpractice unforeseeable? What are the relevant policy considerations? What problems of joint liability, contribution and indemnity arise?

5. In *Thompson* v. *Fox* (1937), 192 Atl. 107 (Sup. Ct. Penn.), the plaintiff was injured by reason of the negligent operation of a motor car by one Taylor on Nov. 21, 1932. He was taken to the defendant physician's hospital where he remained until May, 1933. In Oct., 1933, the plaintiff commenced an action against Taylor for damages, alleging that he had been permanently crippled, etc. On July 25, 1934, the plaintiff settled this action and by formal document released Taylor "from all causes of action . . . arising out of an accident to me caused by J.R. Taylor running an automobile into me on Nov. 21, 1932". On March 4, 1935, the plaintiff commenced action against defendant alleging the negligent and improper treatment of the fractures received in the accident of Nov. 21, 1932. The action was dismissed and this was upheld on appeal. Stern J. said:

> "In the action against Taylor, plaintiff's recovery for the injury to his hip would have included the added damage caused by the alleged negligence of the defendant. Doctors, being human, are apt occasionally to lapse from prescribed standards, and the likelihood of carelessness, lack of judgment or of skill, on the part of one employed to effect a cure for a condition caused by another's act, is therefore considered in law as an incident of the original injury, and, if the injured party has used ordinary care in the selection of a physician or surgeon, any additional harm resulting from the latter's mistake or negligence is considered as one of the elements of the damages for which the original wrongdoer is liable. [Citations omitted.] 'If the negligent actor is liable for another's injury, he is also liable for any additional bodily harm resulting from acts done by third persons in rendering aid which the other's injury reasonably requires, irrespective of whether such acts are done in a proper or negligent manner.' *Restatement of the Law of Torts*, §457.

> Such being the law, for the final condition of his hip plaintiff could have sued, and did sue, Taylor; for the aggravation of the original condition plaintiff could have sued, and did sue, defendant. He could have pursued both actions to judgment. For the same injury, however, an injured party can have

but one satisfaction and the receipt of such satisfaction, either as payment of a judgment recovered or consideration for a release executed by him, from a person liable for such injury, necessarily works a release of all others liable for the same injury and prevents any further proceeding against them. [Citations omitted.]"

Is this way of treating intervening malpractice preferable to that in *Mercer* v. *Gray?*

6. Some Canadian authority for a similar view is the statement of Haines J. in *Kolesar* v. *Jeffries* (1974), 9 O.R. (2d) 41; varied (1976), 12 O.R. (2d) 142; affd on other grounds 77 D.L.R. (3d) 161 (S.C.C.), who suggested that an originally negligent defendant may be held responsible for the later negligence of a doctor or a hospital which aggravates the original injury "unless it is completely outside the range of normal experience".

7. In *Price* v. *Milawski* (1977), 82 D.L.R. (3d) 130 (Ont. C.A.), it was held that one negligent doctor could be liable for the additional loss caused by another negligent doctor. As Mr. Justice Arnup explained, at p. 141:

". . . a person doing a negligent act may, in circumstances lending themselves to that conclusion, be held liable for future damages arising in part from the subsequent negligent act of another, and in part from his own negligence, where such subsequent negligence and consequent damage were reasonably foreseeable as a possible result of his own negligence.

It was reasonably foreseeable by Dr. Murray that once the information generated by his negligent error got into the hospital records, other doctors subsequently treating the plaintiff might well rely on the accuracy of that information, *i.e.,* that the X-ray showed no fracture of the ankle. It was also foreseeable that some doctor might do so without checking, even though to do so in the circumstances might itself be a negligent act. The history is always one factor in a subsequent diagnosis and the consequent treatment. Such a possibility was not a risk which a reasonable man (in the position of Dr. Murray) would brush aside as far-fetched—see *"Wagon Mound" (No. 2), supra, per* Lord Reid at p. 643 G.

The later negligence of Dr. Carbin compunded the effects of the earlier negligence of Dr. Murray. It did not put a halt to the consequences of the first act and attract liability for all damage from that point forward. In my view the trial Judge was correct in holding that each of the appellants was liable to the plaintiff and that it was not possible to try to apportion the extent to which each was responsible for the plaintiff's subsequent operation and his permanent disability."

Does this mean that *Mercer* v. *Gray* is overruled? See also *Powell* v. *Guttman* (1978), 6 C.C.L.T. 183 (Man. C.A.), *per* O'Sullivan J.A.

8. The Criminal Code of Canada, R.S.C. 1970, c. C-34, s. 207 reads:

207. Where a person, by an act or omission, does any thing that results in the death of a human being, he causes the death of that human being notwithstanding that death from that cause might have been prevented by resorting to proper means.

Section 208 is as follows:

208. Where a person causes to a human being a bodily injury that is of itself of a dangerous nature and from which death results, he causes the death of that human being notwithstanding that the immediate cause of death is proper or improper treatment that is applied in good faith.

Is the solution to this problem in fatal cases outlined in the Criminal Code attractive to you? See also *R.* v. *Smith,* [1959] 2 Q.B. 35, [1959] 2 All E.R. 193; *The Queen* v. *Jordan* (1956), 40 Cr. App. R. 152 (C.C.A.U.K.); *People* v. *Lewis* (1899), 57 Pac. 470 (S.C.Cal.). Should the decisions reached in tort cases be consistent with those in criminal cases? If not, which should have a broader view of "causation"? Which do have the broader view?

9. Does the plaintiff who incurs injury have an obligation, similar to that in contract law, to try and "mitigate" his damages by seeking medical attention? For example, an injured plaintiff goes to a masseuse for treatment to relieve her pain instead of seeing a doctor. If the plaintiff shows no appreciable recovery

which she would have had she been given proper medical care, can it be argued
that this was a *novus actus interveniens?* See *Lowrie* v. *Megett* (1974), 11
S.A.S.R. 5. What if the plaintiff seeks no attention at all and the condition gets
worse?

10. If someone commits suicide because of the depression he feels after being
negligently injured, should the original tortfeasor be liable for the death? In
Pigney v. *Pointers Transport Services Ltd.,* [1957] 1 W.L.R. 1121, [1957] 2 All
E.R. 807, an accident victim, suffering from anxiety neurosis hanged himself. He
was not legally insane in that he knew what he was doing and that it was wrong.
Relying on *Polemis*, the court imposed liability because the death was "directly
traceable" to the physical injury. In its reasons, however, the court found that
it was "clearly a matter which could not reasonably have been foreseen". How
would a court treat this problem in *The Wagon Mound (No. 1)* era?

11. The American courts impose liability if the person is insane when he kills
himself but not if a sane person wilfully destroys himself. See *McMahon* v. *City
of New York* (1955), 141 N.Y.S. (2d) 190 (sane); *Daniels* v. *New York, N.H. &
H.R.R. Co.* (1903), 183 Mass. 393, 67 N.E. 424 (insane).

12. Why should sanity or lack of it make a difference? Is suicide by an insane
person more foreseeable? Could the thin-skull rule be applied in this situation?

13. How do these cases compare with the situations where a patient in a
hospital kills himself? Can the hospital be held liable? What does it depend on?
See *Stadel* v. *Albertson,* [1954] 2 D.L.R. 328 (no liability). See also *Lepine* v.
University Hospital Board, [1966] S.C.R. 561 (no liability for non-fatal jump
out of window by epileptic); Roth, "Note" (1967), 5 O.H.L.J. 105. Compare
with *Villemure* v. *L'Hôpital Notre-Dame* (1972), 31 D.L.R. (3d) 454 (S.C.C.).
Where there is a suicide, is it better to hold liable the injurer of the suicide victim,
the people who may have prevented the suicide, both of these, or neither?

E. SHIFTING RESPONSIBILITY

GRANT v. SUN SHIPPING CO. LTD.

House of Lords. [1948] A.C. 549; [1948] 2 All E.R. 238

A stevedore, with other labourers, was employed in the morning in rolling oil
drums along an alleyway between a berthed ship's hatches and the starboard
side. The deck was lit by three clusters of lights, two on the starboard and one
on the port side of the ship. At the same time workmen employed by a company
of ship repairers were at work in the holds and, in the same morning, had removed some of the hatch covers. At noon, when the stevedore left for dinner,
the repairers were still at work but the stevedore heard one of the ship's officers
tell them to see that everything was secure when they finished their work. When
the stevedore and his mates returned, the repairers had completed their work
and gone. They had, however, failed to replace the hatch covers and to refix the
cluster of lights from the port side which they had taken down and left lying on
the deck. As the stevedore rolled up a drum he found himself in darkness. He
saw the port lights on the deck and, believing the hatch covers on, moved over
to get it in order to replace it on the port side of the ship. He fell into the hold
sustaining injuries for which he brought action against the shipowners and the
repairers. At the trial and on appeal, both the shipowners and the repair company were held to be negligent and in breach of statutory obligation: the shipowners, for failing to inspect to see that all was secure, for failure to see that
proper lighting was provided and for failure to see that the hatches were closed;
the repair company for failure to close the hatches and in not replacing the
light which was necessary for those working on the deck. At the trial, the Lord
Ordinary gave judgment against the shipowners only. On appeal the plaintiff
was held not entitled to recover because of his contributory negligence and the

plaintiff appealed. That part of the case exonerating the plaintiff from contributory negligence is omitted.

Lord Du Parcq: . . . My Lords, I regard it as a well-settled principle that when separate and independent acts of negligence on the part of two or more persons have directly contributed to cause injury and damage to another, the person injured may recover damages from any one of the wrongdoers, or from all of them. The Lord Ordinary's view was that "the effect of any negligence of the second defenders was broken by the later negligence of the first defenders". This reasoning seems to me to be akin to that which has led to frequent and determined attempts to establish the so-called "rule of the last opportunity", of which less will be heard since the decision of your Lordships' House in *Boy Andrew (Owners)* v. *St. Rognvald (Owners)*, [1948] A.C. 140. I refer especially to the opinion of Viscount Simon. With the greatest respect for the Lord Ordinary's opinion I think that his reasoning is fallacious. If the negligence or breach of duty of one person is the cause of injury to another, the wrongdoer cannot in all circumstances escape liability by proving that, though he was to blame, yet but for the negligence of a third person the injured man would not have suffered the damage of which he complains. There is abundant authority for the proposition that the mere fact that a subsequent act of negligence has been the immediate cause of disaster does not exonerate the original offender. . .

In the same case, *The Bernina,* Lord Escher M.R. in the Court of Appeal discussed the question "what is the law applicable to a transaction in which a plaintiff has been injured by negligence, and in the course of which transaction there have been negligent acts or omissions by more than one person?" The learned Master of the Rolls said that upon many points as to such a transaction the common law was clear, and stated the first of these points in these words: "If no fault can be attributed to the plaintiff, and there is negligence by the defendant and also by another independent person, both negligences partly directly causing the accident, the plaintiff can maintain an action for all the damages occasioned to him against either the defendant or the other wrongdoer."

My Lords, it was truly said by counsel for the appellants that the case now before your Lordships would in normal times have been one proper for the consideration of a jury. A jury would not have profited by a direction couched in the language of logicians, and expounding theories of causation, with or without the aid of Latin maxims. It would, I think, have been right to instruct them in language similar to that used by Lord Esher in the passage which I have just quoted. For my own part I have no doubt (leaving aside for the moment the question whether fault can be attributed to the pursuer) that the negligence and breach of statutory duty attributable to each of the defenders "partly" and "directly" caused the pursuer injuries. Whether or not a cause is a "direct" cause is sometimes a difficult question, but here the precautions, which the regulations prescribed and ordinary prudence should have dictated, have for their object the prevention of accidents of the very nature of that which befell the pursuer.

[The speeches of Lord Porter and Lord Uthwatt to the same effect are omitted. Lord Oaksey would have barred the plaintiff because of contributory negligence.]

NOTES

1. In *Ostash* v. *Sonnenberg et al.* (1968), 67 D.L.R. (2d) 311 the Alberta Court of Appeal refused to relieve one negligent defendant from liability on the ground that another defendant could have discovered the defect. Chief Justice Smith, citing *Grant* v. *Sun Shipping Co., Ltd.,* stated ". . . my view is that there

were separate acts of negligence on the part of two persons which directly contributed to cause injury and damage to the plaintiffs and that therefore they are entitled to recover from both of them".

2. In *Pittsburg* v. *Horton* (1908), 87 Ark. 576, 113 S.W. 647, a boy of ten, Charlie Copple, picked up a box of dynamite caps which were thrown out by a servant of the defendant. The caps looked like small metal cartridges and appeared empty save for some dirt. The boy carried the caps home where he played with them in the presence of his parents. The boy played with them at home for a week and his mother frequently picked them up from the floor and placed them on the clock shelf where they remained when the boy was not playing with them. The boy's father worked in a mine similar to that of the defendant. After a week the boy carried the caps to school and traded them to the plaintiff, a boy of 13, for some writing paper. The plaintiff, in the belief that the caps were spent cartridges was picking at what he believed to be dirt in one of them when it exploded, tearing his hand so badly it had to be amputated. At the trial the defendant was held liable, but on appeal the judgment was reversed. *Per* Hart J.: "[The mother's] course of conduct broke the causal connection between the original negligent act of appellant and the subsequent injury of the plaintiff. It established a new agency, and the possession by Charlie Copple of the caps or shells was thereafter referable to the permission of his parents, and not to the original taking. Charlie Copple's parents having permitted him to retain possession of the caps, his further acts in regard to them must be attributable to their permission and were wholly independent of the original negligence of appellants."

3. In *Henningsen* v. *Markowitz* (1928), 230 N.Y.S. 313, a criminal statute forbade the sale of air rifles to children. The defendant sold one to a child, 13, whose mother took it away form him and hid it. The boy found it and, while shooting into a target, negligently injured the plaintiff. The defendant was held liable. Is this distinguishable from *Pittsburgh* v. *Horton*? See also *J.B. Hand & Co. Ltd.* v. *Best Motor Accessories Ltd.* (1962), 34 D.L.R. (2d) 282 (Nfld.); *Great Eastern Oil & Import Co., Ltd.* v. *Best*, [1962] S.C.R. 118, 31 D.L.R. (2d) 153.

REVIEW PROBLEM

Dodo manufactured disinfectant, which he packed in large cylindrical cans about three feet high and two feet in diameter and weighing about 100 lbs. each. One day Dodo loaded his two ton truck, which was open at the back, with about 50 of these cans and set out to deliver them to his customers. He failed to fasten a rope or chain around them, as was the custom.

Unbeknownst to Dodo, a youthful adventurer of limited intelligence and decided delinquent tendencies, known in Dodo's neighbourhood as "Dennis the Menace" stowed away on the back of the truck amongst the cans. Dodo made no inspection of his vehicle prior to setting out along the highway towards his first customer's factory, which inspection would undoubtedly have turned up Dennis.

As the truck crossed the bridge over the River Koo, Dennis, the 15-year-old menace, emerged from hiding and slowly pushed one of the cans toward the back edge of the truck six feet away. Dennis went to push the can off the truck and hollered "Depth charges away!" Before Dennis was able to push the can off, however, the truck which was travelling over the 50 miles per hour speed limit hit a bump in the road and the can fell off the truck. The can took a rather strange bounce and landed on top of the three foot railing of the bridge, balanced there for a moment, and then toppled over toward the River Koo, 100 feet below.

Unfortunately, a first year law student named Peter, who had just finished his examinations and had gone fishing for relaxation, was sitting in a rented rowboat on the River Koo, fishing rod in hand. As luck would have it, the 100 lb. can flew right into the rowboat smashing it to bits and tossing Peter into the chilly water. Because of his weakened condition as a result of his examination ordeal, Peter contracted pneumonia and had to stay in bed all summer.

The first day he got out of bed he fell, because he was so frail, and broke his leg. His doctor negligently set it in such a way that he now walks with a limp.

What tort liabilities have arisen?

CHAPTER 10

IMPERFECTLY PROTECTED INTERESTS

Although foreseeability is now the major criterion for determining the limits of tort responsibility, the courts have not extended it into all areas. There remain certain interests that are still imperfectly protected, even though damage to them is expectable. One reason for this time lag is that bodily security must be assured before courts can turn their attention to more ephemeral and less immediate interests. Initially, therefore, the judicial reaction was to deny completely any compensation for mental suffering, for damage to economic interests, or for negligent misstatements. The notion of duty was frequently utilized to explain these immunities, but, on occasion, remoteness and causation language were also invoked. In the last few years, these anachronisms began to collapse under the onslaught of the "neighbour principle" of *Donoghue* v. *Stevenson*. The courts did not, however, sweep away all vestiges of their earlier reticence. Instead, they chipped away at these blanket immunities, moving from the duty rationale, which lends itself to a complete refusal of liability, over to remoteness and proximate cause reasoning, which can be controlled more sensitively. Foreseeability has played an important role in all this, but it has not solved everything. There are still difficult value choices to be made.

A. NERVOUS SHOCK

MARSHALL et al. v. LIONEL ENTERPRISES INC. et al.
Ontario High Court. [1972] 2 O.R. 177

Application to determine a point of law raised by a statement of claim and for an order striking out the claim of a wife based on nervous shock suffered from seeing the aftermath of an accident in which her husband was grievously injured.

Haines J.: . . . A review of the cases dealing with this point of law shows that the history of nervous shock in the common law has been one of evolution and adaptation to the growth of medical science and common knowledge.

The early denial of liability for physical illness caused by shock in *Victorian Railways Com'rs* v. *Coultas* (1888), 13 App. Cas. 222 (P.C.), has been reversed many times in the twentieth century. That decision was based on the ground that such damages would be remote. Sir R. Couch, in delivering judgment, made the following statement (at pp. 225-6):

"Damages arising from mere sudden terror unaccompanied by any actual physical injury, but occasioning a nervous or mental shock, cannot under such circumstances, their Lordships think, be considered a consequence which, in the ordinary course of things, would flow from the negligence of the gate-keeper. If it were held that they can, it appears to their Lordships that it would be extending the liability for negligence much beyond what that liability has hitherto been held to be. Not only in such a case as the present, but in every case where an accident caused by negligence had given a person a serious nervous shock, there might be a claim for damages on account of mental injury. The difficulty which now often exists in case of alleged physical injuries of determining whether they were caused by the negligent act would be greatly increased and a wide field opened for imaginary claims."

The law then at this time was clear and the reason for it was caution.

However, not much later, it was acknowledged that there was liability for shock experienced by a plaintiff through negligent conduct of the defendant but only where such negligence put the plaintiff in fear of his own bodily safety. As early as 1901 the English courts sustained a claim by a barmaid who suffered a miscarriage from fear of personal injury to herself when the defendant's pair-horse was hurtled into her husband's pub: *Dulieu* v. *White & Sons*, [1901] 2 K.B. 669. In giving judgment, Kennedy J., tried to impose the following limitation (at p. 675):

"It is not, however, to be taken that in my view every nervous shock occasioned by negligence and producing physical injury to the sufferer gives a cause of action. There is, I am inclined to think, at least one limitation. The shock, where it operates through the mind, must be a shock which arises from a reasonable fear of immediate personal injury to oneself."

This limitation did not remain in effect for long however and the real question soon became the scope of legal protection where nervous shock is suffered for reasons other than fear for one's own safety. This question was canvassed by the English Court of Appeal in 1924 in *Hambrook* v. *Stokes Brothers*, [1925] 1 K.B. 141. In that case the plaintiff's wife suffered nervous shock which eventually caused her death as a result of seeing a run-away lorry rushing down a road to where she had just left her children. It was held by a majority of the Court of Appeal that, on the assumption that the shock was caused by what the woman saw with her own eyes as distinguished by what she was told by bystanders, the plaintiff was entitled to recover, notwithstanding that the shock was brought about by fear for her children's safety and not by fear for her own.

Bankes L.J., in his reasons for judgment, rejected the *dictum* laid down by Kennedy J. He failed to find any real distinction between the fear of immediate bodily injury to the mother and a natural fear for the well-being of her child. Atkin L.J., would have carried this reasoning even further. On p. 157 he states: "Personally I see no reason for excluding the bystander in the highway who receives injury in the same way from apprehension of or the actual sight of injury to a third party." He, however, viewed the cause of action as created by breach of the ordinary duty to take reasonable care to avoid inflicting personal injuries, followed by damage, even though the type of damage may be unexpected. The question appeared to him to be as to the extent of the duty and not as to remoteness of damage. It should be noted here that the court made the assumption that the injury in this case was caused by what the mother saw rather than what she was later told. The implication may be taken that a new limitation was imposed in that it would be necessary for the plaintiff in such cases to apprehend the danger with his or her unaided senses.

It should also be remembered that this case was decided shortly after the decision in *Re Polemis and Furness, Withy & Co.*, [1921] 3 K.B. 560. That case decided that as long as the damage was directly traceable to the negligent act it was irrelevant that the particular injury was not foreseeable by the defendants.

Sargant L.J. also decided the case on the basis of breach of duty rather than remoteness of damage. It was his feeling that liability for nervous shock could only be reached "by a new and quite unusual link in the chain of causation".

Sargant L.J. therefore felt that there was no duty in this situation and would have dismissed the appeal.

The next major case dealing with the point was *Hay or Bourhill* v. *Young*, [1943] A.C. 92. In this case, the plaintiff, a pregnant fishwife, was getting off a tramcar when a motorcyclist negligently collided with a car about 45 feet away. Plaintiff did not see the accident but claimed that the noise and sight of blood at the scene caused her nervous shock which resulted in a miscarriage.

Lord Thankerton felt that the duty of a motorcyclist on a public road was to drive his cycle with such reasonable care as would avoid the risk of injury to such persons as he could reasonably foresee might be injured by failure to exercise such reasonable care. He noted that it was not settled that such injury includes injury by shock although no direct physical impact or lesion occurs. He then went on to apply the test of proximity or remoteness which he felt required that the injury must be within that which the cyclist ought to have reasonably contemplated as the area of potential danger. He concluded that the fishwife was not in this area due to the distance between her and the actual accident and the fact that there was a tramcar between her and the scene of the accident. He concluded from this that the fishwife plaintiff had failed to establish that at the time of the collision, the cyclist owed any duty to her.

Lord Russell agreed that the cyclist owed no duty to the plaintiff and was therefore not guilty of any negligence in relation to her. He further stated that he preferred the dissenting judgment of Sargant L.J., to the decision of the majority in *Hambrook* v. *Stokes Brothers, supra*. However, it was not necessary to disapprove of that case for the simple reason that the negligence in that case was admitted.

The reasons by Lord Macmillan give to some extent a summary of the development of the law in regard to nervous shock up to this point [p. 103]:

> "It is no longer necessary to consider whether the infliction of what is called mental shock may constitute an actionable wrong. The crude view that the law should take cognizance only of physical injury resulting from actual impact has been discarded, and it is now well recognized that an action will lie for injury by shock sustained through the medium of the eye or the ear without direct contact. The distinction between mental shock and bodily injury was never a scientific one, for mental shock is presumably in all cases the result of, or at least accompanied by, some physical disturbance in the sufferer's system. And a mental shock may have consequences more serious than those resulting from physical impact. But in the case of mental shock there are elements of greater subtlety than in the case of an ordinary physical injury and these elements may give rise to debate as to the precise scope of legal liability."

Lord Macmillan also decided that there was no duty owed by the cyclist to the plaintiff and thus it was not necessary to consider the question of whether injury through mental shock is actionable only when the shock arises out of a reasonable fear of immediate personal injury to oneself. This was admitted not to be the situation on the facts of the case with which he was dealing.

Lord Wright concluded that the cyclist was guilty of no breach of duty to the appellant as well. He did not feel that the cyclist or any reasonable man could reasonably have foreseen the likelihood that anyone placed in the position of the plaintiff could be affected in the manner in which she was.

Lord Porter, enlarging on this point at p. 117, makes the following statement:

> "The duty is not to the world at large. It must be tested by asking with reference to each several complainant: Was a duty owed to him or her? If no one of them was in such a position that direct physical injury could reason-

ably be anticipated to them or their relations or friends normally I think no duty would be owed, and if, in addition, no shock was reasonably to be anticipated to them as a result of the defender's negligence, the defender might, indeed, be guilty of actionable negligence to others but not of negligence towards them."

Lord Porter concludes, however, that "It is not every emotional disturbance or every shock which should have been foreseen." On p. 119 he states:

"In order, however, to establish a duty towards herself, the appellant must still show that the cyclist should reasonably have foreseen emotional injury to her as a result of his negligent driving, and, as I have indicated, I do not think she has done so."

In *Hay or Bourhill* v. *Young, supra*, the court criticized an earlier decision in *Owens* v. *Liverpool Corp.*, [1939] 1 K.B. 394. In that case the court found in favour of a group of mourners in a funeral procession who suffered shock as a result of witnessing the hearse and casket overturned by a negligently driven tramcar. The court in *Hay or Bourhill* v. *Young, supra*, however, did approve of a decision of the High Court of Australia in *Chester* v. *Waverley Corp.* (1939), 62 C.L.R. 1. There it was held that the existence of a duty of care depended on whether a mother's shock, on seeing the dead body of her child recovered from an unguarded street excavation, could be regarded as a risk within the reasonable purview of the defendant municipality. The majority dismissed the action on the ground that it was not reasonably foreseeable. The House of Lords obviously approved of defining the duty which the defendant owed to the plaintiff on the basis of whether it was within the foreseeable risk created.

The use of foreseeability as the test in defining the duty of care was continued by the English Court of Appeal in the case of *King* v. *Phillips*, [1953] 1 Q.B. 429, [1953] 1 All E.R. 617. The fact situation involved a taxi driver who backed his cab negligently and ran into a child on a tricycle immediately behind him, slightly injuring the child. The child's mother, in a house 70 or 80 yards away, heard the child scream and looking out of the window, saw the cab back into the tricycle but she could not see the child. Fear for the child's safety caused nervous shock to the mother.

The majority held that the test of negligence as regards the mother was whether the taxi driver could reasonably have foreseen the risk of damage to her. In the circumstances, they felt the taxi driver could not reasonably have contemplated that, if he backed his taxicab without looking where he was going, he might cause nervous shock to the mother and therefore he owed her no duty of care (*per* Singleton and Hodson, L.JJ.). Denning L.J., felt that there was a duty of care owed by the taxi driver to the mother but that under the circumstances the shock could not have been foreseen by the driver and was therefore too remote as a head of damage.

In stating his reasons, Singleton L.J., made the following statement [at p. 437]:

"I find it difficult to draw a distinction between damage from physical injury and damage from shock; *prima facie*, one would think that, if a driver should reasonably have foreseen either, and damage resulted from the one or from the other, the plaintiff would be entitled to succeed."

Unfortunately, Singleton L.J., found it unnecessary to decide this point for the purposes of the particular case.

Denning L.J., however, at p. 441 makes the following statement: ". . . there can be no doubt since *Bourhill* v. *Young*, [1943] A.C. 92, that the test of liability for shock is foreseeability of injury by shock". But later in the same paragraph, he observes that: "One judge may credit him with more foresight than another. One judge may think that he should have foreseen the shock. Another may not." The differing views of different judges as to foreseeability of nervous shock at various periods of time may go far to explain many of the discrepancies in individual cases. Denning L.J., himself distinguishes the case of *Hambrook* v. *Stokes Brothers*, [1925] 1 K.B. 141, on the basis that while shock may be foreseeable when a lorry goes careening down a hill towards some children, it is not when a taxicab backs up slowly over a tricycle. This distinction has many critics among legal writers.

In the case of *Boardman et al.* v. *Sanderson (Keel and Block Third Party)*, [1964] 1 W.L.R. 1317, also decided by the English Court of Appeal, an eight-year-old boy was injured when the defendant negligently drove over his foot while backing out of a garage. The young boy's father, who to the defendant's knowledge was within earshot, heard the young boy's screams and ran to his assistance. As a result, the father later showed symptoms of nervous shock. In finding the defendant liable to the father, the trial judge, at p. 1320, distinguished *King* v. *Phillips, supra*, as follows:

"In this case the defendant did know that the father was only a few yards away and, therefore, the defendant could reasonably have foreseen, if he were negligent and as a result of that negligence he did injury to the infant, that the father would be immediately upon the scene and might be shocked as, indeed, he was shocked."

This distinction was approved of in the judgment of Ormerod L.J. In a concurring judgment, Danckwerts L.J., also felt that the case satisfied the test of reasonable foreseeability set out by the Privy Council in *Overseas Tankship (U.K.) Ltd.* v. *Morts Dock & Engineering Co. Ltd. (The Wagon Mound)*, [1961] A.C. 388. It would seem, therefore, that any change in the law introduced by this latter case, did not have a significant effect on cases of nervous shock.

Rescuers were added to the category of foreseeable nervous shock victims by the decision of the English Court of Queen's Bench in *Chadwick* v. *British Transport Com'n*, [1967] 2 All E.R. 945. In that case the plaintiff voluntarily took an active part in rescue operations at the scene of a collision between two railway trains in which ninety persons had been killed and many others trapped and injured. As a result of the horror of his experience, the plaintiff suffered a prolonged and disabling anxiety neurosis, necessitating hospital treatment. The decision of Waller J., was that under the circumstances it was reasonably foreseeable that a rescuer other than the railway employees might participate in the rescue operations, that injury by shock to a rescuer was reasonably foreseeable and that damages were recoverable for injury by shock notwithstanding that the shock was not caused by the injured person's fear for his own safety or for the safety of his children. In holding as he did, Waller J., came to the conclusion that the only test of liability was foreseeability of injury by shock.

A Canadian case in which liability for nervous shock was found was *Pollard* v. *Makarchuk* (1958), 16 D.L.R. (2d) 225, 26 W.W.R. 22, a decision of the Alberta Supreme Court. The fact situation here involved a mother and daughter who were passengers in a motor vehicle involved in an accident. The mother suffered severe mental shock on seeing what she believed to be the dead body of her daughter lying on the pavement following the collision. Johnson J.A., clearly felt that a duty of care was owing not to injure Mrs. Makarchuk. He felt that this duty included injury by nervous shock as well as by physical impact. The question for him then became one of remoteness of damages, and in deciding this question the learned trial Judge once again looked to the concept of foreseeability. He concluded at p. 229: "A reasonable man would surely anticipate that an injury to, or death of the daughter in the presence of her mother caused by his negligence would result in mental shock to the mother." He does, however, appear to recant somewhat from this position as shown in his statement on p. 230 which obviously bears the influence of the decision in *Re Polemis and Furness, Withy & Co.*, [1921] 3 K.B. 560:

"There would appear to be no doubt that the doctrine that a person is responsible for the direct consequences of his unlawful act applies, once the duty and its breach are found. In the present case Mrs. Makarchuk's injuries were direct consequences in the sense that they follow directly from the negligence without any other intervening or contributing cause. In such cases, it is probably unnecessary to consider what a reasonable man would be expected to anticipate because he is presumed to intend those consequences."

A Canadian case decided following *The Wagon Mound* case, *supra*, is *Abramzik et al.* v. *Brenner et al.* (1967), 65 D.L.R. (2d) 651, 62 W.W.R. 332, a decision of the Saskatchewan Court of Appeal. The defendant in this case was found to be grossly negligent in driving in front of a freight train while conveying the plaintiff's infant children to a church service. The plaintiff, the mother of the children, suffered a nervous breakdown after being told of the death of her children by her husband. She did not witness the accident or its aftermath personally. Culliton C.J.S., speaking for the Saskatchewan Court of Appeal at p. 654 debated:

". . . whether nervous shock is a substantive tort or whether a particular instance of damage flowing from a particular tort. If the latter, recovery depends upon the question of remoteness. If the former, recovery depends upon a breach of duty."

With all respect to the learned Chief Justice, I must reject this as an unnecessary distinction which only serves to further confuse an already confused area of our law. Negligence requires that there be a duty, a breach of this duty by the defendant and damage to the plaintiff resulting from the breach. Nervous shock is nothing more than a particular type of damage which may be suffered by a plaintiff. If a reasonable man in the position of the defendant could foresee that the defendant might suffer damage as a result of his action then the duty exists. Inserting a concept of remoteness at a later stage serves merely to create a duty for an unforeseeable type of damage. This, in my opinion, is of no particular assistance.

After a careful review of the cases, Culliton C.J.S., comes to the following conclusion at p. 657:

"In my opinion, the test established by the House of Lords in *Hay or Bourhill* v. *Young* is that the plaintiff, to succeed in a claim for damages arising from nervous shock, must prove that the defendant ought, as a reasonable man, to have foreseen nervous shock (as opposed to other physical injury) as a result of his conduct."

He found, however, that the shock experienced by the plaintiff in this particular case was not a type of damage which the defendant ought, as a reasonable person, to have foreseen as a result of her conduct. In so finding, the court did not indicate that any importance was attached to the fact that the plaintiff here received the information from her husband rather than from her own unaided senses.

Aside from the unnecessary distinction mentioned above, the case of *Abramzik et al.* v. *Brenner et al.*, *supra*, provides a relatively clear and simple test for liability in cases of nervous shock. It would seem both logical and necessary that the test be foreseeability of nervous shock rather than just foreseeability of injury. While nervous shock may result in physical damage and while physical injury may often result in nervous shock, the two cannot be so closely linked as to be inseparable. Foreseeability of nervous shock may result from the same facts as does the foreseeability of physical injury or it may result from entirely different facts. For the present at least, I am convinced that foreseeability of the one type of injury cannot be automatically assumed from the foreseeability of the other. For this reason, the test must be the foreseeability of nervous shock itself.

This brings us to the present case. Briefly the facts as alleged are that William Marshall purchased a snowmobile made by Lionel Enterprises Inc. and sold to him by Marineland Sales & Upholstery, and that St. Lawrence Manufacturing Company Inc. manufactured the clutch for the snowmobile. While the machine was in use, the clutch broke and caused grievous injuries to Mr. Marshall. His wife was nearby and when she saw her injured husband, went into considerable shock. The claim being questioned in this motion appears in para. 10 of the statement of claim:

> "10. As a result of the accident of the aforesaid Plaintiff, William Marshall, the Plaintiff, Carolyn Marshall, sustained severe nervous shock which resulted in a state of acute anxiety, which did prevent the said Plaintiff, Carolyn Marshall from continuing her employment, and which said condition is entirely the result of the injuries of William Marshall's which were viewed by the female Plaintiff immediately after the occurrence. The said Plaintiff, Carolyn Marshall has suffered substantial loss of enjoyment of life as a result of the said injuries."

As can be seen, it is alleged that the female plaintiff suffered nervous shock as a result of what she saw with her own senses but this was the aftermath rather than the accident itself. It is also clear that there is no allegation that the female plaintiff was physically injured or indeed, that she was within the ambit of physical risk at the time of the accident. However, in light of the test outlined above, I do not regard these factors as conclusive in any case.

There should exist a duty not to cause nervous shock to others when it can be foreseen as the likely result of certain conduct. Since our state of knowledge is constantly broadening, the scope of the duty of care must expand accordingly. Since it is the knowledge of an average man that is to be attributed to the defendant and since his knowledge is constantly changing it is to be expected that earlier Judges will have discovered no duty where one is found to exist to-day. The arbitrary limits which have been imposed on duty situations in the past could only be justified if they had the effect of elucidating the reasonable foresight of the time.

Although we are concerned here only with the question of the negligent infliction of nervous shock, I should like to refer to some constructive comments in the case of *Purdy* v. *Woznesensky*, [1937] 2 W.W.R. 116, a case in the Saskatchewan Court of Appeal which was dealt with on the basis that the infliction of nervous shock had been intentional. Mackenzie J.A., in reference to the judgment in *Victorian Railways Com'rs* v. *Coultas, supra*, states at p. 124:

> "At that time, 1888, the relationship of nervous shock to physical injury was not known or understood as it is to-day. Consequently their Lordships were exceedingly anxious, as their judgment shows, not to open the door to the presentation of what so far as they could then see might well be imaginary claims. Now that so much more is known about the physical consequences of nervous shock the difficulty with which their Lordships felt themselves confronted in the *Coultas* case can seldom arise and is certainly not present in this case."

Questions will no doubt arise as they have throughout the history of cases like these, as to how far the law can go in compensating victims of nervous shock. Close relatives will no doubt pose little problem but what of sweethearts, fiancees, or perhaps even close friends? And too, what about the unrelated bystander who merely witnesses the carnage? In answer to these nagging worries, I can do little better than to quote the statement of Lord Wright in *Hay or Bourhill* v. *Young*, [1943] A.C. 92 at p. 110:

> "The lawyer likes to draw fixed and definite lines and is apt to ask where the thing is to stop. I should reply it should stop where in the particular case the good sense of the jury or of the judge decides."

The "good sense" of the judge or jury must, of course, take into account the knowledge of the time. It is this type of inquiry which has kept the common law a vibrant and vital force for so many centuries.

I myself would certainly have thought it not beyond the realm of possibility that a reasonable man would foresee nervous shock to a wife who had just come upon the badly injured body of her husband shortly after an accident. However, this question is not before me at this time. It is for the judge and/or jury when this case ultimately comes to trial. What is for me to decide and what I have decided is that the law imposes no predetermined limitations on the position the plaintiff must occupy in order to be compensated for nervous shock.

Accordingly, I must dismiss this motion with costs

Application dismissed.

NOTES

1. According to Mr. Justice Haines, what is the test that should be used to determine whether there is liability for nervous shock? Does he advocate the employment of the "duty", "remoteness" or "proximate cause" technique of limiting liability for negligent conduct? Does it make any difference which approach is used? See *King* v. *Phillips*, [1953] 1 Q.B. 429, [1953] 1 All E.R. 619 (*per* Denning L.J.); *Bourhill* v. *Young* (1944), 8 Camb. L.J. 265; Wright, "Comment" (1943), 21 Can. Bar Rev. 65; Goodhart, "The Shock Cases and Area of Risk" (1953), 16 Mod. L. Rev. 14; J. Williams, "Tort Liability for Nervous Shock in Canada", printed in *Studies in Canadian Tort Law* (1968); Rendall, "Nervous Shock and Tortious Liability" (1962), 2 O.H. L.J. 291; Magruder, "Mental and Emotional Disturbances in the Law of Torts" (1936), 49 Harv. L.Rev. 1033; Havard, "Reasonable Foresight of Nervous Shock" (1956), 19 Mod. L. Rev. 478.

2. What policy reasons can be advanced for using caution before awarding compensation for nervous shock? See *Victorian Railways Commissioners* v. *Coultas* (1888), 13 App. Cas. 222 (P.C.) referred to by Mr. Justice Haines in the principal case. Did it make any sense at all to limit liability for nervous shock only to those cases where there was some impact? Can you swear that you did not strike anyone with your car in the last year? Can you swear that you did not frighten anyone and cause them nervous shock with your car in the last year? The trouble you may have answering the last question may explain the problem the courts faced in this area.

3. The "impact rule" has now been abandoned in the Commonwealth and in most of the United States. See, for example, *Batalla* v. *State* (1961), 10 N.Y. 2d 237, 176 N.E. 2d 729; *Niederman* v. *Brodsky* (1970), 436 Pa. 401, 261 A. 2d 84 overruling *Bosley* v. *Andrews* (1958), 393 Pa. 161, 142 A. 2d 263. The "impact rule" survived longer in the states that contained large, metropolitan areas. Can it be that the danger of fake claims was more prevalent in large cities? Or are big city people expected to have tougher hides?

4. Even though the impact rule has been discarded, liability will not be found for every trivial emotional upset. See *Duwyn* v. *Kaprielian* (1978), 7 C.C.L.T. 121 (Ont. C.A.), at p. 142. Some physical symptoms must be present such as a heart attack, a miscarriage, neurasthenia, or a recognizable psychiatric illness. The temporary emotion of fright or sadness does not yet sound in tort. See Linden, *Canadian Tort Law* (2nd ed., 1977), p. 359.

5. In *Mount Isa Mines* v. *Pusey* (1971), 45 A.L.J.R. 88, Mr. Justice Windeyer stated:

"Sorrow does not sound in damages. A plaintiff in an action of negligence cannot recover damages for a 'shock', however grievous, which was no more than an immediate emotional response to a distressing experience sudden, severe and saddening. It is, however, today a known medical fact that severe emotional distress can be the starting point of a lasting disorder of mind or body, some form of psychoneurosis or a psychosomatic illness. For that, if it be the result of a tortious act, damages may be had. It is in that consequential sense that the term 'nervous shock' has come into the law. In the last reported case on this topic in England – *Hinz* v. *Berry*, [1970] 1 All E.R. 1074 – Lord Denning M.R. said (at p. 1075): 'Damages are recoverable for nervous shock, or, to put it in medical terms, for any recognisable psychiatric illness caused by the breach of duty by the defendant' . . .

Law, marching with medicine but in the rear and limping a little, has today come a long way since the decision in *Coultas's* case (1888), 13 App. Cas. 222, which in recent times has been regularly by-passed by courts. An illness of the mind set off by shock is not the less an injury because it is functional, not organic, and its progress is psychogenic."

6. In the case of *Hinz* v. *Berry, cited in* note 5, *supra*, Mrs. Hinz, the plaintiff, had been married for ten years and had four young children of her own as well as four foster children. In addition, she was pregnant. While the family was on a picnic, during "bluebell time in Kent", Mrs. Hinz witnessed a dreadful accident in which a Jaguar car went out of control, killing her husband and injuring several of her children. It was held at trial that, being of "robust character", she would have recovered from the shock of the death of her husband in a short time had she not witnessed the actual accident. Instead, however, she began to suffer from morbid depression, a recognizable psychiatric illness, and this illness persisted for the five years preceding the trial. Damages of £4000 were awarded to her for compensation for the nervous shock. The defendant appealed this assessment of damages. In dismissing the appeal, Lord Justice Pearson stated:

"Counsel for the defendant has given us a list of five causes of the depressed state, and he says, I think rightly, that these five causes have all been operating from the date of the accident until now. The first factor was her own inevitable grief and sorrow at losing her husband, a good husband who was also a good father to her family. That would have caused much sorrow and mourning in any event. Secondly, there was her anxiety about the welfare of her children who were injured in the accident. Thirdly, there was the financial stress resulting from the removal of this very hardworking breadwinner who took extra work in addition to his normal work. She may well have been in considerable financial difficulty. The fourth factor was the need for adjusting herself to a new life, which may well have been quite unusually severe in this case. Now, all those four factors are not compensatable, that is to say they are not proper subjects to be taken into account in assessing damages according to English law. And then we come to the fifth of the five substantial factors, and that is the shock of witnessing the accident. That is the only factor which is compensatable in the sense that I have explained."

Why should the first four items not be proper matters for compensation? In his concurring judgment, Lord Justice Denning outlined a method for assessing damages:

"Somehow or other the court has to draw a line between sorrow and grief for which damages are not recoverable; and nervous shock and psychiatric illness for which damages are recoverable. The way to do this is to estimate how much the plaintiff would have suffered if, for instance, her husband had been killed in an accident when she was 50 miles away; and compare it with what she is now, having suffered all the shock due to being present at the accident. The evidence shows that she suffered much more by being present. . . ."

Is this a practical test to apply? Is it fair? See also *Alaffe* v. *Kennedy* (1974), 40 D.L.R. (3d) 429, at p. 432; *Cameron* v. *Marcaccini* (1978), 87 D.L.R. (3d) 442 (B.C.).

7. What if a mother, whose child is injured, becomes emotionally upset as a result of having to cope with the child during its period of recuperation? See *Duwyn* v. *Kaprielian, supra,* at p. 143.

8. In *Owens* v. *Liverpool Corporation*, [1939] 1 K.B. 394, [1938] 4 All E.R. 727, 108 L.J.K.B. 155, 55 T.L.R. 246, 160 L.T. 8, the defendants' servant so negligently operated a tramcar that it collided with a hearse in a funeral procession, overturning the coffin and putting it in danger of falling into the road. The hearse was followed by a carriage containing the aged mother of the deceased, an uncle, a cousin and a cousin's husband. Only the uncle saw the actual impact; the others saw the effect after it had happened. All of them sued for damages resulting from "severe shock". The trial judge, while finding that all received injury in the nature of shock dismissed their actions on the ground that there must be apprehension of injury to a human being to found liability for shock. On appeal this judgment was reversed and judgment given for all plaintiffs. "It may be that the plaintiffs are of that class which is peculiarly susceptible to the luxury of woe at a funeral so as to be disastrously disturbed by any untoward accident to the trappings of mourning. But one who is guilty of negligence to another must put up with idiosyncrasies of his victim that increase the likelihood or extent of damage to him: it is no answer to a claim for a fractured skull that its owner had an unusually fragile one." Is this a special case?

9. In addition to the requirement of a "recognisable psychiatric illness", the courts experimented with several other tests for limiting liability for nervous shock. At one time, it was thought that there had to be fear for oneself (*Dulieu* v. *White & Sons*, [1901] 2 K.B. 669; *Austin* v. *Mascarin*, [1942] O.R. 165), fear for oneself or one's children developed through one's own unaided senses (*Hambrook* v. *Stokes Bros.*, [1925] 1 K.B. 141), or one had to be within the area of physical risk (*Waube* v. *Warrington* (1935), 216 Wis. 603, 258 N.W. 497; *Amaya* v. *Home Ice* (1963), 59 Cal. App. 2d 295, 379 P. 2d 513). Eventually, these concepts were replaced by foreseeability as the touchstone of liability (see *Hay (or Bourhill)* v. *Young*, [1943] A.C. 92, Wright, "Comment" (1943), 21 Can. Bar Rev. 65), but this idea has not eliminated all of the problems.

10. In *Brown* v. *Hubar* (1974), 3 O.R. (2d) 448 (Ont. H.C.), for example, in a fact situation resembling *Marshall* v. *Lionel Enterprises*, the foresight principle was used to deny a plaintiff recovery for nervous shock resulting from witnessing the aftermath of an accident. The plaintiff was requested by telephone to come and pick up his daughter as she had been involved in an accident. Upon arriving at the scene he found that she was lying under a blanket on a stretcher, bleeding, and showing no signs of life. He was informed later at the hospital that she was dead. At the time of the accident the plaintiff was recuperating from a recent heart attack. The medical evidence indicated that the recuperation period was considerably prolonged by the shock of the accident. The plaintiff also developed other psychological problems which he claimed resulted from the accident. The plaintiff claimed for damages for the death of his daughter and for his own nervous shock. The defendant admitted negligence. Grant J. pointed out that the plaintiff had served with the Army Medical Corps in World War II, the Korean War and in Indo-China where he had seen many of his friends killed or wounded. His Lordship concluded that the issue was whether or not the nervous shock was foreseeable in the circumstances and stated:

"The plaintiff went to the area where his daughter was lying with some knowledge of the fact that she had been involved in a mishap, although there is no evidence to indicate that he knew she had sustained physical injury. He must have been directing his attention, however, to the welfare of his daughter as he went to the scene. To find her, therefore, as he did was not a complete surprise. It was only after waiting to see the attending doctor at the hospital for over an hour that he became aware of her demise.

I consider it would be unreasonable to conclude that the driver should have foreseen that, as a result of the manner in which he was driving at the time of the collision, the plaintiff would sustain mental shock. There is no evidence to indicate that the defendant knew the plaintiff or the daughter or that he had any knowledge of the state of the plaintiff's health. It is rendered more difficult to come to such conclusion as there is no evidence before the Court of the nature of the driving."

Do you agree with the reasoning of Grant J.? Can this case be reconciled with *Marshall* or are they in direct conflict? Is it significant that the *Marshall* case was a decision on the pleadings that left the ultimate issue of foreseeability to be determined at the trial, whereas the *Brown* case was a decision after a trial? Is the plaintiff's war experience relevant? Is the heart condition significant? Does it make a difference that the plaintiff in *Brown* was a man, while in *Marshall* the plaintiff was a woman? Should the fact of the telephone call, prior to the plaintiff's appearance at the scene, make any difference? Would the result have been the same if the plaintiff had witnessed the accident from start to finish?

11. A father returns to his home to find that an explosion has just demolished it and killed or injured several members of his family. He searches through the rubble to try to help but is restrained and taken to hospital. He suffers severe nervous shock and later becomes quite unstable and badly-adjusted. Is this foreseeable? See *Fenn* v. *Peterborough* (1976), 1 C.C.L.T. 90 (Ont.), *per* R.E. Holland J., at p. 132; affd but damages varied C.A., (1979), 25 O.R. (2d) 399.

12. A mother suffers from nervous shock upon seeing her baby born deformed as a result of her taking thalidomide while she was pregnant. Forseeable? See *S.* v. *Distillers Co.*, [1969] 3 All E.R. 1412.

13. A mother comes upon the scene of an accident in which her child has been injured only slightly. The mother is extra-sensitive because of an experience she had in her youth with another accident involving her brother for which she felt guilty. As a result, she overreacts and suffers emotional upset. Recovery? See *Duwyn* v. *Kaprielian, supra,* at p. 142.

14. A consumer suffers nervous shock as a result of seeing a decomposed mouse in a bag of flour she was using. Liability? *Curll* v. *Robin Hood Multifoods Ltd.* (1974), 56 D.L.R. (3d) 129 (N.S.). What if nervous shock is suffered as a result of opening a package of bread and finding it blue with mold and containing pieces of metal in it? See *Taylor* v. *Weston Bakeries Ltd.* (1976), 1 C.C.L.T. 158 (Sask. Dist. Ct.).

ABRAMZIK v. BRENNER

Saskatchewan Court of Appeal. (1967), 65 D.L.R. (2d) 651

The plaintiffs' three children were being driven to church by defendant neighbour when, as a result of defendant driver's "gross negligence", the car collided with a railroad train and two of plaintiff's children were killed. Some little time later plaintiff husband, also driving to church, arrived at the scene of the accident and saw one of his dead children. He proceeded home to inform his wife. He then returned to the crossing. Several hours later he and his wife went to the hospital to see their third child who was badly injured. In an action by plaintiffs, husband and wife, the evidence showed plaintiff wife was in a state of shock and acute mental depression resulting in hospitalization for five days following the funeral. According to the medical evidence, as a result of the wife's mental reaction "her body processes were slowed down and she lacked incentive to do anything". For about six months she "wandered around, cried and appeared lost". Sirois J., gave the plaintiff wife $5,000 damages. He held that she had met "the requisites" to establish her cause of action: (1) a wrongful act or omission done by the defendant; (2) resultant nervous shock sustained directly; (3) physical injury arising from such shock.

The defendant appealed.

Culliton C.J.S.. . . . While it was once contended that nervous shock was a form of personal injury for which damages could not be recovered, this would not now appear to be correct. I think it may now be said that nervous shock is a form of personal injury for which damages may or may not be recoverable. Whether damages are recoverable depends upon the circumstances in each case. . . .

The first question which arises is whether nervous shock is a substantive tort or whether a particular instance of damage flowing from a particular tort. If the latter, recovery depends upon the question of remoteness. If the former, recovery depends upon a breach of duty. Legal writers and commentators have expressed contrary views, but in my opinion the authoritative view is that nervous shock, other than that flowing from a physical injury suffered by a claimant as a result of a negligent act, is a substantive tort. This, then, poses the problem of what is the duty the breach of which gives rise to a claim for damages for nervous shock.

While mental suffering unaccompanied by physical injury is not the basis for a claim for damages, I think the law is clear that if nervous shock resulting in physical injury is the direct result of a wrongful act, damages are recoverable for such physical injury: *Dulieu* v. *White & Sons*, [1901] 1 K.B. 669; *Wilkinson* v. *Downton*, [1897] 2 Q.B. 57.

There can be no doubt but that an action will lie for the wilful infliction of shock, or a reckless disregard as to whether or not shock will ensue from the act committed: *Janvier* v. *Sweeney*, [1919] 2 K.B. 316; *Purdy* v. *Woznesensky*, [1937] 2 W.W.R. 116. It is where nervous shock is the result of negligence that difficulties arise. In such cases the courts have not been prepared to apply the ordinary principles of liability without qualification or restriction. What, then, is the test that establishes the duty, the breach of which may give rise to a valid claim in damages for nervous shock? [His Lordship summarized the cases.] This summation, however, does not fully answer the question. Is the duty which a plaintiff must establish in seeking to recover damages for nervous shock only that the defendant ought, as a reasonable man, to have foreseen injury to the plaintiff as a result of his conduct, or must the plaintiff establish that the defendant ought, as a reasonable man, to have foreseen nervous shock (as opposed to other physical injury) to the plaintiff as a result of his conduct? . . .

In my opinion, the test established by the House of Lords in *Hay or Bourhill* v. *Young* is that the plaintiff, to succeed in a claim for damages arising from nervous shock, must prove that the defendant ought, as a reasonable man, to have foreseen nervous shock (as opposed to other physical injury) as a result of his conduct. I am strengthened in this view by the statement of Denning L.J., in *King et al.* v. *Phillips*, [1953] 1 Q.B. 429, when at p. 441 he said:

> "Howsoever that may be, whether the exemption for shock be based on want of duty or on remoteness, there can be no doubt since *Bourhill* v. *Young*, [1943] A.C. 92 that the test of liability for shock is foreseeability of injury by shock."

In *Boardman et al.* v. *Sanderson*, [1964] 1 W.L.R. 1317, the English Court of Appeal applied the foreseeability of shock as the test in finding the defendants liable for the shock suffered by the plaintiff. The same test was applied by Lord Denning M.R., in delivering the judgment of the Court of Appeal in *Cook* v. *Swinfen*, [1967] 1 W.L.R. 457, when at p. 461 he said:

> "In these circumstances I think that, just as in the law of tort, so also in the law of contract, damages can be recovered for nervous shock or anxiety state if it is a reasonably foreseeable consequence."

It was contended that the views which I have expressed are contrary to the judgment in *Schneider* v. *Eisovitch*, [1960] 2 Q.B. 430. With respect, I cannot agree with this contention. In that case Paull J., held that the defendant owed a duty to the plaintiff to drive with reasonable care and was in breach of that duty and that the shock which the plaintiff suffered on hearing of her husband's death, being a consequence which flowed from the breach, she was entitled to recover. The liability for shock found by the learned trial judge was based upon the principles established in *Re Polemis and Furness, Withy & Co., Ltd.*, [1921] 3 K.B. 560.

I think I have made it clear that, in my opinion, the plaintiff can only recover damages in respect of nervous shock if it can be proved that the defendant ought, as a reasonable man, to have foreseen nervous shock (as opposed to physical injury) to the plaintiff as the result of his conduct. In the present case I am satisfied the plaintiff Ursula Abramzik did not prove that the shock which she experienced, resulting in her illness, was one which the defendant Julia Brenner ought, as a reasonable person, to have foreseen as a result of her conduct.

The appeal is therefore allowed with costs and the judgment below awarding damages to Ursula Abramzik is set aside.

Appeal allowed.

NOTES

1. Was the concept of foresight actually helpful to the court? Was the result really unforeseeable to the reasonable person?

2. What was the true reason for denying liability in *Abramzik* v. *Brenner*?

3. Do you agree with the result?

4. In *Schneider* v. *Eisovitch*, [1960] 1 All E.R. 169, the plaintiff and her husband were being driven in defendant's motor car when the defendant negligently caused the car to leave the highway and crash into a tree. As a result, the plaintiff's husband was killed and plaintiff rendered unconscious. While in the hospital, plaintiff was informed of her husband's death and this shock, coming on top of the shock she suffered in the accident itself, had serious consequences. In an action for damages for personal injuries brought by plaintiff, the trial Judge indicated that the nervous shock to plaintiff resulted in recurrent attacks of neuro-dermatitis. This was due to three factors: (1) the shock of the accident; (2) the shock on hearing in the hospital that her husband had been killed; (3) the continued strain of adjusting her life after her husband's death. Paull J., found that damages due to (1) were £125; from (2) an additional £275; from (3) an additional £450. He allowed (1) and (2) but refused (3), giving judgment for £400 for damages arising from shock. "It cannot be doubted . . . that if plaintiff had not been injured but had seen her husband killed the resultant shock would have been actionable . . . Once a breach of duty is established the difference between seeing and hearing is immaterial. . . . The fact that the defendant by his negligence caused the death of plaintiff's husband does not give the plaintiff a cause of action for the shock caused to her, but the plaintiff having a cause of action for the negligence of the defendant may add the consequences of shock caused by hearing of her husband's death when estimating the amount recoverable on her cause of action."

Is *Schneider* different from *Abramzik*? *Cf. Alaffe* v. *Kennedy* (1974), 40 D.L.R. (3d) 429, at p. 432.

5. See Glasbeek, "Comment on *Abramzik* v. *Brenner*" (1969), 47 Can. Bar Rev. 96.

6. In *Pollard* v. *Makarchuk* (1958), 16 D.L.R. (2d) 225 (Alta. S.C.), defendant negligently ran into a motor car in which the plaintiff and her daughter were passengers. The daughter was killed and the plaintiff, while sustaining only superficial physical injuries, suffered severe mental shock resulting in a period of hospitalization, as the result of seeing her daughter killed. Johnson J.A., held that the mother could collect damages for the conditions resulting from the shock. "To concede that [defendant] was under a duty not to injure her and at the same time to deny that duty because he injured her in a particular way is lacking in logic. . . . There would appear to be no doubt . . . that a person is responsible for the direct consequences of his act . . . once the duty and its breach are found."

Can *Pollard* be distinguished from *Abramzik*? Are the decisions in *Pollard* and *Schneider* affected by *The Wagon Mound (No. 1)*? See *Andrews* v. *Williams*, [1967] V.R. 831. *Cf. Dietelbach* v. *Public Trustee* (1973), 37 D.L.R. (3d) 621, at p. 624.

7. What if a child, injured slightly in an accident, develops a mental disorder because of the ineffective way its mother looks after it as a result of her own mental problems? See *Duwyn* v. *Kaprielian, supra,* at p. 140. How does this compare with the problem of injuries aggravated by ineffective medical attention? See *ibid.,* at p. 146.

8. X is injured in an accident caused by Y's negligence and in which Y is killed. X blames himself for the accident, becomes severely depressed and then kills himself. Can X's family recover from Y's estate? Would it make any difference if X is not injured at all in the accident? What if X's child was killed in the accident also?

9. Where is the line to be drawn? It is now clear that the plaintiff suffering nervous shock need not necessarily be a close relative of the injured person. For example, in *Dooley* v. *Cammell Laird & Co. Ltd. et al.*, 1 Lloyd's Rep. 271, the plaintiff was using a crane to hoist a heavy load over the hold of a ship in which he knew that fellow workmen were working, when a rope on the sling broke and the load crashed into the hold. No one was injured but the plaintiff suffered nervous shock for which he recovered damages from his employer, the owner of the shipbuilding yard, and from the owners of the sling, Mersey Co. Donovan J. found that "if the driver of the crane concerned fears that the load may have fallen upon some of his fellow workmen, and that fear is not baseless or extravagant, then it is, I think, a consequence reasonably to have been foreseen that he may himself suffer a nervous shock". Would a bystander witnessing this "accident" be able to recover? How does the bystander differ from the plaintiff? What if the bystander, seeing this, leaped to the rescue and suffered nervous shock as a result?

10. In *Chadwick* v. *British Transport Commission*, [1967] 2 All E.R. 945, the plaintiff went to the scene of a railway disaster in which 90 persons were killed to assist in rescue operations. He worked there all night and, as a result, he became psycho-neurotic, no longer took an interest in life and could not work for a considerable time. Mr. Justice Waller observed that he did "not see any objection in principle to damages being recoverable for shock caused other than by fear for one's safety or for the safety of one's children". After asking himself whether "injury by shock was foreseeable", he concluded it was in the light of the "gruesome" circumstances. No emphasis was placed upon the point that the plaintiff, although a stranger, was a "rescuer" and not a mere observer. Could this have been a factor in the decision? Is it more foreseeable that a rescuer would be likely to suffer nervous shock than a mere observer? See Glasbeek, "Comment" (1968), 46 Can. Bar Rev. 299.

11. In the Australian case of *Mount Isa Mines* v. *Pusey* (1971), 45 A.L.J.R. 88, the plaintiff workman heard a loud noise. He hurried to the floor above and

found that two electricians had been horribly burned in an accident resulting from a short circuit. He assisted one of the two. The electrician he assisted died nine days later.

The plaintiff developed symptoms of schizophrenia as a consequence of his involvement. Mr. Justice Windeyer, in a penetrating analysis of what he termed the "blessed, and sometimes overworked, word 'foreseeability' ", concluded that the question was "not whether shock would be likely to produce this particular illness, but whether there was a real risk that a foreseeable accident such as occurred would cause a man in the powerhouse to suffer a nervous shock having lasting mental consequences". He pointed out that the plaintiff was not a relative nor even a friend of the injured person. "He did not know him, except perhaps as a fellow in the power-house." Mr. Justice Windeyer explained that judicial reliance upon relationship was "originally a humane and ameliorating exception to the general denial that damages could be had for nervous shock", but it should not be used to restrict liability to relatives alone. The prime consideration is whether claimants were "neighbours", which category would include both relatives and rescuers, but not "curious strangers" or "mere bystanders". His Lordship felt that the relationship of master and servant between the plaintiff and the defendant could also support the duty. Mr. Justice Walsh agreed that, "there is no rule of law which made it a condition of the respondent's right to recover that he should have been a close relative", although he did feel that "a family relationship" may be "a relevant and important fact in deciding the question whether or not injury of that kind to the plaintiff was reasonably foreseeable".

How does this case compare with *Chadwick* and *Dooley*?

12. Most American courts have consistently denied compensation to people who suffer shock as a result of witnessing the negligent infliction of injury upon others including a near relative. For example, a mother who saw her child run over by a car was denied recovery for her mental suffering. See *Amaya* v. *Home Ice, Fuel & Supply Co.* (1963), 59 Cal. 2d 295, 379 P. 2d 513; *Waube* v. *Warrington* (1935), 216 Wis. 603, 258 N.W. 497; see also *Restatement of Torts, Second,* §§313, 436. Recently there has been a spectacular reversal in California, which may augur a general shift. In *Dillon* v. *Legg* (1968), 441 P. 2d 912 (S.C. Cal.), Mr. Justice Tobriner awarded damages to a mother who witnessed her child being killed when it was run over by the defendant. In coming to this decision, Mr. Justice Tobriner relied on several English cases (*Boardman, Hambrook*), something that is not too frequently done in the United States. The new approach advocated by the Supreme Court of California was as follows:

"Since the chief element in determining whether defendant owes a duty or an obligation to plaintiff is the foreseeability of the risk, that factor will be of prime concern in every case. . . .

We note, first, that we deal here with a case in which plaintiff suffered a shock which resulted in physical injury and we confine our ruling to that case. In determining, in such a case, whether defendant should reasonably foresee the injury to plaintiff, or, in other terminology, whether defendant owes plaintiff a duty of due care, the courts will take into account such factors as the following: (1) Whether plaintiff was located near the scene of the accident as contrasted with one who was a distance away from it. (2) Whether the shock resulted from a direct emotional impact upon plaintiff from the sensory and contemporaneous observance of the accident, as contrasted with learning of the accident from others after its occurrence. (3) Whether plaintiff and the victim were closely related, as contrasted with an absence of any relationship or the presence of only a distant relationship.

The evaluation of these factors will indicate the degree of the defendant's foreseeability: obviously defendant is more likely to foresee that a mother who observes an accident affecting her child will suffer harm than to foretell that a stranger witness will do. Similarly, the degree of foreseeability of the third person's injury is far greater in the case of his contemporaneous observance of the accident than that in which he subsequently learns of it. The defendant is more likely to foresee that shock to the nearby, witnessing mother will cause physical harm than to anticipate that someone distant from the accident will suffer more than a temporary emotional reaction. All these elements, of course, shade into each other; the fixing of obligation intimately tied into the facts, depends upon each case.

In light of these factors the court will determine whether the accident and harm was reasonably foreseeable. Such reasonable foreseeability does not turn on whether the particular defendant as an individual would have in actuality foreseen the exact accident and loss; it contemplates that courts, on a case-to-case basis, analyzing all the circumstances, will decide what the ordinary man under such circumstances should reasonably have foreseen. The courts thus mark out the areas of liability, excluding the remote and unexpected."

Is this a workable approach? How does it compare with that of Mr. Justice Haines in *Marshall* v. *Lionel Enterprises*?

13. A child is struck by a negligently driven automobile and killed. Which of the following people can recover for nervous shock: (1) the father who witnesses the accident from an upstairs window and suffers a heart attack: (2) A brother who hears the brakes being applied while playing in the back yard and then races to the scene immediately? (3) A sister who returns from school an hour later, sees the blood on the street and is then told the sad news? (4) A neighbour who saw the accident from her porch and who was "very close" to the child? (5) A neighbour who saw the accident but who hardly knew the child? (6) The child's mother, who is visiting her sister in New York, and is telephoned the dreadful news? (7) The grandmother in Victoria, B.C., who is informed by telephone? Would your answers to any of the above change if the child merely had its leg broken in the accident? Would any of your answers be different if the child was not hurt at all in the "accident"?

14. What are the policy and administrative problems to be sorted out here? Can you formulate a possible rule to be included in legislation? Should the matter be left to the judge or jury in each case?

15. Legislation dealing with this problem has been enacted in Australia and New Zealand. For example, New South Wales, in its Law Reform (Miscellaneous Provisions) Act, 1944 Part III enacted the following provisions:

INJURY ARISING FROM MENTAL OR NERVOUS SHOCK

3. (1) In any action for injury to the person caused after the commencement of this Act, the plaintiff shall not be debarred from recovering damages merely because the injury complained of arose wholly or in part from mental or nervous shock. . . .

4. (1) The liability of any person in respect of injury caused after the commencement of this Act by an act, neglect or default by which any other person is killed, injured or put in peril, shall extend to include liability for injury arising wholly or in part from mental or nervous shock sustained by —

    (a) a parent or the husband or wife of the person so killed, injured or put in peril; or

    (b) any other member of the family of the person so killed, injured or put in peril where such person was killed, injured or put in peril within the sight or hearing of such member of the family. . . .

5. In this section —

"Member of the family" means the husband, wife, parent, child, brother, sister, half-brother or half-sister of the person in relation to whom the expression is used.

"Parent" includes father, mother, grandfather, grandmother, stepfather, stepmother, and any person standing in loco parentis to another.

"Child" includes son, daughter, grandson, granddaughter, stepson, stepdaughter and any person to whom another stands in loco parentis.

For a general discussion of the operation of the above provisions see *Smee* v. *Tibbetts* (1953), 53 S.R. (N.S.W.) 391; *Anderson* v. *Liddy* (1949), 49 S.R. (N.S.W.) 320.

Would *Abramzik* v. *Brenner* be decided differently under the N.S.W. Act? Does this provision eliminate the administrative problems in this area? Would you favour such a statute in this country?

16. A client goes to a lawyer. The lawyer negligently mishandles her case. She suffers a nervous breakdown. Is this a foreseeable consequence for which she should be compensated? See *Cook* v. *Swinfen*, [1967] 1 W.L.R. 457, at p. 461. See also *Heywood* v. *Wellers*, [1976] 1 All E.R. 300.

17. A travel agent promised to supply an enjoyable vacation to the plaintiff. The holiday did not measure up to advance billing, causing the plaintiff loss of enjoyment, annoyance, disappointment and frustration. Compensable? See *Jarvis* v. *Swan Tours*, [1973] 1 All E.R. 71; *Jackson* v. *Horizon Holidays*, [1975] 3 All E.R. 92. See also Fleming, "Damages for Non-material Losses" in Law Society of Upper Canada, *Special Lectures on New Developments in the Law of Torts* (1973), at p. 1; Fleming, "Distant Shock in Germany (and Elsewhere)" (1972), 20 Am. J. Comp. L. 485.

18. A much beloved dog of an aged passenger is entrusted to an airline's care during a flight. It is put into the baggage compartment. Upon arrival, the dog is dead. The passenger suffers extreme emotional upset. Recovery? See *Newell* v. *Canadian Pacific Airlines* (1976), 14 O.R. (2d) 752 (Co. Ct.).

A man is wrongfully dismissed from his job. He suffers a nervous breakdown as a result. Liability?

19. In *Guay* v. *Sun Publishing Co., Ltd.*, [1953] 2 S.C.R. 216, [1953] 4 D.L.R. 577, the defendant carelessly published in its newspaper a statement that the husband of the plaintiff and two sons had been killed in a motor car accident. The plaintiff, living apart from her husband under a separation agreement, discovered some three or four weeks later that the report was untrue. Eight months later she saw a physician and, in the following month, brought action for damages resulting from shock produced by the defendant's negligence. On appeal to the Supreme Court of Canada, the plaintiff's action was dismissed. Kerwin and Locke JJ., held that no action would lie for damages resulting from negligent speech. Estey J., refused to decide whether there could ever be recovery for physical illness or other injury caused by shock consequent upon negligent mis-statements. Assuming such a duty be found there was no physical harm, apart from grief or shock, and this he considered essential to a cause of action. Cartwright J., Rinfret C.J.C., concurring, dissented and would have given judgment for plaintiff. He felt the case was one in which defendant negligently caused physical injury to the plaintiff's health. He indicated the court was free to follow *Hambrook* v. *Stokes* and should do so. "I think that the existence of liability for shock negligently caused should be determined not by inquiring whether the shock resulted from fear for the personal safety of the claimant but rather by inquiring whether a reasonable person in the position of the defendant would have foreseen that his negligent act would probably result in shock injurious to the health of the claimant."

How does *Guay* fit into the picture?

20. The *Guay* case has been assailed by the authors. See MacIntyre, "A Novel Assault on the Principle of No Liability for Innocent Misrepresentation" (1953), 31 Can. Bar Rev. 770; Head, "Comment" (1952), 30 Can. Bar Rev. 741. Its influence has been weakened by the opinion of Mr. Justice Spence, dissenting, in *J. Nunes Diamonds* v. *Dominion Electric Protection* (1972), 26 D.L.R. (3d) 699 (S.C.C.) and by the Ontario Court of Appeal's reversal (Nov. 16, 1973, unreported) of *Hurley* v. *Sault Star Ltd.* (July 15, 1973, unreported, O'Driscoll J.). See Linden *Canadian Tort Law* (2nd ed., 1977), p. 381 and *Hurley* v. *Sault Star Ltd.*, (Aug. 9, 1974) unreported, *per* Galligan J.

21. A newspaper reports that a child "ran across the pavement into the path of a car and was killed". Suppose that the child was not killed, but the parents on reading the story, suffer nervous shock. Liability? Suppose that the child

was in fact killed by a car, but in circumstances that did not imply negligence on the child's part. The parents suffer severe nervous shock as a result of this misinformation. Liability? *Cf. Hurley* v. *Sault Star Ltd. supra.*

B. ECONOMIC LOSSES

WELLER & CO. v. FOOT AND MOUTH DISEASE RESEARCH INSTITUTE

Queen's Bench Division. [1966] 1 Q.B. 569; [1965] 3 All E.R. 560

Widgery J.: This matter comes before the court in the form of a Special Case, in which the opinion of the court is sought on certain questions of law. The case is a commendably short one, and I think that I should read it in full.

"1. These are consolidated actions in which the plaintiffs in each action at all material times carried on business *inter alia* as auctioneers, in particular as auctioneers of cattle at Guildford and Farnham Markets in the County of Surrey. . . . 3. The defendants at all material times owned and occupied land and premises at Pirbright in the county of Surrey where they carried on experimental work in connexion with foot and mouth disease in cattle [by consent, the following words have been added to that paragraph, namely, 'and had for that purpose imported a virus from Africa']. 4. At the end of the year 1959 and/or in January, 1960, cattle in the vicinity of the defendants' said premises of Pirbright became infected with foot and mouth disease. 5. By their statement of claim each plaintiff alleges that the said cattle became infected with foot and mouth disease as a result of the escape of the said virus from the premises of the defendants. 6. As a result of the said cattle becoming infected with foot and mouth disease the Minister of Agriculture made an order under statutory powers dated Jan. 18, No. 8 of 1960, closing Guildford Market and Farnham Market and as a result both plaintiffs were unable to carry on their business of auctioneers of cattle in the said markets upon a number of market days amounting in all to six. 7. The plaintiffs' claims are based both on breach of an absolute duty arising out of the escape of a dangerous thing from the defendants' premises which the defendants kept at the said premises and on the negligence of the defendants, their servants or agents, in carrying out their work at the said place, and/or in or about the steps taken to prevent escape of the said virus. . . ."

I will begin by considering the plaintiffs' claim in negligence, and for this purpose I will make the assumptions of fact which are most favourable to them, namely, that their loss was foreseeable and that the defendants were guilty of neglect which caused the escape of the virus.

Counsel for the plaintiffs bases his contention on the well-known speech of Lord Atkin in *Donoghue (or McAlister)* v. *Stevenson.* . . . Applying this principle, counsel for the plaintiffs say that, since the defendants should have foreseen the damage to his clients but nevertheless failed to take proper precaution against the escape of the virus, their liability is established. It may be observed that if this argument is sound, the defendants' liability is likely to extend far beyond the loss suffered by the auctioneers, for in an agricultural community the escape of foot and mouth disease virus is a tragedy which can foreseeably affect almost all businesses in the area. The affected beasts must be slaughtered, as must others to whom the disease may conceivably have spread. Other farmers are prohibited from moving their cattle and may be unable to bring them to market at the most profitable time; transport contractors who make their living by the transport of animals are out of work; dairymen may go short of milk, and sellers of cattle feed suffer loss of business. The magnitude of these consequences must not be allowed to deprive the plaintiffs of their rights, but it emphasizes the importance of this case.

The difficulty facing counsel for the plaintiffs is that there is a great volume of authority both before and after *Donoghue* v. *Stevenson* to the effect that a plaintiff suing in negligence for damages suffered as a result of an act or omission of a defendant cannot recover if the act or omission did not directly injure, or at least threaten directly to injure, the plaintiff's person or property but merely caused consequential loss as, for example, by up-setting the plaintiff's business relations with a third party who was the direct victim of the act or omission. The categories of negligence never close, but when the court is asked to recognise a new category, it must proceed with some caution. [His Lordship discussed the authorities denying liability for economic loss.]

. . . I am invited to consider those cases in the light of the more recent decision of the House of Lords in *Hedley Byrne & Co., Ltd.* v. *Heller & Partners, Ltd.,* [1964] A.C. 465. . . . The decision in *Hedley Byrne & Co., Ltd.* v. *Heller & Partners, Ltd.* does not depart in any way from the fundamental that there can be no claim for negligence in the absence of a duty of care owed to the plaintiff. It recognises that a duty of care may arise in the giving of advice even though no contract or fiduciary relationship exists between the giver of the advice and the person who may act on it, and having recognised the existence of the duty it goes on to recognise that indirect or economic loss will suffice to support the plaintiff's claim. What the case does not decide is that an ability to foresee indirect or economic loss to another as a result of one's conduct automatically imposes a duty to take care to avoid that loss.

In my judgment, there is nothing in *Hedley Byrne & Co., Ltd.* v. *Heller & Partners, Ltd.* to affect the common law principle that a duty of care which arises from a risk of direct injury to person or property is owed only to those whose person or property may foreseeably be injured by a failure to take care. If the plaintiff can show that the duty was owed to him, he can recover both direct and consequential loss which is reasonably foreseeable, and for myself I see no reason for saying that proof of direct loss is an essential part of his claim. He must, however, show that he was within the scope of the defendant's duty to take care.

In the present case, the defendants' duty to take care to avoid the escape of the virus was due to the foreseeable fact that the virus might infect cattle in the neighbourhood and cause them to die. The duty of care is accordingly owed to the owners of cattle in the neighbourhood, but the plaintiffs are not owners of cattle and have no proprietary interest in anything which might conceivably be damaged by the virus if it escaped. Even if the plaintiffs have a proprietary interest in the premises known as Farnham Market, these premises are not in jeopardy. In my judgment, therefore, the plaintiffs' claim in negligence fails even if the assumptions of fact most favourable to them are made.

[His Lordship also rejected the argument that the virus was a dangerous thing for the escape of which the defendants should be strictly liable.]

For those reasons, the plaintiffs are unable to succeed on any of the assumptions of fact put forward in the Special Case, and there will accordingly be judgment for the defendants with costs.

NOTES

1. The policy reasons underlying this principle are several. In *Stevenson* v. *East Ohio Gas Co.* (1946), 73 N.E. 2d 200 (C.A. Ohio), the plaintiff sued for loss of wages incurred because the defendant negligently caused a fire which made his work place too dangerous for the plaintiff to work at. The trial court sustained a demurrer which was affirmed on appeal. Mr. Justice Morgan stated:

"While the reason usually given for the refusal to permit recovery in this class of cases is that the damages are 'indirect' or are 'too remote' it is our opinion that the principal reason that has motivated the courts in denying recovery in this class of cases is that to permit recovery of damages in such cases would open the door to a mass of litigation which might very well overwhelm the courts so that in the long run while injustice might result in special cases, the ends of justice are conserved by laying down and enforcing the general rule. . . .

If one who by his negligence is legally responsible for an explosion or a conflagration should be required to respond in damages not only to those who have sustained personal injuries or physical property damage but also to every one who has suffered an economic loss, by reason of the explosion or conflagration, we might well be appalled by the results that would follow. In the instant case the door would be opened to claims for damages based on delay by all those who may have had contracts with The Bishop & Babcock Company either to deliver materials to the company or to receive from the company the products manufactured by it. Cases might well occur where a manufacturer would be obliged to close down his factory because of the inability of his supplier due to a fire loss to make prompt deliveries; the power company with a contract to supply a factory with electricity would be deprived of the profit which it would have made if the operation of the factory had not been interrupted by reason of fire damage; a man who had a contract to paint a building may not be able to proceed with his work; a salesman who would have sold the products of the factory may be deprived of his commissions; the neighbourhood restaurant which relies on the trade of the factory employees may suffer a substantial loss. The claims of workmen for loss of wages who were employed in such a factory and cannot continue to work there because of a fire, represent only a small fraction of the claims which would arise if recovery is allowed in this class of cases.

It is our opinion that the courts generally have reached a wise result in limiting claims for damages in this class of cases to those who may have sustained personal injuries or physical property damage and in refusing to open their doors in such cases to claims of loss of wages and other economic loss based on contract."

2. Mr. Justice Oliver Wendell Holmes once had occasion to deal with this point. In *Robins Dry Dock & Repair Co.* v. *Flint* (1927), 275 U.S. 303, the owners of a ship had entered into a time charter of the ship with A, the charterer. A term of the charter-party provided that the ship was to be docked once every 6 months and payment for hire was to be suspended until the ship was in a proper state of service. In accordance with these terms the ship was delivered to B and dry-docked for repairs. By the negligence of B, the ship's propeller was injured which resulted in a delay while a new one was installed. A now sued B for loss of the use of the steamer from August 1 — August 15. B had no knowledge of the charter-party when the delay began, but, on August 10, A advised B that the latter would be held liable for delay. The Supreme Court of the United States held that A had no cause of action against B. *Per* Holmes J.: "The question is whether [A] has an interest protected by law against unintended injuries inflicted upon the vessel by third persons who know nothing of the charter. . . . Their loss arose only through their contract with the owners — and while intentionally to bring about a breach of contract may give rise to a cause of action . . . no authority need be cited to show that, as a general rule, at least, a tort to the person or property of one man does not make the tort-feasor liable to another merely because the injured person was under a contract with that other unknown to the doer of the wrong. . . . The law does not spread its protection so far."

See 1 Harper and James, *The Law of Torts*, p. 504, where it is suggested that, the defendant, having settled with the owner in the *Robins* case, the "rational explanation" of that case lies in "the reluctance of the court to hold the tortfeasor liable, in addition to the physical damage to the vessel, for the value of *two* bargains."

3. What other policy reasons can you think of that might justify this principle? Are physical losses more worthy of protection than economic losses? Does it make better sense economically to make victims here bear their own losses and encourage them to insure rather than to shift the loss to the wrong-doers? Does this approach discourage a multiplicity of actions and encourage the channelling of several claims into one? See Linden, *Canadian Tort Law* (2nd ed., 1977), p. 369.

4. Economic losses resulting from property damage are compensable, including any profit that would have been earned during the period it is not operational. In *Athabaska Airways Ltd.* v. *Saskatchewan Government Airways* (1957), 12 D.L.R. (2d) 187 (Sask. Q.B.); varied as to damages (1958), 14 D.L.R. (2d) 66 (Sask. C.A.), the defendant negligently damaged one of the plaintiff's planes. The defendant and the plaintiff were competitors and the defendant refused to rent the plaintiff one of its planes as a substitute. The plaintiff there-upon rented a plane from another source and claimed as damages the rental of such plane until the return of its own. The defendant claimed that the rental exceeded the profits that the plaintiff could have made by the use of its own and that such profits were the limits of its liability. Davis J., held the plaintiff could obtain the actual rental paid since the plaintiff's loss was a plane as a "going concern" and the defendant could not insist on the plaintiff adopting a course that would have channelled its business into the defendant's hands.

5. A similar right is recognized in bailees who are felt to have a sufficient possessory interest to assert such a claim if they are deprived of the use of the bailed article. See *Courtenay* v. *Knutson* (1957), 26 D.L.R. (2d) 768 (B.C.).

6. In *Owners of Dredger Liesbosch* v. *Owners of Steamship Edison*, [1933] A.C. 449, the defendants' ship negligently sunk the dredger of the plaintiffs. Be-cause of their lack of financial capital, the plaintiffs were unable to purchase another dredger in order to proceed with the contract they were performing, although one was available. When pressed to continue their work, the plaintiffs hired a dredger which was more expensive to operate. They claimed, *inter alia*, for the additional expense. Lord Wright stated:

"The respondents contend that all that is recoverable as damages is the true value to the owners of the lost vessel as at the time and place of loss. Be-fore considering what is involved in this contention, I think it is desirable to examine the claim made by the appellants, which found favour with the Registrar and Langton J., and which in effect is that all their circumstances, in particular their want of means, must be taken into account and hence the damages must be based on their actual loss, provided that, as the Registrar and the judge have found, they acted reasonably in the unfortunate predica-ment in which they were placed, even though but for their financial embar-rassment they could have replaced the *Liesbosch* at a moderate price and with comparatively short delay. In my judgment the appellants are not en-titled to recover damages on this basis. The respondents' tortious act involved the physical loss of the dredger; that loss must somehow be reduced to terms of money. But the appellants' actual loss in so far as it was due to their im-pecuniosity arose from that impecuniosity as a separate and concurrent cause, extraneous to and distinct in character from the tort; the impecunio-sity was not traceable to the respondents' acts, and in my opinion was out-side the legal purview of the consequences of these acts. The law cannot take account of everything that follows a wrongful act; it regards some subsequent matters as outside the scope of its selection, because 'it were infinite for the law to judge the cause of causes', or consequence of consequences. Thus the loss of a ship by collision due to the other vessel's sole fault, may force the shipowner into bankruptcy and that again may involve his family in suffering, loss of education or opportunities in life, but no such loss could be recovered from the wrongdoer. In the varied web of affairs, the law must abstract some consequences as relevant, not perhaps on grounds of pure logic but simply for practical reasons. In the present case, if the appellants' financial embarrassment is to be regarded as a consequence of the respondents' tort, I think it is too remote, but I prefer to regard it as an independent cause, though its operative effect was conditioned by the loss of the dredger. The question of remoteness of damage has been considered in many authorities and from many aspects, but no case has been cited to your Lordships which would justify the appellants' claim. . . ."

Cf., Freedhoff v. *Pomalift Industries Ltd.,* [1971] 2 O.R. 773 (C.A.).

The principle utilized in assessing the damages in cases such as these was described in the *Liesbosch* case as follows:

". . . The true rule seems to be that the measure of damages in such cases is the value of the ship to her owner as a going concern at the time and place of the loss. In assessing that value regard must naturally be had to her pending engagements, either profitable or the reverse. The rule, however, obviously requires some care in its application; the figure of damage is to represent the capitalized value of the vessel as a profit-earning machine, not in the abstract but in view of the actual circumstances. The value of prospective freights cannot simply be added to the market value but ought to be taken into account in order to ascertain the total value for purpose of assessing the damage, since if it is merely added to the market value of a free ship, the owner will be getting *pro tanto* his damages twice over. The vessel cannot be earning in the open market while fulfilling the pending charter or charters. . ."

7. Economic losses that flow from personal injury are, of course, recoverable from a negligent wrongdoer. Thus, hospital and medical costs, loss of wages and loss of profits are compensable, even though they are "economic" losses, because they result from the physical injury. See *infra,* Chapter 14.

8. Similarly, an action for "pecuniary loss" is available to the dependants of someone who is fatally injured or whose earning ability has been reduced by injury. See Family Law Reform Act, 1978, S.O. 1978, c. 2, s. 60. See also *infra,* Chapter 14.

9. So too, an employer, a parent or a husband may recover any economic losses they suffer as a result of injury to an employee, child or wife. The basis of this action *per quod servitium amisit* is that there has been a loss of services caused to the plaintiff which must be reimbursed. The scope of this protection is far from certain today. It is unclear whether all types of employees are covered or whether only domestic servants are. Similarly, it is unclear whether only expenses and wages paid are recoverable or whether loss of profits are also compensable. See *The King* v. *C.P.R.,* [1947] S.C.R. 185 (S.C.C.); *Kneeshaw and Spawton's Crumpet Co. Ltd.* v. *Latendorff* (1965); 54 D.L.R. (2d) 84 (Alta.), broad view; *cf. Lee* v. *Sheard,* [1956] 1 Q.B. 192; *Inland Revenue Commissioners* v. *Hambrook,* [1956] 2 Q.B. 641; *R.* v. *Richardson,* [1948] S.C.R. 57; *Genereux* v. *Peterson, Howell & Heather (Canada) Ltd.,* [1973] 2 O.R. 558 (C.A.), narrow view; *Nugent* v. *Board of Rosetown School Unit No. 43* (1977), 2 C.C.L.T. 325 (Sask. C.A.). See also Gareth Jones, *"Per Quod Servitium Amisit"* (1958), 75 L.Q.R. 39; Hansen and Mullan, "Private Corporations in Canada: Principles of Recovery for the Tortious Disablement of Shareholder/Employees" in Klar (ed.), *Studies in Canadian Tort Law* (1977), Would a broader or narrower view of these matters encourage employers to be more generous to their employees in the benefits provided to them in case of injury?

10. In Workmen's Compensation cases, if a third person is liable for injury caused a workman, and the workman elects to take compensation, the Board (or the employer if individually liable) is subrogated to the rights of the injured workman or his dependants and may sue in his name or their names or in the name of the Board. See R.S.O. 1970, c. 505, s. 8(4). O.H.I.P. and other private insurers may also be subrogated in similar situations.

11. It is clear that double recovery is not permitted and that the costs incurred are to be paid only once to whomever it is that actually pays them.

12. See Atiyah, "Negligence and Economic Loss" (1967), 83 L.Q. Rev. 248; Harvey, "Economic Losses and Negligence: The Search for a Just Solution"

(1972), 50 Can. Bar Rev. 580; L.L. Stevens, "Negligent Acts Causing Pure Financial Loss: Policy Factors at Work" (1973), 23 U. of T.L.J. 431; Jolowicz, "The Law of Tort and Non-physical Loss" (1972-73), 12 J. Soc. Pub. T.L. 91; James, "Limitations on Liability for Economic Loss Caused by Negligence: A Pragmatic Appraisal" (1972-73), 12 J. Soc. Pub. T.L. 105, reprinted from (1972), 25 Vand. L. Rev. 43; A.V. Alexander, "The Law of Tort and Non-physical Loss: Insurance Aspects" (1972-73), 12 J. Soc. Pub. T.L. 119; J.C. Smith, "Clarification of Duty-Remoteness Problems Through A New Physiology of Negligence: Economic Loss, A Test Case" (1974), 9 U.B.C.L. Rev. 218.

SEAWAY HOTELS LTD. v. GRAGG (CANADA) LTD. AND CONSUMERS GAS CO.

Ontario Court of Appeal (1959), 21 D.L.R. (2d) 264; affg. 17 D.L.R. 292

A gas company, in the course of installing a gas main, negligently cut a feeder line of an electricity company which supplied electric current to plaintiff's hotel about a mile away. The gas company had a plan of the area showing the feeder line. As a result, electric service to the hotel was disrupted. The plaintiff brought action against the gas company for damages caused by negligence.

McLennan J.: . . . As a result of the power being cut off, refrigerators for the storage of food and equipment for cooking and washing would not operate and the air-conditioning, elevators and some lights would not work. The weather was warm and humid. As a result food spoiled and had to be thrown away to the estimated value of $1,274 and the dining room and cocktail bars had to be closed some hours before the usual time at an estimated loss of $1,540. A small claim was also made for loss of rental of rooms and additional miscellaneous loss and two items totalling approximately $350. . . .

Counsel for the defendants argued that even if the defendants were negligent the plaintiff had no right of action in law because liability for negligence only arises where there is a wrong done to the same person who suffers the loss and in this case while the plaintiff suffered loss there was no wrong done to the plaintiff. As he put it, where a wrong is done to the property of the Hydro, which results in loss to the plaintiff by reason of the plaintiff's contractual relationship with the Hydro, no cause of action exists.

As authority for this proposition he relied on three decisions: *Cattle* v. *Stockton Waterworks Co.* (1875), L.R. 10 Q.B. 453; *La Société Anonyme de Remorquage à Hélice* v. *Bennetts,* [1911] 1 K.B. 243 and *Anglo-Algerian S.S. Co.* v. *Houlder Line Ltd.,* [1908] 1 K.B. 659. These three cases undoubtedly establish the proposition that negligence which interferes with contractual rights *only* does not impose liability on the wrongdoer. Different reasons are given for the rule in the cases which I have mentioned and in the American authorities but I do not think it is necessary to discuss those reasons in view of the conclusion to which I have come which is that the principle established by those cases does not apply to this case. In none of these cases was there any damage to the property or person of the plaintiff and the loss for which compensation was sought arose solely by reason of interference with contractual relationships. In this case there was direct damage to the plaintiff's property in the food which was spoiled by reason of the refrigeration equipment failing to operate. It may be, and it is unnecessary to decide, that the other items of damage considered alone might fall within the principle established in those cases. But if an actionable wrong has been done to the plaintiff, he is entitled to recover all the damage resulting from it even if some part of the damage considered by itself would not be recoverable: *Horton* v. *Colwyn Bay & Colwyn Urban District Council*, [1908] 1 K.B. 327, at p. 341. . . . There will therefore be judgment for the plaintiff.

The defendant appealed.

Laidlaw J.A.: . . . The principles which are properly applicable to the particular facts were discussed in *M'Alister (or Donoghue)* v. *Stevenson*, [1932] A.C. 562 and the law has been reviewed with great care in the case of *Bolton* v. *Stone*, [1951] A.C. 850. . . .

I am satisfied that the defendants would know that interference with the duct shown on the plan in their possession before the work of construction was commenced and interference with the supply of electrical energy through that duct would cause damage to the persons entitled to receive that supply of electrical energy. The facts in the case are not in dispute and when the court applies the principles stated in *Bolton* v. *Stone* and elsewhere there can be only one conclusion, namely that the defendants ought reasonably to have foreseen the injury that resulted from interference with the duct. Upon that finding, the judgment against the defendants is correct.

NOTES

1. Is the distinction drawn by the trial judge a significant one? Did the Court of Appeal go any farther than the trial judge? Would the plaintiff have recovered under Mr. Justice McLennan's test if its loss had involved only profits? Under Mr. Justice Laidlaw's test?

2. In *Heeney* v. *Best* (1978), 23 O.R. (2d) 19, varied as to percentage of contributory negligence (25-75) and damages (Ont. C.A. Dec. 10/79) the defendants negligently knocked down some hydro wires cutting off the electricity supply to the plaintiff's barn, where he raised chickens. As a result the oxygen supply was cut off and 32,500 baby chicks died of suffocation. The defendants were held liable for an agreed amount of damages. Mr. Justice Stark at trial explained:

"In the present case and at the present time where electric power is so universally used, any reasonable person should be expected to foresee that if he negligently disrupts that power that damage will ensue to property in some form or other. He cannot be expected to foresee that a chicken-raising farm may be in the immediate neighbourhood. He cannot be expected to foresee that damage to property may be comparatively light as compared to a different form of injury but he can be expected to foresee that damage will follow his negligence. I know of no decision which holds that he must be aware of the detailed specifics of that damage before liability will follow. In this case I hold that the plaintiff has suffered direct damage as a result of the defendant's negligence in the amount of $31,500."

His Lordship also held the plaintiff contributorily negligent (50-50) because he failed to activate an available safety device that night, which would have warned him about the power failure. His Lordship stated:

"The situation at bar is not unlike the plaintiff who negligently fails to make use of a seatbelt; or the plaintiff who allows his smoke detector apparatus to remain idle."

Would there be liability for the loss of profits that would have been earned if the chickens had grown up and been sold in the ordinary course of business? What about the loss of profits to the wholesaler to whom the farmer usually sells his chickens? What about the loss of profits to the local restaurant which has been deprived of chickens to serve to its customers?

3. An electric cable owned by X is negligently cut and, as a result, X has to send its employees home and pay them their wages though they do not work. Liability? See *MacMillan Bloedel Ltd.* v. *Foundation Co. of Canada Ltd.*, [1977]

2 W.W.R. 717 (B.C.), no loss proved because extra productivity made up for the loss incurred.

4. In *SCM (United Kingdom) Ltd.* v. *W.J. Whittall & Son Ltd.,* [1970] 3 W.L.R. 694, [1970] 3 All E.R. 245, (C.A.), the electric supply of the plaintiff's factory was cut off when the defendant negligently damaged an electric cable owned by the electricity board. This caused a 7-hour power failure resulting in damage to the plaintiff's materials and machines as well as loss of profit from one day's production. The Court of Appeal upheld a trial judgment of liability on a preliminary issue. Lord Denning M.R. stated [p. 248 All E.R.]:

> "It is well settled that when a defendant by his negligence causes physical damage to the person or property of the plaintiff, in such circumstances that the plaintiff is entitled to compensation for the physical damage, then he can claim, in addition, for economic loss consequent on it."

In an *obiter dictum,* His Lordship asserted that damages for economic loss that did not flow from the physical loss were not recoverable. He was prepared to rely on *Seaway Hotels* only to the extent that it concerned the spoiling of the food. Lord Denning found that a duty was owed to the plaintiff by the defendants, but that pure financial loss was not compensable because "economic loss is regarded as too remote". Denning M.R. felt that either "*all* who suffered loss of profit should get damages for it, or *none* of them should. It should not depend on the chance whether material damage was done as well." He admitted that there may be "no difference in logic" between economic loss and material damage, but there is a "great deal of difference in common sense. The law is the embodiment of common sense, or, at any rate, it should be. In actions of negligence, when the plaintiff has suffered *no* damage to his person or property, but has only sustained *economic* loss, the law does not usually permit him to recover that loss. The reason lies in public policy." Denning M.R. continued [All E.R. p. 250]:

> "It is not sensible to saddle losses on this scale on to one sole contractor. Very often such losses occur without anyone's fault. A mine may be flooded, or a power failure may occur, by mischance as well as by negligence. Where it is only mischance, everyone grumbles but puts up with it. No one dreams of bringing an action for damages. So also when it occurs by negligence. The risk should be borne by the whole community rather than just on one pair of shoulders, *i.e.,* one contractor who may, or may not, be insured against the risk. There is not much logic in this but still it is the law."

His Lordship concluded by holding that "the contractors are liable for the material damage done to the factory-owners and the loss of profit truly consequent thereon: but not for any other economic loss". Lord Justice Winn agreed, but also stated *obiter* that he would not apply *Seaway Hotels* in any such case as the instant one. He proceeded to forge his own limiting device to avoid the "enormous" losses: "there is no liability for unintentional negligent infliction of any form of economic loss which is not itself consequential upon foreseeable physical injury or damage to property". Lord Justice Buckley, who also upheld the decision on the facts, preferred not to express a concluded opinion upon the other point.

SPARTAN STEEL & ALLOYS LTD. v. MARTIN & CO. (CONTRACTORS) LTD.

Court of Appeal. [1972] 3 All E.R. 557, [1972] 3 W.L.R. 502, [1973] 1 Q.B. 27

The plaintiffs manufactured stainless steel alloys at a factory which was directly supplied with electricity by a cable from a power station. The factory worked 24 hours a day. Continuous power was required to maintain the temperature in a furnace in which metal was melted. The defendant's employees, who were working on a near-by road, damaged the cable whilst using an excavating shovel. The electricity board shut off the power supply to the factory for 14½ hours until the cable was mended. There was a danger that a "melt" in the furnace might solidify and damage the furnace's lining, so the plaintiffs poured oxygen on to the 'melt' and removed it, thus reducing its value by £368. If the supply had not been cut off, they would have made a profit of £400 on the "melt", and £1,767 on another four "melts", which would have been put into the furnace. They claimed damages from the defendants in respect of all three sums. The defendants admitted that their employees had been negligent, but disputed the amount of their liability.

Lord Denning M.R.: . . . The plaintiffs claim all those sums as damages against the defendants for negligence. No evidence was given at the trial, because the defendants admitted that they had been negligent. The contest was solely on the amount of damages. The defendants take their stand on the recent decision in this court of *SCM (United Kingdom) Ltd.* v. *W. J. Whittall & Son Ltd.* [[1970] 3 All E.R. 245.] They admit that they are liable for the £368 physical damages. They did not greatly dispute that they are also liable for the £400 loss of profit on the first melt, because that was truly consequential on the physical damages and thus covered by *SCM* v. *Whittall* . But they deny that they are liable for the £1,767 for the other four melts. They say that was economic loss for which they are not liable. The judge rejected their contention and held them liable for all the loss. The defendants appeal to this court.

Counsel for the plaintiffs raised a point which was not discussed in *SCM* v. *Whittall*. He contended that there was a principle of English law relating to "parasitic damages". By this he meant that there are some heads of damage which, if they stood alone, would not be recoverable; but, nevertheless, if they could be annexed to some other legitimate claim for damages, might yet be recoverable. They are said to be "parasitic" because, like a parasite, in biology, they cannot exist on their own, but depend on others for their life and nourishment. Applying this principle he contended that, even if the economic loss (£1,767) on these four melts, standing alone, would not be recoverable, nevertheless by being attached to the other claim it can be added to it, and recovered as a 'parasite' to it. . . .

I do not like this doctrine of "parasitic damages". I do not like the very word "parasite". A "parasite" is one who is a useless hanger-on sucking the substance out of others. "Parasitic" is the adjective derived from it. It is a term of abuse. It is an opprobrious epithet. The phrase "parasitic damages" conveys to my mind the idea of damages which ought not in justice to be awarded, but which somehow or other have been allowed to get through by hanging on to others. If such be the concept underlying the doctrine, then the sooner it is got rid of the better. It has never been used in any case up until now. It has only appeared hitherto in the textbooks. I hope it will disappear from them after this case. . . .

Counsel for the plaintiffs submitted in the alternative that the views expressed by Winn L.J. and me in *SCM* v. *Whittall* were wrong. He said that if there was any limitation on the recovery of economic loss, it was to be found by restricting the sphere of duty, and not by limiting the type of damages recoverable. In this present case, he said, the defendants admittedly were under a duty to the plaintiffs and had broken it. The damages by way of economic loss were foreseeable, and, therefore, they should be recoverable. He cited several statements from the books in support of his submissions, including some by myself.

At bottom I think the question of recovering economic loss is one of policy. Whenever the courts draw a line to mark out the bounds of *duty*, they do it as a matter of policy so as to limit the responsibility of the defendant. Whenever the courts set bounds to the *damages* recoverable — saying that they are, or are not, too remote — they do it as matter of policy so as to limit the liability of the defendant. . . .

The more I think about these cases, the more difficult I find it to put into its proper pigeon-hole. Sometimes I say: "There was no duty." In others I say: "The damage was too remote." So much so that I think the time has come to discard those tests which have proved so elusive. It seems to me better to consider the particular relationship in hand, and see whether or not, as a matter of policy, economic loss should be recoverable. Thus in *Weller & Co.* v. *Foot and Mouth Disease Research Institute* it was plain that the loss suffered by the auctioneers was not recoverable, no matter whether it is put on the ground that there was no duty or that the damage was too remote. Again, in *Electrochrome Ltd.* v. *Welsh Plastics Ltd.*, it is plain that the economic loss suffered by the plaintiffs factory (due to the damage to the fire hydrant) was not recoverable, whether because there was no duty or that it was too remote.

So I turn to the relationship in the present case. It is of common occurrence. The parties concerned are the electricity board who are under a statutory duty to maintain supplies of electricity in their district; the inhabitants of the district, including this factory, who are entitled by statute to a continuous supply of electricity for their use; and the contractors who dig up the road. Similar relationships occur with other statutory bodies, such as gas and water undertakings. The cable may be damaged by the negligence of the statutory undertaker, or by the negligence of the contractor, or by accident without any negligence by anyone; and the power may have to be cut off whilst the cable is repaired. Or the power may be cut off owing to a short-circuit in the power house; and so forth. If the cutting off of the supply causes economic loss to the consumers, should it as a matter of policy be recoverable? And against whom?

The first consideration is the position of the statutory undertakers. If the board do not keep up the voltage or pressure of electricity, gas or water — or, likewise, if they shut it off for repairs — and thereby cause economic loss to their consumers, they are not liable in damages, not even if the cause of it is due to their own negligence. The only remedy (which is hardly ever pursued) is to prosecute the board before the justices. . . . If such be the policy of the legislature in regard to electricity boards, it would seem right for the common law to adopt a similar policy in regard to contractors. If the electricity boards are not liable for economic loss due to negligence which results in the cutting off of the supply, [neither] should a contractor be liable.

The second consideration is the nature of the hazard, namely, the cutting of the supply of electricity. This is a hazard which we all run. It may be due to a short circuit, to a flash of lightning, to a tree falling on the wires, to an accidental cutting of the cable, or even to the negligence of someone or other. And when it does happen, it affects a multitude of persons; not as a rule by way of physical damage to them or their property, but by putting them to inconvenience, and sometimes to economic loss. The supply is usually restored in a few hours, so the economic loss is not very large. Such a hazard is regarded by most people as a thing they must put up with — without seeking compensation from anyone. Some there are who install a stand-by system. Others seek refuge by taking out an insurance policy against breakdown in the supply. But most people are content to take the risk on themselves. When the supply is cut off, they do not go running round to their solicitor. They do not try to find out whether it was anyone's fault. They just put up with it. They try to make up the economic loss by doing more work [the] next day. This is a healthy attitude which the law should encourage.

The third consideration is this. If claims for economic loss were permitted for this particular hazard, there would be no end of claims. Some might be genuine, but many might be inflated, or even false. A machine might not have been in use anyway, but it would be easy to put it down to the cut in supply. It would be well-nigh impossible to check the claims. If there was economic loss on one day, did the applicant do his best to mitigate it by working harder next day? And so forth. Rather than expose claimants to such temptation and defendants to such hard labour — on comparatively small claims — it is better to disallow economic loss altogether, at any rate when it stands alone, independent of any physical damage.

The fourth consideration is that, in such a hazard as this, the risk of economic loss should be suffered by the whole community who suffer the losses — usually many but comparatively small losses — rather than on the one pair of shoulders, that is, on the contractor on whom the total of them, all added together, might be very heavy.

The fifth consideration is that the law provides for deserving cases. If the defendant is guilty of negligence which cuts off the electricity supply and causes actual physical damage to person or property, that physical damage can be recovered: see *Baker* v. *Crow Carrying Co. Ltd.*, referred to by Buckley L.J. in *SCM* v. *Whittall,* and also any economic loss truly consequential on the material damage: see *British Celanese Ltd.* v. *A.H. Hunt (Capacitors) Ltd.* and *SCM* v. *Whittall.* Such cases will be comparatively few. They will be readily capable of proof and will be easily checked. They should be and are admitted.

These considerations lead me to the conclusion that the plaintiffs should recover for the physical damage to the one melt (£368), and the loss of profit on that melt consequent thereon (£400); but not for the loss of profit on the four melts (£1,767), because that was economic loss independent of the physical damage. I would, therefore, allow the appeal and reduce the damages to £768.

Edmund Davies L.J. (dissenting): . . . For my part, I cannot see why the £400 loss of profit here sustained should be recoverable and not the £1,767. It is common ground that both types of loss were equally foreseeable and equally direct consequences of the defendants' admitted negligence, and the only distinction drawn is that the former figure represents the profit lost as a result of the physical damage done to the material in the furnace at the time when the power was cut off. But what has that purely fortuitous fact to do with legal principle? In my judgment, nothing, and I would seek no stronger support for my answer than the following passage from the judgment of Lord Denning M.R. himself in *SCM* v. *Whittall.*

> "Damage was done to many factories by the cutting-off of the electricity supply. Those who had a stand-by system would not suffer loss. But all others would suffer loss of production and loss of profit. This could be reasonably foreseen. Some of the factories may have suffered material damage as well. But that should not give them a special claim. Either *all* who suffered loss of profit should get damages for it, or *none* of them should. It should not depend on the chance whether material damage was done as well."

Nevertheless, Lord Denning M.R. went on to point out that:

> "In actions of negligence, when the plaintiff has suffered *no* damage to his person or property, but has only sustained *economic loss,* the law does not usually permit him to recover that loss. The reason lies in public policy."

It should, however, be stressed that, as in that case physical damage was sustained, observations regarding the position where the damage is economic only, while clearly commanding the greatest respect, are to be regarded as strictly *obiter.*

[His Lordship then discussed the authorities.]

Having considered the intrinsic nature of the problem presented in this appeal, and having consulted the relevant authorities, my conclusion, as already indicated, is that an action lies in negligence for damages in respect of purely economic loss, provided that it was a reasonably foreseeable and direct consequence of failure in a duty of care. The application of such a rule can undoubtedly give rise to difficulties in certain sets of circumstances, but so can the suggested rule that economic loss may be recovered *provided* it is directly consequential on physical damage. Many alarming situations were conjured up in the course of counsel's arguments before us. In their way, they were reminiscent of those formerly advanced against awarding damages for nervous shock; for example, the risk of fictitious claims and expensive litigation, the difficulty of disproving the alleged cause and effect, and the impossibility of expressing such a claim in financial terms. But I suspect that they (like the illustrations furnished by Lord Penzance in *Simpson & Co.* v. *Thomson*) would for the most part be resolved either on the ground that no duty of care was owed to the injured party or that the damages sued for were irrecoverable *not* because they were simply financial but because they were too remote. . . .

. . . Here too the line has to be drawn where in the particular case the good sense of the judge decides. . . .

Such good sense as I possess guides me to the conclusion that it would be wrong to draw in the present case any distinction between the first, spoilt 'melt' and the four 'melts' which, but for the defendants' negligence, would admittedly have followed it. That is simply another way of saying that I consider the plaintiffs are entitled to recover the entirety of the financial loss they sustained.

I should perhaps again stress that we are here dealing with economic loss which was both reasonably foreseeable and a direct consequence of the defendants' negligent act. What the position should or would be were the latter feature lacking (as in *Weller & Co.* v. *Foot and Mouth Disease Research Institute*) is not our present concern. By stressing this point one is not reviving the distinction between direct and indirect consequences which is generally thought to have been laid at rest by *The Wagon Mound (No. 1),* for, in the words of Professor Atiyah, that case:

> "was solely concerned with the question whether the directness of the damage is a *sufficient* test of liability. . . . In other words *The Wagon Mound* merely decides that a plaintiff cannot recover for unforeseeable consequences even if they are direct; it does not decide that a plaintiff can always recover for foreseeable consequences even if they are indirect."

Both directness and foreseeability being here established, it follows that I regard the learned trial judge as having rightly awarded the sum of £2,535.

Having regard to the route which has led me to this conclusion, it is not necessary for me to express any concluded view regarding the topic of 'parasitic damages'. I content myself with saying that, whatever be the scope of such a concept in other and wholly different branches of the law, I am at present not satisfied that it can be invoked in cases of the type now under consideration.

I would be for dismissing the appeal.

[Lawton L.J. concurred with Denning M.R.]

Appeal allowed.

NOTES

1. In sorting out these problems do you prefer the method employed in *Seaway Hotels, S.C.M. (United Kingdom) Ltd.* or in *Spartan Steel*?

2. In *Dominion Tape of Canada Ltd.* v. *L.R. McDonald & Sons Ltd. et al.,*
[1971] 3 O.R. 627, several bales fell from the defendant's negligently loaded
trailer breaking a hydro pole and causing a power failure whereby the plaintiff,
owner of a manufacturing plant, suffered economic loss through loss of profits
and the necessity to pay employees for time during which they could not work.
Chartrand Co. Ct. J. found that, while the loss of profit was foreseeable, it was
too remote. However, he held that the wages could be recovered as they represented "positive outlays" which constituted "a proximate and direct consequence of the wrongful act of the defendants and [were] not too remote to be
recovered", rather than "negative" ones, consisting of a "mere deprivation of an
opportunity to earn an income".

Is there a logical distinction between lost profits and wages paid? His Honour
had some further comments on the subject:

"Unlike academics, courts have to be practical rather than logical. That one
who causes damages to others by his careless acts or omissions, should bear
the burden of compensation for all those damages, may be a proposition
which appeals by its simplicity, but a literal application of it would generally
bring to the aggrieved mere rhetorical justice: a judgment pompously en-
grossed which cannot be executed for want of sufficient assets on the part of
the judgment debtor, thus turning a trial into a futile exercise and illustrating
the general fact that, existentially, the immoderate and singleminded pursuit
of absolutes is self-defeating.

A good deal of wrongs have tremendous repercussions, and rare are the
litigants who have sufficient means to repair completely their mischiefs, even
if abundantly insured. In the present case, several other plants were also adversely affected by the abrupt stoppage of power, and so were their employees, clients, suppliers, carriers and so on indefinitely, so that it would be
absurd not to sever the concatenation somewhere.

To adapt compensation to the financial measure of the average litigant,
the law seeks to limit the ramifications of liability by different devices. One
is the doctrine of foreseeability which holds that a person is bound to foresee
only the reasonable and probable consequences of the failure to take care,
judged by the standard of the ordinary man, and liable to make good only
that foreseen injury."

See also *British Celanese Ltd.* v. *A.H. Hunt (Capacitors) Ltd.,* [1969] 2 All E.R.
1252; *Electrochrome Ltd.* v. *Welsh Plastics Ltd.,* [1968] 2 All E.R. 205.

3. In *Yumerovski* v. *Dani* (1977), 18 O.R. (2d) 704 (Co. Ct.), the plaintiffs
bought several charter flight tickets from the defendant for their two families.
The defendant drove one of the families to the airport, but on the way an
accident occurred due to the defendant's gross negligence, in which one of the
Yumerovkis was killed. As a result, no one went on the trip. There were no
rebates allowed on the tickets by the airline. McCart C.C.J. reviewed the
authorities and held that the plaintiffs were entitled to the return of the cost of
the tickets and explained:

"Thus, we have a defendant who knew that if the plaintiffs did not board
the charter flight for which they had tickets on June 28, 1973, they would
be unable to recover the cost of those tickets, and who also knew, or is presumed to have known, that if he negligently prevented the father from
making the trip, the plaintiffs would not go. In other words, the defendant
had the knowledge or the means of knowledge that the plaintiffs, individually,
would likely suffer economic loss as a consequence of his negligence, and he
owed the plaintiffs a duty to take care not to cause them such loss by his
negligent act."

What if the defendant was a taxi-driver who did not know the plaintiffs?

4. In *Caltex Oil (Australia) Pty. Ltd.* v. *The Dredge "Willemstad"* (1976), 11
A.L.R. 227, an underwater pipeline was broken by a dredge through the negligence of its operators and the Decca Company which installed the ship's
navigation system. The plaintiff, Caltex, distributed crude oil from the refinery
by means of the pipeline, which they did not own themselves. Caltex claimed

damages against the owners of the dredge and Decca for the costs incurred in arranging for alternative means of transporting petroleum products while the pipeline was being repaired. The trial judge held that this was not recoverable as it was economic loss unrelated to any injury to the property of Caltex. The High Court reversed that decision unanimously.

Gibbs J. declared:

"In my opinion it is still right to say that as a general rule damages are not recoverable for economic loss which is not consequential upon injury to the plaintiff's person or property. The fact that the loss was foreseeable is not enough to make it recoverable. However, there are exceptional cases in which the defendant has knowledge or means of knowledge that the plaintiff individually, and not merely as a member of an unascertained class, will be likely to suffer economic loss as a consequence of his negligence, and owes the plaintiff a duty to take care not to cause him such damage by his negligent act. It is not necessary, and would not be wise, to attempt to formulate a principle that would cover all cases in which such a duty is owed; to borrow the words of Lord Diplock in *Mutual Life & Citizens' Assurance Co. Ltd.* v. *Evatt* [1971] 1 All ER 150; [1971] AC 793 at 809: "Those will fall to be ascertained step by step as the facts of particular cases which come before the courts make it necessary to determine them." All the facts of the particular case will have to be considered. It will be material but not in my opinion sufficient, that some property of the plaintiff was in physical proximity to the damaged property, or that the plaintiff, and the person whose property was injured, were engaged in a common adventure.

In the present case the persons interested in the dredge and the employees of Decca (in particular Mr. Austin) knew that the pipeline led directly from the refinery to Caltex's terminal. They should have known that, whatever the contractual or other relationship between Caltex and AOR might have been, the pipeline was the physical means by which the products flowed from the refinery to the terminal. Moreover the pipeline appeared to be designed to serve the terminal particularly (although no doubt it would have been possible for it to serve other persons as well) and was not like a water main or electric cable serving the public generally. In these circumstances the persons interested in the dredge, and Decca, should have had Caltex in contemplation as a person who would probably suffer economic loss if the pipes were broken. Further, the officers navigating the dredge had a particular obligation to take care to avoid damage to the pipeline, which was shown on the drawing supplied to them for the very purpose of enabling them to avoid it. Decca had a similar obligation to draw the lines on the track plotter chart, in such a way that the navigators would not sail the dredge over the pipeline. In all these circumstances the particular relationship between the dredge and Decca on the one hand, and Caltex on the other, was such that both the dredge and Decca owed a duty to Caltex to take reasonable care to avoid causing damage to the pipeline and thereby causing economic loss to Caltex. It should therefore, in my opinion, be concluded that Caltex is entitled to recover the economic loss resulting from the breach of that duty of care."

5. The Supreme Court of Canada had occasion recently to consider this problem in *Rivtow Marine Ltd.* v. *Washington Iron Works et al.* [1973] 6 W.W.R. 692, which was primarily a products liability case. See *infra*. One of the issues to be resolved was whether the plaintiff charterer could recover for loss of profits suffered when he had to remove from service one of his barges which was fitted with a defective crane manufactured by the defendant. It was held *inter alia* that it could recover this loss.

Mr. Justice Ritchie, after dealing with the authorities, decided that the damages were "recoverable as compensation for the direct and demonstrably foreseeable result of the breach of [the] duty [to warn]. This being the case, I do not find it necessary to follow the sometimes winding paths leading to the formulation of a policy decision."

Mr. Justice Laskin (dissenting on another point) had this to say on this issue:

"Support for such recovery in the present case will not lead to 'liability in an indeterminate amount for an indeterminate time to an indeterminate class', to borrow an often-quoted statement of the late Cardozo J. in *Ultramares Corp.* v. *Touche* (1931), 255 N.Y. 170 at 179; 174 N.E. 441; 74 A.L.R. 1139. The pragmatic considerations which underlay *Cattle* v. *Stockton Waterworks Co.* (1875), L.R. 10 Q.B. 453, will not be eroded by the imposition of liability upon Washington as a negligent designer and manufacturer: *cf.* Fleming James, "Limitations on Liability for Economic Loss Caused by Negligence: A Pragmatic Appraisal" [(1972-73)] 12 J. Soc. Pub. T.L. 105. Liability here will not mean that it must also be imposed in the case of any negligent conduct where there is foreseeable economic loss; a typical instance would be claims by employees for lost wages where their employer's factory has been damaged and is shut down by reason of another's negligence. The present case is concerned with direct economic loss by a person whose use of the defendant Washington's product was a contemplated one, and not with indirect economic loss by third parties, for example, persons whose logs could not be loaded on the appellant's barge because of the withdrawal of the defective crane from service to undergo repairs. It is concerned (and here I repeat myself) with economic loss resulting directly from avoidance of threatened physical harm to property of the appellant if not also personal injury to persons in its employ."

6. In *A.-G (Ontario) et al.* v. *Crompton* (1976), 1 C.C.L.T. 81, the defendant, Grandmont, was negligent in his driving on the highway and got into an accident which caused a fire. The local township fire department put it out, even though it was the province's responsibility to do so since it was a provincial highway. The province had made a contract with the township whereby it agreed to do this. The Attorney General, as representative of the Crown in the right of the province, and the township both sought as damages the cost of fighting the fire.

The court rejected the township's claim but allowed the province to succeed. Mr. Justice Haines explained:

"Clearly, the sine qua non of a claim in tort is the plaintiff's loss. How can it be said that one called upon to perform a contractual obligation has thereby suffered a loss, much less a tortious loss? How, in this case, can it be said that the Township, protected by an agreement with the Crown to provide emergency services for payment, has suffered a loss when called upon to perform those very services? It is not to the law of tort that the Township must look for recovery of its expenses, but rather to its contractual rights. The fact that it did do so and was paid the amount now claimed is ample evidence that its proper expectations have been fulfilled, and need no further gratification in this Court."

The situation with regard to the Crown was entirely different, suggested Mr. Justice Haines:

"The familiar calculus of negligence requires that the plaintiff to succeed establish a duty of care owed the plaintiff, breach by the defendant of that duty, and injury consequent to that breach. In each of these stages, the test of reasonable foresight is applied ultimately to define and delimit the permissible scope of recovery.

On this traditional formulation, I find that Grandmont, measured against the standard of the reasonable man of ordinary prudence, failed to conform to the standard of care required of the driver of a motor vehicle in the circumstances. The duty of care of which he was in breach extended not only to other motorists using the highways, but to all persons foreseeably imperiled by his conduct.

To my mind, the plaintiff Crown, owner of the highway, came squarely within the scope of that duty. It is manifest that a reasonably foreseeable consequence of a head-on collision between automobiles meeting at a combined speed of almost 150 miles per hour is that the wreckage would burst into flame and damage the road surface; that debris and lubricants from the automobiles would be strewn over the road surface to the extreme hazard of high speed traffic. On this view, not only did Grandmont owe a duty to the Crown, but Grandmont's conduct was the proximate cause of the Crown's damages in the sense that they were reasonably foreseeable and not too remote.

. . .

In the present case, . . . the question becomes: can the consequence complained of be fairly regarded as within the risk created by Grandmont's negligence? The common sense answer: the colossal risks created by the negligent operation of a motor vehicle at high speeds on busy modern highways materialized at Grandmont's hands into a hazard which required immediate attention, not only in the interests of the Crown as owner of the highway, whose roadway stood to be damaged, but in the interests of the travelling public, to whom the danger created by the obstructed highway was immediate and severe. The cost of rectification of this perilous situation lies properly with the actor whose negligence brought it about."

Does this case make sense?

STAR VILLAGE TAVERN v. NIELD

Manitoba Queen's Bench. [1976] 6 W.W.R. 80; 71 D.L.R. (3d) 439

Hamilton J.: Plaintiff owns a tavern 1½ miles east of a bridge and across the Red River from Selkirk, Manitoba. On 6th August 1974 the defendant Nield, while operating his co-defendant's vehicle, negligently collided with and damaged the bridge, causing it to be closed for repairs for approximately one month. During the time the bridge was closed, the travelling distance between Selkirk and the tavern became 15 miles. Plaintiff seeks damages from defendants for its economic loss caused by many of its Selkirk patrons suspending their patronage.

. . .

It is now settled law that a person may recover for economic loss caused by another's negligence although there has been no physical damage; see *Hedley Byrne & Co. Ltd.* v. *Heller & Partners Ltd.,* [1964] A.C. 465, [1963] 2 All E.R. 575; *Rivtow Marine Ltd.* v. *Washington Iron Works,* [1973] 6 W.W.R. 692, [1974] S.C.R. 1189, 40 D.L.R. (3d) 530; and *Haig* v. *Bamford,* [1976] 3 W.W.R. 331 (Can.).

The question is whether plaintiff, who suffered damage as a result of defendant's negligence, has a claim in law. As I understand counsel's argument, it is that if plaintiff can show damage and can attribute that damage to defendant's negligence, plaintiff is entitled to succeed. He argues that merely because others might also have a cause of action, plaintiff should not be denied. Cases were cited where a recovery has followed the cutting of gas, telephone or power lines, but none in a situation like the present. This in itself does not mean plaintiff may not succeed. The question is, should he?

The article of C. Harvey on "Economic Losses and Negligence" (1972), 50 Can. Bar Rev. 580, was urged upon me as an indication of the extension of liability. There are many qualifications in the article to which I need not refer, but the objectives are worth exploring. The problem recognized by the courts and by Mr. Harvey is to determine rules or guidelines to define the limits of liability.

The test suggested by Harvey, at p. 600, is:

"*. . . a person should be bound by a legal duty of care to avoid causing economic loss to another in circumstances where a reasonable man in the* *position of the defendant would foresee that kind of loss and would assume responsibility for it.*"

He says at pp. 620-21:

"This principle brings together wider considerations than the reasonable foreseeability formula which, standing alone, is inadequate to control liability in economic loss cases. The addition of reasonable responsibility directs the court's inquiry to the question of whether a reasonable man in the shoes of the defendant would have assumed responsibility for the loss. And that, as every common law lawyer will recognize, is the same as the fundamental question of whether the defendant ought to be made to bear the loss."

To do what Harvey suggests, as I understand him, the judge should say to himself: "If I were this defendant, being a reasonable man, freed from the prejudice of self-interest, would I in these circumstances feel a financial obligation to this plaintiff as a result of my negligence?" In answering that question in this case I would have to say that while I regretted any inconvenience that might have been caused, I could hardly assume the loss. To do so I would equally have to assume loss to all other users of the bridge who had been put to some expense.

If I was to ask the question as if it were asked prior to the accident, a more realistic answer might be given: "If I run into this bridge and cause it to be closed for a month, to whom will I owe compensation?" My answer might be that I would be responsible to the bridge authority, but I would not think of anyone else to whom I owed compensation. I might feel I owed a duty to the public at large not to damage a public thoroughfare, but if through some unintentional though negligent act, I did cause the thoroughfare to be closed, I could hardly feel that I should pay any user of the highway who suffered some loss by having to detour. If I caused a bridge to be closed, I could imagine that everyone who used the bridge might suffer economic loss by having to drive a further distance to their normal destination. It is possible that merchants in the Town of Selkirk lost business usually coming from the east side of the river. While I accept the "neighbour" principle with respect to liability in tort, there are also normal risks of living and doing business which one assumes. Every loss or inconvenience in life cannot give rise to a cause of action.

This test of placing oneself in the shoes of the negligent person before the occurrence of the negligence would seem to fit many of the economic loss situations referred to in the cases. Will I owe a duty to a merchant and should I compensate him if I cut his power line—disrupt his telecommunications; destroy a hydrant and cause water to enter his place of business; give an inaccurate financial statement on which he may rely? One could reasonably answer those questions in the affirmative, but so have the reported cases from which the questions arise.

To answer the question in the affirmative, it appears that there must be some link between the wrongdoer and the person suffering loss. While Harvey would have us abandon former terminology, it appears that the test of foreseeability remains. That test confines the limits of liability within reason. To abandon it places compensation at large and within the limitless discretion of the judiciary. In my opinion, there must be rules for determining the limits of liability so that there will be consistency in the application of the law so that the public, whether as potential litigants, or merely concerned with protecting themselves by caution or by insurance, will have some way of predetermining their liability or freedom therefrom.

In the case at bar, liability of the defendant to this plaintiff is, in my mind, beyond the contemplation of the reasonable wrongdoer.

The test suggested by Harvey was considered by Dickson J. in *Haig* v. *Bamford, supra.* He said at p. 341:

"This 'assumption of responsibility' test is an interesting one, although it is no more objective than a foreseeability test. It would allow the Court to narrow the scope of liability from that resulting from a foreseeability test, but it would still require a policy determination as to what should be the scope of liability."

The Supreme Court of Canada, then, has taken into account the extension of liability, if that is the correct term, resulting from *Hedley Byrne,* supra. It has also considered Harvey's proposals.

The test of foreseeability was defined in *M'Alister (Donoghue)* v. *Stevenson,* [1932] A.C. 562, where Lord Atkin said at p. 580:

"You must take reasonable care to avoid acts or omissions which you can reasonably foresee would be likely to injure your neighbour. Who, then, in law is my neighbour? The answer seems to be—persons who are so closely and directly affected by my act that I ought reasonably to have them in contemplation as being so affected when I am directing my mind to the acts or omissions which are called in question."

This principle was adopted and applied by Ritchie J. at p. 704 in *Rivtow Marine Ltd.* v. *Washington Iron Works,* supra.

Applying the foreseeability test to the case before me, I conclude the plaintiff does not fall within the category of "neighbour" to the defendants. It would not reasonably have been within the contemplation of defendants that they would assume responsibility for any damage caused to the plaintiff. Plaintiff was not sufficiently close to the defendants or their acts of negligence, to be within their reasonable contemplation, either as a neighbour to whom a duty was owed, or as one who ought reasonably to be compensated. To apply the test accepted by the Supreme Court—damage to this plaintiff ought not reasonably to have been in the contemplation of defendants. It was not reasonably foreseeable.

The claim is therefore dismissed with costs. . . .

NOTES

1. Will the foreseeability test adopted by Hamilton J. foster the consistency he advocates? Compare with *Trappa Holdings* v. *Surrey et al.,* [1978] 6 W.W.R. 545 (B.C.), where business loss due to a road blockage was held to be foreseeable in the circumstances.

2. What about the concept he uses that the "plaintiff was not sufficiently close to the defendants, or their acts of negligence to be within their reasonable contemplation"?

3. What about the test propounded in the much-cited article of Professor Harvey?

4. In *Gypsum Carrier Inc.* v. *The Queen; C.N.R.* v. *The Ship "Harry Lundeberg"* (1977), 78 D.L.R. (3d) 175 (Fed. Ct. T.D.), the defendant's ship negligently collided with a bridge owned by the federal Crown, which was used by the plaintiff railway companies under contract with the Crown. As a result of the damage to the bridge, railway traffic over it was suspended for eight days. This required re-routing by the plaintiffs of their trains, which involved extra expense. No claim was made for lost profits. The action of the railways was dismissed. Mr. Justice Collier explained:

"To my mind, economic loss, even though foreseeable, ought not to be recoverable unless it results directly from the careless act. This . . . approach . . . when combined or intermingled with the foreseeability approach . . . in my view, provides some guide as to whether or not recovery may be had."

Since the railways' loss was not a "direct and foreseeable result", there was no liability found. What do you think of this two-pronged test of Mr. Justice Collier? Does it relate to the duty question or to the remoteness issue? Does it make any difference? See also *Hunt* v. *T.W. Johnstone Co. Ltd.* (1976), 69 D.L.R. (3d) 639, 12 O.R. (2d) 623, *per* Hughes J.

JOSEPH C. SMITH, "THE MYSTERY OF DUTY"

in Klar (Ed.), *Studies in Canadian Tort Law* (1977)

Does economic loss raise an issue of extension (will the courts impose a standard of care in regard to activities which can result in pure economic loss?) or does it raise an issue of remoteness (under what circumstances does economic loss fall beyond the limits of legal liability?). If economic loss is an issue of extension then the proposition that there is a general rule that liability in negligence does not extend to economic loss except in limited circumstances is substantially correct. If, however, economic loss raises an issue of remoteness, then we must start from the basic assumption that as far as the extent or perimeters of the law of negligence is concerned, there is no basis or reason for distinguishing between physical damage and pure economic loss. Economic loss is recoverable unless it is too remote. This is to say that non-recovery for economic loss is the exception rather than the rule.

. . .

Which position is the correct one is certainly not clear from the cases. . . .

. . .

In order to decide whether economic loss is a matter of extension or remoteness, we must ascertain why economic loss constitutes a problem, and whether what is at stake is an issue like those raised where we are dealing with questions of extension, or whether it is an issue like those raised where we are dealing with problems of remoteness.

Clearly, economic loss poses a problem because it is often so widespread. In *Cattle* v. *Stockton Waterworks Co.,* Blackburn J. gives the example of a flooded mine:

> ". . . the defendant would be liable, not only to an action by the owner of the drowned mine, and by such of his workmen as had their tools or clothes destroyed, but also to an action by every workman and person employed in the mine, who in consequence of its stoppage made less wages than he would otherwise have done."

Widgery J. in *Weller & Co.* v. *Foot and Mouth Disease Research Institute* makes the same point in regard to economic loss resulting from the escape of foot and mouth virus:

> "It may be observed that if this argument is sound, the defendants' liability is likely to extend far beyond the loss suffered by the auctioneers, for in an agricultural community the escape of foot and mouth disease virus is a tragedy which can foreseeably affect almost all businesses in that area. The affected beasts must be slaughtered, as must others to whom the disease may conceivably have spread. Other farmers are prohibited from moving their cattle and may be unable to bring them to market at the most profitable time; transport contractors who make their living by the transport of animals are out of work, dairymen may go short of milk, and sellers of cattle feed suffer loss of business. The magnitude of these consequences must not be allowed to deprive the plaintiffs of their rights, but it emphasizes the importance of this case."

Questions relating to the radius of recoverability have little in common with the kind of policies at issue where the courts will not impose the law of negligence in particular areas or on certain kinds of conduct. They are, however, precisely the kinds of problems and policy issues which are at stake where questions of remoteness of damages are involved.

Whenever duty of care language is used in regard to a question of remoteness, confusion results because issues of extension and standard of care become confused with the remoteness issue. Assuming that economic loss raises problems of remoteness rather than extension, we should be able to enunciate the following principle:

> Where the courts are able to place strict and carefully defined limits on economic loss, there is no reason for not allowing recovery for the loss merely because it is economic rather than physical.

The problem, in other words, is not that the loss is economic, but that such losses are hard to limit. In the final analysis, the law measures all loss including bodily injury in terms of money. It is escpecially difficult to draw a distinction between pure economic loss and the economic loss incurred as a result of physical damage to chattels, particularly where the chattel is not unique. Recovery for economic loss has never presented a problem for the law of contract because the ambit of the agreement always limits the degree of recovery.

The above stated principle can be tested by an examination of the situations where the courts have and have not given recovery for economic loss. If it can be shown that the courts will award damages for economic loss whenever they are able to limit the radius of recovery by relating the loss to other factors or by the application of a principle that will not result in absurd consequences when applied to other similar situations, and if it can be shown that they will not give recovery where no such limiting factor or principle can be found to achieve that result, then the proposition that recovery for economic loss is the rule rather than the exception, and that economic loss raises issues of remoteness rather than extension, will have been successfully defended.

In order that recovery for economic loss does not result in what Cardozo C.J. aptly describes as "liability in an indeterminate amount for an indeterminate time to an indeterminate class", there must be some limitations on the amount of recovery, the numbers of those who can recover, and the time within which the loss can arise. These limitations must be such that they form a part of the rule of the case when the particular decision is generalized; otherwise, there will be a remoteness problem.

The most common example of economic loss is loss of earnings or earning capacity as the result of negligently caused physical injury. Such losses raise no problem of remoteness, because the amount is limited by prior earning capacity, the class which can recover is limited to those injured, and the damages are limited in regard to time by the date of loss of earnings or earning power and runs to the time when earning power is restored or one would anticipate earnings to cease in the normal event.

Economic loss suffered by the family or dependents of a person killed is recoverable under statute from the person negligently causing the death. Such loss causes no problems of remoteness because the class which can recover is narrowly defined, the damages are limited in terms of amount by the dead person's earning record and capacity, and in regard to time by the estimated length of his working career had it not been foreshortened.

Economic loss suffered as the result of a chattel being damaged is recoverable because such a loss is limited to the owner of the chattel, in amount, by the nature of the chattel and its use, and in time, by the period of its repair or replacement.

Economic loss suffered by an employer as a result of injuries to his employee has been recoverable (providing it comes within the old *actio per quod servitium amisit*) because such loss can be limited in regard to class of persons who can recover, amount, and time. Where such losses can be so limited there is no reason why they need fit into the old *per quod* categories. This certainly has been the trend in Canada, and to some degree in Australia.

A further line of cases allows recovery for economic loss where it is "directly consequential" on physical damage. By relating economic loss to physical damage, certain limitations can be placed on the class of people who can recover, the amount of loss, and the time within which the loss must arise.

The law of negligence allows recovery for economic loss caused by a negligent failure to carry out duties arising from a fiduciary relationship, because the duty relationship itself furnishes the limits to recovery.

In those limited cases where there is recovery in the law of torts for a breach of a promise, the ambit of the promise confines recovery in much the same way as a contract generally limits recovery to the contracting parties, in regard to specific subjects, and within a specified time. In the case of *Baxter & Co.* v. *Jones,* which has been followed in *Myers* v. *Thompson,* and *Kostiuk* v. *Union Acceptance Corp.,* the courts perceived no problems at all in giving recovery for pure economic loss.

Where the law of negligence does not extend to an activity which results in economic loss, the reasons why the courts will not impose a standard of care on such activities have nothing to do with the fact that the loss may be purely economic. In other words, the fact that the loss may be purely economic is irrelevant to the issue of extension.

This argument can be supported by several lines of cases. Arbitrators are not liable if they carry out their responsibilities negligently. University examiners cannot be held liable for negligence. The courts will not interfere with the internal affairs of a business by allowing liability for badly or negligently made business decisions. In all the above cases the loss would be purely economic. Yet this factor does not enter into the judgments. Rather, the court is reluctant to "take upon itself the management of concerns which others may understand far better than the Court does." If the law of negligence was extended to cover the making of evaluative judgments such as those instances in the types of cases above, the effect would be to set up a complex, slow and expensive appeal procedure for such decisions. Reasons such as these have nothing to do with whether the loss is economic or physical. It just so happens that this kind of activity results only in economic loss.

The trend in recent years has been for the courts to broaden the law of negligence to cover more and more areas of human activity. Wherever there has been economic loss which has not raised problems of remoteness because it is limitable in terms of the class which can recover, the amount, and the time, the fact that the loss is economic has not deterred the courts from extending the umbrella of the law of negligence.

The above argument that courts will not be deterred from extending the law of negligence to economic loss, providing no problems of remoteness are raised, is further supported by the recent decision of the Supreme Court of Canada in *Rivtow Marine Ltd.* v. *Washington Iron Works and Walkem Machinery & Equipment Ltd.* The defendants in this case, who negligently designed and manufactured a type of crane being used by the plaintiff charterers of a log barge, failed to warn the plaintiff of the danger of collapse after they became aware of the defects in their design. Recovery was given for the financial loss suffered as a result of having to take the crane out of service in the busiest part of the season when the full danger of the structural defects finally became apparent as the result of the collapse of a similar crane killing a workman. The fact that the loss was economic posed no problem for the Court since it was limited to the charterers, to a specific amount, within a given period of time. The Supreme Court of Canada, however, did not allow recovery for the cost of repairing the barge. The probable grounds are that this loss is better dealt with as a part of the law of contract. If recovery were allowed in tort, a subsequent purchaser would have a better remedy than would the original purchaser as the original contract of purchase could contain contractual limitations on the liability of the manufacturer. Whatever the reason, it cannot be on the grounds of remoteness, as any expenditure incurred to prevent physical damage from occurring is similarly limitable in regard to extent, amount and time of the risk, and therefore is not too remote.

Historically the law has allowed recovery for physical loss but not for economic loss resulting from a negligent misstatement upon which the plaintiff relied. This state of the law reflects certain priorities in our values. Our interest in being able to communicate freely without fear of legal liability is more important than giving recovery for economic loss. Our physical well-being, however, is more important than our interest in communicating freely without concerning ourselves with legal consequences. If there are to be exceptions to the rule that the law will impose no standard of care on us in regard to negligent misstatements creating risks of economic loss, two hurdles must be passed. Firstly, it must be shown that the exception poses no serious limitations on free communication, and secondly, that the economic loss is not too remote, that is, the extenet of recovery will not be out of proportion to the degree of fault incurred by the creation of the risk. The fact that the damages would always present problems of remoteness is a good reason for not extending the law of negligence to cover a particular area of conduct. Both hurdles are passed in the exception to the general rule arising our of *Hedley Byrne.* Requiring professional people to comply with a standard of care in carrying out their professional calling does not impose any serious limitations on freedom of communication, and the economic loss recoverable is not too remote because it is limited to the person to whom the negligent misstatement is made, and the risk is in regard to a very specific loss.

The question at stake in regard to the problem of extension is whether the advantages of giving recovery in negligence outweigh the disadvantages. The answer to this question varies according to the kind of activity involved. There are a few activities which do not create risks of physical damage but only of pure economic loss. But even in these areas this fact is only relevant if the economic loss is always too remote; that would be a good reason for not placing that kind of activity under the umbrella of negligence. Other than this the fact that the loss is economic makes no difference to the advantages or disadvantages of allowing recovery in the law of negligence. Therefore, we may conclude that recovery for economic loss raises policy issues which are at the heart of remoteness problems, rather than policy issues relating to the extension of the law of negligence.

————————

SOLOMON AND FELDTHUSEN, "RECOVERY FOR PURE ECONOMIC LOSS: THE EXCLUSIONARY RULE"

in Klar (Ed.), *Studies in Canadian Tort Law* (1977)

The solution to this dilemma is to abandon attempts to treat all claims for pure economic loss alike. Instead we suggest that categories of cases be identified and that specific limiting formulae be adopted to meet the unique loss distribution and indeterminate class problems within each category. The remaining cases can be dealt with by applying slightly modified principles of remoteness.

Several categories of pure economic loss claims have already been identified, and the courts and legislature have developed specific limiting formulae or guidelines for recovery. Categories include the negligent misstatement cases, the charter cases, the joint maritime venture cases, the *per quod* actions, and statutory fatal accident claims. As indicated earlier, there are numerous unresolved issues within each category, but at least the economic loss issue in each category can be isolated from the economic loss problems posed by other categories of cases. It is beyond the scope of this paper to analyze the limiting formula within any existing category or to develop a specific limiting formula for any proposed category. Our goal is rather to isolate those categories of cases in which specific limiting formulae are required.

Negligence actions brought against public authorities may represent an emerging category of pure economic loss claims. Whether or not a particular public official owes a duty of care to a specific class of the public will depend on the statutory authority from which he derives his power, and on policy considerations relating to administrative law in general. However, once such a duty is found, the English courts at least have little difficulty in allowing claims for pure economic loss, apparently because this is usually the precise type of loss the official was supposed to prevent. Clearly such cases do not pose typical loss distribution or indeterminate class problems and there appears to be no reason to lump them with other kinds of pure economic loss claims.

Products liability cases encompass another category of pure economic loss claims for which a specific limiting formula is required. The principles governing recovery of pure economic loss in products liability cases have not yet crystallized; however, the ambit of recovery appears to be expanding. Damages for physical injury and consequential economic loss caused by a defective product are recoverable in the absence of privity of contract between the manufacturer and the consumer. Pure economic losses, such as the depreciation in the market value of the product, the cost of repair, and the loss in profits caused by taking the product out of service for repair or by the improper functioning of the product are generally not recoverable. There are several alternative approaches to these loss distribution and indeterminate class problems which would allow the courts to expand recovery for pure economic loss within workable guidelines. What has deterred the courts, however, is not so much the nature of the loss, but rather reluctance to make fundamental changes in the law of contract by expanding recovery in negligence. This overlap between contract and tort in the products liability cases is somewhat unique, and regardless of how it is resolved it should not colour recovery of pure economic loss claims in other kinds of cases.

The last category of cases which require special treatment are the utility cases. One insignificant electrical cable, telephone cable, or water main can supply hundreds of potential plaintiffs, and it is probably accurate to state that no other single piece of property influences the economic prospects of so many people. In addition, the potential for physical injury, consequential economic loss, and pure economic loss is enormous! These indeterminate class and distribution of loss problems stem from the nature of utility supply itself, rather than the nature of the loss suffered. Whatever solution is adopted to meet these unique problems should not influence recovery for pure economic loss claims in unrelated fact situations.

In summarizing we suggest that the courts abandon the classification of cases on the ground that the loss claimed is purely economic. Within the categories we have isolated, the existence of a duty of care will depend on the principles developed to deal with the special problems raised by each type of case. The plaintiff's purely economic loss can then be analyzed by applying ordinary remoteness principles.

The cases which do not fit into any of the special categories can be dealt with by applying slightly modified principles of remoteness. A duty of care will be imposed whenever the defendant's conduct creates a foreseeable risk of injury to the plaintiff, and the existence of the duty should not depend upon whether the foreseeable injury is physical or economic. However, as in any negligence case, the type of injury suffered must be foreseeable, or else it will be considered too remote. Given the indeterminate class problem posed by pure economic loss claims, it is necessary to slightly modify the ordinary principles of remoteness. One negligent act can cause a chain reaction of pure economic losses, and it is neither desirable nor practical to compensate each victim. In addition to the foreseeability test of remoteness, therefore, we would add the criterion that pure economic loss, to be recoverable, must in most cases be the direct result of the defendant's negligence. This is not a new criterion, but it is rarely discussed in cases of physical harm because such injuries are almost always direct.

There is considerable judical approval for the limiting factors of foreseeability and directness, although the latter criterion has been subject to some criticism. This criticism is based on the fact that the distinction between direct and indirect injury has never been clearly drawn. However, by adopting Mr. Justice Lawton's definition in *British Celanese Ltd. v. A.H. Hunt Capacitors Ltd.*, this difficulty can be avoided. He defined a direct injury as one which occurred by operation of the law of nature without any further human intervention.

Had this approach been taken in the *Weller* case, the result would have been the same. The auctioneers' pure economic losses were indirect; they occurred when the cattle owners failed to bring their cattle to market because government officials quarantined the cattle. However, in the *Cattle, Bennetts, World Harmony,* and *Margarine Union* cases, the plaintiff would have recovered his pure economic loss. In our opinion this would have been a desirable result. In each case there was no potential problem of indeterminate class, or any reason why the plaintiff rather than the defendant was better able to bear or insure against the loss. In each case the owner could have recovered the loss claimed had he been the one to incur liability for it. From the defendant's point of view it was entirely fortuitous that the plaintiff rather than the owner of the damaged property suffered the loss. In conclusion, we feel that the direct and foreseeable test of remoteness will produce a just result in those cases which do not fall within the special categories.

NOTES

1. Do you find these two articles helpful?
2. How would you handle these cases of pure economic loss?
3. What do you think of the statement of Ruttan J. in *Smith* v. *Melancon,* [1976] 4 W.W.R. 9, at p. 19 (B.C.): "Once negligence is established, damages are recoverable which flow from that negligence, be they physical or economic."
4. Although negligent interference with economic interests creates many difficulties, intentional interference with economic interests has been much more broadly regulated by tort law. Inducing breach of contract intentionally, for example, has long been held tortious. See *Lumley* v. *Gye* (1853), 2 El. & Bl. 216; *Jones* v. *Fabbi et al.* (1973), 37 D.L.R. (3d) 27 (B.C.S.C.); *Torquay Hotel Co. Ltd.* v. *Cousins,* [1969] 1 All E.R. 522; Payne, "Interference With Contract" (1954), 7 Cur. Leg. Prob. 94; Harper, "Interference With Contractual Relations" (1953), 47 Nw. U.L. Rev. 873. An action for deceit has long been countenanced if the defendant, as a result of a fraudulent misrepresentation, deceives the plaintiff causing him economic loss. See *Derry* v. *Peek* (1889), 14 App. Cas. 337; *Goad* v. *Canadian Imperial Bank of Commerce* (1968), 67 D.L.R. (2d) 189 (Ont. H.C.). Another possible theory of liability in the economic area is that of intimidation which lies when a defendant, by threats of violence, forces someone to do something causing economic loss. See *Rookes* v. *Barnard,* [1964]

A.C. 1129; *Stratford* v. *Lindley,* [1965] A.C. 269; *Mintuck* v. *Valley River Band No. 63A* (1977), 2 C.C.L.T. 1 (Man. C.A.). See generally, Heydon, *Economic Torts* (1973). See also Chapter 18, *infra* Business Torts.

REVIEW PROBLEM

In Mississauga, Ontario, on November 10, 1979, a 106-car Canadian Pacific Railway train was derailed, causing one railway car, carrying propane gas, to explode and catch fire and another railway car carrying chlorine gas, to start leaking, endangering the entire neighbourhood. As a result some 240,000 people had to be evacuated from a 50 square mile area for a period of one week, the largest such event in North American history.

Miraculously, no lives were lost as a result of this disaster. No one was even seriously injured. The losses that occurred were almost exclusively economic. The total has been estimated at between $100 million and $150 million dollars.

A host of fascinating legal questions are raised by this incident, but only the questions of extent of liability are to be considered here.

Assuming an admission of liability in negligence, which of the following items of economic loss would be compensable, applying the present Canadian law?:

1. A homeowner, Harold, living quite near the railway line, heard the explosion and saw the railway cars burning a few hundred feet away. Fearing for his own and his children's safety, he packed a few necessities and moved into a motel. He also placed his dog in a kennel at $100 a week.

They ended up staying in the motel for a week, eating all of their meals there and buying several items, such as clothing and personal hygiene products, that they left behind. Harold missed work and lost one week's pay, because he felt he must stay with his children, who were very frightened by the experience. When he finally returned to the house, he found that its exterior was covered in soot and its interior was a mess caused by the water sprayed by the firemen trying to extinguish the fire. His valuable goldfish died. In addition, there was some looting and $10,000 worth of jewellery was taken.

Which, if any, of these individual expenses could Harold recover? Which, if any, are not recoverable?

2. Helping during this disaster were hundred of policemen and firefighters, from the local community, as well as from neighbouring counties. For example, some 600 Peel County Police, some 300 members of the Metropolitan Toronto Police, some members of the Ontario Provincial Police and some officers of the R.C.M.P. participated in the enormous task of protecting the people and property in the area. Are the costs of supplying any of these forces recoverable by the various municipalities and governments which suffered them?

3. Sam owned a grocery store in Mississauga. It had to be closed down for a week as a result of the disaster. Most of his milk and produce to a value of $500 was spoiled and, after he returned, he had to throw it out. He felt duty bound to pay a week's wages of $200 to his one employee. He also lost an estimated $1,000 in profits that he would have earned that week, had he been able to do his usual amount of business.

Which, if any, of these losses are compensable?

4. Louis owned a tavern in Mississauga. As a result of the closure of his tavern, his stock of liquor was not damaged, nor did he have to pay any of his employees any wages, but he still lost $5,000 in profits. Recovery?

5. Can Paul, Louis' bartender, who lived in Toronto and received no pay for the week he could not get to Mississauga to work, recover his lost wages in the amount of $300. Toronto Daily Star suffered loss because it could not deliver its newspapers to Mississauga residents. Recovery?

6. The Max Motor Company has a plant in the area, which was closed down for the week. Its losses included:

   (a) The full wages it was required by the collective agreement to pay all of its hourly employees, in the amount of $100,000;

   (b) The proportion of the annual salaries of its executives, accountants, engineers, etc., totalling $20,000;

(c) The expenses, such as interest and taxes on the real property, the heating and electricity costs, advertising costs, etc., in the amount of $30,000;

(d) The loss of profits that would have been earned on the cars that would have been produced during the week, an amount of $100,000.

7. Would any loss of profits suffered by dealers of the Max Motor Company, who could not deliver the cars they had promised to their customers on time, be recovered?

8. What about compensation to the employees of these dealers who lost commission on these aborted sales?

9. What about any loss suffered by a buyer of a Max car, who had to wait an extra week to get it? What if the buyer is a taxi-driver who depends for his livelihood on his car?

10. Would any of your answers to the above change if it turned out that the authorities overreacted and it is found that there was really danger only to a very few people in the immediate area of the derailment?

C. NEGLIGENT STATEMENTS

HEDLEY BYRNE & CO. LTD. v. HELLER & PARTNERS LTD.

House of Lords. [1964] A.C. 465; [1963] 2 All E.R. 575

Plaintiffs were a firm of advertising agents. Having placed several orders for television time and advertising space in newspapers on behalf of a client, Easipower Ltd., on terms under which plaintiffs became personally liable, they caused their bank, the National Provincial Bank Ltd., to make inquiries concerning the financial position of Easipower Ltd., who was a customer of defendant bankers. The National Bank telephoned the defendants and said they wanted to know in confidence and without responsibility on the part of defendants, the respectability and standing of Easipower Ltd. and whether the latter would be good for an advertising contract for £8,000 to £9,000. Some months later the National Bank wrote to the defendants asking for their opinion in confidence as to the respectability and standing of Easipower Ltd., and whether defendants would consider such company trustworthy to the extent of £100,000 per annum advertising contract. Defendants replied to both inquiries to the effect that Easipower Ltd. was a respectably constituted company, considered good for its normal business requirements. Defendants' letter in reply to the last inquiry of National Bank read: "For your private use and without responsibility on the part of the bank or its officials."

The defendants' replies to National Bank's inquiries were communicated to plaintiff who, relying on these replies placed orders for advertising time and space on behalf of Easipower Ltd. The latter went into liquidation and plaintiff lost over £17,000 on the advertising contracts.

Plaintiff brought action against defendants alleging that defendants' replies to National Bank's inquiries were made negligently and that such negligence created a false impression of Easipower's credit. At the trial, McNair J., found the defendants negligent but dismissed the action on the ground that defendants owed no duty of care to plaintiffs. The Court of Appeal dismissed an appeal by plaintiffs on the ground that they were bound by authority to hold that no duty of care existed and also because they were not satisfied that it would be reasonable to impose on a banker the obligation contended for. The plaintiffs appealed to the House of Lords.

Lord Reid: . . . Before coming to the main question of law it may be well to dispose of an argument that there was no sufficiently close relationship between these parties to give rise to any duty. It is said that the respondents did not know the precise purpose of the inquiries and did not even know whether National Bank, Ltd. wanted the information for its own use or for the use of a customer: they knew nothing of the appellants. I would reject that argument. They knew that the inquiry was in connexion with an advertising contract, and it was at least probable that the information was wanted by the advertising contractors. It seems to me quite immaterial that they did not know who these contractors were: there is no suggestion of any specialty which could have influenced them in deciding whether to give information or in what form to give it. I shall therefore treat this as if it were a case where a negligent misrepresentation is made directly to the person seeking information, opinion or advice, and I shall not attempt to decide what kind of degree of proximity is necessary before there can be a duty owed by the defendant to the plaintiff.

The appellant's first argument was based on *Donoghue (or McAlister)* v. *Stevenson.* That is a very important decision, but I do not think that it has any direct bearing on this case. That decision may encourage us to develop existing lines of authority, but it cannot entitle us to disregard them. Apart altogether from authority I would think that the law must treat negligent words differently from negligent acts. The law ought so far as possible to reflect the standards of the reasonable man, and that is what *Donoghue (or McAlister)* v. *Stevenson* set out to do. The most obvious difference between negligent words and negligent acts is this. Quite careful people often express definite opinions on social or informal occasions, even when they see that others are likely to be influenced by them; and they often do that without taking that care which they would take if asked for their opinion professionally, or in a business connexion. The appellants agree that there can be no duty of care on such occasions, and we were referred to American and South African authorities where that is recognised, although their law appears to have gone much further than ours has yet done. But it is at least unusual casually to put into circulation negligently-made articles which are dangerous. A man might give a friend a negligently-prepared bottle of home-made wine and his friend's guests might drink it with dire results; but it is by no means clear that those guests would have no action against the negligent manufacturer. Another obvious difference is that a negligently-made article will only cause one accident, and so it is not very difficult to find the necessary degree of proximity or neighbourhood between the negligent manufacturer and the person injured. But words can be broadcast with or without the consent or the foresight of the speaker or writer. It would be one thing to say that the speaker owes a duty to a limited class, but it would be going very far to say that he owes a duty to every ultimate "consumer" who acts on these words to his detriment. It would be no use to say that a speaker or writer owes a duty, but can disclaim responsibility if he wants to. He, like the manufacturer, could make it part of a contract that he is not to be liable for his negligence: but that contract would not protect him in a question with a third party at least if the third party was unaware of it.

So it seems to me that there is good sense behind our present law that in general an innocent but negligent misrepresentation gives no cause of action. There must be something more than the mere misstatement. I therefore turn to the authorities to see what more is required. The most natural requirement would be that expressly or by implication from the circumstances the speaker or writer has undertaken some responsibility, and that appears to me not to conflict with any authority which is binding on this House. Where there is a contract there is no difficulty as regards the contracting parties: the question is whether there is a warranty. The refusal of English law to recognise any *jus quaesitum tertio* causes some difficulties, but they are not relevant here. Then there are cases where a person does not merely make a statement, but performs a gratuitous service. I do not intend to examine the cases about that, but at least they show that in some cases that person owes a duty of care apart from any contract, and to that extent they pave the way to holding that there can be a duty of care in making a statement of fact or opinion which is independent of contract.

Much of the difficulty in this field has been caused by *Derry* v. *Peek* (1889), 14 App. Cas. 337. . . . It must now be taken that *Derry* v. *Peek* did not establish any universal rule that in the absence of contract an innocent but negligent mis-representation cannot give rise to an action. It is true that Lord Bramwell said: "To found an action for damages there must be a contract and breach, or fraud": and for the next twenty years it was generally assumed that *Derry* v. *Peek* decided that. But it was shown in this House in *Nocton* v. *Lord Ashburton*, [1914] A.C. 932, that that is much too widely stated. We cannot therefore now accept as accurate the numerous statements to that effect in cases between 1889 and 1914, and we must now determine the extent of the exceptions to that rule.

In *Nocton* v. *Lord Ashburton* a solicitor was sued for fraud. Fraud was not proved, but he was held liable for negligence. Viscount Haldane L.C., dealt with *Derry* v. *Peek* and pointed out that while the relationship of the parties in that case was not enough, the case did not decide "that where a different sort of re-lationship ought to be inferred from the circumstances, the case is to be con-cluded by asking whether an action for deceit will like. . . . There are other obligations besides that of honesty the breach of which may give a right to damages. These obligations depend on principles which the judges have worked out in the fashion that is characteristic of a system where much of the law has always been judge-made and unwritten."

It hardly needed *Donoghue* v. *Stevenson* to show that that process can still operate. Lord Haldane quoted a passage from the speech of Lord Herschell in *Derry* v. *Peek* where he excluded from the principle of that case "those cases where a person within whose special province it lay to know a particular fact has given an erroneous answer to an inquiry made with regard to it by a person desirous of ascertaining the fact for the purpose of determining his course". . . .

Lord Haldane gave a further statement of his view in *Robinson* v. *National Bank of Scotland,* [1916] S.C. (H.L.) 154, [where] he went on to say: "I think, as I said in *Nocton's* case that an exaggerated view was taken by a good many people of the scope of the decision in *Derry* v. *Peek.* The whole of the doctrine as to fiduciary relationships, as to the duty of care arising from implied as well as express contracts, as to the duty of care arising from other special re-lationships which the courts may find to exist in particular cases, still remains, and I should be very sorry if any word fell from me which should suggest that the courts are in any way hampered in recognising that the duty of care may be established when such cases really occur."

This passage makes it clear that Lord Haldane did not think that a duty to take care must be limited to cases of fiduciary relationship in the narrow sense of relationships which had been recognized by the Court of Chancery as being of a fiduciary character. He speaks of other special relationships, and I can see no logical stopping place short of all those relationships where it is plain that the party seeking information or advice was trusting the other to exercise such a degree of care as the circumstances required, where it was reasonable for him to do that, and where the other gave the information or advice when he knew or ought to have known that the inquirer was relying on him. I say "ought to have known" because in questions of negligence we now apply the objective standard of what the reasonable man would have done.

A reasonable man, knowing that he was being trusted or that his skill and judgment was being relied on, would, I think, have three courses open to him.

He could keep silent or decline to give the information or advice sought; or he could give an answer with a clear qualification that he accepted no responsibility for it or that it was given without that reflection or inquiry which a careful answer would require: or he could simply answer without any such qualification. If he chooses to adopt the last course he must, I think, be held to have accepted some responsibility for his answer being given carefully, or to have accepted a relationship with the inquirer which requires him to exercise such care as the circumstances require.

If that is right then it must follow that *Candler* v. *Crane, Christmas & Co.* was wrongly decided. . . . The majority of the Court of Appeal held that they were bound by *Le Lievre* v. *Gould,* [1893] 1 Q.B. 491, and that *Donoghue* v. *Stevenson* had no application. In so holding I think that they were right. The Court of Appeal have bound themselves to follow all *rationes decidendi* of previous Court of Appeal decisions, and, in face of that rule, it would have been very difficult to say that the ratio in *Le Lievre* v. *Gould* did not cover *Candler's* case. . . . So the question which we now have to consider is whether the ratio in *Le Lievre* v. *Gould* can be supported. But before leaving *Candler's* case I must note that Cohen L.J. (as he then was), attached considerable importance to a New York decision, *Ultramares Corporation* v. *Touche,* a decision of Cardozo C.J. But I think that another decision of that great judge, *Glanzer* v. *Shepard,* is more in point because in the latter case there was a direct relationship between the weigher who gave a certificate and the purchaser of the goods weighed, who the weigher knew was relying on his certificate: there the weigher was held to owe a duty to the purchaser with whom he had no contract. The *Ultramares* case can be regarded as nearer to *Le Lievre* v. *Gould.*

In *Le Lievre* v. *Gould* a surveyor, Gould, gave certificates to a builder, who employed him. The plaintiffs were mortgagees of the builders' interest and Gould knew nothing about them or the terms of their mortgage; but the builder, without Gould's authority, chose to show them Gould's report. I have said that I do not intend to decide anything about the degree of proximity necessary to establish a relationship giving rise to a duty of care, but it would seem difficult to find such proximity in this case and the actual decision in *Le Lievre* v. *Gould* may therefore be correct. The decision, however, was not put on that ground: if it had been, *Cann* v. *Willson* (1888), 39 Ch.D. 39, would not have been overruled. Lord Esher M.R., held that there was no contract between the plaintiffs and the defendant and that this House in *Derry* v. *Peek* had "restated the old law that, in the absence of contract, an action for negligence cannot be maintained when there is no fraud". Bowen L.J., gave a similar reason [and] he added that the law of England "does not consider that what a man writes on paper is like a gun or other dangerous instrument; and, unless he intended to deceive, the law does not, in the absence of contract, hold him responsible for drawing his certificate carelessly". So both he and Lord Esher held that *Cann* v. *Willson* was wrong in deciding that there was a duty to take care. We now know on the authority of *Donoghue* v. *Stevenson* that Bowen L.J., was wrong in limiting duty of care to guns or other dangerous instruments, and I think that, for reasons which I have already given, he was also wrong in limiting the duty of care with regard to statements to cases where there is a contract. On both points Bowen L.J., was expressing what was then generally believed to be the law, but later statements in this House have gone far to remove those limitations. I would therefore hold that that ratio in *Le Lievre* v. *Gould* was wrong and that *Cann* v. *Willson* ought not to have been overruled.

Now I must try to apply these principles to the present case. What the appellants complain of is not negligence in the ordinary sense of carelessness, but rather misjudgment in that Mr. Heller, while honestly seeking to give a fair assessment, in fact made a statement which gave a false and misleading impression of his customer's credit. It appears that bankers now commonly give references with regard to their customers as part of their business. I do not know how far their customers generally permit them to disclose their affairs, but even with permission it cannot always be easy for a banker to reconcile his duty to his customer with his desire to give a fairly balanced reply to an inquiry; and inquirers can hardly expect a full and objective statement of opinion or accurate factual information such as skilled men would be expected to give in reply to other kinds of inquiry. So it seems to me to be unusually difficult to determine just what duty, beyond a duty to be honest, a banker would be held to have undertaken if he gave a reply without an adequate disclaimer of responsibility or other warning. It is in light of such considerations that I approach an examination of the case of *Robinson* v. *National Bank of Scotland*. . . .

That case is very nearly indistinguishable from the present case. . . . With regard to the bank's duty Lord Haldane said: ". . . when a mere inquiry is made by one banker of another, who stands in no special relation to him, then, in the absence of special circumstances from which a contract to be careful can be inferred, I think there is no duty excepting the duty of common honesty to which I have referred". I think that by "a contract to be careful" Lord Haldane must have meant an agreement or undertaking to be careful. This was a Scots case and by Scots law there can be a contract without consideration: Lord Haldane cannot have meant that similar cases in Scotland and England would be decided differently on the matter of special relationship for that reason. I am, I think, entitled to note that this was an extempore judgment. So Lord Haldane was contrasting "mere inquiry" with a case where there are special circumstances from which an undertaking to be careful can be inferred. . . .

It appears to me that the only possible distinction in the present case is that there was no adequate disclaimer of responsibility. Here, however, the appellants' bank, who were their agents in making the inquiry, began by saying that "they wanted to know in confidence and without responsibility on our part", *i.e.*, on the part of the respondents. So I cannot see how the appellants can now be entitled to disregard that and maintain that the respondents did incur a responsibility to them. . . .

I am therefore of opinion that it is clear that the respondents never undertook any duty to exercise care in giving their replies. The appellants cannot succeed unless there was such a duty and therefore in my judgment this appeal must be dismissed.

Lord Morris of Borth-y-Gest: . . . My lords, I consider that it follows and that it should now be regarded as settled that if someone possessed of a special skill undertakes, quite irrespective of contract, to apply that skill for the assistance of another person who relies on such skill, a duty of care will arise. The fact that the service is to be given by means of, or by the instrumentaility of, words can make no difference. Furthermore if, in a sphere in which a person is so placed that others could reasonably rely on his judgment or his skill or on his ability to make careful inquiry, a person takes it on himself to give information or advice to, or allows his information or advice to be passed on to, another person who, as he knows or should know, will place reliance on it, then a duty of care will arise. . . .

Lord Devlin: . . . My lords, I approach the consideration of the first and fundamental questions in the way in which Lord Atkin approached the same sort of question — that is, in essence the same sort, though in particulars very different — in *Donoghue* v. *Stevenson*. If counsel for the respondents' proposition is the result of the authorities, then, as Lord Atkin said: "I should consider the result a grave defect in the law and so contrary to principle that I should hesitate long before following any decision to that effect which had not the authority of this House." So before I examine the authorities, I shall explain why I think that the law, if settled as counsel for the respondents says that it is, would be defective. As well as being defective in the sense that it would leave a man without a remedy where he ought to have one and where it is well within the scope of the law to give him one, it would also be profoundly illogical. The common law is tolerant of much illogicality especially on the surface; but no system of law can be workable if it has not got logic at the root of it.

Originally it was thought that the tort of negligence must be confined entirely to deeds and could not extend to words. That was supposed to have been decided by *Derry* v. *Peek*. I cannot imagine that anyone would now dispute that, if this were the law, the law would be gravely defective. The practical proof of this is that the supposed deficiency was, in relation to the facts in *Derry* v. *Peek,* immediately made good by Act of Parliament. Today it is unthinkable that the law could permit directors to be as careless as they liked in the statements that they made in a prospectus.

A simple distinction between negligence in word and negligence in deed might leave the law defective but at least it would be intelligible. This is not, however, the distinction that is drawn in counsel for the respondents' argument and it is one which would be unworkable. A defendant who is given a car to overhaul and repair if necessary is liable to the injured driver (a) if he overhauls and repairs it negligently and tells the driver that it is safe when it is not; (b) if he overhauls it and negligently finds it not to be in need of repair and tells the driver that it is safe when it is not; and (c) if he negligently omits to overhaul it at all and tells the driver that it is safe when it is not. It would be absurd in any of these cases to argue that the proximate cause of the driver's injury was not what the defendant did or failed to do but his negligent statement on the faith of which the driver drove the car and for which he could not recover. In this type of case where, if there were a contract there would undoubtedly be a duty of service, it is not practicable to distinguish between the inspection or examination, the acts done or omitted to be done, and the advice or information given. So neither in this case nor in *Candler* v. *Crane, Christmas & Co.* (Denning L.J. noted the point when he gave the example of the analyst who negligently certifies food to be harmless) has counsel for the respondent argued that the distinction lies there.

This is why the distinction is now said to depend on whether financial loss is caused through physical injury or whether it is caused directly. The interposition of the physical injury is said to make a difference of principle. I can find neither logic nor common sense in this. If irrespective of contract, a doctor negligently advises a patient that he can safely pursue his occupation and he cannot and the patient's health suffers and he loses his livelihood, the patient has a remedy. But if the doctor negligently advises him that he cannot safely pursue his occupation when in fact he can and he loses his livelihood, there is said to be no remedy. Unless, of course, the patient was a private patient and the doctor accepted half a guinea for his trouble; then the patient can recover all. I am bound to say, my lords, that I think this to be nonsense. It is not the sort of nonsense that can arise even in the best system of law out of the need to draw nice distinctions between borderline cases. It arises, if it is the law, simply out of a refusal to make sense. The line is not drawn on any intelligible principle. It just happens to be the line which those who have been driven from the extreme assertion that negligent statements in the absence of contractual or fiduciary duty give no cause of action have in the course of their retreat so far reached.

I shall now examine the relevant authorities and your lordships will, I hope, pardon me if, with one exception, I attend only to those that have been decided in this House, for I have made it plain that I will not in this matter yield to persuasion but only to compulsion. [His Lordship analyzed the cases.] . . .

The real value of *Donoghue* v. *Stevenson* to the argument in this case is that it shows how the law can be developed to solve particular problems. Is the relationship between the parties in this case such that it can be brought within a category giving rise to a special duty? As always in English law the first step in such an inquiry is to see how far the authorities have gone, for new categories in the law do not spring into existence overnight.

It would be surprising if the sort of problem that is created by the facts of this case had never until recently arisen in English law. As a problem it is a by-product of the doctrine of consideration. If the respondents had made a nominal charge for the reference, the problem would not exist. If it were possible in English law to construct a contract without consideration, the problem would move at once out of the first and general phase into the particular; and the question would be, not whether on the facts of the case there was a special relationship, but whether on the facts of the case there was a contract.

The respondents in this case cannot deny that they were performing a service. Their sheet anchor is that they were performing it gratuitously and therefore no liability for its performance can arise. My Lords, in my opinion this is not the law. A promise given without consideration to perform a service cannot be enforced as a contract by the promisee; but if the service is in fact performed and done negligently, the promisee can recover in an action in tort. This is the foundation of the liability of a gratuitous bailee. . . .

. . . In one way or another the law has ensured that in this type of case a just result has been reached. But I think that today the result can and should be achieved by the application of the law of negligence and that it is unnecessary and undesirable to construct an artificial consideration. I agree with Sir Frederick Pollock's note on the case of *De la Bere* v. *Pearson, Ltd.,* where he wrote in *Pollock on Contract* (13th ed.) 140 (note 31) that "the cause of action is better regarded as arising from default in the performance of a voluntary undertaking independent of contract".

My lords, it is true that this principle of law has not yet been clearly applied to a case where the service which the defendant undertakes to perform is or includes the obtaining and imparting of information. But I cannot see why it should not be: and if it had not been thought erroneously that *Derry* v. *Peek* negatived any liability for negligent statements, I think that by now it probably would have been. . . .

I think, therefore, that there is ample authority to justify your lordships in saying now that the categories of special relationships, which may give rise to a duty to take care in word as well as in deed, are not limited to contractual relationships or to relationships of fiduciary duty, but include also relationships which in the words of Lord Shaw in *Nocton* v. *Lord Ashburton* are "equivalent to contract" that is, where there is an assumption of responsibility in circumstances in which, but for the absence of consideration, there would be a contract. Where there is an express undertaking, an express warranty as distinct from mere representation, there can be little difficulty. The difficulty arises in discerning those cases in which the undertaking is to be implied. In this respect the absence of consideration is not irrelevant. Payment for information or advice is very good evidence that it is being relied on and that the informer or adviser knows that it is. Where there is no consideration, it will be necessary to exercise greater care in distinguishing between social and professional relationships and between those which are of a contractual character and those which are not. It may often be material to consider whether the adviser is acting purely out of good nature or whether he is getting his reward in some indirect form. The service that a bank performs in giving a reference is not done simply out of a desire to assist commerce. It would discourage the customers of the bank if their deals fell through because the bank had refused to testify to their credit when it was good.

I have had the advantage of reading all the opinions prepared by your lordships and of studying the terms which your lordships have framed by way of definition of the sort of relationship which gives rise to a responsibility towards those who act on information or advice and so creates a duty of care towards them. I do not understand any of your lordships to hold that it is a responsibility imposed by law on certain types of persons or in certain sorts of situations. It is a responsibility that is voluntarily accepted or undertaken either generally where a general relationship, such as that of solicitor and client or banker and customer, is created, or specifically in relation to a particular transaction. In the present case the appellants were not, as in *Woods* v. *Martins Banks, Ltd.,* [1959] 1 Q.B. 55, the customers or potential customers of the bank. Responsibility can attach only to the single act, *i.e.,* the giving of the reference, and only if the doing of that act implied a voluntary undertaking to assume responsibility. This is a point of great importance because it is, as I understand it, the foundation for the ground on which in the end the House dismisses the appeal. I do not think it possible to formulate with exactitude all the conditions under which the law will in a specific case imply a voluntary undertaking, any more than it is possible to formulate those in which the law will imply a contract. But in so far as your lordships describe the circumstances in which an implication will ordinarily be drawn, I am prepared to adopt any one of your lordships' statements as showing the general rule; and I pay the same respect to the statement by Denning L.J. in his dissenting judgment in *Candler* v. *Crane, Christmas & Co.* about the circumstances in which he says a duty to use care in making a statement exists.

I do not go further than this for two reasons. The first is that I have found in the speech of Lord Shaw in *Nocton* v. *Lord Ashburton* and in the idea of a relationship that is equivalent to contract all that is necessary to cover the situation that arises in this case. Counsel for the appellants does not claim to succeed unless he can establish that the reference was intended by the respondents to be communicated by National Provincial Bank, Ltd. to some unnamed customer of theirs, whose identity was immaterial to the respondents, for that customer's use. All that was lacking was formal consideration. The case is well within the authorities that I have already cited and of which *Wilkinson* v. *Coverdale* is the most apposite example.

I shall therefore content myself with the proposition that wherever there is a relationship equivalent to contract there is a duty of care. Such a relationship may be either general or particular. Examples of a general relationship are those of solicitor and client and of banker and customer. For the former *Nocton* v. *Lord Ashburton* has long stood as the authority and for the latter there is the decision of Salmon J., in *Woods* v. *Martins Bank, Ltd.* which I respectfully approve. There may well be others yet to be established. Where there is a general relationship of this sort it is unnecessary to do more than prove its existence and the duty follows. Where, as in the present case, what is relied on is a particular relationship created *ad hoc,* it will be necessary to examine the particular facts to see whether there is an express or implied undertaking of responsibility.

I regard this proposition as an application of the general conception of proximity. Cases may arise in the future in which a new and wider proposition, quite independent of any notion of contract, will be needed. There may, for example, be cases in which a statement is not supplied for the use of any particular person, any more than in *Donoghue* v. *Stevenson* the ginger beer was supplied for consumption by any particular person; and it will then be necessary to return to the general conception of proximity and to see whether there can be evolved from it, as was done in *Donoghue* v. *Stevenson,* a specific proposition to fit the case. When that has to be done, the speeches of your lordships today as well as the judgment of Denning L.J., to which I have referred — and also, I may add, the proposition in the American *Restatement of the Law of Torts,* Vol. III, p. 122, para. 552, and the cases which exemplify it — will afford good guidance as to what ought to be said. I prefer to see what shape such cases take before committing myself to any formulation, for I bear in mind Lord Atkin's warning, which I have quoted, against placing unnecessary restrictions on the adaptability of English law. I have, I hope, made it clear that I take quite literally the *dictum* of Lord Macmillan, so often quoted from the same case, that "the categories of negligence are never closed". English law is wide enough to embrace any new category or proposition that exemplifies the principle of proximity.

I have another reason for caution. Since the essence of the matter in the present case and in others of the same type is the acceptance of responsibility, I should like to guard against the imposition of restrictive terms notwithstanding that the essential condition is fulfilled. If a defendant says to a plaintiff: "Let me do this for you, do not waste your money in employing a professional, I will do it for nothing and you can rely on me", I do not think that he could escape liability simply because he belonged to no profession or calling, had no qualifications or special skill and did not hold himself out as having any. The relevance of these factors is to show the unlikelihood of a defendant in such circumstances assuming a legal responsibility and as such they may often be decisive. But they are not theoretically conclusive, and so cannot be the subject of definition. It would be unfortunate if they were. For it would mean that plaintiffs would seek to avoid the rigidity of the definition by bringing the action in contract as in *De la Bere* v. *Pearson, Ltd.* and setting up something that would do for consideration. That to my mind would be an undesirable development in the law; and the best way of avoiding it is to settle the law so that the presence or absence of consideration makes no difference. . . .

A man cannot be said voluntarily to be undertaking a responsibility if at the very moment when he is said to be accepting it he declares that in fact he is not. The problem of reconciling words of exemption with the existence of a duty arises only when a party is claiming exemption from a responsibility which he has already undertaken or which he is contracting to undertake. For this reason alone, I would dismiss the appeal.

Lord Pearce: . . . The reason for some divergence between the law of negligence in word and that of negligence in act is clear. Negligence in word creates problems different from those of negligence in act. Words are more volatile than deeds. They travel fast and far afield. They are used without being expended and take effect in combination with innumerable facts and other words. Yet they are dangerous and can cause vast financial damage. . . . If the mere hearing or reading of words were held to create proximity, there might be no limit to the persons to whom the speaker or writer could be liable. Damage by negligent acts to persons or property on the other hand is more visible and obvious; its limits are more easily defined and it is with this damage that the earlier cases were more concerned. . . .

The range of negligence in act was greatly extended in *Donoghue* v. *Stevenson* on the wide principle of the good neighbour — *sic utere tuo ut alienum non laedas.* It is argued that the principles enunciated in *Donoghue* v. *Stevenson* apply fully to negligence in word. . . . But they were certainly not purporting to deal with such issues as, for instance, how far economic loss alone without some physical or material damage to support it, can afford a cause of action in negligence by act. . . . That case, therefore, can give no more help in this sphere than by affording some analogy from the broad outlook which it imposed on the law relating to physical negligence. . . . Economic protection has lagged behind protection in physical matters whether there is injury to person and property. It may be that the size and the width of the range of possible claims has acted as a deterrent to extension of economic protection. . . .

Denning L.J. in his dissenting judgment in *Candler* v. *Crane, Christmas & Co.,* reached the conclusion that in respect of reports and work that resulted in such reports there was a duty of care laid on "those persons such as accountants, surveyors, valuers and analysts, whose profession and occupation is to examine books, accounts and other things and to make reports on which other people — other than their clients — rely in the ordinary course of business". The duty is in his opinion owed (apart from contractual duty to their employer) "to any third person to whom they themselves show the accounts, or to whom they know their employer is going to show the accounts so as to induce him to invest money or take some other action on them". He excludes strangers of whom they have heard nothing and to whom their employer without their knowledge may choose to hand their accounts, and continues: "The test of proximity in these cases is: did the accountants know that the accounts were required for submission to the plaintiff and use by him?" (It is to be noted that these expressions of opinion produce a result somewhat similar to the American *Restatement of the Law of Torts,* Vol. III, p. 122, para. 552.) I agree with those words. In my opinion, they are consonant with the earlier cases and with the observations of Lord Haldane.

It is argued that so to hold would create confusion in many aspects of the law and infringe the established rule that innocent misrepresentation gives no right to damages. I cannot accept that argument. The true rule is that innocent misrepresentation *per se* gives no right to damages. If the misrepresentation was intended by the parties to form a warranty between two contracting parties, it gives on that ground a right to damages. . . . If an innocent misrepresentation is made between parties in a fiduciary relationship it may, on that ground, give a right to claim damages for negligence. There is also, in my opinion a duty of care created by special relationships which, though not fiduciary, give rise to an assumption that care as well as honesty is demanded.

Was there such a special relationship in the present case as to impose on the respondents a duty of care to the appellants as the undisclosed principals for whom National Provincial Bank Ltd. was making the inquiry? The answer to that question depends on the circumstances of the transaction. If, for instance, they disclosed a casual social approach to the inquiry no such special relationship of duty of care would be assumed. To import such a duty the representation must normally, I think, concern a business or professional transaction whose nature makes clear the gravity of the inquiry and the importance and influence attached to the answer. . . . A most important circumstance is the form of the inquiry and of the answer. Both were here plainly stated to be without liability. Counsel for the appellant argues that those words are not sufficiently precise to exclude liability for negligence. . . . I do not . . . accept that, even if the parties were already in contractual or other special relationship, the words would give no immunity to a negligent answer. But in any event they clearly prevent a special relationship from arising. They are part of the material from which one deduces whether a duty of care and a liability for negligence was assumed. If both parties say expressly (in a case where neither is deliberately taking advantage of the other) that there shall be no liability, I do not find it possible to say that a liability was assumed. . . . I would, therefore, dismiss the appeal.

[Lord Hodson agreed.]

NOTES

1. Prior to *Hedley Byrne* the leading English case was *Candler* v. *Crane, Christmas & Co.*, [1951] 2 K.B. 164, [1951] 1 All E.R. 426. Lord Justice Denning's powerful dissent in that case was accepted by the House of Lords in *Hedley Byrne*. The plaintiff had subscribed to shares in a company on the strength of certain negligently prepared accountant's documents. Lord Justice Denning wanted to impose a duty in certain limited circumstances. He criticized the "timorous souls who were fearful of allowing a new cause of action". Lord Asquith (Cohen L.J. concurring), however, clung to the established doctrine denying the existence of a duty of care. In concluding he stated:

"In the present state of our law different rules still seem to apply to the negligent mis-statement, on the one hand, and to the negligent circulation or repair of chattels, on the other, and *Donoghue's* case does not seem to me to have abolished these differences. I am not concerned with defending the existing state of the law or contending that it is strictly logical. It clearly is not — but I am merely recording what I think it is. If this relegates me to the company of 'timorous souls', I must face that consequence with such fortitude as I can command. I am of opinion that the appeal should be dismissed."

2. While the majority in *Candler* referred to the judgment of Cardozo C.J. in *Ultramares Corporation* v. *Touche* (1931), 174 N.E. 441, in which accountants were held not liable for negligence in preparing a financial report of a company on the strength of which a third person advanced money to the company, no reference was made to the earlier judgment of the same judge in *Glanzer* v. *Shepard* (1922), 135 N.E. 275. In that case plaintiff had bought 900 bags of beans from a vendor to be paid for in accordance with the weight as certified by public weighers. The vendor employed and paid the defendant, a public weigher, to weigh the beans telling him the beans had been sold to plaintiff to whom a copy of the certificate was to be given. The plaintiff paid the vendor on the basis of the certified weight and discovering some 12,000 pounds shortage, sued the defendant for the amount overpaid. Cardozo J., held the defendant liable. "It is ancient learning that one who assumes to act, even though gratuitously, may thereby become subject to the duty of acting carefully, if he acts at all. . . . The most common examples of such a duty are cases where action is directed towards the person of another or his property. A like principle applies, however, where action is directed toward the governance of conduct. The controlling circumstance is not the character of the consequence, but its proximity or remoteness in the thought and purpose of the actor. . . . Here the defendants are held, not merely for careless words . . . but for the careless performance of a service — the act of weighing — which happens to have found in the words of a certificate its culmination and its summary."

3. Negligent statements causing property damage, as contrasted with economic loss, never created any problem for the courts. Thus, where negligent advice caused a fire, liability followed. See *Manitoba Sausage Manufacturing Co.* v. *City of Winnipeg* (1976), 1 C.C.L.T. 221 (Man. C.A.). So too, where a model was asked to step back, causing her to fall off the stage, she was allowed to recover for her personal injuries. See *Robson* v. *Chrysler Corp. of Canada* (1962), 32 D.L.R. (2d) 49 (Alta. C.A.). Similarly, negligent statements that cause nervous shock may yield liability. See *contra, Guay* v. *Sun Publishing Co.*, [1953] 2 S.C.R. 216, *supra;* see also Linden, *Canadian Tort Law* (2nd ed., 1977), p. 380.

4. A succinct description of the principle of *Hedley, Byrne* v. *Heller* has been offered by Mr. Justice R.E. Holland in *Toromont Industrial Holdings Ltd.* v. *Thorne, Gunn, Helliwell and Christenson* (1975), 10 O.R. (2d) 65, at p. 86; varied (1975), 14 O.R. (2d) 87 (C.A.) as follows:

"In order for there to be liability for negligent misrepresentation there must be first a duty of care; second, a negligent misrepresentation; third, reliance on the misrepresentation by the plaintiff and fourth, loss resulting from that reliance."
See also *Farmer* v. *Chambers Ltd.*, [1973] 1 O.R. 355, at p. 357 (C.A.).

5. In *Town of The Pas* v. *Porky Packers Ltd.* (1976), 65 D.L.R. (3d) 1 (S.C.C.), a plaintiff, who knew as much about the municipal by-laws as the employees of the municipality, could not recover because he did not "rely" on their advice in spending money to build an abattoir in violation of those by-laws. Mr. Justice Spence explained that the representations must be made "to a person who has no expert knowledge himself by a person whom the representee believes has a particular skill or judgment in the matter, and that the representations were relied upon to the detriment of the representee".
See also *Burstein* v. *Crisp Devine Ltd.*, [1973] 3 O.R. 342, no negligence, alt. ground; *Algee* v. *Surette* (1972), 9 N.S.R. (2d) 60 (C.A.).

6. The reliance must also be reasonable. One cannot, therefore, rely on a gas truck driver's assurance that there is no danger of leaking gas because he was not a skilled service man. See *Kleine* v. *Canada Propane* (1967), 64 D.L.R. (2d) 338 (B.C.). See also *Nunes Diamonds Ltd.* v. *Dominion Electric Protection Co.*, [1971] 1 O.R. 218, at p. 227, *per* Schroeder J.A.; affd [1972] S.C.R. 769. Nor should one rely on an adversary, such as the insurance adjuster of someone you have negligently injured. See *Sulzinger* v. *C.K. Alexander Ltd.*, [1972] 1 O.R. 720 (C.A.), at p. 722, alt. ground. What about contributory negligence here? See *Vartan Garapedian Inc.* v. *Anderson* (1943), 31 A. 2d 371, at p. 374.

7. For a critical examination of the two decisions of Cardozo C.J., see Seavey, "Mr. Justice Cardozo and the Law of Torts" (1939), 52 Harv. L. Rev. 372; 48 Yale L.J. 390; 39 Colum. L. Rev. 20. See, in general, Paton, "Liability in Tort for Negligent Statements" (1947), 25 Can. Bar Rev. 123; Seavey, "*Candler* v. *Crane, Christmas and Co.*, Negligent Misrepresentation by Accountants" (1951), 67 L.Q.Rev. 466; Wilson, "Chattels and Certificate in the Law of Negligence" (1952), 15 Mod. L. Rev. 160; Fridman, "Negligence by Words" (1954) 32 Can. Bar Rev. 638; Fridman, "Negligent Misrepresentation" (1976), 22 McGill L.J. 1; Stevens, "*Hedley Burne* v. *Heller;* Judicial Creativity and Doctrinal Possibility" (1964), 27 Mod. L. Rev. 121; Goodhart, "Liability for Innocent but Negligent Misrepresentations" (1964), 74 Yale L.J. 286; Glasbeek, "Limited Liability for Negligent Misstatement" in Linden, *Studies in Canadian Tort Law* (1968) 115, Harvey, "Economic Losses and Negligence" (1972), 50 Can. Bar Rev. 580; Gordon, "*Hedley Byrne* v. *Heller* in the House of Lords" (1965), 2 U.B.C.L.Rev. 113; Lindgren, "Professional Negligence in Words and the Privy Council" (1972), 46 Aust. L.J. 176; Stevens, "Two Steps Forward & Three Back! Liability for Negligent Words" (1972), 5 N.Z.U.L. Rev. 39; Craig, "Negligent Misstatements, Negligent Acts and Economic Loss" (1976), 92 L.Q.R. 213.

1. What Plaintiffs?

HAIG v. BAMFORD ET AL.

Supreme Court of Canada. [1976] 3 W.W.R. 331,
[1977] 1 S.C.R. 466, 72 D.L.R. (3d) 68

The defendants, who were accountants, prepared a financial statement for a client, knowing that it would be used to persuade investors to invest in the client's business. A serious error was contained in the statement, which showed as income some money that was actually a prepayment on work yet to be done. The defendants also failed to audit the records of the client, although it appeared that one had been done. The plaintiff invested $20,075, relying on the statement. After discovering the error, the plaintiff also invested another $2,500 to assist the client in meeting a payroll.

Dickson J. (Laskin C.J.C., Ritchie, Spence, Pigeon and Beetz JJ. concurring):
This appeal concerns the liability of an accountant to parties other than his
employer for negligent statements. The Court is asked to decide whether there
was in the relationship of the parties to the appeal such kind or degree of
proximity as to give rise to a duty of care owed by the respondents to the
appellant. The damages involved are not large but the question raised is of
importance to the accounting profession and to the investing public.

. . .

The trial Judge found negligence on the part of the accountants. I think the
evidence amply supports that finding. From the expert testimony, it appears
that the engagement of a chartered accountant can be on either an "audit" basis
or a "non-audit" basis. If the engagement is for an audit, the accountant does
what he considers necessary by way of auditing procedures, tests and verification
of internal controls, accounts and records to permit him to give an opinion on
the financial statements. In an engagement of the non-audit type, the accountant
merely helps the client in the preparation of the financial statement on terms
which permit him to accept the client's records and dispense with the checks and
verifications expected in an audit. The product of an audit is a financial statement accompanied by an auditor's report expressing an opinion on the financial
statement. At the end of a non-audit engagement, a financial statement is issued
to which is appended a comment in which the auditor expressly disclaims
responsibility.

. . .

The report would lead the reader to believe that an audit had been done but
the evidence shows that no audit was done. The report is qualified in three
respects but not with respect to liabilities. Gary Lloyd Davidge, then an articled
student in the accountants' office and now a chartered accountant, prepared the
impugned financial statements. He testified that he had been instructed by his
firm not to do an audit; he believed he was acting as accountant and not auditor;
he was not furnished with an audit program. He did not peruse invoices or
purchase orders; he did not inquire as to prepayments or as to the state of contracts; he did not analyze the figures as to sales or work in progress; nor did he
inquire as to internal controls to determine to what extent the controls could be
relied upon to assure the accuracy of the revenue accounts. He left the employ
of the accountants before the statement was delivered to the client, in the belief
that it would be accompanied by a complete disclaimer as had accompanied the
1963 financial statements of Scholler Brothers Millwork. Notwithstanding all of
this, the auditors rendered the quoted opinion in which they said that their
examination had included a general review of the accounting records and other
supporting evidence as they considered necessary in the circumstances. That was
not true. They also expressed the opinion, subject to the three reservations
earlier referred to, that the balance sheet and related statement of profit and
loss fairly presented the financial position of the company at 31st March 1965.
The work done by or on behalf of the accountants did not warrant any such
affirmation. In representing to have done an audit when they were aware that an
audit had not been done, in my view the accountants were guilty of a serious
dereliction of duty. This was more than honest blunder or error in judgment.

III

I come then to the question whether Haig, who received the defective
financial statements and relied on them to his loss, has a right of recovery from
the accountants. MacPherson J. at trial allowed recovery. He held that the
accountants knew or ought to have known that the statements would be used by

a potential investor in the company; although Haig was not, in the Judge's words, "in the picture" when the statement was prepared, he must be included in the category of persons who could be foreseen by the accountants as relying on the statement and therefore the accountants owed a duty to Haig. The Judge applied a test of foreseeability.

The majority in the Court of Appeal for Saskatchewan (Hall J.A. with Maguire J.A. concurring) came to a different conclusion. The majority of the Court were satisfied that the accountants had been informed by Scholler that the statement would be used to induce persons to invest equity capital in the company. Hall J.A. noted that at the time there was no specific person or group in mind as a prospective investor or investors; Haig was not known to the accountants and they were not aware that he had been shown a copy of the statement or that he had been approached to invest in the company. The learned Justice of Appeal observed that the financial statement had been given to Haig without the knowledge of Scholler or the company. With respect, I think this observation is in error as Wiltshire testified that before giving a copy of the statement to Haig he had received Scholler's permission. The point is, however, of no great consequence for if the accountants, at the request of the company, prepared financial statements for distribution to, inter alia, potential investors, and furnished the company with copies for that purpose, I fail to understand why the company or anyone on its behalf would be expected to seek permission of the accountants before releasing a copy. The learned Justice of Appeal concluded that the accountants owed Haig the duty to be honest but that they were not liable to him for negligence and, since the misrepresentation contained in the financial statement was the result of an "honest blunder", the appeal should be allowed with costs. The dissenting Judge, Woods J.A., was of opinion that the accountants knew that the statement was intended for a special purpose, a purpose that would affect the economic interests of those from whom Scholler would attempt to secure funds, and that Haig fell within this category. The outcome of this appeal rests, it would seem, on whether, to create a duty of care, it is sufficient that the accountants knew that the information was intended to be disseminated among a specific group or class, as MacPherson J. and Woods J.A. would have it, or whether the accountants also needed to be apprised of the plaintiff's identity, as Hall and Maguire JJ.A. would have it.

IV

The increasing growth and changing role of corporations in modern society has been attended by a new perception of the societal role of the profession of accounting. The day when the accountant served only the owner-manager of a company and was answerable to him alone has passed. The complexities of modern industry combined with the effects of specialization, the impact of taxation, urbanization, the separation of ownership from management, the rise of professional corporate managers and a host of other factors have led to marked changes in the role and responsibilities of the accountant and in the reliance which the public must place upon his work. The financial statements of the corporations upon which he reports can affect the economic interests of the general public as well as of shareholders and potential shareholders.

With the added prestige and value of his services has come, as the leaders of the profession have recognized, a concomitant and commensurately increased responsibility to the public. It seems unrealistic to be oblivious to these developments. It does not necessarily follow that the doors must be thrown open and recovery permitted whenever someone's economic interest suffers as the result of a negligent act on the part of an accountant. Compensation to the injured party is a relevant consideration but it may not be the only relevant consideration. Fear of unlimited liability for the accountant, "liability in an indeterminate amount for an indeterminate time to an indeterminate class", was considered a relevant factor by Cardozo J. in *Ultramares Corpn.* v. *Touche* (1931), 255 N.Y. 170, 174 N.E. 441 at 444. From the authorities, it appears that several possible tests could be applied to invoke a duty of care on the part of accountants vis-à-vis third parties: (i) foreseeability of the use of the financial statement and the auditor's report thereon by the plaintiff and reliance thereon; (ii) actual knowledge of the limited class that will use and rely on the statement; (iii) actual knowledge of the specific plaintiff who will use and rely on the statement. It is unnecessary for the purposes of the present case to decide whether test (i), the test of foreseeability, is or is not a proper test to apply in determining the full extent of the duty owed by accountants to third parties. The choice in the present case, it seems to me, is between test (ii) and test (iii)—actual knowledge of the limited class or actual knowledge of the specific plaintiff. I have concluded on the authorities that test (iii) is too narrow and that test (ii), actual knowledge of the limited class, is the proper test to apply in this case.

The English authorities: I do not think one can do better than begin with Lord Denning's dissent in *Candler* v. *Crane, Christmas & Co.,* [1951] 2 K.B. 164, [1951] 1 All E.R. 426, which later found favour in *Hedley Byrne & Co.* v. *Heller & Partners,* [1964] A.C. 465, [1963] 2 All E.R. 575. After identifying accountants as among those under a duty to sue care, Lord Denning, in answer to the question "To whom do these professional persons owe this duty?" said (p. 434):

> "They owe the duty, of course, to their employer or client, and also, I think, to any third person to whom they themselves show the accounts, or to whom they know their employer is going to show the accounts so as to induce him to invest money or take some other action on them. I do not think, however, the duty can be extended still further so as to include strangers of whom they have heard nothing and to whom their employer without their knowledge may choose to show their accounts."

And:

> "The test of proximity in these cases is: Did the accountants know that the accounts were required for submission to the plaintiff for use by him?

One can find some support in these words for the position taken by the majority in the Saskatchewan Court of Appeal but their effect is tempered by what appears later in the judgment, p. 435:

> "It will be noticed that I have confined the duty to cases where the accountant prepares his accounts and makes his report for the guidance of the very person in the very transaction in question. That is sufficient for the decision of this case. I can well understand that it would be going too far to make an accountant liable to any person in the land who chooses to rely on the accounts in matters of business, for that would expose him, in the words of Cardozo, C.J., in *Ultramares Corpn.* v. *Touche* [supra], to
>
> "'. . . liability in an indeterminate amount for an indeterminate time to an indeterminate class.'
>
> "Whether he would be liable if he prepared his accounts for the guidance of a specific class of persons in a specific class of transactions, I do not say. I should have thought he might be, just as the analyst and lift inspector would be liable in the instances I have given earlier."

In the case at bar, the accounts were prepared for the guidance of a "specific class of persons", potential investors, in a "specific class of transactions", the investment of $20,000 of equity capital. The number of potential investors would, of necessity, be limited because the company, as a private company, was prohibited by s. 3(o)(iii) of The Companies Act of Saskatchewan, R.S.S. 1965, c. 131, from extending any invitation to the public to subscribe for shares or debentures of the company.

One comes then to the *Hedley Byrne* case, supra. The argument was raised in that case that the relationship between the parties was not sufficiently close to give rise to any duty. Lord Reid dealt with that argument in these words (p. 580):

> "It is said that the respondents did not know the precise purpose of the inquiries and did not even know whether National Provincial Bank, Ltd. wanted the information for its own use of for the use of a customer: they knew nothing of the appellants. I would reject that argument. They knew that the inquiry was in connexion with an advertising contract, and it was at least probable that the information was wanted by the advertising contractors. It seems to me quite immaterial that they did not know who these contractors were: there is no suggestion of any speciality which could have influenced them in deciding whether to give information or in what form to give it. I shall therefore treat this as if it were a case where a negligent misrepresentation is made directly to the person seeking information, opinion or advice, and I shall not attempt to decide what kind or degree of proximity is necessary before there can be a duty owed by the defendant to the plaintiff."

In the present case the accountants knew that the financial statements were being prepared for the very purpose of influencing, in addition to the bank and Sedco, a limited number of potential investors. The names of the potential investors were not material to the accountants. What was important was the nature of the transaction or transactions for which the statements were intended, for that is what delineated the limits of potential liability. The speech of Lord Morris in *Hedley Byrne* included this observation, p. 588:

> "It is, I think, a reasonable and proper inference that the bank must have known that the National Provincial were making their inquiry because some customer of theirs was or might be entering into some advertising contract in respect of which Easipower, Ltd., might become under a liability to such customer to the extent of the figures mentioned. The inquiries were from one bank to another. The name of the customer (Hedleys) was not mentioned by the inquiring bank (National Provincial) to the answering bank (the bank): nor did the inquiring bank (National Provincial) give to the customer (Hedleys) the name of the answering bank (the bank). These circumstances do not seem to me to be material. The bank must have known that the inquiry was being made by someone who was contemplating doing business with Easipower Ltd. and that their answer or the substance of it would in fact be passed on to such person."

Lord Devlin stood on narrow ground, content with the proposition that wherever there is a relationship equivalent to contract there is a duty of care and such relationship may be either *general*, such as that of solicitor and client and of banker and customer, or *particular*, created ad hoc, in which case it becomes necessary to examine the particular facts to see whether there is an express or implied undertaking of responsibility. This reference to "assumption of responsibility" is crucial in cases involving economic loss, according to C. Harvey, "Economic Losses and Negligence" (1972), 50 Can. Bar Rev. 580. Harvey devises a test for imposing a duty of care in cases of economic loss which he phrases as follows (p. 600):

> "(A) *person should be bound by a legal duty of care to avoid causing economic loss to another in circumstances where a reasonable man in the position of the defendant would foresee that kind of loss and would assume responsibility for it.*"

This "assumption of responsibility" test is an interesting one, although it is no more objective than a foreseeability test. It would allow the Court to narrow the scope of liability from that resulting from a foreseeability test, but it would still require a policy determination as to what should be the scope of liability. As Lord Pearce stated in *Hedley Byrne* (p. 615):

> "How wide the sphere of the duty of care in negligence is to be laid depends ultimately on the courts' assessment of the demands of society for protection from the carelessness of others."
>
> . . .

The American authorities: Judgment in the two leading cases was written by Cardozo J. In *Glanzer* v. *Shepard* (1922), 233 N.Y. 236, the defendants, public weighers, at the request of a seller of beans, made a return of the weight and furnished the plaintiff buyer with a copy. The buyer paid the seller on the faith of the certificate which turned out to be erroneous. The buyers were entitled to recover from the weighers. The certificate was held to be the very "end and aim" of the transaction and not something issued in the expectation that the seller would use it thereafter in the operations of his business as occasion might require.

The question whether third parties were protected from the negligence of accountants came before the New York Courts in *Ultramares Corpn.* v. *Touche,* supra. The breach made in the wall of privity by *Glanzer's* case was narrowed in *Ultramares.* In that case, a company showed a balance sheet prepared by the defendants to a factor who advanced money to the company. The factor was unknown to the defendants, and Cardozo J. held that the defendants owed the factor no duty of care. Although the *Ultramares* decision has been followed widely in the United States, it has also been criticized: see Prosser, Law of Torts, 4th ed., pp. 706-709; Hawkins, "Professional Negligence Liability of Public Accountants" (1959), 12 Vand. Law Rev. 797; note, "Accountants' Liability for False and Misleading Statements" (1967), 67 Colum. Law Rev. 1437. *Ultramares* has also been distinguished in a case similar to the one at bar, *Rusch Factors Inc.* v. *Levin* (1968), 284 F. Supp. 85. In *Rusch,* the Court held that the plaintiff investor, who had relied on the financial statement prepared by the defendant, was actually foreseen by the defendant. Pettine J. distinguished *Ultramares* in these words (p. 91):

> "There, the plaintiff was a member of an undefined, unlimited class of remote lenders and potential equity holders not actually foreseen but only foreseeable."

The *Rusch* case was followed by the United States Court of Appeal (Fourth Circuit) in *Rhode Island Hospital Trust National Bank* v. *Swartz* (1972), 455 F. 2d 847. That case mentions that *Rusch* has been followed in Iowa and Minnesota.

The case before us is closer to *Glanzer* than to *Ultramares.* The very end and aim of the financial statements prepared by the accountants in the present case was to secure additional financing for the company from Sedco and an equity investor; the statements were required primarily for these third parties and only incidentally for use by the company. In the *Ultramares* case, Touche would know that the statements were primarily for company use although they might be read in the ordinary course of business by shareholders, investors, banks and countless others.

Prosser, Law of Torts, 4th ed., notes at p. 707 that a duty of reasonable care has been found where a representation is made to a third person with knowledge that he intends to communicate it to the specific individual plaintiff for the purpose of inducing him to act, and that most of the courts have drawn the line there. The following question is posed, however (p. 708):

"But what if the defendant is informed that his representation is to be passed on to some more limited group, as a basis for action on the part of some one or more of them?"

And the answer is in these words (p. 709):

". . . where the group affected is a sufficiently small one, and particularly, as in the case of the successful bidder, only one person can be expected to suffer loss, the guess may be hazarded that the recovery will be allowed. Certificates of expert examination are intended to be exhibited, not hidden under a bushel; and a rule which denies recovery because the defendant who has provided one for such a purpose does not know the plaintiff's name, or the particulars of the transaction, has a very artificial aspect."

The approach taken in the American Restatement of Torts (2d) SS 552 is to permit recovery for loss suffered by the person or one of the persons for whose benefit or guidance the professional person intends to supply the information or knows that the recipient intends to supply it. A duty of care arises if the defendant accountant knows that a third party will receive his statements. This knowledge is not with regard to the specific individual but to a limited class of which he forms a part. An explanatory note in the Restatement shows this:

"A is negotiating with a bank for a credit of $50,000. The bank requires an audit by certified public accountants. A employs B & Company, a firm of accountants, to make the audit, telling them he is going to negotiate a bank loan. A does not get his loan from the first bank but does negotiate a loan with another bank, which relies upon B & Company's certified statements. The audit carelessly overstates the financial resources of A, and in consequence the second bank suffers pecuniary loss. B & Company is subject to liability to the second bank."

(See also (1969), 53 Minn. Law Rev. 1357.)

The Canadian authorities: The *Hedley Byrne* case has been considered by this Court in *Welbridge Holdings Ltd.* v. *Winnipeg,* [1972] 3 W.W.R. 433, [1971] S.C.R. 957, 22 D.L.R. (3d) 470. Recovery for economic loss caused by negligence has been allowed in *Rivtow Marine Ltd.* v. *Washington Iron Works,* [1973] 6 W.W.R. 692, [1974] S.C.R. 1189, 40 D.L.R. (3d) 530, where Ritchie J. said, p. 1213:

". . . I am of opinion that the case of *Hedley Byrne* represents the considered opinion of five members of the House of Lords to the effect that a negligent misrepresentation may give rise to an action for damages for economic loss occasioned thereby without any physical injury to person or property and apart from any contract of fiduciary relationship".

See also *J. Nunes Diamonds Ltd.* v. *Dominion Electric Protection Co.,* [1972] S.C.R. 769, 26 D.L.R. (3d) 699.

V

In summary, Haig placed justifiable reliance upon a financial statement which the accountants stated presented fairly the financial position of the company as at 31st March 1965. The accountants prepared such statements for reward in the course of their professional duties. The statements were for benefit and guidance in a business transaction, the nature of which was known to the accountants. The accountants were aware that the company intended to supply the statements to members of a very limited class. Haig was a member of the class. It is true the accountants did not know his name but, as I have indicated earlier, I do think that is of importance. I can see no good reason for distinguishing between the case in which a defendant accountant delivers information directly to the plaintiff at the request of his employer (*Candler's* case and *Glanzer's* case) and the case in which the information is handed to the employer who, to the knowledge of the accountant, passes it to members of a limited class (whose identity is unknown to the accountant) in furtherance of a transaction the nature of which is known to the accountant. I would accordingly hold that the accountants owed Haig a duty to use reasonable care in the preparation of the accounts.

I am of the view, however, that Haig cannot recover from the accountants the sum of $2,500 which he advanced to the company in December 1965 because by that time he was fully cognizant of the true state of affairs. It cannot be said that the sum was advanced in reliance upon false statements. Haig had the choice of advancing additional money in the hope of saving his original investment. He chose to make a further advance, but the choice was his and not one for which the accountants are liable.

I would allow the appeal, set aside the judgment of the Court of Appeal for Saskatchewan and reinstate the judgment of MacPherson J., subject only to disallowance of the claim of $2,500 the whole with costs in this Court and in the Courts below.

Martland J. (Judson and de Grandpre JJ. concurring):—I agree with the conclusion reached by my brother Dickson that, based upon the finding of the learned trial Judge [reported [1972] 6 W.W.R. 557] which was not disturbed by the Court of Appeal [[1974] 6 W.W.R. 236, 53 D.L.R. (3d) 85], the respondents knew, prior to the completion of the financial statement, that it would be used by Sedco, by the bank with which the company was doing business and by a potential investor in equity capital, the respondents owed a duty of care, in the preparation of that financial statement, to that potential investor (the appellant), even though they were not aware of his actual indentity.

I would dispose of the appeal in the manner proposed by my brother Dickson.

NOTES

1. What do you think the Supreme Court of Canada will do when it is faced with a plaintiff who is in Class (i), foreseeability of the plaintiff who uses a financial statement?

2. In *Whittingham* v. *Crease & Co.* (1977), 6 C.C.L.T. 1 (B.C.), the defendant law firm prepared a will for a testator, who was the father of the plaintiff. The testator had sought to leave his house and the residue of the estate to his son, the plaintiff. The solicitor, in the plaintiff's presence, mistakenly had the wife of the plaintiff sign the will as a witness, which had the legal effect of rendering the bequest to the plaintiff, her husband, void. The residue, therefore, went as on an intestacy and the plaintiff received only a part of the residue, instead of all of it. He sued the solicitor for the difference and recovered.

Mr. Justice Aikins explained his decision as follows:

"While I am not free to make pronouncements on such a broad basis without authority, I am of the opinion that the factual situation in the present case falls fairly within the principles enunciated in *Hedley Byrne* as expounded in *Haig* v. *Bamford.* I hold that in all the circumstances Mr. Cowan was subject to an implied duty to the plaintiff to use reasonable care, skill and diligence in attending to the witnessing of the testator's will.

The facts in the present case differ in one particular and troublesome aspect from those in the general run of cases in which *Hedley Byrne* has been successfully invoked. I have not been referred to a case, nor have I been able to find one, in which the principle of *Hedley Byrne* has been applied where the plaintiff had not acted on the strength of the representation made by the defendant and it was the plaintiff's own act which was the *immediate* cause of the loss.

In this case the plaintiff has suffered a loss but without his having done anything in reliance on the implied representation made by Mr. Cowan. In my opinion there are two reasons, linked to each other, which enable the plaintiff to succeed in this case, notwithstanding that he remained passive and did nothing, relying on Mr. Cowan's implied representation. First, it was unnecessary for the plaintiff to act at all on the implied representation in order to attract the loss which he has suffered; second, Mr. Cowan could reasonably foresee that if he, in the performance of his duty, failed to see to it that the will was properly witnessed, then that neglect would cause the very loss the plaintiff has suffered, without the plaintiff doing anything at all. Granted that there was an implied duty on the part of Mr. Cowan to the plaintiff and that the plaintiff relied on Mr. Cowan fulfilling that duty, it seems to me on principle that it is immaterial that the plaintiff himself did nothing, in reliance on the implied representation made by Mr. Cowan, which brought about his loss. This is so because the negligence of the solicitor caused the loss without there having to be any intervening act by the plaintiff to perfect the chain of causation.

For these reasons I hold on the line of authorities headed by *Hedley Byrne* and on the particular facts in this case that the defendant is liable to the plaintiff in negligence. I wish to make it clear my conclusion rests on the particular facts of this case and that I make no pronouncement on the more general issue of the liability of a solicitor to a third party beneficiary on the ground of negligence in the preparation of a will. . . ."

What does Mr. Justice Aikins mean by the last few words he wrote?

In *Ross* v. *Caunters* (1969), 3 W.L.R. 605, Megarry L.C. followed this case even though the beneficiary knew nothing about the will and did not rely on it.

3. In *Ministry of Housing and Local Government* v. *Sharp*, [1970] 2 Q.B. 223, a clerk in a land registry office negligently issued a clear certificate of search, failing to note an encumbrance. As a result, the Ministry of Housing suffered financial loss. An action was brought against both the registrar and the council of the municipality. The council was held liable, but the action against the registrar was dismissed.

Lord Denning M.R. (dissenting as to the liability of the registrar) stated *inter alia:*

". . . In my opinion the duty to use due care in a statement arises, not from any voluntary assumption of responsibility, but from the fact that the person making it knows, or ought to know, that others, being his neighbours in this regard, would act on the faith of the statement being accurate. That is enough to bring the duty into being. It is owed, of course, to the person to whom the certificate is issued and whom he knows is going to act on it. . . . But is is also owed to any person whom he knows, or ought to know, will be injuriously affected by a mistake, such as the incumbrancer here."

See also *Silva* v. *Atkins* (1978), 20 O.R. (2d) 570, no duty of sheriff to give names similar to names on execution requisition.

4. Mr. Justice Ruttan has also suggested that liability should be imposed for loss suffered by "another person who [the defendant] knows or should know will place reliance on his advice". See *Cari-Van Hotel Ltd.* v. *Globe Estates Ltd.*, [1974] 6 W.W.R. 707, at p. 715 (B.C.), where, in a *dictum,* it was said that an appraiser of real estate could be liable to anyone connected with "any transaction relating to the land" such as a "mortgage, credit rating or sale". There was no negligence found, however, in the case.

5. Where the plaintiff buys a boat in reliance upon the defendant's report concerning the condition of the boat, no liability will be imposed if the defendant does not know and does not reasonably know that it will be relied upon by this person. See *Beebe* v. *Robb* (1977), 81 D.L.R. (3d) 349 (B.C.), *per* Ruttan J.

2. What Defendants?

MUTUAL LIFE AND CITIZEN'S ASSURANCE CO. v. EVATT

Privy Council. [1971] 2 W.L.R. 23; [1971] 1 All E.R. 150

Mr. Evatt, a policy holder in Mutual Life and Citizen's Assurance Company, sought information and advice from the company concerning the financial stability of another company, H.G. Palmer (Consolidated) Ltd. Both H.G. Palmer and Mutual Life were subsidiaries of M.L.C. Ltd. (the second defendant). Mutual Life had the facilities and expertise to provide better information than Mr. Evatt could obtain independently. Mutual Life provided Mr. Evatt with the information that investments could be safely made, with the knowledge that he intended to act in reliance on this information. There was no disclaimer of responsibility. Mr. Evatt not only left his already invested money in H.G. Palmer but he invested more in the company. The advice turned out to be bad and Mr. Evatt suffered financial losses as a result.

Mr. Evatt brought an action against Mutual Life and M.L.C. Ltd. on the basis of the negligent information and advice supplied by them. The defendant companies demurred upon the ground that the facts alleged disclosed no cause of action known to law. The demurrer was dismissed by the Court of Appeal of the Supreme Court of New South Wales, with three judges dissenting. On appeal to the High Court of Australia, this judgment was upheld on a three-two decision. The defendants appealed to the Privy Council.

Lord Diplock (for the majority): . . . Mr. Evatt does not allege that at or prior to the time of his inquiry the company carried on the business of supplying information or advice on investments to its policy holders or to anyone else, or that the company had claimed, professed or represented to him or to anyone else that it possessed any qualification, skill or competence to do so greater than that possessed by the ordinary reasonable man. Nor does he allege that at the time of his inquiry the company undertook or represented to him that it would make use of its facilities to obtain full, complete or up-to-date information concerning the financial affairs of Palmer or that it would obtain and communicate to him the opinion of officers in its employment who were capable of forming a reliable judgment on such information if obtained. Nor does he allege that at the time the company supplied him with the information and advice it represented to him that it had done any of these things.

Counsel for Mr. Evatt concedes that, if in order to establish a duty of care owed by the company to Mr. Evatt it will be necessary to establish one or other of these facts. . . the company's demurrer should succeed. The question in this appeal is whether or not it is so necessary.

The several speeches in *Hedley Byrne & Co. Ltd.* v. *Heller and Partners Ltd.*, [1964] A.C. 465 have lain at the heart of the argument in the courts of Australia and before their Lordship's Board. That case broadened the category of relationships between one man and another which gave rise to a duty at common law to use reasonable skill and care in making statements of fact or of opinion. Prior to *Hedley Byrne* it was accepted law in England that in the absence of contract the maker of a statement of fact or opinion owed to a person whom he could reasonably foresee would rely upon it in a matter affecting his economic interest, a duty to be honest in making the statement. But he did not owe any duty to be careful, unless the relationship between him and the person who acted upon it to his economic detriment fell within the category of relationships which the law classified as fiduciary. *Hedley Byrne* decided that the class of relationships between the maker of the statement and the person who acted upon it to his economic detriment which attracted the duty to be careful was not so limited, but could extend to relationships which though not fiduciary in character possessed other characteristics.

In *Hedley Byrne* itself and in the previous English cases on negligent statements which were analysed in the speeches, with the notable exceptions of *Fish v. Kelly* (1864), 17 C.B.N.S. 194; *Derry v. Peek* (1889), 14 App. Cas. 337 and *Low v. Bouverie,* [1891] 3 Ch. 82, the relationship possessed the characteristics (1) that the maker of the statement had made it in the ordinary course of his business or profession and (2) that the subject-matter of the statement called for the exercise of some qualification, skill or competence not possessed by the ordinary reasonable man, to which the maker of the statement was known by the recipient to lay claim by reason of his engaging in that business or profession.

In the United States of America, where the development of this branch of the common law of negligence had anticipated the English decision in *Hedley Byrne,* [1946] A.C. 465, the *American Restatement of the Law of Torts* (2nd) vol. 3. p. 122, para. 552, which was referred to by Lord Devlin, at p. 531, and by Lord Pearce, at p. 539, specifies as a necessary characteristic of a relationship which gives rise to a duty of care on the part of the maker of the statement that he should be a person who makes it a part of his business or profession to supply for the guidance of others in their business transactions information of the kind contained in the statement and that the statement should be made by him in the course of that business or profession.

A requirement that the existence of a similar characteristic is necessary in order to attract a duty of care is not stated unequivocally in any of the speeches in *Hedley Byrne.* But those speeches, like all judgments under the common law system, must be understood *secundum subjectam materiam.* The fact that the characteristics were present in the relationship between the maker and the recipient of the statement under consideration in *Hedley Byrne* made it unnecessary for those who expressed the reason for their decision of the case to direct their minds to the question whether the terms in which the reasons were expressed would have called for some qualification in their application to cases where those characteristics were absent — as they are in the instant appeal. The speeches in *Hedley Byrne* cannot thus be determinative in themselves of whether or not the presence of these characteristics in the relationship between the maker and the recipient is necessary in order to give rise to a duty of care at common law.

Their Lordships accordingly conceive it to be their task in the instant appeal to examine that question as one of principle in the light of the earlier development of this branch of the law of negligence in the cases which preceded, and were for the most part referred to, in *Hedley Byrne,* as well as in the light of the speeches in *Hedley Byrne* themselves.

The instant appeal is concerned with a statement consisting of "information and advice concerning the financial stability of a certain company . . . and as to the safety of investments therein". In regard to this subject matter *viz.* financial stability and safety of investment, no distinction need be drawn between "information" and "advice" and it is convenient to use the latter word. Such advice to be reliable (*i.e.,* to be of a quality upon which it would be reasonable for the advisee to rely in determining his course of action in a matter which affected his economic interests) calls for the exercise on the part of the adviser of special skill and competence to form a judgment in the subject matter of the advice, which the advisee does not possess himself. The problem to be solved arises in that field of human activity which calls for the services of a skilled man.

The proposition stated in the maxim *spondet peritiam artis et imperitia*

culpae adnumeratur is one of the oldest principles in English law. The duty imposed by law upon those who followed a calling which required skill and competence to exercise in their calling such reasonable skill and competence as was
appropriate to it lies at the origin of the action of assumpsit itself. It was first
applied to artificers "for it is the duty of every artificer to exercise his art right
and truly as he ought" (Fitzherbert *Natura Brevium* (1534) 94 D). It was later
extended to all other occupations which involve the doing of acts calling for
some special skill or competence not possessed by the ordinary man. The
standard of skill and competence was that which is generally possessed by persons who engage in the calling, business or profession of doing acts of that kind
for reward. The duty to conform to the standard was attracted by engaging in
that particular calling, business or profession because by doing so a man holds
himself out as possessing the necessary skill and competence for it. To undertake to do an act requiring special skill and competence for reward was also a
sufficient holding out by the obligor to the obligee. But the doing of the act
gratuitously by a person who did not engage in the calling, business or profession, did not attract the duty to exercise skill and competence: *Shiells* v. *Black-
burne* (1789), 1 in *Hedley Byrne,* [1964] A.C. 465 of Lord Hodson, at p. 510,
and Lord Pearce, at pp. 537-8.

Where advice which calls for the exercise of special skill and competence by
the adviser is not to be based exclusively upon facts communicated to him by
the advisee no relevant distinction can be drawn between the ascertaining by the
adviser of the facts upon which to base his judgment as to the advice to be
given, and the forming of that judgment itself. The need for special skill and
competence extends to the selection of the particular facts which need to be
ascertained in order to form a reliable judgment and to the identification of the
sources from which such facts can be obtained.

As in the case of a person who gratuitously does an act which calls for the
exercise of some special skill and competence, a duty of care which lies upon
an adviser must be a duty to conform to an ascertainable standard of skill
and competence in relation to the subject-matter of the advice. Otherwise
there can be no way of determining whether the adviser was in breach of
his duty of care. The problem cannot be solved by saying that the adviser
must do his honest best according to the skill and competence which he in
fact possesses, for in the law of negligence standards of care are always objective. The passages in the judgment of Cozens-Hardy M.R. in *Parsons* v. *Barclay
& Co. Ltd.* and *Goddard* (1910), 103 L.T. 196, 199 and of Pearson L.J. in the
Court of Appeal, [1962] 1 Q.B. 396, 414-5 in *Hedley Byrne* itself, which were
quoted with approval in the House of Lords make it clear that a banker giving a
gratuitous reference is not required to do his best by, for instance, making enquiries from outside sources which are available to him, though this would make
his reference more reliable. All that he is required to do is to conform to that
standard of skill and competence and diligence which is generally shown by persons who carry on the business of providing references of that kind. Equally it
is no excuse to him to say that he has done his honest best, if what he does falls
below that standard because in fact he lacks the necessary skill and competence
to attain to it.

The reason why the law requires him to conform to this standard of skill and
competence and diligence is that by carrying on a business which includes the
giving of references of this kind he has let it be known to the recipient of the
reference that he claims to possess that degree of skill and competence and is
willing to apply that degree of diligence to the provision of any reference which
he supplies in the course of that business, whether gratuitously so far as the re-

cipient is concerned or not. If he supplies the reference the law requires him to make good his claim.

It would not in their Lordships' view be consonant with the principles hitherto accepted in the common law that the duty to comply with that objective standard should be extended to an adviser who, at the time at which the advice is sought, has not let it be known to the advisee that he claims to possess the standard of skill and competence and is prepared to exercise diligence which is generally shown by persons who carry on the business of giving advice of the kind sought. He has given the advisee no reason to suppose that he is acquainted with the standard or capable of complying with it or that he has such appreciation of the nature and magnitude of the loss which the advisee may sustain by reason of any failure by that adviser to attain that standard as a reasonable man would require before assuming a liability to answer for the loss.

But if it would not be just or reasonable to require him to conform to this objective standard of care which would be incumbent upon a person who carried on the business of giving advice of the kind sought, there is in their Lordships' view no half-way house between that and the common law duty which each man owes his neighbour irrespective of his skill — the duty of honesty. No half-way house has been suggested in the argument in the instant appeal or in any of the decided cases. . . .

In *Low* v. *Bouverie* it was made plain to the defendant, who was trustee of a settlement, that the information sought from him as to circumstances upon the life interest of his *cestui que trust* was required by the inquirer for the purpose of enabling him to make a decision upon a business transaction and that he would rely upon that information. The trustee informed the inquirer of the existence of certain incumbrances but omitted to mention six prior mortgages whose existence he had forgotten, though they were recited in the deed by which he had been appointed trustee of the settlement four years before. The only skill and competence on his part which was called for to enable him to provide accurate information was the ability to appreciate the need to look at the deed of appointment. In their Lordships' view the crucial distinction between this case and those cases which it was held in *Hedley Byrne* gave rise to a duty of care as well as honesty (*viz., Cann* v. *Wilson* (1888), 39 Ch.D. 39; *Le Lievre* v. *Gould*, [1893] 1 Q.B. 491; *Candler* v. *Crane, Christmas & Co.*, [1951] 2 K.B. 164; *Woods* v. *Martins Bank Ltd.*, [1959] 1 Q.B. 55 and *Hedley Byrne* itself), is that the trustee in *Low* v. *Bouverie*, [1891] 3 Ch. 82 did not hold himself out to the inquirer as being prepared to supply in the course of his business information of the kind sought. He had made no claim to any skill or competence which the law could require him to make good.

The carrying on of a business or profession which involves the giving of advice of a kind which calls for special skill and competence is the normal way in which a person lets it be known to the recipient of the advice that he claims to possess that degree of skill and competence and is willing to exercise that degree of diligence which is generally possessed and exercised by persons who carry on the business or profession of giving advice of the kind sought. The *American Restatement of the Law of Tort* (2nd) confines the duty of care in giving advice to persons who make it part of their business to supply advice; though later tentative redrafts suggest that the duty also attaches where the adviser has a financial interest in the transaction — a situation which is not relevant to the instant appeal. Denning L.J. also so confined it in his dissenting judgment in *Candler's* case, [1951] 2 K.B. 164, 179-180, where after stating that the persons subject to a duty of care in giving advice are

> "those persons such as accountants, surveyors, valuers and analysts *whose profession and occupation it is* to examine books, accounts and other things,

and to make reports on which other people — other than their clients — rely in the ordinary course of business," added, "Herein lies the difference between these professional men and other persons who have been held to be under no duty to use care in their statements, such as promoters who issue a prospectus: *Derry* v. *Peek,* 14 App.Cas. 337 (now altered by statute) and trustees who answer inquiries about the trust funds: *Low* v. *Bouverie,* [1891] 3 Ch. 82. Those persons do not bring, and are not expected to bring, any professional knowledge or skill into the preparation of their statements: they can only be made responsible by the law affecting persons generally, such as contract, estoppel, innocent misrepresentation or fraud."

This dissenting judgment was referred to with approval in *Hedley Byrne,* [1964] A.C. 465 in the speeches of Lord Hodson, at p. 509, Lord Devlin, at p. 530, and Lord Pearce, at p. 538.

While accepting this as the common case giving rise to the duty of care their Lordships would not wish to exclude the case where the adviser, although not carrying on the business or profession generally, has, at or before the time at which his advice is sought, let it be known in some other way that he claims to possess skill and competence in the subject-matter of the particular inquiry comparable to those who do carry on the business or profession of advising on that subject-matter and is prepared to exercise a comparable skill and competence in giving the advice. Here too, by parity of reasoning, the law should require him to make good his claim. But the mere giving of advice with knowledge, as in *Low* v. *Bouverie,* [1891] 3 Ch. 82, that the inquirer intends to rely upon it does not, of itself, in their Lordships' view, amount to such a claim.

The converse of this is the case where a person who does carry on a business or profession which involves the giving of advice of the kind sought by the inquirer, does so in circumstances which should let it be known to a reasonable inquirer that he was not prepared to exercise in relation to the particular advice sought that degree of diligence which he would exercise in giving such advice for reward in the course of his business or profession. Casual advice given by a professional man upon a social or informal occasion is the typical example, of which *Fish* v. *Kelly,* 17 C.B.N.S. 194 provides an illustration among the decided cases.

There are two passages in the speeches in *Hedley Byrne,* [1964] A.C. 465 which have been particularly relied upon, in the argument before their Lordships and in the majority judgments in each of the courts below, as amounting to a decision that the law imposes a "duty of care" upon a person who gives advice to another on a subject-matter requiring skill and competence and diligence, so long as he knows or ought to have known that the other intends to rely upon it in a matter affecting his economic interests, notwithstanding that the adviser neither carries on the business of giving advice of that kind nor has let it be known in some other way to the advisee at or before the time his advice is sought that *he claims* to possess a comparable skill and competence and is prepared to exercise a comparable diligence. . . .

In their Lordships' view these additional allegations are insufficient to fill the fatal gap in the declaration that it contains no averment that the company to the knowledge of Mr. Evatt carried on the business of giving advice upon investments or in some other way had let it be known to him that they claimed to possess the necessary skill and competence to do so and were prepared to exercise the necessary diligence to give reliable advice to him upon the subject-matter of his inquiry. In the absence of any allegation to this effect Mr. Evatt was not entitled to assume that the company had accepted any other duty towards him than to give an honest answer to his inquiry nor, in the opinion of their Lordships, did the law impose any higher duty upon them. This is in agreement with the reasoning of Taylor J. in the High Court of Australia with which the judgment of Owen J. is also consistent.

As with any other important case in the development of the common law *Hedley Byrne* should not be regarded as intended to lay down the metes and bounds of the new field of negligence of which the gate is now opened. Those will fall to be ascertained step by step as the facts of particular cases which come before the courts make it necessary to determine them. The instant appeal is an example; but their Lordships would emphasize that the missing characteristic of the relationship which they consider to be essential to give rise to a duty of care in a situation of the kind in which Mr. Evatt and the company found themselves when he sought their advice, is not necessarily essential in other situations — such as, perhaps, where the adviser has a financial interest in the transaction upon which he gives his advice (*cf. W.B. Anderson & Sons Ltd. v. Rhodes (Liverpool) Ltd.*, [1967] 2 All E.R. 850; *American Re-statement of the Law of Torts* 3rd. *Tentative Redraft).* On this, as on any other metes and bounds of the doctrine of *Hedley Byrne* their Lordships are expressing no opinion. The categories of negligence are never closed and their Lordships' opinion in the instant appeal, like all judicial reasoning, must be understood *secundum subjectam materiam.*

For these reasons their Lordships will humbly advise Her Majesty that the appeal be allowed. In accordance with undertakings given when special leave to appeal was granted, there will be no order as to the costs before their Lordships' Board and the orders for costs below will not be disturbed.

Lord Reid and **Lord Morris of Borth-y-Gest** (dissenting): . . . The main question in this appeal is whether the appellant company owed any duty of care to the respondent when, in response to his request for information and advice about the financial stability of another company referred to as Palmer, it gave to him an opinion that Palmer were financially stable. The appellant accepts the principles laid down by the House of Lords in *Hedley Byrne & Co. Ltd.* v. *Heller & Partners Ltd.,* [1964] A.C. 465 that in certain circumstances such a duty can arise although there is no contract between the parties, but maintains that no such duty could arise in the present case. . . .

In our judgment it is not possible to lay down hard and fast rules as to when a duty of care arises in this or in any other class of case where negligence is alleged. When, in the past, judges have attempted to lay down rigid rules or classifications or categories they have later had to be abandoned. But it is possible and necessary to determine the principles which have to be applied in determining whether in given circumstances any duty to take care arises.

In this class of case the first principle is that no duty beyond the duty to give an honest answer can arise when advice is given casually or in a social context, and the reason is that it would be quite unreasonable for the inquirer to expect more in such circumstances and quite unreasonable to impose any greater duty on the adviser. The law must keep in step with the habits of the reasonable man and consider whether ordinary people would think they had some obligation beyond merely giving an honest answer.

It may be going too far to say that a duty to take care can only arise where advice is sought and given in a business or professional context, for there might be unusual cases requiring a wider application of this principle. But for present purposes we think that the appropriate question is whether this advice was given on a business occasion or in the course of the appellant's business activities. The solution of this question may be difficult where advice is given by an individual, but here the advice is alleged to have been given by some individual. If it was given by the company that must mean that the individual who gave the advice must have had general or special authority from the company to give it, or at least that the company must have held him out as authorised to give it. It is not suggested that this company was so limited by its memorandum and articles that it could not give such authority. We are unable to see how a company can authorise the giving of such advice otherwise than as a part of its business activities. So long as a company does not act *ultra vires* it is for the company to determine the scope of its business. It appears to be quite common practice for businesses to perform gratuitous services for their customers with the object of retaining or acquiring their goodwill. If they incur expense in doing so it has never so far as we are aware been suggested that such expense is not a business expense. And we think that where companies do perform such service both they and their customers would be surprised to learn that the company is under no obligation to take any care in the matter.

The ordinary rule, that a defendant can only be liable for loss which was caused by his acts or omissions, appears to us to afford the answer to a number of questions discussed in argument. If the plaintiff acted reasonably in seeking the advice of the defendant and made it clear to the defendant that he intended to rely on the advice with regard to a certain matter, then it could properly be said that by giving the advice the defendant caused the plaintiff to act as he did. If, however, the plaintiff acted unreasonably in taking or following the advice then it was his own fault if he suffered loss and it would be unnecessary to consider whether the defendant owed any duty of care when giving the advice. Accordingly we are only concerned with a case where the plaintiff acted reasonably. In this case the respondent alleges that he was aware that the appellant had special facilities for obtaining the necessary information and was in a position to give reliable and up-to-date advice, and the appellant was aware that he intended to act on the appellant's advice. So, if taking care would have caused the appellant to give different advice, these allegations would enable the respondent to prove that the appellant's failure to take care caused his loss.

Much of the argument was directed to establishing that a person giving advice cannot be under any duty to take care unless he has some special skill, competence, qualification or information with regard to the matter on which his advice is sought. But then how much skill or competence must he have? Even a man with a professional qualification is seldom an expert on all matters dealt with by members of his profession. Must the adviser be an expert or specialist in the matter on which his advice is sought? And when it comes to matters of business or finance where those whose business it is to deal with such matters generally have no recognised formal qualification, how is the sufficiency of the adviser's special skill or competence to be measured? If the adviser is invited in a business context to advise on a certain matter and he chooses to accept that invitation and to give without warning or qualification what appears to be considered advice, is he to be allowed to turn round later and say that he was under no duty to take care because in fact he had no sufficient skill or competence to give the advice?

It must be borne in mind that there is here no question of warranty. If the adviser were to be held liable because his advice was bad then it would be relevant to inquire into his capacity to give the advice. But here and in cases coming within the principles laid down in *Hedley Byrne* the only duty in question is a duty to take reasonable care before giving the advice. We can see no ground for the distinction that a specially skilled man must exercise care but a less skilled man need not do so. We are unable to accept the argument that a duty to take care is the same as a duty to conform to a particular standard of skill. One must assume a reasonable man who has that degree of knowledge and skill which facts known to the inquirer (including statements made by the adviser) entitled him to expect of the adviser, and then inquire whether such a reasonable man could have given the advice which was in fact given if he had exercised reasonable care.

Then it was argued that an adviser ought not to be under any liability to exercise care unless he had, before the advice was sought, in some way held himself out as able and willing to give the advice. We can see no virtue in a previous holding out. If the inquirer, knowing that the adviser is in a position to give informed advice, seeks that advice and the adviser agrees to give it, we are unable to see why his duty should be more onerous by reason of the fact that he had previously done the same for others. And again, if the previous conduct of the adviser is relevant, would it be sufficient that, in order to attract new customers or increase the goodwill of existing customers, he had anticipated a general willingness to do what he could to help inquirers, or must he have indicated a willingness and ability to deal with the precise kind of matter on which the inquirer seeks his assistance?

In our judgment when an inquirer consults a business man in the course of his business and makes it plain to him that he is seeking considered advice and intends to act on it in a particular way, any reasonable business man would realise that, if he chooses to give advice without any warning or qualification, he is putting himself under a normal obligation to take some care. It appears to us to be well within the principles established by the *Hedley Byrne* case to regard his action in giving such advice as creating a special relationship between him and the inquirer and to translate his moral obligation into a legal obligation to take such care as is reasonable in the whole circumstances.

In *Hedley Byrne* their Lordships were not laying down rules. They were developing a principle which flows, as in all branches of the tort of negligence, from giving legal effect to what ordinary reasonable men habitually do in certain circumstances. Admittedly, there is nothing in *Hedley Byrne's* case which governs this case. The principles there indicated must be developed from time to time to cover new cases, and we have attempted to set out what we believe to be a proper development to meet the present case. We are unable to construe the passages from our speeches cited in the judgment of the majority in the way in which they are there construed. In our view they are consistent with and support the views which we have already expressed in the present case. We do not think that it would be useful to quote expressions from speeches used without having in mind circumstances such as we have here. Earlier authorities were explained in that case and, with one exception, we do not propose to add to those explanations.

We must, however, deal with *Low* v. *Bouverie,* [1891] 3 Ch. 82 because the appellant argued that the respondent could not succeed if that case was rightly decided. We do not agree. We see nothing wrong with the decision, although the judgments are to some extent coloured by a view of the effect of *Derry* v. *Peek* (1889), 14 App.Cas. 337 which was held in *Hedley Byrne & Co.'s* case to be erroneous. In *Low* v. *Bouverie,* Low, a moneylender, proposed to lend money to a relative of Bouverie who had interests in a trust of which Bouverie was a trustee. So, at the instigation of the borrower, he wrote to Bouverie asking whether those interests were mortgaged. In reply, Bouverie mentioned two mortgages, but failed to mention others which he had forgotten about. So Low lent money but lost it because the borrower became bankrupt, and there was nothing left of the borrower's interest in the trust after payment of the mortgages which Bouverie had forgotten to mention. In the first place, Bouverie was not acting in any business capacity. He was acting in his private capacity as a trustee in a family trust and we have already said that in our view there is, in general, no duty to take care imposed on an adviser who is not acting in the course of his business or professional activities. And, secondly, it appears from the judgments of Lindley L.J. and Bowen L.J. that Bouverie's letters to Low were not unequivocal statements that there were no other encumbrances. "They are quite consistent with the view that the encumbrances mentioned by the defendant were all he knew of or remembered" (p. 103); "I think that his language would be reasonably understood as conveying an intimation of the state of his belief, without an assertion that the fact was so apart from the limitation of his own knowledge" (p. 106); so it was not reasonable for Low to act on Bouverie's letters without taking further steps to check the information.

We think that the judgments of the majority in the High Court are consistent with the views which we have expressed as to the principles which should govern the present case. We are, therefore, of opinion that the appeal should be dismissed.

NOTES

1. How does *Mutual Life* v. *Evatt* affect the principle of *Hedley Byrne* v. *Heller*? Do you prefer the majority or minority opinion? It should be noted that both dissenting judges had participated in the *Hedley Byrne* case.

2. Should reasonably foreseen reliance on a statement be sufficient to impose a duty of care? See Goodhart, "Comment" (1971), 87 L.Q.Rev. 147; Glasbeek, "Negligent Statements in the Privy Council" (1972), 50 Can. Bar Rev. 128; Pickford, "A Mirage in the Wilderness: *Hedley Byrne* Considered" (1971), 34 Mod. L. Rev. 328, where the author described *Mutual Life* v. *Evatt* as a decision "by a bare majority, on an ill-defined issue, based on very few facts, and conflicting with much that was said on the problem in *Hedley Byrne's* case".

3. In *Patrick L. Roberts* v. *Sollinger Industries Ltd. and Ontario Development Corp.* (1978), 19 O.R. (2d) 44 (C.A.), the plaintiff agreed to install certain equipment for Sollinger Industries. Before installing the equipment, the plaintiff entertained doubts about the financial stability of Sollinger. Sollinger suggested that the plaintiff inquire of the Ontario Development Corporation, which had agreed to lend Sollinger some money. The officer who was contacted told the plaintiff that financing was being made available that would more than cover the plaintiff's contract, even though he knew that Sollinger had not yet completed the paper work for the loan and that the loan was "frozen" because of an unexplained over-run of expenditures. The trial judge found both Sollinger and O.D.C. liable and the Court of Appeal affirmed on liability but varied the damages awarded.

MacKinnon J.A. explained:

"[The defendant] must be held to have accepted responsibility for the foreseeable consequences in light of all the circumstances known to him. This is not the case of a person asking directions from a stranger who might negligently misdirect him; nor was it a casual or perfunctory conversation in which, in the course of exchanging social amenities, some information or advice was lightly requested and lightly given.

Lord Morris in *Hedley Byrne & Co. Ltd.* v. *Heller & Partners Ltd.,* put the principle which I would apply here as follows (p. 503):

Lord Hodson agreed with Lord Morris' statement of principle (p. 514).

At the risk of being repetitious, I would emphasize once again the circumstances surrounding the telephone conversation and the knowledge of the defendant's servant. As Lord Pearce pointed out in *Hedley Byrne & Co. Ltd.* v. *Heller & Partners Ltd.,* "a most important circumstance is the form of the enquiry and of the answer" (p. 539). In my view the form of the inquiry here indicated clearly the concern of the plaintiff and its reasonable reliance on any assurance it might receive. The response, in light of the knowledge of Zuibrycki, gave that assurance negligently.

Although the reasons for judgment in *Hedley Byrne & Co. Ltd.* v. *Heller &*

Partners Ltd., have been criticized for being vague and imprecise, the facts of this case bring it clearly within the most limited application of the principle therein enunciated. The demands of society for protection from the carelessness of others must extend to the facts of this case."

See also *J. Nunes Diamonds* v. *Dominion Electric Protection Co., infra,* and compare the treatment of *Mutual Life* v. *Evatt* by the majority. The minority did not mention *Mutual Life* in their reasons.

4. In *Farish* v. *National Trust et al.,* [1975] 3 W.W.R. 499 (B.C.), Mr. Justice Bouck held a trust company liable for negligent tax advice to a client, in relation to a pension plan changeover, which cost him additional income taxes. His Lordship referred to *Mutual Life* and explained that, when Lord Diplock used the word "profession", he did not mean to confine the class of persons covered to solicitors, accountants or physicians. Rather, he believed, that he "meant to use it in the context of a person that holds himself out to the public as being skilled or knowledgeable in a particular matter. As such, it applies to the National Trust in these proceedings". His Lordship held the trust company to the standard of a solicitor, in giving this legal advice, and found it wanting.

5. In *Sharadan Builders* v. *Mahler et al.* (1978), 22 O.R. (2d) 122 (C.A.), town officials were excused from liability when they did not inform the plaintiff's solicitor about the restrictions of a conservation authority with regard to the issuance of building permits. The court explained that they did not hold themselves out as being "engaged in the business of or otherwise expert in advising upon requirements for building permits other than those imposed by the municipality itself".

6. Real estate agents have been held liable for giving negligent information to purchasers of property. Thus, if an agent negligently misrepresents the costs and revenues of a property he will be liable. See *Dodds* v. *Millman* (1964), 45 D.L.R. (2d) 472 (B.C.). So too, if he carelessly tells a purchaser that a piece of land is an "apartment site" he may be responsible. See *Hopkins* v. *Butts* (1967), 65 D.L.R. (2d) 711 (B.C.). Other types of agents may also be held liable, as where one carelessly advised the sellers of some fruit that a proposed purchaser was creditworthy. See *W.B. Anderson & Sons Ltd.* v. *Rhodes (Liverpool) Ltd.,* [1967] 2 All E.R. 850; *Osman* v. *J. Ralph Moss Ltd.,* [1970] 1 Lloyd's Rep. 313 (C.A.).

7. A real estate agent, acting on the sale of a dairy farm, carelessly fails to tell the purchaser that his quota of milk will be reduced upon the sale because of the Milk Marketing Board's rules. Liability? See *Olsen* v. *Poirier* (1978), 21 O.R. (2d) 642 (Steele J.).

8. A bank manager gratuitously undertakes to "check out" a car that a client plans to buy. He assures the client that there are no problems. The client buys the car. He then learns the car is stolen and must return it. Liability? See *Zahara* v. *Hood & Royal Bank of Canada,* [1977] 1 W.W.R. 359. What if the defendant introduces the plaintiff to someone who sells the plaintiff a stolen car? See *Van der Kuilen* v. *Todd,* [1979] 3 W.W.R. 165.

9. What if a bank carelessly lets a client fraudulently transfer funds from a corporate bank account to his personal account and then withdraw it with a cheque payable to cash? See *Groves-Raffin Construction Ltd.* v. *Bank of Nova Scotia et al.* (1975), 51 D.L.R. (3d) 380 (B.C.).

10. What if an architect's estimate of the cost of a building is beyond the reasonable range of error? See *Saxby and Pokorny* v. *Fowler* (1977), 2 C.C.L.T. 195 (Alta. C.A.).

What if the amount of a pension is negligently represented and an employee, in reliance upon this, leaves his employment prematurely? See *Manuge* v. *Prudential Assurance Co.* (1977), 81 D.L.R. (3d) 360 (N.S.).

Must an engineer tell the owner and the architect about the need for a soil test? See *District of Surrey* v. *Church* (1977), 76 D.L.R. (3d) 721 (B.C.), *per* Munroe J.

Must an insurance agent advise his client that sufficient insurance is taken out to cover the property? See *McCann* v. *Western Farmers Mutual Insurance Co.*

(1978), 20 O.R. (2d) 210. *Cf. Mason* v. *Morrow's Moving & Storage Ltd.* (1977), 2 C.C.L.T. 118 (B.C.).

11. The principles being developed since *Hedley Byrne* furnish an alternative technique for the control of governmental officials by individuals suffering loss as a result of their conduct. For example, a governmental inspector may be held responsible for failing to discover a defect in the foundation of a home. See *Dutton* v. *Bognor Regis U.D.C.,* [1972] 2 W.L.R. 299 (C.A.); *Anns* v. *London Borough of Merton,* [1977] 2 All E.R. 492 (H.L.). Officials dealing with zoning matters can be held liable for providing misinformation, as where someone was negligently told that he could operate a used car business in an area which prohibited such use. See *Windsor Motors Ltd.* v. *Corporation of Powell River* (1969), 68 W.W.R. 173 (B.C.C.A.). Similarly, if a building permit is negligently issued to someone, who begins to build in reliance upon it, and it is later revoked, liability can be imposed. See *Gadutsis et al.* v. *Milne et al.,* [1973] 2 O.R. 503, where Mr. Justice Parker, after distinguishing the *Mutual Life* case as one where it was "not the normal or usual duty of an insurance company to give out financial advice about other companies", concluded:

". . . the employees in the zoning department of the municipality were there to give out information as to zoning. [They] must have known that persons inquiring would place reliance upon what they said. [The employee] gave out incorrect information in the course of employment directly to the person seeking information. Under these circumstances I find that the municipality owed a duty of care . . . that it failed to discharge such duty and that as a consequence, the plaintiffs suffered loss."

See also *H.L. & M. Shoppers* v. *Town of Berwick* (1977), 82 D.L.R. (3d) 23.

12. Health authorities may also run into difficulties if they fail to exercise their powers carefully. In *Collins* v. *Haliburton, Kawartha Pine Ridge District Health Unit,* [1972] 2 O.R. 508, 26 D.L.R. (3d) 73, the defendant authority, after receiving written complaints from his neighbours, notified the plaintiff that his business operations, which he had been carrying on for over a year—namely the freezing, storing, processing and packaging of poultry offal for mink ranchers—constituted an offensive trade under the Public Health Act of Ontario and that it must be carried out elsewhere. This notice, which became known to everyone in the area, caused the ruin of the plaintiff's business. The defendant was found to be negligent in giving the notice, which he should have known would become public knowledge, without making a proper investigation and inspection, and without giving the plaintiff an opportunity to put forward his position.

Mr. Justice Donoghue declared:

"Now if in *Donoghue* v. *Stevenson* the manufacturer of a bottle soft drink owed a duty of care to the purchaser of such drink from a shop to guard such purchaser from noxious material in the drink, it seems to me that the defendant here owed a duty of care to the plaintiff. It it should be said that the defendant here is a public body carrying out specific assigned duties and therefore is not liable for negligence which damaged the plaintiff, I would reply that this distinction was not made in the *Dutton* v. *Bognor* case. . . ."

This action was later dismissed because of a technical defect in the action. See *Collins* v. *Haliburton, Kawartha Pine Ridge District Health Unit (No. 2),* [1972] 3 O.R. 643 (Donoghue J.).

13. Can hydro officials be liable for estimating erroneously the cost of heating an indoor swimming pool? See *Hodgins* v. *Hydro-Electric Power Commn. of Nepean* (1976), 10 O.R. (2d) 713; affd [1976] 2 S.C.R. 501.

14. Plaintiff asks the municipal fire department officials whether a building he plans to buy complies with their fire regulations and is told erroneously that he is "home free". He buys the building. A few months later he is ordered by the fire marshall to comply with the legislation. He spends money in doing so and

sues the municipality for reimbursement. Recovery? See *Jung* v. *Corporation of the District of Burnaby* (1978), 7 C.C.L.T. 113 (B.C.); *cf. Sharadan Builders, supra,* note 5.

15. There are limitations on the ability of tort law to regulate governmental agencies' conduct. An insight into the boundary-line was provided in *Welbridge Holdings Ltd.* v. *Metropolitan Corporation of Greater Winnipeg* (1972), 22 D.L.R. (3d) 470 (S.C.C.). The plaintiffs had begun constructing apartment buildings, when their building permits were revoked because the zoning by-law, which had allowed them to build on the particular site, was voided by a Supreme Court of Canada decision because of procedural irregularities. The plaintiffs sued the municipality for the financial loss it suffered as a result of its carelessness in passing the by-law. In dismissing the appeal and the action, Laskin J. (as he then was) distinguished between the exercise of "administrative" or "business powers" by the municipality, for which liability could be incurred in contract or in tort, and the exercise of "legislative" or "quasi-judicial" powers, for which no liability would be imposed. His Lordship explained:

"Accepting that *Hedley Byrne* has expanded the concept of duty of care, whether in amplification or extension of *M'Alister (or Donoghue)* v. *Stevenson,* [1932] A.C. 562, it does not, nor, in my view, would any underlying principle which animates it, reach the case of a legislative body, or other statutory tribunal with *quasi* judicial functions, which in the good faith exercise of its powers promulgates an enactment or makes a decision which turns out to be invalid because of anterior procedural defects. . . .

Under the considerations on which the *Hedley Byrne* enunciation of principle rests, it cannot be said in the present case either that a special relationship arose between the plaintiff and the defendant or that the defendant assumed any responsibility to the plaintiff with respect to procedural regularity. This would equally be my view if the plaintiff had been the applicant for the rezoning by-law. A rezoning application merely invokes the defendant's legislative authority and does not bring the appellant in respect of his particular interest into any private nexus with the defendant, whose concern is a public one in respect of the matter brought before it. The applicant in such case can reasonably expect honesty from the defendant but not a wider duty. Beyond this, I would adapt to the present case what the late Mr. Justice Jackson said in dissent in *Dalehite* v. *U.S.* (1953), 346 U.S. 15 at p. 59 (a case concerned with the Federal Tort Claims Act, 1946, of the United States), as follows:

'When a [municipality] exerts governmental authority in a manner which legally binds one or many, [it] is acting in a way in which no private person could. Such activities do and are designed to affect, often deleteriously, the affairs of individuals, but courts have long recognized the public policy that such [municipality] shall be controlled soley by the statutory or administrative mandate and not by the added threat of private damage suits.'

(The words in brackets are mine.)

The defendant is a municipal corporation with a variety of functions, some legislative, some with also a *quasi*-judicial component (as the *Wiswell* case determined) and some administrative or ministerial, or perhaps better categorized as business powers. In exercising the latter, the defendant may undoubtedly (subject to statutory qualification) incur liabilities in contract and in tort, including liability in negligence. There may, therefore, be an individualization of responsibility for negligence in the exercise of business powers which does not exist when the defendant acts in a legislative capacity or performs a *quasi*-judicial duty.

Its public character, involving its political and social responsibility to all those who live and work within its territorial limits, distinguishes it, even as respects its exercise of any *quasi*-judicial function, from the position of a voluntary or statutory body such as a trade union or trade association which may have *quasi*-judicial and contractual obligations in dealing with its members: *cf. Abbott* v. *Sullivan*, [1952] 1 All E.R. 226; *Orchard et al.* v. *Tunney*, 8 D.L.R. (2d) 273, [1957] S.C.R. 436. A municipality at what may be called the operating level is different in kind from the same municipality at the legislative or *quasi*-judicial level where it is exercising discretionary statutory authority. In exercising such authority, a municipality (no less than a provincial Legislature or the Parliament of Canada) may act beyond its powers in the ultimate view of a court, albeit it acted on the advice of counsel. It would be incredible to say in such circumstances that it owed a duty of care giving rise to liability in damages for its breach. "Invalidity is not the test of fault and it should not be the test of liability": see Davis, 3 *Administrative Law Treatise* (1958), at p. 487. . . .

Moreover, even if the *quasi*-judicial function be taken in isolation, I cannot agree that the defendant in holding a public hearing as required by statute comes under a private tort duty, in bringing it on and in carrying it to a conclusion, to use due care to see that the dictates of natural justice are observed. Its failure in this respect may make its ultimate decision vulnerable, but no right to damages for negligence flows to any adversely affected person, albeit private property values are diminished or expense is incurred without recoverable benefit. If, instead of rezoning the land involved herein to enhance its development value, the defendant had rezoned so as to reduce its value and the owners had sold it thereafter, could it be successfully contended, when the rezoning by-law was declared invalid on the same ground as By-law 177, that the owners were entitled to recoup their losses from the municipality? I think not, because the risk of loss from the exercise of legislative or adjudicative authority is a general public risk and not one for which compensation can be supported on the basis of a private duty of care. The situation is different where a claim for damages for negligence is based on acts done in pursuance or in implementation of legislation or of adjudicative decrees."

Does the distinction drawn by Laskin J. appeal to you? See also *Berryland Canning Co. Ltd.* v. *The Queen* (1974), 44 D.L.R. (3d) 568 (Fed. Ct.), action against Crown for banning cyclamates dismissed.

16. In *Anns* v. *London Borough of Merton*, [1977] 2 All E.R. 496 (H.L.), Lord Wilberforce drew a similar distinction in the case of a municipality between its "operational" functions and its "discretionary" or "policy" functions. He indicated that this was a "distinction of degree; many 'operational' powers or duties have in them some element of 'discretion'. It can safely be said that the more 'operational' a power or duty may be, the easier it is to superimpose on it a common law duty of care." Do you prefer this language?

17. In *Bowen* v. *City of Edmonton* (1977), 4 C.C.L.T. 105 (Alta. C.A.), an action against a city for negligently replotting a subdivision before it got proper tests of soil stability was dismissed. Clement J.A. explained that the city omitted to do something that was "ancillary to the exercise of a quasi-judicial function". His Lordship stated that he saw no "appreciable distinction between 'legislative powers' and 'judicial or quasi-judicial powers'". He also suggested that no "useful distinction can be drawn between the expression 'operational area' . . . and the expression 'administrative' or 'business powers'". He felt that the resolution of the city was "not of an administrative nature".

Do you agree or disagree? What does all this mean in practical terms?

18. What remedies other than tort suits are available to supervise governmental bodies acting in their *quasi*-judicial or legislative capacities? What is lacking in them that is present in the tort remedy? See Molot, "Tort Remedies Against Administrative Tribunals for Economic Loss" in Law Society of Upper Canada, *Special Lectures in New Developments in the Law of Torts* (1973), at p. 413; Molot, "Administrative Bodies, Economic Loss and Tortious Liability" in Fridman, *Studies in Canadian Business Law* (1971); Goldenberg, "Tort Actions Against the Crown in Ontario" in Law Society of Upper Canada, *Special Lectures in New Developments in the Law of Torts* (1973), at p. 341;

Slutsky, "Liability of Public Authorities for Negligence: Recent Canadian Developments" (1973), 36 Mod. L. Rev. 656.

19. On the question of intentional interference by government officials, see *Roncarelli* v. *Duplessis,* [1959] S.C.R. 121, 16 D.L.R. (2d) 689; *Roman Corporation Ltd. et al.* v. *Hudson's Bay Oil & Gas Ltd. et al.* (1973), 36 D.L.R. (3d) 413 (S.C.C.); *Central Canada Potash* v. *Government of Saskatchewan* (1977), 6 C.C.L.T. 265 (S.C.C.). See generally Linden, "Tort Law's Role in the Regulation and Control of the Abuse of Power", *Law Society of Upper Canada Special Lectures, Abuse of Power* (1979). See *infra,* Chapter 18.

3. The Contractual Context

J. NUNES DIAMONDS LTD. v. DOMINION ELECTRIC PROTECTION CO.

Supreme Court of Canada. (1972), 26 D.L.R. (3d) 699

The (plaintiff) appellant company carried on business as a diamond merchant in Toronto. The company premises were protected from theft by a security system installed and serviced by the defendants. The contract between the two companies explicitly stated that the defendant company D.E.P. was not an insurer of its clients and that liability in the case of the system failing would be limited to $50 liquidated damages.

During the night of June 15, 1961, a robbery occurred and the alarm system failed to function. An investigation followed but it did not unearth the cause of the failure of the alarm system. It appeared that either the system had been circumvented by some unknown method or that there had been complicity on the part of some of the defendant's employees.

The evidence also indicated that, two weeks before the burglary, there had been a false alarm registered by the system, but the cause of this was also unexplained. A year-and-a-half prior to this robbery another diamond company (Baumgold), which also used the D.E.P. system, had been robbed. There, too, the cause of the system's failure had not been determined. Following the Baumgold robbery, Mr. Nunes-Vaz, the President of the plaintiff company, had asked D.E.P. to inspect its system to determine whether or not it was functioning properly. In response, they had sent an unidentified serviceman to check the system. While he was on the premises, Miss Geddes, the company secretary, had asked this serviceman whether the alarm system could be "got through". He replied: "Even our own engineers could not go through the system without setting an alarm." This statement was proved to be inaccurate.

In addition to this oral communication, two letters were sent by D.E.P.'s general manager, R.Y. Atlee, in response to inquiries, to the plaintiffs' insurance brokers. These letters stated that the Baumgold robbery was being investigated but that no conclusions had been reached as yet. They added that "the system performed its functions properly".

The plaintiffs brought an action against the defendants for breach of contract and for negligent misrepresentation. The contract aspect of the action was dismissed at all three levels as there was no evidence that the terms of the contract had been breached in any way. The tort action was based on the statement of the serviceman and on the two letters. (A third statement by an F. Mortimer, who was investigating the Baumgold incident, was given no weight at any level of the proceedings.)

The trial judge, Addy J., [1969] 2 O.R. 473, 5 D.L.R. (3d) 679, dismissed the action, holding that the serviceman's statement was not a representation that could reasonably have been relied upon. The letters were not discussed in any detail at the trial level, but it was held that no misrepresentations, other than that of the serviceman, had been made by the defendant company. In the Court of Appeal, [1971] 1 O.R. 218, 15 D.L.R. (3d) 26, Schroeder J.A. dismissed the plaintiffs' appeal, accepting the findings of Addy J. The plaintiffs appealed to the Supreme Court of Canada.

Pigeon J. (Martland and Judson JJ. concurring): . . . Concerning the statement to Miss Geddes, it appears to me that the courts below correctly held that it was made without actual or apparent authority. Nunes-Vaz himself testified that his request to a D.E.P. executive was: ". . . to send somebody to at least see how our system – if our system was functioning or not, which they did". This is how he finally stated it, thus clearly eliminating his earlier attempt to put it differently in saying that by "would function" he meant "that this system would not be circumvented". In any case, his words must be taken for what they mean, not what he may have intended but did not say. An employee sent in answer to such a request could not reasonably be expected to be qualified for making a statement beyond the purpose of his visit, namely, to ascertain whether the system was functioning. The wording of his statement shows that he was not an engineer. No employee other than a high executive or an engineer could reasonably be presumed to have knowledge of the degree of security afforded by the D.E.P. system. It is abundantly clear that there was no actual authority to make such a statement because it was established policy not to disclose to the subscribers any details of the actual method of operation, except in special cases such as banks and Governments. The trial judge made the following finding that is amply supported by the evidence, bearing in mind that one of the two servicemen who testified before him was the man who made an inspection on June 7, 1961, the day following the false alarm registered two weeks before the break-in [5 D.L.R. (3d) 679 at p. 691, [1969] 2 O.R. 473]:

> "As to the statement by the unidentified serviceman made to Miss Geddes (refer, my finding of fact 6), it seems unreasonable to me to suppose that Mr. Nunes-Vaz would rely on the representation of a mere serviceman as to the security of the system. The person was obviously not an engineer nor was it established that he was an electrician. He was apparently merely a person who periodically checked the current in the safe to see whether the system was operating as it should, by means of a fixed set of tests. I had the opportunity of seeing two such persons who were performing these duties for D.E.P. who gave evidence at the trial and neither one was a person with any particular skill or learning. Both would be classed as unskilled labourers."

Turning now to the letters, it is far from clear that the statement "The system performed its functions properly" was inaccurate. The trial judge's finding was [at p. 685]:

> "8. The method by which the diamonds were removed from the Baumgold safe was never determined, and it is still questionable whether it was by a circumvention of the alarm system or by the complicity of the employees of Baumgold or of the employees of D.E.P., or a combination of any two of the three."

This finding was fully supported by the evidence. . . .

Even on the assumption that the Baumgold incident was really a case of circumvention of the alarm system by compromising the line between the central station and the protected safe cabinet, it is not clear that the statement "The system performed its functions properly" was inaccurate. In so far as the system was designed to set off an alarm only if the current carried on the line to a subscriber's premises deviated by more than some 40 percent, plus or minus, from the regular 25 milliamperes, it could be said that it had not failed to function properly. On the other hand, assuming that such regular flow of current had been maintained by substituting an equivalent resistance for the network in the protected cabinet and thus compromising the connecting line, it can be said that the system, as a whole, had not functioned properly because it had failed to set off an alarm when it was designed to set one, that is when the circuit inside the safe cabinet was broken by removing the front in order to get at the safe. Furthermore, it may be that this is how the statement ought to have been expected to be understood. I will therefore deal with the point on the assumption that the letters contained an inaccurate statement. It is not alleged that it was dishonest, and, at most, it could not be construed as anything more than a representation that the system on the Baumgold premises had not been circumvented.

The appellant relies upon the judgment of the House of Lords in *Hedley Byrne & Co. Ltd.* v. *Heller & Partners Ltd.,* [1964] A.C. 465, in which it was said that there might be, in certain circumstances, a liability for negligent misrepresentation. No finding of negligence was made because it was held that disclaimers of responsibility were sufficient to negative any duty of care which might have existed. The speeches make it clear that it is not every negligent statement which may give rise to a claim in damages. Lord Reid's formulation at p. 486, that is quoted by my brother Spence, was considered by the Privy Council in a recent Australian case, *Mutual Life & Citizens' Assurance Co. Ltd. et al.* v. *Evatt,* [1971] 1 All E.R. 150, and was the subject of the following observations by Lord Diplock at p. 159:

> "This is not the language of statutory codification of the law of tort but of judicial exposition of the reasons for reaching a particular decision on the facts of the case. Read out of the context in which the whole argument in *Hedley Byrne* proceeded, i.e. advice given in the course of a business or profession which involved the giving of skilled, competent and diligent advice, these words are wide enough to sustain the respondent's case in the instant appeal. But in their Lordships' view the reference to "such care as the circumstances require" pre-supposes an ascertainable standard of skill, competence and diligence with which the advisor is acquainted or had represented that he is. Unless he carries on the business or profession of giving advice of that kind he cannot be reasonably expected to know whether any and if so what degree of skill, competence or diligence is called for, and *a fortiori*, in their Lordships' view, he cannot be reasonably held to have accepted the responsibility of conforming to a standard of skill, competence and diligence of which he is unaware, simply because he answers the enquiry with knowledge that the advisee intends to rely on his answer. This passage should in their Lordships' view be understood as restricted to advisors who carry on the business or profession of giving advice of the kind sought and to advice given by them in the course of that business."

On that view, it was decided that the claimant could not recover the loss suffered by reason of erroneous information negligently given by an insurance company concerning the financial stability of an associated company. Lord Diplock said at pp. 160-1:

> "The amendments introduced in the Court of Appeal state the respects in which it is alleged that the company was, and was known by the respondent to be, in a better position [than] he was to give reliable advice on the subject-matter of his enquiry. . . .
>
> In their Lordships' view these additional allegations are insufficient to fill the fatal gap in the declaration that it contains no averment that the com-

pany to the knowledge of the respondent carried on the business of giving advice on investments or in some other way had let it be known to him that they claimed to possess the necessary skill and competence to do so and were prepared to exercise the necessary diligence to give reliable advice to him on the subject-matter of his enquiry. In the absence of any allegation to this effect the respondent was not entitled to assume that the company had accepted any other duty towards him than to give an honest answer to his enquiry nor, in the opinion of their Lordships, did the Law impose any higher duty on them."

D.E.P. did not act in any fiduciary or advisory capacity towards Nunes. Its situation was that of a party contracting to supply specified services. The insurance brokers were those who were giving advice to Nunes. By giving them information, D.E.P. did not cease to be a contractor and become an advisor to the appellant on the matter of burglary protection. If it did make an honest, but inaccurate, statement as to the performance of its system it did not thereby assume responsibility for all damage which might thereafter be sustained by the appellant if its system, on his premises, was circumvented.

This is not a case where a person seeks information from another, whose business it is to give such information. It is not a case of misrepresentation leading to the making of a contract. It is a case in which, the parties having mutually established their respective rights and obligations by contract, it is sought to impose upon one of them a much greater obligation than that fixed by the contract by reason of an alleged misrepresentation as to the infallibility of the system which it provides. In essence, the appellant's position is that, although he had agreed to accept the respondent's system for what it was worth, and that the respondent was not to be an insurer, he can now claim in damages because the respondent had subsequently represented that the system could not be circumvented, and such circumvention had occurred.

Furthermore, the basis of tort liability considered in *Hedley Byrne* is inapplicable to any case where the relationship between the parties is governed by a contract, unless the negligence relied on can properly be considered as "an independent tort" unconnected with the performance of that contract, as expressed in *Elder, Dempster & Co. Ltd.* v. *Paterson, Zochonis & Co. Ltd.*, [1924] A.C. 522 at p. 548. This is specially important in the present case on account of the provisions of the contract with respect to the nature of the obligations assumed and the practical exclusion of responsibility for failure to perform them.

It is an essential basis of the contract between the parties that D.E.P. is not to be in the situation of an insurer. It is in consideration of this stipulation that the charges are established "solely on the probable value of the service", not on the value of the goods intended to be protected. To make the protection company liable, in the case of the failure of its protection system, not for the stipulated nominal damages ($50) but for the full value of the goods to be protected, is a fundamental alteration of the contract.

In my view, the representation relied on by appellant cannot be considered as acts independent of the contractual relationship between the parties. This can be readily verified by asking the question: Would these representations have been made if the parties had not been in the contractual relationship in which they stood? Therefore, the question of liability arising out of those representations should not be approached as if the parties had been strangers, but on the basis of the contract between them. Hence the question should be: May this contract of service be considered as having been turned into the equivalent of a contract of insurance, by virtue of inaccurate or incomplete representations respecting the actual value of the protection service supplied? In my view, there is no doubt that this question should be answered in the negative. There is nothing from which it can properly be inferred that Nunes considered that the contract had been so altered and it is perfectly obvious that D.E.P.'s management never intended to assume such obligations.

Irrespective of my conclusion on that point, I must say that it does not appear to me that Nunes has shown that damages claimed were caused by the statement made and the letters written in October, 1959. In order to support the claim it was suggested that, if not reassured by the statement and the letters as to the value of the protection system, other precautions would have been taken whereby the loss could have been avoided. Those other precautions are: (a) adding another protective device; (b) reducing the inventory; (c) using a bank vault. [Each of these was dismissed by His Lordship.]

The proof in this case has shown that for protection against burglary, Nunes really relied on insurance. It was so well protected that after the break-in its insurers paid $67,000 more than the actual cost of its inventory, as found by the trial judge. This amount being substantially in excess of the additional costs and losses due to the theft, which the trial judge fixed at $22,795.07, Nunes' chartered accountant, Adams, had to negotiate with the Department of National Revenue the allocation of the profit from the "incident" between the taxation years 1960 and 1961. Of course, the existence of indemnity insurance is not a defence available to a tortfeasor. However, this does not necessarily mean that the extent of such protection is not a factor to be borne in mind when considering whether a claimant was really lulled into a false sense of security by misrepresentations as to the value of other protective measures.

The appeal should be dismissed with costs.

Spence J. (dissenting): . . . I propose to deal first with the question of whether the statement to Miss Geddes, and by her transmitted to Mr. Nunes-Vaz, does constitute a representation which binds the respondent. It must be remembered that Mr. Nunes-Vaz requested an examination and I find much importance in the words which he used in making such request, "and then we asked to have somebody check and see to make sure that the system we have would function". And when he was asked by counsel to explain what he meant by the words "would function" he answered, "Well, in case of an attempted burglary that this system would not be circumvented, the system we have had in our premises to protect our . . . ." Therefore, I have no doubt that this employee was sent to the premises of the appellant for the purpose of checking the system to make sure that it would function, that is, that it would not be circumvented, and would protect the appellant's inventory. Neither the appellant company nor its president, Mr. Nunes-Vaz, was in the slightest bit interested in whether wires were all connected or how the system operated electrically. What they were interested in was that the system would operate to sound the alarm warning from any interference with the safe or its surroundings. That is why the appellant had purchased the system and it was the apparent failure of a like system to operate in the case of the Baumgold robbery which was the cause of Mr. Nunes-Vaz's immediate concern. The unnamed employee who Miss Geddes testified she is sure was a full-time employee of the respondent and was not the ordinary inspector who carried out periodic inspections did attend and she believes presented his identification card upon attending the premises and did make an inspection. Mr. Nunes-Vaz was engaged with customers and neither he nor Miss Geddes was capable of understanding the process of the inspection but nothing could be more natural than for Miss Geddes to inquire from the man who was making the inspection whether he could say that the inspection showed that the purpose for which he had been sent to inspect had been accomplished, that is, to determine whether the system would function to protect the inventory. That question, Miss Geddes testified, she put in very ordinary and easily understood language and language which accurately reflected the purpose of the technician's visit:

> "I asked him if this system could be got through because we had heard that maybe this is what had happened.
>
> Q. At Baumgold? A. At Baumgold."

Miss Geddes' evidence is that the precise words used by the person carrying out the inspection in reply to that inquiry were "even our own engineers could not get through the system without setting an alarm". That is the exact assurance that Mr. Nunes-Vaz desired when he made the call. The person who attended on behalf of the respondent and who was said to be a senior man, gave the exact reassurance requested and I cannot understand how it can be said that the appellant and its president, Mr. Nunes-Vaz, to whom the answer was transmitted would not be entitled to rely on the representation made by such employee of the respondent. . . .

In the case of the Atlee letters of October 26, 1959, which I have recited above, no question of the authority to make a representation is in issue. Mr. Atlee was the general manager of the respondent and signed the letters as such.

There remains the question as to whether these two representations, that by the technician to Miss Geddes, and that by Mr. Atlee, are misrepresentations and give a cause of action to the appellant. Of course, the representation made by the unnamed technician or inspector to Miss Geddes is very plainly a misrepresentation. A statement that not even the officers of the respondent company could circumvent the system without causing the alarm to operate was, on the admission of the respondent, a false statement. The said officers of the respondent knew of and testified as to three different methods whereby the system could be circumvented. The representation made in the letters is of a different character and perhaps what was not said is as important as what was said. The statement, "Toronto Police Officials and our people have reached no conclusions as yet. The system performed its function properly" is certainly a suggestion that although the investigation had not been completed the indication was that the system of alarm worked properly but that the burglary had occurred for some other reason. The final paragraph of the letter which reads as follows:

> "You can be assured that there is no relaxing nor will there be, of our principal interest — serving subscribers in all ways consistent with good protection. Every effort will be made to find the answer to the Baumgold matter."

is certainly an indication that investigation will be continued until an answer to the Baumgold matter had been discovered and surely it is the implication from such a statement that the appellant as someone most interested in that investigation will be informed of the result thereof. The evidence is that no officer of the appellant company ever heard any more from the respondent. . . .

The learned trial judge has made a finding of fact fully supportable on the evidence as follows [15 D.L.R. (3d) at p. 685]:

> "8. The method by which the diamonds were removed from the Baumgold safe was never determined, and it is still questionable whether it was by a circumvention of the alarm system or by the complicity of the employees of Baumgold or of the employees of D.E.P., or a combination of any two of the three."

Surely, even this unsatisfactory conclusion of the Baumgold investigation was of the greatest interest to the appellant. If the system could be circumvented *simpliciter* then Mr. Nunes-Vaz has outlined alternative steps which he might take and I have referred to them above. If the Dominion Electric Protection Co. employees were involved in the burglary, that fact was one of the greatest interest to another subscriber to the protection offered by the respondent company. No employee of the respondent was ever determined to have been guilty of any such complicity but immediately after the Baumgold robbery the respondent did discharge four different employees for security reasons. In the light of the finding of the trial judge as to the result of the Baumgold investigation, one cannot understand why this important information should not have been given to the appellant. It was the respondent's position that it was an integral part of the security which it offered its subscribers that no one should know how the system could be circumvented and that therefore it would have been most unwise to have ever admitted to the appellant or any other subscriber that such result could be obtained. The appellant was in a somewhat peculiar position. Only three persons would have had any right to information as to the security of the system: the president, the vice-president, and Miss Geddes, who may be called the informal secretary. Surely, the revelation to them that the system could be circumvented would not have been as dangerous to security generally as the failure to reveal such a fact especially when it was quite possible that knowledge of the fact was current in the underworld, if the Baumgold robbery resulted from circumvention, and that it was even possible that some employees of the respondent had been in complicity with the burglars. Four of the employees had been subsequently discharged as security risks.

It is possible, of course, that misrepresentation may be made by what has been called the "economy of truth", an expression used by Hodgins J.A. in *Kenny* v. *Lockwood*, [1932] 1 D.L.R. 507 at p. 526, [1932] O.R. 141. In this case, I view the failure to inform the appellant of the result of the Baumgold investigation after the general manager of the respondent had forwarded his letters of October 26, 1959, as more than a mere "economy of truth". It is a case of an implied undertaking to further report and then a failure to so further report when most important circumstances should have been reported.

There remains, therefore, the question of whether these representations, which I have found to be misrepresentations, give rise to a cause of action. In this case, no reliance was placed upon any allegation of fraud or deceit and the case must be considered as merely one of innocent misrepresentation. . . .

In considering *Hedley Byrne & Co. Ltd.* v. *Heller & Partners Ltd.*, Schroeder J.A., in giving reasons for the Court of Appeal for Ontario, quoted the paragraph which I have just quoted and expressed the view that the respondent in this case had followed the first course mentioned by Lord Reid, that is, he had kept silent or declined to give the information. With respect, I must express an opposite conclusion. Although Schroeder J.A., excepted from his statement the evidence as to the representation made by the so-called technician since he was of the opinion that it could not bind the company, I am of the opinion that the representation made by the general manager in the two letters dated October 25th which I have quoted was much more than refraining from giving any information or advice. The letters contained the bald statement that the equipment had functioned properly and as I have pointed out certainly implied that a further report would be made when the investigation had been completed, an undertaking which the respondent failed to carry out, and in failing to make such further report, by what has been nicknamed an "economy of truth", in fact misrepresented the situation.

I am, therefore, of the opinion that the respondent here adopted not the first course outlined by Lord Reid but the third course outlined by Lord Reid, *i.e.*, that the respondent simply answered without any qualification. As Lord Reid pointed out, a respondent choosing the last course must be held to have accepted some responsibility for his answer being given carelessly or to have accepted a relationship with the inquirer which required him to exercise such care as the circumstances required. Lord Morris of Borth-y-Gest said at pp. 502-3:

> "My Lords, I consider that it follows and that it should now be regarded as settled that if someone possessed of a special skill undertakes, quite irrespective of contract, to apply that skill for the assistance of another person who relies upon such skill, a duty of care will arise. The fact that the service is to be given by means of or by the instrumentality of words can make no difference. Furthermore, if in a sphere in which a person is so placed that others could reasonably rely upon his judgment or his skill or upon his ability to make careful inquiry, a person takes it upon himself to give information or advice to, or allows his information or advice to be passed on to, another person who, as he knows or should know, will place reliance upon it, then a duty of care will arise."

Lord Devlin, at p. 530, said:

> "I shall therefore content myself with the proposition that wherever there is a relationship equivalent to contract, there is a duty of care."

The learned author of [sic] Fleming, *The Law of Torts*, in the 4th edition (1971), at p. 564, in referring to *Hedley Byrne* v. *Heller & Partners, said:*

> "The sheet anchor of a duty of care is the speaker's assumption of responsibility for what he says. In other words, the recipient must have had reasonable grounds for believing that the speaker expected to be trusted. There is a world of difference, *e.g.*, between casual statements on social or informal occasions and serious communications made in circumstances warranting reliance. Usually, though by no means exclusively, the latter are encountered in the sphere of business or professional affairs, though not necessarily between persons linked by a contractual or fiduciary tie in the conventional sense."

I am of the view that the learned author, in that statement, properly summarized the effect of *Hedley Byrne* v. *Heller & Partners,* and I apply the case and that summary to the facts in the present case. Certainly, the inquiries made by the insurance representatives in their letters replied to by the general manager of the respondent on October 26, 1959, and the inquiry made by Miss Geddes to the unnamed technician were not made on social or informal occasions but were serious communications made in circumstances where the representer could have no other view than that his expert opinion was intended to be relied on.

I am personally of the view that under the circumstances which existed in the present case, that is, that the respondent was supplying to the appellant a very important service under a written contract and the inquiry was whether such service was and could be efficiently performed and the representation was that it was so being performed, the decision in *Nocton* v. *Lord Ashburton* is enough to justify a decision in favour of the appellant. Herein, I think I should note that Addy J. in his reasons, said [5 D.L.R. (3d) at p. 689]:

> "I feel also in the present case that, due to the existence of the contract and also the special knowledge which D.E.P. had, covering the subject-matter of burglar protection systems, a special relation existed between the plaintiff and the defendant. By reason of this D.E.P. would, in my view, be responsible for any misrepresentation pertaining to burglar protection which it negligently made to the plaintiff and which caused damages by inducing the plaintiff to fail to take precautions against burglary which it otherwise would have taken. If, in the ordinary course of business or in professional affairs a person seeks information or advice from another, who is not under

contractual obligation to give this advice, in circumstances in which a reasonable man so asked would know that he was being trusted or that his skill or judgment was being relied on, and the person asked chooses to give the information or advice, without clearly so qualifying his answer to show that he does not accept responsibility, then the person replying accepts the legal duty to exercise such care as the circumstances require in making this reply; and, for a failure to exercise that care, an action will lie if damage results. . . .''

In so far as that paragraph is a statement of facts, I accept it; in so far as it is a statement of law, I agree with it. In the present case, there was no such express denial of responsibility as was found to have saved Heller & Partners in *Hedley Byrne* v. *Heller & Partners.* In my opinion, the appellant is entitled to succeed upon the basis of the doctrine outlined in the latter case even if he thought that *Nocton* v. *Ashburton* did not go far enough to aid it. . . .

The question remains whether para. 16 of the agreement between the appellant and the respondent applies. That paragraph reads simply:

"16. No conditions, warranties or represeniations have been made by Dominion Company, its officers, servants or agents other than those endorsed hereon in writing."

That clause is contained in a written contract dated September 26, 1958. By its words, it refers to conditions, warranties or representations which *have been made* and can have no application whatsoever to representations which were made some 13 months after the date of the contract. Addy J., in giving reasons for judgment at trial, said [at p. 688]:

"At the outset, I would like to make it clear that the plaintiff has not, in my view, contracted itself out of its right to claim damages against the defendant, if such damages can be founded on an action in tort. A clause purporting to provide for exclusion of liability for negligence will be strictly interpreted and, even though it might exempt from liability based on a contractual duty, it will not exempt from liability based on the breach of a general duty of care unless the words to that effect are clear and unequivocal."

With that view I agree and have no hesitation in coming to the conclusion that cl. 16 of the agreement between the appellant and the respondent cannot operate as a bar to a claim based on a tortious misrepresentation made many months after the contract which contained such a clause had been executed.

The agreement between the parties is of importance in so far as it established a relationship between them, and thus provided a basis upon which, in the light of subsequent events, the appellant could rightly assess that the negligent misrepresentations of the respondent were made in breach of a duty of care to the appellant. I cannot agree that the mere existence of an antecedent contract foreclosed tort liability under the *Hedley Byrne* principle.

For these reasons, I have come to the conclusion that the appellant is entitled to succeed upon its claim for actionable misrepresentation. . . .

I would, therefore, allow the appeal and give judgment for the appellant for that amount with costs throughout.

[Laskin J. concurs with Spence J.]

Appeal dismissed.

NOTES

1. What was the basis of the majority decision in this case? How did the minority differ?

SEALAND OF THE PACIFIC LTD. v. ROBERT McHAFFIE LTD. AND ROBERT C. McHAFFIE

British Columbia Court of Appeal. (1975),
51 D.L.R. (3d) 702, [1974] 6 W.W.R. 724

The plaintiff, Sealand, hired McHaffie Ltd., naval architects, to repair their underwater aquarium in Victoria, B.C. Ocean Cement, a supplier of concrete, recommended a product for the job that proved unsuitable. The plaintiff sued the supplier, Ocean Cement, the architect McHaffie Ltd., and McHaffie, an employee of McHaffie Ltd., personally. The Court of Appeal held both Ocean Cement and McHaffie Ltd. liable in contract, but dismissed the personal action in tort against McHaffie.

Seaton J.A.: Sealand also seeks judgment against Mr. McHaffie individually on the basis of a negligent statement, relying on the principle in *Hedley Byrne & Co. Ltd.* v. *Heller & Partners, Ltd.,* [1964] A.C. 465, [1963] 2 All E.R. 575, [1963] 3 W.L.R. 101. Before dealing specifically with that claim, I shall discuss whether Sealand could recover against McHaffie Ltd. on that principle. There was a contract between Sealand and McHaffie Ltd. The statement was made by an employee of McHaffie Ltd. in carrying out that contract and I think that the duty and the liability ought to be discovered in the contract. If additional duties and liabilities are to be attached, it will have the effect of changing the bargain made by the parties. That would be inappropriate. . . .

Now I turn to the claim against Mr. McHaffie. For a statement of part of the principle in *Hedley Byrne* I refer to what Lord Morris of Borth-y-Gest said at pp. 502-3 (A.C.):

> My Lords, I consider that it follows and that it should now be regarded as settled that if someone possessed of a special skill undertakes, quite irrespective of contract, to apply that skill for the assistance of another person who relies upon such skill, a duty of care will arise. The fact that the service is to be given by means of or by the instrumentality of words can make no difference.

Here Mr. McHaffie did not undertake to apply his skill for the assistance of Sealand. He did exercise, or fail to exercise, his skill as an employee of McHaffie Ltd. in the carrying out of its contractual duty to Sealand. Further, while Sealand may have chosen to consult McHaffie Ltd. because it had the benefit of Mr. McHaffie's services as an employee, it was with McHaffie Ltd. that Sealand made a contract and it was upon the skill of McHaffie Ltd. that it relied.

An employee's act or omission that constitutes his employer's breach of contract may also impose a liability on the employee in tort. However, this will only be so if there is breach of a duty owed (independently of the contract) by the employee to the other party. Mr. McHaffie did not owe the duty to Sealand to make inquiries. That was a company responsibility. It is the failure to carry out the corporate duty imposed by contract that can attract liability to the company. The duty in negligence and the duty in contract may stand side by side but the duty in contract is not imposed upon the employee as a duty in tort.

NOTES

1. Do you agree with the reasoning of Seaton J.A.?

2. If the aquarium had collapsed and injured someone, could that person recover against McHaffie personally? If so, why should there be a different result in the two situations? Could it have anything to do with likelihood of the "reasonable reliance" of the plaintiff in *Sealand* on the corporate defendant alone? See Reiter, "Contract, Tort, Relations and Reliance" in Reiter and Swan, *Studies on Contract Law* (1980).

3. An airline contracts with the federal government to supply air traffic

controller services. As a result of a controller's negligence, an airplane crashes. Would there be recovery against the controller personally by the airline? What about an action against him personally by a passenger, who has no contract with the federal government?

4. One scholar has lamented that:

"It would be ironic indeed if, just as in the earlier development of negligence law the *absence* of a contractual relationship was in some circumstances an effective bar to a claim in tort, the *presence* of a contractual relationship between the parties in a negligent misstatement situation should now rigidly rule out tortious liability."

See Symmons, "The Problem of the Applicability of Tort Liability to Negligent Misstatements in Contractual Situations: A Critique of *Nunes Diamonds* and *Sealand* Cases" (1975), 21 McGill L.J. 79, at p. 81.

ESSO PETROLEUM CO. LTD. v. MARDON

Court of Appeal. [1975] 1 All E.R. 203; varied [1976] 2 W.L.R. 583

The Esso company was engaged in the production and distribution of petroleum. In 1961 Leitch, a dealer sales representative with 40 years' experience in the business, induced Esso to acquire a site for a gas station on the basis that it would sell 200,000 gallons per year by the second year. It later became obvious that the station had certain physical deficiencies that reduced its ability to attract customers. In 1963, Mardon, a potential tenant, was assured by Leitch that the "throughput" would be 200,000 gallons in the third year. Based on these assurances, Mardon agreed to take over the station. Despite efforts by Mardon to make the station a success, the business did not prosper, largely because of its inability to attract passing trade. By the third year, the annual throughput was only 86,502 gallons. Mardon was forced to give up the tenancy in 1966. The company sued for arrears of rent and Mardon counterclaimed for damages in negligence.

Lawson J. (at trial): I finally come to what has been the most difficult part of the case, that is, the counterclaim based on the allegations of negligence contained in para 8a of the defence and counterclaim. This involves considering two questions: firstly, in the circumstances of this case did the plaintiffs owe a duty of care to the defendant in relation to the information contained in the statement which I have found was made to him in or about March 1963? Secondly, if such duty were owed, was it broken? I can deal at once with the second question. I am satisfied that the plaintiffs failed to take reasonable care in relation to the relevant statement. Their fatal error lay in the failure to reappraise the 1961 throughput forecast of 200,000 gallons in the light of the physical characteristics of the site as they became plain when its development was completed in 1963 and before the defendant began negotiations for the April 1963 tenancy. Mr. Leitch said, and I accept, that he was disappointed when he saw the results of the building of the showroom. He thought it was, as was the fact, blocking the visibility from Eastbank Street of part of the forecourt. He agreed that the obstruction of the view of the pumps from that street would adversely affect throughput. He also conceded that the site layout was back-to-front and this adversely affected the site's potential. The same view is of course expressed in the plaintiff's internal memorandum of 4th August 1964.

. . .

My finding that the plaintiffs were in breach of duty, if one was owed to the defendant, rests and rests solely on a state of facts as to the site which were apparent to the defendant when he began his negotiations. The plaintiffs' difficulty in relying on this as an answer to the counterclaim based on negligence lies in the fact, which I found, that the defendant's realistic assessment of throughput communicated to the plaintiffs' representatives was 100,000 to 150,000 gallons per annum and that he resiled from his estimate in reliance on the plaintiffs' superior expertise, which so to speak 'sugared' their statement so that he relied on what they told him and not what he himself thought.

I come back to the vital question: did the plaintiffs, in all the circumstances, owe the defendant the duty in relation to the statement made? My answer is, Yes. The reasons why I reach this conclusion can be summarised as follows. In *Nocton* v. *Lord Ashburton* I understand their Lordships to be saying that a duty of care may arise in relation to a statement made when there are special circumstances which give rise to an implied contract in law or to a relationship which equity would regard as fiduciary. Lord Dunedin treats this liability as an aspect of the law of negligence. That I think is an important point because one finds very strong echoes of the same position being taken up in the judgment of Lord Devlin in *Hedley Byrne & Co. Ltd.* v. *Heller & Partners Ltd.* to which I will now come. In the *Hedley Byrne* case, Lord Reid was clearly of opinion that such a duty might arise from a special relationship; and the nature of this he indicated in two passages in his speech. . . . .

[His Lordship discussed *Hedley, Byrne.*]

It seems to me that all their Lordships were all agreed that, apart from a general relationship involving fiduciary aspects such as solicitor and client, bank and customer, the special relationship from which the duty of care in the making of the statements arises, is not limited to particular categories of persons or types of situations. . . . .

[His Lordship discussed *Mutual Life.*]

Subject to one last point which I have to consider, I am satisfied that there was, in the circumstances of this case, a special relationship; and this special relationship I find to have existed, even if one applies the tests indicated by the majority in the *Mutual Life* case. The present was a situation in which in fact the plaintiffs did have a financial interest in the advice they gave. This was advice which was given to the defendant who, as they knew, was asking or seeking information and was in fact given information which would lead him into the decision to enter into the tenancy agreement, the benefit of which the plaintiffs as landlords would have. If one applies the *Mutual Life* minority test, which is expressed in the passage which I have just read, it is clear in my judgment, subject to the final point I an now coming to, that this was a situation in which the plaintiffs owed the defendant a duty of care.

The last point on which the counterclaim could founder is whether the fact that the statement was made in the context of pre-contractual negotiations between the plaintiffs and the defendant, and from which a contract resulted, excludes the duty of care. . . .

It is right to say there is no direct authority on this point which is binding on me. . . .

I have however been referred to *Dillingham Construction Pty* v. *Downs,* an Australian case, a decision of Hardie J sitting in the Supreme Court of New South Wales. This question is discussed by the judge at some length. I think it is sufficient if I read passages from the headnote, having first said that this is a decision which was handed down after the Privy Council had decided the *Mutual Life* case in the way which has been indicated. The facts, putting them very briefly, were that the plaintiffs had entered into a contract to undertake certain works in a New South Wales harbour; these works became much more difficult to carry through at the contract price, because all sorts of snags and difficulties emerged, since there were disused coal workings under the harbour; the defendant knew of the existence of these workings but nothing had been said of them to the plaintiffs. So the plaintiffs alleged, amongst other things, that there was a duty of care on the defendant to give them this information, in the course of making statements in the pre-contractual situation, and that this duty of care had been broken. The relevant passage in the headnote is as follows:

> *"Held:* (1) The policy of the common law is to uphold contracts freely made between parties who are at arm's length and on equal terms. The pre-contract relationship between such parties would not normally qualify as a special relationship of the type which, according to the doctrine of *Hedley Byrne & Co. Ltd.* v. *Heller & Partners Ltd.,* would subject one or other of the parties to a duty of care in the assembly or presentation of facts, figures or other information as to the subject matter of the contract."

Then there is a reference to McNair J's case and to two other Australian cases where the point had arisen but in which no determination was reached about it. Then the headnote goes on:

> "(2) In the present case, in view of the very special nature of the contract and the nature and extent of the specialised knowledge in the possession of the defendant which would have been of the utmost importance to the plaintiffs if it had been imparted to them, the mere fact that the parties were in a pre-contract relationship at the time when the duty was said to have been created and to have been breached, would not in itself necessarily preclude the application of the principle under consideration. (3) Upon a consideration of all relevant factors . . . there was no assumption or acceptance by the defendant, in fact or law, of the task of providing the plaintiffs with accurate or full information . . ."

I am not going to read passages from Hardie J's judgment; they are, in my view, accurately summarised in those passages in the headnote. I find the reasoning and the decision in his case to be very helpful, because it does indicate a view, which I personally hold, that the fact that statements are made in a pre-contractual relationship does not preclude the person to whom the statements are made from relying on the duty of care in the making of the statements by the person who is making them.

The special features of the present case are, of course, that here was the defendant who had himself formed what he thought a realistic estimate of the turnover of this garage; he puts his realistic figure to the plaintiffs, who are the landlords seeking a tenant for their premises, and he is given by them a different estimate which I find to be affected by a failure to take care in relation to its being made. I have given the reasons why I hold that there was a failure to take care. Furthermore, the plaintiffs must have appreciated, and I am sure they appreciated—and in fact they quite frankly said this—that had the statement not been made the defendant would certainly have not entered into the tenancy agreement of 10th April at the rental and on the terms which he did.

As a matter of principle, I cannot think there is anything wrong in holding that the duty of care in relation to the making of statements may arise in a pre-contractual situation. For example, it is well established that a seller of goods which are dangerous, and which are dangerous to the knowledge of the seller, can be liable to the buyer in damages for negligence as well as in damages for breach of the contractual term in relation to the merchantability or fitness of the goods; and the passages to which I have referred in Lord Devlin's speech in *Hedley Byrne* are really on the same lines. The theory that in some way or other the law is different in relation to negligent mis-statements from the law concerning the circulation of dangerous things—the theory that there is a distinction between a negligent statement and some negligence or omission in relation to goods or chattels or land—seems to me to be harking back to the pre-*Hedley Byrne* days when the view was taken, on the basis of cases since overruled—*Le*

Lievre v. *Gould* and the majority decision in *Chandler* v. *Crane, Christmas & Co.*
—that there was no duty of care in relation to the making of statements. What
Hedley Byrne has done, I am quite satisfied, is to indicate that there is really no
difference between the duty of care in relation to the making of a statement and
the duty of care in relation to other situations which, if broken, might give rise
to a cause of action for damages for negligence. Of course, it may well be said, if
my view is right, that I am opening the door very wide indeed and eroding the
principle of caveat emptor and the general principle that contracting parties are
at arm's length. But I fall back on what Lord Reid said in *Hedley Byrne* on this
point:

> "A reasonable man, knowing that he was being trusted or that his skill and
> judgment were being relied on, would, I think, have three courses open to
> him. He could keep silent or decline to give the information or advice sought:
> or he could give an answer with a clear qualification that he accepted no
> responsibility for it or that it was given without that reflection or inquiry
> which a careful answer would require: or he could simply answer without any
> such qualification. If he chooses to adopt the last course he must, I think, be
> held to have accepted some responsibility for his answer being given carefully,
> or to have accepted a relationship with the inquirer which requires him to
> exercise such care as the circumstances require."

Therefore, for those reasons I find for the defendant on his counterclaim for
damages for negligence. I am against him on the other basis of his counterclaim,
but I have indicated sufficiently, I trust, the four walls within which this liability
falls. It follows that the plaintiffs are entitled to £1,103.69, subject to setting off
such damages as the defendant may be entitled to having regard to my findings
on the plaintiffs' liability on the counterclaim.

Judgment for the plaintiffs and judgment for the defendant on the counterclaim.
Defendant's damages to be assessed.

Denning M.R. (on appeal): "This is," said the judge, "a tragic story of wasted
endeavour and financial disaster." It is a long story starting as long ago as 1961,
and finishing in 1967. Since then eight years have been spent in litigation.

. . .

. . . the question arises whether Esso are liable for negligent misstatement
under the doctrine of *Hedley Byrne & Co. Ltd.* v. *Heller & Partners Ltd.*
[1964] A.C. 465. It has been suggested that *Hedley Byrne* cannot be used so as
to impose liability for negligent pre-contractual statements: and that, in a pre-
contract situation, the remedy (at any rate before the Act of 1967) was only in
warranty or nothing. . . .

In arguing this point, Mr. Ross-Munro took his stand in this way. He submitted that when the negotiations between two parties resulted in a contract
between them, their rights and duties were governed by the law of contract and
not by the law of tort. There was, therefore, no place in their relationship for
Hedley Byrne [1964] A.C. 465, which was solely on liability in tort. He relied
particularly on *Clark* v. *Kirby-Smith* [1964] Ch. 506 where Plowman J. held
that the liability of a solicitor for negligence was a liability in contract and not
in tort, following the observations of Sir Wilfrid Greene M.R. in *Groom* v.
Crocker [1939] 1 K.B. 194, 206. Mr. Ross-Munro might also have cited *Bagot*
v. *Stevens Scanlan & Co. Ltd.* [1966] 1 Q.B. 197, about an architect; and other
cases too. But I venture to suggest that those cases are in conflict with other
decisions of high authority which were not cited in them. These decisions show
that, in the case of a professional man, the duty to use reasonable care arises not
only in contract, but is also imposed by the law apart from contract, and is
therefore actionable in tort. It is comparable to the duty of reasonable care

which is owed by a master to his servant, or vice versa. It can be put either in contract or in tort: . . .

To this there is to be added the high authority of Viscount Haldane L.C., in *Nocton* v. *Lord Ashburton* [1914] A.C. 932, 956:

> ". . . the solicitor contracts with his client to be skilful and careful. For failure to perform his obligation he may be made liable at law in contract or even in tort, for negligence in breach of a duty imposed on him."

That seems to me right. A professional man may give advice under a contract for reward; or without a contract, in pursuance of a voluntary assumption of responsibility, gratuitously without reward. In either case he is under one and the same duty to use reasonable care: see *Cassidy* v. *Ministry of Health* [1951] 2 K.B. 343, 359-360. In the one case it is by reason of a term implied by law. In the other, it is by reason of a duty imposed by law. For a breach of that duty he is liable in damages: and those damages should be, and are, the same, whether he is sued in contract or in tort.

It follows that I cannot accept Mr. Ross-Munro's proposition. It seems to me that *Hedley Byrne & Co. Ltd.* v. *Heller & Partners Ltd.* [1964] A.C. 465, properly understood, covers this particular proposition: if a man, who has or professes to have special knowledge or skill, makes a representation by virtue thereof to another—be it advice, information or opinion—with the intention of inducing him to enter into a contract with him, he is under a duty to use reasonable care to see that the representation is correct, and that the advice, information or opinion is reliable. If he negligently gives unsound advice or misleading information or expresses an erroneous opinion, and thereby induces the other side to enter into a contract with him, he is liable in damages. This proposition is in line with what I said in *Candler* v. *Crane, Christmas & Co.* [1951] 2 K.B. 164, 179-180, which was approved by the majority of the Privy Council in *Mutual Life and Citizens' Assurance Co. Ltd.* v. *Evatt* [1971] A.C. 793. And the judges of the Commonwealth have shown themselves quite ready to apply *Hedley Byrne* [1964] A.C. 465, between contracting parties; see in *Sealand of the Pacific Ltd.* v. *Ocean Cement Ltd.* (1973) 33 D.L.R. (3d) 625; and New Zealand *Capital Motors Ltd.* v. *Beecham* [1975] 1 N.Z.L.R. 576.

Applying this principle, it is plain that Esso professed to have—and did in fact have—special knowledge or skill in estimating the throughput of a filling station. They made the representation—they forecast a throughput of 200,000 gallons—intending to induce Mr. Mardon to enter into a tenancy on the faith of it. They made it negligently. It was a "fatal error." And thereby induced Mr. Mardon to enter into a contract of tenancy that was disastrous to him. For this misrepresentation they are liable in damages.

NOTES

1. Does the reasoning in *Esso Petroleum* v. *Mardon* appeal to you? Is it in conflict with *Nunes Diamonds* and *Sealand of the Pacific?* Can the cases be distinguished on the ground of "reasonable reliance"? *Esso* v. *Mardon* has been followed in *Sodd Corp.* v. *Tessis* (1977), 2 C.C.L.T. 245 (Ont. C.A.). Do you agree with the following quote from Reiter, "Contracts, Torts, Relations and Reliance" in Reiter and Swan, *Studies on Contract Law* (1980), p. 310:

> "This is a development that should be applauded and encouraged. The law ought to protect those who rely reasonably on others who appreciate the reliance, and those who form reasonable expectations based upon considered words or acts of others. The evolution of contract and tort into a law of relational obligations permits the courts to consider the important issues of policy that arise in novel cases, freed of the apparent constraints of classical contract and tort doctrine that so often compelled judges to employ indirect

and obtuse methods of reaching socially desirable decisions. The principle of liability advocated in this study allows courts the benefits of the guidance offered by past decisions, but frees them to address the truly difficult issues directly. Moreover, it represents the culmination of a process of growth that began long before various groups of cases were (somewhat arbitrarily) characterized as contractual or tortious and before it was ever suggested that the categories were exclusive or were premises and not conclusions of legal reasoning.

Modern developments now allow it to be stated with confidence that if legal intervention is appropriate, neither contract nor tort doctrine stands in the path of reaching desirable results and of fashioning suitable remedies. As this fact becomes recognized generally, some of the spurious problems thrown up by the rationalization of civil liability—problems of damages, remoteness, limitations, contribution and the like—will recede into irrelevance. The truly difficult problems, problems that raise strong and conflicting policies of freedom to arrange affairs by private contract and concerns for avoiding abuses of power, for preventing some injuries and compensating some victims of others, remain. With the resolution of the pesky doctrinal problems, we shall soon be able to devote our full attention to these more difficult facets of contracts, torts, relations and reliance."

NOTE ON OCCUPIERS' LIABILITY

1. It is pretty well agreed that the Canadian law of occupiers' liability is a mess. (Harris, "Some Trends in the Law of Occupiers' Liability"(1963), 41 Can. Bar Rev. 401, reprinted in *Studies in Canadian Tort Law* (1972). McDonald and Leigh, "The Law of Occupiers' Liability and the Need for Reform in Canada" (1965), 16 U of T.L.J. 55; A.L. MacDonald, "Invitees" (1930), 8 Can. Bar Rev. 344; Friedmann, "Liability to Visitors of Premises" (1943), 21 Can. Bar Rev. 79. See generally Fleming, *The Law of Torts* (5th ed., 1977), p. 432.) Indeed, nowhere else in the law of torts has confusion been as prevalent and injustice as rampant as it has been in disputes arising out of injuries sustained on the land of another. This is understandable, perhaps, for "the history of this subject is one of conflict between the general principles of the law of negligence and the traditional immunity of landowners". (Bohlen, "The Duty of a Landowner Towards Those Entering His Premises of Their Own Right" (1920), 69 U. Pa. L. Rev. 142, 237, 340, at p. 237.) In this clash, Canadian landowners have emerged victorious. Despite significant advances by legislation in the United Kingdom, New Zealand, Alberta and British Columbia (Occupiers' Liability Act, 1957, 5 & 6 Eliz. 2, c. 31, Occupiers' Liability Act, c. 96 (N.Z.), Occupiers' Liability Act, Stat. Alta. (1973), c. 79) and by decisions in the United States (*Rowland* v. *Christian* (1968), 443 P. 2d 561 (Cal.)), Canadian courts have clung to a system of rigid rules and formal categories devised in the last century to protect landowners from unsympathetic juries. True, Canadian judges occasionally complain about the need for categorization, and some have pushed the law ahead to some extent, but they have usually succumbed to authority.

2. Our courts have steadfastly insisted that there were three immutable categories of entrants: (1) trespassers; (2) licensees; and (3) invitees, to whom three distinct duties of care were owed. (*White* v. *Imperial Optical Co.* (1957), 7 D.L.R. (2d) 471 (Ont. C.A.); revg. (1957), 6 D.L.R. (2d) 496.) Authors have attacked this rigid scheme, some urging the creation of additional categories (Friedman, *op. cit.;* Paton, "The Responsibility of an Occupier to Those Who Enter As of Right" (1941), 19 Can. Bar Rev. 1), and others suggesting a reduction in the number of categories. (McDonald and Leigh, *op. cit.*)

3. The first group of entrants are trespassers, who generally are those who enter land without the permission of the occupier. Historically, an occupier has been found liable to a trespasser only if he wilfully injures him or acts in reckless disregard of his presence. (*Haynes* v. *C.P.R.* (1972), 31 D.L.R. (3d) 62 (B.C.C.A.); *Harris* v. *Wong* (1971), 19 D.L.R. (3d) 589 (Sask.); *Robert Addie & Sons*

(Collieries) v. *Dumbreck,* [1929] A.C. 358, at pp. 365 and 370.) Some attempts have been made to circumvent this rule in cases where its application causes unfairness or hardship. A court may, by some device or other, find that a trespasser, particularly if he is a child, has an 'implied license' to be on the premises and is, therefore, owed a duty to be protected. (*Excelsior Wire Rope Co. Ltd. v. Callan,* [1930] A.C. 404.) Recently, however, a new line of cases has developed (*Herrington v. British Railways Bd.,* [1972] A.C. 877; *Pannett v. McGuinness Co. Ltd.,* [1972] 3 W.L.R. 387, [1972] 3 All E.R. 137 (C.A.); *Southern Portland Cement Ltd. v. R.J. Cooper,* [1974] 1 All E.R. 87 (P.C.)), which reject the use of fictions, and suggest instead a new test which requires the occupier to treat the trespasser with "common humanity". The Supreme Court of Canada recently adopted this test in the case of *Veinot* v. *Kerr-Addison Mines Ltd.* 3 N.R. 94, revg. [1973] 1 O.R. 411. In his judgment, Mr. Justice Dickson quoted with approval from Denning M.R.'s reasons for judgment in *Pannett* v. *McGuinness & Co. Ltd. supra.,* in which Lord Denning suggested four factors for a judge to consider in determining whether the occupier is in breach of his duty. These are:

"(1) . . . the gravity and likelihood of the probable injury. . . .

(2) . . . the character of the intrusion. . . .

(3) . . . the nature of the place where the trespass occurs . . . and

(4) . . . the knowledge which the defendant has or ought to have, of the likelihood of trespassers being present. . . ."

A fifth factor which the courts have also considered is the cost to the occupier of removing the danger. It remains to be seen whether the "common humanity" test will allow the courts to reach an equitable compromise "between the demands of humanity and the necessity to avoid placing undue burdens on occupiers". (*Herrington, supra, per* Lord Wilberforce, at p. 920.) See also *Mitchell* v. *C.N.R.,* [1975] 1 S.C.R. 592; But *cf. Wade* v. *C.N.R.* (1977), 3 C.C.L.T. 173 (S.C.C.).)

Mr. Justice R.E. Holland has recently declared that children trespassers need no longer be classified but should be dealt with by the ordinary law of negligence. His Lordship opined, "Too often the occupier shelters behind a policy of insurance rather than a chain link fence." (*Walker* v. *Sheffield Bronze* (1977), 2 C.C.L.T. 97.) It is too early to tell whether this view will ultimately prevail, although it is a consequence devoutly to be wished by most commentators.

4. The distinction between the licensee and the invitee is not always easy to fathom. Generally, a licensee is a person, such as a social guest, who enters the occupiers' land with permission but who is not there for any business or related purpose. The invitee, on the other hand, is a "lawful visitor from whose visit the occupier stands to derive an economic advantage". (Harris, *op. cit.,* at p. 403.) It is often extremely difficult to distinguish between these two groups and, on occasion, courts have classified as invitees students at school (*Phillips* v. *Regina Public School Dist. No. 4 Board of Education* (1976), 1 C.C.L.T. 197 (Sask. Q.B.), certain visitors to public libraries (*Nickell* v. *City of Windsor* (1927), 59 O.L.R. 618, [1927] 1 D.L.R. 379 (C.A.)), hospitals (*Slade* v. *Battersea Hospital,* [1955] 1 W.L.R. 207 (Q.B.D.); *Creighton* v. *Delisle Hospital Board* (1961), 38 W.W.R. (N.S.) 44, 34 D.L.R. (2d) 606 (Sask. Q.B.)) and railroad stations (*Stowell* v. *Railway Executive,* [1949] 2 K.B. 519, [1949] 2 All E.R. 193; *cf. Spencer* v. *G.T.R.* (1896) 27 O.R. 303 (Q.B.)), who did not necessarily bring any economic advantage to the occupier. Some of the cases make little sense.

5. The occupier's duty to a licensee has been to prevent damage from concealed dangers or traps of which he has actual knowledge. (*Addie* v. *Dumbreck, supra, per* Lord Hailsham L.C., at p. 365. See also *Hambourg* v. *T. Eaton Co. Ltd.,* [1935] S.C.R. 430; *Fraser* v. *Ronsten Developments Ltd.* (1969), 4 D.L.R. (3d) 475 (Ont. H.C.)) Whether a dangerous condition on premises is a trap or a concealed danger is not always obvious. For example, what is an obvious danger in daylight may be transformed into a concealed danger after dark. (*Sanders et al.* v. *Frawley Lake Lumber Co. Ltd.* (1972), 25 D.L.R. (3d) 46 (Ont. C.A.). What constitutes 'actual knowledge' of the occupier is also fraught with com-

plexity. In *White* v. *Imperial Optical Co.* [1957] O.W.N. 192, (1957), 7 D.L.R. (2d) 471 (Ont. C.A.) it was held that an occupier must actually know of the condition involved, but that once such knowledge is shown, the question is not whether the occupier knew that the condition constituted a concealed danger, but whether he, as a reasonable person, ought to have realized that it constituted a concealed danger. Thus, the 'actual knowledge' requirement has been so much diluted that imputed knowledge is often considered sufficient. (See *Ellis* v. *Fulham Borough Council,* [1938] 1 K.B. 212, [1937] 3 All E.R. 454 (C.A.); *Pearson* v. *Lambeth Borough Council,* [1950] 2 K.B. 353, [1953] 1 All E.R. 682 (C.A.); *Hawkins* v. *Coulsdon & Purley Urban District Council,* [1954] 1 Q.B. 319, [1954] 1 All E.R. 97; *Slater* v. *Clay Cross Co. Ltd.,* [1956] 2 Q.B. 264, [1956] 2 All E.R. 625; *Jesmer et al.* v. *Bert Katz Real Estate Ltd. et al.* (1973), 33 D.L.R. (3d) 662.)

6. More recently, there has been a blurring of the standard of care owing to licensees and that owing to invitees. In *Bartlett* v. *Weiche Apartments* (1974), 7 O.R. (2d) 263 (C.A.), Mr. Justice Jessup stated that the duty owed to a licensee "is to take reasonable care to avoid foreseeable risk of harm from any unusual danger on the occupier's premises of which the occupier actually has knowledge or of which he ought to have knowledge because he was aware of the circumstances". See also *Hanson* v. *St. John Horticultural Assoc.* [1974] S.C.R. 354; *Alaica* v. *Corporation of the City of Toronto* (1976), 1 C.C.L.T. 212 (Ont. C.A.); *Evans* v. *Forsyth* (1978), 21 O.R. (2d) 210. But *cf. Phillips* v. *Regina Board of Education, supra,* using older formulation.

7. The duty that an occupier owes to an invitee was expressed by Willes J. in *Indermaur* v. *Dames* (1867), L.R. 2 C.P. 311 (Ex. Ct.), at p. 388, as follows:

> ". . . with respect to such a visitor, at least, we consider it settled law that he, using reasonable care on his part, for his own safety, is entitled to expect that the occupier shall on his part use reasonable care to prevent damage from unusual danger, which he knows or ought to know; . . ."

In *Smith* v. *Provincial Motors Ltd.* ((1962), 32 D.L.R. (2d) 405, at p. 412), Ilsley J. suggested that, once it is decided that the entrant is an invitee, four additional questions should be asked: First, was there an unusual danger? Second, did the defendant know or have reason to know about it? Third, did the defendant act reasonably? Fourth, did the plaintiff use reasonable care for his own safety or did he voluntarily incur the risk?

8. The question of what is an unusual danger has been the subject of some controversy. Indeed, it has been suggested that the concept was introduced into our law by mistake. (For a discussion of the problems of "unusual dangers" see Linden, "A Century of Tort Law in Canada: Whither Unusual Dangers, Products Liability and Automobile Accident Compensation?" (1967), 45 Can. Bar Rev. 836.) Nevertheless, such dangers as icy streets (*Foster* v. *Canadian Interurban Properties Ltd.* (1973), 35 D.L.R. (3d) 248 (Sask. Q.B.); *Bilenky* v. *Ukranian Greek Catholic Parish et al.,* [1971] 2 W.W.R. 595; *Such* v. *Dominion Stores* (1963), 37 D.L.R. (2d) 311), stairways (*Campbell* v. *Shelbourne Hotel,* [1939] 2 K.B. 534; *cf. Lucy* v. *Bawden,* [1914] 2 K.B. 318; *Wilkinson* v. *Fairrie* (1862), 1 H. & C. 633. 130 R.R. 700), wet floors (*Campbell* v. *Royal Bank of Canada,* [1964] S.C.R. 85 (S.C.C.); *Tokar* v. *Town of Selkirk & Chorney,* [1974] 3 W.W.R. 612 (Man. Q.B.)), and objects on store floors may be considered "unusual" in some situations but not in others. Held to be unusual dangers recently have been a running lawnmower (*Whaling* v. *Ravenhorst* (1975), 2 C.C.L.T. 114 (Ont. C.A.) and a sliding glass door (*Pajot* v. *Commonwealth Holiday Inns Canada Ltd.* (1978), 20 O.R. (2d) 76, *per* Boland J.). Held not to be unusual dangers, however, have been an irregularity on a walkway (*Johnston* v. *Sentineal* (1977), 80 D.L.R. (3d) 571, *per* Steele J.; *Evans* v. *Forsyth* (1978), 21 O.R. (2d) 210) and ice on a parking lot in winter (*Davies* v. *Day* (1977), 2 C.C.L.T. 91 (Ont. C.A.)).

9. The problems associated with the effect of the invitee's knowledge of the danger led to some strange and draconian results (*London Graving Dock Co. Ltd.* v. *Horton,* [1951] A.C. 737, [1951] 2 All E.R. 1, [1951] 1 T.L.R. 949

(H.L.); *Campbell* v. *Royal Bank of Canada, supra; Letang* v. *Ottawa Electric Railway Co.,* [1926] A.C. 725, [1926] 3 W.W.R. 88, [1926] 3 D.L.R. 457 (P.C.); *Smith* v. *Austin Lifts Ltd.,* [1959] 1 All E.R. 81, [1959] 1 W.L.R. 100 (H.L.), which have now been overruled. Today it is clear that the plaintiff's knowledge is not relevant to whether a danger is an unusual one. See *Mitchell* v. *C.N.R.,* [1975] 1 S.C.R. 592, 50-50 split; *Bartlett* v. *Weiche, supra; Davies* v. *Day, supra; Evans* v. *Forsyth, supra.*

10. In order to mitigate some of the hardships arising from the rigid categorization of entrants, the courts have developed a fourth categoɪy, that of contractual entrant, who is someone, like a patron of a threatre, who pays for the right to enter land. The courts in these situations apply ordinary negligence principles. (*McLenan* v. *Segar,* [1917] 2 K.B. 325; *Brown* v. *B. & F. Theatres,* [1947] S.C.R. 486, [1947] 3 D.L.R. 593, *per* Rand J., at p. 596 (D.L.R.)) A landlord, for example, is now under an "obligation to use reasonable care to keep the premises reasonably safe for his tenant". (*Sinclair* v. *Hudson Coal Co.,* [1966] 2 O.R. 256 (C.A.), *per* Kelly J.A.; *Richardson* v. *St. James Court Apt.,* [1963] 1 O.R. 534, 38 D.L.R. (2d) 25, *per* Aylen J.) Similarly, a patron of a hotel is a contractual entrant. See *Pajot* v. *Commonwealth Holiday Inns Canada Ltd.* (1978), 20 O.R. (2d) 76, *per* Boland J. The duty owed to contractual entrants may be limited by the terms of the contract. (*Blais* v. *Lafontaine* (1972), 21 D.L.R. (3d) 381 (Que. C.A.))

11. The field of occupiers' liability has been complicated further by an overriding distinction between an "activity duty" and an "occupancy duty", which derives from the misfeasance-nonfeasance dichotomy. Thus, if an entrant is injured by "current operations" being carried out by the occupier on the land, the courts may impose the ordinary duty to use reasonable care. (See Harris, *supra,* at p. 409; *Excelsior Wire Rope Co.* v. *Callan,* [1930] A.C. 404. See also *Mitchell* v. *C.N.R.* [1975] 1 S.C.R. 592; *Wade* v. *C.N.R.* (1977), 3 C.C.L.T. 173 (S.C.C.), *per* Laskin C.J.C., dissenting.)

12. It is obvious that, despite some improvements in the law, a complete legislative overhaul of the entire field is required. (*Cf.* Alexander, "Occupiers' Liability: Alberta Proposes Reform" (1970), 9 Alta. L. Rev. 89, who seems to prefer common law reform.)

13. In the United Kingdom, legislation has been enacted, abolishing the distinction between licensees and invitees. The Occupiers' Liability Act of 1957, *supra*, stipulates that "An occupier of premises owes the same duty, the common duty of care' to all his visitors. . ." (s. 2(1)) and that "The common duty of care is a duty to take such care as in all the circumstances of the case is reasonable to see that the visitor will be reasonably safe in using the premises for the purposes for which he is invited or permitted by the occupier to be there" (s. 2(2)). There is also a list of the factors to be considered in determining whether the duty of care has been breached. (See generally North, *Occupiers' Liability* (1971).)

14. The Ontario Law Reform Commission's *Report on Occupiers' Liability* (1972), recommended the adoption of a new Occupiers' Liability Act, which has now been embodied in a Bill of the Legislative Assembly of Ontario, Bill 202, 1979. The two key sections read:

> 3.—(1) An occupier of premises owes a duty to take such care as in all the circumstances of the case is reasonable to see that persons entering on the premises, and the property brought on the premises by those persons are reasonably safe while on the premises.

> (2) The duty of care provided for in subsection 1 applies whether the danger is caused by the condition of the premises or by an activity carried on on the premises.

> (3) The duty of care provided for in subsection 1 applies except in so far as the occupier of premises is free to and does restrict, modify or exclude his duty.

> 4.—(1) The duty of care provided for in subsection 1 of section 3 does not apply in respect of risks willingly assumed by the person who enters on the

premises but in that case the occupier owes a duty to the person to not create a danger with the deliberate intent of doing harm or damage to the person or his property and to not act with reckless disregard of the presence of the person or his property.

(2) A person who is on premises with the intention of committing, or in the commission of, a criminal act shall be deemed to have willingly assumed all risks.

15. The Province of Alberta, following the *Report on Occupiers' Liability* of the Alberta Institute of Law Research and Reform, was the first Canadian province to adopt an Occupiers' Liability Act, S.A. 1973, c. 79. This statute includes the following provisions:

5. An occupier of premises owes a duty to every visitor on his premises to take such care as in all the circumstances of the case is reasonable to see that the visitor will be reasonably safe in using the premises for the purposes for which he is invited or permitted by the occupier to be there or is permitted by law to be there.

6. The common duty of care applies in relation to
 (a) the condition of the premises,
 (b) activities on the premises, and
 (c) the conduct of third parties on the premises.

12. (1) Subject to subsection (2) and to section 13, an occupier does not owe a duty of care to a trespasser on his premises.

(2) An occupier is liable to a trespasser for damages for death or of injury to the trespasser that results from the occupier's wilful or reckless conduct.

13. (1) Where an occupier knows or has reason to know
 (a) that a child trespasser is on his premises, and
 (b) that the condition of, or activities on, the premises create a danger of death or serious bodily harm to that child,
the occupier owes a duty to that child to take such care as in all the circumstances of the case is reasonable to see that the child will be reasonably safe from that danger.

(2) In determining whether the duty of care under sub-section (1) has been discharged consideration shall be given to
 (a) the age of the child,
 (b) the ability of the child to appreciate the danger, and
 (c) the burden on the occupier of eliminating the danger or protecting the child from the danger as compared to the risk of the danger to the child.

(3) For the purposes of subsection (1), the occupier has reason to know that child trespassers are on his premises if he has knowledge of facts from which a reasonable man would infer that children are present or that their presence is so probable that the occupier should conduct himself on the assumption that they are present.

Let us hope that the other provincial legislatures will enact forthwith legislation to modernize and simplify the present law of occupiers' liability.

16. One should not be fooled, however, into thinking that legislation will solve everything. The problems associated with these cases have not all disappeared in Alberta. See *Nasser* v. *Rumford* (1977), 2 C.C.L.T. 209; revd (1977), 4 C.C.L.T. 49 (Alta. C.A.), foreseeability problem; *Epp* v. *Ridgetop Builders Ltd.* (1978), 7 C.C.L.T. 291, wall fell in heavy wind, no liability.

CHAPTER 11

CONDUCT OF THE PLAINTIFF

Despite the presence of a duty, a breach of duty and resulting damage, a plaintiff's claim may still be defeated because of his own conduct. This is a legacy of the individualism of the common law. The rationale behind these defences is that the law should only assist those persons who are deemed worthy of its protection. Thus, anyone who is negligent with regard to his own safety is denied the protection of the law in whole or in part. Similarly, anyone who consents to assume the risk of injury has waived his usual legal rights. There is, also, a growing body of law to the effect that someone engaged in illegal activity may also be barred from recovery. This chapter will examine the defences of contributory negligence, voluntary assumption of risk and illegality.

A. CONTRIBUTORY NEGLIGENCE

BUTTERFIELD v. FORRESTER

King's Bench. (1809), 103 E.R. 926

This was an action on the case for obstructing a highway, by means of which obstruction the plaintiff, who was riding along the road, was thrown down with his horse and injured, &c. At the trial before Bayley J., at Derby, it appeared that the defendant, for the purpose of making some repairs to his house, which was close by the roadside at one end of the town, had put up a pole across this part of the road, a free passage being left by another branch or street in the same direction. That the plaintiff left a public house not far distant from the place in question at 8 o'clock in the evening in August, when they were just beginning to light candles, but while there was light enough left to discern the obstruction at 100 yards distance: and the witness, who proved this, said that if the plaintiff had not been riding very hard he might have observed and avoided it; the plaintiff however, who was riding violently, did not observe it, but rode against it, and fell with his horse and was much hurt in consequence of the accident; and there was no evidence of his being intoxicated at the time. On this evidence Bayley J. directed the jury, that if a person riding with reasonable and ordinary care could have seen and avoided the obstruction; and if they were satisfied that the plaintiff was riding along the street extremely hard, and without ordinary care, they should find a verdict for the defendant, which they accordingly did. The plaintiff moved for a new trial.

Bayley J.: The plaintiff was proved to be riding as fast as his horse could go, and this was through the streets of Derby. If he had used ordinary care he must have seen the obstruction, so that the accident appeared to happen entirely from his own fault.

Lord Ellenborough C.J.: A party is not to cast himself upon an obstruction which has been made by the fault of another, and avail himself of it, if he do not himself use common and ordinary caution to be in the right. In cases of persons riding upon what is considered to be the wrong side of the road, that would not authorize another purposely to ride up against them. One person being in fault will not dispense with another's using ordinary care for himself. Two things must concur to support this action, an obstruction in the road by the fault of the defendant, and no want of ordinary care to avoid it on the part of the plaintiff.

Rule refused.

NOTES

1. What was the reason advanced for denying compensation to the plaintiff? Did causation play a role?
2. Does the defence have a penal basis in that the plaintiff is being punished for his own wrongdoing?
3. Is the defence a deterrent to negligent conduct by potential plaintiffs? Does the defence have the opposite effect on potential defendants, who will be relieved from responsibility for otherwise negligent conduct?
4. For an historical account of contributory negligence, see Malone, "The Formative Era of Contributory Negligence" (1946), 41 Ill. L. Rev. 151. See also James, "Contributory Negligence" (1953), 62 Yale L. J. 691; Bohlen, "Contributory Negligence" (1908), 21 Harv. L. Rev. 151.

DAVIES v. MANN

Exchequer Court. (1842), 10 M. & W. 566; 12 L.J. Ex. 10; 152 E.R. 588

Case for negligence. The declaration stated, that the plaintiff theretofore and at the time of the committing of the grievance thereinafter mentioned, to wit, on, &c., was lawfully possessed of a certain donkey, which said donkey of the plaintiff was then lawfully in a certain highway, and the defendant was then possessed of a certain wagon and of certain horses drawing the same, which said wagon and horses of the defendant were then under the care, government, and direction of a certain then servant of the defendant, in and along the said highway; nevertheless the defendant, by his said servant, so carelessly, negligently, unskilfully, and improperly governed and directed his said wagon and horses, that by and through the carelessness, negligence, unskilfulness, and improper conduct of the defendant, by his said servant; the said wagon and horses of the defendant then ran and struck with great violence against the said donkey of the plaintiff, and thereby then wounded, crushed, and killed the same, &c.

The defendant pleaded not guilty.

At the trial, before Erskine J., at the last Summer Assizes for the county of Worcester, it appeared that the plaintiff, having fettered the fore-feet of an ass belonging to him, turned it into a public highway, and at the time in question the ass was grazing on the off side of a road about eight yards wide, when the defendant's wagon, with a team of three horses, coming down a slight descent, at what the witness termed a smartish pace, ran against the ass, knocked it down, and the wheels passing over it, it died soon after. The ass was fettered at the time, and it was proved that the driver of the wagon was some little distance behind the horses. The learned judge told the jury, that though the act of the plaintiff, in leaving the donkey on the highway so fettered as to prevent his getting out of the way of carriages travelling along it, might be illegal, still, if the proximate cause of the injury was attributable to the want of proper conduct on the part of the driver of the wagon, the action was maintainable against the defendant; and his Lordship directed them, if they thought that the accident might have been avoided by the exercise of ordinary care on the part of the driver, to find for the plaintiff. The jury found their verdict for the plaintiff, damages 40s.

Godson now moved for a new trial, on the ground of misdirection.

Lord Abinger C.B.: I am of opinion that there ought to be no rule in this case. The defendant has not denied that the ass was lawfully in the highway, and therefore we must assume it to have been lawfully there; but even were it otherwise, it would have made no difference, for as the defendant might, by proper care, have avoided injuring the animal, and did not he is liable for the consequences of his negligence, though the animal may have been improperly there.

Parke B.: This subject was fully considered by this court in the case of *Bridge* v. *The Grand Junction Railway Company*, 3 M. & W. 246 where, as appears to me, the correct rule is laid down concerning negligence, namely, that the negligence which is to preclude a plaintiff from recovering in an action of this nature, must be such as that he could, by ordinary care, have avoided the consequences of the defendant's negligence. I am reported to have said in that case, and I believe quite correctly, that "the rule of law is laid down with perfect correctness in the case of *Butterfield* v. *Forrester*, that, although there may have been negligence on the part of the plaintiff, yet unless he might, by the exercise of ordinary care, have avoided the consequences of the defendant's negligence, he is entitled to recover; if by ordinary care he might have avoided them, he is the author of his own wrong". In that case of *Bridge* v. *Grand Junction Railway Co.*, there was a plea imputing negligence on both sides; here it is otherwise; and the judge simply told the jury, that the mere fact of negligence on the part of the plaintiff in leaving his donkey on the public highway, was no answer to the action, unless the donkey's being there was the immediate cause of the injury; and that, if they were of opinion that it was caused by the fault of the defendant's servant in driving too fast or, which is the same thing, at a smartish pace, the mere fact of putting the ass upon the road would not bar the plaintiff of his action. All that is perfectly correct; for, although the ass may have been wrongfully there, still the defendant was bound to go along the road at such a pace as would be likely to prevent mischief. Were this not so, a man might justify the driving over goods left on a public highway, or even over a man lying asleep there, or the purposely running against a carriage going on the wrong side of the road.

[Gurney B., and Rolfe B. concurred.]

Rule refused.

NOTES

1. What explanation for the doctrine of "last clear chance" was offered by the court? Were they influenced by the causation theory?

2. Was the defendant the more culpable of the two parties?

3. Was the doctrine a reaction to the harshness of the contributory negligence doctrine? See MacIntyre, "The Rationale of Last Clear Chance" (1940), 18 Can. Bar Rev. 665; also in Linden *Studies in Canadian Tort Law* (1968), p. 160, and in (1940), 53 Harv. L. Rev. 1225, where the author outlines the development of the doctrine.

4. For a fuller study of the complex theories that were spun by courts about "last clear chance", see *Long* v. *Toronto Railway Company* (1914), 50 S.C.R. 224, 20 D.L.R. 369; *B.C. Electric Ry. Co. Ltd* v. *Loach*, [1916] 1 A.C. 719, 23 D.L.R. 4, 8 W.W.R. 1263 (P.C.); *Gives* v. *C.N.R.*, [1941] 4 D.L.R. 625 (Ont. C.A.); *Davies* v. *Swan Motor Co. (Swansea) Ltd.*, [1949] 2 K.B. 291, [1949] 1 All E.R. 620. See also Goodhart, "The Last Opportunity Rule" (1949), 65 L.Q.Rev. 237.

5. There was much criticism of the "stalemate rule", which denied all recovery to negligent plaintiffs. The "last clear chance" doctrine helped in some cases, but it lacked both flexibility and candour. Reform of this "monstrously unjust" situation was overdue. See Schroeder, "Courts and Comparative Negligence", [1950] Ins. L.J. 791, at p. 794. Agitation began in the law reviews. See McMurchy, "Contributory Negligence – Should the Rule in Admiralty and Civil Law be Adopted?" (1923), 1 Can. Bar Rev. 844; Anglin, "Law of Quebec and Other Provinces" (1923), 1 Can. Bar Rev. 33, at p. 49. Even the Supreme Court of Canada expressed its displeasure with the "stalemate rule" and praised the more equitable principle of "common fault" that was used in Quebec. See *Grand Trunk Pacific Railway* v. *Earl*, [1923] S.C.R. 397, at p. 398 *per* Duff J., at p. 406 *per* Anglin J., and at p. 408 *per* Mignault J. The next year, 1924, the Legislature of Ontario responded and enacted the first Canadian comparative negligence statute (Stat. Ont. 1924, c. 32), most of which is reproduced below as amended.

THE NEGLIGENCE ACT

R.S.O. 1970, c. 296

2. (1) Where damages have been caused or contributed to by the fault or neglect of two or more persons, the court shall determine the degree in which each of such persons is at fault or negligent, and, except as provided by subsections (2), (3) and (4), where two or more persons are found at fault or negligent, they are jointly and severally liable to the person suffering loss or damage for such fault or negligence, but as between themselves, in the absence of any contract express or implied, each is liable to make contribution and indemnify each other in the degree in which they are respectively found to be at fault or negligent.

(2) In any action brought for any loss or damages resulting from bodily injury to, or the death of any person being carried in, or upon, or entering, or getting on to, or alighting from a motor vehicle other than a vehicle operated in the business of carrying passengers for compensation, and the owner or driver of the motor vehicle that the injured or deceased person was being carried in, or upon, or entering, or getting on to, or alighting from is one of the persons found to be at fault or negligent, no damages are, and no contribution or indemnity is, recoverable for the portion of the loss or damage caused by the fault or negligence of such owner or driver except, subject to subsection (4), where such portion of the loss or damage was caused by the gross negligence of the driver of the motor vehicle, and the portion of the loss or damage so caused by the fault or negligence of such owner or driver shall be determined although such owner or driver is not a party to the action.

(3) . . .

(4) In any action founded upon fault or negligence and brought for loss or damage resulting from bodily injury to, or the death of any married person where one of the persons found to be at fault or negligent is the spouse of such married person, no damages are, and no contribution or indemnity is recoverable for the portion of loss or damage caused by the fault or negligence of such spouse, and the portion of the loss or damage so caused by the fault or negligence of such spouse shall be determined although such spouse is not a party to the action.

3. A tort feasor may recover contribution or indemnity from any other tort feasor who is, or would if sued have been, liable in respect of the damage to any person suffering damage as a result of a tort by settling with the person suffering such damage, and thereafter commencing or continuing action against such other tort feasor, in which event the tort feasor settling the damage shall satisfy the court that the amount of the settlement was reasonable, and in the event that the court finds the amount of the settlement was excessive it may fix the amount at which the claim should have been settled.

4. In any action for damages which is founded upon the fault or negligence of the defendant if fault or negligence is found on the part of the plaintiff that contributed to the damages, the court shall apportion the damages in proportion to the degree of fault or negligence found against the parties respectively.

5. If it is not practicable to determine the respective degree of fault or negligence as between any parties to an action, such parties shall be deemed to be equally at fault or negligent.

6. Whenever it appears that any person not already a party to an action is or may be wholly or partly responsible for the damages claimed, such party may be added as a party defendant to the action upon such terms as are deemed just or may be made a third party to the action in the manner prescribed by the rules of practice for adding third parties.

7. In any action tried with a jury, the degree of fault or negligence of the respective parties is a question of fact for the jury.

8. Where the damages are occasioned by the fault or negligence of more than one party, the Court has power to direct that the plaintiff shall bear some portion of the costs if the circumstances render this just.

9. Where an action is commenced against a tort feasor or where a tort feasor settles with a person who has suffered damage as a result of a tort, within the period of limitation prescribed for the commencement of actions by any relevant statute, no proceedings for contribution or indemnity against another tort feasor are defeated by the operation of any statute limiting the time for the commencement of action against such other tort feasor provided,

    (*a*) such proceedings are commenced within one year of the date of the judgment in the action or the settlement, as the case may be; and

    (*b*) there has been compliance with any statute requiring notice of claim against such tort feasor.

NOTES

1. All the other common law provinces and most of the other Commonwealth jurisdictions have now enacted similar legislation. In 1945, England adopted The Law Reform (Contributory Negligence) Act, 8 & 9 Geo. VI, c. 28. In the United States, until recently, comparative negligence legislation was enacted only in a handful of states, but now over 20 states have done so. In Florida, comparative negligence has been adopted by judicial legislation. See *Hoffman* v. *Jones* (1973), 280 So.2d 431(Fla.S.C.). See generally, Schwartz, *Comparative Negligence* (1974). Concerning the operation of s. 5, see Dickson J. dissenting in *Taylor* v. *Asody* (1975), 49 D.L.R. (3d) 724 (S.C.C.).

2. The standard of care demanded of a plaintiff is no different than that expected from a defendant — he must exercise such care for his own safety as a reasonable person would in like circumstances. The contributory negligence issue, like the negligence question, goes to the jury, if there is one in the case. In practice, juries and courts might be a little less demanding of plaintiffs, but there is no differentiation in theory between plaintiffs and defendants. Should there be? See James, "Contributory Negligence" (1953), 62 Yale L.J. 691; James and Dickinson, "Accident Proneness and Accident Law" (1950), 63 Harv. L. Rev. 769.

3. There are numerous cases dealing with the conduct expected of a plaintiff for his own safety. For example, a boater was held contributorily negligent for failing to keep a proper lookout for a waterfall that resulted in a drowning (*Hendricks* v. *The Queen* (1970), 9 D.L.R. (3d) 454 (S.C.C.)). In another case, a pedestrian was held partially to blame for failing to face the traffic and for walking in the middle of the highway at night where she was struck and killed by a motorist (*Lepine* v. *DeMeule et al.* (1973), 30 D.L.R. (3d) 49 (N.W.T.),

affd. with modification of damages (1973), 36 D.L.R. (3d) 388 (N.W.T.C.A.). See also *Lackner* v. *Neath* (1966), 58 D.L.R. (2d) 662 (Sask. C.A.)).

4. There are also many cases where no contributory negligence was found. For example, where a policeman drives at a speed in excess of the speed limit during a chase, he is not contributorily negligent if this is "reasonably necessary to carry out his statutory duty". See Arnup J.A. in *Attorney-General for Ontario* v. *Keller* (1978), 23 O.R. (2d) 143 (C.A.). See also *Rogers* v. *Hill* (1973), 37 D.L.R. (3d) 468 (B.C. C.A.) (hunting accident); *Law* v. *Upton Lathing Ltd.* (1972), 22 D.L.R. (3d) 407 (Ont. C.A.) (warning about reading label).

5. The contributory negligence of children poses many problems. See *Joyal* v. *Barsby* (1965), 55 D.L.R. (2d) 38 (Man. C.A.) (6-year-old not negligent); *Kaplan* v. *Canada Safeway Ltd.* (1968), 68 D.L.R. (2d) 627 (Sask. Q.B.) (3-year-old not negligent); *McEllistrum* v. *Etches*, [1956] S.C.R. 787, 6 D.L.R. (2d) 1. See *supra*, Chapter 4.

6. How should a plaintiff act in an emergency? In *Zervobeakos* v. *Zervo-beakos* (1970), 8 D.L.R. (3d) 377 (N.S. C.A.), the plaintiff was a lodger who wakened to find himself on the second storey of a house imperilled by a fire that had been caused by the negligence of the owner of the house. He exited through a window but slipped from a sloping ledge and fell to the ground sustaining injuries. The plaintiff would probably have been rescued without injury if he had remained at the window and had not ventured outside. The Nova Scotia Court of Appeal held that the plaintiff was not contributorily negligent. McKinnon C.J.N.S. stated that a person placed in a "perilous position" cannot be required to "exercise as much judgment and self-control in attempting to avoid danger as would reasonably be expected of him under ordinary circumstances". Do you agree? What standard should be demanded of a person in danger?

7. A similar approach was taken in *Walls* v. *Mussens Ltd. et al.* (1970), 11 D.L.R. (3d) 245 (N.B. C.A.), where the defendant had negligently caused a fire in the plaintiff's garage. Coming upon the fire, the plaintiff joined with the defendant and others in throwing snow on the fire. The plaintiff failed to use an available fire extinguisher, which might have been able to put out the fire. The court ruled that the plaintiff was not contributorily negligent. Hughes J.A. wrote that the test to be employed is "not whether the plaintiff exercised a careful and prudent judgment in doing what he did, but whether what he did was something an ordinarily prudent man might reasonably have done under the stress of the emergency. . . . The plaintiff's reaction to the emergency was merely to do what the others were doing and I cannot say that it was something an ordinarily prudent man might not reasonably have done in the circumstances." See also *Molson* v. *Squamish Transfer Ltd. et al.* (1970), 7 D.L.R. (3d) 553 (B.C. S.C.), *supra*.

8. Such a view was also expressed by Freedman C.J.M. in *Neufeld* v. *Landry* (1975), 55 D.L.R. (3d) 296 (Man. C.A.), an automobile collision case, as follows:

"... The conduct of the plaintiff driver must be assessed in the light of the crisis that was looming up before her. If in the 'agony of the moment' the evasion action she took may not have been as good as some other course of action she might have taken—a doubtful matter at best—we would not characterize her conduct as amounting to contributory negligence. It was the defendant who created the emergency which led to the accident. It does not lie in his mouth to be minutely critical of the reactive conduct of the plaintiff whose safety he had imperilled by his negligence."

9. A passenger jumped out of an amphibious airplane, which had collided with an obstruction while taxiing along the water, and drowned. He failed to wear a lifejacket that was available to him. Contributory negligence? Voluntary assumption of risk? See *Holomis* v. *Dubuc* (1975), 56 D.L.R. (3d) 351 (B.C.).

10. There is still some disagreement about whether the doctrine of last clear chance survived the passage of comparative negligence legislation. There is no doubt that its use has been very much curtailed, but it is not completely dead.

It will still be invoked on rare occasions. See, for example, *McKee* v. *Malenfant*, [1954] S.C.R. 651, [1954] 4 D.L.R. 785; *Sigurdson* v. *B.C. Electric Co. Ltd.*, [1953] A.C. 291, [1952] 4 D.L.R. 1 (P.C.); *Dugas* v. *Le Clair* (1962), 32 D.L.R. (2d) 459 (N.B. C.A.); *Brooks* v. *Ward* (1956), 4 D.L.R. (2d) 597; *Seniunas* v. *Lou's Transport* (1972), 25 D.L.R. (3d) 277 (Ont. H.C.). See also Linden, *Canadian Negligence Law* (1972), p. 354. Newfoundland, Saskatchewan and Alberta enacted legislation stating when the doctrine is to be used.

   Paradoxically, the doctrine has even been used to deny recovery to a claimant. See *Weeks* v. *Cousins* (1964), 44 D.L.R. (2d) 316 (P.E.I.); *Milligan* v. *MacDougall* (1962), 32 D.L.R. (2d) 57 (P.E.I.). It appears, however, that the jury will not be asked a specific question about the doctrine; rather, last clear chance is treated as part of the causation question. See Schroeder, "Courts and Comparative Negligence", [1950] Ins. L.J. 791, at p. 797.

   11. There is a strong movement to eradicate the doctrine altogether from our law, an eventuality which may one day come to pass. See, for example, Laskin J.A. in *R. A. Beamish Stores Co. Ltd.* v. *F. W. Argue, Ltd.*, [1966] 2 O.R. 615 (C.A.); revd. by S.C.C. in *F. W. Argue* v. *Howe* (1969), 3 D.L.R. (3d) 290; Denning L.J. in *Davies* v. *Swan Motor Co. (Swansea) Ltd.*, [1949] 2 K.B. 291, [1949] 1 All E.R. 620 (C.A.); Henderson J.A. in *Gives* v. *C.N.R.*, [1941] 4 D.L.R. 625 (Ont. C.A.). Mr. Justice Dickson has recently expressed his "gravest doubt" that the last opportunity rule has survived the passage of the contributory negligence acts. See *Hartman* v. *Fisette* (1976), 66 D.L.R. (3d) 516 (S.C.C.).

   12. One consistent opponent of the doctrine was the late Malcolm M. MacIntyre, of the University of British Columbia, who waged war on it in the law reviews. In "The Rationale of Last Clear Chance" (1940), 18 Can. Bar Rev. 665, 53 Harv.L.Rev. 1225, also printed in Linden, *Studies in Canadian Tort Law* (1968), p. 160, he wrote:

> "The whole last clear chance doctrine is only a disguised escape, by way of comparative fault, from contributory negligence as an absolute bar, and serves no useful purpose in jurisdictions which have enacted apportionment statutes. The decisions super-imposing last clear chance upon these statutes, though understandable historical accidents resulting from the greater fault meaning which the phrase 'proximate cause' had acquired during the common-law struggle to escape from the contributory negligence bar, add injustice as well as complexity to an already confused *corpus juris*. Had the statutes not been thus hamstrung, they would have provided the means of doing openly and more completely what the courts have been doing unavowedly and incompletely ever since *Davies* v. *Mann*.
>
> Every vestige of last clear chance must be swept away in favour of apportionment. In the meantime, though the path of doctrine be tortuous, one must welcome piecemeal encroachments . . . on decisions retaining last clear chance despite apportionment legislation, even as one welcomed encroachments on *Butterfield* v. *Forrester* by means of the last clear chance doctrine."

Another attack came in MacIntyre, "Last Clear Chance After Thirty Years Under The Apportionment Statutes" (1955), 33 Can. Bar Rev. 257. Should the doctrine be abolished altogether?

McLAUGHLIN v. LONG

Supreme Court of Canada. [1927] S.C.R. 303; [1927] 2 D.L.R. 186

   The infant plaintiff sustained serious injuries while riding on the defendants' motor truck by reason of an accident caused, as alleged, through negligent driving of the truck by the defendants' servant, Rogers. The defendants conducted a bakery in the city of St. John, and delivered a portion of their goods by motor trucks to points outside the city. The accident in question occurred on a road some miles from the city. The truck plunged off the road, and the infant plaintiff, a boy about ten years of age, who was on the running board, was injured by being jammed between the truck and a tree. Another boy, also being given a ride by Rogers, was seated beside the latter in the truck. He was thrown through the roof of the truck by the impact and landed some feet away. Fortunately he sustained only minor cuts and bruises. The car was badly damaged and the windshield shattered. The boy (by his father as next friend) and his father sued the defendants for damages.

The case was tried before Crockett J. with a jury. The following were some of the questions submitted to the jury at the close of the evidence, with the answers thereto:

1. Q. Was there any negligence on the part of the defendants' chauffeur Rogers? A. Yes.

Q. If so, in what did such negligence consist? A. First, in allowing the boy on the running board of the car. Second, lack of proper attention to his duty of driving the car just previous to and at the time of the accident.

2. Q. Was the injury to the infant plaintiff entirely caused by the negligence set out in your answer to question one? A. No.

3. Q. Was the infant plaintiff guilty of any contributory negligence without which the accident would not have happened? A. Yes.

Q. If so, in what did such negligence consist? A. By staying on the car after having been asked to get off, and by standing on the running board of the car when it was moving.

4. Q. If you find there was any contributory negligence on the part of the infant plaintiff, to what degree was he at fault? A. Twenty-five per cent of the amount that otherwise would have been allowed.

5. Q. Was the infant plaintiff on the running board with the permission and consent of Rogers? A. Yes.

On these findings judgment was given the infant plaintiff for $3,000, being 25 per cent less than his proved damages of $4,000. On appeal, this judgment was sustained by the Supreme Court of New Brunswick: [1926] 3 D.L.R. 918. The defendants appealed and the plaintiff cross-appealed.

Anglin C.J.C.: . . . The contributory negligence of the infant plaintiff as found by the jury was "by staying on the car after having been asked to get off, and by standing on the running-board of the car when it was moving". They had already found the driver negligent "in allowing the boy on the running board of the car". The evidence is consistent only with the view that the boy remained on the running board with the tacit consent of the driver . . . .

With the utmost respect, it would appear that in the courts below the application to a charge of contributory negligence of the maxim, *in lege causa proxima, non remota, spectatur*, was not sufficiently adverted to . . . .

In order to constitute contributory negligence it does not suffice that there should be some fault on the part of the plaintiff without which the injury that he complains of would not have been suffered; a cause which is merely a *sine qua non* is not adequate. As in the case of primary negligence charged against the defendant, there must be proof, or at least evidence from which it can reasonably be inferred that the negligence charged was a proximate, in the sense of an effective, cause of such injury. . . .

We are for these reasons of the opinion that there was no evidence to submit to the jury on the issue of contributory negligence . . . .

In our opinion, within the meaning of s. 2 of the Contributory Negligence Act of New Brunswick (1925, c. 41) damage or loss is "caused" by the fault of two or more persons only when the fault of each of such persons is a proximate or efficient cause of such damage or loss, *i.e.*, only when at common law each would properly have been held guilty of negligence which contributed to causing the injurious occurrence: *Canada Pacific Ry. Co.* v. *Frechette*, [1915] A.C. 871, at p. 879. It follows that the Contributory Negligence Act has no application to the case at bar . . . .

The appeal should be dismissed with costs, and the cross-appeal allowed with costs, and judgment should be entered for the [infant] plaintiff for $4,000.

[Duff, Mignault and Rinfret JJ., concurred with Anglin C.J.C. The concurring judgment of Newcombe J. is omitted.]

NOTES

1. In *Jones* v. *Livox Quarries Ltd.*, [1952] 1 T.L.R. 1377, the plaintiff, contrary to express orders of the defendants not to ride on quarry vehicles, had jumped on the back of a "traxcavator" — a vehicle running on tracks at about 2½ m.p.h. A "dumper", with a speed of about 5 m.p.h., driven by a servant of the defendants, ran into the back of the "traxcavator" and crushed the plaintiff. In an action by the plaintiff against defendants the trial judge found negligence on the driver of the "dumper" and contributory negligence on the part of the plaintiff. He found that the plaintiff, in travelling at an improper place ran the risk "of being thrown off . . . that is I think the risk he ran and no other". The trial judge found the plaintiff responsible for one-fifth of his damage, however, and gave judgment in his favour for four-fifths of the proved damages. On appeal, this judgment was sustained. Denning L.J. said that it was admitted that if the plaintiff had been thrown off, his injury would have been partly due to his own negligence. The argument that because he was crushed, instead, his injury was in no way due to his negligence, was "too fine a distinction for me", citing *In re Polemis*. Denning L.J. also commented on the Canadian decision of *McLaughlin* v. *Long*. He said he could not understand the decision and thought it plain "that the boy's negligence was one of the causes of his injury". "The explanation of the decision may be that in 1926 the doctrine of last opportunity was still influential in Canada, as, indeed, it was here at that time. But it is so no longer, at any rate not here." Hodson L.J. said that the danger to which the plaintiff was exposing himself was not only the danger of falling off but of being injured in the way that occurred.

2. In *Smithwick* v. *Hall & Upson Co.* (1890), 59 Conn. 261, 21 Atl. 924 (S.C. Conn.) the plaintiff, an employee of the defendant, while engaged in storing ice in a building, was warned not to go to the east end of a platform on which he was working since it was not safe to stand there. It was not safe because there was no railing and the platform was made slippery by the broken ice. The plaintiff, notwithstanding this warning, went to the east end. Just then a brick wall of the defendant's building gave way in consequence of the defendant's negligence and fell on the plaintiff. The latter was thrown off the platform to the ground sustaining serious injuries. The trial judge reserved the case for the advice of the Supreme Court on the question of contributory negligence.

Torrance J. held that the failure to heed the warning did not constitute contributory negligence. He reasoned as follows:

"Now the act or omission of a party injured which amounts to what is called contributory negligence, must be a negligent act or omission, and in the production of the injury it must operate as a proximate cause or one of the proximate causes, and not merely as a condition.

In the case at bar the conduct of the plaintiff, as we have seen, was, with respect to the danger from the falling wall, not negligent for the want of knowledge or its equivalent on the part of the plaintiff.

Nor was his conduct, legally considered, a cause of the injury. It was a condition rather.

If he had not changed his position he might not have been hurt. And so, too, if he had never been born, or had remained at home on the day of the injury, it would not have happened; yet no one would claim that his birth or his not remaining at home that day, can in any just or legal sense be deemed a cause of the injury.

The court below has found that the plaintiff's fall in the position in which he stood was due to the giving way of the wall, and that most of his injuries were occasioned by the fall. His position there, upon the facts found, can no more be considered as a cause of the injury, than it could be in a case where the defendant, in doing some act near the platform without the plaintiff's knowledge, had negligently knocked him to the ground, or had negligently hit him with a stone. Had the injury been occasioned by a misstep or slip from the platform by the carelessness of the plaintiff, or for the want of a railing, the causal connection between the change of position and the injury would, legally speaking, be quite obvious; but from a legal point of view no such connection exists between the change of position and the giving way of the wall."

3. In *Hansen* v. *"Y" Motor Hotel Ltd.,* [1971] 2 W.W.R. 705 (Alta. C.A.), the plaintiff's expensive mink jacket was stolen from the defendant's cloakroom. The court found that the manager of the premises knew that his clientele would use this facility and his failure to provide supervision of the cloakroom was such negligence as entitled the plaintiff to recover. The court also ruled that the plaintiff was not contributorily negligent in making use of the cloakroom, even though it was unattended. Do you agree?

If the defendant was negligent in failing to foresee the theft, why was the plaintiff not also negligent in exposing her coat to possible thieves?

4. In *Meyer et al.* v. *Hall et al.* (1972), 26 D.L.R. (3d) 309 (Alta. C.A.), a lodge was destroyed by fire when an automobile, that had been negligently parked without the brake on, moved forward and struck a propane bottle which was held to the side of a building by only one steel strap. Although the trial judge had apportioned liability between the lodge-owner and the motorist, the Court of Appeal ruled that the motorist was entirely to blame for the accident. Additional steps to secure the bottle more adequately would have been required "if this type of accident — being run into by a motor vehicle — was so obvious a hazard that it should have been guarded against". There was no need, however, to guard against the "most unusual conduct" of the driver. In the alternative, the court also relied on last clear chance. Does this case make sense?

5. P, while a passenger on the back of a snowmobile driven by another person, falls off and is run over by a second snowmobile that was following too closely. Is P contributorily negligent for failing to tell the driver that he was not safely seated? See *Ainge* v. *Siemon* (1972), 19 D.L.R. (3d) 531 (Ont. H.C.).

6. Should the defence of contributory negligence be available to a defendant who is in violation of a penal statute?

Usually, the defence is available where the defendant violates a statute. In *Graham* v. *R.* (1978), 90 D.L.R. (3d) 223 (Sask. Q.B.), the contributory negligence defence was employed, even though the defendant was in breach of a statute regarding the maintenance of a highway.

In the U.S., however, there is authority that, in certain situations, the defence may be unavailable to a defendant who violates a statute. See *Dart* v. *Pure Oil Co.* (1947), 223 Minn. 326, 27 N.W. 2d 555 outlining some of the exceptional statutes the violation of which may forbid a defendant in the United States from relying on the defence. They include child labour statutes, legislation prohibiting sale of dangerous articles to minors, protecting intoxicated persons, and other similar legislation. See also Prosser, *Contributory Negligence as a Defense to Violation of Statute* (1948), 32 Minn. L. Rev. 105.

There is little evidence that this theory is applied directly in our law, but there is some indication of an indirect influence. See, for example, *Ball* v. *Richard Thomas & Baldwin's Ltd.,* [1968] 1 All E.R. 389 where the plaintiff workman was injured when standing too near a crane. The court held the plaintiff 25 percent at fault. Davies L.J. stated, "when a breach of statutory duty has been found on the part of the employers, it would be wrong to attribute to the injured workman too large a share of the responsibility for his own injury". See also

Adams et al. v. *Dias* (1968), 70 D.L.R. (2d) 1 (S.C.C.) where the Supreme Court of Canada reversed a finding of contributory negligence. Mr. Justice Ritchie stated, "a driver is in no way relieved from the liability which flows from a failure to take reasonable care simply because another user of the highway is driving in such a fashion as to violate the law, but in my opinion, no motorist is required to anticipate, and therefore keep on the look-out for, such an unusual and expected violation as was manifested by the appellant's course of conduct in the present case".

See generally Cronkite, "Effect of the Violation of a Statute by the Plaintiff in a Tort Action" (1929), 7 Can. Bar Rev. 67; Gibson, "Illegality of Plaintiff's Conduct as a Defence" (1969), 47 Can. Bar Rev. 89; Fridman, "The Wrongdoing Plaintiff" (1972), 18 McGill L.J. 275; Weinrib, "Illegality as a Tort Defence" (1976), 26 U.T.L.J. 28; see *infra*, Section D.

Is this defence available in actions for intentional torts? For actions based on trespass? What is meant by the words "fault or negligence" as used in section 4?

In *Hollebone* v. *Barnard*, [1954] O.R. 236, [1954] 2 D.L.R. 278, the plaintiff was struck by a golf ball driven by the defendant. In an action for damages, presented as an action of "trespass", the jury found (1) that the defendant had not satisfied them that the plaintiff's injuries were suffered without negligence on the part of the defendant; (2) that there was contributory negligence on the part of the plaintiff which caused or contributed to his injuries; (3) that the plaintiff's and the defendant's negligence contributed equally to the plaintiff's injuries. The trial judge held that the Ontario Contributory Negligence Act, directing apportionment of damages in proportion to the degree of fault or negligence found against the parties in an action "founded upon the fault or negligence of the defendant", did not apply to an action based on trespass. In his view a plea of contributory negligence had never been a defence to an action of trespass and the Act was confined "to cases arising in negligence". "[This] is not an action which was founded upon the fault or negligence of the defendant. It is in fact an action which is founded on the alleged trespass of the defendant to the person of the plaintiff. That is something entirely different."

The plaintiff, therefore, recovered the full amount of the damages sustained by him.

8. Compare with *Bell Canada* v. *Cope (Sarnia) Ltd.* (1980), 11 C.C.L.T. 170, where Bell was suing the defendant in both negligence and trespass for cutting one of its live service wires. The defendant was unable to show that it did not damage the wire as a result of its negligence or intentional conduct. The defendant, however, did prove that the plaintiff was negligent in the way it staked the underground wires, among other things. Mr. Justice Linden apportioned liability, two-thirds against Bell and one-third against Cope. Linden J. explained as follows:

"Fault and negligence, as these words are used in the Statute, are not the same thing. Fault certainly includes negligence, but it is much broader than that. Fault incorporates all intentional wrongdoing, as well as other types of substandard conduct. In this case, both intentional and negligent wrongdoing were satisfactorily proved.

Our courts today should, where possible, refrain from deciding important substantive questions, such as whether *The Negligence Act* applies here, on the basis of whether the pleading alleges trespass, or negligence, or both. . . .

The gist of the trespass action today is fault; if it can be established by the defendant that there was no negligence and no intentional interference then the action will fail because no fault exists. Consequently, trespass is based on fault and is no longer a strict liability cause of action. (See *Weaver* v. *Ward* (1616), 80 E.R. 284). I find, therefore, that a trespass action comes within the opening words of section 4 of *The Negligence Act*."

Mr. Justice Linden distinguished *Hollebone* v. *Barnard* as a case based *solely* on trespass. He also declared that, since *Hollebone* v. *Barnard* was a decision of a trial Judge, he was 'not strictly bound by it'. In any event, he felt that it was 'based on an erroneous reliance upon certain early authorities dealing with the

scope of the Negligence Act . . .' which had 'no relevance at all in the interpretation of the meaning of the words "fault or negligence" in this context'."
Which approach do you prefer?

COLONIAL COACH LINES LTD. v. BENNETT & C.P.R. CO.

Court of Appeal. (1967), 66 D.L.R. (2d) 396

Laskin J.A.: A cow escaped from the defendant Bennett's farm through a defective fence along the adjoining right of way of the defendant railway. It proceeded along the right of way and then to a highway adjoining the right of way on the other side. At about four o'clock in the morning the cow collided with the plaintiff's motor coach, and as a result it was killed and the motor coach was damaged. The plaintiff sued Bennett and the railway; Bennett counterclaimed against the plaintiff and the railway for the loss of his cow. After the trial before P.J. McAndrew Co.Ct.J. and a jury, the latter found the plaintiff 35 percent at fault; Bennett 5 percent at fault, and the railway 60 percent at fault. The plaintiff's damages were assessed at $3,000 and those of Bennett at $250.

Following the jury's findings, the trial judge acceded to a submission by counsel for the railway, and on the authority of *Gray Coach Lines Ltd.* v. *C.P.R. Co.,* [1951] O.R. 89, [1951] 1 D.L.R. 807, 66 C.R.T.C. 346, a judgment of this court, dismissed the action against it. He then proceeded to apportion the jury-adjudged 60 percent fault of the railway between the other two parties according to the ratio of the fault of each to their total fault. The result was a determination that the plaintiff was 87½ percent at fault and Bennett 12½ percent. The damages found by the jury were apportioned accordingly. Recovery by Bennett on his counterclaim was allowed, however, in terms of the jury's assignment of fault, against both the railway and the plaintiff who, as between themselves, were declared entitled to contribution and indemnity according to their respective degrees of fault so apportioned.

After the trial judge exonerated the railway, the defendant Bennett sought leave to amend or to serve a third party notice in order to claim indemnity from the railway, under a particular construction of s. 392 of the Railway Act, R.S.C. 1952, c. 234, in respect of his liability to the plaintiff. His original claim of indemnity evaporated when the trial judge absolved the railway of any negligence in law, and hence the attempt to found such a claim on statute. The two-year limitation period had expired, and Bennett's application was refused.

An appeal by the plaintiff and a cross-appeal by Bennett were brought to this court. The plaintiff does not contest the finding of negligence against it, but seeks to have the finding against the railway restored. Failing this, it urges that the 35 percent fault attributed to it exhausted its negligence and that the remaining liability was that of the defendants or of each of them *quoad* the plaintiff. Failing acceptance of either submission, it was contended that the case should be remitted to a jury for a proper apportionment between the plaintiff and Bennett, or that, on consent, this be done by the court; and in this connection it was argued that a finding of 5 percent or 12½ percent fault against Bennett was perverse.

Bennett's cross-appeal is from the dismissal of his application to amend to seek "statutory" indemnity and is pressed only if the jury's finding of negligence against the railway is not reinstated.

The principal question that emerges from the course of the trial and the appeal and cross-appeal is the correctness of the trial judge's ruling that the railway owed no duty to the plaintiff either under ss. 277 and 392 of the Railway Act or at common law. . . .

It follows that the jury's finding of fault against the railway should be reinstated. It is appropriate to add as well that as against the plaintiff the defendant Bennett could not limit his liability to 5 percent of the damages suffered by the plaintiff. The Negligence Act, R.S.O. 1960, c. 261, declares, by s. 2(1), the *joint and several* liability of two or more negligent defendants; and if Bennett was the only defendant at fault, he would be liable for all of the plaintiff's damages subject only to diminution to the extent of the latter's contributory fault.

In the result it becomes unnecessary to solve the problem created in this case, by the jury's apportionment of fault and the consequent exoneration of one of the defendants as a matter of assumed law. There would seem, however, to be much merit in the contention that, in the practical administration of a system of apportionment of fault where multiple parties defendant are involved, an assessment of the degree of contributory negligence of a plaintiff should be taken as referable to all or the one only of the defendants found to be at fault with respect to the cause of action sued upon; that is to say a defendant found to be at fault and disappointed in his expectation of having a co-defendant share, as between themselves, a portion of the liability to an injured plaintiff may well be disentitled to shift additional blame to a plaintiff who has been already fixed with a percentage of fault.

I would allow the plaintiff's appeal, set aside the judgment below so far as it relates to the defendants' liability to the plaintiff, and in its place direct judgment for the plaintiff against the defendants for 65 percent of its damages; the defendants, as between themselves, shall be liable to the plaintiff according to the degrees of fault assessed against them by the jury. The plaintiff is entitled to its costs of the appeal against the defendant railway, and to the costs of the trial on the County Court scale against both defendants who, as between themselves, will bear them according to their respective degrees of fault. The plaintiff's success makes it unnecessary to deal with the defendant Bennett's crossappeal, and I would dismiss it without costs. There should be no costs to or against Bennett in respect of the plaintiff's appeal.

> *Appeal allowed;*
> *cross-appeal dismissed.*

NOTES

1. There are some extremely complicated procedural and mathematical problems arising out of apportionment legislation, which cannot be dealt with here in any depth. In addition to the principal case, see *Lecomte* v. *Bell Telephone*, [1932] 3 D.L.R. 220 (Ont.); *Nesbitt* v. *Beattie*, [1955] O.R. 111, [1955] 2 D.L.R. 91, and compare *Catt* v. *Coveyduck*, [1950] O.W.N. 176. In one recent case, a jury attributed 10 percent of the blame to the defendant, 15 percent to one of the plaintiffs and 75 percent to no one. (See *Houle* v. *B.C. Hydro* (1972), 29 D.L.R. (3d) 510). Can this be? See generally Williams, *Joint Torts and Contributory Negligence* (1951); Gregory, *Legislative Loss Distribution in Negligence Actions* (1936); Schwartz, *Comparative Negligence* (1974). See Klar, "Contributory Negligence and Contribution between Tortfeasors", in Klar (ed.), *Studies in Canadian Tort Law* (1977); Cheyfetz, *Apportionment of Damages Under The Ontario Negligence Act* (1980). See also Chapter 8 on Causation, Section B. Multiple Causes.

2. Dean Wright, in the "Adequacy of the Law of Torts", [1961] Camb. L.J. 44, reprinted in Linden, *Studies in Canadian Tort Law* (1968), wrote: "On the basis of extending liability, everyone welcomed the statutory innovations of the Contributory Negligence Acts. For reasons in this and the following section I

must confess that I have lost some of my original enthusiasm. It is possible that such Acts may result in a serious curtailment of insurance company liability unless attention is paid to the realities of motor-car litigation rather than the common law formalities. Assume that A's and B's cars collide, and A sustains $10,000 damage and B $4,000; in an action with counterclaim both drivers are found equally at fault, and we have a judgment of *A* v. *B* for $5,000 and of *B* v. *A* for $2,000. If, as many Canadian courts do, we set these judgments off, one against the other, as if they were truly personal actions between A and B, it would appear that $3,000 only would be paid by B's insurance company and $11,000 absorbed individually by the parties out of an accident in which there was available insurance, sufficient to cover the total loss of $14,000. It can and has been argued that if we had not 'reformed' our law, a jury might have found at least $10,000 in favour of A or $4,000 in favour of B. It is true that some courts do not set off these judgments. This is an open recognition of the fact that the true parties are not A and B but the two insurance companies. In that event, of course, B's insurance company will pay A the $5,000 and A's insurance company will pay B the $2,000. This is a desirable practice, but in view of the lack of uniformity we have another uncertainty which, in the hands of skilled insurance counsel, leads to settlements discounted by this and other uncertainties."

3. In *Wells* v. *Russell*, [1952] O.W.N. 521, the plaintiff and the defendant motorists collided and the plaintiff brought action for damages; the defendant counterclaimed for damages. At the trial the plaintiff proved damages of $917; the defendant proved damages of $1,350. The trial judge found that both drivers were equally at fault. The operative parts of the formal judgment entered read as follows: "The plaintiff will be entitled to recover $458.50 and the defendant (plaintiff by counterclaim) will recover the sum of $675 and the parties will be entitled to a set-off; 2. This Court doth order and adjudge that the defendant do pay the plaintiff his costs of this action forthwith after taxation thereof; 3. This Court doth further order and adjudge that the plaintiff do pay to the defendant the sum of $216.50; 4. And this Court doth further order and adjudge that the plaintiff do pay to the defendant his costs of the counterclaim forthwith after taxation thereof." The plaintiff appealed from this order contending that a set-off should not have been ordered but that the plaintiff should have been given judgment for $458.50 and the defendant a judgment for $675. Counsel for the defendant supported this appeal, but it was opposed by counsel representing an insurance company subrogated to the rights of the defendant. The Court of Appeal allowed the appeal by varying the judgment to award the plaintiff $458.50 and costs, and to the defendant a judgment of $675 and costs. Laidlaw J.A. pointed out that while it might be convenient to issue judgment in the form adopted here, it was not in accordance with practice, and that the claim and counterclaim were separate actions requiring a judgment in each.

4. In *Lewenza* v. *Ruszezak*, [1960] O.W.N. 40, in an action brought by one motorist against another who made a claim by counterclaim, the plaintiff recovered judgment for $145 and the defendants for $50. Subsequently, the defendants moved to set-off the amount owing to them on the counter-claim against the amount owing by them on the claim. The plaintiff opposed the motion on the ground that he was insured against collision, with a $100 deductible clause, and as his insurer was subrogated to his rights, a portion of the amount due him was due and owing the insurer, who would be deprived of his rights if the set-off were permitted. The order for set-off was made. On appeal, the Court of Appeal reversed this order. The equitable rule of set-off was not applicable for lack of mutuality between the two debts. The order was contrary to principle and authority, as indicated in *Wells* v. *Russell, supra*. In actions of this character insurers frequently had an interest in the recovery made by one or some of the parties, and their rights might be defeated if there should be a departure from recognized practice. *Cf. Schellenberg* v. *Cooks* (1960), 25 D.L.R.

(2d) 607 (Sask.); *Johnny's Taxi* v. *Ostoforoff* (1962), 33 D.L.R. (2d) 85 (Sask. C.A.).

LINDEN & SOMMERS, THE CIVIL JURY IN THE COURTS OF ONTARIO: A POSTCRIPT TO THE OSGOODE HALL STUDY

(1968), 6 Osgoode Hall L.J. 252, at p. 254

THE RESULT OF TRIALS

Critics of the civil jury charge that it is biased in favour of the plaintiff and, consequently, the defendants do not get a fair hearing. This allegation is not borne out by the facts. Table I shows that, although the jury decided wholly in favour of the plaintiff in 48.6 percent of the cases studied, the trial judges alone found completely in the plaintiffs favour 71.7 percent of the time, indicating a more marked inclination on the part of judges to favour the plaintiff, contrary to what has been charged. When one studies the dismissals, however, this trend is modified, for judges alone tended to dismiss law suits more readily than juries did; judges exonerated the defendant in 18.8 percent of the cases, while juries did so only in 2.7 percent of the cases they decided.

Table 1

THE RESULT OF JURY TRIALS COMPARED WITH NON-JURY TRIALS

Type of Case	For Plaintiff Wholly		Apportionment Plaintiff 1–50% At Fault		Apportionment Plaintiff 51–99% At Fault		Case Dismissed		Total	
	No.	%	No.	%	No.	%	No.	%	No.	%
Jury	18	48.6	11	29.7	7	18.9	1	2.7	37	99.9
Non-jury	38	71.7	3	5.6	2	3.7	10	18.8	53	99.8

It is in the treatment of contributory negligence that one of the main distinctions between judge and jury trial is demonstrated; judges rarely apportion negligence, whereas juries do so frequently. Liability was split in 48.6 percent of the jury trials, but only in 9.3 percent of the judge trials. This indicates that judges have hardly taken notice of the comparative negligence legislation which permits liability to be divided, feeling themselves able to decide completely one way or the other on the facts. The jury is less confident of its own powers and chooses rather to divide responsibility between the two parties, a practice that may well accord better with the true position with regard to blameworthiness. This willingness on the part of juries to reduce the awards of plaintiffs shows a lack of bias on their part. As another consequence, however, plaintiffs before juries receive some reparation in 97.2 percent of the decisions, while those before judges do in 81 percent of the cases. This indicates that the jury system does in fact assist to broaden the incidence of tort recovery, but these payments are often reduced in amount because of comparative negligence. Indeed, if the jury trial were jettisoned, the laudable objective of the Negligence Act would be severely undermined, since judges seem so reluctant to avail themselves of it.

NOTES

1. The Report of The Osgoode Hall Study on Compensation for Victims of Automobile Accidents demonstrated that 43 percent of the personal injury victims studied received some tort recovery while in Michigan only 37 percent recovered. See Conard *et al.*, *Automobile Accident Costs & Payments* (1964). This was so even though there was no absolute bar against guest passengers in Michigan as there was at the time in Ontario. Of what relevance is comparative negligence legislation to these results? See Rosenberg, "Comparative Negligence in Arkansas: A 'Before and After' Survey" in *Dollars, Delay and the Automobile* (1968), p. 187.

2. Overall satisfaction with our comparative negligence legislation has been expressed by Mr. Justice Schroeder in these words:

". . . the change effected by our statute was more consonant with the modern needs and concepts of society in a changing world, and better adpated to the requirements and habits of the age in which we live; . . . the doctrines established long before the days of the steam engine, the incandescent lamp, the modern automobile and the jet-propelled airplane, no longer served to promote the welfare of the members of our modern society and needed to be replaced by a law which was better adjusted to the increasing complexities of the daily routine and the greater tempo of life in our day and generation".

He concluded that there is not "a progressive and socially conscious member of the judiciary or of the bar of our province who would wish to repeal the legislation . . . and return to the discarded common-law doctrine of contributory negligence". See "Courts and Comparative Negligence", [1950] Ins. L.J. 791. *Cf.* Davie, *Common Law and Statutory Amendment in Relation to Contributory Negligence in Canada* (1936), reviewed by MacDonald (1936), 14 Can. Bar Rev. 368.

B. THE SEAT BELT DEFENCE

YUAN ET AL. v. FARSTAD ET AL.

British Columbia Supreme Court. (1967), 66 D.L.R. (2d) 295

The deceased was killed and his wife, a passenger, was injured when their vehicle was struck by the defendant's automobile. The defendant was found 100 percent at fault for the collision. The deceased was not wearing the seat belt that was available in his car. His wife had no belt available to her. The court found that, if the deceased had worn the belt, he would have been hurt but he would not have been fatally injured because he would not have hit the steering wheel as violently nor would he have been thrown out of the car.

Munroe J.:

Seat Belt Defence – Contributory Negligence

The defendants submit too, that the deceased was guilty of contributory negligence in that he failed to use the driver's lap seat belt with which his car was equipped. It is not suggested that such failure contributed to the cause of the collision but, rather, that such failure contributed to the injuries sustained by the deceased and to the loss and damages sustained by the plaintiffs herein. Section 2 of the Contributory Negligence Act, R.S.B.C. 1960, c. 74, enacts as follows:

2. Where by the fault of two or more persons damage or loss is caused to one or more of them, the liability to make good the damage or loss shall be in proportion to the degree in which each person was at fault, except that

(*a*) if, having regard to all the circumstances of the case, it is not possible to establish different degrees of fault, the liability shall be apportioned equally; and

(*b*) nothing in this section shall operate so as to render any person liable for any damage or loss to which his fault has not contributed.

It is the submission of the defendants that the deceased, by his failure to use his seat belt, failed to use reasonable care or to take proper precautions for his own safety and thereby contributed to his own injuries. If that is so, the defence of contributory negligence must succeed. [Citations omitted.]

In support of such submission the defendants called as witnesses Captain E.T. Corning, retired captain of the Seattle Police Force, and Dr. Peter Fisher, a Seattle physician and surgeon and specialist in internal medicine. Each of these men has made a study of the effectiveness of seat belts in safeguarding motorists from injuries. Their qualifications and experience entitle them to give opinion evidence. Captain Corning has investigated hundreds of automobile accidents. Based upon his experience and studies, he is firmly of opinion that lap seat belts, when worn, do tend to lessen the severity of injuries in most automobile accidents. Based upon personal observations made at race tracks as well as other studies made by him, Dr. Fisher is of opinion that a lap seat belt will prevent ejection from a vehicle and will lessen the severity of any steering wheel injury because it prevents body displacement. While a lap seat belt has the capability of causing serious abdominal injury, such injury, he said, is so rare as to be improbable and in any case, is correctible by surgery. He concluded that in most cases the injury resulting from failure to use a seat belt is greater than any injury likely to be caused by use thereof. Based upon the evidence of these two experts, which was uncontroverted, and based upon the general knowledge of mankind, it is clear, and I find, that lap seat belts are effective in reducing fatilities and minimizing injuries resulting from automobile accidents. I adopt the view of Mr. Justice Frankfurter who once said, "there comes a point where this court should not be ignorant as judges of what we know as men".

Can a person reasonably anticipate that when driving his car in a city he may be involved in a collision? The answer to that question, I think, must be in the affirmative. That being so, such a person must use reasonable care and take proper precautions for his own safety and such precautions include the use of an available seat belt. It was the practice of the deceased, like so many motorists, to fasten his seat belt when driving upon high speed highways outside the city but not to use the belt when driving within the city, despite common knowledge that collisions between motor vehicles occur almost daily within the city and that avoidable injuries occur when drivers and passengers are thrust forward by the force of the impact and sometimes are ejected from the car. In the face of such knowledge, and despite the apparent absence of any Canadian precedents upon the matter, I am of opinion that a reasonable and prudent driver of a motor vehicle in a city would and should make use of a seat belt provided for his use. I am not unmindful of the fact that in driving without having his seat belt done up, the deceased was committing neither a crime nor any breach of statute. He was lawfully entitled to drive without using his seat belt, but that is not determinative of the issue as to whether or not in so doing he failed to take proper precautions for his safety and thus contributed to his injuries. If he did so fail the defendants are entitled to be relieved of some degree of responsibility for the resulting injuries, as is provided by the Contributory Negligence Act. I do not say that in British Columbia a motorist commits any breach of the law when he fails to use a seat belt. I say only that where a motorist fails to use an available seat belt and where it is shown that the injuries sustained by him would probably have been avoided or of less severity had he been wearing a seat belt, then the provisions of s. 2 of the Contributory Negligence Act are applicable. Since s. 206 of the Motor-vehicle Act was enacted [1966, c. 30, s. 347], all cars manufactured since December 31, 1963, must be equipped with not less than two seat belts for use in the front seat. Such enactment, while it does not make mandatory the wearing of seat belts, does give some legislative sanction to the wearing of same. Although, as I have said, no Canadian authorities were cited to me, the Appeal Court of Wisconsin in *Bentzler* v. *Braun* (1967), 34 Wis. (2d) 362, 149 N.W. 2d 626, being of opinion that a person is safer wearing a seat belt than without one, found a duty, based on common law standards of ordinary care, to use an available seat belt and held that when a causal relationship is shown between the failure to wear a seat belt and the injuries sustained, the jury should be instructed in this regard. So, too, the Appeal Court of California in *Mortensen* v. *Southern Pacific Co.* (1966), 53 Cal. Rptr. 851, held that even where there was no statute which made the installation of belts mandatory, it was a question for the jury to decide whether the defendant's failure to provide seat belts for its employees amounted to negligence.

Having found that the defendant driver was guilty of negligence which was the sole cause of the collision, and that the deceased was guilty of negligence which contributed to his own injuries, it remains to apportion the fault between them, as provided by s. 5 of the Contributory Negligence Act. I apportion such fault 75 percent upon the defendant driver, and 25 percent upon the deceased. The major share of the fault must, I think, be attributed to the defendant driver because notwithstanding the fault of the deceased, the fact remains that he would still be uninjured and alive were it not for the negligence of the defendant driver in causing the collision.

The defence of contributory negligence does not avail against Mrs. Yuan because no causal relationship has been shown between her failure to wear a seat belt and the injuries sustained by her, and because no seat belt was available to her. The Rambler was equipped with two seat belts, one for use by the driver, and one for use by a passenger in the front seat. At the time of the accident, there were two passengers lawfully riding in the front seat; for one of them, no seat belt was available. Seated in the middle it would have been impracticable if not impossible for Mrs. Yuan to use the belt, in view of its position.

NOTES

1. In *McDonnell* v. *Kaiser* (1968), 68 D.L.R. (2d) 104 (N.S.S.C.) Mr. Justice Dubinsky refused to apply the seat belt defence, because (1) it was not pleaded and (2) because he did not believe that he should. His Lordship stated:

"The contention that failure to wear a seat belt constitutes contributory negligence *per se* does not appeal to me. My reading on the subject convinces me that the effectiveness of seat belts is still in the realm of speculation and controversy. In the case before me this defence was not pleaded. I cannot foretell what future cases will present and whether or not the particular circumstances and skilled expert testimony will be such as to warrant revised thinking. What, if anything, will the legislature do on this point? For the time being, there is too much indecision about the matter even among experts. . . . I am not prepared to accept, at this stage, the suggestion that a motorist who drives carefully and lawfully should be stamped with the mark of carelessness, that he has not discharged his duty as a reasonable man, simply because he has not fastened to his person the seat belt. Most people know the true reasons for the slaughter on the highways."

Do you prefer *Yuan* v. *Farstad* or *McDonnell* v. *Kaiser?* Which rule would serve tort law's goal of compensation better? Which one would encourage safe driving? Which one would be more likely to foster the use of seat belts? See Note, (1968), 14 McGill L.J. 332.

2. See Kleist, "Seat Belt Defence — An Exercise in Sophistry" (1967), 18 Hastings L.J. 613, upon which Mr. Justice Dubinsky relied:

" 'Following a collision, no doctor can say exactly what injuries would have been suffered if the victim had worn a seat belt, as compared to those incurred without one. There are too many unknown variables in any given accident to permit a precise answer to this question. The problem is further complicated when one considers the effect of these forces in conjunction with the positions of potential obstacles such as dashknobs, directional-signal levers, etc.

Under such circumstances it does violence to one's sense of justice to say that the innocent injured victim must bear the risk of a wrong guess. It is, therefore, not surprising that the law has not yet placed upon the plaintiff a *duty* to wear seat belts.

. . .

'There is a basic legal fallacy to the seat belt "defence". It fails to take into account the established rule that a motorist has a right to assume that others upon the highway will obey the traffic laws; he need not take protective measures against the mere possibility of some future negligent act by another.

The logic of the seat belt reasoning can be extended indefinitely, and various ridiculous conclusions envisioned. Would not a motorist be guilty of contributory negligence for failing to wear a shoulder harness? for failing to wear a crash helmet? for failing to drive in an armored car? for failing to utilize all of these protective devices simultaneously? If not, why not? They follow the reasoning advanced in the seat belt "defence". As protective measures, they are certainly as valuable as the use of seat belt.' "

Are you frightened by the parade of horribles mooted by the author? What would be so terrible about being expected to wear a helmet, for example, if it can be shown that many lives could be saved thereby? See also Roethe, "Seat Belt Negligence in Automobile Accidents," [1967] Wis. L. Rev. 288; Linden, "Seat Belts and Contributory Negligence" (1971), 49 Can. Bar Rev. 475; Linden, *Canadian Tort Law* (2nd ed., 1977), p. 416 for a discussion and further references; Hicks, "Seat Belts and Crash Helmets" (1974), 37 Mod. L. Rev. 308; K. Williams, "Seat Belts—Contributory Negligence—Position of English Courts" (1975), 53 Can. Bar Rev. 113.

3. There are a few other cases now where courts have applied the seat belt defence. For example, in *Jackson* v. *Millar*, [1972] 2 O.R. 197, revd. on another point, [1973] 1 O.R. 399 (C.A.) revd. on another point [1976] 1 S.C.R. 225 (S.C.C.), a 16-year-old unbuckled passenger was ejected from a vehicle while it was making some rather violent gyrations, caused by the gross negligence of the driver, another youth of 16. At trial Mr. Justice Osler found that there was a seat belt that was in working order available to the plaintiff in the front passenger seat and that he was aware of this. Nevertheless, he did not choose to avail himself of it. Moreover, at the time of the accident he was slouched against the right-hand front door. The court concluded that "if Jackson had remained within the car he would not have suffered the injuries he received", which injuries were caused "principally, if not entirely, by coming into contact with the ground after separating from the automobile". Despite the absence of expert evidence concerning the efficacy of seat belts, His Lordship felt that the facts proven entitled him to find contributory negligence. He explained:

"As a matter of law, therefore, I find that his injuries were contributed to by his own negligence which consisted of failure to make use of a readily available seat belt at a time when he deliberately chose to rest a portion of his weight upon the car door. In the event that the automobile should be subjected to any sort of violent force, these acts and omissions on Jackson's part were such as to ensure the probability of ejection from the car, the very event that occurred."

Mr. Justice Osler allocated 10 percent of the blame to the plaintiff and 90 percent to the defendant. On appeal, Mr. Justice Evans, on this point, stated simply: "I am prepared to accept the conclusion of the trial judge with respect to the finding of contributory negligence on the part of the infant plaintiff." There was no appeal on this point to the Supreme Court.

4. See also *Pasternack* v. *Poulton*, [1973] 2 All E.R. 74 (Q.B. Div.), where an unbelted plaintiff was held 5% responsible for her injuries. His Honour, Judge Kenneth Jones Q.C. refused to follow *MacDonell* v. *Kaiser* and explained that "the factors influencing the advisability of using seat belts . . . were different [in 1971] from what they had been . . . in 1968 or even earlier in 1964". His Honour concluded that the plaintiff "acting reasonably" should have foreseen that "by wearing a seat belt [she] would suffer no, or certainly less, injury if the car were involved in an accident". And see also, *Geier* v. *Kujawa*, [1970] 1 Ll. R. 364: *Haley* v. *Richardson* (1975), 10 N.B.R. (2d) 653 (C.A.).

5. Denning M.R. has placed his stamp of approval on the seat belt defence in *Froom* v. *Butcher*, [1975] 3 All E.R. 520 (C.A.) where he said:

"The cause of the damage

In these seat belt cases, the injured plaintiff is in no way to blame for the accident itself. Sometimes he is an innocent passenger sitting beside a negligent driver who goes off the road. At other times he is an innocent driver of one car which is run into by the bad driving of another car which pulls out on to its wrong side of the road. It may well be asked: why should the injured plaintiff have his damages reduced? The accident was solely caused by the negligent driving by the defendant. Sometimes outrageously bad driving. It should not lie in his mouth to say: "You ought to have been wearing a seat belt.' . . .

I do not think that is the correct approach. The question is not what was the cause of the accident. It is rather what was the cause of the damage. In most accidents on the road the bad driving, which causes the accident, also causes the ensuing damage. But in seat belt cases the cause of the accident is one thing. The cause of the damage is another. The *accident* is caused by the bad driving. The *damage* is caused in part by the bad driving of the defendant, and in part by the failure of the plaintiff to wear a seat belt. If the plaintiff was to blame in not wearing a seat belt, the damage is in part the result of his own fault. He must bear some share in the responsibility for the damage and his damages fall to be reduced to such extent as the court thinks just and equitable. . . .

The sensible practice

It is compulsory for every motor car to be fitted with seat belts for the front seats. The regulations so provide. They apply to every motor car registered since 1st 1965. In the regulations seat belts are called, in cumbrous language, 'body-restraining seat belts.' A 'seat belt' is defined as 'a belt intended to be worn by a person in a vehicle and designed to prevent or lessen injury to its wearer in the event of an accident to the vehicle . . .'

Seeing that it is compulsory to fit seat belts, Parliament must have thought it sensible to wear them. But it did not make it compulsory for anyone to wear a seat belt. Everyone is free to wear it or not, as he pleases. Free in this sense, that if he does not wear it, he is free from any penalty by the magistrates. Free in the sense that everyone is free to run his head against a brick wall, if he pleases. He can do it if he likes without being punished by the law. But it is not a sensible thing to do. If he does it, it is his own fault; and he has only himself to thank for the consequences.

Much material has been put before us about the value of wearing a seat belt. It shows quite plainly that everyone in the front seats of a car should wear a seat belt. Not only on long trips, but also on short ones. Not only in the town, but also in the country. Not only when there is fog, but also when it is clear. Not only by fast drivers, but also by slow ones. Not only on motorways, but also on side roads. On 15th November 1974 the Minister of Transport said in the House of Commons:

'In 1973, 41,000 people were killed or seriously injured in the front seats of cars and light vans. I estimate that a thousand of these deaths and nearly 13,000 serious injuries could have been avoided by the wearing of seat belts . . . In a frontal crash the car stops very rapidly, but the occupants continue to move forward and strike the part of the car in front of them, frequently causing injuries to the head. Quite often they are ejected through the windscreen. Careful study of accident types and injuries led to the estimate that the risk of death or injury is reduced by 50% if a seat belt is worn.'

This material confirms the provision of the Highway Code which contains this advice: 'Fit seat belts in your car and make sure they are always used.' This advice has been in the Highway Code since 1968, and should have been known to Mr. Froom at the time of his accident in November 1972.

The Road Traffic 1972 says that a failure to observe that provision does not render a person liable to criminal proceedings of any kind, but it can be relied on in civil proceedings as tending to establish or negative liability: see s 37(5). Sir George Baker P. in *Freeborn* v. *Thomas* made a comment on the provision about seat belts. He said: '[It] says nothing about passengers, nor does it say "You must always wear a seat belt." It is, if anything, an exhortation to the driver or the owner.' I think that Sir George Baker P. construed the code too narrowly. The Highway Code is a guide for all persons who use the road. 'Make sure they are always used' is sound advice, not only for drivers, but also for passengers.

The government's view is also plain. During the years 1972 to 1974 they spent £2½ million in advertisements telling people to wear seat belts. Very recently a bill was introduced into Parliament seeking to make it compulsory. In this respect England is following the example of Australia, where it has been compulsory for the last three or four years. The bill here has been delayed. So it will not be compulsory yet awhile. But, meanwhile, I think the judges should say plainly that it is the sensible practice for all drivers and passengers in front seats to wear seat belts whenever and wherever going by car. It is a wise precaution which everyone should take."

As for the share of responsibility to be attributed to the unbelted plaintiff, Denning M.R. advised:

"The share of responsibility

Whenever there is an accident, the negligent driver must bear by far the greater share of responsibility. It was his negligence which caused the accident. It also was a prime cause of the whole of the damage. But insofar as the damage might have been avoided or lessened by wearing a seat belt, the injured person must bear some share. But how much should this be? Is it proper to enquire whether the driver was grossly negligent or only slightly negligent? or whether the failure to wear a seat belt was entirely inexcusable or almost forgivable? If such an enquiry could easily be undertaken, it might be as well to do it. In *Davies* v. *Swan Motor Co.* we said that consideration should be given not only to the causative potency of a particular factor, but also its blameworthiness. But we live in a practical world. In most of these cases the liability of the driver is admitted; the failure to wear a seat belt is admitted; the only question is: what damages should be payable? This question should not be prolonged by an expensive enquiry into the degree of blameworthiness on either side, which would be hotly disputed. Suffice it to assess a share of responsibility which will be just and equitable in the great majority of cases.

Sometimes the evidence will show that the failure made no difference. The damage would have been the same, even if a seat belt had been worn. In such cases the damages should not be reduced at all. At other times the evidence will show that the failure made all the difference. The damage would have been prevented altogether if a seat belt had been worn. In such cases I would suggest that the damages should be reduced by 25 per cent. But often enough the evidence will only show that the failure made a considerable difference. Some injuries to the head, for instance, would have been a good deal less severe if a seat belt had been worn, but there would still have been some injury to the head. In such case I would suggest that the damages attributable to the failure to wear a seat belt should be reduced by 15 per cent.

Conclusion

Everyone knows, or ought to know, that when he goes out in a car he should fasten the seat belt. It is so well known that it goes without saying, not only for the driver, but also the passenger. If either the dirver or the passenger fails to wear it and an accident happens—and the injuries would have been prevented or lessened if he had worn it—then his damages should be reduced. Under the Highway Code a driver may have a duty to invite his passenger to fasten his seat belt, but adult passengers possessed of their faculties should not need telling what to do. If such passengers do not fasten their seat belts, their own lack of care for their own safety may be the cause of their injuries. In the present case the injuries to the head and chest would have been prevented by the wearing of a seat belt and the damages on that account might be reduced by 25 per cent. The finger would have been broken anyway and the damages for it not reduced at all. Overall the judge suggested 20 per cent and Mr. Froom has made no objection to it. So I would not interfere.

I would allow the appeal and reduce the damages by £100."

See also *Ulveland* v. *Marini* (1970), 4 C.C.L.T. 102 (B.C.), where a 15% deduction was made against a passenger who wore a lap belt but neglected to fasten the shoulder harness which was available.

6. An admirable summary of the predominant view on this issue has been given by Fulton J. in *Gagnon* v. *Beaulieu*, [1977] 1 W.W.R. 702 (B.C.) as follows:

"(a) Failure, while travelling in a motor vehicle on a street or highway, to wear a seat belt or any part thereof as provided in a vehicle in accordance with the safety standards from time to time applicable is failure to take a step which a person knows or ought to know to be reasonably necessary for his own safety.

(b) If in such circumstances he suffers injury as the result of the vehicle being involved in an accident, and if it appears from the evidence that if the seat belt had been worn the injuries would have been prevented or the severity thereof lessened, then the failure to wear a seat belt is negligence which has contributed to the nature and extent of those injuries.

(c) In the case of this particular form of contributory negligence, the onus is on the defendant to satisfy the court, in accordance with the usual standard of proof, not only that the seat belt was not worn but also that the injuries would have been prevented or lessened if the seat belt had been worn. The court should not find the second of these facts merely by inference from the first, even if that has been established."

His Lordship reduced the damages by 25% in a case where the plaintiff was thrown out of the vehicle.

7. Some courts continue to resist the use of the seat belt defence. One eloquent refusal to employ it was articulated by Sirois J. In *Reineke* v. *Weisgerber et al.,* [1974] 3 W.W.R. 97 (Sask. Q.B.):

"The seat belt, harness and head rest age is still in its infancy. While . . . [those] involved in automobile safety have learned a great deal during the past few years, . . . they still have a long row to hoe before the dust has settled and the public are apprised of what is best in this regard. There have been terrible accidents of which amazingly enough unrestrained people were fortunate enough to walk away from unscathed. And then at the opposite end of the spectrum a fatality may result from a relatively minor collision. I have no doubt that with the number of motor vehicle accidents constantly increasing, with the tempo of research on the upswing, and with ever solicitous legislators always on their guard to do more things "gratuitously" for an ever increasing number of people who cannot think for themselves anymore, legislation will soon come to pass making the wearing of safety gear in vehicles compulsory. However perhaps the remedy lies not *after* something has happened but rather before it has been initiated — such as being more careful in the issuing of operators' licences for one thing. The old saying that an ounce of prevention is worth a pound of cure still makes sense in this area as well as in others. Having said earlier that no final consensus has yet been reached by the research people in the field of automobile safety, the proposition that a person driving down the highway on the proper side of the road is entitled to assume that other persons using the highway will obey the laws of the road still appeals to one and it is not negligence not to strap oneself in a seat like a dummy, a robot or an astronaut."

See also *O'Brien* v. *Covin* (1974), 19 N.S.R. (2d) 659, *per* Hart J. Most of the other cases refusing to apply the seat belt defence are based on a lack of convincing evidence in the case. See *Dame Lynch* v. *Grant,* [1966] Cour supérieure (C.S.) 479 (Que.); *Anders* v. *Sim* (1970), 11 D.L.R. (3d) 366 (Alta.); *Van Spronsen* v. *Gawor,* [1971] 2 O.R. 729 (Colter C.C.J.); *Hunt* v. *Schwanke,* [1972] 2 W.W.R. 541 (Alta. S.C.); *Rigler* v. *Miller* (1972), 26 D.L.R. (3d) 366 (B.C.S.C.); *Dover* v. *Gooddy* (1972), 29 D.L.R. (3d) 639 (P.E.I.S.C.); *Heppell* v. *Irving Oil Co. Ltd.* (1973), 40 D.L.R. (3d) 476 (N.B.C.A.), (defence not pleaded and evidence not showing that injuries would have been less); *Brown* v. *Rafus* (1969), 8 D.L.R. (3d) 649 (N.S.); *Earl* v. *Bourdon* (1975), 65 D.L.R. (3d) 646 (B.C.); *Beaver* v. *Crowe* (1975), 49 D.L.R. (3d) 114 (N.S.)

8. What if the unbelted passenger is unaware of the presence of a seat belt in the vehicle? What if he should reasonably be aware that a belt is there to be used? See *Haley* v. *Richardson* (1975), 10 N.B.R. (2d) 653, at p. 667 (C.A.) *per* Hughes C.J. Is there an obligation on the driver to advise a passenger to wear his seat belt? See *Beaver* v. *Crowe* (1975), 49 D.L.R. (3d) 114 (N.S.).

9. For several years now Canadian legislation has required seat belts for all passengers on all new vehicles sold in Canada as well as a buzzer system which activates when someone does not buckle up.

10. Actually, there is really no dispute among the experts on the value of seat belts in reducing the number and severity of injuries and death. Virtually all agree that they will help in most cases.

In a recent article, Dr. Hodson-Walker, "The Value of Safety Belts: A Review" (1970), 102 Can. Med. Ass. J. 391 surveyed the medical literature and prepared the following table:

TABLE II

Reduction in major and fatal injuries by the use of seat-belts

Authors	No. of injuries studied	Percentage reduction
Tourin and Garrett	9717	35
Backstrom	712	50
Moreland	121	55
Lister and Milsom	893	67
Lindgren And Warg	382	69
Herbert	not stated	80
Gikas and Huelke	79	45
Kihlberg and Robinson	1302	59

He concludes that safety belts reduce the risk of major or fatal injuries by nearly 60 percent. An incidence of abdominal trauma of the order of .5 percent is ascribed to seat belts. However, "they have never been shown to worsen injury and, while themselves producing injuries, they have prevented more serious ones".

11. As one might expect, there are conflicting decisions in the United States over the use of the seat belt defence. See *Bentzler* v. *Braun* (1967), 149 N.W. 2d 626 (Wis.) (*dictum* in favour); *cf. Miller* v. *Miller* (1968), 160 S.E. 2d 65 (N.C.); *Romankewiz* v. *Black* (1969), 167 N.W. 2d 606 (Mich.). One good reason for refusing to invoke the seat belt defence in the United States is the lack of comparative negligence legislation which would require the dismissal of an action by an unbelted plaintiff, rather than merely a reduction in his recovery. This would clearly be too harsh a result. Moreover, some legislatures in the United States have specifically enacted that a failure to use belts shall not be deemed contributory negligence (*e.g.,* Minn., Tenn., Va.).

12. A few jurisdictions have mandated seat belt use with amazing success in reducing the tragic loss of life and limb among their people. Australia has been a pioneer in this regard. The state of Victoria, for example, enacted the Motor Car (Safety) Act, 1970, No. 8074, s. 31 B(1) which says: A person shall not be seated in a motor car, that is in motion, in a seat for which a safety belt is provided unless he is wearing the safety belt and it is properly adjusted and securely fastened. Penalty $20.

13. The Province of Ontario has enacted legislation requiring the use of seat belts, which came into force on January 1, 1976. Section 63(a) of The Highway Traffic Act, as amended, now requires "every person who drives on a highway, a motor vehicle in which a seat belt assembly is provided for the driver, shall wear the complete seat belt assembly in a properly adjusted and securely fastened manner" (s. 63(a)(3)). This obligation is also placed on passengers as well (s. 63 (a)(4)). Drivers are forbidden from driving the vehicle if their youthful passengers (between 2 and 16) are not wearing their seat belts (s. 63(a)(6)). An exception is made for persons who hold a medical certificate, who during their work must get in and out of their vehicles, who are driving in reverse and who are under 16 years of age (s. 63(a)(5)). Nova Scotia has also enacted a similar section, S.N.S. 1974, c. 42, s. 10 amending s. 157(12) of its Motor Vehicle Act, R.S.N.S. 1967, c. 191. A similar provision is in force in British Columbia.

14. Is it wise to use the criminal law to force people to protect themselves against injury? If people want to take the risk of being injured more severely in a crash, why not respect their own judgment? What effect, if any, will this statute have on the courts' use of the seat belt defence in civil cases? See *Froom* v. *Butcher, supra; Brown* v. *Kendrick* (1966), 192 So. 2d 49 (Fla.). The Nova Scotia statute enacts that the "use or non-use of restraint equipment by operators or passengers shall not be evidence of negligence in any civil action" see s. 157(14). Is this wise?

15. Is the use of the contributory negligence principle of tort law a better way of encouraging seat belt use? What are the limitations of tort law in this area? Do people generally have any knowledge of tort law? What is the proper role of the courts in this area? See Weiler, "Legal Values and Judicial Decision-Making" (1970), 48 Can. Bar Rev. 1.

16. There are many proof problems presented by the seat belt defence. There are also some thorny mathematical issues. In *Yuan* v. *Farstad,* should the widow receive 75 percent of her total loss; or 75 percent of the difference between the loss she would have suffered had her husband strapped in and the loss she in fact suffered? Is the 75 percent figure an estimate by the court of the difference between the damages actually suffered and those that would have been suffered if the belt had been worn?

17. What other ways are there of fostering seat belt use? Will advertising help? A few years ago, before mandatory seat belts, the Ontario Government launched a "crusade" to increase seat belt use. Several pamphlets and other printed material were produced and made available for groups who wish to use them. A few conferences were held extolling the virtues of seat belts. It was difficult to perceive any major breakthrough in seat belt use as a result, however.

18. The Co-operators Insurance Association of Guelph, Ontario includes in their accident benefits policy the following clause:

"Seat-Belts — If the insured automobile is equipped with seat-belts and an injured insured is using a properly fastened and properly installed CSA or SAE approved seat-belt at the time of accidental collision or upset, the principal sum shall be deemed to be increased by 25 percent. The insurer's findings as to use, fastening and installation shall be final and conclusive."

Do you think this would have any effect?

19. It may be that before long seat belts will become obsolescent and be replaced by airbag devices that inflate on impact to restrain the occupant of a vehicle. Because these will operate automatically, the importance of the seat belt defence may well diminish. There are still many technical problems that will have to be overcome before these devices come into general use. See Arthur D. Little, Inc., *The State of The Art of Traffic Safety* (1966), p. 215; *Road and Track*, December 1969, at p. 52.

20. Should it be contributory negligence for a motorcyclist not to wear a safety helmet? Would it make any difference if the wearing of such a helmet was required by law? See Highway Traffic Act, R.S.O. 1970, c. 202, s. 62(1); *O'Connell* v. *Jackson*, [1971] 3 All E.R. 129 (15 percent reduction for not wearing crash helmet); *cf. Hilder* v. *Associated Portland Cement Co.*, [1961] 3 All E.R. 701 (not contributory negligence, but no proof of cause, and not required by law).

21. Should it be contributory negligence to drive in a small, foreign car that you know will be badly smashed up if it collides with a larger car? See *Hunt* v. *Schwanke*, [1972] 2 W.W.R. 541, at p. 543.

22. With regard to problems of imputed negligence, see *Mills* v. *Armstrong: The Bernina* (1888), 13 App. Cas. 1, 4 T.L.R. 360 (ship passenger and master); *Oliver* v. *Birmingham & Midland Motor Omnibus Co. Ltd.*, [1933] 1 K.B. 35, 48 T.L.R. 540 (grandfather and child); *Kaplan* v. *Canada Safeway Ltd.* (1968), 68 D.L.R. (2d) 627 (Sask. Q.B.) (parent and child); *Krahn* v. *Bell* (1930), 24 Sask. L.R. 365, [1930] 4 D.L.R. 480 (bailment); *Flamant* v. *Knelson*, [1971] 4 W.W.R. 454 (B.C.) (employer and employee); *Mallet* v. *Dunn*, [1949] 2 K.B. 180, [1949] 1 All E.R. 973 (husband and wife); see s. 2(2) and (3), Negligence Act, *supra* and *Enridge* v. *Cooper* (1966), 57 D.L.R. (2d) 239 (B.C.) (husband's recovery cut down); *cf. Cowle* v. *Filion* (1956), 6 D.L.R. (2d) 258 (Ont.); see also *Drinkwater* v. *Kimber*, [1952] 2 Q.B. 281, [1952] 1 All E.R. 701. See MacIntyre, "The Rationale of Imputed Negligence" (1944), 5 U. of T.L.J. 368; Klar, "Contributory Negligence and Contribution Among Tortfeasors", in Klar (ed.), *Studies in Canadian Tort Law* (1977), p. 154.

C. VOLUNTARY ASSUMPTION OF RISK

HAMBLEY v. SHEPLEY

Ontario Court of Appeal. (1967), 63 D.L.R. (2d) 94

Laskin J.A.: . . . This case, which appears to be a novel one on its facts, concerns the claim of a policeman to recover damages for personal injuries. On radio instructions, he used his police cruiser as a roadblock against the defendant, a motorist, who was escaping arrest. The defendant's car, then being driven at high speed and in the wrong lane, proceeded into an intersection against the traffic lights and struck the police cruiser, which was athwart the intersection, before the plaintiff could get out. The trial judge dismissed the action on the ground that the policeman was barred under the principle of *volenti non fit injuria*.

The neat question for determination is whether that principle applies against a person whose injuries occur in the discharge by him of a public duty (see s. 47 [am. 1966, c. 118, s. 15] of the Police Act, R.S.O. 1960, c. 298) so as to absolve an otherwise negligent defendant whose conduct caused those injuries. In my opinion, the *volenti* doctrine — in negligence cases, perhaps more properly referred to as the doctrine of voluntary assumption of risk — is inapplicable to such a case.

The trial judge reached his conclusion by analogizing the case of a policeman using a gun (instead of a motor vehicle) to stop and arrest an escaping armed prisoner. No doubt, consent, on the principle of *volenti,* may be a defence to an intentional tort, but I do not think it follows from the illustration used by the trial judge that a policeman is necessarily without civil remedy against a person who assaults him, albeit this occurs in the course of effecting an arrest. However, I need not pursue such a question here.

The doctrine of *volenti* or voluntary assumption of risk as a defence in negligence actions has two correlative effects; it means that the plaintiff is agreeable to bearing the injurious consequences of the defendant's negligent conduct, and that the defendant is relieved of any duty of care to the plaintiff in respect of the particular risk of harm: see Fleming, *Law of Torts,* 3rd ed., p. 256. Clearly, the plaintiff in the present case knew of the risk of harm to which he might be exposing himself, but it would be a reversion of the rigid mid-19th century conception of *volenti* to hold that he thereby accepted that risk so as to absolve the defendant of any duty of care towards him. It seems to me that just as the doctrine of *volenti* no longer immunizes an employer from common law liability to an employee who in carrying out his duties of employment is injured because of an unsafe working system of which he is aware, so the doctrine should have no application to a policeman who is aware of a risk of injury which in fact befalls him in the discharge of the duties of his office . . . [Citations omitted.]

There is not, of course, the relationship between policeman and member of the public that exists between employee and employer, and I do not press any perfect analogy; but neither the policeman nor the employee can reasonably be charged with sufferance of injury resulting from negligence simply because each persists in his employment in full awareness of the risk: see *Merrington* v. *Ironbridge Metal Works Ltd.,* [1952] 2 All E.R. 1101. I agree with the view of Fleming, *op. cit.,* at p. 259 that "the defence [of *volenti*] cannot succeed unless the evidence permits a genuine inference that the plaintiff consented not merely to the risk of injury, but to the lack of reasonable care which may produce that risk". I do not see in the present case any such consent as is last referred to, and I so hold aside entirely from the contention made in some textbooks and cases that the doctrine only applies where the parties have first come into some association, such as that of driver and passenger, or occupier and visitor: see Fleming, *op. cit.,* at p. 263; and *cf. Car & Gen'l Ins. Corp. Ltd.* v. *Seymour and Maloney,* [1956] S.C.R. 322, 2 D.L.R. (2d) 369.

The more pertinent question in this case is whether the plaintiff was guilty of contributory negligence, which was also pleaded in defence. The plaintiff, notwithstanding his public duty, is not relieved of the obligation to take reasonable care for his own safety if he would seek to impose liability upon another for negligence resulting in personal injuries. It was urged in the present case that the plaintiff should be in no worse position with respect to alleged contributory negligence than the rescuing policeman in *Haynes* v. *Harwood,* [1935] 1 K.B. 146, who went to the aid of children imperilled by the defendant's negligence; and see also *Ward* v. *T.E. Hopkins & Son Ltd.,* [1959] 3 All E.R. 225. I do not, however, see the two situations as exactly parallel. A crystallized situation of peril into which a rescuing policeman thrusts himself is different from one in which the anticipation of peril to himself leaves him still time or room to act for his own safety.

The issue on this point in the present case is hence whether on the facts the plaintiff acted reasonably in the way he met an anticipated risk of harm from the defendant's negligent, and even reckless operation of his motor vehicle. In *Bittner et al.* v. *Tait-Gibson Optometrists Ltd.,* [1964] 2 O.R. 52, 44 D.L.R. (2d) 113, this court determined that a policeman who, seeing lights in defendant's premises while on patrol duty, slipped on a patch of ice near the store front as he approached the entrance door, was not guilty of contributory negligence. That was because he had no reason to suspect the presence of ice at the doorway when the street was otherwise clear of ice; and McLennan J.A. for the court added that "if there was a risk the end to be achieved outweighed that risk".

Here the plaintiff had good reason to know that the defendant was not approaching with care; his communicating radio kept him informed of the course of the pursuit of the defendant by other policemen. He never did reach the intersection to which he was originally directed to set up a roadblock because, hearing over the radio of the route being taken by the defendant, he found himself close to the intersection of a road which the defendant had entered, and he determined to cut him off at that intersection which the defendant was then approaching from a half-mile away. The plaintiff intended to stop in the intersection and then get out of his car after unfastening his seat belt and putting on the revolving red top light with which police cruisers are equipped. He got as far as stopping his car in the intersection when he was struck.

I am not prepared on the foregoing facts to find the plaintiff guilty of negligence contributing to his personal injuries as contrasted with damage to the police cruiser (for which no claim is made in this suit). Weighing what the plaintiff properly set out to do against the danger to which he was exposing himself in doing it, I would not regard his failure to get out of his car in time to avoid personal injuries as failure to act reasonably for his own safety. To hold otherwise would be to say that he should have abandoned his plan to stop the defendant at the particular intersection. This was not a case of the plaintiff delaying his exit from his car or confronting the defendant's approaching car on foot. His judgment as to his ability to get clear in time should not be held against him merely because it turned out to be wrong.

I would allow the appeal, set aside the judgment below, and in its place direct judgment for the plaintiff for the general and special damages assessed by the trial judge. The plaintiff is entitled to his costs here and below.

Appeal allowed.

NOTES

1. See also *City of Sarnia* v. *Shepley et al.* (1969), 4 D.L.R. (3d) 315 for the city's action for damage to the radio. Lang Co. Ct. J. stated:

"As found in the *Hambley* v. *Shepley* case the plaintiff in that case knew of the risk involved in blocking the intersection. In so far as this case is concerned, Hambley was instructed by his superiors to block the intersection and he and his superiors knew of the risk of damages to the cruiser and radio and probably could be said to have consented thereto but there is no evidence the plaintiff consented to be relieved of any duty or care to the plaintiff or to the legal risk of injury or damage. Further, under the circumstances here the plaintiff consciously and deliberately faced the risk of damage to cruiser and radio to apprehend a criminal and to protect possibly several citizens from injury or death and in such circumstances the rule *volenti non fit injuria* does not apply. *Volenti non fit injuria* is not the equivalent of *scienti non fit injuria*."

2. The defence of voluntary assumption of risk may arise either by express

agreement or it may be implied from the conduct of the parties. See *Dokuchia*
v. *Domansch,* [1944] O.W.N. 461, at p. 464; *Regal Oil* v. *Campbell,* [1936]
S.C.R. 311, at p. 320. The situations of express consent will not be dealt with
here but are left to courses on contract. See *A.E. Farr Ltd.* v. *The Admiralty,*
[1953] 2 All E.R. 542; Cootes, *Exception Clauses* (1964). These consent terms
are often printed on signs or on tickets handed to people. See, for example,
Alderslade v. *Hendon Laundry,* [1945] 1 K.B. 189; Cumming, "Judicial Treatment of Disclaimer Clauses in Sale of Goods Transactions in Canada" (1972),
10 O.H.L.J. 281. One recent case demonstrating the effectiveness of an express
agreement is *Birch* v. *Thomas,* [1972] 2 All E.R. 905 (C.A.), where the defendant, the driver of an uninsured motor vehicle, had a notice in his car windshield stating that all passengers rode at their own risk. He informed the plaintiff of the presence of the notice and its contents when the plaintiff entered the
automobile. The Court of Appeal unanimously held that the maxim *volenti
non fit injuria* applied and the plaintiff could not recover for personal injuries
suffered through the defendant's negligent driving. See also *White* v. *Blackmore,*
[1972] 3 All E.R. 158 (C.A.); *Bennett* v. *Tugwell,* [1971] 2 All E.R. 248
(Q.B.D.); compare with *Leva* v. *Lam* (1972), 25 D.L.R. (3d) 513 (Ont. C.A.),
where liability was imposed on a parking lot owner for damage caused to a
patron's car by his employee while trying to park it on the lot, even though the
ticket read:

> "Charges are for use of parking space only. The company assumes no
> responsibility for loss through fire, theft, collision or otherwise to the car or
> its contents, whether due to negligence or otherwise.
> Cars parked at owner's risk."

3. The traditional requirements for a defendant to establish the non-contrac-
tual defence of voluntary assumption of risk were "(1) that the plaintiff clearly
knew and appreciated the nature and character of the risk he ran and (2) that
he voluntarily incurred it". See Lamont J. in *Kelliher* v. *Smith,* [1931] S.C.R.
672, at p. 679, quoting from *C.P.R.* v. *Frechette,* [1915] A.C. 871, p. 880.
Another explication of the theory was given by Gillanders J.A. in *Harrison* v.
Toronto Motor Car et al., [1945] O.R. 1, at p. 9, to the effect that the plaintiff
to be barred must not only have "perceived the existence of the danger, but
also fully appreciated it and voluntarily assumed the risk, and that is a question
of fact". Consequently, when some people died of carbon monoxide poisoning
because of a defective muffler, they were held not to be *volenti* because they
were unaware that the muffler was broken. See *Kowton* v. *Public Trustee of
Alberta* (1966), 57 W.W.R. 370.

4. As for the question of free choice, see *Rush* v. *Commercial Realty Co.*
(1929), 145 A. 475 (S.C.N.J.), where it was held that the plaintiff, who fell
through the floor while using a dangerous privy, was not *volens.* The New Jersey
court felt that she "had no choice, when impelled by the calls of nature but to
use the facilities placed at her disposal . . . she was not required to leave the
premises and go elsewhere". This issue of free choice used to prevent rescuers
from recovery. (See Goodhart, "Rescue and Voluntary Assumption of Risk"
(1934), 5 Camb. L.J. 192.) But this is no longer the case. In *Ward* v. *T.E.
Hopkins & Son Ltd.,* [1959] 3 All E.R. 225 (C.A.) Morris C.J. stated that if a
rescuer

> "actuated by an impulsive desire to save life, acts bravely and promptly
> and subjugates any timorous over-concern for his own well-being or comfort,
> I cannot think that it would be either rational or seemly to say that he freely
> and voluntarily agreed to incur the risks of the situation which had been
> created by A's negligence."

Do you agree that in these situations the "choice" is not really voluntary? In
the case of employees exposing themselves to risks on the job the courts have
been reluctant to hold them *volenti,* on the ground that their choice is rarely
free. See, for example, *Burnett* v. *British Waterways Ltd.,* [1972] 1 W.L.R.
1329 (Q.B.).

5. More recently, the ambit of the defence of *volenti* has been narrowed

considerably so as to require evidence of an express or an implied agreement to exempt the defendant of any liability for injury suffered. This is a complicated issue that will be dealt with in more depth below, in connection with the problem of willing passengers. One recent case that is demonstrative of the modern judicial attitude to *volenti* is *Lagasse et al.* v. *Rural Municipality of Ritchot et al.,* [1973] 4 W.W.R. 181 (Man. Q.B.). The plaintiff's husband was a tractor-operator who agreed to plow some snow on a lake at the request of the defendant municipality. While plowing the snow, the ice gave way and the tractor sunk into the lake, drowning the plaintiff's husband. In deciding if *volenti non fit injuria* applied, Matas J. quoted the statement of Denning M.R. in *Nettleship* v. *Weston:*

> "This brings me to the defence of *volenti non fit injuria.* . . . In former times this defence was used almost as an alternative defence to contributory negligence. Either defence defeated the action. Now that contributory negligence is not a complete defence, but only a ground for reducing the damages, the defence of *volenti non fit injuria* has been closely considered, and, in consequence, it has been severely limited. Knowledge of the risk of injury is not enough. Nor is a willingness to take the risk of injury. Nothing will suffice short of an agreement to waive any claim for negligence. The plaintiff must agree, expressly or impliedly, to waive any claim for that injury that may befall him due to the lack of reasonable care by the defendant: or more accurately, due to the failure of the defendant to measure up to the standard of care that the law requires of him. . . ."

Matas J. concluded:

> "Nothing in [the deceased's] words or conduct, either express or by necessary implication, showed that he gave a real consent to the assumption of risk without compensation or that he absolved the defendants from the duty to take care."

His Lordship went on, however, to reduce the widow's recovery by 25 percent because of her husband's contributory negligence.

6. *Volenti* has not disappeared, however. In *Benjamin et al.* v. *Boutilier* (1971), 17 D.L.R. (3d) 611 (N.S.S.C.), the defendant was operating a bulldozer; to backfill around the plaintiff's house. The conditions were wet and the defendant warned the plaintiff that it was dangerous to fill closer than seven feet to the house. The plaintiff instructed the defendant to proceed, regardless of the conditions. Damage resulted to the foundation of the house when a rock rolled off a mound and collided with the wall. The court found that the operator-defendant was negligent in proceeding with the work when his common sense told him it was dangerous. The court dismissed the action, however, because the plaintiff had voluntarily consented to take the risk.

7. If someone assumes a particular risk, it does not mean that he is barred from recovering if he is injured as a result of some other risk which he did not assume. For example, a passenger on the back of a snowmobile may assume the "risk of falling off", but he does not thereby necessarily assume the "risk of being run over by another [snowmobile]". See *Ainge* v. *Siemon* (1972), 19 D.L.R. (3d) 531 (Ont. H.C.) *per* Addy J.; see also *Rootes* v. *Skelton* (1967), 116 C.L.R. 383 (water-skier may assume risk of hitting obstruction, but not boat driver's negligence in failing to warn about such an obstruction).

8. One vivid case, on this issue, is *Deskau et al.* v. *Dziama et al.* (1973), 36 D.L.R. (3d) 36 (Ont. H.C.), where the defendant and a number of friends drove to a gravel road on which there was a series of sharp hills. The group divided into two for the purposes of taking turns riding with the defendant who negotiated the hills at very high speed in an attempt to cause the vehicle to leave the ground as he crested each hill. On the second turn the car went out of control and crashed. Both passengers were seriously injured and sued the defendant alleging gross negligence. In dismissing their action, Keith J. stated that the plaintiffs had voluntarily assumed the inherent risks:

> "The nature of the risk that these plaintiffs voluntarily assumed was unlimited in the circumstances. Any one of many things could and was likely

to bring about disaster. For example, as happened in this case, the defendant was apparently momentarily stunned when his head hit the steering wheel on the return of the vehicle from its free flight on the third crest, immediately interfering with his power to control the vehicle, even if nothing broke when the car being subjected to such abuse, hit the ground. There was the distinct possibility of striking a stone or a rut in this gravel road, which would throw the car out of control. . . . One need not further elaborate on the possibilities inherent in this venture that would mean nothing but disaster and serious injury, if not death. . . .In my view, this is one of those cases in which the doctrine is applicable, and therefore I do not propose to discuss the alternative defence raised in this case of contributory negligence, since that defence can only arise in cases where the circumstances do not justify the application of the doctrine of *volenti*."

9. P is injured while giving a driving lesson to D as a result of the latter's negligence? Does P voluntarily assume the risk of an accident? Does it depend on the type of accident that occurs? Is P contributorily negligent, rather than *volens*? Compare *Nettleship* v. *Weston*, [1971] 3 W.L.R. 370 with *Lovelace* v. *Fossum et al. (No. 1)* (1972), 24 D.L.R. (3d) 561 (B.C.S.C.). Does a student pilot assume the risk of a crash? See *Stephens* v. *Gittens* (1974), 15 N.S.R. (2d) 63.

10. See generally James, "Assumption of Risk" (1952), 61 Yale L.J. 141; Bohlen, "Voluntary Assumption of Risk" (1906), 20 Harv. L. Rev. 14; Green, "Assumed Risk as a Defense" (1961), 22 La. L. Rev. 77; Wade, "The Place of Assumption of Risk in the Law of Negligence" (1961), 22 La. L. Rev. 5; Payne, "Assumption of Risk and Negligence" (1957), 37 Can. Bar Rev. 950; Hertz, "Volenti Non Fit Injuria: A Guide" in Klar (ed.) *Studies in Canada Tort Law* (1977), p. 101.

1. Sports

FINK v. GREENIAUS

Ontario High Court of Justice. (1974), 2 O.R. (2d) 541

Van Camp J.: This is an action brought by the plaintiff, Sondra Fink, for damages for personal injuries sustained by her as a result of a collision on a ski hill with the defendant, another skier. . . .

The collision took place on April 5, 1970, a Sunday, at about 4 o'clock in the afternoon at the Alpine Ski Club near Collingwood, at which both the plaintiff and the defendant were guests. It was in evidence that it was a clear, dry, cold day and there was no evidence in any way to indicate that visibility was difficult, even at this time of day. To understand the evidence, it is necessary to know something of the ski-run on which the accident occurred. The evidence leaves something to be desired as to the nature of this run, but it would seem that it was a wide, gentle run about three-quarters of a mile long with trees on either side which, about two-thirds of the way down, levels off to a plateau or crest and then continues on into sections slightly angled to right and to left to the bottom of the hill where the tows are. The right arm continues without interruption but the left arm called the "Chute" drops steeply from the lip or crest of the plateau into a bowl. The two arms are divided by trees which commence above the lip of the plateau. It is the arm called the Chute which is the one where the accident occurred. It is a short hill which most of the skiers used as the common way to get to the base terminal of the lift. The hill, called the Alpine Run and its continuation in the Chute, was graded an intermediate run. When I say it drops steeply, I am talking of a drop of such a nature that a skier closer than 15 ft. to the lip of the drop would not be visible to the skier coming from above and the skier below the drop could not see those above until they were within a few feet of the edge of the drop. The ski-run was between 100 and 150 ft. wide. It was possible for a lower intermediate skier to ski straight over the drop and it would seem that the grade was not that steep as it continued to the bottom. There was some evidence to indicate that other runs from the top of the hill merged into the plateau.

Mrs. Fink — and I will, from now on, refer to her as the plaintiff — had been skiing since about 11 o'clock that morning; had stopped for lunch about 1 o'clock and had started her run at this time in the afternoon from the top to the right; had come to the plateau, had skied out to the edge about the middle and then had crossed to the right side to check the skiers who were coming from above and who were below the edge of the hill. After a few minutes, she had continued skiing down the Chute, moving from the right side to the left side of the hill at a shallow angle to the horizontal of the hill at a slow to medium speed, not overly fast, traversing the hill as was her custom. When she was about seven yards from the trees on the left side and below the lip of the plateau at a horizontal distance of some 10 to 15 ft., she was hit from behind and to the left by the defendant.

The defendant had come as a guest of a member of the ski patrol and had arrived about 9:30 that morning, and had been skiing all day except for the lunch-hour break some time between 12 and 2. It was his first time at this club. He had been on the other runs including one other like this run and another that was a little harder that they used more. He had skied several times in the morning and the afternoon with his host, Frank Sloane and began this run again with Frank Sloane, intending to go straight down the Alpine Run and the Chute to the bottom. He was skiing down the fall-line with short turns to slow down. It was his evidence that it was impossible to do it without such turns. The run had been busy earlier but it was not at this time. It took him about one and a half to two minutes to reach the lip of the plateau. He did not slow for it. He became airborne as he went over the edge. As he came across the plateau, he could see beyond the edge of the plateau but not the slope immediately below the lip of the plateau and he saw the plaintiff just as he came over the edge. He tried to swerve but did not have time to do so, collided with the plaintiff and ended up some 20 to 25 ft. downhill from the plaintiff. The plaintiff, who had fallen where she was hit, had not swerved or changed her path as she had crossed the hill to the point of collision. . . .

[The Justice discussed the evidence and the sport of skiing in general.]

It is the question of the definition of the duty owed by skiers on the ski hill that, for the first time, seems to be before the court. Surprising as it may seem, in view of the thousands of skiers each year in this country who indulge in it, ranging from beginners to experts, counsel were able to refer me to only one case in which the question had come before the court and so consequently it is necessary to look to cases relating to other sports in order to have some assistance in the definition. The general definition of negligence with which one begins is that it is the failure to exercise that degree of care which certain circumstances demand. The omission to do something which a reasonable and prudent man, guided by those considerations which ordinarily regulate the conduct of our affairs, would do in any particular situation or the doing of something which that man would not do in that situation.

Negligence is relative to the circumstances; the standard of care is measured by the conduct of the average man. In a very careful review of the cases, counsel have referred me to a number of cases which may be grouped in three divisions; those in which a spectator claims against the operator of the sports facility;

those in which a spectator claims against a participant, and those in which a participant claims against another participant. . . .

[The Justice outlined the authorities.]

I hold that the defendant skier owed a duty of care to his fellow skier not to act in reckless disregard of the other's safety. . . .

[The Justice considered the evidence of negligence and concluded that the defendant's conduct was negligent.]

I have been invited to set forth rules of the road for skiing but I cannot see that it is my function. It is a matter either for the legislature or for the different ski clubs and ski resorts to establish. I am not saying that this type of skiing would be negligent in all circumstances. I am simply stating that, on this particular hill at this time and with the type of terrain and with these other skiers to be expected, the conduct of the defendant constituted negligence.

There then arises the question of whether the plaintiff, by her conduct, has also been negligent and that her negligence has contributed to her injuries. I have the fact that she was proceeding where there was a steep drop, a rapid drop in the terrain. She was proceeding below that drop where — and where she should have known by her use of the trail that — she was not obvious to the skiers coming from above; that she should have known from her use of the trail that it was the custom and, in fact, she did know that it was the custom for certain skiers to ski straight over the edge of the drop. In fact, her reason for stopping at the edge of the plateau before she proceeded to traverse it in a partial horizontal or crosswise fashion was to see if there were other skiers coming from above. Her statement was that she saw others and assumed that they would slow and she commenced to cross, but it does not seem compatible with her reason for stopping and looking. She pointed out that she did not feel she was taking a chance because she had looked both ways and she pointed out also that one can traverse any run if you check that no one is coming. I cannot find that her rate of speed in crossing this hill was in any way a factor that caused the collision. Whether she had been going quickly or whether she had been standing still in that position when the defendant arrived there, the same collision would have occurred but I must find that her conduct in traversing the bowl when she was not visible to skiers coming from above, when she knew that she was not visible, when she knew that certain skiers proceeded directly across the centre line of the bowl, over the lip of the plateau, when she also would know that at this time of the day some of them would not have as quick reflexes, when there were open to her other methods of proceeding down the incline means that she also has been negligent and that her negligence in this respect contributed to the accident. I realize that there is evidence that others also traversed this bowl and traversed it as she was doing, but I cannot find that the fact that others used the same method meant that at that time of day, having looked to see who was coming, she was not negligent.

I have been referred to Mr. Linden's book on *Canadian Negligence Law* (1972), where he considers, at p. 380, the doctrine of voluntary assumption of risk and where he has pointed out that it is a defence. At p. 368 he states that:

> "There have been attempts to subsume voluntary assumption of risk within the duty issue. In other words, it has been argued that no duty of care is owed to one who consents to a risk. Canadian courts have evinced an attraction towards this approach, on occasion, but they have not adopted it. It is preferable to treat *volenti* as a defence for several reasons."

and at pp. 380-1:

> "When the courts say that the risk of being hit by a puck or a golf ball is assumed by the plaintiff, that is not what they mean; they should explain in-

stead that there is no negligence in such a case. Any talk of voluntary assumption of risk is superfluous. *Volenti* is not invoked unless someone is negligent and he wants to avoid liability on the basis of the consent of his victim."

The same approach was used by Lord Diplock and Lord Justice Sellers in the above *Wooldridge* v. *Sumner* case, *supra*. There was no evidence before me to support a finding that the plaintiff had voluntarily assumed the risk of the negligence that has been found. There was no express agreement to assume the risk nor can I imply it from the mere presence of the plaintiff on the slopes. The defendant has now showed that the plaintiff fully appreciated the nature of the risk she ran in crossing the slope; there was no evidence that she had released him from his responsibility. . . .

By reason of the contributory negligence which I have found, and by reason of the fact that I find both the plaintiff and defendant equally responsible for the injuries that she has sustained, the judgment will be for one-half of the total damages.

NOTES

1. Do you agree with the result in the case? The reasoning? Skiers often receive tickets when they pay for admission to ski areas. One such ticket reads:
"The holder of this ticket as a condition of being permitted to use the facilities of the area agrees: (1) To assume all risk of personal injury or loss of or damage to property;. . . ."
Does this ticket form part of a contract by which the skier assumes the risk of damage or injury caused by the negligence of the ski area's management? See *Wilson* v. *Blue Mountain Resorts Ltd.* (1975), 4 O.R. (2d) 713.

2. Participants in sports and recreational activities are often barred by *volenti*. One of the classic cases on the point is *Murphy* v. *Steeplechase Amusement Co.* (1929), 250 N.Y. 479, 166 N.E. 173, where the plaintiff was injured when he was thrown to the floor on an amusement ride called the "flopper". He testified that he "took a chance" in going on the ride. Cardozo C.J. denied liability and said:
"*Volenti non fit injuria.* One who takes part in such a sport accepts the dangers that inhere in it so far as they are obvious and necessary, just as a fencer accepts the risk of a thrust by his antagonist or a spectator at a ball game the chance of contact with the ball. . . . The antics of the clown are not the paces of the cloistered cleric. The rough and boisterous joke, the horse-play of the crowd, evokes its own guffaws, but they are not the pleasures of tranquility. The plaintiff was not seeking a retreat for meditation. Visitors were tumbling about the belt to the merriment of onlookers when he made his choice to join them. He took the chance of a like fate, with whatever damage to his body might ensue from such a fall. The timorous may stay at home."

3. In *Gillmore* v. *London County Council*, [1938] 4 All E.R. 331 (K.B.D.) the plaintiff had joined a class in physical training organized by the defendant council, and had paid a small fee upon joining. The exercises were performed in a hall which was used for dances and of which the floor was fairly highly polished. While performing an exercise in which the members of the class were hopping on one leg and making lunges at another member in an endeavour to compel that other to put his raised foot on the ground, the plaintiff slipped and suffered injury. The whole class at the time were wearing rubber shoes.
Lord Justice du Parcq stated:
"That leads me to the question whether anything can remain here of the defence *volenti non fit injuria* — that is, that the plaintiff cannot complain because he agreed to take the risk, and was willing to run any risk there was. It is plain, in my view, on the evidence, that he did nothing of the sort. He trusted to those who had invited him and to those who were, so to speak, in command. It never occurred to him that he was being asked to do anything

dangerous in a dangerous place. Of course, he took certain risks. Anybody who plays a game which involves any bodily violence or is content to hop about on one leg lunging at somebody else takes certain risks, and, if he fell down in the normal way, he cannot complain, just as anybody who is unfortunate enough to break his collar-bone on the football field in the ordinary way has no right to claim damages at law against anybody else. Here, however, there was added danger, in my view. He did not assume the risk willingly. I think that it did not occur to him that there was an added danger, and with that added danger there, he was entitled to assume that it was safe. I do not think that it was safe, and, on that ground, the warranty being as I have stated it, I think that the plaintiff succeeds. I suppose that, by adopting the same reasoning, one might say that there was a failure on the part of the defendants or their agents to take reasonable care."

4. A participant, although he may assume the ordinary risks of a sporting event, does not assume the risk of the organizer's negligence. See *White* v. *Blackmore*, [1972] 3 All E.R. 158 (C.A.), *per* Denning M.R. (dissenting on another point):

"No doubt the visitor takes on himself the risks inherent in motor racing, but he does not take on himself the risk of injury due to the defaults of the organisers. People go to race meetings to enjoy the sport. They like to see the competitors taking risks, but they do not like to take risks on themselves. Even though it is a dangerous sport, they expect, and rightly expect, the organisers to erect proper barriers, to provide proper enclosures, and to do all that is reasonable to ensure their safety. If the organisers do everything that is reasonable, they are not liable if a racing car leaps the barriers and crashes into the crowd: see *Hall* v. *Booklands Auto-Racing Club*. But, if the organisers fail to take reasonable precautions, they cannot excuse themselves from liability by invoking the doctrine of volenti non fit injuria; for the simple reason that the person injured or killed does not willingly accept the risks arising from their want of reasonable care:"

See also *Reese* v. *Coleman*, [1976] 3 W.W.R. 739 (Sask.) *per* McPherson J., *cf. Magee* v. *Prairie Dusters Motorcycle Club*, [1975] W.W.D. 165 (Sask.) *per* Bence C.J.Q.B.

5. Spectators at sporting events are often denied compensation for their injuries on the basis of *volenti*. In *Elliot* v. *Amphitheatre Ltd.*, [1934] 3 W.W.R. 225, the defendant was excused from liability when a puck flew over the boards of its hockey rink and hit an 18-year-old spectator in the eye. McDonald C.J.K.B. observed that the proprietor was not an insurer and that the "spectators assume the risk peculiar to that form of entertainment". The plaintiff, who was a hockey player himself, chose to sit in the front row, outside the protection of the screens that had been installed at both ends of the rink, which was the customary method of building hockey arenas. See also *Wooldridge* v. *Sumner*, [1962] 2 All E.R. 978; *Wilks* v. *Cheltenham Home Guard Motorcycle*, [1971] 2 All E.R. 369, no liability to spectators at motorcycle scramble.

6. Compare with *Payne* v. *Maple Leaf Gardens*, [1949] O.R. 26, [1949] 1 D.L.R. 369, where a spectator sitting next to the boards was injured when one player attacked another to take away his stick. In an action against the arena proprietors and the offending player the plaintiff failed at the trial. On appeal he obtained judgment against the offending player. While spectators assumed the risk of accidents "it cannot be properly held [they] assumed the risk of injuries resulting directly from negligence or improper conduct on the part of one of the players. Such a player could not properly say that they assumed a risk created by his own wrong-doing". See also *Klyne* v. *Bellegarde* (1978), 92 D.L.R. (3d) 747 (Sask. Q.B.), no *volenti* by fan against use of hockey sticks by players but two-thirds contributory negligence for not guarding against them.

7. In *Murray* v. *Harringay Arena, Ltd.*, [1951] 2 K.B. 529, [1951] 2 All E.R. 320, the infant plaintiff, aged six years, was taken by his father to see an ice-hockey match at the defendant's arena. The only available seats were in the front row at one side. There was netting eight feet, nine inches high at the ends

of the arena but on the sides only a wooden barrier three feet high. In the course of play, a puck was struck out of the arena and hit plaintiff in the eye. In an action for damages the plaintiff failed to recover. The Court of Appeal held that the liability of the defendant depended on an implied term of the contract (which Singleton L.J. assumed the infant plaintiff to have entered with the defendant), that the defendant had taken reasonable care to see that the premises were fit for the purpose for which it was used. The trial judge had found that (1) there was no negligence or failure to take customary precautions on defendant's part; (2) the plaintiff as a spectator voluntarily undertook the risks incidental to the game. With these reasons the court agreed.

If, as Williams, *Joint Torts and Contributory Negligence* (1951) argues voluntary assumption of risk requires "agreement", how can a child of six make a valid agreement? See Williams, *op. cit.,* p. 132.

See also *Agar* v. *Canning* (1965), 54 W.W.R. 302 (Man. Q.B.), *supra*. See generally Siskind, "Liability for Injuries to Spectators" (1968), 6 O.H. L.J. 305.

8. Golf has been the subject of some litigation. In *Ellison* v. *Rogers et al.* (1968), 67 D.L.R. (2d) 21, the plaintiff golfer was hit by a golf ball that had been hooked onto his fairway by the defendant. His actions against the golfer and the club were both dismissed. Mr. Justice Brooke of the High Court of Ontario concluded:

"I think that the normal risk assumed in the case of a spectator is precisely the same thing in the case of the use of a golf course by a player and described as the danger usually found in carrying out the function for which (the golfer), the invitee, is upon the property. Further that the action of other golfers is not a risk for which the proprietor of the golf course is liable if it is the normal risk of the game."

9. It is possible, however, for both a golf club and a golfer to be held liable for injuries caused to someone during a golf game. In *Ratcliff* v. *Whitehead,* [1933] 3 W.W.R. 447, the defendant hit a golf ball directly at a group of golfers from a distance of only 40-80 yards. Mr. Justice Adamson felt that this risk was not assumed. "If it were to be found that it is a risk incidental to the game to have balls driven almost directly at one, it would, to say the least, interfere with the alleged pleasure and healthfulness of the game." He further stated that "every one knows that a golf ball does not always go in exactly the direction intended, in fact for most people it rarely does". See also *McLeod* v. *Roe,* [1947] 1 D.L.R. 135, at p. 148; revd. on another ground, [1947] 3 D.L.R. 241 (S.C.C.).

10. Are *Ellison* v. *Rogers* and *Ratcliff* v. *Whitehead* in conflict? Does it matter if the golfer was obeying the rules of the game? What if there were no rules at all? What if the plaintiff had never been on a golf course in his life?

11. Is the real issue of these decisions the standard of care rather than *volenti?* See *Vander Linden* v. *Kellet* (1972), 21 D.L.R. (3d) 256, no negligence when plaintiff injured while riding a horse.

2. Willing Passengers

CAR & GENERAL INSURANCE CORPORATION, LTD. v. SEYMOUR & MALONEY

Supreme Court of Canada. [1956] S.C.R. 322; 2 D.L.R. (2d) 369; affg. [1955] 4 D.L.R. 104; revg. [1955] 1 D.L.R. 824

Plaintiff, Miss Seymour, met defendant Maloney, in a restaurant in Halifax. It was arranged that defendant and his brother would take plaintiff and her friend, Miss Spencer, to Windsor in defendant's car. The party set out with defendant driving, but due to a change in plan they arrived at Chester at 2 a.m. En route some two bottles of rum were consumed, chiefly by defendant. The following morning they had breakfast, including a bottle of rum, of which defendant had the larger share. After breakfast defendant procured more liquor and they set out for Windsor by a gravel road but soon abandoned it and drove towards Halifax. Defendant kept drinking as he drove. His passengers complained that he was driving too fast but he would not slow down. Plaintiff asked defendant to let his brother drive but defendant refused. Some time later a Buick car, owned by Mrs. Sweeney, overtook and passed them, and shortly after defendant passed the Buick and stopped. Defendant signalled the Buick to stop and went back to find out the year model of the Buick about which he was arguing with his brother. At this time the evidence showed defendant was sweating profusely, his eyes were glassy and his talk thick and heavy. The stop occurred at Ingramport. Shortly after this, defendant overtook the Buick at an extremely fast speed and a few minutes later his car went off the road and turned upside down. Plaintiff was seriously injured.

Plaintiff brought action against defendant, and the latter claimed over against the third party, an insurance company.

At trial, MacDonald J. held that the defence of voluntary assumption of risk had been established and dismissed the action. His Lordship also held that, if this defence had not been applied, he would have held the plaintiff 25 percent contributorily negligent. On appeal to the Nova Scotia Court of Appeal, it was held that the plaintiff had not voluntarily assumed the risk of the accident and that she was entitled to judgment for 75 percent of her damages against the defendant and the third party insurance company. The third party appealed to the Supreme Court of Canada, which upheld the decision of the Nova Scotia Court of Appeal.

Rand J.: This action arises out of injuries to the young woman plaintiff through an accident while in an automobile driven by the respondent Maloney. Two defences are raised, assumption of risk, and contributory negligence. The risk lay in the fact that Maloney, at the time of and for some time prior to the occurrence, was, in some degree under the influence of alcohol, and the question of its assumption in such circumstances comes before us directly for the first time. It is an important question and calls for an examination of that conception.

The form in which the principle has traditionally been stated is that if a person is aware of all the facts of a danger and voluntarily exposes himself to it, he is held to have accepted the risk of any resulting injury. It seems to have originated in matters between master and servant involving hazardous conditions, the simplest case being that of entering upon work inherently dangerous. The next step was taken in *Priestley* v. *Fowler*, which extended the risk to the negligence of a fellow servant. In the developing conceptions of duty, the scope of the assumption was reduced by the requirement of reasonably safe working conditions including statutory provision for machinery and other protection. Complications of the principle are presented by the multiplying risks of modern modes of carrying on business and of social life, and among them is that of the relation between a driver of an automobile and a gratuitous passenger. In several provinces the judgment of the legislature has been expressed in an absolute denial of any claim against the operator; but in Nova Scotia where gross negligence has, as here, been found, the question is at large.

The risk in this case arises out of a special relation which, in turn, results from an undertaking in the original sense of that word: Maloney accepts from the respondent Seymour a commitment of herself to a quasi-custody which he assumes for a purpose involving special hazards under his control or within his general responsibility on terms which include one relating to care in executing the purpose. The degree of care on his part engaged or the risk on hers assumed, qualified or unqualified, may be expressly stipulated, and if so, it would be as determinative during the course of the undertaking as if consideration had passed; but in the generality of cases this term including qualifications is to be implied from the total circumstances. The initial question is whether the undertaker is capable, as if it were in contract, of entering into such an engagement; if he is, what is to be implied as to continued fitness and ability to carry it out until the relation is ended or modified? If he is not originally capable, the passenger acts alone; if self-caused incapacity develops during the performance, its effect will depend on the original terms. No other aspects of the relation are brought into discussion; it is not argued, for instance, that there was a joint venture which would introduce new elements. . . .

I demur to the usual form of the question by which the principle is raised; did the injured person assume the risk that has brought about the injury? The injured person is generally the passenger but it might be the operator not only of automobiles but of airplanes and other machines. So put, the question tends to disguise the governing fact that the other party is setting up in defence the acceptance of the risk as a term of the undertaking, the burden of proving which lies upon him. In such commitments the question ought, I think, rather to be, can the defendant reasonably be heard to say, as an inference from the facts, that the risk of injury from his own misconduct was required by him to be and was accepted by the complainant as such a term?. . . .

If A is driving an automobile for private purposes from X to Y and is hailed on the road by B who requests a lift toward Y, what would most likely be said by A if the question of misconduct of either during the trip was at that moment raised? I think he would ordinarily say, or at least it could reasonably be found that he implies — as he does when asked to allow a licensee to pass over his land — "You may come along, but you must take my skill and care and the risk of my ordinary conduct as I myself am doing, from which I am not likely to but might have a minor lapse." At the same time it would equally be understood that he would not engage in reckless or grossly careless driving. . . .

If, on the other hand, A, for his own purpose, takes the initiative by inviting B — assuming always the absence of any special circumstances or notice — then it could be deemed to be unreasonable for A to urge that he did not intend to assure B that he could expect the ordinary care of prudent drivers to be exercised in operating the machine. The question, as before, is what conditions as terms can A reasonably claim to have laid down, and B reasonably held to have accepted. If the driver was a beginner, that again, would be a special circumstance. These examples illustrate the fact that the basic understanding must be reduced to an actual or constructive exchange of terms under which the commitment of the interests of both is brought. . . .

Neither at . . . Halifax, from which they originally set out nor at Chester can his [defendant's] capacity to engage for the journey and for careful driving to the destination, Windsor, be successfully challenged; is it then to be implied that he did so engage? Or was the engagement subject to the condition that he should not render himself incapable through liquor either of reaching Windsor or of driving safely or, put conversely, that the respondent would take the risk of any negligence which could be attributed to that eventuality?

. . . They had originally tried out a gravelled road from Chester in a more direct line to Windsor but after going some miles turned back to the paved road and the route via Halifax. The young woman was, therefore, in a section of country with which she was not familiar and in surroundings by which she was most likely to be intimidated. The answer to her request to him to let the brother drive is significant: it was to the effect that he knew what he was doing and did not want to be interfered with.

In that situation the *prima facie* implication of reasonable care in the original undertaking — subject to the provisions of the statute — is confirmed and that of any such qualifying condition rebutted.

These considerations are, in my opinion, substantially the same as those underlying *Dann* v. *Hamilton*, [1939] 1 K.B. 509, where Asquith J. on facts almost identical found against the driver. The decision has been the object of some criticism. In *Insurance Com'r.* v. *Joyce* (1948), 77 C.L.R. 39 at p. 57, Dixon J. dissenting, after an analysis of the principle in terms of relations, observes, "If he knowingly accepts the voluntary services of a driver affected by drink, he cannot complain of improper driving caused by his condition, because it involves no breach of duty."

That conclusion depends on the terms of the undertaking and so far as it implies the determination to be unilateral I am unable to agree with it. Of the judgment in *Dann* v. *Hamilton* he says: "No doubt the issue his Lordship propounded for decision was one of fact but, with all respect, I cannot but think that the plaintiff should have been precluded. Every element was present to form a conscious and intentional assumption of the very risk for which she suffered."

For the reasons already given, I cannot concur in the validity of that criticism. It fails, in my opinion, to give sufficient emphasis to the original undertaking in which the passenger has primarily the interest and the driver, the responsibility, and in the performance of which itself the risk resides. The unilateral formula, adequate to the early situations, is both inadequate and inappropriate to a bilateral relation in which two persons are co-operating in complementary actions. It confines the enquiry into the fact sought to the external conditions evident to the passenger, paying — apparently — no regard to the elements of the undertaking or the governing role of the driver. In the other view the court starts with his original acceptance of responsibility, whatever it may have been, and from the subsequent circumstances finds whether the undertaking has been carried out according to its terms.

In the light of these considerations, Maloney has not established his case that the passenger at any time accepted the continuing journey, or gave him any reason to infer that she did, on the terms that she released him from responsibility for care and would take the risk of any consequences resulting from the effects on him of liquor. Nor has he shown that any condition arose which modified that responsibility within the terms of the original undertaking.

There remains the question of contributory negligence. . . . In this case the failure charged against the plaintiff is that she maintained herself in a situation fraught with too great possibility of danger. On that question I am unable to say that the finding of either the fact or the degree of fault by the trial judge and by the Appeal Division is wrong.

I would, therefore, dismiss the appeal with costs.

Kellock J.: . . . In my opinion, the learned trial judge does not address his mind to the proper point of time, namely, the inception of the defendant's undertaking which, at the latest, was the commencement of the journey at Chester on the morning of the accident. I have had the advantage of reading the opinion of my brother Rand and agree with him that that was the relevant time. In this view, I do not think it arguable that the situation was then such as *necessarily* to lead to the conclusion either that the plaintiff agreed to take upon herself the whole risk or that the defendant accepted her into his automobile on such a footing.

If this be so, then, again in agreement with my brother Rand, I do not understand how the defendant has established that, by reason of anything thereafter occurring, the terms of his undertaking were altered. The result is, as was the view of the court below, that the present is a case of contributory negligence on the part of the plaintiff, who "did not in her own interest take reasonable care of herself and contributed by this want of care, to her own injury". . . . The plaintiff had full opportunity to leave the car while it was stopped at In-gramport and she then had the knowledge of the facts and an appreciation of the risk to herself in continuing, which the learned trial judge has above described.

I would therefore dismiss the appeal with costs.

[Locke, Cartwright and Abbott JJ. agreed.]

NOTES

1. In *Miller* v. *Decker*, [1957] S.C.R. 624, 9 D.L.R. (2d) 1, the defendant, owner and driver of a motor car, and the plaintiff, together with a number of friends, agreed early in the evening that they would first go to a beer parlour and then on to a dance. At the beer parlour all of them had considerable to drink and all became intoxicated. Later, they drove to the dance hall and after they left the dance hall the defendant's car, due to his intoxication, was in-volved in a serious accident. In an action brought for damages, the defendant was found guilty of gross negligence (as required by statute in British Columbia for liability to a gratuitous passenger). The action was dismissed on the ground of voluntary assumption of risk and this judgment was upheld on appeal. On further appeal to the Supreme Court of Canada, a majority of three sustained the judgment dismissing the action.

Rand J. for the majority reasoned as follows: . . .

"From these facts the inference is clear that the three were acting together in a common purpose and that the drinking of each was an encouragement to the same act in the others. Being fully aware of the most likely conse-quences of this indulgence, each voluntarily committed himself to the spe-cial dangers which they then entered upon.

In that situation I cannot think that any difficulty arises in the application of the principles of liability for negligence. As between themselves there is no doubt of what would have been required by Decker in the interchange that is to be constructed between these young men as they sat down at the beer table to begin 'to make an evening of it'. That he would have required the other two to assume the risks all were able to foresee and would have partici-pated in creating, to take the same risks that he was taking, is unquestion-able. The conditions then existing, their inevitable development, and the ob-vious hazards were theirs equally and jointly; and one can imagine the rea-sonable response of Decker, had his mind still been clear enough, if either of them has let fall a suggestion that he would be responsible for their safety: they would have been told to get into another car.

It is equally clear that Miller is to be taken to have accepted that require-ment. This would have been obvious if he had remained sober and in com-mand of his faculties; and having, by his voluntary acts, co-operated in creat-ing and placing himself in the midst of the mounting dangers, his intoxication does not qualify his acceptance.

In this case, to treat either the question whether the assumption of the risk was a requirement of Decker or whether it was accepted by Miller as to be decided at the moment of setting out from the dance hall, would, in view of their conditions, be futile; one could not then rationally propose terms nor the other accept them: and only from the circumstances in which they moved to the fulfilment of their purpose around the beer table is the answer in either case to be drawn. The terms are to be inferred, then, on the under-standings which the ordinary persons of their age, aware of their situation and as it would develop, as reasonable and prudent young men, would have proposed, and accepted. That standard is imposed on those whose minds are clear and those who deliberately commit themselves to the vortex of such risks can claim no greater indulgence. . . ."

Abbott J., dissenting, observed: . . .

"It is clear from the judgments in this court in the *Seymour* case that for a negligent driver to be completely relieved from liability, the plaintiff must have agreed expressly or by implication to exempt the defendant from liability for damages suffered by plaintiff and occasioned by the negligence of the defendant during the carrying out of the latter's undertaking. In other words, to constitute a defence there must have been an expressed or implied bargain between the parties whereby the plaintiff gave up his right of action for negligence. . . .

It is not without significance, I think, that we were referred to no case decided in England since the passing of the *Law Reform (Contributory Negligence) Act*, 1945 (Imp.), c. 28, in which the doctrine of voluntary assumption of risk has been applied to relieve a defendant completely from civil liability for the consequences of his own negligence. . . .

In the instant case I am of opinion that the proper point of time at which appellant might be said to have voluntarily assumed the risk was when the three young men set out in respondent's car to visit the beer parlour. At that time no drinks had been consumed and the respondent John Decker stated that, as he was the driver, he had only intended to take one or two drinks. These good intentions as so often happens were not lived up to, but to paraphrase the words of Kellock J. in the *Seymour* case, *supra*, at p. 378 D.L.R., p. 332 S.C.R., I do not think that the situation was then such as *necessarily* to lead to the conclusion either that the appellant agreed to take upon himself the whole risk or that the respondent accepted him into his automobile on such a footing. Moreover, in my opinion the evidence established that after some two hours spent in the beer parlour appellant was in no condition to give such an undertaking."

Mr. Justice Abbott would have permitted 50 percent recovery in the case.

2. In *Lehnert* v. *Stein*, 36 D.L.R. (2d) 159 (S.C.C.); on appeal from 31 D.L.R. (2d) 673 (Man. C.A.), the defendant had been drinking at noon, and again at dinner time in the evening. He then proceeded to the Ivanhoe Restaurant where he had another drink. At the restaurant he met the plaintiff and invited her to go to a night club in the suburbs of Winnipeg. The plaintiff had one drink with the defendant before leaving the Ivanhoe at 9 p.m. At the night club the defendant, a well-known habitué, was served four drinks totalling ten ounces of whisky in less than two hours. The plaintiff had one drink only. At 11 p.m. the defendant started to drive the plaintiff home and at 11.05 p.m., driving at a high rate of speed, he lost control of the car and hit two power poles. The plaintiff was seriously injured and brought an action for damages.

The trial judge found that on leaving the night club the plaintiff was fully aware of the risk of an accident; that "defendant required her to accept the risk" in the sense, as explained by him, that had he "been asked to assume the safety of the plaintiff at the time of leaving the [night club] and had he been sober, he would have entered into no such undertaking". He further found that the plaintiff accepted the risk. As a result, he held the plaintiff's action failed on the basis of *volenti non fit injuria*. In the event he were wrong on the *volens* finding the trial judge assessed the plaintiff's fault at 75 percent as against the defendant's 25 percent.

On appeal, a majority (3:2) reversed the trial judgment; found the doctrine of *volens* did not apply; and although the plaintiff was guilty of contributory negligence, the fault was apportioned as 25 percent to the plaintiff and 75 percent to the defendant. Miller C.J.M., speaking for the majority, held that the time to determine *volens* was when the plaintiff got into the defendant's car at Ivanhoe. At that time the plaintiff did not know how much drinking the defendant had done and did not assume any risk of drunkenness because there was then no risk. On leaving the night club, even though the defendant was noticeably drunk, this did not make the plaintiff *volens*, but only contributorily negligent. The proper test of *volens* is not whether the plaintiff willingly ran the risk of intoxicated driving but whether she consented to absolve the defendant from the duty of care. Tritschler J.A., dissenting, agreed with the trial judge. "The leaving of the [night club] was unquestionably the proper time at which to assess the question of *volenti*." "Had defendant not been drunk, and had his mind been clear enough to appreciate a suggestion by plaintiff that he would be responsible for her safety, he would have told her to take a bus or taxi or to walk." Guy J.A., dissenting, said that using the hypothetical questions of Rand J., in the *Seymour* case, based on the evidence in this case, the "imaginary" conversation at the Ivanhoe might be as follows: "Defendant: 'How would you like . . . to come with me to the [night club]? We'll take my car. You know how I drive and you have often said 'go slower' and you know I don't pay any attention; but think of the fun! Are you willing to assume the risks in order to have a gay time?' Plaintiff: 'I'm always scared of an accident when I'm with you but you have never had one and for the sake of the gay evening I'm going to go. I will assume whatever risk there is of an accident.' "

On further appeal to the Supreme Court of Canada the judgment of the Manitoba Court of Appeal was sustained by a majority (4:1). All members of the court agreed that "the critical point of time" was when the plaintiff left the night club. Cartwright J., writing for the majority, stated that *Car & General Insurance Corp.* v. *Seymour and Maloney*

". . . establishes that where a driver of a motor vehicle invokes the maxim *volenti non fit injuria* as a defence to an action for damages for injuries caused by his negligence to a passenger, the burden lies upon the defendant of proving that the plaintiff, expressly or by necessary implication, agreed to exempt the defendant from liability for any damage suffered by the plaintiff occasioned by that negligence. . . .

There is nothing in the reasons delivered in this court in *Miller* v. *Decker*, 9 D.L.R. (2d) 1, [1957] S.C.R. 624, to throw any doubt on the principles enunciated in the *Seymour* case. In *Miller* v. *Decker* the majority were of the view that an agreement of the nature defined in the *Seymour* case should be implied from the active encouragement by the plaintiff of the defendant's conduct which resulted in disaster while the minority took the contrary view. The difference of opinion was not as to the applicable law but as to what inference of fact should be drawn from the primary facts. . . .

There is a most useful discussion as to when the defence of *volenti non fit injuria* is admitted in Mr. Glanville Williams' work *Joint Torts & Contributory Negligence*, 1951. At p. 296 the learned author points out that "the scope of the defence has been progressively curtailed since the end of the last century, so that at the present day it is allowed only when there is a positive agreement waiving the right of action."

I wish to adopt the following passages at p. 308 of the last mentioned work:

"It is submitted that the key to an understanding of the true scope of the *volens* maxim lies in drawing a distinction between what may be called physical and legal risk. Physical risk is the risk of damage in fact; legal risk is the risk of damage in fact for which there will be no redress in law. . . . To put this in general terms, the defence of *volens* does not apply where as a result of a mental process the plaintiff decides to take a chance but there is nothing in his conduct to show a waiver of the right of action communicated to the other party. To constitute a defence, there must have been an express or implied bargain between the parties whereby the plaintiff gave up his right of action for negligence."

On the facts of the case at bar the plaintiff, although apprehensive that the defendant would drive negligently and that an accident might result, decided to take a chance and go with him, that is to say, employing the phraseology of the passages just quoted, she thereby incurred the physical risk. In my opinion, there is nothing to warrant a finding that she decided to waive her right of action should she be injured or that she communicated any such decision to the defendant."

3. There is a fourth case in the Supreme Court of Canada, *Eid* v. *Dumas* (1969), 5 D.L.R. (3d) 561, where the plaintiff got the defendant to drive him somewhere after work. The plaintiff, over the defendant's objections, kept him awake until 4 a.m., when he finally fell asleep at the wheel and ran into a culvert, injuring the plaintiff. Mr. Justice Ritchie, speaking for the majority, held that the plaintiff was not *volens*, since he had not "taken upon himself the whole risk of being injured", nor did the defendant accept him into his automobile on any such footing. There was no reason to expect that there was any risk of his going to sleep at the wheel, since he was sober, the trip was only 30 miles and he could have stopped if he was too tired to continue. Mr. Justice Ritchie did not even feel that he was guilty of any contributory negligence. Martland J., although agreeing that the plaintiff was not *volens,* dissented on the issue of contributory negligence.

Professor Weiler has suggested that this decision has tacitly overruled *Miller* v. *Decker.* See "Groping Towards a Canadian Tort Law" (1974), 21 U. of T.L.J. 267, at p. 287. Do you agree? Certainly, the court did not express any such intention. See also *Mabey* v. *Robertson* (1970), 8 D.L.R. (3d) 84 (Alta. C.A.).

4. Since the Supreme Court has reformulated the Canadian law of *volenti,* there has been a flurry of decisions. Most of them have tended to hold that there was no assumption of the risk. In many of these cases, the plaintiff is a young person, a woman or someone who might be considered vulnerable or not in a position of equality with the driver. See *Simpson* v. *Parry* (1968), 65 W.W.R. 606 (B.C.S.C.) (17-year-old in back seat neither *volens* nor contributorily negligent); *Dorn* v. *Stevens* (1963), 39 D.L.R. (2d) 761 (16-and 17-year-olds held 50 percent to blame for going with unlicenced driver); *Prior* v. *Kyle* (1965), 55 W.W.R. 1 (B.C.C.A.) (16-year-old 25 percent to blame for failing to object to race in car); *Rondos* v. *Wawrin* (1968), 62 W.W.R. 369 (14-year-old 50 percent at fault for driving in stolen vehicle); *Van der Zouwen* v. *Koziak et al.* (1972), 25 D.L.R. (3d) 354 (Alta. C.A.) (plaintiff asleep); *Stevens* v. *Hoeberg* (1973), 29 D.L.R. (3d) 673 (woman, with several men, drank beer).

5. In some of the cases the courts seem to have leaned over backwards in avoiding the *volenti* doctrine. See *Lackner* v. *Neath* (1966), 57 W.W.R. 496 (Sask. C.A.) (plaintiff standing on bumpers of two cars while one being pushed by the other, 60 percent to blame); *Carnegie* v. *Trynchy* (1966), 57 W.W.R. 305 (Alta. S.C.) (girl's recovery reduced 50 percent, even though she speed-clocked the car in a drag race); *McDonald* v. *Dalgleish,* [1973] 2 O.R. 826, (25% fault). Occasionally, a plaintiff who drinks along with the driver (*Marasek* v. *Condie* (1958), 12 D.L.R. (2d) 252 (Alta.), 15% negligent), or even one who buys some of the liquor has been held not to be *volenti,* but merely contributorily negligent. See *Atwell* v. *Gertridge* (1958), 12 D.L.R. (2d) 669 (N.S.) (45% reduction).

6. Some courts have indicated that this defence should be avoided in passenger cases where possible, because it has in great measure lost its validity. Chief Justice MacKeigan has written that "for the *volenti* defence to succeed the Canadian law now requires proof that a bilateral bargain was actually made, expressly or by necessary implication from the facts, with the onus on the defendant to advance such proof, a burden especially difficult to discharge in passenger gross negligence cases". See *Crossan* v. *Gillis* (1979), 7 C.C.L.T. 269 (N.S.C.A.). See also *Ferris* v. *Stubbs* (1978), 89 D.L.R. (3d) 364 (N.B.C.A.).

7. There is a group of cases in which *volenti* is still employed. They are usually cases in which the conduct of the plaintiff is "extreme" (*Skinner* v. *Shawara* (1960), 67 Man. R. 90, at p. 104), involving something like "active encouragement" or "common purpose". See *Deauville* v. *Reid* (1967), 52 M.P.R. 218, at p. 223 (common intention to make a night of drinking); *Champagne* v. *Champagne* (1969), 67 W.W.R. 764 (B.C.S.C.) ("double-minded dedication to the achievement of drunkenness"); *Schwindt* v. *Giesbrecht* (1958), 13 D.L.R. (2d) 770 (Alta S.C.) (when stopped by the R.C.M.P. on the highway,

plaintiff incited driver to give them a "run for it" and got agreement of other passengers to chip in and share the fine, if they were caught); *Pepper* v. *Hoover* (1976), 71 D.L.R. (3d) 129 (Alta.) (high speed police chase); *Conrad* v. *Crawford,* [1972] 1 O.R. 134; *Boulay* v. *Wild,* [1972] 2 W.W.R. 234 (Alta. C.A.); *Allen* v. *Lucas* (1972), 25 D.L.R. (3d) 218 (Sask. C.A.) ("common purpose" to avoid apprehension by police); *Tomlinson* v. *Harrison,* [1972] 1 O.R. 670 (*ex turpi causa* also used); *Frehlick* v. *Andersen* (1961), 27 D.L.R. (2d) 46 (B.C.) *Kinney* v. *Haveman,* [1977] 1 W.W.R. 405 (B.C.).

8. It is no easy task to decide which approach a court will take in a specific case. In *Halliday* v. *Essex* (1972), 2 D.L.R. (3d) 293 (Ont. H.C.), for example, the plaintiff and a group of friends decided to spend a "drinking week-end" at a cottage. Late one night, the group, all of whom were intoxicated, went for a drive. An accident ensued. Lacourcière J. ruled that the plaintiff did not impliedly agree to "release the defendant from his responsibility for care" because he was drunk and "was in no position to appreciate the nature and extent of the risk and to freely release the defendant of his obligation to drive safely". The plaintiff was found to be 40 percent contributorily negligent. On the other hand, in *Conrad* v. *Crawford* (1972), 22 D.L.R. (3d) 386 (Ont. H.C.), the plaintiff, the defendant and a friend went on a beer-drinking joy-ride in the defendant's car. All three became intoxicated. When the defendant's driving attracted the attention of the police, he attempted to elude them. He lost control of his car and crashed into a telephone pole, injuring the plaintiff. Although the defendant was adjudged guilty of gross negligence, Mr. Justice Hughes denied recovery to the plaintiff because the defendant had shown that he "not only assumed the physical, but the legal risk". "The inference to be drawn from the circumstances of the whole transaction is that the plaintiff . . . agreed, by necessary implication of his conduct and the evidence he gave, to exempt the defendant . . . from liability for any damage suffered by him or as a result of the latter's negligence." It was a "pre-concerted expedition" with "encouragement" to continue drinking.

9. A third recent case is *Priestly* v. *Gilbert* (1974), 1 O.R. (2d) 365 (Ont. C.A.), where the plaintiff was severely injured when the car which the defendant was driving, and in which he was a passenger, went out of control and collided head-on with an approaching vehicle. Both young men had drunk to excess. In determining whether the maxim applied, Schroeder J.A., for the court, stated: "On the facts and circumstances disclosed by the record it appears to us that the plaintiff must be taken by implication, to have consented to the physical and legal risk of injury involved. This may be inferred from the joint venture undertaken by these friends of long standing, involving, as it did, the consumption by them of copious quantities of spirits and beer and the driving of his motor vehicle by the respondent Gilbert when he might, as he did, become hopelessly intoxicated and grossly impaired." The court dismissed the contention that the plaintiff's intoxicated state precluded the implication that he had consented to take the legal risk.

10. The process of reasoning in these cases has been described as a "bit fanciful" by Gordon, "Drunken Drivers and Willing Passengers" (1966), 82 L.Q.Rev. 62, also at (1966), 14 Chitty's L.J. 203. Do you agree? Can you think of a test to distinguish the cases? One effort at distinguishing these cases was made by Lieff J. in *McDonald* v. *Dalgleish,* [1973] 2 O.R. 826, at p. 837, where he said: "One can distinguish between the cases which might be determined 'the common enterprise' type of situation . . . and those cases which may be referred to as the 'drive home' cases." Another attempt to rationalize the cases focuses on the "degree of involvement by the plaintiff in the drinking or wrongdoing. Where the plaintiff's conduct is really serious or where he has encouraged or fully become a part of the dangerous activity, he may be said to have been *volens.*" See Linden, *Canadian Tort Law* (2nd ed., 1977), p. 439. Can it fairly be said that, "assumption of risk may be implied from a situation in which the plaintiff encourages the defendant to involve himself in the risk-creating activity but apparently not if the plaintiff merely becomes part of the dangerous activity in a

rather passive way". See Hertz, "Volenti Non Fit Injuria: A Guide" in Klar (ed.), *Studies in Canadian Tort Law* (1977), p. 122.

Can you do better than any of these three efforts?

11. See James, "Assumption of Risk" (1952), 61 Yale L.J. 141:

"The doctrine of assumption of risk, however it is analyzed and defined, is in most of its aspects a defendant's doctrine which restricts liability and so cuts down the compensation of accident victims. It is a heritage of the extreme individualism of the early industrial revolution. But quite aside from any questions of policy or of substance, the concept of assuming the risk is purely duplicative of other more widely understood concepts, such as scope of duty or contributory negligence. The one exception is to be found, perhaps, in these cases where there is an actual agreement. Moreover, the expression has come to stand for two or three distinct notions which are not at all the same, though they often overlap in the sense that they are applicable to the same action.

Except for express assumption of risk, therefore, the term and the concept should be abolished. It adds nothing to modern law except confusion. For the most part the policy of individualism it represents is outmoded in accident law; where it is not, that policy can find full scope and far better expression in other language."

12. See also Wade, "The Place of Assumption of Risk in the Law of Negligence" (1961), 22 La. L. Rev. 5:

"The expression, assumption of risk, is a very confusing one. In application it conceals many policy issues, and it is constantly being used to beg the real question. Accurate analysis in the law of negligence would probably be advanced if the term were eradicated and the cases divided under the topics of consent, lack of duty, and contributory negligence. Then the true issues involved would be more clearly presented and the determinations, whether by judge or jury, could be more accurately and realistically rendered.

But the term appears to be here to stay. There is little indication that the courts have shown any tendency to relinquish its use. Though it overlaps other fields there is a unifying idea in the cases coming within its circle — the idea that the plaintiff has deliberately subjected himself to the danger. To speak of assumption of risk in this situation is a natural thing to do. Persons with no legal background often use the term when speaking of factual situations like those in which the courts use it.

The advantages of the use of the expression, assumption of risk, are forensic and administrative. Assumption of risk often affords a quick and easy way of talking about the issue without undertaking an analysis of the total problem. It offers the court another legal device for use in handling a negligence case and thus increases the freedom of action of the deciding agency — whether trial judge, jury, or appellate court. Much of the time it does not prevent the court from reaching the correct result. Its disadvantages lie primarily in its obfuscatory nature. It may either prevent an accurate analysis by the court of the real problems involved in reaching the decision, or permit the court to write an opinion which elides or covers up the real basis of the decision."

13. The defence of *volenti* is often held unavailable to a defendant who is himself in violation of a statute. Where the defendant breaches legislation requiring that a highway be kept in good repair, the offender cannot rely on a voluntary assumption of risk: *Greer* v. *Mulmur* (1926), 59 O.L.R. 259, at p. 265, *per* Masten J.A. and at p. 267, *per* Riddell J.A. dissenting. See also *Jesson* v. *Livingstone,* [1929] 2 D.L.R. 474, at p. 479 (Sask. C.A.), *per* McKay J.A.; *Baddeley* v. *Granville* (1887), 19 Q.B.D. 423. Similarly, if the plaintiff is injured at work because of a violation of the Factories Act, *volenti* cannot be invoked by the employer so as to thwart the policy of protecting workmen from injury: *McClemont* v. *Kilgour Mfg. Co.* (1913), 27 O.L.R. 305, at p. 312, *per* Teetzel J. See also *Rodgers* v. *Hamilton Cotton Co.* (1887), 23 O.R. 425, at p. 435. On the other hand, the fact that the criminal code or a speeding statute is contra-

vened by a defendant does not render inapplicable the *volenti* defence, because these statutes are not aimed at the highly desirable social goal of worker safety with which consent cannot interfere: see *Miller v. Decker*, [1957] S.C.R. 624, at p. 634, *per* Kellock J. Recently, it has been established that an employer may rely on *volenti* where the statute is violated, not by the employer himself, but by one of his workmen: see *I.C.I. Ltd. v. Shatwell*, [1964] 2 All E.R. 999 (H.L.). See also Atiyah, "Causation, Contributory Negligence and *Volenti Non Fit Injuria*" (1965), 43 Can. Bar Rev. 609.

D. ILLEGALITY

TOMLINSON v. HARRISON

Ontario High Court of Justice. [1972] 1 O.R. 670

The plaintiff, the defendant and a third person, after having drunk a large quantity of beer, stole a car. They went for a drive, with the defendant at the wheel, drinking beer as they roared along at 100 m.p.h. They were spotted by a police cruiser which gave chase. In trying to elude apprehension, the car went off the road and the plaintiff was injured. Mr. Justice Addy held that the action was barred both because of the principle of *ex turpi causa non oritur actio* and voluntary assumption of risk.

Addy J.: . . . the defendant Harrison, among other defences, raised the defence of *ex turpi causa non oritur actio.*

It appears clear that at least the following offences were committed that afternoon and evening: the theft of two cars; drinking while driving; reckless or dangerous driving; driving while intoxicated, or at least when the driver's ability to drive was impaired; escaping or attempting to escape apprehension by the police.

In considering the defence of *ex turpi*, the first question, of course, is whether the plaintiff was or was not a party to any of these offences and, secondly, whether the accident occurred as a result of the commission of the offence in question and as a natural consequence of the commission of same. . . . In a civil case, where a finding that one of the parties committed a criminal act is an element of the case such a fact need not be established beyond the reasonable doubt in accordance with the standard of proof required in criminal cases, but merely on a balance of probabilities in accordance with the standard in civil cases. . . .

Applying this test, I find that the plaintiff was an active party to the theft of both cars, that, by supplying drinks to the driver Harrison from the back seat of the car she became a party to the offence of drinking while driving and contributed to, and was a party to the offence of driving while intoxicated or impaired, and reckless or dangerous driving for, notwithstanding the evidence of the police to the effect that, in the short time that they observed the car, they did not notice that anything in the actual driving showed a lack of ability to drive. . . .

As to the offence of escaping apprehension the plaintiff was not, of course, driving the car. There is no evidence whatsoever that she, in any way, resisted or objected to the attempt to escape. . . .[I]n the absence of any evidence that the common purpose no longer existed and that she had disassociated herself from the actual attempt to escape, I find that, on a balance of probabilities she was a party to the attempt to escape apprehension.

Counsel for the plaintiff, as to the defence of "*ex turpi* as well as to the defence of *volenti non fit injuria*", to which I shall refer later, argued most forcibly that his client was so intoxicated as to be totally unable to either agree to commit any criminal act or to consent to assume the risk which ultimately resulted in the accident. . . .

There is really no evidence whatsoever that the plaintiff was so drunk as to be unable to give the necessary consent for a defence of *volenti non fit injuria* to succeed or to be unable to understand the nature of the criminal acts and thereby escape a defence of *ex turpi.*

In civil cases, as well as in criminal cases, a person is presumed to intend the natural consequences of his or her acts. The onus is on any person alleging drunkeness as an answer, to establish, on a balance of probabilities, that drunkeness in fact existed to the degree required at the relevant time.

In the absence of any positive evidence to the contrary, I find that the plaintiff must have known, or must be presumed to have known what she was doing and that the above-mentioned unlawful acts were in fact unlawful. . . .

As previously stated, there is no evidence of any expressed words of encouragement on the part of the plaintiff to the defendant to speed up and escape the police as in the case of *Schwindt* v. *Giesbrecht, Doe and Doe* (1958), 13 D.L.R. (2d) 770, 25 W.W.R. 18, but there certainly is ample evidence of a common enterprise and the attempt to elude the police, having regard to the conduct of the parties, must necessarily be held to be a common one to which all three agreed, with presumably full knowledge of the possible consequences.

I therefore conclude that there was a common intention to pursue not only an unlawful purpose but a criminal purpose at the time of the accident and the damage suffered by the plaintiff was a direct and readily foreseeable result of that common purpose. (*R.* v. *Baldessare* (1930), 22 Cr. App. R. 70.) It follows that, on the principle of *ex turpi causa non oritur actio,* the action of the plaintiff must fail. . . .

I feel that the defence of *ex turpi* is part and parcel of the law torts in the province and is available as a defence when all the necessary elements are present. When two criminals are pursuing a joint criminal venture and, in the attainment of the criminal object, one of them happens to be injured, and when the occurrence from which the injury results is a natural and probable consequence of the attempt to attain the criminal object, I fail to see why our courts should give any relief to one of them who happens to be injured in the process, or how, or why our courts, in such a case, should proceed to apply to the conduct of one of them the test of what a reasonable man would do in those circumstances in order to give some relief to the other. Although there might possibly be some question whether today, in this jurisdiction, the defence of *ex turpi* is available as between two parties involved in an unlawful act constituting a mere breach of a penal statute or a minor offence of the nature of those formerly known at common law as misdemeanours, it is available, as in the present case, between two parties involved in the commission of an indictable offence.

Where, of course, the defence of *ex turpi* exists, it is not necessary for a court to ask itself whether the plaintiff did expressly or impliedly renounce any legal right of action against the defendant, as must be done in the case of a defence of *volenti non fit injuria.* However, since counsel argued the possible defence of *volenti* most extensively, and in the eventuality of a higher court not sharing my view as to the application of the doctrine of *ex turpi*, consideration should be given to the question of whether a defence of *volenti non fit injuria* would prevail in the circumstances of this case. . . .

In the case at bar, drinking with the driver while the car is proceeding on the highway and handing bottles of beer forwards so that the driver may drink with full knowledge that the driver was intoxicated or at the very least impaired, in my view, identifies the plaintiff with the driver's conduct and necessarily leads to the inference that the plaintiff voluntarily assumed the risk. . . .

The case before me is far from being one where the passenger passively accepts a gratuitous ride in a car driven by a person who is in fact and who appears to be intoxicated. There was a joint venture created from the very beginning when it was decided in the tavern to steal a car in order to get to Ottawa and the active participation of the plaintiff throughout continued the joint dangerous venture until the moment of the accident. The unfortunate result could easily have been foreseen and was a natural consequence of the many reckless actions taken up to that moment. The case is one which, in my view, falls in the category of these referred to as joint dangerous ventures or common dangerous enterprises. . . .

On the circumstances of this case I, therefore, find that the plaintiff was *volens,* in the sense that she must at law be presumed to have had a full knowledge of the risk, to have agreed to incur it and to absolve the defendant Harrison from any legal liability arising as a result of his actions in pursuing their joint venture.

NOTES

1. Is this a clever way of dealing with cases such as these? Is it more ingenuous than some of the above cases dealing with *volenti*? What is wrong with this approach? Is this the old "stalemate rule" creeping back into the law? See Gibson's eloquent plea, "Illegality of Plaintiff's Conduct as a Defence" (1969), 47 Can. Bar Rev. 89:
> "There is no justification, either in policy or in law, for introducing the *ex turpi causa* defence to the law of tort."

See also Wright, "Comment", [1946] 3 D.L.R. 172. Compare with Dean Fridman's solution in "The Wrongdoing Plaintiff" (1972), 18 McGill L.J. 275. See also Weinrib, "Illegality as a Tort Defence" (1976), 26 U.T.L.J. 28.

2. In *Tallow et al.* v. *Tailfeathers et al.,* [1973] 6 W.W.R. 732 (Alta. C.A.), a group of young men stole a car following heavy drinking. Predictably, serious injury and death ensued when a car crash ended the revelry. The majority of the Alberta Court of Appeal ruled that the plaintiff's action must be dismissed on the ground of voluntary assumption of risk. Mr. Justice Clement concurred but preferred to rest his decision on *ex turpi causa*. During the course of a long and learned opinion, these comments appeared:
> ". . . I understand that the positive law, of which Lord Mansfield spoke in the context of an immoral or illegal act, [in a contract setting] is one that prohibits the commission of an act that has such a quality of turpitude that it must be regarded as anti-social. The cause of action must arise out of the commission of that act, and the participation of the claimant in the act.
>
> Thus, the applicability of the rule is dependent on behaviour on the part of the plaintiff which in its nature and degree is inimical to the interests of society, and on his claim against the defendant 'arising' out of that behaviour. Both must concur to warrant denial of his claim. Judgment must be based, not on the social and legal structure of a past century, but on the present changes and changing conditions of society and the proliferating controls of conduct in the pervasive juridical system by which it is governed. . . ."

3. In *Bigcharles et al.* v. *Merkel et al.,* [1973] 1 W.W.R. 324 (B.C.S.C.), the plaintiff's husband, with four other thieves, broke and entered a building, the premises of a furniture company. The defendant, an employee of the company, was aroused by the noise. He armed himself with a rifle, went to the storage room, turned on the lights and saw the burglars, who immediately exited through a window. The defendant inexplicably fired one shot after them. It struck and killed the deceased, whose wife brought an action for damages. Mr. Justice Seaton accepted the defendant's evidence that he did not intend to hit the deceased, but held that the act of shooting was nevertheless negligent in the circumstances, since it could not be "justified as preventing crime, preventing

a continuance of a breach of the peace, a step in an arrest, protection of property, repelling a trespasser, protection of himself or those under his care, or preventing breaking in or breaking out of a dwelling". His Lordship rejected the defence of voluntary assumption of risk on the ground that the most the plaintiff might have had was "knowledge of the possibility of a wrongful act." His Lordship also indicated that the widow was not barred from recovery because of "public policy". Since counsel for the plaintiff conceded that the deceased was also "at fault", His Lordship held that because the deceased's fault was "much the greater", his family could recover only 25 percent of the loss, 75 percent of the blame being attributed to the deceased.

Should this case have been decided on the ground of *ex turpi causa*? What if the plaintiff had survived and had sued on his own behalf?

4. In *Teece et al.* v. *Honeybourn et al.* (1975), 54 D.L.R. (3d) 549 (B.C.), the deceased, Teece, was one of four suspects who entered a stolen car which was under police surveillance. The suspects attempted to drive away but were blocked in a lane by two police cruisers. They then tried to flee on foot, and the four policemen in the cruisers got out and gave chase after the suspects ignored calls to surrender. During the course of the pursuit, the defendant Honeybourn, heard a shot and saw one of his fellow officers apparently go down as if hit. He drew his revolver and ran after the deceased. He caught up with him and, in the ensuing struggle to effect an arrest, Honeybourn's gun discharged, killing Teece.

The plaintiffs, the father and grandmother of the deceased, brought an action framed in assault and negligence under the Families Compensation Act, R.S.B.C., c. 138, against the four officers. The action against the three officers other than Honeybourn failed, but Honeybourn was held negligent to the extent of 20%, and Teece contributorily negligent to the extent of 80%. In addressing the issue of illegality, which was pleaded as a defence, Rae J. declared:

> "The defence pleads *ex turpi causa non oritur actio*. This is a defence more commonly put forward in a case of contract. It has seemingly been only rarely applied in cases of tort, and that only where the plaintiff and the defendant have each been engaged, for example, in a common criminal enterprise at the time of the infliction of the alleged wrong. The defence refers me to cases such as *Tomlinson* v. *Harrison et al.* (1971), 24 D.L.R. (3d) 26, [1972] 1 O.R. 670 (H.C.), where both the parties were involved in turpitude. A case to the same general effect is *Tallow et al.* v. *Tailfeathers et al.* (1973), 44 D.L.R. (3d) 55, [1973] 6 W.W.R. 732 (Alta. App. Div.). The principle is founded on public policy. It would be contrary to public policy, it seems to me, to apply it in the case before me to exclude the claim of the plaintiffs. It may seem somewhat anomalous that where the defendants, as here, were not involved as participants in the criminal wrongdoing, they may not have the advantage of the defence, whereas, were they so involved, they might have that advantage. But that appears to be the law. (See Fleming, *Law of Torts* 4th ed. (1971), p. 232; Salmond, *Law of Torts*, 16th ed. (1973), para. 190, and *National Coal Board* v. *England*, [1954] A.C. 403 at pp. 418-20, 424-5 and 428-9.)"

See also *Smith* v. *Jenkins* (1970), 119 C.L.R. 397, *cf. Craft* v. *Stocks and Parkes (Bldg.) Pty. Ltd.,* [1975] 2 N.S.W.L.R. 156 (C.A.); varied (1976), 51 A.L.J.R. 184.

5. In *Murphy* v. *Culhane,* [1976] 3 All E.R. 533 (C.A.), a motion to strike out defences was rejected by Denning M.R., who stated, when a "burglar breaks into a house and the householder, finding him there, picks up a gun and shoots him, using more force maybe than is reasonably necessary . . . [t]he householder might well have a defence either on grounds of *ex turpi causa non oritur actio* or *volenti non fit injuria*". See also *Cummings* v. *Granger,* [1976] 3 W.L.R. 842 (C.A.) *per* Denning M.R. Does this new concept frighten you? Or is it a necessary development?

6. In *Lewis* v. *Sayers* (1971), 13 D.L.R. (3d) 543 (Ont. Dist. Ct.), an intoxicated owner of a vehicle allowed an intoxicated friend to drive them both on a short trip in the course of which the driver negligently collided with a parked

car. The defence of *volenti* did not apply because there was no bargain, express or implied, to give up his right of action. Gould D.C.J., nevertheless, apportioned liability 50-50 on the ground that the Ontario Negligence Act covered such conduct. He explained:

"The defendant relied mainly upon the maxim *ex turpi causa non oritur actio* and this matter was argued at length and requires serious consideration. If the defendant should succeed in establishing either of these special defences, my previous findings as to negligence and respective degrees of fault would be of no importance, as the plaintiff would be absolutely debarred from recovering against the defendant. I was referred to the article on this subject by Mr. Dale Gibson printed in 47 Can. Bar Rev. 89 (1969), and to a long list of cases, many of which are referred to in the article. . . .

These cases, of course, make it very clear that the maxim *ex turpi causa non oritur actio* under proper circumstances applies and is frequently used in our courts.

The two Manitoba cases of *Ridgeway* v. *Hilhorst* and *Rondos* v. *Wawrin*, although different in their facts from the present case, both suggest that the *ex turpi causa* doctrine might apply here. An important consideration, however, is that the Manitoba statute which corresponds to s. 4 of the Ontario Negligence Act is worded differently, in that it refers only to negligence rather than to fault or negligence. The result would appear to be that the Ontario statute applies to a considerably wider range of situations than the Manitoba Act. Section 4 of the Ontario Negligence Act reads as follows:

4. In any action for damages that is founded upon the fault or negligence of the defendant if fault or negligence is found on the part of the plaintiff that contributed to the damages, the court shall apportion the damages in proportion to the degree of fault or negligence found against the parties respectively.

It appears to me that in a case to which, by reason of its facts, s. 4 of the Negligence Act applies, the Ontario Legislature has quite deliberately substituted for the *ex turpi causa* rule a positive direction that the court shall make a finding as to the degree of fault or negligence to be attributed to each party and shall apportion the damages accordingly. I realize of course that s. 4 was enacted primarily to do away with the absolute defence formerly available in cases of contributory negligence, but the wording is equally apt in relation to the defence now under discussion, to which the added words 'fault or' seem to apply with particular force. The defence *ex turpi causa non oritur actio* seems necessarily to involve a situation where both parties are alleged to be at fault, and so long as it is remembered that s. 4 applies only where the fault of each has contributed to the damages, in my opinion the section leaves no room for the application of the maxim."

Do you agree? Why not rely on *ex turpi causa* and then apportion in accordance with the Negligence Act? Is there anything that forbids this? If *ex turpi causa* were handled in this way, how would it differ from ordinary contributory negligence? Should this illegality defence be allowed to survive as a complete bar to recovery?

7. In *Bond* v. *Loutit*, [1979] 2 W.W.R. 154 (Man. Q.B.), Hamilton J. refused to use the *ex turpi causa* defence where the plaintiff was injured when a car he helped steal was later involved in an accident because the theft of the car was not connected to the negligence causing the accident. The court felt that this defence, which was based on "public policy", had only limited application.

CHAPTER 12

STRICT LIABILITY

As must have become apparent in preceding chapters, negligence frequently involves no moral fault and consists merely in a failure to conform to certain standards of conduct. Only a slight shifting of emphasis is required to impose liability where not only is there no moral wrongdoing, but no failure to observe a standard of care, however highly pitched. There are certain types of conduct which, although they cannot be styled wrongful, are either so fraught with danger, or so unusual in a given community, that it is felt that the risk of loss should be shifted from the person injured to the person who, merely by engaging in such conduct, created the risk which resulted in harm. The extent to which the growth of such liability is due to a feeling that certain inevitable risks of harm can better be distributed than to leave it on the shoulders of the injured person is shown by modern Workmen's Compensation Acts. The haphazard advance of judicial decisions in the same direction must have become evident in earlier chapters in connection with the part played by *"res ipsa loquitur"* and other devices which, while preserving the language of "fault", frequently produce results far removed from that concept. The present chapter is devoted to the cases which have consciously admitted the principle of liability for non-negligent and unintended harms.

A. ORIGIN AND SCOPE

RYLANDS v. FLETCHER

House of Lords. (1868), L.R. 3 H.L. 330; 37 L.J. Ex. 161:
affg. L.R. 1 Ex. 265

Fletcher brought an action against Rylands and Horrocks to recover damages for injury to his mines caused by water flowing into them from a reservoir built on the defendants' land. The declaration alleged negligence on the part of defendants. When the case came on for trial, it was referred to an arbitrator who was later asked to state a special case for the consideration of the Court of Exchequer.

The special case stated the material facts as follows: Fletcher was, with the permission of the landowners and the lessee, Lord Wilton, working coal mines and had worked the mines up to a spot where old passages of disused mines and a vertical shaft filled with rubbish were encountered. Rylands and Horrocks owned a mill near the land under which Fletcher's mines were being worked. With Lord Wilton's permission they constructed a reservoir on Lord Wilton's land in order to supply water to their mill. They employed competent engineers and contractors to construct the reservoir and Rylands and Horrocks did not know that coal had ever been worked under or near the site of the reservoir. The site chosen, however, was over old coal mines which communicated with the workings of Fletcher. While there was no negligence on the part of the defendants, the contractors did encounter old shafts while building the reservoir and it was found that they did not use reasonable care to provide sufficient supports for the reservoir when filled with water.

The reservoir was completed early in December, 1860, and was partially filled with water. On the 11th of December one of the old shafts gave way and the water in the reservoir flowed into the old mine workings and large quantities of the water found their way into Fletcher's workings and flooded them.

The question for the court was whether the plaintiff was, on these facts, entitled to recover damages from the defendants.

The Court of Exchequer (Pollock C.B. and Martin B., Bramwell B. dissenting) gave judgment for the defendants: (1865), 3 H. & C. 774. The plaintiff brought error in the Exchequer Chamber.

Blackburn J.: . . . The plaintiff, though free from all blame on his part, must bear the loss unless he can establish that it was the consequence of some default for which the defendants are responsible. The question of law therefore arises, What is the obligation which the law casts on the person who, like the defendants, lawfully brings on his land something which, though harmless whilst it remains there, will naturally do mischief if it escape out of his land? It is agreed on all hands that he must take care to keep in that which he has brought on the land and keeps there, in order that it may not escape and damage his neighbours, but the question arises whether the duty which the law casts upon him, under such circumstances, is an absolute duty to keep it in at his peril, or is, as the majority of the Court of Exchequer have thought, merely a duty to take all reasonable and prudent precautions, in order to keep it in, but no more. If the first be the law, the person who has brought on his land and kept there something dangerous, and failed to keep it in, is responsible for all the natural consequences of its escape. If the second be the limit of his duty, he would not be answerable except on proof of negligence, and consequently would not be answerable for escape arising from any latent defect which ordinary prudence and skill could not detect.

Supposing the second to be the correct view of the law, a further question arises subsidiary to the first, *viz.*, whether the defendants are not so far identified with the contractors whom they employed, as to be responsible for the consequences of their want of care and skill in making the reservoir in fact insufficient with reference to the old shafts of the existence of which they were aware, though they had not ascertained where the shaft went to.

We think that the true rule of law is, that the person who for his own purposes brings on his lands and collects and keeps there anything likely to do mischief if it escapes, must keep it in at his peril, and, if he does not do so, is *prima facie* answerable for all the damage which is the natural consequence of its escape. He can excuse himself by showing that the escape was the consequence of *vis major,* or the act of God; but as nothing of this sort exists here, it is unnecessary to inquire what excuse would be sufficient. The general rule, as above stated, seems on principle just. The person whose grass or corn is eaten down by the escaping cattle of his neighbour, or whose mine is flooded by the water from his neighbour's reservoir, or whose cellar is invaded by the filth of his neighbour's privy, or his habitation is made unhealthy by the fumes and noisome vapours of his neighbour's alkali works, is damnified without fault of his own; and it seems but reasonable and just that the neighbour, who has brought something on his own property which was not naturally there, harmless to others so long as it was confined to his own property, but which he knows to be mischievous if it gets on his neighbour's, should be obliged to make good the damage which ensues if he does not succeed in confining it to his own property. But for his act in bringing it there no mischief could have accrued, and it seems but just that he should at his peril keep it there so that no mischief may accrue, or answer for the natural and anticipated consequences. And upon authority, this we think is established to be the law whether the things so brought be beasts, or water, or filth, or stenches.

The case that has most commonly occurred, and which is most frequently to be found in the books, is as to the obligation of the owner of cattle which he has brought on his land, to prevent them escaping and doing mischief. The law as to them seems to be perfectly settled from early times; the owner must keep them in at his peril, or he will be answerable for the natural consequences of their escape; that is with regard to tame beasts, for the grass they eat and trample upon, though not for any injury to the person of others, for our ancestors have settled that it is not the general nature of horses to kick, or bulls to gore, but if the owner knows that the beast has a vicious propensity to attack men, he will be answerable for that too. . . . These authorities, and the absence of any authority to the contrary, justify Williams J., in saying as he does in *Cox* v. *Burbidge,* that the law is clear that in actions for damage occasioned by animals that have not been kept in by their owners, it is quite immaterial whether the escape is by negligence or not.

As has been already said, there does not appear to be any difference in principle between the extent of the duty cast on him who brings cattle on his land to keep them in, and the extent of the duty imposed on him who brings on his land, water, filth, or stenches, or any other thing which will, if it escape, naturally do damage to prevent their escaping and injuring his neighbour, and the case of *Tenant* v. *Goldwin,* 1 Salk. 21, 360, is an express authority that the duty is the same, and is, to keep them in at his peril. [Blackburn J. discussed this case, in which a defendant was held liable for the seepage of filth from a privy on his premises to the plaintiff's premises.] As Lord Raymond in his report, 2 Ld. Raym. at p. 1092 said: "The reason of this case is upon this account, that every one must so use his own as not to do damage to another; and as every man is bound so to look to his cattle as to keep them out of his neighbour's ground, that so he may receive no damage; so he must keep in the filth of his house or office that it may not flow in upon and damnify his neighbour. . . ."

No case has been found in which the question as to the liability for noxious vapours escaping from a man's works by inevitable accident has been discussed, but the following case will illustrate it. Some years ago several actions were brought against the occupiers of some alkali works at Liverpool for the damage alleged to be caused by the chlorine fumes of their works. The defendants proved that they at great expense erected contrivances by which the fumes of chlorine were condensed and sold as muriatic acid, and they called a great body of scientific evidence to prove that this apparatus was so perfect that no fumes possibly could escape from the defendants' chimneys. On this evidence it was pressed upon the jury that the plaintiff's damage must have been due to some of the numerous other chimneys in the neighbourhood; the jury, however, being satisfied that the mischief was occasioned by chlorine, drew the conclusion that it had escaped from the defendants' works somehow, and in each case found for the plaintiff. No attempt was made to disturb these verdicts on the ground that the defendants had taken every precaution which prudence or skill could suggest to keep those fumes in, and that they could not be responsible unless negligence were shown. . . . The uniform course of pleading in actions on such nuisances is to say that the defendant caused the noisome vapours to arise on his premises, and suffered them to come on the plaintiff's, without stating that there was any want of care or skill in the defendant, and that the case of *Tenant* v. *Goldwin, supra,* showed that this was founded on the general rule of law, that he whose stuff it is must keep it that it may not trespass. . . .

But it was further said by Martin B. that when damage is done to personal property, or even to the person, by collision, either upon land or at sea, there must be negligence in the party doing the damage to render him legally responsible; and this is no doubt true, and as was pointed out by Mr. Mellish during his argument before us, this is not confined to cases of collision, for there are many cases in which proof of negligence is essential, as, for instance, where an unruly horse gets on the footpath of a public street and kills a passenger: *Hammack* v. *White,* 11 C.B.N.S. 588; or where a person in a dock is struck by the falling of a bale of cotton which the defendant's servants are lowering: *Scott* v. *London Dock Company,* 3 H. & C. 596; and many other similar cases may be found. But we think these cases distinguishable from the present. Traffic on the highways, whether by land or sea, cannot be conducted without exposing those whose persons or property are near it to some inevitable risk; and that being so, those who go on the highway, or have their property adjacent to it, may well be held to do so subject to their taking upon themselves the risk of injury from that inevitable danger; and persons who by the licence of the owner pass near to warehouses where goods are being raised or lowered, certainly do so subject to the inevitable risk of accident. In neither case, therefore, can they recover without proof of want of care or skill occasioning the accident; and it is believed that all the cases in which inevitable accident has been held an excuse for what *prima facie* was a trespass, can be explained on the same principle, *viz.,* that the circumstances were such as to show that the plaintiff had taken that risk upon himself. But there is no ground for saying that the plaintiff here took upon himself any risk arising from the uses to which the defendants should choose to apply their land. He neither knew what these might be, nor could he in any way control the defendants, or hinder their building what reservoirs they liked, and storing up in them what water they pleased, so long as the defendants succeeded in preventing the water which they there brought from interfering with the plaintiff's property.

The view which we take of the first point renders it unnecessary to consider whether the defendants would or would not be responsible for the want of care and skill in the persons employed by them, under the circumstances stated in the case.

We are of opinion that the plaintiff is entitled to recover, but as we have not heard any argument as to the amount, we are not able to give judgment for what damages. The parties probably will empower their counsel to agree on the amount of damages; should they differ on the principle the case may be mentioned again.

[Rylands and Horrocks appealed to the House of Lords.]

The Lord Chancellor (Lord Cairns): . . . My Lords, the principles on which this case must be determined appear to me to be extremely simple. The defendants, treating them as the owners or occupiers of the close on which the reservoir was constructed, might lawfully have used that close for any purpose for which it might in the ordinary course of the enjoyment of land be used; and if, in what I may term the natural user of that land, there had been any accumulation of water, either on the surface or under ground, and if, by the operation of the laws of nature, that accumulation of water had passed off into the close occupied by the plaintiff, the plaintiff could not have complained that that result had taken place. If he had desired to guard himself against it, it would have lain upon him to have done so by leaving, or by interposing, some barrier between his close and the close of the defendants in order to have prevented that operation of the laws of nature. . . .

On the other hand, if the defendants, not stopping at the natural use of their close, had desired to use it for any purpose which I may term a non-natural use for the purpose of introducing into the close that which in its natural condition was not in or upon it, for the purpose of introducing water either above or below ground in quantities and in a manner not the result of any work or operation on or under the land; and if in consequence of their doing so, or in consequence of any imperfection in the mode of their doing so, the water came to escape and to pass off into the close of the plaintiff, then it appears to me that that which the defendants were doing they were doing at their own peril; and if in the course of their doing it the evil arose to which I have referred, the evil, namely, of the escape of the water and its passing away to the close of the plaintiff and injuring the plaintiff, then for the consequence of that, in my opinion, the defendants would be liable. . . .

My Lords, these simple principles, if they are well founded, as it appears to me they are, really dispose of this case.

[Lord Cairns then quoted from Blackburn J.'s opinion in the Exchequer Chamber.] My Lords, in that opinion I must say I entirely concur. Therefore, I have to move your Lordships that the judgment of the Court of Exchequer Chamber be affirmed, and that the present appeal be dismissed with costs.

Lord Cranworth: My Lords, I concur with my noble and learned friend in thinking that the rule of law was correctly stated by Mr. Justice Blackburn in delivering the opinion of the Exchequer Chamber. If a person brings, or accumulates, on his land anything which, if it should escape, may cause damage to his neighbour, he does so at his peril. If it does escape and cause damage, he is responsible, however careful he may have been, and whatever precautions he may have taken to prevent the damage.

In considering whether a defendant is liable to a plaintiff for damage which the plaintiff may have sustained, the question in general is not whether the defendant has acted with due care and caution, but whether his acts have occasioned the damage. This is all well explained in the old case of *Lambert* v. *Bessey*, reported by Sir Thomas Raymond: Sir T. Raym. 421. And the doctrine is founded on good sense. For when one person, in managing his own affairs, causes, however innocently, damage to another, it is obviously only just that he should be the party to suffer. He is bound *sic uti suo ut non laedat alienum.* This is the principle of law applicable to cases like the present, and I do not discover in the authorities which were cited anything conflicting with it. . . .

The defendants, in order to effect an object of their own, brought on to their land, or on to land which for this purpose may be treated as being theirs, a large accumulated mass of water, and stored it up in a reservoir. The consequence of this was damage to the plaintiff, and for that damage, however skilfully and carefully the accumulation was made, the defendants, according to the principles and authorities to which I have adverted, were certainly responsible.

I concur, therefore, with my noble and learned friend in thinking that the judgment below must be affirmed, and that there must be judgment for the defendant in error.

NOTES

1. Why was the defendant not held liable for the negligence of the contractor, as he would be today? Why was there no trespass? Why was there no liability for nuisance?

2. Are the opinions of Mr. Justice Blackburn and Lord Cairns in accord? What is the difference between them? What is the rule in *Rylands* v. *Fletcher?*

3. In addition to the term strict liability, the phrases "absolute liability" and "liability without fault" have been used to describe this doctrine. Which is the best phrase? See Bohlen, "The Rule in Rylands v. Fletcher" (1911), 59 U. Pa. L. Rev. 298, 373, 423; Stallybrass, "Dangerous Things and the Non-Natural User of Land" (1929), 3 Camb. L.J. 376; Thayer, "Liability Without Fault" (1916), 29 Harv. L. Rev. 801; Prosser, "The Principle of Rylands v. Fletcher" printed in *Selected Topics on the Law of Torts* (1953), at p. 135; Gregory, "Trespass to Negligence to Absolute Liability" (1951), 37 Va. L. Rev. 359; Fridman, "The Rise and Fall of Rylands v. Fletcher" (1956), 34 Can. Bar Rev. 810; V.C. MacDonald, "Rylands v. Fletcher and Its Limitations" (1923), 1 Can. Bar Rev. 140; Goodhart, "The Rule in Rylands v. Fletcher" (1947), 63 L.Q. Rev. 160; Morris, "Absolute Liability for Dangerous Things" (1948), 61 Harv. L.Rev. 515; Winfield, "The Myth of Absolute Liability" (1926), 42 L.Q. Rev. 37; Linden, "Whatever Happened to *Rylands* v. *Fletcher?"* in Klar (ed.) *Studies in Canadian Tort Law* (1977), p. 325.

1. Non-natural User

RICKARDS v. LOTHIAN

Privy Council. [1913] A.C. 263; 82 L.J.P.C. 42

The defendant was the occupier of a business building and leased part of the second floor to the plaintiff. On the fourth floor was a men's lavatory containing a basin. The lavatory was provided for the use of the tenants and persons in their employ. The plaintiff's stock in trade was found seriously damaged one morning by water. Such water came from the basin on the fourth floor and examination showed that the waste pipe had been plugged with various articles such as nails, penholders, string and soap and that the water tap had been turned full on. The defendant's caretaker had found the lavatory in proper order at 10.20 p.m. the previous evening.

The plaintiff brought action against the defendant alleging carelessness in construction and management, and also for allowing large quantities of water to escape and to flow into the plaintiff's premises. At the trial the jury found the defendant negligent in not providing further equipment against flooding. They also found that "this was the malicious act of some person". The trial judge entered judgment for the plaintiff, which judgment was set aside by the Supreme Court of Victoria and judgment entered for the defendant. By a majority, this judgment, in turn, was reversed by the High Court of Australia. The defendant, by leave of the High Court appealed to the Judicial Committee of the Privy Council.

Lord Moulton: . . . The arguments on behalf of the plaintiff in the Courts of Appeal were mainly directed to bring the case under one of two well-known types of action, namely: (1) it was contended that the defendant ought to have foreseen the probability of such a malicious act and to have taken precaution against it, and that he was liable in damages for not having done so. (2) It was contended that the defendant was liable apart from negligence on the principles which are usually associated with the well-known case of *Fletcher* v. *Rylands.* [Lord Moulton then found there was no evidence of negligence on which to find liability.]

The principal contention, however, on behalf of the plaintiff was based on the doctrine customarily associated with the case of *Fletcher* v. *Rylands.* It was contended that it was the defendant's duty to prevent an overflow from the lavatory basin, however caused, and that he was liable in damages for not having so done, whether the overflow was due to any negligent act on his part or to the malicious act of a third person.

The legal principle that underlies the decision in *Fletcher* v. *Rylands* was well known in English law from a very early period, but it was explained and formulated in a strikingly clear and authoritative manner in that case and therefore is usually referred to by that name. It is nothing other than an application of the old maxim *"Sic utere tuo ut alienum non laedas."*

It will be seen that Blackburn J., with characteristic carefulness, indicates that exceptions to the general rule may arise where the escape is in consequence of *vis major,* or the act of God, but declines to deal further with the question because it was unnecessary for the decision of the case then before him. A few years later the question of law thus left undecided in *Fletcher* v. *Rylands* came up for decision in a case arising out of somewhat similar circumstances.

[His Lordship dealt with the case of *Nichols* v. *Marsland* (1876-77), 2 Ex. D.1 and quoted from the opinion of Mellish L.J. to this effect:]

"A defendant cannot, in our opinion, be properly said to have caused or allowed the water to escape, if the act of God or the Queen's enemies was the real cause of its escaping without any fault on the part of the defendant. If a reservoir was destroyed by an earthquake, or the Queen's enemies destroyed it in conducting some warlike operation, it would be contrary to all reason and justice to hold the owner of the reservoir liable for any damage that might be done by the escape of the water. We are of opinion therefore that the defendant was entitled to excuse herself by proving that the water escaped through the act of God."

Their Lordships are of opinion that all that is there laid down as to a case where the escape is due to *"vis major* or the King's enemies" applies equally to a case where it is due to the malicious act of a third person, if indeed that case is not actually included in the above phrase. To follow the language of the judgment just recited — a defendant cannot in their Lordships' opinion be properly said to have caused or allowed the water to escape if the malicious act of a third person was the real cause of its escaping without any fault on the part of the defendant. . . .

But there is another ground upon which their Lordships are of opinion that the present case does not come within the principle laid down in *Fletcher* v. *Rylands.* It is not every use to which land is put that brings into play that principle. It must be some special use bringing with it increased danger to others, and must not merely be the ordinary use of the land or such a use as is proper for the general benefit of the community . . . . This is more fully expressed by Wright J., in his judgment in *Blake* v. *Woolf,* [1898] 2 Q.B. 426. In that case the plaintiff was the occupier of the lower floors of the defendant's house, the upper floors being occupied by the defendant himself. A leak occurred in the cistern at the top of the house which without any negligence on the part of the defendant caused the plaintiff's premises to be flooded. In giving judgment for the defendant Wright J. says: "The general rule as laid down in *Rylands* v. *Fletcher* is that *prima facie* a person occupying land has an absolute right not to have his premises invaded by injurious matter, such as large quantities of water which his neighbours keep upon his land. That general rule is, however, qualified by some exceptions, one of which is that, where a person is using his land in the ordinary way and damage happens to the adjoining property without any default or negligence on his part, no liability attaches to him. The bringing of water on to such premises as these and the maintaining of a cistern in the usual way seems to me to be an ordinary and reasonable user of such premises as these were; and, therefore, if the water escapes without any negligence or default on the part of the person bringing the water in and owning the cistern, I do not think that he is liable for any damage that may ensue."

The provision of a proper supply of water to the various parts of a house is not only reasonable, but has become, in accordance with modern sanitary views, an almost necessary feature of town life. It is recognized as being so desirable in the interests of the community that in some form or other it is usually made obligatory in civilized countries. Such a supply cannot be installed without causing some concurrent danger of leakage or overflow. It would be unreasonable for the law to regard those who install or maintain such a system of supply as doing so at their own peril, with an absolute liability for any damage resulting from its presence even when there has been no negligence. It would be still more unreasonable if, as the respondent contends, such liability were to be held to extend to the consequences of malicious acts on the part of third persons. In such matters as the domestic supply of water or gas it is essential that the mode of supply should be such as to permit ready access for the purpose of use, and hence it is impossible to guard against wilful mischief. Taps may be turned on, ball-cocks fastened open, supply pipes cut, and waste-pipes blocked. Against such acts no precaution can prevail. It would be wholly unreasonable to hold an occupier responsible for the consequences of such acts which he is powerless to prevent, when the provision of the supply is not only a reasonable act on his part but probably a duty. Such a doctrine would, for example, make a householder liable for the consequences of an explosion caused by a burglar breaking into his house during the night and leaving a gas tap open. There is, in their Lordships' opinion, no support either in reason or authority for any such view of the liability of a landlord or occupier. In having on his premises such means of supply he is only using those premises in an ordinary and proper manner, and, although he is bound to exercise all reasonable care, he is not responsible for damage not due to his own default, whether that damage be caused by inevitable accident or the wrongful acts of third persons. . . .

The appeal must therefore be allowed and judgment entered for the defendant in the action with costs in all the courts, and the plaintiff must pay the costs of this appeal, and their Lordships will humbly advise His Majesty accordingly.

NOTES

1. What is the *ratio decidendi* of this case? Are there two?

MIHALCHUK v. RATKE ET AL.

Saskatchewan Queen's Bench. (1966), 57 D.L.R. (2d) 269

MacPherson J.: The plaintiffs in each of these actions claim damages for injury to their crops of rape by reason of the escape or drift of the herbicide 2-4D from the land of the defendant. . . .

Mr. Ratke by verbal contract hired Nipawin Air Services Ltd. to spray this field and others. The operation commenced about 6:00 a.m. on June 22, 1965.

Bordering the barley field on the east is a road allowance of 66 ft. and beyond that lie the fields of the plaintiffs which were damaged. The barley field was a mile long. Each of the rape fields affected was one-half a mile long. Mr. Mihalchuk's field was triangular in shape and extended, at one corner, considerably farther east than that of Mr. Kwasnuik.

The aircraft was a high wing monoplane, beneath the wings of which is slung a boom on each side. The herbicide is ejected under pressure from nozzles in the booms. The pilot flew the aircraft straight north and south across the barley field guided by two other employees of Nipawin Air Services Ltd., who were on the ground as markers. The markers located themselves in the centre of each pass. The pilot aimed his craft over them at a speed of 90 to 100 m.p.h. and at a height which would put the boom eight to ten feet above the ground. The swath of the spray seems to have been about 80 ft. wide.

The purpose of the operation, of course, was to kill weeds growing in the Ratke's barley. In the Meadow Lake area where this occurred, rape is a common crop. It constantly volunteers, however, in fields of cereal crops where it is a weed and must be killed. 2-4D does the trick. Rape is very sensitive to this herbicide, which does not affect the cereals.

The spray mixture itself was composed of fuel oil into which was mixed the 2-4D in the proportion of 4½ ozs. of 2-4D to one-half gallon of oil per acre. Oils have a lower surface tension than water and thus the drops are smaller when the substance is sprayed under pressure. An oil drop can be very small and light and is capable of drifting great distances. Furthermore, oil does not evaporate as quickly as water.

In the early morning of June 22, 1965, there was a light breeze blowing from the west. If there was any drift from the spray laid down by the plane it would naturally drift over the land of the plaintiffs where the two rape crops were growing.

There does not seem to be any doubt there was such a drift. Damage to these crops was apparent immediately. There was not a general destruction, but symptoms of herbicide damage was more apparent on the west side of the rape fields adjoining the sprayed barley. The damage became less as one proceeded easterly into the rape, until it virtually disappeared in the most easterly part of Mr. Mihalchuk's field. . . .

I have . . . positive evidence that there was damage to the rape caused by 2-4D under such circumstances that it could only have come from the spray laid down by the aircraft. Rape is extremely sensitive to 2-4D. Tiny oil droplets are capable of travelling great distances. There must therefore have been an invisible drift. No other conclusion is possible on these facts.

The plaintiffs put their claim for the liability of the defendants on three grounds: first, the rule in *Rylands* v. *Fletcher* (1868), L.R. 3 H.L. 330, affg. L.R. 1 Ex. 265; secondly, negligence; and thirdly, nuisance.

The rule in *Rylands* v. *Fletcher* is stated in *Salmond on Torts,* 14th ed., p. 441, as follows:

> "The occupier of land who brings and keeps upon it anything likely to do damage if it escapes is bound at his peril to prevent its escape, and is liable for all the direct consequences of its escape, even if he has been guilty of no negligence."

Cases applying the rule have ranged from the bursting of reservoirs to the wandering of gypsies (*Att'y-Gen'l* v *Corke,* [1933] Ch. 89) to the spread of a set fire (*Curtis et al.* v. *Lutes,* [1953] 4 D.L.R. 188, [1953] O.R. 747) to noxious fumes (*Heard and Heard* v. *Woodward* (1954), 12 W.W.R. 312) to the escape of a racing car (*Aldridge and O'Brien* v. *Van Patter et al.,* [1952] 4 D.L.R. 93, [1952] O.R. 595). So far as counsel and I have been able to discover, the rule has not yet been considered with respect to the drift of a herbicide, which, recognizing the widespread use of these substances, may be rather surprising.

In all respects save one (and I shall discuss it presently) the rule seems clearly to apply to the facts as I have found them. The herbicide 2-4D is a substance which can readily do mischief or cause damage if it is not handled with care. It was brought on or to their land by the defendants. Some of it drifted or escaped onto the lands of the plaintiffs. The nature of the damage caused indicates that not a great deal of the substance escaped, but not much is required to injure the rape plant.

The one aspect of the rule in *Rylands* v. *Fletcher* which has given me pause is whether the application of herbicide by aircraft was a natural or non-natural user of the land of the defendants. Lord Cairns L.C. in the House of Lords' judgment in *Rylands* v. *Fletcher* (L.R. 3 H.L. at p. 340) laid down that only where the defendant's use was non-natural was liability absolute. This has given rise to vast judicial and editorial discussion. The most acid comment was by Lord Macmillan in *Read* v. *J. Lyons & Co., Ltd.*, [1947] A.C. 156, when he said at p. 174: ". . . in consequence of some non-natural user of that land, whatever precisely that may mean". The author of *Salmond on Torts*, 14th ed., p. 450, suggests that no definition of "natural user" is possible or even desirable. The authors of *Winfield on Torts*, 7th ed., p. 452, say that the uncertainty of the phrase is only typical of the English law of tort.

The most frequently quoted and most useful comment on the point is that of Lord Moulton in *Rickards* v. *Lothian*, [1913] A.C. 263 at p. 280:

> "It is not every use to which land is put that brings into play that principle. [The principle of *Rylands* v. *Fletcher*.] It must be some special use bringing with it increased danger to others, and must not merely be the ordinary use of the land or such a use as is proper for the general benefit of the community."

The natural use of the lands of the defendants here quite plainly is the growth and production of crops. Involved in this use, undoubtedly, is the control of weeds which volunteer themselves. The male defendant would not be the successful farmer he is if he did not attempt such control. There are, however, many ways to kill weeds. The ancient and completely safe method was the hoe which would be absurdly impractical in modern agriculture.

The argument of the defence counsel was that since the purpose of the defendant was to kill weeds, and such is an admittedly good agricultural purpose, then it follows that what was done was a natural user. The fallacy of this argument is that it would justify any method employed to achieve the end. The key, in my view, is the method not the purpose.

The defendants' method was to spray from an aircraft using oil as a carrier for the 2-4D. Only a small proportion of the land in the Meadow Lake area has the herbicide sprayed from the air. This was an unusual operation. The neighbours gathered to watch. As against the usual boom-spraying behind a tractor this method brought with it increased danger to others because of the speed and height of the aircraft and the oil mixture.

In the result I conclude that because of its unusual nature and increased danger to others, the defendants' operation was a special use and not a natural use of their land.

The principle of *Rylands* v. *Fletcher* therefore applies and the defendants are liable.

Having so found there is no necessity to consider the claim of nuisance which may or may not have been adequately pleaded.

Because of the possibility of further litigation between the defendants and the aircraft company I have avoided discussing whether or not the latter may have been negligent. The plaintiff did not plead *res ipsa loquitur*.

NOTES

1. Would the court have reached the same result if most of the farmers in the area sprayed in this way as a result of advances in the technology of herbicide

application? See *Cruise* v. *Niessen,* [1977] 2 W.W.R. 481; revd [1978] 1 W.W.R. 688, *cf.* Solomon J. at p. 483, in [1977] 2 W.W.R. with Matas J.A. (dissenting) at p. 694 in [1978] 1 W.W.R. See also *Bridges Brothers Ltd.* v. *Forest Protection Ltd.* (1976), 72 D.L.R. (3d) 335 (N.B.Q.B.), liability for damage by spraying based on nuisance theory but not *Rylands* v. *Fletcher.*

2. What is the real meaning of "non-natural use"? What factors should the court consider in making its determination? Is there a difference between the use of water for domestic as contrasted with commercial purposes? Is an oil well a non-natural use of land near Toronto? Is it a non-natural use near Calgary? Is a water reservoir like the one in *Rylands* v. *Fletcher* a non-natural use of land in an arid region in Texas? See *Turner* v. *Big Lake Oil Co.* (1936), 128 Tex. 155, 96 S.W. 2d 221 (S.C. Tex.). Is the storage or manufacture of dynamite *ever* a natural use of land? What about nuclear testing? See Seavey, "Torts and Atoms" (1958), 46 Calif. L. Rev. 3.

3. In *Attorney-General* v. *Corke,* [1933] Ch. 89, the defendant, owner of a disused brick-field, permitted a number of gypsies to occupy it and live in caravans and tents. The gypsies threw slop water about in the neighbourhood of the field, and allowed accumulations of filth, etc. An injunction was granted against the defendant, Bennett J., stating that *Rylands* v. *Fletcher* applied. While it was not unlawful to license caravan dwellers, it was "abnormal", and as such persons have habits of life which are offensive to those persons with fixed homes, it was likely that the injuries sustained would occur. For criticisms of this case, see 11 Can. Bar Rev. 693, 49 L.Q.Rev. 158.

4. In *Shiffman* v. *Order of St. John,* [1936] 1 All E.R. 557, a 30-foot flag-pole erected by the defendants in Hyde Park fell and injured some children in the vicinity. While Atkinson J. found the defendants negligent, he stated that liability could also be placed on *Rylands* v. *Fletcher.* "The defendants erected something exceptional, something which would be easily caused to fall and something which, if it fell, was likely to do mischief to others."

If the defendant's tree falls on the plaintiff's property, is this a non-natural use of land attracting strict liability? See *Bottoni* v. *Henderson* (1978), 21 O.R. (2d) 369 (Steele J.). What if the roots of a tree damage the plaintiff's property? Compare *Crosty* v. *City of Burlington* (1978), 21 O.R. (2d) 753 (Co. Ct.), where it was held that there was no absolute liability under the Local Improvement Act in relation to tree root damage.

5. In *Saccardo* v. *Hamilton,* [1971] 2 O.R. 479, at p. 492, Mr. Justice Osler, as an alternative ground of his decision, held that Christmas decorations that fell from above injuring the plaintiff were under *Rylands* v. *Fletcher* because they were "dangerous things". Are Christmas decorations in the street "non-natural" in Hamilton, Ontario, during the Christmas season?

6. In *St. Anne's Well Brewery Co.* v. *Roberts* (1928), 140 L.T. 1, 44 T.L.R. 703, Scrutton L.J. discussed the question of liability for damage caused by a brick wall on the defendant's land that fell on the plaintiff's property. It was argued that *Rylands* v. *Fletcher* applied, but Scrutton L.J. stated that the doctrine did not apply to "the normal use of land". "One of the most normal uses of land, it appears to me, is to put buildings on it. . . ."

7. In *Gertsen* v. *Municipality of Metropolitan Toronto et al.* (1974), 2 O.R. (2d) 1, the defendants used organic matter as land fill in a residential area. As it decomposed, it generated methane gas which escaped onto adjoining lands and into the plaintiff's garage. One day, when the plaintiff turned on the ignition of his car, an explosion occured destroying the garage, damaging the car and injuring the plaintiff. Mr. Justice Lerner imposed liability on negligence, nuisance and strict liability theories. He explained that the gas was a "dangerous substance" which "escaped onto the plaintiff's land and caused them damage". Therefore, *prima facie,* liability should follow without proof of negligence. He went on to explain that if the

> "potential source of mischief is an accepted incident of some ordinary purpose to which the land is reasonably applied by the occupier, the *prima facie* rule of absolute responsibility for the consequences of its escape must give

way. In applying this qualification, the courts have looked not only to the thing or activity in isolation, but also to the place and manner in which it is maintained and its relation to the surroundings. Time, place and circumstance, not excluding purpose, are most material. The distinction between natural and non-natural use is both relative and capable of adjustment to the changing patterns of social existence."

In deciding whether the garbage fill was a natural or non-natural use of land, Mr. Justice Lerner stressed that the purpose was "selfish and self-serving" and not justifiable on any "overriding public welfare theory" which was to the "general benefit of the community". In the light of the "time, place and circumstances and not excluding purpose", he held that the activity was a "non-natural use of the land".

8. In *O'Neill* v. *Esquire Hotels Ltd.* (1972), 30 D.L.R. (3d) 589 (N.B.C.A.) it was held, *inter alia,* that propane gas that was brought on to the premises of a hotel was not a non-natural use of land. The system was "being operated to provide gas for cooking purposes for the benefit of all the occupants of the hotel", including the deceased, who was killed in an explosion caused by the gas. Is this case in conflict with *Gertsen?*

9. In *Dahlberg* v. *Naydiuk* (1969), 10 D.L.R. (3d) 319 (Man. C.A.), the plaintiff argued, among other things, that the defendant, who shot him accidentally while deer hunting, was liable under *Rylands* v. *Fletcher.* In rejecting this argument, Mr. Justice Dickson observed:

"Deer hunting is a perfectly legal activity. I do not think it can properly be said that the act of hunting big game is inherently dangerous, an enterprise which has unusual hazards in itself. A loaded fire-arm in the hands of an experienced hunter is safer than a moving automobile in the hands of some drivers. Hunting may become dangerous if a hunter is not qualified to handle his rifle or if he does not exhibit proper respect for the force he has at his disposal, or if his mind does not travel at the same rate as his reflex to shoot. But if a hunter does all that a reasonably prudent hunter would do, under the circumstances in which he is placed, to avoid an accident, neither the law nor current social thinking has arrived at the position of imposing absolute liability, irrespective of fault."

10. In *MacDonald* v. *Desourdy Construction et al.* (1972), 27 D.L.R. (3d) 144 (N.S.S.C.), the plaintiff's residence was damaged by blasting operations conducted by the defendants. Mr. Justice Dubinsky held the defendants strictly liable, commenting that he could not "see how anyone can possibly describe similar operations as not being . . . 'extra hazardous' or 'inherently dangerous' ". See also *Jackson* v. *Drury Construction* (1974), 4 O.R. (2d) 735 (C.A.).

11. *Rylands* v. *Fletcher* is sometimes applied in cases of fire damage. The decision depends on whether the fire resulted from some exceptionally dangerous conduct or from some ordinary activity. Thus, if the fire stems from a defect in ordinary domestic wiring (*Collingwood* v. *Home & Colonial Stores,* [1936] 3 All E.R. 200) or from an ordinary fireplace (*Sochacki* v. *Sas,* [1947] 1 All E.R. 344), no liability will follow on this theory. See also *Balfour* v. *Barty-King,* [1957] 1 Q.B. 496, [1957] 1 All E.R. 156 (blow lamp); *Ayoub* v. *Beaupré* (1964), 45 D.L.R. (2d) 411 (S.C.C.). As to fires started to clear land, see *Dean* v. *McCarty* (1846), 2 U.C.Q.B. 448; *Furlong* v. *Carroll* (1882), 7 O.A.R. 145, *cf. Gogo* v. *Eureka Sawmills,* [1944] 4 D.L.R. 689. See also the Accidental Fires Act, R.S.O. 1970, c. 4, which declares that "no action shall be brought against any person in whose house or building or on whose land any fire accidentally begins, nor shall any recompense be made by him for damages suffered thereby; but no agreement between landlord and tenant is defeated or made void by this Act". This Act does not foreclose *Rylands* v. *Fletcher* actions, however. See *Musgrove* v. *Pandelis,* [1919] 2 K.B. 43; *Mason* v. *Levy Auto Parts of England Ltd.,* [1967] 2 Q.B. 530; *Attorney-General for Canada* v. *Diamond Waterproofing Ltd.* (1974), 4 O.R. (2d) 489 (C.A.), (flammable naptha vapours found non-natural use); *McAuliffe* v. *Hubbell* (1931), 66 O.L.R. 349, [1931] 1 D.L.R. 835 (onus on plaintiff to show "accidental" fire). See

generally Ogus, "Vagaries in Liability for the Escape of Fire", [1961] Camb. L.J. 104.

12. In *Schubert* v. *Sterling Trusts Corp. et al.,* [1943] O.R. 438, Hogg J. held the defendants liable for the deaths of a husband and wife who died when gas escaped into their apartment from a neighbouring one while it was being fumigated. Several theories, including negligence and *Rylands* v. *Fletcher* were relied upon by the court. Was this a non-natural use of land? At p. 445 Mr. Justice Hogg spoke of the "increased danger to others". Is this the key to the riddle of *Rylands* v. *Fletcher?* See Wright, "The Law of Torts: 1923-1947" (1948), 26 Can. Bar Rev. 46, at pp. 75 *et seq.*

13. The American Law Institute in its first *Restatement of Torts* § 519 articulated the principle thus:

> . . . one who carries on an ultrahazardous activity is liable to another whose person, land or chattels the actor should recognise as likely to be harmed by the unpreventable miscarriage of the activity for harm resulting thereto from that which makes the activity ultrahazardous, although the utmost care is exercised to prevent the harm.

See also § 520, which defines "ultrahazardous" as follows:

An activity is ultrahazardous if it

(a) necessarily involves a risk of serious harm to the person, land or chattels of others which cannot be eliminated by the exercise of the utmost care, and

(b) is not a matter of common usage.

Is this principle broader or narrower than *Rylands* v. *Fletcher?* Is it both broader and narrower?

14. See Ehrenzweig, "Negligence Without Fault" (1951), reprinted at (1966), 54 Cal. L. Rev. 1422 for this comment about the *Restatement* rule:

> "With its liability for *'ultrahazardous activities'* the American Law Institute has taken a further and, potentially at least, decisive step towards the recognition of a new rationale of enterprise liability. Courageously abandoning the language of the traditional strict liabilities (where there is still much talk of presumptions of negligence or violations of duty), Section 519 of the *Restatement* advocates a new liability for foreseeable, though unavoidable, consequences of lawful, though hazardous, conduct. . . .
>
> This rule, while not adopted by the courts, seems to express the missing rationale of the 'negligence' liability of mechanical enterprise for unpreventable calculable harm. But section 520 expressly excludes from the liability under section 519 all activities which are a 'matter of common usage'. The scope of this exception is obscure. Oilwells are covered because 'the dangers incident thereto are characteristic of oil lands and not of lands in general'. On the other hand, railroads, and thus probably the very enterprise here discussed are excluded as 'of common usage' and, therefore, within the generally recognized domain of the negligence rule. Yet, in our search for a rationale of enterprise liability for negligence, the *Restatement* rule remains a significant attempt at formulating dormant thought. . . . *Anticipation of harm at the time of the start of the activity rather than the time of the injurious conduct determines the scope of liability.* It is this determination which reveals the rationale of the non-fault liabilities discussed: these *liabilities are the price which must be paid to society for the permission of a hazardous activity."*

See also Ehrenzweig, "Assurance Oblige — A Comparative Study" (1950), 15 Law & Cont. Prob. 445; Keeton, "Conditional Fault in the Law of Torts" (1959), 72 Harv. L. Rev. 401; Fletcher, "Fairness and Utility in Tort Theory" (1972), 85 Harv. L. Rev. 537.

15. More recently, although not yet approved by the Institute, the section in the *Restatement of Torts, Second,* has been redrafted by discarding the term "ultrahazardous" and by replacing it with the phrase "abnormally dangerous". The new § 520 that has been recommended reads as follows:

In determining whether an activity is abnormally dangerous, the following factors are to be considered:

(a) whether the activity involves a high degree of risk of some harm to the person, land or chattels of others;

(b) whether the gravity of the harm which may result from it is likely to be great;

(c) whether the risk cannot be eliminated by the exercise of reasonable care;

(d) whether the activity is not a matter of common usage;

(e) whether the activity is inappropriate to the place where it is carried on; and

(f) the value of the activity to the community.

Does this balancing operation sound familiar? In what way is this new principle different from negligence liability?

16. Should this doctrine be applied in air crash cases? Should the same rule be applied to protect; (1) a passenger who is killed in a crash, (2) the owner of an aircraft destroyed in a mid-air collision, and (3) the owner of a building into which an aircraft crashes?

17. In its infancy air traffic was considered an ultrahazardous activity. Should this still be so? What are the considerations? Compare Orr, "Is Aviation Ultrahazardous?" (1954), 21 Ins. Couns. J. 48 with Vold, "Strict Liability for Airplane Crashes" (1953), 5 Hastings L.J. 1.

18. Passengers killed during international air travel are now subject to the Warsaw Convention provisions which provide for an almost strict liability up to a certain maximum amount. See Carriage By Air Act, R.S.C. 1970, c. C-14 as amended; Rosevear, "The Future of the Warsaw Convention" (1968), 14 McGill L.J. 161. On domestic flights negligence law now applies, see *Malone* v. *T.C.A., supra.*

19. Ground damage used to be governed by strict liability but the position is no longer so clear. Compare *Rochester Gas & Electric Corp.* v. *Dunlop* (1933), 266 N.Y.S. 469 with *Southern California Edison Co.* v. *Coleman* (1957), 150 Cal. App. 2d 829, 310 P. 2d 504. Should there be a difference depending upon whether the flight is a normal commercial flight or an experimental flight like stunt flying or rocket testing? Under The Aeronautics Act, R.S.C. 1970, c. A-3, detailed rules and regulations to control flying in Canada have been enacted. Should tort liability flow from a breach of one of these provisions?

LINDEN, WHATEVER HAPPENED TO RYLANDS v. FLETCHER?

in Klar (Ed.) *Studies in Canadian Tort Law* (1977)

Enough has been said to demonstrate that Canadian courts, in these strict liability cases, are concerned with more than non-natural use, mischief and escape as outlined in *Rylands* v. *Fletcher*. Although these phrases are still frequently employed in the cases, there are also references to increased danger or extra-hazardous activities, concepts that resemble the notions of abnormal danger and ultra-hazardous activities, embedded in the American jurisprudence. The latter concepts are a more appropriate foundation for strict liability today than the archaic language of *Rylands* v. *Fletcher*. They provide a better reason for adopting a different standard of care to regulate a particular group of activities.

Those who create extraordinary peril to society should be treated in an extraordinary way. Rather than being subject to negligence law, which applies to the ordinary risks of society, they should be subject to strict liability, which applies to dangers out of the ordinary. When it also appears that the activity is pursued for profit or for the purposes of the actor, it is hard to avoid the conclusion that liability should be strict. Further, when one realizes that such activities are usually, though not always, conducted by business enterprises or by governments who can well afford to furnish compensation for the victims of their actions, either directly or though insurance, the case for strict liability becomes unanswerable.

This philosophy of strict liability is consistent with the main purpose of tort law. Compensation, which remains the prime aim of tort law, is awarded to more victims under strict liability theory than under negligence theory. Deterrence is achieved because the enterpriser should exercise "super-care" in order to avoid being held strictly liable, rather than the ordinary care he would be required to exercise under the negligence standard. The educational aims of tort law are promoted by teaching society that certain types of activities, which are more perilous than others, labour under special responsibilities. Moreover, the psychological needs of the victims of these enterprises (and of society generally) are provided for by individual court actions that dramatize the "rights" and "wrongs" of this group of human encounters. Market deterrence, *a la* Calabresi, is achieved by forcing these enterprisers to pay all the costs of the accidents generated by their activities, whether or not they are negligently caused. Lastly, the ombudsman role of tort law is served by focussing attention on the kinds of things that may go wrong with these unique activities, fostering public re-assessment of the value of these pursuits and the way they are regulated.

Mr. Justice Windeyer of Australia has recognized what has become of *Rylands* v. *Fletcher,* and has suggested that, although strict liability was not "called into existence in 1866 for the purpose of ensuring that industrial enterprises make good the harm they do", that is the "socially beneficial result" of the doctrine today. His Lordship explained further:

"Actions for negligence dominate the work of common law courts today, mainly because railway trains, motor-cars and industrial machinery, have so large a place in men's lives. But to regard negligence as the normal requirement of responsibility in tort, and to look upon strict liability as anomalous and unjust, seems to me to mistake present values as well as past history. In an age when insurance against all forms of liability is commonplace, it is surely not surprising or unjust if law makes persons who carry on some kinds of hazardous undertakings liable for the harm they do, unless they can excuse or justify it on some recognized ground. That is, I think the position today in the countries of the common law. In England, and in those countries which have the common law as it is in England, this comes about through the principle of *Rylands* v. *Fletcher.*"

Such a view of *Rylands* v. *Fletcher* is full of potential for the future. It furnishes a solid basis for tort liability—that of strict liability—which can regulate certain types of abnormally hazardous activities, for which negligence law provides insufficient protection. The concept lies hidden in the cases, waiting to be discovered. It has survived for more than a century, and one could forecast that it will be alive, hopefully, in an altered form, a century from now. If it is re-oriented in the way suggested, one could forecast that the future of *Rylands* v. *Fletcher* will be one of steady growth and continuing service to society, not one of decay and ultimate eclipse.

And that is what has happened to *Rylands* v. *Fletcher.*

OTTO E. LANG, THE ACTIVITY-RISK THEORY OF TORT: RISK, INSURANCE AND INSOLVENCY

(1961), 39 Can. Bar Rev. 53

The basic proposition and starting point is that activity should bear the risks of harm which it produces. Unless the act is sufficiently worthwhile to pay for the increase in risks which accompany it, the act should not be done at all. In the words of Bramwell J.: "If the reward which he gains for the use of the machine will not pay for the damage, it is mischievous to the public and ought to be suppressed, for the loss ought not to be borne by the community or the injured person." In simple cases, this means that if the actor who receives (or controls) all the benefits from an act also has to pay for harm resulting from the increase in risk, then the proper decision about whether to do the act is more likely to be made. This is the defence of the old law's theory of strict liability in trespass. Putting a person or thing in motion obviously increases the risk of harm to others. This risk includes some harm which is likely, some which is only possible and some which is quite unlikely. The mover ought to pay even for the unlikely if it occurs. The risk of it happening was apparent and if modern terminology is to be used, the mover could be said to be at fault for having acted, knowing this sort of harm could result, and indeed, would result sooner or later if the activity was repeated. In this sense, he could be accused of intending the harm (or risk) while regretting it (or hoping the worst would not materialize).

This liability should remain on the actor even if his decision to act is perfectly reasonable. This only means that the benefits — which generally accrue to him — outweigh the risks of harm. Out of the benefits, he should pay for that harm, especially since this removes the difficult determination of what is exactly reasonable in all the circumstances. . . .

The general objective is to have activity more completely bear its risks. Strict liability is helpful to this end and also removes the expense of determining negligence. A schedule of damages would save further expense. Premium assessment could provide the necessary deterrent more equitably than the present system. In assumpsit and joint-activity situations, the activity-risk theory is not applicable but the desirability of insurance, the need to guard against insolvency, and economic advantages through inexpensive insurance all argue for the schedule of damages, strict or even absolute liability, and compulsory insurance. The end result may be general society insurance with activity and special assessment premiums, some contribution from taxation, and compensation without regard to cause but according to a modest, rigid schedule.

NOTES

1. A similar view was recently expressed by Denning M.R. in *Nettleship* v. *Weston,* [1971] 3 All E.R. 581, at p. 586:

"The high standard thus imposed by the judges is, I believe, largely the result of the policy of the Road Traffic Acts. Parliament requires every driver to be insured against third-party risks. The reason is so that a person injured by a motor-car should not be left to bear the loss on his own, but should be compensated out of the insurance fund. The fund is better able to bear it than he can. But the injured person is only able to recover if the driver is liable in law. So the judges see to it that he is liable, unless he can prove care and skill of a high standard: see *The Merchant Prince,* [1892] P. 179 . . . and *Henderson* v. *Henry E. Jenkins & Sons Ltd.* [[1969] 3 All E.R. 756, [1970] A.C. 282]. Thus we are, in this branch of the law, moving away from the concept: 'No liability without fault.' We are beginning to apply the test: 'On whom should the risk fall?' Morally the learner-driver is not at fault; but legally she is liable to be because she is insured and the risk should fall on her."

2. The Pearson Commission has suggested that strict liability should be imposed on the controllers of things and operations that are:

(1) unusually hazardous things, like explosives and flammable liquids, or
(2) things that pose a risk of serious and extensive casualties, like dams, bridges and stadiums.

The Commission proposed that a detailed list of the things and operations subject to strict liability be enacted in a statutory instrument so as to provide certainty as well as some flexibility. See *Report of the Royal Commission on Civil Liability and Compensation for Personal Injury* (1978).

CODE CIVIL DE LA PROVINCE DE QUÉBEC

Art. 1054. Elle est responsable non seulement du dommage qu'elle cause par sa propre faute, mais encore de celui causé par la faute de ceux dont elle a le contrôle, et par les choses qu'elle a sous sa garde.

Le père, et après son décès, la mère, sont responsables du dommage causé par leurs enfants mineurs;

Les tuteurs sont également responsables pour leurs pupilles;

Les curateurs ou autres ayant légalement la garde des insensés, pour le dommage causé par ces derniers;

L'instituteur et l'artisan, pour le dommage causé par ses élèves ou apprentis, pendant qu'ils sont sous sa surveillance;

La responsabilité ci-dessus a lieu seulement lorsque la personne qui y est assujettie ne peut prouver qu'elle n'a pu empêcher le fait qui a causé le dommage;

Les maîtres et les commettants sont responsables du dommage causé par leurs domestiques et ouvriers dans l'exécution des fonctions auxquelles ces derniers sont employés. (He is responsible not only for the damage caused by his own fault, but also for that caused by the fault of persons under his control and by things he has under his care;

The father and, after his decease, the mother, are responsible for the damage caused by their minor children;

Tutors are responsible in like manner for their pupils;

Curators or others having the legal custody of insane persons, for the damage done by the latter;

Schoolmasters and artisans, for the damage caused by their pupils or apprentices while under their care.

The responsibility attaches in the above cases only when the person subject to it fails to establish that he was unable to prevent the act which has caused the damage.

Masters and employers are responsible for the damage caused by their servants and workmen in the performance of the work for which they are employed.)

Art. 1055. Le propriétaire d'un animal est responsable du dommage que l'animal a causé, soit qu'il fût sous sa garde ou sous celle de ses domestiques, soit qu'il fut égaré ou échappé.

Celui qui se sert de l'animal en est également responsable pendant qu'il en fait usage.

Le propriétaire d'un bâtiment est responsable du dommage causé par sa ruine, lorsqu'elle est arrivée par suite du défaut d'entretien ou par vice de construction. (The owner of an animal is responsible for the damages caused by it, whether it be under his own care or under that of his servants, or has strayed or escaped from it.

He who is using the animal is equally responsible while it is in his service.

The owner of a building is responsible for the damage caused by its ruin, where it has happened from want of repairs or from an original defect in its construction.)

NOTES

1. See Crépeau, "Liability for Damage Caused by Things — From The Civil Law Point of View" (1962), 40 Can. Bar Rev. 222; Dunlop, "Liability for Damage Caused by Things — From The Common Law Point of View" (1962), 40 Can. Bar Rev. 240.

NOTE ON LIABILITY FOR ANIMALS

Damage done by animals has long been a subject of concern to tort law. Certain concepts of strict liability have been utilized for years to resolve cases where dangerous animals caused injury. There are two types of dangerous animals. First, there are *ferae naturae,* animals that are dangerous as a group. Included in their number are lions, elephants, zebras, bears and the like. If damage is done by any of these creatures, strict liability is automatically imposed. Second, there is another group of animals that are dangerous as individuals, even though they may be members of a species which is considered harmless. These *mansuetae naturae,* as these harmless animals are called, include dogs, cats, horses and the like. Where an individual animal of this *mansuetae naturae* group is known to be dangerous, and it harms someone, strict liability will be imposed. This action has been called the *scienter* action. It is from this notion that the mythical legal principle that "every dog is entitled to one bite" emerged. It is not necessarily so, because *scienter* may exist even where a dog has not yet bitten anyone, as for example where a dog is constantly barking at, chasing and trying to bite passersby.

Strict liability will also be imposed for cattle that trespass on neighbouring land. See Fleming, *The Law of Torts* (5th ed., 1977), p. 340.

In addition to these strict liability doctrines, animals may render their owners liable on a negligence theory. The owner of a dog who bites a child will be held responsible if he could reasonably have foreseen such an event occurring and if he failed to take reasonable steps to prevent it. See *Draper* v. *Hodder,* [1972] 2 All E.R. 210 (C.A.). For the effect of legislation prohibiting animals from running at large, see *Wolfe* v. *Dayton* (1976), 55 D.L.R. (3d) 552 (B.C.).

Damage done by cattle straying on Canadian roads is now regulated by negligence law, although, in England, under *Searle* v. *Wallbank,* [1947] A.C. 341, no duty of care is owed for such conduct. The old English rule was decisively rejected in Canada by *Fleming* v. *Atkinson,* [1959] S.C.R. 513, 18 D.L.R. (2d) 81. In the Court of Appeal, Mr. Justice Roach declared:

"It is now over 200 years since Thomas Gray wrote his famous lines descriptive of rural England at eventide, 'The lowing herd winds slowly o'er the lea'. The lea no doubt included such highways as then traversed the landscape. As I read the modern English cases the herd may still wander along those same highways without the owner being subject to civil liability for the injuries they may cause. No longer in this Province does 'the ploughman homeward plod his weary way'. He goes now in his tractor, oft-times along the highway. The farmer whose land adjoins the King's Highway can in this modern era scarcely know the meaning of 'the solemn stillness' of which Gray wrote. No longer can he be conscious of the beetle wheeling his droning flight. What he hears, instead, is the whir of motor cars wheeling their way at legalized speed along the adjoining highway. The common law of England may have been adequate in Gray's day. The Courts in England have held that it is still adequate, but surely it must be apparent that today in this Province it is not."

See the recommendation in the "Report of the Committee on the Law of Civil Liability for Damage Done by Animals" (1953), Cmd. 8746. On this topic generally, see Williams, *Liability for Animals* (1939); North, *Modern Law of Animals* (1972).

2. Escape

READ v. J. LYONS & CO. LTD.

House of Lords. [1947] A.C. 156; [1946] 2 All E.R. 471

The defendants operated, on behalf of the Ministry of Supply, a factory for the manufacture of high explosive shells. The plaintiff, under the National Service Acts, was directed by the Ministry, in whose employ she was considered to be, to work at the defendants' plant as an inspector in the filling of shells. In the course of her work an explosion took place seriously injuring the plaintiff. The latter sued, alleging no negligence, and based her claim on the ground that the defendants carried on the manufacture of shells which to their knowledge were dangerous things.

At the trial, [1944] 2 All E.R. 98, Cassels J. gave judgment for the plaintiff, holding that "defendants were under a strict liability to the plaintiff . . . and it was unnecessary to aver negligence because they were dealing with dangerous things which got out of control and did damage to the plaintiff". He held that liability for damage arising from dangerous animals was merely an instance of strict liability of *Rylands* v. *Fletcher* and that escape from defendants' premises was unnecessary to the general principle. The defendants appealed.

In the Court of Appeal, [1945] K.B. 216; [1945] 1 All E.R. 106, the judgment was reversed and the action dismissed. Scott L.J. delivered an elaborate judgment in which he refuted the argument that the American Law Institute's *Restatement of Torts,* ss. 519-20 (defining "ultrahazardous activities" and recognizing a liability for harm caused to "person, land or chattels" by such "activity") represented English law. He held that the principle of *Rylands* v. *Fletcher*, in common with cattle-trespass and nuisance, involved "interference with an existing proprietary right of the plaintiff". "The vital feature in *Rylands* v. *Fletcher* . . . was the defendant's interference with the plaintiff's right to enjoy his land without interference by the defendant." Du Parq L.J. said that the "mediaeval principle" of *Rylands* v. *Fletcher* was not to be extended; that in the dangerous animal cases it was "more accurate to speak of presumed negligence", and the present case was one which depended on the rules governing an occupier's liability to persons coming on the premises. The plaintiff appealed to the House of Lords.

Viscount Simon L.C.: . . . The classic judgment of Blackburn J., besides deciding the issue before the court and laying down the principle of duty between neighbouring occupiers of land on which the decision was based, sought to group under a single and wider proposition other instances in which liability is independent of negligence, such, for example, as liability for the bite of a defendant's monkey. See also the case of a bear on a chain on the defendant's premises. There are instances, no doubt, in our law in which liability for damage may be established apart from proof of negligence, but it appears to me logically unnecessary and historically incorrect to refer to all these instances as deduced from one common principle. . . .

Now, the strict liability recognized by this House to exist in *Rylands* v. *Fletcher* is conditioned by two elements which I may call the condition of "escape" from the land of something likely to do mischief if it escapes, and the condition of "non-natural use" of the land. This second condition has in some later cases, which did not reach this House, been otherwise expressed, *e.g.*, as "exceptional" user, when such user is not regarded as "natural" and at the same time is likely to produce mischief if there is an "escape". Dr. Stallybrass, in a learned article in 3 Cambridge Law Review, p. 376, has collected the large variety of epithets that have been judicially employed in this connection. *The American Restatement of the Law of Torts, III,* s. 519, speaks of "ultrahazardous activity", but attaches qualifications which would appear in the present instance to exonerate the respondents. It is not necessary to analyse this second condition on the present occasion, for in the case now before us the first essential condition of "escape" does not seem to me to be present at all. "Escape", for the purpose of applying the proposition in *Rylands* v. *Fletcher,* means escape from a place which the defendant has occupation of, or control over, to a place which is outside his occupation or control. . . .

In these circumstances it becomes unnecessary to consider other objections that have been raised, such as the question of whether the doctrine of *Rylands* v. *Fletcher* applies where the claim is for damages for personal injury as distinguished from damages to property. . . . On the much litigated question of what amounts to "non-natural" use of land, the discussion of which is also unnecessary in the present appeal, I content myself with two further observations. The first is that when it becomes essential for the House to examine this question it will, I think, be found that Lord Moulton's analysis in delivering the judgment of the Privy Council in *Rickards* v. *Lothian* is of the first importance. The other observation is as to the decision of this House in *Rainham Chemical Works, Ltd.* v. *Belvedere Fish Guano Co.,* [1921] 2 A.C. 465, to which the appellant's counsel in the present case made considerable reference in support of the proposition that manufacturing explosives was a "non-natural" use of land.

I think it not improper to put on record, with all due regard to the admission and *dicta* in that case, that if the question had hereafter to be decided whether the making of munitions in a factory at the government's request in time of war for the purpose of helping to defeat the enemy is a "non-natural" use of land, adopted by the occupier "for his own purposes", it would not seem to me that the House would be bound by this authority to say that it was. In this appeal the question is immaterial, as I hold that the appellant fails for the reason that there was no "escape" from the respondents' factory. I move that the appeal be dismissed with costs.

Lord Macmillan: . . . In my opinion, the appellant's statement of claim discloses no ground of action against the respondents. The action is one of damages for personal injuries. Whatever may have been the law of England in early times I am of opinion that, as the law now stands, an allegation of negligence is in general essential to the relevancy of an action of reparation for personal injuries.

The process of evolution has been from the principle that every man acts at his peril and is liable for all the consequences of his acts to the principle that a man's freedom of action is subject only to the obligation not to infringe any duty of care which he owes to others. The emphasis formerly was on the injury sustained and the question was whether the case fell within one of the accepted classes of common law actions; the emphasis now is on the conduct of the person whose act has occasioned the injury and the question is whether it can be characterized as negligent. I do not overlook the fact that there is at least one instance in the present law in which the primitive rule survives, namely in the case of animals *ferae naturae* or animals *mansuetae naturae* which have shown dangerous proclivities. The owner or keeper of such an animal has an absolute duty to confine or control it so that it shall not do injury to others and no proof of care on his part will absolve him from responsibility, but this is probably not so much a vestigial relic of otherwise discarded doctrine as a special rule of practical good sense. At any rate, it is too well established to be challenged. But such an exceptional case as this affords no justification for its extension by analogy. . . .

The doctrine of *Rylands* v. *Fletcher,* as I understand it, derives from a conception of the mutual duties of adjoining or neighbouring landowners and its congeners are trespass and nuisance. If its foundation is to be found in the injunction *sic utere tuo ut alienum non laedas,* then it is manifest that it has nothing to do with personal injuries. The duty is to refrain from injuring not *alium* but *alienum.* The two prerequisites of the doctrine are that there must be the escape of something from one man's close to another man's close and that which escapes must have been brought on the land from which it escapes in consequences of some non-natural use of that land, whatever precisely that may mean. Neither of these features exists in the present case. I have already pointed out that nothing escaped from the defendants' premises, and, were it necessary to decide the point, I should hesitate to hold that in these days and in an industrial community it was a non-natural use of land to build a factory on it and conduct there the manufacture of explosives. I could conceive it being said that to carry on the manufacture of explosives in a crowded urban area was evidence of negligence, but there is no such case here and I offer no opinion on the point.

Your Lordships' task in this House is to decide particular cases between litigants and your Lordships are not called on to rationalize the law of England. That attractive, if perilous field, may well be left to other hands to cultivate. It has been necessary in the present instance to examine certain general principles advanced on behalf of the appellant because it was said that consistency required that these principles should be applied to the case in hand. Arguments based on legal consistency are apt to mislead, for the common law is a practical code adapted to deal with the manifold diversities of human life and as a great American judge has reminded us "the life of the law has not been logic: it has been experience". For myself, I am content to say that, in my opinion, no authority has been quoted from case or text-book which would justify your Lordships, logically or otherwise, in giving effect to the appellant's plea. I should, accordingly, dismiss the appeal.

Lord Porter: . . . Normally at the present time in an action of tort for personal injuries if there is no negligence there is no liability. To this rule, however, the appellant contends that there are certain exceptions, one of the best known of which is to be found under the principle laid down in *Rylands* v. *Fletcher.* . . . To make the rule applicable, it is at least necessary for the person whom it is sought to hold liable to have brought on to his premises, or, at any rate, to some place over which he has a measure of control, something which is dangerous in the sense that, if it escapes, it will do damage. Possibly a further requisite is that to bring the thing to the position in which it is found is to make a non-natural use of that place. Such at any rate, appears to have been the opinion of Lord Cairns, and this limitation has more than once been repeated and approved. . . .

In all cases which have been decided, it has been held necessary, to establish liability, that there should have been some form of escape from the place in which the dangerous object has been retained by the defendant to some other place not subject to his control. . . .It was urged on your Lordships that it would be a strange result to hold the respondents liable if the injured person was just outside their premises but not liable if she was just within them. There is force in the objection, but the liability is itself an extension of the general rule, and, in my view, it is undesirable to extend it further. . . .

I would add that, in considering the matter now in issue before your Lordships, it is not, in my view, necessary to determine whether injury to the person is one of those matters in respect of which damages can be recovered under the rule. Atkinson J. thought it was: *Shiffman* v. *Order of St. John*, [1936] 1 All E.R. 557, and the language of Fletcher Moulton L.J. in *Wing* v. *L.G.O. Co.*, [1909] 2 K.B. 652, . . . is to the same effect, and . . . in *Miles* v. *Forest Rock Granite Co. Ltd.*, 34 T.L.R. 500, the Court of Appeal applied the rule in *Rylands* v. *Fletcher* in support of a judgment in favour of the plaintiff in respect of personal injuries. Undoubtedly, the opinions expressed in these cases extend the application of the rule and may some day require examination. For the moment it is sufficient to say that there must be escape from a place over which a defendant has some measure of control to a place where he has not. In the present case there was no such escape and I would dismiss the appeal.

[Concurring opinions were also given by Lord Simonds and Lord Uthwatt.]

NOTES

1. What did the House of Lords actually decide in *Read* v. *Lyons*?

2. Does the requirement of escape make any sense? Can you think of any policy reasons in support of it? What can be said against the requirement? See *Musgrove* v. *Pandelis,* [1919] 2 K.B. 43; Attorney-*General for Canada* v. *Diamond Waterproofing Ltd.* (1974), 4 O.R. (2d) 489 (C.A.), *per* Schroeder J.A. See also Linden, "Whatever Happened to *Rylands* v. *Fletcher*?" *supra,* where at p. 334 this appears:

> "This requirement of escape makes little sense. Where two people are injured by the same type of conduct, their tort recovery should not depend on whether they were on the land or off the land upon which the activity was conducted. Such distinctions are ludicrous. Indeed, it might be argued that a preferable differentiation, if one were required, would allow the person on the land to recover but deny compensation to the person off the land. A more rational treatment, however, would be to ignore the escape limitation, as the Americans have done."

3. Did the House of Lords actually decide that there could never be any liability for personal injuries under *Rylands* v. *Fletcher*? Are the statements to this effect binding on the English courts? Are they binding on the Canadian courts? In *Perry* v. *Kendricks Transport Ltd.,* [1956] 1 W.L.R. 85, at p. 92 Lord Justice Parker stated:

> "I feel bound to approach the matter upon the basis that the facts here bring the case within the rule in *Rylands* v. *Fletcher:* nor do I think it is open to this court to hold that the rule only applies to damage to adjoining land or to a proprietary interest in land and not to personal injury. It is true that in *Read* v. *Lyons & Co. Ltd.,* Lord MacMillan, Lord Porter and Lord Simonds all doubted whether the rule extended to cover personal injuries, but the final decision in the matter was expressly left over, and as the matter stands at present, I think we are bound to hold that the defendants are liable in this case, quite apart from negligence, unless they can bring themselves within one of the well-known exceptions to the rule."

See also *Benning* v. *Wong* (1969), 122 C.L.R. 249 where Barwick C.J. said:

> "Personal injuries sustained by reason of the escape to the plaintiff's land of a dangerous thing or substance brought to land by a defendant are, in my opinion, to be included in the damages caused by such escape."

4. In *Deyo* v. *Kingston Speedway Ltd.,* [1954] O.R. 223, two spectators at a stock car race were injured, one fatally, when a racing car went out of control. The action was dismissed on the ground that they were trespassers at the time. Mr. Justice Roach relying on *Read* v. *Lyons,* stated that there was "no escape from the lands occupied by and under the control of the respondent corporation".

5. Compare with *Aldridge* v. *Van Patter,* [1952] O.R. 595, [1952] 4 D.L.R. 93, where the defendant, Western Fair, was in occupation of a park on which there was a grandstand and race-track. For a fee, it licensed the defendant Wilmer to conduct stock-car racing on the race-track. A car driven by the defendant Van Patter, while engaged in racing, crashed through a rail fence and injured the two plaintiffs who were in the park and proceeding to a wicket to buy a ticket to see the races. In an action against the three defendants for damages, Spence J. held: (1) Wilmer and Western Fair liable under the principle of *Rylands* v. *Fletcher.* Despite Lord Macmillan's *dictum,* in *Read* v. *Lyons,* this doctrine extended to personal damages sustained "by anyone to whom the probability of such damage would naturally be foreseen"; (2) Wilmer and Western Fair liable in nuisance; (3) all three defendants liable for negligence. See also *Hale* v. *Jennings, infra.*

6. Is *Rylands* v. *Fletcher* limited to adjusting disputes between adjoining landowners? See Newark, "The Boundaries of Nuisance" (1949), 65 L.Q.Rev. 480, at p. 488. See also *Wing* v. *London General Omnibus Co.,* [1909] 2 K.B. 652, where Fletcher Moulton L.J. spoke of cases under *Rylands* v. *Fletcher* as being in reality cases of nuisance, which he defined as "excessive use of some private right whereby a person exposes his neighbour's property or person to danger".

7. In *Charing Cross Electricity Supply Co.* v. *Hydraulic Power Co.,* [1914] 3 K.B. 772, the defendant's hydraulic mains, under a public street, burst and damaged the plaintiff's cables, also laid under the street. The defendant was held liable. See Lord Sumner at p. 779: "I think that this present case is also indistinguishable from *Rylands* v. *Fletcher.* Two grounds of distinction have been suggested. It is said that the doctrine of *Rylands* v. *Fletcher* is applicable between the owners of adjacent closes, which are adjacent whether there be any intermediate property or not; and that it is a doctrine depending upon the ownership of land and the rights attaching to the ownership of land, under which violations of that species of right can be prevented or punished. In the present case, instead of having two adjacent owners of real property, you have only two neighbouring owners, not strictly adjacent, of chattels, whose chattels are there under a permission which might have been obtained by the private licence of the owners of the soil, though in fact obtained under parliamentary powers; hence the two companies are in the position of co-users of a highway or at any rate of co-users of different rooms in one house, and *Rylands* v. *Fletcher* does not apply. The case depends on doctrines applicable to the highways, or houses let out in tenements. I am unable to agree with any of these distinctions, though they have been pressed upon us by both learned counsel with great resource and command of the authorities. *Midwood* v. *Manchester Corporation,* [1905] 2 K.B. 597, is not decided as a case of a dispute arising between the owners of two adjacent closes. The case is treated as one between a corporation, whose business under the roadway is exactly similar to that of the defendant corporation here, and injured occupiers of the premises. If the distinction drawn between the present case and that of adjacent landowners in *Rylands* v. *Fletcher* be a good one, it either was not taken in *Midwood* v. *Manchester Corporation,* or was taken and treated as of no importance. Further I am satisfied that *Rylands* v. *Fletcher* is not limited to the case of adjacent freeholders. I shall not attempt to shew how far it extends. It extends as far as this case, and that is enough for the present purposes."

8. In *Sochacki* v. *Sas,* [1947] 1 All E.R. 344, Lord Goddard C.J., in a *dictum* relating to fires, said that if a fire spreads, the person responsible for it "may be liable not merely to an adjoining owner who suffers damage, but to any other person who suffers damage. If I happen to be on somebody else's land at a time when a fire spreads to that land and my motor car or property is destroyed, I have just as much right against the person who improperly allows the fire to escape from his land as the owner of the land on which I happen to be." See also *Vaughan* v. *Halifax-Dartmouth Bridge Commission* (1961), 29 D.L.R. (2d) 523 (N.S.C.A.).

9. In *Dokuchia* v. *Domansch,* [1945] O.R. 141, [1945] 1 D.L.R. 757, the plaintiff was riding in a truck with the defendant. The truck stalled and the defendant had the plaintiff lie on the fender and pour gasoline into the carburettor. The truck went a short distance when an explosion occurred. The plaintiff was thrown off the truck and the truck ran over him. In an action for damages the plaintiff obtained a judgment based on an assessment of comparative fault, 20 percent to plaintiff, 80 percent to defendant. On appeal this judgment was upheld. Laidlaw J.A. affirmed the judgment on the ground that the handling of gasoline involved the principle of *Rylands* v. *Fletcher.* The rule was not confined to landowners but made the owner of a dangerous thing liable for "any mischief thereby occasioned"; and it was immaterial whether damage be caused on or off the defendant's premises.

10. In *Ekstrom* v. *Deagon and Montgomery,* [1946] 1 D.L.R. 208, [1945] 2 W.W.R. 385 (Alta.), the defendant had his stalled truck towed to the front of the plaintiff's garage where he began to look for the trouble. He obtained the plaintiff's permission to use an electric light on the end of an extension cord. While draining his fuel tank the fumes took fire and the plaintiff's garage was burned. Parke J. held the defendant liable without proof of negligence. This was not a natural user of the garage premises by the defendant even though the plaintiff might conceivably have done exactly the same thing on his own premises. "If a person brings on his own land a dangerous substance which escapes and injury results to another and for which he thus becomes liable, how much more so would a person who takes a dangerous article on another person's property and causes damage to the latter be liable?" See also *Crown Diamond Paint Co. Ltd.* v. *Acadian Holding Realty Ltd.,* [1952] 2 S.C.R. 161; *Jackson* v. *Drury Construction* (1974), 4 O.R. (2d) 735 (C.A.).

B. DEFENCES

PETERS v. PRINCE OF WALES THEATRE (BIRMINGHAM) LTD.

Court of Appeal. [1943] K.B. 73; [1942] 2 All E.R. 533

Defendants leased to plaintiff a shop in a building which contained a theatre and, over the plaintiff's shop, a rehearsal room. In the latter, at the time the lease was granted, there was, to plaintiff's knowledge, a sprinkler system installed as a precaution against fire. The system extended to plaintiff's shop. In a thaw, following a severe frost, water poured from the sprinklers in the defendant's rehearsal room and damaged plaintiff's stock. Plaintiff brought action claiming (a) negligence and (b) liability under *Rylands* v. *Fletcher.* At the trial negligence was negatived but plaintiff obtained judgment on the latter ground. Defendants appealed.

The judgment of the court (Scott, MacKinnon and Goddard L.JJ.) was read by Goddard L.J. [The court agreed with the finding that the defendant had not been negligent.]

. . . This is not a case of the escape of water brought on the premises merely for domestic purposes, and the sprinkler system cannot be treated as analogous to ordinary water-closets, lavatories and baths. It is a system in which there is potential danger of the escape of an enormous quantity of water. Accordingly [the trial judge] held that the case was not within the exception to the rule which has been established by a series of cases of which . . . *Rickards* v. *Lothian* [is] perhaps the leading example. . . .

Carstairs v. *Taylor* (1871), L.R. 6 Exch. 217, established the first exception to *Rylands* v. *Fletcher.* . . . The plaintiff occupied the ground floor of a warehouse and the defendant, from whom he hired it, occupied the upper floor. Rain water percolated into the plaintiff's floor owing to the guttering being rendered defective by rats, but no negligence was found. It was held that the plaintiff had no cause of action. Kelly C.B. put his judgment on the ground of *vis major.* Bramwell B. with whom Pigott B. concurred, relied on the roof being for the common protection of both plaintiff and defendant and the collection of water running from it was for their joint benefit. The decision of Martin B. was that one who takes a floor in a house must be held to take the premises as they are and cannot complain that the house was not constructed differently. . . .

We agree with the criticism of Hallet J. of the passage in Charlesworth's *Law of Negligence,* p. 552, where it is stated that "Water brought on the premises for business purposes, as opposed to domestic purposes gives rise to the liability in *Rylands* v. *Fletcher,* whether or not there is negligence." That is too wide a statement. It is not the purpose to which the water is being put which is decisive. It is that the plaintiff takes the premises as they are, and, accordingly, consents to the presence there of the installed water system with all its advantages and disadvantages.

Applying the principles which we have endeavoured to deduce from the authorities to the present case, the plaintiff took a lease from theatre proprietors of part of the building in which they carried on their theatre. When he took it the sprinkler system was installed and he knew of it. It is not to be supposed that the defendants would have consented to have let to him had he stipulated for the removal of that system. He took the place as he found it for better or worse. Indeed, if common benefit, be the material consideration, although, in our opinion, it is not, considering that theatres are generally regarded as buildings exposed to more than ordinary risk of fire, it may well be for the benefit of tenants in the building that the most effective apparatus should exist for dealing with this danger. It is, however, on the implied consent of the plaintiff to the presence of this installation that we base our decision that the doctrine of *Rylands* v. *Fletcher* does not apply. The appeal must be allowed, and judgment entered for the defendants.

NOTES

1. Assuming that the escape from a sprinkler system would have involved liability as between two adjoining owners, could one owner have enjoined the use of a sprinkler before the escape because he did not "consent" to its presence? Even if a tenant "consents" to the presence of a sprinkler does he "consent" to the escape of water from it? May not "consent" be more relevant to the manner in which a plaintiff comes within the area of danger created by something which does not require the consent of anyone for its continuance? See *Elfassy* v. *Sylben Investments* (1978), 21 O.R. (2d) 609, where Reid J. held that a sprinkler system was not an "inherently dangerous thing" and that, in any event, it was installed for the benefit of the plaintiff and with his knowledge, acquiescence and consent.

2. In *Holinaty* v. *Hawkins* (1965), 52 D.L.R. (2d) 289 (Ont. C.A.), the plaintiff, owner of a garage, entered into a contract with the defendant company to remove existing underground tanks and to replace them with larger tanks. The defendant company entered into a subcontract with Hawkins to do the excavation work which all parties knew would involve the use of dynamite. As a result of blasting, the plaintiff's building was damaged. In an action for damages against the company and Hawkins, the trial judge held that *Rylands* v. *Fletcher* was inapplicable since the plaintiff had consented to the use of dynamite. On appeal this was reversed. "While . . . the plaintiff consented . . . to the use of dynamite . . . [he did not] consent to its improper or excessive use, [nor did he] knowingly and willingly assume the risk of loss or damage which would flow from such use." The court also found Hawkins negligent and the company liable for the negligence of its independent contractor in the use of a "dangerous thing". Compare with *Gilson* v. *Kerrier R.D.C.,* [1976] 1 W.L.R. 904 (C.A.).

3. In *Frederic* v. *Perpetual Investments Ltd. et al.* (1969), 2 D.L.R. (3d) 50 (Ont.), carbon monoxide gas escaped from the landlord's garage up into the apartment of his tenant, causing her to suffer chronic carbon monoxide poisoning. The landlord relied mainly on the defence of "caveat lessee".

Stark J. pointed out that the problem here was not with the demised premises but the penetration of the gas from outside:

"The defendant placed chief reliance upon the 'caveat lessee' doctrine. That is to say, the general principle of the law enunciated over and over again in the cases and in the texts and expressed for example by Aylesworth, J.A., [quoting from *Salmond's Law of Torts,* 10th ed., pp. 500-2] in *MacDonald* v. *Town of Goderich,* [1949] O.R. 619 at p. 629, [1949] 3 D.L.R. 788 at p. 793, is that:

'Apart from any express contract to that effect, a landlord owes no duty, either towards his tenant or towards any other person who enters on the premises during the tenancy, to take care that the premises are safe either at the commencement of the tenancy or during its continuance.'

As Chief Justice Erle so graphically put it in *Robbins* v. *Jones* (1863), 15 C.B. (N.S.) 221 at p. 240, 143 E.R. 768: '. . . fraud, apart, there is no law against letting a tumbledown house . . .'

In the particular facts of this case, however, in my view liability does rest upon the landlord for two very different reasons, both of which properly emerge from the plaintiff's pleading. In the first place, it must be borne in mind that there was nothing inherently defective in the premises occupied by this tenant. The injuries arose because the landlord in conducting his garage undertaking on his own premises directly below the tenant, failed to keep within the bounds of this neighbouring property the dangerous gaseous fumes. Thus, it appears to me that the rule in *Fletcher* v. *Rylands* (1866), L.R. 1 Ex. 265, is applicable. In *Salmond on Torts,* 14th ed., p. 441, the rule formulated thus:

'The occupier of land who brings and keeps upon it anything likely to do damage if it escapes is bound at his peril to prevent its escape, and is liable for all the direct consequences of its escape, even if he has been guilty of no negligence.'

A fortiori, it would seem that he should be liable if his negligence in failing to close and seal openings to the plaintiff's apartment directly above his garage undertaking permitted easy ingress for the gaseous fumes. . . ."

The landlord was also held liable in negligence and for breach of the covenant of quiet enjoyment.

4. For discussions of the defences to strict liability actions under *Rylands* v. *Fletcher,* see Linden, *Canadian Tort Law* (2nd ed., 1977), p. 460; Fleming, *The Law of Torts* (5th ed., 1977), p. 329.

HALE v. JENNINGS BROTHERS

Court of Appeal. [1938] 1 All E.R. 579

Plaintiff was the owner of a shooting-gallery on ground leased from defendants for that purpose. Defendants occupied the adjoining ground on which they erected, as amusement proprietors, a chair-o-plane — a contrivance that whirled customers around in attached chairs at a considerable rate of speed. While a patron, one Crampton, was riding in a chair and fooling about in it, the chair came loose and struck and injured the plaintiff. In an action for damages, evidence showed that the chairs and equipment were properly made and maintained and that the defendants had done everything possible to stop this particular patron from fooling with the mechanism. The trial judge found defendants were not negligent and dismissed the action on the ground that *Rylands* v. *Fletcher* did not apply since although "the chair-o-plane was something of an unusual danger", it "was not essentially dangerous in itself. It is dangerous . . . only if it is not in a proper state of repair, or if passengers on it behave recklessly." Plaintiff appealed.

Scott L.J.: . . . The behaviour of Crampton in causing the chair to become detached, was in my view just the kind of behaviour which ought to have been anticipated as being a likely act with a percentage of users of the apparatus. People go there in a spirit of fun. Many of them are ignorant, and many of them are wholly unaware of the dangers incidental to playing with the chairs in that sort of way, and they cause a danger that they do not in the least realize. That kind of accident does not come within the exceptions to the rule at all. The apparatus is dangerous within the meaning of the rule because it is intended to be used by that sort of person; and is likely to produce this very danger. I consider that the rule in *Rylands* v. *Fletcher* applies to the facts of this case, because the apparatus was set up by the defendants for the purpose of profit. It was a non-natural user of the land. It was inherently dangerous, and the defendants have to take the risk of any damage which may result from it. For these reasons, I think that the judgment of the county court judge should be reversed.

[The judgments of Slesser and Clauson L.JJ. to the same effect are omitted.]

NOTES

1. Why did the court not dismiss the case on the basis of the conduct of the third person, as in *Rickards* v. *Lothian*? Is the reasoning of the court on this point familiar?

2. In *Perry* v. *Kendricks Transport Ltd.,* [1956] 1 W.L.R. 85, [1956] 1 All E.R. 154, the defendants had placed on their parking ground a disused coach from which the petrol had been drained and a cap screwed over the entrance pipe. The plaintiff, a boy of ten, was injured, as he approached the parking ground, by an explosion of petrol fumes from this coach. In an action for damages, the trial judge found that the cap had been removed by some unknown person and that a lighted match had been thrown in the tank by one of two boys who hurried away as the plaintiff approached. He dismissed the action. On appeal, the court held that the case was within *Rylands* v. *Fletcher*, but the defendants were not liable since the escape was caused by the act of a stranger. It was argued that the act of a young child could not be a *novus actus interveniens*. The court held that if the act causing the escape was one which could not reasonably have been anticipated and was one over which the defendants had no control, then the real cause of the escape was not due to the defendants' action in having the dangerous thing on its premises, nor of any failure on its part to keep the thing, nor to any latent or·patent defect in protective measures. "The real cause is the act of the stranger, for whose acts the occupier of the land is in no sense responsible, because he cannot control them."

3. As to "act of God" see *Greenock* v. *Caledonian Ry.,* [1917] A.C. 556, and compare *McDougall* v. *Snider* (1913), 29 O.L.R. 448, before that decision, with *Smith* v. *Ont. and Minnesota Power Co.* (1918), 44 O.L.R. 43, following it.

NORTH WESTERN UTILITIES, LTD. v. LONDON GUARANTEE & ACCIDENT CO. LTD.

Privy Council. [1936] A.C. 108; 105 L.J.P.C. 18

The defendant maintained, pursuant to statute, a 12 inch gas main some 3½ feet below the surface of the street in Edmonton. The municipality in constructing a storm sewer immediately beneath the defendant's main had weakened the latter so that it sagged and finally sprung a leak. A year later gas from this main percolated through the soil and entered the plaintiff's building, where it caught fire and destroyed the building. An action for damages against the defendant was dismissed at the trial, but on appeal to the Supreme Court of Alberta judgment, for damages to be assessed, was entered for the plaintiff. The defendant appealed to the Judicial Committee of the Privy Council.

Lord Wright M.R.: . . . That gas is a dangerous thing within the rules applicable to things dangerous in themselves is beyond question. Thus the appellants who are carrying in their mains the inflammable and explosive gas are *prima facie* within the principle of *Rylands* v. *Fletcher*: that is to say, that though they are doing nothing wrongful in carrying the dangerous thing so long as they keep it in their pipes, they come *prima facie* within the rules of strict liability if the gas escapes; the gas constitutes an extraordinary danger created by the appellants for their own purposes, and the rule established by *Rylands* v. *Fletcher* requires that they act at their peril and must pay for damage caused by the gas if it escapes, even without any negligence on their part. The rule is not limited to cases where the defendant has been carrying or accumulating the dangerous thing on his own land; it applies equally in a case like the present where the appellants were carrying the gas in mains laid in the property of the City (that is in the sub-soil) in exercise of a franchise to do so: *Charing Cross Electricity Supply Co.* v. *Hydraulic Power Co.,* [1914] 3 K.B. 772.

This form of liability is in many ways analogous to a liability for nuisance, though nuisance is not only different in its historical origin but in its legal character and many of its incidents and applications. But the two causes of action often overlap, and in respect of each of these causes of action the rule of strict liability has been modified by admitting as a defence that what was being done was properly done in pursuance of statutory powers, and the mischief that has happened has not been brought about by any negligence on the part of the undertakers. As an illustration of this well known doctrine, reference may be made to *Green* v. *Chelsea Waterworks Co.,* 70 L.T. 547, 549, where Lindley L.J. said of *Rylands* v. *Fletcher:* "That case is not to be extended beyond the legitimate principle on which the House of Lords decided it. If it were extended as far as strict logic might require, it would be a very oppressive decision." By the same reasoning the rule has been held inapplicable where the casualty is due to an act of God; or to the independent or conscious volition of a third party, as in *Box* v. *Jubb,* 4 Ex.D. 76, which was approved by the Judicial Committee in in *Rickards* v. *Lothian;* and not to any negligence of the defendants. In *Box* v. *Jubb* the act which caused the escape of the water was a malicious (which their Lordships think means no more than conscious or deliberate) act of a third person. It was said by Kelly C.B.: "I think the defendants could not possibly have been expected to anticipate that which happened here, and the law does not require them to construct their reservoir and the sluices and gates leading to it to meet any amount of pressure which the wrongful act of a third person may impose." . . .

It is not here intended to enumerate all the defences which might be available to a defendant in this class of action: but the two defences mentioned are both material in this case. Reference was made to a further possible defence based on the contention that the appellants and the owners of the property destroyed had a common interest in maintaining the potentially dangerous installations, or that these owners had consented to the danger. It is true that in proper cases such may be good defences but they do not seem to have any application to a case like the present, where the appellants are a commercial undertaking, though no doubt they are acting under statutory powers, while those whose property has been destroyed are merely individual consumers who avail themselves of the supply of gas which is offered. These facts do not constitute a common interest or consent in any relevant sense.

Where undertakers are acting under statutory powers it is a question of construction, depending on the language of the statute, whether they are only liable for negligence or whether they remain subject to the strict and unqualified rule of *Rylands* v. *Fletcher.* Thus in *Charing Cross Electricity Supply Co.* v. *Hydraulic Power Co.,* it was held (following the previous decision in *Midwood & Co.* v. *Manchester Corporation,* [1905] 2 K.B. 597) that the defence of statutory authority was limited by a clause in the statutory Order providing that nothing therein should exonerate the Corporation from liability for nuisance. In *Hammond* v. *St. Pancras Vestry,* L.R. 9 C.P. 316, where the Act imposed on the Vestry the duty of properly cleansing their sewers, it held that as these words were susceptible of meaning either that an absolute duty was imposed or that the duty was only to exercise due and reasonable care, the latter meaning was to be preferred, since the absolute duty could not be held to be imposed save by clear words. That case was followed in *Stretton's Derby Brewery Co.* v. *Mayor of Derby,* [1894] 1 Ch. 431.

It accordingly now becomes necessary to consider the meaning of ss. 11 and 13 of the Alberta Water, Gas, Electric and Telephone Company Act, cited above. . . . [It was found that the Act did not impose an absolute duty to maintain.] But in any event, the question is not eventually material in this case, for, even if the section applies to maintenance, and is absolute in its terms, the duty it imposes is still no more than the duty under the rule in *Rylands* v. *Fletcher,* according to which the appellants would not be liable for damage caused, without default on their part, by the independent act of a third party. Then, whether or not s. 13 applies to maintenance, and whether or not it imposes, where it does apply, a liability unqualified in terms, the position is the same for purposes of this case: the appellants' real defence was that the damage was caused by the act of the city, for which they were not responsible and could not control, and that they were guilty of no negligence in the matter. That defence could be equally good on any view of the effect of s. 13; and the same reasoning applies to s. 11, if indeed that section is open at all to the respondents in this case.

It accordingly becomes necessary to consider the issues of fact which have occupied the greater part of the hearing of this appeal, as they seem to have done in the courts below. The respondents have contended that the original construction of the pipe line was improper, and that the damage was solely caused thereby; the appellants have contended that not only was their original construction proper but the breaking of the pipe was solely due to the ground beneath it being let down by the new sewerage works constructed by the city in 1931. [The defendant was found not to have been negligent in the original construction.]

There remains the further point, which is, that assuming that the city in fact let down the ground and caused the pipe to break, still the appellants should have foreseen and guarded against the risk of their pipes being affected. . . .

The authorities already cited herein show that, though the act of a third party may be relied on by way of defence in cases of this type, the defendant may still be held liable in negligence if he failed in foreseeing and guarding against the consequences to his work of that third party's act. . . .

In truth, the gravamen of the charge against the appellants in this matter is that though they had the tremendous responsibility of carrying this highly inflammable gas under the streets of a city, they did nothing at all in all the facts of this case. If they did not know of the city works, their system of inspection must have been very deficient. If they did know they should have been on their guard; they might have ascertained what work was being done and carefully investigated the position, or they might have examined the pipes likely to be affected so as to satisfy themselves that the bed on which they lay was not being disturbed. Their duty to the respondents was at the lowest to be on the watch and to be vigilant: they do not even pretend to have done as much as that. In fact, so far as it appears, they gave no thought to the matter. They left it all to chance. It is, in their Lordships' judgment, impossible for them now to protest that they could have done nothing effective to prevent the accident: and in any case their Lordships cannot accept that as the true view.

In the result their Lordships agree with the decision on this point of the Appellate Division, and are of opinion that the appeal should be dismissed.

NOTES

1. What is the holding of this case?
2. With regard to the effect of statutory authorization, see Lord Russell C.J. in *Price* v. *South Metropolitan Gas Co.* (1895), 65 L.J.Q.B. 126:

> "It is clear that where a gas company such as this, having statutory authority to lay pipes, does so in the exercise of its statutory powers, the 'wild beast' theory referred to in the well-known case of *Fletcher* v. *Rylands* is inapplicable."

And see Lord Blackburn in *Geddis* v. *Proprietors of Bann Reservoir* (1878), 3 App. Cas. 430, at p. 455:

> "It is now thoroughly well established that no action will lie for doing that which the Legislature has authorized, if it be done without negligence, although it does occasion damage to anyone; but an action does lie for doing that which the Legislature has authorized, if it be done negligently."

Most of these statutory authorization cases are nuisance cases, but they are equally applied in *Rylands* v. *Fletcher* situations. See *dictum* in *Charles R. Bell Ltd.* v. *City of St. John's* (1965), 54 D.L.R. (2d) 528, at p. 555.

3. See also *Dunne et al.* v. *North Western Gas Board et al.,* [1964] 2 Q.B. 806 (C.A.), where a break in a gas main caused by a burst water main resulted in the escape of gas into the sewers. An explosion occurred on a highway, injuring the plaintiffs. With regard to the Gas Board and the Liverpool Corporation which controlled the water main, Sellers L.J. made these comments as to the applicability of *Rylands* v. *Fletcher:*

> ". . . But clearly in so far as gas and water were brought into this locality they were so brought under statutory authority and for the general benefit of the public for whom such facilities were obviously provided. They escaped and did damage without any negligence on the part of the defendants or of anyone else. It is not a case of an independent contractor having been negligent, as was the case in *Rylands* v. *Fletcher,* which brought about a decision in wide terms imposing liability on a landowner for things which escaped from his land, whereas in the present time the defendants' liability in that case could simply have been based on the defendants' failure of duty to take reasonable care to protect the adjacent mines which were known to be there or which ought to have been discovered with reasonable care, and in respect of such a duty it is no answer to say that the failure was that of an independent contractor. The water in that case escaped through negligence and the occupier's duty to his neighbour was not performed.
>
> The present case is therefore on its facts different from *Rylands* v. *Fletcher* in that respect, and in all the circumstances it scarcely seems accurate to hold that this nationalised industry collects and distributes gas for its 'own purposes.'
>
> Gas, water and also electricity services are well-nigh a necessity of modern life, or at least are generally demanded as a requirement for the common good, and one or more are being taken with considerable despatch to every village and hamlet in the country with either statutory compulsion or

sanction. It would seem odd that facilities so much sought after by the community and approved by their legislators should be actionable at common law because they have been brought to the places where they are required and have escaped without negligence by an unforeseen sequence of mishaps. A sequence of events may be just as unforeseeable and unavoidable, and as extraneous to an individual or a supplier of services, as an act of God is recognised to be."

4. The decision in *Dunne* was approved of in *Benning* v. *Wong* (1969), 43 A.L.J.R. 467. There, injury was caused to the plaintiff by the escape of gas from pipelines laid by the Australian Gas Light Co. in a public street and under statutory powers. Menzies J. distinguished the *North Western Utilities* case as one in which a finding of negligence was made. He stated the general proposition as follows:

". . . It was, I think, a correct understanding of the rule in *Rylands* v. *Fletcher* that led to the decision in *Green* v. *Chelsea Waterworks Co.* (1894), 70 L.T. 547, that *Rylands* v. *Fletcher* does not apply to the escape of what has been brought to the point where it escapes by the authority of an Act of Parliament. If a person acts in accordance with statutory authority in bringing a dangerous substance to his premises, why should he be absolutely liable if it escapes? The rule in *Rylands* v. *Fletcher* was established to meet the case of one proprietor putting others in jeopardy by taking the risk of bringing something dangerous to his premises, but, if the bringing was within a statutory authority which it was intended, should be exercised, the reason for the rule has no application. If it were to be established that a dangerous thing, brought upon premises by statutory authority, escaped through the negligence of the person who brought it, that would be another matter, but it would not be a matter within *Rylands* v. *Fletcher,* rather it would depend upon the principles enunciated in *Geddis* v. *Proprietors of the Bann Reservoir* (1878), 3 App. Cas. 430. This is what the decisions show."

See also *Boxes Ltd.* v. *British Waterways Board,* [1971] 2 L1.R. 183 (C.A.).

5. In *Danku* v. *Town of Fort Frances* (1976), 73 D.L.R. (3d) 377 (Fitzgerald D.C.J.), a municipal sewer system backed up as a result of a break in a private sewer system owned by a trailer park which was joined to the public system. In relieving the municipality of liability but holding the trailer park responsible under *Rylands* v. *Fletcher,* Fitzgerald D.C.J. stated:

"While there is an increasing tendency toward collective responsibility for the misfortunes of others as opposed to individual accountability, the move in this direction, being a departure from common law philosophy, had been accomplished by legislation rather than by case law. It is probably better that in the realm of property law it should remain so. Thus, in the absence of negligence or actionable nuisance for which a municipality is accountable there appears to be no reason why the municipality should not be entitled to the benefit of the recognized exception to *Rylands* v. *Fletcher* that strict liability for the escape of dangerous things does not apply to a person, corporate or otherwise, lawfully carrying on an undertaking which the Court determines to be for the general benefit of the community at large. Particularly is this so if the person is a municipality carrying on such an undertaking by the authority of a statute which does not in specific words deprive the municipality of protection: see *Winfield, op. cit.* at p. 428.

I find as fact that in the case before me the municipality was lawfully and without negligence operating a sewage disposal network. I find that unknown to the municipality a third party caused a blockage to form in that system causing the escape of effluent which damaged the property of the plaintiffs and that the municipality responded when notified and corrected the condition without delay. I find that the sewerage system owned and operated by the municipality was an undertaking lawfully carried on by the municipality for the general benefit of the community at large and that it is therefore exempt from the strict liability to which, in the absence of statutory relief expressly or by necessary implication afforded to it, it would otherwise be liable under the rule in *Rylands* v. *Fletcher*.

. . .

There is a fundamental difference between the defendants in this matter. The defendant municipality operates its sewage system solely for the benefit of the entire population. Unlike the supply of utilities even those who do not connect to the system benefit by the disposal of noxious waste which would otherwise pollute and contaminate the area with what is so graphically described in the original Anglo-Saxon of the judgment in *Rylands* v. *Fletcher* as 'filth' and 'stenches'.

The defendant Walleye on the other hand operates its system both for its own private purposes and for the benefit of a particular segment of the community; namely, its tenants. The system is operated as part of a scheme devoted to private profit and is therefore not within the exception to the rule in *Rylands* v. *Fletcher* relating to the general benefit of the community. If the effect is to impose a heavier burden on such a commercial enterprise than upon the municipality one may reconcile it in the words of Lord Wright, previously quoted, that the result is 'reasonable according to the ordinary usages of mankind living in . . . a particular society'.

In this case the defendant Walleye constructed upon its land a sewer which collected not only the waste from habitations located on its property but also waste from a sizeable commercial laundromat. In my view it does so at its peril if by reason of a defect in its sewage disposal system a substance or combination of substances escapes with resulting damage to neighbouring landowners. It is only just that if the loss must fall somewhere it be upon the person conducting an enterprise for the purpose of profit rather than upon its completely innocent neighbour. That, I perceive to be the philosophy behind the rule in *Rylands* v. *Fletcher* and I believe it to be perfectly applicable to the case at bar. I therefore find the defendant Walleye liable to the plaintiffs for the damages suffered by them.

Since the liability of the defendant Walleye is totally disposed of by the application of the rule in *Rylands* v. *Fletcher* it is unnecessary for me to decide if the involuntary discharge of sand from its system could also be an actionable nuisance."

Does this distinction make sense to you? What if the municipality alone was the cause of the flooding?

6. The onus of proving absence of negligence lies on the defendant. See *Manchester Corp.* v. *Farnworth,* [1930] A.C. 171; *Lawrysyn* v. *Town of Kipling* (1966), 55 D.L.R. (2d) 471 (Sask. C.A.). But *cf. Benning* v. *Wong, supra,* where majority felt onus was on plaintiff, not defendant.

7. The word negligence is not used in the ordinary sense here; the courts have narrowed its meaning. "If the damages could be prevented it is, within the meaning of this rule, negligence not to make such reasonable exercise of powers," See *Geddis* v. *Proprietors of Bann Reservoir* (1878), 3 App. Cas. 430, at p. 455. Similarly, it has been suggested that "it is negligence to carry out work in a manner which results in damage, unless it can be shown that that, and that only, was the way in which the duty could be performed". See *Provender Millers* v. *Southampton County Council,* [1940] 1 Ch. 131, at p. 140.

8. Other techniques of minimizing the importance of this defence are described in Linden, "Strict Liability, Nuisance and Legislative Authorization" (1966), 4 O.H. L.J. 196:

"The importance of the defence of legislative authority is on the wane. Only rarely does the legislation authorizing activity expressly deal with the question of tort liability. This has left the judiciary in a position to fabricate legislative intention where none really exists, which path has created considerable confusion. Part of this confusion results from a changed attitude toward activities authorized by legislation and the need to compensate the victims of progress. Because the historical and policy reasons which prompted the creation of the immunity have ceased to be influential, the courts have commenced to circumscribe its operation. However, rather than leading a direct frontal attack on the immunity, the courts have used subterfuge and have created several judicial techniques whereby invocation of the immunity can be avoided. At the same time lip service is paid to the received doctrine. . . .

[T]here were certain factors that courts weigh in deciding whether to rely on the immunity or one of the techniques for its avoidance. The immunity will tend to be invoked and recovery denied where a plaintiff is seeking to gain increased compensation by avoiding a statutory compensation scheme, where the defendant is a non-profit making operation, where the authority is by statute rather than by an inferior legislative enactment, where an injunction is sought, and where a particularly important industry is involved. On the other hand, courts will tend to avoid the immunity and impose nuisance or strict liability where the defendant is a profit-making organization, where the legislative authority is a by-law or governmental contract, where the defendant's conduct was reprehensible and where loss could be easily avoided. Although the best solution to this problem is for legislatures to consider this aspect of tort liability when legislation is drafted, experience dictates that this will not be done. The judiciary, as always, is left to do its best to reconcile the conflicting interests. It would be helpful if in so doing they would refuse to rely on fictions and disclose the true basis of their decisions. If this is done one can prophesy that the future of the immunity will be shortlived."

9. In *Vaughn* v. *Halifax-Dartmouth Bridge Commission* (1961), 29 D.L.R. (2d) 523 (N.S.C.A.), the defendant commission was by statute authorized to construct, operate and maintain a bridge, across an arm of the sea, connecting Halifax and Dartmouth. In the course of painting the bridge, the plaintiff's car, parked in a parking lot of the dockyard authorities about 60-70 feet south of the bridge, sustained damage from many flecks of paint which hardened. It was admitted that the paint came from the painting of the bridge. The plaintiff brought an action for damages based alternatively on negligence, nuisance, and strict liability for the escape of dangerous things. The defendant pleaded that the paint was properly used in exercise of its statutory powers to maintain the bridge. The plaintiff obtained judgment at the trial. The trial judge found the case came under *Rylands* v. *Fletcher* or nuisance; that painting was necessary for the maintenance of the bridge and was done without negligence, and that it was practically impossible to prevent dripping and blowing of paint. He found, however, that the defendant had not taken all proper means to see that no unnecessary harm was occasioned the plaintiff since he could have given notice before painting and could have stationed men to remove paint from the cars as it fell.

On appeal, the judgment was upheld. All members of the court negatived nuisance as a cause of action since the plaintiff was not in possession or occupation of land. Ilsley C.J. held that the plaintiff could recover on the basis of *Rylands* v. *Fletcher*, which he expressly denied was confined to property damage or interests in land. In the absence of statutory authorization the erection and maintenance of this bridge was a "non-natural" use of land. He based this on the ground that the inevitable escape of paint even after all precaution had been taken constituted a non-natural use. Assuming that, he concluded the defendant had not discharged the onus of showing that in practical feasibility the defendant's statutory duty could not have been performed without damage to the plaintiff, *e.g.*, by warning those parked cars, etc. Currie J. held that *Rylands* v. *Fletcher* did not apply since the erection and maintenance of the bridge was a natural user of land and the statutory right to maintain it was paramount to any right of the plaintiff to park his car. The only question to his mind was whether the defendant should have given the plaintiff notice that it intended to paint in the "relevant area". [It was in evidence that winds might carry the paint 300-400 feet.] With some doubt he felt it should and its failure was "actionable negligence". MacDonald J. indicated that the trial judge's approach "may well be erroneous" since the plaintiff had no interest in land which, in his view, was essential to a *Rylands* v. *Fletcher* liability, as well as nuisance. To him the proper form of action was in negligence. The defendant owed a duty of care because of the foreseeable risk from dropping paint and "in establishing breach of that duty he would be aided by the admitted fact that painting operations were carried on . . . and that paint which alit on his car came from the bridge. These facts . . . would constitute a *prima facie* case of negligence to which the defence of statutory authority — though relevant — would fail." MacDonald J. had earlier stated that the "defendant had not discharged the onus of showing the damage was inevitable or of negativing 'negligence' in the sense in which that term is used in relation to statutory authorization".

If this is an action for negligence, on whom is the burden of proof? Assume the possibility of a jury; how should it be charged? What if the plaintiff parked where he did in the mistaken belief the wind would change? Is this contributory negligence — apportionable — or what? If the plaintiff's car was in a central "metropolitan" parking lot, could all the car owners sue — or leave their cars at home? See also *Gertsen* v. *Municipality of Metropolitan Toronto et al., supra.*

10. Strict liability has not developed beyond this point in the Commonwealth. Should it be expanded to cover other hazardous activities? Automobile accidents claim 5,000 Canadian lives each year. Should strict liability be utilized in claims arising out of car crashes? What are the arguments pro and con? Defective products injure and even kill many Canadians each year. Should strict liability be imposed on the manufacturers of these products? See *infra,* Chapters 13 and 15.

A NOTE ON VICARIOUS LIABILITY

1. One form of strict liability arises when a "servant" is guilty of tortious conduct in the course of his employment. In such a situation, the servant's "master" is called upon to make good the loss, even though he is not personally at fault. He is said to be vicariously liable. The theory of vicarious liability was developed through the use of various fictions attempting to implicate the master. In reality, however, it was probably the desire to spread the losses that inevitably occur in industry among a larger group than the victims that fostered its growth. It is strange, however, that the fault principle seems to have worked its way back into this area. For example, a master may reimburse himself at the expense of the servant, whose negligence gave rise to the master's vicarious responsibility. See *Lister* v. *Romford Ice & Cold Storage Co. Ltd.,* [1957] A.C. 555, [1957] 1 All E.R. 125 (H.L.).

2. There are limits upon the employers' liability for the acts of their employees. The master must be in a position to exercise "detailed control" over the "manner in which [the servant] shall do his work". See *Performing Right Society Ltd.* v. *Mitchell & Booker (Palais de Danse) Ltd.,* [1924] 1 K.B. 762; *cf. T.G. Bright & Co. Ltd.* v. *Kerr,* [1939] S.C.R. 63, [1939] 1 D.L.R. 193; *Egginton* v. *Reader,* [1936] 1 All E.R. 7. More recently this test has been enlarged and is being displaced by "something like an 'organization test'." See *Co-operators Insurance Association* v. *Kearney,* [1965] S.C.R. 106, 48 D.L.R. (2d) 1, *per* Spence J.; *Armstrong* v. *Mac's Milk* (1975), 7 O.R. (2d) 478 (Lerner J.); *Kennedy* v. *C.N.A. Assur. Co.* (1978), 20 O.R. (2d) 674 (Linden J.); Magnet, "Vicarious Liability and the Professional Employee" (1978-9), 6 C.C.L.T. 208.

3. For the master to be held vicariously liable, the servant must have been in the course of his employment. See *Battistoni* v. *Thomas,* [1932] S.C.R. 144, [1932] 1 D.L.R. 577; *Hoar* v. *Wallace,* [1938] O.R. 666, [1938] 4 D.L.R. 774 (Ont. C.A.); *C.P.R.* v. *Lockhart,* [1942] A.C. 591, [1942] 3 D.L.R. 529 (P.C.).

4. Vicarious liability can even extend to intentional torts perpetrated by employees while on the job. See *Griggs* v. *Southside Hotel Ltd. & Berman,* [1947] O.R. 674, [1947] 4 D.L.R. 49 (Ont. C.A.); *Petersson* v. *Royal Oak Hotel Ltd.,* [1948] N.Z.L.R. 136; *Jennings* v. *C.N.R.,* [1925] 2 D.L.R. 630 (B.C.C.A.). It also may be used in cases of fraud. See *Lloyd* v. *Grace, Smith & Co.,* [1912] A.C. 716 (H.L.).

5. There are some difficult problems concerning the transfer of a servant. In other words, who bears the responsibility for the act of a servant temporarily loaned to another person? Here, too, control has been the key notion. See *Century Insurance Co.* v. *N.I.R.T.B.,* [1942] A.C. 509; *Mersey Docks* v. *Coggins,* [1947] A.C.1. This perplexing issue often arises in cases of operating room accidents. See *Aynsley et al.* v. *Toronto General Hospital,* [1969] 2 O.R. 829 (Ont. C.A.); affd. (1972), 25 D.L.R. (3d) 241 (S.C.C.), for a consideration of whether an anaesthetist or a hospital should bear the vicarious responsibility for the act of a senior resident. See Linden, "Changing Patterns of Hospital Liability in Canada" (1967), 5 Alta. L. Rev. 212. See generally Atiyah, *Vicarious Liability in the Law of Torts* (1967). A recent fascinating case, dealing with some of these issues, is *Morgans* v. *Launchbury et al.,* [1972] 2 All E.R. 606 (H.L.).

6. It has recently been held that a hospital has a non-delegable duty to treat its patients and, consequently, it will be liable for the torts of its specialist staff members, even though they are not employees of the hospital. See *Yepremian* v. *Scarborough General Hospital* (1978), 20 O.R. (2d) 510 (R.E. Holland J.), at p. 534.

CHAPTER 13

PRODUCTS LIABILITY

This is an age of consumption. The production of goods and the construction of buildings are among the most important activities in our economy. In Canada billions of dollars worth of goods are manufactured each year and the amount continues to rise. Without any doubt, these products bring many benefits to our citizenry.

Sometimes, however, consumers and users of these goods are injured. Coca-Cola bottles explode. Steering mechanisms on cars jam. Airplanes crash. Financial losses are thereby incurred.The job of tort law is to decide which of these losses will be shifted to the manufacturers (or other persons in the chain of distribution) and which will lie where they fall. It is no easy task. These articles are becoming more complex and sophisticated than ever before. Component parts of automobiles and television sets, for example, may come thousands of miles across the sea. Goods produced in one country can be sold in every corner of the earth. In response to the social necessities of the times, tort law has developed (albeit slowly) to reflect the felt needs of the society at the time.

Recently, the United States has witnessed a revolution in the way defective product claims are treated in the courts. The American consumer has won a substantial measure of protection through many decisions adopting the theory of strict liability in tort. In Canada, we have not yet seen a corresponding development, despite the marked similarity of both products and distribution techniques in the two countries. In contrast to the United States, very few cases have been brought in Canada. Whether we should follow the American lead to broader protection for the consumer or whether we should cling to our present approach is one of the recurring questions asked in this chapter. Whether tort law can effectively serve contemporary Canadian society in this area is another underlying question.

A. CONTRACT THEORY

SALE OF GOODS ACT

R.S.O. 1970, c. 421, s. 15

Subject to this Act and any statute in that behalf, there is no implied warranty or condition as to the quality or fitness for any particular purpose of goods supplied under a contract of sale, except as follows:

1. Where the buyer, expressly or by implication, makes known to the seller the particular purpose for which the goods are required so as to show that the buyer relies on the seller's skill or judgment, and the goods are of a description that it is in the course of the seller's business to supply (whether he is the manufacturer or not), there is an implied condition that the goods will be reasonably fit for such purpose, but in the case of a contract for the sale of a specified article under its patent or other trade name there is no implied condition as to its fitness for any particular purpose.

2. Where goods are bought by description from a seller who deals in goods of that description (whether he is the manufacturer or not), there is

an implied condition that the goods will be of merchantable quality, but if the buyer has examined the goods, there is no implied condition as regards defects that such examination ought to have revealed.

3. An implied warranty or condition as to quality or fitness for a particular purpose may be annexed by the usage of trade.

4. An express warranty or condition does not negative a warranty or condition implied by this Act unless inconsistent therewith.

NOTES

1. The action by the buyer of goods against a seller for breach of warranty is a curious one, with characteristics of both contract and tort. Professor Ames suggested that the action was originally in tort, upon the case for breach of assumed duty, with overtones of misrepresentation and deceit. See "History of Assumpsit" (1888), 2 Harv. L. Rev. 1, at p. 8. However, in *Stuart* v. *Wilkins* (1778), 1 Douglas 18, 99 E.R. 15, it was held that assumpsit would be for breach of an express warranty as a part of the contract of sale. After that warranties came to be considered as part of the contract of sale. With the development of commerce the courts completely reversed the old notion of *caveat emptor* and by a process of creating "implied" terms gave effect to the view that a vendor should stand behind his product and that a buyer could rely on his seller selling only "good" merchandise. The common law development was codified in the English Sale of Goods Act, 1893 (56 & 57 Vict., c. 71), which has been adopted in the Canadian provinces.

2. A detailed consideration of the operation of these implied terms is left to the course on commercial law. See generally Ziegel, "The Sellers' Liability for Defective Goods at Common Law" (1966), 12 McGill L.J. 183; Kessler, "The Protection of the Consumer under Modern Sales Law" (1964), 74 Yale L.J. 262; Prosser, "The Implied Warranty of Merchantable Quality" (1943), 21 Can. Bar Rev. 446; Waddams, *Products Liability* (1974); Waddams, "Implied Warranties and Products Liability" in *Special Lectures on New Developments in the Law of Torts* (1973); Waddams, "Strict Liability, Warranties and the Sale of Goods" (1969), 19 U. of T.L.J. 157; Waddams, "The Strict Liability of Suppliers Goods" (1974), 37 Mod. L. Rev. 154; Fridman, *Sale of Goods in Canada* (2nd ed., 1979); Atiyah, *Sale of Goods* (5th ed., 1975); Linden, *Canadian Tort Law* (2nd ed., 1977) p. 469.

3. One serious shortcoming of the Sale of Goods Act is that it is frequently rendered inapplicable by the fine print in standard form contracts. Here are the terms from a typical contract for the purchase of an automobile:

"I expressly agree that there are no conditions or warranties (either legal or conventional or contractual, including any legal warranty for latent defects) the warranty printed on the back hereof being hereby expressly accepted in lieu of all other warranties, conditions or representations express or implied, statutory or otherwise made by the dealer, its officers, agents or employees or the manufacturer, on the motor vehicle, chassis or parts furnished hereunder nor shall any agreement collateral hereto be binding upon the dealer unless such condition, warranty, representation or collateral agreement shall be endorsed hereon in writing. The obligation of the dealer under any condition, warranty, representation or collateral agreement which may be endorsed hereon in writing shall be limited to repair or replacement of parts and shall in no event extend to liability for consequential damages.

The front and back of this purchase order and agreement comprises the entire agreement affecting this purchase and no other agreement or understanding of any nature concerning the same has been made or entered into or will be recognized. I acknowledge that I have read the matter printed on the front and back of this purchase order and agreement and I agree to the matter printed on the back hereof to the same extent as if it were printed above my signature."

On the back of the purchase order these clauses appear:

"The manufacturer warrants each new motor vehicle (including original equipment placed thereon by the manufacturer except tires), chassis or part manufactured by it to be free from defects in material or workmanship under normal use and service. Its obligation under this warranty being limited to making good at its factory any part or parts thereof which shall, within 24 months after delivery of such vehicle to the original purchaser or before such vehicle has been driven 24,000 miles, whichever event shall first occur, be returned to it with transportation charges prepaid and which its examination shall disclose to its satisfaction to have been thus defective; this warranty being expressly in lieu of all other warranties expressed or implied, and all other obligations or liabilities on its part, and it neither assumes nor authorizes any other person to assume for it any other liability in connection with the sale of its vehicles. This warranty shall not apply to any vehicle which shall have been repaired or altered outside of an authorized service station in any way so as in the judgment of the manufacturer to affect its stability and reliability, nor which has been subject to misuse, negligence or accident."

4. Many American courts have rendered invalid exculpatory provisions such as these on the ground that they offend against public policy. See *Henningsen* v. *Bloomfield Motors Inc.* (1960), 32 N.J. 358, 161 A. 2d 69. The Canadian and English courts have not been so protective of the consumer. In *Castle* v. *Davenport-Campbell Co.,* [1952] 3 D.L.R. 540 (Ont. C.A.), Mr. Justice Hogg relieved the defendant from liability for damage caused by a defective oil pump that it had installed:

"The learned trial judge held that under the terms of the service contract entered into between the appellant and the respondent Davenport-Campbell Co. Ltd. to which I have referred, that company was protected from any liability in the matter in view of a term of the contract which reads as follows: 'We will not be responsible for delay or inability to perform service due to conditions beyond our control or for loss or damage caused directly or indirectly by such service for any reason.'

I think that the providing of a new pump and attaching it to the oil burner is to be regarded as part of the service rendered under the contract. It is to be observed that the clause which I have quoted refers to damage caused, not only directly but indirectly, by any service provided by the Davenport company. These words, in my opinion, are broad enough to include the procuring and installing of the new pump as part of the appellant's heating equipment, and I think Wells J. was right in dismissing the action against the Davenport company."

5. One device that Commonwealth courts have utilized to give some protection to consumers is the doctrine of fundamental terms, which makes it difficult for a party to contract out of the very root of a contract. The principle was articulated by Lord Justice Denning in *Karsales (Harrow) Ltd.* v. *Wallis*, [1956] 1 W.L.R. 936 (C.A.):

"The law about exempting clauses, however, has been much developed in recent years, at any rate about printing exempting clauses, which so often pass unread. Notwithstanding earlier cases which might suggest the contrary, it is now settled that exempting clauses of this kind, no matter how widely they are expressed, only avail the party when he is carrying out his contract in its essential respects. He is not allowed to use them as a cover for misconduct or indifference or to enable him to turn a blind eye to his obligations. They do not avail him when he is guilty of a breach which goes to the root of the contract. It is necessary to look at the contract apart from the exempting clauses and see what are the terms, express or implied, which impose an obligation on the party. If he has been guilty of a breach of those obligations in a respect which goes to the very root of the contract, he cannot rely on the exempting clauses."

Recently, the force of this doctrine has been diluted in the United Kingdom. See *Suisse Atlantique (etc.)* v. *Rotterdamsche Kolen Centrale*, [1967] A.C. 361.

See, generally, Cumming, "The Judicial Treatment of Disclaimer Clauses in Sales of Goods Transactions in Canada" (1972), 10 O.H. L.J. 281. See also *Heffron* v. *Imperial Parking Co.* (1974), 3 O.R. (2d) 722 (*per* Estéy J.A.); *R.G. McLean Ltd.* v. *Canadian Vickers Ltd.* [1971] 1 O.R. 207; *Murray* v. *Sperry Rand Corp.* (1979), 23 O.R. (2d) 456 (Reid J.).

6. In Ontario, s. 44a of the Consumer Protection Act, R.S.O. 1970, c. 82, was enacted under an Act to Amend the Consumer Protection Act, S.O. 1971, c. 24, s. 2, in an attempt to prevent sellers from contracting out of the warranties established by the Sale of Goods Act.

> **44**a. (1) In this section, "consumer sale" means a contract for the sale of goods made in the ordinary course of business to a purchaser for his consumption or use, but does not include a sale,
>
> > (*a*) to a purchaser for resale;
> > (*b*) to a purchaser whose purchase is in the course of carrying on business;
> > (*c*) to an association of individuals, a partnership or a corporation;
> > (*d*) by a trustee in bankruptcy, a receiver, a liquidator or a person acting under the order of a court.
>
> (2) The implied conditions and warranties applying to the sale of goods by virtue of *The Sale of Goods Act* apply to goods sold by a consumer sale and any written term or acknowledgement, whether part of the contract of sale or not, that purports to negative or vary any of such implied conditions and warranties is void and, if a term of a contract, is severable therefrom, and such term or acknowledgement shall not be evidence of circumstances showing an intent that any of the implied conditions and warranties are not to apply.

What effect is this section likely to have on the above exculpatory clauses? Compare with Consumer Protection Act, Stat. Man. 1969, c. 4, s. 58(1), which includes the warranties of the Sale of Goods Act in every sale and hire-purchase "notwithstanding any agreement to the contrary".

7. Another important inadequacy of these warranties is the requirement, before they are employed, of privity of contract between the supplier and the plaintiff, something that is often lacking. The concept of privity may, however, be stretched on occasion to bring the plaintiff within its purview. See *Algoma Truck Sales Ltd.* v. *Bert's Auto Supply* (1968), 68 D.L.R. (2d) 363; *Traders Finance Corporation Ltd.* v. *Haley et al.* (1966), 57 D.L.R. (2d) 15.

MURRAY v. SPERRY RAND CORP. ET AL.

Ontario High Court. (1979), 23 O.R. (2d) 456

A farmer purchased a forage harvester for cutting and chopping hay and grass crops. The farmer had no direct negotiations with the manufacturer but relied on performance specifications set out in the manufacturer's brochure. The retailer endorsed these representations. It was clear that the machine never operated with an output anything near what the brochure promised and, as a result, the farmer suffered economic loss.

One of the issues facing the court was whether the manufacturer could be liable to the ultimate purchaser.

Reid J.: It is, in my opinion, the law that a person may be liable for breach of a warranty notwithstanding that he has no contractual relationship with the person to whom the warranty is given: *Shanklin Pier Ltd.* v. *Detel Products Ltd.*, [1951] 2 K.B. 854; *Traders Finance Corp. Ltd.* v. *Haley; Haley* v. *Ford Motor Co. of Canada Ltd.* (1966), 57 D.L.R. (2d) 15, at p. 18; affirmed . . . 62 D.L.R. (2d) 329 . . . .

. . . [T]he brochure was put out to entice sales. I can see no other purpose for it. It contained a number of warranties that were proven to be inaccurate. The breach of these creates liability upon the dealer. I can see no legal basis for differentiating between dealer and manufacturer in relation to collateral warranties. The manufacturer initiated the affirmations; it was the manufacturer who apparently prepared and certainly published the brochure. The dealer would perforce have to rely on the manufacturer.

The dealer induced a sale through the use of the brochure and thus acquired liability. Should the manufacturer who published the brochure in an obvious attempt to induce sales be shielded from liability because it had no direct contact with plaintiff?

In *Shanklin,* McNair, J. was dealing with a case in which a paint manufacturer made representations concerning the qualities of its paint to pier owners. Owners caused the paint to be specified in a contract for painting the pier. The painting contractors therefore purchased the paint and applied it to the pier. The paint failed. The owners sued the manufacturers; a mirror image of this case.

McNair, J. held that the representations were warranties given by manufacturers to owners. The defence submitted . . . that "in law a warranty could give rise to no enforceable cause of action except between the same parties as the parties to the main contract in relation to which the warranty was given".

McNair, J. said . . . :

"In principle his submission seems to me to be unsound. If, as is elementary, the consideration for the warranty in the usual case is the entering into of the main contract in relation to which the warranty is given, I see no reason why there may not be an enforceable warranty between A and B supported by the consideration that B should cause C to enter into a contract with A or that B should do some other act for the benefit of A."

In other words, manufacturers would have been liable if they had supplied the paint directly to the owners and were equally liable in supplying the paint indirectly.

I see no significant difference between the oral warranties given by the paint manufacturer in that case and the written warranties given by the harvester manufacturer in this. The intention was the same in both cases, *viz.,* to induce the recipient of such representations to purchase the product described. I see no real difference either in the way in which the representations were placed before the prospective purchasers. Dissemination of a sale brochure through dealers is a well-known and normal method of distribution for manufacturers whose products are not sold directly to the public. Through the brochure, the manufacturer presents his case to the potential customer just as directly as he would if they were sitting down together to discuss the matter.

Plaintiff's purchase from the dealer in this case seems clearly to be "some other act for the benefit of the manufacturer" contemplated by McNair, J."

[His Lordship concluded by holding the manufacturer liable to the plaintiff.]

NOTES

1. What was the exact basis of liability here? Was it contract? Was it tort? Is it clear?

2. Compare with *Traders Finance Corp.* v. *Haley; Haley* v. *Ford Motor Co. of Canada Ltd.* (1966), 57 D.L.R. (2d) 15; affd (1967), 62 D.L.R. (2d) 329 (Alta. C.A.), where a purchaser approached the Ford Motor Company directly and verbal warranties were given to the effect that certain trucks were suitable for a specified purpose. The trucks were then sold to the purchaser through a dealer. When it later became clear that the representation of Ford was inaccurate, the plaintiff sued Ford directly. The court seemed to regard the dealer who actually sold the trucks as simply a conduit and made a finding that Ford was, in fact, the true vendor. Is this case distinguishable from the *Murray* case above?

3. The American courts reached a similar result to that in *Murray* much earlier. In *Baxter* v. *Ford Motor Co.* (1932), 12 P. 2d 409, the Washington Supreme Court imposed liability on the Ford Motor Company for representations made in their brochure to the effect that the glass of their windshields was shatter proof which turned out to be false. The court explained the rationale for imposing liability on the manufacturer in this way:

"Since the rule of caveat emptor was first formulated, vast changes have taken place in the economic structures of the English speaking peoples. Methods of doing business have undergone a great transition. Radio, billboards, and the products of the printing press have become the means of creating a large part of the demand that causes goods to depart from factories to the ultimate consumer. It would be unjust to recognize a rule that would permit manufacturers of goods to create a demand for their products by representing that they possess qualities which they, in fact, do not possess, and then, because there is no privity of contract existing between the consumer and the manufacturer, deny the consumer the right to recover if damages result from the absence of those qualities, when such absence is not readily noticeable."

4. What practical advantages accrue to a consumer as a result of these decisions? What is the effect of allowing purchasers of defective products to sue the manufacturers directly, on a strict liability basis, in addition to or instead of the retailer?

5. A pharmaceutical company prints a brochure which accompanies all its birth control pills sold by druggists on prescription which states that they are "effective and safe". A woman, relying on this, takes the pills for several years and suffers a debilitating stroke as a result. What argument in her favour would you advance on the basis of the above decisions?

6. The Supreme Court of Canada has recently, under the Quebec Civil Code, extended the warranty liability of a manufacturer to a third party buyer of an automobile. See *G.M.* v. *Kravitz,* [1979] 1 S.C.R. 790. Should the common law follow this course? *Maughan* v. *International Harvester* (Mar. 27, 1980).

LOCKETT v. A. & M. CHARLES, LTD.

King's Bench Division. [1938] 4 All E.R. 170; 55 T.L.R. 22

Action for damages for breach of contract and/or breach of duty. The plaintiffs, who were husband and wife, stopped for lunch at a hotel owned by the defendant company. The meal included whitebait, and the female plaintiff, having swallowed a mouthful of the whitebait, refused to eat the remainder. She was subsequently taken ill, and it was contended that the illness was due to the fact that the food supplied was unfit for human consumption, and that there was a breach of an implied term of the contract under which the meal was supplied. There was also a claim in tort, but the case was ultimately rested on a breach of warranty alone.

Tucker J.: . . . With regard to the female plaintiff's position in respect of breach of warranty, every proprietor of a restaurant is under a duty to take reasonable care to see that the food which he supplies to his guests is fit for human consumption. If he does not take such reasonable steps, and if he is negligent, a person who buys the food which he supplies can recover damages from him based on his negligence. As, however, there is no allegation of such negligence in this case, it must be assumed that the proprietor of the hotel and his servants could not be at fault in any way, and either plaintiff can recover only if he or she establishes that there was a contract between him or her and the proprietor of the hotel.

Counsel for the defendants submitted that, where a man and a woman be they husband and wife or not, go into a restaurant and the man orders the dinner, *prima facie* the only inference is that the man alone makes himself liable in contract to the proprietor of the hotel. He agreed that every case must depend on its own circumstances, and that there might very easily be circumstances in which that inference could not be drawn, and that there might be a case where it was quite apparent that the woman was going to pay, and that in fact, to use counsel's expression, she was in charge of the proceedings. Counsel also agreed that, where somebody orders a private room at a hotel, entertains a large party, and makes arrangements beforehand, there is no question but that he is the only person who is contracting with the hotel, and that his guests who attend have no contractual relationship with the proprietor of the hotel. Counsel, however, argues that, in the ordinary case where a man and a woman go into a hotel, it is naturally assumed that the man is going to pay for the meal, and that he is the one making the contract, unless there is evidence to the contrary.

In this particular case, there is very little evidence to show precisely what happened in the hotel in that respect. . . . The evidence is that both plaintiffs ordered, or had, whitebait. . . . It is what may be described as completely neutral evidence, and simply a case where a man and a woman sat down at a table and ordered their food, and I think that I am entitled to assume that the man asked the woman what she would have, and that she accordingly ordered her meal. There was no specific evidence as to who actually paid for the lunch, but everybody is agreed in fact that the husband did.

Counsel for the plaintiffs is, in my opinion, right when he submits that, when persons go into a restaurant and order food, they are making a contract of sale in exactly the same way as they are making a contract of sale when they go into a shop and order any other goods. I think that the inference is that the person who orders the food in a hotel or restaurant *prima facie* makes himself or herself liable to pay for it, and when two people — whether or not they happen to be husband and wife — go into a hotel and each orders and is supplied with food, then, as between those persons and the proprietor of the hotel, each of them is making himself liable for the food which he orders, whatever may be the arrangement between the two persons who are eating at the hotel. On the facts in this case, it is, in my opinion, right to hold that there was a contract implied by the conduct of the parties between the plaintiff, Mrs. Lockett, and the defendants when she ordered and was supplied with the whitebait at the Hotel de Paris. . . .

Where there is no evidence to indicate to the proprietor of the hotel what the relationship between the parties is, and where there is no evidence that one or the other is in charge of the proceedings, and yet, one or the other takes on himself the position of a host entertaining his guests, the proper inference of law is that the person who orders and consumes the food is liable to pay for it as between himself and the proprietor of the restaurant. If that is so, it follows beyond all doubt that there is an implied warranty that the food supplied is reasonably fit for human consumption. I hold that the whitebait delivered in this case were not reasonably fit for human consumption, and that there was a breach of warranty. Accordingly I give judgment for the male plaintiff for the agreed sum of £99. 8s., and for Mrs. Lockett for £100.

NOTES

1. The courts have expanded the operation of the implied warranties to some third persons by a variety of devices. For example, in *Greenberg* v. *Lorenz* (1961), 173 N.E. 2d 773 (N.Y. C.A.), the defendant sold the father of the plaintiff a can of salmon for consumption in the family home. The tinned fish contained some pieces of sharp metal which injured the child's teeth and mouth.

The Court of Appeal, while noting that warranty sounded in contract and required privity of contract which would have prevented recovery by the infant
plaintiff, pointed out the unfairness of the rule and the growing bibliography in
the United States against this requirement. The court reached the conclusion
that "as to food and household goods the presumption should be made" that
the purchase was made for all members of the household, and imposed liability
on the defendant even in the absence of negligence. The dissenting judge pointed out that while he agreed with the result, he felt that the question was one for
the legislature and, as it had been before the New York Law Revision Committee for three years and nothing had been done, he felt the law should not be
changed in such a radical way by judicial legislation.

2. The courts have also extended the implied warranties by analogy to cover
situations not strictly within the terms of the statute. One such case is *Dodd* v.
Wilson, [1946] 2 All E.R. 691. The defendant, a veterinary surgeon, inoculated
the plaintiff's cattle. Many of the cattle became ill because of something wrong
in the toxoid used by the defendant who purchased it from the third party to
the action, who bought it in turn from the manufacturer, the fourth party.
The plaintiff sued the defendant, but alleged no negligence. The fourth party
admitted a warranty to the third and the third to the defendant. The question
in issue was the liability of the defendant to the plaintiff. The court held that
although the Sale of Goods Act did not apply, there was an implied condition
of the contract between the plaintiff and the defendant that the toxoid should
be reasonably fit for the purpose. The court felt that if the plaintiff had asked
the defendant whether the toxoid was "safe" the latter would have said: "Of
course, that goes without saying", since he obtained it, knew where it came
from and "would have a remedy against those third parties if, in colloquial
language, they 'let him down' ". The plaintiff obtained judgment against
the defendant; the defendant against the third party; and the third against
the fourth party for the same sum.

3. Plaintiff using pay telephone suffers electric shock. Although defendant
not negligent liability was imposed on the basis of an implied warranty that the
"equipment was reasonably safe for use." *Hart* v. *Bell Telephone* (1979), 10
C.C.L.T. 335.

4. The American Uniform Commercial Code. s. 2-318, reads:

Third Party Beneficiaries of Warranties Express or Implied

A seller's warranty whether express or implied extends to any natural person who is in the family or household of his buyer or who is a guest in his
home if it is reasonable to expect that such person may use, consume or be
affected by the goods and who is injured in person by breach of the warranty.
A seller may not exclude or limit the operation of this section.

There have been further legislative developments along these lines in
Saskatchewan and New Brunswick as well as several recommendations for reform in other places. See *infra* Section G.

B. TORT THEORY

WINTERBOTTOM v. WRIGHT

Court of Exchequer. (1842), 10 M. & W. 109; 152 E.R. 402

The defendant contracted with the Postmaster-General to supply mail coaches to carry the mail and to see that the coaches would be "kept in a fit, proper,
safe, and secure state and condition for said purpose". One Atkinson, knowing
of such contract, agreed to supply horses and drivers to the Postmaster-General

to move the coaches. The plaintiff was one of the drivers provided by Atkinson. While driving a coach that was provided and serviced by the defendant, the plaintiff was thrown to the ground and lamed for life, when the coach broke down because of a latent and negligent defect. The defendant demurred to the plaintiff's action on the case.

Lord Abinger C.B.: . . . Here the action is brought simply because the defendant was a contractor with a third person; and it is contended that thereupon he became liable to everybody who might use the carriage. If there had been any ground for such an action, there certainly would have been some precedent of it; but with the exception of actions against innkeepers, and some few other persons, no case of a similar nature has occurred in practice. That is a strong circumstance, and is of itself a great authority against its maintenance. It is however contended, that this contract being made on behalf of the public by the Postmaster-General, no action could be maintained against him, and therefore the plaintiff must have a remedy against the defendant. But that is by no means a necessary consequence — he may be remediless altogether. There is no privity of contract between these parties; and if the plaintiff can sue, every passenger, or even any person passing along the road, who was injured by the upsetting of the coach, might bring a similar action. Unless we confine the operation of such contracts as this to the parties who entered into them, the most absurd and outrageous consequences, to which I can see no limit, would ensue. Where a party becomes responsible to the public, by undertaking a public duty, he is liable, though the injury may have arisen from the negligence of his servant or agent. So, in cases of public nuisances, whether the act was done by the party as a servant, or in any other capacity, you are liable to an action at the suit of any person who suffers. Those, however, are cases where the real ground of the liability is the public duty, or the commission of the public nuisance. There is also a class of cases in which the law permits a contract to be turned into a tort; but unless there has been some public duty undertaken, or public nuisance committed, they are all cases in which an action might have been maintained upon the contract. Thus, a carrier may be sued either in assumpsit or case; but there is no instance in which a party, who was not privy to the contract entered into with him, can maintain any such action. The plaintiff in this case could not have brought an action on the contract; if he could have done so, what would have been his situation, supposing the Postmaster-General had released the defendant? That would, at all events have defeated his claim altogether. By permitting this action, we should be working this injustice, that after the defendant had done everything to the satisfaction of his employer, and after all matters between them had been adjusted, and all accounts settled on the footing of their contract, we should subject them to be ripped open by this action of tort being brought against him.

Alderson B.: I am of the same opinion. . . . If we were to hold that the plaintiff could sue in such a case, there is no point at which such actions would stop. The only safe rule is to confine the right to recover to those who enter into the contract; if we go one step beyond that, there is no reason why we should not go fifty. The only real argument in favour of the action is, that this is a case of hardship; but that might have been obviated if the plaintiff had made himself a party to the contract. . . . Our judgment must therefore be for the defendant.
[Gurney B. concurred.]

Rolfe B.: The breach of the defendant's duty, stated in this declaration, is his omission to keep the carriage in a safe condition; and when we examine the mode in which that duty is alleged to have arisen, we find a statement that the defendant took upon himself, to wit, under and by virtue of the said contract, the sole and exclusive duty, charge, care, and burden of the repairs, state, and condition of the said mail-coach, and, during all the time aforesaid, it had become and was the sole and exclusive duty of the defendant, to wit, under and by virtue of his said contract, to keep and maintain the said mail-coach in a fit, proper, safe, and secure state and condition. The duty, therefore, is shewn to have arisen solely from the contract; and the fallacy consists in the use of that word "duty". If a duty to the Postmaster-General be meant, that is true; but if a duty to the plaintiff be intended (and in that sense the word is evidently used), there was none. This is one of those unfortunate cases in which there certainly has been *damnum,* but it is *damnum absque injuria;* it is, no doubt, a hardship upon the plaintiff to be without a remedy, but by that consideration we ought not to be influenced. Hard cases, it has been frequently observed, are apt to introduce bad law.

Judgment for the defendant.

NOTES

1. It is sometimes said that *Winterbottom* v. *Wright* was an action by the plaintiff, a third party, on the contract between the defendant and the Postmaster-General. There is, however, ample evidence to the contrary, particularly the concluding sentence of Lord Abinger's opinion.

2. *Winterbottom* v. *Wright* has been described as a "fishbone in the throat of the law", "a thorn in the side of progress". Do you agree?

3. Professor Seavey has written that future law students will look upon *Winterbottom* v. *Wright* as "an interesting illustration of judicial frailty or, if they favour the economic interpretation of judicial opinion, as an example of the protective judicial legislation given the manufacturers until they became sufficiently strong as a group to pay for the consequences of their employees' mistakes". See "Mr. Justice Cardozo and the Law of Torts" (1939), 52 Harv. L. Rev. 372, 379. Do you subscribe to this view?

4. Herbert Spencer (1820-1903), the British sociologist and scientist, was a classical liberal and social Darwinist. He believed that the fittest would survive in the competitive economic struggle and that the progress of civilization would result from this. Spencer opposed government intervention on behalf of the poor on the ground that the government should only protect its people, not satisfy their wants. In his book, *Social Statics* (1851), he wrote:

"Pervading all nature we may see at work a stern discipline, which is a little cruel that it may be very kind. That state of universal warfare maintained throughout the lower creation, to the great perplexity of many worthy people, is at bottom the most merciful provision which the circumstances admit of. . . . The poverty of the incapable, the distresses that come upon the imprudent, the starvation of the idle, and those shoulderings aside of the weak by the strong, which leave so many in shallows and in miseries, are the decrees of a large, farseeing benevolence. It seems hard that an unskilfulness which with all its efforts he cannot overcome, should entail hunger upon the artisan. It seems hard that a labourer incapacitated by sickness from competing with his stronger fellows, should have to bear the resulting privations. It seems hard that widows and orphans should be left to struggle for life or death. Nevertheless, when regarded not separately, but in connection with the interests of universal humanity, these harsh fatalities are seen to be full of the highest beneficence — the same beneficence which brings to early graves the children of diseased parents, and singles out the low-spirited, the intemperate, and the debilitated as the victims of an epidemic. . . ."

Is *Winterbottom* v. *Wright* consistent with this philosophy?

5. Over the years there emerged three exceptions to the rule of *Winterbottom* v. *Wright*. The first was where the article was inherently dangerous or dangerous in itself. One of the leading cases was *Thomas* v. *Winchester* (1852), 6 N.Y. 397, where the defendant druggist sold to A what was purported to be extract of dandelion. He negligently delivered belladonna, a dangerous poison. B, who was not a party to sale, was poisoned by the drug. The defendant was held liable on the ground that there must be an exception to the rule of non-liability where the article sold is "inherently dangerous to life or health". The second exception was where the defendant knew that the article was dangerous by reason of some defect (although not dangerous in itself) and failed to warn the plaintiff (*Heaven* v. *Pender* (1883), 11 Q.B.D. 503). See *Lewis* v. *Terry* (1896), 111 Cal. 39, 43 P. 398. The third was where something known to be unsafe was represented as safe by the defendant, on a theory resembling fraud or deceit. See *Langridge* v. *Levy* (1837), 2 M. & W. 519.

6. There was a significant breakthrough in 1916 when Mr. Justice Cardozo of the New York Court of Appeals, in *MacPherson* v. *Buick Motor Co.*, (1916), 217 N.Y. 382, 111 N.E. 1050, greatly expanded the first exception. The plaintiff was injured when the spoke on the wheel of a car, bought from a dealer and manufactured by the defendant, crumbled into fragments. Mr. Justice Cardozo stated:

". . . We hold, then, that the principle of *Thomas* v. *Winchester* is not limited to poisons, explosives, and things of like nature, to things which in their normal operation are implements of destruction. If the nature of a thing is such that it is reasonably certain to place life and limb in peril when negligently made, it is then a thing of danger. Its nature gives warning of the consequences to be expected. If to the element of danger there is added knowledge that the thing will be used by persons other than the purchaser, and used without new tests, then, irrespective of contract, the manufacturer of this thing of danger is under a duty to make it carefully. . . .

Precedents drawn from the days of travel by stagecoach do not fit the conditions of travel today. The principle that the danger must be imminent does not change, but the things subject to the principle do change. They are whatever the needs of life in a developing civilization require them to be."

7. A similar position was reached shortly afterwards in the Canadian case of *Buckley* v. *Mott* (1920), 50 D.L.R. 408 (N.S.S.C.), where the plaintiff was injured by some powdered glass which found its way into a chocolate cream bar that he had purchased from a retailer. In the suit against the manufacturer, it was contended that no duty was owed the plaintiff, since he was a stranger to the contract between the manufacturer and the retailer. Mr. Justice Drysdale rejected this argument and remarked:

"In the American courts it is held that where defendants manufacture and put a dangerously faulty article in its stock for sale, they are therein negligent, and liable to an action for such negligence, it being the proximate cause of injury to the plaintiff without any reference to contract relation existing between him and the plaintiff. . . . [T]here was a duty to the public not to put on sale such a dangerous article as the chocolate bar in question; that the defendants were guilty of negligence in this respect, which was the proximate cause of plaintiff's injuries."

8. Not long after this, in *Ross* v. *Dunstall* (1921), 62 S.C.R. 393, 63 D.L.R. 63, the Supreme Court of Canada had occasion to cite the *MacPherson* v. *Buick Motor Co.* case, but it was treated merely as another case of the "inherently dangerous thing" exception. Since the *Ross* case involved a defective gun, there was no need to expand the exception, as was done in *MacPherson* and in *Buckley* v. *Mott*. All of this occurred in Canada before the House of Lords finally discovered *MacPherson* and transformed the English law of products liability.

———————

M'ALISTER (or DONOGHUE) v. STEVENSON

House of Lords. [1932] A.C. 562

Plaintiff brought action to recover damages from defendant, a manufacturer of aerated waters, for injuries she suffered as a result of consuming part of the contents of a bottle of ginger-beer, manufactured by defendant, and which contained the decomposed remains of a snail. The bottle of ginger-beer had been purchased from a retailer for her by a friend. The bottle was of dark opaque glass sealed with a metal cap. The plaintiff claimed that it was defendant's duty to have a system of work and inspection sufficient to prevent snails from getting into ginger-beer bottles.

The defendant objected that the plaintiff's claim disclosed no cause of action. The Lord Ordinary overruled the objection. The Second Division by a majority, Lord Hunter dissenting, reversed this judgment and dismissed the action. The plaintiff appealed.

Lord Atkin: [His Lordship's reasons, as they refer to the concept of duty and the "neighbour principle", are reproduced *supra*, Chapter 7.] There will, no doubt, arise cases where it will be difficult to determine whether the contemplated relationship is so close that the duty arises. But in the class of case now before the court I cannot conceive any difficulty to arise. A manufacturer puts up an article of food in a container which he knows will be opened by the actual consumer. There can be no inspection by any purchaser and no reasonable preliminary inspection by the consumer. Negligently in the course of preparation he allows the contents to be mixed with poison. It is said that the law of England and Scotland is that the poisoned consumer has no remedy against the manufacturer. My Lords, if this were the result of the authorities, I should consider the result a grave defect in the law and so contrary to principle that I should hesitate long before following any decision to that effect which had not the authority of this House. I would point out that in the assumed state of the authorities not only would the consumer have no remedy against the manufacturer, he would have none against anyone else, for in the circumstances alleged there would be no evidence of negligence against anyone other than the manufacturer, and except in the case of a consumer who was also a purchaser no contract and no warranty of fitness, and in the case of the purchase of a specific article under its patent or trade name, which might well be the case in the purchase of some articles of food or drink, no warranty protecting the purchaser-consumer. There are other instances of articles of food and drink where goods are sold intended to be used immediately by the consumer, such as many forms of goods sold for cleaning purposes, when the same liability must exist. The doctrine supported by the decision below would not only deny a remedy to the consumer who was injured by consuming bottled beer or chocolates poisoned by the negligence of the manufacturer, but also the user of what should be a harmless proprietary medicine, an ointment, a soap, a cleaning fluid or cleaning powder. I confine myself to articles of common household use, where everyone, including the manufacturer, knows that the articles will be used by persons other than the actual ultimate purchaser — namely, by members of his family and his servants, and in some cases, his guests. My Lords, I do not think so ill of our jurisprudence as to suppose that its principles are so remote from the ordinary needs of civilized society and the ordinary claims which it makes upon its members as to deny a legal remedy where there is so obviously a social wrong. [A detailed examination of the case law is omitted.]

I do not find it necessary to discuss at length the cases dealing with duties where the thing is dangerous, or, in the narrower category, belongs to a class of things which are dangerous in themselves. I regard the distinction as an unnatural one so far as it is used to serve as a logical differentiation by which to distinguish the existence or non-existence of a legal right. In this respect I agree with what was said by Scrutton L.J., in *Hodge & Sons* v. *Anglo-American Oil Co.* (1922), 12 Ll.L. Rep. 183, 187, a case which was ultimately decided on a question of fact. "Personally, I do not understand the difference between a thing dangerous in itself, as poison, and a thing not dangerous as a class, but by negligent construction dangerous as a particular thing. The latter, if anything, seems the more dangerous of the two; it is a wolf in sheep's clothing instead of an obvious wolf." The nature of the thing may very well call for different degrees of care, and the person dealing with it may well contemplate persons as being within the sphere of his duty to take care who would not be sufficiently proximate with less dangerous goods; so that not only the degree of care but the range of persons to whom a duty is owed may be extended. But they all illustrate the general principle. . . .

It is always a satisfaction to an English lawyer to be able to test his application of fundamental principles of the common law by the development of the same doctrines by the lawyers of the courts of the United States. In that country I find that the law appears to be well established in the sense in which I have indicated. The mouse had emerged from the ginger-beer bottle in the United States before it appeared in Scotland, but there it brought a liability upon the manufacturer. I must not in this long judgment do more than refer to the illuminating judgment of Cardozo J., in *MacPherson* v. *Buick Motor Co.,* in the New York Court of Appeals (1916), 217 N.Y. 382; 111 N.E. 1050, in which he states the principles of the law as I should desire to state them, and reviews the authorities in other States than his own. . . .

My Lords, if your Lordships accept the view that this pleading discloses a relevant cause of action you will be affirming the proposition that by Scots and English law alike a manufacturer of products, which he sells in such a form as to show that he intends them to reach the ultimate consumer in the form in which they left him with no reasonable possibility of intermediate examination, and with the knowledge that the absence of reasonable care in the preparation or putting up of the products will result in an injury to the consumer's life or property, owes a duty to the consumer to take that reasonable care.

It is a proposition which I venture to say no one in Scotland or England who was not a lawyer would for one moment doubt. It will be an advantage to make it clear that the law in this matter, as in most others, is in accordance with sound common sense. I think that this appeal should be allowed.

Lord Macmillan: . . . It humbly appears to me that the diversity of view which is exhibited in such cases as *George* v. *Skivington* on the one hand and *Blacker* v. *Lake & Elliot, Ltd.,* on the other hand — to take two extreme instances — is explained by the fact that in the discussion of the topic which now engages your Lordships' attention two rival principles of the law find a meeting place where each has contended for supremacy. On the one hand, there is the well established principle that no one other than a party to a contract can complain of a breach of that contract. On the other hand, there is the equally well established doctrine that negligence apart from contract gives a right of action to the party injured by that negligence — and here I use the term negligence, of course, in its technical legal sense, implying a duty owed and neglected. The fact that there is a contractual relationship between the parties which may give rise to an action for breach of contract, does not exclude the co-existence of a right of action founded on negligence as between the same parties, independently of the contract, though arising out of the relationship in fact brought about by the contract. Of this the best illustration is the right of the injured railway passenger to sue the railway company either for breach of the contract of safe carriage or for negligence in carrying him. And there is no reason why the same set of facts should not give one person a right of action in contract and another person a right of action in tort. . . .

The exceptional case of things dangerous in themselves, or known to be in dangerous condition, has been regarded as constituting a peculiar category outside the ordinary law both of contract and of tort. I may observe that it seems to me inaccurate to describe the case of dangerous things as an exception to the principle that no one but a party to a contract can sue on that contract. I rather regard this type of case as a special instance of negligence where the law extracts a degree of diligence so stringent as to amount practically to a guarantee of safety. . . .

[His Lordship then referred to *MacPherson* v. *Buick Motor Co.*, quoting Mr. Justice Cardozo, and wrote the passage printed *supra*, Chapter 7.]

To descend from these generalities to the circumstances of the present case, I do not think that any reasonable man or any twelve reasonable men would hesitate to hold that if the appellant establishes her allegations the respondent has exhibited carelessness in the conduct of his business. For a manufacturer of aerated water to store his empty bottles in a place where snails can get access to them and to fill his empty bottles without taking any adequate precautions by inspection or otherwise to ensure that they contain no deleterious foreign matter may reasonably be characterized as carelessness without applying too exacting a standard. But, as I have pointed out, it is not enough to prove the respondent to be careless in his process of manufacture. The question is, Does he owe a duty to take care, and to whom does he owe that duty?

Now I have no hesitation in affirming that a person who for gain engages in the business of manufacturing articles of food and drink intended for consumption by members of the public in the form in which he issues them is under a duty to take care in the manufacture of these articles. That duty, in my opinion, he owes to those whom he intends to consume his products. He manufactures his commodities for human consumption; he intends and contemplates that they shall be consumed. By reason of that very fact he places himself in a relationship with all the potential consumers of his commodities, and that relationship which he assumes and desires for his own ends imposes upon him a duty to take care to avoid injuring them. . . .

It must always be a question of circumstances whether the carelessness amounts to negligence, and whether the injury is not too remote from the carelessness. I can readily conceive that where a manufacturer has parted with his produce and it has passed into other hands it may well be exposed to vicissitudes which may render it defective or noxious for which the manufacturer could not in any view be held to be to blame. It may be a good general rule to regard responsibility as ceasing when control ceases. So, also where between the manufacturer and the user there is interposed a party who has the means and opportunity of examining the manufacturer's product before he re-issues it to the actual user. But where, as in the present case, the article of consumption is so prepared as to be intended to reach the consumer in the condition in which it leaves the manufacturer, and the manufacturer takes steps to ensure this by sealing or otherwise closing the container so that the contents cannot be tampered with, I regard his control as remaining effective until the article reaches the consumer and the container is opened by him. The intervention of any exterior agency is intended to be excluded and was in fact in the present case excluded. . . .

Lord Buckmaster (dissenting): . . . The general principle of these cases is stated by Lord Sumner in the case of *Blacker* v. *Lake & Elliot, Ltd.,* in these terms: "The breach of the defendant's contract with A to use care and skill in and about the manufacture or repair of an article does not of itself give any cause of action to B when he is injured by reason of the article proving to be defective."

From this general rule there are two well known exceptions: (1) In the case of an article dangerous in itself; and (2) where the article not in itself dangerous is in fact dangerous, by reason of some defect or for any other reason, and this is known to the manufacturer. Until the case of *George* v. *Skivington* I know of no further modification of the general rule. . . .

So far . . . as the case of *George* v. *Skivington* and the *dicta* in *Heaven* v. *Pender* are concerned, it is in my opinion better that they should be buried so securely that their perturbed spirits shall no longer vex the law. One further case mentioned in argument may be referred to, certainly not by way of authority, but to gain assistance by considering how similar cases are dealt with by eminent judges of the United States. That such cases can have no close application and no authority is clear, for though the source of the law in the two countries may be the same, its current may well flow in different channels. The case referred to is that of *Thomas* v. *Winchester.* There a chemist issued poison in answer to a request for a harmless drug, and he was held responsible to a third party injured by his neglect. It appears to me that the decision might well rest on the principle that he, in fact, sold a drug dangerous in itself, none the less so because he was asked to sell something else, and on this view the case does not advance the matter.

In another case of *MacPherson* v. *Buick Motor Co.,* where a manufacturer of a defective motor-car was held liable for damages at the instance of a third party, the learned judge appears to base his judgment on the view that a motor-car might reasonably be regarded as a dangerous article.

In my view, therefore, the authorities are against the appellant's contention, and, apart from authority, it is difficult to see how any common law proposition can be formulated to support her claim.

The principle contended for must be this: that the manufacturer, or indeed the repairer, of any article, apart entirely from contract, owes a duty to any person by whom the article is lawfully used to see that it has been carefully constructed. All rights in contract must be excluded from consideration of this principle; such contractual rights as may exist in successive steps from the original manufacturer down to the ultimate purchaser are *ex hypothesi* immaterial. Nor can the doctrine be confined to cases where inspection is difficult or impossible to introduce. This conception is simply to misapply to tort doctrines applicable to sale and purchase.

The principle of tort lies completely outside the region where such considerations apply, and the duty, if it exists, must extend to every person who, in lawful circumstances, uses the article made. There can be no special duty attaching to the manufacture of food apart from that implied by contract or imposed by statute. If such a duty exists it seems to me it must cover the construction of every article, and I cannot see any reason why it should not apply to the construction of a house. If one step, why not fifty? Yet if a house be, as it sometimes is, negligently built, and in consequence of that negligence the ceiling falls and injures the occupier or any one else, no action against the builder exists according to the English law, although I believe such a right did exist according to the laws of Babylon. Were such a principle known and recognized, it seems to me impossible, having regard to the numerous cases that must have arisen to persons injured by its disregard, that, with the exception of *George* v.

Skivington, no case directly involving the principle has ever succeeded in the courts, and, were it well known and accepted, much of the discussion of the earlier cases would have been waste of time, and the distinction as to articles dangerous in themselves or known to be dangerous to the vendor would be meaningless. . . . I am of opinion that this appeal should be dismissed.

[Lord Tomlin agreed with Lord Buckmaster. The judgment of Lord Thanker-ton, agreeing in the result with Lord Atkin and Lord MacMillan, is ommitted.]

NOTES

1. Was there *actually* a snail in the bottle of ginger beer? Do we know? Was there ever a trial on the merits? The following excerpt from Heuston, *"Donoghue* v. *Stevenson* in Retrospect" (1957), 20 Mod. L. Rev. 1, may cast some light on these intriguing questions:

". . . There have been curious uncertainties about two elements of the case — its title and its facts. The full title in the *Law Reports* read *'M'Alister (or Donoghue) (Pauper)* v. *Stevenson'.* The terminology of Scots law is a perpetual source of fascination to all who live south of the Tweed. It appears to be the Scots practice to name a married woman in legal documents by her maiden as well as by her married surname 'with the (infelicitous) disjunctive "or" interposed'. Despite this, it is her married surname alone which is used in citing the case: *Donoghue* v. *Stevenson* is the correct form. Secondly, there has been some dispute about the facts. Now the issue before all the courts was a purely legal one: as Lord Atkin said, it was 'Do the averments made by the pursuer in her pleadings, if true, disclose a cause of action?' or, in the perhaps more appropriate phraseology of Lord Thankerton, 'the only question in this appeal is whether, taking the appellant's averments *pro veritate,* they disclose a case relevant in law so as to entitle her to have them remitted for proof'. The House, as we have seen, answered this question in the affirmative. Now the pursuer's averments were that she had entered a café in Paisley occupied by one Minchella; and that a friend who accompanied her bought from Minchella some refreshment for both of them. The refreshment consisted of two slabs of ice-cream, each of which was placed in a tumbler, and over which was then poured part of the contents of a bottle of ginger-beer. The ginger-beer had been manufactured by the defender Stevenson, and bought from him by Minchella. It was contained in a bottle made of dark opaque glass. When the pursuer had partly finished the confection, her friend attempted to replenish her glass by pouring into it the remains of the contents of the bottle. As she was doing this a decomposed snail floated out. The appellant averred that as a result of the nauseating sight of the snail and the impurities in the ginger-beer which she had already consumed, she had suffered from shock and severe gastro-enteritis. Now there has been a persistent rumour (which has found support even in the Court of Appeal) that when the case went back to the Court of Session 'to do as shall be just and consistent with this judgment' it was discovered that there never had been a snail in the bottle at all. This is not so. The truth is that the issue of fact was never decided: the defender died before proof and the pursuer in consequence compromised the action and received £ 100 in settlement of her claim."

See also Heuston, R.F.V., *"Donoghue* v. *Stevenson:* A Fresh Appraisal", [1971] Current Leg. Prob. 37.

2. Was the House of Lords wise in taking this step? Was it proper for them to rely on American authority, *i.e. MacPherson* v. *Buick Motor Co.?*

C. WHAT PRODUCTS?

GRANT v. AUSTRALIAN KNITTING MILLS, LTD.

Privy Council. [1936] A.C. 85; 52 T.L.R. 38

The plaintiff purchased from a retailer a suit of woollen underwear made by the defendants. After wearing the underwear the plaintiff had a severe attack of dermatitis caused by the presence of an unreasonable amount of chemicals left in the underwear in the course of manufacture. The plaintiff obtained judgment against the retailer for breach of warranty, and the Privy Council held that the doctrine of *res ipsa loquitur* applied in the plaintiff's favour. The decision also clarified the doctrine of "control" as used in the *Donoghue* case, saying that it merely emphasized the fact that the article must reach the consumer exactly as it left the manufacturer.

Lord Wright: . . . The presence of the deleterious chemical in the pants, due to negligence in manufacture, was a hidden and latent defect, just as much as were the remains of the snail in the opaque bottle; it could not be detected by any examination that could reasonably be made. Nothing happened between the making of the garments and their being worn to change their condition. The garments were made by the manufacturers for the purpose of being worn exactly as they were worn in fact by the appellant: it was not contemplated that they should be first washed. It is immaterial that the appellant has a claim in contract against the retailers, because that is a quite independent cause of action, based on different considerations, even though the damage may be the same. Equally irrelevant is any question of liability between the retailers and the manufacturers on the contract of sale between them. The tort liability is independent of any question of contract.

It was argued, but not perhaps very strongly, that *Donoghue's* case was a case of food or drink to be consumed internally, whereas the pants here were to be worn externally. No distinction, however, can be logically drawn for this purpose between a noxious thing taken internally and a noxious thing applied externally: the garments were made to be worn next the skin: indeed Lord Atkin specifically puts as examples of what is covered by the principle he is enunciating things operating externally, such as "an ointment, a soap, a cleaning fluid or cleaning powder." . . . .

Mr. Green further contended on behalf of the manufacturers that if the decision in *Donoghue's* case were extended even a hair's-breadth, no line could be drawn, and a manufacturer's liability would be extended indefinitely. He put as an illustration the case of a foundry which had cast a rudder to be fitted on a liner: he assumed that it was fitted and the steamer sailed the seas for some years; but the rudder had a latent defect due to faulty and negligent casting, and one day it broke, with the result that the vessel was wrecked, with great loss of life and damage to property. He argued that if *Donoghue's* were extended beyond its precise facts, the maker of the rudder would be held liable for damages of an indefinite amount, after an indefinite time, and to claimants indeterminate until the event. But it is clear that such a state of things would involve many considerations far removed from the simple facts of this case. So many contingencies must have intervened between the lack of care on the part of the makers and the casualty that it may be that the law would apply, as it does in proper cases, not always according to strict logic, the rule that cause and effect must not be too remote: in any case the element of directness would obviously be lacking. Lord Atkin deals with that sort of question in *Donoghue's* case where he refers to *Earl* v. *Lubbock:* he quotes the common-sense opinion of Mathew L.J.: "It is impossible to accept such a wide proposition, and, indeed, it is difficult to see how, if it were the law, trade could be carried on."

In their Lordships' opinion it is enough for them to decide this case on its actual facts.

No doubt many difficult problems will arise before the precise limits of the principle are defined: many qualifying conditions and many complications of fact may in the future come before the courts for decision. It is enough now to say that their Lordships hold the present case to come within the principle of *Donoghue's* case and they think that the judgment of the Chief Justice was right in the result and should be restored as against both respondents, and that the appeal should be allowed, with costs here and in the courts below, and that the appellant's petition for leave to adduce further evidence should be dismissed, without costs.

They will humbly so advise his Majesty.

NOTES

1. Although some of the original statements in *Donoghue* v. *Stevenson* seemed to limit the type of products to "articles of food and drink" or "articles of common household use", other language referred generally to "manufactured products". It soon became apparent, as the principle case indicates, that the class of products could not sensibly be confined. Today virtually every product under the sun is subject to the *Donoghue* v. *Stevenson* principles. See Linden, *Canadian Tort Law* (2nd ed., 1977), p. 482.

2. For a time, buildings and fixtures contained therein were the only "products" that were excepted from the operation of *Donoghue* v. *Stevenson*. See *Bottomley* v. *Bannister*, [1932] 1 K.B. 458; *Otto* v. *Bolton and Norris*, [1936] 2 K.B. 46, [1936] 1 All E.R. 960; *Davis* v. *Foots*, [1940] 1 K.B. 116; *Travers* v. *Gloucester Corporation*, [1947] 1 K.B. 71, [1946] 2 All E.R. 506. The theory upon which this exception was based was that the necessary "proximity" was lacking since an examination of real property, which would disclose any defects, could easily be made. See Atkinson J. in *Otto* v. *Bolton, supra*.

3. Can you think of any reasons why the law with regard to real property should be any different from the law dealing with chattels? What about the gravity of the risk? What about the frequency of defect and injury? What about loss distribution? What about deterrence? Who are the potential defendants? Are they likely to be solvent or insured? What about other types of regulation? Is tort law equipped to supervise housing construction?

4. There was one prophetic *dictum* to the contrary. In *Johnson* v. *Summers*, [1939] 2 D.L.R. 665, [1939] 1 W.W.R. 362 (Man.), the plaintiff, a housemaid, was injured when a hot water radiator weighing about 400 pounds fell from the wall causing her serious injury. The radiator had been installed by the defendant, a steam fitter, for a previous owner about two or three years earlier. An action based on negligence failed because the plaintiff did not show that the defendant's method of installation was the cause of the injury. Adamson J., on the assumption that there had been such proof, indicated his willingness to hold defendant liable. "I can see no reason why the legal liability for negligently erecting a heavy fixture in a cottage should be different from negligently erecting a similar fixture in a railway coach or in a large motor bus. There is no principle upon which such a distinction can be made. Such a distinction is not made in some strong Courts in the United States: *MacPherson* v. *Buick Motor Co*. With all due respect, simply to say that one is realty and the other is a chattel is in itself not very illuminating. . . . An alleged ground for this supposed distinction between realty and a chattel seems to be the suggestion that there is always opportunity for inspection and possibility of discovery of a defect in realty, whereas that is not always so in a chattel. We all know that that is not the case. How many persons going into a house, whether purchasers, tenants, servants or others, proceed to test all the heavy fixtures for hidden defects and dangers?

We all know that this is not done, so why base a distinction upon it? . . . In this case the plaintiff, in entering this house for her day's work, could not be expected to, nor did anybody ever intend, that she should test all the heavy fixtures for defects, nor does anyone suppose that she was qualified or could possibly discover any defects that existed." Adamson J., stated that the Manitoba Court was not bound by *Otto* v. *Bolton* but did consider itself bound by the principle of *Donoghue* v. *Stevenson,* which he felt to be of general application.

5. Eventually, the courts abandoned this anomaly. See *Billings* v. *Riden,* [1957] 3 W.L.R. 496, [1957] 3 All E.R. 1, visitor to premises recovered from negligent repairer; *Sharpe* v. *Sweeting & Son Ltd.,* [1963] 2 All E.R. 455 (Nield J.), tenant's wife injured by collapsing canopy allowed to recover from builder; *Gallagher* v. *McDowell Ltd.,* [1961] N.I. 26, tenant, whose high-heeled shoe went through hole in floor, recovered from building contractor. One of the clearest expositions of the current law and its evolution is contained in the following case.

DUTTON v. BOGNOR REGIS URBAN DISTRICT COUNCIL

Court of Appeal. [1972] 2 W.L.R. 299

A builder was given permission by the defendant council to build a house on a particular site on condition that the foundations be inspected by one of council's building inspectors before being covered up. The conditions were met, and the house was completed and sold. The plaintiff bought it from the original purchaser in 1960. Shortly thereafter serious defects developed in the internal structure of the house which were found to be the result of the foundations being built on the site of an old "rubbish tip", causing them to be unsound. An action was brought against the builder for negligence in the construction of the house and against the council for negligence in the inspection of the foundations. While the action against the builder was settled before trial, Lord Denning M.R. discussed the duty of a builder to a purchaser of a house. [Only that portion of the decision is excerpted here. The liability of the council is dealt with elsewhere.]

Lord Denning M.R.:

The Position of the Builder

. . . In the 19th century, and the first part of this century, most lawyers believed that no one who was not a party to a contract could sue on it or anything arising out of it. They held that if one of the parties to a contract was negligent in carrying it out, no third person who was injured by that negligence could sue for damages on that account. The reason given was that the only duty of care was that imposed by the contract. It was owed to the other contracting party, and to no one else. Time after time counsel for injured plaintiffs sought to escape from the rigour of this rule. But they were met invariably with the answer given by Alderson B. in *Winterbottom* v. *Wright* (1842) 10 M. & W. 109, 115:

> "If we were to hold that the plaintiff could sue in such a case, there is no point at which such actions would stop. The only safe rule is to confine the right to recover to those who enter into the contract: if we go one step beyond that, there is no reason why we should not go fifty."

So the courts confined the right to recover to those who entered into the contract. If the manufacturer or repairer of an article did it negligently, and someone was injured, the injured person could not recover: see *Earl* v. *Lubbock,*

[1905] 1 K.B. 253, *Blacker* v. *Lake and Elliot Ltd.* (1912), 106 L.T. 533. If the landlord of a house contracted with the tenant to repair it and failed to do it — or did it negligently — with the result that someone was injured, the injured person could not recover: see *Cavalier* v. *Pope,* [1906] A.C. 428. If the owner of land built a house on it and sold it to a purchaser, but he did his work so negligently that someone was injured, the injured person could not recover: see *Bottomley* v. *Bannister,* [1932] 1 K.B. 458. Unless in each case he was a party to the contract.

That 19th century doctrine may have been appropriate in the conditions then prevailing. But it was not suited to the 20th century. Accordingly it was done away with in *Donoghue* v. *Stevenson,* [1932] A.C. 562. But that case only dealt with the manufacturer of an article. *Cavalier* v. *Pope* (on landlords) and *Bottomley* v. *Bannister* (on builders) were considered by the House in *Donoghue* v. *Stevenson,* [1932] A.C. 562, but they were not overruled. It was suggested that they were distinguishable on the ground that they did not deal with chattels but with real property; see per Lord Atkin at p. 598 and Lord Macmillan at p. 609. Hence they were treated by the courts as being still cases of authority. So much so that in 1936 a judge at first instance held that a builder who builds a house for sale is under no duty to build it carefully. If a person was injured by his negligence, he could not recover: see *Otto* v. *Bolton & Norris,* [1936] 2 K.B. 46.

The distinction between chattels and real property is quite unsustainable. If the manufacturer of an article is liable to a person injured by his negligence, so should the builder of a house be liable. After the lapse of 30 years this was recognised. In *Gallagher* v. *N. McDowell Ltd.,* [1961] N.I. 26, Lord MacDermott C.J., and his colleagues in the Northern Ireland Court of Appeal held that a contractor who built a house negligently was liable to a person injured by his negligence. This was followed by Nield J. in *Sharpe* v. *E.T. Sweeting & Son Ltd.,* [1963] 1 W.L.R. 665. But the judges in those cases confined themselves to cases in which the builder was only a contractor and was not the owner of the house itself. When the builder is himself the owner, they assumed that *Bottomley* v. *Bannister* [1932] 1 K.B. 458 was still authority for exempting him from liability for negligence.

There is no sense in maintaining this distinction. It would mean that a contractor who builds a house on another's land is liable for negligence in constructing it, but that a speculative builder, who buys land and himself builds houses on it for sale, and is just as negligent as the contractor, is not liable. That cannot be right. Each must be under the same duty of care and to the same persons. If a visitor is injured by the negligent construction, the injured person is entitled to sue the builder, alleging that he built the house negligently. The builder cannot defend himself by saying: "True I was the builder; but I was the owner as well. So I am not liable." The injured person can reply: "I do not care whether you were the owner or not, I am suing you in your capacity as builder and that is enough to make you liable."

We had a similar problem some years ago. The liability of a contractor doing work on land was said to be different from the liability of an occupier doing the selfsame work. We held that each was liable for negligence: see *Billings (A.C.) & Sons* v. *Riden,* [1957] 1 Q.B. 46 and our decision was upheld by the House of Lords, [1958] A.C. 240: see also *Miller* v. *South of Scotland Electricity Board,* [1958] S.C. 20, 37-38.

I hold, therefore, that a builder is liable for negligence in constructing a house — whereby a visitor is injured — and it is no excuse for him to say that he was the owner of it. In my opinion *Bottomley* v. *Bannister,* [1932] 1 K.B. 458 is no longer authority. Nor is *Otto* v. *Bolton & Norris,* [1936] 2 K.B. 46.

They are both overruled. *Cavalier* v. *Pope,* [1906] A.C. 428 has gone too. It was reversed by the Occupiers' Liability Act 1957, s. 4 (1).

Sacks L.J.: . . . Next came the suggestion that because the plaintiff in the present action was not the original purchaser from the building owner but was next in the line of succession in purchasers the relationship between her and the building owner was not sufficiently proximate. That suggestion overlooks the very essence of the *Donoghue* v. *Stevenson* decision. As regards hidden defects the fact that there have been intermediate purchasers or users is not in point where the defect can only come to light at the stage when the plaintiff is injuriously affected. Here again there is no distinction in this respect between a defect in a house and a defect in a chattel, so that suggestion also has no substance. . . .

NOTES

1. The result in the principal case had been reached ten years earlier in the Ontario case of *Lock* v. *Stibor* (1962), 34 D.L.R. (2d) 704, where it was held that a social visitor to a new house, who was injured when a carelessly installed cupboard fell off the kitchen wall striking her on the back of the neck, could recover from both the vendor and the builder. Richardson J. distinguished *Otto* v. *Bolton* on the ground that in that case the blobs on the ceiling were "plainly to be seen" by "anybody making a proper inspection" whereas, in this case, the danger was hidden and "would not be discovered by reasonable examination". Richardson J. concluded:

"It is said that the alleged grounds for the distinction between realty and chattel seems to be the suggestion that there is always opportunity for inspection and possibility of discovery of a defect in realty whereas that is not always so with a chattel. This, in my opinion, is not the case because if that is the ground for the distinction, how could a layman be expected to inspect the brakes of his automibile after they had been repaired by a garageman?"

2. Professor R.J. Gray has called *Lock* v. *Stibor* "a potential Ontario breakthrough toward *Donoghue* v. *Stevenson* rationalization in the swampy terrain of landlord's and owner's tort liability". See "Tort Liability of Landlords", *Special Lectures of the Law Society of Upper Canada* (1965), at p. 290. He also suggests that perhaps Richardson J. was "indulging in a little corporate veil-lifting", because the vendor and the builder, both corporations, "were really the same parties wearing different corporate cloaks and the careless workman who installed the cabinet was an employee of both companies".

3. In the U.S., the law regulating building contractors has followed the law of manufacturers' liability, but has tended to lag a generation or so behind. A similar path was followed. Exceptions were created to the general no-privity rule. Then the general rule was changed and negligence theory adopted. In recent years, the liability of builders in the U.S. has begun to move in the direction of strict liability in tort, the prevailing theory now used in defective chattel cases. See Prosser, *Handbook of The Law of Torts* (3rd ed., 1971), p. 639.

4. The Ontario Law Reform Commission has recently recommended that builders and vendors be required to sell new houses that are (a) fit for habitation, (b) built of proper material and in a good and workmanlike manner, and (c) free from latent defects in construction. See "Report on Trade Sale of New Houses" (1968). The Report does not deal with liability to third parties in tort. And see Carr, "Latent Defects in New Houses: Who Pays?" (1971), 29 U.T. Fac. L. Rev. 84.

D. WHAT DEFENDANTS?
HASELDINE v. C.A. DAW & SON, LTD.

Court of Appeal. [1941] 2 K.B. 343; [1941] 3 All E.R. 156

Defendant, Daw, owned a block of flats which he leased to tenants. Access to the flats on the upper floors was by a hydraulic lift in the occupation and control of Daw. Daw made a contract with A. & P. Stevens, Ltd., a firm of engineers, under which the latter agreed once a month to adjust, clean and lubricate the mechanism of the lift, to provide packing, etc., and to report whenever repairs were necessary. The engineers reported in November, 1939, that the rams of the lift, some 35 years old, were badly worn, and suggested two visits a month to grease the rams. This was arranged. At no time did the engineers report that the lift was dangerous. On June 18, 1940, an employee of the engineers repacked the bottom gland of the lift but failed to replace the gland properly on the worn ram. As a result, on the following day, the plaintiff, a solicitor's clerk, while using the lift to visit a client on the fifth floor, was injured when the lift fell to the bottom of the well, the fall being caused by a fracture of the gland which had been improperly placed by the engineers' employee. The plaintiff sued defendant Daw and the firm of engineers. At the trial he obtained judgment against both defendants who then appealed. [That part of the case dealing with the liability of the landlord is omitted. The landlord's appeal was allowed.]

Goddard L.J.: . . . I now turn to the question of the liability of A. & P. Stevens, Ltd., which depends, I think entirely, on whether the principle of *M'Alister (or Donoghue)* v. *Stevenson* applies to the case of a repairer as it does to a manufacturer of chattels, when, from the nature of the case, it appears that there is no reasonable opportunity for the examination of the chattel after the repair is complete and before it is used, and when the use by persons other than the person with whom the repairer contracted must be contemplated or expected. The plaintiff contends that it does, and that this view has been taken on more than one occasion by courts of first instance. A. & P. Stevens, Ltd., contend that it is the principle of *Earl* v. *Lubbock*, [1905] 1 K.B. 253, which governs this case, and that *M'Alister (or Donoghue)* v. *Stevenson* expressly recognizes the correctness of that decision. I believe that this is the first time that the question has come before an appellate court, and, accordingly, one must examine with care the principle on which *M'Alister (or Donoghue)* v. *Stevenson* depends.

It is to be observed that the two noble and learned Lords who formed the minority in that case thought that the decision must necessarily apply to a repairer. I think that one may say that this appears to have been one of the reasons for their dissent. Lord Buckmaster said: "The principle contended for must be this: that the manufacturer, *or indeed the repairer* of any article, apart entirely from contract, owes a duty to any person by whom the article is lawfully used to see that it has been carefully constructed." The italics are mine. Lord Tomlin expressed the same view. Taken alone the sentence states the proposition too widely, for it omits the all-important qualification that the liability is said to exist only where there is no reasonable opportunity for inspection of the chattel between its leaving the hands of the manufacturer or repairer and its consumption or use. . . .

If then, there was any doubt about the governing principle of *M'Alister (or Donoghue)* v. *Stevenson*, Lord Wright has dissipated it. The manufacturer was held liable, not because he was interested in his product being used as it left his factory, but because he had no reason to contemplate an examination by the retailer or ultimate buyer before use. . . .

On what sound principle, then, can the case of a repairer be distinguished from that of a maker of an article? Of course, the doctrine does not apply to the repair of any article any more than to its manufacture. If I order my tailor to make me a suit, or a watchmaker to repair my watch, no one would suppose that anyone but myself was going to use the suit or watch. If the tailor left a large needle in the lining, and it injured a persón to whom at the same time I lent the coat, I should think that the latter could not recover against the tailor. The relationship would be altogether too remote, and many of the suggested difficulties of *M'Alister (or Donoghue)* v. *Stevenson* disappear if it is realized that the decision was, as I venture to believe, essentially one on the question of remoteness. The case of a lift repairer, however, is very different. A lift in a block of flats is there to be used by the owner and his servants, the tenants and their servants, and all persons resorting thereto on lawful business. Blocks of flats and offices are frequently owned by limited companies who would be contracting parties with the lift engineers. In such a case, the employer would be the one "person" who could by no possibility use the lift. If the repairers do their work carelessly or fail to report a danger of which, as experts they ought to be aware, I cannot see why the principle of *M'Alister (or Donoghue)* v. *Stevenson* should not apply to them. . . . It follows that, where the facts show that no intermediate inspection is practicable or is contemplated, a repairer of a chattel stands in no different position from that of a manufacturer, and does owe a duty to a person who, in the ordinary course, may be expected to make use of the thing repaired.

It is said, however, that it is not right that a repairer who, as in the present case, has stipulated with the person who employs him that he shall not be liable for accidents should none the less be made liable to a third person. The answer to this argument is that the duty to the third party arises not out of the contract, but independently of it. It is, for instance, a common thing nowadays for a garage proprietor to stipulate that customers' cars are driven by him only at the sole risk of the customer. If, however, while driving a customer's car, the garage proprietor runs into and injures a pedestrian, the contract he has made affords no answer to the latter's claim. To hold the repairer liable in the circumstances of the present case in no way enlarges the liability of a contractor or repairer who, being employed to do certain work, does it properly and hands it over to the person who employed him. If a danger be thereby created, it is for the employer to guard against it. For instance, an owner of property engages a contractor to erect an obstruction across a drive or private road where none has before existed. He does what he is employed to do exactly in the way his employer desires. Next day a tradesman approaching the house in the dark runs into the unexpected obstruction and is injured. He has no claim against the contractor, because it is the employer who created the danger, and on whom lies the duty of guarding or warning against it.

To render the contractor or repairer liable, there must be (1) a want of care on his part in the performance of the work he was employed to do, and (2) circumstances which show that the employer will be left in ignorance of the danger which the lack of care has created. Suppose a lift repairer told the owner that a part was worn out, so that, while he could patch it up, he could not leave it in a safe condition. If he were told to do the best he could, and an accident then happened, I cannot conceive that the repairer would be held liable. He has fulfilled his duty by warning the employer, and, if the latter, in spite of that, chooses to allow the lift to be used, the liability rests on him. The accident would be caused, not by the carelessness of the repairer, but by the employer's disregard of the warning given to him. In the present case, Daw is not liable to the plaintiff, because he had a right to rely on the work and reports of the experts he employed, and no examination of their work after completion was contemplated. It would, I venture to think, be a strange and unjust result if the plaintiff, who has been injured directly by the careless performance of the work, is to be left without a remedy. In my opinion, the appeal of A. & P. Stevens, Ltd., should be dismissed.

Scott L.J.: . . . I cannot refrain from noticing a curious repetition of history. Lord Atkin's exposition of principle has met with the same unfair criticism, although less in degree, as that which Lord Esher's exposition [in *Heaven* v. *Pender*, 11 Q.B.D. 503, 509] evoked: see *per* Scrutton L.J. in *Farr* v. *Butters Bros. & Co.*, [1932] 2 K.B. 613, 614, and Prof. Stallybrass in his last edition (the ninth) of Sir John Salmond's *Torts*, at p. 459. It is because the critics have fallen into the error, as in the case of Lord Esher, of assuming that Lord Atkin was intending to formulate a *complete* criterion, almost like a definition in the prolegomena to a new theory of philosophy. Does not such criticism miss the real value of attempts to get at legal principle? The common law of England has throughout its long history developed as an organic growth, at first slowly under the hampering restrictions of legal forms of process, more quickly in Lord Mansfield's time, and in the last one hundred years at an ever increasing rate of progress as new cases, arising under new conditions of society, of applied science and of public opinion, have presented themselves for solution by the courts.

It is worth noticing that in *Donoghue* v. *Stevenson* Lord Buckmaster treated the repairer as in *consimili casu* to the manufacturer. He recognized that the principle which he denied to the common law must, if it exists at all, apply to the repairer as well as to the manufacturer. The fact that he regarded that similarity as a reason for rejecting the principle does not lessen the force of the reasons for saying that, if it does apply to the one, it must also apply to the other. . . .

Clauson L.J. (dissenting): . . . The principles to be found in the opinions of the majority of their Lordships in *Donoghue* v. *Stevenson*, were discussed and further expounded by the Judicial Committee of the Privy Council in *Grant* v. *Australian Knitting Mills Ltd.*, [1936] A.C. 85. Their Lordships' judgment clarifies the question, which was much discussed before us, as to the relationship, if any, between the manufacturer or repairer of an article, on the one hand, and, on the other, the persons to whom the immediate customer of the manufacturer or repairer intends, in the way of his trade or business, to give permission to use the article. . . .

The crucial point seems to me to be whether, in the case of repair of a machine which the man who orders the repairs is intended, in the way of his trade or business, to permit others to use without any reference to the repairer, the reasonable man would regard it as reasonably contemplated by the parties that the repairer is to remain liable, after he has delivered over the machine to his immediate employer, to any one but that employer for the damage traceable to his negligence which may be occasioned, while that employer is working the machine, to such persons as the employer may happen to permit to use it. In the present case there is no evidence or, indeed, suggestion, that the repairer took any action, such as Lord Thankerton found in *Donoghue* v. *Stevenson*, to bring himself into direct relationship with the injured plaintiff, or that any step whatever was taken by the repairer or his employer to bring into being any relationship between the repairer and the potential users. I venture to repeat, with slight verbal alterations to suit the facts of the present case, the words of Mathew L.J., in *Earl* v. *Lubbock*, [1905] 1 K.B. 259, words approved, as I read it, by Lord Atkin in *Donoghue* v. *Stevenson*, and by their Lordships of the Privy Council in *Grant* v. *Australian Knitting Mills, Ltd.*: "The argument of counsel for the plaintiff was that the defendant had been negligent in the performance of the contract (*scil.* to repair the machine) with the owner of the machine, and that it followed as a matter of law that any one who sustained an injury traceable to that negligence had a cause of action against the defendant. It is impossible to accept such a wide proposition, and, indeed, it is difficult to see how, if it were the law, trade could be carried on. No prudent man would contract to make or repair what the employer intended to permit others to use in the way of his trade."

For these reasons, I feel unable to hold that the plaintiff has established any such relationship between himself and the engineers, as entitles him to recover damages against them in respect of his injuries, and, accordingly, in my judgment, the appeal of those defendants should . . . be allowed.

NOTES

1. Under the principle of *stare decisis* was the Court of Appeal bound to decide *Haseldine* v. *Daw* as it did? Was the decision one of logic, values, or both?

2. Does this decision encourage repairers to be more careful in their work? Do you know? Do repairers know the law? Do they obey it? Do we have any evidence?

3. What do you think of the warning sounded by Mathew L.J. in *Earl* v, *Lubbock* and echoed by Lord Justice Clauson in his dissent? Were they right?

4. In *Marschler* v. *G. Masser's Garage,* [1956] O.R. 328, 2 D.L.R. (2d) 484, Mr. Justice Lebel in a *dictum* chose to follow *Haseldine* v. *Daw* while indicating his sympathy in these words:

"The legal position of the repairer of chattels which are by their nature dangerous when in use is a precarious one and there seems to be a dearth of authority in Canada on the subject. I say the position is precarious because unlike the position in contract he may be, and sometimes is, held liable to persons who are complete strangers to him. His responsibility may extend to an indefinite number of persons for indefinite amounts of money over indefinite periods of time, for the person who repairs the brake of a motor vehicle, for instance, must be assumed to know that if his work is done carelessly that vehicle may cause injury and damage not only to the person with whom he made his contract to repair, but also to others who may be passengers in the vehicle or lawfully upon the highway."

Is there any reason why a repairer's position should be any less "precarious" than that of a manufacturer?

5. The range of possible defendants has expanded beyond manufacturers and repairers. Liability has been imposed on a dairy (*Shandloff* v. *City Dairy,* [1936] O.R. 579) and a bottling company (*Saddlemire* v. *Coca Cola,* [1941] 4 D.L.R. 614 (Ont. C.A.); *Mathews* v. *Coca Cola,* [1944] 2 D.L.R. 355 (Ont. C.A.); *Cohen* v. *Coca Cola* [1967] S.C.R. 469) even though they did not actually manufacture their product. Those who assemble products are treated like manufacturers. (*MacPherson* v. *Buick Motor Co.* (1916), 111 N.E. 1050; *Murphy* v. *St. Catharines General Hospital et al.* (1964), 41 D.L.R. (2d) 697). A wholesaler (*O'Fallon* v. *Inecto Rapid,* [1939] 1 W.W.R. 264; affd [1940] 2 W.W.R. 714 (B.C.)) and a distributor who places his label on a product (*Watson* v. *Buckley,* [1940] 1 All E.R. 174) may be responsible even though they did not participate in the production of the article. See Linden, *Canadian Tort Law* (2nd ed., 1977), p. 484.

6. How should the producer of a defective component part be treated? Should the plaintiff be permitted to sue him directly? Should the plaintiff be allowed his options? See *Evans* v. *Triplex Glass,* [1936] 1 All E.R. 283 (defective windshield). But *cf. Goldberg* v. *Kollsman Instruments* (1963), 191 N.E. 2d 81 (altimeter maker absolved, airplane manufacturer held liable).

7. In *Pack* v. *County of Warner* (1964), 44 D.L.R. (2d) 215 (Alta C.A.) the plaintiff cattle breeder had some of his bulls sprayed for lice by a county employee. The spray was purchased from a distributor which recommended its use for this purpose, despite the fact that a manufacturer's label on the bottle contained a warning about its toxicity. This warning was not read by the county

employee. The bulls were ruined as a result. An action against the employee, the county and the distributor succeeded against all three on the basis of their negligence. See also *Clay* v. *Crump & Sons,* [1964] 1 Q.B. 533, [1964] 3 All E.R. 687 (C.A.), where an architect, a building contractor and a demolition contractor were all held liable when one wall of a building, that had been left standing, fell on a workman, injuring him.

8.   Should liability for negligence be imposed on someone who rents a chattel? (See *White* v. *John Warwick,* [1953] 1 W.L.R. 1285; *Chapman* v. *Sadler,* [1929] A.C. 584.) A donor of a chattel? (See *Hawkins* v. *Coulsdon U.D.C.,* [1954] 1 Q.B. 319, at p. 333.) An endorser of a product? See *Hanberry* v. *Hearst Corp.* (1969), 276 Cal. App. 2d 680, 81 Cal. Reptr. 519; Carlin, "Liability of a Product Endorser" (1969), 15 N.Y.L.F. 835.

9.   The range of possible claimants to whom *Donoghue* v. *Stevenson* extends has also been widened over the years. The word "consumer" was liberally interpreted to include not only the purchasers of products and their families but also anyone who could reasonably come into contact with them. Consumer is not used in any narrow sense but includes anyone who could be considered one's "neighbour" in the broadest sense. For example, a manufacturer of a carcinogenic substance used by employees in a customer's rubber factory will be liable to those employees if they contract cancer, if it should have realized that the substance involved a real risk of causing cancer to those employees. See *Wright* v. *Dunlop Rubber Co. Ltd., et al.* (1973), K.I.R. 255 (C.A.). See Linden, *Canadian Tort Law* (2nd ed., 1977), p. 487.

"You don't complain to the retailer about side effects. You write directly to the manufacturer."*

E. INTERMEDIATE INSPECTION

We have seen that virtually all types of defendants may be held liable for negligence in the production, assembly, application and distribution of virtually all types of products. But we have not considered when any one of these defendants will be relieved of responsibility because of the intervening conduct of another one of these defendants.

Lord Atkin's formulation of the principle of *Donoghue* v. *Stevenson* contained two requirements which have been largely misunderstood; the duty was to be owed only where (1) the products were "intended to reach the consumer in the form in which they left him", and (2) there was "no reasonable possibility of intermediate examination". These words, until recently, have been slavishly followed as if embodied in a statute, despite the fact that Lord Atkin was merely alluding to the traditional problems of proof of causation and of intervening cause.

PHILLIPS v. CHRYSLER CORPORATION OF CANADA LTD. AND ROXBURGH MOTORS LTD.

Ontario High Court. (1962), 32 D.L.R. (2d) 347

The deceased was killed and some passengers in the car injured when the car went out of control and crashed into another vehicle. The steering mechanism of the 1957 Dodge vehicle had jammed prior to the collision. The accident occured about 18 months after its purchase and after it had travelled some 14,000 miles. Nine months had elapsed since the last time the distributor had serviced the vehicle, but in the meantime at least one other garage had looked after the car. The evidence did not explain what the defect was nor what the cause of the jamming was. Actions were brought against the manufacturer for breach of warranty and negligence.

Landreville J.: . . . Generally, in line with the cases quoted, I have come to the following conclusions. If the consumer or plaintiff claims inherent defect or defective and improper material or adjustments, there must be an element of time and nature involving the thing which precludes any other cause from having intervened. This may range from a sealed bottled product down to a motor vehicle of very old vintage in the hands of a fifth owner. In the first, tampering with the inside product or the expectation of examination by the distributor is not likely. In the second, a wide range of "ifs" may have taken place.

In our case, I must resolve the enigma to the loss of [sic] the plaintiffs. The enigma is one of fact, not one of law as the doctrine of *res ipsa loquitur* is not applicable here. I cannot find that the sales contract nor its warranties render the defendants contractually liable. Nor can I find in tort that a reasonable and probable cause of the accident was the defective gear box, its components or its adjustment supplied by the defendants. There are too many unanswered "ifs" in the case of the plaintiffs. . . .

I find as a fact that too many months have elapsed, too many miles have been travelled by that product claimed to have been defective, from the time it has left the possession, the control, the responsibility of the vendors. As to the defendant Chrysler, this has strong application particularly. The inspection and servicing is left to the distributor. Moreover, it buys steering assemblies as a unit and I cast doubt on the practicality of the liability of a vendor who himself buys a sealed and assembled product. On the defendant Roxburgh Motors, it strikes me as unreasonable to hold it liable for misalignment, misadjustment or wrong parts installed, unless the owner can with a degree of plausibility, establish the non-tampering of the product by a third party. There is not here that exclusion of the possibility and probability of interference by another garage or mechanic. (*Bell* v. *Travco Hotels Ltd.,* [1953] 1 All E.R. 638.) It is a sophism to believe that because an accident has happened someone is liable. Again I state that the plaintiffs have failed to establish by a preponderance of evidence that the defendants are, mechanically speaking, responsible for the condition of the car. The older the car the weaker the likelihood and the cited cases have all that underlying principle.

NOTES

1. What was the reason for the decision dismissing the action? If you had been the plaintiffs' lawyer, do you think that you could have got a different result?

2. Why did *res ipsa loquitur* not apply in this case? Should it have been applied?

3. The problems of proof in a defective products case can be overwhelming. The cost of experts can be enormous. Some courts appear to have put the obligation of proving subsequent interference upon the manufacturer or repairer. See *Marschler* v. *Masser's Garage,* [1956] O.R. 328. Is this a wise course?

4. In the past some courts have gone overboard in the strength of the evidence they demand. In *Ferstenfeld* v. *Kik Cola* (1939), 77 Que. S.C. 165, one reason why the court refused to impose liability was that the bottle of soda pop in question had been opened in the store and transported across a crowed street for the plaintiff. The court admitted that it was "unlikely" that the deleterious substance got in at that time, but it felt that the "possibility" was not excluded. This strict view is on the wane.

HASELDINE v. C.A. DAW & SON, LTD.

Court of Appeal. [1941] 2 K.B. 343; [1941] 3 All E.R. 156

Goddard L.J.: . . . I pause here for a moment to say that I think that it is generally considered that, when Lord Atkin used the expression "reasonable possibility" with relation to inspection, he meant possibility in a commercial sense, and, as I ventured to say in *Paine* v. *Colne Valley Electricity Supply Co., Ltd., and British Insulated Cables, Ltd.,* [1938] 4 All E.R. 803, the word "probability" might perhaps be used instead. One should, I think, ask oneself the question: "In the circumstances of any particular case, ought the purchaser, or, in the case of repairs, the person for whom the repairs were done, to have made inspection for himself?"

Apart from the question whether *Earl* v. *Lubbock* is good law, the contention of these defendants, as I understand it, is that the true principle underlying *M'Alister (or Donoghue)* v. *Stevenson* is that it was to the interest of the manufacturer that his goods should reach the consumer unopened, and that it was his intention that they should, and that this was the reason for privity or proximity or direct relationship, call it what you will, being established between the manufacturer and the ultimate consumer. On the other hand, it is said that the governing factor is the possibility or probability or contemplation that an inspection will take place before the goods are put into use. For my part, I think that the latter proposition is the truth, and for this conclusion I find support in the advice of the Judicial Committee in *Grant* v. *Australian Knitting Mills, Ltd.,* [1936] A.C. 85. The *corpus delicti* in that case was a pair of underpants. Had they been washed before use, no ill effects would have resulted. I cannot see that it matters one iota to a manufacturer whether a purchaser washes them before use or not, from the point of view of his interest in the sale. I can well understand, however, that a canner of food or a manufacturer of mineral water has an interest in his products not being opened by anyone but the consumer, as the product would otherwise be injured. Equally I have no doubt that some rather particular people would have new underclothes washed before using them. However, in *Grant's* case, Lord Wright disposed of the matter in a sentence: "It was not contemplated that they should be first washed."

If then, there was any doubt about the governing principle of *M'Alister (or Donoghue) v. Stevenson,* Lord Wright has dissipated it. The manufacturer was held liable, not because he was interested in his product being used as it left his factory, but because he had no reason to contemplate an examination by the retailer or ultimate buyer before use....

NOTES

1. The five word phrase used by Lord Atkin — reasonable possibility of intermediate examination — was not meant to be oracular. Other synonymous phrases appeared in the reasons. For example, Lord Atkin himself elsewhere used the words "there can be no inspection by the consumer". Lord MacMillan stated that where "a party who has the means and opportunity of examining the manufacturer's produce before he re-issues it to the actual user is interposed", no liability would follow.

2. Gradually the standard was relaxed, as depicted in the language of Lord Goddard in *Haseldine v. Daw.* One recent statement of the principle was that of the late Chief Justice Porter in *Shields v. Hobbs Manufacturing,* [1962] O.R. 355, at p. 359; affd. 34 D.L.R. (2d) 307, when he stated that a duty would exist if it were "apparent on the balance of probabilities that there would be no intermediate inspection . . .". Another helpful dictum from *Stewart v. Lepage Inc.,* [1955] O.R. 937 suggests that the manufacturer would be liable if " . . . in the ordinary course of business and in the manner in which the goods are distributed, there is no reasonable probability that there will be intermediate examination". See generally Linden, *Canadian Tort Law* (2nd ed., 1977), p. 488.

3. What are the courts trying to do with these phrases? If someone who is supposed to inspect a negligently made article fails to do so or does so negligently, should the manufacturer be relieved of liability altogether? Is there a better way to handle the problem? See *Grant v. Sun Shipping Co., Ltd.,* [1948] A.C. 549, [1948] 2 All E.R. 238 (H.L.).

IVES v. CLARE BROTHERS LTD. ET AL.

High Court of Ontario. [1971] 1 O.R. 417

Wright J. (orally): . . . The basic facts are simple enough. The plaintiff was bound to take gas service from Twin City Gas. In January, 1967, he bought a Clare Hecla Gas Furnace Model G.101 from the supplier and installer. This was manufactured by the defendant Clare Brothers Limited and shipped assembled. It was installed by the supplier. Its installation was inspected by the defendant Twin City Gas on its own behalf and, as I understand it, on behalf of the Minister charged with the administration of the Energy Act, 1964 (Ont.), c. 27.

I find as a fact that there were three service calls answered by Twin City Gas with respect to the Clare Hecla Gas Furnace thus installed. These were:

(1) On December 3, 1967, there was a leakage which was tightened up at the time.

(2) On January 8, 1968, there was a gas odour call. The plaintiff's wife had felt ill for two or three days and the plaintiff had "felt bad". When the

Twin City Gas service man came he had a meter in his hand. On entering the house he called out: "Open all doors and windows because there is definitely gas in the house." On that occasion the service man did not tell the plaintiff there were a few screws loose which were tightened. The service man apparently reported that he found nothing.

(3) On April 2, 1968, there was a "no heat" call. There was no pilot light. The service man relit it and said: "There must have been a back draft."

At no time was the plaintiff given any warning of danger.

On Wednesday morning, April 3, 1968, the plaintiff testified that he felt unwell and called his employer to be excused from work. From then on he was in distress and helpless in his home. A paper-boy heard moaning on Thursday and again on Friday. He then entered and found Mr. Ives on his back in the living-room, having suffered the injuries giving rise to his damages.

A Government inspection and a joint inspection followed. In addition to the facts that I have already found, I find:

(1) The prototype of the Clare Hecla Gas Furnace Model G.101 had been approved by the Canadian Gas Association after testing.

(2) It was in general use in Ontario and particularly satisfactory compared to many other furnaces.

(3) It had, to the knowledge of the defendant Clare Bros. Ltd., the defect of losing screws in shipment and in use, particularly the four screws attaching the draught head to the heat exchanger.

(4) The defect which the furnace of the plaintiff Ives had in April, 1968, was that these four screws were loose and that, as a result, there was a gap between the draught head and the heat exchanger, which allowed air from the furnace blower to "pressurize" the combustion chamber, upset the burner and caused carbon monoxide to be produced.

(5) The carbon monoxide thus produced was the cause of the plaintiff's injuries and damages.

[His Lordship discussed the doctrine of "articles dangerous in themselves" and the onus of disproof it places upon the defendants.]

I find that the defendant Twin City Gas was negligent in that it and its service men on three occasions failed to appreciate, as was their duty, the serious and cumulative effect of the reasons which gave rise to their three service calls, failed to remedy the defects indicated by the customer's complaints, and failed to warn the plaintiff of the danger which they should have detected. These were duties owed to the customer who might have been saved from injury by their performance.

I find that the defendant Clare Bros. Ltd. was negligent in that it manufactured and supplied a defective furnace which was, in design and in particular, a peril by reason of the fact that the screws used did not, in some furnaces known to it and in the plaintiff's furnace, ensure that there would not be a gap leading to the production and emission in the home of carbon monoxide, in that it failed to warn customers, suppliers and service men of this danger of which it had been made aware, and in that it failed to provide other means to hold the gaps closed. These were duties owed to the consumer who might have been saved from injury by their performance.

It was strongly urged by Mr. Outerbridge that even if his client, the defendant Clare Bros. Ltd., had been negligent, there had in fact been inspection which broke the chain of causation from that negligence to the damage and thus completely exonerated the negligent manufacturer — a doctrine of forgiveness of sin by inspection. I must say I marvel at the redemptive effect of intermediate inspection. Despite the many cases which have paid heed to this doctrine, and its affinity to Lord Dunedin's "conscious act of another volition",

I find it hard to relate it in this case to the sensible proportionate rule of the Negligence Act, R.S.O. 1960, c. 261. In *Shields* v. *E. V. Larson Co. Ltd. et al.,* [1962] O.R. 355, at p. 357, 32 D.L.R. (2d) 273 at p. 275; affirmed [1962] S.C.R. 716, 34 D.L.R. (2d) 307, Porter C.J.O. discusses the questions of the opportunity to inspect and the Negligence Act and says: "If there were no duty, there would be no negligence. The Negligence Act, R.S.O. 1960, c. 261, adds nothing to the duty. It merely eliminates contributory negligence as a complete defence, and provides for apportionment of the damages."

Here I find that both the remaining defendants had duties and were negligent and that their acts of negligence led to the damage. They caused or contributed to the cause. The Negligence Act applies.

Mr. Outerbridge also put his argument in the form that the proximate cause or the *causa causans* was the negligence of the defendant Twin City Gas. It is true that liability under most insurance policies only arises if the risk insured against is the proximate cause of the loss, and that there can only be one proximate cause for that purpose (despite the assertions of Laidlaw J.A. in *Ford Motor Co. of Canada Ltd* v. *Prudential Ass'ce Co. Ltd. et al.,* [1958] O.W.N 295, 11 D.L.R. (2d) 7, [1958] I.L.R. 294; reversed on appeal [1959] S.C.R. 539, 18 D.L.R. (2d) 273, [1956-60] I.L.R. 566). Lord Dunedin in *Dominion Natural Gas Co.* v. *Collins, supra,* speaks of "proximate cause", but I venture the view that where there are duties on two or more parties and negligence by each causing or contributing to the cause of damage, it is the Negligence Act and not the doctrine of proximate cause which is applied. If this is so, then inspection may cease to be the gospel of redemption it sometimes appears to be, but will continue to be, as it should be, a significant element of fact in considering liability.

I find each of the defendants, Clare Bros. Ltd. and Northern & Central Gas Corp. Ltd., equally negligent and give judgment for the plaintiff against them for $22,000.

NOTES

1. What do you think of this treatment of the issue of intermediate inspection?

2. In *Kubach* v. *Hollands,* [1937] 3 All E.R. 907, 51 T.L.R. 1024, a school teacher requested the defendant, a retail chemist, to supply manganese dioxide suitable for use in a classroom for the preparation of oxygen. The defendant sold a powder which he had purchased from the manufacturer as manganese dioxide but which was a mixture of two chemicals. The manufacturer had sold the defendant the chemicals with notice that "they must be examined and tested by user before use". The defendant made no examination or test nor did he advise the schoolteacher that a test was desirable. The plaintiff, one of the chemistry students, was injured when the powder purchased from the defendant, used to make oxygen, caused an explosion. The defendant was held liable to the plaintiff for negligence. See also *Pease* v. *Sinclair Oil Co.* (1939), 104 F. 2d 183.

3. In *Saccardo* v. *City of Hamilton et al.,* [1971] 2 O.R. 479 (H.C.), the plaintiff was injured when a Christmas decoration fell on him from a hydro pole during a strong wind. The decorations had been installed by the defendant contractor who followed the defendant manufacturer's instructions. The contractor accepted the verbal assurances of the manufacturer that no secondary method of securing the decorations had been found necessary in the past. The contractor was held liable for negligence in the tending of the decorations, but the action against the manufacturer was dismissed, Osler J. stating:

"... the actual installation of the article provided was something over which the supplier had no control. Even assuming that the installer relied upon the method of installation recommended by the supplier and was entitled to rely on that method, it is apparent that improper execution of the method could in itself result in failure of the decoration to remain properly in place and the sort of episode that occurred here. The loss of control by the supplier, therefore, and the intervening actions of the installer in erecting and placing the decorations effectively insulate the supplier from responsibility to the plaintiff. . ." .

Is this decision consistent with *Ives* v. *Clare Bros.?* If the recommended method had been proven to be negligent, would the liability have been apportioned?

4. Should inspection and approval by a goverment inspector relieve a contractor of its duty to persons who may be injured by its negligence? See *Buckner* v. *Ashby & Horner Ltd.*, [1941] 1 K.B. 321 affd. at p. 337 where the plaintiff tripped over a protruding "sole plate" built by the defendant and broke his foot while leaving an air raid shelter. The plate had been inspected by a works supervisor of the City of London, who failed to discover any defect. It was held by Atkinson J.: . . .

"... that the plaintiff must fail in this case. The defendant's contractual obligation was to do the work to the satisfaction of the corporation. The defendants knew that there would be an expert inspection of their work and that they would not be able to discharge their contractual obligation until after that examination. There was an examination and their work was passed. It may very well be said that the inspection was perfunctory and hurried, but none the less there was an intervening conscious agency which might and should have averted the mischief. I think that the defendants were well entitled to take it for granted that when once their work had been examined and passed by people competent to examine it, their responsibility would cease."

See *contra*, *Dutton* v. *Bognor Regis Urban District Council*, [1972] 2 W.L.R. 299 (C.A.), in which Denning M.R. would have held both the builder and the inspector liable for negligence in the construction of the house. The inspector failed to make a proper inspection and, therefore, did not discover a defect in the foundations which subsequently led to damage to the house. See also *Ostash* v. *Sonnenberg et al.* (1968), 67 D.L.R. (2d) 311 (Alta. C.A.), *supra*.

5. In *Taylor* v. *Rover Co., Ltd.*, [1966] 2 All E.R. 181, the plaintiff was injured in the course of his employment by the first defendant, when a splinter of steel flew from a chisel he was using. The chisel had been manufactured by the second defendant. Some three or four weeks earlier the first defendant's leading hand had been injured when a small piece had flown off the chisel and cut his cheek. Assuming the second defendant manufacturer to have been responsible for the improper heat-hardening of the chisel, Baker J. held the second defendant not liable to the plaintiff since the first defendant, through their leading hand, had actual knowledge of the defect in the chisel. His Lordship stated:

"This was not carelessness which failed to reveal the defect, the defect was known. This was a dangerous chisel. A piece had flown and cut Mr. Jones's cheek. Secondly, this guilty chisel ought then to have been taken out of circulation; it was the keeping of the chisel in circulation with the knowledge that it was dangerous that caused the accident. It seems to me, therefore, that, in this case, the second defendant cannot be liable to the plaintiff. . . ."

How does *Taylor* v. *Rover Co. Ltd.* differ from *Buckner* v. *Ashby & Horner?* Is this a sensible basis upon which to distinguish when a manufacturer will be insulated and when it will not?

6. In *Smith* v. *Inglis Ltd.* (1978), 6 C.C.L.T. 41 (N.S.C.A.), the plaintiff received an electric shock from his refrigerator, which had been manufactured by the defendant, when he touched his oven with one of his hands at the same time as his other hand was touching the refrigerator. The shock resulted from two things: (1) an electrical defect in the fridge caused by the negligence of the manufacturer, and (2) the absence of a third prong on the plug of the fridge, which had been cut off by a third person sometime earlier. The key issue was whether the removal of the third prong was a *novus actus interveniens* isolating the manufacturer from liability for its prior negligence. MacKeigan C.J.N.S.

refused to insulate the defendant explaining:

". . . Related questions are whether provision, as a safety feature, of the third prong satisfied or discharged the manufacturer's duty to make a reasonably safe refrigerator and whether generally the damage was too remote, unforeseeable by the manufacturer. None of these closely intertwined questions of causation, duty, and remoteness of damage elicits, it seems to me, an answer favouring absolution of the respondent from liability on the facts of this case.

Many persons involved, . . . did not realize the serious danger involved in removing a third or grounding plug or in nullifying its purpose by using an easily obtained adaptor which can receive a three-prong plug and then be plugged into a usual two-prong household wall-plug. The evidence shows that everyone in the business knew or should have known that prongs are often cut off and adaptors used. The respondent should thus have foreseen that this might happen.

I must express the hope that the public may be instructed on this issue by advertising or otherwise, and that [the] legislature may, as in some other jurisdictions, by statute prohibit the sale of adaptors and the removal of third prongs, require manufacturers to provide three-prong plugs, where appropriate, as the respondent did, and to affix notices to appliances notifying users of the risk in nullifying this safety feature."

The plaintiff was held contributorily negligent by the court. MacKeigan C.J.N.S. observed as follows:

"With his knowledge of building and of electrical hazards, the appellant should in my opinion have checked the plug when he bought the refrigerator and had it installed. He must have been aware of the danger of using a two-prong plug in a three-hole outlet and did not reasonably guard against the danger.

The appellant must thus share responsibility for the damage he suffered. It is not possible to establish the degree of fault, which should thus be apportioned equally between him and the respondent—Contributory Negligence Act, R.S.N.S. 1967, c. 54, s. 1(1)".

Following this decision, Inglis sued the serviceman, who cut off the third prong, and the retailer, who sold the refrigerator to the plaintiff with the two prongs, for contribution and indemnity. This action was dismissed because the negligence of these two parties related to the removal of the third prong which was "in effect imputed to Smith . . . in finding him contributorily negligent. In other words, responsibility for the portion of his damage that related to the ground prong removal was assigned to him." Consequently, stated the court, "it cannot be said that their respective faults contributed to the damage". See *South Shore et al.* v. *Inglis Ltd.*, Mar. 30/79 (N.S.).

Does this make sense? What would have been the result if Smith, instead of suing only the manufacturer, had also sued the serviceman who removed the third prong and the store which sold the refrigerator to him with only two prongs?

7. With regard to a possible intermediate inspection by the plaintiff himself, see also *Shields* v. *Hobbs Manufacturing Co.*, [1962] S.C.R. 716, where a manufacturer sold negligently made electrical equipment to the deceased's employer. The deceased was electrocuted when, in violation of a statute requiring a test by grounding before using the machine, he began to install it. The majority of the court permitted the widow to recover 50 percent of her damages because the deceased was contributorily negligent in failing to ground the machine. As for the liability of the manufacturer, Chief Justice Kerwin explained simply that there was "no apparent reason for any person . . . to open and examine the box". The minority of the court felt that, since the grounding of the machine was ordained by law, it was an examination that was reasonably contemplated. Hence there was no "direct relation" and no duty owed to the deceased by the manufacturer. Do you prefer the majority or the minority? See also *Billings* v. *Riden*, [1958] A.C. 240.

Would there be a different decision if the deceased had known about the defect? See *Farr* v. *Butters*, [1932] 2 K.B. 606. What if he had been hired by the machine's owner to fix the defect and was killed while trying to do so? Compare with *Daley* v. *Gypsy Caravan Co.*, [1966] 2 N.S.W.R. 22 (C.A.).

8. In the United States an intermediary's negligent failure to discover a defect in a product does not relieve the defendant of responsibility. *Rosebrock* v. *G.E. Co.* (1923), 236 N.Y. 227, 140 N.E. 571. The same is true for other foreseeable intervening negligence. On the other hand, where a defect is actually discovered by an intervening agency, liability is generally not imposed. Is this a sensible distinction? Can you see any problems with it? See *Stultz* v. *Benson Lumber Co.* (1936), 6 Cal. 2d 688, 59 P. 2d 100.

9. All automobile manufacturers require their dealers to conduct detailed pre-delivery inspections on all new vehicles. By so instructing their dealers, are the car producers relieved of all liability for negligently-included defects that are not discovered on this inspection? Should they be? Is it reasonably foreseeable that a dealer will fail to discover a defect? Or that he will discover it, but fail to notify the purchaser? Compare with the problems raised in *Ford Motor Co.* v. *Wagoner* (1946), 183 Tenn. 392, 192 S.W. 2d 840; and *Comstock* v. *General Motors Corp.* (1959), 358 Mich. 163, 99 N.W. 2d 627.

10. The defendant made and installed an escalator in a department store. It was defective. Several accidents occurred and customers suffered minor injuries. These were reported to the owner of the department store, but he did not tell the defendant. The plaintiff was seriously injured later by reason of the defect. Is defendant liable? See *Dragen* v. *Otis Elevator Co.* (1963), 189 A. 2d 693.

11. What policies are served by relieving the first defendant of responsibility in these cases? What policies are served by holding everyone jointly liable? Which solution do you prefer?

12. How is the goal of deterrence of careless conduct best served? Will we be able to encourage the dominant party in the transaction to supervise the operations of the others? Is this good? What are the dangers of such a policy?

13. How is the goal of loss distribution best served? Is the plaintiff in any better position under joint liability? Does he not usually sue everyone in any event?

14. Do we need the special language of intermediate inspection in products cases? Are these problems the same ones as those dealt with under proximate cause, remoteness and duty?

15. Can you articulate a verbal test that will solve the questions raised in these cases? What about the terms risk and foresight?

F. THE STANDARD OF CARE: NEGLIGENCE

RAE AND RAE v. T. EATON CO. (MARITIMES) LTD. ET AL.

Nova Scotia Supreme Court. (1961), 28 D.L.R. (2d) 522

A mother handed her 10-year-old daughter a discarded can containing artificial "snow", used for spraying Christmas trees and for stencilling, with instructions to put it in the garbage. Instead of doing so the child began to play with it outside, operating the push button on top of the can which had the effect of releasing the "snow" under pressure of a propellant gas which was contained in the can. When the nozzle became clogged she resorted to banging the can hard against a concrete wall. After several such bangings the can suddenly "exploded" and the top of the can was driven into her eye which was so badly injured that it had to be removed. The evidence indicated however that the force of the "explosion" was quite slight and if the top of the container had struck her anywhere other than the eye there would have been little or no damage. The label on the can advertised that it was "Safe — Harmless — Easy to use" but warned that it should not be punctured, thrown in a fire or stored near heat. An action for damages was joined in tort against the manufacturer of the product, the distributor thereof, and the retail store from which it was purchased.

Patterson J.: . . . As I have said, the main use of the container was to spray artificial snow on Christmas trees and it also had a use in making stencils. I have no doubt that it was for these purposes that it was sold by Eatons and purchased by Mrs. Rae. When used for these purposes it was entirely harmless and I have no doubt that its explosion was caused by the unusual treatment it received when it was banged against the wall. I, however, have no doubt that there was an "explosion" of a kind. It was not just merely the case of a person hitting a stone wall or other hard substance with an empty beer bottle with the result that there was the noise of breaking glass and pieces of glass being driven into the body of the person. In that case, whatever happened to the bottle or its particles would be caused by the external force applied. In this case it does not seem to have been questioned that the banging given to the container resulted in the release of an internal force — but whether it was this force that drove a part of the container into the eye of the plaintiff, is not so clear. As, however, the sound of what was apparently an explosion was contemporaneous with the injury, I think I am justified in holding that a released internal force drove or helped to drive the cap of the container into the eye of the plaintiff. . . .

As I have already said, I think the force which was created when the freon gas was liberated was slight. There was certainly nothing inherently dangerous in the container and its contents and it was only when the gas was liberated in the most unusual circumstances of this case that any damage resulted. . . . [Authorities discussed re dangerous things.]

If in fact the container were a dangerous thing when it came into the hands of Eatons, I feel that Eatons had no way in reason of knowing it was dangerous. They had handled millions of such containers or similar ones and had had no complaints, although this in itself may not be a conclusive answer to plaintiff's case. The dangerous quality, if any, of the container could have been ascertained only by a chemical examination of its contents. The container was supplied to Eatons in the condition in which the manufacturer or distributor expected it to reach the hands of the ultimate customer and in order for Eatons to have discovered the inherent danger, if any, it would virtually have had to destroy the container. At least there is no evidence that Eatons knew or by a reasonable examination could have discovered that the container held other than a mild propellant, and that in its normal use, or in reasonable foreseeable use, it was harmless.

The only danger, if any, that Eatons knew of or by the exercise of reasonable care could have known of were dangers mentioned in the warning which, for those dangers, was ample. Eatons had no reasonable way of knowing that a repeated or severe banging would set off a mild explosion or an explosion of such a nature that might in reason result in harm to anyone using or near to the container. . . .

The particulars of the negligence alleged against Eatons are:

(a) That Eatons did not inform the purchaser of the container that it was dangerous under certain circumstances. The answer to that is that Eatons, as I said, did not know nor had it a reasonable opportunity of knowing that the container was dangerous in circumstances other than were covered by the warning;

(b) that Eatons knew that the container might be used by children and failed to warn the purchaser of the inherent explosive danger in the container.

This must fail, for as I have already said, Eatons did not know of the explosive danger in the container nor could it have learned of the explosive danger, if any, except by virtually destroying the container.

The plaintiffs' claim against Eatons based on negligence must fail.

However, in contract the plaintiffs (assuming there is privity between the plaintiffs and Eatons) claim that Eatons fraudulently represented the container to be "safe and harmless" when it was purchased by Mrs. Rae. This claim must fail for so far as Eatons knew the container was safe and harmless, except against the dangers contained in the warning.

Again the plaintiffs claim that the damages suffered were due to the negligence of Eatons in the manufacture of the container. The answer to this is of course that Eatons did not manufacture the container.

The plaintiffs also invoke s. 16(a) of the Sale of Goods Act, R.S.N.S. 1954, c. 256, and allege that there was an implied warranty that the said container was safe and harmless. Said s. 16(a) is as follows:

> 16. Subject to this Act, and any statute in that behalf, there is no implied warranty or condition as to the quality or fitness, for any particular purpose, of goods supplied under a contract of sale, except as follows:
>
> (a) where the buyer, expressly or by implication, makes known to the seller the particular purpose for which the goods are required, so as to show that the buyer relies on the seller's skill or judgment and the goods are of a description which it is in the course of the seller's business to supply (whether he be the manufacturer or not) there is an implied condition that the goods shall be reasonably fit for such purpose; provided that, in the case of a contract for the sale of a specified article under its patent or other trade-name, there is no implied condition as to its fitness for any particular purpose.

Even assuming that Mrs. Rae had made known to Eatons the particular purpose for which she had purchased the container, which would be its ordinary use, Eatons could not be liable, for it is clear that the container was reasonably fit for the purposes for which it was sold, that is, for the only purposes that Eatons, in the absence of some express knowledge, would know of.

The action against Eatons must in my opinion be dismissed. . . .

I shall first deal with the claim against Aerocide [the manufacturer], I think the plaintiffs may succeed if they can show that Aerocide did not exercise a reasonable care — a care it owed in duty to all those whom it might reasonably foresee would use the container for the purposes not so different for which it was contemplated to be used and that lack of that reasonable care caused the damage complained of by the plaintiff. The usual case of this nature is where there has been shown to be a defect of such a nature in manufacture that the exercise of reasonable care could have avoided and that it was this defect that caused the injuries complained of. As I said, I am satisfied that there was no defect in the manufacture of the container and that every reasonable precaution was taken to prevent its causing harm when used for the purposes for which it was intended to be used. In the well-known case of *M'Alister (or Donoghue) v. Stevenson*, [1932] A.C. 562, a manufacturer was held liable for damages to the plaintiff who suffered damages as the result of [her] drinking the contents of the ginger-beer bottle — in which was a part of a decomposed dead snail. In effect the decision is that the manufacturer intended the contents of the bottle for human consumption and that it owed a duty to use reasonable care to assure to the consumer thereof that the contents were fit for human consumption, and that it was negligence if it had failed in its duty to use reasonable care to see that its drink was fit for human consumption. In the present case there is not, to my mind, any such negligence shown — and the burden is on the plaintiff to show such negligence — either in the manufacture of the container or of the supplying of it. The container was subjected to two different types of tests and for the purposes for which it was intended or could in reasonable foreseeability be used was harmless — except for excessive heat, which had nothing to do with the cause of injury.

In this respect I find that there was no breach of any duty that the manufacturer owed to the ultimate user of the container. . . .

Was there a duty on the manufacturer to have a label on the container which warned of the possibility of an explosion such as happened?

It might now be relevant to inquiry what caused the explosion. Certainly it is clear that in the ordinary or incidental use of the container there is nothing to indicate that an explosion would have happened. It is not the case of the container falling from a Christmas tree or dropping from an arm's height or from a shelf, or being subjected to a treatment that one might reasonably expect. An examination of the container seems to confirm the evidence of the plaintiff and of Cathcart that the container was banged at least half a dozen times. The most severe dent and the one which probably set off the explosion was just beneath the opening. Apparently the other bangs alone would not bring about the explosion. It was either the last bang or the accumulative effect of the bangs which brought about the explosion. Nor is it at all clear just why the banging did cause an explosion. Mr. Mitchell seems to say that the top being knocked off this allowed the freon gas to escape and when it did so, it expanded. He also says that the noise of an explosion is not a criterion of the force of its released energy, or words to that effect. Plaintiffs' solicitor suggests that the cubic contents of the container were so reduced by the dents that as a result there was an increased internal pressure which in turn forced the top of the container off. On the evidence, to my mind, it is not at all clear just what caused the explosion, though, as I have found, I think the explosion had something to do with supplying the force that drove the cap of the container into the eye of the plaintiff.

The possibility of the container ever exploding was, it seems to me, remote, and even if it did explode, the chances of its injuring anyone were still more remote. The danger of the container exploding and causing injury to life, limb or property was only at least a mere possibility and so remote that I do not think that the manufacturer was not using due care when he released the container to the market without its first seeing that there was thereon a label giving warning of its explosive possibility. I do not think a reasonable man would foresee the risk of harm to anyone from the container, apart from these dangers that were warned against on the label. I do not think that Aerocide could be reasonably expected to anticipate an explosion of the container, or that if it did explode, harm would ensue. I have therefore reached the conclusion that the evidence does not sustain proof of any negligence on the part of Aerocide.

I do not think the evidence discloses any negligence on the part of Thompson [the distributor]. The containers, when they came to him, were sealed, and there was no way of his examining their contents without destroying the containers themselves or at least making them useless. Nor do I think that it was established that this container C/1 was sold to Eatons by Thompson. According to the evidence, it may have been shipped direct from Aerocide to Eatons. . . .

The action will therefore be dismissed against all the defendants, and I suppose with costs, on which I will hear counsel when the order is taken out. If I might be permitted to do so, I feel that I should suggest that, considering the tragedy in the plaintiff's life and indeed in her whole household, defendants might well in goodness of heart forego their claim for costs.

NOTES

1. What is the standard of care demanded of (1) Eatons, the retailer. (2) Aerocide, the manufacturer, (3) Thompson, the distributor?

2. The problem of "abnormal use", discussed in this case, is sometimes considered to be a "defence" that a manufacturer can raise in a products liability case. What do we really mean when we use the phrase "abnormal use"? Can we express this notion with more familiar language used in other contexts? Why not merely say that the defendant was not negligent? What about the notion of voluntary assumption of risk? Could we, in such a case, conclude that the plaintiff was contributorily negligent and merely reduce the damages rather than dismiss the action altogether? See Noel, "Defective Products: Abnormal Use, Contributory Negligence and Assumption of Risk" (1972), 25 Vand. L. Rev. 93.

3. Another case in which the language of "abnormal use" was employed is *Yachetti* v. *John Duff & Sons Ltd. and Paolini*, [1943] 1 D.L.R. 194, where the plaintiff was infected with trichinosis from eating sausages which she had purchased from Paolini, a meat pedlar. Paolini had originally bought the fresh pork from the defendant meat packing company. The evidence indicated that the plaintiff had eaten some of the meat before it was properly cooked and that, if it had been heated to a temperature greater than $131^\circ F.$, the possibility of her being infected by trichinosis would have been eliminated. The evidence disclosed that there was no economical way of testing the raw meat for trichinosis before selling it without destroying the product and that the meat had been inspected and approved by government inspectors.

An action was brought against the manufacturer for negligence and against the vendor under s. 15 of the Sale of Goods Act.

Greene J. dismissed the action against both defendants, holding *inter alia* that the manufacturer was not negligent and that the vendor did not violate the Sale of Goods Act. His Lordship explained that the "normal use of fresh pork is to eat it after cooking", and that the plaintiff's use of the pork raw or only partially cooked was "abnormal". He concluded that as the plaintiffs "did not notify the defendant Paolini that they desired to make an abnormal use of the fresh pork sausages purchased from him . . . they cannot invoke the provisions of the Sale of Goods Act". What do you think of this decision?

4. In a note "The Nature of Recovery for Trichinosis in Pork", 16 Temple L.Q. 80, 86 (1941), it is said: "It is submitted, however, that a recovery should be allowed despite the impossibility of detection, such recovery to be limited only by a finding of the fact that the meat had not been properly cooked. The basic reason underlying the rule is a social one. Assuming that the packer could not detect trichinae, and that the consumer did make proper preparation of the meat, it would seem that the loss should be borne by whoever is better able to afford it. It is submitted that the same basic philosophy which justifies workmen's compensation laws (also a case of liability without fault) should govern the case. When one remembers the comparative rarity of the disease, it becomes apparent that the burden on the packers is not a staggering one, but is one that they should assume in the interests of public welfare. They may be compensated by raising the price of their products, thus passing on the burden to the consuming public, and the burden would then be in the nature of a hidden insurance premium." Do you agree?

5. There are a number of other negligence cases dealing with what may be described as "abnormal use" problems. What about someone who stirs a decorating compound with his finger? See *Schfranek* v. *Benjamin Moore & Co.* (1931), 54 F. 2d 76. What about standing on a chair? See *Phillips* v. *Ogle Aluminum Furniture Inc.* (1951), 106 Cal. App. 2d 650, 295 P. 2d 857. What about someone using hair dye without making a patch test contrary to the directions on the bottle? See *Taylor* v. *Jacobson* (1958), 336 Mass. 709, 147 N.E. 2d 770. See also *Ingham and another* v. *Emes*, [1955] 2 All E.R. 740 (C.A.).

6. In *Phillips* v. *Ford Motor Co. et al.*, [1971] 2 O.R. 637, at p. 653, Mr. Justice Schroeder wrote that "our courts do not, in product liability cases, impose on manufacturers, distributors or repairers, as is done in some of the States of the American union, what is virtually strict liability. The standard of care exacted of them under our law is the duty to use reasonable care in the circumstances and nothing more."

1. Violation of Statute

DOHERTY v. S. S. KRESGE

Supreme Court of Wisconsin. (1938), 227 Wis. 661; 278 N.W. 437

Plaintiff's wife ate a turkey sandwich in defendant's restaurant in Duluth, Minnesota. That evening she was ill, and about three weeks later she died. There was evidence that her death was caused by food poisoning, and that other people had been poisoned by eating turkey in defendant's restaurant at about the same time. The Supreme Court found the evidence sufficient to justify the conclusion that she died because of eating unwholesome food served by defendant. Defendant appeals from judgment for plaintiff.

Fairchild J.: . . . It is plain upon this record that there is no evidence of actual negligence in selection, preparation, or serving of food by defendant's restaurant, and the question is whether under the laws of Minnesota anything more is required to sustain a recovery than that unwholesome food was sold and that damage resulted. Section 3789, Mason's Minnesota Statutes 1927, constituting a portion of the Pure Food Act, reads as follows: "It shall be unlawful for any person to manufacture, sell, use, transport, offer for sale or transportation, or have in possession with intent to use, sell, or transport any article of food which is adulterated, . . . unwholesome, poisonous or deleterious within the meaning of this act."

Meshbesher v. *Channellene Oil & Mfg. Co.*, 107 Minn. 104, 119 N.W. 428, 430, 131 Am. St. Rep. 441, was an action involving the pure food statute. The Minnesota court considered that the allegations of the complaint failed to state a cause of action except for breach of the statute. In other words, there were no independent allegations of negligence. The court held that the complaint and findings of fact of the trial court brought the cause within the rule that where a statute for the protection or benefit of individuals prohibits a person from doing an act or imposes a duty upon him if he disobeys the prohibition or neglects to perform the duty, he is liable to those for whose protection the statute was enacted for damages resulting proximately from such disobedience or neglect. It was there said: "The fact that the trial court did not find that the defendant knew that the oil was impure does not affect the question of its liability; for it was bound to know whether the article, which it sold to be retailed to the customers of the purchaser . . . was sound, wholesome, and complied with the statute."

We construe that decision as holding that the liability of defendant for selling unwholesome food exists independently of any showing of actual negligence. The statute is apparently held to create a species of statutory tort arising out of a failure, however innocent, to comply with a specific mandate of a statute designed to promote public health and safety. . . .

We are of the opinion that the law of Minnesota has created a tort liability in favor of a person injured by the eating of unwholesome, poisonous, or deleterious food sold to him; that under the law this liability exists independently of any showing of culpability other than a showing of a violation of the statute. We thus reach the conclusion that death resulting as found by the jury in the case at bar under the Minnesota law constitutes death by wrongful act and creates a cause of action under s. 9657. Had deceased lived she could have maintained an action for damages resulting to her from her illness. Having died, this cause of action for wrongful death is in the statutory beneficiaries.

Judgments affirmed.

NOTES

1. The Food and Drugs Act, R.S.C. 1970, c. F-27, s. 4 prohibits any sale of "an article of food that (a) has in or upon it any poisonous or harmful substance; (b) is unfit for human consumption; (c) consists in whole or part of any filthy, putrid, disgusting, rotten, decomposed, or diseased animal or vegetable substance; (d) is adulterated; or (e) was manufactured, prepared, preserved, packaged or stored under unsanitary conditions". Do you think that *Doherty* v. *S.S. Kresge* would be decided the same way by a Canadian court?

2. In *Curll* v. *Robin Hood Multifoods Ltd. et al.* (1974), 56 D.L.R. (3d) 129 (N.S.), the plaintiff suffered nervous shock when she found a partially decomposed mouse in a bag of flour manufactured by the defendant Robin Hood and sold to her by the second defendant, Ernst. Cowan C.J.T.D. awarded damages against both defendants. His Lordship relied *inter alia* on s. 4 of the Food and Drugs Act and stated:

"The Food and Drugs Act does, in my opinion, apply to the sale by the manufacturer to the defendant Carl Ernst, and creates a duty on the part of the manufacturer, which is owed not only to the original purchaser, the defendant, Carl Ernst, but also to anyone who, like the female plaintiff, is a consumer of the food whom the manufacturer should have in contemplation. This duty is in addition to the duty which I find exists at common law based on the decision in *Donoghue* v. *Stevenson* . . . ."

See also *Taylor* v. *Weston Bakeries Ltd.* (1976), 1 C.C.L.T. 158 (Sask. Dist. Ct.).

3. In *Heimler* v. *Calvert Caterers Ltd.* (1975), 4 O.R. (2d) 667; affd (1975), 8 O.R. (2d) 1 (C.A.), His Honour Judge Stortini imposed liability on someone who supplied food, which was contaminated with typhoid, to a guest at a wedding. There was a finding of negligence in the case, but His Honour went on in a dictum to discuss the impact of a violation of the Food and Drugs Act. His Honour somehow fell prey to the reasoning that the federal Food and Drugs Act could not constitutionally confer a civil cause of action on the plaintiff and, therefore, he refused to hold that a civil cause of action had been created. He did, however, suggest that "the provisions of the federal statute may be relevant in establishing a standard of care in the civil action."

When the case came before the Ontario Court of Appeal, it was affirmed on the ground of negligence. Mr. Justice Evans stated:

"[W] e do not find it either necessary or convenient to deal with the other interesting and intriguing points dealt with by the trial Judge in his judgment. But our failure to comment or our silence with respect to those items is not to be taken as an affirmation of his views on these other issues."

What did Evans J.A. mean by this statement? Do you think he would have preferred the treatment afforded the statute in *Curll* v. *Robin Hood Multifoods Ltd.?*

4. The Hazardous Products Act, R.S.C. 1970, c. H-3, s. 3(1), forbids the sale of certain hazardous products such as children's toys or furniture painted with material containing lead. Certain other products such as glues, polishes containing petroleum distillates and bleaches and cleansers containing chloride or other acidic substances cannot be sold except as authorized by the regulations. Suppose someone sells a child's toy painted with a lead substance and a child dies as a result. Liability?

5. The Canadian judiciary and bar have only rarely relied on the copious penal legislation in civil actions for defective products. There is one *dictum*, in *Yachetti* v. *John Duff, supra*, where Mr. Justice Greene evinced an aversion toward a civil action based on a violation of statute in these words:

"It is frequently a difficult matter to decide as to whether the violation of a penal statute founds an action for negligence. Assuming for the moment that the sale of fresh pork infested with trichinae is a violation of the above statutes, I would hesitate to find that these statutes impose a liability for breach apart from knowledge on the part of the vendor. It would be very harsh legislation if so applied to the circumstances under consideration when it is impossible as a matter of practical procedure for the vendor to find out whether the pork is infected with trichinae or not. The result would be to prohibit the sale of fresh pork. . . ."

Does this attitude appeal to you? See generally Linden, *Canadian Tort Law* (2nd ed., 1977), p. 212.

6. What policies are served by imposing civil liability for breach of statutes such as these? Does it have anything to do with encouraging more caution in the production and distribution of products? Does it have anything to do with the social welfare or loss distribution goals of tort law? What about the desirability of consistency between criminal and civil law? What about the difficulty of setting standards in these cases? Anything else?

7. Why, do you think, have the Canadian courts been so slow to invoke these statutory violations in products liability cases? Is there a lack of knowledge about the existence of these statutes? Are there theoretical problems associated with the use of penal legislation here? See Chapter 6. Negligence and Violation of Criminal Statutes, *supra.* What force should the evidence of a breach of a pure food statute be given? Are there, in cases of federal statutes, any constitutional problems? See *Transport Oil Co.* v. *Imperial Oil Co.,* [1935] O.R. 111, [1935] 1 D.L.R. 751; affd. [1935] O.R. 215, [1935] 2 D.L.R. 500. See again *Vapour* case, *supra,* Chapter 6.

2. Warning

LAMBERT ET AL. v. LASTOPLEX CHEMICALS CO. LTD. ET AL.

Supreme Court of Canada. (1971), 25 D.L.R. (3d) 121

The plaintiff, an engineer, was injured by an explosion which occurred when the vapour from a floor sealer, which he was applying in his recreation room, was ignited by the pilot light of his furnace. The furnace was located in the room next to the recreation room. Although it was summer at the time, the plaintiff had turned down the thermostat on the furnace, but he had not extinguished the pilot light because he was unaware that leaving it on could create a danger of fire or explosion.

At trial, judgment was given for the plaintiff, but this decision was reversed on appeal. The plaintiff appealed to the Supreme Court of Canada.

Laskin J.: . . . The three labels on the cans of the respondent's product contained, respectively, the following cautions: (1) The largest label, rectangular in shape, which bore the name and description of the product, contained on its end panel, in addition to drying time information, the words "Caution inflammable! Keep away from open flame!". Along the side of this panel, vertically and in small type, were the words "Danger — harmful if swallowed, avoid prolonged skin contact, use with adequate ventilation, keep out of reach of children". (2) A diamond-shaped red label with black lettering, issued in conformity with packing and marketing regulations of the then Board of Transport Commissioners for Canada and having shipping in view, had on it in large letters the following: "Keep Away From Fire, Heat And Open-Flame Lights", "Caution", "Leaking Packages Must be Removed to a Safe Place", "Do Not

Drop". (3) A third label, rectangular in shape, contained a four-language caution, which was in the following English version: "Caution, Inflammable — Do not use near open flame or while smoking. Ventilate room while using".

The evidence disclosed that a lacquer sealer sold by a competitor of the respondent contained on its label a more explicit warning of danger in the following terms: "Danger — Flammable", "Do Not Smoke, Adequate Ventilation To The Outside Must Be Provided. All Spark Producing Devices And Open Flames (Furnaces, All Pilot Lights, Spark-Producing Switches, Etc.), Must Be Eliminated, In Or Near Working Area".

A comparison of the cautions on the two competing products shows that the labels of the respondent did not warn against sparks, or specifically against leaving pilot lights on, in or near the working area. In neither case was any point made of the rapid spread of vapours from the products.

The appellants founded their action against the respondent on negligence, including in the specifications thereof failure to give adequate warning of the volatility of the product, and it was argued throughout on that basis and on the defence, *inter alia*, that the male appellant was the author of his own misfortune. The hazard of fire was known to the manufacturer, and there is hence no need here to consider whether any other basis of liability would be justified if the manufacturer was unaware or could not reasonably be expected to know (if that be conceivable) of particular dangers which its product in fact had for the public at large or for a particular class of users.

Manufacturers owe a duty to consumers of their products to see that there are no defects in manufacture which are likely to give rise to injury in the ordinary course of use. Their duty does not, however, end if the product, although suitable for the purpose for which it is manufactured and marketed, is at the same time dangerous to use; and if they are aware of its dangerous character they cannot, without more, pass the risk of injury to the consumer.

The applicable principle of law according to which the positions of the parties in this case should be assessed may be stated as follows. Where manufactured products are put on the market for ultimate purchase and use by the general public and carry danger (in this case, by reason of high inflammability), although put to the use for which they are intended, the manufacturer, knowing of their hazardous nature, has a duty to specify the attendant dangers, which it must be taken to appreciate in a detail not known to the ordinary consumer or user. A general warning, as for example, that the product is inflammable, will not suffice where the likelihood of fire may be increased according to the surroundings in which it may reasonably be expected that the product will be used. The required explicitness of the warning will, of course, vary with the danger likely to be encountered in the ordinary use of the product.

In my opinion, the cautions on the labels affixed to the container cans of Supremo W-200 lacked the explicitness which the degree of danger in its use in a gas-serviced residence demanded. A home owner preparing to use that lacquer sealer could not reasonably be expected to realize by reading the three cautions that the product when applied as directed gives off vapours to such a degree as likely to create a risk of fire from a spark or from a pilot light in another part of the basement area. This was the view of the trial judge, who also concluded that any special knowledge possessed by the male appellant did not make the cautions sufficient *vis-à-vis* him. The Court of Appeal expressly differed from the trial judge in this latter respect, holding (in its words) that "having regard to the plaintiff's knowledge as to the dangers inherent in the application of this product in an enclosed space the warning given by the [manufacturer] was equal to the requirements of the situation", and that his failure to turn off the pilot lights after having turned down the thermostat was an error of judgment, exonerating the manufacturer from liability.

The question of special knowledge of the male appellant was argued in this court as going to the duty of the respondent to him and not to his contributory negligence. What was relied on by the respondent as special knowledge was the fact that the male appellant had qualified as a professional engineer, he knew from his experience that a lacquer sealer was inflammable and gave off vapours, and hence knew that it was dangerous to work with the product near a flame. This, however, does not go far enough to warrant a conclusion that the respondent, having regard to the cautions on the labels, had discharged its duty to the male appellant.

I do not think that the duty resting on the respondent in this case can be excluded as against the male appellant, or anyone else injured in like circumstances, unless it be shown that there was a voluntary assumption of the risk of injury. That can only be in this case if there was proof that the male appellant appreciated the risk involved in leaving the pilot lights on and willingly took it. The record here does not support the defence of *volenti*. On the evidence, there was no conscious choice to leave the pilot lights on; rather, it did not enter the male appellant's mind that there was a probable risk of fire when the pilot lights were in another room. There is thus no basis in the record for attributing an error of judgment to the male appellant. Nor do I think there is any warrant for finding — and this would go only to contributory negligence — that he ought to have known or foreseen that failure to turn off the pilot lights would probably result in harm to himself or his property from his use of the lacquer sealer in the adjoining area.

I would, therefore, allow the appeal, set aside the judgment of the Court of Appeal and restore the judgment of Morand J. in favour of the appellants. They should have their costs throughout.

Appeal allowed.

NOTES

1. What do you think of the degree of explicitness required in the warning in this case?

2. A manufacturer of weed killer warns that it should not be allowed to "contact flowers, vegetables, shrubs or other desirable plants . . .". An invisible spray from the weed killer floats, without wind, for a quarter of a mile and damages the plaintiff's crops. Is the warning sufficient? See *Ruegger* v. *Shell Oil Co.*, [1964] 1 O.R. 88 (Ferguson J.). A warning on a propane heater says "Keep combustible material at least three feet away from front of camp heater". A tent is ignited by the heater, which was not kept three feet away from the canvas. Liability? Compare *Affeldt* v. *B.D. Wait Co.* (Jan. 7, 1980), *per* Osler J.

3. Following the *Lambert* case, do you think that the *Rae* v. *T. Eaton Co.* case might be decided differently? How would you argue *Rae* today?

4. A helpful insight into the law regarding warnings has been offered by Clement J.A. in *Lem* v. *Borotto Sports* (1976), 58 D.L.R. (3d) 465; affd 69 D.L.R. (3d) 276 (Alta. C.A.):

"... the duty to warn of danger is subject to the same limitation of scope and extent as are other duties of care recognized in tort. I wish to emphasize this limit on the principle, as in my view it is in the end decisive of the present issue. The limitation is the reasonably foreseeable in the circumstances of the particular case: *Glasgow Corp.* v. *Muir et al.,* [1943] A.C. 448 at p. 457; *Kauffman* v. *Toronto Transit Com'n* (1960), 22 D.L.R. (2d) 97 at p. 105, [1960] S.C.R. 251 at p. 261, 80 C.R.T.C. 305. It embraces dangers that are known or ought reasonably to be known to the manufacturer in the use of his product, which is to say dangers that are reasonably foreseeable. I am addressing myself here to a product which is not itself defective, nor which in itself is dangerous to use. In respect of such dangers the duty of the manufacturer is to give adequate warning, that is to say explicit warning, not only as to such that would arise out of the contemplated proper use of the product, but also as to such that might arise out of reasonably foreseeable fault on the part of the purchaser in its contemplated use. Abnormal use in the sense of putting the product to a use for which it is not intended is not in question here. The duty of care of which the duty to give warning is an aspect, grows more exacting with the degree of danger of injury or damage arising from its misuse, and accordingly the reach of foreseeability is extended further as the circumstances may reasonably require. This obligation extends equally to the distributor or seller as the circumstances may require, and as to the seller exists independently of any obligations arising out of the contract of sale. On the other side of the scale, the dangers of use or misuse may be sufficiently apparent or well known to the ordinary prudent person that a warning in respect of them should be taken to be unnecessary in law. . . ."

5. Would the result in *Lambert* have been any different if the lacquer in question was not sold to the general public but only to expert painters who were usually aware of the danger from pilot lights? *Cf. Murphy* v. *St. Catharines General Hospital* (1964), 41 D.L.R. (2d) 697, at p. 711.

6. In *Austin* v. *3M Canada* (1974), 7 O.R. (2d) 200, it was held that, because it was common knowledge among auto repairers that the use of a disc on a grinder at 8,000 r.p.m.'s was dangerous, there was no need to warn them about this. According to McCart C.C.J., "the plaintiff was not a member of the general public" and the discs "carried no danger in their ordinary use in the hands of a reasonably competent auto-repair man". What if the person using the machine was a believer in do-it-yourself, but had not yet had any experience in the automobile field? Would it make any difference if the machine was sold only wholesale to auto mechanics or at the Canadian Tire store?

7. Does a manufacturer of matches have to warn about the danger of fire? Does a knife producer have to caution consumers that it will cut? If the situation in *Yachetti* v. *John Duff & Sons* came up again, would *Lambert* be of any help to the plaintiff? Does the renter of a boat have to warn about the danger of falling off if one rides on its bow? See *Schulz* v. *Leeside Developments* (1978), 6 C.C.L.T. 248 (B.C.C.A.).

8. A detailed warning appears on a product but the print is so small that it is barely visible without a magnifying glass. The consumer does not notice it and is injured. Liability? What if the warning is not printed on the product itself but is included in a pamphlet that accompanies the product? *Cf. O'Fallon* v. *Inecto,* [1939] 1 D.L.R. 805; affd. [1940] 4 D.L.R. 276 and *Holmes* v. *Ashford,* [1950] 2 All E.R. 76. Does it depend on the type of product and the class of consumers it is meant for?

9. If a product is used by or around children should a more stringent warning requirement arise? What if a product is frequently used by illiterate people or persons not familiar with the language in general use in the country?

10. In testimony before an American Senate investigating committee in 1966, a representative of the National Urban League stated:

"In the neighbourhoods from whence this group comes, low income, lack of education, rural backgrounds, racial discrimination, ill health, poor housing, and other problems combine to produce families or partial families whose economic position is precarious, both for the gainfully employed and those dependent upon public assistance. Whatever the source of income, the details of its use are critical in determining whether effective steps can be taken to help break the cycle of poverty, ill health, and related afflictions.

Thanks to poor education, they may not be able to read labels or advertisements. They lack the training which would lead to comparison shopping, price comparison, and the effective questioning of the practices of retail purveyors. Bound to local neighbourhoods, they do not travel in search of better bargains, nor are they exposed to information such as newspaper advertisements which would inform them of the possibility of better bargains. Compensating for lack of achievement, they often-times aspire to consume highly visible status-giving goods, and so become susceptible to fraudulent or high-powered advertising, with consequent ensnarement in heavy installment debts, legal entanglements, and repossession claims.

Lacking the ability to consume wisely, the impoverished are subjected to a variety of exploitive forces. Retail goods are marked up in price, often to higher levels than in more affluent communities. Unlabeled and outdated merchandise is sold to purchasers who do not exercise quality control."

11. What if the warning is explicit enough, and printed in large letters, but it is nevertheless not read by the consumer? Should there be no liability? Or should liability be apportioned? *Cf. Law* v. *Upton Lathing Ltd.*, [1972] 1 O.R. 155 (C.A.); *Schmitz* v. *Stoveld* (1974), 11 O.R. (2d) 17; *Lem* v. *Borotto Sports* (1976), 58 D.L.R. (3d) 465; affd 69 D.L.R. (3d) 276 (Alta. C.A.).

12. In *Allard* v. *Manahan et al.*, [1974] 3 W.W.R. 588 (B.C.S.C.), the plaintiff's husband was killed while using a rented power actuated tool to fire nails through 2 x 4 lumber into a cement wall. The accident happened when a nail curved out of the side of the wood, rather than entering the concrete, ricochetted and struck the deceased in the head. The evidence indicated that, while a special guard which would have prevented this accident, was available, the common practice was to use only the standard guard, one of which was attached to the tool used by the deceased. Macfarlane J. held that, as the deceased was fully experienced in the use of the tool and could easily have read the manufacturer's manual, which described the special guard, the rental company was not liable in negligence for failing to provide him with a special guard or for failing to warn him of the dangers involved. He further held that the danger was not reasonably foreseeable to either the manufacturer or the distributor as such an accident had never been known to have occurred before, even though the special guard was almost never used during such use of the tool. The defendants were therefore not liable in negligence to the plaintiff. What do you make of this case?

13. Does anyone, in addition to the manufacturer, owe a duty to warn about dangers inherent in the use of products? X employs Y to install some inflammable material. X advises Y to read the label, which clearly warns about the danger. Y fails to do so, lights a cigarette and starts a fire which damages X's property. Is X contributorily negligent for failing to warn Y about the danger from fire? See *Law* v. *Upton Lathing Ltd.*, *supra*.

14. Federal and provincial legislative enactments sometimes require that warning labels be placed on certain products. See, for example, the Food and Drugs Act, R.S.C. 1970, c. F-27 as amended, s. 25(1) (b), which authorizes regulations to be enacted with respect to labelling, etc. Such regulations have been proclaimed and they contain many detailed instructions for distributors of food and drugs. For example, s. C.01.003 declares that "no person shall sell a drug that is not labelled as required by these regulations". Such labels must contain "adequate directions for use of the drug" (C.01.004(5)(d)) as well as other information that is outlined in the regulations. All the information must be contained on "both the inner and the outer labels" of the product.

15. The Hazardous Products Act, R.S.C. 1970, c.H-3, s. 7(a) and the regulations enacted thereunder require the following symbols to be placed on certain products which are described as hazardous:

Poison

Corrosive

Flammable

Explosive

The Act also requires that specified products contain clear and easily-read warnings setting out the proper instructions for use of the product, the primary and secondary hazards arising from such use and the necessary first aid treatments in case of injury. Breaches of the Act may be punished on summary conviction by a fine of $1,000 or six months in prison or both, or as indictable offences by up to two years imprisonment.

Should tort liability be imposed for violations of the Act? If a manufacturer meets the requirements set out in the legislation, but a person is still injured by the product, can a cause of action against the manufacturer succeed? How foolproof are the pictorial symbols and the warnings printed on labels? Are they specific enough?

16. Regulations under the Hazardous Products Act (S.O.R. 70-95, s. 33), now require aerosol spray cans to carry the warning that an explosion may occur if the can is heated. They also require a warning not to place in hot water, or near radiators, stoves or other sources of heat. How would these new requirements affect a case such as *Rae* v. *T. Eaton Co.* if it arose again?

17. The Pharmacy Act, R.S.O. 1970, c. 345, s. 46 enacts that no person shall sell any poison unless the word "poison" is "legibly and conspicuously displayed on the outer surface of the container". Donaldson, a druggist, violates this section and sells a bottle containing poison to Peter without the required label. Peter, not realizing the danger, drinks the poison and dies. Is Donaldson liable in tort to Peter's widow? Would it make any difference if Donaldson was not aware that the bottle contained poison? Would it make any difference if he had placed a label on the bottle but it had later fallen off without his knowledge? *Cf. Antoine* v. *Duncombe* (1906), 8 O.W.R. 719 (no liability).

18. Sometimes, the regulations specify the wording that must be printed on the label. For example, s. C.01.028 of the regulations under the Food and Drugs Act forbids the sale of strychnine unless the label carries a "caution to the effect that the drug should be kept out of the reach of children". Is this an adequate warning for purposes of tort law? If a child ingests some strychnine, could liability be imposed under *Lambert* even though the drug company printed these words, but no more, on its strychnine product? See also s. C.01.029-s.C.01.032.

19. Is labelling enough? In 1966 there were 35,596 accidental poisonings in Canada. Over 75 percent of these involved children 4 years old or under, and 40 percent of the deaths occurred in this age group (13 out of 32). See *Publication of Department of National Health and Welfare, 1966.* Will more and better labels have much of an impact in reducing child injuries and death? Can you think of another approach?

20. Ontario Regulation 362/72, as amended, passed pursuant to the Pharmacy Act, R.S.O. 1970, c. 345, requires that prescription drugs be dispensed in child-resistant packages which have been certified and designated as such by the Canadian Standards Association. The Regulation is subject to certain exceptions, such as where the prescribing doctor or the pharmacist feels it is inadvisable to use these packages or where they are unavailable. Should this Regulation be expanded to cover non-prescription drugs and other harmful substances?

21. Would a court hold civilly liable to the parents of a poisoned child a druggist who failed to use one of these child-resistant containers? What are the legal difficulties? What are the policy considerations involved?

22. If someone distributes a product that he thinks is safe at the time and he later learns that it is dangerous, is he obligated to warn his former customers? See *Algoma Truck Sales Ltd.* v. *Bert's Auto Supply* (1968), 68 D.L.R. (2d) 363 and the following case.

3. Extent of Liability

RIVTOW MARINE LIMITED v. WASHINGTON IRON WORKS AND WALKEM MACHINERY AND EQUIPMENT LTD.

Supreme Court of Canada. [1973] 6 W.W.R. 692, 40 D.L.R. (3d) 530

Washington Iron Works designed and manufactured a special type of crane which the plaintiff used on its log barge. Walkem was the agent and distributor of the crane in British Columbia. When another Washington crane collapsed, killing its operator, the plaintiff withdrew its crane from service, examined it, found cracks and carried out extensive repairs. It was discovered that both defendants had been aware of the existence of the cracks on cranes of this type, but they had failed to warn the plaintiff.

The plaintiff sued for the cost of repairing the crane and for the economic loss suffered while the barge and crane were idle. Ruttan J., the trial judge, refused to award the cost of repairs but gave judgment for the difference between the loss of use of the barge and crane during their busy season and the loss that would have resulted if a warning had been promptly given which would have allowed the crane to be fixed during their slow period. An appeal by the defendant to the British Columbia Court of Appeal was allowed and the claim was dismissed. The plaintiff appealed to the Supreme Court of Canada, a majority of which restored the decision of the trial judge.

Ritchie J. (Fauteux C.J.C., Abbott, Martland, Judson, Spence and Pigeon JJ. concurring):

In its appeal to this Court the appellant asked for judgment for the cost of repairs to the cranes and for loss of use of the barge, and for its actual losses due to the barge's inactivity based on "coastal operations", in accordance with the claim advanced in the statement of claim.

It appears to me to follow from the trial judge's analysis of the evidence and from the admissions made by the respondents, that both Washington and Walkem knew of the potential danger involved in the continued use, without extensive repairs and alterations, of the pintle-type cranes which Washington had designed and installed on the *Rivtow Carrier*, and that both respondents were seized with this knowledge in ample time to have notified the appellant and given it an opportunity to have the repairs effected at a slack period in its activities rather than having to remove its barge and tug from service at one of the most profitable periods of the year, thus incurring substantial damage to which it need not have been exposed if it had known of the inherent dangers resulting from faults in the design of the cranes at the time when the respondents first became aware that these were a common feature of cranes of this type.

In my opinion the knowledge of the danger involved in the continued use of these cranes for the purpose for which they were designed carried with it a duty to warn those to whom the crane had been supplied, and this duty arose at the moment when the respondents or either of them became seized with the knowledge.

In the present case, the respondents not only knew the purpose for which the cranes were to be used, but they had become aware of their inadequacy for that purpose without modification and repair, and although there was no contractual relationship between the manufacturer and the appellant, the respondents both knew the appellant as one who was using the cranes for their intended purpose in reliance on their advice and, having regard to their knowledge of the business in which the *Rivtow Carrier* was engaged, they must have known approximately the dates when it would be at the peak of its activities and that, by withholding their knowledge of the risk, they were exposing the appellant to the direct consequence of losing the services of the barge for at least a month during one of its busiest seasons.

The learned trial judge posed the question lying at the heart of this appeal in the following terms [p. 119]:

"I turn to consider the claim for economic loss for non-use of the carrier which is sought under the headings of 'negligence in design' and 'failure to warn'. . . .

The problem here is that recovery is sought not for physical or property loss suffered directly by the purchaser of the chattel, but for economic loss suffered to a third person who is user of that chattel."

In the Court of Appeal Tysoe J.A. stated the question even more succinctly at p. 743, where he said:

"The question is, assuming Walkem and Washington come within the proximity of relationship and the rule of liability contemplated in *M'Alister (Donoghue)* v. *Stevenson, supra,* is Rivtow entitled to recover for the *character of harm* suffered by it?". . . .

As I have indicated, the judgment of the Court of Appeal in this case appears to me to proceed on the assumption that Walkem and Washington owed a duty of care to the appellant as being a person "so closely and directly affected" by the faulty design of the cranes that they ought reasonably to have had it in contemplation as being so affected in directing their mind to the known defects which are here called in question.

Proceeding on this assumption, I take it that the Court of Appeal would have treated the respondents as being liable for damages attributable to personal injury or damage to property resulting from defects in the cranes, but Tysoe J.A., in concluding his reasons for judgment at p. 596, said:

"In my opinion the law of British Columbia as it exists today is that neither a manufacturer of a potentially dangerous or defective article nor other person who is within the proximity of relationship contemplated in *M'Alister (Donoghue)* v. *Stevenson* is liable in tort, as distinct from contract, to an ultimate consumer or user for damage arising in the article itself, or for economic loss resulting from the defect in the article, but only for personal injury and damage to other property caused by the article or its use. It is my view that to give effect to the claims of Rivtow it would be necessary to extend the rule of liability laid down in the *Donoghue* case beyond what it now is. I do not feel that this court would be justified in extending it so that it covers the character of damage suffered by Rivtow. I think that, if that is to be done, it must be left to a higher court to do it."

Tysoe J.A.'s conclusion was based in large measure on a series of American cases, and particularly *Trans World Airlines Inc.* v. *Curtiss-Wright Corpn.* (1955), 148 N.Y.S. 2d 284, where it is pointed out that the liability for the cost of repairing damage to the defective article itself, and for the economic loss flowing directly from the negligence, is akin to liability under the terms of an express or implied warranty of fitness and, as it is contractual in origin, cannot be enforced against the manufacturer by a stranger to the contract. It was, I think, on this basis that the learned trial judge disallowed the appellant's claim for repairs and for such economic loss as it would, in any event, have sustained even if the proper warning had been given. I agree with this conclusion for the same reasons; but while this finding excludes recovery for damage to the article and economic loss directly flowing from Washington's negligence and faulty design, it does not exclude the additional damage occasioned by breach of the duty to warn of the danger.

In the present case, both Washington as manufacturer and Walkem as its representative, knew that the appellant relied on them for advice concerning the operation of the pintle cranes and in my opinion a clear duty lay upon them both to warn the appellant of the necessity for repairs as soon as they had become aware of the defects and the potential danger attendant thereon.

As in the case of *Ross* v. *Dunstall, supra,* the duty to warn in the present case was born of the respondent's knowledge of all the circumstances, and the additional damage sustained through the barge's inactivity during the period of "coastal operations" was solely attributable to the negligent breach of this duty.

That liability for this damage does not flow from negligence in design and manufacture is illustrated by the fact that Walkem, which was not a party to such negligence, is equally liable with Washington for failing to warn the appellant. The difference between the two types of liability and consequent damage is that one may arise without the manufacturer having any knowledge of the defect, whereas the other stems from his awareness of the danger to which the defect gives rise. . . .

[His Lordship quoted at length from *Lambert* v. *Lastoplex Chemicals Co., supra.*]

Finding as I do that there was in this case a breach of a duty to warn which constituted negligence on the part of both respondents, and that the economic loss solely attributable to the interruption of the appellant's business during "coastal operations" was the immediate consequence of that breach, I come to consider the question of whether such damage is recoverable in an action for negligence.

Neither the case of *M'Alister (Donoghue)* v. *Stevenson* nor that of *Grant* v. *Australian Knitting Mills Ltd.* contains any suggestion that the plaintiffs in those actions would have been precluded from recovery for economic loss if such had been claimed, but, as I have indicated, I agree with the learned trial judge that those cases are not authority for holding the manufacturer liable for damage to the defective cranes or for the loss which the appellant would have sustained if it had been properly warned.

The cases of *Cattle* v. *Stockton Waterworks Co.* (1875), L.R. 10 Q.B. 453, and *Société Anonyme de Remorquage à Hélice* v. *Bennetts,* [1911] 1 K.B. 243, which have been referred to in the reasons for judgment of the learned trial judge at pp. 120 and 121, were at one time considered as limiting the range of liability for negligence so as to exclude economic loss altogether, but in my view the judgment of Blackburn J., in the former case, indicates that redress for the proximate and direct consequences of negligent acts were not excluded. . . .

The question of whether damages can be recovered in an action for negligence for economic loss, occasioned otherwise than by reason of personal injury or damage to property of the plaintiff, was the subject of extensive review in the House of Lords in the case of *Hedley Byrne & Co.* v. *Heller & Partners Ltd.,* [1964] A.C. 465, [1963] 2 All E.R. 575. . . .

. . . I am of opinion that the case of *Hedley Byrne* represents the considered opinion of five members of the House of Lords to the effect that a negligent misrepresentation may give rise to an action for damages for economic loss occasioned thereby without any physical injury to person or property, and apart from any contract or fiduciary relationship, and that under the circumstances of that case the plaintiff would have been entitled to recover its economic loss had it not been for the warning which was implicit in the defendant's express denial of responsibility.

In the present case there is no suggestion that liability should be based on negligent misrepresentation and to this extent the *Hedley Byrne* case is of no relevance. I refer to it for the sole purpose of indicating the view of the House of Lords that where liability is based on negligence the recovery is not limited to physical damage but extends also to economic loss. The case was recently distinguished in this Court in *J. Nunes Diamonds Ltd.* v. *Dominion Electric Protection Co.,* [1972] S.C.R. 769, 26 D.L.R. (3d) 699, where Pigeon J., speaking for the majority of the Court said at p. 777:

"Furthermore, the basis of tort liability considered in *Hedley Byrne* is inapplicable to any case where the relationship between the parties is governed by a contract, unless the negligence relied on can properly be considered as 'an independent tort' unconnected with the performance of that contract . . . This is specially important in the present case on account of the provisions of the contract with respect to the nature of the obligations assumed and the practical exclusion of responsibility for failure to perform them."

In the present case, however, I am of opinion that the failure to warn was "an independent tort" unconnected with the performance of any contract either express or implied.

In the course of the exhaustive argument which he presented on behalf of the appellant, Mr. Locke referred to a number of recent decisions in the Court of Appeal of England to illustrate the development of the thinking in that Court on the question of recovery for pure economic loss in an action for negligence where no physical damage has been sustained by the plaintiff.

[His Lordship discussed some of the recent U.K. decisions on the issue of economic losses.]

I am conscious of the fact that I have not referred to all relevant authorities relating to recovery for economic loss under such circumstances, but I am satisfied that in the present case there was a proximity of relationship giving rise to a duty to warn, and that the damages awarded by the learned trial judge were recoverable as compensation for the direct and demonstrably foreseeable result of the breach of that duty. This being the case, I do not find it necessary to follow the sometimes winding paths leading to the formulation of a "policy decision".

It will be seen that I prefer the reasoning and conclusion of the trial judge to those of the Court of Appeal and, for the reasons which I have indicated, I reject the suggestion of Tysoe J.A. that this conclusion involves an extension of the rule in *M'Alister (Donoghue)* v. *Stevenson*, where the liability was based on a different ground.

For all these reasons I would set aside the judgment of the Court of Appeal and restore the judgment rendered at trial by Ruttan J.

The appellant will have its costs in this court and the costs of the respondents' cross-appeal in the Court of Appeal.

Laskin J. (dissenting in part) (Hall J. concurring): This is the first occasion upon which this court has been called upon to determine whether recovery may be had in a negligence action for economic loss which stands alone and is not consequent upon physical injury. The trial judge [74 W.W.R. 110] awarded damages for loss of earnings suffered by the appellant for a certain down period required for repairs to the pintle crane, but he denied recovery for the cost of repairs to make the faultily designed and manufactured crane fit for service. In this view he is sustained in the reasons of my brother Ritchie which I have had an opportunity to read. I agree with the award of damages so far as it goes, but I would enlarge it to include as well the cost of repairs.

I would do this because I do not agree that the liability of the respondents should be rested on the one basis of a failure to warn of the probability of injury by reason of the defective design of the crane. The failure to warn is, of course, the only basis upon which, on the facts herein, liability could be imposed upon Walkem. However, Washington, as the designer and manufacturer of the crane, was under an anterior duty to prevent injury which foreseeably would result from its negligence in the design and manufacture of this piece of equipment. If physical harm had resulted, whether personal injury or damage to property (other than to the crane itself), Washington's liability to the person effected, under its anterior duty as a designer and manufacturer of a negligently-produced crane, would not be open to question. Should it then be any less liable for the direct economic loss to the appellant resulting from the faulty crane merely because the likelihood of physical harm, either by way of personal injury to a third person or property damage to the appellant, was averted by the withdrawal of the crane from service so that it could be repaired?

Two new points are involved in this question. The first is whether Washington's liability for negligence should embrace economic loss when there has been no physical harm in fact, and the second is whether the appellant is a proper plaintiff to recover for economic loss and as well the cost of repairing the defective crane.

A manufacturer's liability in negligence for physical harm extends to ensuing economic loss by the person who has suffered the physical harm: see *British Celanese Ltd.* v. *A. H. Hunt (Capacitors) Ltd.,* [1969] 1 W.L.R. 959, [1969] 2 All E.R. 1252; *S.C.M. (United Kingdom) Ltd.* v. *W. J. Whittall & Son Ltd.,* [1971] A.C. 337, [1970] 3 All E.R. 245. There is no doubt that the appellant in the present case was within the ambit of risk of physical harm through the collapse of the defectively designed and manufactured crane; damage to the barge which it had under charter was a foreseeable consequence of Washington's negligence. It is said, however, that a manufacturer's liability for negligence does not extend to economic loss where no physical harm results, even in a case where physical harm is threatened. It is true that economic interests, ordinarily protected in contract as promised advantages, were for long protected in tort in only limited classes of cases, as for example, cases of intentional torts, such as deceit and interference with contract relations, *per quod* actions by a master for injury to his servant by a defendant's negligence and statutory fatal accidents actions by dependants of a person whose death was caused by negligence of another. To these classes a new member has been admitted; the doctrine of *Hedley Byrne & Co.* v. *Heller & Partners Ltd.,* [1964] A.C. 465, [1963] 2 All E.R. 575, which has been considered in this court and has been applied in other courts in Canada, shows that economic or pecuniary loss is not outside the scope of liability for negligence.

The present case is not of the *Hedley Byrne* type, as the reasons of my brother Ritchie show, but recovery for economic loss alone is none the less supported under negligence doctrine. It seems to me that the rationale of manufacturers' liability for negligence should equally support such recovery in the case where, as here, there is a threat of physical harm and the plaintiff is in the class of those who are foreseeably so threatened: see Fleming, *Law of Torts,* 4th ed., 1971, pp. 164-5, 444-5.

Support for such recovery in the present case will not lead to "liability in an indeterminate amount for an indeterminate time to an indeterminate class", to borrow an often-quoted statement of the late Cardozo J. in *Ultramares Corpn.* v. *Touche* (1931), 255 N.Y. 170 at 179, 174 N.E. 441, 74 A.L.R. 1139. The pragmatic considerations which underlay *Cattle* v. *Stockton Waterworks Co.* (1875), L.R. 10 Q.B. 453, will not be eroded by the imposition of liability upon Washington as a negligent designer and manufacturer: *cf.* Fleming James, "Limitations on Liability for Economic Loss Caused by Negligence: A Prag-

matic Appraisal" (1972), 12 Jo. Soc. Pub. T.L. 105. Liability here will not mean
that it must also be imposed in the case of any negligent conduct where there is
foreseeable economic loss; a typical instance would be claims by employees for
lost wages where their employer's factory has been damaged and is shut down
by reason of another's negligence. The present case is concerned with direct
economic loss by a person whose use of the defendant Washington's product
was a contemplated one, and not with indirect economic loss by third parties,
for example, persons whose logs could not be loaded on the appellant's barge
because of the withdrawal of the defective crane from service to undergo repairs.
It is concerned (and here I repeat myself) with economic loss resulting directly
from avoidance of threatened physical harm to property of the appellant if not
also personal injury to persons in its employ.

In advancing its claim for the cost of repairs as well as for loss of earnings,
the appellant relied, *inter alia,* upon a passage in the reasons for judgment of
Lord Denning M.R. in *Dutton* v. *Bognor Regis Urban District Council,* [1972]
1 Q.B. 373, [1972] 1 All E.R. 462, at 474 (*sub nom. Dutton* v. *Bognor Regis
United Building Co.*), which is as follows:

"The damage done here was not solely economic loss. It was physical damage
to the house. If Mr. Tapp's submission were right, it would mean that if the
inspector negligently passes the house as properly built and it collapses and injures a person, the council are liable; but if the owner discovers the defect in
time to repair it — and he does repair it — the council are not liable. That is an
impossible distinction. They are liable in either case.

I would say the same about the manufacturer of an article. If he makes it
negligently, with a latent defect (so that it breaks to pieces and injures someone),
he is undoubtedly liable. Suppose that the defect is discovered in time to prevent
the injury. Surely he is liable for the cost of repair." . . .

In brief, given the case of a manufacturer who is under a duty not to expose
consumers or users of its products to an unreasonable risk of harm (and I would
place builders of houses under the same duty), what are the limits on the kind
or range of harm for which liability will be imposed if there is a breach of duty?
One type of answer has been to invoke the notion of remoteness which may relate to physical harm no less than to economic loss: *cf. Seaway Hotels Ltd.* v.
Consumers' Gas Co., [1959] O.R. 581, 21 D.L.R. (2d) 264 (C.A.); and *Spartan
Steel & Alloys Ltd.* v. *Martin & Co. (Contractors) Ltd.,* [1973] 1 Q.B. 27,
[1972] 3 All E.R. 557. Another, and more usual answer since *MacPherson* v.
Buick Motor Co. (1961), 217 N.Y. 382, 111 N.E. 1050, and *M'Alister (Donoghue)*
v. *Stevenson,* [1932] A.C. 562, has been to deny manufacturers' liability unless
physical harm has resulted from the breach of duty. Put another way, liability
has been denied on the ground that there is no duty to a consumer or user in
respect of economic loss alone. It seems to me that this restriction on liability
has in it more of a concern to avoid limitless claims for economic loss from any
kind of negligence than a concern for the particular basis upon which manufacturers' liability for negligence rests. That liability rests upon a conviction
that manufacturers should bear the risks of injury to consumers or users of their
products when such products are carelessly manufactured because the manufacturers create the risk in the carrying-on of their enterprises, and they will be
more likely to safeguard the members of the public to whom their products are
marketed if they must stand behind them as safe products to consume or to use.
They are better able to insure against such risks, and the cost of insurance, as a
business expense, can be spread with less pain among the buying public than
would be the case if an injured consumer or user was saddled with the entire
loss that befalls him.

This rationale embraces, in my opinion, threatened physical harm from a negligently designed and manufactured product resulting in economic loss. I need not decide whether it extends to claims for economic loss where there is no threat of physical harm or to claims for damage, without more, to the defective product.

It is foreseeable injury to person or to property which supports recovery for economic loss suffered by a consumer or user who is fortunate enough to avert such injury. If recovery for economic loss is allowed when such injury is suffered, I see no reason to deny it when the threatened injury is forestalled. Washington can be no better off in the latter case than in the former. On the admitted facts, a crane on another person's barge, of similar design to that installed on the appellant's barge, had collapsed, killing its operator. It was when this fact came to its notice that the appellant took its crane out of service. Its crane had the same cracks in it that were found in the collapsed crane, and they were due to the same faulty design in both cases. Here then was a piece of equipment whose use was fraught with danger to person and property because of negligence in its design and manufacture; one death had already resulted from the use of a similar piece of equipment that had been marketed by Washington. I see nothing untoward in holding Washington liable in such circumstances for economic loss resulting from the down time necessary to effect repairs to the crane. The case is not one where a manufactured product proves to be merely defective (in short, where it has not met promised expectations) but rather one where by reason of the defect there is a foreseeable risk of physical harm from its use and where the alert avoidance of such harm gives rise to economic loss. Prevention of threatened harm resulting directly in economic loss should not be treated differently from post-injury cure.

Liability of Washington to make good the appellant's loss of profits being established, it remains to consider its liability for the cost of repairs. It is unnecessary in this case to see this cost as necessarily a foreseeable consequence of the breach of anterior duty resting upon Washington. It can stand on another footing. A plaintiff injured by another's negligence is required to act reasonably to mitigate his damages. If his damages are economic damages only, mitigation may involve him in repairing the defect which brought them about. It may not be open to him to do that because the tortfeasor is in control of the matter that invites repair or correction, as in the *Seaway Hotels* and *Spartan Steel* cases already cited. But where the defective product which threatened injury has been in use by the plaintiff, it may be reasonable for him, upon learning of the threat of likely injury from its continued use, to expend money for its repair to make it fit for service. Such an expenditure then becomes part of the economic loss for which Washington must respond. No question was raised in this case about the reasonableness of the appellant's conduct in suspending use of the crane nor about the reasonableness of having it repaired nor of the reasonableness of the cost of repair.

I would, accordingly, allow the appeal, set aside the judgment of the British Columbia Court of Appeal and restore the judgment of Ruttan J., but would vary it to add the cost of repair of the crane to the amount of economic loss for which he found Washington liable. I agree with the disposition as to costs made by my brother Ritchie.

NOTES

1. For which losses did the majority award damages and for which losses did they deny damages? On what theory did they rest the disposition of the case? Were both defendants treated identically?

2. Which losses did the minority think should be compensated and on what

theory? Were the two defendants handled differently? On this basis, should Washington be liable for *all* of the loss of business?

3. Do you prefer the reasoning of the majority or the minority? See Waddams, "Comment" (1974), 52 Can. Bar Rev. 96; Harvey, "Comment" (1974), 37 Mod. L. Rev. 320; Binchy, "Negligence and Economic Loss: The Canadian Tabula Rasa" (1974), 90 L.Q.Rev. 181.

4. Is the concept of loss distribution, espoused by Mr. Justice Laskin, appealing to you? Is it dangerous? Will it lead inevitably to strict liability or to social insurance?

5. An automobile manufacturer negligently produces a vehicle, which, as a result of the defect, is involved in a collision and is damaged. Is the manufacturer liable for the cost of repairing the vehicle? See *Fuller* v. *Ford Motor Co.* (1978), 22 O.R. (2d) 764 (*per* Houston C.C.J.).

6. Does someone who buys some heaters have an action in negligence against their manufacturer, with whom he has no contract, if the heaters do not function properly, but no other loss is incurred? See *Ital-Canadian Investments* v. *North Shore Plumbing & Heating,* [1978] 4 W.W.R. 289 (B.C.).

4. Negligence in Design

Occasions may arise when someone is injured not as a result of a defectively *produced* product but as a result of a defectively *designed* product. In other words, no error has been made during the actual manufacture of the article, but the article itself is not all it might have been. It is here that the skill and imagination of the lawyer is put to the test more than anywhere else. It is here too that the courts must decide whether they will intrude into what is normally thought of as an area of legislative regulation.

MICKLE v. BLACKMON

Supreme Court of South Carolina
(1969), 252 S.C. 202, 166 S.E. 2d 173

On May 29, 1962, 17-year-old Janet Mickle was a passenger in a 1949 Ford automobile driven by Kennith Hill, which was in collision with an automobile driven by Larry Blackmon. The collision threw Janet forward against the gearshift lever. The knob on the end of the lever shattered upon the impact, and she was impaled on the lever, which penetrated to her spine and caused injuries which left her permanently paralyzed. She brought action against the Ford Motor Company, which had manufactured the car, as well as other defendants. The jury returned a verdict of $312,000 against Ford. The trial court granted Ford's motion for judgment notwithstanding the verdict, and plaintiff appealed.

Brailsford J.: . . . Plaintiff's case against Ford rests upon the claim that Ford was negligent in the design and placement of the gearshift lever, which, without an adequate protective ball or knob, created an unreasonable risk of injury to a passenger upon the happening of a collision; and that this risk was realized when the protective knob shattered on the impact of plaintiff's body and she was impaled on the spear-like lever. Ford, while defending the suitability of its gearshift lever assembly at the time of the production and initial sale of the car, disclaims any duty to manufacture an automobile in which it is safe to have a collision, or to exercise care to minimize the collision-connected hazards presented to occupants by the design of the passenger compartment. Ford urges that its only duty in this respect is to manufacture a product which is free of latent defects and reasonably fit for its intended use, and that such use does not include colliding with other vehicles or objects. . . .

There is scant authority on the specific issue which Ford tenders, *i.e.,* whether the manufacturer of an automobile owes a duty in the design and composition of his product to avoid creating unreasonable risks of injury to passengers in a collision of the automobile with another object. Stated differently, does the manufacturer owe a duty of care to reasonably minimize the risk of death or serious injury to collision victims who, quite predictably, will upon impact be forcefully thrown against the interior of the car or outside of it?

Whether Ford owed such a duty is a question of law. If not, plaintiff has no case against Ford. If so, whether Ford breached this duty to plaintiff's injury is a question of fact, unless, of course the evidence is susceptible of only one reasonable inference.

It is a matter of common knowledge that a high incidence of injury-producing motor vehicle collisions is a dread concomitant of travel upon our streets and highways, and that a significant proportion of all automobiles produced are involved in such smashups at some time during their use. Thus, an automobile manufacturer knows with certainty that many users of his product will be involved in collisions, and that the incidence and extent of injury to them will frequently be determined by the placement, design and construction of such interior components as shafts, levers, knobs, handles and others. By ordinary negligence standards, a known risk of harm raises a duty of commensurate care. We perceive no reason in logic or law why an automobile manufacturer should be exempt from this duty. . . .

Having resolved the legal question of Ford's duty to exercise care in plaintiff's favor, we now examine the sufficiency of the evidence to support the jury's factual finding that there was a breach of that duty. . . .

[The 1949 Ford was equipped with a manual transmission, mounted on the right side of the steering shaft below the wheel. It was a slender cylindrical steel rod, on which a white plastic knob or ball was mounted. This knob was made of a material known as tennite butyrate, which would deteriorate under exposure to the ultraviolet rays of sunlight. Hairline cracks had developed, which caused the knob to shatter easily upon impact. The addition of carbon to the material, coloring it black, would have prevented the deterioration.]

It is implicit in the verdict that the gearshift level presented an unreasonable risk of injury if not adequately guarded. At the time of plaintiff's injury the knob on the Hill car continued to serve its functional purpose as a handhold, but it had become useless as a protective guard. It is inferable that the condition of the knob did not arise from ordinary wear and tear, but from an inherent weakness in the material of which Ford was aware when the selection was made. In the light of the insidious effect on this material of exposure to sunlight in the normal use of an automobile, it could reasonably be concluded that Ford should have foreseen that many thousands of the one million vehicles produced by it in 1949 would, in the course of time, be operated millions of miles with gearshift lever balls which, while yet serving adequately as handholds, would furnish no protection to an occupant who might be thrown against the gearshift lever. The jury could reasonably conclude that Ford's conduct, in manufacturing a needed safety device of a material which could not tolerate a frequently encountered aspect of the environment in which it would be employed, exposed many users of its product to unreasonably great risk of harm. Therefore, the issue of Ford's negligence was submissible under elementary common law principles, unless other considerations relied upon by Ford require a different conclusion. . . .

Reversed and remanded as to defendant Ford Motor Company, Inc.

NOTES

1. In coming to its decision, the court relied on the leading case of *Larsen* v. *General Motors Corp.* (1968), 391 F. 2d 495, where F.R. Gibson, Circuit Judge,

in a case where a steering column in a Corvair was thrust rearward in a collision and injured the plaintiff, stated:

"Where the manufacturer's negligence in design causes an unreasonable risk to be imposed upon the user of its products, the manufacturer should be liable for the injury caused by its failure to exercise reasonable care in the design. These injuries are readily foreseeable as an incident to the normal and expected use of an automobile. While automobiles are not made for the purpose of colliding with each other, a frequent and inevitable contingency of normal automobile use will result in collisions and injury-producing impacts. No rational basis exists for limiting recovery to situations where the defect in design or manufacture was the causative factor of the accident, as the accident and the resulting injury, usually caused by the so-called "second collision" of the passenger with the interior part of the automobile, all are foreseeable. Where the injuries or enhanced injuries are due to the manufacturer's failure to use reasonable care to avoid subjecting the user of its products to an unreasonable risk of injury, general negligence principles should be applicable. The sole function of an automobile is not just to provide a means of transportation, it is to provide a means of safe transportation or as safe as is reasonably possible under the present state of the art.

We do agree that under the present state of the art an automobile manufacturer is under no duty to design an accident-proof or fool-proof vehicle or even one that floats on water, but such manufacturer is under a duty to use reasonable care in the design of its vehicle to avoid subjecting its user to an unreasonable risk of injury in the event of a collision. Collisions with or without fault of the user are clearly foreseeable by the manufacturer and are statistically inevitable.

The intended use and purpose of an automobile is to travel on the streets and highways, which travel more often than not is in close proximity to other vehicles and at speeds that carry the possibility, probability, and potential of injury-producing impacts. The realities of the intended and actual use are well known to the manufacturer and to the public and these realities should be squarely faced by the manufacturer and the courts. We perceive of no sound reason, either in logic or experience, nor any command in precedent, why the manufacturer should not be held to a reasonable duty of care in the design of its vehicle consonant with the state of the art to minimize the effect of accidents. The manufacturers are not insurers but should be held to a standard of reasonable care in design to provide a reasonably safe vehicle in which to travel. *Ford Motor Company* v. *Zahn, supra.* Our streets and highways are increasingly hazardous for the intended normal use of travel and transportation. While advances in highway engineering and non-access, dual highways have considerably increased the safety factor on a miles traveled ratio to accidents, the constant increasing number of vehicles gives impetus to the need of designing and constructing a vehicle that is reasonably safe for the purpose of such travel. At least, the unreasonable risk should be eliminated and reasonable steps in design taken to minimize the injury-producing effect of impacts.

This duty of reasonable care in design rests on common law negligence that a manufacturer of an article should use reasonable care in the design and manufacture of his product to eliminate any unreasonable risk of foreseeable injury. The duty of reasonable care in design should be viewed in light of the risk. While all risks cannot be eliminated nor can a crash-proof vehicle be designed under the present state of the art, there are many common-sense factors in design, which are or should be well known to the manufacturer that will minimize or lessen the injurious effects of a collision. The standard of reasonable care is applied in many other negligence situations and should be applied here."

See also *Dyson* v. *G.M.* (1969), 298 F. Supp. 1064 (E.D.Pa.), roof gave way during rollover; *Grundmanis* v. *British Motor Corp.* (1970), 308 F. Supp. 303 (E.D. Wis.), fuel tank location and design; *Frericks* v. *G.M.* (1974), 313 A. 2d 494.

2. The Canadian courts have also been willing to impose liability for negligence in design. In *Phillips* v. *Ford Motor Co. et al.*, [1970] 2 O.R. 714; revd. on other grounds [1971] 2 O.R. 637 (C.A.), the former Mayor of Toronto, Nathan Phillips, while driving with his wife in their Lincoln Continental, attempted to apply the brakes. They did not work and the car collided with a post, injuring the former Mayor and his wife. They sued Ford, the manufacturer, and Elgin, the dealer.

In imposing liability both on the manufacturer and the dealer, Mr. Justice Haines held that there was an inadequate fail-safe system. When the power brakes worked properly, 25 pounds of force could bring the vehicle to a stop at 30 m.p.h., but when they did not, 250 pounds of force was necessary. Because Ford and Elgin knew or should have known of this, they negligently failed to warn Mr. Phillips. Mr. Justice Haines stated:

"A manufacturer who designs and puts a product on the market is liable to the ultimate consumer to ensure that the goods so marketed are free from defects which arise from negligence or lack of care on the part of the manufacturer. In a situation where there is no opportunity to inspect the product purchased, the manufacturer owes a duty to all purchasers to take reasonable care, and where the product is a dangerous or potentially dangerous thing, the duty of care so owed approximates an absolute liability. [Citation omitted.]

Persons who supply, distribute, sell or import a product owe a similar duty of care to the ultimate consumer to ensure that the product does not contain defects which result from the negligence of such supplier, distributor, vendor or importer. . . .

It is my opinion that the defendant Ford Motor Company of Canada Limited failed in its duty as manufacturer, designer, importer, supplier and vendor of the vehicle in question. Although not specifically pleaded, counsel for Ford raised the defence that if there was any negligence in design or manufacture of the Lincoln automobile in question, it was the responsibility of Ford of the United States and not Ford of Canada. I found this quite startling in view of the fact that Ford of Canada imports a great many automobiles and parts from Ford of the United States for sale and distribution to the Canadian public. I ventured the opinion to him in argument that when purchasing a Ford product from a dealer in Canada, a purchaser really would not know whether it was made in Canada by Ford of Canada or in the United States by Ford of the United States and that the Canadian public would be astounded by the proposition that when damages were sustained by a defective Ford product sold by Ford of Canada, they would be met with the defence that Ford of Canada could not be held responsible because of the fact that Ford of the United States had manufactured the vehicle. I asked counsel for the defendant Ford to reconsider his position. He took time and replied that it was a considered defence which he wished to raise. Therefore I must deal with it.

It is my opinion based upon the principles enunciated in *Donoghue* v. *Stevenson* and the more recent cases, *supra,* that this defence must fail. If the Canadian consumer is to receive any degree of protection from negligently designed products, Ford of Canada must be held liable, not only for importing, distributing and supplying such vehicle, but must also share in the responsibility for the design of such vehicle. The basis of such liability is that they, Ford of Canada, designed, manufactured, imported, distributed and sold a Lincoln automobile which had an inadequate fail-safe system. I think Stable J. summed this up in *Watson* v. *Buckley, supra,* by saying that a distributor cannot escape liability by pleading that the initial mistake was made by someone for whose actions, he, the distributor, is not responsible.

Turning to Elgin Motors, there is some question as to whether Ford or Elgin actually sold the car to Mr. Phillips. The transaction was between friends and usual business procedure was not adopted. I do not think it is necessary to go further into this argument. Elgin Motors pleaded that it was the vendor of the car to the plaintiff, Nathan Phillips, and therefore, it must be taken to have a duty of care to both the plaintiffs, within the principles of *Donoghue* v. *Stevenson* and the cases which hold a vendor-supplier liable.

It is my opinion therefore that the defendant, Elgin Motors, owed a duty as vendor of the Lincoln automobile in question to ensure that the product sold was not defective in its design. Elgin Motors failed in this respect.

Furthermore, the law places an onus on persons in the position of repairers within the principles of *Donoghue* v. *Stevenson, supra,* to ensure that the repair work carried out is not done negligently in such a manner as may cause injury to the person with whom he has contracted to repair or to any person who may be injured or damaged as a consequence of such negligence. [Citations omitted.]

It is my opinion that as repairers, Elgin Motors must be taken to have known or ought to have known of the inadequate fail-safe system in the vehicle, and should have brought this to the attention of the plaintiffs, especially in view of the tremendous amount of trouble Mr. and Mrs. Phillips had encountered with the braking system. Furthermore, I refer back to Mr. Grover's statement concerning "real trouble". This statement indicates knowledge at least on the part of Grover, as to the inherent danger involved in the design of this particular car; but Phillips was not warned of the danger.

Both defendants had a duty to warn the plaintiffs of the danger in the event of power brake failure. Both defendants knew or ought to have known the potential hazards of the fail-safe systems installed in the particular vehicle and to at least inform the plaintiffs as to the amount of pressure required to lock the wheels without the assistance of the power booster. . . . The defendants were negligent in failing to warn Phillips of the danger which would result in the event of power brakes failure, a danger enhanced by the inadequate fail-safe system. . . ."

On appeal, the majority of the Ontario Court of Appeal reversed on procedural grounds and ordered a new trial. Mr. Justice Schroeder felt that the plaintiff had not established negligence and that, therefore, the action should have been dismissed. Mr. Justice MacKay agreed but added that "whatever Phillips pressed his foot on, it was not the brake pedal and that he was mistaken in thinking that he had done so". Phillips launched an appeal, but eventually the case was settled with Phillips paying the defendants $5,000 in costs.

See also *Rivtow Marine Ltd., supra, per* Mr. Justice Laskin; *Davie* v. *New Merton Mills*, [1959] A.C. 604 at p. 626; *Carpini* v. *Pittsburgh & Weirton Bus. Co.* (1954), 216 F. 2d 404 (3d Cir.), recognizing that there can be liability for negligence in design.

3. A gas company which installs a gas cooking range with a defectively designed connector may be negligent in failing to recognize that fact, even though it was actually designed by someone else. See *Lemesurier* v. *Union Gas et al.* (1976), 8 O.R. (2d) 152.

4. Although several American cases, including the principal case, hold that liability follows for negligence in design, when an automobile is constructed without being reasonably crashworthy so as to protect its occupants from injury during a "second collision", there are cases which do not. See *Evans* v. *G.M.* (1966), 359 F. 2d 822 (7th Cir.); *Shumard* v. *G.M.* (1967), 270 F. Supp. 311 (S.D. Ohio). Which is the better rule in your view? See Nader and Page, "Automobile Design and the Judicial Process" (1967), 55 Calif. L. Rev. 645; Katz, "Liability of Automobile Manufacturers for Unsafe Design of Passenger Cars" (1956), 69 Harv. L. Rev. 863; Katz, "Negligence in Design: A Current Look," [1965] Ins. L.J. 5; Noel, "Negligence of Design or Directions for Use of a Product" (1962), 71 Yale L.J. 816; Noel, "Recent Trends in Manufacturers' Negligence as to Design, Instruction or Warnings" (1965), 19 S.W.L.J. 43.

5. A manufacturer produces a car that can travel 115 m.p.h. Some fool drives it at that speed and crashes into another car. Should the manufacturer (as well as the fool) be liable on the basis of negligence in design? *Cf. Schemel* v. *G.M.* (1967), 384 F. 2d 802 (7th Cir.).

6. An automobile producer designs a car with its gas tank in the rear. The vehicle is struck from behind. The gas tank ruptures and bursts into flames, burning an occupant. Is the manufacturer liable? *Cf. Shumard* v. *G.M., supra,* note 4 (no liability); *Badorek* v. *G.M.* (1970), 11 Cal. App. 3d 902, 12 Cal. App. 3d 447, 90 Cal. Rptr. 305 (liability).

7. Some recent cases have held that manufacturers may be held strictly liable for second accident injuries. See *infra. The Restatement of Torts, Second,* § 402A has been applied in determining liability in these cases. See, for example, *Dyson* v. *G.M., supra,* note 1; *Wright* v. *Massey-Harris Inc.* (1966), 68 Ill. App. 2d 70, 215 N.E. 2d 465; *Stephan* v. *Sears, Roebuck & Co.* (1970) 266 A. 2d 855 (N.H.); *Badorek* v. *General Motors Corp., supra,* note 6; *Turner* v. *G.M.* (1974), 514 S.W. 2d 497. In such cases the issue is still whether the defendant has designed a reasonably fit and safe product, and so is virtually a question of negligence. See generally Fritz, *"Badorek* v. *General Motors Corp."* (1971), 16 So. Dak. L. Rev. 504; Perry, "Strict Liability for Enhanced Injuries Caused by Unreasonable Defective Design" (1971), 13 Wm. and Mary L. Rev. 242; Gram, "Torts Strict Liability in the Second Accident Case" (1971), 20 Kan. L. Rev. 179.

8. There has been some legislative activity in the area of automobile design and safety. In 1965, a young attorney called Ralph Nader published a book *Unsafe At Any Speed,* which dramatized the danger of the "second collision". (See also O'Connell and Meyers, *Safety Last* (1966).) Shortly thereafter the U.S. Senate held some well-publicized hearings on the problem. In 1966, Congress responded by enacting the National Traffic and Motor Vehicle Safety Act of 1966 which, *inter alia,* required that certain safety features be built into all American-built cars. The Canadian Government was slow to follow suit, but it did not matter very much since the American manufacturers incorporated these safety features into all the cars they produced, including the ones destined for the Canadian market. In 1970, the Canadian Parliament passed the Motor Vehicle Safety Act, R.S.C. 1970, c. 26 (1st Supp.), which empowered the government, by means of the device of a national safety mark without which a vehicle could not be sold in Canada, to require the inclusion of safety features in automobiles sold or produced in Canada. Consequently, all vehicles now sold in Canada contain safety features such as collapsible steering columns, seat-belts, head-rests, shatterproof glass, side-view mirrors, reinforced doors, better padding and knob design, *etc.* There has been close co-operation between the Canadian and the U.S. governments and the automobile industry in the development of these regulations.

9. Is there still a role for tort law to play in helping to improve the design of automobiles? Should courts be involved in this type of problem? What are the dangers to the courts, the public, the bar? See Weiler, "Legal Values and Judicial Decision-Making" (1970), 49 Can. Bar Rev. 1. In the *Larsen* case (*supra,* note 1), when the defendant argued that the courts should not intrude into questions involving vehicle design because Congress had enacted legislation in the area, F.R. Gibson, Circuit Judge, stated:

"It is apparent that the National Traffic Safety Act is intended to be supplementary of and in addition ot the common law of negligence and product liability. The common law is not sterile or rigid and serves the best interests of society by adapting standards of conduct and responsibility that fairly meet the emerging and developing needs of our time. The common law standard of a duty to use reasonable care in light of all the circumstances can at least serve the needs of our society until the legislature imposes higher standards or the courts expand the doctrine of strict liability for tort. The Act is a salutary step in this direction and not an exemption from common law liability."

Do you agree?

10. In his article "Negligence in Design: A Current Look", [1965] Ins. L.J. 5, Harold Katz contended that the civil law suit has been "history's great persuader of the socially irresponsible". Do you agree?

11. Is there any social benefit in bringing a products liability suit that fails? Should a lawyer launch an action that is unlikely to win in order to educate the public? Is this ethical? Does it depend on whether the client has been told about the weakness of the case but wants to proceed notwithstanding this? What are the dangers of this type of activity by counsel? See generally Linden, "Tort Law as Ombudsman" (1973), 51 Can. Bar Rev. 155, at p. 167.

G. STRICT LIABILITY IN TORT

GREENMAN v. YUBA POWER PRODUCTS INC.

Supreme Court of California
(1963), 53 Cal. 2d 57, 377 P. 2d 897

A wife bought for her husband a shopsmith combination power tool that could be used as a saw, drill and wood lathe. While the husband was using the shopsmith, the piece of wood he was working on flew out of it, hitting him on the forehead. In an action against the retailer and manufacturer, the jury found for the plaintiff against the manufacturer but dismissed the action against the retailer. Both the manufacturer and the plaintiff appealed.

Traynor J.: A manufacturer is strictly liable in tort when an article he places on the market, knowing that it is to be used without inspection of defects, proves to have a defect that causes injury to a human being. Recognized first in the case of unwholesome food products, such liability has now been extended to a variety of other products that create as great or greater hazards if defective. [Citations omitted.]

Although in these cases strict liability has usually been based on the theory of an express or implied warranty running from the manufacturer to the plaintiff, the abandonment of the requirement of a contract between them, the recognition that the liability is not assumed by agreement but imposed by law [Citations omitted.] and the refusal to permit the manufacturer to define the scope of its own responsibility for defective products [Citations omitted.] make clear that the liability is not one governed by the law of contract warranties, but by the law of 'strict liability in tort'. Accordingly, rules defining and governing warranties that were developed to meet the needs of commercial transactions cannot properly be invoked to govern the manufacturer's liability to those injured by its defective products unless those rules also serve the purposes for which such liability is imposed.

We need not recanvass the reasons for imposing strict liability on the manufacturer. They have been fully articulated in the cases cited above. (See also 2 Harper and James, *Torts*, §§ 28.15-28.16, pp. 1569-1574; Prosser, "Strict Liability to the Consumer", 69 Yale L.J. 1099; *Escola* v. *Coca Cola Bottling Co.*, 24 Cal. 2d 453, 461 [150 P. 2d 436], concurring opinion.) The purpose of such liability is to insure that the costs of injuries resulting from defective products are borne by the manufacturers that put such products on the market rather than by the injured persons who are powerless to protect themselves. Sales warranties serve this purpose fitfully at best. (See Prosser, "Strict Liability to the Consumer", 69 Yale L.J. 1099, 1124-1134.) In the present case, for example, plaintiff was able to plead and prove an express warranty only because he read and relied on the representations of the Shopsmith's ruggedness contained in the manufacturer's brochure. Implicit in the machine's presence on the market, however, was a representation that it would safely do the jobs for which it was built. Under these circumstances, it should not be controlling whether plaintiff selected the machine because of the statements in the brochure, or because of the machine's own appearance of excellence that belied the defect lurking beneath the surface, or because he merely assumed that it would safely do the jobs it was built to do. It should not be controlling whether the details of the sales from manufacturer to retailer and from retailer to plaintiff's wife were such that one or more of the implied warranties of the sales act arose. (Civ. Code, § 1735.) 'The remedies of injured consumers ought not to be made to depend upon the intricacies of the law of sales.' [Citations omitted.] To establish the manufacturer's liability it was sufficient that plaintiff proved that he was injured while using the Shopsmith in a way it was intended to be used as a result of a defect in design and manufacture of which plaintiff was not aware that made the Shopsmith unsafe for its intended use.

The judgment is affirmed.

NOTES

1. The development of strict liability in the United States has been described by the late Dean Prosser as the "most rapid and spectacular overthrow of an established rule in the entire history of the law of torts". See Prosser, "The Fall of the Citadel" (1966), 50 Minn. L. Rev. 791. See also Wade, "Strict Tort Liability of Manufacturers" (1965), 19 S.W. L.J. 5; Dickerson, "The A B C's of Products Liability" (1969), 36 Tenn. L. Rev. 439.

2. Nearly two decades before Greenman, Mr. Justice Traynor had articulated this heresy, in a concurring opinion in *Escola* v. *Coca Cola Bottling Co. of Fresno* (1944), 150 Pac. 2d 436. The majority of the court had held that *res ipsa loquitur* applied and permitted the plaintiff, who was injured when a Coca Cola bottle exploded in her hand, to recover in negligence. Mr. Justice Traynor wrote:

". . . I concur in the judgment, but I believe the manufacturer's negligence should no longer be singled out as the basis of a plaintiff's right to recover in cases like the present one. In my opinion it should now be recognized that a manufacturer incurs an absolute liability when an article that he has placed on the market, knowing that it is to be used without inspection, proves to have a defect that causes injury to human beings. *MacPherson* v. *Buick Motor Co.,* 217 N.Y. 382; 111 N.E. 1050, established the principle, recognized by this court, that irrespective of privity of contract, the manufacturer is responsible for an injury caused by such an article to any person who comes in lawful contact with it. . . . In these cases the source of the manufacturer's liability was his negligence in the manufacturing process or in the inspection of component parts supplied by others. Even if there is no negligence, however, public policy demands that responsibility be fixed wherever it will most effectively reduce the hazards to life and health inherent in defective products that reach the market. It is evident that the manufacturer can anticipate some hazards and guard against the recurrence of others, as the public cannot. Those who suffer injury from defective products are unprepared to meet its consequences. The cost of an injury and the loss of time or health may be an overwhelming misfortune to the person injured, and a needless one, for the risk of injury can be insured by the manufacturer and distributed among the public as a cost of doing business. It is to the public interest to discourage the marketing of products having defects that are a menace to the public. If such products nevertheless find their way into the market it is to the public interest to place the responsibility for whatever injury they may cause upon the manufacturer, who, even if he is not negligent in the manufacture of the product, is responsible for its reaching the market. However intermittently such injuries may occur and however haphazardly they may strike, the risk of their occurrence is a constant risk and a general one. Against such a risk there should be general and constant protection and the manufacturer is best situated to afford such protection. . . .

As handicrafts have been replaced by mass production with its great markets and transportation facilities, the close relationship between the producer and consumer of a product has been altered. Manufacturing processes, frequently valuable secrets, are ordinarily either inaccessible to or beyond the ken of the general public. The consumer no longer has means or skill enough to investigate for himself the soundness of a product, even when it is not contained in a sealed package, and his erstwhile vigilance has been lulled by the steady efforts of manufacturers to build up confidence by advertising and marketing devices such as trademarks. . . . Consumers no longer approach products warily but accept them on faith, relying on the reputation of the manufacturer or the trade mark. . . . Manufacturers have sought to justify that faith by increasingly high standards of inspection and a readiness to make good on defective products by way of replacements and refunds. . . . The manufacturer's obligation to the consumer must keep pace with the changing relationship between them; it cannot be escaped because the marketing of a product has become so complicated as to require one or more intermediaries. Certainly there is greater reason to impose liability on the manufacturer than on the retailer who is but a conduit of a product that he is not himself able to test. . . .

The manufacturer's liability should, of course, be defined in terms of safety of the product in normal and proper use, and should not extend to injuries that cannot be traced to the product as it reached the market."

3. In 1965 the American Law Institute in the *Restatement of the Law of Torts, Second,* felt able to include the following section as a statement of existing law in the United States: 402A. (1) One who sells any product in a defective condition unreasonably dangerous to the user or consumer or to his property is subject to liability for physical harm thereby caused to the ultimate user or consumer, or to his property if (a) the seller is engaged in the business of selling such a product, and (b) it is expected to and does reach the user or consumer without substantial change in the condition in which it is sold. (2) The rule stated in subsection (1) applies although (a) the seller has exercised all possible care in the preparation and sale of his product, and (b) the user consumer has not bought the product from or entered into any contractual relation with the seller.

The Institute expressed no opinion whether this rule might apply to persons other than users or consumers; to the seller of a product expected to be processed or otherwise substantially changed before it reaches the user or consumer; or to the seller of a component part of a product to be assembled.

4. Some American courts utilized the concept of warranty to move into a regime of strict liability for defective products. In *Henningsen* v. *Bloomfield Motors Inc. et al.* (1960), 32 N.J. 358, 161 A. 2d 69, the plaintiff was injured when something went wrong with the steering gear of the 1955 Plymouth her husband had bought for her for Christmas. Although the actions against the dealer and the manufacturer in negligence were dismissed, the jury found that there had been a breach of the implied warranty of merchantability. Francis J. affirmed and stated:

"There is no doubt that under early common-law concepts of contractual liability only those persons who were parties to the bargain could sue for a breach of it. In more recent times a noticeable disposition has appeared in a number of jurisdictions to break through the narrow barrier of privity when dealing with sales of goods in order to give realistic recognition to a universally accepted fact. The fact is that the dealer and the ordinary buyer do not, and are not expected to, buy goods, whether they be foodstuffs or automobiles, exclusively for their own consumption or use. Makers and manufacturers know this and advertise and market their products on that assumption; witness, the "family" car, the baby foods, etc. The limitations of privity in contracts for the sale of goods developed their place in the law when marketing conditions were simple, when maker and buyer frequently met face to face on an equal bargaining plane and when many of the products were relatively uncomplicated and conducive to inspection by a buyer competent to evaluate their quality. [Citation omitted.] With the advent of mass marketing, the manufacturer became remote from the purchaser, sales were accomplished through intermediaries, and the demand for the product was created by advertising media. In such an economy it became obvious that the consumer was the person being cultivated. Manifestly, the connotation of "consumer" was broader than that of "buyer". He signified such a person who, in the reasonable contemplation of the parties to the sale, might be expected to use the product. Thus, where the commodities sold are such that if defectively manufactured they will be dangerous to life or limb, then society's interests can only be protected by eliminating the requirement of privity between the maker and his dealers and the reasonably expected ultimate consumer. In that way the burden of losses consequent upon use of defective articles is borne by those who are in a position to either control the danger or make an equitable distribution of the losses when they do occur. . . .

Most of the cases where lack of privity has not been permitted to interfere with recovery have involved food and drugs. [Citations omitted.] In fact, the rule as to such products has been characterized as an exception to the general doctrine. But more recently courts, sensing the inequity of such limitation, have moved into broader fields: . . . [Citations omitted.]

We see no rational doctrinal basis for differentiating between a fly in a bottle of beverage and a defective automobile. The unwholesome beverage may bring illness to one person, the defective car, with its great potentiality for harm to the driver, occupants, and others, demands even less adherence to the narrow barrier of privity. . . .

Under modern conditions the ordinary layman, on responding to the importuning of colorful advertising, has neither the opportunity nor the capacity to inspect or to determine the fitness of an automobile for use; he must rely on the manufacturer who has control of its construction, and to some degree on the dealer who, to the limited extent called for by the manufacturer's instructions, inspects and services it before delivery. In such a marketing milieu his remedies and those of persons who properly claim through him should not depend "upon the intricacies of the law of sales". The obligation of the manufacturer should not be based alone on privity of contract. It should rest, as was once said, upon 'the demands of social justice'. . . .

Accordingly, we hold that under modern marketing conditions, when a manufacturer puts a new automobile in the stream of trade and promotes its purchase by the public, an implied warranty that it is reasonably suitable for use as such accompanies it into the hands of the ultimate purchaser. Absence of agency between the manufacture and the dealer who makes the ultimate sale is immaterial."

5. The American Uniform Commercial Code, ss. 2-318, expanded the protection of the implied conditions of sales law to other members of the family or household of the buyer and his guests. A few states have gone further and extended the operation of the implied warranties to any person who may "reasonably be expected to use, consume or be affected by the goods and who is injured". There has been much controversy about the conflicting merits of the warranty approach as contrasted to the strict liability in tort theory. See Franklin, "When Worlds Collide: Liability Theories and Disclaimers in Defective Products Cases" (1966), 18 Stan. L. Rev. 974; Speidel, "The Virginia Anti-privity Statute: Strict Liability Under the U.C.C." (1965), 51 Va. L. Rev. 804; Titus, "Restatement (Second) Torts, Section 402A and the U.C.C." (1970), 22 Stan. L. Rev. 713.

DUNHAM v. VAUGHAN & BUSHNELL MFG. CO.

Supreme Court of Illinois.
(1969), 42 Ill. 2d 339, 247 N.E. 2d 401

The plaintiff bought a claw hammer from defendant Belknap which was fabricated by the defendant Vaughan. While using the hammer, 11 months later, a chip broke off the hammer and stuck the plaintiff in the eye, destroying his eyesight. Both defendants were held liable in a jury action. This was affirmed by the intermediate Appeal Court and by the Supreme Court of Illinois.

Schaeffer J.: The basic theory of the defendants in this court is that the requirements of strict liability, as announced in *Suvada* v. *White Motor Co.*, 32 Ill. 2d 612, 210 N.E. 2d 182, were not established, because the testimony of the experts showed that the hammer contained no defect. *Suvada* required a plaintiff to prove that his injury resulted from a condition of the product which was unreasonably dangerous, and which existed at the time the product left the manufacturer's control. But the requirement that the defect must have existed when the product left the manufacturer's control does not mean that the defect must manifest itself at once. The defective "aluminum brake linkage bracket", with which the court was concerned in ruling upon the legal sufficiency of the complaint in *Suvada,* was alleged to have been installed in the tractor not later than March of 1957; it did not break until June of 1960.

Although the definitions of the term "defect" in the context of products liability law use varying language, all of them rest upon the common premise that those products are defective which are dangerous because they fail to perform in the manner reasonably to be expected in light of their nature and intended function. So, Chief Justice Traynor has suggested that a product is defective if it fails to match the average quality of like products. (Traynor, "The Ways and Meanings of Defective Products and Strict Liability", 32 Tenn. L. Rev. 363 (1965).) The *Restatement* emphasizes the viewpoint of the consumer and concludes that a defect is a condition not contemplated by the ultimate consumer which would be unreasonably dangerous to him. (*Restatement, Torts (Second)* § 402A, comment g.) Dean Prosser has said that "the product is to be regarded as defective if it is not safe for such a use that can be expected to be made of it, and no warning is given". (Prosser, "The Fall of the Citadel," 50 Minn. L. Rev. 791, 826). Dean Wade has suggested that apart from the existence of a defect "the test for imposing strict liability is whether the product is unreasonably dangerous, to use the words of the *Restatement.* Somewhat preferable is the expression 'not reasonably safe' ". (Wade, "Strict Tort Liability of Manufacturers", 19 S.W. L.J. 5, 15.) See also, Dean Keeton, "Products Liability — Liability without Fault and the Requirement of a Defect", 45 Tex. L. Rev. 855, 859.

The evidence in this case, including both the General Services Administration specifications and tests and the testimony of the experts as to "work hardening" or "metal failure", shows that hammers have a propensity to chip which increases with continued use. From that evidence it would appear that a new hammer would not be expected to chip, while at some point in its life the possibility of chipping might become a reasonable expectation, and a part of the hammer's likely performance. The problems arise in the middle range, as Chief Justice Traynor has illustrated: "If an automobile part normally last five years, but the one in question proves defective after six months of normal use, there would be enough deviation to serve as a basis for holding the manufacturer liable for any resulting harm. What if the part lasts four of the normal five years, however, and then proves defective? For how long should a manufacturer be responsible for his product?" . . .

The answers to these questions are properly supplied by a jury, and on the record that is before us this case presents only the narrow question whether there is sufficient evidence to justify the jury's conclusion that the hammer was defective. The record shows that it was represented as one of "best quality" and was not put to a use which was regarded as extraordinary in the experience of the community. The jury could properly have concluded that, considering the length and type of its use, the hammer failed to perform in the manner that would reasonably have been expected, and that this failure caused the plaintiff's injury.

Strict liability, applied to the manufacture of the hammer, Vaughan & Bushnell, extends as well to the wholesaler, Belknap Hardware and Mfg. Co., despite the fact that the box in which this hammer was packaged passed unopened through Belknap's warehouse. The strict liability of a retailer arises from his integral role in the overall producing and marketing enterprise and affords an additional incentive to safety. (See *Vandermark* v. *Ford Motor Co.* (1964), 61 Cal. 2d 256, 37 Cal. Rptr. 896, 391 P. 2d 168.) That these considerations apply with equal compulsion to all elements in the distribution system is affirmed by our decision in *Suvada* v. *White Motor Co.*, 32 Ill. 2d 612, 617, 210 N.E. 2d 182. See, *Restatement (Second), Torts* (1965) § 402A, comment f.

The defendant's objections to the instructions to the jury were adequately disposed of in the opinion of the appellate court. The judgment of the appellate court is affirmed.

NOTES

1. The problem of deciding when a product is "defective" is no easy matter. See, in general, Wade, "Strict Tort Liability of Manufacturers" (1965), 19 S.W.L. Rev. 5; Keeton, "Products Liability: Liability Without Fault and the Requirement of a Defect" (1963), 41 Tex. L. Rev. 855; Traynor, "The Ways and Meanings of Defective Products and Strict Liability" (1965), 32 Tenn. L. Rev. 362; Freedman, " 'Defect' in the Product: The Necessary Basis for Products Liability" (1966), 33 Tenn. L. Rev. 323; Dickerson, "Products Liability: How Good Does a Product Have to Be" (1967), 42 Ind. L.J. 301; Rheingold, "Proof of Defect in Product Liability Cases" (1971), 38 Tenn. L. Rev. 325; Calabresi and Hirschoff, "Toward a Test for Strict Liability" (1972), 81 Yale L.J. 1054; Henderson, "Judicial Review of Manufacturer's Conscious Design Choices: The Limits of Adjudication" (1973), 73 Colum. L. Rev. 1531; Shapo, "A Representational Theory of Consumer Protection: Doctrine, Function and Legal Liability for Product Disappointment" (1974), 60 Va. L. Rev. 1109; Wade "On the Nature of Strict Tort Liability for Products" (1973), 44 Miss. L. J. 825.

2. Some jurisdictions have now rejected the *Restatement's* "unreasonably dangerous" requirement in causes of action based on strict liability in tort. In *Cronin* v. *I.B.E. Olson Corporation* (1972), 8 Cal. 3d 121, 501 P. 2d 1153, 104 Cal. Rptr. 433, the plaintiff was seriously injured when his bread truck collided with another vehicle. The bulk of his injuries resulted from the breaking of an aluminum safety latch which was located just behind the driver's seat and which was designed to hold the bread trays in place. The loaded trays, driven forward by the abrupt stop and impact of the truck, struck the plaintiff in the back and hurled him through the windshield. The evidence indicated that the latch was defective in that the metal was very porous and weak and, therefore, could not withstand any force exerted upon it. In an action by the plaintiff against the supplier of the truck, the Supreme Court of California unanimously held that all that was required to succeed in the action was proof that the product was defective and that it was not necessary to establish that the product was unreasonably dangerous. Sullivan J. stated that such an interpretation of *Restatement* § 402A ". . . has burdened the injured plaintiff with proof of an element which rings of negligence . . ." and ". . . represents a step backward in the area pioneered by this court. . . .". In discussing this issue, Sullivan J. explained: ". . . We recognize that the words 'unreasonably dangerous' may also serve the beneficial purpose of preventing the seller from being treated as the insurer of its products. However, we think that such protective end is attained by the neces-

sity of proving that there was a defect in the manufacture or design of the product and that such defect was a proximate cause of the injuries. Although the seller should not be responsible for all injuries involving the use of its products, it should be liable for all injuries proximately caused by any of its products which are adjudged 'defective' ".

See also *Glass et al.* v. *Ford Motor Co. et al.* (1973), 123 N.J. Super. 599, 304 A. 2d 562.

3. One perplexing problem that remains is that of the treatment of side-effects of drugs under a strict liability regime. In *Cochrane* v. *Brooke* (1966), 409 P. 2d 904, for example, the plaintiff suffered a loss of vision after using a drug called chloroquine in the treatment of her arthritis. The Supreme Court of Oregon held that the product was "pure and not defective". The plaintiff suffered from "an idiosyncracy which caused her to be peculiarly susceptible to this uncommon reaction". Sloan J. concluded:

"The far reaching consequences that may ensue if we were to take so bold a step as to impose the absolute liability suggested by plaintiff are beyond the ability of a court to know or comprehend. It is, indeed, easy for compassion to dictate an absolute liability against the makers of a product that can cause blindness. But once the liability is imposed, it could not be judicially limited only to cases involving disastrous consequences. An upset stomach caused by taking aspirin would, as well, entitle the user to his measure of damages. We can agree with the plaintiff that social justice might require that the price of the drugs should include an amount sufficient to create a fund to compensate those who suffer unanticipated harm from the use of a beneficial drug. But this kind of a system of compensation is beyond the power of a court to impose."

4. In *Casagrande* v. *F.W. Woolworth Co.* (1960), 340 Mass. 552, 165 N.E. 2d 109, the plaintiff suffered irritation in her armpits after using a deodorant called "MUM", which she had used many times before. The evidence was that not more than one in two thousand could show a sensitive reaction. Although the court agreed that there was an implied warranty of merchantability, it did not think that "a significant number of other persons would be hurt by the deodorant". A directed verdict for the defendant followed. What if 1 person in 200 had an allergic reaction? What if it were 1 in 20? What if, instead of a skin irration, death ensued to 1 in 2,000 persons? What if it were in 20,000? 1 in 200,000? Is this balancing process familiar?

5. Some people are allergic to penicillin. Should a manufacturer of penicillin be held liable to someone who sustains a reaction? Should the doctor be liable? Should a warning be given? In *Davis* v. *Wyeth Laboratories Inc.* (1968), 399 F. 2d 121 (9th Cir.), it was held that the defendant manufacturers, who failed to warn all recipients of the Sabin polio vaccine that there was a slight possibility (1 in a million) that serious injury could result from receiving the vaccine, could be strictly liable. The failure to warn "rendered the drug unfit in the sense that it was thereby rendered unreasonably dangerous".

6. The thalidomide tragedy is still fresh in the minds of many people. In the early 1960's many children, whose mothers had ingested the drug thalidomide between the 4th and 6th week of pregnancy, were born with phocomelia of the arms, legs and other deformities. Thalidomide, sold in Canada under the name Kevadon and Talimol, was very effective as a sleep-inducing agent, a depressant and an anti-nauseant. The only trouble with it was that it could produce deformed babies. Is this a "defect" in the drug? Should there be liability? What percentage of the users of thalidomide would be between the 4th and 6th week of pregnancy? Would the victims be any better off under strict liability than under negligence? See generally Keeton, "Products Liability — Drugs and Cosmetics" (1972), 25 Vand. L. Rev. 131; Bennett, "The Liability of the Manufacturers of Thalidomide to the Affected Children" (1965), 39 A.L.J. 256; Whitmore, "Allergies and Other Reactions Due to Drugs and Cosmetics" (1965), 19 S.W. L.J. 76.

7. Should a cigarette manufacturer be liable strictly if one of its heavy-

smoking customers contracts lung cancer as a result of their product? There were several cases brought in the United States, but the result of the litigation was inconclusive. See Wegman, "Cigarettes and Health: A Legal Analysis" (1966), 51 Cornell L.Q. 678. See *Green* v. *American Tobacco Co.* (1969), 409 F. 2d 1166 (5th Cir.) (no liability); *Pritchard* v. *Liggett & Myers Tobacco Co.* (1961), 295 F. 2d 292 (3rd Cir.) (liability). Now that smokers are aware of the dangers of smoking, should they be permitted to recover from a cigarette producer?

8. After many years of heavy drinking, Paul contracts cirrhosis of the liver. He sues the company that bottled the brand of Scotch he specialized in. Can he recover under strict liability?

9. Peter is a big butter-eater. His arteries are full of cholesterol. If he suffers a heart attack, can he recover from his dairy under strict liability?

10. There are many similar problems. For example, a blood transfusion may cause hepatitis. Sugar may seriously poison a diabetic. What should courts do with these problems? Franklin, "Tort Liability for Hepatitis: An Analysis and a Proposal" (1972), 24 Stan. L. Rev. 439.

11. As in negligence liability, the strict liability doctrine has been extended to cover all consumers or users of the product including members of the family, guests, and even bystanders. See Noel, "Defective Products: Extension of Strict Liability to Bystanders" (1970), 38 Tenn. L. Rev. 1.

12. The problem of intermediate examination and intervening negligence has not evaporated. If a defect is not discovered by some third person who had a reasonable opportunity to do so, is the manufacturer relieved of strict liability? See *Duckworth* v. *Ford Motor Co.* (1962), 211 F. Supp. 888 (Pa.). If a defect is discovered by a third person, who does not take steps to prevent harm, is the manufacturer strictly liable? See *Halpern* v. *Jad Construction Co.* (1960), 202 N.Y.S. 2d 945.

13. Even where the product is serviced by a dealer, some courts have been extremely reluctant to relieve manufacturers of liability. In *Vandermark* v. *Ford Motor Co.* (1964), 61 Cal. 2d 206, 391 P. 2d 168, it was held that the obligation of the maker to supply a safe automobile could not be delegated to a dealer. Do you agree with this decision? What are its dangers? What are its benefits?

14. The plaintiff still bears the onus of proof. He must establish that he was injured by the product, that it was defective and that the defect was present when the product was sold by the defendant. If this is so, is the plaintiff any better off under strict liability than he is under negligence liability with *res ipsa loquitur?* Does the lawyer have to do any less work?

15. Does tort law have any effect in fostering care by manufacturers? Does strict liability help more than negligence liability in this regard? A drug called MER/29 was used to combat cholesterol in the arteries. One of its side-effects was that it caused eye cataracts to develop. A great many law suits were launched in the United States (including criminal proceedings) against Richardson-Merrell, which was the North American distributor of MER/29 as well as Thalidomide. Most of these actions have been settled. Assessing the impact of this litigation, Reingold, "The MER/29 Story — An Instance of Successful Mass Disaster Litigation" (1968), 56 Cal. L. Rev. 116, concluded:

"... the impact of the MER/29 disaster upon the manufacturer, Richardson-Merrell, is unmeasurable. Its stock fell disastrously; its earnings and profits declined; earned surplus usually available for expansion was used to pay off claims after the insurance was exhausted; and the company's standing with its regulatory agency, the FDA, fell considerably. The company was not hurt, however, in the eyes of its purchasing public, the medical profession, which continued to prescribe its other products, as is discussed in the next section below. Responding to these adverse effects, Richardson-Merrell undoubtedly took steps to avoid 'another MER/29' within its system."

On the other hand, a Report of the Chairman and President to Richardson-Merrell Stockholders, dated June 20, 1967, stated as follows:

"Notwithstanding the difficulties of predicting the results of this multiple litigation, it continues to be our best judgment (in view of the probability that such litigation will be spread over a number of years, and the product liability insurance carried by the Company, and the opinion of legal counsel as to realistic estimate of the merits of these claims and lawsuits) that they will not significantly affect our daily operations or our aggressive programs for growth or materially impair our strong financial position."

A New York stockbrokers' bulletin, dated December 3, 1968, confirms that the value of Richardson-Merrell stock "which had been selling between 25 and 35 times earnings, plunged to a 15 times multiple in 1962". The "fears proved groundless", however, according to these brokers, who suggested that the stock, then selling at 22.7 times earnings, was "undervalued" and, therefore, was a good buy.

16. Who bore the cost of settling the MER/29 and Thalidomide actions? The stockholders? The managers? The government? The public? The customers of Richardson-Merrell? The victims? All of these? Would you buy any stock in Richardson-Merrell? Would you buy any of their products?

17.   As for the American law on this topic, see generally Hursh & Bailey, *American Law of Products Liability* (1974); Frumer & Friedman, *Products Liability* (1974).

A NOTE ON THE CANADIAN POSITION

Despite the revolution that is proceeding apace in the United States, the Canadian courts have so far clung to negligence liability. To be sure, *res ipsa loquitur,* statutory negligence and other devices have been utilized to widen liability. Nevertheless, the big jump to strict liability has not been taken. The reasons for this are hard to determine. Perhaps Canadian industry, being less developed than American, needed more protection. Perhaps our judges are less willing to intrude on what they believe is a legislative responsibility. Perhaps our bar has not been as bold in advancing new theories of liability. In any event, the time is drawing near when our courts will have to choose which path they will follow.

The Canadian courts have so far largely ignored the issue. There are two little-known *dicta* of Mr. Justice Riddell indicating that he favoured a form of strict liability for defective products, but these have not been adopted by the courts. Whether this will continue to be the case remains to be seen. In the case of *Shandloff* v. *City Dairy Ltd. et al.,* [1936] O.R. 579, [1936] 4 D.L.R. 712, the plaintiff purchased a bottle of chocolate milk from a retail merchant to whom the milk had been supplied by City Dairy Ltd. The bottle contained particles of glass which caused injury to the plaintiff. Without citing any authorities and without the support of his brethren, Mr. Justice Riddell declared: "It is good sense and should be good law, that anyone manufacturing for public consumption an article of food should be held to warrant to the consumer that it is free from hidden defects, which are or may be dangerous; and it is no hardship to hold the vendor of food as warranting to the purchaser and consumer in the same way."

But Mr. Justice Riddell was only a voice crying in the wilderness. Five years later in the case of *Arendale et al.* v. *Canada Bread Company Ltd.,* [1941] O.W.N. 69, [1941] 2 D.L.R. 49, the plaintiff was injured by particles of glass in a loaf of bread made and supplied by Canada Bread Company Ltd. There was in that case evidence called by the defendant to show the process of manufacture, that its machinery and equipment were the best and most modern available, designed to safeguard the ingredients entering into the finished loaf, and that a high degree of care was used to prevent glass or other foreign substances from getting into the bread. The learned trial judge found that the plaintiff had failed to prove that the glass was in the bread at the time it was delivered by Canada Bread Company Ltd. to the plaintiff, and accordingly dismissed the action. The Court of Appeal reversed the finding of fact as to the glass being in the bread at the time of delivery and reversed the judgment.

Riddell J.A., at p. 70, expressed the opinion that: ". . . when one manufactures for human consumption any article, fluid or solid, he putting it on the market gives an implied warranty that it contains no deleterious substance; and that if the ultimate consumer is injured by the presence of such deleterious substance he is entitled to damages unless the manufacturer proves that it was there introduced by some agency other than his own — in other words he must prove that this deleterious article did not obtain entrance through his act or negligence but that of some other. The onus is on the manufacturer so to prove." His fellow judges decided the case on other grounds.

Although the pure doctrine of strict liability in tort has not been adopted in Canada, there survives a concept that resembles this theory in some ways — inherently dangerous things or things dangerous in themselves. Under this doctrine, which applies to such things as guns, poison and explosives, a higher standard of care is required than is ordinarily demanded. There are some who contend that this notion should be jettisoned, but somehow it clings to life. Mr. Justice Patterson of the Nova Scotia Supreme Court has expressed the current Canadian law in *Rae* v. *T. Eaton Co.* (1961), 28 D.L.R. (2d) 522, at p. 528, thus:

". . . The test of liability is not whether the product sold was or was not a 'dangerous thing', but considering its nature and all relevant circumstances whether there has been a breach of duty by the manufacturer which he owed to the injured person. The duty is to use that due care that a reasonable person should use under all circumstances. And one of the most important circumstances — and often the controlling circumstance - is the character of the article sold and its capacity to do harm."

Mr. Justice Middleton explained the notion in *Shandloff* v. *City Dairy*, [1936] O.R. 579, at p. 590: "The lack of care essential to the establishment of such a claim increases according to the danger to the ultimate consumer, and where the thing is in itself dangerous, the care necessary approximates to, and almost becomes, an absolute liability."

This theory was given a boost, at least in food cases, by Evans J.A. in *Heimler* v. *Calvert Caterers Ltd.* (1975), 8 O.R. (2d) 1 (C.A.), a case in which a supplier of contaminated food was held liable to someone who contracted typhoid. His Lordship stated:

"The standard of care demanded from those engaged in the food-handling business, is an extremely high standard and as Middleton, J.A., observed in *Shandloff* v. *City Dairy Ltd. and Moscoe*, [citations omitted] the lack of care essential to the establishment of such a claim increases according to the danger to the ultimate consumer, and where the thing is in itself dangerous, the care necessary approximates to and almost becomes an absolute liability. While the facts in the *Shandloff* case are considerably different to the present situation, the same principle is applicable. The degree of care is extremely high."

In relation to dangerous products such as herbicide, it has been suggested by Mr. Justice Nicholson of P.E.I. that a manufacturer will be held liable in negligence to those suffering damage therefrom unless it establishes that it took "all reasonable and possible care to ensure that the product was safe and reasonably fit for the purpose of controlling weeds . . .". Mr. Justice Nicholson felt that the manufacturer should have known about the "possibility of the damage to the turnip crop". See *Willis* v. *F.M.C. Machinery & Chemicals et al.* (1976), 68 D.L.R. (3d) 127 (P.E.I.).

Another remnant of the inherently dangerous article theory is that the onus of proof is shifted to the manufacturer and the other defendants. For example, in *Ives* v. *Clare Bros. Ltd.*, [1971] 1 O.R. 417, responsibility was attached for a defective gas furnace that caused injury to a homeowner by leakage of gas. Mr. Justice Peter Wright of the Ontario High Court stated:

"Once it is established that injury or damages have been caused by the usage of natural gas through an installation made, installed or serviced by others, the onus of proving that there is no negligence is on each defendant who made, installed or serviced the installation. In other words, the position of an innocent gas user harmed by the use of gas is analogous to that of a pedestrian under s. 106(1) of the Highway Traffic Act."

His Lordship indicated that he was prepared to extend this theory even to ordinary products in these words:

"Although I find this a sure ground for determination of legal problems in the use of natural gas, which our legislation and regulations establish to be hazardous, I would not find it unjust or illogical in the modern world of faceless plants and suppliers to apply it to the case of manufacturers and distant powers generally distributing their products in our society. It seems to be a recognition of the position of the lonely hurt citizen in the face of power so great and so remote that the common injured consumer cannot reasonably be expected to discover the secrets and complexities which may have caused him harm. I do not assert that that is the law of products' liability generally, but I shall not be shocked or surprised when higher authority free to do so avers it to be the law."

Both the producers and the service people were unable to "discharge the burden" and, consequently both were held liable.

It is difficult to tell whether this special category of dangerous articles will eventually disappear or whether it will be expanded to include other products. The concept is not dissimilar to the rule of *Rylands* v. *Fletcher* and it does improve the legal position of the consumer. It would undoubtedly be neater to promote product safety without reliance on such an artificial distinction. Nevertheless, as long as the tradition of bolder judicial approaches is lacking, perhaps this device, which permits an indirect response to a felt social need, is preferable to the *status quo*.

See Stallybrass, "Dangerous Things and Non-Natural User" (1929), 3 Camb. L.J. 376.

NOTES

1. Should the Canadian courts adopt the American theory of strict liability in tort for defective products? See Calabresi, *The Costs of Accidents* (1970); Ison, *The Forensic Lottery* (1967); Weiler, "Defamation, Enterprise Liability and Freedom of Speech" (1967), 17 U. of T.L.J. 278. See also Stradiotto, "Products Liability in Tort", Law Society of Upper Canada, *Special Lectures on New Developments in the Law of Torts* (1973), at p. 174; Thompson, "Manufacturers Liability" (1970), 7 Alta. L. Rev. 305, at p. 314; compare with Linden, *Canadian Tort Law* (2nd ed., 1977).

2. In *Valeri* v. *Pullman Co.* (1914), 218 F. 519 (D.C. U.S.), Mr. Justice Augustus N. Hand commented upon an argument in favour of strict liability as follows:

"My own feeling is that protection to the public lies not so much in extending the absolute liability of individuals, as in regulating lines of business in which the public has a particular interest in such a way as reasonably to insure its safety. In other words, pure food laws, and rigorous inspection of meats, canning factories, and other sources of food supply, would seem to me a much more effective way of protecting the public than by the imposition of the liability of an insurer upon those who furnish food. The former method corrects the evil at its source. The latter method only imposes an obligation in cases which *ex hypothesi* cannot be guarded against by the individual by the exercise of due care. It shifts the loss from the person immediately suffering the injury to a person who has neglected no precaution in supplying the food. This certainly is not in accord with the general tendencies of the common law. I am inclined to think that the imposition of such an obligation would tend to lead in the long run to the prosecution of unfounded claims, rather than to the protection of individuals or the public."

3. Professor Marcus Plant in an article entitled "Strict Liability of Manufacturers for Injuries Caused By Defects in Products — An Opposing View" (1957), 24 Tenn. L. Rev. 938, wrote:

"It takes very few words to demonstrate that the proposed rule is completely out of accord with modern concepts of justice and legal policy. For more than 150 years the accepted legal basis of tort liability in Anglo-American law has been the general philosophy that, except for intentional wrongdoing, a person should be accorded freedom of action, subject only to the limitation that in exercising this freedom he must use the care which can be expected of a reasonably prudent man. He must meet this social standard; if he does not, he will be held liable for the injuries which he causes. If he fulfills this obligation, however, he is not liable, even though he does in fact cause injury to the person or property of another. In other words, the members of society are protected against injuries resulting from the failure to use due care but they are not guarded against any and all injuries resulting from the voluntary actions of other persons. Whereas primitive law stressed security, modern law stresses freedom of action.

The extent to which this philosophy has contributed to the enormous economic and social progress of this country can probably never be determined with any precision, but that its influence has been profound cannot be doubted. It has enhanced the atmosphere of encouragement to the man who generates new ideas and has a venturesome temperament."

4. Commenting on the deterrence rationale of strict liability, Professor Plant wrote:

"The existing rule of liability based on fault constitutes substantial incentive for a manufacturer to use all known methods of inspection and manufacture to make the product safe. This is particularly true in the light of the willingness of modern courts to allow the question of due care to go to the jury. Unless the manufacturer can prove that he used all of the modern methods available for testing and inspection he is virtually certain to be found negligent and held liable.

Furthermore, what is probably a more powerful incentive to make products as safe as possible lies in the desire of manufacturers to avoid the danger that their products will develop a reputation for being unsafe or defective and therefore be unacceptable to the purchasing public. Every manufacturing executive with whom the writer has discussed this matter regards it as a potential disaster when one of its products is found to be defective and the cause of an injury. The element which is most disturbing to manufacturers is not the potential judgment of legal liability but the injury which is done to the reputation of the product and its producer. While it may be conceivable that the imposition of strict liability could increase in some small measure the pressure upon a few backward manufacturers to make their products safe, it is doubtful that it will add very much to existing pressures."

5. With regard to the loss distribution rationale for strict liability, Professor Plant argued:

"It should be recognized immediately that if this is the motivation for adoption of the rule, its proponents are not primarily concerned with the question of what constitutes justice for the manufacturer. Their principal concern is with what is sometimes euphemistically called 'social engineering', which frequently turns out to be crass expediency seeking its ends without any particular regard for basic principles. In this instance they ask the manufacturer to assume the burden and pass it on simply because they consider him to be in a position to do so. But if this approach is sound, why should we not carry the process still further? If the manufacturer can pass on to society the cost of all injuries arising from product defects, why should he not also be required to pass on to society the losses arising from all other injuries incurred in the course of manufacturing activity? For example, suppose an automobile manufacturer has a delivery truck which carries motors from one plant to another, and that this truck, while being operated with due care, injures a pedestrian. Isn't this as much a 'cost of production' element as an injury arising from a product defect? Ought we not to hold that manufacturer strictly liable for that injury and respond to his protests with the easy answer that he should charge a price for his product which will take into account that a certain number of such injuries are inevitably going to occur because of his industrial activity? If this general policy is expedient for injuries arising from product defects, it is equally expedient for any others. Yet it has not been argued persuasively that such a policy should be followed.

But a more fundamental question is involved. Is it sound to assume that manufacturers in general are in a position to distribute the risk of all product injuries through the price mechanism? There is substantial reason to doubt that such a generalization is valid as to all industries or for all manufacturers in a specific industry. Of course, if one is speaking of a monopoly industry in which the price of the product is or can be dictated by one or a few members, there is a possibility of adjusting price to cover any cost item. Even in a monopoly industry, however, there are likely to be limitations on this possibility. For example, certain products are subject to what economists call an 'elastic demand', *i.e.*, a slight increase in price will cause a sharp reduction in demand or will turn consumers to a substitute product. In such industries the product's price is by no means as adjustable as is assumed by the proponents of strict liability.

The fact is, however, that most of our manufacturing industries are not monopolies in which the manufacturers can dictate price. In these industries prices are determined by a host of factors. The intensity of competition, the stage of the business cycle, the facility with which capital can move in and out of the industry, changes in public desires and tastes, and technological developments in the field are only a few of the variables constantly influencing price and causing price fluctuations. As a result of these economic factors it may often be a matter of pure chance as to whether a given manufacturer or industry can adjust its price structure to absorb a new cost thrust upon it. In the case of an individual, an increase may mean pricing himself out of the market. In the case of an industry a substantial general addition to price may have a devastating effect upon marginal producers. . . .

The point attempted to be made here is that it is not sound thinking to assume, as a general basis for policy determination, that manufacturers are always in an economic position to pass on to the public the risks arising from non-negligently caused product defects. Some manufacturers may be, but it would be astonishing if all are in this fortunate situation. A great deal of economic analysis needs to be done before the validity of this hypothesis can be demonstrated.

If the imposition of strict liability for product defects is to be founded on the expediency and desirability of distributing or (pardon the expression) socializing loss over the general consuming public, would it not be a more honest course and would it not be more economically and socially desirable, frankly to establish a governmental mechanism through which such losses could be fairly distributed through taxation? The writer does not advocate such a step, but it is preferable to adoption of a legal doctrine which seeks to accomplish the same result by throwing this burden on manufacturers in general where its incidence will be determined by chance or by unsystematic and capricious factors. It is dubious social policy to single out a particular group in society and make its members or some of its members bear the cost of what may be a very commendable reform, while everyone else in society operates under an entirely different legal doctrine and philosophy.''

6. **The Pearson Commission** (*Report of the Royal Commission on Civil Liability and Compensation for Personal Injury* (1978)) has suggested the adoption of a regime of strict liability for the producers of defective products. A product would be considered defective "when it does not provide the safety which a person is entitled to expect, having regard to all the circumstances including the presentation of the product". The Commission did not recommend any maximum amount for liability, nor was it willing to exclude liability for developmental risks. See Fleming, "The Pearson Report: Its Strategy" (1979), 42 Mod. L. Rev. 249.

7. Legislative developments are overtaking judicial creativity. The Province of Saskatchewan has extended the liability of manufacturers of consumer products to any persons who "may reasonably be expected to use, consume or be effected by a consumer product" . . . for any "personal injuries" suffered that are "reasonably foreseeable as liable to result from a breach". (See Consumer Products Warranties Act, 1977, Stat. Sask., c. 15, s. 5, s. 27.)

New Brunswick has gone even further enacting legislative strict liability upon suppliers of "consumer products" that are "unreasonably dangerous to person or property because of a defect in design, material or workmanship" for "consumer loss" if the loss is "reasonably foreseeable" at the time of his supply. A consumer loss is one not suffered in a business capacity. (See Consumer Product Warranty and Liability Act 1978, S.N.B. c. C-18.1, not yet in force.)

The Ontario Law Reform Commission, in its excellent Report on Products Liability (1979), has urged the enactment of a statute imposing strict liability on business suppliers of defective products, at least for personal injury or damage to property and any economic loss directly consequent thereon.

Similar developments are taking place in Quebec and have been recommended by the E.E.C. (1976) and the Strasbourg Convention (Council of Europe) (1976). It is, therefore, clear that whether we like it or not, there is a momentum building for legislative reform, which will probably supplant the parallel, though slower, development of the law of products liability.

8. What about a no-fault solution? See O'Connell, *Ending Insult to Injury: No-Fault Insurance for Products and Services* (1975).

REVIEW PROBLEM

In October of 1961, Mrs. Mala went to her doctor, Dr. Donald, complaining about insomnia and inability to conceive. In order to relax her he gave her several sample bottles of a new drug called "Thalidimo" which was manufactured by the Thalidimo Company Ltd. in Toronto. Mrs. Mala, according to his instructions, took one of these pills each day until December 23rd. Each time she did, she had severe pain, a pins and needles feeling, in her left arm and left leg. There was a warning on the bottle of Thalidimo that the pills might cause peripheral neuritis, the symptoms of which are pins and needles.

On November 16, 1961, at a medical convention in Hamburg, Germany, one Dr. Lenz announced that he believed that the drug "Thalidimo" was connected with the increased number of deformed children born in Germany. After further investigation, on December 1st the German government withdrew the drug from the market in Germany. The British government followed suit the next day, as did several other governments. The Thalidimo Company Ltd. in Toronto, after sending two people to Germany to investigate, decided not to withdraw the drug for the time being. Instead, on December 5th the company sent Drug Warning letters to every doctor in Canada. The Drug Warning letter said that there had been some discussion about the relation of the drug Thalidimo and certain congenital deformities in children, but that the evidence of causal relation was uncertain at this time. It concluded with these words: "Thalidimo should not be administered to pregnant women."

Mrs. Mala again visited Doctor Donald on December 23, 1961, at which time he told her that she had become pregnant on Nov. 1st, and that she should discontinue the Thalidimo pills. He had read the Drug Warning Letter on December 6, but had done nothing then.

On March 1, 1962, when the mounting scientific information demonstrated that Thalidimo could cause deformity if taken in the fifth or sixth week of pregnancy, the drug was withdrawn from the Canadian market. Mrs. Mala carried full term and gave birth to a deformed child, Rosa, on July 17, 1962. As a result of all this, Mrs. Mala's mental and physical condition deteriorated and remains poor.

At the trial, without a jury, the Thalidimo Company Ltd. admitted that they had not tested the drug on pregnant animals nor on pregnant women. Various drug industry experts testified that they did not suspect that any drug could affect the development of the foetus, and that no one in the industry did any testing on pregnant women or on animals. Dr. Lenz, on the other hand, testified that he had written several articles in German in which he warned that the foetus could be affected by drugs and that fuller testing procedures should be used. Mrs. Mala proved conclusively that the pills she took in her fifth and sixth week of pregnancy caused the deformity of her daughter.

On this evidence the trial judge dismissed the action of Mrs. Mala and of her daughter Rosa against the Thalidimo Company Ltd. and Dr. Donald. The Court of Appeal affirmed the decision.

You have been appointed to the Supreme Court of Canada and have been asked by the Chief Justice of Canada to write the opinion of the Court. Do so.

CHAPTER 14

ASSESSMENT OF DAMAGES FOR PERSONAL INJURIES AND DEATH

The assessment of damages is one of the most important aspects of tort law and yet it has received, until recently, only scant attention from scholars. The basic aim of the law here is to measure and provide compensation for the unique loss suffered by each individual claimant. As noble as this attempt may be, problems are created. It is a costly and time-consuming process. Moreover, it is very hard to achieve any precision. In recent years, the complexities have multiplied with the advent of tax laws, liability insurance and widespread social legislation. Many tough questions are being asked about the future of tort damages. Should the jury be involved? Should lump sum awards be continued? Should pain and suffering be compensated for? These and other questions are by no means academic because they affect the very underpinnings of tort law.

This chapter is meant to provide only a glimpse of a very large and complex area by raising a few of the fundamental issues.

A. GENERAL PRINCIPLES

CHARLES, "JUSTICE IN PERSONAL INJURY AWARDS"
in Klar (ed.), *Studies in Canadian Tort Law* (1977)

The general objectives of the law in the area of personal injuries can be stated without too much difficulty or disagreement. It is readily agreed that the injured person should be compensated for the loss he has suffered, and where he has died from his injuries, his dependants should be compensated for their loss. There is also public agreement that the law in this area, as in others, should operate uniformly and produce predictable results, while at the same time being fair to both plaintiff and defendant. The average citizen would probably think it reasonable that where the loss suffered by the victim can be quantified in monetary terms with reasonable accuracy, the plaintiff should be compensated to the full extent of his loss. In situations where the loss is of such a nature that it cannot be objectively determined, the plaintiff should nevertheless be awarded damages on the basis of principles which can be rationally supported and which can produce results considered by the public to be generally fair and just.

But while such broad objectives can be enunciated and agreed upon without too much difficulty, their very general nature provides little guidance when a court is required to place a dollar value on particular kinds of personal injuries in specific circumstances. Is it possible for a court, using the existing rules for the assessment of damages, to arrive at a monetary figure which accurately reflects the loss? There is obviously a need for more specific rules or principles, the application of which by the court will enable the law to reach the broad objectives previously suggested. How far have our courts progressed in developing a scientific statement of the law of damages? What are the new problems with which they are forced to cope in their assessment of the amount of compensation to which the plaintiff is entitled? The answers to these questions form the basis of the following discussion of the law of damages.

Although it is necessary for the plaintiff in a personal injury case to establish the liability of the defendant before the question of damages can be considered by the court, the calculation of losses suffered by the plaintiff is of equal, if not greater, importance to both the plaintiff and the defendant. Yet in spite of this obvious truism, most law teachers, students and lawyers, spend relatively little time studying the many problems involved in the calculation of damages, or the rules and principles used by the court in their assessment of the loss suffered. It has been said that "Questions of damages—and particularly their magnitude—do not lend themselves so easily to discourse. Professors dismiss them airily as matters of trial administration. Judges consign them uneasily to juries with a minimum of guidance, occasionally observing loosely that there are no rules of assessing damages in personal injury cases."

In personal injury cases, as with other torts situations, the law, by virtue of the principle of *restitutio in integrum,* seeks to place the victim in the same position he was in before the accident occurred. Since perfect compensation in the sense of physical reconstruction of the victim to his pre-accident condition is generally impossible, the initial premise upon which damage awards are based is that damages should be computed so that the dollars awarded will be an adequate compensation for the loss which was suffered by the injured party. To the extent that money damages can make the victim whole again, the award of compensation is considered to be the fairest solution to both plaintiff and defendant. The plaintiff recovers his losses to a reasonable extent and the defendant is penalized only to the extent that he has to compensate the plaintiff, either personally or through his insurance company. As a matter of practical policy the courts refuse to determine compensation on the basis of the amount of money the plaintiff would have been willing to pay himself in order to avoid the injury or be relieved of it. Such damages, even if measurable and accepted as adequate by the plaintiff, would be so high as to be socially unacceptable.

If it is considered important that justice be done between the parties in relation to the liability question, it is equally important that justice also be done insofar as the assessment of damages is concerned. The generally declining use of juries in personal injury cases in Canada means that the task of awarding proper damages falls more often on the shoulders of the judge. As plaintiffs' counsel present more detailed and sophisticated evidence of losses suffered by their clients as a result of the defendant's acts, judges are forced to think more and more about the principles upon which their damage awards are to be determined. Faced with arguments relating to collateral benefits, inflation, income tax, cost of future case, loss of amenities and loss of expectation of life in complex cases involving severe loss, Canadian judges have been forced in recent years to articulate more clearly than ever before the principles governing the proper assessment of personal injury losses. Such an undertaking raises the question whether the assessment of damages as a process is susceptible to a rational analysis. Perhaps it is so elusive that it must be left to the individual judge to decide, on the basis of his own personal intuition, what level of compensation is fair to both parties. Is it even possible for our judges to formulate principles which can be articulated in an open manner? The degree to which they are, or will be, successful in creating socially acceptable guidelines may be an important factor in the overall public evaluation and acceptance of the tort system as the primary instrument for the provision of compensation to injured persons.

. . .

To establish a cause of action the plaintiff must first prove that he or she suffered injury that was not too remote or, in other words, an injury that was reasonably foreseeable. Damages, on the other hand, are awarded on the basis of losses which result from that injury. Compensability depends, not upon the severity of the injury, but on the consequences to the individual affected by the tortious act. Courts have recognized the fact that different kinds of consequences can ensue from a tortious act. They have done so by establishing several distinct heads of damage:

(a) the physical injury itself and the pain and suffering associated with it up to the time of trial;
(b) disability and loss of amenities before trial;
(c) loss of earnings before trial;
(d) expenses incurred before trial;
(e) pain and suffering expected to be suffered in the future (after trial) either temporarily or permanently;
(f) loss of amenities after trial;
(g) loss of life expectancy;
(h) loss of earnings to be suffered after the trial and into the foreseeable future, and
(i) cost of future care and other expenses.

In the case of personal injury actions resulting in the death of the victim, the law permits an action by the dependants as a class, as well as by the estate, against the wrongdoer. In an action by the dependants, the loss suffered is in most cases primarily financial, but it can also include, as in the case of the death of a parent, loss of guidance and education as well. The common law does not presently recognize loss in the form of grief or *solatium.*

a) SPECIAL AND GENERAL DAMAGES

Some of the damages or losses suffered by the plaintiff will have manifested themselves prior to trial and thus will be capable of precise calculation by the court. Expenses such as physician fees, hospital bills, payment for housekeeping assistance, and lost wages can be easily pinpointed. They are usually agreed to by counsel and designated as special damages. The bulk of the plaintiff's loss, however, might well extend far into the future and be incapable of precise calculation. Pecuniary loss, involving loss of future wages and costs of future medical care, are dealt with separately by the court under the heading of general damages. Losses incurred between the date of the writ and the date of the trial have caused some difficulty. The practice of the courts does not appear to be uniform, with some tribunals treating lost wages as special damages, while others have added them to lump sum awards as general damages.

b) LUMP SUM OR PERIODIC PAYMENTS

Canadian courts have adopted the traditional view that an award of periodic payments is not possible unless both parties consent or it is authorized by statute. The accepted practice is to award a lump sum, in spite of the fact that many of the difficulties encountered by the courts in the determination of damages stem from the necessity of awarding a once-and-for-all payment. Courts are thus forced in many cases to look far into the future and to struggle with a host of unknown factors such as the degree of improvement or deterioration in the victim's physical condition, the economic future the victim might have expected insofar as this relates to loss of future earnings, as well as future costs, particularly medical costs.

Although modern no-fault compensation schemes show a decided preference for a plan based upon periodic payments, the United Kingdom Law Commission has recently concluded that periodic payments should not be introduced into the existing fault system as an alternative mode of compensation. This decision was arrived at after consultation with the public and interested groups and left the Commission in no doubt that "the introduction of a system of periodic payments would meet with vehement opposition" from insurance interests, organizations representing plaintiffs' interests, the Bar Council and the Law Society itself.

The lump sum award procedure appears to have developed without a conscious regard for alternatives, but it appears to have certain attractions for the plaintiff, insurance companies, and courts alike. Even in those countries where choice is possible, claimants appear to prefer a lump sum award. Not only does it give them more flexibility in planning their future, but psychologically a bird in the hand appears to be more satisfying than one in the bush. From the court's point of view the desire to determine disputes with a degree of finality, and to avoid the increased administrative load associated with supervision of periodic payments tends to discourage the use of such payments. For the same reason insurance companies prefer to close their books on a claim and avoid the need to carry cash reserves to cover future payments or increases in awards. There would probably also be some difficulty establishing insurance rates on a short-term basis as well.

Those who advocate periodic payments do so not only because this mode of payment permits a more accurate determination of damages over a long period of time, but in addition such a system eliminates the chance that the victim will not invest his award wisely but will dissipate it and become a charge on society. Unfortunately, little is known about how victims spend their damage awards. If the lump sum awarded is to be retained, one way to protect the successful claimant from his own weakness would be to establish some form of trusteeship to invest, manage and dispurse funds as required by the victim. Periodic payments should be variable, if the effects of inflation are to be adequately countered. This may well require a detailed judicial statement of the assumptions underlying the awards, particularly the future variables such as the degree of disability and the wage rates to be applied. Although much has been written about the difficulties created by the present lump sum award procedure, there is little evidence of a desire within the judiciary or the profession to adopt a periodic payment plan within the existing tort fault system.

NOTES

1. Which of the nine heads of damage listed by Dean Charles are considered special damages and which are general damages? Another way of considering damages is that they may be pecuniary or non-pecuniary. Which of the nine heads of damage are pecuniary and which are non-pecuniary?

2. See *British Transport Commission* v. *Gourley,* [1956] A.C. 185, [1955] 3 All E.R. 796 where Lord Reid stated:

"The general principle on which damages are assessed is not in doubt. A successful plaintiff is entitled to have awarded to him such a sum as will, so far as possible, make good to him the financial loss which he has suffered and will probably suffer as a result of the wrong done to him for which the defendant is responsible. It is sometimes said that he is entitled to *restitutio in integrum,* but I do not think that this is a very accurate or helpful way of stating his right. He cannot in any real sense be restored, even financially, to his position before the accident. If he had not been injured he would have had the prospect of earning a continuing income, it may be, for many years, but there can be no certainty as to what would have happened. In many cases the amount of that income may be doubtful even if he had remained in good health, and there is always the possibility that he might have died or suffered from some incapacity at any time. The loss which he has suffered between the date of the accident and the date of the trial may be certain, but his prospective loss is not. Yet damages must be assessed as a lump sum once and for all, not only in respect of loss accrued before the trial, but also in respect of prospective loss. Such damages can only be an estimate, often a very rough estimate, of the present value of his prospective loss."

3. What do you think of the idea of a lump sum award, which cannot be altered afterwards? What are the advantages and disadvantages of such a scheme?

4. There is seldom any trouble with regard to special damages. However, on occasion, a court may hold that a claimant is trying to recoup costs that are too extravagant. In *Alexandroff* v. *The Queen in Right of Ontario* (1967), 64 D.L.R. (2d) 673; affd. [1970] S.C.R. 753, for example, a claim of $3,844.55 for a two-month holiday in Hawaii on the recommendation of a doctor, while undoubtedly "salubrious", was found to be "asking too much of the defendant", and was reduced by $2,000. Similarly, a claim for $1,295, the cost of seven suits at $185 that were prematurely worn, because of a brace the plaintiff had to wear, was reduced by $700.

5. In *Shearman* v. *Folland*, [1950] 2 K.B. 43, the English Court of Appeal indicated that an injured person might not be able to recover the full cost of a lengthy nursing home stay, but that the normal cost of food and rent should be deducted from this, if they are not incurred. Because the evidence was incomplete, the court deducted only the cost of food at £1 per week for the 55 week period of convalescence.

6. If a keen sailor, as a result of a serious injury to a hand, finds he cannot handle his sailboat without some expensive new equipment, should he be able to recover the actual cost of such equipment from the defendant? Or should it be considered as part of the general damage award? See *Hayes* v. *Nanaimo Shipyard Ltd.*, [1972] 5 W.W.R. 337 (B.C.C.A.).

7. There used to be some difficulty encountered when relatives or friends expended money to assist or to visit injured people, but most of the problems have been resolved in Ontario, where The Family Law Reform Act, 1978, S.O. 1978, c. 2, permits relatives to recover "expenses reasonably incurred for the benefit of the injured person", "a reasonable allowance for travel expenses actually incurred in visiting the injured person during his treatment for recovery" and a "reasonable allowance for loss of income or the value of services where a claimant provides nursing, housekeeping or other services". See s. 60 (2), (a) (b) (c), *infra*.

8. There was also some problem with women being allowed to recover for medical expenses they incurred on the ground that they were "necessaries" which the husband, not the wife, was obligated to provide. See *Oliversen* v. *Mills* (1964), 50 D.L.R. (2d) 768 (B.C.). This foolishness has now been laid to rest by Mr. Justice Haines in *Lang* v. *Gambareri*, [1968] 2 O.R. 736, 70 D.L.R. (2d) 464. See also Family Law Reform Act, 1978, S.O. 1978, c. 2, s. 65.

9. Loss of past income, which is part of the special damages, is normally compensable without any difficulties. Loss of future income, which is part of the general damages, causes more trouble. It is clear that a person with a large income is entitled to full reimbursement for its loss. In *Smith* v. *London & S.W. Ry. Co.* (1870), L.R. 6 C.P. 14, Mr. Justice Blackburn stated: "If a person fires across a road when it is dangerous to do so and kills a man who is in the receipt of a large income he will be liable for the whole damage, however great, that may have resulted to his family, and cannot set up that he could not have reasonably expected to injure anyone but a labourer." Conversely, a person with a small income or no income will be paid only what he actually lost. For some cases dealing with loss of earnings, see *Ferguson* v. *Wink et al.*, [1973] 2 W.W.R. 539 (B.C.S.C.); *Morton* v. *Elston*, [1973] 2 W.W.R. 758 (B.C.C.A.).

10. In Munkman, *Damages for Personal Injuries and Death* (5th ed., 1973), p. 61, the author writes:

"There are two ways of looking at the assessment of damages for the loss of future earnings. One way is to concentrate on *earning capacity*, and value this as a capital asset destroyed or diminished by the accident. Thus Windeyer J., said in *Teubner* v. *Humble* (1963), 108 C.L.R. 491 (High Court of Australia):

> 'I think that the damage arises really from the destruction of a faculty or skill, and that this is the best way in which to consider its assessment.'

It must be remembered that it is an asset of limited duration, like leasehold property or an annuity, and has to be valued accordingly. To make this valuation the court must find as a fact (i) for what period, on a balance of chances, earning ability is reduced and (ii) what, on average, the reduction in earnings will be over that period. Suppose it is £2 a week for 10 years. Then we have to find the value of an annuity of £100 a year for 10 years, and this is not 10 times £100 because, if a fund were set aside at once to pay the annuity, interest would be earned until the fund was exhausted. Annuity tables are worked out allowing for this interest, and may show that the cost of a 10-year annuity is 7 times £100, so we call this '7 years' purchase'.

The other, more old-fashioned approach is to look at the *actual amount of future earnings,* and make an estimated deduction to reduce it to its 'present value', because instead of being received over many years it is received as an immediate lump sum which can be invested and used. This is called 'discounting' the total. Of course if one takes the RATE of earnings instead of the sum total, it can be valued as an annuity by multiplying the rate by so many years' purchase, just as if the case were approached on the basis of earning capacity. The two approaches are not always clearly distinguished in the authorities. The older cases tend to speak in terms of actual future earnings, while the modern practice — except where the injuries are of short duration — is to speak in terms of earning capacity. However, both approaches are legitimate. It will be more convenient to start with total earnings and discount the total where the loss is for a short period such as 18 months, or where there are successive periods with varying rates of loss and the valuation of successive annuities would be awkward. The theoretical difference between loss of earning capacity and loss of earnings is not significant in practice, except where there is an unused earning capacity, a special case to which Prof. Street (*Principles of Law of Damages,* 1962, p. 44) has rightly drawn attention and which is discussed later.

In either case there are many permutations. There may be a total loss of earnings for life; or a permanent partial loss of earnings, either at a fixed rate or at a rate slowly tapering off as the plaintiff becomes readjusted; or a loss, total or partial or tapering, for a limited period. If there is a tapering loss, it will be necessary to estimate an average over the period."

11.   There are a number of helpful works on the law of damages. See generally, in Canada, Goldsmith, *Damages for Personal Injuries and Death in Canada* (1973-77), and 1978 Digest; *Special Lectures of the Law Society of Upper Canada on Assessment of Damages for Personal Injuries* (1958); Carter, "Assessment of Damages for Personal Injuries or Death in the Courts of the Common-law Provinces" (1954), 32 Can. Bar Rev. 713. In England, see Kemp, *The Quantum of Damages in Personal Injury Claims* (4th ed., 1975); Munkman, *Damages for Personal Injuries and Death* (5th ed., 1973); Mayne and McGregor, *Damages* (13th ed., 1972); Street, *Principles of the Law of Damages* (1962); Ogus, *The Law of Damages* (1973); Luntz, *Assessment of Damages for Personal Injury and Death* (1974). In the United States, see Belli, *Modern Damages* (1959-63); Fuchsberg, *Damages* (1965); McCormick, *Damages* (1935). See also Samuels "Damages in Personal Injuries Cases: A Comparative Law Colloquium Report" (1968), 17 Int. & Comp. L.Q. 443.

12.   Where a trial is conducted by a judge with a jury, the quantum of damages is decided by the jury. In provinces like Ontario and British Columbia jury trials are as common as trials without a jury, but in the other provinces jury trials are less common. The jury, if it is required to decide the amount of the award, will be charged by the presiding judge on the law. There is some conflict over whether any dollar figures may be mentioned to the jury by the

judge and by counsel. See Schroeder, "The Charge to the Jury" in Law Society of Upper Canada, *Special Lectures on Jury Trials* (1959).

B. THE TOOLS OF ASSESSMENT

GRAY v. ALANCO DEVELOPMENTS, LTD.

Court of Appeal, [1967] 1 O.R. 597

By **The Court** (Mackay, Kelly and Evans JJ.A.): This action for damages arising out of an automobile accident was tried by Haines J., sitting with a jury. The jury determined liability 75 percent and 25 percent in favour of the plaintiff and assessed his damages as follows:

Special damages	7,600.60
Past loss of wages	9,736.59
General damages	71,000.00

The appeal by the defendant is against both the finding of liability and the award of general damages. At the close of the argument, the appeal as to liability was dismissed for reasons stated by the court at that time. Judgment was reversed on the appeal against the quantum of general damages.

The grounds of appeal in respect of these damages were:

1. The damages assessed by the jury were excessive;
2. The learned trial judge erred in charging the jury that he would advise them of his view of the range of damages if invited and in accepting such an invitation and advising the jury what possible ranges thus undoubtedly stressing portions of the evidence; . . . .

We are of the opinion that on the evidence the award of $71,000 for general damages was so excessive as to warrant interference by this court, and the appeal must be allowed, the verdict as to general damages set aside and a new trial directed, limited to the assessment of general damages.

As there appears to be some divergence of view among the trial judges of this court as to whether it lies within the province of either counsel or trial judges to express to the jury their personal views as to the proper quantum of general damages or to state to the jury the amount of such damages claimed in the statement of claim, we think it desirable that we should consider the question raised by the second ground of appeal and express our opinion thereon. In this case the questioned direction of the learned trial judge was made under the following circumstances.

During the course of his charge to the jury, the learned trial judge stated:

"If you find that you would like to come back and ask me as to what my view, as to the minimum or maximum award might be having regard to what is given in other cases, if you really need that assistance — I am not suggesting that you do — but if you need that assistance, I am prepared to answer the question on the understanding that you are perfectly entitled to disagree with me, and will disagree with me if you don't accept it, then I will give you that minimum or maximum amount but only then. I want you to grapple with this question yourselves, but you are entitled to come back in my view, so long as you thoroughly understand that anything I say is not intended to impose my will upon you. You must not accept it unless you believe that it is right, because you must come to your conclusions independently and therefore anything I say at that time will be only something that you may take into consideration or may not, as you see fit."

Although counsel for the defendant had taken strong objection to this invitation to the jury, when the jury later returned and asked for some guidance as to the range of general damages the learned trial judge after carefully warning them that they were not bound by his opinion said:

> "It is for you, but my opinion is that the lower limit would be in the neighbourhood of $20,000, the upper limit in the neighbourhood of $35,000."

The only case to which we have been referred where a trial judge of his own motion mentioned amounts to the jury is *Bradenburg* v. *Ottawa Electric R. Co.* (1909), 19 O.L.R. 34 (C.A.) at pp. 37-8, *per* Moss C.J.O.:

> "It is urged that the jury may have been improperly influenced by that part of the charge in which the learned trial judge, in directing the attention of the jury to the consideration of what would be a fair and reasonable compensation, mentioned $25,000 as a sum that might appear large to a man who was earning only a few hundred dollars a year, while to a man earning $6,000 a year it was not so much, and also referred to the sum claimed as $50,000. But, reading the charge as a whole, and that is the proper manner to deal with it, and having regard to the further explanations given when the jury were recalled, it seems plain that they were not left under the impression that they were directed as to the amount they were to fix. They were clearly instructed and doubtless fully understood, that it was only by way of illustration that any sum was spoken of, and that they were not to consider it as an instruction or even an indication of the judge's own view.
>
> It was further objected that counsel for the plaintiff, in opening to the jury, should not have named the sum claimed in the statement of claim.
>
> It is not easy to see how the bare mention of something that is fully set out in a pleading can be supposed unduly to affect the mind of a jury. One can scarcely believe that twelve intelligent men could be mislead or influenced by a mere statement of that kind. In this Province it has not been considered objectionable to inform the jury as to the amount of damages claimed: see *Misener* v. *Toronto and York Radial R.W. Co.* (1908), 11 O.W.R. 1064, at p. 1068. And it is questionable whether to-day the courts in England would regard the incident so seriously as in the instance referred to by Lord Halsbury in *Watt* v. *Watt*, [1905] A.C. 115, at p. 118, though they may still discountenance the practice."

It is to be noted that the learned trial judge in the present case did not use figures as an illustration as was done in the *Bradenburg* case, but gave the figures as being his personal view as to the range within which the quantum of damages should fall. [Other cases reviewed.]

In dealing with the disclosure of the amount claimed as general damages in the statement of claim, we are of the opinion that such disclosure is not permissible and does violence to the fundamental right of a litigant in a jury trial to have the quantum of his damages assessed by a jury in the course of a trial properly conducted. The jurors are sworn to reach a verdict solely on the evidence. The amount claimed in the statement of claim is not evidence. It is merely an opinion (frequently extravagant) of the draftsman of the pleading of his view of the maximum amount that a jury might award. It is not evidence properly before a jury. It is an unsworn, unsupported and biased observation.

In considering the practice of counsel or trial judges expressing their views as to the quantum of damages to be allowed, we believe the following principles to be applicable.

Counsel in addressing the jury are limited to reviewing and commenting on the evidence and to the making of submissions which may properly be supported by the evidence adduced. They are not entitled to express their personal opinions on the evidence. The trial judge, however, may not only review and comment on the evidence but he may also, provided that he warns the jury that the facts are within their exclusive jurisdiction and that they do not have to accept his views, express his personal views on the evidence and the credibility of the witness, but he may not go outside the evidence.

In an injury case evidence is usually given by the injured party and by doctors as to the nature and extent of the injuries; the degree of pain and suffering and the extent of the limitation of the enjoyment of the amenities of life resulting, or likely to result from the injuries, but evidence may not be given by such witnesses as to the monetary value to be placed upon such loss. To permit the trial judge to express such an opinion would be to sanction the admission of opinion evidence unsupported by qualified evidence but based solely upon the judge's personal experience derived from the evidence or verdicts in other cases. This would be tantamount to countenancing his usurpation of functions committed exclusively to the jury. Litigants exercising their right to have their cases tried by a jury are entitled to the jury's verdict uninfluenced by anything extraneous to the evidence, proper submissions of counsel thereon, the instructions of the judge as to the law and his summing up of the evidence together with his comments thereon and the credit to be given to it.

Aside from the legal objections to the practice there are practical considerations that weigh against it. In *Ward* v. *James,* [1965] 1 All E.R. 563, Lord Denning M.R., delivering the judgment of a court of five judges, at p. 575, said:

"CAN THE JURY BE GIVEN MORE GUIDANCE?

The other remedy that has been suggested is that the jury should be given more guidance. Two possible ways are put forward: (i) by referring them to awards in comparable cases; (ii) by telling them the conventional figure. I will take them in order.

(i) *Comparable cases.* Before 1951 it was not the practice for counsel to refer the court or the jury to awards in comparable cases. It is obvious that counsel could not call witnesses to give the figures in other cases. Nor could counsel give figures himself from his own experience or from the books. If counsel sought to refer to·any comparable case, it would be rejected out of hand on the ground that it was *res inter alios acta.* Since the case of *Bird* v. *Cocking & Sons, Ltd.,* [1951] 2 T.L.R. 1260, a change has set in. When the case is tried by a judge alone, or heard on appeal by the Court of Appeal, counsel is allowed to refer to awards in comparable cases. This is because we now recognize that the award is basically a conventional figure, and in order to arrive at it, it is relevant to refer to comparable cases. If this be so before a judge alone, or the Court of Appeal, why should it not also be so in trial by jury? Why should the jury not receive the same guidance as a judge?

This sounds well in theory, but in practice it is open to strong objection. During the argument before us both counsel agreed that it would not do. See what would happen! Each counsel would refer the jury to cases which he believed were comparable, but which were not really so. Speeches would be taken up with the one counsel citing analogies and the other destroying them. Then the judge would have to review them all again in his summing-up. The inevitable result would be that the minds of the jury would be distracted from the instant case and left in confusion. If counsel cannot refer the jury to comparable cases, neither can the judge. He cannot, on his own initiative, drag out from the books, or from his own experience, other awards (and tell the jury of them) when counsel have not had an opportunity of commenting on them, or distinguishing them. All in all, I am quite satisfied that the present practice should be maintained where the jury are not told of awards in comparable cases.

(ii) *Conventional figures.* Another suggestion is that the jury should be told of the conventional figures in this way, that the judge should be at liberty in his discretion to indicate to the jury the upper and lower limits of the sum which in his view it would be reasonable to award. Thus in the case of loss of a leg, he might indicate that the conventional figure is between £4,000 and £6,000. This proposal has many attractions. It would give the jury the guidance which they at present lack. But here again we come up against a serious objection. If the judge can mention figures to the jury, then counsel must also be able to mention figures to them. Once that happened, we get into the same trouble again. Each counsel would, in duty bound, pitch the figures as high or as low as he dared. Then the judge would give his views on the rival figures. The proceedings would be in danger of developing into an auction. The objections are so great that both counsel before us agreed that counsel ought not to be at liberty to mention figures to the jury. If this be so, I think that the judge should not do so either. Apart from this, it seems to me that, if the judge were at liberty to mention the upper and lower limits, then in order to be of any real guidance, they would have to be somewhat narrow limits. It would be no use his telling the jury (as judges have done in the past) for the loss of a leg: "Do be reasonable. Don't give as much as £100,000, or as little as £100." The judge would have to come nearer home and say: "The conventional figure in such a case as this is between £4,000 and £6,000." But if he can give them narrow limits of that kind, there is little point in having a jury at all. You might as well let the judge assess the figure himself. I come to the conclusion, therefore, that we must follow the existing practice, and we cannot sanction any departure from it."

We are also aware that judges may vary considerably in their individual appraisal of the proper quantum of damages, for example, for pain and suffering, or for loss of the amenities of life, in any particular case, so that if the practice followed in the present case were to be generally pursued, juries might well be given varying ranges of figures from case to case, having regard to the views entertained by the judge charged with the trial.

What has been stated is applicable to those headings of general damages where there can be no evidence as to the value in monetary terms of the loss sustained, for example damages, claimed for pain and suffering or the loss or diminution of the amenities of life. . . .

[New trial ordered.]

NOTES

1. For a comment on this case, see Watson (1970), 48 Can. Bar Rev. 565.

2. Suppose that the trial judge, instead of giving a top and bottom figure, merely said that (1) the figure mentioned by an actuary was too high, and (2) that if they gave only $5,000, they would be cheap. *Cf., Byron v. Williams* (1968), 67 D.L.R. (2d) 111 (S.C.C.).

3. If the judge cannot give figures and the lawyer cannot give figures, how is the jury able to determine what is a reasonable amount?

4. Once made, it is extremely difficult to upset a jury's damage award. It is not enough to overturn a jury's award that the appellate court merely feels it is too high or too low. A jury assessment may only be upset if the appellate tribunal believes that no 12 people acting reasonably could have given it, if the jury took into account matters they ought not to have considered or if it misunderstood or disregarded its duty. See generally *Davey et al. v. McManus Petroleum Ltd.,* [1949] O.R. 374 (C.A.). If an assessment of damages is made by a trial judge alone, a court of appeal may interfere with it if the trial judge applied a wrong principle of law or if the award is so ordinately high or low that it must be a wholly erroneous estimate of the damage. It is sometimes said that there should be no interference unless the award "shocks the conscience". (See *Alexandroff v. The Queen,* [1970] S.C.R. 753, at p. 770). The Supreme Court

has expressed its reluctance to interfere with the assessments by provincial courts of appeal except in the most exceptional circumstances (as where there has been an error in principle), because it is felt that they are in a better position to decide on the basis of the local environment. See *Gorman* v. *Hertz Drive Yourself Stations* (1965), 54 D.L.R. (2d) 133 (S.C.C.); *Hossack* v. *Hertz Drive Yourself Station* (1965), 54 D.L.R. (2d) 148 (S.C.C.); *Stannard et al.* v. *Kidner* (1973), 34 D.L.R. (3d) 650 (S.C.R.); *Hood* v. *Hood* (1971), 19 D.L.R. (3d) 669, [1972] S.C.R. 244 (S.C.C.): *Fanjoy* v. *Keller* (1973), 38 D.L.R. (3d) 81 (S.C.C.).

5. For an eloquent defence of the jury see Haines, "The Future of the Civil Jury" in Linden, *Studies in Canadian Tort Law* (1968). See also *Special Lectures of the Law Society of Upper Canada,* "Jury Trials" (1959); Joiner, *Civil Justice and the Jury* (1962); Devlin, *Trial by Jury* (1956); Cornish, *The Jury* (1968).

C. GENERAL DAMAGES

ANDREWS v. GRAND & TOY ALBERTA LTD. ET AL.

Supreme Court of Canada. (1978), 3 C.C.L.T. 225

Dickson J.: This is a negligence action for personal injury involving a young man rendered a quadriplegic in a traffic accident for which the respondent Anderson and his employer, Grand & Toy Alberta Ltd., have been found partially liable. Leave to appeal to this court was granted on the question whether the Appellate Division of the Supreme Court of Alberta erred in law in the assessment of damages. At trial Kirby J. awarded $1,022,477.48 [[1974] 5 W.W.R. 675, 54 D.L.R. (3d) 85]; the Appellate Division reduced that sum to $516,544.48 [[1976] 2 W.W.R. 385, 64 D.L.R. (3d) 663].

The amounts awarded in each court under each of the several heads of damages are set out below:

Pecuniary Loss

(a) Cost of Future Care	Trial	Appellate Division
— special equipment	$ 14,200	$ 14,200
— monthly amount	4,135	1,000
— contingencies	20%	30%
— capitalization rate	5%	5%
— life expectancy	45 years	45 years
	$735,594	$164,200
(b) Loss of Prospective Earnings		
— level of earnings	$ 830	$ 1,200
— basic deduction to avoid duplication between the award for future care and that part of the lost earnings that would have been spent on living expenses	440	—
Net	$ 390	$ 1,200
— contingencies	20%	20%
— work span	30.81	30.81
— capitalization rate	5%	5%
Total	$ 59,539	$175,000

Non-Pecuniary Loss
    — pain and suffering
    — loss of amenities
    — loss of expectation of life $150,000 $100,000

Special Damages . . . . $ 77,344 $ 77,344

    Liability is not an issue. The trial judge found that the fault was entirely that of the respondents. The Appellate Division (McDermid J.A. dissenting on this issue) found the appellant James Andrews 25 per cent contributorily negligent. Those findings do not arise for discussion in this appeal. Nor does the question of special damages.

    This court is called upon to establish the correct principles of law applicable in assessing damages in cases such as this where a young person has suffered wholly incapacitating injuries and faces a lifetime of dependency on others. The question of "million-dollar" awards has not arisen in Canada until recently, but within the past several years four such cases have been before the courts, namely, (i) the case at bar; (ii) *Thornton* v. *Bd. of School Trustees of School District No. 6.' (Prince George),* in which the award at trial was $1,534,058.93, reduced on appeal to $649,628.87; (iii) *Arnold* v. *Teno,* also under appeal to this court, in which the award for general damages at trial was $950,000, reduced on appeal to $875,000; (iv) *McLeod* v. *Hodgins* (not reported), in which Robins J. of the Ontario High Court awarded at trial an amount of $1,041,197, of which $1,000,000 was general damages.

    Let me say in introduction what has been said many times before, that no appellate court is justified in substituting a figure of its own for that awarded at trial simply because it would have awarded a different figure if it had tried the case at first instance. It must be satisfied that a wrong principle of law was applied, or that the overall amount is a wholly erroneous estimate of the damage: *Nance* v. *B.C. Electric Ry. Co.,* [1951] A.C. 601, 2 W.W.R. (N.S.) 665, [1951] 3 D.L.R. 705, [1951] 2 All E.R. 448.

    The method of assessing general damages in separate amounts, as has been done in this case, in my opinion, is a sound one. It is the only way in which any meaningful review of the award is possible on appeal and the only way of affording reasonable guidance in future cases. Equally important, it discloses to the litigants and their advisers the components of the overall award, assuring them thereby that each of the various heads of damage going to make up the claim has been given thoughtful consideration.

    The subject of damages for personal injury is an area of the law which cries out for legislative reform. The expenditure of time and money in the determination of fault and of damage is prodigal. The disparity resulting from lack of provision for victims who cannot establish fault must be disturbing. When it is determined that compensation is to be made, it is highly irrational to be tied to a lump-sum system and a once-and-for-all award.

    The lump-sum award presents problems of great importance. It is subject to inflation; it is subject to fluctuation on investment; income from it is subject to tax. After judgment new needs of the plaintiff arise and present needs are extinguished; yet, our law of damages knows nothing of periodic payment. The difficulties are greatest where there is a continuing need for intensive and expensive care and a long-term loss of earning capacity. It should be possible to devise some system whereby payments would be subject to periodic review and variation in the light of the continuing needs of the injured person and the cost of meeting those needs. In making this comment I am not unaware of the negative recommendation of the British Law Commission (Law Com. 56—

Report of Personal Injury Litigation—Assessment of Damages) following strong opposition from insurance interests and the plaintiffs' bar.

The apparent reliability of assessments provided by modern actuarial practice is largely illusionary, for actuarial science deals with probabilities, not actualities. This is in no way to denigrate a respected profession; but it is obvious that the validity of the answers given by the actuarial witness, as with a computer, depends upon the soundness of the postulates from which he proceeds. Although a useful aid and a sharper tool than the "multiplier-multiplicand" approach favoured in some jurisdictions, actuarial evidence speaks in terms of group experience. It cannot and does not purport to speak as to the individual sufferer. So long as we are tied to lump-sum awards, however, we are tied also to actuarial calculations as the best available means of determining amount.

In spite of these severe difficulties with the present law of personal injury compensation, the positive administrative machinery required for a system of reviewable periodic payments and the need to hear all interested parties in order to fashion a more enlightened system both dictate that the appropriate body to act must be the legislature, rather than the courts. Until such time as the legislature acts, the courts must proceed on established principles to award damages which compensate accident victims with justice and humanity for the losses they may suffer.

I proceed now to a brief recital of the injuries sustained by the appellant James Andrews in the present case. He suffered a fracture with dislocation of the cervical spine between the fifth and sixth cervical vertebrae, causing functional transection of the spinal cord but leaving some continuity; compound fracture of the left tibia and left humerus; fracture of the left patella. The left radial nerve was damaged. The lesion of the spinal cord left Andrews with paralysis involving most of the upper limbs, spine and lower limbs. He has lost the use of his legs, his trunk, essentially his left arm and most of his right arm. To add to the misery, he does not have normal bladder, bowel and sex functions. He suffers from spasticity in both upper and lower limbs. He has difficulty turning in bed and must be re-positioned every two hours. He needs regular physiotherapy and should have someone in close association with him at all times, such as a trained male orderly. The only functioning muscles of respiration are those of the diaphragm and shoulders. There is much more in the evidence but it need not be recited. Andrews is severely if not totally disabled. Dr. Weir, a specialist in neurosurgery, said of Andrews' condition that "there is no hope of functional improvement." For the rest of his life he will be dependent on others for dressing, personal hygiene, feeding and, indeed, for his very survival. But, of utmost importance, he is not a vegetable or a piece of cordwood. He is a man of above average intelligence and his mind is unimpaired. He can see, hear and speak as before. He has partial use of his right arm and hand. With the aid of a wheelchair he is mobile. With a specially-designed van he can go out in the evening to visit friends, or to the movies, or to a pub. He is taking driving lessons and proving to be an apt pupil. He wants to live as other human beings live. Since 31st May 1974 he has resided in his own apartment with private attendant care. The medical long-term care required is not at a sophisticated level, but rather at a practical care level.

Andrews was 21 years of age and unmarried on the date of the accident. On that date he was an apprentice carman employed by the Canadian National Railways in the city of Edmonton.

I turn now to consider assessment of the damages to which Andrews is entitled.

1. PECUNIARY LOSS

(a) Future Care

(i) Standard of Care

While there are several subsidiary issues to be decided in this case, there is one paramount issue: in a case of total or near-total disability, should the future care of the victim be in an institutional or a home-care environment? The trial judge chose home care. The Appellate Division agreed that home care would be better but denied it to him. McGillivray C.J.A., who delivered the judgment of the court on this issue, said [pp. 422-23]:

> "All the evidence called supports the proposition that psychologically and emotionally Andrews would be better in a home of his own, where he could be lord of the manor, as it were."

Some evidence even indicated the medical superiority of a home environment.

The trial judge found that it would take $4,135 per month to provide care for Andrews in a home environment. The Appellate Division considered that this standard of care was unreasonably and unrealistically high. Without giving any reason for selecting the particular figure chosen, the Appellate Division substituted $1,000 per month. Obviously, here is the heart of the controversy. On other matters there was substantial agreement between the lower courts.

In my opinion, the court of appeal erred in law in the approach it took. After the statement quoted above, that Andrews would be better psychologically and emotionally in a home of his own, McGillivray C.J.A. referred to some of the evidence supporting that proposition. He quoted the following passage from the evidence of Dr. Weir:

> "Well, I think that the greatest problem they have and the greatest burden of their affliction is the fact that they are all depressed because not only have they lost the potential for many normal and enjoyable human activities, in fact up until the present they pretty well have been converted into life-long inhabitants of a hospital institution; and an institution is an institution, it is virtually a life sentence and has been to this date. I would say that if you really, you know, if you wanted to give him the optimal potential it would be in a home environment in which he had some, in which he had the control of it to the same extent that the rest of us have control over our own homes and dwelling places. I don't really think that any hospital or medical institution has the potential to give someone that same feeling that they are in fact the lords and masters of their own castle."

[The justice noted that Andrews had said he would not live in an institution, and quoted exerpts from the evidence.]

With respect, I agree that a plaintiff must be reasonable in making a claim. I do not believe that the doctrine of mitigation of damages, which might be applicable, for example, in an action for conversion of goods, has any place in a personal injury claim. In assessing damages in claims arising out of personal injuries, the ordinary common law principles apply. The basic principle was stated by Viscount Dunedin in *Admiralty Commrs.* v. *S.S. Susquehanna,* [1926] A.C. 655 at 661 (cited with approval in *H. West & Son* v. *Shephard,* [1964] A.C. 326 at 345, [1963] 2 All E.R. 625), in these words:

> "... the common law says that the damages due either for breach of contract or for tort are damages which, so far as money can compensate, will give the injured party reparation for the wrongful act".

The principle was phrased differently by Lord Dunedin in the earlier case of *Admiralty Commrs.* v. *S.S. Valeria* (No. 2), [1922] 2 A.C. 242 at 248, but to the same effect:

". . . in calculating damages you are to consider what is the pecuniary sum which will make good to the sufferer, so far as money can do so, the loss which he has suffered as the natural result of the wrong done to him."

The principle that compensation should be full for pecuniary loss is well established: see McGregor on Damages, 13th ed. (1972), pp. 738-39, para. 1097:

"The plaintiff can recover, subject to the rules of remoteness and mitigation, full compensation for the pecuniary loss that he has suffered. This is today a clear principle of law."

To the same effect, see Kemp and Kemp, Quantum of Damages, 3rd ed. (1967), vol. 1, at p. 4: "The person suffering the damage is entitled to full compensation for the financial loss suffered." This broad principle was propounded by Lord Blackburn at an early date in *Livingstone* v. *Rawyards Coal Co.* (1880), 5 App. Cas. 25 at 39, in these words:

"I do not think there is any difference of opinion as to its being a general rule that, where any injury is to be compensated by damages, in settling the sum of money to be given for reparation of damages you should as nearly as possible get at that sum of money which will put the party who has been injured, or who has suffered, in the same position as he would have been in if he had not sustained the wrong for which he is now getting his compensation or reparation."

In theory a claim for the cost of future care is a pecuniary claim for the amount which may reasonably be expected to be expended in putting the injured party in the position he would have been in if he had not sustained the injury. Obviously, a plaintiff who has been gravely and permanently impaired can never be put in the position he would have been in if the tort had not been committed. To this extent, restitutio in integrum is not possible. Money is a barren substitute for health and personal happiness, but to the extent, within reason, that money can be used to sustain or improve the mental or physical health of the injured person it may properly form part of a claim.

Contrary to the view expressed in the Appellate Division of Alberta, there is no duty to mitigate, in the sense of being forced to accept less than real loss. There is a duty to be reasonable. There cannot be "complete" or "perfect" compensation. An award must be moderate and fair to both parties. Clearly, compensation must not be determined on the basis of sympathy or compassion for the plight of the injured person. What is being sought is compensation, not retribution. But, in a case like the present, where both courts have favoured a home environment, "reasonable" means reasonableness in what is to be provided in that home environment. It does not mean that Andrews must languish in an institution which on all evidence is inappropriate for him.

The reasons for judgment of the Appellate Division embodied three observations which are worthy of brief comment. The first [p. 424]:

". . . it is the choice of the respondent to live in a home of his own, and from the point of view of advancing a claim for damages, it is a most salutary choice, because it is vastly the most expensive."

I am not entirely certain as to what is meant by this observation. If the import is that the appellant claimed a home life for the sole purpose of inflating his damage claim, then I think the implication is both unfair and unsupported by evidence. There is no doubt upon the medical and other evidence that a home environment would be salutary to the health of the appellant and productive of good effects. It cannot be unreasonable for a person to want to live in a home of his own.

The next observation:

"Secondly, it should be observed that in many cases, particularly in Alberta, where damages have been awarded, the persons injured were going to live with their families. Here, the evidence (in spite of the fact that the respondent's mother advanced a claim for $237 which represented a towing charge for the motor cycle and parking, taxis and bus fare expended on visits to her son in the hospital for approximately a nine-month period prior to the issue of the statement of claim) is that the respondent and his mother were not close before the accident, and matters proceeded on the footing that the mother's natural love and affection should have no part in Andrews' future. Again, this situation is the most expensive from the point of view of the respondent."

The evidence showed that the mother of the appellant James Andrews was living alone in a second-floor apartment and that relations between Andrews and his mother were strained at times. This should have no bearing in minimizing Andrews' damages. Even if his mother had been able to look after Andrews in her own home, there is now ample authority for saying that dedicated wives or mothers who choose to devote their lives to looking after infirm husbands or sons are not expected to do so on a gratuitous basis. The second observation is irrelevant.

The third observation was made in these words:

"Thirdly, it should be observed that the learned trial Judge has referred with approval to the English authorities which held that full compensation for pecuniary loss must be given. It does not, however, follow that every conceivable expense, which a plaintiff may conjure up is a pecuniary loss. On the evidence, then, should this Court consider that Andrews should live in a home of his own for the next 45 years at the expense of the appellant?"

I agree that a plaintiff cannot "conjure up" "every conceivable expense". I do not think that a request for home care falls under that rubric.

Each of the three observations seems to look at the matter solely from the point of view of the respondents and the expense to them. An award must be fair to both parties, but the ability of the defendant to pay has never been regarded as a relevant consideration in the assessment of damages at common law. The focus should be on the injuries of the innocent party. Fairness to the other party is achieved by ensuring that the claims raised against him are legitimate and justifiable.

The Appellate Division relied upon *Cunningham* v. *Harrison,* [1973] Q.B. 942, [1973] 3 All E.R. 463. In that case, as a result of an accident, the plaintiff was permanently paralyzed in his body and all four limbs. The trial judge found that the plaintiff was a self-opinionated person who should, if possible, live in some dwelling of his own where he would be looked after by a housekeeper and the persons who did the nursing. The Court of Appeal held that the plaintiff's entitlement to reasonable expenses for nursing and accommodation appropriate to a normal person should not be increased by reason of his exceptional personality. The Court of Appeal, in reducing the award from £72,616 to £59,316, took into account three factors: (i) the difficulty of obtaining a housekeeper and nurses; (ii) that ground floor flats specially designed for handicapped persons were being built in the borough; (iii) that the plaintiff might accept the aid of statutory and voluntary organizations at much less cost. None of these factors is significant in the present case. Although it reduced the award, the court nevertheless affirmed that the award included provision for a housekeeper and nursing services and also for extra accommodation. The case does not stand for the proposition that though home care is better it will not be provided because the cost is excessive. In the present case, the Appellate Division asked [p. 425]:

"If Andrews does have a home of his own, however, should he not so locate that orderly services from existing hospitals could be available to him at night and in the daytime for his hygienic and getting-up periods? Is it to be assumed that in a province such as Alberta, orderly service could not be given outside the four walls of an institution if the subject of the service is a nearby resident?"

The respondents did not raise the possibility about which the court speculated. There was no evidence as to the feasibility of such a proposal, no evidence as to the availability or cost of out-patient care.

With respect to Andrews' disinclination to live in an institution, the court commented [p. 425]:

"He might equally say that he would not live in Alberta, as he did not wish to face old friends, or for any other reason, and that he wished to live in Switzerland or the Bahamas."

Andrews is not asking for a life in Europe or in the Caribbean. He asks that he be permitted to coninue to live in Alberta and to see his old friends, but in his own home or apartment, not in an institution.

The court then expressed the view that the standard accepted by the trial judge was the equivalent of supplying a private hospital. The term "private hospital" is both pejorative and misleading. It suggests an extravagant standard of care. The standard sought by the appellant is simply practical nursing in the home. The amount Andrews is seeking is, without question, very substantial, but essentially it means providing two orderlies and a housekeeper. The amount is large because the victim is young and because life is long. He has 45 years ahead. That is a long time.

In reducing the monthly amount to $1,000 the Appellate Division purported to apply a "final test", which was expressed in terms of the expenses that reasonably-minded people would incur, assuming sufficient means to bear such expense. It seems to me difficult to conceive of any reasonably-minded person of ample means who would not be ready to incur the expense of home care, rather than institutional care, for himself or for someone in the condition of Andrews for whom he was responsible. No other conclusion is open upon the evidence adduced in this case. If the test enunciated by the Appellate Division is simply a plea for moderation then, of course, no one would question it. If the test was intended to suggest that reasonably-minded people would refuse to bear the expense of home care, there is simply no evidence to support that conclusion.

The Appellate Division, seeking to give some meaning to the test, said that it should be open to consider "standards of society as a whole as they presently exist" [p. 426]. As instances of such standards the court selected the daily allowances provided under The Workers' Compensation Act, 1973 (Alta.), c. 87, s. 56, and the federal Pension Act, R.S.C. 1970, c. P-7, s. 28. The standard of care expected in our society in physical injury cases is an elusive concept. What a legislature sees fit to provide in the cases of veterans and in the cases of injured workers and the elderly is only of marginal assistance. The standard to be applied to Andrews is not merely "provision", but "compensation", i.e., what is the proper compensation for a person who would have been able to care for himself and live in a home environment if he had not been injured? The answer must surely be home care. If there were severe mental impairment or [if this were a case of] an immobile quadriplegic, the results might well be different; but, where the victim is mobile and still in full control of his mental facilities, as Andrews is, it cannot be said that institutionalization in an auxiliary hospital represents proper compensation for his loss. Justice requires something better.

Other points raised by the Appellate Division in support of its reversal of the trial judge may be briefly noted:

(a) "It seems to me probable that . . . there will be, at government expense, people employed to look after quadriplegics. In the United States there are now a few institutions which have special apartments as part of the hospital setting, where patients can receive attention and at the same time have privacy" [p. 429]. There is no evidence that the government of Alberta at present has any plans to provide special care or institutions for quadriplegics. Any such possibility is speculation.

(b) ". . . will the respondent, in fact, operate from a home of his own?" [p. 430]. The court expressed the fear that Andrews would take the award, then go into an auxiliary hospital and have the public pay. It is not for the court to conjecture upon how a plaintiff will spend the amount awarded to him. There is always the possibility that the victim will not invest his award wisely but will dissipate it. That is not something which ought to be allowed to affect a consideration of the proper basis of compensation within a fault-based system. The plaintiff is free to do with that sum of money as he likes. Financial advice is readily available. He has the flexibility to plan his life and to plan for contingencies. The preference of our law to date has been to leave this flexibility in the plaintiff's hands: see Fleming, "Damages: Capital or Rent?" (1969), 19 U. of T. Law Jour. 295. Save for infants and the mentally incompetent, the courts have no power to control the expenditure of the award. There is nothing to show that the dangers the Appellate Division envisaged have any basis in fact.

In its conclusion, the Appellate Division held that the damages awarded by the trial judge were "unreasonably and unrealistically high" [p. 430], and that an award which would result in the appellant receiving approximately $1,000 a month for cost of care would be entirely adequate and would constitute a generous award. The Appellate Division further reduced the award by 30 per cent for potential contingencies. Why $1,000?

The main issue at trial was the choice between home care and institutional care. There is no question but that Andrews could be taken care of in an auxiliary hospital, but both courts below concluded that home care was the appropriate standard. The trial judge made an award reflecting the cost of home care. The Appellate Division made an award related neither to home care nor to institutional care. The effect is to compel a youthful quadriplegic to live the rest of his life in an auxiliary hospital. In my opinion, the Appellate Division failed to show that the trial judge applied any wrong principle of law or that the overall amount awarded by him was a wholly erroneous estimate of the damage. With great respect, the irrelevant considerations which the Appellate Division took into account were errors in law.

Is it reasonable for Andrews to ask for $4,135 per month for home care? Part of the difficulty of this case is that 24-hour orderly care was not directly challenged. Counsel never really engaged in consideration of whether, assuming home care, such care could be provided at lesser expense. Counsel wants the court, rather, to choose between home care and auxiliary hospital care. There are unanimous findings below that home care is better. Although home care is expensive, auxiliary hospital care is so utterly unattractive and so utterly in conflict with the principle of proper compensation that this court is offered no middle ground.

The basic argument, indeed, the only argument, against home care is that the social cost is too high. In these days the cost is distributed through society through insurance premiums. In this respect, I would adopt what was said by Salmon L.J. in *Fletcher* v. *Autocar and Transporters Ltd.,* [1968] 2 Q.B. 322, [1968] 1 All E.R. 726 at 750, where he stated:

"Today, however, virtually all defendants in accident cases are insured.

This certainly does not mean compensation should be extravagant, but there is no reason why it should not be realistic . . . It might result in some moderate increase in premium rates, which none would relish, but of which no-one, in my view, could justly complain. It would be monstrous to keep down premiums by depressing damages below their proper level, i.e., a level which ordinary men would regard as fair—unprejudiced by its impact on their own pockets."

I do not think the area of future care is one in which the argument of the social burden of the expense should be controlling, particularly in a case like the present, where the consequences of acceding to it would be to fail in large measure to compensate the victim for his loss. Greater weight might be given to this consideration where the choice with respect to future care is not so stark as between home care and an auxiliary hospital. Minimizing the social burden of expense may be a factor influencing a choice between acceptable alternatives. It should never compel the choice of the unacceptable.

(ii) Life Expectancy

At trial, figures were introduced which showed that the life expectancy of 23-year-old persons in general is 50 years. As McGillivray C.J.A. said in the Appellate Division, it would be more useful to use statistics on the expectation of life of quadriplegics. A statistical average is helpful only if the appropriate group is used. At trial, Dr. Weir and Dr. Gingras testified that possibly five years less than normal would be a reasonable expectation of life for a quadriplegic. The Appellate Division accepted this figure. On the evidence I am willing to accept it.

(iii) Contingencies of Life

The trial judge did, however, allow a 20 per cent discount for "contingencies and hazards of life". The Appellate Division allowed a further 10 per cent discount. It characterized the trial judge's discount as being for "life expectancy" or "duration of life", and said that this ignored the contingency of "duration of expense", i.e., that despite any wishes to the contrary, Andrews in the years to come may be obliged to spend a great deal of time in hospital for medical reasons or because of the difficulty of obtaining help. With respect, the Appellate Division appears to have misunderstood what the trial judge did. The figure of 20 per cent as a discount for contingencies was arrived at first under the heading of "Prospective Loss of Earnings" and then simply transferred to the calculation of "Costs of Future Care". It was not an allowance for a decreased life expectancy, for this had already been taken into account by reducing the normal 50-year expectancy to 45 years. The "contingencies and hazards of lie" in the context of future care are distinct. They relate essentially to duration of expense and are different from those which might affect future earnings, such as unemployment, accident, illness. They are not merely to be added to the latter so as to achieve a cumulative result. Thus, so far as the action taken by the Appellate Division is concerned, in my opinion, it was an error to increase by an extra 10 per cent the contingency allowance of the trial judge.

This whole question of contingencies is fraught with difficulty, for it is in large measure pure speculation. It is a small element of the illogical practice of awarding lump-sum payments for expenses and losses projected to continue over long periods of time. To vary an award by the value of the chance that certain contingencies may occur is to ensure either over-compensation or under-compensation, depending on whether or not the event occurs. In light of the considerations I have mentioned, I think it would be reasonable to allow a discount for contingencies in the amount of 20 per cent, in accordance with the decision of the trial judge.

(iv) Duplication with Compensation for Loss of Future Earnings

It is clear that a plaintiff cannot recover for the expense of providing for basic necessities as part of the cost of future care while still recovering fully for prospective loss of earnings. Without the accident, expenses for such items as food, clothing and accommodation would have been paid for out of earnings. They are not an additional type of expense occasioned by the accident.

When calculating the damage award, however, there are two possible methods of proceeding. One method is to give the injured party an award for future care which makes no deduction in respect of the basic necessities for which he would have had to pay in any event. A deduction must then be made for the cost of such basic necessities when computing the award for loss of prospective earnings, i.e., the award is on the basis of net earnings and not gross earnings. The alternative method is the reversal, i.e., to deduct the cost of basic necessities when computing the award for future care and then to compute the earnings award on the basis of gross earnings.

The trial judge took the first approach, reducing loss of future earnings by 53 per cent. The Appellate Division took the second. In my opinion, the approach of the trial judge is to be preferred. This is in accordance with the principle which I believe should underlie the whole consideration of damages for personal injuries: that proper future care is the paramount goal of such damages. To determine accurately the needs and costs in respect of future care, basic living expenses should be included. The costs of necessaries when in an infirm state may well be different from those when in a state of health. Thus, while the types of expenses would have been incurred in any event, the level of expenses for the victim may be seen as attributable to the accident. In my opinion, the projected cost of necessities should, therefore, be included in calculating the cost of future care, and a percentage attributable to the necessities of a person in a normal state should be reduced from the award for future earnings. For the acceptability of this method of proceeding see the judgment of this court in *Regina* v. *Jennings,* [1966] S.C.R. 532 at 540-41, 57 D.L.R. (2d) 644, affirming [1965] 2 O.R. 285, 50 D.L.R. (2d) 385 at 418 (sub nom. *Jennings* v. *Cronsberry*), and also *Bisson* v. *Powell River* (1967), 62 W.W.R. 707 at 720-21, 66 D.L.R. (2d) 226, affirmed without written reasons 64 W.W.R. 768, 68 D.L.R. (2d) 765 n (Can.).

(v) Cost of Special Equipment

In addition to his anticipated monthly expenses, Andrews requires an initial capital amount for special equipment. Both courts below held that $14,200 was an appropriate figure for the cost of this equipment. In my opinion, this assessment is correct in principle, and I would therefore accept it.

(b) Prospective Loss of Earnings

We must now gaze more deeply into the crystal ball. What sort of a career would the accident victim have had? What were his prospects and potential prior to the accident? It is not loss of earnings but, rather, loss of earning capacity for which compensation must be made: *Regina* v. *Jennings,* supra. A capital asset has been lost: what was its value?

(i) Level of Earnings

The trial judge fixed the projected level of earnings of Andrews at $830 per month, which would have been his earnings on 1st January 1973. The Appellate Division raised this to $1,200 per month, a figure between his present salary and the maximum for his type of work of $1,750 per month. Without doubt the value of Andrews' earning capacity over his working life would have been higher than his earnings at the time of the accident. Although I am inclined to view even that figure as somewhat conservative, I would affirm the holding of the Appellate Division that $1,200 per month represents a reasonable estimate of Andrews' future average level of earnings.

(ii) Length of Working Life

Counsel for the appellants objected to the use of 55 rather than 65 as the projected retirement age for Andrews. It is agreed that he could retire on full pension at 55 if he stayed with his present employer, Canadian National Railways. I think it is reasonable to assume that he would, in fact, retire as soon as it was open for him to do so on full pension.

One must then turn to the mortality tables to determine the working life expectancy for the appellant over the period between the ages of 23 and 55. The controversial question immediately arises whether the capitalization of future earning capacity should be based on the expected working life span prior to the accident, or the shortened life expectancy. Does one give credit for the "lost years"? When viewed as the loss of a capital asset consisting of income-earning capacity rather than a loss of income, the answer is apparent: it must be the loss of that capacity which existed prior to the accident. This is the figure which best fulfils the principle of compensating the plaintiff for what he has lost: see Mayne and McGregor on Damages, 12th ed. (1961), at p. 659; Kemp and Kemp, Quantum of Damages, vol. 1 (Supp.), c. 3, p. 28; *Skelton* v. *Collins* (1966), 39 A.L.J.R. 480, 115 C.L.R. 94. In the instant case, the trial judge refused to follow the *Oliver* v. *Ashman,* [1962] 2 Q.B. 210, [1961] 3 All E.R. 323, approach, the manifest injustice of which is demonstrated in the much-criticized case of *McCann* v. *Sheppard,* [1973] 1 W.L.R. 540, [1973] 2 All E.R. 881, and in this I think the judge was right. I would accept his decision that Andrews had a working life expectancy of 30.81 years.

(iii) Contingencies

It is a general practice to take account of contingencies which might have affected future earnings, such as unemployment, illness, accidents and business depression. In the *Bisson* case, supra, which also concerned a young quadriplegic, an allowance of 20 per cent was made. There is much support for the view that such a discount for contingencies should be made: see, e.g., *Warren* v. *King,* [1964] 1 W.L.R. 1, [1963] 3 All E.R. 521; *McKay* v. *Bd. of Govan School Unit No. 29,* 64 W.W.R. 301, [1968] S.C.R. 589, 68 D.L.R. (2d) 519. There are, however, a number of qualifications which should be made. First, in many respects, these contingencies implicitly are already contained in an assessment of the projected average level of earnings of the injured person, for one must assume that this figure is a projection with respect to the real world of work, vicissitudes and all. Second, not all contingencies are adverse, as the above list would appear to indicate. As is said in *Bresatz* v. *Przibilla,* 108 C.L.R. 541, [1963] A.L.R. 218, in the Australian High Court, at p. 544: "Why count the possible buffets and ignore the rewards of fortune?" Finally, in modern society there are many public and private schemes which cushion the individual against adverse contingencies. Clearly, the percentage deduction which is proper will depend on the facts of the individual case, particularly the nature of the plaintiff's occupation; but generally it will be small: see J.H. Prevett, "Actuarial Assessment of Damages: The Thalidomide Case—I" (1972), 35 Modern Law Rev. 140 at 150.

In reducing Andrews' award by 20 per cent Kirby J. gives no reasons. The Appellate Division also applied a 20 per cent reduction. It seems to me that actuarial evidence could be of great help here. Contingencies are susceptible to more exact calculation than is usually apparent in the cases: see A.T. Traversi,

"Actuaries and the Courts" (1956), 29 Australian Law Jour. 557. In my view, some degree of specificity, supported by evidence, ought to be forthcoming at trial.

The figure used to take account of contingencies is obviously an arbitrary one. The figure of 20 per cent which was used in the lower courts (and in many other cases), although not entirely satisfactory, should, I think, be accepted.

(iv) Duplication of the Cost of Future Basic Maintenance

As discussed, since basic needs such as food, shelter, and clothing have been included in the cost of future care, a deduction must be made from the award for prospective earnings to avoid duplication. The injured person would have incurred expenses of this nature even if he had not suffered the injury. At trial evidence was given that the cost of basics for a person in the position of Andrews prior to the accident would be approximately 53 per cent of income. I would accept this figure and reduce his anticipated future monthly earnings accordingly to a figure of $564.

(c) Considerations Relevant to Both Heads of Pecuniary Loss

(i) Capitalization Rate: Allowance for Inflation and the Rate of Return on Investments

What rate of return should the court assume the appellant will be able to obtain on his investment of the award? How should the court recognize future inflation? Together these considerations will determine the discount rate to use in actuarially calculating the lump sum award.

The approach at trial was to take as a rate of return the rental value of money which might exist during periods of economic stability, and consequently to ignore inflation. This approach is widely referred to as the Lord Diplock approach, as he lent it his support in *Mallett* v. *McMonagle,* [1970] A.C. 166, [1969] 2 All E.R. 178. Although this method of proceeding has found favour in several jurisdictions in this country and elsewhere, it has an air of unreality. Stable, non-inflationary economic conditions do not exist at present, nor did they exist in the recent past, nor are they to be expected in the foreseeable future. In my opinion, it would be better to proceed from what known factors are available rather than to ignore economic reality. Analytically, the alternate approach to assuming a stable economy is to use existing interest rates and then make an allowance for the long-term expected rate of inflation. At trial the expert actuary, Mr. Grindley, testified as follows:

> "Yes, as I mentioned yesterday, I was comfortable with that assumption— 5 per cent interest—because it produces the same result as, for example, 8 per cent interest and 3 per cent inflation . . .
>
> "I would be happy to use either of the following two packages of assumption: either an 8 per cent interest rate combined with provision for amounts which would increase 3 per cent in every year in the future, or a 5 per cent interest rate and level amount, level amounts, that is, no allowance for inflation."

One thing is abundantly clear: present interest rates should not be used with no allowance for future inflation. To do so would be patently unfair to the plaintiff. It is not, however, the level of inflation in the short term for which allowance must be made, but that predicted over the long term. It is this expectation which is built into present interest rates for long-term investments. It is also this level of inflation which may at present be predicted to operate over the lifetime of the plaintiff to increase the cost of care for him at the level accepted by the court, and to erode the value of the sum provided for lost earning capacity.

In *Bisson* v. *Powell River,* supra, the British Columbia Court of Appeal held that there had been a misdirection, or non-direction amounting to misdirection, in the trial judge's charge to the jury with respect to quantum of damages for the plaintiff's personal injuries. Bull J.A. listed several instances of misdirection, including failure to instruct the jury that although they might give some thought to possibilities of future inflation it was wrong to include any built-in inflation factors in the actuarial calculations with respect to the sums for future care and loss of prospective earnings. An appeal to this court was dismissed, Cartwright C.J.C. giving short oral reasons as follows [p. 768, W.W.R.] :

> "We are all of opinion that the court of appeal were right in holding that they were justified in setting aside the assessment of damages made by the jury. In such circumstances they had jurisdiction under R. 36 of the British Columbia court of appeal Rules to reduce the damages instead of ordering a new trial. We find ourselves unable to say that in fixing the amount of damages the court of appeal erred in principle or that the figure at which they arrived was such as to represent a wholly erroneous estimate."

In my opinion, this cannot be taken as an express endorsement by this court of the method of calculation expressed by Bull J.A. When discussing this issue, Bull J.A. stated that the correct procedure was to use a capitalization rate of 5 or 6 per cent, since there was evidence that 6 per cent was a normal and available rate of return on first-class securities, and not to build in any inflation rate at all. With respect, I cannot understand how thought is to be given to the possibility of inflation in calculating the award if no inflation factor is to be built into the calculation of the award. In his judgment, Bull J.A. further states, at p. 723:

> "If inflationary trends appear, it may well be that the use to which the money is put, whatever it may be, will itself increase its own amount as part of an inflationary process. It is well known that interest rates, or the 'wages' of money, rise in times of inflation."

One might offer two comments: First, the words "If inflationary trends appear" reflect economic conditions in 1967, when serious inflation was only on the horizon. During the past ten years, inflation has become one of the most serious Canadian problems. This court, in *Reference Re Anti-Inflation Act,* [1976] 2 S.C.R. 373, 68 D.L.R. (3d) 452, 9 N.R. 541, recognized the Anti-Inflation Act, 1974-75-76 (Can.), c. 75, as a measure necessary to meet a situation of economic crisis imperilling the well-being of the people of Canada as a whole. Second, the passage immediately above-quoted accepts the proposition that interest rates or the "wages" of money rise in times of inflation. This rise is attributable, at least in part, to the erosion of the dollar. Accepting the highly unlikely proposition that the appellant will be able to invest for the balance of his lifetime at current high rates the capital sum awarded to him, this investment will provide him with a constant number of dollars each year, but the services which those dollars will provide will become more costly by the year. If current high interest rates abate with a reduction of inflationary pressures and return, say, to the 1967 rates of 5 or 6 per cent, it is obvious that re-investment from time to time in later years of the equities or fixed income securities comprising the capital sum will be at rates which fall far short of those at present available. Then, even the number of dollars the appellant gets will be less than *even the present cost of care.* With respect, the economic analysis in *Bisson* proceeds on the erroneous basis that the cost of services decreases as the rate of inflation decreases. On the contrary, a decrease in the rate of inflation merely results in a lower rate of increase in the cost of these services.

In *Schroth* v. *Innes,* [1976] 4 W.W.R. 225, 71 D.L.R. (3d) 647 (B.C. C.A.), Bull J.A., delivering the judgment of the court, repeated his views on this matter.

Again, the relevance of inflation was recognized in principle but was excluded from the calculation of the award. At p. 236, Bull J.A. states, ". . . it is today's money to which the respondent Shiels is entitled in damages." With respect, we are not concerned only with today's money. The real concern is in determining what that money will provide in the way of services over the next 45 years.

Bull J.A. voiced his disapproval of any recognition for inflation, whether by building in an inflation factor while using current rates of return or by using a hypothetical "stable state". The learned judge attempted to refute the conclusion that inflation should be included. He said, at p. 239:

> "With the greatest deference, I do not agree with the basic premises of those conclusions. To me what was really said was that current interest rates, much higher than those prevailing in the old days of the so-called 'stable economy', exist only because of an existing inflated economy and the current fear of future inflation; and hence should not be used unless future inflation estimates or factors are fed into the computer also. That may well be so in England but I am not prepared to accede to that proposition with respect to this country. I think it general knowledge that interest rates in Canada for many years have reached higher levels because of the desire and need to attract new capital from abroad to create and service our expanding industrial and commercial economy. But I content myself with saying that I am satisfied that the current high rates of interest (which have been with us for years with only modest variations up and down) reflect today the present value of already inflated money in exactly the same way as do current high wages and prices generally. They live together, and the use of a high level of wages as one side of the coin and a low level of interest for the other is, in my respectful view, wrong."

In my opinion, this analysis is manifestly in error. Fear of future inflation is not confined to England. It is such as to have constituted a national emergency in this country. The current high rates of interest do not merely reflect the present value of already inflated money. They reflect the present expectation of *future* inflation. This is not the only factor which determines the existing interest rate, but it is without doubt one of the major factors. In my opinion, recognition of this fact must be made in the calculations of a damage award.

The approach which I would adopt, therefore, is to use present rates of return on long-term investments and to make some allowance for the effects of future inflation. Once this approach is adopted, the result, in my opinion, is different from the 5 per cent discount figure accepted by the trial judge. While there was much debate at trial over a difference of a half to one percentage point, I think it is clear from the evidence that high quality long-term investments were available at time of trial at rates of return in exess of 10 per cent. On the other hand, evidence was specifically introduced that the former head of the Economic Council of Canada, Dr. Deutsch, had recently forecast a rate of inflation of 3½ per cent over the long-term future. These figures must all be viewed flexibly. In my opinion, they indicate that the appropriate discount rate is approximately 7 per cent. I would adopt that figure. It appears to me to be the correct result of the approach I have adopted, i.e., having regard to present investment market conditions and making an appropriate allowance for future inflation. I would, accordingly, vary to 7 per cent the discount rate to be used in calculating the present value of the awards for future care and loss of earnings in this case. The result in future cases will depend upon the evidence adduced in those cases.

(ii) Allowance for Tax

In *Regina* v. *Jennings,* supra, this court held that an award for prospective income should be calculated with no deduction for tax which might have been attracted had it been earned over the working life of the plaintiff. This results from the fact that it is earning capacity and not lost earnings which is the subject of compensation. For the same reason, no consideration should be taken of the amount by which the income from the award will be reduced by payment of taxes on the interest, dividends, or capital gain. A capital sum is appropriate to replace the lost capital asset of earning capacity. Tax on income is irrelevant either to decrease the sum for taxes the victim would have paid on income from his job, or to increase it for taxes he will now have to pay on income from the award.

In contrast with the situation in personal injury cases, awards under The Fatal Accidents Act, R.S.A. 1970, c. 138, should reflect tax considerations, since they are to compensate dependants for the loss of support payments made by the deceased. These support payments could only come out of take-home pay, and the payments from the award will only be received net of taxes: see the contemporaneous decision of this court in *Keizer* v. *Hanna.*

The impact of taxation upon the income from the capital sum for future care is mitigated by the existence of s. 110(1)(*c*)(iv.1) [en. 1973-74, c. 14, s. 35] of the Income Tax Act, 1970-71-72 (Can.), c. 63, in respect of the deduction of medical expenses, which provides that medical expenses in excess of 3 per cent of the taxpayer's income include "remuneration for one full-time attendant upon an individual who was a taxpayer . . . in a self-contained domestic establishment in which the cared-for person lived." This exemption, I should think, permits a deduction for the payment of one full-time attendant for seven days a week, regardless of whether this attendance is provided by several attendants working over 24-hour periods, or one person working 24-hour shifts seven days a week.

The exact tax burden is extremely difficult to predict, as the rate and coverage of taxes swing with the political winds. What concerns us here is whether some allowance must be made to adjust the amount assessed for future care in light of the reduction from taxation. No such allowance was made by the courts below. Elaborate calculations were provided by the appellant to give an illusion of accuracy to this aspect of the wholly speculative projection of future costs. Because of the provision made in the Income Tax Act, and because of the position taken in the Alberta courts, I would make no allowance for that item. The Legislature might well consider a more generous income tax treatment of cases where a fund is established by judicial decision and the sole purpose of the fund is to provide treatment or care of an accident victim.

One subsidiary point should be affirmed with respect to the determination of the present value of the cost of future care. The calculations should provide for a self-extinguishing sum. To allow a residual capital amount would be to overcompensate the injured person by creating an estate for him. This point was accepted by the lower courts and not challenged by the parties.

2. NON-PECUNIARY LOSS

Andrews used to be a healthy young man, athletically active and socially congenial. Now he is a cripple, deprived of many of life's pleasures and subjected to pain and disability. For this, he is entitled to compensation. But the problem here is qualitatively different from that of pecuniary losses. There is no medium of exchange for happiness. There is no market for expectation of life. The monetary evaluation of non-pecuniary losses is a philosophical and policy exercise more than a legal or logical one. The award must be fair and reasonable, fairness being gauged by earlier decisions; but the award must also of necessity be arbitrary or conventional. No money can provide true restitution. Money can provide for proper care: this is the reason that I think the paramount concern of the courts when awarding damages for personal injuries should be to ensure that there will be adequate future care.

However, if the principle of the paramountcy of care is accepted, then it follows that there is more room for the consideration of other policy factors in the assessment of damages for non-pecuniary losses. In particular, this is the area where the social burden of large awards deserves considerable weight. The sheer fact is that there is no objective yardstick for translating non-pecuniary losses, such as pain and suffering and loss of amenities, into monetary terms. This area is open to widely extravagant claims. It is in this area that awards in the United States have soared to dramatically high levels in recent years. Statistically, it is the area where the danger of excessive burden of expense is greatest.

It is also the area where there is the clearest justification for moderation. As one English commentator has suggested, there are three theoretical approaches to the problem of non-pecuniary loss (A.I. Ogus, "Damages for Lost Amenities: For a Foot, a Feeling or a Function?" (1972), 35 Modern Law Rev. 1). The first, the "conceptual" approach, treats each faculty as a proprietary asset with an objective value, independent of the individual's own use or enjoyment of it. This was the ancient "bot", or tariff system, which prevailed in the days of King Alfred, when a thumb was worth 30 shillings. Our law has long since thought such a solution unsubtle. The second, the "personal" approach, values the injury in terms of the loss of human happiness by the particular victim. The third, or "functional" approach, accepts the personal premise of the second, but rather than attempting to set a value on lost happiness it attempts to assess the compensation required to provide the injured person "with reasonable solace for his misfortune". "Solace" in this sense is taken to mean physical arrangements which can make his life more endurable rather than "solace" in the sense of sympathy. To my mind, this last approach has much to commend it, as it provides a rationale as to why money is considered compensation for non-pecuniary losses such as loss of amenities, pain and suffering, and loss of expectation of life. Money is awarded because it will serve a useful function in making up for what has been lost in the only way possible, accepting that what has been lost is incapable of being replaced in any direct way. As Windeyer J. said in *Skelton* v. *Collins*, supra, at p. 131:

> "He is, I do not doubt, entitled to compensation for what he suffers. Money may be a compensation for him if having it can give him pleasure or satisfaction . . . But the money is not then a recompense for a loss of something having a money value. It is given as some consolation or solace for the distress that is the consequence of a loss on which no monetary value can be put."

If damages for non-pecuniary loss are viewed from a functional perspective, it is reasonable that large amounts should not be awarded once a person is properly provided for in terms of future care for his injuries and disabilities. The money for future care is to provide physical arrangements for assistance, equipment and facilities directly related to the injuries. Additional money to make life more endurable should then be seen as providing more general physical arrangements above and beyond those relating directly to the injuries. The result is a coordinated and interlocking basis for compensation, and a more rational justification for non-pecuniary loss compensation.

However one may view such awards in a theoretical perspective, the amounts are still largely arbitrary or conventional. As Denning L.J. said in *Ward* v. *James*, [1966] 1 Q.B. 273, [1965] 1 All E.R. 563, there is a great need in this area for assessability, uniformity and predictability. In my opinion, this does not mean that the courts should not have regard to the individual situation of the victim. On the contrary, they must do so to determine what has been lost. For example, the loss of a finger would be a greater loss of amenities for an amateur pianist than for a person not engaged in such an activity. Greater compensation would be required to provide things and activities which would function to make up for this loss. But there should be guidelines for the translation into monetary terms of what has been lost. There must be an exchange rate, albeit conventional. In *Warren* v. *King,* supra, at p. 528, the following dictum of Harman L.J. appears, which I would adopt, in respect of the assessment of non-pecuniary loss for a living plaintiff:

> "It seems to me that the first element in assessing such compensation is not to add up items as loss of pleasures, of earnings, of marriage prospects, of children and so on, but to consider the matter from the other side, what can be done to alleviate the disaster to the victim, what will it cost to enable her to live as tolerably as may be in the circumstances?"

Cases like the present enable the court to establish a rough upper parameter on these awards. It is difficult to conceive of a person of his age losing more than Andrews has lost. Of course, the figures must be viewed flexibly in future cases in recognition of the inevitable differences in injuries, the situation of the victim, and changing economic conditions.

The amounts of such awards should not vary greatly from one part of the country to another. Everyone in Canada, wherever he may reside, is entitled to a more or less equal measure of compensation for similar non-pecuniary loss. Variation should be made for what a particular individual has lost in the way of amenities and enjoyment of life, and for what will function to make up for this loss, but variation should not be made merely for the province in which he happens to live.

There has been a significant increase in the size of awards under this head in recent years. As Moir J.A., of the Appellate Division of the Alberta Supreme Court, has warned: "To my mind, damages under the head of loss of amenities will go up and up until they are stabilized by the Supreme Court of Canada": *Hamel* v. *Prather,* [1976] 2 W.W.R. 742 at 748, 66 D.L.R. (3d) 109. In my opinion, this time has come.

It is customary to set only one figure for all non-pecuniary loss, including such factors as pain and suffering, loss of amenities and loss of expectation of life. This is a sound practice. Although these elements are analytically distinct, they overlap and merge at the edges and in practice. To suffer pain is surely to lose an amenity of a happy life at that time. To lose years of one's expectation of life is to lose all amenities for the lost period, and to cause mental pain and suffering in the contemplation of this prospect. These problems, as well as the fact that these losses have the common trait of irreplaceability, favour a composite award for all non-pecuniary losses.

There is an extensive review of authorities in the court of appeal judgment in this case as well as in the *Thornton* and *Teno* cases, to which I have referred. I need not review these past authorities. What is important is the general picture. It is clear that until very recently damages for non-pecuniary losses, even from very serious injuries such as quadriplegia, were substantially below $100,000. Recently, though, the figures have increased markedly. In *Jackson* v. *Millar,* [1976] 1 S.C.R. 225, 59 D.L.R. (3d) 246, this court affirmed a figure of $150,000 for non-pecuniary loss in an Ontario case of a paraplegic. However, this was done essentially on the principle of non-interference with awards allowed by provincial Courts of Appeal. The need for a general assessment with respect to damages for non-pecuniary loss, which is now apparent, was not as evident at that time. Even in Ontario, prior to these recent cases, general damages allocable for non-pecuniary loss, such as pain and suffering and loss of amenities, were well below $100,000.

In the present case, $150,000 was awarded at trial, but this amount was reduced to $100,000 by the Appellate Division. In *Thornton* and *Teno*, $200,000 was awarded in each case, unchanged in the provincial Courts of Appeal.

I would adopt as the appropriate award in the case of a young adult quadriplegic like Andrews the amount of $100,000. Save in exceptional circumstances, this should be regarded as an upper limit of non-pecuniary loss in cases of this nature.

Total Award

This is largely a matter of arithmetic. Of course, in addition, it is customary for the court to make an overall assessment of the total sum. This, however, seems to me to be a hangover from the days of global sums for all general damages. It is more appropriate to make an overall assessment of the total under each head of future care, prospective earnings, and non-pecuniary loss, in each case in light of general considerations such as the awards of other courts in similar cases and an assessment of the reasonableness of the award.

In the result I would assess general damages for the appellant Andrews as follows:

1. PECUNIARY LOSS

    (a) Cost of future care

— special equipment	$14,200
— amount for monthly payments (monthly amount $4,135; life expectancy 45 years; contingencies 20 per cent; capitalization rate 7 per cent)	557,232

    (b) Prospective loss of earnings

(monthly amount $564; work span 30.81 years: contingencies 20 per cent; capitalization rate 7 per cent)	69,981

2. NON-PECUNIARY LOSS

— compensation for physical and mental pain and suffering endured and to be endured, loss of amenities and enjoyment of life, loss of expectation of life	100,000
Total General Damages	$741,413
Rounded off at	$740,000

To arrive at the total damages award, the special damages of $77,344 must be added to give a final figure of $817,344.

The appellant Andrews will have judgment for 75 per cent of that amount, that is, $613,008.

The appellants should have their costs in this court and in the trial court. The respondents should have their costs in the court of appeal as they achieved substantial success in that court in respect of the finding of contributory negligence on the part of Andrews.

Appeal allowed.

NOTES

1. This case was the first of a trilogy whereby the Surpreme Court of Canada has sought to reconstruct the Canadian law of damages for personal injuries. See Charles, "A New Handbook on the Assessment of Damages in Personal Injury Cases from the Supreme Court of Canada" (1977-78), 3 C.C.L.T. 344. See also Charles, "Justice in Personal Injury Awards: The Continuing Search for Guidelines" in Klar (ed.), *Studies in Canadian Tort Law* (1977), p. 37.

2. The second case of the trilogy was *Thornton* v. *Board of School Trustees of School District No. 57 (Prince George) et al.* (1978), 3 C.C.L.T. 257 (S.C.C.), where a 15-year-old student in B.C. was rendered quadriplegic when he fractured his back doing gymnastics at school. Mr. Justice Dickson made these comments during the course of his reasons for judgment:

"The observation that the large award was warranted by reason of change in medical evidence, not change in legal principle, is worthy of note. It recognizes the revolution in rehabilitative and physical medicine in recent years. The current enlightened concept is to dignify and accept the gravely injured person as a continuing, useful member of the human race, to whom every assistance should be afforded with a view to his re-integration into society. Formerly, the gravely handicapped were relegated to institutions where they could look forward to little other than an early demise. They die, according to Dr. Ezzedin, because 'there is nothing to help them to live.'"

As for the damages to be awarded for future care, Mr. Justice Dickson stated:

"In my opinion, the Court of Appeal erred in law in the approach it took toward the standard of care. According to the medical evidence, the very length of life of the youthful quadriplegic is directly proportional to the nature of the care provided. With home care the injured person can be expected to live a normal, or almost normal, life-span. With institutional care it can be expected that he will not live a normal life-span. It is difficult, indeed impossible, to fashion a yardstick by which to measure 'reasonableness' of cost in relation to years of life. It is sufficient, I think, for the purposes of the present case, to say that before denying a quadriplegic home care on the ground of 'unreasonable' cost something more is needed than the mere statement that the cost is unreasonable. There should be evidence which would lead any right-thinking person to say: 'That would be a squandering of money—no person in his right mind would make any such expenditure.' Alternatively, there should be evidence that proper care can be provided in the appropriate environment at a firm figure less than that sought to be recovered by the plaintiff.

In the case at hand a number of expert witnesses, all highly qualified, representing various disciplines, appeared before the court and advocated a particular type of care. In general terms, they would be aware of the cost of that care. Is it to be supposed that, as responsible people, they would recommend a particular standard of care if they thought that standard wildly extravagant or foolish? If there be a body of opinion holding that view then the burden was on the respondents to make that opinion known during trial. The defence did not call any evidence to rebut either the standard of care or the cost of care evidence tendered on behalf of the appellant. I think the award of the trial judge for cost of future care should stand. His judgment, if I may say so, shows thoughtful and anxious consideration of every aspect of this difficult case."

In relation to non-pecuniary loss, Mr. Justice Dickson observed:

". . . *Pain and Suffering, Loss of Amenities, Loss of Expectation of Life*

It will be recalled that, under this heading, the trial judge assessed the sum of $200,000. The Court of Appeal was of the opinion that the amount awarded by the trial judge, though generous, was not so inordinately high as to constitute a wholly erroneous award. The court considered that there was little to distinguish the condition of the appellant in this case from that of the appellant in the *Andrews* case. The Court of Appeal made no reduction under this head in the sum of $200,000.

The award under non-economic related heads of damage should be a conventional Canadian award, adjusted to meet the specific circumstances of the individual case. I am in agreement with the Court of Appeal that the pain and suffering, loss of amenities, loss of enjoyment of life and loss of expectation of life experienced by Thornton are essentially similar to that experienced by Andrews. Both were active young men with an abundance of life's pleasures before them. Both are now quadriplegics, although both are mentally unimpaired and both are mobile when provided with proper assistance. For the reasons expressed by me in *Andrews* I would reduce the award for non-pecuniary loss to $100,000."

In summary, he awarded the following damages:

"GENERAL DAMAGES

A. Pecuniary Loss

I. *Cost of Future Care*

   (a) Initial capital outlay for:

Home	$ 45,000
Econo-van motor vehicle	8,500
Home-care equipment	12,000

   (b) Capitalized annual cost of future care (monthly amount of $4,305; life expectancy of 49 years; contingencies at 20%; capitalization rate at 7%)   586,989

II. *Loss of Future Earnings*

   ($407 per month; workspan of 43 years; contingencies at 10%; capitalization rate at 7%)   61,254

B. Non-Pecuniary Loss

   Compensation for physical and mental pain and suffering endured and to be endured, loss of amenities and enjoyment of life and loss of expectation of life . . . .   <u>100,000</u>

   TOTAL GENERAL DAMAGES . . . .   <u>$813,743</u>

                           Rounded off at . . <u>$810,000</u>

To arrive at the total damages awarded, the special damages of $49,628, which includes $7,500 to be held in trust for the appellant's mother, must be added to give a final figure of $859,628."

3. The third case of the trilogy was *Arnold* v. *Teno* (1978), 3 C.C.L.T. 272, where a 4½-year-old girl ran onto the road after buying an ice cream from a vending truck and was struck and rendered virtually totally disabled for life. Mr. Justice Spence commented upon the award of the court as follows:

"There remains for consideration the question of the quantum of damages. The problem of quantum of damages in serious personal injury cases is a most difficult one and has been considered by this court in not only the present appeal but, as I have said, in two other appeals argued just prior to the argument in the present appeal, namely, *Andrews* v. *Grand & Toy Alta. Ltd.* and *Thornton* v. *Bd. of School Trustees of School District No. 57*. In all three cases, the plaintiffs suffered extremely serious personal injuries. There are, however, very considerable differences in the three appeals. In the first place, the plaintiff in the present appeal was, at the time of her injuries, a 4½-year-old little girl. In *Andrews* v. *Grand & Toy Alta. Ltd.*, the plaintiff was, at the time of the accident, a young man 21 years of age, gainfully employed. In *Thornton* v. *Bd. of School Trustees of School District No. 57*, the plaintiff was, at the time of the accident, a 15-year-old boy. Therefore, in *Andrews* the court had a good basis for a consideration of the important topic in the fixing of the quantum of damages, that is, the loss of income, and even in *Thornton,* with a youth of Gary Thornton's age, the court had much more solid ground upon which to proceed. On the other hand, as I have said, the plaintiff in the present appeal was a 4½-year-old girl at the time of the accident. Secondly, the injuries in both the *Andrews* and *Thornton* cases resulted in conditions of quadriplegia with no impairment of mental faculties. The injuries to the present plaintiff, as I shall show hereafter, were very different, consisting chiefly of injuries to the brain with resultant physical disabilities and with a very considerable mental impairment. There are other differences between the three appeals but the above recital is sufficient to demonstrate that no general formulation can be used to reach a common result.

A similarity of verdicts may well be considered desirable and of some assistance in the settlement of future cases prior to judical consideration of them, or in the assessment of the damages allowed upon such consideration, but it must be realized that that goal of similarity is one quite impossible to attain and that each case of assessment of damages for personal injuries must be determined in the consideration of the individual circumstances, the personality of the plaintiff, and many other particular aspects of each case.

. . .

. . . It should be stressed that in such a case as the present one, and indeed in the other personal damage actions to which I have referred above, the prime purpose of the court is to ensure that the terribly injured plaintiff should be adequately cared for during the rest of her life. That end having been attained, other elements of damage are of lesser importance.

. . .

I am of the view that annual amounts should only be calculated from the time the infant plaintiff would have reached 20 years of age until she would have reached the normal retirement age in industry today of 65 years. Moreover, when we assume that the plaintiff would have been a wage earner, we must also consider that all wage earners are faced with possibilities of failure through illness short of death, financial disasters, personality defects, and other causes. I, therefore, believe that we should allow a 20 per cent contingency deduction from the $7,500 to make a net annual loss of income of $6,000, and then calculate the present value of payments of $6,000 commencing at the time the infant plaintiff whould have attained the age of 20 years and continuing until she would have reached 65 years. That present value, in my view, should be calculated at the same discount rate of 7 per cent as the present value of the amount provided for future care for the reasons which I have discussed above. This calculation appears hereafter in my summary.

There remains the assessment of the quantum of non-pecuniary damages. These damages are spoken of as 'compensation' for pain and suffering, loss of amenities of life, loss of expectation of life—a grant of largely subjective considerations the very naming of which indicates the impossibility of precise assessments. I have recited above in very complete detail the evidence and report of a pre-eminent medical specialist. I repeat his conclusion: 'This accident has produced one of the most disabled children I have ever seen'. The learned trial judge in his global award of $950,000 assigned $200,000 as non-pecuniary damages. The Court of Appeal, despite vigorous attacks on that amount by counsel for all defendants, confirmed that amount. The same counsel launched the same attack in this court.

The real difficulty is that an award of non-pecuniary damages cannot be 'compensation'. There is simply no equation between paralyzed limbs and/ or injured brain and dollars. The award is not reparative: there can be no restoration of the lost function. There can be no doubt that awards for non-pecuniary damages in the immediate past have been increasing apace in their amounts. In the case of many verdicts in the United States, it may well be said that they have been soaring. The reasons are probably many. Firstly, I have pointed out the impossibility of accurate assessment. Then there must be many cases of what really are expressions of deep sympathy for the terribly injured plaintiff and a mistaken feeling that his or her sore loss of the amenities of life may be assuaged by the feeling of satisfaction from a pocketful of money. There might even be some element of punishment for the wrongdoer or, the most irrelevant of considerations, a measuring of the depth of the defendant's purse. Certainly, such awards, which one may well characterize as exorbitant, fail to accord with the requirement of reasonableness, a proper gauge for all damages.

I repeat my view expressed earlier that in these cases of very serious personal injuries the prime purpose in fixing an award of damages is the provision of adequate reasonable care for the plaintiff for the rest of the plaintiff's life. This I have attempted above by providing a fund from which may be drawn annually the necessary sum for care and attention and by an award for loss of future income from which she may supply the ordinary necessities of life. I have reached these two amounts without regard for any social impact of the admittedly, and necessarily, large award. Indeed, the social burden may only be borne by a proper and reasonable assessment of the amounts. Under the present common law system of liability for fault, there can be no excuse for foisting on the public the burden of caring for the plaintiff or supplying her with the necessities of life. However, that accomplished, and I hope I have accomplished it, one may and should have regard for the social impact of very large and, as I have said, non-compensatory awards for non-pecuniary damages. The very real and serious social burden of these exorbitant awards has been illustrated graphically in the United States in cases concerning medical malpractice. We have a right to fear a situation where none but the very wealthy could own or drive automobiles because none but the very wealthy could afford to pay the enormous insurance premiums which would be required by insurers to meet such exorbitant awards.

One solution might be that discussed in some English cases, i.e., to confine the non-pecuniary damages to 'an arbitrary conventional sum'. This solution I seek to avoid. Rather, I adopt the course taken by my brother Dickson in *Andrews,* that is, to fix the non-pecuniary damages by reference to a rational basis for them. If one realizes, as did my brother Dickson, that it is impossible to compensate for the losses of the various elements involved in non-pecuniary damages and that it is reasonable, none the less, to make an award, then gauge that award by attempting to set up a fund from which the plaintiff may draw, not to compensate for those losses, but to provide some substitute for those amenities. As Harman L.J. put it so well in *Warren* v. *King,* [1963] 3 All E.R. 521 at 528: 'what can be done to alleviate the disaster to the victim, what will it cost to enable her to live as tolerably as may be in the circumstances?'

I am in respectful agreement with Dickson J. that there should be uniformity, always allowing flexibility to meet each differing individual case, in awards for non-pecuniary damages. Perhaps one should say that there must be upper limits with awards lower in some cases and higher in exceptional cases. Dickson J. has found $100,000 as being the upper limit in both *Andrews* and *Thornton.* As I have pointed out, those were both cases of young men turned into quadriplegics by the accidents but whose mental faculties were unimpaired and who, by use of wheelchairs and appropriate automotive vehicles, will be able to get about amongst their fellow men.

The infant plaintiff Diane Teno, although not completely paralyzed, is so disabled that her very limited ability to walk is accomplished in such an awkward fashion as to cause her continual embarrassment. Her left arm is very clumsy, her right is useless because of spastic weakness, her speech is impaired and nearly unintelligible and her mental impairment has reduced her to the 'dull normal range'. I am of the opinion that such a condition justifies a very generous award to permit the infant plaintiff to find some way by which her life may be made a little more tolerable. Moreover, the infant plaintiff in the present appeal has a life expectancy of 66.9 years while Andrews has a life expectancy of only 45 years and Thornton only 49 years. Therefore, despite the fact that the infant plaintiff, unlike Andrews and Thornton, will not need the frequent actual treatment required by the latter two, such as turning in bed every two hours, the other circumstances to which I have referred justify the allowance of the same sum of $100,000 to her under this heading of non-pecuniary damages.

The result of these reasons I would summarize as follows:

Firstly, the respondent Orville Teno is entitled to retain his judgment against all the defendants for special damages fixed at $14,979.62 of which sum he is to hold $7,500 in trust for his wife, Yvonne Teno.

Secondly, the respondent Diane Teno is entitled to the following sums:

(1) *For future care*
To provide a fund of $21,000 per annum for
57 years calculated at a discount rate of 7 per
cent $294,387.00

To provide an additional sum of $6,000 per
annum commencing in 1984 (when she attains
the age of 19 years) and continuing for the
balance of her life . . . . $ 54,735.00
(This sum will have generated a fund of
$82,708 by 1984.)

(2) *Loss of future income* . . . . $ 54,272.00
(Fixed at $6,000 per year for 45 years com-
mencing in 1984 when this sum at a discount
rate of 7 per cent will have accumulated a
fund of $82,008.)

(3) *Non-pecuniary damages* $100,000.00
(4) *Management fee* . . . . $ 35,000.00

TOTAL damages of Diane Teno $538,394.00
rounded out at . . . . $540,000.00"

4. Professor Charles has summarized the effect of these three cases (and the *Keizer* v. *Hanna* case) in his article, "A New Handbook on the Assessment of Damages in Personal Injury Cases from the Supreme Court of Canada" (1977-78), 3 C.C.L.T. 344, at p. 346, as follows:

"The rules or principles of law to be applied in the assessment of damages in personal injury cases as enunciated by the Supreme Court in *Andrews, Thornton, Teno* and *Keizer* may be summarized as follows:

(1) The judge should assess damages using an itemization approach rather than a global approach.
(2) Courts should continue to use actuarial evidence as long as lump sum payments are made, but with the realization that actuarial predictions are not as accurate in relation to individual cases as they might seem to be.
(3) General principles:
    (a) The mitigation of damage principle has no place in personal injury cases.
    (b) There should be full compensation for pecuniary loss.
    (c) The law cannot provide perfect or complete compensation and the plaintiff has a duty to be reasonable in his claim.
    (d) The award must be moderate and fair to both parties.
    (e) Compensation must not be determined on the basis of sympathy for the victim but neither should the court try to punish the defendant.
(4) The primary or guiding principle in total disability cases is to ensure that

the injured plaintiff should be adequately cared for during the rest of his or her life.

(5) A lump sum should be awarded to cover all non-pecuniary losses such as (i) pain and suffering, (ii) loss of amenities, and (iii) loss of enjoyment of life. The upper limit in most total disability cases will be $100,000 unless exceptional circumstances exist.

(6) In computing lost future earnings, the court should take into account various factors that might increase or decrease the plaintiff's earning capacity. This will, in most cases, result in a reduction of the amount computed, but, in most cases, the percentage reduction will be small.

(7) When capitalizing to present value, courts should recognize the effects of inflation upon damage awards and the fact of high interest rates. This can best be done by adopting a discount rate of 7 per cent in relation to sums awarded for cost of future care and loss of future earnings.

(8) Allowance for tax:
  (a) In non-fatal injury cases the effect of taxation is not to be considered in computing loss of future earnings or in relation to taxation of the award.
  (b) In fatal injury cases the effect of taxation upon the lost dependency is to be taken into account.

(9) Credit should be given for the "lost years". Capitalization of future earning capacity should be based on the expected working life span prior to the accident rather than the shortened life span.

(10) In computing the future loss earnings of a very young child, it is not proper to assume that the child will necessarily adopt the vocation of the parent and to calculate lost future earnings on this basis.

(11) In cases where the plaintiff is mentally incapable of handling his or her own affairs, it is proper to add a management fee to the damage award.

(12) The cost of providing basic necessities should be deducted from the award for loss of future income rather than from the award for cost of future care.

It is clearly the intention of the Supreme Court of Canada that the principles and rules concerning assessment of damages in personal injury cases, which it has taken pains to lay down in the four cases under review, should form the basis upon which lower courts can, and should, approach the problem of personal injury claims."

See also Bisset-Johnson, "Damages for Personal Injuries—The Supreme Court Speaks" (1978), 24 McGill L.J. 316; Feldthusen & McNair, "General Damages in Personal Injury Suits: The Supreme Court's Trilogy" (1978), 28 U. of T.L.J. 381.

5. Do you agree with the sentiments expressed by Mr. Justice Dickson about the defects in the methods used to calculate damages for personal injuries and the need for legislative action? Mr. Justice Keith, the trial judge in the *Arnold* v. *Teno* case, admitted that "setting a dollar figure by way of compensation for personal injuries must be one of the most inexact sciences known to man rather in the category of economic or weather forecasting". See (1974), 7 O.R. (2d) 276.

6. Is the concept of "home care" adopted by Mr. Justice Dickson a sound one?

Contrast with *Cunningham* v. *Harrison*, [1973] 3 W.L.R. 97 (C.A.), where £56,00 general damages were awarded to a quadriplegic. On the question of whether he should be allowed money to purchase his own bungalow and special nursing care because his personality was such that he could not live in a nursing home, Denning M.R. said:

"For his own sake, it would be better for him to be on his own. But should it all be charged on the defendant? Is it often said that a wrongdoer must take his victim as he finds him. But I do not think that should be carried to the length here claimed.

There should be moderation in all things, even in a claim for personal injuries. Let him have all such reasonable expenses as are appropriate to a normal person so placed, but let them not be increased by his special personality."

Which approach to this issue do you prefer?

7. What do you think about the maximum figure of $100,000 established for non-pecuniary losses? Why should there be a maximum for this type of loss but not for pecuniary loss?

8. Mr. Justice Wright has eloquently described the goal of the courts in assessing non-pecuniary damages for loss of amenities in *V. v. C.,* [1972] 2 O.R. 723, as follows:

[Courts provide] "money solace for the blinded who will miss the pleasures of sight; the legless who cannot enjoy his walking excursions; the fly fisherman who cannot fish; the athlete who cannot play; the deafened who cannot hear loved music; the dancer, the chess player, the sport, indeed, all these who have or should have enjoyed life in their own way but can do so no longer by reason of the injuries".

Are these matters less important than pecuniary losses?

9. The suggested maximum for non-pecuniary damages has not been uniformly adhered to by all courts across Canada. The Ontario Court of Appeal in *Fenn* v. *Peterborough* (1979), 9 C.C.L.T. 1 awarded $125,000 under this head and explained:

"In this case there are two factors which justify an award somewhat higher than $100,000. Firstly, the trial in this case (the point in time as of which damages are to be assessed) took place approximately a year and a half after the latest of the trials in the trilogy of cases decided by the Supreme Court. It is apparent that during that time there has been an appreciable erosion in the value of money. Secondly, it appears that Sandra Fenn has suffered substantially more pain than any of the plaintiffs in *Teno, Andrews* and *Thornton*. We do not in any way wish to minimize the suffering of the plaintiffs in any of those three cases. Assuredly, any of these plaintiffs suffers terribly with the dawn of each new day which renews the recognition of cold reality. However, unlike the other plaintiffs, Sandra Fenn suffered excruciating, prolonged, raw physical pain which requires an increase in her assessment of damages. Taking into account these two additional factors, an appropriate figure for general damages would be $125,000."

Similarly, Mr. Justice Fulton in *Lindal* v. *Lindal,* [1978] 4 W.W.R. 592 (B.C.) expressed the view that the door was open to awards in excess of $100,000 for non-pecuniary loss and awarded an amount of $135,000 on the ground that the injuries were more serious than in *Andrews.*

10. The discount rate of 7 percent used in *Andrews* has come under severe attack. The Ontario Court of Appeal in *Fenn* v. *Peterborough, supra,* has indicated that the 7 percent figure adopted by the Supreme Court of Canada was not the discount rate as "a matter of law". It approved instead a figure of 3 percent which it said was supported by the expert evidence in the case before it as the difference between the inflation rate and the probable investment return. See also *Julian* v. *Northern & Central Gas Corp.* (1978), 5 C.C.L.T. 148 (Ont.). What is the importance of the percentage used?

What do you think about the reduction of 20 percent for the contingencies of life? In *Lan* v. *Wu* (1978), 7 C.C.L.T. 314 (B.C.), Mr. Justice Bouck refused to deduct anything for contingencies, saying that "there is hardly a shred of acceptable evidence which indicates life will get worse in the years to come. If anything it should get better."

11. How was the question of income tax handled by the Supreme Court? Is it possible that an award should be increased, rather than decreased, because it may be taxed in future? On the matter of income tax and damage awards, see Bale, *"British Transport Commission* v. *Gourley,* Reconsidered" (1966), 44 Can. Bar Rev. 66 and (1966), 44 Can. Bar Rev. 724; Vineberg, "Deductability of Income Taxes in Measuring Compensation for Personal Injuries" (1956), 34 Can. Bar Rev. 940; Jolowicz, "Damages and Income Tax", [1959] Camb. L.J. 86;

Iverach, "Tax Considerations in Damage Awards—Is *The Queen* v. *Jennings* the Final Rule in Canada?" (1973), 11 Alta. L. Rev. 153.

12. How much should a court award to a thalidomide child who is born with flippers for arms and no legs? What if the child has normal legs but only flippers for arms? See *S and another* v. *Distillers Co. (Biochemicals), Ltd.; J and another* v. *Distillers Co. (Biochemicals), Ltd.,* [1969] 3 All E.R. 1412, where Mr. Justice Hinchcliffe assessed £52,000 for the former and £32,000 for the latter. Because of a settlement only 40 percent of these amounts were paid by the defendant. Mr. Justice Hinchcliffe explained his award as follows:

"It is on this evidence that the court has to determine what in all the circumstances of the case is fair and reasonable compensation not only for the plaintiffs but also for the defendants. In every case where a person has been severely injured by the negligence of another the assessment of damages is not an easy matter. Mathematical accuracy is impossible, and there is no yardstick by which the court can measure the disability. But an assessment has to be made, and a fair and moderate value has to be placed on the disability and on the consequential loss. Actuarial aids are sometimes helpful, but they are not the be-all and end-all of this difficult matter. In the long run it is the court which takes into consideration all the circumstances of the case, that is to say, the deprivation, the loss of earning capacity and the cost of special expenses, and then decides what is fair compensation to both parties. The assessment of the global sum is based on experience and by the application of reasonable common sense and according to social standards as reflected in the general level of awards by the courts. In these two cases the problem is more difficult since there are no awards in comparable cases to guide the court. These children were born deformed, they have never known what it is to have their limbs or to be accepted by their fellow creatures; they will never know what it is to play games with other children, to be treated as normal.

. . .

Never can there have been two cases where there are so many imponderable factors. It is fair to say that the court is asked to speculate on every aspect of damage. If ever there was a case where a broad view should be taken as to what is just and reasonable compensation, this is it. . . .

In my judgment, a fair and reasonable sum to award R.S. for general damages is £32,000. Actuarial calculations to which evidence was directed do not disclose a very different figure from my finding. I take the 5 percent table for reasons that I have given. I take special care at £250 a year: annuity value required £3,200. I take the loss of wages at £1,500 a year; annuity value £10,700 after allowing for *Gourley*. One gets a total of £13,900. For loss of amenities . . .

I award R.S. £18,000, making a total of £31,900. It is not so very far away from my global sum. The third check on the figure of £32,000 is that, if it was invested carefully, it would be sufficient to keep R.S. free from financial worry and would go some way towards ameliorating the discomfort and deprivations that he is bound to suffer.

. . .

So far as D.J. is concerned I award him £52,000. To test this figure by the actuarial calculations, again I take the 5 percent table. Special care I put at £1,000; annuity value £13,200, but I think that this should be discounted a little because the help will not always be required full-time. I take the view that the fair figure for the annuity value would be £10,400. Loss of wages I take at £1,500 and, allowing for *Gourley*, the figure is £13,200. The total of these two sums is £23,600. For loss of amenities, . . . I award the sum of £28,000, making a total of £51,600. Of course the award is for £52,000. This sum properly invested will also give adequate security."

13. The cases brought on behalf of the thalidomide children in England and elsewhere in the world raised many legal issues. Among them was the question of the proper amount of damages to be awarded. On the basis of this assessment by Mr. Justice Hinchcliffe, over 60 cases were settled in the United Kingdom. In 1973, a furor developed in the United Kingdom press and in Parliament over the lack of compensation for the other 350 or so thalidomide children. Finally, after many draft offers by Distillers were rejected, the defendants agreed to pay some £20,000,000 for the benefit of the children. An amount of £6,000,000 was to be distributed among the children as private money, based on 40 percent of Hinchcliffe J.'s guidelines, adjusted upwards by 33 percent because of inflation. These individual figures would be determined initially by a Panel of Assessment, composed of seven barristers, with an appeal to a judge. The balance of £14,000,000 is to be paid over a seven year period into a trust fund on behalf of all the thalidomide children. In Australia, after protracted litigation, similar settlements have been arrived at. Elsewhere in the world, agreements in varying amounts were also reached. See *Suffer the Children: The Story of Thalidomide* (1979), for the full story as written by the staff of the London Sunday Times. See also Sjöström and Nilsson, *Thalidomide and the Power of the Drug Companies* (1973).

14. In Canada, there were some 74 thalidomide children born. An action on behalf of 8 of them, brought in Ohio against Richardson-Merrell, the American distributor, was settled in 1968 for an undisclosed amount said to include, however, an annuity that would provide financial security to the children. In 1971, 12 more cases on behalf of Canadian children were settled on largely the same basis. In 1973, a class action was commenced in Ohio on behalf of the remaining uncompensated Canadian children and another action was started in New Jersey for most of the Quebec children. The federal government wrote to the parents of each of the known children informing them of their rights. In Alberta, counsel was appointed by the government to assist the Alberta children and a settlement on their behalf was promptly reached. Eventually all the remaining claims were settled for lump sums, ranging from $100,000 to $999,000. See *Suffer the Children, supra,* p. 136.

15. Was the award of Mr. Justice Hinchcliffe an "adequate" one? What would be an adequate sum for a thalidomide child? Should a lump sum award be allowed in such a case? What are the advantages and disadvantages? Why do you think that most of the Canadian children sued in the United States? What would be the advantages of such a course?

16. As for the matter of the use of actuarial evidence, see Prevett, "Actuarial Assessment of Damages: the Thalidomide Case" (1972), 35 Mod. L. Rev. 140, 257. See also *White et al.* v. *Parkin,* [1974] 3 W.W.R. 509 (B.C.), where Berger J. stated that the practice in British Columbia justifies the use of actuarial evidence. His Lordship disagreed with Mr. Justice Winn in an English decision, who suggested that such evidence was "imprecise" and "non-scientific". Berger J. concluded:

"He preferred to rely on instinct. But so long as we make lump sum awards, once and for all, in personal injury cases, the methods we use will necessarily be imprecise and non-scientific. Nothing in [the U.K. cases] convinces me that we would be any better off by trying to work out a multiplicand and then choosing a multiplier and getting a total in that way, as the English courts do; indeed. . . on the whole we would be worse off. This is not to say that I adopt the assumptions made by the actuary regarding inflation and interest rates. I must take the long view about such matters."

17. How much compensation should be paid for a broken leg that eventually mends? The damages can vary from as little as $1,000 or so to as much as $20,000, depending on whether there is any continuing disability. Should someone who earns their living in physical work receive more general damages than someone with a sedentary job? Should someone who likes sports receive more than someone who does not engage in sport? Should an older person who mends more slowly receive more than a younger person, who heals quickly?

18. Should we compensate people who suffer "whiplash" injuries? These are extremely common, resulting usually from rear-end collisions which make up about one-half of all reported accidents. Sometimes, the plaintiff merely has a stiff neck for a few days, but on other occasions the trauma can be serious. Consider the case of *Fanjoy* v. *Keller* (1973), 38 D.L.R. (3d) 81 (S.C.C.), where the plaintiff, a physician, suffered a whiplash injury that caused considerable pain and discomfort resulting in a loss of enjoyment of life as well as a reduction of earnings. In his judgment, restoring the general damage award of $25,000 granted by the trial judge, Spence J. stated:

". . . it is my reluctant conclusion that the learned Justices of Appeal simply regarded the appellant's injury as an ordinary kind of whiplash. There can be no exact alignment of the awards necessary to compensate plaintiffs in these personal injury cases. Each case must stand on its own feet and be determined upon the evidence given in the particular case. The evidence in this case showed that this was not ordinary whiplash but was a very disabling injury which had already persisted for three years and which the orthopaedic surgeon thought might continue for another two or three years. The injury was suffered by a man who was engaged in a highly-skilled profession and the exercise of the skills in that profession required him to engage in movements which were made most difficult and sometimes impossible by the disability which he suffered."

See Ashe, "Medico-Legal Aspects of Whiplash Injuries to the Neck" (1957), 4 Med. Trial Techniques 55; Seletz, "Whiplash Injuries — A New Concept and the Medico-Legal Implications" (1959-60), 6 Med. Trial Techniques 59.

19. See also *Darmanin* v. *Szczesny*, [1970] 3 O.R. 724 (C.A.), where a 22-year-old female school teacher suffered such an injury in a rear-end auto collision. She suffered a 10 percent restriction in movement of her neck to the left and required physiotherapy and drugs to alleviate arm and neck pain which she might suffer for up to three years. A jury awarded general damages of $1,000. In allowing her appeal, and ordering a new trial, Aylesworth J.A. stated, "The injury fortunately was not extensive as such injuries go. . . . We are all of the opinion that that award is so inordinately low as to require our interference. It is of no consequence that every member of the court, had he been sitting as a trial judge without a jury, would have allowed more, but what is important is that taking into consideration all of the evidence the conscience of the court is shocked as to the inadequacy of the award."

20. How much should be awarded to someone who has lost a kidney due to an accident? In *Gambino* v. *Di Leo* (1971), 17 D.L.R. (3d) 167, Mr. Justice Osler awarded $20,000 to the infant plaintiff, relying in large measure on the increased danger to the plaintiff's life if the other kidney were injured or became diseased. In *Tier* v. *Wierzbicki*, [1973] 3 O.R. 193, Mr. Justice Lerner, basing his decision on *Gambino*, awarded $25,000 to a 12-year-old boy who lost a kidney after being run down by a horse. See also *Urbanski* v. *Patel* (1978), 84 D.L.R. (3d) 650. Are these amounts fair? Would it be better if the case could be reopened in case of further injury to the remaining kidney? What difficulties would this create?

21. What if someone loses one eye? See *Klyne* v. *Bellegarde* (1978), 92 D.L.R. (3d) 747 (Sask.) ($18,000). What if someone is blinded completely? See *Crossman* v. *Stewart* (1977), 5 C.C.L.T. 45 (B.C.) ($65,000). What if someone loses a tooth? See *Gagnon* v. *Stortini* (1974), 4 O.R. (2d) 270 ($1,200); Ten teeth?

22. Should there be compensation for cosmetic injuries, such as scarring, when a person's capacity to work has not been impaired thereby? In *Charters* v. *Brunette* (1974), 1 O.R. (2d) 13 (C.A.), a 15-year-old female was injured in a motorcycle accident. She spent 49 days in the hospital, had to use crutches for three weeks, and was left with scarring on her leg as a result of a large graft of skin taken from her buttock. The trial judge's assessment of $1,000 for pain and suffering for this injury was said to be excessively low. With regard to loss of amenities, plaintiff became so conscious of her appearance that she would not expose her lower leg and wore only slacks. She largely gave up sports

which she used to enjoy. The trial assessment of $3,000 on this head was said to be too low, because it overlooked the "subjective or emotional impact of her disfigurement — something quite apart from her disinclination to expose the scar". Chief Justice Gale felt that the plaintiff suffered an "emotional shock" and that it was not necessary for a "traumatic neurosis" to be present in order to award damages for this. The total general damages were reassessed at $9,500. Would it have made any difference if the plaintiff were a 15-year-old male? What if the plaintiff were a grandparent of 70?

23. Mental disability that results from physical injury is compensable under the thin-skull rule. See *supra.* A plaintiff, as a result of a fractured patella, developed a paranoid illness and depression that rendered him totally disabled. How much general damages should he receive? See *Kovach* v. *Smith et al.,* [1972] 4 W.W.R. 677 (B.C.) ($40,000 general, including lost earnings past and future). What about traumatic neurosis? *Krahn* v. *Rawlings* (1977), 2 C.C.L.T. 92 (Ont. C.A.).

24. If someone's physical capacity to engage in sexual activity is damaged in an accident, should they be compensated? What if they are mentally disabled in the accident in such a way that they cannot participate in sexual activity? See *Meglio* v. *Kaufman Lumber Ltd.* (1977), 2 C.C.L.T. 81 (Ont.) Cory J. disagreeing with Wright J. in *V.* v. *C.,* [1972] 2 O.R. 723, at p. 732 (part of general damages but not loss of amenities). What if the injured person can perform sexually but it hurts to do so? (*Gray* v. *LaFleche,* [1950] 1 D.L.R. 337 (Man.).)

25. What if someone is deprived of sexual enjoyment because of an injury to his spouse so that the spouse is unable to participate in sexual activity? It used to be that an action would lie for loss of consortium by the husband if there was a total loss of it, but not if there was only a partial loss. See *V.* v. *C., supra,* at p. 731; *cf. Finney* v. *Callender* (1971), 20 D.L.R. (3d) 301 (B.C.C.A.); *Dietelbach* v. *Public Trustee* (1973), 37 D.L.R. (3d) 621 (B.C.). A wife's right to consortium, however, was never recognized by the courts. See *Dietelbach, supra; Best* v. *Samuel Fox & Co.,* [1952] A.C. 716 (H.L.). This right has now been abolished in Ontario. See Family Law Reform Act, 1978, S.O. 1978, c. 2, s. 69(3): "No action shall be brought by a married person for the loss of the consortium of his or her spouse or for any damages resulting therefrom."

Section 60 of the same Act, however, enables certain relatives to sue for pecuniary loss they suffer as a result of injury (or death) of their relatives. The definition of "pecuniary loss" includes "loss of guidance, care and companionship that the claimant might reasonably have expected to receive from the injured person if the injury had not occurred". Will the courts now permit any compensation to a spouse for the inability of the other spouse to engage in sex on the ground that this is an aspect of "companionship"?

26. Should there be a different general damage award for a victim who is unconscious than there is for a victim who is aware of his injury? In the case of *H. West & Son Ltd.* v. *Shephard,* [1964] A.C. 326, Lord Morris of Borth-y-Gest had this to say:

"Certain particular questions have been raised. How are general damages affected, if at all, by the fact that the sufferer is unconscious? How are they affected, if at all, if it be the fact that the sufferer will not be able to make use of any money which is awarded?

The first of these questions may be largely answered if it is remembered that damages are designed to compensate for such results as have actually been caused. If someone has been caused pain then damages to compensate for the enduring of it may be awarded. If, however, by reason of an injury someone is made unconscious either for a short or a prolonged period, with the result that he does not feel pain, then he needs no monetary compensation in respect of pain because he will not have suffered it. Apart from actual physical pain it may often be that some physical injury causes distress or fear or anxiety. If, for example, personal injuries include the loss of a leg, there may be much physical suffering; there will be the actual loss of the leg (a loss the gravity of which will depend on the particular circumstances of the particular case); and there may be (depending on particular circumstances) elements of consequential worry and anxiety. One part of the affliction (again depending on particular circumstances) may be an inevitable and constant awareness of the deprivations which the loss of the leg entails. These are all matters which judges take into account. In this connexion also the length of the period of life during which the deprivations will continue will be a relevant factor. To the extent to which any of these last-mentioned matters depend for existence on an awareness in the victim it must follow that they will not exist and will not call for compensation if the victim is unconscious. An unconscious person will be spared pain and suffering, and will not experience the mental anguish which may result from knowledge of what has in life been lost, or from knowledge that life has been shortened. The fact of unconsciousness is therefore relevant in respect of, and will eliminate, those heads or elements of damage which can only exist by being felt or thought or experienced. The fact of unconsciousness does not, however, eliminate the actuality of the deprivations of the ordinary experiences and amenities of life which may be the inevitable result of some physical injury.

If damages are awarded to a plaintiff on a correct basis, it seems to me that it can be of no concern to the court to consider any question as to the use that will thereafter be made of the money awarded. It follows that if damages are assessed on a correct basis, there should not then be a paring down of the award because of some thought that a particular plaintiff will not be able to use the money. In assessing damages there may be items which will only be awarded if certain needs of a plaintiff are established. A particular plaintiff may have provision made for some future form of transport: a particular plaintiff may have to have provision made for some special future attention or some special treatment or medication. If, however, some reasonable sum is awarded to a plaintiff as compensation for pain endured or for the loss of past or future earnings or for ruined years of life or lost years of life, the use to which a plaintiff puts such sum is a matter for the plaintiff alone. A rich man, merely because he is rich and is not in need, is not to be denied proper compensation: nor is a thrifty man merely because he may keep and not spend."

Lord Tucker agreed with Lord Morris of Borth-y-Gest. Lord Pearce, the third member of the majority, stated:

"The loss of happiness of the individual plaintiffs is not, in my opinion a practicable or correct guide to reasonable compensation in cases of personal injury to a living plaintiff. A man of fortitude is not made less happy because he loses a limb. It may alter the scope of his activities and force him to seek his happiness in other directions. The cripple by the fireside reading or talking with friends may achieve happiness as great as that which, but for the accident, he would have achieved playing golf in the fresh air of the links. To some ancient philosophers the former kind of happiness might even have seemed of a higher nature than the latter, provided that the book or the talk were such as they would approve. Some less robust persons on the other hand are prepared to attribute a great loss of happiness to a quite trivial event. It would be lamentable if the trial of a personal injury claim put a premium on protestations of misery and if a long face was the only safe passport to a large award. Under the present practice there is no call for a parade of personal unhappiness. A plaintiff who cheerfully admits that he is as happy as he was, may yet receive a large award as reasonable compensation for the grave injury and the loss of amenity over which he has managed to triumph."

Lord Reid dissented and observed:

"There are two views about the true basis for this kind of compensation. One is that the man is simply being compensated for the loss of his leg, or the impairment of his digestion. The other is that his real loss is not so much his physical injury as the loss of those opportunities to lead a full and normal life which are now denied to him by his physical condition—for the multitude of deprivations and even petty annoyances which he must tolerate. Unless I am prevented by authority I would think that the ordinary man is, at least after the first few months, far less concerned about his physical injury than about the dislocation of his normal life. So I would think that compensation should be based much less on the nature of the injuries than on the extent of the injured man's consequential difficulties in his daily life. It is true that in practice one tends to look at the matter objectively and to regard the physical loss of an eye or a limb as the subject for compensation. But I think that is because the consequences of such a loss are very much the same for all normal people. If one takes the case of injury to an internal organ, I think that the true view becomes apparent. It is more difficult to say there that the plaintiff is being paid for the physical damage done to his liver or stomach or even his brain, and much more reasonable to say that he is being paid for the extent to which that injury will prevent him from living a full and normal life and for what he will suffer from being unable to do so.

If that is so, then I think it must follow that if a man's injuries make him wholly unconscious so that he suffers none of these daily frustrations or inconveniences, he ought to get less than the man who is every day acutely conscious of what he suffers and what he has lost. I do not say that he should get nothing. This is not a question that can be decided logically. I think that there are two elements, what he has lost and what he must feel about it, and of the two I think the latter is generally the more important to the injured man. To my mind there is something unreal in saying that a man who knows and feels nothing should get the same as a man who has to live with and put up with his disabilities, merely because they have sustained comparable physical injuries. It is no more possible to compensate an unconscious man than it is to compensate a dead man. The fact that the damages can give no benefit or satisfaction to the injured man and can only go to those who inherit the dead man's estate would not be a good reason for withholding damages which are legally due. But it is, in my view, a powerful argument against the view that there is no analogy between a dead man and a man who is unconscious and that a man who is unconscious ought to be treated as if he were fully conscious.

It is often said that it is scandalous that it should be cheaper to kill a man than to maim him, and that it would be monstrous if the defendant had to pay less because in addition to inflicting physical injuries he had made the plaintiff unconscious. I think that such criticism is misconceived. Damages are awarded not to punish the wrong-doer but to compensate the person injured, and a dead man cannot be compensated. Loss to his estate can be made good, and we can give some compensation to those whom he leaves behind. Perhaps we should do more for them — but not by inflating the claim of the dead man's executor, for then the money may go to undeserving distant relatives or residuary legatees or even to the Treasury if he dies intestate and without heirs."

Lord Devlin also dissented and explained his view as follows:

"Loss of consciousness, however caused, whether by the injury itself or produced by drugs or anaesthetics, means that physical pain is not experienced and so has not to be compensated for; and this must be true also of mental pain. Then there is or may be a temporary or permanent loss of a limb, organ or faculty. Whether it is the limb itself that is lost or the use of it is immaterial. What is to be compensated for is the loss of use and deprivation thereby occasioned. This deprivation may bring with it three consequences. First, it may result in loss of earnings and they can be calculated. Secondly, it may put the victim to expense in that he has to pay others for doing what he formerly did for himself; and that also can be calculated. Thirdly, it produces loss of enjoyment, loss of amenities as it is sometimes called, a diminution in the full pleasure of living. This is incalculable and at large. This deprivation with its three consequences is something that is personal to the victim. You do not, for instance, put an arbitrary value on the loss of a limb, as is commonly done in an accident insurance policy. You must ascertain the use to which the limb would have been put, so as to ascertain what it is of which the victim has actually been deprived.

What has to be considered in the present case is the method of compensation for the third of these consequences, loss of enjoyment or pleasure. There is here an almost total loss of use of all the faculties or limbs, but compensation under this head must be assessed in the same way as it would be for a partial loss of a single limb or faculty. The degree is different, but not the principle.

There are two ways in which this loss of enjoyment can be considered. It can be said that from beginning to end it is really all mental suffering. Loss of enjoyment is experienced in the mind and nowhere else. It may start with acute distress at the inability to use a limb in games or exercise as before or just in getting about, and may end with a nagging sense of frustration. If this is the true view, then total unconsciousness as in *Wise* v. *Kaye* relieves all mental suffering, and nothing can be recovered for a deprivation which is not being experienced.

The other way to look on the deprivation of a limb is as the loss of a personal asset, something in the nature of property. A limb can be put both to profitable use and to pleasurable use. In so far as it is put to profitable use, the loss is compensated for by calculating loss of earnings and not by assessing mental pain. On the same principle, it can be said, a sum must be assessed for loss of pleasurable use irrespective of whether there is mental suffering or not. . . .

My lords, as might be expected, English law has not come down firmly in favour of either of these two ways to the exclusion of the other. It favours a compound of both, as was agreed in argument and as I shall show later by reference to the authorities. The elements to be compounded have been called the objective and the subjective. The loss of property element is objective; it requires some sort of valuation that is in no way dependent on the victim's sense of loss. The other element is subjective because it depends entirely on mental suffering actually experienced. Is the main — or, at least, a very substantial — element in the compound, the objective, so that an evaluation must be made of it with an addition for mental suffering when proved? Or is the main element suffering laid on an objective bedrock, so that some sum is always recoverable even where there is no mental suffering at all? . . .

I turn now to consider the part which the objective element should play in the total award. If this were a matter on which the House could gain no guidance from the authorities, I could see much scope for argument about the relative importance of the objective and the subjective. But slowly and painfully English law has evolved ways of assessing the incalculable and it is important that they should be followed and applied as far as possible so that the law may be coherent. I am satisfied on the authorities that the objective element should be rated low. They are not authorities that are directly applicable; if they were, there would be no division of opinion in this House. But they are authorities which in my opinion cannot be evaded without grave injury to the structure of the law of damages for personal injuries and so I think they ought to be followed and applied. As they are also the authorities which permit the objective element to be considered at all, I must examine them with some care.

This is not a problem that has arisen very frequently. Deprivation is almost always accompanied by knowledge of it in the victim. So the traditional way of assessing compensation has been by reference to the feelings of the victim. I cannot agree that judges and juries usually approach the matter by asking themselves objectively what is the value of a leg; they think of what it must feel like to be a cripple and they award what is often called a solatium. Until medicine had progressed sufficiently to keep unconscious persons alive for an indefinite period, there was never any need in the case of the living for drawing a hard and fast distinction between the objective and the subjective. The problem arose only in the case of the dead when a sum had to be awarded to compensate for loss of expectation of life. What has to be compensated for in this assessment is a total loss of enjoyment of all the faculties, a complete loss of the pleasure of living. When the victim knows his fate, he will suffer from the distress which, except in the most saintly or philosophical, is caused by the prospect of death; and for that clearly he must be compensated. But what if he never knows his fate? It has been decided that he still must have some compensation, which should be moderate."

27. The Supreme Court of Canada has adopted the "objective view" of the majority in *The Queen in the Right of the Province of Ontario* v. *Jennings et al.* (1966), 57 D.L.R. (2d) 644, where Mr. Justice Cartwright stated simply that "damages for loss of amenities of life are not to be reduced by reason of the fact that the injured person is unconscious and unaware of his condition".

28. The Australian courts have chosen to reject the majority view in *West* v. *Shephard*, preferring a more "subjective view" of damages where the plaintiff is unconscious. In *Skelton* v. *Collins* (1966), 39 A.L.J.R. 480, the plaintiff, a 19-year-old, suffered severe brain damage which left him unconscious and with a life expectancy of only six months after the trial. An award of only £1,500 general damages was affirmed by Mr. Justice Taylor, who explained that "a person who is obliged for the rest of his life to live with his incapacity, fully conscious of the limitations which it imposes upon his enjoyment of life, is entitled to greater compensation than one who, although deprived of his former capacity is spared, by insensibility, from the realization of his loss and the trials and tribulations consequent upon it".

Mr. Justice Windeyer agreed and stressed that damages are "compensatory" not "punitive". He continued:

". . . . A man whose capacity for activity, mental or physical is impaired, so that no longer can he get satisfaction and enjoyment from things that he was accustomed to do and cannot do what he had planned or hoped to do, has not lost a thing the value of which for him can be measured in money by any process of calculation or estimation that I can understand. This consequence of an injury may be called by the convenient phrase, 'loss of amenities', or be described more elaborately and in more elegant words. However described, it is not a loss of something in the same sense that loss of a possession or of earning capacity is. A man who loses a limb, his eyesight, or his mind, does not lose a thing that is his, as his ox or his ass or his motor car is his, but something that is a part of himself, something that goes to make up his personality. I am not prepared to carry Cartesian doctrine so far as to distinguish here between injuries to body and mind. I am unable myself to understand how monetary compensation for the deprivation of the ability to live out life with faculties of mind and body unimpaired can be based upon an evaluation of a thing lost. It must surely be based upon solace for a condition created not upon payment for something taken away. . . .

I do not for a moment doubt that a man who has been deprived of the opportunity to live his life as he would have wished, and for as long as he might have expected, may, if he retains sufficient intellectual capacity to know his misfortune, feel distressed and frustrated. He is, I do not doubt, entitled to compensation for what he suffers. Money may be a compensation for him if having it can give him pleasure or satisfaction. If his expected years of life have been made less, money may enable him to cram more into the time that remains. If he has been deprived of the ability to do some things that he had enjoyed doing or had hoped to do, then money may enable him to enjoy other things instead. But the money is not then a recompense for a loss of something having a money value. It is given as some consolation or solace for the distress that is the consequence of a loss on which no monetary value can be put. . . .

In my view, his Honour, having thus held that on the evidence there was not even a chance that the additional sum could be used for the advantage of the plaintiff, ought not to have awarded it. It could not bring any advantage or consolation to the plaintiff. Consolation presupposes consciousness and some capacity of intellectual appreciation. If money were given to the plaintiff he could never know that he had it. He could not use it or dispose of it. It would simply go to his legal personal representatives on his death. It would be of no more benefit to him personally than sending the defendant to gaol would be. He is not, like Samson Agonistes, aware and able to bemoan his fate 'to live a life half dead, a living death' . His existence is in very truth a living death. . . ."

Mr. Justice Windeyer concluded:

"I can only hope that some day the law will provide some better way of meeting the consequences of day-to-day hazards than by actions for negligence and a measuring of damages by unprovable predictions, metaphysical assumptions and rationalized empiricism."

29. Which approach to this problem do you prefer? Should a person who is oblivious to his injury be awarded the same amount of damages as one who knows of his condition? No damages are awarded for pain and suffering to the unconscious victim, whereas these damages are granted to the conscious victim. Is such a distinction sufficient? No damages for pain and suffering were awarded either in *Skelton* or in *Jennings*.

30. Can a trial judge tell a jury to give the plaintiff an award that includes an amount to enable her to "buy pleasure", such as a trip, so as to offset the pain she has suffered? See *Parlee* v. *Sun Oil Co. Ltd.* (1977), 3 C.C.L.T. 159 (Ont. C.A.).

31. The problem of compensation for loss of expectation of life creates many difficulties. The loss of the right to a normal life span was recognized by the House of Lords in *Rose* v. *Ford,* [1937] A.C. 826, when Lord Wright stated: "A man has a legal right that his life should not be shortened by the tortious act of another." This right was allowed both to the victim himself or to his estate, if the victim died. Canadian legislators, however, wishing to reduce windfall benefits to the estates of deceased persons, abolished this right where the victim died. See for example Trustee Act, R.S.O. 1970, c. 470, s. 38(1). See also Wright, "The Abolition of Claims for Shortened Expectation of Life" (1938), 16 Can. Bar Rev. 193. Thus, all provinces, except Manitoba, allow damages for loss of expectation of life only to a surviving victim. Alberta has recently abolished the right of an estate to recover damages for loss of expectation of life, among other things, but has permitted $3,000 in damages to be awarded "for bereavement" to the spouse and minor children. See The Survival of Actions Act, 1978 Alta., c. 35. Is this a good idea?

The English courts have set a relatively low conventional figure that is to be allowed for loss of expectation of life. See *Benham* v. *Gambling,* [1941] A.C. 157. Canadian courts have also sought to limit the amounts to be awarded under this heading as well, but there has been considerable conflict in the cases. Most recently, the Supreme Court of Canada in *Crosby* v. *O'Reilly,* [1974] 6 W.W.R. 475 tried to dispell the confusion in the area by rejecting a maximum of $10,000 and permitting variations within a narrow range depending on the circumstances. The confusion has not been dissipated, however, and some members of the Manitoba Court of Appeal felt compelled to call for legislative intervention to resolve the mess. See *Pollock* v. *Milbery et al.,* [1976] 2 W.W.R. 481. See Charles, "Justice in Personal Injury Awards", *supra,* at p. 91; Kahn-Freund, "Expectation of Happiness" (1942), 5 Mod. L. Rev. 81.

32. Another problem that arises is whether there should be compensation for the "lost years" in cases of shortened life expectancy. The question is whether loss of earnings and pain and suffering should be awarded only for the reduced post-accident life expectancy or for the full pre-accident life expectancy. Here too, there is disagreement. The *Andrews* case indicates that the Canadian courts award compensation for "the lost years". So do the Australian courts. See *Skelton* v. *Collins* (1966), 115 C.L.R. 194. But the British courts do not. See

Wise v. *Kaye*, [1962] 1 Q.B. 638 (C.A.); Fleming, "The Lost Years" (1963), 50 Calif. L. Rev. 598.

33. Should the courts be granting such large sums of money to these injured people? What if they squander the money and are left impecunious after a few years? Would it be better to award periodic payments, as is done by workmen's compensation and victims of crime plans? See Fleming, "Damages: Capital or Rent" (1969), 19 U. of T.L.J. 295. Would it be wise to separate the liability part of the trial from the damages part? See Winn J. in *Stevens* v. *William Nash Ltd.*, [1966] 3 All E.R. 156 (C.A.); *Report of the Committee on Personal Injuries Litigation* (1968), U.K. Cmnd. 3691, at p. 485.

34. Should any damages at all be awarded for non-pecuniary losses such as pain and suffering and loss of amenities of life? The abolition of such awards in motor vehicle cases has been advocated by the Ontario Law Reform Commission in its *Report on Motor Vehicle Accident Compensation* (1973). In Australia, the abolition of non-pecuniary damages in all cases has been suggested. See *Report on Compensation and Rehabilitation in Australia* (1974). See also O'Connell and Simon, *Payment for Pain and Suffering: Who Wants What, When & Why?* (1972), also at [1971] U. Ill. L. Forum 1; Fleming, "Damages for Non-Material Losses" in Law Society of Upper Canada, *Special Lectures on New Developments in the Law of Torts* (1973); Dunlop, "The High Price of Sympathy: Damages for Personal Injuries" (1967), 17 U. of T.L.J. 51; Cooper, "Assessing Possibilities in Damage Awards—The Loss of a Chance or the Chance of a Loss" (1973), 37 Sask. L. Rev. 193.

35. The Pearson Commission made several recommendations in relation to damages for personal injuries. Among the suggestions were the following: (1) Damages for loss of expectation of life as a separate head of damage should be abolished. (2) Damages for non-pecuniary loss should not be allowed for the first three months after the injury. (3) The Commission was equally divided about whether there should be a maximum on the non-pecuniary damages in the range of five times the annual industrial earnings. (4) Non-pecuniary damages should not be permitted where the victim is permanently unconscious. (5) Loss of income should be awarded for the pre-accident life expectancy. (6) The court should be able to award periodic payments instead of lump sums. What do you think of these? See *Report of Royal Commission on Civil Liability and Compensation for Personal Injury* (1978).

36. In *V.* v. *C.*, [1972] 2 O.R. 723, Mr. Justice Wright had some critical things to say about damages for non-pecuniary losses:

"It does not follow that progress is extending the heads and amounts of general damages. It may well be in our society that the increase in the awards for non-pecuniary losses is not advancing justice but adding to injustice.

If we take the three cases of the soldier, the careless child, and the victim of a negligent driver, who are separately disabled physically to exactly the same extent, we can see clearly that the one who is favoured and who alone is compensated for non-pecuniary losses is the victim of negligence.

We now provide in one way or another for the treatment and life-time care of each of the three from funds which organized society provides, but to the victim of negligence we give from car-owner's premiums or from public funds an estimated lump sum covering as well, compensation for pain and suffering, past and to come, lost earnings for the past and for the future, and something for his lost amenities. The injury is the same. The sources of compensation are collective funds provided by our society. But the financial position of that victim is rendered by his general damages, far better than that of the soldier or the child, for whom society has more responsibility. And if the victim of negligence chooses to squander the damages awarded, he or she may still enjoy the widespread yet stinted welfare of the State.

Under modern conditions, money compensation for non-pecuniary losses seems to be based on the suppositions that we each have the right to be happy and free from pain and owe a duty to preserve those felicities to each of our fellow citizens, and that money can compensate for their loss and in some way ease the pain. . . . We cannot in the courts change the inequalities of today, but need not add to them for tomorrow if we are presented with choice."

37. What can be said in favour of this type of award? Does it foster one's respect for individual human dignity? Does it diminish the claimant's sense of having been wronged? Does it serve to underscore our sense of responsibility for our actions?

JAFFE, DAMAGES FOR PERSONAL INJURY: THE IMPACT OF INSURANCE

(1953), 18 Law and Cont. Prob. 219

When the defendant's conduct is reprehensible, damages are an apt instrument of punishment. The criminal law is often a clumsy and ineffective device for dealing with unsocial activity. The engines of public prosecution may be too ponderous or too busy with high crimes. The tort law serves as a useful supplement or alternative. To pay money to one's victim is a salutary humiliation. The victim is the focus of the communal sense of having been wronged. The receipt of money particularly from the wrongdoer assuages a justified sense of outrage. It is true that here the law does operate without any adequate premise for measurement . . . as society holds that punishment serves a useful function. It is perhaps possible to provide a measure by relating monetary punishment to the size of the defendant's income. Many courts arbitrarily restrict punitive damages, probably a wise expedient in an area where there is no guide to judgment.

Rationalization becomes more obscure and wavering when the defendant's conduct is merely negligent rather than willful. It is customarily said that the purpose of a tort action is compensation rather than punishment, particularly where the gist of the action is negligence. When the plaintiff's damage is restricted to mental distress the courts have quite consistently denied any recovery but once given physical injury as a predicate, pain and suffering is allowed as "parasitic damage". The court will invariably admit that there is no measure for its valuation but it is thought that justice nevertheless demands its equation into money. . . .

But why we may ask *should* the plaintiff be compensated in money for an experience which involves no financial loss? It cannot be on the principle of returning what is his own. Essentially that principle rests on an economic foundation: on maintaining the integrity of the economic arrangements which provide the normally expectable basis for livelihood in our society. Pain is a harm, an "injury", but neither past pain nor its compensation has any consistent economic significance. The past experience is not a loss except in so far as it produced present deterioration. It will be said, however, that these arguments betray a limited, a Philistine view of the law's concern, one that the law has happily transcended. This objection mistakes the argument. Of course the law is concerned, and properly so, with other than economic interests. The criminal law and the tort law *in so far as punitive* (that is to say in so far as the conduct of the plaintiff warrants punishment) is much concerned with the protection of non-economic interests; and to punishment may be added judicial remedies of a preventive character such as the injunction against nuisances, invasions of privacy, etc., and legislative devices such as zoning.

I am aware, however, that though the premise may elude detection, some deep intuition may claim to validate this process of evaluating the imponderable. One who has suffered a violation of his bodily integrity may feel a sense of continuing outrage. This is particularly true where there has been disfigurement or loss of a member (even though not giving rise to economic loss). Because our society sets a high value on money it uses money or price as a means of recognizing the worth of non-economic as well as economic goods. If, insists the plaintiff, society really values my personality, my bodily integrity, it will signify its sincerity by paying me a sum of money. Damages thus may somewhat reestablish the plaintiff's self-confidence, wipe out his sense of outrage. Furthermore, though money is not an equivalent it may be a consolation, a solatium. These arguments, however, are most valid for disfigurements or loss of member giving rise to a continuing sense of injury. (And in such cases there may be potential economic injury which cannot be established.) It is doubtful that past pain figures strongly as present outrage. And even granting these arguments there must be set over against them arbitrary indeterminateness of the evaluation. Insurance aside, it is doubtful justice seriously to embarass a defendant, though negligent, by real economic loss in order to do honor to plaintiff's experience of pain. And insurance present, it is doubtful that the pooled social fund of savings should be charged with sums of indeterminate amount when compensation performs no specific economic function. This consideration becomes the stronger as year after year the amounts set aside for the security account become a larger proportion of the national income.

It is not supposed, however, that even were the reasons of the best — and mine I am sure will fail to satisfy many — the courts will forthwith deny the right of the plaintiff to have these intangibles valued. But putting aside for the moment their bearing on legislation, I would suggest that they are not irrelevant to the judicial creation of new remedies and new items of damage; nor to the judical administration of present items of damage.

D. COLLATERAL SOURCES

Accident victims now have available to them several sources of compensation in addition to the tortfeasor. They may receive money from a variety of public and private schemes that reimburse them for their hospital, medical, wage and other losses. In Canada, we have a plethora of programs such as O.H.I.P., Canada Pension Plan, Unemployment Insurance, Workmen's Compensation, and general welfare. In addition, there are an assortment of private sources of aid to accident victims. Needless to say, these various sources of payment have created many problems for the courts in assessing damages.

There are three possible methods of handling these collateral benefits: (1) accumulation, which allows the injured person to keep the collateral source funds and to collect in full from the wrongdoer as well. This, of course, permits double recovery, something that many people object to; (2) subrogation, which provides for the reimbursement of the collateral source by the wrongdoer. Under this method, the claimant receives only one payment, the tortfeasor pays for the loss, but the fund receives a type of windfall; (3) set-off or deduction, under which the collateral payment is deducted from what the defendant has to pay. This technique avoids double recovery, but it gives the defendant a windfall and denies the plaintiff the benefits of his own insurance.

All three treatments of collateral sources have their deficiencies, yet all of them are used in different situations. The first, accumulation, is now the most popular in Canada and the U.S. (See *infra, Boarelli* and *Gill* cases.) The second, subrogation, is frequently provided for in legislation. (See, for example, R.R.O. 1970, O. Reg. 443, s. 55, under the Hospital Services Commission Act, R.S.O. 1970, c. 209, which grants subrogation rights to the Commission. See also *Re Ledingham* v. *Di Natale*, [1973] 1 O.R. 291, 3 D.L.R. (3d) 18 (C.A.) noted by Fleming in (1974), 52 Can. Bar Rev. 103; see also Workmen's Compensation Act, R.S.O. 1970, c. 505, s. 8). Often, insurance companies contract for subrogation rights in the policies they issue. The third, deduction, still has a following in the U.K. and among many scholars, but it is waning in popularity. Deduction may be provided for in legislation or by contract (see material on no-fault insurance, *infra*).

It is doubtful whether we shall ever reach a consensus on a uniform treatment of these collateral sources, and perhaps we should not. There are many different types of programs, designed for varying purposes, and perhaps it is best that they be treated individually, in accordance with their specific aims. The material that follows will give an introduction to the types of problems encountered. For a more thorough analysis of the problems see McInnes, *Collateral Benefits in the Assessment of Damages in Tort Actions* (1973), Law Society Special Lectures; Fleming, "The Collateral Source Rule and Loss Allocation in Tort Law" (1966), 54 Calif. L. Rev. 1478; Cooper, "A Collateral Benefits Principle" (1971), 49 Can. Bar Rev. 501; Ganz, "Mitigation of Damages by Benefits Received" (1962), 25 Mod. L. Rev. 559.

BOARELLI v. FLANNIGAN

Court of Appeal. [1973] 3 O.R. 69

Dubin J.A.: This appeal raises a matter of considerable public importance. The immediate issue is whether welfare payments received by the plaintiff while unemployed as a result of injuries received in a motor vehicle accident caused by the defendant should be deducted from the amount that the plaintiff would otherwise have recovered as loss of income.

Apart from welfare payments, in our modern society persons injured as a result of the tortious conduct of others have benefits available to tide them over during their period of unemployment far beyond those ever contemplated in the early days of the common law. As Lord Wilberforce put it in *Parry* v. *Cleaver*, [1970] A.C. 1 at pp. 38-9:

> "The injured plaintiff is liable to taxation on his earnings. He may be protected by an elaborate structure of social welfare arrangements entitling him to industrial injuries benefit, unemployment pay, sickness benefit and other payments of constantly changing nature and amount. Apart from any private insurance he may have taken out, he may be covered by an 'insurance' scheme in his employment. This may be voluntary or compulsory, contributory or non-contributory; it may be partly transferred from a previous employment and may be transferable to a future employment; the true element of insurance in the arrangements may be considerable or very slight. If he is injured in a large-scale catastrophe, and sometimes even when he is not, a fund may be raised by public subscription out of which he may receive very large sums indeed. He may receive help from private benefaction. . . . In many cases even now, and possibly in most cases in the future, the whole of his loss, so far as measurable in money terms, may be covered, independently of any claim against the 'wrongdoer'."

Such benefits have come to be known as collateral benefits, and I do not think that the matter of welfare payments can be isolated from the broader issue as to what consideration, if any, should be given to collateral benefits in the assessment of damages for loss of income and loss of earning capacity in actions founded in tort. Since these are matters which are frequently arising in our courts and have been the subject of considerable judicial conflict, I think it necessary to deal with this subject now.

In the instant case the plaintiff appealed from the judgment pronounced by the Honourable Mr. Justice Haines after a trial before him and a jury. The plaintiff appealed solely in relation to the quantum of the award of damages under two items; loss of income and general damages.

On the argument the court was of the unanimous view that the award of general damages ought not to be interfered with, leaving the sole issue in the appeal as one relating to the assessment of the plaintiff's loss of income. By reason of the injuries the evidence disclosed that the plaintiff was unable to work from the time of his accident to the date of trial. The evidence further disclosed that the plaintiff was on welfare for much of the time of his period of unemployment, was still on welfare at the date of trial, and was receiving $127.50 every two weeks.

In his charge to the jury the learned trial judge instructed them that, in determining what amount the plaintiff was entitled to for loss of income at the date of trial, they were to take into consideration what he received as welfare and invited the jury to deduct from what they would otherwise have assessed as loss of income, the amount of the welfare payments.

On appeal, counsel for the plaintiff sought leave to introduce additional material. The additional material disclosed that the solicitors for the Municipality of Metropolitan Toronto advised the defendant shortly after the accident that the plaintiff was being provided relief assistance and that he had executed an assignment of any moneys that he was to receive as a result of the accident in favour of the Municipality of Metropolitan Toronto to the extent of the moneys received by way of welfare assistance and a copy of this assignment was included in the material filed in the Court of Appeal. It was further disclosed that a total of approximately $6,000 had been paid to the plaintiff up to the time of trial. Although this material was available to both counsel for the plaintiff and for the defendant at the time of trial, it was not drawn to the attention of the learned trial judge. Because it was so material to the issues, leave was granted to file this additional information and the same was taken into consideration in determining the issues before us. It was not seriously contended by counsel for the defendant that, if the material had been placed before the judge and jury at trial, the welfare payments should have been deducted.

It is, therefore, apparent that the judgment below cannot stand and must be set aside.

However, it was obviously the view of the learned trial judge in this case that welfare payments received by a plaintiff in the absence of an obligation to repay should be deducted from the amount that the defendant would otherwise have had to compensate the plaintiff for. The Honourable Mr. Justice Hughes in the case of *Kingscott* v. *Megaritis et al.*, [1972] 3 O.R. 37, 27 D.L.R. (3d) 310 (H.C.), arrived at the same conclusion. In that case the learned trial judge made a very careful analysis of the present state of the law in this province and appears to have felt that he was compelled to arrive at that conclusion by the judgment of this court in *Menhennet* v. *Schoenholz*, [1971] 3 O.R. 355, 20 D.L.R. (3d) 395. It is to be observed in the reasons for judgment delivered by this court in *Menhennet* v. *Schoenholz* that the court relied at least in part on the judgment of *Browning* v. *War Office*, [1962] 3 All E.R. 1089 (C.A.). Prior to the date of the judgment of this court in the *Menhennet* case the majority of the House of Lords in *Parry* v. *Cleaver, supra,* rejected the majority judgment in *Browning* v. *War Office.* I am advised that the judgment in *Parry* v. *Cleaver* was not brought to the attention of the Court of Appeal when the judgment in *Menhennet* v. *Schoenholz* was delivered. Although the judgment in the *Menhennet* case did not directly deal with welfare payments and, in that sense could be distinguishable from the case at bar, I am of the view that the matters raised in the *Menhennet* case should now be considered afresh.

In considering the development in the common law courts as to whether collateral benefits should be considered in the assessment of damages in actions founded in tort, it is apparent that, in the absence of any statutory direction, the common law has treated such matters as one depending upon justice, reasonableness and public policy. But not being content to leave the matter as one dependent on such considerations, an effort has been made to envelop the issues within the framework of some recognized judicial maxims, which on analysis now appear to be far too confining to meet the complexity of modern society. The determination has often been placed as being dependent on the doctrine of remoteness, or as being an issue of *causa causans* or *causa sine qua non.* It has also been said on many occasions that damages awarded in negligence cases for personal injury are not to be "punitive", still less are they to be a reward; they are to be compensatory only and these propositions are said to be applicable to both special damages as well as general damages. However, as Lord Pearce observed in the case of *Parry* v. *Cleaver, supra,* at p. 33:

> "The word 'punitive' gives no help. It is simply a word used when a court thinks it unfair that a defendant should be saddled with liability for a particular item. There is nothing punitive in calling on a defendant to pay that which the law says is a just recompense for the injury the plaintiff has caused."

It has also been said that the defendant must take a plaintiff as he finds him and that all that the defendant is obligated to repay is the actual loss suffered by the plaintiff, but no more than his loss. If that were so, then one would take into consideration on the credit side every benefit that the injured party obtained following the accident to assist him during the period of his incapacity, but that has never been the common law.

Moneys received by an injured party as a result of a private or public benevolence have never been taken into consideration in assessing damages for loss of income or earning capacity.

In the case of *Redpath* v. *Belfast and County Down Railway,* [1947] N.I. 167 at p. 170, where the company sought to bring into account sums received from distress funds, Andrew L.C.J. said that the plaintiff's counsel had submitted:

> ". . . that it would be startling to the subscribers to that fund if they were to be told that their contributions were really made in ease and for the benefit of the negligent Railway Company. To this last submission I would only add that if the proposition contended for by the defendants is sound the inevitable consequence in the case of future disasters of a similar character would be that the springs of private charity would be found to be largely, if not entirely, dried up."

Lord Reid in *Parry* v. *Cleaver, supra,* at p. 14, commenting on this case further observed as follows:

> "It would be revolting to the ordinary man's sense of justice, and therefore contrary to public policy, that the sufferer should have his damages reduced so that he would gain nothing from the benevolence of his friends or relations or of the public at large, and that the only gainer would be the wrong-

doer. We do not have to decide in this case whether these considerations also apply to public benevolence in the shape of various unconvenanted benefits from the welfare state, but it may be thought that Parliament did not intend them to be for the benefit of the wrongdoer."

It is this latter matter which falls squarely to be decided in this appeal.

In addressing myself as to whether welfare payments received by an injured party while unemployed as a result of an accident or other injury under such statutes as the General Welfare Assistance Act, R.S.O. 1970, c. 192, or Family Benefits Act, R.S.O. 1970, c. 157, I view these payments as benefits provided to persons in need, independent of any cause of action such person may have or assert, and as a benefit provided to him not in diminution of any claim the injured person may have for damages. Answering the query of Lord Reid, I do not think that the Legislature intended them to be for the benefit of the wrongdoer. . . .

It is helpful, I think, to recall that the plaintiff's right of action is complete at the time when his injuries are sustained. It is apparent that, if a person were to have been recompensed immediately upon the suffering of his injury, there would have been no need for him having to obtain any assistance, pursuant to our present social welfare statutes. Merely because such damages cannot be determined at that time should not affect the result. I do not think that there is any difference in principle between benefits received under our present social welfare legislation and those received by way of private or public benevolence. In such case it may be said that the injured party has received a reward as a result of the injury. If that is so, in my view, it is no concern of the defendant and such matters should be dealt with by the appropriate legislative authority. In many statutes a right of subrogation for moneys received from an unsuccessful defendant is established. In this way the loss is borne by the tortfeasor and the question of overlapping compensation is thereby avoided. However, in my opinion, it is for the appropriate legislative authority to determine whether the right of subrogation should be included in those statutes which are now silent in this respect.

[His Lordship then referred to the language in *The Queen in Right of the Province of Ontario* v. *Jennings*, [1966] S.C.R. 532, which he felt "equally appropriate" here, see *infra* p. 605.]

Similarly, I would hold that the plaintiff's claim for damages and loss of earnings should not be reduced by reason of having received unemployment insurance benefits. On this matter I would adopt what was said in the following language of Ritchie J., in *Bourgeois* v. *Tzrop* (1957), 9 D.L.R. (2d) 214 at pp. 224-5:

"The wrongdoer should not get the benefit of the fortuitous circumstance that the plaintiff's employment entitled him to unemployment insurance benefits. It therefore, is my conclusion the principle that a wrongdoer is not entitled to the benefit of a policy of insurance for which he has paid nothing extends, in claims at common law for negligence, to unemployment insurance benefits paid to an injured party as a result of his being unemployed because of injuries suffered by reason of the negligence of a wrongdoer."

In short, I view benefits received under the present social welfare legislation, where the statute does not require that such payments be taken into account, as being intended to confer a benefit independent of any legal liability in another person to compensate the injured party. The benefit is available equally to persons who have no cause of action, and the funds so provided shall not be used to reduce the normal obligation of the person at fault to compen-

sate the victim. . . . It has been urged in a very learned article by Professor K.D.
Cooper, "A Collateral Benefits Principle", 49 Can. Bar Rev. 510 at p. 502
(1971):

> ". . . that there is a crucial distinction to be made in this respect between
> benefits which are intended to compensate a specific pecuniary loss (which
> should be deducted) and benefits intended for other purposes, such as to
> compensate non-pecuniary loss, (which should not be deducted). . . ."

But with respect to the learned author, if such was the test, the benefits received from accident insurance policies should be deducted, since unlike payments under social welfare legislation, which may only incidentally be available
to an injured party, such payments are intended specifically to compensate the
injured party for pecuniary loss.

However, moneys received as a result of a private insurance plan to cover
the contingency of an accident have never been set off against the damages
which the defendant must otherwise pay. That principle was established in
Bradburn v. *Great Western R. Co.* (1874), L.R. 10 Ex. 1, and has never been
seriously challenged. The legal premise upon which such set off was refused is
set forth by Asquith L.J. in *Shearman* v. *Folland*, [1950] 2 K.B. 43 at p. 46,
where he said as follows:

> "If the wrongdoer were entitled to set off what the plaintiff was entitled to
> recoup or had recouped under his policy, he would in effect be depriving
> the plaintiff of all benefit from the premiums paid by the latter, and
> appropriating that benefit to himself."

But what are the principles which should govern in determining whether
collateral benefits, available and provided to an injured party during his period
of incapacity and emanating from sources other than welfare statutes, should
be deducted in the assessment of damages in such cases as this?

It would appear that, prior to the judgment of the Court of Appeal in
Browning v. *War Office*, [1962] 3 All E.R. 1089, generally speaking, such
benefits were regarded as *res inter alios* and not deducted. The majority of the
court in *Browning* v. *War Office* viewed the failure to deduct benefits received
by way of public or private charity, or benefits received under a private contract of insurance, as anomalies and ought not to be extended to the variety of
collateral benefits now available.

It also appeared that the majority of the court in that case relied heavily on
the judgment in the House of Lords in *British Transport Com'n* v. *Gourley*,
[1956] A.C. 185. In the *Gourley* case the House of Lords held that, in determining damages for future loss of earnings, the defendant must compensate the
plaintiff for his net loss only, and therefore the incidence of taxation was to be
considered in determining the amount of the award.

Since the Supreme Court of Canada in the case of *The Queen in right of the
Province of Ontario* v. *Jennings, supra,* rejected the principle of the *Gourley*
case and held it to be inapplicable in this country, I am of the view that the
majority judgment of *Browning* v. *War Office* ought not to have had any effect
in determining the issue here. I would have preferred the vigorous dissenting
judgment of Donovan J. in the *Browning* case, who held that the refusal of the
courts to set off payments received from public or private benevolence or from
insurance policies were not anomalies, but founded on principle to be applied
to other types of benefits. . . .

In *Parry* v. *Cleaver*, [1970] A.C. 1, the majority of the House of Lords held
that the pension received by a police constable under a statutory pension plan,
which entitled him as of right to a pension on being discharged from the police
on disablement, was not to be considered in the amount to be assessed for his

loss. After pointing out that the *Gourley* case was not at all decisive of the issue, and that moneys received from private insurance plans were never deductible, Lord Reid, at pp. 14-5, goes on to say as follows:

"Then I ask — why should it make any difference that he insured by arrangement with his employer rather than with an insurance company? In the course of the argument the distinction came down to be as narrow as this: if the employer says nothing or merely advises the man to insure and he does so, then the insurance money will not be deductible; but if the employer makes it a term of the contract of employment that he shall insure himself and he does so, then the insurance money will be deductible. There must be something wrong with an argument which drives us to so unreasonable a conclusion.

It is said to make all the difference that both the future wages of which he has been deprived by the fault of the defendant, and the benefit which has accrued by reason of his disablement come from the same source or arise out of the same contract. This seems to be founded on an idea of remoteness which is, I think, misconceived. Remoteness from the defendant's point of view is a familiar conception in connection with damages. He pays damages for loss of a kind which he might have foreseen but not for loss of a kind which was not foreseeable by him. But here we are not dealing with that kind of remoteness. No one has ever suggested that the defendant gets the benefit of receipts by the plaintiff after his accident if they are of a kind which he could have foreseen, but not if they are of a kind which he could not have foreseen, or vice versa. That the plaintiff may, in consequence of the defendant's fault, receive benefit from benevolence or insurance is no more or no less foreseeable or remote than that he may get a benefit from a pension to be paid by his employer. If remoteness has any relevance here it is quite a different kind of remoteness — the connection or absence of connection between the source of the benefit and the source of the wages. But what has that got to do with the defendant? It is rational to make the extent of the defendant's liability depend on remoteness from his point of view — on what he knew or could or should have foreseen. But it is, to my mind, an irrational technicality to make that depend on the remoteness or closeness of relationship between the plaintiff's source of loss and source of gain. Surely the distinction between receipts which must be brought into account and those which must not must depend not on their source but on their intrinsic nature."

In considering those collateral benefits which an injured party receives, pursuant to his contract of employment, I would approach it in the manner that Lord Pearce did in *Parry* v. *Cleaver, supra,* at p. 37, where he was dealing with the question of pensions. He put the test this way.

"If one starts on the basis that *Bradburn's* case (1874), L.R. 10 Ex. 1, decided on fairness and justice and public policy, is correct in principle, one must see whether there is some reason to except from it pensions which are derived from a man's contract with his employer. These, whether contributory or non-contributory, flow from the work which a man has done. They are part of what the employer is prepared to pay for his services. The fact that they flow from past work equates them to rights which flow from an insurance privately effected by him. He has simply paid for them by weekly work instead of weekly premiums.

Is there anything else in the nature of these pension rights derived from work which puts them into a different class from pension rights derived from private insurance? Their 'character' is the same, that is to say, they are intended by payer and payee to benefit the workman and not to be a subvention for wrongdoers who will cause him damage."

I would also adopt, as Lord Pearce did, the following test as set forth in the

American Restatement of the Law of Torts (1939), vol. 4, p. 616, para. 920, where the general principle is stated:

> "Where the defendant's tortious conduct has caused harm to the plaintiff or to his property and in so doing has conferred upon the plaintiff a special benefit to the interest which was harmed, the value of the benefit conferred is considered in mitigation of damages, where this is equitable."

In the para. (e), pp. 620-1, however, dealing with "benefits received from third persons" it is stated that:

> "The rule . . . does not apply where, although a benefit is received because of the harm, such benefit is the result of the forethought of the plaintiff or of a gift to him by a third person. . . . Where a person has been disabled and hence cannot work but derives an income during the period of disability from a contract of insurance or from a contract of employment which requires payment during such period, his income is not the result of earnings but of previous contractual arrangements made for his own benefit, not the tortfeasor's."

Therefore, with respect to collateral benefits obtained, pursuant to collective bargaining agreements or private contracts of employment, I would view such benefits as part of the wage package and the benefits received as having been paid for by the employee, and I do not think that they should be treated any differently than a benefit received from a private insurance plan. For that reason, I would not now approve the judgment of *Rados et al.* v. *Neumann*, [1971] 2 O.R. 269, 17 D.L.R. (3d) 521, where the amount of moneys received by the injured party from a sickness and accident insurance policy paid by the employer was deducted from the amount otherwise payable by the defendant. I would prefer the judgment of Grant J., as noted in *Menhennet* v. *Schoenholz*, [1971] 3 O.R. 355, 20 D.L.R. (3d) 395, in the case of *Zuzek* v. *Fenton and Moore* [unreported]. However, I think it safe to assume in present society that such benefits are included in the wages which the employee receives and for which he must work, rather than requiring proof of such facts in every case. It is well known that in the determination of a remuneration to be paid to employees "fringe benefits" are considered in arriving at a total wage benefit package, and the amount of the weekly salary or wage is dependent upon the cost of the totality of the benefits.

I cannot conclude that there is any equitable principle which should permit a tortfeasor to obtain the advantage of benefits earned by the person who has been injured. It is for the contracting parties to determine whether such benefits are to be subrogated and it is of no concern of the party otherwise liable in damages.

But what of a payment made *ex gratia*? It is clear that an *ex gratia* payment from a relative or friend has never been the subject of deduction. In my view, I see no difference in principle if the *ex gratia* payment emanated from the employer.

In the case of *Myers and City of Guelph* v. *Hoffman*, [1955] O.R. 965, 1 D.L.R. (2d) 272, a police officer, who was injured by the negligence of the defendant, continued to receive his salary or wages from the municipality, which payment was made voluntarily by them, and for which he was not legally obligated to repay. The issue arose as to whether such payments should be taken into consideration in determining the amount of damages which the police officer was entitled to. At p. 975 O.R., pp. 281-2 D.L.R., McRuer C.J.H.C. stated as follows:

> "A wrongdoer is not entitled to the benefit of a payment made *ex gratia* which some beneficient person or corporation may have seen fit to make to

the victim of his wrongdoing. If the donor wishes to trust to the honour of the donee to repay the amount so paid instead of taking an undertaking to do so that is his business and the mere form of the payment cannot enure to the benefit of the wrongdoer. I think the fact that Myers was paid by the corporation puts him in a stronger position than if he had received *ex gratia* payments from a benevolent third party. His future relations with his employer have been directly affected and the moral obligation to reimburse that employer is great. The payments were not paid as wages or salary for services rendered; in fact he had no earning-power during the time the payments were made. They were in law purely *ex gratia* gifts made because he had been injured while on duty."

In that case the learned Chief Justice had before him the undertaking of counsel for the plaintiff to repay the amount paid to him as salary by the municipality while he was disabled out of any compensation received, and the order made by him was conditional that the undertaking be carried out. Indeed, there have been many other cases where, in an effort to avoid what the courts regard as a reward to the injured party, such an order has been made, even in the absence of such an undertaking. However, I do not view that type of order as being essential to the *ratio* of the case, and I am of the respectful opinion that a moral obligation of the recipient of an *ex gratia* payment should be left to the recipient's own good conscience.

That brings me to consideration of the judgment of this court in *Menhennet* v. *Schoenholz, supra.* In that case the injured party received a payment from his employer which was described as sick pay. The court was of the opinion that there was no evidence to show that this was a payment obligatory on the employer's part, payment for which benefit had been negotiated or accepted by the union for an employee in lieu of an increase in his hourly wage. It is to be observed that it is implicit in that judgment that, if it had been shown that the payment therein was a fringe benefit as part of the total wage package, the said sum would not have been deducted, which is consistent with the views that I have heretofore expressed. However, relying on the principles in *Browning* v. *War Office, supra,* on the assumption that the payment was *ex gratia*, the court held that the amount should be deducted.

As pointed out in *Parry* v. *Cleaver, supra,* the source of the payment is no longer relevant and, therefore, the fact that it is the employer in one case and a friend in another, who is the donor, should not affect the result. In my opinion, therefore, such *ex gratia* payments made by an employer should not be deducted from the award of damages which would otherwise prevail.

In my opinion, what I have said is consistent with the public policy expressed in the Fatal Accidents Act, R.S.O. 1970, c. 164, s. 3(3):

> 3(3) In assessing the damages in an action brought under this Act there shall not be taken into account any sum paid or payable on the death of the deceased or any future premiums payable under a contract of insurance.

Prior to the introduction of this long standing provision of the Fatal Accidents Act, the matters provided for in s. 3(3) were, of course, deducted in the assessment of damages in actions brought under the Fatal Accidents Act.

I find comfort in the views that I have expressed above in the recent judgment of the Supreme Court of Canada in the case of *Canadian Pacific Ltd. et al.* v. *Gill et al.* (unreported), which has just come to my attention. In that case the Supreme Court of Canada was called upon to consider, amongst other matters, whether the present value of a pension received by a widow under the Canada Pension Plan, R.S.C. 1970, c. C-5, should have been deducted from the damages to be awarded. The action was brought under the British Columbia Family Compensation Act, which is that province's counterpart of our Fatal Accidents

Act. Section 4(4) of the British Columbia Family Compensation Act is a provision similar to that of s. 3(3) of the Fatal Accidents Act of Ontario.

After citing with apparent approval certain passages from the decision in *Parry* v. *Cleaver, supra,* the court held that the principles set forth in *Parry* v. *Cleaver*, although dealing with a personal injury case and not a claim under a fatal accidents statute, were of assistance in determining whether the present value of the pension should have been deducted from the award of damages otherwise payable, having regard to the provisions of s. 4(4) of the British Columbia statute.

The Supreme Court of Canada concluded that such payments were so much of the same nature as contracts of insurance that they should also be excluded from consideration when assessing damages under the provisions of the British Columbia statute.

After considering the above authorities, I have come to the conclusion that the collateral benefits, which I have discussed above, should not be taken into account in assessing damages for loss of earnings or earning capacity in personal injury actions.

In the result, I would allow the appeal to the extent of directing a new trial limited to the assessment of the special damages for loss of wages. The order as to payment of costs of the first trial shall be deleted. In all other respects, judgment below is confirmed. There will be no costs of this appeal.

Appeal allowed, assessment of damages ordered.

NOTES

1. In *Canadian Pacific* v. *Gill*, [1973] 4 W.W.R. 593 (S.C.C.), the widow of someone killed in a car crash sued for damages under the B.C. Families' Compensation Act. The trial judge gave judgment for 50 percent of the damages, but deducted from the recovery the present value of the pension which the widow and children were receiving from the Canada Pension Plan. The Court of Appeal set aside the deduction and the Supreme Court of Canada affirmed. Mr. Justice Spence felt that, like in the U.K., the payments under the Canada Pension Plan were akin to those made under a "contract of assurance" and were not to be deducted. He explained:

"It is true that the state pension in the United Kingdom is not an exact counterpart of the Canada Pension Plan, but it is on a like basis, that is, persons in the class of pensionable persons are required by statute to make a contribution to the pension plan; the employer makes contribution, and then a pension is payable on retirement or upon becoming disabled, or a pension is payable to the widow and dependent children upon the death of the contributor. The plan, therefore, is an exact substitute for a privately arranged insurance policy made between the deceased person and an insurance company, with the benefits payable upon the death or disablement of the insured. There is an element of risk to both the contributor under the Canada Pension Plan and to the Government which pays the benefits under the Plan. It may well be that a person who is a contributor may make but a few payments and then become disabled and be paid pension amounts over a long period; on the other hand, the contributor may contribute for a very long number of years and then upon retirement die within a few months so that very little pension benefit is obtained.

There are, of course, many forms of insurance and surely one of them may be considered to be the social insurance now exemplified by the Canada Pension Plan. Insofar as the word "contract" is concerned, there is, in result, a contract between the contributor to the Canada Pension Plan and the Government which, by virtue of the statute, exacts from such contributor weekly deductions from his wages. One must keep in mind the evident remedial character of s. 4(4) of The Families' Compensation Act. I am therefore of the opinion that pensions payable under the Canada Pension Plan are so much of the same nature as contracts of insurance that they also should be excluded from consideration when assessing damages under the provisions of that statute."

2. A similar result was reached in *White et al.* v. *Parkin et al.*, [1974] 3 W.W.R. 509 (B.C.S.C.), where Berger J. refused to deduct the Canada Pension Plan payments from an award since it was "in the broad sense, a form of insurance". His Lordship continued: ". . . Mr. White and his employer made the contributions. He was to get a pension if he became totally disabled. Now he is totally disabled. Why on earth should we assume that Parliament enacted the Canada Pension Plan to defray a wongdoer's liability in a case like this?" See also *Plachta* v. *Richardson* (1974), 4 O.R. (2d) 654; *Meeks* v. *White* (1974), 39 D.L.R. (3d) 126 (N.S.C.A.); *Chiasson* v. *Paul* (1975), 12 N.B.R. (2d) 432 (C.A.).

3. In *Turenne* v. *Chang* (1962), 36 D.L.R. (2d) 197 (Man. C.A.), the plaintiff, a member of a religious order, claimed one year's loss of pay as damages. The plaintiff had directed her salary be paid to the order from which she received her board and maintenance. Defendant's argument that the plaintiff as a consequence suffered no loss, failed. "It is basic that a person may do what he wishes with his earnings. . . . It would be wrong to permit the defendant tortfeasors to invoke this arrangement for the purpose of reducing their own liability."

4. In *Stead* v. *Elliott* (1963), 39 D.L.R. (2d) 170 (N.S.), it was held that a father suing to recover medical expenses incurred for his child, injured by the defendant's negligence, could recover such expenses even though they had been paid under an accident insurance policy.

5. In *Cunningham* v. *Harrison*, [1973] 3 W.L.R. 97 (C.A.), it was held that the damages awarded were not to be reduced by *ex gratia* payments made by an employer to an injured employee. Denning M.R. also thought that where a wife looked after an injured husband, he should be able to recover the value of those services and hold the amount in trust for her.

6. Most of the older conflicting cases are now rendered obsolete by the *Boarelli* and *Gill* decisions. See Wright and Linden, *The Law of Torts: Cases, Notes and Materials* (5th ed., 1970), pp. 523 *et seq.*

7. Are we now headed in the right direction? If you were a legislator, how would you prefer to treat each of the various social insurance programs now in existence? If you were an insurance company executive, what provisions, if any, would you try to include in your policies?

E. FATAL ACCIDENTS

THE TRUSTEE ACT

R.S.O. 1970, c. 470

38. (1) Except in cases of libel and slander, the executor or administrator of any deceased person may maintain an action for all torts or injuries to the person or to the property of the deceased in the same manner and with the same rights and remedies as the deceased would, if living, have been entitled to do, and the damages when recovered shall form part of the personal estate of the deceased; providing that if death results from such injuries no damages shall be allowed for the death or for the loss of the expectation of life, but this proviso is not in derogation of any rights conferred by The Fatal Accidents Act.

(2) Except in cases of libel and slander if a deceased person committed a wrong to another in respect of his person or property, the person wronged may maintain an action against the executor or administrator of the person who committed the wrong. . . .

FAMILY LAW REFORM ACT, 1978

Stat. Ont. 1978, c. 2

60.—(1) Where a person is injured or killed by the fault or neglect of another under circumstances where the person is entitled to recover damages, or would have been entitled if not killed, the spouse, as defined in Part II, children, grandchildren, parents, grandparents, brothers and sisters of the person are entitled to recover their pecuniary loss resulting from the injury or death from the person from whom the person injured or killed is entitled to recover or would have been entitled if not killed, and to maintain an action for the purpose in a court of competent jurisdiction. R.S.O. 1970, c. 164, s. 3 (1), *amended.*

(2) The damages recoverable in a claim under subsection 1 may include:

(a) actual out-of-pocket expenses reasonably incurred for the benefit of the injured person;

(b) a reasonable allowance for travel expenses actually incurred in visiting the injured person during his treatment or recovery;

(c) where, as a result of the injury, the claimant provides nursing, housekeeping or other services for the injured person, a reasonable allowance for loss of income or the value of the services; and

(d) an amount to compensate for the loss of guidance, care and companionship that the claimant might reasonably have expected to receive from the injured person if the injury had not occurred.

(3) In an action under subsection 1, the right to damages is subject to any apportionment of damages due to contributory fault or neglect of the person who was injured or killed. *New.*

(4) Not more than one action lies under subsection 1 for and in respect of the same occurrence, and no such action shall be brought after the expiration of two years from the time the cause of action arose. R.S.O. 1970, c. 164, s. 5; 1975, c. 38, s. 1.

61.—(1) An action under subsection 1 of section 60 in respect of a person who is killed shall be commenced by and in the name of the executor or administrator of the deceased for the benefit of the persons entitled to recover under subsection 1 of section 60. R.S.O. 1970, c. 164, s. 3, *part, amended.*

(2) If there is no executor or administrator of the deceased, or if there is an executor or administrator and no such action is, within six months after the death of the deceased, brought by the executor or administrator, the action may be brought by all or any of the persons for whose benefit the action would have been if it had been brought by the executor or administrator.

(3) Every action so brought is for the benefit of the same persons and is subject to the same regulations and procedure, as nearly as may be, as if it were brought by the executor or administrator. R.S.O. 1970, c. 164, s. 7.

62.—(1) Where an action is commenced under section 60, the plaintiff shall, in his statement of claim, name and join the claim of any other person who is entitled to maintain an action under section 60 in respect of the same injury or death and thereupon such person becomes a party to the action.

(2) A person who commences an action under section 60 shall file with the statement of claim an affidavit stating that to the best of his knowledge, information and belief the persons named in the statement of claim are the only persons who are entitled or claim to be entitled to damages under section 60. R.S.O. 1970, c. 164, s. 6 (1,2), *amended.*

63.—(1) The defendant may pay into court one sum of money as compensation for his fault or neglect to all persons entitled to compensation without specifying the shares into which it is to be divided. R.S.O. 1970, c. 164, s. 4.

(2) Where the compensation has not been otherwise apportioned, a judge may, upon application, apportion it among the persons entitled.

(3) The judge may in his discretion postpone the distribution of money to which minors are entitled and may direct payment from the undivided fund. R.S.O. 1970, c. 164, s. 8.

64.—(1) In assessing the damages in an action brought under this Part, the court shall not take into account any sum paid or payable as a result of the death or injury under a contract of insurance.

(2) For the purposes of this Part, damages may be awarded for reasonable expenses actually incurred for the burial of the person in respect of whose death the action is brought. R.S.O. 1970, c. 164, s. 3 (2,3), *amended.*

NOTES

1. These two statutes have their counterparts in each of the provinces of Canada. The purpose of the Trustee Act is to permit tort actions both by and against the estate of a deceased person. According to the early common law, personal actions died with the deceased so that the estate could neither sue nor be sued. By virtue of the Trustee Act, which was first enacted in 1886 in Ontario, this is no longer the case.

2. The purpose of the Family Law Reform Act or the Fatal Accidents Act, as it is sometimes called, is to create a legal right of action by the dependants of the deceased for their individual losses as a result of the death. At common law, if someone was wrongfully killed, no tort liability arose. See *Baker* v. *Bolton* (1808), 1 Camp. 493; *The Amerika,* [1917] A.C. 38. In 1846, however, Lord Campbell's Act granted limited protection to some dependants of the deceased. The Family Law Reform Act or the Fatal Accidents Act are successor statutes, upon which dependants of the deceased now sue.

3. In Canada, the damages under the Trustee Act, if death is instant, are usually fairly low, being largely the expenses incurred by the estate because of the death. However, if there is pain and suffering for a considerable time before death, the amounts can be quite substantial. Normally, the greater damage sum is awarded under the Family Law Reform Act or the Fatal Accidents Act action for the loss of support by the dependants.

4. Full discussion of the Trustee Act is left to the courses on civil procedure. Detailed consideration of the Family Law Reform Act is also left to courses on damages, injuries to relations or family law. See, generally, Fleming, *The Law of Torts* (5th ed., 1977), p. 647; Prosser, *Handbook of the Law of Torts* (4th ed., 1971), p. 898.

SCHROEDER, THE CHARGE TO THE JURY

Special Lectures of the Law Society of Upper Canada
on Jury Trials (1959)

Awarding damages in an action brought under The Fatal Accidents Act always involves peculiar difficulty for a jury. They should be told that the action is a statutory one and that under the statute

> . . . such damages may be awarded as are proportioned to the injury resulting from such death to the persons respectively for whom and for whose benefit the action is brought.

This should be enlarged upon and the jury should be told that the measure of damage is the pecuniary loss suffered by these dependants as a result of the death. No damages are to be given for the mental suffering they have undergone, or by way of solatium for their wounded feelings, or the pain and suffering of the deceased. The pecuniary loss means the actual financial benefit of which the dependants have, in effect, been deprived whether the benefit was a result of a legal obligation or of what may reasonably have been expected to take place in the future. It is the amount of the pecuniary benefit which it is reasonably probable that the dependants would have received if the deceased had remained alive.

It is important to point out that in ascertaining the pecuniary loss in cases in which the deceased lived with the dependants as in the case of a husband or a son, it is necessary to take into account the cost of maintaining the deceased. There must also be taken into account the expectation of life of the deceased and of each of the persons claiming to be dependants under the statute. When the income of the deceased was derived from his own earnings, it then becomes necessary to consider what, but for the accident which terminated his existence, would have been his reasonable prospects of his life work and remuneration; and also how far these, if realized, would have conduced to the benefit of the individuals claiming compensation. Here again the jury must be asked to take into account all the uncertainties and the exigencies of mortal existence; the proneness of human beings to accident or death from illness; the probability of the surviving spouse remarrying; these and other considerations should be drawn to the jury's attention because here again, they cannot be expected to award the full amount of a perfect compensation. In cases in which a husband claims damages under The Fatal Accident Act in respect of the death of his wife, he is, of course, not entitled to damages of a purely sentimental character but he may recover for the loss of the household and other services which she was accustomed to perform for him and which would have to be replaced by hired services. The jury, however, must be asked to take into account the cost of the wife's maintenance, because it is an element to be considered in determining the actual pecuniary loss to the husband. Children claiming damages arising out of the death of their mother are entitled to compensation for the loss that they have sustained of the care and moral training of their mother as an element of damage.

NOTES

1. A helpful discussion of the way damages are assessed in a fatal accident case is provided by Pepper, "Fatal Accidents" in Law Society of Upper Canada, *Special Lectures on Damages for Personal Injuries* (1958). He describes how the court must first work out the dependency, which is the net annual contribution made to his relatives by the deceased. The next step is to find the *multiplier* which is the number of years this annual contribution would be made. By combining these figures, a capital sum, which is the present value of the future payments, may be determined. This capital sum must then be reduced because of the contingencies of life, *i.e.*, a widow may remarry, the deceased may have died from some other cause, etc.

KEIZER v. HANNA ET AL.

Supreme Court of Canada. (1978), 3 C.C.L.T. 316

Dickson J. (Laskin C.J.C., Martland, Ritchie, Beetz and Pigeon JJ. concurring): ... There are two issues: (i) the deductibility of income tax in arriving at an award of damages; and (ii) quantum. Although as a member of the court I shared in the decision in *Gehrmann* v. *Lavoie*, [1976] 2 S.C.R. 561, 59 D.L.R. (3d) 634, I have concluded, upon reading the reasons for judgment to which I have referred, and upon further reflection, that de Grandpré J. is correct in law and that the impact of income tax should be taken into account in assessing a damage award under The Fatal Accidents Act, R.S.O. 1970, c. 164.

On point (ii), however, "quantum", I have come to a conclusion other than that arrived at by my brother de Grandpré. I would allow the appeal, and like my brother Spence, award the amount of $100,000 claimed in the statement of claim but deduct therefrom the amount of $6,500 for insurance benefits already received by the appellant under the accident and death benefits provision found in Sched. E of the deceased's insurance policy. In the result, the award of general damages would amount to $93,500.

The accident in which Mr. Keizer was killed occurred on 16th July 1973. At that date he was 33 years of age with a life expectancy of 38.55 years. He was a tool room foreman for the town of Renfrew, capable, conscientious, industrious and in good health. He had been married for 9 years to the appellant, who at the date of his death was 27 years of age with a life expectancy of 49.60 years. Mr. and Mrs. Keizer had one child, an infant of six months.

The trial judge projected average earnings of $15,000 for a working expectancy of 31 years [7 O.R. (2d) 327, 55 D.L.R. (3d) 171]. From this figure he deducted $3,200 for income tax, $1,800 for personal use and $3,000 for personal support leaving disposable income for dependants in the amount of $7,000. The judge made a deduction for income tax with which the Court of Appeal agreed [10 O.R. (2d) 597, 64 D.L.R. (3d) 193] and which, in my view, was proper. The Court of Appeal did not question the judge's finding that the deceased would expend $1,800 for his personal use and $3,000 for his personal support. Thus, as a result, $7,000 would be available as disposable income for dependants. The evidence was that he contributed his pay cheque weekly to his family, reserving only nominal sums and odd-job earnings for his own use. Having concluded that $7,000 per year would have been available to the appellant and her child each year, the judge said [p. 336]:

> "Actuarial tables filed as ex. 1 herein at 9% and 10% compound interest show the present value of $1 to age 65 for the male as $9.9375 and $9.1381 respectively. I believe a more realistic interest rate would be the approximate amount of 6½% which would materially inflate these figures; for example, at 4% the factor is 18.66461. One must consider income tax as a reality of modern life and its depreciating impact along with the contingencies hereinbefore alluded to is reflected in my assessment. Under the provisions of the Fatal Accidents Act I award the plaintiff the sum of $120,000, of which sum I apportion $17,500 for the infant Mitchel Stephen."

It is difficult, if not impossible, to know what use, if any, the trial judge made of actuarial tables to which he was referred. It would seem, however, that he proceeded on an exhausting fund basis, with a discount rate of approximately 6½ per cent. He made an allowance in respect of the income tax which the deceased would have had to pay on his earnings had he lived, and he further reduced the award by a contingency allowance. He referred to the contingencies which might bear on assessment, as follows [pp. 333-34]:

"(a) Possibility of remarriage;
(b) Possibility of widow's death before expiry of joint expectancy period;
(c) Possibility of deceased's dying under other circumstances prior to expiry of said joint expectancy period;
(d) Possibility of deceased husband's retiring before expiry of joint expectancy period;
(e) Acceleration of inheritance to widow—bearing in mind likelihood of increased inheritance in event death had not occurred;
(f) Possibility the infant child may not be a burden to the father or require additional benefits for the full period of his calculated working life."

On the question of prospects of remarriage, the judge adopted the apt comments of Phillimore J. in *Buckley* v. *John Allen & Ford (Oxford) Ltd.,* [1967] 2 Q.B. 637, [1967] 1 All E.R. 539, including the statement that judges should act on evidence rather than guesswork, and, there being no evidence of any existing interest or attachment, he concluded [p. 335]: "I therefore accord no material significance to this prospect by way of deduction." He did not say that he is according no weight to the contingency.

As to the possibility of the early demise of either husband or wife, the judge said [p. 335]:

> "All of the evidence indicates excellent health prospects and I rule that relatively little real significance can be attached to this contingency by way of reduction."

Again, it is not a question of refusing to consider a particular contingency. The judge considered the contingency, but decided it merited little significance. I do not think he can be faulted on this account.

With respect to the possibility of acceleration of the inheritance to the appellant, the judge had this to say [p. 335]:

> "So far as the acceleration of her inheritance is concerned, I am readily satisfied that same should have no reducing effect as in these circumstances. I am assured it is more than offset by the substantial loss she has suffered in future realization from this source."

Finally, the possibility that the infant child might not be a burden during his father's working life—on this point, the judge said that he would give this fact material consideration in considering his award. These are his words [p. 335]:

> "Unquestionably, there is the probability that the child Mitchel Stephen would not have been a burden to his father for anything like the 30 years or so of his working expectancy and I give this fact material consideration in considering this award."

The quantum of the award came before the Court of Appeal for Ontario. In that court, reference was made by Arnup J.A., for the court, to the six contingencies to which the trial judge referred. Arnup J.A. observed that the trial judge might have added [p. 604]: "Possibility of incapacity to earn, occasioned by industrial or other accident, or by illness." He then continued:

> "Having listed these contingencies, the trial Judge decided he should make no deduction for any of them. In so doing, he erred. A contingency, in the context of damages under the *Fatal Accidents Act,* is obviously an event that may or may not happen. A defendant is entitled to have contingencies taken into account by way of reduction from the result that would be reached if every contingency turned out favourably to the dependants, although due weight must be given in each case to the probability, or otherwise, of the contingent event actually happening."

I have been unable to find in the trial judgment any statement by the trial judge that he had decided he should not make any deduction for any of the contingencies. The evidence, as I read it, is to the contrary. It is true that the trial judge might have considered the possibility of the deceased husband becoming unable to earn, but I do not think it can be said that failure to express himself on this point amounts to reversible error. The award of $120,000 exceeded the amount claimed of $100,000 but that does not preclude an award of $100,000.

In making a gross award of $65,000 the Court of Appeal was content with the following cryptic statement [p. 604]:

> "In my view, the appropriate award of general damages in all of the circumstances of this case, as disclosed by the evidence, would have been $65,000."

The judgment does not assist us, or the parties, by explaining why $65,000 should be considered to be the appropriate award. From this amount the Court of Appeal deducted the $6,500, to which I have referred, and directed that

$10,000 be paid into court for the infant. In the result, the widow would receive from the defendants for her support and maintenance for the next 50 years the sum of $48,500. This, plus $6,500 already received, totals $55,000.

It is, of course, true that a trial judge must consider contingencies tending to reduce the ultimate award and give those contingencies more or less weight. It is equally true that there are contingencies tending to increase the award, to which a judge must give due weight. At the end of the day the only question of importance is whether, in all the circumstances, the final award is fair and adequate. Past experience should make one realize that if there is error in the amount of an award it is likely to be one of inadequacy.

In my opinion, in the circumstances of this case, an award of $55,000 to the appellant can only be described as niggardly. The appellant is entitled to an award of such amount as will ensure her the comforts and station in life which she would have enjoyed but for the untimely death of her husband. If one is speaking of contingencies, I think it is not unreasonable to give primary attention to the contingencies, and they are many, the occurrence of which would result in making the award, in the light of events, entirely inadequate. An assessment must be neither punitive nor influenced by sentimentality. It is largely an exercise of business judgment. The question is whether a stated amount of capital would provide, during the period in question, having regard to contingencies tending to increase or decrease the award, a monthly sum at least equal to that which might reasonably have been expected during the continued life of the deceased.

The proper method of calculating the amount of a damage award under The Fatal Accidents Act is similar to that used in calculating the amount of an award for loss of future earnings, or for future care, in cases of serious personal injury. In each, the court is faced with the task of determining the present value of a lump sum which, if invested, would provide payments of the appropriate size over a given number of years in the future, extinguishing the fund in the process. This matter has been discussed in detail in the decisions of this court in *Andrews* v. *Grand & Toy Alta. Ltd.*, *Thornton* v. *Bd. of School Trustees of School District No. 57 (Prince George)* and *Arnold* v. *Teno*, which are being delivered with the decision in the present case.

The object here is to award a sum which would replace present day payments of $7,000 per year for a future period of 31 years, with some reduction for contingencies. The trial judge used a discount rate of 6½ per cent without explaining this choice except to say that it was a "more realistic" rate than 9 or 10 per cent. As I have said in *Andrews* and *Thornton,* in my opinion the discount rate should be calculated on the basis of present rates of return on long-term investments with an allowance for the effects of future inflation. Evidence on these matters was not introduced at trial in the present case. However, the 6½ per cent rate chosen by the judge can be tested by the fact that present day investment rates reach about 10½ per cent, and Dr. Deutsch of the Economic Council of Canada forecasted an inflation rate of about 3½ per cent over the long-term future. These two figures suggest that an appropriate discount rate is approximately 7 per cent. This is only marginally different from the rate used by the trial judge. Ignoring, for the moment, the other factors to be taken into consideration, the sum required to produce $7,000 per year for 31 years, payable monthly, discounted at 6½ per cent, is slightly less than $95,000. The award should be reduced somewhat to account for contingencies although, as I have mentioned, this amount would probably not be large. On the other hand, in order to yield the sum required net of taxes a greater sum would obviously be called for. The resulting amount would not reach the figure of $120,000 which the trial judge chose. However, the sum of $100,000, the amount claimed, can be justified with reasonable allowance made for income tax impact and contingency deduction.

I would allow the appeal, set aside the judgment of the Court of Appeal and direct that the appellant recover from the defendants the sum of $93,500. Out of that sum there should be paid to Marilyn E. Keizer the sum of $78,500, and there should be paid into court to the credit of the infant, Mitchel Stephen Keizer, the sum of $15,000, to be paid out to the said infant when he attains the age of 18 years, or upon further order of a judge of the County Court of the county of Renfrew. The appellant is also entitled to her award of $1,600 under the provisions of The Trustee Act, R.S.O. 1970, c. 470, in respect of funeral expenses and the value of an automobile.

I would allow the appellant her costs at trial against both defendants and her costs in this court and in the Court of Appeal against the defendant Buch.

Appeal allowed.

NOTES

1. Do you agree with the Supreme Court that income tax should be treated differently in fatal accident cases? Spence J. disagreed on this point in the Supreme Court, preferring to remain true to the earlier decision of the court in *Gehrmann* v. *Lavoie*, [1976] 2 S.C.R. 561, which he had delivered.

2. Will the method of calculation differ under the new Ontario legislation? What amount, if any, would be granted in this case for "guidance, care and companionship"? Are these new items or were they included in the calculations before? See *Lewis* v. *Todd* (1978), 5 C.C.L.T. 167 (Ont. C.A.).

3. In *May* v. *Municipality of Metropolitan Toronto*, [1969] 1 O.R. 419, Mr. Justice Addy awarded $37,500 to a widow, 54 years of age at the date of the accident, for the loss of her husband, killed at age 58, who earned about $11,000 yearly, but spent about $5,125 of this on himself each year. The joint life expectancy was 15 years.

4. In *Yuan et al.* v. *Farstad et al.* (1967), 66 D.L.R. (2d) 295, a doctor, 33 years of age, was killed, leaving a wife, 28 years of age, and two children. He was just starting out on his career and had earned only $5,206 in 1965. The joint life expectancy was 29 years. Mr. Justice Munroe assessed the damages under the Families' Compensation Act at $85,000 apportioned $55,000 to the widow and $15,000 each to the two children. Under the Administration Act, $1,917.89 special damages were awarded including $750 for funeral expenses, although the actual cost of burial was $1,276. Was it right that the Yuan family was awarded more than the May family?

5. In *MacDonnell* v. *Maple Leaf Mills Ltd.* (1972), 26 D.L.R. (3d) 106 (Alta. C.A.), a 32-year-old mechanic was killed, leaving a 28-year-old wife and six children between the ages of two and 14 years at the date of trial. On the basis that he would contribute about $7,000 per year to the family, the court affirmed an award, under the Fatal Accidents Act, of $80,000, apportioned $50,000 to the widow and the balance divided among the children in amounts of $4,500 to the oldest three, $5,000 to the next two and $6,500 to the two-year-old. See also *McColl* v. *Osterhout*, [1968] 2 O.R. 562 (C.A.).

6. In *Wiksech* v. *General News Co.*, [1948] O.R. 105, [1948] 1 D.L.R. 753, the defendant's servant driving a motor truck, struck and killed one Wiksech. His wife brought action under the Fatal Accidents Act on behalf of herself and an infant child. At the trial both the defendant's servant and Wiksech were found negligent and the jury found the degree of negligence of Wiksech to be 40 percent as against 60 percent to defendant's servant. Judgment was given in favour of the widow and child for 60 percent of the damages they had sustained in the death of Wiksech. On appeal it was argued that the Ontario Negligence Act had been changed since the decision in *Littley* v.

Brooks, in particular by substituting the words "plaintiff" and "defendant" for the word "party" and, therefore, as the plaintiff was not in fault, full damages should be recoverable. The court sustained the trial judgment. Under the Negligence Act (Ontario) "damages to be paid by the defendant are only those proportionate to his degree of fault". The benefits of the Act are not confined to the case where there is contributory negligence on the part of a living plaintiff. The question under the Act is "whether there was negligence not only upon the part of the one against whom an action has been brought, but also on the part of the person suffering the injury".

7. In *Julian* v. *Northern and Central Gas Corp. Ltd.* (1978), 5 C.C.L.T. 148 (Ont.) *per* Southey J., $415,000 was assessed under Fatal Accident Act for deceased dentist.

VANA v. TOSTA ET AL.

Supreme Court of Canada. [1968] S.C.R. 71; revg. (1966), 54 D.L.R. (2d) 15; revg. (1964), 45 D.L.R. (2d) 574

Haines J. (Trial Judge): I now assess the damages. [After reviewing the evidence relating to the personal injuries suffered by the plaintiffs and assessing damages in respect thereto, the trial judge continued as follows:]

This leaves the assessment under the Fatal Accidents Act, R.S.O. 1960, c. 138, for the death of Melania Vana.

Her husband is 47 years of age and his life expectancy is 26.76 years. Melania Vana was 37 years at the time of her death and her life expectancy was 40.28 years. Their joint expectancy was 25 years. At 3% it would take $21,182 to produce $100 per month for the joint expectancy, and at 6% the sum of $15,757.

Prior to the accident, the plaintiff, his wife and family lived together in a house in Brecksville, Ohio. The plaintiff went to work each day and earned a net weekly salary of $93. His wife looked after the household and the children. She found the time to work for a local caterer as a part-time waitress earning on the average $30 per week which she contributed to the household. Also she managed to create a bank account to be used for the college education of the children. With the death of his wife, the plaintiff was faced with the problem of replacing her services. As might be expected, he found this impossible on his salary. He required someone to do the housework, get the meals and do all those things which his wife had performed about the house on a 24 hour basis. In addition, he required some one with sufficient education and understanding to train and guide his children. Enquiry disclosed that it would cost at least $50 per week for a housekeeper, which he could not afford, and he did not enquire as to the cost of obtaining someone who would substitute for his wife in the duties of training and guiding the children. His position is very similar to what is encountered in any household where the wife-mother is removed by death. Faced with the problem of replacing her services by strangers, able and willing to undertake and discharge the obligations of a wife-mother, it becomes readily apparent that such services are frequently beyond the means of the average wage-earner. In practice, it often takes two people to replace the wife, because a stranger who would undertake the menial tasks is rarely suited to discharge those more exacting duties in the education and training of the children. In this case the plaintiff persuaded his 75-year-old mother to come and live in his home. She can perform only some of the duties of the late Mrs. Vana and it is unlikely she can continue this work for very long. Mr. Vana has promised to pay her $30 per week but so far has been unable to pay anything because of the heavy expenses he has incurred as a result of the accident and subsequent litigation.

It is difficult to estimate the cash value of wife-mother services, but one need not be a home economist to appreciate their worth. They are and must be worth considerable. The amount varies with each individual household. The high cost of replacement of the services by strangers only serves to enhance one's appreciation of these services, even after making the necessary deductions because the plaintiff would not have to clothe the wife-mother substitute nor give her pocket money.

The plaintiff has incurred the following pecuniary losses:

1. Loss of the wife's contribution of $1,500 a year to the household for a period which I estimate at least 10 years. It may well be that she would have worked much longer. She was in good health.
2. The expense of employing a housekeeper and perhaps another person on at least a part-time basis to train and guide his children, all of which services were rendered gratuitously by the wife.
3. The expense of providing board and lodging for those he employs to replace his wife's services.
4. The expense of furnishing a room and providing the amenities for those he employs.
5. Extra expenses which may be incurred from time to time in providing those countless little services that would have been provided by his wife that will not be provided by those he employs.

The losses sustained by the children are deserving of special mention. Nancy, at 13, and Steven, at 10, are entering the most formative and critical years of their lives. They have been deprived of the care, education, training and counsel of their mother. Granted, the plaintiff must endeavour to substitute in place of his wife but in the rearing of children, especially girls, a mother can bring to the solution of problems understanding, sympathy and guidance not afforded by a father. In their mental, moral and physical development they were entitled to the assistance and guidance of both parents. Now they have only one, and I consider the loss of their mother one of the greatest losses these children could sustain.

Counsel for the defendants objects that this loss is merely sentimental and one that does not attract damages under the Fatal Accidents Act. Fortunately, our courts have long held to the contrary. In *St. Lawrence & Ottawa R. Co.* v. *Lett* (1885), 11 S.C.R. 422, Sir W. J. Ritchie C.J. makes it quite clear that such damages are recoverable, that they are substantial, and that no court should be deterred in awarding them because of the difficulty in their estimation. Social science has contributed greatly to our thinking since 1885, and serves to enhance what was said by the learned Chief Justice. The loss of a parent, the disruption of a home, the failure to receive sound and adequate guidance, understanding and maternal interest during one's minority can and often does result in impairment of development. Adolescents encounter difficult problems in adjusting to the complexities of modern living and in the preparation for a responsible adult life. Constantly they are besieged with a multitude of stimuli, much of which is erotic and spurious. The choice of good companions and the appreciation of the real from the second rate — all of these are matters in which every young person needs the guidance of two understanding parents. One thing is painfully apparent to those on the Bench when dealing with the offences of youth, and that is the broken home. The absence of one or sometimes both parents in this critical time of a young person's life seems to be a common denominator in youthful misconduct.

To the extent to which a monetary award can make restitution, it is the duty of the court to provide it.

Finally, I must consider the matter of remarriage. I have seen the plaintiff and have studied him closely throughout the trial. I think remarriage unlikely.

Under the Fatal Accidents Act, I award for the death of Melania Vana, the sum of $35,000 and apportion $10,000 to the infant, Nancy, and $5,000 to the infant, Steven and the balance of $20,000 to the plaintiff. Although Nancy is three years older than Steven, I think this girl's loss of her mother is greater than Steven's loss. The plaintiff can try to make up for lost maternal care to his son but cannot do so in the same measure with his daughter.

[On appeal to the Ontario Court of Appeal, the damages under the Fatal Accidents Act were reduced as follows: George Vana, $10,000; Nancy Vana, $2,000; and Steven Vana, $1,500. The Court of Appeal refused to follow *St. Lawrence & Ottawa Ry. Co.* v. *Lett*, because it had not been followed in England. There was a further appeal to the Supreme Court of Canada.]

Spence J. (Supreme Court of Canada): In reducing the award by $10,000 the Court of Appeal erred in placing far too much emphasis on the possibility of remarriage and in taking into account any services the appellant's mother and mother-in-law might contribute to maintaining the home. It is trite law that a wrongdoer cannot claim the benefit of services donated to the injured party. In the present case it amounts in my judgment to conscripting the mother and mother-in-law to the services of the appellant and his children for the benefit of the tortfeasor and any reduction of the award on this basis is and was an error in principle. There being error in principle, the amount awarded by the Court of Appeal is reviewable in this court: *Widrig* v. *Strazer et al.*

The next question is whether the $20,000 awarded by the learned trial judge should be restored or varied and whether the amount fixed by the Court of Appeal should stand. I am of opinion that the $20,000 awarded was excessive and not justified by the evidence. I am also of opinion that the Court of Appeal erred in cutting the award in two for the reasons given in the judgment of MacKay J.A. Mr. Justice MacKay pointed out that the evidence is indefinite as to how much of the wife's earnings were used for herself and how much might reasonably be expected to enure to the benefit of the husband and children. It is significant to observe that the wife's earnings only totalled about $1,500 per year and that the husband was a man in moderate circumstances. Out of the sum of $1,500 a year, the mother put aside about $200 a year for the future benefit of the two children. It must be realized that what she expended out of the balance for her own maintenance was, under the circumstances of a moderate income family, a contribution to what would ordinarily have been provided by her husband. The husband was under the duty of supporting his wife in accordance with their circumstances in life, and the case cannot be considered as one where the earnings of the wife which she retained for herself were quite apart from any contribution made by her husband for her support, but rather as one where her earnings in part contributed to her support as well as to that of the balance of the family and the loss of those earnings was, therefore, a pecuniary loss to the husband. The situation resembles somewhat that dealt with by Ritchie J. in *Corrie* v. *Gilbert*. In that case he said at p. 464:

> "It is unusual in this court on an appeal such as this to reject both the award of the jury and that of the Court of Appeal, but there is no doubt that under s. 46 of the Supreme Court Act it is empowered to give the judgment that the court whose decision is appealed against should have given, and for the reasons which I have stated, I do not think the award made by either of the courts below should be affirmed."

However, after reviewing the evidence as a whole and giving due weight to the possible remarriage, remote as it may be, and what it will cost to hire a housekeeper and the other factors involved, I have reached the conclusion that an award of $14,000 should be made and I would vary the judgment appealed from accordingly.

I deal next with that part of the judgment of the Court of Appeal for Ontario which would reduce the award under The Fatal Accidents Act to the daughter Nancy Vana from $10,000 to $2,000 and the award under the said Fatal Accidents Act to the son Steven Vana, from $5,000 to $1,500.

Before setting these amounts, the learned judges in appeal said:

> "The conclusion I have reached is that the learned trial judge erred in principle in that he took into consideration matters that cannot be classed as pecuniary loss, that he failed to allow for the contingencies of life to which I have referred; that he made assumptions in the absence of evidence and disregarded evidence that would tend to mitigate or lower the damages."

This statement followed immediately the consideration of the damages awarded to the two children under the provisions of The Fatal Accidents Act. If the initial words which I have quoted are taken to mean that the judgment of Ritchie C.J. in this court in *St. Lawrence & Ottawa Railway Company* v. *Lett* is no longer law, then I must, with respect, express disagreement. . . .

Despite anything that was said in *Grand Trunk Railway Company* v. *Jennings* or comments made in the Australian and New Zealand cases, the decision of this court in *St. Lawrence & Ottawa Railway Company* v. *Lett* is unaffected and remains good law in Canada. I am, therefore, in agreement with my brother Ritchie when he expresses that view in his reasons for judgment. . . .

Nancy Vana was 12½ years of age at the time of the accident in which her mother died, and Steven Vana was a little less than 10 years of age. In my view, awards of $1,000 and $500, respectively, to those two children for the loss of the care and guidance of their mother made as of the year 1963 were, to use the words of Danckwerts L.J. in *Naylor* v. *Yorkshire Electricity Board*, "a purely conventional assessment" and therefore were in error of principle. In such circumstances as I have already pointed out, it becomes the duty of this court to assess what would be an amount awarded upon a proper principle.

I am of the opinion that the award of the learned trial judge in the sums of $10,000 and $5,000 was unreasonable in that it was so "inordinately high as to be a wholly erroneous estimate of the damages": *Davies et al.* v. *Powell Duffryn Associated Collieries Ltd.* The award should be based upon a realistic assessment of the evidence of the particular circumstances of the case under consideration. It would not be proper to be guided by any criterion such as the necessity of finding "a very moderate figure" as recommended by Viscount Simon L.C. in *Benham* v. *Gambling*. . . .

What is that evidence in the present case? Without going into detail, I shall summarize it. The deceased woman was a good wife and industrious helpmate to her husband, and was a good mother to her children. No attempt was made by her husband to show that she was any extraordinary paragon but he gave such evidence without elaboration as would justify the aforesaid conclusion. In my view, to require the establishment of any different situation by the plaintiff would only encourage the gross exaggeration of evidence in an attempt to bolster claims and result in the exaggeration of the verdict to which Lord Roche referred. The *St. Lawrence & Ottawa Railway Company* v. *Lett* case established that these two children under these circumstances suffered the pecuniary loss from their mother's early death without the care, education and training (and I would also add the guidance, example and encouragement) which only a mother can give. I have already expressed the view that to allow damages under these circumstances attributable to such pecuniary loss of only $1,000 to a girl of 12 years of age and $500 to a boy of 9 years of age is a "purely conventional assessment" and is, therefore, an error in principle. I would increase the amount of the award for this loss to the daughter Nancy Vana from $1,000 to $2,000 and to the son Steven Vana from $500 to $1,000. This would result in the total award to Nancy Vana under the provisions of The Fatal Accidents Act being fixed at $3,000 and the total award to Steven Vana under the provisions of The Fatal Accidents Act being fixed at $2,000.

[Cartwright and Hall JJ. agreed with Spence J. Ritchie and Judson JJ. dissented in part.]

NOTES

1. What do you think of the way the damages for the loss of a wife and mother were assessed here? Is the amount too much, too little or just about right? Will this calculation change under the new Ontario Act?

2. The awards for loss of a wife and mother are usually quite low. See *Alaffe* v. *Kennedy* (1974), 40 D.L.R. (3d) 429 ($10,000 to husband). If the woman has a job outside the home, the amount will be higher. See *Thompson* v. *Toorenburg* (1972), 29 D.L.R. (3d) 608 ($27,500 to husband, $5,000 to child); *Carney* v. *Lewis et al.* (1969), 68 W.W.R. 573 ($17,500 to husband); *Kovats* v. *Ogilvie* (1970), 17 D.L.R. (3d) 343 (B.C.C.A.) ($20,000 to husband, $3,000 and $3,500 to children).

3. Are the courts undervaluing women? Can you think of a fairer way to assess the damages for the loss of a wife and mother? What about trying to allocate a dollar value to each of the services usually performed by a woman who is running a home and raising children?

4. As cold-hearted as the courts appear in assessing damages for the loss of a wife and mother, they are even more so in evaluating the life of a child. There are actually cases in the books where courts have decided that an action by parents for the wrongful death of a young child would be dismissed because no damages "either actual or prospective" were incurred. See *Barnett* v. *Cohen*, [1921] 2 K.B. 461 (4-year-old). See also *Pedlar* v. *Toronto Power Co.* (1913), 29 O.L.R. 527; 30 O.L.R. 581 (two-year-old); *Cashin* v. *Mackenzie*, [1951] 3 D.L.R. 495 (5-year-old); *Nickerson* v. *Forbes* (1956), 1 D.L.R. (2d) 463 (N.S.C.A.) (child nearly six). The theory behind these cases is that there is little likelihood of "pecuniary benefit or advantage" to the parents of a young child. See *Alaffe* v. *Kennedy, supra,* note 2 (4-month-old child), *per* Gillis J., at p. 437. As the children grow older, because the courts feel that there is more likelihood of material gain to the parents apparently, small amounts of damages may be granted. See *Courtemanche* v. *McElwain* (1962), 37 D.L.R. (2d) 595, where the Ontario Court of Appeal upheld a judgment awarding $1,500 to a father and mother for the death of a seven-year-old son. The court seemed to be satisfied with evidence showing plans for educational advancement of the boy "and the expectation and feeling" that he would ultimately be of pecuniary assistance to the parents. Somewhat larger amounts are awarded for teenagers. In *French* v. *Blake,* [1971] 3 W.W.R. 705 (B.C.C.A.), the parents of a 15-year-old girl, who had been performing household duties for them, received $4,000 in a fatal accident claim, since there was a "reasonable expectation of pecuniary advantage" (*per* Maclean J.A.). In *Child* v. *Stevenson,* [1973] 4 W.W.R. 322 (B.C.C.A.), two awards of $5,000 and one of $7,500 were upheld for the loss of boys of 15, 16 and 17.

5. Dissatisfaction with this method of assessing damages for the loss of children has led some American courts to pioneer a new approach. In *Wycko* v. *Gnodtke* (1960), 361 Mich. 331, 105 N.W. 2d 118, Smith J. affirmed a jury award of $14,000 for the death of a child. He rejected the "child-labour measure of damages" and adopted instead the "pecuniary value of the life" test:

"The pecuniary value of a human life is a compound of many elements. The use of material analogies may be helpful and inoffensive. Just as with respect to a manufacturing plant, or industrial machine, value involves the costs of acquisition, emplacement, upkeep, maintenance service, repair, and renovation, so, in our context, we must consider the expenses of birth, of food, of clothing, of medicines, of instruction, of nurture and shelter. Moreover, just as an item of machinery forming part of a functioning industrial plant has a value over and above that of a similar item in a showroom, awaiting purchase, so an individual member of a family has a value to others as part of a functioning social and economic unit. This value is the value of mutual society and protection, in a word, companionship. The human companionship thus afforded has a definite, substantial, and ascertainable pecuniary value and its loss forms a part of the 'value' of the life we seek to ascertain. We are, it will be noted, restricting the losses to pecuniary losses, the actual money value of the life of the child, not the sorrow and anguish caused by its death. This is not because these are not suffered and not because they are unreal. The genius of the common law is capable, were it left alone, of ascertaining such damages, but the legislative act creating the remedy forbids. Food, shelter, clothing, and companionship, however, are obtainable on the open market, have an ascertainable money value. Finally if, in some unusual situation, there is in truth, or reasonably forthcoming, a wage-profit capability in the infant (an expectation of an excess of wages over keep, the measure heretofore employed) the loss of such expectation should not be disregarded as one of the pecuniary losses suffered. In such case, however, the assessment is made as a matter of fact and not of fiction. It is true, of course, that there will be uncertainties in all of these proofs, due to the nature of the case, but we are constrained to observe that it is not the privilege of him whose wrongful act caused the loss to hide behind the uncertainties inherent in the very situation his wrong has created. . . .

Error, then, there was. But the error into which the court was betrayed was the direct and natural result of this court's insistence upon the continued employment of the child-labour standard of pecuniary loss. Whatever the situation may have been in 1846, as the children brought home their wages from plant, mine, and mill, today their gainful employment is an arrant fiction and we know it. The trial judge may have been on sound ground as a matter of economies in saying that he didn't think the deceased child had a $14,000 earning capacity. But we are not dealing in economics. We are dealing with a fiction, the fiction that under today's conditions, not those of 1846, the minor child is a breadwinner. He is not. He is an expense. A blessed expense, it is true, but nevertheless an expense. . . .

The fiction now employed as the measure of pecuniary loss should be abandoned. It perpetuates an attitude towards the value of a child's life completely repudiated by modern legislation and the enlightened child-welfare policies of this jurisdiction. It does violence to the intent of the act, which is to grant a recovery whenever a death 'of a person' is caused by the wrongful act of another. The child is a person and is not to be read out of the act by judicial acquiescence in the Chief Baron's theory that his life has no pecuniary value save as that of a wage-earner. The bloodless bookkeeping imposed upon our juries by the savage exploitations of the last century must no longer be perpetuated by our courts."

What do you think of this approach? Can you devise a better one?

6. Is it really possible to place a value upon human life? Should there be a minimum figure of say $10,000 or $25,000 that should be awarded for the loss of any life, with the right to recover more if greater loss can be established? Should there be a maximum placed on these awards? Do you feel comfortable with the notion that different human beings are worth different amounts of money if they are killed? Does it make any sense that you may recover for pain and suffering for a cut on your finger but not for the loss of your child? Why not provide compensation for the grief associated with the loss of a loved

one? See the Survival of Actions Act, 1978, Alta., c. 35, where $3,000 damages "for bereavement" are allowed to a spouse and minor children of a deceased.

7. What damages, if any, should be assessed for "wrongful life"? Suppose, for example, a sterilization procedure is done improperly and a pregnancy and unplanned birth of a child ensues. Should the cost of raising such child be recoverable? See *Doiron* v. *Orr* (1978), 20 O.R. (2d) 71, where Garrett J. denied compensation for this because he found such a claim "grotesque". What about recovery for the pain and suffering undergone by the mother? See *Cryderman* v. *Ringrose,* [1978] 3 W.W.R. 481 (Alta.), where $5,000 awarded and *Doiron* v. *Orr,* where $1,000 assessed but not awarded because no negligence found. Compare with the position under the civil law of Quebec, *Cataford* v. *Moreau* (1978), 7 C.C.L.T. 241, where Deschênes C.J. permitted damages to the mother for the equivalent of pain and suffering, but did not allow anything to the child. See Rodgers-Magnet, "Action for Wrongful Life" (1979), 7 C.C.L.T. 242; Tedeschi, "On Tort Liability for Wrongful Life", [1966] Israel L. Rev. 513. *Cf. Troppi* v. *Scarf* (1971), 18 N.W. 2d 511 (Mich.), where damages were allowed for cost of rearing child.

CHAPTER 15

AUTOMOBILE ACCIDENT COMPENSATION

Probably the most important function of tort law at present is its role in adjusting the disputes arising out of automobile accidents. Certainly tort lawyers spend more of their time working on these cases than any other. There has been much dissatisfaction expressed about the way tort law handles these losses. This debate, over the future of the tort suit in automobile cases, is global and seems to be endless. Books and reports have been written. Articles abound. There has been a recent breakthrough in Canada, but the voices calling for reform have not been stilled. Automobile accident compensation plans and social insurance schemes will continue to be debated in the press, in the law reviews, at bar meetings and in legislatures for many years to come. It is, therefore, appropriate to expose students to some of what has been written in this area. The discussion is important not only to sort out the best way of administering car crash losses, but it also raises the whole matter of the role of tort law in the welfare state.

A. THE TORT SYSTEM AND ITS INADEQUACIES

KEETON AND O'CONNELL, BASIC PROTECTION FOR THE TRAFFIC VICTIM

(1969)

Serious shortcomings beset the automobile claims system operating in each of our states. In each there is need for re-examination and reform of the whole set of laws, institutions, insurance arrangements, and customary practices currently used in determining who among the hundreds of thousands of annual traffic victims will receive compensation and how much each will receive. The most striking of the shortcomings can be stated in five points.

First, measured as a way of compensating for personal injuries suffered on the roadways, the system we have falls grievously short. Some injured persons receive no compensation. Others receive far less than their economic losses. Partly this gap is due to the role of fault in the system — to the need for the injured person to assert both that another was at fault in causing the accident and that he himself was legally blameless. In advancing these contentions a traffic victim faces severe problems of proof. Nearly always he finds it difficult to show what actually happened, and occasionally he cannot even identify the person responsible, because the accident was hit and run. Another major factor contributing to the gap between amounts of loss and amounts of compensation is that a person legally responsible for an injury may be financially irresponsible — uninsured and with inadequate assets of his own available to satisfy a claim. The size of the accumulated gap from these two and other causes varies significantly from state to state. Probably it is somewhat smaller in the states with compulsory motor vehicle liability insurance (Massachusetts, New York, and North Carolina) than in others. But even in these states it is still substantial.

15-1

Second, the present system is cumbersome and slow. Prompt payments of compensation for personal injuries are extraordinary indeed. And delays of several years before final payment — or determination that no payment is due — are common, especially in metropolitan areas. The backlog of automobile personal injury cases presents a serious community problem of delay in the courts, affecting other kinds of cases as well. And often justice delayed is justice denied. An injured person needing money to pay his bills cannot wait, as can an insurance company, through the long period necessary to press and recover his claim, and he may be forced to settle for an inadequate amount in order to obtain immediate recovery.

Third, the present system is loaded with unfairness. Some get too much — even many times their losses — especially for minor injuries. To avoid the expenses and risks of litigation insurance companies tend to make generous settlements of small claims. This largesse comes out of the pockets of all who are paying premiums as insured motorists. Others among the injured, as we have just suggested, get nothing or too little, and most often it is the neediest (those most seriously injured) who get the lowest percentage of compensation for their losses. Their larger claims are more vigorously resisted, and their more pressing needs induce them to give up more in return for prompt settlement. This disparity between losses and compensation is not explained by differences in fault in different cases. It is true that under the theory of the present system, in general, only an injured person innocent of fault is entitled to recover, and then only against a motorist who was at fault. But the practical results are more often inconsistent with this theory than consistent. In short, the results are branded unfair by the theory of the system itself, and one searches in vain for any substitute standard of fairness that gives these results a clean bill of health.

Fourth, operation of the present system is excessively expensive. It is burden enough to meet the toll of losses that are inescapable when injuries occur. It is intolerable to have to meet the additional burden of administrative waste built into our methods of shouldering inescapable costs. To some extent, it is true, costs of administration are part of the inescapable burden. But because of the role of fault in the present system, contests over the intricate details of accidents are routine. Often these contests are also exercises in futility, since all drivers must continually make split-second judgments and many accidents are caused by slight but understandable lapses occurring at unfortunate moments. Such contests, and all the elaborate preparations that must precede them, wastefully increase the costs of administration. In cases of relatively modest injury, the expense of the contest often exceeds the amount claimed as compensation. All this expense, of course, is added to automobile insurance costs and, together with mark-up for the insurers through whose treasuries the premium dollars must pass, is reflected in the premium of every insured.

Fifth, the present system is marred by temptations to dishonesty that lure into their snares a stunning percentage of drivers and victims. To the toll of physical injury is added a toll of psychological and moral injury resulting from pressures for exaggeration to improve one's case or defense and indeed for outright invention to fill its gaps or cure its weaknesses. These inducements to exaggeration and invention strike at the integrity of driver and injured alike, all too often corrupting both and leaving the latter twice a victim — injured and debased. If one is inclined to doubt the influence of these debasing factors, let him compare his own rough-and-ready estimates of the percentage of drivers who are at fault in accidents and the percentage who admit it when the question is put under oath. Of course the disparity is partly accounted for by self-deception, but only partly. And even this self-deception is an insidious undermining of integrity, not to be encouraged.

This, in capsule, is the way the present automobile claims system looks when we stand back and view its performance in gross. It provides too little, too late, unfairly allocated, at wasteful cost, and through means that promote dishonesty and disrespect for law.

NOTES

1. There are several practitioners' books dealing with automobile law. See Horsley and O'Donnell, *Manual of Motor Vehicle Law* (2nd ed., 1974); Phelan, *Highway Traffic Law* (3rd ed., 1969); Wunder, *Conduct of a Personal Injury Action* (1970); Shannon, *Motor Vehicle Offences* (1964).

2. In 1965, the *Report of the Osgoode Hall Study on Compensation for Victims of Automobile Accidents* was published. Based on personal interviews with 590 personal injury victims of car crashes that occurred in 1961, in the County of York, it demonstrated that only 42.9 percent of the respondents received tort compensation, whereas 57.1 percent received no tort recovery. Part of the reason for this poor recovery record was that, in that year, Ontario guest passengers were barred from recovery against their hosts. Consequently, 66.3 percent of the injured passengers received no tort recovery and this lowered the percentage of those who recovered. Since that time, the Ontario law has been amended so as to permit recovery by guest passengers, a step that should have broadened considerably the incidence of recovery.

The Osgoode Hall Study also showed that there was significant delay, especially in the serious injury cases, with only 46.6 percent of the cases settled after one year and 12 percent still awaiting trial after two and a half to three and a half years after the accident. Consequently, even though most cases are settled relatively promptly, and even though there may be some good reasons for delay, too many cases take too long to finish.

The Study also demonstrated that only a small fraction of the injury cases reach litigation. A Writ of Summons was issued in only 13.4 percent of the cases, and only 1.2 percent of them ever reached a trial on the merits. Consequently, it is apparent that the present auto accident compensation system is predominantly one of negotiation rather than litigation. It should be noted that a lawyer was consulted in only 37.3 percent of the cases, so that some of these negotiations are proceeding without any legal advice. See Generally, Ross, *Settled out of Court* (1970).

The non-tort recovery sources cannot be ignored. The Osgoode Hall Study disclosed that some 46 percent of all the money recovered by accident victims came from non-tort sources. Hospital bills were paid in 94.5 percent of the cases. This would be even higher today. Although in 1961, medical expenses were very poorly covered, they are rarely a problem today because of universal medicare programs that are in operation across Canada. The major problem in 1961, and today, is replacement of income.

After all the sources of recovery were taken into account, only 7.2 percent of the Osgoode Hall Study respondents ended up with over $500 out-of-pocket losses and only 2.4 percent lost more than $2,000. When asked for their opinions, 40.2 percent of the respondents expressed dissatisfaction with the size of their tort recovery, 47.9 percent opposed the fault system while 42.2 percent favoured it, and yet 70 percent favoured compensation for pain and suffering. See Linden, "Peaceful Coexistence and Automobile Accident Compensation" (1966), 9 Can. Bar J. 5, for a summary of the findings.

3. There have been some other statistical studies of auto accident compensation systems, the findings of which were not too dissimilar to those of the Osgoode Hall Study. See Conard et al., *Automobile Accident Costs and Payments* (1964); *Report of the British Columbia Royal Commission on Automobile Insurance* (1968); Harris and Hartz, *Report of a Pilot Survey of the Financial Consequences of Personal Injuries Suffered in Road Accidents in the City of Oxford During 1965* (1968); U.S. Department of Transportation, *Automobile Insurance and Compensation Study: Economic Consequences of Automobile Accident*

Injuries (1970). The five studies listed above were relied upon and summarized in the Ontario Law Reform Commission, *Report on Motor Vehicle Accident Compensation* (1973). See also Ison, *The Forensic Lottery* (1967); Atiyah, *Accidents, Compensation and the Law* (2nd ed., 1975).

4. The original landmark of social science research in this area was the Columbia Report of 1932. See "Compensation for Automobile Accidents: A Symposium" (1932), 32 Colum. L. Rev. 785. See also Conard, "The Economic Treatment of Automobile Injuries" (1964), 63 Mich. L. Rev. 279; Morris and Paul, "The Financial Impact of Automobile Accidents" (1962), 110 U. Pa. L. Rev. 913; Franklin, Chanin and Mark, "Accidents, Money and the Law: A Study of the Economics of Personal Injury Litigation" (1961), 61 Colum. L. Rev. 1; Zeisel, Kalven and Buchholz, *Delay in Court* (1959); Hunting and Neuwirth, *Who Sues in New York City?* (1962); *Dollars, Delay and the Automobile Victim* (1968); Linden, "The Processing of Automobile Claims" [1967] Ins. Couns. J. 50; Linden, "Automobile Cases in the British Columbia Courts" (1967), 3 U.B.C.L. Rev. 194; U.S. Department of Transportation, *Automobile Accident Litigation* (1970).

5. How reliable are statistical reports from foreign jurisdictions? How old must a statistical study be before it becomes out-dated? Does it depend on the pace and nature of the development in the jurisdiction under study? How important are statistics in our consideration of a question such as this?

6. Leon Green, one of America's foremost torts professors, has written in *Traffic Victims — Tort Law and Insurance* (1958):

> "The courts are powerless to reconstruct a rational process for general use. They have reached a dead end. As a means of giving adequate protection against the machines of the highway, negligence law has run its course. Something better must be found."

GRIFFITHS, DON'T ABOLISH TORT LAW IN AUTO ACCIDENT COMPENSATION

(1969), 12 Can. Bar J. 187

The criticism of the delay in disposing of claims by reason of congested court lists may be more valid in the United States than in Ontario or other Canadian provinces. Statistics indicate that the delay in the courts in the American metropolitan areas average 31 months and is said to be as much as 6 years in Cook County, Illinois. Professor Allen M. Linden suggested that it takes more than 2 years in Toronto and an average of 1 year in Vancouver to get an automobile case to trial. This is in contrast to the statement of the Law Society's Special Committee on Trial of Damage Actions which reported in 1962 that an Ontario claimant could bring his case to trial within 6 to 9 months from the commencement of proceedings and that trials within 3 to 4 months are not unusual. In York County the average period was from 3 to 12 months.

The criticism of delay may be valid but the proposed remedy, *i.e.*, a drastic change in the tort law, is not responsive to the problem.

In my view there are probably three principal reasons for delay. First, during the last few years delays have been occasioned, particularly in Toronto, by the substantial increase in criminal cases which take precedence for trial over civil cases. These criminal cases at times literally "clog" our courts. Is this a reason for changing the substantive criminal law?

The second reason is the lack of sufficient judges available to try these cases. In Ontario in the past few years there has been an increase in all forms of court business which is commensurate with the population increase. Delay has developed due to our failure to provide the facilities and personnel needed to keep pace with this growth.

The third reason for delay reflects unfavourably on the bar. A small percentage of lawyers, both for the plaintiff and the defence, are dilatory, disorganized and inefficient in moving their clients' auto claims forward to final disposition. This is a defect which surely can be corrected and the bar as a whole must redouble its efforts to find ways to increase the speed and efficiency of dealing with automobile tort cases.

There are occasions when competent plaintiff's counsel have valid reasons for delaying the final disposition of the plaintiff's claim. In personal injury cases of a severe nature it is frequently difficult to obtain, until considerable time has elapsed, a final medical prognosis sufficient to enable counsel to assess the value of the general damages of the plaintiff. In such cases it is my experience that the plaintiffs are rarely financially destitute or prejudiced by the delay. A great majority are supported by some form of sick benefit plan provided by their employers whereby they recover a portion, if not all, of their income. Hospital and medical expenses are almost invariably paid for by some other agency. Moreover, the insurance industry itself, in an effort to overcome any criticism for the delay in payment to the needy victim, has developed a plan, supported by the majority of insurance companies in Ontario, where in cases of clear liability, advanced payments are made on behalf of the defendant to the claimant to cover his loss of income, medical and other expenses as they are incurred. The claimant is then free to proceed to trial when his injury has "matured" if the offer of general damages made by the defendant's insurer appears inadequate.

NOTES

1. See Linden, "The Law's Delay" (1971), 5 Law Society of Upper Canada Gazette 96, at p. 97, where this appears: "In the same way as justice delayed may be justice denied, justice hurried may also be justice denied." Is there anything to this?

McRUER, THE MOTOR CAR AND THE LAW

printed in Linden, *Studies in Canadian Tort Law* (1968)

THE FAILURE OF TORT LAW

What concerns those engaged in the administration of justice most is whether the courts of justice are really exercising their true functions with respect to injuries arising out of motor vehicle accidents under the conditions that in fact exist. We ask ourselves three questions:

(1) Is the law of torts, as we conceive it to be, appropriate to meet the changed conditions of 1965?

(2) What is the real function that the courts are in fact performing in this field of tort law?

(3) Are the present processes of the courts the best method that can be devised to provide just compensation for injuries sustained through the operation of motor vehicles on the highways?

To answer the first question one must examine the process by which liability and compensation are determined in the motor vehicle cases that now come before the courts. In Ontario either party has a right to trial by jury in a motor vehicle accident case. This right is not always exercised but, whether the case is tried by a judge sitting alone or by a judge and jury, the tribunal of fact has to determine liability arising out of conditions that were never dreamed of when the concepts of negligence were forged in the common law courts.

The court is asked to come to a conclusion on what the fictional reasonable and prudent man would have done in circumstances which more often than not required split second decisions. Witnesses are asked to tell, months or years after the event, with great accuracy, their observation of events prior to and leading up to an accident when they had no occasion whatever to make any observations because no accident was anticipated. The evidence in the ordinary intersection case affords the best example of the unreality of evidence of this character. It would require several witnesses observing the accident armed with directors and stop watches to give the sort of evidence witnesses are continually asked to give in these cases. The witness is asked how far he was from the intersection when he looked to the left, where he was when he sounded his horn and where he was when he applied the brakes. A great part of the evidence in actions arising out of motor vehicle accidents is in fact reconstruction and too often reconstruction with an eye on the result. Dean Wright has said:

> "Lawyers supporting the trial jury are willing to admit that in the ordinary automobile accident the case that is actually tried by a jury is a case that never in fact took place, and is the result of conjectural recall, imagination, colourful dramatization, and pure inventiveness."

I do not think Dean Wright has over-stated the case, but I would apply his comments with equal force to those cases tried by a judge without a jury.

The violence of motor vehicle accidents is such that in many cases, the witnesses who might have some knowledge of how the accident happened are either killed or suffer from traumatic amnesia to such an extent that they are unable to relate any of the events leading up to or following the accident. In such cases the parties who are justly entitled to compensation may be entirely deprived of any relief because the evidence on their behalf has been extinguished by the force of the accident, or, on the other hand, liability may be imposed for the same reason where there is no fault.

The difficulties of the courts do not end with the uncertainties and imponderables in determining liability. A just and fair assessment of damages presents equal, if not greater, difficulties and equal speculation.

Many cases are comparatively simple but where there has been a serious injury or a fatal injury the judgment of the court, final as it is, must in respect of general damages be based largely on conjecture.

What is just compensation for a child that has lost an eye, or a young wife and family that have lost the breadwinner, or a farmer that has lost an arm, or a young mother that is paralyzed for life? Often the compensation is determined by the limitation of the defendant's insurance policy. In the case of the child who has lost an eye it may, through accident or disease, lose the other eye. The court is asked to take that into consideration. What does that mean in dollars and cents? Likewise, the young farmer who has lost his arm may be so handicapped that he has to give up his farm but he may become a drover and he may be much better off financially. How can a just result be arrived at by considering unknown and speculative factors? Although these difficulties arise in assessing damages in all personal injury cases, they are particularly emphasized in motor vehicle cases as they were emphasized in the common law employers' liability cases. In those cases the difficulties were resolved in Ontario by providing for disability allowances payable out of the compensation fund according to the continuance of the disability.

All the hazards of proof of liability in motor vehicle accident cases and the difficulties in assessing damages have united with the growth of casualty insurance during the last 50 years to reduce the use of the processes of administering justice to little more than an instrument in the adjustment of claims, be they adjustments between individuals or between individuals and insurance companies or between individuals and the Department of Transport.

This is amply demonstrated by the experience in the County of York in the Province of Ontario, which is quite typical of that throughout the Province. In the year 1964, which was not an unusual year, 458 actions arising out of motor vehicle accidents were entered for trial for the Winter Assizes — of these 19 were tried and 128 were settled: 438 were entered for the Spring Assizes — of these 25 were tried and 116 were settled; 548 were entered for the Autumn Assizes — of these 26 were tried and 103 were settled.

Actions not disposed of at a particular Assize were either among those that were re-set down for trial at the next Assize or were disposed of without further reference to the court. The proportion re-set down cannot be readily ascertained. The experience of the year 1964 was quite similar to previous years. It is a fair estimate that less than 15 percent of actions commenced that arise out of motor vehicle accidents are ever tried.

These facts show that the normal processes of the courts really do not function in this field of law to serve the public according to their intended purposes. . . .

Suggestions have been made from time to time that there should be some form of pre-trial after actions have been entered for trial to make sure that the action is ready for trial and to bring plaintiffs and defendants together with a view to promoting a settlement. The adoption of such a proposal, instead of expediting trials would provide a means of delay, increase costs and give greater opportunity to put pressure on one side or the other to bring about a settlement. Such pre-trial procedure is just a further prostitution of the judicial process. The judicial function is not to intimidate litigants into settlement but to preside over trials and decide cases. It is quite true that when the presiding judge has heard sufficient of the facts at the trial he may sometimes by wise suggestion enable parties to adjust their difficulties, but that is a usefulness that a judge should reserve for exceptional cases. The problems arising out of motor vehicle accidents cannot be solved by merely aggravating the misuse of the courts.

Motor vehicle accident facts demonstrate quite clearly the pressure of the "felt necessities of the time" in this realm of tort law. In Ontario, with a population of about 8,000,000, there is one registered motor vehicle for every four of the population. In the year 1964 there were 54,560 persons injured in motor vehicle accidents and 1,424 persons were killed. The increase during the last ten years in persons killed and injured has been over 100%, and during the last two years it has been 14% annually.

In these circumstances the orderly judicial process of applying the law of torts and the law of evidence has proved quite inadequate to provide prompt and just service to the public in determining liability and just compensation. Since the processes of law have not afforded injured persons effective means of relief they have been forced to resort to the well-known methods used in the Middle East in the retail trade — bargaining. The ordinary judicial procedure has become only a tool used in the bargaining procedure. One of the unfortunate things in this procedure is that the injured person arrives late and is seldom in an equal bargaining position. He has been recovering from his injuries and he has already been weighed down with anxiety through financial loss due to the accident. In addition, the facts as related may or may not be true. He is faced with all the uncertainties of a lawsuit, a split verdict and a very considerable risk as to costs — a risk that can be greatly increased by the defendant paying money into court. In addition, the accident may have destroyed his best evidence. In the result, in considerably over 90 percent of the cases liability is not determined and compensation is not fixed by any legal procedure but by a mere process of negotiation.

NOTES

1. Is Mr. Justice McRuer justified in disapproving of the use of litigation as an "instrument in the adjustment of claims"? What is so nasty about suing someone in order to get him to "agree" to pay what he owes?

MARRYOTT, TESTING THE CRITICISMS OF THE FAULT CONCEPT

in *Justice and the Adversary System*
(1968)

One of the criticisms of the tort system is that the question of who was at fault is difficult to determine. This difficulty, it is said, causes unjustified expense and results in too many wrong determinations being made. It is argued that accidents happen so quickly and arise from such complex circumstances that the people involved really do not know what happened.

We should, I suggest, not accept such assertions without a reasonable effort to test their validity. One of the purposes of this paper is to tell you about my efforts to perform such a test.

Our studies indicate that a large proportion of all automobile accidents are uncomplicated events in which the fault determination is very easy and that many of the more complex accidents can be accurately analyzed, by people trained to do such work, on the basis of the physical facts, even when the impressions of the witnesses are confused. The final positions of the cars, the tire marks, the location and extent of the damage, frequently established very clearly how the accident happened and who was at fault.

This brings me to the point of describing my little bit of research. I wanted to find out, if I could, what proportion of automobile liability cases reported to Liberty Mutual Insurance Company were such that a decision of who was at fault was easy and uncomplicated. The experiment consisted of two parts. First we looked at the "file" on each of 229 accidents reported to our Andover, Massachusetts office beginning on March 1, 1967, looking at the reports in numerical sequence. Then we did the same thing as to 123 cases in our Natick office — beginning with April 1, 1967. The total is 352.

In some cases the "file" consisted of an accident report alone. These were the cases in which the accident was so insignificant, or in which the facts, as originally reported, so clearly indicated who was at fault, as to justify a decision that no further investigation need be made. In the other cases an appropriate investigation had been made.

This is what we found:

In 25 cases the policyholder struck a stationary object other than a parked car.

In 64 cases parked cars were involved. In 24 of these the policyholder backed into the other car. In 21 cases our policyholder struck the parked car in some way other than by backing into it.

In 16 cases the other car struck our parked car other than by backing into it.

In one case the policyholder said he was struck in the rear by the other car. In the same case the claimant said the policyholder backed into him while he was parked. We recorded that case as "fault questionable".

In 29 other cases backing into a moving car was involved. In 18 of these our policyholder backed into the claimant and was clearly at fault. In 9 other cases the other car backed into ours and was clearly at fault.

There were 79 "rear enders" other than those included above. In 44 of these the policyholder struck the other car from the rear and was judged to be clearly at fault. In 35 of these the claimant struck our car from the rear and was judged to be clearly at fault.

There were 78 intersection cases — 22% of the total number. Of these the policyholder was judged clearly at fault in 16 cases, and probably at fault in 19 cases. The claimant was thought to be clearly at fault in 22 cases and probably at fault in 10 cases. 11 were "questionable".

Only one pedestrian case showed up and in this one the policyholder was judged to be clearly at fault.

Six cases involved a car that was pulling out from a parked position. The policyholder was judged clearly at fault in 4, the claimant in 1 and 1 was "questionable".

There were 14 "sideswipe" cases, *i.e.*, the cars were going in the same direction. Our policyholder was held clearly at fault in 6. The claimant was held to be clearly at fault in 5. Three cases were "questionable".

In 32 cases the cars were going in opposite directions. In 16 of these the policyholder's car crossed the center line and was judged to be clearly at fault. In 12 the claimant crossed the center line and was held to be clearly at fault. Four cases were classed as "questionable".

23 cases fell into the "miscellaneous" slot. The policyholder was clearly at fault in 3, and probably at fault in 4. The claimant was held clearly at fault in 8 and probably at fault in 5. Three were "questionable".

Three cases were found that involved a question of being "under the influence".

One case involved a defect in the vehicle.

No cases attributable to road defect (other than ice and snow) were found.

No cases involving speeding in excess of 10 miles over the limit were found.

The summary is:

Policyholder clearly at fault	201	57.1%
Claimant clearly at fault	125	35.5%
Fault questionable	26	7.4%
	352	100.0%

NOTES

1. Is this a "reliable" study? Is it scientific? Is it unbiased? Mr. Marryott, when he wrote this article, was associated with the Liberty Mutual Insurance Company.

2. Sometimes injured people, because of economic pressure, may settle their claims for less than they would ultimately receive if they went to trial. The economic factors that influence them in doing this, such as the legal costs, the delay and the risk of losing are discussed in Phillips and Hawkins, "Some Economic Aspects of the Settlement Process: A Study of Personal Injury Claims" (1976), 39 Mod. L. Rev. 497. Do these factors sometimes help a claimant to get more than he would be entitled to at trial? What do you think about this? Is it a deficiency only in the tort system, or is it a defect in the entire legal system? What can be done about this?

BLUM AND KALVEN, PUBLIC LAW PERSPECTIVES ON
A PRIVATE LAW PROBLEM –
AUTO COMPENSATION PLANS

(1965) printed in (1964), 31 U. Chi. L. Rev. 646

We turn to consider fault as a criterion of liability. We do so with only the most modest of expectations. The whole concept of fault, even in our torts system, is so closely tied to views on personal responsibility – and hence to values that have deep cultural and religious roots – that we must limit our discussion of it here to very narrow confines. We have no intention of developing an adequate brief on its behalf. Our purpose is merely to counteract the fashionable tendency to dismiss it out of hand as being an untenable principle.

There have been various objections to fault as a criterion for liability, but in oversimplified fashion they can be schematized as three general points: (1) We can never get enough facts about a particular accident to know whether fault was present or not; (2) even if we had a full history of the event we would be unable to rationally apply the fault criterion because it is unintelligible; and (3) even if we knew the history of the event and understood what fault meant, we would be deciding cases on the basis of an unsound and arbitrary criterion.

The objection based on the difficulties of proof is a familiar one in all litigation, but it is urged as presenting special and decisive difficulties for the auto accident. There is the threat of evidence deteriorating because of the time it may take to get to trial. There is the sheer absence of competent witnesses at the crucial time of the event. And there is the emphasis under the fault criterion on split-second time sequences which place extra burdens on the capacity of witnesses to perceive, recall and narrate. These difficulties cumulate, we are told, so that the actual trial almost necessarily involves an imperfect and ambiguous historical reconstruction of the event, making a mockery of the effort to apply so subtle a normative criterion to the conduct involved. An impenetrable evidentiary screen thus makes fault unworkable as a criterion whatever its merits as a concept.

But does not this objection run the risk of proving too much? All adjudication is vulnerable to the inadequacies of evidence and the consequent exploitation of the situation by the skill of counsel. From prosecutions for murder to adjudications of the validity of family partnerships for income tax purposes, the law has had to wrestle with these difficulties. Auto accidents are at least more public than many other legal situations and they almost invariably do leave physical traces. The witness to an auto accident is asked for observations likely to be well within his daily experience. The law can tolerate a goodly margin of error, and the threshold of distortion which this line of attack on liability for fault must establish before it becomes a persuasive reason for throwing over the system is high. We remain skeptical that the evidentiary aspects of the auto accident are so peculiar as to be set apart from the evidentiary aspects of all other controversies that are brought to law.

The objections to fault as being an unintelligible concept also run the risk of proving too much. One needs a generous view of the meaning of a legal principle. We should be at least as charitable toward negligence as we are toward procedural due process, fraud, or gross income. All the big ideas of law are imprecise and have a core meaning which moves toward ambiguity at the margin. Except intuitively, there seems no way of measuring the relative clarity of such ideas. When we place negligence in the context of law's other big ideas, it looks at home. A simple test of its intelligibility is whether we can put easy cases so as to compel virtually complete agreement on the presence or absence of fault. We would all readily recognize that the negligence concept could pass this test were it not for the fact that our impressions of it are derived so much from the reading of appellate decisions with their marginal fact situations. The negligence concept, after all, has been employed by generations of lawyers and judges as though it makes sense. They were able to argue in terms of it and to array cases inside and outside the line. The decades of apparently rational discussion at the bar are paralleled by the decades of law school teaching. Every law student has been exposed to the experience of locating the relevant variables involved and of ranking the cases through varying a fact in one direction or the other.

But the critic can rightly say that law students do not decide cases, while juries do. The negligence concept is too vague, asserts the critic, to guide the judgment of juries. The result is that juries allocate liability on the basis of all kinds of legally irrelevant but humanly sympathetic grounds, and that the legal criterion in fact evaporates at the level of actual jury behavior.

Normally on a point such as this there is little evidence other than lawyer anecdotes. However, in this instance the University of Chicago Law School Jury Project does have some directly relevant data. In an extensive survey of the way judge and jury would decide the same personal injury case, the project found that in 80% of all cases the judge and jury agreed on liability or no liability. In 10% of the cases the jury found for the plaintiff where the judge would have found for the defendant. And, surprisingly, in the remaining 10% of the cases the judge would have found for the plaintiff where the jury found for the defendant. In brief, the jury would have found for the plaintiff in precisely the same number of cases as the judge. The upshot seems to be that whatever hidden rules the jury is in fact following when it operates under the negligence formula, its rules must be very similar to those governing the judge. It is thus difficult to make any special argument about the failure of this negligence criterion to control the jury.

This, however, does not dispose of the issue completely since the critic may now press his final objection to the intelligibility of the fault principle — the difficulty of controlling even the behavior of judges by so expansible a standard as negligence. In fact he may well say that our Jury Project evidence confirms his worst fears that fault is inherently a quixotic criterion, that is infinitely expansible and is constantly changing its meaning. He will tell us that what is now regarded as negligence would have astonished judges and juries of a century ago. The challenge is that within established and apparently unchanging doctrine, the concept of negligence has greatly expanded its boundaries and will continue to do so.

The difficulty with this line of objection is that it presupposes that where a jury instructed under negligence has found negligence and the judge concurs there is available the judgment of some third party bystander who fails to find negligence and who over time would increasingly be in disagreement with the official results. Without this ideal bystander how can one say that negligence was found by the law and the community when negligence does not exist? At a deep level all that the negligence formula ever required was that the actor be held liable only when the community judged that the risk he took was not a reasonable one. It is possible, although there is no evidence here, that the community is gradually becoming more stringent in its judgments about the reasonableness of risks in the operation of autos. In a formal sense no matter how harsh these judgments become the system would remain essentially a negligence system. In a realistic sense, however, it is conceivable that a point could be reached where negligence in auto accidents became only a fiction. Whatever might lie in the future, it seems clear to us that we are not approaching such a point today.

The third objection, that even the fault theory is an unsound criterion, has several facets. The first is that the law exaggerates the contribution of the actor's fault to an accident. On a larger view the actor's role is frequently dwarfed by other causally contributing factors, such as road engineering, traffic density, car design, traffic regulations, and the performance of other cars just before the accident. The precise challenge is whether an admitted flaw in the actor's conduct, looked at in the context of other causes, is a sufficient basis for determining whether the accident victim is to get compensation.

This challenge appears to mirror the proposition sometimes advanced in criminal law that the individual actor's contribution to the crime is overshadowed by such other contributing factors as poor education, poverty, broken home, and so forth. The difficulty with this approach either in tort or in crime is that it is hard to see what else the law could do but single out the conduct of the individual actor. Speaking statistically, we can of course say that road engineering or broken homes are significant causes of accidents or crimes. But this does not help dispose of the individual case, and the law is charging the actor for a flaw in conduct that the mass of mankind — including those who come from broken homes or drive on poorly engineered highways — could have avoided. Although never philosophical about causation, the law has clearly recognized that any actor is but one of an infinity of causes of a particular event. It has dealt with the actor because he was a reachable cause and because his contribution to the event was relevant and decisive. Even if we conceded that the law always overrates the contribution of the actor, there is nothing in the auto accident field that gives this perception any special force.

The critic of the fault criterion might shift his emphasis and follow another line in pressing the point about the incommensurability of the actor's flaw and the consequences the law attaches to it. Negligence covers a multitude of sins, ranging from the grave to the trivial; and the critic can stress that there is no correlation whatsoever between the gravity of the sin and the magnitude of the damage caused. If tort damages were viewed as a system of fines, everyone would agree that the incidence of sanctions would be absurd, and it would be the rare case in which the punishment fits the crime. The difference in conduct between the negligent and the non-negligent drivers is too slight to support the huge difference in consequences that the fault principle attaches.

Does it matter for tort law that the punishment does not fit the crime? A sufficient answer is that the purpose of tort law is to compensate and not to punish; and this is well understood throughout the community and by the typical defendant. But the critic's point probably over-estimates the lack of correlation between risk and damage. On the average we are likely to find that the magnitude of harm caused correlates fairly well with the magnitude of the risk taken — in fact, the magnitude of the potential harm bears a direct relationship to the magnitude of the risk taken. The critic's point in any event is especially weak in the case of auto accidents inasmuch as virtually everyone is well aware that an auto in motion can maim or kill. It is true that on occasion the law has recognized the point as when it limited liability for a slip of the pen in the *Ultramares* case. The fact that no such limitation has been imposed in auto accident situations suggests that the law deliberately declines to follow the policy in the case of the auto. Be that as it may, it is improper to invert the process of judgment and argue that a small amount of harm somehow indicates a small degree of negligence. The key concept for the law here is risk; and what is constant in these situations is the amount of negligent risk taken — and this is a factor which, as Holmes noted almost a century ago, is independent of the harm that actually occurs.

Another facet of the objection to fault as a principle builds on the not implausible assumption that all drivers are at some time or other clearly negligent.

Most negligent conduct, however, is not actionable inasmuch as it does not cause harm. Whether a given negligent act causes harm seems to be largely a matter of chance. Since all drivers are in the same boat morally and only chance distinguishes them, it has been urged that all drivers ought to pay for the damages inflicted by drivers as a class, and that it is unjustifiable to place the burden solely on those whom chance did not favor.

The popular impression that all drivers are alike in being occasionally negligent is very likely an overestimation, for it fails to take account of the many minor adjustments in conduct which are made when men engage in what seems to be essentially the same risky behavior. Driving eighty miles an hour is not a constant risk, and presumably all recognize that such a speed in the city entails a markedly higher risk than in the open country. But driving eighty miles an hour in the city does not represent a constant risk either, and those who drive at this speed under similar conditions might well do so with differing degrees of reserve or caution. It is not unlikely that there are grades of prudence even among the negligent risk takers. These minor differentiations in all probability partially account for which of the negligent drivers in fact get into accidents. And even if we grant that there is a large factor of chance as to which of the negligent drivers do cause accidents, it does not follow that the recruitment of drivers to accidents is a random process. Under the laws of chance, the drivers who take relatively more risks of a given magnitude are more likely to become involved in accidents than their fellow drivers who take relatively fewer risks of the same magnitude.

The last challenge to fault as a principle echoes the recurring suggestion in much contemporary writing about tort law that a proper criterion for choice between competing rules is the sheer number of losses that would be shifted. We should always prefer, we are told, the rule that results in shifting the largest number of losses off victims. Using this criterion at the most general level, it could be said that the basic difficulty with the common law fault rule in the world of the auto is that it leaves too many victims of auto accidents uncompensated. And we are offered empirical studies to prove that this is indeed the case.

If the earlier objections to fault run the risk of proving too much, this one runs the risk of begging the question. It should be abundantly clear that the common law never has had information about the incidence of recovery which would follow from the application of its liability rules. What is more important, it has had no expectations about incidence of recovery, and could not have cared less. Its commitment to fault as a basis for shifting losses is independent of any estimates of how many losses will thus be shifted.

No empirical study of gaps in loss shifting, insofar as they rest on the absence of liability, can be relevant. The striking point is that under the common law system it is intended that some victims will have to bear their own losses.

As familiar as all this is, it marks a critical point of departure. The question frequently now heard is: "By what arrangement can we most expeditiously maximize the shift of losses?" There is a profound difference between this and the old-fashioned question: "What losses should be shifted and what losses should the victim bear?" Under the logic of the common law, there is no meaningful way of answering the first question unless the second question has already been answered. We agree with that logic.

B. ARE THE VICTIMS OF AUTO
ACCIDENTS DIFFERENT?

LINDEN, PEACEFUL COEXISTENCE AND
AUTOMOBILE ACCIDENT COMPENSATION
(1966), 9 Can. Bar J. 5

. . . [W] hy single out motor accident victims for special treatment over other victims of adversity? Injuries resulting from automobile accidents are worthy of special treatment because, as Judge Marx, a dedicated proponent of reform, has written, "The automobile accident victim . . . is a very marked social problem, both because of his number and because of the source of his injury." Indeed automobile accidents kill almost 50,000 people and injure over a million each year in North America. Governments have long recognized this by the enactment of special legislation making owners of automobiles responsible for the negligence of their drivers, creating unsatisfied judgment funds, requiring compulsory liability insurance and the like. Criminal and quasi-criminal legislation has been passed regulating traffic, enacting rules of the road and requiring certain equipment on motor vehicles. Moreover, the legal profession bears a special responsibility because it is already heavily committed to participation in both civil and criminal cases arising from automobile accidents. Accordingly, it is looked to for leadership in this field, while it plays no role in the economic or social treatment of bathtub or cancer victims. Another factor which distinguishes automobile victims is that the machinery for loss-distribution and loss-spreading is already available in the almost universal liability insurance that is prevalent in Canada. No longer are we forced to choose one of the two *individuals* involved in an accident to bear the total losses produced; we are now able to allocate all of the costs generated by an activity to a *group* of persons selected in advance through the insurance device.

ISON, TORT LIABILITY AND SOCIAL INSURANCE
(1969), 19 U. of T. L.J. 614

There are two possible explanations of why motor vehicle compensation plans have come to be advocated. First, the sudden drama of the event, the exposure to public view, the system of prosecutions, tort claims, the availability of statistical data, traffic safety campaigns, rising casualty figures, and increasing insurance premiums have all combined to focus public attention on road accidents. Hence motor vehicle accidents feature in the press and in political debate, and any proposal for a motor vehicle compensation plan is assured of a sympathetic audience. Second, a plan of motor vehicle accident compensation can be administered by insurance companies whereas a more comprehensive plan of sickness and injury compensation can only be implemented efficiently by the development of a social insurance system administered by government. Hence the advocates of a compensation plan limited to motor vehicle accidents can hope for support from the insurance industry. In the United States, this support is already coming. In other words, the advocacy of compensation plans limited to motor vehicle accidents seems to be justified by nothing more virtuous than a timid concession to predictions of political feasibility.

Of course it can be argued that for good social cost accounting, the cost of accident compensation should be charged on those who engage in accident causing activities. But, as I will try to show, this can be achieved more efficiently by an advanced system of social insurance than by a proliferation of separate plans, each of which compensates a different category of misfortunes classified according to their cause.

Furthermore, there is really no rational ground for distinguishing between deaths and disabilities caused by accidents and those resulting from sickness or disease.

So far in Canada we have dealt with compensation for disablement and death by a proliferation of separate plans involving separate administrative structures. Thus we have Workmen's Compensation, the Canada Pension Plan, compensation for the victims of crimes of violence, the Saskatchewan Automobile Insurance Plan, sick pay, life insurance, personal accident insurance, and welfare. Expensive enquiries into complex issues of causation are often required to determine under which plan, if any, the victim is entitled to compensation. There is surely no point in aggravating these problems by adding to the list another plan and another administrative structure.

BLUM AND KALVEN, PUBLIC LAW PERSPECTIVES ON A PRIVATE LAW PROBLEM — AUTO COMPENSATION PLANS

(1965), printed in (1964), 31 U. Chi. L. Rev. 641

Nor will we do more than mention several differences, which some observers have urged as critical, between the industrial accident situation and the auto accident situation. It is said that while the industrial accident is relatively fixed and easy to investigate, the auto accident is more transient and difficult to investigate. The result is that there are likely to be great differences in the opportunities for policing fraudulent claims in the two areas. It is also said that damages are more amenable to scheduling in the one case than in the other, both because the range and variety of physical injuries is more restricted in the industrial accident and because the injured personnel are drawn from a fairly homogeneous economic group. These are acute observations, and they do point up specific difficulties which would be encountered in administering a compensation plan, but they do not cut deep enough to put to rest Jeremiah Smith's challenge of fundamental inconsistency.

There are three residual differences which lead us to deny the analogy to workmen's compensation. First, there is a great difference between the common law system for industrial accidents which workmen's compensation was created to replace and the common law system for auto accidents which exists today. Under the law of fifty years ago, we are told, the ability of the injured employee to recover was greatly circumscribed by the well-known trilogy of employer defenses — assumption of risk, contributory negligence, and the fellow servant rule. The old law has looked to some like a conspiracy to throw the losses of industrial accidents onto employees as a class at a time when they were conspicuously less well off than their employers. There is no comparable harshness in the law which confronts the auto accident claimant today. In the same vein, the whole "welfare" support for workmen's compensation is considerably diluted today in the auto accident area. First party insurance and social legislation have come on the scene and have greatly reduced the likelihood that the auto accident victim and his family will bear the full brunt of the accident.

A second difference is that the enterprise situation made possible a popular myth as to how the cost of workmen's compensation was to be borne. The widespread image was that by placing the cost of workmen's compensation on employers the cost would be passed on to consumers of their products through operation of market forces. The result was thought to be that not only social justice but economic justice would be accomplished; and this view of the matter was crystalized in the slogan that the cost of products should reflect the blood of workmen. Although there are good reasons today for doubting whether consumers do bear the cost of workmen's compensation, for our immediate purposes it is enough that there is no one in the auto situation who occupies a role which the employer was popularly thought to play in the industrial accident situation — no one, that is, who could be regarded as being in a position to pass on the costs to consumers via the market.

A third difference challenges the view that workmen's compensation offers a competing doctrine of tort liability. There is no doubt that this is the traditional view; workmen's compensation was enacted to repeal and replace common law tort rules, and it was challenged and ratified in court on that premise. We wish to suggest here a considerably different view of the history and rationale. In retrospect, we are impressed that workmen's compensation can best be understood as a kind of "fringe benefit" incorporated by law into the basic employment contract. The law in effect compelled the employer to provide, as a term of employment, an industrial accident policy for his employees.

GRIFFITHS, DON'T ABOLISH TORT LAW IN AUTO ACCIDENT COMPENSATION

(1969), 12 Can. Bar J. 187

Has the volume of deaths and injuries inflicted by the automobile in the 20th century created such a socio-economic problem as to warrant a complete about turn in the common law fault concept? The assertion by the critics that the loss of life and limb caused by the automobile creates a special and distinct social problem does not, I submit, stand up under close examination.

The National Safety League of Canada reports that in 1967 there were a total of 11,474 fatalities in Canada due to accidents. Of these 5,412 were due to motor vehicles and the balance of 6,184 were due to falls, drowning, fire and explosion, suffocation, poisoning, machinery, blows from falling or projected objects, firearms, aircraft and assorted other causes.

While the automobile, of all types of accidents, is the largest single offender, do the families of the other victims (home, public, non-motor vehicle, industry) who were killed in 1967 face less of a social and economic burden than the families of the victims of the auto accident? Why should those killed in automobile accidents be singled out for special treatment? What about death due to disease and natural cause? Does not the economic impact of the loss of a breadwinner who died from heart disease or cancer affect society just as much as the loss by one who dies in a motor vehicle accident?

And what of the victim of accidents arising from other activities in places such as the home, the office, the school? Is it socially just that the individual who slips and injures himself while leaving his home will recover nothing but if he deliberately propels himself out onto the street into the path of a moving vehicle and is thus injured, he will be entitled to compensation, on the concept of payment to all irrespective of fault?

Surely the tort system was not intended to perform the social welfare service of taking care of the needy. If we are to talk the idiom of social welfare then the problem is to be analyzed within social welfare framework. Our efforts should be devoted towards the assistance of all victims of misfortune and an attack on the structure of the tort system and the judicial administration is irrelevant.

SOMERVILLE, THE MOTORISTS' COMPENSATION BOARD

(1962), 5 Can. Bar J. 357

... [A]ccording to a news report, 37 persons in Ontario died accidentally over the Labour Day weekend, but only 26 of them in highway accidents. Upon what rational grounds should the dependents of two-thirds of them be compensated irrespective of fault and the other one-third get nothing? Why should the dependents of a reckless driver be compensated while those of a drowning victim who ignored warnings against undertow get nothing? A friend of mine supplied an apt slogan, "It's not who you know, but how you go"....

BLUM AND KALVEN, PUBLIC LAW PERSPECTIVES ON A PRIVATE LAW PROBLEM – AUTO COMPENSATION PLANS

(1965) printed in (1964), 31 U. Chi. L. Rev. 641

From the very beginning the proponents of plans have insisted that the auto accident be viewed as an instance of human misfortune calling for a welfare remedy. When the situation is looked at in this manner, it immediately becomes apparent that the problem is bigger than that which the proponents started out to solve. The welfare universe is not limited to victims of auto accidents but includes victims of all other kinds of human misfortune. We can think of no ground for singling out the misfortune of auto accident victims for special welfare treatment.

The social security perspective also has the merit of bringing to the surface the profound question of why the state should do anything about human misfortune. We infer that those who urge the state to intervene have mixed motives. To some extent they favor sumptuary legislation in behalf of prudence. They are willing to restrict the power of the individual to choose because they distrust every man's capacity to make prudent judgments about privately carrying accident insurance. But more important, they are concerned over the financial ability of people to absorb misfortune. They see that by no means is everyone prosperous enough to buy adequate insurance against misfortune. The attraction of financing protection through the tax mechanism is that the necessary funds can be collected on some progressive tax basis, so that the richer will pay the costs for the poorer. Intervention by the state thus is sought in order to mitigate the evils of poverty. We are tempted to hazard the grand generalization that at the root of most of our major social issues lies the concern with what is thought to be poverty. The automobile compensation plan is no exception....

The old common law issue of justice apart, the social security approach to the problem of the auto accident victim has some distinctive disadvantages of its own. If economic considerations have a bearing on accident causing behavior, this approach would seem to run the greatest risk of lessening deterrence. Neither drivers nor pedestrians would perceive any relationship between their taxes and their conduct in respect to automobiles. The approach also has the disadvantage of supplanting the private insurance industry in a major sector of its activities, and replacing it with taxation and government administration of welfare benefits. Such a development would add to the power of the government and weaken what is now an important private pool of power. Finally, the approach calls for one more — and perhaps an irreversible — reduction in the area of individual autonomy.

It is not comfortable for us to end by repeating all the well-aired objections to social security. We are aware that we are a long way from home. And it is no accident that we have travelled so far from the tort world from which we began. Private law cannot borrow goals from public law fields without accepting the obligation to make a proper public law analysis. In the case of automobile compensation plans, such an analysis shows that the special problem cannot be solved adequately without solving a larger problem. This much, at least, we have learned from this venture in applying public law perspectives to an important private law problem.

NOTES

1. Are those pressing to reform the auto accident system too limited in their objectives? Should they be urging compensation for all accident victims? All sickness and injury victims? All victims of misfortune in society? All poor people?

2. Are there any good logical reasons for limiting their objectives? Economic reasons? Political reasons?

C. WHO SHOULD PAY THE COSTS OF AUTO ACCIDENTS?

CALABRESI, THE DECISION FOR ACCIDENTS: AN APPROACH TO NON-FAULT ALLOCATION OF COSTS

(1965), 78 Harv. L. Rev. 713

Many recent writers have tended to focus on compensation as the main purpose of accident law. Were this emphasis proper, that would be no justification for limiting compensation to accidents and not spreading it across the board to illness, old age, and all the troubles of this planet. Of course, we do spread compensation beyond accidents to some extent, but it is the fact that we only do it "to some extent" that is crucial. Why is compensation for illness — even in highly welfaristic countries — much less complete than compensation for accidents? And why is the accident field kept a separate entity, where methods that achieve a fair degree of compensation spreading are used, but which would be woefully inefficient if compensation spreading were the only aim? Surely, if the type of cost reduction with which we are concerned is solely or principally that accomplished by diminishing secondary costs — social and economic dislocations — then a generalized system of social insurance covering all types of severe injuries would be the only efficient system.

The answer is that accidents are not the same as diseases. There are ways to reduce the primary cost of accidents — their number and severity — that can, indeed must, be an important aim of whatever system of law that governs the fields. One way is to discourage those activities that result in accidents and to substitute safer ones for them. Another is to encourage care in the course of an activity. "Activity" and "care" are not, of course, mutually exclusive categories. If "activity" is defined narrowly or if "care" is broadly viewed, the concepts tend to merge. The activity of driving is not thought to be careless although a predictable number of accidents result from it. Driving through a busy intersection without brakes is careless and not an activity. Between these relatively clear cases the distinction becomes more difficult, as, for example, navigating without radar. In addition, an activity may properly be defined as the doing of something by an actuarial class, which may tend to do it carelessly. Treating the problems of accident law in terms of activities rather than in terms of careless conduct is the first step toward a rational system of resource allocation. The question is to what extent an economically rational system is our goal. . . .

Our society is not committed to preserving life at any cost. In its broadest sense, this rather unpleasant notion should be obvious. Wars are fought. The University of Mississippi is integrated. But what is more interesting to the study of accident law, though perhaps equally obvious, is that lives are used up when the *quid pro quo* is not some great moral principle but "convenience". Ventures are undertaken that, statistically at least, are certain to cost lives. Thus, we build a tunnel under Mont Blanc because it is essential to the Common Market and cuts down the traveling time from Rome to Paris, though we know that about a man per kilometer of tunnel will die. We take planes and cars rather than safer, slower means of travel. And perhaps most telling, we use relatively safe equipment rather than the safest imaginable because — and it is not a bad reason — the safest costs too much.

Of course, it is rarely known who is to die. Indeed, in the uncustomary case of an individual — a known individual rather than a statistical unknown — in a position of life or death, we are apt to spend very much more to save him than in any conceivable money sense he is worth. And while I do not doubt this is as it should be, it seems odd that we should refuse to apply the same standards of "value beyond any price" when we deal with the same man's life as part of a statistic. But odd or not, it is the case.

A decision balancing lives against money or convenience when made in the broadest terms is not purely an economic one. The decision whether the Mont Blanc tunnel is worth building is not based solely on whether the revenue received from tolls through the completed tunnel will pay for the construction costs, including compensation of the killed and maimed. Neither is the decision whether to allow prostitution based solely on whether it can pay its way. Such a pure free enterprise solution has never been acceptable. It was in fact rejected by even the most classical of classical economists, though they felt it necessary to explain the rejections in terms of a theory that is as narrow or broad as any society, welfaristic or free enterprise, cares to make it. The real issue, whether or not expressed in terms of these economists "hidden social costs" or "hidden social savings" theory, is how often a decision for or against an activity is to be allowed regardless of whether it can pay its way. Such decisions operate, on the one hand, to create subsidies for some activities that could not survive in the market place, and on the other, to bar some activities that can more than pay their way. The frequency with which decisions to ignore the market are made tells something about the nature of a society — welfare or *laissez-faire*. What is clear is that in virtually all societies such decisions to overrule the market are made, but are made only sometimes.

Characteristically, in the field of accident law the decision whether or not to take lives in exchange for money or convenience is sometimes made politically or collectively without a balancing of the money value of the lives taken against the money price of the convenience, and sometimes made through the market on the basis of such a value. The reasons for this varying approach are not entirely reasons of principle. Great moral issues lend themselves to political determination. These questions must necessarily be decided in whatever political way our society chooses to decide moral questions. But "rotary mowers versus reel mowers", "one method of making steel as against another" are questions difficult of collective decision. For one thing, they occur too frequently. Every choice of product and use hides within it a decision regarding safety and expense. The dramatic cases we resolve politically. We ban the general sale of fireworks regardless of the ability or willingness of the manufacturer to pay for all of the injuries that result. But we cannot deal with all issues involved in all activities through the political process. For most, the market place serves as the tough testing ground. A manufacturer is free to employ a process even if it occasionally kills or maims if he is able to show that consumers want his product badly enough to enable him to compensate those he injures and still make a profit. Economists would say that except in those few areas of collective decision, this is the best way to decide if the activity is worth having.

All this is just saying, in a slightly different way, that one of the functions of accident law is to reduce the cost of accidents, by reducing those activities that are accident prone. Activities are made more expensive, and thereby less attractive, to the extent of the accidents they cause. In the extreme cases they are priced out of the markets: the market mechanism may thus eliminate an otherwise useful activity because it maims too many.

CALABRESI, THE COSTS OF ACCIDENTS
(1970)

The general deterrence approach operates in two ways to reduce accident costs. The first and more obvious one is that it creates incentives to engage in safer activities. Some people who would engage in a relatively dangerous activity at prices that did not reflect its accident costs will shift to a safer activity if accident costs *are* reflected in prices. The degree of the shift will depend on the relative difference in accident costs and on how good a substitute the safer activity is. Whatever the shift, however, it will reduce accident costs, since a safer activity will to some degree have been substituted for a dangerous one.

The second and perhaps more important way general deterrence reduces accident costs is that it encourages us to make activities safer. This is no different from the first if every variation in the way an activity is carried out is considered to be a separate activity, but since that is not how the term activity is used in common language, it may be useful to show how general deterrence operates to cause a given activity to become safer. Taney drives a car. His car causes, on the average, $200 per year in accident costs. If a different kind of brake were used in the car, this would be reduced to $100. The new kind of brake costs the equivalent of $50 per year. If the accident costs Taney causes are paid either by the state out of general taxes or by those who are injured, he has no financial incentive to put in the new brake. But if Taney has to pay, he will certainly put the new brake in. He will thus bear a new cost of $50 per year, but it will be less than the $100 per year in accident costs he will avoid. As a result, the cost of accidents to society will have been reduced by $50.

NOTES

1. Professor Calabresi's work triggered a remarkable debate in the law reviews with Professors Blum and Kalven of the University of Chicago, all of which is rewarding reading. See Blum and Kalven, *Public Law Perspectives on a Private Law Problem — Auto Compensation Plans* (1965), reprinted in (1964), 31 U. Chi. L. Rev. 641; Calabresi, "Fault Accidents and the Wonderful World of Blum and Kalven" (1965), 75 Yale L. J. 216; Blum and Kalven, "The Empty Cabinet of Dr. Calabresi: Auto Accidents and General Deterrence" (1967), 34 U. Chi. L. Rev. 239; Calabresi, "Views and Overviews" (1967), U. Ill. L.F. 600; Blum and Kalven, "A Stopgap Plan for Compensating Auto Accident Victims", [1968] Ins. L. J. 661; Calabresi, *The Costs of Accidents* (1970); Blum and Kalven, "Ceilings, Costs and Compulsion in Auto Compensation Legislation" (1973), Utah L. Rev. 341. See also Posner, *Economic Analysis of Law* (1972), p. 84.

2. Professors Blum and Kalven argue in their article "The Empty Cabinet of Dr. Calabresi: Auto Accidents and General Deterrence", *supra:*

"The difficulty with general deterrence as a justification for shifting non-fault auto accident losses to motorists is that it is too fragile to carry the weight that would be put on it. Where the burdens are clear, certain, and not trivial, something more than conjecture about possible patterns of behavior is needed as a countervalue. To put the disagreement in a nutshell: when we know as little as we appear to know now about the prophecies of general deterrence, it is unjust to tax motorists on behalf of it."

KEETON AND O'CONNELL, BASIC PROTECTION FOR THE TRAFFIC VICTIM

(1965)

When we recognize that the law may distribute losses rather than merely shift them, one significant possibility that is presented is to place the burden of bearing an assigned share of the losses resulting from accidents on those who benefit most from motoring; that is, to adopt explicitly the principle that motoring should be required to pay its way in society.

a. *Fairness.* One ground of support for such a requirement is an unabashed appeal to one's sense of fairness. Is it not fair that the burdens and costs of an activity be borne by those who benefit from it and, insofar as feasible, in proportion to the benefit each receives? Occasionally society subsidizes some activity instead of requiring it to pay its way. For example, our society commonly subsidizes municipal transit systems. In this example, however, a subsidy seems fair because all the citizens of the community, including nonusers of public transportation, benefit directly or indirectly from its availability; moreover, experience has demonstrated that a subsidy may be essential if the system is to function at all.

It can be argued, of course, that motoring also indirectly benefits the whole community and is often indirectly subsidized. To the extent that gasoline taxes do not cover the costs of building and maintaining roads, and to the extent that tax-supported activities of the police and the courts are devoted to the consequences of motoring, such an indirect subsidy does exist. Our society's treatment of automobiles does not, however, simply underwrite a definite and definable loss as it does in the case of municipal transportation; we expect motoring to pay its own way, at least to the extent that the costs of purchasing and operating cars are to be borne by motorists themselves. Should not the costs of damage caused by cars also be treated as part of the costs of operating them? In answering this question consider first losses resulting from unavoidable accidents — unavoidable in the sense that they occur without substandard conduct either of the victim or of anyone against whom he might claim. It has been implicit in our automobile law that losses caused by non-negligent motoring are to be borne by the victims. Yet it is not the theory that the victims deserve to bear these losses. Leaving the loss on the victim in a particular case is rather an incidental consequence of finding no sufficient reason to shift the loss to another. The harshness of this result becomes especially evident once it is recognized that the alternatives include not only the unpalatable shifting of the whole loss to another equally blameless party but also the distribution of the loss among a larger group, all of whom are potentially victims of mischance. No one can know where or when any particular accident will occur, but we do know that there will be unavoidable accidents if we permit motoring to continue. The cost of compensating losses from such accidents can be allocated to motoring generally by requiring drivers, as part of their motoring costs, to pay insurance premiums from which a pool of funds can be drawn to compensate victims of these accidents. In cases of this type, the imposition of this relatively slight burden on many motorists seems much fairer than causing some particular motorist or victim to bear the whole burden.

Somewhat different considerations are raised by avoidable accidents brought about by the substandard conduct of one or both of the parties involved. It may be argued that it is unfair to treat such accidents as part of the costs of motoring, as opposed to treating them as part of the costs of engaging in substandard conduct. For example, it may seem unfair to add to the costs borne by every motorist in order to provide a fund for compensation of a loss caused by the exceptional conduct of a motorist who uses his vehicle as a weapon, deliberately running another down. The loss caused by such an intentional injury, it may be argued, should be treated as a cost of the particular motorist's deliberate misconduct and not as a cost of motoring in general. It might be thought to follow that loss caused by a motorist's careless driving should also be treated as a cost of his carelessness and not as a cost of motoring. The extent to which this argument is persuasive depends to a considerable degree on the standard of carelessness applied. If the standard is one that drivers generally can meet if they try, then the analogy between cases of careless injury and cases of intentional injury is rather close. If, on the other hand, the standard is one that drivers generally cannot hope to meet, then the analogy to intentional injury is weak and the analogy to injuries caused without substandard conduct is strong. As the definition of negligence is broadened to include instances of conduct not morally blameworthy, the argument becomes stronger for treating such losses as costs of motoring to be distributed equitably among motorists through insurance, rather than to be borne by either of the parties to the particular accident. In fact, the standard of negligence has been broadened beyond a standard that drivers can meet if only they will try. And as this trend continues, the argument becomes more cogent that the judgment against a motorist ought not to end the matter but rather should be one step in a system that treats losses sustained by accident victims as inevitable costs of motoring and distributes them generally through insurance. . . .

We propose a new allocation of the burden of motoring injuries. It is an allocation guided by the two principles that motoring should pay its way and that negligent motorists should pay their way. It is not a sacrifice of one principle to the other, but an accommodation of the two. Motorists generally will pay a share of the burden, and negligent motorists will pay a somewhat larger share. We do not argue that this is the only allocation one might reach under the general direction of these principles. We do believe that one who accepts these principles must be dissatisfied with present automobile claims systems and that commitment to these principles will move one in the general direction we have gone, if not to our proposed solution in all its details. One who believes that motoring generally ought to bear at least a part of the cost of motoring accidents, and yet also believes that fault has a place in an automobile claims system, will in all likelihood end up somewhere near our proposal.

D. THE CANADIAN BREAKTHROUGH:
PEACEFUL COEXISTENCE

OTTO E. LANG, THE NATURE AND POTENTIAL OF THE SASKATCHEWAN INSURANCE EXPERIMENT

(1962), 14 U. Fla. L. Rev. 352

At the heart of the Saskatchewan operation is a government-owned corporation, the Saskatchewan Government Insurance Office, popularly called SGIO.

This office competes in many fields of the insurance business, but these activities are secondary to its operation with respect to automobile insurance.

The involvement of SGIO in the automobile injury field can best be understood by breaking it down into three categories: low level universal coverage without regard to fault, medium compulsory and monopoly coverage using standard liability, and unlimited competitive extension coverage. The most famous category is that provided for in Part II of the Automobile Accident Insurance Act. In this part, statutory liability is imposed upon SGIO, which must compensate persons injured or the dependents or next-of-kin of those killed as the result of the operation of a motor vehicle in Saskatchewan as well as Saskatchewan residents injured while riding in Saskatchewan-registered vehicles in the United States or Canada.

The most important characteristic of this statutory compensation is that no question is asked as to the manner in which the accident occurred. This is a clear application of a theory of strict liability, since those active in operating and owning automobiles contribute to the fund, which pays for the resulting harm without raising the standard question of fault in tort law. This is compulsory insurance combined with strict liability, and the inelegance with which the premiums are assessed does not justify an allegation that the question of liability is being ignored. Liability is attached to activity in accordance with the theory of strict liability.

A second distinctive feature of statutory compensation is a complete disregard for the income or status of the person killed or injured. Thus the payment for any person leaving a primary dependent is $5,000 plus $1,000 for every secondary dependent up to a maximum of $10,000. The death of an adult without dependents entitles his parents to a division of $1,000. The payment for a child under fifteen years of age is graduated upwards from $100 for a child under seven years old, with an added $100 for each additional year of age.

Weekly indemnities of $25 may be provided for temporary disability for a maximum of 104 weeks. There is a schedule of payments for permanent disability; $4,000 is the payment for total disability, and lesser amounts are provided for partial disability according to its severity. A short excerpt from the 1960 schedule will illustrate the approach.

CLASS I – SHOULDER AND FOREARM

Disability	Degree of Impairment of:	
	Upper Extremity	Whole Body
Shoulder:		
1. Amputation:		
(a) disarticulation at shoulder (or loss above deltoid insertion)	100%	85%
(b) between shoulder and elbow	100%	50%
(c) below elbow or loss of entire hand	80%	40%
2. Limitation of motion:		
(a) total ankylosis (arm at side):		
scapula fixed	80%	40%
scapula free	60%	30%

The second involvement of SGIO in automobile insurance differs greatly from the first. It is a simple compulsory insurance for damage to one's own vehicle and for property damage and public liability up to certain common medium-range maximums, including several deductibles at the lower ranges. The feature that makes the Saskatchewan approach distinct from that employed in other jurisdictions in which compulsory insurance has been adopted is the additional requirement that this insurance be effected with SGIO. The Saskatchewan Government Insurance Office is, therefore, a monopoly insurer in this major area of automobile insurance. Its potential liability is reduced by any amounts that may be paid by it under Part II of the act in the pattern previously outlined. The obligation to compensate an insured for damage to his own vehicle is straightforward insurance involving no question of his liability. In so far, however, as property damage and public liability are concerned, the principles of liability from tort law are retained. The SGIO is liable only to the extent that its insured are liable.

The monopoly feature eliminates some disputes that might otherwise arise among parties or their respective insurers. This is true as to the vehicle itself, since the same company insures the owner's possible loss as well as the liability of anyone who is at fault in regard to the vehicle. In regard to personal injuries, the liability and fault problems of the tort law are allowed to inflict themselves upon claimants and raise especially difficult and undesirable problems when the insurance office shields itself behind the shelter given to actors against gratuitous passengers. Insurance for this group is so desirable, and could be obtained so cheaply if included in an owner's premium, that owners would usually be glad to pay for it.

Because of its monopolistic position, SGIO is liable for hit-and-run drivers and operators of stolen cars, subject only to rights of subrogation against the drivers. . . .

The third category of involvement of SGIO in automobile insurance is in the purely competitive field of extension insurance beyond that which is compulsory and automatic under the act. In this category the Saskatchewan position is the same as that of most jurisdictions in North America. The insurance is completely voluntary, and there is full competition in the free enterprise sense. This may be subject to some important qualifications as a result of SGIO's favorable position through its contracts in handling the other basic types of insurance under Part II and the comprehensive and liability category, the publicity it receives, its rate leadership, and its novel experiment. At the present time approximately fifty percent of the extension insurance sold in Saskatchewan is effected through SGIO. . . .

In this area of extension insurance, then, SGIO is in no different position from that of any independent private company except as far as savings may result from its monopolistic operation in other categories. Questions of fault arise in Saskatchewan as frequently as in other parts of North America, whether between different insurance companies or between an insurance company and an uninsured individual. The fault question also arises beyond the limits of whatever extension insurance happens to have been written. In extension insurance, all of the companies operating in Saskatchewan employ a deterrent feature by increasing rates in successive years after an accident in which the insured was at fault. They do it in a rather inelegant way, without much attention to the degree of fault or the seriousness of the accident.

NOTES

1. The Saskatchewan plan was enacted in 1946 by a C.C.F. (now N.D.P.) Government. It was the first major reform of auto accident compensation in the English-speaking world. Strangely, however, no other jurisdiction followed this bold pioneering effort for over 20 years. Can you think of any reasons why there was such reticence? See Linden, "Peaceful Coexistence and Automobile

Accident Compensation" (1966), 9 Can. Bar J. 5, where the following appears: "Unfortunately, the humanitarian desire of providing compensation for the injured has been stifled because reformers have frequently proposed a special administrative tribunal to allocate these costs, urged the abolition of the civil jury and have tried to supplant the private insurance companies with government insurance. Anyone who disapproves of boards, supports the jury or dislikes socialism is normally driven to defend the present system, despite its admitted shortcomings." Is this a possible explanation?

2. Many academics wrote articles and books calling for reform. Some of them designed new plans that they hoped would be adopted. One such scheme was devised by the late Professor Albert Ehrenzweig of Berkeley in his book, *Full Aid Insurance for the Traffic Victim* (1954), also in (1955), 43 Calif. L. Rev. 1. There are three steps in his plan. First, a new form of insurance, full aid insurance, which provides recovery independent of fault up to certain minimum amounts, is created. If the driver or owner carries such insurance, he is then relieved by statute of any common law liability for negligence. It is left optional with drivers, however, whether they insure or not and, if they do insure, whether they take out full aid insurance. Second, an uncompensated injury fund is set up, to be administered by the private insurance companies, from which the victim of an accident can recover the same statutory minimum amounts in the event he is injured by a car not carrying full aid insurance. This fund is to be financed partly by taxation, and partly by a series of "tort fines". The third step involves criminal fines, which are to be levied against both drivers and victims who are seriously (criminally) negligent, whether or not they are covered by full aid insurance.

Professor Ehrenzweig suggests that his Full Aid Plan will achieve the following goals: (1) insurance will remain voluntary; (2) it will lead to no impairment of safety incentives and quite possibly to an increase in them; (3) there will be no legislative interference with the common law of torts; (4) there will be no increase in expense to the insuring public and quite possibly a saving; (5) there will be an easy determination of awards and an equality among them; and (6) there will be the widest possible coverage of the public.

3. Professor Leon Green also developed a plan in his book *Traffic Victims: Tort Law and Insurance* (1958). He urged an end to tort liability and the creation of "compulsory motor vehicle comprehensive insurance". This plan would compensate everyone regardless of fault on the basis of common law damages, except that there would be no payment for pain and suffering and a deductible feature of $100. The courts were to adminster the plan.

4. Another effort at solving the problem was that of Morris and Paul, "The Financial Impact of Automobile Accidents" (1962), 110 U. Pa. L. Rev. 913. It was a plan to assist in economic disaster cases only. Their objective was to leave the existing tort system substantially intact and to simply augment it with an insurance feature for hardship cases. "Its objective," they said, "is to give limited help to those who have been seriously injured, irrespective of their fault, by a system of supplementary insurance — but only when their reimbursement from established sources has fallen disastrously short of the 'tangible loss' inflicted by the accident."

The fund was to be collected from motorists, possibly via a gasoline tax. Supplementary payments would be made to those whose "unreimbursed medical expenses and earning losses total more than $800". Payments would be limited to 85 percent of the medical expense and there would be a $600 per month maximum for earning losses.

As a corollary proposal to reduce what they regarded as the overpayment of small claims and to help finance the disaster fund, they proposed three changes in cases involving tangible losses under $800: (1) abolition of the right to damages for pain and suffering; (2) abolition of the collateral source rule; (3) recovery of reasonable legal expense.

5. There have been scores of other efforts at reform, too numerous to consider here. Among the most important were Keeton and O'Connell, *Basic Pro-*

tection for the Traffic Victim: A Blueprint for Reforming Automobile Insurance (1965), in which a draft statute was drawn by the authors. See also bibliographies in Conard et al., *Automobile Accident Costs and Payments* (1964), pp. 15-19; Keeton and O'Connell, *supra*, at pp. 543-566; Rokes, *Compendium of Automobile Indemnification Proposals* (1968); *Compensation and Rehabilitation in Australia* (1974), p. 347. And see symposia at (1971), 71 Colum. L. Rev. 189 *et seq.*; (1973), Utah L. Rev. 341.

6. One of the most important developments on the road to reform was the *Final Report on Automobile Insurance of the Select Committee of the Ontario Legislature* published in 1963. The Committee expressed its dissatisfaction with the present system of auto insurance and urged the adoption of a "limited accident benefits" scheme, which would provide "no fault" benefits to all accident victims, up to a certain level, without depriving them of their right to sue. Both the insurance industry and the organized bar supported the recommendations. Further studies were commissioned including a costing one by a technical committee of civil servants and a statistical one by the Osgoode Hall Law School on the position of accident victims under the present law. Finally, legislation was enacted in Ontario to permit limited accident benefits to be written on a *voluntary* basis as of January 1, 1969. Most of the other provinces did likewise around that time. The pressure mounted for a mandatory plan. The Canadian Bar Association, at its annual convention in Ottawa on September 3, 1969, passed the following Ontario-sponsored resolution: "Be it resolved that the accident insurance benefits presently available in the standard automobile policy be made mandatory in all such policies and in all provinces." Shortly thereafter, the Government of Ontario made the no-fault coverage mandatory as of January 1, 1972. The history of these developments is traced in Linden, "Automobile Insurance — Canadian Style" (1972), 21 Cath. U. L. Rev. 369; Linden, "Automobile Insurance Breakthrough in Canada" (1969), 1 Transp. L. Rev. 171. See also Atkey, "Perspectives for Non-fault Accident Compensation in Ontario" (1966), 5 Western L. Rev. 1; Linden, "Automobile Accident Compensation in Ontario — A System in Transition" (1966-67), 15 Am. J. Comp. L. 301; Conard, "The Economic Treatment of Automobile Injuries" (1964), 63 Mich. L. Rev. 279; Conard and Ethan, "New Hope for Consensus in the Automobile Injury Impasse" (1966), 52 A.B.A.J. 533.

7. After five years of operation, a further study was done by a Select Committee of the Ontario Legislative Assembly, under the chairmanship of Vernon Singer, Q.C. The Select Committee, in an interim report, made many recommendations, including enriching the accident benefits, abolishing the guest passenger section, requiring compulsory third party insurance, providing that third party coverage be for an unlimited amount, as well as many others. See Select Committee on Company Law, *First Report on Automobile Insurance* (1977). Many of these suggestions were swiftly acted upon by the Ontario government, which was undoubtedly spearheaded by the Honourable Larry Grossman, Q.C., minister responsible for insurance at the time, who had been a member of the Select Committee. The amendments to the benefits came into effect July 1, 1978. Since that time, the Select Committee, under its new chairman, James Breithaupt, Q.C., has also issued a *Second Report* (1978) and a *Third Report* (1979). See *infra*.

8. The Ontario plan, as amended, provides compensation, regardless of fault, to any "insured person . . . who sustains bodily injury or death, directly and independently of all other causes, by an accident arising out of the use or operation of an automobile". An "insured person" includes any occupant of the insured vehicle, any person who is struck in Canada by the insured automobile, and the insured and members of his family injured while occupants of another vehicle or while they are pedestrians. (Is a T.T.C. streetcar, which strikes a pedestrian, to be treated as an "automobile" or as "railway rolling stock that runs on rails" and, as such, exempted from the no-fault scheme? See *Punja* v. *T.T.C.* (1978), 21 O.R. (2d) 697, *per* Linden J., revd by Divisional Court, (1979), 24 O.R. (2d) 812.)

The benefits are substantial. All reasonable expenses incurred within four years from the date of the accident for necessary medical, surgical, dental, chiropractic, hospital, professional nursing, ambulance service, and rehabilitation care to a limit of $25,000 per person will be paid. The insurer, however, is not liable for any portion of these expenses that are "payable or recoverable under any medical, surgical, dental, or hospitalization plan or law". In addition, funeral expenses up to the amount of $1,000 per person will be reimbursed. Death benefits are payable in the amount of $10,000 for a head of the household, $10,000 for a spouse of the head of the household and $2,000 for dependants. If the head of a household dies, leaving two or more survivors, an additional $1,000 is payable for each survivor other than the first.

Weekly disability benefits are forthcoming during the time when a person "suffers substantial inability to perform the essential duties of his occupation or employment". To qualify, this inability must occur within 30 days of the accident and the person must have been employed at the date of the accident. (See *Sansone* v. *State Farm,* April 20, 1979 (C.A.)). These payments will stop after 104 weeks, however, unless it is established that such injury continuously prevents such person from engaging in any occupation or employment for which he is reasonably suited by education, training or experience. In such a case, these weekly benefits will run for the duration of such inability.

The amount of the weekly benefit is 80 percent of the gross weekly earnings, subject to a maximum of $140 per week. For a housekeeper who is unable to perform any of his or her duties, by reason of incapacity, the payment is $70 per week to a maximum of 12 weeks.

Tort rights are preserved for losses over the amount of these benefits. See Insurance Amendment Act, 1971, Stat. Ont., Vol. 2, c. 84, ss. 14, 15. See also O.Reg. 162/78. Payments made under the no-fault plan, however, are deducted from any tort recovery, but not if they are payments by the plan of another province. See Insurance Act, R.S.O. 1970, c. 224 as amended, s. 237(2); *MacDonald* v. *Proctor* (1977), 19 O.R. (2d) 745 (Ont. C.A.). This coverage currently costs $15 per vehicle annually.

For an excellent description of the operation of the Ontario plan, see Rachlin, "Accident Benefits—Revisited" (1979), 13 Law Soc. of Up. Can. Gaz. 51; Kavanagh, "Ontario Automobile Accident Benefits" (1973), 6 Ottawa L. Rev. 285.

9. In Alberta a scheme much the same as that in Ontario is in operation. See generally Laycraft, "Reforming the Automobile Tort System" (1971), 9 Alta. L. Rev. 22; Linden, "Automobile Accident Compensation in Alberta" (1968), 6 Alta. L. Rev. 219; Report of Alberta Automobile Insurance Board on I.B.C. "Variplan" Proposal (1976).

10. The Province of British Columbia has had a compulsory no-fault scheme with slightly different benefits since January 1, 1970. When the New Democratic Party formed a new government, however, it established the Insurance Corporation of British Columbia which has had a monopoly in the field of auto insurance since March 1, 1974. The basic contours of the earlier scheme were unaffected by the government takeover of the industry although there were some minor changes. See Schmitt, *Automobile Insurance in British Columbia* (1977), 35 Advocate 497, for a thorough examination of the legislation.

11. The Province of Manitoba also has a government-run, compulsory no-fault auto insurance plan. "Autopac", as it is called, has been operated by the Manitoba Public Insurance Corporation since November 1, 1971. The scheme closely resembles the Saskatchewan plan, after which it was modelled. For a brief description, see Linden, "Automobile Insurance — Canadian Style" (1972), 21 Cath. U. L. Rev. 369, at p. 383; Green, "A Fish Out of Water — Classical Fault on the Highway" (1970), 35 Sask. L. Rev. 2.

12. In the Atlantic provinces, no-fault benefits are available to motorists on an optional basis. These plans are under review at present. New Brunswick introduced a new plan similar to Ontario's in 1975. See MacArthur, *Brief on Automobile Insurance* (1973).

13.   The right to sue in tort has not been interfered with, (except for a set-off of the no-fault benefits to eliminate double recovery) in any Canadian province, save for Quebec. See *infra.* Tort law survives even in the three western provinces where the government has entered the auto insurance business.

14.   Can you think of any ways that the Canadian no-fault schemes could be improved?

15.   In its *Report on Motor Vehicle Accident Compensation* (1973), the Ontario Law Reform Commission had these comments to make about the Canadian-type schemes:

"The idea that a no-fault compensation scheme can co-exist with the fault system is practically, but not ideologically, acceptable. The two schemes are premised on such different philosophies of compensation that one can only reconcile their co-existence as a practical compromise between the strongly held views of those who regard no-fault as an essential reform and the equally strongly held views of those who regard the fault system as a fundamental requirement of justice."

Is this "practical compromise" reached across Canada ideologically unacceptable to you?

16.   What do you think of the following observation in Linden, "Peaceful Coexistence and Automobile Accident Compensation" (1966), 9 Can. Bar J. 5:

"It is now possible, however, to provide basic compensation for all accident victims without discarding the jury trial, without the necessity of creating another board, and without submitting to 'creeping socialism'. Further, there is no need to jettison the present tort system with its reliance on the fault doctrine. In other words, an accommodation is possible — let there be peaceful coexistence between tort law and the automobile accident compensation plan. The best features of both systems could be retained and the worst of both mitigated. Full and immediate compensation may be provided to all injury victims for medical, rehabilitation, and burial costs and subsistence income regardless of fault. At the same time, the tort system would remain available to those who wished to press their claims against negligent motorists to secure additional reparation."

17.   See also Glasbeek & Hasson, "Fault—The Great Hoax" in Klar (ed.), *Studies in Canadian Tort Law* (1977):

"A not-so-explicit admission of defeat is revealed by recent developments related to the next most important area of carnage in our society, namely, the motor vehicle accident cases. All Canadian provinces have created, side by side with their much-vaunted *fault* system, a so-called *no-fault* scheme. The point of the *no-fault* scheme is to ensure that compensation will be available to all victims of car accidents. In addition, the tort system is supposed to continue to flourish. It is hard to perceive the logic of this kind of arrangement unless it is in terms of a tacit admission of intellectual bankruptcy by the proponents of *fault* doctrine.

The rationales of a *fault* system are, as we have seen, that it may appease, provide for ethical compensation, ethical retribution, specific deterrence or general deterrence. If we can ignore the appeasement aspect as one of the possible purposes of the *fault* system (and we suggest it is a *raison d'etre* fairly classified as frivolous), we are left with the basic notion that the *fault* system is geared towards regulating the conduct of people in society. Inasmuch as motor car drivers' conduct is to be regulated by the payment of compensation to victims, it ought to follow that, if the *fault* system is working, sufficient compensation is being paid out to sufficient victims to keep the motor car drivers' behaviour under acceptable control and, if this were so, the number of accidents would never be a problem. That this is not so is apparent from the fact that society has recognized that there are so many victims of accidents who were not compensated a *no-fault* scheme had to be introduced, *i.e.,* a scheme which does not rely on finding any kind of relationship between the need to compensate and the need to find *fault*.

We recognize that it may be that society still believes the *fault* system regulates people's behaviour sufficiently and has only instituted minimal compensatory schemes because accidents occur as a result of behaviour which is totally acceptable. Our reply is that this is simply unlikely to be true. Under the *fault* system many people do not recover, not because a driver was not at *fault* (even by the precepts of the doctrine as interpreted by the courts) but mainly because they do not know that they have a cause of action, they do not have the money to pursue it, or the costs involved in a tort cause of action outweigh the value of the compensation they seek. If this is so, even if it is only partially so, it follows that unredressed victims under a *fault* system are victims of behaviour which the *fault* system ought to have eradicated. It is in this sense that we say the strange mixture of *fault* and *no-fault* which has become prevalent in our provincial jurisdiction is an admission that the *fault* system does not work as it ought to. How has it come about that society has accepted this kind of a mixture, this irrational scheme? It is our suggestion that the prevailing concept of *fault*—that no one should be compensated unless somebody has been found to be culpable in some way—is so deeply ingrained that it is very hard for people who set up new schemes to get rid of the *idée fixe* that compensation has to be tied to some kind of *fault*-finding. That, at least in part, must explain why *no-fault* schemes are so niggardly. Society has recognized that victims of motor car accidents should be compensated without having to prove any kind of wrongdoing by anyone, yet, having gone that far, society has kept the benefits available at an absurdly low level. A direct comparison can be made with the much-complained-about workmen's compensation schemes. Niggardly though those schemes seem to some —especially injured workers—they are vastly superior to anything that any *no-fault* scheme which is in part based on *fault* has yet provided.

We are also willing to say here, without trying to sketch it out in any kind of detail because the point is not fundamental to our argumentation, that there are powerful lobbies who have a vested interest in retaining a *fault* scheme for motor vehicle accidents. In particular, we suggest that lawyers have a very high financial stake in continuing the negligence system in its present form. Although motor vehicle litigation does not make up an overwhelming proportion of lawyers' work, it does comprise a considerable fraction thereof, and for some people it is a major part of their business. It is very remunerative work. Further, lawyers are aided in their support of the system by their deeply-held belief that the adversary system is best suited to the resolution of all difficulties in society, especially where the trial takes the form of dispute resolution before a jury. Furthermore, lawyers (and many other people) have a fascination for the spectacular. By this we mean that the *fault* system is designed to occasionally permit a person to recover a great amount. Under the heading of pain and suffering courts are entitled to award damages well in excess of the actual losses suffered by the injured person in respect of earning capacity, lost business opportunities and expenses related to rehabilitation and medical treatment. This head of compensation is part of the compassionate face of the law of torts. To us, it seems an unwarranted distortion of an already cruel system. Study after study has shown that the most seriously injured people are under-compensated and the less seriously injured are over-compensated. The latter are frequently given settlements or receive settlements because of their nuisance value rather than because they have established an adequate amount of *fault* or, indeed, have established that they have lost the amount they claim. Their compensation will result— if the *fault* system does in any way exact ethical retribution, deter specifically and deter in general—in overkill and be immoral, inasmuch as the defendant supposedly bears the burden of the loss because of his blameworthiness. Seriously injured people, because the quantum of their damages could be very great, are fought very hard by insurers. As a result, there is a long delay before they recover anything, and they are frequently under-compensated. Inasmuch as the amount of the award does not reflect the amount of *fault* on the defendant's part, the system is once again ineffectual. It is hard to understand how this kind of compensatory scheme can be defended. There seems to us to be no reason that any person should be over-compensated. There seems to be no reason why anybody should be under-compensated. And, most importantly, there should be no reason at all why most people should not be compensated at all. It is to be remembered at all times that these people who claim that the large awards show how compassionate they are and what deep laudable feelings they have for social and human values, are willing to permit 50 percent of all people who are the victims of motor car accidents not to recover any compensation from the tort system at all. It is true that the *no-fault* schemes come in and give accident victims an absolute pittance. This apparently satisfies the *fault* proponents' conscience. We believe this kind of scheme to be totally irrational."

Do you agree or disagree with this assessment of the current peaceful coexistence schemes? What do you think of the following observations of Blum and Kalven?

BLUM AND KALVEN, THE EMPTY CABINET OF DR. CALABRESI: AUTO ACCIDENTS AND GENERAL DETERRENCE

(1967), 34 U. Chi. L. Rev. 239

A first reaction might well be that such arrangements are politically ingenious but wholly unprincipled. The absence of clear principle is suggested by twin circumstances: the proponents have argued the need for a compensation plan on the weaknesses of the common law fault criterion and have viewed some aspects of common law damages as excessive; they nevertheless end up by keeping the fault system alive and giving common law damages. The cleverness of the arrangement is that it makes possible a plan under which no victim as a victim can be worse off than he was at common law and under which some function is still left for the tort system. Thus any sense of grievance over the proposed change is abated for those parties most likely to complain — the victims and the lawyers.

On fuller examination, however, it appears there need be no inconsistency in the two level arrangement; and further, whatever the practical motivation for such plans, the two level concept may be the route to a sound solution to the whole problem. The key lies in the separation of two functions of tort damages that have always been tied together in the past — the welfare function of providing relief for the injured and the corrective justice function of righting a private wrong. So long as the functions are lumped together, the welfare function is likely to be seen as dominant given present concerns. By separating the functions, the two level plans may test sharply whether the corrective justice function is worth preserving.

In our earlier essay we found it instructive to think about the tort field being overlaid by the adoption of a broad social security system that covered a large variety of human ills and misfortunes. And we maintained that, insofar as we are concerned with compensation of victims, there is no alternative superior to extension of social security. It alone can provide a coherent and equal treatment of deserving beneficiaries, and it alone is capable of furnishing a rationale for distributing burdens and for determining benefits. What the two level plans ultimately put in issue is whether even under such extensive welfare guarantees there is a function left over for the tort system. . . . One point, however, is of special interest to us. In large part corrective justice is concerned not with deterring the wrongdoer, but with satisfying the victim's feeling of indignation. If the victim recovers only from the fund, he will not gain the satisfaction of seeing his wrong righted. . . .

To us there remains great force in the notion that no one should be worse off because of the wrongdoing of another so long as the wrongdoer, or his insurer, is in a position to make redress. The law ought not to break sharply with the moral traditions of the society, as it would do were it no longer to recognize fault and personal responsibility. And we would urge that not all reflection of moral values should be left to the criminal law. The tort system can share some of the burden of satisfying indignation.

The two level arrangement, whereby welfare underwriting for all accidents is supplied by social security and the tort system is left "on top" of that underwriting, has one paramount advantage. It permits the society to make independent judgments on matters that cannot be cleanly handled together — the setting of welfare payment levels and the setting of corrective justice damage levels. On the one side, welfare payments should be set by some general standard deemed appropriate for victims of all misfortunes. They clearly should not be set differently for victims of auto accidents and other victims. And they should, as a matter of policy, be set without contagion from common law damages and the settlement practices of insurance companies. On the other side, it should be observed that there is a basic compatibility between pain and suffering as a recognition of the dignitary aspects of accident injuries and a liability system keyed to fault. From a welfare point of view awards for pain and suffering may well be regarded as a quixotic luxury; from a corrective justice point of view such damages may be at the heart of the matter.

E. NEW STIRRINGS: THREE ALTERNATIVE APPROACHES

1. Mixed No-Fault Plans: Tort Action Survives

KEETON AND O'CONNELL, BASIC PROTECTION FOR THE TRAFFIC VICTIM

(1965)

PRINCIPLES UNDERLYING THE PROPOSED REFORM

There are two principal features of our proposal: (1) Development of a new form of compulsory automobile insurance (called basic protection insurance), which in its nature is an extension of the principle of medical payments coverage. It compensates all persons injured in automobile accidents without regard to fault for all types of out-of-pocket personal injury losses up to limits of $10,000 per person. Whenever an insured's automobile is in an accident and he, or a guest, is injured, his own insurance company will compensate him or his guest. (2) Enactment of legislation granting to basic protection insureds an exemption from tort liability to some extent — an exemption eliminating tort liability entirely in those cases in which damages for pain and suffering would not exceed $5,000 and other tort damages would not exceed the $10,000 limit of basic protection coverage. In all other cases, the effect of the exemption is to reduce the tort liability of basic protection insureds by approximately these same amounts.

Although this new coverage is like workmen's compensation in calling for payments on a basis of liability without fault and for periodic payments as losses occur, it is nonetheless very different in other important respects. Unlike workmen's compensation acts generally, the proposed basic protection act preserves tort actions for cases of severe injury — cases in which tort damages exceed the tort exemption. Also, the basic protection plan does not require a separate marketing system or a separate system of administrative machinery like a workmen's compensation board. Rather, we propose that the new coverage be marketed through the same channels of private enterprise now used for automobile liability insurance and that claims be processed through present institutions and procedures — including jury trial of not only the tort claims that are preserved but also the more substantial basic protection claims (involving at least $5,000 of *economic loss*). Further, the proposed act does not provide a schedule of fixed benefits for each specific type of injury, as does workmen's compensation. Rather, reimbursement is based only on actual losses as they accrue. Thus, basic protection insurance bears more similarity to current tort liability insurance than to workmen's compensation insurance. The closest analogy in present insurance, however, is medical payments coverage.

The basic protection proposal, then, is a blueprint for prompt reimbursement of losses month by month as they occur, for reimbursement at reduced overhead and administrative cost because of the avoidance of a multitude of contests over fault and the value of pain and suffering in cases of less severe injury, and for reimbursement through standards and procedures that minimize inducements to dishonesty and causes of disrespect for law in day-to-day practical application.

NOTES

1. The Keeton-O'Connell proposal heated up the automobile insurance debate in the mid-1960's. The authors included in the book a proposed statute, which enabled individual legislators to introduce the plan into their various state legislatures in the U.S. Although no state has actually adopted the Keeton-O'Connell plan, a few have enacted legislation that was inspired by its basic principle, which is to provide *some* no-fault benefits in return for the removal of *some* tort rights. Abolishing part of the tort claim permits some of the premium dollar to be diverted into no-fault benefits, while keeping the cost of insurance within manageable limits. See Gibson, "Non-fault Automobile Insurance" (1968), 11 Can. Bar J. 172 for a comparison of Keeton and O'Connell with the Canadian voluntary schemes in force at that time. See also Linden, Book Review (1966), 44 Can. Bar Rev. 696.

2. A comparison of Keeton and O'Connell's Basic Protection and the Saskatchewan scheme was made by Kalven, "A Schema of Alternatives to the Present Auto Accident Tort System" (1968), 1 Conn. L. Rev. 33. He observes:

"The dilemma posed by the reluctance to place the full cost of accidents on drivers and the parallel reluctance to lower awards was solved with spectacular ingenuity some years ago by the Province of Saskatchewan. In many ways the Saskatchewan plan has offered the most interesting model yet put forward. In effect, it is a two-level system. At the lower level the damages for all accident victims are underwritten at a modest level of damages; at the second level, the common law tort action is kept alive over and beyond this basic recovery. The beauty of this scheme is that under it, no plaintiff can be worse off than he was under the common law. All victims will still receive whatever they would have gotten at common law and some victims will receive more.

It is, I think, an especially good question to put to Professors Keeton and O'Connell as to why they do not claim the Saskatchewan plan as their model since they too propose a two-level system and keep the tort system alive over and beyond their initial basic protection. Indeed, they not only do not claim the Saskatchewan plan as a precedent, they remain virtually silent about it. The reasons, I think, are not hard to find. Although their plan leaves the common law action alive, it is not true that all victims will be as well off under it as they were under the common law. The most distinctive feature of the Keeton-O'Connell plan is the adaptation it makes of the two-level plan model. The best way of putting their plan in perspective is to lay it next to the Saskatchewan plan and to note the differences. One of the difficulties I have with the Keeton-O'Connell plan is simply that when such a comparison is made, I find it less intelligible and less attractive than the Saskatchewan model."

3. About two dozen American states have now adopted some type of no-fault scheme. A few of them, such as Arkansas, Delaware, Maryland, Oregon, South Carolina, South Dakota, Texas, Virginia and Wisconsin, have enacted plans similar to those in Canada in that they do not eliminate any of the tort rights. These schemes are sometimes called "add-on" plans.

Another group of states, including Colorado, Connecticut, Florida, Georgia, Hawaii, Kansas, Kentucky, Massachusetts, Michigan, Minnesota, Nevada, New Jersey, New York, Pennsylvania and Utah, have enacted no-fault plans that have interfered, to some extent, with the right to sue. Various thresholds, described either by type of injury, or amount of monetary loss or both, must be crossed before any tort reparation is permitted.

For example, the New York plan limits damages for non-pecuniary losses only to cases of serious injury such as death, dismemberment, significant disfigurement, a compound or comminuted fracture, or where the expenses exceed $500. In Michigan, recovery for non-pecuniary loss is limited to cases of death, serious disability or disfigurement. Some of these provisions have been challenged on constitutional grounds over the years.

4. A strong influence on the development of these plans in the United States is the Uniform Motor Vehicle Accident Reparations Act (UMVARA) which was approved by the National Conference of Commissioners on Uniform State Laws in 1972. It eliminates tort liability for general damages unless the accident causes death, significant permanent injury, serious permanent disfigurement, or more than six months of complete inability to work. Even if a person qualifies under one of these thresholds, the first $5,000 of general damages is not recoverable. See for a short description of most of the new U.S. plans, Kircher, "Automobile Accident Reparation Legislation (Current Status)" (1973), 9 The Forum 15. See also Spangenberg, "No Fault Fact, Fiction and Fallacy" (1973), 44 Miss. L.J. 15; Schwarz, "Faulty No-Fault: Let the Consumer Beware" (1973), 22 Cath. U.L. Rev. 746. See also O'Connell and Henderson, *Tort Law, No-Fault and Beyond* (1975) for a description of various U.S. schemes; O'Connell, "Operation of No-Fault Auto Laws: A Survey of Surveys" (1977), 56 Neb. L. Rev. 23; U.S. Department of Transportation, *State No-Fault Automobile Experience, 1971-1977,* (1977);

5. Some of the concepts incorporated in these new American plans have spilled over into Canada in recent years. For example, in Nova Scotia the *Report of the Royal Commission on Automobile Insurance* (1973), recommended a no-fault plan which would pay no-fault benefits at the same level as in Ontario. However, it urged the abolition of the right to sue in tort except for two situations: (1) where the economic losses exceeded the amounts payable by no-fault, and (2) where the non-economic losses involved the death of a person, serious impairment of body functions or serious disfigurement or where a person is intentionally injured. The right to sue in tort for property damage is also to be virtually eliminated.

6. Another major proposal being advanced in Canada is called Variplan, which was developed by the Insurance Bureau of Canada (I.B.C.), an association which includes as members most Canadian insurers. It has gone through various mutations over the period of a year or so. Variplan resembles very closely the American UMVARA plan.

Under the I.B.C. plan economic loss is compensable on a compulsory, first-party, no-fault basis. The right to sue is retained to the extent that the economic loss incurred is in excess of the amounts paid under the no-fault benefits. The tort remedy is also permitted for non-pecuniary losses, but only in the event of death or serious permanent injury, which includes substantial disfigurement and severe and prolonged disability (over six months).

The benefits available as compensation for economic loss are in excess of the benefits available under all government plans or other types of insurance. Medical and rehabilitation expenses, to the extent that they are not covered by other plans, are payable to a maximum of $20,000 per person. Income loss is to be compensated weekly at the rate of 80 percent of gross income loss, the maximum allowable gross income being $250 per week or $13,000 per year. Such benefits are payable for a maximum of three years, even if the individual is permanently incapacitated through the injury. Benefits provided under such plans as Workmen's Compensation or an employer's wage continuation plan are subtracted from gross earnings before the calculation is made. Payments under the Unemployment Insurance program or the Canada Pension Plan are only deducted if they were being received before the occurrence of the accident. There is a waiting period of seven days for which no income loss compensation is payable.

In the event of the death of the head of the household or the spouse of the head of the household, $5,000 is payable in death benefits. This lump sum payment may be increased by $1,000 for each surviving dependant beyond the first on the death of the head of the household. $1,000 is paid for the death of a dependant child under the age of 18. Reimbursement for funeral expenses to a maximum of $1,000 is also available.

In the case of property damage, the right to sue in tort is largely abolished. Collision coverage is not compulsory, but where it is purchased, recovery is permitted under one of three different property damage plans which are available. Plan A, or Broad Collision Coverage, provides insurance coverage for loss or damage to one's automobile and loss of use arising from collision or upset with another vehicle, subject to a standard deductible clause. Plan B, Basic Collision, provides the same type of coverage as in Plan A with the exception that there will be no deductible if the insured vehicle is parked and is struck by an identified vehicle. Under Plan C, Limited Collision, insurance is provided against loss or damage to the vehicle which arises from collision with another identified vehicle. Payments are only made under this plan under the circumstances and to the extent set forth in the Recovery Rules. Recovery for loss of use under all plans is limited to $15 per day for a maximum of 15 days.

The Recovery Rules apply where an insured motor vehicle sustains damage in a collision with another identified motor vehicle. The insured owner recovers from his own insurer his loss or damage, deductible to the extent allowed by the rules. Under Rule 1, the insured is entitled to 100 percent recovery if his vehicle is struck under a number of specified circumstances which would tend to indicate that the other driver was at fault, such as being struck while parked or struck from the rear. Under Rule 2, no recovery is available if no other vehicle is involved in the collision or if the owner of the other vehicle is entitled to payment under Rule 1. Rule 3 entitles the insured to 50 percent recovery where the circumstances are not within either Rule 1 or Rule 2. Additional coverages may be purchased at the option of the insured.

The plan is to be administered through the private insurance companies. If a dispute arises between the insured and his insurer it is to be submitted to a tribunal of independent representatives of each party under s. 102 of the Ontario Insurance Act. The decision of this tribunal may be appealed to the courts.

I.B.C. claims that some savings in premiums can be achieved by the adoption of Variplan. So far, however, no provincial government has adopted it.

7. Is the I.B.C. plan an improvement over the present Canadian schemes? Does it take away more than it gives? T.H. Rachlin, in his paper "The I.B.C. Proposal With Respect to Personal Injuries Claims" (1974), 8 Law Society Gazette 48, gives the following examples of the I.B.C. plan in operation:

> "1. A vehicle driven by a drunk driver mounts a sidewalk, strikes a pedestrian and then crashes into a building. The pedestrian has fractured bones and much pain and suffering but no serious permanent injury. The pedestrian can receive no compensation for his injuries. The building owner is entitled to sue for the full amount of the damage to his building.
> 2. A person is in excruciating pain for weeks or months, but if there is no

serious permanent injury then he receives no compensation for this.

3. A student is temporarily disabled so he loses one or more years of schooling and as a result loses future earnings as well as forfeiting prepaid tuition and he can receive no compensation for this.

4. The pedestrian struck by the drunk driver is a teacher who receives two fractured legs and a fractured left arm. He has several operations and is hospitalized for three months. He is able to return to work after five months. He is left with continuing intermittent pain and a slight limp and he cannot fully straighten his left arm. He is right handed. He has had much pain and suffering and has lost many of the pleasures of life. Because his work is not physically demanding, his ability to earn a livelihood is not affected. While acknowledging that his injuries are permanent, his doctor says he will not be left with any serious permanent injury. OHIP pays his hospital and medical bills in full. A wage continuation plan available through his employer pays his salary in full during his time off work. He has contributed to the premiums of both OHIP and the wage continuation plan. He receives not one cent of IBC no-fault benefits and his right to sue the drunk driver for compensation for his injuries is completely taken away."

Do you favour a plan that yields such results?

8. For the same insurance premium should a person who earns $13,000 per year receive more than one who earns $6,500 per year on a no-fault basis? Does this discriminate against the poor?

9. See, for a thorough analysis of I.B.C., "Symposium on No-Fault Insurance" (1974), 8 Law Society Gazette 17 *et seq.*

10. A variation of the I.B.C. scheme, which was thought to be dead, has been resurrected by the Ontario Legislative Assembly's Select Committee, *Second Report on Automobile Insurance* (1978), p. 63. The Select Committee has sketched out a no-fault scheme, which would furnish generous compensation for economic loss to all auto accident victims regardless of fault. There would be no limit for medical costs but there would be a reasonable maximum on the amount of the weekly benefits paid. Death benefits would also be paid. There would also be provision for a limited amount of non-economic loss to be paid on a no-fault basis. It would take the form of a modest lump sum payment based on a fixed scale, as in New Zealand.

The right to sue would be eliminated, except for certain serious cases where it was felt to be unfair to limit the recovery to the amount set out on a scale. As in Variplan and UMVARA, a victim would be allowed to sue in tort for his non-economic losses to a maximum of $100,000 if he can establish (i) "serious and permanent injury resulting in substantial and medically demonstrable permanent impairment affecting the resumption of customary activities; or (ii) permanent loss of important bodily function; or (iii) significant permanent scarring or disfigurement". A method of dealing with vehicle damage on a no-fault basis was also outlined. Costing studies were not done.

What do you think of this scheme? Does it furnish a better or a worse deal for accident victims? For insurance consumers? For insurance companies? For lawyers?

11. The Pearson Commission, after five years of study, made some recommendations with regard to the reform of the auto accident compensation system in Britain. See the *Report of the Royal Commission on Civil Liability and Compensation for Personal Injury* (1978). The Report suggests that a no-fault scheme be established for automobile accident victims which would pay them benefits on the same level as injured workmen are paid. It urges that the plan be administered by the Department of Health and Social Security and be financed by a new tax levy on gasoline. (1 p. per gallon). The present right to tort damages would survive, but the claimant would not be permitted to recover any non-pecuniary damages for the first three months following the injury. What do you think of this compromise proposal? Why should the scheme be operated by a government department rather than the private insurance companies? Why finance the

scheme out of a gasoline tax? What do you think of the "deductible" feature in relation to non-pecuniary damages? See Fleming, "The Pearson Report: Its 'Strategy'" (1979), 42 Mod. L. Rev. 249; Weir, "The Pearson Commission Report", [1978] Camb. L.J. 222; Ogus, Corfield & Harris, "Pearson: Principled Reform or Political Compromise" (1978), 7 Industrial L.J. 143; Allen, Bourn and Holyoak (ed.), *Accident Compensation After Pearson* (1979).

"No fault, my foot! It's your fault!"

Drawing by Weber; © 1974; The New Yorker Magazine, Inc.

2. Accident Insurance: 'Pure' No-fault: Tort Action Disappears

ONTARIO LAW REFORM COMMISSION, REPORT ON MOTOR VEHICLE ACCIDENT COMPENSATION

(1973)

An integrated, more appropriate and more efficient system should, we think, replace the tort action and the diversity of other collateral schemes as the source of compensation for losses resulting from the activity of motoring.

The elements of an improved reparation system should include the following:

(1) Reparation should be made without regard to fault for all pecuniary losses arising out of personal injury, death, or property damage occasioned by a motor vehicle.

(2) First party accident insurance rather than third party liability insurance should be the basis of the system, ensuring compensation to all accident victims, although liability insurance would remain necessary for extra-provincial operation of Ontario vehicles. The insurance should be compulsory and provide adequate compensation by insuring against all pecuniary loss, but only pecuniary loss, arising out of:

    (a) personal injury,

    (b) deprivation of support to dependants through a fatal injury to an insured person, and

    (c) damage to tangible property, including motor vehicles.

(3) There should be no compensation for non-pecuniary losses, for example, damages for pain and suffering, loss of amenities of life, and shortened expectation of life. While damages for non-pecuniary losses may serve some valid purpose, they serve it for such a small percentage of accident victims, and have such offsetting disadvantages, that the net benefit to be derived from sacrificing them in a system that provides compensation for all pecuniary losses is overwhelming.

(4) Pecuniary losses should be paid as they accrue. Thus, medical, hospital and other expenses should be paid from time to time as they are incurred. Compensation for loss of time should be paid on a monthly basis.

Periodic payments represent the best method of taking account of such factors as:

(a) improvement or deterioration in the physical condition of the accident victim requiring more or less intensive treatment;

(b) increase or decrease in the price of medical, hospital and other forms of treatment or service made necessary by the condition of the accident victim;

(c) variation in the earning capacity of the accident victim;

(d) inflation;

(e) the subsequent death of the accident victim.

(5) The motor vehicle accident policy should be the primary source of compensation, thereby ensuring that the costs of motor vehicle accidents are allocated to the activity of motoring.

(9) An administrative board should be established to supervise the underwriting and compensation aspects of the no-fault plan. It should also be concerned with accident prevention, emergency services and rehabilitative treatment.

PRIVATE OR PUBLIC UNDERWRITING

The arguments for and against underwriting by a Crown agency range from the purely pragmatic, relating primarily to the efficiency of the compensation scheme, to the more broadly based and philosophical, relating to general economic and political philosophy.

Any determination of the question of public *versus* private underwriting would have to take into account a variety of factors, such as the cost of each method of underwriting, and the ability of each to pass a maximum proportion of the premium dollar into the hands of accident victims; ease of integration into the existing medical and hospital insurance scheme; effective utilization of premium income; comparative expertise in administering an insurance scheme and ability to safeguard the interests of insured persons.

While we make no recommendation as to which method of underwriting is preferable, we do recommend that careful consideration be given to the question of public underwriting, private underwriting, or mixed public and private underwriting. . . .

(c) LOST TIME

An injury may prevent a person from engaging, or engaging fully, in normal activities, particularly the activity whereby the person earns his or her income. Where a person's ability to earn is limited, the plan should pay what he or she would have earned but did not because of the injury. As it would appear that such payments would not be taxable unless the insurance premiums had been paid by the recipient's employer, the payment should be net loss after calculation of tax except in cases where the payment will be taxable. The limit under the compulsory policy should be $1,000 per month, but individuals wishing increased coverage for their own income should be permitted to obtain it for themselves.

Partially or wholly disabled persons who are not earning an income (housewives, retired persons, unemployed persons) have nevertheless suffered the loss of a valuable asset. We recommend that the housewife and the retired person should receive payments based on what they could reasonably expect to earn if they chose to seek employment rather than devoting their time to non-paying activity. The unemployed person should, within the time when he or she could reasonably have expected to obtain employment, be entitled to payments based on earning capacity as well.

A permanently disabled child should receive a modest payment for lost time but as he or she grows up, should receive payments in lieu of earned income on a reasonable basis — what the individual would have been capable of earning, if that is determinable.

Payments for lost time should continue for as long as the person's earning capacity remains limited. To encourage rehabilitation, lost time payments should not be reduced on a dollar for dollar basis as the accident victim recovers his or her earning capacity. Rather a formula should be used which would permit a net benefit to be derived from a return to gainful employment.

(d) DEATH BENEFITS

Death benefits should be paid in respect of every fatal injury occasioned to an insured person. These benefits should include reasonable funeral expenses up to $1,000. In addition, where the deceased is survived by dependants, a lump sum payment of $1,000 should be made to meet their necessary expenses pending determination and commencement of an appropriate continuing periodic payment in respect of the losses this group may have suffered by being deprived of the support of the deceased.

A monthly allowance in respect of loss of support should be paid for the benefit of the dependants of the deceased and should be calculated with a view to permitting them to continue to live in a fashion reasonably approximating that in which they were being maintained by the deceased. The limit of this allowance under compulsory coverage should be $1,000 per month, but additional coverage should be available on an optional basis.

In households where both spouses earn income from employment, the family income should be considered as the appropriate guide for calculating a monthly payment in the event of the death of one, or both. . . .

An adjustment in the allowance should be made when minor children reach majority unless they are continuing their education or are otherwise dependent by reason of infirmity. In the case of a child who is continuing his or her education, the adjustment in the family allowance should be made whenever the child ceases to be a full-time student at a school or university.

A widow who remarries should receive one year's payments in a lump sum and thereafter the allowance should cease except where there are children in which case it should be reduced by half but continue on the basis described in the preceding paragraph.

(e) COLLISION AND PROPERTY DAMAGE

The major item of property loss that arises in connection with the use or operation of motor vehicles is collision damage — damage inflicted on the vehicles themselves.

Some of this damage is now compensated entirely on a no-fault basis through the medium of collision insurance. Most one-car accidents are dealt with in this fashion and some two-car collisions under knock-for-knock agreements. In most cases where there is more than one vehicle involved in a collision, the accident must be investigated by at least two insurers. Since most Ontario vehicles carry public liability and property damage insurance, and three quarters of them carry collision insurance the issue frequently is not whether the damage will be compensated, but by which insurer. To make no-fault the universal method of dealing with this type of loss would thus be largely a case of standardizing the method of distributing this loss among motorists.

The sacrifice in adopting a no-fault approach as the exclusive means of dealing with collision damage would lie in giving up the right to full compensation.

Collision insurance carried by motorists today provides for the insured to bear the risk of the first 25, 50 or 100 dollars in damage. This is called the "deductible" portion of the loss, which would be prohibitively expensive to insure. It is nevertheless possible under present law for the insured to obtain compensation for this loss provided someone is to blame for it and the claim is deemed worth pursuing. The collision insurer is subrogated to the rights of the insured against any "wrongdoer" to the extent that the insurer has paid the collision loss.

No-fault insurance, like collision insurance, would be prohibitive in cost in the absence of a deductible portion. Yet abolishing the right to recover against another driver on the basis of fault would mean that this deductible portion would simply have to be borne by the motorist suffering the loss. In other words, the vehicle owner would become a self-insurer to the extent of the deductible portion of the collision loss. It seems entirely likely, however, that the administrative cost savings resulting from the reduced need for investigation, and the abolition of negotiation and litigation based on fault would make the sacrifice worthwhile.

We recommend that collision coverage continue to be optional. It is a measurable, limited interest of the vehicle owner alone that is at stake, and thus it does not seem justified to force the decision to insure on the owner. It should, however, be made abundantly clear to owners that they can look to no one for compensation if they choose not to carry collision coverage.

Other property damaged through the use or operation of a vehicle, except other vehicles and their contents, should be compensated for, up to a certain limit, by the policy of the owner of the vehicle. This limit should be determined on the basis of underwriting experience.

3. EXCLUSIONS

We recommend that the following be excluded from coverage by the no-fault policy:

(a) loss or damage deliberately inflicted by the claimant on his or her own person or property;

(b) loss or damage suffered by a claimant in the course of committing a criminal offence (other than a driving offence) or in the course of escaping or avoiding lawful arrest.

Some plans now in existence also exclude loss or damage suffered while a person is under the influence of alcohol or a drug. It is our view, however, that this type of misbehaviour is best penalized by the criminal process and that the deterrent of deprivation of compensation is too drastic.

NOTES

1. This is not the first time such a scheme has been suggested. See *The Report of the British Columbia Royal Commission on Automobile Insurance* (Wooton Commission) (1968); Ison, "Highway Accidents and the Demise of Tort Liability" (1969), 47 Can. Bar Rev. 304; see also American Insurance Association, *Report of Special Committee to Study and Evaluate the Keeton-O'Connell Basic Protection Plan and Automobile Accident Reparations* (1968); New York Insurance Department, *Automobile Insurance . . . For Whose Benefit?* (1970).

2. Under the O.L.R.C. proposal, what compensation would be paid to a

young unmarried person with an unsightly scar on the cheek? What would a young lawyer who lost a leg receive?

3. Do you agree that there should be no compensation for non-pecuniary losses? Should everyone be treated in the same way, regardless of whether they were responsible for the accident? If the same premium were to be paid by all motorists for the new coverage, should someone who earns $1,000 per month or more receive a larger monthly sum than someone who earns less than that?

4. The O.L.R.C. made no estimate of the cost of the scheme that it proposed. Nor did it do any statistical studies of its own. Nor did it consult with members of the legal profession or the insurance industry. It is plain that the O.L.R.C. hoped that they could save some money by simplifying the administration of the scheme and by eliminating the right to general damages. Do you approve of saving money in this way?

5. Do you prefer the O.L.R.C. plan or the I.B.C. proposal? Do you prefer either of them to the present Canadian system? For a critique of the O.L.R.C. plan, see Linden, "Faulty No-Fault: A Critique of the Ontario Law Reform Commission Report on Motor Vehicle Accident Compensation" (1975), 13 O.H.L.J. 449; *Cf.* Hasson, "Blood Feuds, Writs and Rifles—A Reply to Professor Linden" (1976), 14 O.H.L.J. 445; Dunlop, "No-Fault Automobile Insurance and the Negligence Action: An Expensive Anomaly" (1975), 13 O.H.L.J. 439.

6. In the Province of Quebec, a "pure" no-fault scheme has been in effect since Mar. 1, 1978. Pursuant to the *Report of the Committee of Inquiry on Automobile Insurance* (Gauvin Committee) (1974), the Parti Quebecois government created a new agency, called Régie del'Assurance Automobile du Québec, to supply compensation to all Quebec victims of auto accidents regardless of fault.

The right to sue in tort was completely abolished. In its place, a compensation system was enacted which pays all reasonable expenses incurred by those injured in car accidents including $1,000 for funeral expenses. In addition, an income replacement indemnity is payable to those victims who are unable to work as a result of an accident. The minimum amount is $80 per week, plus an additional $10 per week for each dependant to a maximum of $120 per week. The maximum indemnity is 90 percent of net income, which is calculated after certain deductions are made from a maximum gross annual salary of $20,000. These payments may be made for up to 5 years and then may continue until retirement with appropriate deductions for other benefits received. No payments are made for the first 7 days.

Death benefits are also payable. The surviving spouse is entitled to 55 percent of the pension the deceased person could have received had he been disabled. Additional percentages are furnished for dependants, up to a maximum of 80 percent. Here too, the minimum pension is $80 to $120 per week, depending on the number of dependants. If there are no dependants, the estate receives $2,000 and if minor children are killed, the parents receive $4,000.

An interesting feature of this plan is the payment of a lump sum indemnity up to a maximum of $20,000 if a victim sustains injury, disfigurement, dismemberment or loss of enjoyment of life.

As for appeal rights, there is a right of reconsideration by the Régie. Following that, a dissatisfied claimant may appeal to the Commission des Affaires Sociales.

Compensation funds are also established for accidents involving hit-and-run drivers, certain accidents off the highway and for unsatisfied judgments up to a maximum of $50,000.

Quebec citizens are covered by the plan if they are involved in accidents while outside their home province. Non-residents of Quebec are covered for collisions that occur in Quebec but benefits are provided to them only to the extent that they are not responsible for the accident. The decision of the Régie about the percentage of responsibility may be contested in the courts. See *What Non-Residents Should Know About Quebec Auto Insurance* (1979).

The fund is financed from contributions from automobile owners, automobile drivers, interest earned from the investment of accumulated funds and a portion of the taxes collected under the Fuel Tax Act.

See Quebec Government, *General Guide to Quebec Auto Insurance* (1979), Projet de loi No 67, Dec. 22/77.

7. If we had a universal health care plan and a generous guaranteed annual income scheme, would there be any need for a no-fault scheme for auto accident victims?

BLUM AND KALVEN, PUBLIC LAW PERSPECTIVES ON A PRIVATE LAW PROBLEM – AUTO COMPENSATION PLANS

(1965), printed in (1964), U. of Chi. L. Rev

A second major alternative for meeting the costs of additional coverage under a compensation plan is to posit an arrangement under which the potential victims insure themselves against injury regardless of third party fault. In theory damages could be measured as at common law; but to avoid any distractions which may come from being so unrealistic, we will assume that damages are to be fixed by schedule. By carrying such insurance, the victims create a fund which would be available to cover their losses. This arrangement would achieve the objective of shifting the loss off the immediate victim. All victims would be covered under it and they would shift their losses to the insurance fund.

It will be readily perceived that there are at least three lines of objection to this scheme. The first becomes evident when we translate it back into common law liability for auto accidents and substitution of a plan of compulsory accident insurance for victims. The objection then goes to the old point that no one should be compelled to pay premiums to insure against losses caused by the fault of another. While we find this to be a congenial argument against the arrangement offered, it need not detain us because the other objections are much more powerful. A second line of objection derives from the traditional presumption against sumptuary legislation. Everyone is already at liberty to spend his resources for auto accident insurance, but it is difficult to see why the state should intervene and compel him to do so. Although we would not reject out of hand all sumptuary legislation, we do urge that there is some merit in calling a spade a spade. It is at this place that an infrequently noticed detail of the Columbia plan becomes striking. The draftsmen explicitly considered and rejected the desirability of having their proposed compensation fund cover injuries in single car accidents. Since there was agreement that a driver should always be covered if he crashed into another car, it seemed odd not to protect him where he crashed into a tree. The draftsmen nevertheless decided that inclusion of the single car accident would change the basic rationale of the plan and would raise serious constitutional doubts about it. They recognized that such an extention of plan would in effect call for compelling each operator of an auto to insure himself against damages in an accident in which no other auto operator was involved. The heart of the matter was that it seemed anomalous to prevent a person from driving unless he insured himself against damages he might sustain from smashing into a tree. We call attention to the puzzle whether the single car accident should be covered by a plan because it highlights the awkwardness of creating a compensation fund that forces victims to insure themselves.

A third line of objection to our first party insurance model is the least theoretical and most decisive. It has often been observed that proponents of plans usually rely on financing a compensation fund through use of liability insurance, and there has been a call to be more imaginative about the use of insurance.

However, it is not habit alone which keeps the plans tied to liability insurance. The main (if not only) alternative to liability insurance is accident insurance, and difficulty in using it is very basic: There is no practical way of enforcing a system of compulsory auto accident insurance. Everyone in the society is a potential auto accident victim and therefore the usual arrangement of making insurance a license prerequisite is not available. Moreover, even if some way could be found to solve the enforcement problem, the administrative costs of selling insurance to the entire population would be prohibitive. It would be uneconomic in the extreme to single out accidents from so narrow a source and require that that risk alone be covered by a separate insurance policy for each person or family unit.

These practical difficulties suggest that if compulsory accident insurance is thought desirable, a mechanism akin to taxation might be utilized to collect the premiums. We thus come to the major alternative of social insurance.

3. Social Insurance: Government Schemes Treating All Accident Victims Alike

ATIYAH, ACCIDENTS, COMPENSATION AND THE LAW
(2nd ed., 1975)

It is difficult to resist the conclusion that the right path for reform is to abolish the tort system so far as personal injuries and disabilities are concerned, and to use the money at present being poured into the tort system to improve the social security benefits, and the social services generally. . . .

A reasonable working plan would be to bring diseases and natural disabilities and non-industrial accidents under the industrial injuries system. . . .

It may very well be that this could be done without another penny being levied from the taxpayer or the premium payer because if all the tort compensation money (including the vast sums swallowed up in administering the tort system) were levied in the form of a new social security contribution, the proceeds might be sufficient for the purpose. In addition the criminal injuries compensation system could be merged into the industrial injury system.

The cost of a scheme along these lines would of course have to be worked out with great care, but it is desirable to emphasize that if proposals for reform start with the social security system, and not with the tort system, the cost of the changes need impose no extra charge on the public if it is felt that the proportion of national income devoted to these welfare purposes is adequate at present. Most people who have examined the failings of the tort system as a method of compensating for personal injuries have proposed various ways in which tort compensation could be extended (for example by an expansion of 'strict' liability) but as the small proportion of accident victims who today receive tort compensation has come to be more recognized, the enormous cost of expanding tort liability coverage has become intimidating. Clearly, this is to start at the wrong end. The right place to start is with the social security system if only because this extends to the whole population, while tort law only compensates a small proportion of victims of accidents and only a negligible number of victims of disease. The lawyer's traditional attitude which thinks of the courts as the 'ordinary' or 'regular' courts dealing with the 'ordinary' law, while social security is somehow a 'special' or 'extraordinary' system of laws and tribunals, must be revised to bring it into line with the facts. Since the great majority of victims of accident and disease have to do without tort compensation at present, it is clear that even to abolish tort liability altogether and put nothing else in its place, would only be to inflict on some the hardships which at present most have to endure. For example, to abolish tort liability for industrial accidents would not affect the great majority of industrial accident victims who at present make do, and have to make do, with industrial injury and disablement benefits. In one sense, therefore, the entire cost of the tort system is a bonus, an extra sum of money which could be used to supplement the social security system in whatever ways are felt to be necessary. Since the most striking weakness of the social security system is its failure to cope adequately with the long-term disabled (other than the industrially disabled) this is the point at which more money is clearly and urgently needed. As we have already indicated, this money could be derived, without additional cost to the public from the insurance premiums at present devoted to meeting tort liability for road and industrial accidents. Even if this money is inadequate to cover the cost of expanding the industrial injuries system to all people disabled by injury or sickness, a start could be made in this direction. Although a radical equalization of benefits would clearly be justifiable in principle a more practical course might be a gradual increase in the extent and value of the non-industrial injury benefits and a gradual introduction of disability benefits for non-industrial disability.

. . .

Of course, any scheme along these lines would leave quite inadequately compensated the really high income earners who, if they receive tort compensation at all, now receive compensation in full, at least in theory. But we have already given reasons for suggesting that this is one of the unsatisfactory aspects of the tort system. If society provides compensation up to a reasonable earnings-related maximum (tax free) it is surely doing all that can be asked of it; although it might be better still to eliminate the tax concession, and raise the benefits still further with the amount thus saved. If people want additional protection above these levels this should be a matter for private insurance though it is to be hoped that insurance companies might come forward more readily with proposals for such insurance. This does not mean that the earnings-related principle should not be extended; on the contrary, it clearly does need extending both in amount and in the length of time for which such benefits are payable. What above all else cries out for reform is the unfairness produced by the lack of integration of the various compensation systems. For example, the element of double compensation would be an extraordinary waste of money however comprehensive the compensation systems were, but it is surely indefensible to compensate some people twice over *for the same loss or disability,* while refusing any compensation to others. How for example can we justify paying compensation *twice* to a man who loses an eye in an industrial accident merely for the disability itself, while we refuse any compensation for the disability itself to a man who is totally blinded by disease? How can we justify giving tax free social security benefits to people who continue to receive full wages while they are off sick, when the level of long-term sickness benefits is still so low?

Then there is the difficulty of justifying payments made under one system but refused by another. How can we justify giving damages for lost support to a young childless widow, for example, when the social security system refuses any assistance at all to a childless widow under forty, unless she is an industrial widow, or unless, indeed she is quite destitute or incapable of work. Surely society must decide whether it thinks a widow is entitled to support irrespective of her capacity for work, and regulate its compensation systems accordingly.

And finally there is the difficulty—which we have already discussed at length —of justifying the different treatment accorded by the law at present to the victims of disease, and the victims of accidents, and among the latter class as between the victims of fault caused and non-fault caused accidents. Gone is the time when a new system for road accidents or for any other special category of unfortunates can be justified. The selection of the victims of crime for special treatment only a few years ago was a hopeless anachronism, creating yet more anomalies and inconsistencies. There are already far too many special cases. What is surely needed is a single comprehensive system based on the existing social security system, but with benefits as adequate as society can afford.

NOTES

1. Professor Atiyah's book contains a brilliant critique of tort law as well as a thorough analysis of all the various non-tort sources of compensation in England. It is worthy of serious study by anyone interested in this field. See Linden, Book Review (1971), 49 Can. Bar Rev. 146. See also Elliott and Street, *Road Accidents* (1968).

2. One paradoxical feature of Professor Atiyah's book is that, although he is willing to abolish tort suits in personal injury cases, he recoils from doing so in property damage cases because "it is possible that people would find this inequitable in certain circumstances". Do you think it is more "inequitable" to abolish the property damage suit or the personal injury claim?

3. A similar reform plan has been advocated by Professor Ison for years, see *The Forensic Lottery* (1967); Ison, "Contemporary Developments and Reform in Personal Injury Compensation" in Law Society of Upper Canada Special Lectures, *New Developments in the Law of Torts* (1973), p. 521; Ison, "Human Disability and Personal Income" in Klar (ed.), *Studies in Canadian Tort Law* (1977); Ison, "The Politics of Law Reform in Personal Injury Compensation" (1977), 27 U. of T.L.J. 385.

KALVEN, A SCHEMA OF ALTERNATIVES TO THE PRESENT AUTO ACCIDENT TORT SYSTEM

(1968), 1 Conn. L. Rev. 33

For all of us who are moved by welfare concerns when we look at the victims of auto accidents, the social insurance alternative has some attractive advantages. It gives a coherent group of beneficiaries defined not by the accident of being hit by an automobile, but by the fact that they suffered a misfortune. It does recognize a commonality in misfortune of the man hit by an auto and the man hit by cancer. Again, it provides a rational and coherent way of paying for the insurance fund by charging it broadly to the population as a whole, in effect, as a cost of living. Further, it provides through taxation an unbeatably economical and efficient method of collecting premiums, and, finally — and this is worth noting in view of the complexity of the Keeton-O'Connell proposal — it provides an intelligible issue of policy to put to the public.

There are also, however, as I am sure you anticipate, some impressive disadvantages, at least two of which deserve mention. First, we are eliminating an important source of private power in the society and concentrating great additional power in the state itself. And this is not a change to be made lightly. Second, there is the point that Professor Calabresi has urged recently, a point borrowed from the economist. If you take the cost of auto accidents and put them under a social security scheme, you externalize these costs, that is you free the accident-causing activity from any concern with the cost of that activity; you remove all economic discipline from the field of accidents or, to put this in Professor Calabresi's idiom, you eliminate the possibilities of general deterrence.

FRANKLIN, REPLACING THE NEGLIGENCE LOTTERY: COMPENSATION AND SELECTIVE REIMBURSEMENT

(1967), 53 Va. L. Rev. 774

SUMMARY OF PROPOSAL FOR SOCIAL INSURANCE WITH SELECTIVE REIMBURSEMENT

The victim's exclusive legal remedy is to come from a government operated fund. The fund will compensate for all medical expenses. It will also pay eighty-five percent of lost income up to a maximum of 125 dollars per week. There is a deductible in all cases and the possibility of a further reduction to as little as seventy-five percent if a court determines that the victim's injury was caused by his "serious misconduct". There are no awards for pain and suffering. All persons may take out first party insurance against any loss not covered by the fund, although no insurance of any type is compulsory.

The fund is to be created from a general tax base plus a sum collected from private motorists, representing a percentage of the fund's anticipated (or actual) payouts due to private motoring accidents. Separate administrative measures not related to the fund are to be developed to make careless motorists and traffic law violators pay higher fees. The fund is entitled to reimbursement against individual enterprises without regard to fault for all payouts resulting from harms caused in part by business activities. There is no other reimbursement. ...

In brief, I see several gains from the proposed plan. The focus would be on treatment of all victims in terms of economic loss. Reparation is achieved quickly and does not depend on fault or the actor's solvency. Such compensation and deterrence would be separated, substandard conduct could be punished without reference to the welfare of victims.

The plan, with its flexible reparation levels, would permit awards high enough to be meaningful while avoiding moral hazards and trivial cases. Where it would be efficient and avoid lottery problems, selective reimbursement is used to foster self-imposed deterrence. Some enterprises that are now strictly liable for common-law damages would pay less under the plan; others would be reimbursing more frequently than they are now held liable but in smaller amounts. In private activities, administrative measures replace reimbursement. Motorists' group fund assessment and individual penalties for substandard conduct would be handled much as licenses and fines are now handled.

Faster medical treatment would reduce permanent disabilities and lessen the drain on our productive capacity. The personal injury bar would become smaller but today's broad need for attorneys would make reallocation relatively easy. The burden on the judiciary would be greatly reduced. Finally, the insurance industry would no longer operate in the motor vehicle area in which they now claim large losses. Instead, they would continue to write enterprise reimbursement liability insurance and could develop new policies to supplement the fund's first party protections. The need for compulsory insurance would disappear.

The foregoing proposal is in no way a final or fully elaborated plan. Virtually every figure mentioned is a rough estimate that must await research and be judged within the current political temper of a particular jurisdiction. I do, however, contend that enough has been said to show that a broad social insurance plan combined with selective reimbursement can best serve the several goals of accident law.

NOTES

1. Why does Franklin suggest a reduction in recovery where the claimant is guilty of "serious misconduct"?

2. Does this plan deal adequately with "market or general deterrence"?

3. The only jurisdiction to date that has adopted a social insurance solution to the problem of automobile accident compensation is New Zealand. Pursuant to the Report of a Royal Commission set up to study the problem entitled, *Compensation for Personal Injury in New Zealand* (1967), the government, in 1972, enacted legislation (New Zealand Accident Compensation Act), to do much of what was proposed beginning on April 1, 1974. Although it did not go "all the way", it nearly did. Compensation for both economic and some non-economic losses resulting from personal injury accidents is provided to two groups of people.

Under the first scheme, the Earner's Scheme, persons who have been ordinarily resident in New Zealand for at least 12 months, and who are self-employed or who are employees, are eligible for continuous coverage whereby they are insured in respect of personal injury by accident 24 hours a day. A person who is not eligible for continuous cover may still be covered for accidents arising out of and in the course of his employment. Although non-earners are not yet covered by this scheme, the government has announced that it is planning to do so soon. The second scheme, the Motor Vehicle Accident Scheme, provides coverage for all those suffering personal injury in motor vehicle accidents. The right to sue in tort is abolished for the people covered by the new plan, but it remains available for those who are not so protected. Income losses are compensated at a rate of 80 percent of the amount of the lost earning capacity. The earnings of a person who is partially incapacitated on a temporary basis are deducted from his regular earnings and he receives 80 percent of the difference. In the case of permanent incapacity, periodic payments of 80 percent of his permanent loss of earning capacity are made. If the condition of the individual deteriorates his benefits may be increased. They cannot, however, be decreased if his condition subsequently improves. There is a one-week waiting period before any benefits become payable but if the injury occurs during employment, the employer must pay the employee his wages for one full week. In the case of motor vehicle injuries, potential earning capacity may be compensated if the individual is under 21 or can prove that he was training for a career or profession. Medical and rehabilitation expenses are fully payable under the plan to the extent that they are not already covered by the state plan.

Death benefits to a widow or widower who was totally dependent on the deceased amount to a lump sum payment of $1,000, plus one-half of the earnings-related compensation that the deceased would have received had he survived and suffered total loss of earning capacity. Totally dependent minor children receive lump sum payments of $500 per child to a maximum of $1,500, plus 1/16 of the amount which the deceased would have been entitled to. If the dependency is partial, lesser amounts are paid. The total amount payable must not be more than the amount the deceased would have received if he had survived. Dependent widows and widowers who remarry become ineligible for periodic payments but receive a lump sum benefit equal to two years of the earnings-related payments which they would otherwise have received.

One of the striking features of the New Zealand scheme is that, although the tort claim is gone, general damages may be recovered under the scheme to a limited degree. In addition to the earnings-related periodic payments, a lump sum of up to $5,000 (N.Z.) is payable to persons suffering permanent loss or impairment of any bodily function in accordance with a schedule. In addition, further lump sum compensation for non-economic loss may be awarded, subject to a maximum of $7,500 (N.Z.), at the discretion of the Commission for loss "of amenities or capacity for enjoying life, including loss from disfigurement" and for "pain and mental suffering, including nervous shock and neurosis". The loss must be of sufficient nature, duration and intensity to justify payment.

The plan is administered by the Accident Compensation Commission which receives its policy guidelines from the Minister of Labour. Three Commissioners are appointed with three-year terms. Private insurance companies and other organizations act as agents of the A.C.C. for the purpose of receiving and dealing with claims. Assessments as to the degree of incapacity, appeals and other such matters are dealt with by the A.C.C.

4. For detailed descriptions of this plan see Palmer, "Compensation for Personal Injury: A Requiem for the Common Law in New Zealand" (1973), 21 Am. J. Comp. L. 1; Palmer, "Abolishing the Personal Injury Tort System: the New Zealand Experience" (1971), 9 Alta L. Rev. 169; Szakatz, "Community Responsibility for Accidental Injuries: The New Zealand Accident Compensation Act" (1973), 8 U.B.C.L. Rev. 1; Harris, "Accident Compensation in New Zealand: A Comprehensive Insurance System" (1974), 37 Mod. L. Rev. 361; Palmer, "Accident Compensation in New Zealand: The First Two Years" (1977), 25 Am. J. Comp. L. 1; Franklin, "Personal Injury Accidents in New Zealand and the United States: Some Striking Similarities" (1975), 27 Stan. L. Rev. 653.

5. An Australian Royal Commission has issued a report entitled *Compensation and Rehabilitation in Australia* (1974), which urges a complete social insurance solution to the problem of accidents and illness. It is proposed that the tort action be abolished. In its place a scheme will be established to compensate, without regard to fault, all economic losses resulting from physical and mental incapacities, whether caused by sudden injury, medical misadventure, congenital defect and eventually, sickness. Minor injuries, short-term illnesses and non-work-related diseases such as heart conditions and cancer, however, would be excluded from the plan. The five guiding principles of community responsibility, comprehensive entitlement, complete rehabilitation, real compensation and administrative efficiency underlie the proposal.

The economic losses covered would include lost income, rehabilitation services, travelling allowances, prosthetic devices and other similar expenses. For lost income the insured receives weekly benefits equal to a percentage of his taxable weekly earnings to a maximum of $500 per week. The benefits are then taxed as income. Notional weekly earnings of $50 per week are attributed to non-earners or persons earning less than that sum. An assessment may be made, where necessary, for lost potential earnings. Health benefits are to be provided through the existing medical care scheme and a new plan to be set up in conjunction with the scheme.

A person who is totally incapacitated on either a temporary or a permanent basis receives 85 percent of his lost income for the duration of the incapacity. Permanent partial disabilities are compensated according to the seriousness of the disability by calculating a percentage of the amount that would be available to the individual if he was totally disabled. Such a calculation is made by using the median method through which a notional and average figure of earnings is substituted for the individual's actual earnings, so that the income base is raised for lower earners. The degree of impairment is determined by a medical assessor using a guide issued under the plan. Impairments of less than 10 percent are not compensated. No general damages would be paid, except where significant cosmetic impairment is suffered, a lump sum of up to $10,000 is payable.

In the case of a temporary partial incapacity which forces an individual to take a lower paying job for a period of time, a convalescent allowance is payable which increases the wages received to the amount normally received as weekly earnings. Such compensation is limited to a maximum amount of 50 percent of the individual's normal average earnings and is payable for no more than 26 weeks.

In the case of injury, there is a seven-day waiting period before compensation begins. The waiting period in the case of sickness is 21 days (with some exceptions). Payments are periodic and may be adjusted for inflation according to changes in the Consumer Price Index. There is discretion to commute the benefits to a lump sum if this appears to be in the best interests of the individual.

Widows may only receive full death benefits on the death of their husbands if they are continuing to maintain the family home for dependent children, caring for aged or infirm relatives, or over the age of 55 when widowed or unable to engage in suitable gainful work because of general background or length of marriage. A widow who is entitled under the plan receives a lump sum of $1,000 plus periodic payments equal to 60 percent of the amount her husband would have received had he been totally incapacitated. For the purposes of this calculation the minimum earnings of the deceased are set at $100 per week. If the widow remarries she receives a lump sum equal to one year's benefits. A widow who does not qualify under the plan for full benefits receives $1,000 plus 60 percent of her husband's total incapacity benefits for 12 months or until she remarries, whichever is the earlier.

Children of a deceased are presumed to be dependent until they stop attending school on a full-time basis or until they reach 20 years of age, whichever occurs earlier. Fifteen percent of the amount which the deceased parent would have received for total incapacity is payable on the child's behalf. Death benefits are not subject to a waiting period. Funeral benefits may be paid at the discretion of the administrators.

With certain specified exceptions, compensation under the plan is limited to those between the ages of 18 and 65. Australians who are abroad are fully covered for a 12-month period. Visitors to Australia who are employed in the country are fully covered. Non-employed visitors are fully covered for injury but must purchase sickness coverage. Victims of criminal violence, volunteers engaged in rescue work and persons injured through recreational activity are included under the plan, as are persons injured or killed through suicide or deliberate self-injury. There is, however, no coverage available for persons injured while engaged in murder, piracy, hijacking or the wilful infliction of grievous bodily harm.

It is proposed that the plan be administered through a social welfare policy group which is part of a department of government responsible to a senior Minister. Such a department is to coordinate the whole area of social welfare planning, programmes and policies. Compensation and money benefits will be provided through a central benefits and compensation department and medical and vocational rehabilitation will be administered through a division of this department. In addition it is proposed that a National Safety Office be established to coordinate safety programmes.

Implementation of this scheme has been halted since the election of a different national government in Australia which apparently does not wish to proceed with such a programme in the current economic and political climate.

6. The search for a better method of auto accident compensation is worldwide. See U.S. Dept. of Transportation, *Comparative Studies in Automobile Accident Compensation* (1970); Tunc, *Traffic Accident Compensation: Law and Proposals* (1971); Tunc, "Traffic Accident Compensation in France: The Present Law and a Controversial Proposal" (1966), 79 Harv. L. Rev. 1409; Harris, "The Law of Torts and the Welfare State", [1963] N.Z.L.J. 171; Yadin, "Outline of an Automobile Compensation Plan for Israel" (1964), 13 Am. J. Comp. L. 286; Suzman, "Motor Vehicle Accidents: Proposal for a System of Collective Responsibility Irrespective of Fault" (1955), 72 S. Afr. L.J. 374; Hellner, "Tort Liability and Insurance" (1962), 6 Scand. Stud. in Law 129; Kretzmer, "No-fault Comes to Israel" (1976), 11 Israel L. Rev. 288.

7. A major study of the entire social insurance and tort systems has been advocated in this country. If such a commission were set up, what would you suggest as solutions to the many issues raised here? Should tort liability be eliminated completely or partially? Should strict liability replace fault liability?

8. In the United Kingdom, an injured workman has the choice of claiming workers compensation benefits on a no-fault, but limited, basis or of suing in tort for common law damages. Many opt for the latter course. Should the tort remedy be available as an *alternative* to injury victims? Should it be permitted

to survive as an *additional* remedy over and above no-fault or social welfare payments?

9. Should general damages be permitted? Should payments be periodic or in lump sums? Should there be a maximum amount of tort damages? Should there be a minimum amount of loss suffered before a tort action is permitted? Should there be a schedule of benefits for each type of injury? How should collateral source benefits be handled?

10. Should the jury decide the cases, a judge alone, or a board, or an arbitrator? Should the government run the scheme, should private insurers do it or should there be a mixture of public and private administration?

11. Does tort law serve any social purpose in the 1980's? Should it be preserved for any type of situation? If so, which? Read Chapter 1 again. If tort law is retained, should it be codified? See Gibson, *Righting Wrongs* (1975).

CHAPTER 16

DEFAMATION

Tort law protects one's interest in preserving his good reputation. The law of defamation permits actions for libel and slander against those who seek to damage the reputation of another. It is a complicated area, full of confusion and even absurdity. Part of this stems from the convoluted history of the action, but some of it also flows from the real difficulties involved in balancing the interest in free speech, which we all cherish, with the interest in a good name, which we also all prize.

The material that follows seeks to introduce some of the main issues in the field, but it is by no means complete. Each jurisdiction has its own unique legislative provisions and its own distinct procedural requirements. There is literally an avalanche of cases, all of which cannot be included in a work such as this.

A. WHAT IS DEFAMATORY?

MURPHY v. LA MARSH et al.

British Columbia Court of Appeal.
[1971] 2 W.W.R. 196; affg (1970), 73 W.W.R. 114

Wilson C.J.S.C. [at trial] : The plaintiff Murphy was formerly employed as a radio newsman in the press gallery at Ottawa reporting for his radio station the doings of Parliament and the Government of Canada and general political news, including the public and private actions of politicians who were in the public eye.

The defendant Julia (more usually called Judy) LaMarsh is the author of, and the defendant McClelland and Stewart Limited is the publisher of, a book of political reminiscences called *Memoirs of a Bird in a Gilded Cage,* first published in 1968.

The first edition of this book, 10,000 copies, contained statements about the plaintiff which he says are defamatory and upon which this lawsuit is based. It is necessary to cite the impugned passage. . . .

> "A brash young radio reporter, named Ed Murphy (heartily detested by most of the Press Gallery and the members), had somehow learned that Maurice Lamontagne (then Secretary of State, and a long-time friend and adviser of the Prime Minister) had purchased furniture but had not paid for it. . . ."

In subsequent editions (25,000 copies) the words "heartily detested by most of the Press Gallery and the members" were deleted and they are also omitted from a paperback edition of which 50,000 copies are being circulated by another publisher.

The passage just cited ("heartily detested by most of the Press Gallery and the members") is alleged to be libellous. The plaintiff also claims that the latter part of the extract cited [omitted here] considered in its context, imputes to the plaintiff a disreputable action, the hounding of Mr. Lamontagne out of office, and is therefore libellous.

Miss LaMarsh was Member of Parliament for Niagara Falls from 1960 to 1968 and was, from 1963 to 1968, a Minister in a Government headed by Mr. Lester Pearson as Prime Minister and consisting of members of the Liberal political party.

Miss LaMarsh's memoirs were, her publisher tells me, expected to be a lively and colourful account of her political career. A good deal of the book fits readily into that definition and if Mr. Murphy's head is left bloody it is not the only one.

The first question is whether or not it is libel to say of a man in Mr. Murphy's occupation that he was "heartily detested" by most of his colleagues and by most Members of Parliament.

Plaintiff's counsel has not argued that the word "brash" is defamatory. I have given some thought to this conception—that the word "brash" is the governing word in the sentence and that the words "heartily detested by most of the Press Gallery and the members" are only inserted to reflect the reaction of those persons to Mr. Murphy's brashness. I have come to the conclusion that this interpretation of what Miss LaMarsh has said will not stand analysis—the statement, in parenthesis, that Mr. Murphy was heartily detested is an independent clause, emphasized by the parenthesis, and not clearly related to the quality of brashness. I do not say that brashness cannot arouse detestation. "Brash", in Canada bears, I think, more the American meaning stated in *Webster's Dictionary,* 1966 of "bumptious", "tactless", "loudly assertive", rather than the English meaning given in the *Oxford Dictionary* of "bold", "rash" or "impudent". But I do not think Miss LaMarsh has asserted that Mr. Murphy is detested because of his brashness; I think she has merely said he is detested by majorities of two groups of people.

These are the people best placed to know and value him, his associates in the press gallery and the Members of Parliament with whom he must associate and about whom he writes.

Ordinarily a libel is more specific than the one alleged here. A shameful action is attributed to a man (he stole my purse), a shameful character (he is dishonest), a shameful course of action (he lives on the avails of prostitution), a shameful condition (he has the pox). Such words are considered defamatory because they tend to bring the man named, according to the classic definition, into hatred, contempt or ridicule. The more modern definition, given by Lord Atkin, in *Sim* v. *Stretch* 52 TLR 669, 80 Sol J 703, [1936] 2 All ER 1237, at 1240, is words tending "to lower the plaintiff in the estimation of right-thinking members of society generally." Perhaps "words likely to cause a man to be detested" might also, although not an all-inclusive definition, fit into the class of defamatory words.

The difference between this and other cases I have read or tried is that no shameful action or characteristic or condition is directly attributed to Mr. Murphy. It is only said of him that he is heartily detested. A fairly careful search of authority has revealed to me no case in which the libel alleged has been couched in such terms—an allegation of bad repute without some direct supporting charge of wrongdoing or bad character.

It is obvious that any decision as to whether or not such words as were used here are libellous must be approached with care. Under proper circumstances I think it must generally be open to writers to express of certain persons opinions as to their popularity or unpopularity, perhaps to say they are by some classes of people liked or disliked. The words used, the circumstances, the person who comments, the person upon whom the comment is made, must all be considered. It may be permissible, for instance, in certain circumstances, to say of a politician that he is losing his popularity, even though such words will certainly not help him in his career and may well hurt him.

The first thing to consider is the nature of the operative word "detested" and this was much discussed at the trial. The *Oxford Dictionary* gives to the word "detests" the meanings "hate", "abominate", "abhor", "dislike intensely". *Webster's Dictionary,* I think, is more up to date in its definitions when it says, "Detest indicates very strong aversion but may lack the actively hostile male-violence associated with hate."

I would say, for instance, that Hamlet hated, or thought he ought to hate Claudius, the murderer of his father and the defiler, as Hamlet thought, of his mother but that he detested Polonius as a sycophant and a tedious moralizing bore ("These tedious old fools": Act II scene 2).

But "detest" remains a strong word. While it may express the feeling one has toward a boor, a bore or a braggart, it may also express the feeling one has toward an unscrupulous reporter, a reporter whose actions have displayed bad character. I do not think that the reasoning in *Capital & Counties Bank* v. *Henty* (1882) 7 App Cas 741, 52 LJQB 232, applies here. The words used are not, as in that case, capable of a harmless meaning and alternatively and rather vaguely of a bad meaning, so that the harmless meaning should be preferred. They are disparaging in any sense, more disparaging in one sense than the other and it seems to me that in those circumstances, where it is clear that right-thinking persons can and probably will properly interpret them as defamatory, there must be liability. The tendency to defame is there.

No wrong or evil is directly attributed to Mr. Murphy but it is said of him that most men who have most to do with him in his occupation heartily detest him. I have no doubt that the ordinary reader, who is not perhaps inclined to such an analysis of words as I have here attempted would, after reading this, think "There must be something wrong or bad about this man Murphy to make these people detest him." Since I think this is the test to be applied, I think the words are defamatory. The effect is the same as would have resulted if it had been said, "He bears a bad reputation among his associates."

The witnesses Charles Lynch and John Webster, speaking as reporters, think otherwise. I am basing my opinion on my conception of what the legendary "right-thinking man" would take the words to mean and I would not want to exclude either witness from that class. I have no reason to doubt the honesty or the correctness of their evidence as reflecting their own opinions. But I must remember that neither Mr. Lynch nor Mr. Webster is an ordinary everyday reader of books attaching to the words in question their conventional effect. Mr. Lynch says that he would, as an employer of newsmen, be interested in a man described as heartily detested by most of the press gallery (which he calls a competitive jungle) and the House, because detestation is a price, a mark of success in press gallery writing, and political approval a warning of failure. Mr. Webster says that to be disliked by a politician may be a badge of honour to a reporter. This evidence has a considerable bearing on the question of damages, which I shall come to later. But the esoteric meaning attached by these initiates to the effect of detestation is not one that would spring to the mind of the ordinary citizen who reads the book, and it is from that level that I must form my opinion. . . .

I should deal with one case relied on by the defendant. *Robinson* v. *Jermyn* (1814) 1 Price 11, 145 ER 1314. The defendants were proprietors of or subscribers to a room called "the Cassino" which they frequented, presumably for social purposes. They posted a regulation of the Cassino reading thus, "The Rev. John Robinson, and Mr. James Robinson, inhabitants of this town, not being persons that the proprietors and annual subscribers think it proper to associate with, are excluded this room." They were sued by the Rev. Robinson for libel. Thomson, C.B. said at p. 16:

> "The demurrer to these pleas involves the material question, whether the publication of the words laid in the declaration are properly the subject matter of an action, and whether, under the circumstances, they amount to a libel. The words are, 'The Rev. John Robinson and Mr. James Robinson, not being persons that the proprietors or annual subscribers think it proper to associate with, are excluded this room.' It seems to me to be a material allegation in this declaration that the plaintiff was officiating minister, but there is certainly nothing affecting him in his clerical character in these words. It then goes on to state, that the words were published in one of the written regulations of the room. Now the principal ground on which this action can be supported is, that it does in substance contain an averment, that these plaintiffs were not fit for common association—that they were not proper persons for general society; and nothing will help this declaration, unless it can be collected from it, that such an insinuation was the object of the words. Now it does not seem to me, that such an imputation can be inferred. It seems merely that these defendants did not think that the plaintiffs were proper persons to be associated with by them; but that may proceed from other causes than such as must appear on the face of the declaration, to have been insinuated, to constitute a libel. There might be reasons assigned not at all affecting the moral character of the plaintiffs; for the defendants may not have thought them agreeable or sociable. They may have considered them troublesome and officious; or, for some other such reasons, improper for their society."

I think this case is clearly distinguishable. The defendants were, in the first place, stating their own opinion, not purporting to report that of other persons. The words were not defamatory. They merely indicated a disinclination by the subscribers to associate with certain persons. It is true that here, as there, the opinion in question was that of a certain body of people, not of society generally. But it seems to me that the mild assertion by persons directly interested of a disinclination to associate with certain other persons is a far cry from a bold statement that a man is heartily detested by most of his associates. If, in this case, Miss LaMarsh had expressed her own detestation of the plaintiff I would have though little of it but it is a different matter when she attributes, without foundation, detestation of Mr. Murphy to his associates.

The defence does not plead that the words written are true but does plead that they are fair comment, that they merely state an opinion.

One may properly ask "fair comment on what?". The comment is not an opinion on the quality of his reporting, in the nature of fair literary criticism, it is a bald statement, irrelevant to the subject under consideration. It adds nothing to Miss LaMarsh's argument. It is a gratuitous, defamatory observation delivered publicly and serving no purpose in the context which contains it.

I do not assert that a statement as to the popularity or unpopularity of an individual, as to whether he is liked or disliked, may not in certain circumstances be a statement of opinion. But where an allegation is made that a man is heartily detested by the majorities of two bodies, I think one has a statement of fact rather than opinion. I do not see how the statement can be classed as comment fair or unfair because comment must, according to the authorities, be based on a substratum of fact, and no facts are given here to justify the comment. Such evidence as I have heard negatives the idea that Murphy was detested as alleged and indicates that Miss LaMarsh made no inquiries to ascertain whether or not he was detested in the gallery and the House.

There was no express malice in what Miss LaMarsh wrote. The real object of the whole passage was not to defame Mr. Murphy but generously to defend Mr.

Lamontagne and Mr. Tremblay, her former associates. I accept her statement that she scarcely knew Murphy and that her mention of him was casual. It was also careless because she made no inquiries to establish the truth of her statement.

I find the innuendo that Murphy hounded Mr. Lamontagne out of public life unfounded. In so far as Miss LaMarsh may be said to have accused any one person of hounding Mr. Lamontagne out of public life her accusation is, I think, directed at a much more eminent figure.

I now come to consider damages. To what extent has Mr. Murphy suffered as a result of the defamation?

On the surface he appears to have prospered. He is a featured performer on what is known as a "hot line" or open-line radio programme. He sits in a studio before a microphone surrounded by telephones. He introduces subjects for discussion—some of his listeners telephone him and discuss the subjects, agreeing or disagreeing with Mr. Murphy's views. Or a listener may, by telephone, raise a subject upon which Mr. Murphy, and other listeners, may express views. I am assured by Mr. Webster, an acknowledged expert, that controversy is an important and desirable element in these discussions.

I have wondered a little about Mr. Murphy's conduct since bringing this action. One would think that a man who felt he had been libelled would desire to restrict the circulation of that fact and avoid drawing attention to it. But Mr. Murphy told, as he says, the news media that he had commenced an action and that Miss LaMarsh was to be served with the writ on the day she was served. As a result reporters and photographers were present, Mr. Murphy himself was present, at the Georgia Hotel when the writ was served on Miss LaMarsh and headlines and photographs of the service of the writ on Miss LaMarsh consequently appeared on the front page of the *Vancouver Province*. This appears to me strange conduct for a man who thought he had been wronged and who might reasonably have considered at that stage the possibility that a retraction might be made and that his suit might be settled without further publicity.

Again, Mr. Murphy's employer during and after the trial, which attracted a great deal of newspaper and radio publicity, published large newspaper advertisements of its radio station with photographs of Mr. Murphy and the assertion "Murphy stirs things up." The statement that the publication of these advertisements contemporaneously with the reports of the trial was entirely accidental is one to be taken with more than a grain of salt. Conceding that Mr. Murphy himself did not publish these advertisements, there is still left an impression that the lawsuit has not been hurtful to Murphy professionally.

Mr. Ross, a highly respected member and former president of the press gallery, said that a statement that a newsman was detested by most of the gallery and members would count against that newsman with him. I believe him, but I must say without, I hope, too much cynicism, that I am inclined also to consider the contrary opinion of Mr. Lynch, who is engaged, *inter alia,* in the business of hiring and firing newsmen. I think that contentiousness is part of the essence of the sort of reporting Mr. Murphy has done and that what harm might be done Mr. Murphy by the libel among professional people of Mr. Ross's way of thinking would be compensated for by the good that might be done him among employers of Mr. Lynch's and Mr. Webster's way of thinking. Furthermore, I doubt that a statement of this kind by a retired politician in a book containing other polemic matter, some of it directed at pressmen (p. 15, drunken newspapermen; p. 19, scruffy newsmen; p. 55, snide editorial; p. 57, a reporter thoroughly disliked; p. 161, reporters awaiting a chance to cloak their reports with parliamentary immunity against libel suits) would be given great weight one way or the other by an experienced employer of reporters.

I revert to the conduct of his present employer as the best guide to damage done to Murphy professionally and state that the employer's advertisement, during the publicity of the trial, of Mr. Murphy as a man who "stirs things up" does not suggest that Mr. Murphy has been injured in his profession.

I have in mind that the objectionable passage was, so soon as the writ was issued, deleted from later editions of the book.

But I have said that Murphy's name has been tarnished in the mind of the ordinary reader, and this by a casual and careless mis-statement. While I think that his actual monetary loss in the conduct of his profession is inconsiderable, I still feel that he is entitled to be compensated for damage done to his name in the minds of ordinary readers and (*vide* Pearson, L.J. in *McCarey* v. *Assoc. Newspapers Ltd.* [No. 2] [1965] 2 QB 86, at 104, [1965] 2 WLR 45, [1964] 3 All ER 947) the injury to his feelings. But I think that the libel is not of a major kind and that the damage is not great because the ordinary reader, unacquainted with Murphy, will probably have forgotten the passage complained of by the time he has turned the next page. I fix his damages at $2,500. Both defendants are liable for their joint tort. Costs will follow the event.

Maclean J.A. in the Court of Appeal (Taggart J.A. concurring):

In my view the learned trial Judge was correct when he held that the words are defamatory and that the effect is the same as would have resulted if it had been said, "He bears a bad reputation among his associates." It must be remembered too that his associates were the members of the Press Gallery, and that the members of the House of Commons were persons with whom Murphy was in daily contact.

In my view any reasonable reader, on reading the words complained of, would conclude that there must be something very wrong with a person when his associates hold him in such poor regard.

The learned trial Judge was correct when he found that the "tendency" to defame was present.

[McFarlane J.A. agreed.]

Appeal dismissed.

[Leave to appeal to the Supreme Court of Canada was refused at [1971] S.C.R. IX.]

NOTES

1. Chief Justice Wilson relied on at least three verbal formulations of the test for defamation. What are they? What do you think of each of them? Which is the broadest and which the narrowest?

2. Two other word formulae were used in *Youssoupoff* v. *Metro-Goldwyn-Mayer Pictures Ltd.* (1934), 50 T.L.R. 581. The defendants produced a film depicting the influence of a person called Rasputin, allegedly a monk, on the Czar and Czarina of Russia that led to the destruction of that country. During the course of the film, Rasputin either raped or seduced a Princess Natasha. The plaintiff, Princess Irina Alexandrova of Russia, sued for libel on the ground that she would be reasonably taken to be the ravaged woman. She succeeded before a jury and the defendant's appeal was dismissed. Scrutton L.J. explained as follows:

"There have been several formulae for describing what is defamation. The learned Judge at the trial uses the stock formula 'calculated to bring into hatred, ridicule, or contempt' and because it has been clearly established some time ago that that is not exhaustive because there may be things which are defamatory which have nothing to do with hatred, ridicule, or contempt, he adds the words 'or causes them to be shunned or avoided'. I, myself, have always preferred the language which Mr. Justice Cave used in *Scott* v. *Sampson*, 8 Q.B.D. 491, a false statement about a man to his discredit. I think that satisfactorily expresses what has to be found. It has long been established that, with one modification, libel or no libel is for the jury and the Court very rarely interferes with a finding by the jury that a particular statement is libel or no libel. The only exception is that it has been established with somewhat unfortunate results that a Judge may say: 'No reasonable jury could possibly think this is a libel, and consequently I will not ask the jury the question whether it is libel or not.' . . .

Fortunately, however, in this case we have not to deal with that exception because it is not suggested that the Judge in this case could have withdrawn the question of this libel from the jury on the point that it was not capable of a defamatory meaning . . . If libel alone is for the jury . . . why is it said that the jury in this case have come to a wrong conclusion? I desire to approach this argument seriously if I can, because I have great difficulty in approaching it seriously . . . This is the argument as I understand it: 'To say of a woman that she is raped does not impute unchastity.' From that we got to this, which was solemnly put forward, that to say of a woman of good character that she has been ravished by a man of the worst possible character is not defamatory. That argument was solemnly presented to the jury, and I only wish the jury could have expressed, and that we could know, what they thought of it, because it seems to me to be one of the most legal arguments that were ever addressed to, I will not say a business body, but a sensible body.

That, really, as I understand it, is the argument upon which is based the contention that no reasonable jury could come to the conclusion that to say of a woman that she had been ravished by a man of very bad character when as a matter of fact she never saw the man at all and was never near him is not defamatory of the woman.

I really have no language to express my opinion of that argument. . . ." What are the two other formulae used here? What do you think of them? What are the respective roles of judge and jury?

3. Lord Justice Slesser, in the *Youssoupoff* v. *M.-G.-M.* case, used another formulation of the test—she has "suffered in social reputation and in the opportunities of receiving respectful consideration from the world". What do you think of this test?

4. Professor Fleming has suggested that defamation "tends to lower a person in the estimation of his fellow men by making them think less of him"—*The Law of Torts* (5th ed., 1977), p. 528. What is your view of this test?

5. Would the result of this case have been different if Miss LaMarsh had written instead: "I detest Ed. Murphy"?

6. What damage was caused by the defamatory statement? Was Murphy's reputation harmed or was it actually enhanced by Miss LaMarsh's reference to him in her book? What do you think of the way the court dealt with the damages here? What about punitive damages?

7. In *Warren* v. *Green* (1958), 25 W.W.R. 563, Mr. Justice Cairns held that calling a doctor a "quack" is defamatory. His Lordship stated:

"There are many instances where words used would not be defamatory, which if used in another setting would be so, such as the using of words which might reflect on a person's ancestry, or other words which might be considered terms of endearment, but it depends on the manner in which these expressions are voiced, and the circumstances under which they are expressed . . . . It is also most important to consider what persons hearing such words would, or might reasonably be expected to, understand from them, apart from a deliberate intention of the utterer."

Is it defamation if a doctor is called a "quack" in jest by another doctor, who is an old friend?

8. Is it defamation to call a lawyer a "shyster"? See *Nolan* v. *Standard Publishing Co.* (1923), 67 Mont. 212, 216 P. 571. What if a fellow lawyer jokingly says to the plaintiff, "You old shyster, you"?

9. Is it defamatory in the presence of a third party to call someone a liar? (See *Penton* v. *Calwell* (1945), 70 C.L.R. 219). What if the mayor of a city publicly charges a lawyer and his developer clients with "deception" and a "breach of faith"? (See *Fraser* v. *Sykes*, [1974] S.C.R. 526). Is a cartoon in a newspaper,

depicting a politician gleefully pulling off the wings from flies with obvious enjoyment, libellous? (See *Vander Zalm* v. *Times Publishers, et al.,* Munroe J., [1979] 2 W.W.R. 673 (B.C.) (revd C.A. Feb. 15, 1980)). Is it libellous to say of someone who permanently left the Soviet Union that he is a "defector" and a "traitor"? (See *Gouzenko* v. *Harris et al.* (1976), 1 C.C.L.T. 37 (Ont.), *per* Goodman J.).

10. The standard of measurement in defamation cases is sometimes said to be the "right-thinking members of society generally". (See Lord Atkin in *Sim* v. *Stretch,* [1936] 2 All E.R. 1237.) This has been somewhat diluted, however, for a person may be defamed in the eyes of citizens who are not "right-thinking" at all. Nowadays, the courts look at what people of "fair average intelligence" would think. (See *Slayter* v. *Daily Telegraph* (1908), 6 C.L.R. 1) or what "ordinary decent folk in the community, taken in general" would feel. (See *Gardiner* v. *Fairfax* (1942), 42 S.R. (N.S.W.) 171). Another standard suggested by Holmes J. and adopted by the *Restatement of Torts, Second* § 559 is this: "If the advertisement obviously would hurt the plaintiff in the estimation of an important and respectable part of the community, liability is not a question of majority vote." (See *Peck* v. *Tribune Co.* (1909), 214 U.S. 185, at p. 190.)

11. In *Grant* v. *Reader's Digest Assoc. Inc.* (1945), 151 F. 2d 733, a statement that the plaintiff, a lawyer, "recently was a legislative representative for the Massachusetts Communist Party", was held capable of a defamatory meaning in that it implied plaintiff was in sympathy with the Party's objects and methods. L. Hand, J., said that a man may value his reputation among those who do not embrace "the prevailing moral standards". Whether "right-thinking" people might shun, despise or condemn a lawyer acting for the Communist Party was not the issue. "It is enough if there be some, as there certainly are, who would feel so, even though they would be 'wrong-thinking' people if they did."

12. Is it defamatory to say of the plaintiff that he has informed the police about a crime which led to his being shunned and avoided by certain criminal elements? See *Mawe* v. *Pigott* (1869), Ir. Rep. 4 C.L. 54. See also *Byrne* v. *Deane,* [1937] 1 K.B. 818, golf club member told police about illegal gambling machines, which caused other members to think less of him.

13. Donald calls Peter a "scab". Peter is a member of a union. Defamatory? See *Murphy* v. *Plasterers' Union,* [1949] S.A.S.R. 98. Would it make any difference if Peter was a general manager or a foreman, and not a union member?

14. In *Dominion Telegraph Co.* v. *Silver and Payne* (1882), 10 S.C.R. 238, it was held defamatory to have said of the plaintiffs, wholesale clothiers, that their business had "failed" and that their "liabilities [were] heavy". Is it actionable to say that X is in "dire financial straits"? See *Katapodis* v. *Brooklyn Spectator* (1941), 287 N.Y. 17, 38 N.E. 2d 112. What about stating that Y refuses to pay his just debts? See *Thompson* v. *Adelberg and Berman* (1918), 181 Ky. 487, 205 S.W. 558.

15. If one accuses a kosher butcher of selling bacon, is this actionable? See *Braun* v. *Armour & Co.* (1930), 173 N.E. 845 (N.Y.). What if someone says of a retailer that he is a price-cutter? See *Meyerson* v. *Hurlburt* (1938), 98 F. 2d 232.

16. Is it actionable to call someone a "Communist" or a "Communist rubber stamp"? See *Dennison et al.* v. *Anderson et al.,* [1946] O.R. 601 (C.A.). What if it is alleged that the plaintiff is a "near-Communist" or that he takes the side of the Communist Party? See *Braddock* v. *Bevins,* [1948] 1 K.B. 580, [1948] 1 All E.R. 450 (C.A.). Is it defamatory to be called a Red? A Pinko? A fellow-traveller? A Socialist? See *Slatyer* v. *Daily Telegraph* (1908), 6 C.L.R. 1. A radical? Does it matter if the plaintiff is a professor, a lawyer or a businessman? Does the place and time of the utterance make any difference?

17. Is it defamatory to say that someone is a Nazi? A Fascist? An arch-reactionary? A member of the Klu Klux Klan? A supporter of Ronald Reagan?

18. Can it ever be actionable to say of someone that he is a member of the Liberal Party of Canada? The Progressive Conservative Party? The N.D.P.? Social Credit?

19. Dick refers to Peter, a white man, as a "coloured gentleman". Can this be

actionable? See *Upton* v. *Times-Democrat Publishing Co.* (1900), 104 La. 141, 28 S. 2d 970. What if a black person is described as white? Is it defamatory to say that someone is a Jew? A German? An Indian? A Métis? A "Newfie"? A "Paki"?

20. Is it defamatory to say that someone is suffering from mental illness? From cancer? From venereal disease? See *French (Oscar)* v. *Smith,* [1923] 3 D.L.R. 902 (Ont.).

21. In *French (Elizabeth)* v. *Smith,* [1923] 3 D.L.R. 904 (Ont.), the defendant said of the plaintiff, "I knew of five fellows who took Lizzie French behind the church and screwed her." Liability? What if it is said of Miss X, a single woman, that she "fools around"? What if this is said of Mrs. Y, a married woman, or of Mr. Y, a married man? What if this is said of Mr. Z, a bachelor? Could it be defamatory if it is said of a woman or a man that they do *not* "fool around"? What if it is said of a mature woman that she is a virgin?

22. Is it defamatory to indicate that "Pandora is a divorcee"? That she is "separated from her husband"? What about, "Pandora is living common-law with Paul"? Is this statement defamatory of Paul?

23. Is it defamatory to say of someone that he is a homosexual? Or that a woman is a lesbian? Or that a person has had a sex change operation?

24. Portnoy, a homosexual, is shunned by his fellow homosexuals when they are told by the defendant that Portnoy has fallen in love with a woman. Liability?

25. Is it possible to defame someone without using words at all? What if a picture of the plaintiff is printed alongside a picture of a gorilla so as to indicate the resemblance between the two pictures? See *Zbyszko* v. *New York American* (1930), 228 App. Div. 277, 239 N.Y.Supp. 411.

26. In *Burton* v. *Crowell Publishing Co.* (1936), 82 F. 2d 154 (U.S.C.A. 2d Cir.), the defendant published an ad for Camel cigarettes featuring a photograph of the plaintiff, which, because of a blurring, made it appear that he was indecently exposed. Although the plaintiff had agreed to the ad generally, he had not approved of this particular picture. In allowing the plaintiff's claim, Learned Hand J. said: "The gravamen of the wrong in defamation is not so much the injury to reputation, measured by the opinion of others, as the feelings, that is, the repulsion or light esteem, which those opinions engender . . . [B]ecause the picture . . . was calculated to expose the plaintiff to more than trivial ridicule, it was prima facie actionable, . . . [even though] it did not assume to state a fact or an opinion. . . ."

See also *Mazatti* v. *Acme Products Ltd.,* [1930] 4 D.L.R. 601 (Man.), where the plaintiff was alleged to have given a testimonial in an advertisement for a product called Keeno, a patent medicine, which was supposed to have cured him of constipation, dizzy spells and indigestion. Liability was imposed since this was "humiliating to the plaintiff, and tended to and did subject him to ridicule".

27. The defamatory statement must be spoken "of and concerning the plaintiff". And this must normally be pleaded and proved. Thus, if the plaintiff is not specifically identified, he must show that he was the person who would be reasonably understood by a sensible reader to have been defamed. See *Morgan* v. *Odham's Press,* [1971] 1 W.L.R. 1239; *Youssoupoff* v. *M.-G.-M.* (1934), 50 T.L.R. 581. A gossip columnist mistakenly writes that the "estranged wife of the Prime Minister was seen smoking pot". Could she sue?

28. This problem of identifying the person defamed arises in cases of group defamation. If someone says "all lawyers are thieves", an individual lawyer could not say that this defamation was "of and concerning him". If the group being defamed, however, is a relatively small one, an individual member of the group may be allowed to recover. What if Donald says that X got one of the four Jones girls in trouble? Can any of them recover? See *Albrecht* v. *Burkholder* (1889), 18 O.R. 287. See also *Browne* v. *Thomson & Co.,* [1912] S.C. 359, one of 7 people could sue; *Neiman-Marcus* v. *Lait* (1952), 13 F.R.D. 311, 15 salesmen could sue but not 382 saleswomen; *Ortenberg* v. *Plamondon* (1914), 35 Can. L.T. 262 (Que.), one of 75 families could sue; *Fraser* v. *Sykes,* [1974] S.C.R. 526, one of 3 can sue.

29. A fine explanation of the principles involved here was given in *Knupffer* v. *London Express Newspaper,* [1944] A.C. 116 (H.L.), where some defamatory things were said of a group called Young Russia, a pro-Nazi organization, of which the plaintiff was a member. There were 2,000 other members in the world, 24 of whom were in Britain. The action was dismissed and Lord Atkin explained:

"I venture to think that it is a mistake to lay down a rule as to libel on a class, and then qualify it with exceptions. The only relevant rule is that in order to be actionable the defamatory words must be understood to be published of and concerning the plaintiff. It is irrelevant that the words are published of two or more persons if they are proved to be published of him, and it is irrelevant that the two or more persons are called by some generic or class name. There can be no law that a defamatory statement made of a firm, or trustees, or the tenants of a particular building is not actionable, if the words would reasonably be understood as published of each member of the firm or each trustee or each tenant. The reason why a libel published of a large or indeterminate number of persons described by some general name generally fails to be actionable is the difficulty of establishing that the plaintiff was, in fact, included in the defamatory statement, for the habit of making unfounded generalizations is ingrained in ill-educated or vulgar minds, or the words are occasionally intended to be a facetious exaggeration. Even in such cases words may be used which enable the plaintiff to prove that the words complained of were intended to be published of each member of the group, or, at any rate, of himself. Too much attention has been paid, I venture to think, in the textbooks and elsewhere to the ruling of Willes, J., in 1858 in *Eastwood* v. *Holmes,* 1 F. & F. 347, a case at nisi prius . . . His words: 'it only reflects on a class of persons' are irrelevant unless they mean 'it does not reflect on the plaintiff', and his instance, 'All lawyers were thieves' is an excellent instance of the vulgar generalizations to which I have referred. It will be as well for the future for lawyers to concentrate on the question whether the words were published of the plaintiff rather than on the question whether they were spoken of a class. I agree that in the present case the words complained of are, apparently, an unfounded generalization conveying imputations of disgraceful conduct, but not such as could reasonably be understood to be spoken of the appellant."

30. Only living people can be defamed; if someone says defamatory things about a deceased person, no action lies by the estate. A corporation and a municipality may also be defamed. See Fleming, *The Law of Torts* (4th ed., 1977), p. 531. See also *City of Prince George* v. *B.C. Television* (1978), 85 D.L.R. (3d) 755 (B.C.); but see *Church of Scientology of Toronto* v. *Globe and Mail* (1978), 84 D.L.R. (3d) 239 (Ont.).

31. Words may appear innocent on the surface but may be defamatory to people who are aware of extrinsic facts. In such a case, the plaintiff must plead and prove this, which is called the "innuendo". See Libel and Slander Act, R.S.O. 1970, c. 243, s. 21. An example of such a situation is the publication of the apparent good news that Mrs. M has given birth to twins. Mrs. M. succeeds in libel when she pleads and proves that she was married only four weeks before, the innuendo being that she has given birth to illegitimate children. See *Morrison* v. *Ritchie & Co.* (1902), 4 F. (Ct. of Sess.) 645, 39 Sc. L.R. 432. Similarly, to publish a photograph identifying one woman as Mrs. X becomes libellous when another woman proves that she is the real Mrs. X and that she has been defamed because of this. *Cf. Cassidy* v. *Daily Mirror Newspapers* [1929] 2 K.B. 331 (C.A.).

32. Because of the lack of protection defamation law affords minority groups who are unfairly defamed, legislation has been enacted to furnish some protection to the victims of what has been called "hate propaganda".

Under the Criminal Code, s. 281.2(1), "Every one who, by communicating statements in any public place, incites hatred against any identifiable group [distinguished by colour, race, religion, or ethnic origin] where such incitement is likely to lead to a breach of the peace"; or, (2) "Every one who, by communicating statements, other than in private conversation, wilfully promotes hatred against any identifiable group" is guilty of an offence. It is a defence for the accused to prove that the "statements communicated were true"; or "in good faith, he expressed or attempted to establish by argument an opinion upon a religious subject"; or "the statements were relevant to any subject of public interest, the discussion of which was for the public benefit [and he believed] on reasonable grounds [that they were true]" or "in good faith, he intended to point out, for the purpose of removal, matters producing or tending to produce feelings of hatred towards an identifiable group in Canada."

For a further discussion of the problem of group defamation, see Riesman, "Democracy and Defamation: Control of Group Libel" (1942), 42 Colum. L. Rev. 727; Fenson, "Group Defamation: Is the Cure too Costly?" (1964), 1 Man. L.S.J. 255; Arthurs, "Hate Propaganda—An Argument Against Attempts to Stop it by Legislation" (1970), 18 Chitty's L.J. 1; Cohen, "The Hate Propaganda Amendments: Reflections on a Controversy" (1971), 9 Alta. L. Rev. 103; Burns, "Defamatory Libel in Canada, A Recent Illustration of a Rare Crime" (1969), 17 Chitty's L.J. 213.

33. The Criminal Code also seeks to penalize "defamatory libel" against an individual. Section 262(1) states: "A defamatory libel is matter published, without lawful justification or excuse, that is likely to injure the reputation of any person by exposing him to hatred, contempt or ridicule, or that is designed to insult the person of or concerning whom it is published." Section 262(2) enacts: "A defamatory libel may be expressed directly or by insinuation or irony (a) in words legibly marked upon any substance, or (b) by any object signifying a defamatory libel otherwise than by words." If the libeller knows the libel is false he is liable to imprisonment for five years; otherwise it is a two-year maximum penalty. See *R.* v. *Georgia Straight Publishing Ltd.,* [1970] 1 C.C.C. 94, 4 D.L.R. (3d) 383 (B.C.).

Can you discern any difference between the criminal definition of libel and that developed by tort law? Is it preferable to reduce libel by tort actions or by criminal prosecutions? See generally LaMarsh, "Abuse of Power by the Media" in Law Society of Upper Canada Special Lectures, *Abuse of Power* (1979).

34. See generally, Williams, *The Law of Defamation in Canada* (1976); Gatley, *Libel and Slander* (7th ed., 1974); Duncan & Neill, *Defamation* (1978); Williams, "Decorum in Defamation" in Klar (ed.), *Studies in Canadian Tort Law* (1977).

B. LIBEL OR SLANDER?

Actionable defamation has long recognized a basic distinction between the written word (libel) and the spoken word (slander). The legal consequences of this distinction, originally emanating in the seventeenth century from the different functions of the common law courts which dealt with slander (a bequest from the Ecclesiastical Courts), and the Court of Star Chamber, which dealt with libel, have often led to unjust and anomalous results.

Libel, generally, includes writings, signs, pictures, statues, films, and even conduct implying a defamatory meaning. It is actionable without proof of damage since general damages are presumed. Libel is also a crime in many jurisdictions.

Slander is communicated orally and is not actionable *per se,* so that an action lies only if special damages are pleaded and proved. There are, however, four classes of slanderous statements that are actionable *per se* and do not require proof of special damages.

Although this "damage" rule is untenable on policy grounds and often generates unquestionably absurd results, the doctrine is well settled in the law and can only be changed by legislative reform. Because of its wholly arbitrary nature, the libel-slander distinction had led to a good deal of disrespect for the law of defamation in general.

Alberta, Manitoba, New Brunswick, Nova Scotia and Prince Edward Island have enacted legislation, suggested by the Uniformity Commissioners in 1944, that treats libel and slander alike. "Defamation" is defined as "libel or slander". Moreover, it is enacted that "An action lies for defamation and in an action for defamation, where defamation is proved, damage shall be presumed." See ss. 2(h) and 3.

A.P. HERBERT, THE UNCOMMON LAW (1935)
CHICKEN v. HAM

Now, my Lords, you are aware that by the mysterious provisions of the English law a defamatory statement may be either a slander or a libel, a slander being, shortly, a defamation by word of mouth, and a libel by the written or printed word; and the legal consequences are in the two cases very different. A layman, with the narrow outlook of a layman on these affairs, might rashly suppose that it is equally injurious to say at a public meeting, 'Mr. Chicken is a toad', and to write upon a postcard, 'Mr. Chicken is a toad'. But the unselfish labours of generations of British jurists have discovered between the two some profound and curious distinctions. For example, in order to succeed in an action for slander the injured party must prove that he has suffered some actual and special damage, whereas the victim of a written defamation need not; so that we have this curious result, that in practice it is safer to insult a man at a public meeting than to insult him on a postcard, and that which is written in the corner of a letter is in law more deadly than that which is shouted from the house-tops. My Lords, it is not for us to boggle at the wisdom of our ancestors, and this is only one of a great body of juridical refinements handed down to us by them, without which few of our profession would be able to keep body and soul together.

MELDRUM v. AUSTRALIAN BROADCASTING CO., LTD.
Supreme Court of Victoria. [1932] V.L.R. 425

The plaintiff brought an action for defamation alleging in the statement of claim that the defendant "wrote a script" and "read out" the words on the script into a broadcasting apparatus. The words were capable of bearing a defamatory meaning and some of them might have been actionable without proof of special damage if they were a "slander"; others could not have been actionable as a "slander" without proof of special damage. No special damages were alleged. The defendant moved to strike out the statement of claim or to have it amended by striking out those parts which referred to a writing or script and those parts of the words which could not support an action of slander without proof of special damage.

Cussen A.C.J.: There are a few cases in relation to circumstances more or less allied to the present case. In *The Case De Libellis Famosis, or of Scandalous Libels* (1605), 5 Co. Rep. 125a, it is said that a libel *in scriptis* may be published (1) *verbis aut cantilenis,* as where it is maliciously repeated or sung in the presence of others; (2) *traditione,* where the libel or any copy of it is delivered over. In *John Lamb's Case* (1610), 9 Co. Rep. 59b, a bill was exhibited in the Star Chamber for publishing two libels, and it was resolved that to be convicted in such a case a person "either ought to be a contriver of the libel, or a procurer of the contriving of it, or a malicious publisher of it, knowing it to be a libel"; and it is added that if after a person has heard or read a libel he repeats it or any part of it in the hearing of others, or after knowing it to be a libel he reads it to others, that is an unlawful publication of it. I think that in the above passage "malicious" means merely "without lawful justification or excuse".

It seems that the cases in the Star Chamber were criminal cases, and to them no doubt the general rule was applied that in the case of a misdemeanour all offenders are principals, and that as a libel, at all events on publication, is a misdemeanour, "all who are in any degree accessory to the publication of a libel, and by any means whatever conduce to the publication, are considered as principals in the act of publication"; Starkie on *Slander and Libel* (3rd ed.) p. 692. See further *R.* v. *Paine* (1696), 5 Mod. Rep. 163, and Hawkins, *Pleas of the Crown*, title "Libels", under the heading "Who are liable to be *punished* for a libel." I do not say that the fact that those were criminal cases necessarily renders them altogether inappropriate authorities here, but the fact must be borne in mind.

The above cases were by the Court of Appeal (Lord Esher, M.R., Bowen, L.J. and A.L. Smith, L.J.) applied in *Forrester* v. *Tyrrell* (1893), 1 T.L.R. 257, to an action for damages to libel. The defendant in that case read a defamatory letter out at a lodge meeting, after he had read it to himself. He said that he did not read it out with a malicious mind against the plaintiff, but the Court said that was immaterial because, as it was libellous and he published it after reading it over, malice was presumed. The Court also said that the law laid down in Coke's Reports already cited had been treated as law ever since. Nothing was said as to a possible distinction between criminal and civil cases. It will be noticed that those who heard what was read out would also be aware that there was a document purporting to contain, and in fact containing, the matter read out. On the other hand, in *Osborn* v. *Thomas Boulter & Son*, [1930] 2 K.B. 226, there are dicta by Scrutton, L.J., and Slesser, L.J., that in their opinion a similar publication would be a slander, and a dictum by Greer, L.J., which I think inclines the other way . . .

In the present case there is no allegation in the statement of claim to indicate that the listeners would understand that the person who was according to the allegations reading from a script was in fact doing so, or even that he was repeating from memory what he had read in a script. A similar position would be created if persons on one side of a partition or out of sight of another person uttering words heard them without any reason to think that they were being read. A blind man, too, might not know if reading was taking place, though of course the fact could be conveyed to him. Two questions may be asked—(1) Were the Court, in *Forrester* v. *Tyrrell,* right in applying the statement as to reading out, in the old cases in the Star Chamber, to an action for damages; or, in other words, was that case rightly decided? (2) Does *Forrester's* Case apply to an action for damages where it may be said that as far as the listeners were concerned what was heard was not indicated as being the publication of a libel? To answer these questions it is desirable to consider the reason or origin of the distinction that whereas defamatory written matter when published is, apart from special defences, actionable without proof of special damage—it being sometimes said that damage is presumed—defamatory oral matter is, except in certain special circumstances, not actionable without such proof.

The modern view is that this distinction is not based on principle, but on historical grounds. The story is told with great care and at great length in Holdsworth's *History of English Law*, Vol. VIII; see particularly at pp. 335-336. See also Jenk's *Digest of English Civil Law*, Vol. II, pp. 501-3; and, for the history to the year 1300, Pollock & Maitland, *History of English Law*, Vol. II, pp. 535-7. The action for defamatory words was developed as an action on the case, and by the end of the sixteenth century was well established. The action for defamatory writings was, notwithstanding the rise and progress of printing, not well established as an actionable wrong in the Common Law Courts until well on in the seventeenth century; but libel as a ground for inducement or for bill or confession in the Star Chamber as a criminal matter, tending to a breach of the peace, even if the publication was to the party defamed, was well known for a long time before this. Although the Star Chamber sometimes gave damages as well as inflicted punishments, when, in 1641, it was abolished and much of its jurisdiction taken over by the Common Law Courts, "libel" as a cause of action still retained many of the characteristics attached to it as a crime. At p. 364 Holdsworth says: "Now in considering the question whether defamation should give rise to an action in tort without proof of special damage, the Judges had before them the following three facts: firstly, such defamation was a crime; secondly, the development of the action on the case had made this action a wholly unsatisfactory remedy for the tort of defamation; thirdly, if the prevalent habit of duelling was to be suppressed, some better remedy must be provided . . . I cannot help thinking that it was the combined weight of all these three reasons which induced them to reform the law by drawing this distinction. However that may be, the cases make it quite clear that this distinction was drawn in the latter half of the seventeenth century." In the case of the action for defamatory words, which as I have said was much earlier, the Judges found it necessary by various devices to check the flood of actions, with which the decay of the borough and manor, etc., Courts and the practical supersession of the Ecclesiastical Courts threatened to overwhelm them. These devices are set out at p. 353 of Holdsworth's book, and at p. 361 he deals at greater length than I can do with the origin of the distinction above-mentioned. It seems plain that it is, as I have said, almost entirely due to historical reasons. Later, when these historical reasons were forgotten or overlooked, Judges and counsel tried to find some principle or principles upon which the distinction could be explained. It was said that compared with spoken words writing was more permanent, and more durable in effect; was capable of greater diffusion, particularly through newspapers; was likely to effect more damage; and showed more deliberation and malice in the defendant. There is no doubt in certain circumstances some force in each of these statements, though most of them are dependent on casual happenings; a writing may be torn up at once, an oral slander may be committed to writing and preserved, much more damage may be caused by some slanders than by some libels; and if broadcasting had been invented before printing the argument might have been the other way. The last statement, that a writing shows more deliberation and malice in fact, may be said to be generally true. It is a consideration derived from the fact that at common law libel was first dealt with entirely, and afterwards to some extent, as a crime.

It follows from what I have said that I cannot satisfactorily deduce from any recognized principle the rule which should be applied to the present case, and that I must do what in the past the Judges often did in connection with the wrongs of libel and slander—give a decision which on the whole seems to be right when applied to the circumstances of the particular case. Though such a proceeding is scarcely conceivable in these days, I do not say that the cases in Coke might not apply to the present circumstances if one were considering a prosecution and not an action.

If the facts here had been in all respects substantially the same as in *Forrester's* Case, I should, notwithstanding what was said later by Scrutton, L.J., and Slesser, L.J., have felt bound either to follow it or to refer, if requested, the matter to the Full Court; but I am not prepared to say that where there is nothing to show that the listeners would regard what they heard as the reading of a libel the publication should in this action be considered as anything but the publication of a slander. It must be remembered that though in cases of defamation damages will sometimes be presumed, damage, as in actions on the case generally, is of the gist of the action; and the important matter in a case like the present is what the listeners would understand, and not what the speaker, whether a reader or not, meant.

The result of what I have said is that I think the references to the script or writing and to the reading of it out should be deleted, and also that in setting out the defamatory matter the statement of claim should be confined to those words which are appropriate to an action for slander—which I understand to be words so closely connected with as to be inseparable from the words first mentioned.

[The plaintiff appealed.]

McArthur J.: But for the decision of the Court of Appeal in 1893 in the case of *Forrester* v. *Tyrrell* (1893), 1 T.L.R. 257, which plaintiff's counsel relied upon as being a decision directly in point, I would have had no hesitation in saying that in a civil action for damages the reading out to a third person or persons of written words defamatory of the person defamed constituted a slander and not a libel.

In that most accurate of text-books, the third edition of *Bullen and Leake's Precedents of Pleadings,* at p. 301, the distinction between libel and slander is as follows: "Libel consists in the publication by the defendant, by means of printing, writing, pictures, or the like signs, of matter defamatory to the plaintiff: 3 Bl. Com. 125. Slander consists in the publication by the defendant, by means of words spoken, of matter defamatory to the plaintiff: 3 Bl. Com. 123." . . . .

It was suggested that *Forrester* v. *Tyrrell* might be distinguished from the present case on the facts inasmuch as in that case it was clear that the hearers knew that the defendant was reading from a written document, whereas in the present case the hearers would not necessarily know whether the speaker was reading from a written document or not. In my opinion this distinction is quite immaterial. I cannot see how it can be said that when the hearers know that the speaker is reading from a written document it is a libel, and when they do not know it it is a slander . . . .

The distinction lies solely, in my opinion, in the mode of publication. Written defamatory words may, of course, be communicated to third persons by word of mouth; but, when so communicated, it is slander and not libel no matter whether the speaker openly reads out the written words, or whether he learns them off by heart and recites them or sings them; so long as the communication is by word of mouth it is, in my opinion, slander and not libel. If, on the other hand, the defamatory words are communicated to the third persons by means of printing, writing, pictures, signs, etc., it is libel and not slander.

It is suggested that this view will not stand the test when it is attempted to apply it to defamation by means of pictures, signs, sculptures, and the like so far at all events as the liability of persons other than those who produced such drawings, etc., is concerned. I do not agree with this. If the defendant showed to a third person, so that he could and did read them, written words defamatory of the plaintiff, though not written by the defendant, it would admittedly be a libel. Similarly, if the defendant showed to a third person a picture or sign or piece of sculpture which was defamatory of the plaintiff, though not painted or executed by the defendant, it would, in my opinion, be a libel. If, on the other hand, the defendant verbally described to a third person the defamatory picture, sign, or piece of sculpture, so as to comunicate to a third person by word of mouth the defamatory nature thereof, it would, in my opinion, be a slander and not libel.

It is also said that curious results may be brought about if the law is as I have stated. One instance given is that no one can be "libelled", as distinguished from "slandered", to a blind man—except perhaps by means of Braille writing, which, however, for the purpose of this discussion we may leave out of account—and therefore in no case can the plaintiff recover damages from the publication to a blind man of defamatory matter, without proof of special damage (except, of course, for the publication of defamatory matter of a particular nature for which actions of slander may be brought without proof of special damage). The other instance given was this: showing a document containing written defamatory matter to a third person so that he can and does read it would be a libel, whereas merely reading it to him would be a slander, and not a libel. For the one an action may be brought without proof of special damage, whereas for the other it is necessary to prove special damage. But in each of these instances this peculiarity (if it be a peculiarity) is not due to the definition of libel and slander as such, or to the fundamental distinction between libel and slander as I have stated it, but to the distinction which the law has made between actionable libel and actionable slander—a distinction which some writers have thought unsatisfactory.

In the present case it is quite clear that the statement of claim alleges that the defamatory words complained of were published by means of words spoken, and not by means of writing; and therefore, if it discloses a cause of action at all, it discloses, in my opinion, a cause of action of slander and not libel. The allegation that prior to such publication the defendant's agent "wrote a script" from which he read out the alleged defamatory words is irrelevant and, I think, embarrassing, and should be struck out.

I agree with the order made by the learned Acting Chief Justice, and I am therefore of opinion that the appeal should be dismissed with costs.

[Judgments to the same effect of Mann and Lowe, JJ., are omitted.]

NOTES

1. In *Lawrence* v. *Finch* (1931), 66 O.L.R. 451, [1931] 1 D.L.R. 689, Riddell J.A., expressed his preference for the view that a person who dictates defamatory matter to a stenographer which is later transcribed, publishes a slander only.

2. In *Ostrowe* v. *Lee* (1931), 256 N.Y. 505, 175 N.E. 505, Cardozo, J., held that publication to a stenographer in such a case is libel. "Many things that are defamatory may be said with impunity through the medium of speech. Not so, however, when speech is caught up on the wing and transmuted into print. What gives the sting to the writing is its permanence of form. The spoken word dissolves, but the written one abides and 'perpetuates the scandal' . . . There is a publication of a libel if a stenographer reads the notes that have been taken by another. Neither the evil nor the result is different when the notes that he reads have been taken by himself . . . . Let us assume a case where words, unaccompanied by special damage, are libellous if written, but are not slanderous *per se*. Let us assume that the defamer has a grudge that will be served by defaming his victim in the thought of a particular person. Let us assume that this person is also his stenographer. With that mind he dictates the defamatory words and instructs the stenographer to preserve and read what has been written. By hypothesis, the one defamed is without a remedy for slander. By hypothesis, too, a writing has been created at the instance of the defamer and lodged in the custody of the very person whose mind was to be poisoned. The outrage is without redress if the libel is not published when written out and read."

3. In *Youssoupoff* v. *Metro-Goldwyn-Mayer Pictures Ltd.* (1934), 50 T.L.R. 581, a talking-moving-picture was held to be libel and not slander.

"So far as the photographic part of the exhibition is concerned, that is a permanent matter to be seen by the eye, and is the proper subject of an action for libel, if defamatory. I regard the speech which is synchronized with the photographic reproduction and forms part of one complex, common exhibition, as an ancillary circumstance, part of the surroundings explaining that which is to be seen."

4. How should television be treated?

5. In Ontario, The Libel and Slander Act, R.S.O. 1970, c. 243 provides in s. 2 that "Defamatory words in a newspaper or in a broadcast shall be deemed to be published and to constitute libel." Section 1 as amended provides: "(1) In this Act, (a) "broadcasting" means the dissemination of writing, signs, signals, pictures and sounds of all kinds, intended to be received by the public either directly or through the medium of relay stations, by the means of, (i) any form of wireless radioelectric communication utilizing Hertzian waves, including radio-telegraph and radiotelephone, or (ii) cables, wires, fibre-optic linkages or laser beams, and "broadcast" has a corresponding meaning.

This legislation reflects the belief that the potential for harm to reputation by means of radio and television is enormous and that they should be treated like the written word.

6. Which of the following are libel and which are slander?
    (a) Speaking into a loudspeaker to a huge crowd at Maple Leaf Gardens.
    (b) The sign language used by deaf-mutes. See *Gutsole* v. *Mathers* (1836), 1 M & W. 495, 501.
    (c) Hanging somebody in effigy. See *Eyre* v. *Garlick* (1878), 42 J.P. 68.
    (d) An unmarried couple is met with a charivari, consisting of guns being fired, bells being rung and shouting, according to local custom with newly married people. See *Varner* v. *Morton* (1919), 52 N.S.R. 180, 46 D.L.R. 597.
    (e) A defamatory statue. See *Monson* v. *Tussauds, Ltd.,* [1894] 1 Q.B. 671 (C.A.).

7. The Ontario Libel and Slander Act, s. 1(2) provides that "any reference to words in this Act shall be construed as including a reference to pictures, visual images, gestures and other methods of signifying meaning". Does this enactment affect any of your answers to the above questions?

8. The *Restatement of Torts, Second,* § 568, reads as follows:

"(1) Libel consists of the publication of defamatory matter by written or printed words, or by its embodiment in physical form, or by any other form of communication which has the potentially harmful qualities characteristic of written or printed words.

(2) Slander consists of the publication of defamatory matter by spoken words, transitory gestures, or by any form of communication other than those stated in Subsection (1).

(3) The area of dissemination, the deliberate and premeditated character of its publication, and the persistence of the defamation are factors to be considered in determining whether a publication is a libel rather than a slander." What is your view of this suggestion?

9. The four types of slander actionable *per se* are the following:

(1) *Imputation of the commission of a crime.* The crime must be a serious one, punishable by a prison term, and not merely a provincial offence. See *McDonald* v. *Brekelmans,* [1971] 3 W.W.R. 107 (B.C.), saying someone would "pocket the money" from a grant is not an accusation of crime. A general accusation of criminality may suffice; it is not necessary to specify, therefore, a particular crime. See *Curtis* v. *Curtis* (1834), 10 Bing. 477; *Webb* v. *Beavan* (1883), 11 Q.B.D. 609.

(2) *Imputation of a loathsome disease.* To say that someone is suffering from a venereal disease is so likely to cause him to be ostracized that it is actionable *per se.* See *French (Oscar)* v. *Smith,* [1923] 3 D.L.R. 902, 53 O.L.R. 28; *Houseman* v. *Coulson,* [1948] 2 D.L.R. 62 (Sask.). It is not actionable *per se,* however, to say that someone suffered from a venereal disease in the past. See *Halls* v. *Mitchell,* [1928] S.C.R. 125. Leprosy was among the loathsome diseases referred to here, because it seemed lasting and incurable. What about saying someone is incurably insane?

(3) *Imputation of unchastity to a woman.* To accuse a woman of unchastity has been considered serious enough to make it actionable *per se.* See *French (Elizabeth)* v. *Smith* (1922), 53 O.L.R. 31; [1923] 3 D.L.R. 904. It is not actionable *per se* to say of a man, however, that he is unchaste. See *Hickerson* v. *Masters* (1921), 226 S.W. 1072. It is actionable *per se* to call a woman a lesbian. See *Kerr* v. *Kennedy,* [1942] 1 K.B. 409. So too, to say of a man that he is homosexual. See *Nowark* v. *Maguire* (1964), 255 N.Y.S. 2d 318. Does any of this make sense anymore in the 1980's? The Ontario Libel and Slander Act, R.S.O. 1970, c. 243, s. 17 reads:

> "In an action for slander for defamatory words spoken of a woman imputing unchastity or adultery, it is not necessary to allege in the plaintiff's statement of claim or to prove that special damage resulted to the plaintiff from the utterance of such words, and the plaintiff may recover damages without averment or proof of special damage."

(4) *Imputation of unfitness to practice one's trade or profession.* Slandering someone in relation to his trade, profession, office or other employment activity is actionable *per se* because it is clearly calculated to damage a person in a pecuniary way. This applies only to remunerative activities, however, and not to positions of honour that do not yield financial benefits. See *Alexander* v. *Jenkins,* [1892] 1 Q.B. 797 (C.A.). The person being defamed must be occupying the office at the time of the publication. At one time the words had to be in the way of his calling. See *Hopwood* v. *Muirson,* [1945] 1 All E.R. 453 (C.A.). But this has now been abrogated by legislation both in the U.K. and Canada. The Ontario Libel and Slander Act, R.S.O. 1970, c. 243, s. 18 states:

> "In an action for slander for words calculated to disparage the plaintiff in any office, profession, calling, trade or business held or carried on by him at the time of the publication thereof, it is not necessary to allege or prove special damage, whether or not the words are spoken of the plaintiff in the way of his office, profession, calling, trade or business, and the plaintiff may recover damages without averment or proof of special damage."

Is the test for whether the words were "calculated to disparage the plaintiff in his calling" an objective or subjective one?

10. With other types of slander the plaintiff must prove special damages before he can succeed. This is often no easy matter. It is not enough to show damage to a reputation; there must also be demonstrated some pecuniary loss. The purpose of this requirement is to reduce the number of trivial slander claims. To prove that the plaintiff has lost the society of his friends or that he was made ill as a result of the slander has been held not to amount to special damage. See *Palmer* v. *Solmes* (1880), 30 U.C.C.P. 481. This decision may, however, be open to review. See Fleming, *The Law of Torts* (5th ed., 1977), p. 525.

C. PUBLICATION

McNICHOL v. GRANDY

Supreme Court of Canada. [1931] S.C.R. 696; [1932] 1 D.L.R. 225

The defendant and the plaintiff met in the dispensary of the plaintiffs' drug store. In the course of the conversation the defendant spoke in a loud and angry tone and uttered words defamatory of the plaintiff. An employee of the plaintiff, Kathleen Wilson, went to the dressing room adjoining the dispensary, and her attention was attracted by the loud tones of the defendant which could be heard through the wall. She listened carefully and overheard the entire conversation by reason of a small hole (which had been cut by firemen in a recent fire) in the wall between the two rooms.

At the trial of an action for slander, the trial judge withdrew the case from the jury on the ground that there was no evidence of publication. The Court of

Appeal for Manitoba reversed this judgment and ordered a new trial. The defendant appealed.

Lamont J.: In an action of slander the onus is upon the plaintiff to prove publication in fact by the defendant, in this sense, that it is publication for which the defendant is responsible. Where statements defamatory of a plaintiff have been uttered by a defendant and overheard by a third person the first inquiry in determining the defendant's responsibility is: Did he intend that anyone but the plaintiff should hear his defamatory utterances? In ascertaining his intention we must proceed in accordance with the fundamental principle referred to by Swinfen Eady, L.J., in the case of *Huth* v. *Huth,* [1915] 3 K.B. 32, that a man must be taken to intend the natural and probable consequences of his act in the circumstances. In that case the defendant sent through the post in an unclosed letter a written communication which the plaintiffs alleged was defamatory of them. The communication was taken out of the envelope and read by a butler who was a servant in the house at which the plaintiffs were staying. The butler did this out of curiosity and in breach of his duty. It was held that there was no publication by the defendant and that the case was properly withdrawn from the jury by the trial judge. The basis of the decision was that, although there had been publication to the butler, it was not publication for which the defendant was responsible, because there was no evidence that he knew or had reason to suspect or should have contemplated that a letter addressed to the plaintiffs and enclosed in an envelope "but unsealed and unstuck down" would, in the ordinary course, be likely to be opened by the butler or any other servant before being delivered to the defendant's wife. In his judgment Bray, J., said: "In my opinion it is quite clear that, in the absence of some special circumstances, a defendant cannot be responsible for a publication which was the wrongful act of a third person. He cannot be said, except in special circumstances, to have contemplated it. It was not the natural consequence of his sending the letter, or writing, in the way in which he did."

To the same effect was the decision in *Powell* v. *Gelston,* [1916] 2 K.B. 615. There a communication containing libellous matter was addressed by the defendant to F.W.P. in answer to inquiries made by him. It was opened by F.W.P.'s father, on whose behalf the inquiries had been made, but of this the defendant was unaware. The communication was not seen by F.W.P. It was held that there was no publication by the defendant to the father because the jury found that the defendant did not "know or expect that the letter might probably be opened or seen by a third person other than the person to whom it was addressed."

The same principle was applied in *Keogh* v. *Dental Hospital,* [1910] I.R. 2 K.B., 577, where Lord O'Brien, L.C.J., stated the ground for determining the defendant's responsibility in the following words: "I think there was no evidence fixing responsibility upon the defendants. No doubt they may have known that the plaintiff practised dentistry work, but they did not know, nor might they have known, nor was there any presumption that they knew, that the plaintiff had a clerk who, in his absence, was authorized to open letters addressed to him."

On the other hand, there is a long line of authorities represented by *Delacroix* v. *Thevenot* (1817), 2 Starkie 63, and *Gomersall* v. *Davies* (1898), 14 Times L.R. 430, in which it has been held that, where a defendant, knowing that the plaintiff's letters were usually opened by his clerk, sent a libellous letter addressed to the plaintiff which was opened and read by the clerk lawfully and in the usual course of business, there was publication by the defendant to the plaintiff's clerk. In *Powell* v. *Gelston,* [1916] 2 K.B. 615, Bray, J., said: "Several cases were cited—*Delacroix* v. *Thevenot, Gomersall* v. *Davies* and *Sharp* v. *Skues* (1909), 25 Times L.R. 336. They show that where to the defendant's knowledge a letter is likely to be opened by a clerk of the person to whom it is addressed the defendant is responsible for the publication to that clerk. As Lord Ellenborough said in *Delecroix* v. *Thevenot,* it must be taken that such a publication was intended by the defendant. On the other hand, in *Sharp* v. *Skues* (1909), 25 Times L.R. 336, Cozens-Hardy, M.R., said: 'It would be a publication if the defendant intended the letter to be opened by a clerk or some third person not the plaintiff, or if to the defendant's knowledge it would be opened by a clerk; but the jury had negatived this in the clearest terms, and under these circumstances it was impossible to hold that some act done by a partner or a clerk of the plaintiff by his direction and for his own convenience when absent from the office could be a publication'."

Then we have the further line of cases which show that where a letter containing defamatory matter concerning the plaintiff has been negligently dropped by the defendant and picked up and read by a third person, the defendant will be held responsible for publication to the person picking it up and reading it: *Weld-Blundell* v. *Stephens,* [1920] A.C. 956. Also where a letter intended for one person was by mistake sent to another *Thompson* v. *Dashwood* (1883), 11 Q.B.D. 43. The defendant in these cases was held responsible because the publication was directly due to his want of care.

The facts in the case at bar clearly distinguished it from the case of *Huth* v. *Huth,* [1915] 3 K.B. 32, upon which the appellant relied. There the publication to the butler resulted from a breach of duty on his part which the defendant could not reasonably be called upon to foresee; while in the case before us the publication to Kathleen Wilson took place while she was performing her duties in the usual course of business, and was not brought about by any improper act of hers.

Then can it be said that the defendant's ignorance (if he was ignorant, for he did not testify) of the presence of Miss Wilson in the dressing room, affords any answer to the plaintiff's claim? Applying the principles set out in the above authorities, we must take it that he intended the natural and probable consequences of his act. The natural and probable consequence of uttering the words used was that all persons of normal hearing who were within the carrying distance of his voice would hear what he said. When, therefore, it was established as a fact that Miss Wilson did overhear him utter the slanderous statements charged against him a *prima facie* case of publication by him was made out and, in order to displace that *prima facie* case the onus was on him to satisfy the jury, not only that he did not intend that anyone other than the plaintiff should hear him, but also that he did not know and had no reason to expect that any of the staff or any other person might be within hearing distance, and that he was not guilty of any want of care in not foreseeing the probability of the presence of someone within hearing range of the speaking tones which he used.

[The judgments of Anglin, C.J.C., and Duff, J., to the same effect are omitted. The appeal was dismissed.]

NOTES

1. Suppose the defendant was speaking in Greek to the plaintiff, who was also Greek, and the person listening knew no Greek at all, though she actually heard every word spoken. Publication? See *Economopoulos* v. *A.G. Pollard Co.* (1914), 105 N.E. 896 (Mass.).

2. Defamatory material must be published or else there is no liability. In other words, the defamation must be communicated to a third person. It need not be told to a crowd of people, but at least one person, other than the defamed individual, must hear and understand it. It is not actionable to say defamatory things to a person about himself. The jury must decide whether there has been a

publication. They should be permitted to infer one, even where there is no specific evidence that the credit information that was requested was sent or received. See *Gaskin* v. *Retail Credit Co.*, [1965] S.C.R. 297.

3. What if defamatory words are spoken to an individual in the presence of others, but they do not actually hear what was said? See *Sheffill* v. *Van Densen* (1859), 13 Gray (Mass.) 304. What if a 3-year-old child, who cannot understand the word, hears someone call his mother a "thief"? See *Sullivan* v. *Sullivan* (1892), 48 Ill. App. 435.

4. The Libel and Slander Act, R.S.O. 1970, c. 243, s. 2 states:
   Defamatory words in a newspaper or in a broadcast shall be deemed to be published and to constitute libel.
What is the effect of this section?

5. Which, if any, of the following are publications?

(a) X dictates a defamatory letter to his secretary, who types it up. X then burns it. See *Osborn* v. *Thomas Boulter & Son*, [1930] 2 K.B. 226; *Pullman* v. *Hill & Co.* [1891] 1 Q.B. 524 (C.A.).

(b) P, a 14-year-old boy, gets a letter accusing him of theft. He shows it to his older brother seeking his advice. See *Hedgepeth* v. *Coleman* (1922), 111 S.E. 517. What if the recipient of the letter is a middle-aged woman? See *Hills* v. *O'Bryan*, [1949] 2 D.L.R. 716 (B.C.).

(c) Perry, who is illiterate, receives a defamatory letter and asks his wife to read it to him. Would it make any difference if the defendant is aware or unaware of Perry's illiteracy? See *Jackson* v. *Staley* (1885), 9 O.R. 334 (C.A.).

(d) Donald hears a defamatory statement being made by Dick. He repeats it to Ezra, saying, "Have you heard the rumour?" Publication by Donald? See *Houseman* v. *Coulson*, [1948] 2 D.L.R. 62 (Sask.). What if a newspaper prints a defamatory story that it picks up from the C.P. wire service. Publication by the newspaper? What if Derek sells a magazine knowing it contains a defamatory article?

6. It is clear that some fault is required in relation to the publication of defamatory matter. If the defendant did not intend a publication and if he could not by reasonable care have avoided it, he will not be held liable. If he was negligent, however, he will be. Thus, if someone speaks defamatory words without any reason to think that he can be overheard, there is no liability. See *Hall* v. *Balkind*, [1918] N.Z.L.R. 740. Compare with *Theaker* v. *Richardson*, [1962] 1 W.L.R. 151 (C.A.), where defendant wrote a letter to plaintiff in which he accused her of being "a lying low-down brothel-keeping whore and thief". Defendant put the letter in the plaintiff's letter box, whereupon her husband picked it up and opened it. In an action for libel, based on publication to plaintiff's husband, the jury found in answer to two questions, (1) that defendant anticipated that someone other than plaintiff would open and read the letter, and (2) it was a natural and probable consequence of defendant's writing and delivery of the letter that plaintiff's husband would open it and read it. Judgment for £500 was given plaintiff. This judgment was upheld on appeal. The majority felt there was evidence on which the jury could find as they did. Ormerod L.J., dissented. In his opinion, there was no evidence on which a jury could find that defendant should have anticipated that someone other than the plaintiff would read the letter and it was not a natural and probable consequence for plaintiff's husband to make the mistake which he said he made.

7. In *Byrne* v. *Deane*, [1937] 1 K.B. 818, [1937] 2 All E.R. 204, some members of a golf club placed a poster containing material defamatory of plaintiff on the wall of the club. Defendants, proprietors of the club, were held liable to plaintiff since, having knowledge of the poster and the power to remove it, their failure so to do constituted publication. The Court of Appeal held that failure to remove defamatory matter may amount to publication where removal is simple and easy. On the other hand, it would be difficult if not impossible to draw an inference of "volition" from failure to remove deeply chiselled defamation from stonework of a building.

8. In *Duke of Brunswick* v. *Harmer* (1849), 14 Q.B. 185, 117 E.R. 75,

defendant's newspaper published a libel of the plaintiff. Seventeen years later an agent of plaintiff purchased a copy of the newspaper at the newpaper office. In an action brought for libel seven months after such purchase, defendant pleaded the Statute of Limitations (21 Jac.I, c. 16, s. 3) which provided that an action for libel must be brought within six years from the date when the cause of action arose. The court held that the statute was no bar since by the sale of a copy the defendant had made a distinct and separate publication which gave rise to a separate cause of action. But *cf. Thomson* v. *Lambert,* [1938] S.C.R. 253, limiting causes of action to one.

9. The American *Restatement of Torts* in s. 578, Comment (b) states the following rule: "Each time a libellous article is brought to the attention of a third person, a new publication has occurred, and each publication is a separate tort. Thus, each time a libellous book or paper or magazine is sold, a new publication has taken place which . . . will support a separate action for damages against the seller."

An increasing number of American decisions, like the Supreme Court of Canada, now support the "single publication" rule to the effect that "where large distributions of published matter are involved, the cause of action accrues, for the purpose of the statute of limitations, upon the first publication, when the issue goes into circulation generally": *Hartmann* v. *Time, Inc.* (1946), 64 F. Supp. 671; *Winrod* v. *Time, Inc.* (1948), 334 Ill. App. 59, 78 N.E. 2d 708; *Ogden* v. *Association of U.S. Army* (1959), 177 F. Supp. 498. There is now a Uniform Single Publication Act, which has been adopted by several states, including California and Pennsylvania.

10. In Canada, several provinces provide by legislation for a short period of limitation in the case of libel in local newspapers or broadcasts. Thus, in Ontario, The Libel and Slander Act, R.S.O. 1970, c. 243, provides in s. 5(1) that no action for libel in a newspaper or broadcast lies unless plaintiff, "within six weeks after the alleged libel has come to his knowledge", has given notice in writing specifying the defamatory matter complained of.

By the Ontario Act, s. 6, actions for libel in a newspaper or a broadcast must be commenced within three months after the libel has come to the knowledge of the person defamed, but if an action is brought within that time, such action may include a claim for any other libel against the plaintiff by the defendant in the same newspaper or broadcast from the same station within a period of one year before the commencement of the action. Section 5(1) and s. 6 apply only to newspapers printed and published in Ontario and to broadcasts from a station in Ontario (s. 7).

11. In *L'Abbe* v. *Southam Press Ltd.* (1971), 18 D.L.R. (3d) 410 (Ont.), the court ruled that the plaintiff could claim for libels within one year before the commencement of the action, even when he had failed to inform the publisher of their defamatory nature at the time of publication as required by s. 5(1), provided that this requirement was fulfilled for the specific publication that was the basis of the cause of action.

D. BASIS OF LIABILITY

E. HULTON & CO. v. JONES

House of Lords. [1910] A.C. 20; 79 L.J.K.B. 198;
101 L.T. 831; 26 T.L.R. 128

The plaintiff, Mr. Thomas Artemus Jones, a barrister practising on the North Wales Circuit, brought the action to recover damages for the publication of an alleged libel concerning him contained in an article in the *Sunday Chronicle,* a newspaper of which the defendants were the printers, proprietors, and publishers. The article which was written by the Paris correspondent of the paper, purported to describe a motor festival at Dieppe, and the parts chiefly complained of ran thus: "Upon the terrace marches the world, attracted by the motor races—a world immensely pleased with itself, and minded to draw a wealth of inspiration —and, incidentally, of golden cocktails—from any scheme to speed the passing hour . . . 'Whist! there is Artemus Jones with a woman who is not his wife, who must be you know—the other thing!' whispers a fair neighbour of mine excitedly into her bosom friend's ear. Really, is it not surprising how certain of our fellow-countrymen behave when they come abroad? Who would suppose, by his goings on, that he was a churchwarden at Peckham? No one, indeed, would assume that Jones, in the atmosphere of London would take on so austere a job as the duties of a churchwarden. Here, in the atmosphere of Dieppe, on the French side of the Channel, he is the life and soul of a gay little band that haunts the Casino and turns night into day, besides betraying a most unholy delight in the society of female butterflies." The defendants alleged that the name chosen for the purpose of the article was a fictitious one, having no reference to the plaintiff, and chosen as unlikely to be the name of a real person, and they denied that any officer or member of their staff who wrote or printed or published or said before publication the words complained of knew the plaintiff or his name or his profession, or his association with the journal or with the defendants, or that there was any existing person bearing the name of or known as Artemus Jones. They admitted publication, but denied that the words were published of or concerning the plaintiff. On the part of the plaintiff the evidence of the writer of the article and of the editor of the paper that they knew nothing of the plaintiff, and that the article was not intended by them to refer to him, was accepted as true. At the trial witnesses were called for the plaintiff, who said that they had read the article and thought that it referred to the plaintiff. The jury returned a verdict for the plaintiff with 1750*l.* damages. The defendants' appeal to the Court of Appeal, and a further appeal to the House of Lords, were dismissed.

Lord Loreburn L.C.: Libel is a tortious act. What does the tort consist in? It consists in using language which others knowing the circumstances would reasonably think to be defamatory of the person complaining of and injured by it. A person charged with libel cannot defend himself by shewing that he intended in his own breast not tc defame, or that he intended not to defame the plaintiff, if in fact he did both. He has none the less imputed something disgraceful and has none the less injured the plaintiff. A man in good faith may publish a libel believing it to be true, and it may be found by the jury that he acted in good faith believing it to be true, and reasonably believing it to be true, but that in fact the statement was false. Under those circumstances he has no defence to the action, however excellent his intention. If the intention of the writer be immaterial in considering whether the matter written is defamatory, I do not see why it need be relevant in considering whether it is defamatory of the plaintiff. The writing, according to the old form must be malicious, and it must be of and concerning the plaintiff. Just as the defendant could not excuse himself from malice by proving that he wrote it in the most benevolent spirit, so he cannot shew that the libel was not of and concerning the plaintiff by proving that he never heard of the plaintiff. His intention in both respects equally is inferred from what he did. His remedy is to abstain from defamatory words.

NOTES

1. The law on this point has been summed up as follows: "The question is not so much who was aimed at as who was hit." See *Corrigan* v. *Bobbs-Merrill Co.* (1920), 126 N.E. 260 (N.Y.), a case involving a supposedly fictitious book which referred to a New York City magistrate without realizing it. The court explained: "The fact that the publisher has no actual intention to defame a

particular man or indeed to injure anyone does not prevent recovery of compensatory damages by one who connects himself with the publication."

2. It used to be that malice was required for slander, a carryover from the ecclesiastical law. See Veeder, "History and Theory of the Law of Defamation" (1904), 4 Colum. L. Rev. 33. In 1825, however, the law began to imply malice, distinguishing between "malice in fact and malice in law". See *Bromage* v. *Prosser* (1825), 107 E.R. 1051. Eventually, malice became a fiction only and defamation became strictly actionable without proof of intention or negligence. See *Morrison* v. *Ritchie & Co.* (1902), 4 F. (Ct. of Sess.) 645, 39 Scot. L.R. 432, liability when birth of twins announced mistakenly without knowledge of marriage four weeks before.

3. In *Newstead* v. *London Express Newspaper Ltd.,* [1940] 1 K.B. 377 (C.A.), the defendant published a story about a bigamy trial and wrote that "Harold Newstead, 30-year old Camberwell man, who was jailed for nine months, liked having two wives at once". These words were true of a man called Henry Newstead, a barman of Camberwell, but the plaintiff, Harold Cecil Newstead, a hairdresser in Camberwell about 30 years of age, sued, alleging the words were defamatory of him. During the course of the judgment Sir Wilfred Greene M.R. stated:

"After giving careful consideration to the matter, I am unable to hold that the fact that defamatory words are true of A, makes it as a matter of law impossible for them to be defamatory of B, which was in substance the main argument on behalf of the appellants. At first sight this looks as though it would lead to great hardship. But the hardships are in practice not so serious as might appear, at any rate in the case of statements which are *ex facie* defamatory. Persons who make statements of this character may not unreasonably be expected, when describing the person of whom they are made, to identify that person so closely as to make it very unlikely that a judge would hold them to be reasonably capable of referring to someone else, or that a jury would hold that they did so refer. This is particularly so in the case of statements which purport to deal with actual facts. If there is a risk of coincidence it ought, I think, in reason to be borne not by the innocent party to whom the words are held to refer, but by the party who puts them into circulation. In matters of fiction, there is no doubt more room for hardship. Even in the case of matters of fact it is no doubt possible to construct imaginary facts which would lead to hardship. There may also be hardship if words, not on their faces defamatory, are true of A, but are reasonably understood by some as referring to B, and as applied to B are defamatory. But such cases must be rare. The law as I understand it is well settled, and can only be altered by legislation."

4. In *Lee* v. *Wilson and MacKinnon* (1935), 51 C.L.R. 276, [1935] V.L.R. 113, the defendant newspaper in reporting a trial stated that the prisoner had charged "detective Lee" of the local police force with taking a bribe. There were two constables, A.L. Lee and Clifford Lee on the force, and both were known as "detective Lee". Both brought actions for libel, and they were tried together. At the trial evidence was offered that the reference was to a third constable Lee of the motor vehicles department. The High Court of Australia held that the evidence was properly excluded and both plaintiffs could recover damages.

CASSIDY v. DAILY MIRROR NEWSPAPERS, LIMITED

Court of Appeal. [1929] 2 K.B. 331; 98 L.J.K.B. 595; 141 L.T. 404;
45 T.L.R. 485

Scrutton L.J.: The facts in this case are simple. A man named Cassidy, who for some reason also called himself Corrigan and described himself as a General in the Mexican Army, was married to a lady who also called herself Cassidy or Mrs. Corrigan. Her husband occasionally came and stayed with her at her flat, and her acquaintances met him. Cassidy achieved some notoriety in racing circles and in indiscriminate relations with women, and at a race meeting he posed, in company with a lady, to a racing photographer, to whom he said he was engaged to marry the lady and the photographer might announce it. The photographer, without any further inquiry, sent the photograph to the *Daily Mirror* with an inscription: "Mr. M. Corrigan, the race horse owner, and Miss X" —I omit the name—"whose engagement has been announced," and the *Daily Mirror* published the photograph and inscription. This paper was read by the female acquaintances of Mrs. Cassidy or Mrs. Corrigan, who gave evidence that they understood from it that the lady was not married to Mr. M. Corrigan and had no legal right to take his name, and that they formed a bad opinion of her in consequence. Mrs. Cassidy accordingly brought an action for libel against the newspaper setting out these words with an innuendo, meaning thereby that the plaintiff was an immoral woman who had cohabited with Corrigan without being married to him.

At the trial counsel for the defendants objected that the words were not capable of a defamatory meaning. McCardie, J., held that they were; the jury found that they did reasonably bear a defamatory meaning and awarded the plaintiff 500*l*. damages. . . .

The real questions involved were: (1) Was the alleged libel capable of a defamatory meaning? (2) As the defendants did not know the facts which caused the friends of Mrs. Cassidy to whom they published the words to draw defamatory inferences from them about the plaintiff, were they liable for those inferences?

Now the alleged libel does not mention the plaintiff, but I think it is clear that words published about A may indirectly be defamatory of B. For instance, "A is illegitimate". To persons who know the parents those words may be defamatory of the parents. Or again, "A has given way to drink; it is unfortunately hereditary"; to persons who know A's parents these words may be defamatory. Or "A holds a D. Litt. degree of the University at X, the only one awarded". To persons who know B, who habitually describes himself (and rightly so) as "D. Litt. of X", these words may be capable of a defamatory meaning. Similarly, to say that A is a single man or a bachelor may be capable of a defamatory meaning if published to persons who know a lady who passes as Mrs. A and whom A visits. . . .

In my view the words published were capable of the meaning "Corrigan is a single man", and were published to people who knew the plaintiff professed to be married to Corrigan; it was for the jury to say whether those people could reasonably draw the inference that the so-called Mrs. Corrigan was in fact living in immoral cohabitation with Corrigan, and I do not think their finding should be interfered with.

But the second point taken was that the defendants could not be liable for the inference drawn, because they did not know the facts which enabled some persons to whom the libel was published, to draw an inference defamatory of the plaintiff. This was rested on some dicta of Brett, L.J., in *Henty's* case, 5 C.P.D. 539, that the evidence which made apparently innocent statements defamatory must be, "known both to the person who wrote the document and to the persons to whom it was published." This, I think, was originally obiter, and, since the decision in *E. Hulton & Co.* v. *Jones,* is no longer law. . . .

In my view, since *E. Hulton & Co.* v. *Jones,* it is impossible for the person publishing a statement which, to those who know certain facts, is capable of a defamatory meaning in regard to A, to defend himself by saying: "I never heard of A and did not mean to injure him." If he publishes words reasonably capable of being read as relating directly or indirectly to A and, to those who know the facts about A, capable of a defamatory meaning, he must take the consequences of the defamatory inferences reasonably drawn from his words.

It is said that this decision would seriously interfere with the reasonable conduct of newspapers. I do not agree. If publishers of newspapers, who have no more rights than private persons, publish statements which may be defamatory of other people, without inquiry as to their truth, in order to make their paper attractive, they must take the consequences, if on subsequent inquiry, their statements are found to be untrue or capable of defamatory inferences. No one could contend that "M. Corrigan, General in the Mexican Army", was "a source in whom we have full confidence." To publish statements first and inquire into their truth afterwards, may seem attractive and up to date. Only to publish after inquiry may be slow, but at any rate it would lead to accuracy and reliability.

In my opinion the appeal should be dismissed with costs. . . .

Greer L.J. (dissenting): In my view, notwithstanding the case of *E. Hulton & Co.* v. *Jones,* the law still is as it was laid down by Brett, L.J., in *Henty's* case, 5 C.P.D. 514. If extrinsic facts are relied upon for the purpose of converting that which would otherwise be an innocent statement of fact into a defamatory libel, the extrinsic facts must be known both to the person who framed the alleged libel and to the persons to whom it was published. In this case I take it as common ground that those who were responsible for the publication of the photograph and the words in question did not know that Corrigan was a married man. . . . If it could be said in this case that those responsible for the publication in question knew or ought to have known that Corrigan was a man who had a wife living at the time, or was a man with whom there was a lady living and claiming to be his wife, it may be that the question whether the words were or were not defamatory ought to have been left to the jury; but there was no evidence from which it is reasonable to conclude that they knew or ought to have known that he was a married man. They were surely entitled to suppose that, as he said he was engaged to marry the lady in question, he was not in fact a married man, unless they knew to the contrary. . . .

The decision of the House of Lords in *E. Hulton & Co.* v. *Jones,* which was very much relied upon by the respondents, does not, in my opinion, afford sufficient authority for deciding the present case in favour of the plaintiff. In that case the words complained of appeared in form to relate to an existing individual who was named. The words, if applied to an existing person, were clearly defamatory, and the House of Lords, affirming the Court of Appeal, held that the mere fact that the writer did not intend to injure the plaintiff afforded no defence to the action. It seems clear that the writer took the risk of making defamatory statements about an individual by name when he ought to have known that it was possible that there might be a person bearing that name who would be understood to be meant by the words which were used. Lord Loreburn in giving judgment pointed out that a person charged with libel cannot defend himself by showing that he intended in his own breast not to defame, or that he intended not to defame the plaintiff, if in fact he did both, and that his remedy was to abstain from using defamatory words. In the present case no defamatory words were used about anybody, and the defendants are, in my judgment, entitled to succeed, not because in his own mind the writer did not intend to defame, but because in fact he has not used language which reasonable persons either have or could have interpreted as defamatory of the plaintiff . . . .

Russell L.J.: Liability for libel does not depend on the intention of the defamer; but on the fact of defamation. If you once reach the conclusion that the published matter in the present case amounts to or involves a statement that Mr. Corrigan is an unmarried man, then in my opinion those persons who knew the circumstances might reasonably consider the statement defamatory of the plaintiff. The statement being capable of a meaning defamatory to the plaintiff, it was for the jury upon the evidence adduced to decide whether the plaintiff had been libelled or not.

It was said that it would be a great hardship on the defendants if they were made liable in consequence of a statement innocent on its face and published by them in good faith. The answer to this appeal for sympathy seems to be to point out that, in stating to the world that Mr. Corrigan was an unmarried man (for that construction is the foundation of their liability), they in fact stated that which was false. From a business point of view no doubt it may pay them not to spend time or money in making inquiries, or verifying statements before publication; but if they had not made a false statement they would not now be suffering in damages. They are paying a price for their methods of business.

Appeal dismissed.

NOTES

1. How does this case differ from *Hulton* v. *Jones*? Should the two different situations be treated differently, as suggested by Greer L.J. in dissent?

2. Professor Fleming has summarized the law regarding fault in this area as follows: "There is no liability for intentionally defamatory matter published accidentally, but there is for accidentally defamatory matter published intentionally." *Law of Torts* (5th ed., 1977), p. 543. Does this distinction make any sense at all?

3. What do you think about Professor Weiler's comments in "Defamation, Enterprise Liability and Freedom of Speech" (1967), 17 U. of T.L.J. 278, at p. 285:

"If any distinction, for purposes of fault as opposed to strict liability, is possible in this area, it should be between those statements which are defamatory of the plaintiff on their face, and those which are innocent on their face and defamatory only by reason of extrinsic facts that are not reasonably knowable to the defendant. Such a distinction is the present basis of the developing doctrine of libel per quod in the United States. This doctrine limits the incidence of liability for libellous statements innocent on their face by requiring the proof of 'special' damages as a condition of liability. Although this is an indirect and rather irrational way of achieving the result of a lesser incidence of defamatory liability (and perhaps justified only in terms of a somewhat misconceived deference for precedent), there is a real basis in fact to the distinction. Those statements which are defamatory on their face (and for which liability depends on their truth) can be seen by the defendant 'publisher' to be a dangerous and harmful instrumentality as far as the plaintiff's reputation is concerned. It may not be unfair to require the defendant, who can fairly know the risk he is running, to bear the responsibility for the harm he causes if his (reasonable) belief that the statement is true proves unfounded. This is of course subject to the caveat that the issue of fault regarding the truth of the statement will become privileged if the interests of the parties concerned make it imperative that the statement be made (and thus the occasion becomes privileged). On the other hand, with regard to statements which are innocent on their face, the defendant is in no position to decide whether he will run the risks in making the particular statement, if it should prove to be untrue. Surely we ought not to be required to run this risk as to all statements we make, however innocent they seem, and thus another rationale must be found for strict liability."

The American legal commentators have not been silent on this subject and alternative doctrines have been suggested and occasionally accepted by their courts. See Prosser, "Libel Per Quod" (1960), 46 Va. L. Rev. 389; Eldredge, "The Spurious Rule of Libel Per Quod" (1966), 79 Harv. L. Rev. 733; Prosser, "More Libel Per Quod", *ibid.*, at p. 1629.

VIZETELLY v. MUDIE'S SELECT LIBRARY

Court of Appeal. [1900] 2 Q.B. 170; 69 L.J.Q.B. 645; 16 T.L.R. 352

A book published in October, 1898, by Messrs. Archibald Constable & Co., called *Emin Pasha: his Life and Work,* contained a passage defamatory of the plaintiff. The latter brought action against the publishers for libel which action was settled by the publishers paying 100*l.* damages, apologizing and undertaking to withdraw the libel from circulation. In the issue of the Publishers' Circular for November 12, 1898, the publishers inserted a notice requesting that all copies of "The Life and Work of Emin Pasha" be returned immediately as they wished to cancel a page and insert another in its place. A similar note appeared on the same date in the *Athenaeum* newspaper.

In March, 1899, it came to plaintiff's knowledge that defendants, proprietors of a circulating library, were lending copies of the book as originally published and selling surplus copies. The plaintiff brought action for libel against defendants.

At the trial it appeared that no one in defendants' business had seen the notices which the publishers had circulated although defendants took both papers in which the notices appeared. A managing director of defendants testified that it was impossible for defendants to have all books that they circulated read. On cross-examination he said there was no one other than himself and his co-directors who exercised any supervision over the books; they did not employ a reader and although on one or two occasions they had books which contained a libel they had never before been subject to an action; it was cheaper for them to run an occasional risk of an action than to have a reader.

Grantham, J., in summing up directed the jury to consider whether, having regard to the evidence, the defendants had used due care in the management of their business. The jury found a verdict for plaintiff, damages 100*l.* The defendants appealed.

Romer L.J.: The law of libel is in some respects a very hard one. In the remarks which I am about to make I propose to deal only with communications which are not privileged. For many years it has been well settled law that a man who publishes a libel is liable to an action, although he is really innocent in the matter, and guilty of no negligence. That rule has been so long established as to be incapable of being altered or modified, and the Courts, in endeavouring to mitigate the hardship resulting from it in many cases, have only been able to do so by holding that, under the circumstances of cases before them, there had been no publication of the libel by the defendant. The result, in my opinion, has been that the decisions on the subject have not been altogether logical or satisfactory on principle. The decisions in some of the earlier cases with which the Courts had to deal are easy to understand. Those were cases in which mere carriers of documents containing libels, who had nothing to do with and were ignorant of the contents of what they carried, have been held not to have published libels. Then we have the case of *Emmens* v. *Pottle,* in which vendors of newspapers in the ordinary course of their business sold a newspaper which contained libel was prima facie a publication of it, but the Court there held that there was no publication of the libel under the circumstances which appeared from the special findings of the jury, those findings being (1.) that the defendants did not know that the newspapers at the time they sold them contained libels on the plaintiff; (2.) that it was not by negligence on the defendants' part that they did not know that there was any libel in the newspapers; and (3.) that the defendants did not know that the newspaper was of such a character that it was likely to contain libellous matter, nor ought they to have known so. Lord Esher M.R. in this Court was of opinion that, though the vendors of the newspapers, when they

sold them, were prima facie publishers of the libel, yet, when the special findings
of the jury were looked at, the result was that there was no publication of the
libel by the defendants. Bowen L.J. put his judgment on the ground that the
vendors of the newspapers in that case were really only in the same position as
an ordinary carrier of work containing a libel. The decision in that case, in my
opinion, worked substantial justice; but, speaking for myself, I cannot say that
the way in which that result was arrived at appears to me altogether satisfactory;
I do not think that the judgments very clearly indicate on what principle Courts
ought to act in dealing with similar cases in future. That case was followed by
other cases, more or less similar to it, namely, *Ridgway* v. *Smith & Son, Mallon*
v. *W.W. Smith & Son,* and *Martin* v. *Trustees of the British Museum.* The result
of the cases is I think that, as regards a person who is not the printer or the first
or main publisher of a work which contains a libel, but has only taken, what I
may call, a subordinate part in disseminating it, in considering whether there has
been publication of it by him, the particular circumstances under which he
disseminated the work must be considered. If he did it in the ordinary way of
his business, the nature of the business and the way in which it was conducted
must be looked at; and, if he succeeds in shewing (1.) that he was innocent of
any knowledge of the libel contained in the work disseminated by him, (2.) that
there was nothing in the work or the circumstances under which it came to him
or was disseminated by him which ought to have led him to suppose that it contained a libel, and (3.) that, when the work was disseminated by him, it was not
by any negligence on his part that he did not know that it contained the libel,
then, although the dissemination of the work by him was prima facie publication
of it, he may nevertheless, on proof of the before-mentioned facts, be held not
to have published it. But the onus of proving such facts lies on him, and the
question of publication or non-publication is in such a case one for the jury.
Applying this view of the law to the present case, it appears to me that the jury,
looking at all the circumstances of the case, have in effect found that the
defendants published the libel complained of, and therefore the defendants are
liable, unless that verdict is disturbed. Looking at the special circumstances of
the case which were brought to the attention of the jury, I cannot say that they
could not reasonably find as they did. The only remaining question is whether
the summing-up and direction of the learned judge were such as would justify us
in sending down the case for a new trial. I find no misdirection in point of law,
and though, with great respect to the learned judge, I do not think that all he
said was correct, or justified by the evidence, the jury had the facts fully put
before them, and on the whole I do not think that there was anything in the
summing-up which caused the jury to come to an erroneous conclusion, or
which would justify us in granting a new trial. For these reasons I think the
application must be dismissed.

Application dismissed.

NOTES

1. Does this case make sense to you? Why treat libraries differently than
newspapers or book publishers?

2. In *Bottomley* v. *F.W. Woolworth & Co. Ltd.* (1932), 48 T.L.R. 521
(C.A.), defendant sold large quantities of an American magazine called *Detective
Story Magazine,* which contained material defamatory of the plaintiff. The action
was dismissed at trial and on appeal Scrutton L.J. relying on *Vizetelly* stated:
"There was no evidence to justify the jury's finding that there was anything in
the magazine which ought to have led the defendants to suppose that it contained
libel."

3. In *Balabanoff* v. *Fossani* (1948), 81 N.Y.S. 2d 732, the court stated: "It is

a good defense to a libel action for a vendor or distributor of a newspaper or other periodical to show that he had no knowledge of the libelous matter and that there were no extraneous facts which should have put him on guard. Such vendor or distributor is liable, however, if he had knowledge that the newspaper or periodical contained libelous matter."

4. How should local radio or T.V. stations be treated when they merely broadcast what is supplied to them by national networks without checking the material? What if they rent their facilities to someone who defames the plaintiff? See *Kelly* v. *Hoffman* (1948), 61 Atl. 2d 143, where Burling J. stated:

"The defendant-respondent as a radio broadcasting company which leased its facilities is not liable for a defamatory statement during a radio broadcast by the person hired by the lessees and not in the employ of the radio broadcasting company, the words being carried to the radio listeners by its facilities, if it could not have prevented publication by the exercise of reasonable care."

Wachenfeld J. dissented and explained:

"The defamation when transmitted by radio cannot effectively be eradicated by retraction or any other procedure. The utterance once made, the damage ensues. It could not have been made except for the use of the facilities and the equipment owned, maintained and provided by the broadcasting company. Its responsibility to the party injured should be definite, clear and absolute."

See also *Summit Hotel Co.* v. *N.B.C.* (1939), 8 Atl. 2d 302 (Pa.).

5. Some relief has been afforded the media for publishing defamatory material in error. The Ontario Libel and Slander Act, R.S.O. 1970, c. 243, s. 5(2), for example, allows recovery only of "actual damages" if an alleged libel was "published in good faith", that it "took place in mistake or misapprehension of the facts" and a "full and fair retraction" is published immediately. Pursuant to s. 9, newspapers and broadcasters may also plead in mitigation of damage that the libel was done "without actual malice and without gross negligence" and that a "full apology" was made "at the earliest opportunity".

6. As to defamation by a telegraph company, see *Dominion Telegraph Co.* v. *Silver* (1882), 10 S.C.R. 238; *Kahn* v. *Gt. Northwestern Telegraph Co.* (1930), 39 O.W.N. 11 and 143. See Smith, "Liability of a Telegraph Company for Transmitting a Defamatory Message" (1920), 20 Colum. L. Rev. 30, 369; also 29 Mich. L. Rev. 339.

7. In *Allan* v. *Bushnell T.V. Co. Ltd.* (1969), 4 D.L.R. (3d) 212, the Ontario Court of Appeal ruled that, in the absence of any relationship analogous to that of principal and agent, a television station is not bound by the malice or gross negligence of a news agency that supplies the station with reports.

E. DEFENCES

1. Truth

FLEMING, THE LAW OF TORTS
(5th ed., 1977), p. 544

At common law, truth is a complete answer to a civil action for defamation and the only defence known by the name of "justification". Actionable defamation consists in a *false* statement impairing another's reputation. "The law will not permit a man to recover damages in respect of an injury to a character which he either does not, *or ought not,* to possess." This is an expression of policy rather than a corollary of the principle that the gist of the civil action is compensation for damage suffered, for the latter leaves open whether the law protects security of an existing or only of a deserved reputation. In contrast, the criminal law of libel, as formulated by the Star Chamber with the object of preventing breaches of the peace, directed its attention to the insult offered, and it was therefore no defence to a prosecution either that publication was to the person defamed or that the allegations were true. For, "as the woman said, she would never grieve to have been told of her red nose if she had not one indeed." This was epitomized in the saying, attributed to Lord Mansfield, "The greater the truth, the greater the libel."

Truth is a matter of defence or, alternatively expressed, the falsity of defamation is presumed until dispelled by the defendant. Casting the burden on him rather than the plaintiff has the effect, if not the purpose, of inhibiting defamatory speech. For in practice, it acts not only as a serious deterrent against dissemination of falsehoods but, in view of the difficulties of adducing legal proof of truth in all factual particulars, constitutes also a powerful brake on public debate by underscoring the wisdom of caution and self-censorship.

. . .

What is Justification
Justification must be as broad as the defamatory imputation itself. The defendant must prove the truth of all material statements contained in the libel; there must be a substantial justification of the whole. A charge that the plaintiff is an habitual liar can only be justified by proof than on repeated occasions he made false statements without an honest belief in their truth. An allegation that the plaintiff was convicted of a crime cannot be proved true by showing that he was convicted, though the conviction was quashed. Yet it is sufficient that the statement is true in substance. Justification need not conform to the exact letter of the accusation, provided the gist of it is proved to be correct: it must 'meet the sting' of the libel. Erroneous details which do not aggravate the defamatory allegation may be ignored. Thus to say of someone that he has been convicted of travelling in a train without a ticket and fined £9 with 3 weeks' imprisonment in default may be justified by establishing that he was sentenced to 2 weeks' imprisonment in default. But if the defamation consists of several distinct allegations, all must be justified *seriatim,* and if the defendant fails in regard to any of them, he will be entitled to a verdict and costs, although the unproved charge could have caused no appreciable damage in view of the truth of the rest. Hence, where the plaintiff was described as a blackmailer, liar, and swindling sharepusher and was alleged to have entered the country illegally, the defendant was held liable in the amount of £50, because he was unable to prove the last, and relatively least infamous, of the charges. With a view to encouraging a less literal interpretation, England, New South Wales, Tasmania and New Zealand have enacted that the defence of justification shall not fail merely because every charged is not proved true, if the untrue elements do not materially injure the plaintiff's reputation, having regard to the truth of the remaining charges.

Repetition of a libel cannot be justified merely by proving that it was a true report of what was said by someone else: otherwise too glib an excuse would be at hand for perpetuating and spreading calumnies under the facile guise of cautioning that 'it is rumoured' or 'I was told'. Not even expressions of doubt or disbelief furnish excuse, though the unqualified contradiction of a rumour may be immune if its defamatory sting is thereby drawn. Again, with respect to such common news item as that a prosecution has been launched against the plaintiff or that the police are inquiring into his affairs, the threshold question must be whether it was reasonably capable of being understood as nothing but a factual report that a charge was made (and implying at worst that there were grounds for suspicion) or of actually suggesting guilt. The former may be justified for all practical purposes by simply establishing the accuracy of the report, but the latter demands nothing less than proof of guilt in order to meet the sinister slant implanted into the story. This important distinction at once allows sufficient latitude for fearless reporting of 'straight news', while exacting a toll from the less responsible press for the luxury of pregnant headlines and sensational embellishments.

If a defendant seeks to justify all the defamatory matters, and these consist partly of statements of fact and partly of comment, he must under that plea prove not only the truth of the facts but also the comment. Not that he would assume the higher burden of seeking to justify comment as being true, unless the defence of fair comment were precluded, e.g. because the comment was inspired by malice. But how can statements of *opinion* ever be proved true? Literally this is of course impossible, but the defendant apparently acquits himself by establishing that the comment is "accurate, i.e. actually justified by, in the sense of being implicit in, the facts which are stated and proved to be true." In other words, the facts must warrant the imputation, and they do not, unless the jury agree with the defendant that it is a conclusion which *ought* to be drawn from those facts.

NOTES

1. The Ontario Libel and Slander Act, R.S.O. 1970, c. 243, s. 23 reads: "In an action for libel or slander for words containing two or more distinct charges against the plaintiff, a defence of justification shall not fail by reason only that the truth of every charge is not proved if the words not proved to be true do not materially injure the plaintiff's reputation having regard to the truth of the remaining charges."

2. Absolute Privilege

On grounds of public policy, the common law has recognized that certain occasions require that an absolute privilege be granted to participants so that they may speak freely without fear of any liability for defamation. In many jurisdictions the legislature has enshrined these immunities in legislation.

The doctrine of absolute privilege is justified on the ground that there are occasions when society is best served by individuals speaking and writing without restraint, even at the expense of another's reputation and good name. Because of the potential for abuse of such blanket privileges, the law has been loathe to permit reliance on them and has interpreted their scope narrowly.

(a) *Judicial Proceedings*

An absolute privilege to speak and write without legal liability for defamation flows to judges, juries, witnesses, and parties while participating in judicial proceedings. This is because ". . . the law takes the risk of their abusing the occasion and speaking maliciously as well as untruly . . . in order that their duties may be carried on freely and without fear of any action being brought against them . . .". (*More* v. *Weaver,* [1928] 2 K.B. 520 (C.A.).)

A witness's testimony is absolutely privileged, however, only if it is relevant to the issues before the bar. Although relevance has been interpreted rather expansively lest a witness withhold evidence out of fear of uttering defamatory words, if, in an aside, he says "Have you heard that Jones has run off with Mrs. Brown", that statement will not be privileged. See *More* v. *Weaver, supra.* Communications made within the solicitor and client relationship are absolutely privileged, provided they are reasonably related to the preparation of a case for trial, on the ground that a solicitor must have full disclosure of all the facts within the client's knowledge. *Watson* v. *M'Ewan,* [1905] A.C. 480; *Nixon* v. *O'Callaghan* (1927), 60 O.L.R. 76. But *cf. Minter* v. *Priest,* [1930] A.C. 558.

A statutory board or tribunal which has "similar attributes" to a court is included within the absolute privilege. *Royal Aquarium* v. *Parkinson,* [1892] 1

Q.B. 431 (C.A.). Thus, a hearing before the Ontario Workmen's Compensation Board was held to be a judicial proceeding within the meaning of the rule (*Halls* v. *Mitchell,* [1928] S.C.R. 125), while a petition to a board of licence commissioners regarding a licence application was not (*Willcocks* v. *Howell* (1884), 5 O.R. 360). In *O'Connor* v. *Waldron,* [1935] A.C. 76, the Privy Council held that an inquiry under the Combines Investigation Act of Canada is not an absolutely privileged occasion as it is not a "judicial" proceeding. "The question . . . in every case is whether the tribunal in question has similar attributes to a court of justice or acts in a manner similar to that in which such courts act." Apparently, the fact that the inquiry determined "no rights, nor the guilt or innocence of anyone" was considered as determinative, even though it might have the powers of a court regarding summoning witnesses and administering oaths, etc. See also *Perry* v. *Heatherington* (1972), 24 D.L.R. (3d) 127 (B.C.); *Duquette* v. *Belanger* (1973), 38 D.L.R. (3d) 613 (Fed. Ct.).

This absolute privilege extends to the reporting of judicial proceedings. The Libel and Slander Act, R.S.O. 1970, c. 243, s. 4, states that, "A fair and accurate report without comment in a newspaper or in a broadcast of proceedings publicly heard before a court of justice, if published in the newspaper or broadcast contemporaneously with such proceedings, is absolutely privileged unless the defendant has refused or neglected to insert in the newspaper in which the report complained of appeared or to broadcast, as the case may be, a reasonable statement of explanation or contradiction by or on behalf of the plaintiff".

This privilege, however, does not cover reports of pleadings filed in law suits. In *The Gazette Printing Company* v. *Shallow* (1909), 41 S.C.R. 339, plaintiff sued defendant, newspaper publishers, for a libel contained in certain pleadings filed in the course of an action instituted in the Superior Court of Quebec, and published in defendant's newspaper. The defendant claimed the publication was privileged within the rule governing the fair report of judicial proceedings. The Supreme Court of Canada held the publication was not made under any privilege and the reasons for subjecting the interests of individuals to the public interest in the administration of justice, which found expression in the privilege to report public judicial proceedings, did not extend to preliminary statements formulated by the parties themselves, and upon which no judicial action has been, or may ever be, taken. "It is obviously undesirable that, by the simple expedient of commencing an action and filing a claim, anybody should be able to secure to himself the protection of the law in the dissemination of the most outrageous libel."

(b) *Parliamentary Proceedings*

In order to foster frank and vigorous debate in our democratic institutions, an absolute privilege surrounds all statements by Members of Parliament made on the floor of the House of Commons in the exercise of their duties.

Reports of these debates are also protected but to a lesser extent. The Libel and Slander Act, R.S.O. 1970, c. 243, s. 3(1), provides that 'A fair and accurate report in an newspaper or in a broadcast or . . . proceedings . . . open to the public . . ." of any legislative or administrative body or any commission of inquiry in the British Commonwealth "is privileged, unless it is proved that the publication thereof was made maliciously".

It appears that only a qualified privilege attaches to statements by members of lesser legislative bodies, including local city councils. See *Royal Aquarium* v. *Parkinson, supra.*

There is considerable controversy whether absolute privilege protects communications between senior members of the executive arm of government. Although it appears that such a privilege protects Ministers of the Crown (*Chatterton* v. *Secretary of State for India*, [1895] 2 Q.B. 189 (C.A.)), it is not clear how far down the chain it extends (*Isaacs (M.) & Sons Ltd.* v. *Cook*, [1925] 2 K.B. 391; *Jackson* v. *Mcgrath* (1947), 75 C.L.R. 293). See generally Becht, "The Absolute Privilege of the Executive in Defamation" (1962), 15 Vand. L. Rev. 1127. See also Veeder, "Absolute Immunity in Defamation: Legislative and Executive Proceedings" (1910), 10 Colum. L. Rev. 131.

(c) *Other*

The common law protects communication between husband and wife with an absolute immunity. Whether this proposition is supported on the technical grounds of want of publication, because of the fiction that the husband and wife are one person, or on grounds of social policy, the rule is well embedded in the law and reflects a healthy respect for the sanctity of confidentiality in the marital relationship.

The common law flounders in confusion and the legislature hesitates to decide whether an absolute immunity attaches to members of the army, police, and national security agencies for their secret and less than secret reports about their own members and other individuals. See Fleming, *The Law of Torts* (5th ed., 1977), p. 553.

If the plaintiff consents to the publication of defamatory material about himself, he will be barred from recovery. See *Jones* v. *Brooks,* [1974] 2 W.W.R. 729, 45 D.L.R. (3d) 413 (Sask.). This defence, however, is narrowly construed and must be given for each publication separately. Thus if someone agrees to discuss on a radio programme certain information that is defamatory of himself, he does not thereby consent to defamatory comment on the programme afterwards. See *Syms* v. *Warren* (1976), 71 D.L.R. (3d) 558 (Man. Q.B.).

3. Qualified Privilege

Qualified privilege is a partial immunity that attaches to certain occasions. Thus, communications that pertain to the legitimate purpose of the occasion, made without malice, are excused from liability for defamation.

Qualified privilege usually arises "where the person who makes [the] communication has an interest or a duty, legal, social or moral, to make it to the person to whom it is made, and the person to whom it is so made has a corresponding interest or duty to receive it". See *Adam* v. *Ward*, [1917] A.C. 309, at p. 334, *per* Lord Atkinson.

Another general description is that a publication is privileged when it is "fairly made by a person in the discharge of a public or private duty, whether legal or moral, or in the conduct of his own affairs, in matters where his interest is concerned". See *Toogood* v. *Spyring* (1834), 149 E.R. 1044, *per* Baron Parke.

There are several broad areas of qualified privilege:

(a) *Protection of One's Own Interest*

SUN LIFE ASSURANCE COMPANY OF CANADA ET AL. v. DALRYMPLE

Supreme Court of Canada. [1965] S.C.R. 302, 50 D.L.R. (2d) 217

Spence J.: This is an appeal from the judgment of the Court of Appeal for Ontario pronounced on November 5, 1964, on an appeal from the judgment of Richardson J. at trial dismissing the plaintiff's action.

This is an action against the Sun Life Assurance Company of Canada and three employees thereof, W.G. Attridge, the director of agencies, and A.G. Dennis and Blythe Moore, two supervisors of agencies, for damages for alleged slander uttered by the three employees on the 13th, 14th and 15th of January 1960 in the course of their duties for their employer.

At the close of the plaintiff's evidence at the trial, the defendant moved to dismiss the action on the ground that the alleged slanders were uttered on an occasion of privilege and that there was no evidence of express malice. After a very lengthy argument, the trial judge held that the alleged slanders were uttered on occasions of qualified privilege and that the plaintiff had failed to adduce sufficient evidence of express malice to justify sending the case to the jury.

The Court of Appeal for Ontario in an oral judgment given at the close of the argument, presumed without deciding that the trial judge had been correct in holding that the occasions were occasions of qualified privilege but differed with the trial judge in holding that there was both extrinsic and intrinsic evidence of express malice giving a sufficient probability to warrant the question of malice or not being put to the jury. The defendants appealed to this Court.

Considerable argument in this Court was concerned with the question of whether the alleged slanders were or were not spoken on occasions of qualified privilege. The occasion advanced by counsel for the appellant was that the individual defendants as company officers were concerned with what they believed to be a wholesale resignation of agents in the Peterborough branch territory including the district offices in Peterborough, Trenton and Oshawa. That situation was one with which they could validly be concerned as it was said in evidence that a very large sum of money must be expended to establish a branch agency of the company and train the agents. Statements which are fairly made by a person in the conduct of his own affairs in matters where his own interest is concerned are *prima facie* privileged: *Toogood* v. *Spyring,* at p. 193; *Halls* v. *Mitchell, per* Duff J. at p. 132; Gatley on Libel and Slander, 5th ed., p. 253.

. . .

There is a further grave question whether the statements made by the three individual defendants were so irrelevant to the proper protection of their employer's interest that the privilege was lost. Certainly, statements irrelevant to protecting the interests will result in loss of privilege: *Adam* v. *Ward, per* Lord Loreburn, at pp. 320-1, Lord Dunedin, pp. 326-7, and Gatley, *op. cit.,* pp. 267ff.

Were the comments irrelevant? The comments may be generally described as being an attempt to show to the agents that their loyalty to the plaintiff was one not justified in their own interests. The defendants Dennis and Moore attempted this by saying to the agents that this man whom they admired so much was one who had previously made a threat to resign and that then he had waited until his pension had vested so that he would suffer no financial loss upon his resignation, while they, on the other hand, having had much shorter employment, would, if they resigned, have no benefit from vested pensions and that in addition the plaintiff was a troublemaker not only within the company but in dealing with others outside the company. It might well be that if these comments were justified in evidence given by the defendants, or reasonable grounds for them found, these comments would not be irrelevant to the attempt to retain the agents in the service of the company. The agents' loyalty to the plaintiff was certainly a very moving factor. It was not the sole factor. The loyalty was inspired in a very material fashion by the plaintiff's resolute insistence of non-interference with the opportunity for profit in the Peterborough branch and that, of course, was to the pecuniary advantage of the agents as well as the plaintiff. It was argued that these defendants coming to the Peterborough branch territory with the purpose of retaining in the organization the agents then on staff, could have carried out that purpose by assuring the staff proper co-operation of head office and the appointment of a new manager who would work for the interest of the company and of those agents. This argument, how-ever, is not convincing. As I say, it was the loyalty of the agents to the manager who had just resigned which was the matter of prime importance and unless that loyalty were broken it would seem of little use to make rosy prophesies of what his successor would do.

I am, in summary, of the view that the alleged slanders were all uttered on occasions of qualified privilege. However, it would seem that the Court of Appeal were, with respect, correct in their view that there was both extrinsic and intrinsic evidence of malice.

"Malice" of course does not necessarily mean personal spite or ill-will; it may consist of some indirect motive not connected with the privilege: . . . .

Firstly, it must be determined what evidence of malice is sufficient to go to the jury. Whether the defendant was actuated by malice is, of course, a question of fact for the jury but whether there is any evidence of malice fit to be left to the jury is a question of law for the judge to determine. . . . .

Although upon an occasion held to be one of qualified privilege the court will not look too narrowly on the language used in the alleged slander, ... the slander if utterly beyond and disproportionate to the facts may provide evidence of express malice: . . . .

Moreover, as Lord Porter pointed out in the judgment quoted and adopted by Cartwright J. in *Jerome* v. *Anderson, supra,* at p. 299, one piece of evidence tending to establish malice is sufficient evidence on which a jury could find for the plaintiff and therefore if more than a mere scintilla, it should be submitted to the jury for its finding of fact.

Express malice must be found against each one of the three defendants: *Egger* v. *Viscount Chelmsford et al.,* per Lord Denning M.R., at p. 412:

> "It is a mistake to suppose that, on a joint publication, the malice of one defendant infects his co-defendant. Each defendant is answerable severally, as well as jointly, for the joint publication: and each is entitled to his several defence, whether he be sued jointly or separately from the others. If the plaintiff seeks to rely on malice to aggravate damages, or to rebut a defence of qualified privilege, or to cause a comment, otherwise fair, to become un-fair, then he must prove malice against each person whom he charges with it. A defendant is only affected by express malice if he himself was actuated by it: or if his servant or agent concerned in the publication was actuated by malice in the course of his employment."

Of course, the express malice which actuated any of the three individual defen-dants will make the corporate defendant liable since the statement was made by the employee in the course of his employer's business.

The Court of Appeal for Ontario in its judgment said, in part:

> "Because as a result of this unanimous view, there must, in the opinion of this Court, be a new trial, we refrain from more specific comment on the evidence so that the matter may in fairness to both parties be left at large for disposition in the new trial."

I have come to the conclusion, with respect, that such a course is a proper one under the circumstances and, therefore, I shall only state that I am convinced that there is both extrinsic and intrinsic evidence of express malice on the part of each of the three individual defendants. . . .

For these reasons, I would dismiss the appeal with costs.

NOTES

1. A qualified privilege attaches to statements made in defence of one's own interests, both economic and personal. One is entitled, therefore, to defend oneself against attacks on his own character. One is also permitted to protect the financial interests of his employer, for presumably one has a personal stake in his employer's well-being. See *Penton* v. *Calwell* (1945), 70 C.L.R. 219.

2. The privilege is limited to information that is reasonably related to a refutation of the original attack. See *Loveday* v. *Sun Newspaper* (1958), 59 C.L.R. 503. As in self-defence, one cannot abuse the occasion of an attack to completely destroy another person's reputation. See *Douglas* v. *Tucker,* [1952] 1 D.L.R. 657. Some latitude is allowed, however, so that if a third person's character is besmirched incidentally, in the defence of one's own reputation, the privilege is still available to the publisher. See *Loveday* v. *Sun Newspaper, supra; Mowlds* v. *Fergusson* (1940), 64 C.L.R. 206.

3. The privilege protects the communication as long as it is made only to those who have an interest or duty to receive it, but the law has not "restricted the right . . . within any narrow limits". See *Adam* v. *Ward,* [1917] A.C. 309, (C.A.), at p. 328.

4. In *Pleau* v. *Simpson-Sears Ltd.* (1976), 2 C.C.L.T. 28 (Ont. C.A.), the plaintiff's wallet was stolen and, shortly thereafter, forged cheques began appearing in his name. The defendant posted notices to its employees near the cash registers, which were visible to customers, to detain Pleau and call security if he presented a cheque. A friend of the plaintiff saw one of these notices and told the plaintiff, who sued. The action was dismissed by a jury and this was affirmed on appeal. Evans J.A. said:

"As to privilege, there is no doubt on the facts that there was a reciprocity of interest between the management of the defendant company and its employees to safeguard the defendant against loss from the passing of cheques bearing the forged name of the plaintiff. The defendant company had an interest to protect, an interest which would be sterile without a consequential interest to pass on to its employees the complaint received from the police."

As to the abuse of privilege Lacourciere J.A. observed:

"In my view, the only question in this appeal is whether the publication complained of went beyond the exigencies of the privileged occasion so as to constitute 'publicity incommensurate to the occasion' . . . .

. . . publication of the impugned notice on a large placard exposed to public view would undoubtedly have removed the qualified privilege of the occasion. One can think of many such excesses. But this was not the case: the photographs exhibited indicate a typewritten slip attached to a cash register, obviously for the private information of the cashier. The notices were of reasonable size, unlikely to attract the public's attention. It was not an uncommon practice, as appears from the evidence of the operating superintendent of the store. . . .

While the burden was on the respondent company in the first instance to establish the existence of a qualified privilege for the publication, once established, the burden was on the appellant as plaintiff to prove that it had been abused by excessive publication (Prosser, Law of Torts, 3rd. ed. (1964), p. 823). I am of opinion that the number and size of the notices and their location on the cash registers were reasonable in the circumstances and did not exceed the privilege of the occasion. While the respondent company would have no interest in publishing the notice to the public at large, it would seem to me that it adopted a reasonable and appropriate mode of publication to reach its large, changing staff of cashiers: the visibility of the notices to some members of the public at a limited number of cash registers constituted, at the most, a publication necessarily incidental to the protected publication to the staff."

Brooke J.A. dissented and remarked:

"Perhaps the notice was a convenient way to remind its staff, but one wonders why a list to be consulted before cheques were accepted would not have been just as convenient, and assure some privacy to the individual concerned. The communication was not restricted by this method of publication to staff alone, but was, on the contrary, publicly displayed and a notice to all who looked at it in a place where so many were intended to look when they purchased goods in this large store, or likely to look when simply passing by the area of the cash register. The evidence was that some 800 customers a day made their way through the store. There is, of course, the added dimension that the occasion was really a continuing one. This was a continuing publication in the sense that, unlike a letter to an individual or words spoken privately but overheard, it was a notice continuously displayed in 37 locations in this busy place.

The rule is that if the occasion is privileged the communication may be protected. An occasion of the publication of words found to be defamatory of the plaintiff may be privileged if the publication was made as a result of a private or public duty or made in the conduct of one's own affairs: *Adam* v. *Ward*, [1917] A.C. 309, and *Toogood* v. *Spyring* (1834), 1 Cr.M. & R. 181, 149 E.R. 1044 at 1048. But to be privileged the communication is one that is made to another to whom there is a duty to publish or who has an interest in receiving the communication.

. . .

I have no doubt that the defendant acted honestly and in the conduct of its own affairs in passing important information to its employees. In addition, the communication by the defendant to its employees of this information was justified as a public duty in response to the request of the police to assist them in catching a thief. But on neither ground was there justification to publish the information in a manner which amounted to publication to any member of the public who might attend at the store and pass in the vicinity of the cash register, nor could this publication to the public be considered as necessary, incidental to, or reasonably necessary to the publication to staff. The members of the public who went to the store had no interest in the information that was of such a character that would make it a matter of common convenience for the welfare of society that the communication to them should be protected at the cost of the plaintiff's reputation."

Which side do you prefer? Would you have sued if you were Pleau? What do you think motivated Pleau to bring this action?

5. On the question of the onus of proof of malice, see also *Netupsky* v. *Craig* (1972), 28 D.L.R. (3d) 742 (S.C.C.), onus on plaintiff.

(b) *Common Interest or Mutual Concern*

BEREMAN v. POWER PUBLISHING CO.

Supreme Court of Colorado. (1933), 2 P. 2d 749

Butler Justice: E.W. Bereman sued The Power Publishing Company, a corporation, Earl Hoage, C.A. Magnuson, Casey's Superior Laundry Company, a corporation, and Sam J. Kortz for damages for an alleged libel. The court nonsuited him and rendered judgment dismissing the action. He seeks a reversal of that judgment.

The alleged libel was published in the Colorado Labor Advocate, the offical publication of the Colorado State Federation of Labor and other labor organizations. . . .

[The article accused plaintiff, and two other members of the Laundry Drivers Union, of having turned traitor to the Union by leaving the only union laundry in the city and taking employment with a non-union one; and further, with soliciting former customers without advising them that they were working for a non-union laundry. The tone and temper of the article are represented by the statement: "These three labor spies have sold their manhood, if they ever possessed any, for a paltry few dollars."]

The trial court held that the publication was qualifiedly privileged. We are in accord with that holding. The article complained of appeared in the official publication of the labor organizations. The Labor Advocate is published weekly in the interests of organized labor, to keep union members informed concerning matters affecting their interests. The publishers of the article and those to whom it was addressed had a common interest in the matters to which it related. The article, therefore, was qualifiedly privileged. . . .

The law on this branch of the case is settled in this state. In *Melcher* v. *Beeler,* . . . we said at page 241 of 48 Colo., 110 P. 181, 184; ". . . A communication made bona fide upon any subject-matter in which the party communicating has an interest, or in reference to which he has a duty, is privileged, if made to a person having a corresponding interest or duty, although it contains incriminatory matter, which, without this privilege, would be slanderous and actionable; and this, though the duty be not a legal one, but only a moral or social duty of imperfect application [obligation] ."

The communication being qualifiedly privileged, no right of action arose unless the publishers were actuated by express malice, and the burden of proving express malice was on the plaintiff. The presumption is that the communication was made in good faith and without malice. . . .

In considering the extent of the publication in the present case, we must bear in mind the nature of the Colorado Labor Advocate and of the communication published therein.

The very life of labor unions depends upon the loyalty of their members. Unions have the power and the right to expel disloyal members, and before the trial that power and right were exercised in this very case. Nothing could be of greater practical interest to labor union members than information concerning acts of disloyalty. It is necessary that they be informed thereof in some manner in order that they may protect themselves against conduct injurious to the cause of organized labor and that, if not exposed, might tend to disrupt a union. Due to the number of labor unions and the large number of their members, it is impracticable to send sealed communications to all. Obviously, it was necessary to adopt some other method of communicating information of interest to organized labor. The Labor Advocate was established to furnish that information. It is not a newspaper of general circulation, its circulation being confined almost exclusively to members of labor unions.

That communications published in papers devoted to particular organizations are not to be treated the same as communications in newspapers of general circulation, is attested by the authorities. Thus, in *Redgate* v. *Roush,* 61 Kan. 480, 59 P. 1050, it was held, quoting from the syllabus: "Where the officers of a church, upon inquiry, find that their pastor is unworthy and unfit for his office, and thereupon, in the performance of what they honestly believe to be their duty towards other members and churches of the same denomination, publish, in good faith, in the church papers, the result of their inquiry, and there is a reasonable occasion for such publication, it will be deemed to be privileged and protected under the law. Where the publication appears to have been made in good faith, and for the members of the denomination alone, the fact that it incidentally may have been brought to the attention of others than members of the church will not take away its privileged character. In such case, and where the plaintiff seeks damages, it devolves upon him to establish actual malice." . . .

The publication in the present case did not go beyond the reasonable requirements of the occasion. The case presents a situation wholly unlike that in *Bearman* v. *People,* 91 Colo. 486, 16 P.2d 425. There, a communication reflecting on a doctor on a hospital staff was directed to the president of the hospital association, but 10,000 printed copies were delivered or mailed to persons having no connection with or interest in the hospital. . . . The following example illustrates the dividing line between what is permissible and what is not: Where an inquiry is made as to the responsibility of another, an answer properly communicated is qualifiedly privileged. See *Melcher v. Beeler, supra.* But a publication of the answer in a newspaper of general circulation would be an excessive publication, and would deprive the communication of its qualifiedly privileged character.

A communication may lose its qualifiedly privileged character by the use of language of a defamatory nature not warranted by the occasion that called forth the publication. [Citation omitted.] Some of the words in the article in question are in bad taste, no doubt. Less offensive words might have been selected. But we must not overlook the fact that disloyalty to a union is fraught with such possibilities of disaster to the union cause that loyal union members may be excused for referring to it in strong terms of condemnation. The conduct of the plaintiff not unnaturally suggested to the minds of union members such words as "traitor," "spies," and "despicable." Instances are not wanting where disloyalty to secret societies and other organizations, both political and nonpolitical, has been condemned in language not less forceful. The condemnatory words in the article before us were applied to the drivers in connection with the facts stated; they were not intended to apply to the drivers generally or in connection with any other matter. Discussing the question when defamatory words in a communication may be considered as affording, by themselves, evidence of malice, Odgers, in his work on Libel and Slander (5th Ed.), says at page 254: "But the test appears to be this. Take the facts as they appeared to the defendant's mind at the time of publication; are the terms used such as the defendant might have honestly and bona fide employed under the circumstances? If so the judge should stop the case. For if the defendant honestly believed the plaintiff's conduct to be such as he described it, the mere fact that he used strong words in so describing it is no evidence of malice to go to the jury."

In view of all the circumstances, we do not believe that the qualifiedly privileged character of the article in question was lost by reason of the language used.

The action of the trial court in dismissing the suit was right.

The judgment is affirmed.

NOTES

1. This qualified privilege extends to members of a church to discuss church affairs (See *Slocinski v. Radwan* (1929), 144 A. 787), and to members of a lodge, social club or fraternity. (See *Hayden v. Hasbrouck* (1912), 84 A. 1087.) In *Cleagman v. Lord Ellesmere et al.,* [1932] 2 K.B. 431, it was held that because a Jockey Club was obliged to publish notice of the plaintiff's suspension in their own racing periodical, the occasion was privileged. However, several newspapers which had printed the story were not privileged, since there was "no general interest to the public or duty owed to the public to publish matters which concern a section of the public only". But see Libel and Slander Act, R.S.O. 1970, c. 243, s. 3(4).

2. People who share a common business interest may discuss amongst themselves matters of mutual economic concern in a privileged setting. Shareholders, for example, are privileged to exchange information about employees or customers freely without attracting tort liability unless they are malicious. See *Telegraph Newspaper v. Bedford* (1934), 50 C.L.R. 632.

3. Several lawyers, defending actions for different clients being sued by the same plaintiff, regarding the same subject matter, are privileged to exchange

information. See *Spielberg* v. *A. Kuhn & Bros.* (1911), 116 P. 1027. Similarly, creditors of the same debtor have a qualified privilege to consult together in furtherance of their common interest. See *Smith Brothers & Co.* v. *W.C. Agee & Co.* (1912), 59 So. 647.

4. Members of professional associations may discuss matters of joint concern as long as they do so fairly and amongst themselves. See *Thompon* v. *Amos* (1949), A.L.J. 98; *Guise* v. *Kouvelis* (1947), 74 C.L.R. 102. Here, as in the other privileged situations, there must be an interest *both* in the recipient of the information and the disseminator of it.

5. In Britain, there was once recognized a common interest among voters in elections to communicate under the protection of a qualified privilege (see *Braddock* v. *Bevins,* [1948] 1 K.B. 580 (C.A.)), but this has now been abrogated by statute. See Defamation Act, 1952, s. 10 which provides:

"A defamatory statement published by or on behalf of a candidate in any election to a local government authority or to Parliament shall not be deemed to be published on a privileged occasion on the ground that it is material to a question in issue in the election, whether or not the person by whom it is published is qualified to vote at the election."

6. The Canadian law did not recognize such a privilege. In *Bureau* v. *Campbell,* [1928] 3 D.L.R. 907 (Sask. C.A.), Martin, J.A., at p. 931 said: "The contention that a political meeting is a privileged occasion is one which is too broad for consideration. . . . There is no reciprocity of interest between the candidate and the hearers at the public meeting. The candidate and those who speak for him are endeavouring by what they say to procure as many votes as possible, and may very well have a motive for attacking opponents and in making defamatory statements about them: but it cannot be said that there is any duty, legal, social or moral, to make such defamatory statements."

(c) *Moral or Legal Duty to Protect Another's Interest*

WATT v. LONGSDON

Court of Appeal. [1930] 1 K.B. 130; 98 L.J.K.B. 711;
142 L.T. 4; 45 T.L.R. 619

Scrutton L.J.: The Scottish Petroleum Company, which carried on business, amongst other places, in Morocco, had in Casa Blanca, a port in Morocco, a manager named Browne, and a managing director named Watt. The Company had in England a chairman named Singer, who held a very large proportion of shares in the company, and also another director, Longsdon, a young man under thirty years of age. The latter had been in Morocco in business and friendly relations with Watt and Browne, and was a friend of Mrs. Watt, who had nursed him in an illness. The company went into voluntary liquidation in November, 1927, and Longsdon was appointed liquidator. In April, 1928, Mrs. Watt was in England, and her husband in Casa Blanca. It is not clear, and there is no evidence, what the effect of the liquidation had been on the actual employment of Watt and Browne, that is, whether they, or either of them still received a salary. Watt's directorship was, under the Companies Act, in a state of suspended animation. Under these circumstances, Longsdon in England received at the beginning of May from Browne in Casa Blanca a letter stating that Watt had left for Lisbon to look for a job, that he had left a bill for 88*l.* for whisky unpaid, and that he had been for two months in immoral relations with his housemaid who was now publicly raising claims against him for money matters. The woman was described as an old woman, stone deaf, almost blind, and with dyed hair. A number of details were given which Browne said Watt's cook had corroborated. The information was mixed up with an allegation that Watt had been scheming to compromise or seduce Mrs. Browne. The letter concluded: "From a letter shown to me by Mr. Watt, I know how bitterly disappointed Mrs. Watt is, and how very much troubled she is. It would therefore perhaps be better not to show her this letter as it could only increase most terribly her own feelings in regard to her husband. These awful facts might be the cause of a breakdown to her, and I think she has enough to cope with at present. Mr. Singer, however, should perhaps know." On May 5, Longsdon, without making inquiries, sent Browne's letter on to Singer, the chairman of the board of directors. At the trial Watt's counsel put in Longsdon's answer to interrogatory 5 that he believed the statements in the letter to be true. On May 5 Longsdon wrote a long letter to Browne, in which he said that he had long suspected Watt's immorality, but had no proof; that he thought it wicked and cruel that Mrs. Watt, a very old friend of the writer's, should be in the dark when Watt might return to her—did not Browne agree?—that he (Longsdon) would not speak until he had a sworn statement in his possession, "and only with such proof would I speak, for an interferer between husband and wife nearly always comes off the worst." Could Browne get a sworn statement? "It may even be necessary for you to bribe the woman to do such, and if only a matter of a few hundred francs I will pay it and of course the legal expenses." Longsdon's letter describes one of the women who was to make this sworn statement as "a prostitute all her life", a description not contained in Browne's letter. Watt returned to England in May. Without waiting for the sworn statement, on May 12, Longsdon sent the letter to Mrs. Watt. Mr. and Mrs. Watt separated, and Mrs. Watt instituted proceedings for divorce, which apparently are still pending.

　　Mr. Watt then instituted proceedings against Longsdon for libel—namely (1) the publication of Browne's letter to Singer; (2) the publication of the same letter to Mrs. Watt; (3) Longsdon's letter of May 5 to Browne. The claim alleged: "The plaintiff, the defendant, and one E.A. Browne were at all material times in the employment in Morocco of the Scottish Petroleum Company, Ltd., a company now in liquidation, of which one W.M.G. Singer was chairman and had a controlling interest therein," and the defence admitted it: "The facts alleged in paragraph 1 of the statement of claim are admitted." The plaintiff also put in at the trial the defendant's answers to interrogatories that his only information on the subject was derived from Browne's letter, that he made no further inquiries, and that he believed that all the statements in Browne's letter, and in the defendant's letter of May 12 were true. The defendant did not justify but pleaded privilege. The case was tried before Horridge, J., and a jury. The learned judge held that all three publications were privileged, and that there was no evidence of malice fit to be left to the jury. He therefore entered judgment for the defendant. The plaintiff appeals.

　　The learned judge appears to have taken the view that the authorities justify him in holding that if "there is an obvious interest in the person to whom a communication is made which causes him to be a proper recipient of a statement," even if the party making the communication had no moral or social duty to the party to whom the communication is made, the occasion is privileged . . . . He has therefore found in the present case that the occasion of each of the three communications, to Singer, to the wife, and to Browne, was privileged and that there is no evidence of excess of communication or of malice to be left to the jury. "No nice scales should be used," as Lord Dunedin said in *Adam* v. *Ward,* [1917] A.C. 309, 330.

　　By the law of England there are occasions on which a person may make defamatory statements about another which are untrue without incurring any legal liability for his statements. These occasions are called privileged occasions. A reason frequently given for this privilege is that the allegation that the speaker has "unlawfully and maliciously published", is displaced by proof that the speaker had either a duty or an interest to publish, and that this duty or interest confers the privilege. But communications made on these occasions may lose their privilege: (1) they may exceed the privilege of the occasion by going beyond the limits of the duty or interest, or (2) they may be published with express malice, so that the occasion is not being legitimately used, but abused. A very careful discussion of the way in which these two grounds of loss of privilege should be considered will be found in Lord Dunedin's judgment in *Adam* v. *Ward,* [1917] A.C. 309. The classical definition of "privileged occasions" is that of Parke, B., in *Toogood* v. *Spyring,* 1 C.M. & R. 181, a case where the tenant of a farm complained to the agent of the landlord, who had sent a workman to do repairs, that the workman had broken into the tenant's cellar, got drunk on the tenant's cider, and spoilt the work he was sent to do. The workman sued the tenant. Parke, B., gave the explanation of privileged occasions in these words: "In general, an action lies for the malicious publication of statements which are false in fact, and injurious to the character of another (within the well-known limits as to verbal slander), and the law considers such publication as malicious, unless it is fairly made by a person in the discharge of some public or private duty, whether legal or moral, or in the conduct of his own affairs, in matters where his interest is concerned. In such cases, the occasion prevents the inference of malice, which the law draws from unauthorized communications, and affords a qualified defence depending upon the absence of actual malice. If fairly warranted by any reasonable occasion or exigency, and honestly made, such communications are protected for the common convenience and welfare of society; and the law has not restricted the right to make them within any narrow limits."

It will be seen that the learned judge requires: (1) a public or private duty to communicate, whether legal or moral; (2) that the communication should be "fairly warranted by any reasonable occasion or exigency"; (3) or a statement in the conduct of his own affairs where his interest is concerned. Parke, B., had given several other definitions in slightly varying terms. For instance, in *Cockayne* v. *Hodgkisson* (1833), 5 C. & P. 543, 548, he had directed the jury: "Where the writer is acting on any duty, legal or moral, towards the person to whom he writes, or where he has, by his situation, to protect the interests of another, that which he writes under such circumstances is a privileged communication." This adds to the protection of his own interest, spoken of in *Toogood* v. *Spyring,* the protection of the interests of another where the situation of the writer requires him to protect those interests. This, I think, involves that his "situation" imposes on him a legal or moral duty. The question whether the occasion was privileged is for the judge, and so far as "duty" is concerned, the question is: Was there a duty, legal, moral, or social, to communicate? As to legal duty, the judge should have no difficulty; the judge should know the law; but as to moral or social duties of imperfect obligation, the task is far more troublesome. The judge has no evidence as to the view the community takes of moral or social duties. All the help the Court of Appeal can give him is contained in the judgment of Lindley, L.J., in *Stuart* v. *Bell,* [1891] 2 Q.B. 341, 350: "The question of moral or social duty being for the judge, each judge must decide it as best he can for himself. I take moral or social duty to mean a duty recognized by English people of ordinary intelligence and moral principle, but at the same time not a duty enforceable by legal proceedings, whether civil or criminal. My own conviction is that all or, at all events, the great mass of right-minded men in the position of the defendant would have considered it their duty, under the circumstances, to inform Stanley of the suspicion which had fallen on the plaintiff." Is the judge merely to give his own view of moral and social duty, though he thinks a considerable portion of the community hold a different opinion? Or is he to endeavour to ascertain what view "the great mass of right-minded men" would take?

It is not surprising that with such a standard both judges and text-writers treat the matter as one of great difficulty in which no definite line can be drawn. . . .

In 1855, in *Harrison* v. *Bush,* 5 E. & B. 344, 348, Lord Campbell, C.J., giving the judgment of the Court of Queen's Bench accepted a principle stated thus: "A communication made *bona fide* upon any subject matter in which the party communicating has an interest, or in reference to which he has a duty, is privileged, if made to a person having a corresponding interest or duty, although it contain criminatory matter which, without this privilege, would be slanderous and actionable." This is the first of a series of statements that both parties, the writer and the recipient, must have a corresponding interest or duty. Lord Esher, M.R., says in *Pullman* v. *Hill & Co.,* [1891] 1 Q.B. 524, 528: "An occasion is privileged when the person who makes the communication has a moral duty to make it to the person to whom he does make it, and the person who receives it has an interest in hearing it. Both those conditions must exist in order that the occasion may be privileged." Lord Atkinson in *Adam* v. *Ward,* [1917] A.C. 309, 334, expresses it thus: "It was not disputed, in this case on either side, that a privileged occasion is, in reference to qualified privilege, an occasion where the person who makes a communication has an interest or a duty, legal, social, or moral, to make it to the person to whom it is made, and the person to whom it is so made has a corresponding interest or duty to receive it. This reciprocity is essential."

With slight modifications in particular circumstances, this appears to me to be well established law, but, except in the case of communications based on common interest, the principle is that either there must be interest in the recipient and a duty to communicate in the speaker, or an interest to be protected in the speaker and a duty to protect it in the recipient. Except in the case of common interest justifying intercommunication, the correspondence must be between duty and interest. There may, in the common interest cases, be also a common or reciprocal duty. It is not every interest which will create a duty in a stranger or volunteer. This appears to fit in with the two statements of Parke, B., already referred to, and with the language of Erle, C.J., in *Whiteley* v. *Adams,* 15 C.B. (N.S.) 392, 418, that the communication was made in the discharge of some social or moral duty, or on the ground of an interest in the party making or receiving it. This is approved by Lindley, L.J., in *Stuart* v. *Bell,* [1891] 2 Q.B. 341, but I think should be expanded into "either (1) a duty to communicate information believed to be true to a person who has a material interest in receiving the information, or (2) an interest in the speaker to be protected by communicating information, if true, relevant to that interest, to a person honestly believed to have a duty to protect that interest, or (3) a common interest in and reciprocal duty in respect of the subject matter of the communication between speaker and recipient." . . .

In my opinion Horridge, J., went too far in holding that there could be a privileged occasion on the ground of interest in the recipient without any duty to communicate on the part of the person making the communication. But that does not settle the question, for it is necessary to consider, in the present case, whether there was, as to each communication, a duty to communicate, and an interest in the recipient.

First as to the communication between Longsdon and Singer, I think the case must proceed on the admission that at all material times Watt, Longsdon and Browne were in the employment of the same company, and the evidence afforded by the answer to the interrogatory put in by the plaintiff that Longsdon believed the statements in Browne's letter. In my view on these facts there was a duty, both from a moral and a material point of view, on Longsdon to communicate the letter to Singer, the chairman of his company, who, apart from questions of present employment, might be asked by Watt for a testimonial to a future employer. Equally, I think Longsdon receiving the letter from Browne, might discuss the matter with him, and ask for further information, on the ground of a common interest in the affairs of the company, and to obtain further information for the chairman. I should therefore agree with the view of Horridge, J., that these two occasions were privileged, though for different reasons. Horridge, J., further held that there was no evidence of malice fit to be left to the jury, and, while I think some of Longsdon's action and language in this respect was unfortunate, as the plaintiff has put in the answer that Longsdon believed the truth of the statements in Browne's and his own letter, like Lord Dunedin in *Adam* v. *Ward,* I should not try excess with too nice scales, and I do not dissent from his view as to malice. As to the communications to Singer and Browne, in my opinion the appeal should fail, but as both my brethren take the view that there was evidence of malice which should be left to the jury, there must, of course, be a new trial as to the claim based on these two publications.

The communication to Mrs. Watt stands on a different footing. I have no intention of writing an exhaustive treatise on the circumstances when a stranger or a friend should communicate to husband or wife information he receives as to the conduct of the other party to the marriage. I am clear that it is impossible to say he is always under a moral or social duty to do so; it is equally impossible to say he is never under such a duty. It must depend on the circumstances of each case, the nature of the information, and the relation of speaker and recipient. It cannot, on the other hand, be the duty even of a friend to communicate all the gossip the friend hears at men's clubs or women's bridge parties to one of the spouses affected. On the other hand, most men would hold that it was the moral duty of a doctor who attended his sister in law, and believed her to be suffering from a miscarriage, for which an absent husband could not be responsible, to communicate that fact to his wife and the husband. . . . If this is so, the decision must turn on the circumstances of each case, the judge being much influenced by the consideration that as a general rule it is not desirable for any one, even a mother in law, to interfere in the affairs of man and wife.

Using the best judgment I can in this difficult matter, I have come to the conclusion that there was not a moral or social duty in Longsdon to make this communication to Mrs. Watt such as to make the occasion privileged, and that there must be a new trial so far as it relates to the claim for publication of a libel to Mrs. Watt. The communications to Singer and Browne being made on a privileged occasion, there must be a new trial of the issue as to malice defeating the privilege. There must also be a new trial of the complaint as to publication to Mrs. Watt, the occasion being held not to be privileged. The plaintiff must have the costs of this appeal; the costs of the first trial must abide the result of the second trial, the issues being separated.

[The judgments of Greer and Russell, L.JJ., are omitted.]

NOTES

1. One of the leading cases in this area is *Adam* v. *Ward, supra,* where an M.P. made certain charges against a senior army officer. The Army Council made an official investigation, exonerated the officer, and, incidentally, made remarks defamatory of the M.P. The Council's report was found to be privileged since it had been made in the discharge of a public duty. Although the Council released the information to the public press, this was held not to be an abuse, having regard to the fact that the accusation had been made in the Parliament. See also *Lacarte* v. *Board of Education of Toronto,* [1959] S.C.R. 465.

2. Courts are more inclined to find a qualified privilege where statements are made in response to specific inquiries, than when they are volunteered. For

example, if a previous employer gives a character reference regarding a discharged employee at the request of a prospective employer, he is more likely to be protected than if he volunteers the information. See *Toogood* v. *Spyring* (1834), 1 Cr. M. & R. 181. Similarly, a businessman who comments on the financial standing of a buyer at the request of another stands in a better position than if the comments were unsolicited. See *Robshaw* v. *Smith* (1878), 38 L.T. 423.

3. An inquiry is not always required, however, Certain relationships generate a duty to inform even without any request to do so. For example, defamatory statements by a father to his daughter about a prospective husband are privileged because of his moral obligation as a father. See *Bordeaux* v. *Jobs* (1913), 6 Alta. L. Rev. 440, *per* Harvey C.J. An employer may also tell his employee certain things related to his work. See *Cooke* v. *Wildes* (1855), 5 E. & B. 328.

4. Mercantile agencies that collect and sell credit information for profit to their customers are denied qualified privilege on the ground that it is not in the public interest to protect those who trade for profit in the characters of other people. See *Macintosh* v. *Dun,* [1908] A.C. 390. This view has been much criticized and has been accordingly modified in *London Assoc. for Protection of Trade* v. *Greenlands Ltd.,* [1916] 2 A.C. 15, where a qualified privilege was accorded to credit reports by a mutual trade protective society, which was a co-operative service, rather than a business run for profit. See also *Howe* v. *Lees* (1910), 11 C.L.R. 361; *Todd* v. *Dun* (1888), 15 O.A.R. 85; *Robinson* v. *Dun* (1897), 24 O.A.R. 287. How would you handle the dissemination of information about the creditworthiness of consumers?

(d) *Public Interest*

THE GLOBE AND MAIL LTD. v. BOLAND

Supreme Court of Canada. [1960] S.C.R. 203; 22 D.L.R. (2d) 277

Cartwright J.: This is an appeal from a judgment of the Court of Appeal for Ontario [17 D.L.R. (2d) 313] allowing the plaintiff's appeal from the judgment of Spence, J. The action is for damages for libel. At the conclusion of the plaintiff's case counsel for the defendant stated that he did not intend to call evidence and moved for a dismissal of the action. The learned trial judge held that the words complained of were published on an occasion of qualified privilege and that there was no evidence of malice to go to the jury and accordingly dismissed the action.

The Court of Appeal, in a unanimous judgment delivered by LeBel, J.A., allowed the appeal and directed a new trial on the ground that there was evidence upon which the jury might find express malice. As I read his reasons, the learned Justice of Appeal neither affirms nor rejects the view of the learned trial judge that it was established that the words were published on an occasion of qualified privilege.

In my opinion the order made by the Court of Appeal was right but as there is to be a new trial I think it desirable to say something as to the appellant's plea of qualified privilege.

The respondent was a candidate for election in Parkdale riding in the general election held in Canada on June 10, 1957. The words complained of appeared on May 27, 1957, as an editorial in all issues of *The Globe & Mail,* a daily newspaper published by the appellant. They read as follows:

SHABBY TACTICS

"One of the less creditable episodes of the election campaign occurred on Thursday evening in Parkdale constituency, in Toronto, when Mr. John Boland, self-styled independent Conservative candidate, introduced an issue which does not exist in this election. McCarthy-style, he put forward an ex-Communist in an attempt to show the Liberals are 'Soft on Communism'. The results were far from edifying.

The reason for this disgusting performance was undoubtedly to mislead the so-called New Canadian vote in that riding, in the hope that their anti-Communist fears might be translated into an anti-Liberal anti-Conservative prejudice. An election won by such tactics would be a degradation to the whole democratic system of Government in Canada. Let us have no more of that sort of thing, this time or ever."

In the statement of claim it is alleged that the defendant falsely and maliciously published this editorial of and concerning the plaintiff and that in its plain and ordinary meaning it is defamatory of him. In paras. 6 to 15 inclusive a number of innuendoes are alleged.

In the statement of defence publication is admitted. The defences pleaded are, (1) that the words complained of in their natural and ordinary meaning are no libel, (ii) that the said words do not bear and were not understood to bear and are incapable of bearing or being understood to bear the meanings alleged in paras. 6 to 15 of the statement of claim, (iii) a plea of qualified privilege, and (iv) the defence of fair comment, pleaded in the form of the "rolled-up" plea.

The plea of qualified privilege is set out in paras. 3 and 4 of the statement of defence which read as follows:

"3. The defendant says that the words complained of were published in the following circumstances—

During the campaign preceding the Federal Elections of June 10, 1957, the Plaintiff, as a Candidate for election, was seeking the support of the electors in Parkdale Rising in the City of Toronto, as an Independent Conservative Candidate. The plaintiff, as part of his campaign, introduced the issue that the Liberal Government was employing pro-communists in the Department of External Affairs and was soft on Communism. This issue was further developed at a Public Meeting held at Parkdale Collegiate Auditorium on 23rd May, 1957, when one, Pat Walsh, addressed the meeting in the interest of the Plaintiff. The raising of this issue by the Plaintiff was the subject of discussion and comment in the Public Press.

4. By reason of such circumstances it was the duty of the Defendant to publish and in the interests of the Public to receive communications and comments with respect to the Candidature of the Plaintiff and by reason of this the said words were published under such circumstances and upon such occasion as to render them privileged."

The rule as to the burden of proof where a defence of qualified privilege is set up is accurately stated in Gatley on *Libel & Slander,* 4th ed., p. 282, as follows: "Where a defence of qualified privilege is set up, it is for the defendant to allege and prove all such facts and circumstances as are necessary to bring the words complained of within the privilege, unless such facts are admitted before or at the trial of the action. Whether the facts and circumstances proved or admitted are or are not such as to render the occasion privileged is a question of law for the judge to decide."

The learned trial judge found that the facts alleged in para. 3 of the statement of defence were proved and, for the purposes of this appeal, I will assume the correctness of that finding. He then went on to hold as a matter of law that these facts established the existence of an occasion of qualified privilege. The learned judge based this conclusion primarily on the decision of Mackay, J., as he then was, the trial judge in *Dennison et al.* v. *Sanderson* reported in appeal at [1946] 4 D.L.R. 314, O.R. 601, and of Kelly, J., the trial judge in *Drew* v. *Toronto Star Ltd. & Atkinson* reported in appeal at [1947] 4 D.L.R. 221, O.R. 730. In the view of the learned trial judge in neither of these cases did the Court of Appeal disapprove of the statements made by the learned judges presiding at the trials to the effect that statements made in a newspaper during an election campaign as to the fitness, or otherwise, for office of candidates offering themselves for election were made on occasions of qualified privilege. The learned trial judge continued: "Therefore in my view we have two judges of this Court who have found that the publication of comment in newspapers as to candidates for election to public office, and made during the course of an election campaign, are uttered on occasions of qualified privilege and the opinion of neither one of those has been disturbed on appeal. Apart from the authority I would be much inclined to come to the same opinion. Surely no section of the public has a clearer duty to publish, for the information and guidance of the public, political news and comment, even critical comment, during a Federal election in Canada than the great Metropolitan daily newspaper such as the defendant. Just as certainly the public, every citizen in Canada, has a legitimate and vital interest in receiving such publications. At this point I do not intend to deal with either the *bona fides* of the publication or with the alleged over-extension of the publication thereof, to both of which I shall refer later, but only with the question whether the occasion was one of qualified privilege. I have come to the conclusion that a Federal election in Canada is an occasion upon which a newspaper has a public duty to comment on the candidates, their campaigns and their platforms or policies, and Canadian citizens have an honest and very real interest in receiving their comments, and that therefore this is an occasion of qualified privilege."

With respect, I am of opinion that this is an erroneous statement of the law. It is directly opposed to the unanimous judgment of this Court in *Douglas* v. *Tucker,* [1952] 1 D.L.R. 657, 1 S.C.R. 275, particularly at pp. 665-7 D.L.R. pp. 287-8 S.C.R. (which does not appear to have been brought to the attention of the learned judge) and to *Duncombe* v. *Daniell* (1837), 8 Car. & P. 222, 173 E.R. 470, 2 Jur. 32, 1 W.W. & H. 101; which was approved and followed in *Douglas* v. *Tucker.*

An attempt was made to distinguish the case at bar from *Duncombe* v. *Daniell* and *Douglas* v. *Tucker* on the ground that in each of those two cases the libel referred to the private life rather than the conduct in public affairs of the plaintiff; but the judgments in both of those cases proceeded on the basis that the defamatory statement made about the candidate would, if true, have been relevant to the question of his fitness for office and was such as the electors had an interest in hearing. In my opinion there is nothing in this suggested distinction which renders the principle of *Douglas* v. *Tucker* inapplicable to the case at bar.

With respect it appears to me that, in the passage from his reasons quoted above, the learned trial judge has confused the *right* which the publisher of a newspaper has, in common with all Her Majesty's subjects, to report truthfully and comment fairly upon matters of public interest with a *duty* of the sort which gives rise to an occasion of qualified privilege.

It is well to bear in mind the following passages from the judgment of Lord Shaw in *Arnold* v. *The King Emperor* (1914), 30 T.L.R. 462 at p. 468, quoted by LeBel, J.A., (p. 316): "'The freedom of the journalist is an ordinary part of the freedom of the subject, and to whatever lengths the subject in general may go, so also may the journalist, but, apart from statute-law, his privilege is no other and no higher. The responsibilities which attach to his power in the dissemination of printed matter may, and in the case of a conscientious journalist do, make him more careful; but the range of his assertions, his criticisms, or his comments is as wide as, and no wider than, that of any other subject. No privilege attaches to his position.'"

To hold that during a Federal election campaign in Canada any defamatory statement published in the press relating to a candidate's fitness for office is to be taken as published on an occasion of qualified privilege would be, in my opinion, not only contrary to the great weight of authority in England and in this country but harmful to that "common convenience and welfare of society" which Baron Parke described as the underlying principle on which the rules as to qualified privilege are founded. (See *Toogood* v. *Spyring* (1834), 1 C.M. & R. 181 at p. 193, 149 E.R. 1044.) It would mean that every man who offers himself as a candidate must be prepared to risk the loss of his reputation without redress unless he be able to prove affirmatively that those who defamed him were actuated by express malice. I would like to adopt the following sentence from the judgment of the Court in *Post Pub. Co.* v. *Hallam* (1893), 59 Fed. 530 at p. 540: "We think that not only is such a sacrifice not required of every one who consents to become a candidate for office, but that to sanction such a doctrine would do the public more harm than good." And the following expression of opinion by the learned author of Gatley (*op. cit.*), p. 254: "It is, however, submitted that so wide an extension of the privilege would do the public more harm than good. It would tend to deter sensitive and honourable men from seeking public positions of trust and responsibility, and leave them open to others who have no respect for their reputation."

The passages just quoted recall the words of Cockburn, C.J., in *Campbell* v. *Spottiswoode* (1863), 3 B. & S. 769 at p. 777, 122 E.R. 288: "It is said that it is for the interest of society that the public conduct of men should be criticized without any other limit than that the writer should have an honest belief that what he writes is true. But it seems to me that the public have an equal interest in the maintenance of the public character of public men; and public affairs could not be conducted by men of honour with a view to the welfare of the country, if we were to sanction attacks upon them, destructive of their honour and character, and made without any foundation." The interest of the public and that of the publishers of newspapers will be sufficiently safeguarded by the availability of the defence of fair comment in appropriate circumstances . . .

At the new trial, in view of the state of the pleadings it should be taken that, as a matter of law, the defence of qualified privilege is not open to the defendant. I would dismiss the appeal with costs.

NOTES

1. For an account of the second trial and subsequent appeal, ordering a third trial, see *Boland* v. *Globe and Mail Ltd.*, [1961] O.R. 712, 29 D.L.R. (2d) 401.

2. In *Banks* v. *The Globe and Mail Ltd.*, [1961] S.C.R. 474, 28 D.L.R. (2d) 343, the trial judge and the Ontario Court of Appeal held that the publication in a newspaper of statements concerning a director of a labour union which had called a strike affecting eight Canadian owned vessels, was made on an occasion of qualified privilege. The strike had lasted many months and before it was settled the eight ships had been transferred to a Foreign Registry. The existence of a subject matter of such wide public interest was held by the lower courts to support a plea of qualified privilege. "There is no more efficient organ for informing the public and for disseminating to the public intelligent comment on such matters of public interest, than a great metropolitan newspaper . . . . The members of the public have a real, a vital—I might go so far as to say—a paramount interest in receiving those comments." The Supreme Court of Canada, however, pointed out that the Ontario courts had confused the *right* of any individual, or newspaper, to comment fairly upon matters of public interest, with a *duty* of the sort which gives rise to an occasion of privilege. No such duty existed here and there was, as explained in the *Boland* case, no qualified privilege.

3. In *Jones* v. *Bennett* (1968), 2 D.L.R. (3d) 291 (S.C.C.), Premier W.A.C. Bennett of B.C., at a public meeting of some of his Social Credit supporters in Victoria, B.C., sought to justify his government's suspension of Jones, a member of a provincial commission. During the course of his speech, which was covered by the press, the Premier spoke some defamatory remarks about Jones, implying that he was unfit for office because of dishonesty. Jones sued. The defence

sought to invoke the defence of qualified privilege. The Supreme Court, however, held that he could not rely on the privilege, even though the subject was clearly one of public interest. Cartwright C.J.C. stated:

"It is, of course, a perfectly proper proceeding for a member of the Legislature to address a meeting of his supporters at any time but if in the course of addressing them he sees fit to make defamatory statements about another which are in fact untrue, it is difficult to see why the common convenience and welfare of society requires that such statements should be protected and the person defamed left without a remedy unless he can affirmatively prove express malice on the part of the speaker."

His Lordship indicated that, even if there were a qualified privilege, the defendant lost it because he was aware of the presence of reporters in the audience, who would publicize his remarks to the general public. The defence of fair comment was also rejected because the "sting of the words" were held not to be comment at all. Do you agree with this disposition of the matter?

4. Compare with *Stopforth* v. *Goyer* (1979), 8 C.C.L.T. 172 (Ont. C.A.), where Jean-Pierre Goyer, when a Minister of the federal Crown, said of one of his civil servants that he gave him "misinformation" and that he was "grossly negligent". The Ontario Court of Appeal, without citing *Jones* v. *Bennett,* held that "the electorate, as represented by the media, has a real and *bona fide* interest in the demotion of a senior civil servant for an alleged dereliction of duty . . . and the appellant had a corresponding public duty and interest in satisfying that interest of the electorate". How would you handle such a situation if you had your choice?

5. What do you think of this principle? In the United States, there is a constitutionally protected privilege to discuss matters of public concern. As long as there is no malice, one may, therefore, criticize public officials (*New York Times* v. *Sullivan* (1964), 376 U.S. 254), or public figures (*Curtis Publishing* v. *Butts* (1967), 388 U.S. 130) without attracting liability for defamation. See also *Gertz* v. *Welsh* (1974), 418 U.S. 323. Should such a concept be imported into Canada?

6. Much of the evil of this rule has been minimized by legislation. Several Canadian provinces permit recovery against newspapers and broadcasting stations that is limited to actual damage if the statement complained of was published in "good faith" and under "mistake" and a full retraction is published. This privilege is "not to apply to the case of a libel against any candidate for public office . . . unless the retraction of the charge is made editorially in a conspicuous manner, at least five days before the election." See The Libel and Slander Act, R.S.O. 1970, c. 243, s. 5. Similarly, the defence of fair comment may be available to the publisher. See *infra.*

7. A privilege is recognized, in the interest of the general public, to report crime to the police. See *Foltz* v. *Moore-McCormack Lines* (1951), 189 F. 2d 537. Similarly, one can report the conduct of public officers to their superiors, (see *Nuyen* v. *Slater* (1964), 127 N.W. 2d 369), or to one's M.P. (*R.* v. *Rule,* [1937] 2 K.B. 375 (C.A.)). So too, a teacher can be reported to a school board in a privileged context. *Fuson* v. *Fuson* (1933), 57 S.W. 2d 42. But one is not privileged to write in a book called the *Children's Crusade,* an account of the Company of Young Canadians, which defames someone, merely because the public would be interested in such an account, there being no "valid social reasons" to do so. See Dubin J.A. in *Littleton* v. *Hamilton* (1974), 4 O.R. (2d) 283 (C.A.).

8. Should a defendant be liable for mistakenly reporting defamatory information to the wrong authority, believing honestly and reasonably that it was the proper agency to receive it? In *Hebditch* v. *MacIlwaine,* [1894] 2 Q.B. 54 (C.A.), it was held that no privilege protected a group of ratepayers who complained about certain election irregularities to the wrong body, which had no duty or interest in receiving the information. Compare with *McIntyre* v. *McBean* (1856), 13 U.C.Q.B. 534, where parents who complained to the wrong authority about a teacher's moral character were excused from liability since it was found commendable to do this as long as the information was "well-founded, or that they

had good reason to believe it was, and that they acted in sincerity and good faith, not maliciously and without just cause or excuse". Similarly, in *Kerr* v. *Davison* (1873), 9 N.S.R. 354, it was held that a privilege exists if a communication is made to a person "not in fact having such interest or duty, but who might reasonably be and is supposed by the party making the communication to have such an interest or duty".

4. Fair Comment

Fair comment on matters of public concern or interest is protected from liability for defamation provided it is based on fact. These matters fall within two main categories; first, those in which the public has a legitimate interest, such as government activity, political debate, and proposals by public figures, and public affairs generally; second, works of art displayed in public such as theatrical performances, music and literature. In a democratic and culturally vibrant society, a discussion of these matters must be unfettered.

Fair comment must be based on fact. The facts must be included in the communication, or they must be indicated with sufficient clarity to lay a proper foundation for the comment being made. See *Kemsley* v. *Foot,* [1952] A.C. 345, at p. 357.

The comments can not be presented so that they appear to be allegations of fact. The ordinary unprejudiced reader must take them to be comments based on facts for the defence to hold. See *Clarke* v. *Norton,* [1910] V.L.R. 494. Thus, if the "sting of the words complained of do not appear to be comment at all", the defence will fail. *Jones* v. *Bennett,* [1969] S.C.R. 277. In other words, to say that someone did something dishonourable is a fact whereas to say that someone did a particular thing and that that was dishonourable is a statement of fact and a comment.

It is a question of fact for the jury to decide whether the communication is fact or comment, unless the judge withdraws the question from them. See *Jones* v. *Skelton,* [1963] 1 W.L.R. 1362.

Unless the facts upon which the comment is based are true and undistorted, the comment cannot be "fair". The truth of the facts, therefore, is essential, not to prove that the statements were justified, but that the comment was a fair one.

Although the comment must be fair, this does not necessarily mean that it must be reasonable. Even the unreasonable are allowed to express their views. The test for the jury is whether they might reasonably regard the opinion as one that no fair-minded person could possibly have promulgated. The jury must not substitute their own opinion on the subject. See *McQuire* v. *Western Morning News,* [1903] 2 K.B. 100 (C.A.); *Masters* v. *Fox* (1978), 85 D.L.R. (3d) 64 (B.C.), fair comment defence fails because no fair-minded person could draw the inference from the facts. In other words, as long as the comment represents a legitimate opinion honestly held, it will be protected.

The Libel and Slander Act, R.S.O. 1970, c. 243, s. 24, states:

> In an action for libel or slander for words consisting partly of allegations of fact and partly of expression of opinion, a defence of fair comment shall not fail by reason only that the truth of every allegation of fact is not proved if the expression of opinion is fair comment having regard to such of the facts alleged or referred to in the words complained of as are proved.

McQUIRE v. WESTERN MORNING NEWS COMPANY

Court of Appeal. [1903] 2 K.B. 100; 72 L.J.K.B. 612; 88 L.T. 757;
19 T.L.R. 471

The statement of claim stated that the plaintiff was an actor and theatrical manager, and the defendants were the owners of a newspaper called the *Western Morning News;* that on June 24, 1901, the plaintiff and a travelling company under his management appeared at the Theatre Royal, Plymouth, in a musical play written and composed by the plaintiff, entitled "The Major"; that, in the edition of the defendant's newspaper dated June 25, 1901, the defendants falsely and maliciously caused to be printed and published of and concerning the plaintiff, and of him as such actor and manager, and also as such author and composer as aforesaid, the words following: "A three act musical absurdity entitled 'The Major', written and composed by Mr. T.C. McQuire, was presented last evening before a full house by the author's company. It cannot be said that many left the building with the satisfaction of having seen anything like the standard of play which is generally to be witnessed at the Theatre Royal. Although it may be described as a play, 'The Major' is composed of nothing but nonsense of a not very humorous character, whilst the music is far from attractive. This comedy would be very much improved had it a substantial plot, and were a good deal of the sorry stuff taken out of it which lowers both the players and the play. No doubt the actors and actresses are well suited to the piece, which gives excellent scope for music-hall artists to display their talent. Among Mr. McQuire's company there is not one good actor or actress, and, with the exception of Mr. Ernest Braime, not one of them can be said to have a voice for singing. The introduction of common, not to say vulgar, songs does not tend to improve the character of the performance, and the dancing, which forms a prominent feature, is carried out with very little gracefulness"; and that by the said words the defendants meant, and were understood to mean, and the meaning of the said words was, that the said play was dull, vulgar, and degrading, that the members of the plaintiff's company were incompetent as actors, singers, and dancers, that they were music-hall artists, and that the plaintiff was himself incompetent both as an actor and composer as aforesaid.

The defence admitted the publication by the defendants of the matter complained of, but pleaded that it was published by them in the ordinary course of their business as public journalists, and without any malice to the plaintiff, and that it was a fair and bona fide criticism upon the play referred to in the statement of claim and its performance, which were matters of public interest, and was therefore no libel.

Evidence was given at the trial on both sides with regard to the nature of the play in question and its performance . . . There was no evidence of any personal malice towards the plaintiff, or of any indirect motive, on the part of the writer of the criticism or of anyone responsible for the management of the defendant's newspaper. The learned judge left the question whether the criticism complained of was or was not a libel to the jury, who found a verdict for the plaintiff with 100*l.* damages. Defendants appealed.

Collins M.R.: This raises a very important question as to what are the limits of "fair comment" on a literary work, and as to what are the respective provinces of the judge and jury with respect thereto. One thing, however, is perfectly clear, and that is that the jury have no right to substitute their own opinion of the literary merits of the work for that of the critic, or to try the "fairness" of the criticism by any such standard. "Fair", therefore, in this collocation certainly does not mean that which the ordinary reasonable man, "the man on the

Clapham omnibus", as Lord Bowen phrased it, the juryman common or special, would think a correct appreciation of the work; and it is of the highest importance to the community that the critic should be saved from any such possibility. In principle, therefore, there would be nothing to leave to the jury unless there was some element in the criticism which might support an inference of unfairness in some other sense. No doubt this element might be, and has been, described in various ways and different instances of it given; but, broadly, I think Mr. Duke is right in contending that, in the case of a literary work at all events, it is something that passes out of the domain of criticism itself. Criticism cannot be used as a cloak for mere invective, nor for personal imputations not arising out of the subject-matter or not based on fact. "If," says Lord Ellenborough in *Carr* v. *Hood,* 1 Camp. 354; 10 R.R. 701, reported in a note to *Tabbart* v. *Tiffer,* 1 Camp. 350; 10 R.R. 698, "the commentator does not step aside from the work or introduce fiction for the purpose of condemnation he exercises a fair and legitimate right . . . Had the party writing the criticism followed the plaintiff into domestic life for the purposes of slander that would have been libellous;" and, in another passage: "Shew me an attack on the moral character of this plaintiff, or any attack upon his character unconnected with his authorship, and I shall be as ready as any judge who ever sat here to protect him." In *Merivale* v. *Carson,* 20 Q.B.D. 275, Bowen, L.J., says: "In the case of literary criticism it is not easy to conceive what would be outside that region"—*i.e.* of fair comment— "unless the writer went out of his way to make a personal attack on the character of the author of the work which he was criticizing. In such a case the writer would be going beyond the limits of criticism altogether, and therefore beyond the limits of fair criticism . . . Still, there is another class of cases in which, as it seems to me, the writer would be travelling out of the region of fair criticism—I mean if he imputes to the author that he has written something which in fact he has not written. That would be a misdescription of the work." I think "fair" embraces the meaning of honest and also of relevancy. The view expressed must be honest and must be such as can fairly be called criticism. I am aware that the word "moderate" has been used in this connection—*Watson* v. *Walter,* L.R. 4 Q.B. 73—with reference to comment on the conduct of a public man; but I think it is only used to express the idea that invective is not criticism. It certainly cannot mean moderate in the sense that that which is deemed by a jury, in the case of a literary criticism, extravagant, and the outcome of prejudice on the part of an honest writer is necessarily beyond the limit of fair comment: see *Merivale* v. *Carson,* 20 Q.B.D. 275. No doubt in most cases of this class there are expressions in the impugned document capable of being interpreted as falling outside the limit of honest criticism, and, therefore, it is proper to leave the question to the jury, and in all cases where there may be a doubt it may be convenient to take the opinion of a jury. But it is always for the judge to say whether the document is capable in law of being a libel. It is, however, for the plaintiff, who rests his claim upon a document which on his own statement purports to be a criticism of a matter of public interest, to shew that it is a libel —*i.e.,* that it travels beyond the limit of fair criticism; and therefore it must be for the judge to say whether it is reasonably capable of being so interpreted. If it is not, there is no question for the jury, and it would be competent for him to give judgment for the defendant . . . The comment, in order to be within the protection of the privilege, had to be fair—*i.e.,* not such as to disclose in itself actual malice. It also had to be relevant; otherwise it never was within it, and the judge could hold as a matter of law that the privilege did not extend to it . . . and in such case the only defence was truth. These factors were, I think, intended to be covered compendiously by the epithet "fair". In other words, it was intended to exclude those elements which took the comment out of, or prevented it from falling within, the privilege of the occasion. The result is that the question of "fair comment" is no more exclusively for the jury in one view of the nature of the right than in the other. In my opinion, there is in this case no evidence on which a rational verdict for the plaintiff can be founded, and the defendants are therefore entitled to have judgment entered for them. In this view it is not ncessary to consider the grounds on which a new trial is asked for; but if there was any evidence fit to be considered by a jury, I am clearly of opinion that the verdict was against the weight of evidence.

[Stirling and Mathew, L.JJ., concurred, and judgment was entered for defendants.]

NOTES

1. In *Cherneskey* v. *Armadale Publishers Ltd.* (1978), 7 C.C.L.T. 69 (S.C.C.), two law students wrote a letter to the editor which the Saskatoon Star-Phoenix published, complaining about the racist attitude of a local alderman. He sued the newspaper for libel. The law students did not testify at the trial and the newspaper staff testified that they did not agree with the contents of the letter. The trial judge withheld from the jury the defence of fair comment; this was reversed by the Saskatchewan Court of Appeal; the Supreme Court of Canada affirmed the trial judge, with Dickson, Spence and Estey, JJ. dissenting.

Mr. Justice Ritchie, for the majority, explained:

". . . each publisher in relying on the defence of fair comment is in exactly the same position as the original writer . . .

. . . the newspaper and its editor cannot sustain a defence of fair comment when it has been proved that the words used in the letter are not an honest expression of their opinion and there is no evidence as to the honest belief of the writers."

This was a reaffirmation of the traditional scope of the defence, which is available in discussion of matters of public interest, if (1) the facts upon which the comment is based are true, (2) the comment is fair and (3) the person making the statement honestly believes it.

Mr. Justice Dickson disagreed fundamentally. He expressed his concern as follows:

"The important issue raised in this appeal is whether the defence of fair comment is denied a newspaper publishing material alleged to be defamatory unless it can be shown that the paper honestly believed the views expressed in the impugned material. It does not require any great perception to envisage the effect of such a rule upon the position of a newspaper in the publication of letters to the editor. An editor receiving a letter containing matter which might be defamatory would have a defence of fair comment if he shared the views expressed, but defenceless if he did not hold those views. As the columns devoted to letters to the editor are intended to stimulate uninhibited debate on every public issue, the editor's task would be an unenviable one if he were limited to publishing only those letters with which he agreed. He would be engaged in a sort of censorship, antithetical to a free press. One can readily draw a distinction between editorial comment or articles, which may be taken to represent the paper's point of view, and letters to the editor in which the personal opinion of the paper is, or should be, irrelevant. No one believes that a newspaper shares the views of every hostile reader who takes it to task in a letter to the editor for error of omission or commission, or that it yields assent to the views of every person who feels impelled to make his feelings known in a letter to the editor. Newspapers do not adopt as their own the opinions voiced in such letters, nor should they be expected to. . . .

It is not only the right but the duty of the press, in pursuit of its legitimate objectives, to act as a sounding board for the free flow of new and different ideas. It is one of the few means of getting the heterodox and controversial before the public. Many of the unorthodox points of view get newspaper space through letters to the editor. It is one of the few ways in which the public gains access to the press. By these means, various points of view, old and new grievances and proposed remedies get aired. The public interest is incidentally served by providing a safety valve for people.

Newspapers will not be able to provide a forum for dissemination of ideas if they are limited to publishing opinions with which they agree. If editors are faced with the choice of publishing only those letters which espouse their own particular ideology, or being without defence if sued for defamation, democratic dialogue will be stifled. Healthy debate will likely be replaced by monotonous repetition of majoritarian ideas and conformity to accepted taste. In one-newspaper towns, of which there are many, competing ideas will no longer gain access. Readers will be exposed to a single political, economic and social point of view. In a public controversy, the tendency will be to suppress those letters with which the editor is not in agreement. This runs directly counter to the increasing tendency of North American newspapers generally to become less devoted to the publishers' opinions and to print, without fear or favour, the widest possible range of opinions on matters of public interest. The integrity of a newspaper rests not on the publication of letters with which it is in agreement, but rather on the publication of letters expressing ideas to which it is violently opposed.

I do not wish to overstate the case. It is my view, however, that anything which serves to repress competing ideas is inimical to the public interest. I agree that the publisher of a newspaper has no special immunity from the application of general laws, and that in the matter of comment he is in no better position than any other citizen. But he should not be in any worse position. That, I fear, will be the situation if one fails to distinguish between the writer of a letter to the editor, and the editor, or if one compresses into one statement the several steps in the requisite process of analysis of the defence of fair comment."

Mr. Justice Dickson preferred to adopt a new, more liberal test, from *Duncan and Neill on Defamation (1978),* for the scope of fair comment:

"(a) the comment must be on a matter of public interest;

(b) the comment must be based on fact;

(c) the comment, though it can include inferences of fact, must be recognisable as comment;

(d) the comment must satisfy the following *objective* test: could any man honestly express that opinion on the proved facts?

(e) even though the comment satisfies the objective test the defence can be defeated *if the plaintiff proves that the defendant was actuated by express malice."*

His Lordship explained further:

". . . If the analysis set out in Duncan and Neill is accepted, and I suggest it should be, it is readily apparent that newspapers need not be in any different position from the rest of the population. Once a comment which is defamatory (in the sense of lowering the subject's reputation) is shown to be objectively fair, the only question is whether it was published with malice. This will depend on whether there is appropriate evidence of malice, which will be different depending upon whether the newspaper, or its staff, writes the comment, or whether the newspaper publishes comments written by others."

In response to this concern Mr. Justice Ritchie had this to say:

"This does not mean that freedom of the press to publish its views is in any way affected, nor does it mean that a newspaper cannot publish letters expressing views with which it may strongly disagree. Moreover, nothing that is here said should be construed as meaning that a newspaper is in any way restricted in publishing two diametrically opposite views of the opinion and conduct of a public figure. On the contrary, I adopt as descriptive of the conclusion which I have reached, the language used by Brownridge J.A., in the following excerpt from his reasons for judgment in the Court of Appeal where he said at p. 192 of the Report:

'What it does mean is that a newspaper cannot publish a *libellous* letter and then disclaim any responsibility by saying that it was published as fair comment on a matter of public interest but it does not represent the honest opinion of the newspaper.'"

2. Do you think that newspapers should be free to publish defamatory material in their letters to the editor section? Some of the provincial Attorneys-General have indicated that they are planning legislation in this issue. In Ontario s. 25 is to be added to the Libel and Slander Act as follows:

Where the defendant published defamatory matter that is an opinion expressed by another person, a defence of fair comment shall not fail for the reason only that the defendant or the person who expressed the opinion, or both, did not hold the opinion, if a person could honestly hold the opinion.

What does this do to *Cherneskey* v. *Armadale Publishers*?

3. In *Barltrop* v. *C.B.C.* (1978), 86 D.L.R. (3d) 61 (N.S.C.A.), the radio show "As It Happens" broadcasted some information about a doctor who was alleged to have "sold" his evidence, which was said to be contrary to public health, to an inquiry. Because the facts upon which the comment were based were found to be false, it was held not to be fair comment and $20,000 damages were awarded.

4. In *Slim* v. *Daily Telegraph*, [1968] 2 Q.B. 157, Denning M.R., though holding defendants liable because of false facts, had this to say:

"The right of fair comment is one of the essential elements which go to make up our freedom of speech. We must even maintain this right intact. It must not be whittled down by legal requirements. When a citizen is troubled by things going wrong, he should be free to write to the newspaper; and the newspaper should be free to publish this letter. It is often the only way to get things put right. The matter must, of course, be one of public interest. The writer must get his facts right; and he must honestly state his real opinion. But that being done, both he and the newspaper should be clear of any liability. They should not be deterred by fear of libel actions."

See also *Holt* v. *Sun Publishing Co.* (1978), 83 D.L.R. (3d) 760, former M.P. Simma Holt collected $2,000 because comments about her were not based on facts.

5. Is the control of the media through defamation law a valuable contribution by tort law to Canadian society in the 1980's? What alternative methods of supervision exist?

REVIEW PROBLEM

X, a solicitor, has acted for Mrs. Y previously, but is not presently so engaged. He learns from someone that Mr. Y has been engaging in homosexual activities. Knowing that Mrs. Y would dearly like a divorce from her husband, he informs her of the allegations by a letter dictated to his stenographer, advising Mrs. Y that this would be a ground for divorce, if true. Mr. Y, believing the letter to his wife to be a bill that he knew was due, opens the letter and reads it. He subsequently sues for defamation.

Was there publication? Is the occasion privileged? Was the privilege lost? Can X raise any other points in his defence?

CHAPTER 17

NUISANCE

McLAREN, NUISANCE IN CANADA
in Linden (ed.), *Studies in Canadian Tort Law* (1968)

Canadian courts have readily accepted the distinction in the modern law between private and public nuisance. At its simplest, private nuisance is definable as an interference of an indirect or consequential nature with the use and enjoyment of land by the occupier thereof. When a wrong of this nature becomes the object of litigation, the fundamental issue before the court is whether the degree of interference complained of is such that it should not be tolerated by the "ordinary occupier" in the position of the plaintiff. If the court accepts that the degree of interference is unwarranted, then liability follows as a matter of course. There is no concern with a comparison of the plaintiff's position with that of any other member of society. It is of no consequence to the question of liability that other members of the community have or have not suffered interference emanating from the same source. In short, private nuisance is exclusively a civil wrong.

Public nuisance, on the other hand, has a schizophrenic character. Basically it refers to a rather motley group of criminal or quasi-criminal offences which involve actual or potential interference with the public convenience or welfare. In substance, they range from the placing of obstructions on a public highway or a navigable river to the running of an odious institution such as a brothel. Since a public nuisance may be committed and its effects may be felt almost anywhere, it has no obvious connection with interference with interests in land. Further, as this type of nuisance is by definition detrimental to the public interest, the initiative in proceeding against the perpetrator lies with an official representative of that interest. If a criminal action is considered appropriate the offender will be charged under the Criminal Code with committing an indictable offence and if found guilty subjected to the prescribed penalty. In the case of civil proceedings the provincial attorney-general is responsible for starting an action to enjoin the continuance of the public nuisance. As long as suffering or inconvenience is general and uniformly injurious, there is no place for independent intervention by private citizens, whether it be an individual or group effort. Certainly they have the right to complain to the appropriate authorities in an attempt to stir the latter to positive action, but they cannot take upon themselves the role of champions of the public interest. In this sense a public nuisance is solely within the ambit of administrative discretion.

Public nuisance, however, has another face. It sometimes transpires that an act or omission which may be characterized as a public nuisance in the criminal sense causes substantial damage to a particular private individual. For instance, he may experience an aggravated degree of inconvenience and financial expenditure in circumventing an obstruction on the highway, or he may suffer a significant diminution in profits because of the proximity of his business to a bawdy house. The knowledge that the offending structure is a public nuisance, and thus ripe for official action may be of little consolation to him. Even if proceedings are

17-1

initiated by the appropriate authorities, a successful outcome will only benefit him insofar as it excises the source of future damage. He is still left with the sober reality of the loss incurred as a result of the defendant's conduct prior to trial. It is for this reason that a private individual has traditionally been allowed a civil action in certain circumstances. If he is a land occupier and the damage he incurs relates to his use and enjoyment of land, then his course of action is clear. He simply frames his action in private nuisance. The fact that the *casus delicti* is a public nuisance is in most cases irrelevant. Where, however, his complaint is not directly related to an interest in land, he is compelled to initiate a civil action for public nuisance. In order to succeed in this venture he has to persuade the court that the injury or damage he has suffered places him in an adverse position as compared with other members of the public. In short he has to prove damage that is special to him.

Given this basic dichotomy in both substance and procedure, it is quite evident that the use of the term "nuisance" to describe both areas of liability has no inherent rational quality. Indeed the connection can only be explained in terms of a quirk of legal history. It so happened that judges sympathetic to the idea of a limited form of civil recovery for the injurious effects of a group of heterogeneous misdemeanours found a springboard for creativity in a tenuous analogy between certain of the offences in question and situations already covered by private nuisance. Since the association of the two is historical rather than functional, an explanation of the peculiar nuances of both is desirable.

A. PUBLIC NUISANCE

HICKEY v. ELECTRIC REDUCTION CO. OF CANADA

Supreme Court of Newfoundland. (1970), 21 D.L.R. (3d) 368

Furlong C.J.: We are dealing with a preliminary objection in law which has been pleaded by the defendants in para. 6 of their defence:

> 6. The defendant will object that the Statement of Claim is bad in law and discloses no cause of action against the defendant on the grounds that the damages claimed by the plaintiffs are too remote in law.

In his argument counsel for the defendant, F.J. Ryan, Q.C., says in effect that an action in nuisance does not lie on the part of the plaintiffs because the facts as pleaded disclose nothing on which to ground an action for private nuisance, but merely give grounds for argument that the actions of the defendant resulted in the creation of a public nuisance the remedy for which is not at the disposal of the plaintiffs. He further takes the position that even if the plaintiffs had a right of action their damages are too remote to sustain the action.

On the pleadings it is apparent that the plaintiffs' attack was a two-pronged one, in negligence, and in nuisance, but counsel for them, Mr. Robert Wells, accepted the position that there was no case in negligence and confined his argument to his claim in nuisance.

In dealing with an objection in point of law we have to proceed on the assumption that the facts as pleaded by the plaintiffs are established. If the objection is not sustained and the trial of the issues take place, then, of course, the pleaded facts require proof.

For our present purposes then, I am assuming that the plaintiffs' assertion is true in substance, and that is, that the defendant discharged poisonous material into the waters of Placentia Bay, from its plant at Long Harbour, Placentia Bay, polluting the waters of the bay, poisoning fish "and rendering them of no commercial value".

So at the outset, we are put on inquiry to consider whether the facts disclose the creation of a tortious act, that is to say, the creation of a private nuisance, or the commission of a criminal act, which is to say, a public nuisance. The former is a civil wrong, actionable at the suit of an affected person.

The latter has been defined by Sir James Stephen in his *Digest of the Criminal Law,* 9th ed. (1950) (using the term "common nuisance"), in these words at p. 179:

> A common nuisance is an act not warranted by law or an omission to discharge a legal duty, which act or omission obstructs or causes inconvenience or damage to the public in the exercise of rights common to all His Majesty's subjects.

Salmond, *The Law of Torts,* 15th ed. (1969), expresses it more succinctly at p. 64:

> A public or a common nuisance is a criminal offence. It is an act or omission which materially affects the reasonable comfort or convenience of life of a class of Her Majesty's subjects . . .

and he adds:

> A public nuisance falls within the law of torts only in so far as it may in the particular case constitute some form of tort also. Thus the obstruction of a highway is a public nuisance; but if it causes any special and peculiar damage to an individual, it is also a tort actionable at his suit.

What has happened here? The defendants by the discharge of poisonous waste from its phosphorous plant at Long Harbour, Placentia Bay, destroyed the fish life of the adjacent waters, and the plaintiffs, as all other fishermen in the area suffered in their livelihood. I have said "all other fishermen", but the resulting pollution created a nuisance to all persons—"all Her Majesty's subjects" —to use Stephen's phrase. It was not a nuisance peculiar to the plaintiffs, nor confined to their use of the waters of Placentia Bay. It was a nuisance committed against the public.

A somewhat similar occurrence happened at a fishing settlement in Labrador, at Little Grady Island, in 1927, when a whaling company erected a factory at Watering Cove on Big Grady Island and polluted the waters adjacent to the premises of a fishing establishment on the former island. In the event an action was taken by the fishery owners against the whaling company. The case was heard in this Court in 1929 by Kent, J., and his judgment has remained unchallenged. He found that amongst other things, that there was serious pollution of the fishing waters from the waste materials of the whale factory. The case is *McRae* v. *British Norwegian Whaling Co., Ltd.,* [1927-31] Nfld. L.R. 274. After declaring at p. 282 that:

> It is an established principle that the right to fish in the sea and public navigable waters is free and open to all. It is a public right that may be exercised by any of the King's subjects, and for any interference with it the usual remedies to vindicate a public right must be employed.

he proceeded to apply the principle to the facts before him at pp. 283-4:

> The plaintiffs in the present action must, therefore, in order to succeed on this cause of complaint, show that the injury inflicted upon them by the acts of the defendants, insofar as they affect the right of fishing in the public navigable waters in the vicinity of Little Grady Island, is, in regard to them, particular direct and substantial, over and above the injury thereby inflicted upon the public in general. It is not enough for the plaintiffs to show that

their business is interrupted or interfered with, by the public nuisance, to enable them to maintain a private action against the defendants in respect thereof, for such interruption or interference is not a direct but merely a consequential damage resulting to them from the nuisance. Neither is it an injury peculiar to the plaintiffs themselves, but is suffered by them in common with everyone else whose right to fish in these public waters is affected by the nuisance. The plaintiffs' right, as one of the public, to fish may be affected to a greater extent than that of others, but they have no ground of complaint different from anyone else who fishes or intends to fish in these waters. If the nuisance took the form of obstructing the right of the plaintiffs as adjacent land owners, of access from their land to the public navigable waters, the injury would be peculiar to themselves, not because it interrupted their right to fish in common with others in the public waters, but because it interrupted their right of access to these waters, which is an incident to the occupation of property adjacent to the sea and would therefore be an interference with a right peculiar to themselves and distinct from their right as one of the public to fish in the public waters. For these reasons I have come to the conclusion that the plaintiff's have failed to establish their right to maintain a private action in respect of the pollution by the defendants of these public navigable waters.

A somewhat similar situation arose in New Brunswick in 1934 in *Fillion* v. *New Brunswick International Paper Co.,* [1934] 3 D.L.R. 22, 8 M.P.R. 89. The waste from a paper mill into the Restigouche River in that Province polluted the waters of a bay where the plaintiff, with others, carried on smelt fishing. An action was taken in nuisance against the owners of the paper-mill and that part of the case was dismissed, Baxter, J., saying at p. 26:

> Assuming then, that the defendant's act constituted a public nuisance, and if it is wrongful I do not see how it can be anything else, the plaintiff has suffered differently from the rest of the public only in degree. That is not enough to entitle him to recover. Nearly all of the cases in which this principle has been invoked concern the obstruction of a highway, but *Ashby* v. *White,* 2 Ld. Raym. 938, at p. 955, 92 E.R. 126, *per* Holt, C.J., and the case of *Williams* in 5 Co. Rep. 72(b), 77 E.R. 163, show that the *ratio decidendi* is that it is inexpedient that there should be multiplicity of actions and that where a nuisance or injury is common to the whole public the remedy is by indictment but that no private right of action exists unless there is a special or particular injury to the plaintiff. *Iveson* v. *Moore,* 1 Ld. Raym. 486, 91 E.R. 1224, is perhaps the leading case. It is unnecessary to trace its application through a long series of cases under Expropriation Acts which often turn upon the language of a particular statute. In the present case the plaintiff's rights were only those which he possessed as one of the public and he suffered exactly the same interference as any other who assumed to exercise the public right of fishing. The jury have so found. Lord Haldane in *A.G.B.C.* v. *A.G. Can.,* 15 D.L.R. at p. 315, assimilates the right of public fishing to that of navigation or "the right to use a navigable river as a highway." He also held in *A.G. Can.* v. *A.G. Que., Re Quebec Fisheries* (1920), 56 D.L.R. 358, at p. 361, that the right of fishing in tidal waters is "a public and not a proprietary right." It follows that on this branch of the case the plaintiff can not succeed.

I think it is clear that the facts, as we have them, can only support the view that there has been pollution of the waters of this area of Placentia Bay which amounts to a public nuisance. If I am right in this view then the law is clear that a private action by the plaintiffs is not sustainable.

Counsel for the plaintiffs, Mr. Robert Wells, argued that when a public nuisance has been created anyone who suffers special damage, that is direct damage has a right of action. I am unable to agree to this rather wide application of Salmond's view that a public nuisance may become a tortious act. I think the right view is that any person who suffers peculiar damage has a right of action, but where the damage is common to all persons of the same class, then a personal right of action is not maintainable. Mr. Wells suggests that the plaintiff's right to outfit for the fishery and their right to fish is a particular right and this right having been interfered with they have a cause of action. This right which they enjoy is a right in common with all Her Majesty's subjects, an interference with which is the whole test of a public nuisance; a right which can only be vindicated by the appropriate means, which is an action by the Attorney-General, either with or without a relator, in the common interest of the public.

Rose et al. v. *Miles,* [1814-23] All E.R. Rep. 580, which has been cited is not in point, as the judgment of Lord Ellenborough, C.J., clearly shows [at p. 581], "This is something substantially more injurious to this person, than to the public at large," and Dampier, J., said "The present case admits of this distinction from most other cases, that here the plaintiff was interrupted in the actual enjoyment of the highway." With great respect I hold that view that that judgment was applicable only to the particular facts of that case, and can only support the general proposition that a peculiar and particular damage, distinct from that of the general public, is necessary to sustain an action.

I think the law as stated by Kent, J., in the *McRae* case remains unchallenged. In this case the facts are indistinguishable and what Mr. Justice Kent said is fully applicable.

In the light of what I have said it becomes unnecessary to deal at length with the further point raised by the defendant, that the remoteness of damage must bar the plaintiffs' action. Mr. Wells suggests that this is a point applicable only to an action in negligence and plays no part in an action in nuisance. He fails to convince me that this is so. I would only say that to sustain an action the damages asserted must be direct and not consequential. There have been several recent judgments dealing with this point: *SCM (U.K.) Ltd.* v. *W.J. Whittall & Son Ltd.,* [1970] 3 All E.R. 245, was decided in the Court of Appeal, and though the action here was in negligence, I would be prepared to adopt the view of Lord Denning, M.R., that economic loss without direct damage is not usually recoverable at law. Similar considerations apply in this case; I think it would be a matter of extreme difficulty to say what direct damages the plaintiffs could pin-point as deriving from the defendant's operations. In negligence the damages would not likely be recoverable, and I think that this is equally so in an action in nuisance.

It is clear then, that the objection raised by the defendant's pleading should be upheld; this disposes of the sufficiency of the plaintiff's cause of action, and their claims must be dismissed, so that the judgment goes for the defendant, with costs.

Action dismissed.

NOTES

1. Do you agree that the fishermen of Placentia Bay suffered no special damage and thus should be denied recompense for public nuisance? Why do Attorneys-General not take a more active role in cases such as these on behalf of the public?

2. Compare with *Burgess* v. *M/V Tamano* (1973), 370 F. Supp. 247 (U.S.D.C. Maine), where oil was discharged into a bay affecting commercial fishermen, clam diggers and other local businessmen. The court found that the fishermen suffered particular damage, but that the businessmen did not. Gignoux D.J. said:

"The commercial fishermen and clam diggers in the present cases clearly have a special interest, quite apart from that of the public generally, to take fish and harvest clams from the coastal waters of the State of Maine. The injury of which they complain has resulted from defendants' alleged interference with *their* direct exercise of the public right to fish and to dig clams.

It would be an incongruous result for the Court to say that a man engaged in commercial fishing or clamming, and dependent thereon for his livelihood, who may have had his business destroyed by the tortious act of another, should be denied any right to recover for his pecuniary loss on the ground that his injury is no different in kind from that sustained by the general public. Indeed, in substantially all of those cases in which commercial fishermen using public waters have sought damages for the pollution or other tortious invasion of those waters, they have been permitted to recover. [Citations] These cases are no more than applications of the more general principle that pecuniary loss to the plaintiff will be regarded as different in kind 'where the plaintiff has an established business making a commercial use of the public right with which the defendant interferes . . . .' "

As to the businessmen, Judge Gignoux stated:

"Unlike the commercial fishermen and clam diggers, the Old Orchard Beach businessmen do not assert any interference with *their* direct exercise of a public right. They complain only of loss of customers indirectly resulting from alleged pollution of the coastal waters and beaches in which they do not have a property interest. Although in some instances their damage may be greater in degree, the injury of which they complain, which is derivative from that of the public at large, is common to all businesses and residents of the Old Orchard Beach area. In such circumstances, the line is drawn and the courts have consistently denied recovery."

3. In *Esso Petroleum* v. *Southport Corp.*, [1954] 2 Q.B. 182 (C.A.); revd [1956] A.C. 212 (H.L.), some oil was discharged into the water by a ship and washed up on the plaintiff's shore, causing considerable damage. Many issues were discussed in the case, but on the issue of public nuisance Denning M.R. had this to say:

". . . [I]t is, in my opinion, a public nuisance to discharge oil into the sea in such circumstances that it is likely to be carried on to the shores and beaches of our land to the prejudice and discomfort of Her Majesty's subjects. It is an offence punishable by the common law. Furthermore, if any person should suffer greater damage or inconvenience from the oil than the generality of the public, he can have an action to recover damages on that account, provided, of course, that he can discover the offender who discharged the oil. This action would have been described in the old days as an action on the case, but it is now simply an action for a nuisance. I realize that by a statute passed in 1922 the discharge of oil in navigable waters has been made an offence punishable summarily; but that does not mean that it is not also a public nuisance by the common law."

Lord Radcliffe agreed with this view that the discharged oil "may possibly have constituted a public nuisance from which the respondent suffered special damage . . .".

See also *National Harbours Board* v. *Hildon Hotel (1963) Ltd.* (1967), 61 W.W.R. 75 (B.C.), public nuisance to discharge oil into bay.

4. See generally Prosser, "Private Action for Public Nuisance" (1966), 52 Va. L. Rev. 997; Estey, "Public Nuisance and Standing to Sue" (1972), 10 Osgoode Hall L.J. 563; Rothstein, "Private Action for Public Nuisance: The Standing Problem" (1974), 76 W. Va. L. Rev. 453; Morrison, "The Nuisance Action: A Useful Tool for the Environmental Lawyer" (1974), 23 U.N.B.L.J. 21; McLaren, "The Law of Torts and Pollution" in Special Lectures of the Law Society of Upper Canada, *New Developments in the Law of Torts* (1973); Sax, *Defending the Environment—A Strategy for Citizen Action* (1970); McLaren, "Common Law Nuisance and the Environmental Battle" (1972), 10 Osgoode Hall L.J. 505.

MINT v. GOOD

Court of Appeal. [1951] 1 K.B. 517, [1950] 2 All E.R. 1159,
94 Sol. Jo. 822

The plaintiff, a boy, was injured by the collapse of a wall adjoining the high-way. The wall was owned by the defendant who had leased the premises to a tenant. The trial judge found that, although the wall was a nuisance, the land-lord was not liable for it. The appeal was allowed.

Denning L.J.: The law of England has always taken particular care to protect those who use a highway. It puts on the occupier of adjoining premises a special responsibility for the structures which he keeps beside the highway. So long as those structures are safe, all well and good; but if they fall into disrepair, so as to be a potential danger to passers-by, then they are a nuisance, and, what is more, a public nuisance; and the occupier is liable to anyone using the highway who is injured by reason of the disrepair. It is no answer for him to say that he and his servants took reasonable care; for, even if he has employed a competent indepen-dent contractor to repair the structure, and has every reason for supposing it to be safe, the occupier is still liable if the independent contractor did the work badly: see *Tarry* v. *Ashton.*

The occupier's duty to passers-by is to see that the structure is as safe as reasonable care can make it; a duty which is as high as the duty which an occupier owes to people who pay to come on to his premises. He is not liable for latent defects, which could not be discovered by reasonable care on the part of anyone, nor for acts of trespassers of which he neither knew, nor ought to have known: see *Barker* v. *Herbert;* but he is liable when structures fall into dangerous disrepair, because there must be some fault on the part of someone or other for that to happen; and he is responsible for it to persons using the highway, even though he was not actually at fault himself. That principle was laid down in this court in *Wringe* v. *Cohen,* where it is to be noted that the principle is confined to "premises on a highway", and is, I think, clearly correct in regard to the respon-sibility of an occupier to passers-by.

The question in this case is whether the owner, as well as the occupier, is under a like duty to passers-by. I think that in many cases he is. The law has shown a remarkable development on this point during the last sixteen years. The three cases of *Wilchick* v. *Marks and Silverstone, Wringe* v. *Cohen,* and *Heap* v. *Ind, Coope & Allsopp Ld.,* show that the courts are now taking a realistic view of these matters. They recognize that the occupying tenant of a small dwelling-house does not in practice do the structural repairs, but the owner does; and that if a passer-by is injured by the structure being in dangerous disrepair, the occupier has not the means to pay damages, but the owner has, or, at any rate, he can insure against it. If a passer-by is injured by its falling on him, he should be entitled to damages from someone, and the person who ought to pay is the owner, because he is in practice responsible for the repairs. This practical respon-sibility means that he has de facto control of the structure for the purpose of repairs and is therefore answerable in law for its condition. Parliament has long made owners responsible under the Public Health Acts for nuisances arising from defects of a structural character: see s. 94 of the Public Health Act, 1875, and s. 93 (*b*) of the Public Health Act, 1936; and the common law now also in many cases makes them responsible for public nuisances due to the disrepair of the structure.

This seems to me to be a logical consequence of the cases to which we have been referred. In *Wilchick* v. *Marks and Silverstone* the landlord had covenanted to repair; in *Heap* v. *Ind, Coope & Allsopp Ltd.,* he had not covenanted to repair, but had reserved a right to enter. In the present case he has not reserved a right to enter, but he has in practice always done the structural repairs. I cannot think that the liability of the owner to passers-by depends on the precise terms of the tenancy agreement between the owner and the tenant, that is to say, on whether he has expressly reserved a right to enter or not. It depends on the degree of control exercised by the owner, in law or in fact, for the purpose of repairs. If a landlord is liable when he reserves an express right to enter, he is also liable when he has an implied right; and even if he has no strict right, but has been given permission to enter whenever he asked, it should make no difference. The landlord has in practice taken the structural repairs on himself and should be responsible for any disrepair.

That is sufficient for the decision of this case, but I venture to doubt whether in these days a landlord can in all cases exempt himself from liability to passers-by by taking a covenant from a tenant to repair the structure adjoining the highway. I know that in *Pretty* v. *Bickmore* a landlord managed to escape liability for a coal-plate which was, at the beginning of the lease, in dangerous disrepair because he took from the tenant a covenant to repair. I doubt whether he would escape liability today. Again, suppose that a landlord of small houses took from weekly tenants a covenant to repair the structure, and then did not trouble to enforce the covenant or to repair himself? Could he escape liability by so doing? I doubt it. It may be that in such cases the landlord owes a duty to the public which he cannot get rid of by delegating it to another. These questions do not however arise here because there was no such covenant. In this case the judge found that the condition of the wall was a nuisance, and that a reasonable examination of the wall by a competent person would have detected the condition in which it was. That means that the duty of the landlord was not fulfilled. His duty was to see that the structure was as safe as reasonable care could make it. It was not so safe.

I agree, therefore, that the appeal should be allowed, and judgment entered accordingly.

NOTES

1. This principle has even been extended to people who are on private land near the highway. See *Harrold* v. *Watney*, [1898] 2 Q.B. 320 (C.A.). It will not be invoked, however, if the person hurt is a long way from the road. See *Hardcastle* v. *South Yorkshire Ry.* (1859), 157 E.R. 761.

2. There are cases such as this, where there is a public nuisance, which demand proof of negligence before recovery will be allowed. See *Cowan* v. *Harrington*, [1938] 3 D.L.R. 271. See also *Hagen* v. *Goldfarb* (1961), 28 D.L.R. (2d) 746 (N.S.). If this is nuisance, why should proof of negligence be necessary?

3. In *Ware* v. *Garston Haulage Co.,* [1944] K.B. 30 the plaintiff motorcyclist at night collided with a truck, which was left unlighted and unattended on a highway. He later died as a result of injuries sustained and an action was brought on behalf of his family based on negligence and nuisance. Scott L.J. held that there was a nuisance and explained: "If anything is placed on a highway which is likely to cause an accident through being an obstruction to those who are using the highway on their lawful occasions . . . and an accident results, there is an actionable nuisance." This case was criticized by Laskin (1944), 22 Can. Bar Rev. 468.

4. *Ware* v. *Garston Haulage* was explained in *Maitland* v. *Raisbeck,* [1944] 1 K.B. 689 (C.A.), where a bus collided with the back of a slow-moving truck, whose rear light had gone out. Greene M.R. observed:

> "We must approach this question of nuisance on the footing of the county court judge's finding that there was no negligence on the part of the second defendants in respect of the extinction of this rear light. In other words, we assume that the rear light went out for some reason not referable to any

negligence on the part of the second defendants. It was, therefore, a misfortune which occurred to the lorry without any fault by them. It is argued that, apart from the driver's knowledge or lack of knowledge that the light was out, and apart from any suggestion of negligence, the mere fact that the light was out at the time, of necessity turned the lorry into a nuisance on the highway. That is a proposition which the county court judge refused to accept, and in my opinion, he was right in doing so. Every person who uses the highway must exercise due care, but he has a right to use the highway, and, if something happens to him which, in fact, causes an obstruction to the highway, but is in no way referable to his fault, it is wrong to suppose that ipso facto and immediately a nuisance is created. A nuisance will obviously be created if he allows the obstruction to continue for an unreasonable time or in unreasonable circumstances, but the mere fact that an obstruction has come into existence cannot turn it into a nuisance. It must depend on the facts of each case whether or not a nuisance is created. If that were not so, it would seem that every driver of a vehicle on the road would be turned into an insurer in respect of latent defects in his machine."

How does this case affect *Ware* v. *Garston Haulage?* See also *Arm River Enterprises* v. *McIvor* (1978), 85 D.L.R. (3d) 758, slow moving vehicle not public nuisance.

5. In *Newell* v. *Smith* (1971), 20 D.L.R. (3d) 598 (N.S.), the defendants blocked up a roadway preventing the plaintiffs from having access to their property. Whenever the blockage was removed, it would be replaced by the defendants. Liability was found by Justice Dubinsky on the ground that the plaintiffs suffered "particular damage and substantial inconvenience . . ." and their damage was found to be "quite distinct from the general inconvenience endured by them in common with the public at large".

B. PRIVATE NUISANCE

PUGLIESE ET AL. v. NATIONAL CAPITAL COMMISSION

Ontario Court of Appeal. (1977), 3 C.C.L.T. 18;
affd but answer varied (1979), 25 N.R. 498, 8 C.C.L.T. 69 (S.C.C.)

The plaintiffs sued because their ground water table below their properties was substantially lowered by the construction of a collector sewer on nearby lands owned by the N.C.C. As a result, they claimed, their properties were damaged because of subsidence. They also contended that there was damage caused as a result of drilling and blasting. An application under Rule 124 was referred to the Court of Appeal, in accordance with s. 35 of the Judicature Act. The court agreed, *inter alia,* to answer the following question: "Does an owner of land have a right to the support of water beneath his land, not flowing in a defined channel, and does the owner have a right of action in negligence or nuisance . . . for any damage resulting from the abstraction of such water?" The court found that both negligence and nuisance were available to the plaintiffs.

As to nuisance **Howland J.A.** wrote: Nuisance is a separate field of tortious liability and not merely an offshoot of the law of negligence. A nuisance may be caused by an intentional or by a negligent act. Negligence is not a prerequisite to an action for nuisance. A negligent act may, however, be a constituent element of a nuisance or may itself constitute a nuisance.

In Salmond on The Law of Torts, 16th ed. (1973), p. 51, the following is stated as a definition of "private nuisance" which has received judicial approval:

"Private nuisances, at least in the vast majority of cases, are interferences for a substantial length of time by owners or occupiers of property with the use or enjoyment of neighbouring property": *Cunard* v. *Antifyre Ltd.,* [1933] 1 K.B. 551 at 557.

At the outset a question arose whether the alleged facts in the present actions could give rise to a right of action in nuisance because the interference with the plaintiffs' use and enjoyment of their lands resulted from the removal of water rather than from an invasion of their property by some substance, as is usually the case in actions for nuisance. I am satisfied, however, from a consideration of the authorities that there is a sound basis for allowing recovery for nuisance in these circumstances: . . . .

In determining whether a nuisance exists, it is not sufficient to ask whether an occupier has made a reasonable use of his own property. One must ask whether his conduct is reasonable considering the fact that he has a neighbour. As Lord Wright pointed out in *Sedleigh-Denfield* v. *O'Callaghan*, [1940] A.C. 880 at 903, [1940] 3 All E.R. 349:

> "A balance has to be maintained between the right of the occupier to do what he likes with his own, and the right of his neighbour not to be interfered with. It is impossible to give any precise or universal formula, but it may broadly be said that a useful test is perhaps what is reasonable according to the ordinary usages of mankind living in society, or more correctly in a particular society."

The matter is also well summarized in Fleming, The Law of Torts, 4th ed. (1971), p. 346, as follows:

> " 'Liability is imposed only in those cases where the harm or risk to one is greater than he ought to be required to bear under the circumstances.' [Restatement of the Law of Torts, 1934, para. 822, comment *j*.]
>
> "The paramount problem in the law of nuisance is, therefore, to strike a tolerable balance between conflicting claims of landowners, each invoking the privilege to exploit the resources and enjoy the amenities of his property without undue subordination to the reciprocal interests of the other. Reconciliation has to be achieved by compromise, and the basis for adjustment is reasonable user. Legal intervention is warranted only when an excessive use of property causes inconvenience beyond what other occupiers in the vicinity can be expected to bear, having regard to the prevailing standard of comfort of the time and place. Reasonableness in this context is a two-sided affair. It is viewed not only from the standpoint of the defendant's convenience, but must also take into account the interest of the surrounding occupiers. It is not enough to ask: Is the defendant using his property in what would be a reasonable manner if he had no neighbour? The question is, is he using it reasonably, having regard to the fact that he has a neighbour?
>
> "Both the utility of his own conduct and the gravity of the harm to which he exposes others are important factors in this evaluating process."

Nuisances of a minor character arising from the ordinary use and occupation of residential property, such as the burning of weeds and the making of repairs, if performed reasonably and not to an excessive degree, are not actionable. As Bramwell B. said in *Bamford* v. *Turnley* (1862), 3 B. & S. 66, 122 E.R. 27 at 33:

> "It is as much for the advantage of one owner as of another; for the very nuisance the one complains of, as the result of the ordinary use of his neighbour's land, he himself will create in the ordinary use of his own, and the reciprocal nuisances are of a comparatively trifling character. The convenience of such a rule may be indicated by calling it a rule of give and take, live and let live."

Beyond this point it is necessary to ask if the conduct of an occupier of land has been reasonable vis-à-vis his neighbour. The taking of all reasonable care is not a defence to an action for nuisance. If an operation cannot by the exercise of reasonable care and skill be prevented from causing a nuisance, then it cannot lawfully be undertaken unless there is either a statutory authorization or the consent of those injured: . . . .

In *Storms* v. *M.G. Henniger Ltd.; Gonu* v. *M.G. Henniger Ltd.*, supra, this court held that the excavation of sand and gravel was a natural user of the land, and there was no right of action in damages with reference to the resulting flow of subterranean water. There remains open the question whether there might be a right of action in nuisance in the present actions if there was unreasonable user of the lands of the NCC.

The test for determining whether a nuisance was created is not whether the drainage of a very large quantity of water for the construction of the LCS was a reasonable user of the NCC lands when looked at from the point of view of the NCC. Rather it is a question whether it was reasonable so far as the plaintiffs were concerned.

Counsel for the plaintiffs contended that the pumping of the excessive amount of water by the defendants was unlawful, not in the sense that it was a statutory violation of s. 37 of The Ontario Water Resources Act, but as an unnatural, and therefore an unlawful, user of the lands of the NCC. In my opinion, it would be for the trial judge to determine whether the abstraction of a very large quantity of water causing damage to the plaintiffs' properties through subsidence, more particularly if it were abstracted in a negligent manner, constituted a nuisance. Did it subject the plaintiffs' lands to damage beyond that which they could reasonably be expected to tolerate? In my opinion, the alleged conduct on the part of the defendants, if established at the trial, could constitute an excessive user of the lands of the NCC. I am of the opinion that interference with a right to the support of underground water can give rise to a cause of action in nuisance as well as in negligence.

[The Court, therefore, answered the question as follows:]

1. An owner of land does not have an absolute right to the support of water beneath his land not flowing in a defined channel, but he does have a right not to be subjected to interference with the support of such water amounting to negligence or nuisance.

2. Such an owner does have a right of action:

    (a) in negligence for damages resulting from the abstraction of such water; or

    (b) in nuisance for damages for unreasonable user of the lands in the abstraction of such water.

NOR-VIDEO SERVICES LTD. v. ONTARIO HYDRO

Ontario Supreme Court. (1978), 4 C.C.L.T. 244

The plaintiff cable television company sued Ontario Hydro for locating one of its electrical power installations where it would interfere with its transmission and reception of T.V. broadcast signals. The plaintiff was the only supplier of T.V. to a small northern community in Ontario named Atikokan. The defendant needed a new transformer and power transmission line and, after considering several sites, chose one next to the plaintiff's receiving tower because it was the most economical and convenient location available. The defendant had been made aware of the possible difficulties but assured the plaintiff that there would be no problem. They built the system and it interfered with the T.V. reception. Remedial efforts by Hydro were made, but in vain. Robins J. found the defendants liable in nuisance, but awarded only minimal damages because there was no proof of any large losses.

Robins J.: The interest which Nor-Video complains has been interfered with or invaded, and allegedly unreasonably so, is, in nuisance terms, its interest in the use and enjoyment of its land. The harm suffered is not, as in most nuisance cases, of a physical nature to land or tangible property nor is it personal discomfort, annoyance or inconvenience. The gravamen of the complaint is the inability to use and enjoy property to the same extent and with the same result as before Hydro's intervention; or, put another way, the plaintiff's complaint is that the interference with TV broadcast reception prevents it from freely enjoying its property and putting it to its full business use. Nor-Video, in short, contends that television reception is an integral part of the beneficial enjoyment of its property and it is entitled to nuisance to protection against the unreasonable and substantial interference with or invasion of such an interest.

Hydro's response to this contention is twofold. It says firstly that the reception of television does not constitute an interest in the use and enjoyment of land recognized in the law of nuisance and accordingly legal protection is not afforded against its interference. And secondly, it says, that, in any event, the plaintiff has applied its property to so abnormally sensitive a use that interference with it cannot amount to nuisance.

On the first submission Hydro finds support in dictum in a case arising out of a somewhat similar factual situation: *Bridlington Relay Ltd.* v. *Yorkshire Electricity Bd.,* [1965] Ch. 436, [1965] 1 All E.R. 264. There Buckley J. (p. 270) took "judicial notice of the widespread reception of television in domestic circles . . . on the footing that in those circles television is enjoyed almost entirely for what I think must be regarded as recreational purposes . . ." and proceeded to observe (p. 271) that:

"There are, of course, many reported cases in which something adversely affecting the beneficial enjoyment of property has been held to constitute a legal nuisance; but I have been referred to no case in which interference with a purely recreational facility has been held to do so. Considerations of health and physical comfort and well being appear to me to be on a somewhat different level from recreation considerations. I do not wish to be taken as laying down that in no circumstances can something which interferes merely with recreational facilities or activities amount to an actionable nuisance. It may be that in some other case the court may be satisfied that some such interference should be regarded, according to such 'plain and sober and simple notions' as Sir J.L. Knight Bruce, V.-C., referred to in a well-known passage in his judgment in *Walter* v. *Selfe* (1851), 4 De G. & Sm. 315 at p. 322, as detracting from the beneficial use and enjoyment by neighbouring owners of their properties to such an extent as to warrant their protection by the law. For myself, however, I do not think that it can at present be said that the ability to receive television free from occasional, even if recurrent and severe, electrical interference is so important a part of an ordinary householder's enjoyment of his property that such interference should be regarded as a legal nuisance particularly, perhaps if such interference affects only one of the available alternative programmes."

From this it is argued that since the interference in this case is to a "recreational facility" it cannot constitute a sufficient interference with ordinary beneficial enjoyment as to amount to a legal nuisance. With deference I cannot agree. Whatever may have been the situation in England at the time of *Bridlington,* in my opinion it is manifest that in Canada today television viewing is an important incident of ordinary enjoyment of property and should be protected as such. It is clearly a principal source of information, education and entertainment for a large part of the country's population; an inability to receive it or an unreasonable interference with its reception would to my mind undoubtedly detract from the beneficial use and ownership of property even applying the test of "plain, sober and simple notions" referred to in the above passage. See note 81 L.Q.R. 181.

"A balance has to be maintained between the right of the occupier to do what he likes with his own and the right of his neighbour not to be interfered with. It is impossible to give any precise or universal formula, but it may broadly be said that a useful test is perhaps what is reasonable according to the ordinary usages of mankind living in society, or, more correctly, in a particular society. The forms which nuisance may take are protean": *Sedleigh-Denfield* v. *O'Callagan,* [1940] A.C. 880, [1940] 3 All E.R. 349 at 364 (H.L.) per Lord Wright.

The notion of nuisance is a broad and comprehensive one which has been held to encompass a wide variety of interferences considered harmful and actionable because of their infringement upon or diminution of an occupier's interest in the undisturbed enjoyment of his property. I can see no warrant for refinements in approach which would preclude from protection the interest in TV reception even assuming it to be a recreational amenity. In this day and age it is simply one of the benefits and pleasures commonly derived from domestic occupancy of property; its social value and utility to a community, perhaps even more so to a remote community such as the one in this case, cannot be doubted. The category of interests covered by the tort of nuisance ought not to be and need not be closed, in my opinion, to new or changing developments associated from time to time with normal usage and enjoyment of land. Accordingly I would reject the defendant's submission and hold that television reception is an interest worthy of protection and entitled to vindication in law.

This brings me to Hydro's next contention which is that Nor-Video has devoted its property to an unusually sensitive use and cannot by so doing make a nuisance out of conduct or activity which would otherwise be harmless. As a matter of general legal principle it is undisputed that an interference with something of abnormal sensitiveness or delicacy does not of itself constitute a nuisance. The law does not extend protection through nuisance to hypersensitive individuals or industries; it is against interferences to what objectively can be considered ordinary uses of property or enjoyments of life that protection is afforded.

"A man cannot increase the liabilities of his neighbour by applying his own property to special uses, whether for business or pleasure": . . . .

The question here is whether, as a matter of fact, the plaintiff's use of its property is of so "delicate" or "sensitive" a nature or constitutes so "special" or "abnormal" a use that injury to it is not actionable in nuisance. It is my opinion that the use to which Nor-Video put its property cannot and ought not to be so characterized. As I view this matter its position, in substance, is comparable to that of owners of domestic antennas who, but for the prohibitive cost involved, could, if they wished, receive the programmes of distant stations by erecting an antenna of similar height. A community antenna system, over-simply stated, provides TV viewers of the community with the advantage of more channels at an affordable cost. But the nature of the apparatus involved is not significantly different or more susceptible to TVI than the installations of the ordinary home-owner and in my view should be treated as being in the same category.

In *Bridlington,* it was said that the cable operator "could not succeed in a claim for damages for nuisance if what I may call an ordinary receiver of television by means of an aerial mounted on his own house could not do so." Accepting that, and with the greatest respect for the contrary view indicated there, I do not appreciate why a domestic owner could not succeed in a nuisance claim or, more particularly, why his claim should be defeated on the ground of extra-sensitive use of property. If, to take an example, Hydro should install in a residential district (zoning bylaws aside) a new device to improve electrical services which resulted in the obliteration of TV in the area, I would not think that claims brought against it in nuisance should fail solely on the ground that the TV antennas of the residents amounted to an abnormally sensitive use of their land. To the contrary, as I see the matter, the residents were simply maintaining a commonplace domestic facility and using their property, in terms of modern society, in a normal, and by no means exceptional, manner.

Interference with a CATV system has the same net result and, in my view, should be treated in the same fashion. I do not believe it can be concluded at the present time that a cable operation, federally licensed and regulated, creates so exceptionally sensitive or vulnerable a condition or should be regarded as so special or abnormal an enterprise that it cannot seek the protection of the law of nuisance, particularly, I might add, against a defendant who by the exercise of reasonable care and foresight and without significant sacrifice to its project could have avoided the harm complained of. It provides, especially in the context of this case, the facility needed for an important aspect of a householder's ordinary enjoyment of his property and should be entitled to protection against unreasonable interference. . . .

I move now to consider whether the conduct which caused the interference with Nor-Video's interest in the beneficial use of its land was of a type that should subject Hydro to liability.

Just as all interferences with use and enjoyment of land are not actionable, so all types of conduct causing such interferences do not constitute actionable wrongs. The complaint in this case is not that Hydro acted intentionally in invading the plaintiff's interest or that it engaged in the type of malevolent or unreasonable conduct devoid of or containing comparatively little social or economic utility such as is found in the line of cases of which *Hollywood Silver Fox Farm, Ltd.* v. *Emmett*, [1936] 2 K.B. 468, [1936] 1 All E.R. 825 is a classic example. Nor is it argued that the invasion was the consequence of an abnormally dangerous activity to which the rule in *Rylands* v. *Fletcher* [(1868), L.R. 3 H.L. 330] should apply and for which Hydro should be held strictly liable.

The complaint on which Nor-Video's case rests is that proprietary interests entitled to protection were invaded by Hydro's action in constructing high power electrical installations in locations where it knew or should have known that to do so would adversely affect the cable system. (The further contention that the installations were improperly designed or maintained is not, as I indicated, supported by the evidence).

It is manifest that Hydro is an important public utility which has been granted wide statutory powers to enable it to perform its highly essential undertakings: The Power Commission Act, R.S.O. 1970, c. 354 (renamed The Power Corporation Act, 1973 (Ont.), c. 57). But it has not been granted immunity from tort liability and, in my opinion, such immunity cannot be implied from a reading of s. 24 of the Act. It was neither inevitable, nor necessary, that the plaintiff be detrimentally affected by Hydro's fulfilment of its legislative mandate. This occurred because Hydro failed to recognize, as it should in my opinion, that by its site selection it created an unreasonable risk to the activity conducted by the cable company on neighbouring lands. The locations in question were discretionary and not prescribed by statute; they did not constitute the only feasible places for Hydro's works. The fact that the acquisition and use of these sites was later retroactively authorized by Order in Council pursuant to s. 24 does not, in my view, render them mandatory locations so as to authorize a nuisance or afford Hydro any greater immunity from action than that extended by s. 24(5) which operates only to prevent it from being "restrained by injunction or other process or proceeding".

Without repeating the findings I set forth earlier, it can, in short, be stated that in planning and embarking on its project in the locations in question Hydro failed properly to apprehend or calculate a perceptible risk to the plaintiff's legitimate interests. It was bound in the circumstances prevailing in the instant case to do so. In planning its own undertaking it was required to act carefully and take into account the likelihood of unreasonably detrimental consequences to the plaintiff. Legislative authority cannot in my opinion be involved as a defence in this case: see, *Hammersmith & City Ry. Co.* v. *Brand* (1869), L.R. 4 H.L. 171; *Manchester Corpn.* v. *Farnsworth,* [1930] A.C. 171 (H.L.); *Metropolitan Asylum Dist. Managers* v. *Hill* (1881), 6 App. Cas. 193 (H.L.); *Geddis* v. *Bann Reservoir Proprietors* (1878), 3 App. Cas. 430 (H.L.); *Guelph Worsted Spinning Co.* v. *Guelph; Guelph Carpet Mills Co.* v. *Guelph* (1914), 30 O.L.R. 466, 18 D.L.R. 73; and generally, for a comprehensive collection and analysis of the authorities, Linden "Strict Liability, Nuisance and Legislative Authorization" (1966), 4 Osgoode Hall L.J. 196.

The defendant's conduct in my view constitutes negligence in the usual sense of failing to take due care to avoid a foreseeable risk. But even if not, it amounts to conduct unreasonable enough to complete the tort of nuisance—there are elements of "fault" and "foreseeability" present sufficient to satisfy the tort: *The Wagon Mound (No. 2),* supra, per Lord Reid at p. 716. The defendant by the placement of its electrical installation commandeered, at least partially, the plaintiff's beneficial use of its property and thereby imposed a burden on it which it ought not to be required to bear without compensation for those damages it may establish. It is not without significance that Hydro obtained a substantial saving in cost by utilizing the locations it did and, in the circumstances, its submission that it should bear no liability even if it put the plaintiff out of business entirely seems to me patently unfair. In the balancing of interests appropriate to this department of the law the social utility of Hydro's undertaking does not provide, as argued, justification for the infringement in this case of private interests; nor can it be said here that the cost of compensation will impair a public utility's ability to achieve its statutory duty or impose undue hardship on it.

To sum up, it is my conclusion that an interest entitled to protection has been unreasonably invaded by conduct which forms the basis for liability and the tort of nuisance has been accordingly established.

NOTES

1. What role did negligence play in the reasoning of the court? Was a finding of negligence necessary before liability could be imposed?

2. Do you agree with the court's reasoning on the issue of "unusually sensitive use"? Is the cable T.V. station's user no different than that of an ordinary person who watches T.V. at home? What if this action had been brought by one T.V. viewer?

3. In *Noyes* v. *Huron & Erie Mortgage Corp.,* [1932] O.R. 426, the plaintiff had a large signboard on one building which he illuminated with advertising material with a "projectoscope" from another building. The defendant, which had premises across the street, illuminated its building in such a way that the reflection of light made it difficult to read the plaintiff's signboard. It was held that the plaintiff's use was of an "exceptional and delicate nature" and not in the "class of ordinary or usual business entitled to protection from interference

by a neighbouring owner in the exercise of his reasonable rights on his own property".

What if an ordinary citizen in an apartment was unable to sleep as a result of these activities?

4. In *O'Regan* v. *Bresson* (1977), 3 C.C.L.T. 214 (N.S. Co. Ct.), a plaintiff with an asthmatic condition was denied recovery against a stable operator on the basis of his "abnormal sensitiveness", but the owner of the property was permitted to recover.

APPLEBY v. ERIE TOBACCO CO.

Divisional Court of the Supreme Court of Ontario. (1910),
22 O.L.R. 533

The plaintiff, a merchant in Windsor, complained of noxious odours coming from the defendants' tobacco factory and interfering with the plaintiff's enjoyment of his premises in the vicinity of the factory. The plaintiff claimed an injunction in respect of these odours and other matters. At the trial the claim for an injunction was dismissed but a reference granted to assess damages. Plaintiff appealed.

Middleton J.: The odour from the tobacco arises chiefly from the processes of steaming, steeping, and stewing which it undergoes, and the boiling of sugar, licorice, and other ingredients with which it is mixed before it is reduced to "plug tobacco" ready for the market. These odours cannot be prevented if the manufacture is to go on, and, upon the evidence, the defendants appear to be doing their best to prevent injury to their neighbours.

Many witnesses were called for the plaintiff who describe the odour as a "most sickening smell", a "very bad smell", "very, very offensive", and "very nauseating". Some say that it produces vertigo and dizziness, others nausea and headache. Some do not find any evil result beyond that incident to the disagreeable nature of the odour. The defendants produce a number of witnesses, many of whom say that the odour is "not unhealthy"; others say that it "does not affect" them; and one enthusiastic lover of the weed describes it as "just splendid".

Upon the whole evidence, there can be no doubt that there is a strong odour that to many, if not most, is extremely disagreeable. . . .

Now, it is to be borne in mind that an arbitrary standard cannot be set up which is applicable to all localities. There is a local standard applicable in each particular district, but, though the local standard may be higher in some districts than in others, yet the question in each case ultimately reduces itself to the fact of nuisance or no nuisance, having regard to all the surrounding circumstances. This is shown by the oftenquoted passage in Lord Halsbury's judgment in *Colls* v. *Home and Colonial Stores, Limited,* [1904] A.C. 179, at p. 185; "A dweller in towns cannot expect to have as pure air, as free from smoke, smell and noise as if he lived in the country, and distant from other dwellings, and yet an excess of smoke, smell and noise may give a cause of action, but in each of such cases it becomes a question of degree, and the question is in each case whether it is a nuisance which will give a right of action."

In *Rushmer* v. *Polsue and Alfiere Limited,* [1906] 1 Ch. 234; [1907] A.C. 121, this principle is applied to the case of a printing office established in a neighbourhood devoted to printing, next door to the plaintiff's residence, and which rendered sleep impossible. Cozens Hardy, L.J., [1906] 1 Ch. at p. 250, sums up the situation in a way that commended itself to the Lords. It was, he says, contended "that a person living in a district specially devoted to a particular trade cannot complain of any nuisance by noise caused by the carrying on of any branch of that trade without carelessness and in a reasonable manner. I cannot assent to this argument. A resident in such a neighbourhood must put up with a certain amount of noise. The standard of comfort differs according to the situation of the property and the class of people who inhabit it . . . But whatever the standard of comfort in a particular district may be, I think the addition of a fresh noise caused by the defendant's works may be so substantial as to cause a legal nuisance. It does not follow that because I live, say, in the manufacturing part of Sheffield, I cannot complain if a steam-hammer is introduced next door, and so worked as to render sleep at night almost impossible, although previous to its introduction my house was a reasonably comfortable abode, having regard to the local standard; and it would be no answer to say that the steam-hammer is of the most modern approved pattern and is reasonably worked. In short . . . it is no answer to say that the neighbourhood is noisy, and that the defendant's machinery is of first-class character." . . .

It is plain, in this case, that the defendants' manufactory does constitute a nuisance. The odours do cause material discomfort and annoyance and render the plaintiff's premises less fit for the ordinary purposes of life, even making all possible allowances for the local standard of the neighbourhood.

The remaining question is: must an injunction follow? . . . The working rule, stated by A.L. Smith, L.J., in *Shelfer* v. *City of London Electric Lighting Co.*, [1895] 1 Ch. 287, at p. 322, as defining the cases in which damages may be given in lieu of an injunction, shows that here an injunction is the proper remedy. No one should be called upon to submit to the inconvenience and annoyance arising from a noxious and sickening odour for a "small money payment", and the inconvenience and annoyance cannot be adequately "estimated in money." The cases in which damages can be substituted for an injunction sought to abate a nuisance of the first class must be exceedingly rare.

The injunction should, therefore, go, restraining the defendants from so operating their works as to cause a nuisance to the plaintiff by reason of the offensive odours arising from the manufacture of tobacco: the operation of this injunction to be stayed for six months to allow the defendants to abate the nuisance if they can do so, or to make arrangements for the removal of that part of the business causing the odour.

NOTES

1. In *Oakley* v. *Webb* (1916), 38 O.L.R. 151, the character of a neighbourhood prevented noise from a stone-cutting establishment from being held an actionable nuisance. There was a railway yard behind the plaintiff's property. There was also a yard 150 feet away where horses and vans were kept. What if the stone-cutting establishment was situated in Forest Hill Village? Does this make sense or does it discriminate against those who cannot afford to live in a "good" neighbourhood? See Lloyd, "Noise as a Nuisance" (1974), 82 U. Penn. L. Rev. 567.

2. In *Thompson Schwab* v. *Costaki*, [1956] 1 All E.R. 652 (C.A.), the plaintiffs who occupied homes on a good residential street in London, obtained an injunction against the defendant's use of an adjoining house for prostitution. The practice of soliciting men in nearby streets and bringing them to the house constituted a substantial interference with the comfortable enjoyment of the plaintiffs' homes.

3. In *Shuttleworth* v. *Vancouver General Hospital*, [1927] 2 D.L.R. 573, the defendant opened a hospital for communicable diseases across the street from the plaintiff's house, 110 feet away. The court refused to interfere. It felt that seeing human suffering would not unduly hamper the plaintiff's enjoyment and comfort. It was merely a matter of "sentiment". Moreover, the fear of possible

infection, because it was unfounded in fact, could not be a basis for liability. The depreciation in the value of the land flowed not from a "legal wrong" but from an unfounded "sentiment of danger". Compare with *Everett* v. *Paschall* (1910), 61 Wash. 47, 111 P. 879, where plaintiff obtained an injunction against the operation of a tuberculosis sanitarium in a residential district. The evidence showed that although there was no actual danger to those in the vicinity, there was a depreciation in sale value due to the dread of tuberculosis. "The question is, not whether the fear is founded in science, but whether it exists; nor whether it is imaginary, but whether it is real, in that it affects the movements and conduct of men. Such fears are actual, and must be recognized by the courts as other emotions of the human mind."

4. Is a funeral home on a quiet residential street a nuisance? See Noel, "Unaesthetic Sights as Nuisance" (1939), 25 Cornell L.Q. 1.

5. Can the dust and noise from a gravel quarry amount to a nuisance? See *Muirhead* v. *Timbers Bros. Sand & Gravel* (1977), 3 C.C.L.T. 1 (Ont.).

6. What about the noise and dust of a building being demolished or built next door? See *Andreae* v. *Selfridge & Co. Ltd.,* [1938] Ch. 1, [1937] 3 All E.R. 255 (C.A.).

7. The plaintiff's house is next to a golf course. In the summer golf balls are constantly landing on his property (53 in one year). Nuisance? Trespass? See *Segal* v. *Derrick Golf & Winter Club* (1977), 2 C.C.L.T. 222 (Alta.).

8. If a blasting operation causes cracks in the rock permitting water to be polluted from a nearby piggery, does an action for nuisance lie? What about *Rylands* v. *Fletcher* here? See *Jackson* v. *Drury Construction Co.* (1974), 4 O.R. (2d) 735 (C.A.), *per* Dubin J.A.

THE MAYOR, ALDERMEN AND BURGESSES OF THE BOROUGH OF BRADFORD v. PICKLES

House of Lords. [1895] A.C. 587, 64 L.J.Ch. 759, 73 L.T. 353, 11 T.L.R. 555

The plaintiffs, carrying on a waterworks project pursuant to statute, derived their water from sources on land adjoining that of the defendant which was on a higher level. The plaintiffs claimed an injunction to restrain the defendant from sinking a shaft on his land for the professed purpose of working minerals on his lands, but in reality, as the plaintiffs alleged, for the sole purpose of injuring the plaintiffs in an endeavour to induce them to purchase his land, or to give him some other compensation. A statute authorizing the original waterworks project made it unlawful for any one "to divert, alter or appropriate in any other manner than by law they may be legally entitled any of the waters supplying or flowing" from the sources on the plaintiffs' lands. North, J., granted an injunction. On appeal the judgment was reversed. Plaintiffs appealed. The Court of Appeal dismissed the plaintiffs' action and the latter appealed.

Lord Halsbury, L.C.: In the case of *Chasemore* v. *Richards,* 7 H.L.C. 349, it became necessary for this House to decide whether an owner of land had a right to sink a well upon his own premises, and thereby abstract the subterranean water percolating through his own soil, which would otherwise, by the natural force of gravity, have found its way into springs which fed the River Wandle, the flow of which the plaintiff in that action had enjoyed for upwards of sixty years. The very question was then determined by this House, and it was held that the landowner had a right to do what he had done whatever his object or purpose might be, and although the purpose might be wholly unconnected with the enjoyment of his own estate.

The only remaining point is the question of fact alleged by the plaintiffs, that the acts done by the defendant are done, not with any view which deals with the use of his own land or the percolating water through it, but is done, in the language of the pleader, "maliciously". I am not certain that I can understand or give any intelligible construction to the word so used. Upon this supposition on which I am now arguing, it comes to an allegation that the defendant did maliciously something that he had a right to do. If this question were to have been tried in old times as an injury to the right in an action on the case, the plaintiffs would have had to allege, and to prove, if traversed, that they were entitled to the flow of the water, which, as I have already said, was an allegation they would have failed to establish.

This is not a case in which the state of mind of the person doing the act can affect the right to do it. If it was a lawful act, however ill the motive might be, he had a right to do it. If it was an unlawful act, however good his motive might be, he would have no right to do it. Motives and intentions in such a question as is now before your Lordships seem to me to be absolutely irrelevant. But I am not prepared to adopt Lindley, L.J.'s view of the moral obliquity of the person insisting on his right when that right is challenged. It is not an uncommon thing to stop up a path which may be a convenience to everybody else, and the use of which may be no inconvenience to the owner of the land over which the path goes. But when the use of it is insisted upon as a right, it is a familiar mode of testing that right to stop the permissive use, which the owner of the land would contend it to be, although the use may form no inconvenience to the owner.

So, here, if the owner of the adjoining land is in a situation in which an act of his, lawfully done on his own land, may divert the water which would otherwise go into the possession of this trading company, I see no reason why he should not insist on their purchasing his interest from which this trading company desires to make profit.

For these reasons, my Lords, I am of the opinion that this appeal ought to be dismissed.

Lord Ashbourne: . . . The plaintiffs have no case unless they can shew that they are entitled to the flow of the water in question, and that the defendant has no right to do what he is doing. Putting aside the statutes, the defendant's rights cannot be seriously contested. The law stated by this House in *Chasemore* v. *Richards* cannot be questioned. Mr. Pickles has acted within his legal rights throughout; and is he to forfeit those legal rights and be punished for their legal exercise because certain motives are imputed to him? If his motives were the most generous and philanthropic in the world, they would not avail him when his actions were illegal. If his motives are selfish and mercenary, that is no reason why his rights should be confiscated when his actions are legal.

[Judgments of Lord Watson, and Lord Macnaghten to the same effect are omitted.]

NOTES

1. Should the landowner out of pure "spite" be permitted to erect a fence on his own land so high and of such a nature as to block out the light and the view from his neighbour's windows? In *Knowles* v. *Richardson* (1669), 1 Mod. 55, Twisden, J., stated: "Why may not I build up a wall that another man may not look into my yard. Prospects may be stopped, so you do not darken the light." And see *McBean* v. *Wyllie* (1902), 14 Man. R. 135, holding that merely cutting off a view of a river was not actionable.

2. In the United States the protection of "spite fences" is being broken down not only by statute, but by development of the case law. In *Hornsby* v. *Smith* (1941), 191 Ga. 491, 13 S.E. 2d 20, defendant erected an eight foot heavy plank fence along the line of his property (vacant lots and a house) adjoining plaintiff. Plaintiff alleged that there was no benefit to defendant and that the fence was

built solely to injure plaintiff by obstructing the view and cutting off light. In an action for damages and an injunction defendant demurred on the ground that the facts showed no cause of action. The demurrer was overruled. "It is our opinion that malicious use of property resulting in injury to another is never a 'lawful use', but is in every case unlawful. The right to the use of property is therefore a qualified rather than absolute right. When one acting solely from malevolent motive does injury to his neighbour, to call such conduct the exercise of an absolute legal right is a perversion in terms." So also in *Barger* v. *Barringer* (1909), 66 S.E. 439 (N.C.): "The law would be untrue to its soundest principles if it declared that wanton and needless infliction of injury can ever be a legal right . . . We are not aware that this Court has ever extended the right of ownership in property so far as to authorize an owner to use it for the express purpose of creating a nuisance and no other."

3. In Ontario, municipalities have power to prescribe "the height and description of lawful fences" by The Municipal Act, R.S.O. 1970, c. 284, s. 354, para. 19.

HOLLYWOOD SILVER FOX FARM, LIMITED v. EMMETT

King's Bench Division. [1936] 2 K.B. 468, [1936] 1 All E.R. 825,
105 L.J.K.B. 829, 155 L.T. 288, 52 T.L.R. 611

Captain Chandler purchased a twenty-acre lot with a view to commencing business as a breeder of silver foxes. On his lot he erected a notice-board inscribed "Hollywood Silver Fox Farm". Defendant Emmett owned the field to the northeast which he was about to develop as a building estate and, feeling the notice-board detrimental to such development, he asked Captain Chandler to remove it. When this request was refused, defendant Emmett warned Captain Chandler that if the notice-board was not removed he would, during the breeding season, shoot with black powder as near as he could to the breeding pens and "I guarantee," he said, "that you will not raise a single cub." Shortly thereafter Captain Chandler formed the plaintiff company.

Silver foxes breed between January and May and, during the breeding season, the vixens are extremely nervous and any loud or unusual noises may either put the vixen off mating, produce a miscarriage, or, where she has whelped, may cause her to kill and devour her young. In April, defendant sent his son to discharge a 12-bore gun loaded with black powder on the border of his land near the vixens' pens. The same thing occurred on three following evenings. On the last occasion, defendant, in reply to Captain Chandler's protests, asked him if he intended to remove the notice-board, saying that he was acquainted with the law and knew he had a right to shoot as he pleased on his own land. The plaintiff's solicitors wrote the defendant demanding an undertaking for the discontinuance of the discharge of guns near the breeding pens, the defendant replying that the shooting was for the purpose of keeping down rabbits.

The plaintiff brought an action alleging nuisance. At the trial the judge found that defendant had sent his son to shoot near the pens not for the purpose of killing rabbits but for the purpose of frightening the vixens, and for no other purpose. He also found that plaintiff had sustained serious loss by the harm created among the breeding silver foxes.

MacNaghten J.: . . . Mr. Roche submitted that the defendant was entitled to shoot on his own land, and that even if his conduct was malicious he had not committed any actionable wrong. In support of his argument, Mr. Roche relied mainly on the decision of the House of Lords in the case of *Bradford Corporation* v. *Pickles.* . . .

. . . . there is authority for the view that in an action for nuisance by noise the intention of the person making the noise must be considered. In the case of

Gaunt v. *Fynney,* L.R. 8 Ch. 8, 12, Lord Selborne, delivering the judgment of the Court, said: "A nuisance by noise (supposing malice to be out of the question) is emphatically a question of degree." The parenthetical statement, "supposing malice to be out of the question," clearly indicated that his Lordship thought that in the case of an alleged nuisance by noise where the noise was made maliciously different considerations would apply from those applicable where the defendant had, in the words of Lord Holt, "occasion" to make the noise. In *Christie* v. *Davey,* [1893] 1 Ch. 316, 326, the plaintiffs, Mr. and Mrs. Christie, and the defendant lived side by side in semi-detached houses in Brixton. Mrs. Christie was a teacher of music, and her family were also musical, and throughout the day sounds of music pervaded their house and were heard in the house of their neighbours. The defendant did not like the music that he heard, and by way of retaliation he took to making noises himself, beating trays and rapping on the wall. The action came on for trial before North, J., who delivered judgment in favour of the plaintiffs and granted an injunction restraining the defendant from causing or permitting any sounds or noises in his house so as to vex or annoy the plaintiffs or the occupiers of their house. In the course of his judgment, he said at page 326, after dealing with the facts as he found them, "The result is that I think I am bound to interfere for the protection of the plaintiffs. In my opinion the noises which were made in the defendant's house were not of a legitimate kind. They were what, to use the language of Lord Selborne in *Gaunt* v. *Fynney* 'ought to be regarded as excessive and unreasonable." I am satisfied that they were made deliberately and maliciously for the purpose of annoying the plaintiffs." Then come the significant words: "If what has taken place had occurred between two sets of persons both perfectly innocent, I should have taken an entirely different view of the case. But I am persuaded that what was done by the defendant was done only for the purpose of annoyance, and in my opinion it was not a legitimate use of the defendant's house to use it for the purpose of vexing and annoying his neighbours."

The cases to which I have referred were decided before the decision of the House of Lords in *Bradford Corporation* v. *Pickles;* and the question therefore arises whether those cases must now be considered as overruled. It is to be observed that in *Allen* v. *Flood,* Lord Watson discussed fully the case of *Keeble* v. *Hickeringill,* and said with reference to that case: "No proprietor has an absolute right to create noises upon his own land, because any right which the law gives him is qualified by the condition that it must not be exercised to the nuisance of his neighbours or of the public. If he violates that condition he commits a legal wrong, and if he does so intentionally he is guilty of a malicious wrong, in its strict legal sense."

In my opinion the decision of the House of Lords in *Bradford Corporation* v. *Pickles* has no bearing on such cases as this. I therefore think that the plaintiff is entitled to maintain this action. I think also that in the circumstances an injunction should be granted restraining the defendant from committing a nuisance by the discharge of firearms or the making of other loud noises in the vicinity of the Hollywood Silver Fox Farm during the breeding season—namely, between January 1 and June 15—so as to alarm or disturb the foxes kept by the plaintiffs at the said farm, or otherwise to injure the plaintiff company.

NOTES

1. Do you agree that the motive behind the conduct should be a relevant consideration in deciding whether there has been a nuisance? If the defendant's son was really shooting rabbits, would the result have been different? What if he shot rabbits day and night without ever going to sleep?

2. Defendant keeps telephoning the plaintiff and bothering him in the middle of the night and first thing in the morning. During one particular hour 30 calls were made. Nuisance? In *Motherwell* v. *Motherwell,* [1976] 6 W.W.R. 550 (Alta. C.A.), Clement J.A. stated:

> "It is clear to me that the protracted and persistent harrassment of the brother and the father in their homes, and in the case of the brother as well in his office, by abuse of the telephone system is within the principle of private nuisance as it has been recognized in the authorities I have referred to. The question is whether the calls amounted to undue interference with the comfortable and convenient enjoyment by the plaintiffs of their respective premises. I can conceive that persistent and unwanted telephone calls could become a harassment even if the subject matter is essentially agreeable. The deliberate and persistent ringing of the telephone cannot but affect the senses in time and operate on the nervous system as the evidence discloses. No special damage is required to support an injunction: it is the loss of the amenities of the premises in substantial degree that is involved."

Would this be actionable as an invasion of privacy? Would it be actionable as an intentional infliction of mental suffering?

RUSSELL TRANSPORT LTD. v. ONTARIO MALLEABLE IRON CO. LTD.
Ontario High Court. [1952] O.R. 621, [1952] 4 D.L.R. 719

Defendant had been carrying on the business of a foundry at its present site in the City of Oshawa, Ontario, since 1907. Plaintiffs bought land in the vicinity in 1949 which it used, in connection with its business of transporting new motor vehicles by truck, as a marshalling-yard for vehicles to be transported. In 1951 complaints were received that the finish on motor cars transported by them was contaminated and damaged, and the cause was traced to particles of iron, manganese sulphide and other materials incident to foundry operation. Faced with a demand by its customers that motor vehicles must be removed from its marshalling yard, plaintiffs brought action for nuisance to recover damages and for an injunction.

McRuer C.J.H.C. [After a lengthy examination of the scientific evidence dealing with the nature and effect of tests made to establish the source of the damage to the vehicles on plaintiffs' land.] : The irresistible conclusion on the evidence is, and I so find, that the defendant emits from its plant particles of iron and iron oxide together with other matters which settle on the plaintiffs' lands, rendering the plaintiffs' property unfit for the purpose for which it was purchased and developed. The plaintiffs have therefore suffered and will continue to suffer material and substantial damage to their property unless the emission of injurious substances is abated. . . .

Salmond on *Torts,* 10th ed., pp. 228-31, summarizes in a comprehensive manner "Ineffectual Defences" as follows:

1. It is no defence that the plaintiffs themselves came to the nuisance.

2. It is no defence that the nuisance, although injurious to the plaintiffs, is beneficial to the public at large.

3. It is no defence that the place from which the nuisance proceeds is a suitable one for carrying on the operation complained of, and that no other place is available in which less mischief would result.

4. It is no defence that all possible care and skill are being used to prevent the operation complained of from amounting to a nuisance. Nuisance is not a branch of the law of negligence.

5. It is no defence that the act of the defendant would not amount to a nuisance unless other persons acting independently of him did the same thing at the same time.

6. He who causes a nuisance cannot avail himself of the defence that he is merely making a reasonable use of his own property. No use of property is reasonable which causes substantial discomfort to others or is a source of damage to their property.

In opening his argument Mr. Sedgwick stated that the principal defences relied on by the defendant were a reasonable use of its land, and prescriptive right.

It is argued that the plaintiffs established their marshalling-yard in an industrial area unsuitable for a business of that character. In the first place, the facts do not support this contention even if there were a sound basis of law for it. . . . It was not until the business had been carried on for nearly 2 years that either the plaintiffs or the defendant became aware of the nuisance. . . .

Any argument based on the fact that the nuisance may have existed before the plaintiffs purchased their property is completely answered by the statement of Lord Halsbury in *Fleming* v. *Hislop* (1886), 11 App. Cas. 686 at pp. 696-7, where he said: "If the Lord Justice Clerk means to convey that there was anything in the law which diminished the right of a man to complain of a nuisance because the nuisance existed before he went to it, I venture to think that neither in the law of England nor in that of Scotland is there any foundation for any such contention. It is clear that whether the man went to the nuisance or the nuisance came to the man, the rights are the same, and I think that the law of England has been settled, certainly for more than 200 years, by a judgment of Lord Chief Justice Hide."

The last proposition that I have quoted from *Salmond* requires some qualification, but only a very limited one. Counsel bases his whole argument on the defence of reasonable use of the defendant's lands on a passage from the judgment of Thesinger, L.J., in *Sturges* v. *Bridgman* (1879), 11 Ch.D. 852 at p. 865, where the learned Lord Justice in dealing with two hypothetical cases said: "As regards the first, it may be answered that whether anything is a nuisance or not is a question to be determined, not merely by an abstract consideration of the thing itself, but in reference to its circumstances; what would be a nuisance in Belgrave Square would not necessarily be so in Bermondsey; and where a locality is devoted to a particular trade or manufacture carried on by the traders or manufacturers in a particular and established manner not constituting a public nuisance, judges and juries would be justified in finding, and may be trusted to find, that the trade or manufacture so carried on in that locality is not a private or actionable wrong."

This statement of the law has been applied with caution in some cases arising out of an alleged nuisance producing sensible personal discomfort, but it is not to be broadly applied nor is it to be isolated from the general body of law on the subject. It was an expression used in a case arising out of noise and vibration.

The judgment of the Lord Chancellor in *St. Helen's Smelting Co.* v. *Tipping* (1865), 11 H.L.C. 642 at p. 650; 11 E.R. 1483, is the classic authority in all cases similar to the one before me: "My Lords, in matters of this description it appears to me that it is a very desirable thing to mark the difference between an action brought for a nuisance upon the ground that the alleged nuisance produces material injury to the property, and an action brought for a nuisance on the ground that the thing alleged to be a nuisance is productive of sensible personal discomfort. With regard to the latter, namely, the personal inconvenience and interference with one's enjoyment, one's quiet, one's personal freedom, anything that discomposes or injuriously affects the senses or the nerves, whether that may or may not be denominated a nuisance, must undoubtedly depend greatly on the circumstances of the place where the thing complained of actually occurs. If a man lives in a town, it is necessary that he should subject himself to the consequences of those operations of trade which may be carried on in his immediate locality, which are actually necessary for trade and commerce, and also for the enjoyment of property, and for the benefit of the inhabitants of the town and of the public at large. If a man lives in a street where there are numerous shops, and a shop is opened next door to him, which is carried on in a fair and reasonable way, he has no ground for complaint, because to himself individually there may arise much discomfort from the trade carried on in that shop. But when an occupation is carried on by one person in the neighbourhood of another, and the result of that trade, or occupation, or business, *is a material injury to property,* then there unquestionably arises a very different consideration. I think, my Lords, that in a case of that description, the submission which is required from persons living in society to that amount of discomfort which may be necessary for the legitimate and free exercise of the trade of their neighbours, would not apply to circumstances *the immediate result of which is sensible injury to the value of the property."* (The italics are mine.)

Even if on any argument a doctrine of reasonable use of the defendant's lands could be expanded to cover a case where there is substantial and material injury to the plaintiffs' property I do not think it could be applied to this case. "Reasonable" as used in the law of nuisance must be distinguished from its use elsewhere in the law of tort and especially as it is used in negligence actions. "In negligence, assuming that the duty to take care has been established, the vital question is, 'Did the defendant take reasonable care?' But in nuisance the defendant is not necessarily quit of liability even if he has taken reasonable care. It is true that the result of a long chain of decisions is that unreasonableness is a main ingredient of liability for nuisance. But here 'reasonable' means something more than merely 'taking proper care'. It signifies what is legally right between the parties, taking into account all the circumstances of the case, and some of these circumstances are often such as a man on the Clapham omnibus could not fully appreciate": Winfield on *Torts,* 5th ed., p. 448. "At common law, if I am sued for a nuisance, and the nuisance is proved, it is no defence on my part to say, and to prove, that I have taken all reasonable care to prevent it": *per* Lindley, L.J., in *Rapier* v. *London Tramways Co.,* [1893] 2 Ch. 588, at pp. 599-600. This is not to be interpreted to mean that taking care is never relevant to liability for nuisance. In some cases if the defendant has conducted his trade or business as a reasonable man would have done he has gone some way toward making out a defence, but only some of the way: *Stockport Waterworks Co.* v. *Potter* (1861), 7 H. & N. 160; 158 E.R. 433.

On the other hand, if the defendant has taken no reasonable precautions to protect his neighbour from injury by reason of operations of his own property the defence of reasonable user is of little avail.

The evidence shows that in so far as the emissions from the cupola are responsible for the injury to the plaintiffs, and I think they are in large measure responsible for the injury complained of, the defendant has adopted no method of modern smoke or fume control . . . The defendant has considered the installation of a fume control system in the cupola but has refrained from doing anything pending the outcome of this action. . . .

To give effect to the defence of reasonable user of the defendant's lands in this case would be to expand the doctrine of law involved in this defence far beyond any authority in British jurisprudence.

Although in this case there is no admission that the defendant has violated the plaintiffs' legal right by damaging the motor vehicles stored on their property, I find as a fact that it has done so, and I cannot find that the storing of automobiles in the open air on the lots in question is a particularly delicate trade or operation. The finish of an automobile is designed to resist reasonable atmospheric contamination and it would be manifestly unjust to hold that property owners in the vicinity of the defendant's plant have no legal right to have their automobiles protected from the emissions from the defendant's foundry simply because they do not keep them under cover.

The defence of prescriptive right remains to be dealt with. The defendant pleads that it and its predecessors in title have for a period of 40 years and more before the commencement of the action enjoyed as of right and without interruption the right to do those things which the plaintiffs claim gives them a right of action, and their claim is therefore barred by the Limitations Act, R.S.O. 1950, c. 207 . . .

In asserting the defence of prescription the onus rests on the defendant. . . . The defendant must not only show that it has exercised the right to deposit the substances herein complained of on the plaintiffs' lands, for the prescribed period, but that the exercise of the right amounted to a nuisance actionable at the instance of the plaintiffs and their predecessors in title for the full period of 20 years: . . . .

Even if on any view of the evidence it could be considered that iron oxide and iron particles were being emitted from the defendant's plant for a period of 20 years next preceding the issue of the writ in this action, to the same extent and in the same manner as they are now being emitted, I think the defence of prescriptive right would still fail. In order to obtain a prescriptive right, the enjoyment of the right must not be secret and the servient owner must have either actual or constructive knowledge of it.

The evidence clearly shows that neither the plaintiffs nor the defendant's officers had any knowledge that any injurious particles were being deposited on the plaintiffs' lands as emissions from the defendant's plant until late in the autumn of 1951. . . .

The history of the plaintiffs' property . . . shows that for more than 20 years prior to the commencement of the action it was low-lying vacant land, formerly the site of a disused foundry . . . . I do not think it can be said that the evidence could warrant me in finding that for the whole period of 20 years prior to 1952 the plaintiffs or their predecessors in title could have maintained an action against the defendant for nuisance . . . .

The form of the relief is one that has given me considerable concern . . . on a case of this character in considering the plaintiffs' damages the diminution of the value of the plaintiffs' property cannot be taken into consideration in assessing the damages as the continuation of the nuisance gives rise to a new cause of action from day to day . . . . It is, therefore, clear that a judgment for damages only would not afford the plaintiffs adequate relief . . . .

Judgment will therefore go for an injunction that the defendant, its servants and agents, be restrained from discharging or allowing to be discharged from its works in the pleadings mentioned any substance, gas or matter in such a manner or to such an extent as to occasion damage to the plaintiffs' property or the buildings thereon and/or motor vehicles or vehicles of like character that may be thereon; provided, however, that the operation of the injunction will be suspended until January 1, 1953.

There will be a reference to the County Judge of the County of Ontario to fix the amount of damages that the respective plaintiffs have suffered and will suffer until the injunction becomes effective.

NOTES

1. On the question of whether an injunction will be granted, see *Black* v. *Canadian Copper Co.* (1917), 12 O.W.N. 243; *McKie* v. *The K.V.P. Co.,* [1948] 3 D.L.R. 201 (Ont.); Read, "Equity and Public Wrongs" (1973), 11 Can. Bar Rev. 73.

2. When actual damage was suffered as a result of a sewer backup, liability in nuisance was imposed in *Royal Anne Hotel* v. *Ashcroft,* [1979] 2 W.W.R. 462 (B.C.C.A.).

HAMMERSMITH AND CITY RAILWAY COMPANY v. BRAND

House of Lords. (1869), L. R. 4 H.L. 171, 38 L.J.Q.B. 265, 21 L.T. 238

The plaintiffs claimed damages for vibration caused by the operation of the defendant railway which had been empowered by statute to make and maintain the railway. A special case was stated for the opinion of the Court of Queen's Bench. That Court held the defendant not liable. The Court of Exchequer Chamber reversed this judgment. On an appeal to the House of Lords, the judges were summoned. All the judges, with the exception of Blackburn, J., advised the House that in their opinion the statute afforded no immunity to the railway for creating a nuisance.

Lord Chelmsford: The question raised for the opinion of the Court below was, whether the plaintiffs in the action, who are owners of a house adjacent to the Hammersmith and City Railway, were entitled to compensation from the railway company for injury to their house from the vibration caused by the passage of trains over the line in the ordinary use of the railway, without negligence, whereby the house was depreciated in value. . . .

If the cases of *Rex* v. *Pease,* 4 B. & Ad. 30, and *Vaughan* v. *The Taff Vale Ry. Co,* 5 H. & N. 679, were rightly decided, this question has been determined. It was established by those cases "that when the Legislature has sanctioned the use of a locomotive engine there is no liability for any injury caused by using it so long as every precaution is taken consistent with its use." . . .

. . . we do not expect to find words in an Act of Parliament expressly authorizing an individual or a company to commit a nuisance or to do damage to a neighbour. The 86th section gives power to the company to use and employ locomotive engines, and if such locomotives cannot possibly be used without occasioning vibration and consequent injury to neighbouring houses, upon the principle of law that *Cuicunque aliquis quid concedit, concedere videtur et id sine quo res ipsa esse non potuit,* it must be taken that power is given to cause that vibration without liability to an action. The right given to use the locomotive would otherwise be nugatory, as each time a train passed upon the line and shook the houses in the neighbourhood actions might be brought by their owners, which would soon put a stop to the use of the railway. I therefore think, notwithstanding the respect to which every opinion of Mr. Baron Bramwell is entitled, that the cases of *Rex* v. *Pease* and *Vaughan* v. *The Taff Vale Railway Company* were rightly decided.

The plaintiffs' remedy by action being taken away, the question remains whether they are entitled to receive compensation from the company for the injury done to their house, a question which must be decided entirely by the provision of the Acts of Parliament relating to the subject. . .

I am compelled very reluctantly, in a case where real damage has been sustained, though not to a very large amount, to come to the conclusion that the Legislature has not provided for the case of these respondents, but has left them without remedy, and that the judgment of the Court of Exchequer Chamber ought, therefore, to be reversed.

Lord Cairns: It appears to me that the effect of the legislation on this subject is to take away any right of action on the part of the landowner against the railway company for damage that the landowner has sustained. It must be taken, I think, from the statements in this case that the railway could not be used for the purpose for which it was intended without vibration. It is clear to demonstration that the intention of Parliament was that the railway should be used. If, therefore, it could not be used without vibration, and if vibration necessarily caused damage to the adjacent landowner, and if it was intended to preserve to the adjacent landowner his right of action, the consequence would be that action after action would be maintainable against the railway company for the damage which the landowner sustained; and after some actions had been brought, and had succeeded, the Court of Chancery would interfere by injunction, and would prevent the railway being worked—which, of course, is a *reductio ad absurdum,* and would defeat the intention of the Legislature. I have, therefore, no hesitation in arriving at the conclusion that no action would be maintainable against the railway company.

[The judgment of Lord Colonsay is omitted.]

NOTES

1. In *C.P.R.* v. *Roy,* [1902] A.C. 220, the liability for fire caused by sparks from a railway locomotive was considered. The Privy Council held that the operation of the railway being authorized by statute, there could be no liability unless the railway was operated negligently.

2. The Railway Act, R.S.C. 1970, c. R-2, s. 338 now imposes strict liability for fires.

MANAGERS OF THE METROPOLITAN ASYLUM DISTRICT v. HILL

House of Lords. (1881), 6 App. Cas. 193, 50 L.J.Q.B. 353, 44 L.T. 653

A statute authorized local boards to erect buildings for the care of the sick, etc. A hospital for the reception of patients suffering from small-pox and other infectious and contagious diseases was erected near the plaintiff's property. It was found at the trial that such hospital was a nuisance and an injunction against its continuance was granted.

As a result of a series of appeals, the question of the right in law to maintain the hospital in its existing condition was brought before the House of Lords.

Lord Watson: I do not think that the Legislature can be held to have sanctioned that which is a nuisance at common law, except in the case where it has authorized a certain use of a specific building in a specified position, which cannot be so used without occasioning nuisance, or in the case where the particular plan or locality not being prescribed, it has imperatively directed that a building shall be provided within a certain area and so used, it being an obvious or established fact that nuisance must be the result. In the latter case the onus of proving that the creation of a nuisance will be the inevitable result of carrying out the directions of the Legislature, lies upon the persons seeking to justify the nuisance. Their justification depends upon their making good these two propositions—in the first place, that such are the imperative orders of the Legislature; and in the second place, that they cannot possibly obey these orders without infringing private rights. If the order of the Legislature can be implemented without the directions of the Legislature lies upon the person seeking to justify the and, on the other hand, it is insufficient for their protection that what is contemplated by the statute cannot be done without nuisance, unless they are also able to shew that the Legislature has directed it to be done. Where the terms of the statute are not imperative, but permissive, when it is left to the discretion of the persons empowered to determine whether the general powers committed to them shall be put into execution or not, I think the fair inference is that the Legislature intended that discretion to be exercised in strict conformity with private rights, and did not intend to confer licence to commit nuisance in any place which might be selected for the purpose . . .

It appears to me that, in making provision with regard to asylums in the Metropolis, the Legislature has done nothing more than is requisite to place the authorities to whom it has committed the execution of that part of the Act, upon the same level as individuals in so far as the right of third parties are concerned, but with the right, which individuals have not, to defray the costs by rates levied from the public.

NOTES

1. In *Chadwick* v. *City of Toronto* (1914), 32 O.L.R. 111, the defendant municipality was authorized by statute to operate a pumping station. The machinery was at first operated by steam, but later electrical power was substituted, and as a result, the noise and vibration caused by the motors constituted a serious interference with the plaintiff's enjoyment of his property. In an action based on a nuisance, it was held that the statute afforded no defence. See Meredith, C.J.O.: "The evidence established, no doubt, that for the supplying of water to consumers in the northern part of the city a high level pumping station is essential, and, if it had been shown that the machinery for pumping could not be operated unless driven by electrical power, I should hold that the use of that mode of operating the machinery at the appellant's pumping station was authorized by the legislation to which I have referred, and that no action lay for such injury as that of which the respondents complain; and it may be, though it is unnecessary to express any opinion upon the point, that, if, though not absolutely impracticable to use any other than electrically driven machinery, it was commercially impracticable to do so, the same result would follow. It is not open to question that it is practicable to operate the machinery by means of steam power, and that was the mode adopted and in use until electrical power was substituted for it." The Court felt that as the water was necessary for municipal purposes, it was justified in granting damages in lieu of an injunction, pursuant to the provisions of the Judicature Act,

2. In *Manchester* v. *Farnworth*, [1930] A.C. 171, Viscount Dunedin stated:

"When Parliament has authorized a certain thing to be made or done in a certain place, there can be no action for nuisance caused by the making or doing of that thing if the nuisance is the inevitable result of the making or doing so authorized. The onus of proving that the result is inevitable is on those who wish to escape liability for nuisance, but the criterion of inevitability is not what is theoretically possible but what is possible according to the state of scientific knowledge at the time, having also in view a certain common sense appreciation, which cannot be rigidly defined, of practical feasibility in view of situation and of expense."

See also *Temple* v. *City of Melville* (1978), 7 C.C.L.T. 1 (Sask.), onus on defendant to exculpate self.

3. Municipalities are not excused from nuisance liability on the ground that their activities are for the benefit of the public at large. See *Royal Anne Hotel* v. *Ashcroft*, [1979] 2 W.W.R. 462 (B.C.C.A.). But see Chapter 12, Section B, *supra*.

4. See generally on this question Linden, "Strict Liability, Nuisance and Legislative Authorization" (1966), 4 Osgoode Hall L.J. 196. See also *supra*, Chapter 12, Section B. *supra*.

CHAPTER 18

BUSINESS TORTS

There is a whole range of business activity that is regulated by tort law. Business interests, like personal and property interests, have cried out for the protection of tort law, and it has responded. Much of the early law in this area has now been taken over by legislation, such as the Combines Investigation Act, the labour relations acts, the Copyright Act and others. There remains, however, a broad sphere of activity that has been relatively untouched by legislation, where tort law still plays a role in preventing undesirable business practices.

These problems are being exacerbated nowadays by the fierce competition in the Canadian business community, by the aggressiveness of so many of the modern entrepreneurs and by the increasing sophistication of consumers and others who are eager to call on the courts to assist them in combatting the improper tactics used in the marketplace. It is a field that is growing in importance for tort lawyers and Canadians generally.

The material in this section is meant to serve only as an introduction to a vast and complex field. Law school curricula normally deal with many of these problems in courses on labour law, copyrights, patents and trade marks, competition law and others. See generally Heydon, *Economic Torts* (1973).

A. DECEIT

DERRY v. PEEK
House of Lords. (1889), 14 A.C. 337, 58 L.J.Ch. 864, 61 L.T. 265

The directors of a tramway company issued a prospectus which asserted that they were empowered to use steam-powered cars. They did not actually have this authority, but the directors honestly believed they would get it as a matter of course. The governmental consent was never obtained, however, and, as a result, the company went into liquidation. The plaintiff had invested in the company shares on the strength of the assertion in the prospectus and sued the directors for deceit. The House of Lords dismissed his claim.

Lord Herschell: My Lords, in the statement of claim in this action the respondent, who is the plaintiff, alleges that the appellants made in a prospectus issued by them certain statements which were untrue, that they well knew that the facts were not as stated in the prospectus, and made the representations fraudulently, and with the view to induce the plaintiff to take shares in the company.

"This action is one which is commonly called an action of deceit, a mere common law action." This is the description of it given by Cotton, L.J., in delivering judgment. I think it important that it should be borne in mind that such an action differs essentially from one brought to obtain rescision of a contract on the ground of misrepresentation of a material fact. The principles which govern the two actions differ widely. Where rescission is claimed it is only necessary to prove that there was misrepresentation; then, however honestly it may have been made, however free from blame the person who made it, the contract, having been obtained by misrepresentation, cannot stand. In an action of deceit, on the contrary, it is not enough to establish misrepresentation alone; it is conceded on all hands that something more must be proved to cast liability upon the defendant, though it has been a matter of controversy what additional elements are requisite. I lay stress upon this because observations made by learned judges in actions for rescission have been cited and much relied upon at the bar by counsel for the respondent. Care must obviously be observed in applying the language used in relation to such actions to an action of deceit. Even if the scope of the language used extend beyond the particular action, which was being dealt with, it must be remembered that the learned judges were not engaged in determining what is necessary to support an action of deceit, or in discriminating with nicety the elements which enter into it. . . .

. . .

I now arrive at the earliest case in which I find the suggestion that an untrue statement made without reasonable ground for believing it will support an action for deceit. In *Western Bank of Scotland* v. *Addie,* L.R. 1 H.L. Sc. 145, the Lord President told the jury "that if a case should occur of directors taking upon themselves to put forth in their report statements of importance in regard to the affairs of the bank false in themselves and which they did not believe, or had no reasonable ground to believe to be true, that would be a misrepresentation and deceit." Exception having been taken to this direction without avail in the Court of Session, Lord Chelmsford in this House said: "I agree in the propriety of this interlocutor. In the argument upon this exception the case was put of an honest belief being entertained by the directors, of the reasonableness of which it was said the jury, upon this direction, would have to judge. But supposing a person makes an untrue statement which he asserts to be the result of a bona fide belief in its truth, how can the bona fides be tested except by considering the grounds of such belief? And if an untrue statement is made founded upon a belief which is destitute of all reasonable grounds, or which the least inquiry would immediately correct, I do not see that it is not fairly and correctly characterized as misrepresentation and deceit."

I think there is here some confusion between that which is evidence of fraud, and that which constitutes it. A consideration of the grounds of belief is no doubt an important aid in ascertaining whether the belief was really entertained. A man's mere assertion that he believed the statement he made to be true is not accepted as conclusive proof that he did so. There may be such an absence of reasonable ground for his belief as, in spite of his assertion, to carry conviction to the mind that he had not really the belief which he alleges. If the learned Lord intended to go further, as apparently he did, and to say that though the belief was really entertained, yet if there were no reasonable grounds for it, the person making the statement was guilty of fraud in the same way as if he had known what he stated to be false, I say, with all respect, that the previous authorities afford no warrant for the view that an action of deceit would lie under such circumstances. A man who forms his belief carelessly, or is unreasonably credulous, may be blameworthy when he makes a representation on which another is to act, but he is not, in my opinion, fraudulent in the sense in which that word was used in all the cases from *Pasley* v. *Freeman* down to that with which I am now dealing. Even when the expression "fraud in law" has been employed, there has always been present, and regarded as an essential element, that the deception was wilful either because the untrue statement was known to be untrue, or because belief in it was asserted without such belief existing. . . .

I think the authorities establish the following propositions: First, in order to sustain an action of deceit, there must be proof of fraud, and nothing short of

that will suffice. Secondly, fraud is proved when it is shewn that a false representation has been made (1) knowingly, or (2) without belief in its truth, (3)
recklessly, careless whether it be true or false. Although I have treated the second
and third as distinct cases, I think the third is but an instance of the second, for
one who makes a statement under such circumstances can have no real belief in
the truth of what he states. To prevent a false statement being fraudulent, there
must, I think, always be an honest belief in its truth. And this probably covers
the whole ground, for one who knowingly alleges that which is false, has
obviously no such honest belief. Thirdly, if fraud be proved, the motive of the
person guilty of it is immaterial. It matters not that there was no intention to
cheat or injure the person to whom the statement was made . . . .

[His Lordship analyzed the evidence.]

I quite admit that the statements of witnesses as to their belief are by no
means to be accepted blindfold. The probabilities must be considered. Whenever
it is necessary to arrive at a conclusion as to the state of mind of another person,
and to determine whether his belief under given circumstances was such as he
alleges, we can only do so by applying the standard of conduct which our own
experience of the ways of men has enabled us to form; by asking ourselves
whether a reasonable man would be likely under the circumstances so to believe.
I have applied this test, with the result that I have a strong conviction that a
reasonable man situated as the defendants were, with their knowledge and means
of knowledge, might well believe what they state they did believe, and consider
that the representation made was substantially true.

Adopting the language of Jessel, M.R., in *Smith* v. *Chadwick,* 20 Ch. D. at p.
67, I conclude by saying that on the whole I have come to the conclusion that
the statement, "though in some respects inaccurate and not altogether free from
imputation of carelessness, was a fair, honest and bona fide statement on the
part of the defendants, and by no means exposes them to an action for deceit."

I think the judgment of the Court of Appeal should be reversed.

NOTES

1. Following this decision legislation was enacted in England imposing a
stricter responsibility on those who issue prospectuses. See now Companies Act,
1948, s. 38. In Canada, detailed legislative provisions now govern the area of
corporate fund raising. See Ontario Securities Act, R.S.O. 1970, c. 426. The
common law principles, however, survive in other contexts.

2. The importance of this action has diminished since *Hedley Byrne* v. *Heller,*
[1964] A.C. 465 has been decided, because it is far more difficult to prove fraud
than it is to establish negligence. Would the plaintiff in *Derry* v. *Peek* be successful today? See *supra,* Chapter 10, Section C.

PEEK v. GURNEY

House of Lords. (1873), L.R. 6 H.L. 377, 43 L.J.Ch. 19

Defendants issued a prospectus, making an offering of stock in an intended
company, which contained fraudulent misrepresentations of fact. Plaintiff did
not acquire stock in the company as an original allottee but purchased his stock
on the market. When the company was wound-up plaintiff was placed on the list
of contributories and later took proceedings to recover the amount by which he
had been damnified by reason of defendants' false representations. At the hearing
judgment was given defendants and the plaintiff appealed.

Lord Cairns: The prospectus was issued on the 12th or 13th of July, 1865,
and a copy was received or was obtained by the appellant. It is not proved from

whom he obtained it. The object of the prospectus on the face of it is clearly to invite the public to take shares in the new company. The prospectus is, as is usual in such cases, an invitation, and there is appended to it a form of application for shares, which was to be filled up, and upon which form the invitation was to be answered. It is a prospectus in this shape, addressed to the whole of the public, no doubt, and any one of the public might take up the prospectus and appropriate it in that way to himself by answering it upon the form upon which it is intended by the prospectus that it should be answered. The appellant, however, did not take up and did not appropriate the prospectus in this way. For reasons which it is unnecessary to inquire into he declined to take, or at all events he did not originally take any shares in the company. The allotment of shares began on the 24th of July; it appears to have been completed on the 28th of July; and it is stated that two or three times the number of shares to be had in the company were applied for. The allotment having been completed, the prospectus, as it seems to me, had done its work; it was exhausted. The share list was full; the directors had obtained from the company the money which they desired to obtain. The appellant subsequently, upon the 17th of October, several months afterwards, bought 1,000 shares at a premium of something over 7*l.*, and again, still later, on the 6th of December, he bought 1,000 other shares at a premium of something over 6*l.* He bought them on the Stock Exchange, and he, of course, did not know in the first instance from whom he bought them. In point of fact, it appears that as to the greater part of them they were shares which had originally been allotted to one of the old partners, Samuel Gurney, by whom they were transferred to a nominee for himself, in whose name they were registered; they were then sold upon the market, and re-sold apparently several times, because the premium seems to have risen from a much smaller to a much larger sum, and ultimately they were sold, at the premium which I have stated, to the appellant, and were registered in his name.

Now, my Lords, I ask the question, How can the directors of a company be liable, after the full original allotment of shares, for all the subsequent dealings which may take place with regard to those shares upon the Stock Exchange? If the argument of the appellant is right, they must be liable *ad infinitum,* for I know no means of pointing out any time at which the liability would, in point of fact, cease. Not only so, but if the argument be right, they must be liable, no matter what the premium may be at which the shares may be sold. That premium may rise from time to time from circumstances altogether unconnected with the prospectus, and yet, if the argument be right, the appellant would be entitled to call upon the directors to indemnify him up to the highest point at which the shares may be sold, for all that he may expend in buying the shares. My Lords, I ask, is there any authority for this proposition? I am aware of none.

During the course of the argument I took the liberty of putting to the learned counsel for the appellant a case which I think was not answered, and to which, so far as I know, no answer can be given that would be favourable to the appellant. I put the case of a person having built a house and desiring to sell it. He comes to me and wishes me to purchase it; he describes it as a highly advantageous purchase, and makes statements of fact to me with regard to the house which are untrue and are misrepresentations; but I decline to purchase, and our overtures come to an end. He subsequently sells it to some other person, upon what terms I know not. That other person completes the purchase, and that other person, desiring to raise money on mortgage, applies to me to lend him money. I lend him money upon a mortgage of the house. The facts stated to me originally turn out to be untrue, and are so material as that the house, not being as represented, becomes comparatively worthless. I then apply to the original vendor, remind him of what he told me, and complain to him that my money lent upon mortgage has been lost, and I commence an action against him for damages to recover my loss. I ask, could such an action be maintained? I know of no authority for it, and I am of opinion that an action of that kind would not lie.

My Lords, I take the rule on this point to have been happily stated in some expressions of my noble and learned friend the late Lord Chancellor (Lord Hatherley), when he was Vice-Chancellor, in the case of *Barry* v. *Croskey,* 2 J. & H. 117 . . . In giving judgment, the Vice-Chancellor stated what he understood to be the principles applicable to such a case. First, that "every man must be held responsible for the consequences of a false representation made by him to another, upon which that other acts, and, so acting, is injured or damnified; Secondly, every man must be held responsible for the consequences of a false representation made by him to another, upon which a third person acts, and so acting, is injured or damnified, provided it appear that such false representation was made with the intent that it should be acted upon by such third person in the manner that occasions the injury or loss." And thirdly, he continues: "But to bring it within the principle, the injury, I apprehend, must be the immediate and not the remote consequence of the representation thus made. To render a man responsible for the consequences of a false representation made by him to another upon which a third person acts, and so acting is injured or damnified, it must appear that such false representation was made with the direct intent that it should be acted upon by such third person in the manner that occasions the injury or loss." . . .

I am of opinion that the appellant in this case has entirely failed to connect himself with the representations made in the prospectus, of which in my opinion an original allottee might have complained, but of which the present appellant cannot, I think, complain.

NOTES

1. How would you articulate the principle decided in this case? How does it compare with the principle in *Haig* v. *Bamford,* [1972] 6 W.W.R. 557; revd [1974] 6 W.W.R. 236 (Sask. C.A.), *supra,* Chapter 10, Section C.

2. See Keeton, "Ambit of a Fraudulent Representor's Responsibility" (1938), 17 Texas L. Rev. 1.

YOUNG v. McMILLAN ET AL.

Supreme Court of Nova Scotia. (1894), 40 N.S.R. 52

Meagher J.: The plaintiffs bought from the defendant one-half of a fishing boat and her gear for $105. They now seek to recover back that sum and damages, on the ground of a false representation alleged to have been made to them by the defendant, with the intention that they should act upon it, and that they did act upon it. The representation relied on was that he had paid $210 for her, while the fact was that he only paid $150 for her . . . .

I am quite convinced that even if the defendant made the alleged statement in the terms claimed . . . it had not the remotest effect in inducing the purchase, nor in determining the price paid. I say this quite apart from what I may say as to the burden of proof.

It was incumbent upon the plaintiffs to show how the representation in question affected them and that they acted on the faith of it, and but for it, would not have purchased at the price paid, or at all; or, at all events, to show a state of facts from which those inferences could fairly be drawn. In other words, that if the truth had been stated they would not have purchased.

Caveat emptor applies to such a sale, and therefore the purchaser had no right to rely upon the vendor's representations as to what he had paid for the boat, etc. They were apparently strangers to each other; at all events, they were not intimately acquainted, and it ought to have been apparent to the plaintiffs that no reason existed why the defendant should sell to them on the same terms as he bought, and therefore there was greater ground for caution on their part . . . .

A misrepresentation, to support an action, must in its nature be material and be a determining ground of the transaction; or, at least, a material inducement to it.

Sugden on *Vendors,* p. 3, says: "An action cannot be maintained against a vendor for having falsely affirmed that a particular person bid a particular sum for the estate, although the purchaser was thereby induced to purchase it, and was deceived in the purchase."

There does not seem to me to be any difference between the case there put and the present one. See *Vernon* v. *Keys* (1810), 12 East 631, affirmed in (1812), 4 Taunt. 489, where the defendant, while negotiating with the plaintiff for the latter's interest in their joint business, falsely and deceitfully represented to the plaintiff that the parties with whom he was about to enter into partnership in the same business would not consent to his giving the plaintiff more than a certain sum, whereas the fact was they had authorized him to buy on the best terms he could. Mansfield, C.J., said "The question is whether the defendant is bound to disclose the highest price he chooses to give, or whether he be not at liberty to do that, as a purchaser, which every seller in this town does every day, who tells every falsehood he can to induce a buyer to purchase."

I am afraid a very substantial proportion of the sales made in the stores from day to day would be liable to be set aside if untrue statements as to what the vendors paid for the articles sold constituted a ground for their rescission.

In Kerr on *Fraud and Mistake,* last edition, p. 51, it is said: "The representations of a vendor of real estate to the vendee, as to the price which he has paid for it, are in respect of the reliance to be placed on them to be regarded generally in the same light as representations respecting its value, or the offers which have been made for it. A purchaser is not justified in placing confidence in them. They constitute what is regarded as ordinary 'dealers' talk'." . . .

Statements by a vendor concerning the value of the thing sold, former offers for it, etc. have everywhere been regarded as statements to be distrusted by the intending purchaser.

In *Medbury* v. *Watson* (1843), 6 Met. 259, the Court said: "But in actions on the case for deceit founded on false affirmations, there has always existed the exception that naked assertions, though known to be false, are not the ground of action as between vendor and vendee; and in regard to affirmations and representations respecting real estate, the maxim of *caveat emptor* has ever been held to apply. When, therefore, a vendor of real estate affirms to the vendee that his estate is worth so much, that he gave so much for it, that he has been offered so much for it, or has refused such a sum for it, such assertions, though known to him to be false, and though uttered with a view to deceive, are not actionable. They are the mere affirmation of the vendor, on which the vendee cannot place confidence, and will not excuse his neglect in not examining it for himself and ascertaining what the facts are and what credit is to be given to the assertions."

The Court, after referring to the distinction to be observed between a false affirmation by the vendor to the vendee, where the maxim *caveat emptor* applies, and the false representation of a third person, said: "In the one, the buyer is aware of his position, he is dealing with the owner of the property, whose aim is to secure a good price, and whose interest it is to put a high estimate on his estate, and whose great object is to induce the purchaser to make the purchase, etc."

In *Hemmer* v. *Cooper* (1864), 8 Allen 334, an action for deceit in an exchange of real estate, the Court said: "The representations of a vendor of real estate to the vendee, as to the price which he paid for it, are to be regarded in the same light as representations respecting its value. A purchaser ought not to rely upon them, for it is settled that, even when they are false and uttered with a view to deceive, they furnish no ground of action."

The real inducement to the purchase from the plaintiffs' standpoint was their belief that they could make more money fishing than in bricklaying. . . . They were then earning $9.00 a day bricklaying, and, therefore, they must have had exaggerated notions of the profits to be made fishing.

The plaintiffs have failed to substantiate their case, both on the facts and the law. The defendant will have judgment with costs.

NOTES

1. Compare the following statement of Learned Hand J., in *Vulcan Metals Co.* v. *Simmons Manufacturing Co.* (1918), 248 Fed. 853: "There are some kinds of talk which no sensible man takes seriously, and if he does he suffers from his credulity. If we were all scrupulously honest, it would not be so; but, as it is, neither party usually believes what the seller says about his own opinions and each knows it. Such statements, like the claims of campaign managers before election, are rather designed to allay the suspicion which would attend their absence than to be understood as having any relation to objective truth. It is quite true that they induce a compliant temper in the buyer, but it is by a much more subtle process than through the acceptance of his claims for his wares."

2. Do you agree with the principle embodied in these decisions? Does anyone really rely on this type of statement? If they do, should they be protected? Just how big a lie like this can a seller tell a buyer and still get away with it? Compare with *Clarke* v. *Dickson* (1859), 6 C.B. N.S. 453.

3. Although untruths as to the price paid for or the value of an item have been dealt with leniently by the courts, because they are considered to be mere puffing, false representations as to the condition of articles may be actionable. See *Abel* v. *McDonald* (1964), 45 D.L.R. (2d) 198 (Ont. C.A.).

4. A passive failure to disclose the truth is usually not considered to be a misrepresentation, unless there is some fiduciary obligation on the representor to do so, but active concealment or statements that are only half-true may be actionable. See Fleming, *The Law of Torts* (5th ed., 1977), p. 617.

B. INDUCING BREACH OF CONTRACT

LUMLEY v. GYE

Queen's Bench. (1853), 118 E.R. 749, 2 E. & B. 216, 22 L.J. Q.B. 463

Miss Johanna Wagner was a well-known opera singer. She agreed to perform for the season at the Queen's Theatre, which the plaintiff managed. The defendant Gye persuaded Miss Wagner to breach her contract with the plaintiff. As a result, she failed to perform at the Queen's Theatre, causing loss to the plaintiff, who sued Gye.

Erle J.: The authorities are numerous and uniform, that an action will lie by a master against a person who procures that a servant should unlawfully leave his service . . . If it is objected that this class of action for procuring a breach of contract of hiring rests upon no principle, and ought not to be extended beyond the cases heretofore decided . . . the answer appears to me to be, that the class of cases referred to rests upon the principle that the procurement of the violation of the right is a cause of action, and that, when this principle is applied to a violation of a right arising upon a contract of hiring, the nature of the service contracted for is immaterial. It is clear that the procurement of the violation of a right is a cause of action in all instances where the violation is an actionable wrong, as in violations of a right to property, whether real or personal, or to personal security: he who procures the wrong is a joint wrong-doer, and may be sued, either alone or jointly with the agent, in the appropriate action for the wrong complained of. Where a right to the performance of a contract has been violated by a breach thereof, the remedy is upon the contract against the contracting party; and, if he is made to indemnify for such breach, no further recourse is allowed; and, as in case of the procurement of a breach of contract the action is for a wrong and cannot be joined with the action on the contract, and as the act itself is not likely to be of frequent occurrence nor easy of proof, therefore the action for this wrong, in respect of other contracts than those of hiring, are not numerous; but still they seem to me sufficient to shew that the principle has been recognized. . . .

He who maliciously procures a damage to another by violation of his right ought to be made to indemnify; and that, whether he procures an actionable wrong or a breach of contract. He who procures the nondelivery of goods according to contract may inflict an injury, the same as he who procures the abstraction of goods after delivery; and both ought on the same ground to be made responsible. The remedy on the contract may be inadequate, as where the measures of damage is restricted; or in the case of non-payment of a debt where the damage may be bankruptcy to the creditor who is disappointed, but the measure of damages against the debtor is interest only; or, in the case of the non-delivery of the goods, the disappointment may lead to a heavy forfeiture under a contract to complete a work within a time, but the measure of damages against the vendor of the goods for non-delivery may be only the difference between the contract price and the market value of the goods in question at the time of the breach. In such cases, he who procures the damage maliciously might justly be made responsible beyond the liability of the contractor . . .

The result is that there ought to be, in my opinion, judgment for the plaintiff.

NOTES

1. In a companion case, *Lumley* v. *Wagner* (1852), 42 E.R. 687, an injunction was granted preventing Miss Wagner from singing for Gye and prohibiting Gye from accepting her services.

2. The principle in *Lumley* v. *Gye* has been followed consistently ever since. See *Bowen* v. *Hall* (1881), 6 Q.B.D. 333 (C.A.); *Jasperson* v. *Dominion Tobacco Co.*, [1923] A.C. 709. For a more recent case see *Fabbi* v. *Jones* (1972), 28 D.L.R. (3d) 224 (S.C.C.), where a dairy was held liable to a trucker for inducing a breach of his contract to carry milk for certain milk producers. Laskin J. stated:

> ". . . [T]he conduct of the defendants in the first action went beyond merely incidental interference with Jones' contracts with the producers in pursuit of the defendants' own interests. This is not a case where the defendants merely caused a breach of contract, although knowing of its existence, in pursuit of a different object of their own, but one where there was an intentional and knowing procurement of the breach through pressure on the contracting producers in pursuance of the same object as that realized by Jones in consummating his contracts with the producers. . . ."

3. If there is no contract breach induced, then this action is unavailable. See *Ruest* v. *Nichols* (1974), 7 O.R. (2d) 53.

4. The defendant can induce a breach of contract directly by persuading a contracting party not to honour his legal obligation. One can also induce a

breach of contract indirectly by preventing the performance of the contractual obligation by some unlawful act, *i.e.*, if the defendant had locked Miss Wagner up, making it impossible for her to perform. See Fleming, *op. cit., supra*, p. 678. See also *Torquay Hotel* v. *Cousins et al.*, [1969] 2 Ch. D. 10 (C.A.).

5. There is nothing that prevents robust competition, however, as long as a contractual breach is not induced thereby and as long as illegal methods are not used. Thus, if an employee has no term of employment, or if his contract is terminable at will, he may be lured away from his employer without anyone incurring any legal liability. In *Triangle Film Corp.* v. *Artcraft Pictures Corp.* (1918), 250 F. 981, Learned Hand J. stated: "Nobody has ever thought, so far as we can find, that in the absence of some monopolistic purpose every one has not the right to offer better terms to another's employee, so long as the latter is free to leave. The result of the contrary would be intolerable, both to such employers as could use the employee more effectively and to such employees as might receive added pay." Do you agree?

6. What if a new supplier of certain articles goes around to various stores and offers his goods to them for 25 percent less than they are paying his chief competitor? They take up his offer and, as a result, the competitor goes into bankruptcy. Liability? Any difference if the stores had a 10-year contract with the original supplier? What if the new supplier's sole motivation was putting the old one out of business out of spite? See *infra, Tuttle* v. *Buck.*

7. Can there be liability for *negligently* inducing breach of contract? In *McLaren* v. *B.C. Institute of Technology* (1978), 7 C.C.L.T. 192, Taylor J. held there could not be. He explained:

"No such cause of action has hitherto been declared to exist; the question is whether it might be declared to exist today. In answering this question little assistance can be derived from general statements of the philosophical basis on which the law of negligence is founded. It has long been clear that the very broad words used by Lord Atkin in *M'Alister (Donoghue)* v. *Stevenson* in defining the "good neighbour" concept of duty of care, while they provide justification for the existence of this tort, are not to be taken as defining its scope. Only certain prescribed categories of negligent conduct are in fact actionable in law. Other types of conduct, although clearly in violation of the spirit of Lord Atkin's rule, have never been actionable; there is foreseeability of harm resulting to someone whose welfare ought to be in the mind of the person contemplating the potentially injurious act or omission, but the law recognizes no duty of care or, at least, no right of action for its breach. The distinction between actionable and non-actionable negligence is not to be drawn from the moral or philosophical basis of the tort; it is to be found rather in the policy of the law, that is to say in what the Courts consider logical and reasonable in their task of defining and developing the rules by which members of contemporary society are to be governed in their relations with each other.

That the categories of negligence continue to be open in the fifth decade after *M'Alister (Donoghue)* v. *Stevenson*, supra, is quite clear from the continuing extension of the law into the field of negligent mis-statement in the wake of the decision of the House of Lords in *Hedley Byrne & Co.* v. *Heller & Partners Ltd.*, [1964] A.C. 465, [1963] 2 All E.R. 575. Is it possible then that the Courts would be prepared today to add to the calendar of actionable negligence the further category for which the plaintiff argues on this application? If it is possible then the plaintiff is entitled to raise the issue in his pleadings, no matter how slim the chance of success.

The categories of actionable negligence in existence before establishment of the principles enunciated in *Hedley Byrne* are thought to have related to conduct capable of physical injury or damage, although recovery was not necessarily limited to physical results of breach of the duty of care. The development of a cause of action for negligent mis-statement involved extension of the tort of negligence to cases in which no physical injury or damage but only "economic injury" could result, but not all negligent misstatement is actionable. The defendant must be a person possessing special skills, the statement must involve the use of those skills and he must know that reliance may be placed on his skill and judgment by those to whose attention his statement will be brought. A person possessing special skills who makes a statement in the course of his calling on which he knows that others may rely must be careful what he says. The duty is created by his own conduct.

How much further is it necessary for the Courts to go in order to impose a duty of care on those who may cause foreseeable, unintentional harm of an "economic" character through interference in, or damage to, contractual rights of others, specifically rights enjoyed under a contract of employment? Here the duty of care would arise, not from the special position of the potential defendant (the actor) as a person possessing, and choosing to exercise, particular skills, but from the nature of the contractual relationships into which the potential plaintiff has entered. The duty imposed on one party would be created, and defined, by the nature of the contractual arrangements which the other party had chosen to make. In a society which grants its members freedom of contract, the opportunity for creation of contractual rights and obligations is, of course, unlimited. The existence of a right of action for damages for negligent interference in contractual relations would enable those who exercise the freedom of contract to impose an equally limitless variety of duties of care on third parties. This does not appear to be another step in the extension of the concept of actionable negligence which would flow logically from the existence of a duty of care on those who choose to exercise special skills in their own business. The movement is not a step but a leap in quite a different direction. This is not the manner in which the law has historically made its progress.

I cannot conclude that there is any real possibility that a right of action for negligent conduct inducing breach of contract, or causing interference with contractual relations, exists or, more precisely, could be found to exist at this point in the development of the law."
Do you agree with this analysis? Do you think there should be an expansion into this area?

8. See generally Sayre, "Inducing Breach of Contract" (1923), 36 Harv. L. Rev. 663; Carpenter, "Interference with Contractual Relations" (1928), 41 Harv. L. Rev. 728; Payne, "Interference with Contract" (1954), 7 Cur. Leg. Prob. 94.

9. If an employer discharges an employee without just cause, that employee has an action for wrongful dismissal and may receive compensation in lieu of notice. It has been argued that this is a tort action, although most authorities treat it as a breach of an implied term of the contract of employment. See B. McDonald, "Wrongful Dismissal: Tortious Breach of Contract", in Law Society of Upper Canada Special Lectures, *New Developments in Torts* (1973).

BRIMELOW v. CASSON

Chancery Division. [1924] 1 Ch. 302, 93 L.J.Ch. 256, 130 L.T. 725

Plaintiff was the owner of a burlesque troupe—the King Wu Tut Tut Revue—which was on tour fulfilling engagements at various theatres. Defendants were members of an actors' Joint Protection Committee which was making attempts to obtain better wages for chorus girls since it had been shown that the lack of a living wage had driven many girls to prostitution. The Committee had fixed a minimum wage of 2*l.* 10*s.* per week. Plaintiff paid his girls 1*l.* 10*s.* It was proved that one of the plaintiff's chorus girls, in order to obtain a living, was living, to plaintiff's knowledge, in immorality with an abnormal, deformed dwarf.

In order to improve the lot of this troupe, defendants persuaded the proprietors of several theatres not to permit plaintiff the use of their buildings and to break existing contracts or refuse to make contracts until higher wages were paid. Plaintiff brought action against defendants for an injunction. . . .

Russell J.: In my opinion, it is true to say that the evils which the Joint Protection Committee and the associations represented by it anticipate as the result of a company being run by a manager paying insufficient salaries are to be found in the plaintiff's company. *Prima facie* interference with a man's contractual rights and with his right to carry on his business as he wills is actionable; but it is clear on the authorities that interference with contractual rights may be justified; *a fortiori* the inducing of others not to contract with a person may be justified. . . .

My task here is to decide whether, in the circumstances of this case, justification existed for the acts done. Let me summarize the salient facts of the present case. The plaintiff is carrying on a business which involves the employment for wage of persons engaged in the theatrical calling, a calling in which numberless persons of both sexes are engaged in different classes of work throughout the country. The unions, or associations, formed for the purpose of representing and advancing the interests of those persons in connection with their different classes of work, and the interests of the calling as a whole, have ascertained by experience, and no one could doubt the fact, that it is essential for the safeguarding of those interests that there should be no sweating by employers. They have found by experience that the payment of less than a living wage to chorus girls frequently drives them to supplement their insufficient earnings by indulging in misconduct for the purpose of gain, thus ruining themselves in morals and bringing discredit on the theatrical calling. With the object of protecting those girls and of safeguarding the interests of the theatrical calling and its various members they have fixed standards of minimum wages, the minimum wage for chorus girls being fixed by the Actors' Association at the sum of 2*l*. 10*s*. a week. They find that the plaintiff is paying to his chorus girls wages on which no girl could with decency feed, clothe, and lodge herself, wages far below the minimum fixed by the Actors' Association. They have had previous experience of the plaintiff, and they cause fresh inquiries to be made, with the result that they are satisfied that many, if not all, the results anticipated by them to flow from such underpayment are present in the plaintiff's company. They desire in the interest of the theatrical calling and the members thereof to stop such underpayment with its evil consequences. The only way they can do so is by inducing the proprietors of theatres not to allow persons like the plaintiff the use of their theatres, either by breaking contracts already made or by refusing to enter into contracts. They adopt this course as regards the plaintiff as the only means open to them of bringing to an end his practice of underpayment which, according to their experience, is fruitful of danger to the theatrical calling and its members. In these circumstances, have the defendants justification for their acts? That they would have the sympathy and support of decent men and women I can have no doubt. But have they in law justification for those acts? As has been pointed out, no general rule can be laid down as a general guide in such cases, but I confess that if justification does not exist here I can hardly conceive the case in which it would be present. These defendants, as it seems to me, owed a duty to their calling and to its members, and, I am tempted to add, to the public to take all necessary peaceful steps to terminate the payment of this insufficient wage, which in the plaintiff's company had apparently been in fact productive of those results which their past experience had led them to anticipate. "The good sense" of this tribunal leads me to decide that in the circumstances of the present case justification did exist.

NOTES

1. Do you agree that this conduct was justified in the circumstances?

2. What if parents persuade their child to break an engagement to marry a person of bad moral character? *Gunn* v. *Barr,* [1926] 1 D.L.R. 855 (Alta. C.A.).

3. These problems frequently arise in the context of labour relations and, consequently, detailed treatment thereof is left to the course on Labour Law. Sometimes if there is collective action taken, a claim may be launched on the basis of civil conspiracy. This is a complex and specialized area of the law that cannot be dealt with here. See Carthy and Millar, "Civil Conspiracy" in Law Society of Upper Canada Special Lectures, *New Developments in the Law of Torts* (1973). See also *Allen* v. *Flood,* [1898] A.C. 1 (H.L.); *Quinn* v. *Leathem,* [1901] A.C. 495 (H.L.); *Croften Hand Woven Harris Tweed Co.* v. *Veitch,* [1942] A.C. 435 (H.L.); *Mogul Steamship* v. *McGregor & Co.* (1889), 23 Q.B.D. 598.

C. INTIMIDATION

ROOKES v. BARNARD

House of Lords. [1964] A.C. 1129, [1964] 1 All E.R. 367

The plaintiff was dismissed from his employment at B.O.A.C. when the defendants, union members and a union official, threatened to go on an illegal strike, in violation of their collective agreement, if the plaintiff was not let go. The House of Lords permitted recovery, holding that it was unlawful to threaten a breach of contract.

Lord Devlin: My Lords, in my opinion there is a tort of intimidation of the nature described in chapter 18 of Salmond on the Law of Torts, 13th ed. (1961), p. 697. The tort can take one of two forms which are set out in Salmond as follows:

"(1) *Intimidation of the plaintiff himself*
  Although there seems to be no authority on the point, it cannot be doubted that it is an actionable wrong intentionally to compel a person, by means of a threat of an illegal act, to do some act whereby loss accrues to him: for example, an action will doubtless lie at the suit of a trader who has been compelled to discontinue his business by means of threats of personal violence made against him by the defendant with that intention . . . .
(2) *Intimidation of other persons to the injury of the plaintiff*
  In certain cases it is an actionable wrong to intimidate other persons with the intent and effect of compelling them to act in a manner or to do acts which they themselves have a legal right to do which cause loss to the plaintiff: for example, the intimidation of the plaintiff's customers whereby they are compelled to withdraw their custom from him, or the intimidation of an employer whereby he is compelled to discharge his servant, the plaintiff. Intimidation of this sort is actionable, as we have said, in certain classes of cases; for it does not follow that, because a plaintiff's customers have a right to cease to deal with him if they please, other persons have a right as against the plaintiff to compel his customers to do so. There are at least two cases in which such intimidation may constitute a cause of action:—
    (i) When the intimidation consists in a threat to do or procure an illegal act;
    (ii) When the intimidation is the act, not of a single person, but of two or more persons acting together in pursuance of a common intention."

As your Lordships are all of opinion that there is a tort of intimidation and on this point approve the judgments in both courts below, I do not propose to offer any further authorities or reasons in support of my conclusion. I note that no issue on justification was raised at the time and there is no finding of fact upon it. So your Lordships have not to consider what part, if any, justification plays in the tort of intimidation.

Your Lordships are here concerned with the sort of intimidation which Salmond puts into the second category, and with the first of Salmond's two cases. The second case is, so Salmond later observed, "one form of the tort of conspiracy." That form is the *Quinn* v. *Leathem* type, so that it is no use to the appellant here. He relies upon "a threat to do or procure an illegal act," namely, a breach of contract. Doubtless it would suit him better if he could rely on the procuring of a breach of contract, for that is a tort; but immunity from that is guaranteed in terms by section 3. So he complains only of the threat to break the service contracts and the breach would undoubtedly be an act actionable by B.O.A.C. though it is neither tortious nor criminal. He does not have to contend that in the tort of intimidation, as in the tort of conspiracy, there can be, if the object is injurious, an unlawful threat to use lawful means. I do not think that there can be. The line must be drawn according to the law. It cannot be said that to use a threat of any sort is per se unlawful; and I do not see how, except in relation to the nature of the act threatened, i.e., whether it is lawful or unlawful, one could satisfactorily distinguish between a lawful and an unlawful threat.

This conclusion, while not directly in point, assists me in my approach to the matter to be determined here. It is not, of course, disputed that if the act threatened is a crime, the threat is unlawful. But otherwise is it enough to say that the act threatened is actionable as a breach of contract or must it be actionable as a tort? My Lords, I see no good ground for the latter limitation. I find the reasoning on this point of Professor Hamson (which Sellers L.J. sets out in his judgment though he does himself accept it) very persuasive. The essence of the offence is coercion. It cannot be said that every form of coercion is wrong. A dividing line must be drawn and the natural line runs between what is lawful and unlawful as against the party threatened. If the defendant threatens something that that party cannot legally resist, the plaintiff likewise cannot be allowed to resist the consequences; both must put up with the coercion and its results. But if the intermediate party is threatened with an illegal injury, the plaintiff who suffers by the aversion of the act threatened can fairly claim that he is illegally injured.

Accordingly, I reach the conclusion that the respondents' second point fails and on the facts of this case the tort of intimidation was committed.

NOTES

1. In *Morgan* v. *Fry et al.*, [1968] 2 Q.B. 710, Lord Denning, M.R., said at p. 724:

"According to the decision in *Rookes* v. *Barnard* [1964] A.C. 1129, [1964] 2 W.L.R. 269, [1964] 1 All E.R. 367, the tort of intimidation exists, not only in threats of violence, but also in threats to commit a tort or a breach of contract. The essential ingredients are these: there must be a threat by one person to use unlawful means (such as violence or a tort or a breach of contract) so as to compel another to obey his wishes; and the person so threatened must comply with the demand rather than risk the threat being carried into execution. In such circumstances the person damnified by the compliance can sue for intimidation."

2. In *J.T. Stratford & Son Ltd.* v. *Lindley*, [1965] A.C. 269, Lord Denning outlined his views of the tort of intimidation as follows:

"The fifth point is whether the defendants were guilty of the tort of intimidation. Such a tort has long been known in cases of threats of violence. If one man says to another, 'I will hit you unless you give me £5,' or 'unless you give the cook notice,' or 'unless you stop dealing with your butcher'; and the party so threatened submits to the threat by paying over the £5, or by giving notice to the cook, or by ceasing to deal with the butcher, then the party damnified by the threat—the payer of the £5, or the cook or the butcher, as the case may be—has a cause of action for intimidation against the person who made the threat. But it is essential to the cause of action that the person threatened should comply with the demand. If he has the courage to resist it and replies saying, 'You can do your worst. I am not going to pay you £5,' or, 'I am not going to give notice to the cook,' or 'I am not going to stop dealing with the butcher,' then the party threatened has no cause of action for intimidation. Nor has the cook. Nor the butcher. For they have suffered no damage by the threat. But in that case, if the threatener carries out his threat—if he commits his act of violence—the party threatened can sue for the unlawful act. He can sue for assault. He need not, however, wait for it. He can sue in advance for an injunction to prevent the threat being carried out. Another thing that is essential to the cause of action is that the threat should be a coercive threat. It must be coupled with a demand. It must be intended to coerce a person into doing something that he is unwilling to do or not doing something that he wishes to do. It must be capable of being expressed in the form, 'I will hit you *unless* you do what I ask,' or 'if you do what I forbid you to do.' A bare threat without a demand does not to my mind amount to the tort of intimidation. If a man says to another, 'I am going to hit you when I get you alone,' it is undoubtedly a threat; and an injunction can be obtained to restrain him from carrying out his threat. But the threat itself does not give rise to a claim for damages. It is only when he delivers the blow that it is actionable: and then as an assault, not as intimidation.

Very recently it has become clear that the tort of intimidation exists not only in threats of violence, but also in threats to commit a tort or a breach of contract. The essential ingredients are the same throughout: there must be a coercive threat to use unlawful means, so as to compel a person into doing something that he is unwilling to do, or not doing something that he wishes to do: and the party so threatened must comply with the demand rather than risk the threat being carried into execution. In such case the party damnified by the compliance can sue for damages for intimidation."

3. In England, *Rookes* v. *Barnard* has been abrogated by statute. See Trade Union and Labour Relations Act, 1974, s. 13(1)(b). Its principle survives in Canada, however.

4. In *Central Canada Potash Co. Ltd.* v. *Attorney-General for Saskatchewan* (1975), 57 D.L.R. (3d) 7; revd [1977] 1 W.W.R. 487 (Sask. C.A.); revd (1978), 6 C.C.L.T. 265 (S.C.C.), Mr. Justice Disbery, at trial, imposed liability for the tort of intimidation in the amount of $1,500,000. On appeal this was reversed. The Supreme Court affirmed the dismissal of the civil action, but reversed on the constitutional issue.

The plaintiff company was in the mining business in Saskatchewan and had an agreement to supply potash to its United-States-based shareholder. As a result of over-production of potash and a drastic drop in world prices, the potash industry in New Mexico, which had been the major producer in the past, became depressed. A deal was made between the Government of Saskatchewan and the Government of New Mexico to control the production and sale of potash. Under the scheme, each producer in Saskatchewan was allowed, under a licence from the Minister, to sell a certain amount of potash. The object was to limit the supply of potash in world markets and to control its price. The scheme was changed to some extent in 1971 to control, through an export association, all exports of potash.

The plaintiff company objected to this scheme on the ground that it interfered with its contractual obligations with its United-States-based shareholder. An application for a licence permitting it to comply with its contract was refused, and the Deputy Minister, by letter to the plaintiff company, threatened to cancel its existing licence because it was exceeding its quota in order to meet its contractual obligation. The plaintiff company yielded to the threat and, then, commenced this action for declarations that the regulations passed under the Act were *ultra vires* the provincial legislature, and that all actions pursuant to them were null and void. In addition, the plaintiff sought damages for intimidation.

The trial judge declared the marketing scheme *ultra vires* and awarded $1,500,000 damages for the tort of intimidation against the Government of Saskatchewan. During the course of his lengthy judgment, Mr. Justice Disbery remarked:

"It is quite clear from the cases that the threat complained of must be a threat to do an act which is in itself illegal. So to make a coericive threat to sue on an overdue promissory note or to disinherit a child of the intimidator would not be actionable because the intimidator has the legal right to sue or to disinherit. On the other hand where a debtor threatened his creditor that he would pay no part of his debt unless the creditor accepted a lesser sum in full satisfaction, such threat was illegal: *D. & C. Builders Ltd.* v. *Rees,* [1966] 2 Q.B. 617 at p. 625. *Salmond on Torts,* 15th ed. (1969), p. 488, states that "The wrong of intimidation includes all those cases in which harm is inflicted by the use of unlawful threats whereby the lawful liberty of others to do as they please is interfered with."

Lord Reid pointed out in the *Rookes* case that [at p. 374] 'Threatening a breach of contract may be a much more coercive weapon than threatening a tort, particularly when the threat is directed against a company or corporation . . .". Again, in the *Rookes* case at p. 375, Lord Reid said:

"Intimidation of any kind appears to me to be highly objectionable. The law was not slow to prevent it when violence and threats of violence were the most effective means. Now that subtler means are at least equally effective I see no reason why the law should have to turn a blind eye to them. We have to tolerate intimidation by means which have been held to be lawful, but there I would stop.'

The Courts are always open to do justice according to the law as given to them by the people's representatives in Parliament and the Legislatures. The Courts have always been opposed to persons seeking 'to do their own justice' in whatever way they themselves desire to adopt. The cult of the heaviest clout, which is too often seen in the world today, is, of course, the very antithesis of the rule of law. . . .

Two-party intimidation exists where the intimidator for some purpose of his own threatens his victim with an unlawful act unless the victim does (or refrains from doing) an act in such a way as to cause damage to himself, in order to avoid what, in the eyes of the victim, would be a greater evil to himself if he refused and the intimidator carried out his threat."

The Saskatchewan Court of Appeal reversed this decision and the Supreme Court of Canada affirmed, even though the scheme was found by the Supreme Court to be *ultra vires* the provincial government. Mr. Justice Martland, on the issue of civil liability, explained:

"If the course of conduct which the person making the threat seeks to induce is that which the person threatened is obligated to follow, the tort of intimidation does not arise . . . Here the Deputy Minister was seeking to induce conformity with the prorationing plan which had been created by legislation which it was his duty to enforce . . . It would be unfortunate, in a federal state such as Canada, if it were to be held that a government official, charged with the enforcement of legislation, could be held to be guilty of intimidation because of his enforcement of a statute whenever a statute whose provisions he is under a duty to enforce is subsequently held *ultra vires.*"

5. In *Mintuck* v. *Valley River Band No. 63A* (1977), 2 C.C.L.T. 1 (Man. C.A.), the plaintiff was prevented from working part of the farm, which he leased from the federal government, as a result of harassment by the defendants including vehicles on the road blocking his access, stray cattle roaming on the farm damaging the crops, defendants driving trucks over the farm under the pretext they were hunting game and, occasionally, he was threatened

in person and over the telephone and even by firearms. The objective of all of this was to get him to abandon his lease rights. He did not. His action was successful at trial on the basis of inducing breach of contract. This was affirmed on appeal, but on different grounds. Mr. Justice Matas rested the liability on "the tort of intimidation and unlawful interference with economic interests". O'Sullivan J.A. said that there was no breach of any contract caused by the acts of the defendant, but the band was "guilty of the two-party torts of intimidation and unlawful interference with economic interests". See also *Gershman* v. *Manitoba Vegetable Producers' Marketing Bd.,* [1976] 4 W.W.R. 406, 69 D.L.R. (3d) 114 (Man. C.A.).

6. What if, as a result of certain threats by a defendant, the plaintiff is frightened and suffers a heart attack. What basis of liability, if any, is available? See *supra,* Chapter 2.

D. INTERFERENCE WITH ADVANTAGEOUS BUSINESS RELATIONS

TUTTLE v. BUCK

Supreme Court of Minnesota. (1909), 119 N.W. 946

The plaintiff alleged that the defendant banker opened a rival barber shop in order to destroy the plaintiff's barber shop business. The plaintiff contended that the defendant, who was influential and wealthy, was not serving any purpose of his own but was maliciously seeking to put the plaintiff out of business and drive him out of town. The defendant influenced many of the plaintiff's former customers not to patronize the plaintiff any longer. It was alleged that, as a result, the plaintiff's business was ruined. A demurrer by the defendant was overruled at trial and the defendant appealed.

Elliott J.: It has been said that the law deals only with externals, and that a lawful act cannot be made the foundation of an action because it was done with an evil motive. In *Allen* v. *Flood,* [1898] A.C. 1, Lord Watson said that, except with regard to crimes, the law does not take into account motives as constituting an element of civil wrong. In *Mayor of Bradford* v. *Pickles,* [1895] A.C. 587, Lord Halsbury stated that if the act was lawful, "however ill the motive might be, he had a right to do it." In *Raycroft* v. *Tayntor,* 68 Vt. 219; 35 A. 53; 33 L.R.A. 225; 54 Am.St. Rep. 882, the court said that, "when one exercises a legal right only, the motive which actuates him is immaterial." In *Jenkins* v. *Fowler,* 24 Pa. 308, Mr. Justice Black said that "malicious motives made a bad act worse, but they cannot make that wrong which, in its own essence, is lawful." . . .

Such generalizations are of little value in determining concrete cases. They may state the truth, but not the whole truth. Each word and phrase used therein may require definition and limitation. Thus, before we can apply Judge Black's language to a particular case, we must determine what act is "in its own essence lawful". What did Lord Halsbury mean by the words "lawful act"? What is meant by "exercising a legal right"? It is not at all correct to say that the motive with which an act is done is always immaterial, providing the act itself is not unlawful. Numerous illustrations of the contrary will be found in the civil as well as the criminal law.

We do not intend to enter upon an elaborate discussion of the subject, or become entangled in the subtleties connected with the words "malice" and "malicious". We are not able to accept without limitations the doctrine above referred to, but at this time content ourselves with a brief reference to some general principles.

It must be remembered that the common law is the result of growth, and that its development has been determined by the social needs of the community which it governs. It is the resultant of conflicting social forces, and those forces which are for the time dominant leave their impress upon the law. It is of judicial origin, and seeks to establish doctrines and rules for the determination, protection, and enforcement of legal rights. Manifestly it must change as society changes and new rights are recognized. To be an efficient instrument, and not a mere abstraction, it must gradually adapt itself to changed conditions. Necessarily its form and substance have been greatly affected by prevalent economic theories.

For generations there has been a practical agreement upon the proposition that competition in trade and business is desirable, and this idea has found expression in the decisions of the courts as well as in statutes. But it has led to grievous and manifold wrongs to individuals, and many courts have manifested an earnest desire to protect the individual from the evil which result from unrestrained business competition. The problem has been to so adjust matters as to preserve the principle of competition and yet guard against its abuse to the unnecessary injury to the individual. So the principle that a man may use his own property according to his own needs and desires, while true in the abstract, is subject to many limitations in the concrete. Men cannot always, in civilized society, be allowed to use their own property as their interests or desires may dictate without reference to the fact that they have neighbours whose rights are as sacred as their own. The existence and well-being of society require that each and every person shall conduct himself consistently with the fact that he is a social and reasonable person. The purpose for which a man is using his own property may thus sometimes determine his rights . . . .

Many of the restrictions which should be recognized and enforced result from a tacit recognition of principles which are not often stated in the decisions in express terms. Sir Frederick Pollock notes that not many years ago it was difficult to find any definite authority for stating as a general proposition of English law that it is wrong to do a wilful wrong to one's neighbour without lawful justification or excuse. But neither is there any express authority for the general proposition that men must perform their contracts. Both principles, in this generality of form and conception, are modern, and there was a time when neither was true. After developing the idea that law begins, not with authentic general principles, but with the enumeration of particular remedies, the learned writer continues: "If there exists, then, a positive duty to avoid harm, much more must there exist the negative duty of not doing wilful harm, subject, as all general duties must be subject, to the necessary exceptions. The three main heads of duty with which the law of torts is concerned, namely, to abstain from wilful injury, to respect the property of others, and to use due diligence to avoid causing harm to others, are all alike of a comprehensive nature." Pollock, *Torts* (8th ed.), p. 21. He then quotes with approval the statement of Lord Bowen that "at common law there was a cause of action whenever one person did damage to another, wilfully and intentionally, without just cause or excuse."

In *Plant* v. *Woods,* 176 Mass. 492; 57 N.E. 1011; 51 L.R.A. 339; 79 Am. St. Rep. 330, Mr. Justice Hammond said: "It is said also that, where one has the lawful right to do a thing, the motive by which he is actuated is immaterial. One form of this statement appears in the first headnote in *Allen* v. *Flood,* as reported in [1898] A.C. 1, as follows: 'An act lawful in itself is not converted by a malicious or bad motive into an unlawful act so as to make the doer of the act liable to a civil action.' If the meaning of this and similar expressions is that where a person has the lawful right to do a thing irrespective of his motive, his motive is immaterial, the proposition is a mere truism. If, however, the meaning is that where a person, if actuated by one kind of a motive, has a lawful right to do a thing, the act is lawful when done under any conceivable motive, or that an act lawful under one set of circumstances is therefore lawful under every conceivable set of circumstances, the proposition does not commend itself to us as either logically or legally accurate." . . .

It is freely conceded that there are many decisions contrary to this view; but, when carried to the extent contended for by the appellant, we think they are unsafe, unsound, and illy adapted to modern conditions. To divert to one's self the customers of a business rival by the offer of goods at lower prices is in general a legitimate mode of serving one's own interest, and justifiable as fair competition. But when a man starts an opposition place of business, not for the sake of profit to himself, but regardless of loss to himself, and for the sole purpose of driving his competitor out of business, and with the intention of himself retiring upon the accomplishment of his malevolent purpose, he is guilty of a wanton wrong and an actionable tort. In such a case he would not be exercising his legal right, or doing an act which can be judged separately from the motive which actuated him. To call such conduct competition is a perversion of terms. It is simply the application of force without legal justification, which in its moral quality may be no better than highway robbery.

Nevertheless, in the opinion of the writer this complaint is insufficient. It is not claimed that it states a cause of action for slander. No question of conspiracy or combination is involved. Stripped of the adjectives and the statement that what was done was for the sole purpose of injuring the plaintiff, and not for the purpose of serving a legitimate purpose of the defendant, the complaint states facts which in themselves amount only to an ordinary every day business transaction. There is no allegation that the defendant was intentionally running the business at a financial loss to himself, or that after driving the plaintiff out of business the defendant closed up or intended to close up his shop. From all that appears from the complaint he may have opened the barber shop, energetically sought business from his acquaintances and the customers of the plaintiff, and as a result of his enterprise and command of capital obtained it, with the result that the plaintiff, from want of capital, acquaintance, or enterprise, was unable to stand the competition and was thus driven out of business. The facts thus alleged do not, in my opinion, in themselves, without reference to the way in which they are characterized by the pleader, tend to show a malicious and wanton wrong to the plaintiff.

A majority of the justices, however, are of the opinion that, on the principle declared in the foregoing opinion, the complaint states a cause of action, and the order is therefore affirmed.

NOTES

1. There were several well-known early cases which established this principle. In *Keeble* v. *Hickeringill* (1706), 11 East 574, 103 E.R. 1127, a defendant was held liable for maliciously firing guns which frightened ducks away from the plaintiff's pond, preventing him from taking them.

2. Another famous old decision is *Tarleton* v. *M'Gawley* (1793), 170 E.R. 153, where the defendant fired on some African natives with whom the plaintiff was hoping to trade. This frightened them away, causing economic loss to the plaintiff. The plaintiff was awarded damages.

3. In *Temperton* v. *Russell*, [1893] 1 Q.B. 715 (C.A.), the court recognized that an action could lie for interference with economic relations which were merely prospective or potential, as well as for inducing actual breaches of contracts. See Lord Esher at p. 728.

4. Someone buys a radio from a department store. It is defective. He gets a picket sign saying "X Co. cheated me. Will they cheat you?" and parades around

in front of the store. Business is hurt. Actionable? Should an injunction be issued. See *Canadian Tire Co. Ltd.* v. *Desmond* (1972), 24 D.L.R. (3d) 642 (Ont.). See also *Hubbard* v. *Pitt,* [1975] 3 All E.R. 1 (C.A.), where Lord Denning allowed picketing to continue to communicate information as long as it was peaceful and the words on the placards were true.

5. Would liability be imposed if an officer of a company, without proper authorization, instructs its bank to stop honouring cheques signed by the plaintiff? See *Volkswagen Canada Ltd.* v. *Spicer* (1978), 91 D.L.R. (3d) 42 (N.S.C.A.).

6. See generally Holmes, "Privilege, Malice and Intent" (1894), 8 Harv. L. Rev. 1; Ames, "How Far an Act May be a Tort Because of Wrongful Motive of the Actor" (1905), 18 Harv. L. Rev. 411; Gutteridge, "Abuse of Rights" (1933), 5 Camb. L. J. 22.

7. To launch a totally unfounded lien claim as a form of "legal blackmail" to obtain a settlement is actionable and punitive damages may be awarded against the defendant. See *Guilford Industries Ltd.* v. *Hankinson Management Services Ltd.* (1973), 40 D.L.R. (3d) 398 (B.C.). There is also an action called slander of title. See *White* v. *Mellin,* [1895] A.C. 154; see also Ontario Libel & Slander Act, R.S.O. 1970, c. 243. See Wood, "Disparagement of Title and Quality" (1942), 20 Can. Bar Rev. 296, 430. Actions for infringement of copyright and passing off are beyond the scope of this book. See *Canadian Shredded Wheat Co. Ltd.* v. *Kellogg Co. of Canada Ltd.,* [1938] 2 D.L.R. 145 (P.C.); Fox, *Canadian Law of Copyright* (2nd ed., 1967); Fox, *Canadian Law of Trade Marks and Unfair Competition* (3rd ed., 1972).

E. ABUSE OF POWER

RONCARELLI v. DUPLESSIS

Supreme Court of Canada. [1959] S.C.R. 121, 16 D.L.R. (2d) 689

Plaintiff was the proprietor of a restaurant in a busy section of Montreal which in 1946, through its transmission to him from his father, had been continuously licensed for the sale of liquor for thirty-four years. While his application for annual renewal was before the Quebec Liquor Commission on December 4th of that year, his existing licence was cancelled and his application for renewal rejected. He was also informed that no future licence would ever issue to him. Plaintiff brought action against the defendant, who was, at all relevant times, the Prime Minister and Attorney-General of the Province of Quebec, for damages resulting to him as a result of the cancellation.

The material facts showed that plaintiff had been an adherent of a religious sect known as Witnesses of Jehovah whose activities in the Province of Quebec had resulted in property damage, meetings forcibly broken up and large-scale arrests (over one thousand) of men and women who had been distributing literature deemed offensive and insulting to the religious beliefs of the predominantly Roman Catholic population. The plaintiff being a person of some means had been accepted as a bondsman on bail in about 380 cases of arrest. Stepped-up pressures against Jehovah's Witnesses in November, 1946, resulted in requiring cash bail on these arrest cases and at the same time investigations were set on foot into the activities of the plaintiff who, as the holder of a "privilege" granted by the Province, was regarded with disfavour as using profits gained from such "privilege" to promote the disturbance of settled beliefs in the community.

Mr. Archambault, the General Manager of the Quebec Liquor Commission, telephoned Mr. Duplessis on November 21st and advised him of Roncarelli's activities in supplying bail. At no time had Roncarelli taken part in the distribution of tracts. In fact, it was accepted that he, apart from giving bail and being an adherent of the sect, was free from any relation that, in the language of Rand, J. "could be tortured into a badge of character pertinent to his fitness or unfitness to hold a liquor licence."

Mr. Duplessis told Mr. Archambault that the matter was serious and that he would like to have the identity of the person furnishing bail and liquor licensee put beyond doubt. A few days later, Mr. Archambault communicated again to Mr. Duplessis reporting the investigation had established the identity. On December 4th, the licence was revoked.

At the trial Mr. Duplessis agreed that reports of newspaper interviews with him concerning the Roncarelli permit were correct. Those reports indicated that Mr. Duplessis had said that it was he, in his capacity as Attorney-General, who had ordered the cancellation of Roncarelli's permit and that it should be cancelled for all time. The following extract indicates the nature of Mr. Duplessis's evidence:

> "Non, je n'ai pas donné un ordre à M. Archambault, je viens de conter ce qui s'est passé. Le Juge Archambault m'a mis au courant d'un fait que je ne connaissais pas, je ne connaissais pas les faits, c'est lui qui m'a mis au courant des faits. Je ne sais pas comment un peut appeler ça quand le Procureur Général, qui est à la tête d'un département, parle à un officier, même à un officier supérieur, et qu'il émet une opinion, ce n'est pas directement un ordre, c'en est un sans l'être. Mais c'est à la suggestion de Juge Archambault, après qu'il eut porté à ma connaissance des faits que j'ignorais, que le décision a été prise . . . Si j'avais dit au Juge Archambault: 'Vous ne le ferez pas', il ne l'aurait probablement pas fait. Comme il me suggérit de le faire et qu'après réflexion et vérification je trouvais que c'était correct, que c'etait conforme à mon devoir, j'ai approuvé et c'est toujours un ordre que l'on donne. Quand l'officier supérieur parle, c'est un ordre que l'on donne, même s'il accepte la suggestion de l'officier dans son départment, c'est un ordre qu'il donne indirectement."

In An Act Respecting Alcoholic Liquor, R.S.Q. 1941, c. 255, a Quebec Liquor Commission was created, the only member of which was the General Manager. By s. 9(e) the Commission was authorized to "grant, refuse, or cancel permits for the sale of alcoholic liquor." The Commission by s. 12 could only be sued with the consent of the Attorney-General. Sec. 35, prescribed for the expiration of every permit on April 30th of each year and, dealing with cancellation, provides that the "Commission may cancel permits at its discretion."

At the trial before Mackinnon, J. ([1952] 1 D.L.R. 680) he found that defendant ordered Mr. Archambault to cancel the plaintiff's permit and that the defendant's order was the determining factor in the cancellation; that the Commission acted arbitrarily in its disregard of the rules of reason and justice in cancelling the permit; that the defendant had failed to show that he had any authority in law to interfere with the administration of the Commission. He awarded plaintiff judgment for $8,123.53. On appeal to the Court of Queen's Bench (Appeal Side), ([1956] Que. Q.B. 447) defendant's appeal was allowed and the plaintiff's action dismissed. The plaintiff appealed to the Supreme Court of Canada; included in the appeal was a claim for an increase in the damages awarded at the trial.

Rand J.: . . . In these circumstances, when the *de facto* power of the Executive over its appointees at will to such a statutory public function is exercised deliberately and intentionally to destroy the vital business interests of a citizen, is there legal redress by him against the person so acting? . . .

The provisions of the statute, which may be supplemented by detailed Regulations, furnish a code for the complete administration of the sale and distribution of alcoholic liquors directed by the Commission as a public service, for all legitimate purposes of the populace. It recognizes the association of wines and liquors as embellishments of food and its ritual and as an interest of the public. As put in Macbeth, the "sauce to meat is ceremony", and so we have restaurants, cafés, hotels and other places of serving food, specifically provided for in that association.

At the same time the issue of permits has a complementary interest in those so catering to the public. The continuance of the permit over the years, as in this case, not only recognizes its virtual necessity to a superior class restaurant but also its identification with the business carried on. The provisions for assignment of the permit are to this most pertinent and they were exemplified in the continuity of the business here. As its exercise continues, the economic life of the holder becomes progressively more deeply implicated with the privilege while at the same time his vocation becomes correspondingly dependent on it.

The field of licensed occupations and businesses of this nature is steadily becoming of greater concern to citizens generally. It is a matter of vital importance that a public administration that can refuse to allow a person to enter or continue a calling which, in the absence of regulation, would be free and legitimate, should be conducted with complete impartiality and integrity; and that the grounds for refusing or cancelling a permit should unquestionably be such and such only as are incompatible with the purposes envisaged by the statute: the duty of a Commission is to serve those purposes and those only. A decision to deny or cancel such a privilege lies within the "discretion" of the Commission; but that means that decision is to be based upon a weighing of considerations pertinent to the object of the administration.

In public regulation of this sort there is no such thing as absolute and untrammelled "discretion", that is that action can be taken on any ground or for any reason that can be suggested to the mind of the administrator; no legislative Act can, without express language, be taken to contemplate an unlimited arbitrary power, exercisable for any purpose, however capricious or irrelevant, regardless of the nature or purpose of the statute. Fraud and corruption in the Commission may not be mentioned in such statutes but they are always implied as exceptions. "Discretion" necessarily implies good faith in discharging public duty; there is always a perspective within which a statute is intended to operate; and any clear departure from its lines or objects is just as objectionable as fraud or corruption. Could an applicant be refused a permit because he had been born in another Province, or because of the colour of his hair? The ordinary language of the Legislature cannot be so distorted.

To deny or revoke a permit because a citizen exercises an unchallengeable right totally irrelevant to the sale of liquor in a restaurant is equally beyond the scope of the discretion conferred. There was here not only revocation of the existing permit but a declaration of a future, definitive disqualification of the appellant to obtain one: it was to be "forever". This purports to divest his citizenship status of its incident of membership in the class of those of the public to whom such a privilege could be extended. Under the statutory language here, that is not competent to the Commission and *a fortiori* to the Government or the respondent: *McGillivray* v. *Kimber* (1915), 26 D.L.R. 164, 52 S.C.R. 146. There is here an administrative tribunal which, in certain respects, is to act in a judicial manner; and even on the view of the dissenting Justices in *McGillivray*, there is liability: what could be more malicious than to punish this licensee for having done what he had an absolute right to do in a matter utterly irrelevant to the *Alcoholic Liquor Act*? Malice in the proper sense is simply acting for a reason and purpose knowingly foreign to the administration, to which was added here the element of intentional punishment by what was virtually vocation outlawry.

It may be difficult if not impossible in cases generally to demonstrate a breach of this public duty in the illegal purpose served; there may be no means, even if

proceedings against the Commission were permitted by the Attorney-General, as
here they were refused, of compelling the Commission to justify a refusal or
revocation or to give reasons for its action; on these questions I make no observation; but in the case before us that difficulty is not present: the reasons are
openly avowed.

The act of the respondent through the instrumentality of the Commission
brought about a breach of an implied public statutory duty toward the appellant;
it was a gross abuse of legal power expressly intended to punish him for an act
wholly irrelevant to the statute, a punishment which inflicted on him, as it was
intended to do, the destruction of his economic life as a restaurant keeper
within the Province. Whatever may be the immunity of the Commission or its
members from an action for damages, there is none in the respondent. He was
under no duty in relation to the appellant and his act was an intrusion upon the
functions of a statutory body. The injury done by him was a fault engaging
liability within the principles of the underlying public law of Quebec: *Mostyn* v.
Fabrigas (1774), 1 Cowp. 161, 98 E.R. 1021, and under art. 1053 of the *Civil
Code*. That, in the presence of expanding administrative regulation of economic
activities, such a step and its consequences are to be suffered by the victim without recourse or remedy, that an administration according to law is to be superseded by action dictated by and according to the arbitrary likes, dislikes and
irrelevant purposes of public officers acting beyond their duty, would signalize
the beginning of disintegration of the rule of law as a fundamental postulate of
our constitutional structure. An administration of licences on the highest level of
fair and impartial treatment to all may be forced to follow the practice of "first
come, first served", which makes the strictest observance of equal responsibility
to all of even greater importance; at this stage of developing government it would
be a danger of high consequence to tolerate such a departure from good faith in
executing the legislative purpose . . . .

It was urged by Mr. Beaulieu that the respondent, as the incumbent of an
office of state, so long as he was proceeding in "good faith", was free to act in a
matter of this kind virtually as he pleased. The office of Attorney-General
traditionally and by statute carries duties that relate to advising the Executive,
including here, administrative bodies, enforcing the public law and directing the
administration of justice. In any decision of the statutory body in this case, he
had no part to play beyond giving advice on legal questions arising. In that role
his action should have been limited to advice on the validity of a revocation for
such a reason or purpose and what that advice should have been does not seem
to me to admit of any doubt. To pass from this limited scope of action to that
of bringing about a step by the Commission beyond the bounds prescribed by
the Legislature for its exclusive action converted what was done into his personal
act.

"Good faith" in this context, applicable both to the respondent and the
General Manager, means carrying out the statute according to its intent and for
its purpose; it means good faith in acting with a rational appreciation of that
intent and purpose and not with an improper intent and for an alien purpose; it
does not mean for the purposes of punishing a person for exercising an
unchallengeable right; it does not mean arbitrarily and illegally attempting to
divest a citizen of an incident of his civil status. . . .

The damages suffered involved the vocation of the appellant within the
Province. Any attempt at a precise computation or estimate must assume probabilities in an area of uncertainty and risk. The situation is one which the Court
should approach as a jury would, in a view of its broad features; and in the best
consideration I can give to them, the damages should be fixed at the sum of
$25,000 plus that allowed by the trial Court.

NOTES

1. See generally Law Society of Upper Canada Special Lectures, *Abuse of Power* (1979), p. 80.

2. In *Farrington* v. *Thompson,* [1959] V.R. 286, some police officers, purporting to exercise their power under the Licensing Act which provided that conviction of a third offence would render a licence forfeited, required the plaintiff to close down his hotel. There was no third conviction, according to the judge, and the jury found that the defendants failed to exercise due care in ascertaining whether a third conviction had been obtained. The court found, nevertheless, that the defendants were liable for "misfeasance in a public office". Mr. Justice Smith said that "if some other public officer does an act, which, to his knowledge, amounts to an abuse of his office, and thereby causes damage to another person, then an action in tort for misfeasance in a public office will lie" (*ibid.;* see also Molot, "Tort Remedies Against Administrative Tribunals for Economic Loss", Law Society of Upper Canada Special Lectures, *New Developments in the Law of Torts* (1973), p. 425). There was apparently sufficient knowledge of lack of jurisdiction to satisfy the court that liability was called for.

3. There is authority to the effect that an unintentional error in the exercise of discretion is not actionable. See *Harris* v. *Law Society of Alberta,* [1936] S.C.R. 88. More recent authority, however, seems to be relaxing the requirement of intention. In *McGillivray* v. *Kimber* (1950), 52 S.C.R. 146, a pilot, licensed at Sydney, Nova Scotia, under the Shipping Act, was dismissed from the service by the Sydney Pilotage Authority before his licence expired. Although the minority of the court felt that malice had to be proven for liability for a quasi-judicial act, the majority decided that the Authority was responsible. It had failed to abide by the statutorily required procedures of giving the plaintiff notice and an opportunity to be heard. Mr. Justice Anglin stated: "They committed an unwarranted and illegal act which subjected them to liability to the plaintiff for such damages as he sustained as a natural and direct consequence thereof." Mr. Justice Idington observed that "the respondents were acting entirely without jurisdiction and so acting must be held liable".

4. The courts of Quebec have been most diligent in this area. In *Lapointe* v. *Le Roi* (1924), 87 B.R. 170, the petitioner, who was holder of a fishing licence, had it revoked by the Minister who lacked the statutory power to do so. The court ordered the Minister to compensate the petitioner for his loss. Another case is *Leroux* v. *City of Lachine,* [1942] C.S. 352, where a licence permitted the plaintiff to operate a dance hall. The city revoked the licence, without permitting him an opportunity to be heard. The court awarded damages on the ground that this was an "unwarranted and negligent action" on the defendant's part, amounting to an abuse of rights.

5. Professor Klar has indicated that there is considerable confusion in delineating the scope of these various economic torts and has asked, "Why have specific nominate torts when you can lump practically all of the factual situations into a tort of unlawfully interfering with economic interest? Is that, after all, not the gist of every action in the area of economic torts?" See Note on *Mintuck* (1977), 2 C.C.L.T. 2. How would you answer Professor Klar's question? See also Burns, "Tort Injury to Economic Interests—Some Facets of Legal Response" (1980), 58 Can. Bar Rev.

6. In *Beaudesert Shire* v. *Smith* (1966), 40 A.L.J.R. 211, a landowner took water for irrigation from a pool in a river. The defendant destroyed the pool by removing gravel from the riverbed and thereby damaged the landowner's crops. He sued and recovered, the court explaining "independently of trespass, negligence or nuisance, but by an action upon the case, a person who suffers harm or loss as the inevitable consequence of the unlawful intentional, and positive acts of another is entitled to recover damages from that other". What do you think of this idea? Fleming has termed it a "spurious principle, destitute of all authority". See *The Law of Torts* (5th ed., 1977), p. 689. Would it make a

difference whether the defendant knew about the consequences of his acts or was totally unaware of them?

7. Is this a valuable role for Canadian tort law to play in the 1980's?

INDEX